THE OFFICIAL®

RINKER

• PRICE GUIDE TO •

COLLECTIBLES

THE OFFICIAL®

RINKER

• PRICE GUIDE TO •

COLLECTIBLES

FOURTH EDITION

HOUSE OF COLLECTIBLES

THE CROWN PUBLISHING GROUP • NEW YORK

Copyright © 2000 by Rinker Enterprises, Inc.

House of Collectibles and the HC colophon are trademarks of Random House, Inc.

Published by: House of Collectibles
                The Crown Publishing Group
                New York, NY

Distributed by The Crown Publishing Group, a division of Random House, Inc., New York, and simultaneously in Canada by Random House of Canada Limited, Toronto.

www.randomhouse.com

Manufactured in the United States of America

ISSN: 1094-3862

ISBN: 0-676-60159-6

10 9 8 7 6 5 4 3 2 1

Fourth Edition: September 2000

RINKER ENTERPRISES, INC.

HARRY L. RINKER
President

DENA C. GEORGE
Associate Editor

DANA G. MORYKAN
Senior Editor

KATHY WILLIAMSON
Associate Editor

NANCY BUTT
Librarian

VIRGINIA REINBOLD
Controller

RICHARD SCHMELTZLE
Support Staff

ABOUT THE AUTHOR — HARRY L. RINKER

Harry L. Rinker is one of the most forthright, honest, and "tell-it-like-it-is" reporters in the antiques and collectibles field today. He is the King of Collectibles, the last of the great antiques and collectibles generalists.

Rinker is president of Rinker Enterprises, Inc., a firm specializing in providing consulting, editorial, educational, photographic, research, and writing services in the antiques and collectibles field. He also directs the Institute for the Study of Antiques & Collectibles, serving as the principal instructor for its seminars and conferences.

Rinker is a prolific antiques and collectibles writer. Other House of Collectibles titles by Rinker include *Dinnerware of the 20TH Century: The Top 500 Patterns*, *Silverware of the 20TH Century: The Top 250 Patterns*, and *Stemware of the 20TH Century: The Top 200 Patterns*. Rinker also is author of *Price Guide to Flea Market Treasures, Fifth Edition* and *Hopalong Cassidy: King of the Cowboy Merchandisers*. He is co-author with Dana G. Morykan of *Garage Sale Manual & Price Guide* and with Norman Martinus of *Warman's Paper*.

Rinker on Collectibles, a weekly syndicated column, appears in trade and daily newspapers from coast to coast. Often highly opinionated and controversial, it is one of the most widely read columns in the antiques and collectibles trade.

Rinker is a frequent television and radio guest. He often refers to himself as the "national cheerleader for collectibles and collecting." His television credits include *Oprah*, *NBC—Today Show*, *ABC—TV Good Morning America*, *CNBC—TV Steals and Deals*, and *MPT Wall Street Week With Louis Rukeyser*. *Whatcha Got*, a ninety-second antiques and collectibles daily feature, is distributed to radio stations by the Minnesota News Network. Rinker also does weekly call-in radio shows for KFGO (Fargo, North Dakota), KLTF (Little Falls, Minnesota), WSAU (Wausau, Wisconsin), and WNPV (Lansdale, Pennsylvania). He can be heard the second and fourth Wednesdays of each month on KROC (Rochester, Minnesota).

Each year Rinker lectures and/or makes personal appearances in over a dozen cities across the United States, sponsored by trade publications, antiques malls, show promoters, and others. In 1996 Rinker and James Tucker co-founded the National Association of Collectors.

Rinker is a dedicated accumulator, a collector of collections. He is continually adding new items to over 250 different collections. Among collectibles collectors, he is best known for his collections of Hopalong Cassidy memorabilia and jigsaw puzzles, the latter exceeding 5,000 examples.

"One great thing about spending time with Harry is that you come away with some great 'Harry' stories. People who have met him trade these stories like bubble gum cards. Each person tries to have the most outrageous story to tell. I brought back some good ones."

Connie Swaim, Editor, Eastern Edition, *AntiqueWeek*

"He was brash, he was iconoclastic, he was funny, and above all, he was thought provoking."

Cheryl York-Cail, *Unravel the Gavel*

ABBREVIATIONS

3D = three-dimensional
4to = 8" x 10"
8vo = 5" x 7"
12mo = 3" x 5"
ADS = autograph document signed
adv = advertising or advertisement
ALS = autograph letter signed
AOG = all over gold
AP = album page signed
approx = approximately
AQS = autograph quotation signed
C = century
c = circa
cov = cover or covered
CS = card signed
cts = carats
d = depth or diameter
dec = decorated or decoration
dj = dust jacket
dwt = penny weight
DS = document signed
ed = edition
emb = embossed
ext = exterior
FDC = first day cover
FH = flat handle
folio = 12" x 16"
ft = foot or feet
ftd = footed
g = gram
gal = gallon
ground = background
h = height
HH = hollow handle
hp = hand painted
illus = illustrated, illustration, or illustrator
imp = impressed
int = interior
j = jewels
K = karat or kilobyte
l = length
lb = pound

litho = lithograph or lithographed
LS = letter signed
mfg = manufactured, manufacturer, or manufacturing
mg = milligram
MIB = mint in box
MIP = mint in package
MISB = mint in sealed box
mkd = marked
mm = millimeter
MOC = mint on card
NM = near mint
NMIB = near mint in box
NMOC = near mint on card
No. = number
NOS = new old stock
opal = opalescent
orig = original
oz = ounce
pat = patent
pc(s) = piece or pieces
pkg = package or packaging
pp = printed pages
pr = pair
PS = photograph signed
pt = pint
qt = quart
rect = rectangular
sgd = signed
SP = silver plated
sq = square
SS = sterling silver
ST = stainless
TLS = typed letter signed
unmkd = unmarked
unsgd = unsigned
Vol = Volume
vol = volumes
w = width
wg = white gold
yg = yellow gold
# = number

CONTENTS

INTRODUCTION

Welcome to the fourth edition of *The Official Rinker Price Guide to Collectibles.* This starship continues to explore new frontiers in the collecting universe, boldly going where no collectibles price guide has gone before. This edition has explored a number of new frontiers and recharted almost all of the known worlds, making the map of the collecting universe easier to follow than before.

As the 21st century begins, the dramatic shift in the antiques and collectibles market continues. Antique prices are extremely stable. There is no longer a need for an annual antiques price guide. Collectibles are the hot portion of the antiques marketplace. They are trendy. Collectible pricing is in a constant state of flux. If you fail to keep up with these price shifts annually, you are at a decided disadvantage whether auctioneer, collector, dealer, decorator, or simple enthusiast.

How does the *The Official Rinker Price Guide to Collectibles* differ from other general antiques and collectibles price guides? First, it focuses on the heart of today's antiques, collectibles, and desirables market—the period between 1920 and the present. Between 80% and 85% of all the material found at auctions, flea markets, antiques malls, shops, and shows dates from this period. Further, today's collectors are primarily 20th-century collectors.

Each year the percentage of individuals collecting 18th- and 19th-century material compared to the whole grows less and less. While there will always be collectors for this early material, they will need deep pocketbooks. Pre-1920 antiques are expensive. Most post-1920 antiques, collectibles, and desirables are both affordable and readily available.

Second, it is comprehensive. This book is filled with the things with which your parents, you, and your children lived and played. Nothing is missing. You will find furniture, decorative accessories, and giftware along with the traditional character and personality items, ceramics, glass, and toys. It is a complete document of the 20th-century American lifestyle.

Third, because *The Official Rinker Price Guide to Collectibles* is an annual publication, it is capable of responding more quickly to market changes and developments. It contains dozens of categories not found in its only competitor. Categories are constantly being restructured and reorganized so that they accurately reflect how things are collected in today's antiques and collectibles market.

I will never be accused of complacency because of what this book contains—no same-old, same-old here. Every category is put to the test. If it no longer has collecting validity, it is dropped or merged into a general category. A dozen new categories appear for the first time, another indication of how rapidly the collectibles market changes.

Fourth, over the years I have developed a reputation in the trade for being extremely opinionated and outspoken. I call 'em like I see 'em. I am not a member of the "if you can't say something nice, don't say anything at all" school.

As a reporter, my job is to present the facts and to interpret them. You will not find any artificial price propping in this book. If prices within a category are being manipulated or highly speculative, I spell it out. Whether you agree or not is not the issue. Unlike the good news price guides, the *The Official Rinker Price Guide to Collectibles* is designed to make you think.

ANTIQUES, COLLECTIBLES, & DESIRABLES

The Official Rinker Price Guide to Collectibles contains antiques, collectibles, and desirables. This being the case, why doesn't this book have a different title? The answer is twofold. When most individuals think of things made in the 20th century, they think of collectibles. People do not like to admit that objects associated with their childhood have become antiques. Further, not everyone, especially manufacturers of contemporary collectors' editions and giftware, separates collectibles and desirables into two different categories. They prefer them lumped together.

What is an antique, a collectible, and a desirable? An antique is anything made before 1945. A collectible is something made between 1945 and the late 1970s. Antiques and collectibles have a stable secondary resale market. A desirable is something made after 1980. Desirables have a speculative secondary resale market.

As each year passes, the number of people who disagree with my definition of an antique lessens. The year 1945 is an important dividing line. Life in America in 1938 was very different than life in America in 1948. The immediate post–World War II period witnessed the arrival of the suburbs, transfer of wartime technology, e.g., injection molding, into domestic production, television, women in the work force, a global view, and, most importantly, the birth of the Baby Boomers.

Today, there are three generations of adult collectors who grew up in the post-1945 time period—those whose childhood (by my definition the period between ages 7 and 14) occurred between 1945 and 1960, between 1960 and the mid-1970s, and between the mid-1970s and the late 1980s. Half of today's population was born after 1960. All they know about John F. Kennedy is what they read in history books. They cannot answer the question: Where were you when you heard JFK was shot?

I used to define a collectible as something made between 1945 and 1962. I have now extended the end date to the late 1970s. The reason is Rinker's Thirty-Year Rule: "For the first thirty years of anything's life, all its value is speculative." It takes thirty years to establish a viable secondary resale market. Some early 1970s objects, especially in vintage clothing, costume jewelry, and movie, music, and television memorabilia, have achieved a stable secondary market. The number is only going to increase.

Will there come a time when I have to move the antique date forward? The answer is yes. I strongly suspect that by 2010, material from the 1950s will definitely be considered antique. However, 2010 is ten years in the future. In the interim, a collectible remains an object made between 1945 and the late 1970s.

America is a nation of collectors. There are more collectors than non-collectors. However, not everyone collects antiques and collectibles. Many individuals collect contemporary objects ranging from Hallmark ornaments to collectors' edition whiskey bottles. These are the desirables. It is as important to report on the market value of desirables as it is antiques and collectibles.

I do not care what someone collects. All I care about is that they collect. The joy of collecting comes from the act of collecting. I resent those who make value judgments relative to what is and is not worth collecting. I know Avon collectors who are far more caring, willing to share, and knowledgeable of the history and importance of their objects than wealthy collectors whose homes are filled with Colonial period furniture and accessories. There is no room for snobbery in today's collecting community. You will find none in this book.

Manufacturers of desirables market them as collectibles. They are not collectibles as I define the term. Desirables have not stood the test of time. Some undoubtedly will become collectibles and even eventually antiques. However, the vast majority will not. Their final resting place is more likely to be a landfill than a china cabinet or shelf.

The Official Rinker Price Guide to Collectibles reports on objects in play, i.e., things that are currently being bought and sold actively in the secondary market. Desirables are as much in play as antiques and collectibles. Hence, they belong in this book.

ORGANIZATION

Categories: Objects are listed alphabetically by category beginning with Abingdon Pottery and ending with Zsolnay pottery. In the past decade, dozens of collectible subcategories, e.g., Barbie and Star Wars, have evolved as full-blown, independent collecting categories. This book's categories clearly illustrate the manner in which objects are being collected at the beginning of the 21st century.

If you have trouble locating an object, check the index. We strive to make it as comprehensive as possible. Collectibles are multifaceted, i.e., they can be assigned to more than one category. A 1949 C&O Railroad calendar picturing Chessie and her kittens playing with a toy train would be equally at home in the Advertising Character, Calendar, Cat, Illustrator, Railroad, or Toy Train categories. Such objects have been extensively cross-referenced. Do not give up after checking your first and second classification choices. Most post-1920 objects cross over into six or more collecting categories.

Category Introduction: An object has many values. Financial is only one of them. The pleasure of owning an object and the nostalgic feelings it evokes are others.

It is a proven fact that the more that is known about an object, the more its value increases. It is for this reason that the histories found in this book are more substantial than those found in other general price guides. Every object has multiple stories attached to it—who made it, when it was made, how it was made, how it was used, why it was saved, etc. The histories answer many of these questions.

Occasionally one or two additional pieces of information—collecting tips and/or market trends—are included with the history. You will not find these insider tips in other general price guides. Of all the information found in this book, these may prove to be the most valuable of all.

References: In many cases, you will find the information you seek in this book. What happens when you do not? Where do you turn next? The answer is the references listed in this book.

Each reference listing contains the name of the author, complete title, edition if appropriate, publisher, and publishing date of the book. This information will enable you to purchase the book, locate it at a library, or have the location of a copy researched through interlibrary loan.

Two principal criteria—availability and quality of information, descriptions, and pricing—were used to select the books that are listed. Almost every book listed is still in print. An occasional exception was made for a seminal work in the category.

Unfortunately, the antiques and collectibles field is plagued with price guides that are nothing more than poorly done point-and-shoot priced picture books or whose prices in no way reflect true market values. They are not listed as references in this book even though they are in print.

Accuracy of information is one of the main hallmarks of this book. Nothing is gained by referencing a source that does not adhere to these same high standards. *The Official Rinker Price Guide to Collectibles* is designed to earn your trust. Carefully selecting the references is only one example of that commitment.

David J. Maloney, Jr.'s *Maloney's Antiques & Collectibles Resource Directory*, published by Antique Trader Books, now part of Krause, is the most important reference book, next to this one of course, in the field. Buy it. I wear out a copy a year. If you use it properly, so will you.

Periodicals and Newsletters: A list of general antiques and collectibles trade periodicals with full addresses and telephone numbers is part of this book's front matter. The periodicals and newsletters listed within a category relate specifically to that category. They are the first place to turn when looking for further information about that category.

Collectors' Clubs: Collectors' clubs play a vital role in the collecting field. They put collectors in touch with one another. Their newsletters contain information simply not found elsewhere. Their annual conventions allow for an exchange of information and objects. Their membership lists are often a who's who within the category.

Trying to keep track of the correct mailing address for a collectors' club is a full-time job. A club's address changes when its officers change. In some clubs, this occurs annually. The address provided has been checked and double-checked. Hopefully, it is current.

A few individuals and manufacturers have created collectors' clubs as sales fronts. With a few exceptions, e.g., Royal Doulton, these are not listed. The vast majority of clubs listed have an elected board of directors and operate as non-profit organizations.

Reproduction Alert: Reproductions (an exact copy of a period piece), copycats (a stylistic reproduction), fantasy items (in a shape or form that did not exist during the initial period of manufacture or licensing), and fakes (deliberately meant to deceive) are becoming a major problem within the antiques and collectibles field. It would require a book more than double the size of this one to list all the objects that fall within these categories.

Reproduction alerts have been placed throughout the book to serve as a reminder that problems exist more than to document every problem that exists. Do not assume that when no reproduction alert appears, the category is free of the problem. Assume every category has a problem. Make any object you are purchasing prove to you that it is right.

The *Antique & Collectors Reproduction News* (PO Box 12130, Des Moines, IA 50312, annual subscription $32) is a publication devoted to keeping track of current reproductions, copycats, fantasy items, and fakes. Consider subscribing.

Listings: The object descriptions and value listings are the heart and soul of this book. Listings contain the details necessary to specifically identify an object. Unlike some price guides whose listings are confined to one line, this guide sets no limit other than to provide the amount of information needed to do the job right. While this approach results in fewer listings, it raises the accuracy and comprehension level significantly. Better to be safe than sorry.

Each category's listings are only a sampling of the items found in that category. Great care has been taken to select those objects that are commonly found in the market. A few high-end objects are included to show the price range within a category. However, no price guide has value if the list-ed objects cannot be found or are priced so high few can afford them.

If you do not find the specific object you are seeking, look for comparable objects similar in description to the one that you own. A general price guide's role is to get you into the ballpark and up to the plate. Great care has been taken in each category to provide listings that represent a broad range of items within a collecting category. Ideally, when looking for a comparable, you should find two or more objects that fit the bill.

The listing format is quick and easy to use. It was selected following a survey of general price guide users. Surprisingly, it allows for more listings per page than an indented system.

Auction Price Boxes: While the values provided in this price guide come from a wide variety of sources, people continually ask, "What does it sell for at auction?" A partial answer to this question is found in the Auction Prices boxes scattered throughout this book.

The assumption is that the highest values are achieved at auction. This is not the case. Dealers purchase a large percentage of objects sold at auction. This is why all auction prices are carefully evaluated and adjusted when necessary before being used in the general listings of this price guide.

The auction boxes are also designed to introduce you to auction houses with which you may not be familiar. There are hundreds of great regional and specialized auction houses conducting catalog sales throughout the United States. I am pleased to help you make their acquaintance.

Index: The index is a road map that shows you the most direct route to the information you are seeking. Take a moment and study it. Like any road map, the more you use it the more proficient you will become.

When researching your object, always start with the broadest general category. If this proves unsuccessful, try specific forms of the object and/or its manufacturer. Remember, because of their multifaceted nature, 20th-century collectibles are at home in multiple categories. Perseverance pays.

Illustrations: Great care has been taken in selecting the illustrations that appear in this book. They are not just fill. Illustrations indicate the type of object or objects commonly found in the category. They come from a variety of sources—auction houses, authors, field photography, and mail and trade catalogs.

This book provides caption information directly beside or beneath the illustration. You do not have to hunt for it in the text listings as you do in some other guides.

The Rinker Enterprises staff works hard to change the illustrations that appear in each edition. This is why you should retain and not discard previous editions of this book, titled *The Official Rinker Price Guide to Collectibles.* When saved in series, they are a valuable identification and priced picture book to collectibles.

PRICE NOTES

The values in this book are based on an object being in very good to fine condition. This means that the object is complete and shows no visible signs of aging and wear when held at arm's length. If the value is based on a condition other than very good or fine, the precise condition is included in the descriptive listing.

Prices are designed to reflect the prices that sellers at an antiques mall or collectibles show would ask for their merchandise. When an object is collected nationally, it is possible to determine a national price consensus. Most of the objects in this book fall into that category. There are very few 20th-century collectibles whose values are regionally driven. Even racing collectibles, once collected primarily in the South, have gone national.

There are no fixed prices in the antiques and collectibles market. Value is fluid, not absolute. Price is very much of the time and circumstance. Change either, change the price. *The Official Rinker Price Guide to Collectibles* is a price guide. That is all it is—a guide. It should be used to confirm, not set prices.

Must the original box or packaging accompany an object for it to be considered complete? While some would argue that the answer is yes, especially for post-1980s material, this book is based on the assumption that the box and object are two separate entities. If the price given includes the box, the presence of the box is noted in the description.

Prices represent the best judgment of the Rinker Enterprises staff after carefully reviewing all the available price source information related to the collecting category. It is not required that an object actually be sold during the past year to be listed in this book. If this policy was followed, users would have a distorted view of the market. Sales of common objects are rarely documented. A book based solely on reported prices would be far too oriented toward the middle and high ends of the market.

Instead, each category's listings have been carefully selected to reflect those objects within the category that are currently available in the antiques and collectibles market. Commonly found objects comprise the bulk of the listings. A few hard-to-find and scarce examples are included. These show the category's breadth and price range.

PRICE SOURCES

The values found in this book come from a wide variety of sources—auctions, dealers, direct sale catalogs and lists, field research, the Internet, private individuals, and trade periodicals. All prices are carefully reviewed and adjusted to reflect fair market retail value.

Several criteria are used in deciding what sources to track. All sections of the country must be represented. This is a national, not a regional, price guide. The sources must be reliable. Listings must be specific. Prices must be consistent,

not only within the source but when compared to other national price sources. There must be a constant flow of information from the sources. Auctions held by collectors' clubs at their annual conventions are the one exception.

ADVISORS

While not creating a formal Board of Advisors for this fourth edition, I did request information from experts for a few categories. When the listings in a category are exclusively from this information, I have included their name and address in an "Advisor" heading at the bottom of the category introduction.

However, do not assume for one moment that I lacked or failed to seek advice from hundreds of antiques mall managers, appraisers, auctioneers, authors, dealers, private collectors, show promoters, and others during the preparation of this book. During the twenty-plus years in which I have been actively involved in the antiques and collectibles field, I have established a network of individuals upon whom I can call whenever a question arises. In many cases, my contacts within a collecting category are several individuals strong.

AMERICANA VERSUS INTERNATIONALISM

Americana, defined as things typical of America, is an obsolete term. It should be dropped from our collecting vocabulary.

First, the entire world is rapidly becoming Americanized. American movies, music, and television play as major a role outside as they do inside America. Burger King, Foot Locker, McDonald's, and Toys 'R Us have gone global. Barbie has a far higher worldwide recognition factor than any human personality.

Second, foreign collectors are not content to only collect objects produced and licensed in their countries. America is the great mother lode of 20th-century collectibles. When African, European, Far Eastern, or South American collectors want Star Wars memorabilia, they come to America to buy. The role played by foreign buyers in the antiques and collectibles market continues to increase.

Third, thanks to the Internet, most individuals need only turn on their computers to sell and buy collectibles anywhere in the world. The Internet is not limited by international boundaries. It is turning us into world citizens no matter what our personal preferences.

Finally, many "American" goods are manufactured offshore or contain parts that were made abroad. Defining something as being distinctly American is no longer easy. We live in an age when new designs can be copied within days of their appearance. Foreign manufacturers are quick to make products that look like the American form.

Let's delete "Americana" and send it to the trash bin.

A BUYER'S GUIDE, NOT A SELLER'S GUIDE

The Official Rinker Price Guide to Collectibles is a buyer's guide. Values reflect what someone should expect to pay for an object he wishes to purchase.

This book is not a seller's guide. Do not be mistaken and assume that it is. If you have an object listed in this book and wish to sell it, expect to receive 30% to 40% of the price listed if the object is commonly found and 50% to 60% if the object is harder to find. Do not assume that a collector will pay more. In the 2000s antiques and collectibles market, collectors expect to pay what a dealer would pay for merchandise when buying privately.

Also, there is no guarantee that you will do better at auction. First, you will pay a commission for selling your goods. Second, dealers buy the vast majority of antiques and collectibles sold at auction. They certainly are not going to resell them for what they paid for them.

The method most likely to result in your selling objects for the values found in this book is to become an antiques dealer. This is not as easy as it sounds. Selling antiques and collectibles is hard work.

There is no one best way to sell antiques and collectibles. Much depends on how much time, effort, and money you wish to expend.

In the final analysis, a good price is one for which the buyer and seller are equally happy. Make as many of your purchases as possible win-win deals. Keep your focus on the object, not the buying and selling process.

COMMENTS INVITED

Every effort has been made to make this price guide useful and accurate. Your comments and suggestions, both positive and negative, are needed to make the next edition even better. Send them to: Rinker Enterprises, Inc., 5093 Vera Cruz Road, Emmaus, PA 18049.

ACKNOWLEDGMENTS

The bridge crew of the starship Rinker Enterprises remains unchanged. The crew is experienced and remains committed to bringing you the highest quality product available. Dana Morykan, my Number One, piloted the starship during the preparation of this book. She was ably assisted by Kathy Williamson and Dena George in the preparation of listings and selection and scanning of the illustrations. Nancy Butt was responsible for checking the reference information that appears in the category introductions. As in the past, this book represents their combined efforts and mine. Credit belongs to all, not to one.

Also, my appreciation to Virginia Reinbold for charting a black route for my starship rather than the more traditional red one. Richard "Cap" Schmeltzle does a top-notch job as our maintenance crew chief.

Because of this able crew, I was able to increase my field appearances, thus providing me with an even broader insight of the national market. Many of these appearances involved my participation in verbal appraisal clinics. There is no better way to find out what objects are in peoples' homes, what they want to know about, and make certain this is the book that best answers their needs.

The success of this book relies heavily on cooperation from hundreds of auctioneers, auction houses, collectors, dealers, trade publications' staffs, and others associated with the antiques and collectibles industry. Virtually every request for help was answered. Whenever possible, I have thanked you personally. For those I missed, please accept these printed thanks until next we meet.

This past year produced great media exposure. Television appearances ranged from *Home Matters* to *Martha Stewart Living*. I now work on a regular basis with six radio stations, KFGO (Fargo, ND), KLTF (Little Falls, MN), KROC (Rochester, MN), WGEE (Green Bay, WI), WNPV (Lansdale, PA), and WSAU (Wausau, WI), doing an hour-long version of **Whatcha Got,** my antiques and collectibles radio call-in show. The shows on KFGO and KROC are broadcast live on the Internet. Several syndicated news stories and articles appearing in national periodicals touted the book. Readership for "Show & Tell," my regular column in *Country Home* magazine, continues to grow. To everyone in the media, thanks for your support.

This past year House of Collectibles was transferred from Random House's Ballantine Publishing Group to its Crown Publishing Group. Linda Loewenthal, Laura Paczosa, and Liz Matthews made certain the transition was a smooth one. As the final pages of this edition were being prepared and continuing its commitment to the long-term growth of this title, Laura informed us that the contract for this book's fifth edition was in the mail.

It is an honor to have the Rinker Enterprises titles in the same division as the Kovels. We look forward to working with the editorial, production, promotion, and sales staffs at Crown. Our initial experience has shown them to be a highly professional support team. As always, we especially appreciate their willingness to include us in the decision-making process.

Finally, my thanks to all who have purchased previous editions of this book. I appreciate your vote of confidence. As I have in the past, I pledge my efforts and those of the Rinker Enterprises staff to ensuring that this and future editions of *The Official Rinker Price Guide to Collectibles* continue to earn your support and loyalty.

Rinker Enterprises, Inc.
5093 Vera Cruz Road
Emmaus, PA 18049

Harry L. Rinker
Author
June 2000

STATE OF THE MARKET

There was more change in the antiques and collectibles marketplace in the 1990s than the previous nine decades combined. The typical 2000 collector is very different from the typical 1990 collector. The personal computer and the Internet introduced important new selling, buying, and information sources. The market became extremely trendy, changing constantly as taste changed. The age of blue chip antiques is over. Brash new players ate established traditional players whole, e.g., eBay's purchase of Butterfield & Butterfield.

Breathe a sigh of relief. No new instruments of change appear on the horizon. The critical issue now is how will the implementation of change impact on the antiques and collectibles trade. The impact will continue to be major. The trade is being redefined over a vast spectrum, ranging from what is and is not worth collecting to how objects are bought and sold.

While the antiques and collectibles market is stronger than ever, the boom market is over. Prices are strong, but stable. "Steady" best describes the market at the moment. Market confidence is at an all-time high across the board. Credit the current strong American economy. Individuals appear quite willing to spend their disposable income on antiques and collectibles.

It is time to divide the post-1945 period into three distinct collecting periods, 1945 to 1963, 1964 to 1980, and the 1980s and 1990s. The death of JFK is the watershed that divides the first period from the second. The psychedelic era and the Vietnam War dominate the second. I do not like using decade years to define periods because I think they are artificial. At the moment, the decades of the 1980s and 1990s lack clear definition, largely because we are still too close to them. In time, perhaps a more appropriate year to mark the end of the second period and beginning of the third will emerge. For the moment, I am going to stick with 1980.

It is critical to remember that when defining a collecting period, I concentrate not on the generation born during that period but those who grew up in the period. I was born in 1941 but grew up in the first of the post-1945 collecting periods. The first Baby Boomers, who have now turned fifty, grew up in the second half of that period.

While not ancient history, the 1950s became a great deal older perception-wise when the 21st century began than when it was still part of the 20th century. The movie, music, and television stars of the era are dying. This past year Gene Autry, Clayton Moore (The Lone Ranger), and Roy Rogers joined Bill Boyd in the great corral in the sky. Their passing heralded the end of the TV cowboys who dominated the tube in the late 1940s through the mid-1950s.

The psychedelic Sixties is the hot decade of the moment. But, watch out for the 1970s. There are plenty of signs it is hot and getting hotter. It will seriously challenge the 1960s for market dominance by 2002 or 2003 and should be the clear winner by 2006 or 2007. This is continued proof that much of the market is nostalgia driven. As individuals mature, they become obsessed with buying back their childhood.

The market is now very decade driven. When an object speaks to a decade, i.e., you look at it and think, now that is Fifties, Sixties, etc., it sells at a far stronger price than generic utilitarian objects from the same time. Think pink and black. It is the 1950s. Think avocado and rust. It is the late Sixties, early Seventies. You get the picture.

This phenomenon is not decorator driven. Decorators continue to emphasize Country, Post-War Modernism, and traditional Colonial with a little French Provincial and Mediterranean added for good measure. Decade decorating is a mass movement that promises to challenge Country for decorating dominance. Heaven help us all if the decorators adopt it and try to make it their own.

Corporate consolidation achieved record levels in 1999 and the first quarter of 2000. Krause Publications purchased Landmark Specialty Publications. It merged Number One with Number Two. Krause's antiques and collectibles virtual empire of trade periodicals, publishing, shows, etc., appears unassailable. Having said this, the question I hear most often is: "Who will buy Krause?" Last year, I would have said impossible. Now, I am not so certain.

In the auction community, eBay bought Butterfield & Butterfield and Kruse, both from under the nose of Amazon. Phillips purchased Selkirk's in St. Louis. When the price fixing investigation of Christie's and Sotheby's was made public, rumors immediately flew about eBay offering to buy Sotheby's and what would Amazon do to stop it. Should the market be concerned that Internet companies less than ten years old have become so powerful that they can purchase institutions in the trade that are more than half a century old? Yes, it should. The management of these Internet companies has little to no antiques and collectibles field experience. Profit and the bottom line rule. What is good for the trade is a secondary consideration.

As eBay's influence continues to go, the key word is "alliances." Skinner's linked its fortunes to Yahoo. Sloan's "merged" with Antique Networking. Sotheby's announced it was developing a joint site with Amazon while developing its own independent second site. Sotheby's has signed up hundreds of other auction houses and dealers as Internet "partners" on its sight. Many auction houses and dealers have opted to go it alone, a questionable decision in an Internet that is so crowded that it is hard to find even the established players.

The Internet is more than eBay, a situation still poorly understood by many. Alternate auction sites such as Yahoo and Amazon are not going away. Watch for several major eBay auction alternatives to be in place within two years. Direct sale, i.e., antiques and collectibles Internet storefront sites, continue to attract new sellers and buyers. Check out antiqnet.com, carters.com.au, collectoronline.com, icollector.com, kaleden.com, rubylane.com, and tias.com. Do not be surprised if one or more of these sites merge during the next year. Tias recently purchased AntiqueAlley.

So much focus has been placed on the existing players that few are asking, "Who is waiting in the wings?" Large publishing houses, e.g., Germany's Bertlesman, media giants such at England's Daily Mail Group and Murdoch, and giant Internet companies, such as Microsoft, are just a few possibilities. In five years, expect many of the current players to be replaced by new entities.

There is no question that the Internet has introduced a new level of internationalism to the antiques and collectibles trade from ownership of Internet sites to worldwide buyers. This past year I made trips to Australia, Canada, and Germany to talk with corporations and individuals about antiques and collectibles on the Internet. In March 2000 a group from Australia flew to Rinker Enterprises in Vera Cruz, Pennsylvania, to meet with a second group who came from Canada and England to talk about cooperative Internet ventures.

The Internet also is profoundly affecting collecting categories. It has redefined the concept of scarcity. Many objects thought scarce by collectors are turning out to be extremely common. Examples have flooded the market in several categories, collapsing existing market pricing, especially for readily found items. It is common for final Internet sale prices to be significantly below book. Check Hummel sales. Putting aside the large number of items that go unsold, most prices are less than half the values found in Robert Miller's *The No. 1 Price Guide to M.I. Hummel: Figurines, Plates, More....*, the established price guide to Hummels.

Having stated this, it is fair to question how accurately Internet prices reflect market price, at least for now. Prices asked for the same objects at antiques and collectibles flea markets, malls, and shows remain closer to established book prices. Not everyone has access to the Internet.

The Internet is contributing to the Americanizing of the world. American, not English, is the language of the Internet. Cheap telephone access currently provides Americans with a tremendous Internet advantage. This will change significantly in the next two to three years.

After 1945, the entire world was influenced by three things—American movies, music, and television. During my trip to Australia, I purchased a number of post-1945 Australian collectibles based on licensed American television shows. The prices for lady head planters corresponded exactly to American book prices. I learned from an antiques mall owner that anodized aluminum is hot. He said every airline stewardess who visited his shop seeking material to take home and resell asked about it.

This past year provided more than ample proof that the Internet will not replace traditional buy-sell sources. Antiques and collectibles flea markets, malls, trade publications and periodicals, shops, and shows survived. Yet, these traditional sources have learned that the key to survival is to find ways to incorporate the Internet into their traditional operations. Companies, such as Go2Sell.com, are contracting with malls to place Internet consignment operations within their facilities.

Show and mall owners and promoters discovered that antiques and collectibles no longer sell themselves. They must now schedule promotions that turn a visit to their venues into an event. Offering verbal appraisal clinics a la "The Antiques Road Show" and educational seminars are just two examples.

This past year was the best year ever for antiques and collectibles exposure in the national media. Led by PBS's "The Antiques Road Show," more than half a dozen antiques and collectibles television programs can now be found on cable television. Everyone is getting in on the act. I now do five weekly antiques and collectibles radio call-in shows. Do not assign this trend too much importance. Nothing is trendier than the media. Antiques and collectibles programming is hot now. It will not be in ten, maybe even as few as five years. Just look at Fox's "Personal FX."

Kudos to Jim and Yvonne Tucker for staging another highly successful antiques and collectibles educational seminar in January 2000 in Orlando. As I did in last year's "State of the Market Report," I encourage everyone to consider joining either the National Association of Collectors or the Antiques and Collectibles Dealers Association. Information about both is available by calling 1-800-287-7127.

As I hinted at last year, several Rinker Enterprises information blocks can now be accessed on the Internet at www.kaleden.com. Currently, you will find a pictorial price guide, past issues of "The Rinker Report," and ninety-second "Whatcha Got" audio clips. There will be more. Do not forget to check out www.rinker.com where you will find "Rinker on Collectibles" columns, my travel schedule, and a host of other information.

My and Rinker Enterprises' future is more than the computer screen I am staring at as I write this State of the Market report. While there is no question that the computer will play an increasing role, so too will an increased personal appearance schedule, consulting commitments to several key trade players, and a growing list of new books, columns, and articles; possibly even a newsletter.

When do I sleep? When you are having this much fun, you do not need sleep.

ANTIQUES & COLLECTIBLES PERIODICALS

Rinker Enterprises receives the following general and regional periodicals. Periodicals covering a specific collecting category are listed in the introductory material for that category.

NATIONAL MAGAZINES

*Antique Trader's Collector
   Magazine & Price Guide*
PO Box 1050
Dubuque, IA 52004-1050
(800) 334-7165
web: traderpr@mwci.net

Antiques & Collecting Magazine
1006 South Michigan Avenue
Chicago, IL 60605
(800) 762-7576
fax: (312) 939-0053
e-mail: LightnerPb@aol.com

Collectors' Eye
6 Woodside Avenue
Suite 300
Northport, NY 11768
(516) 261-4100
fax: (516) 261-9684
web: www.collectorseye.com

Collectors' Showcase
7134 South Yale Avenue
Suite 720
Tulsa, OK 74136
(800) 310-7047
e-mail: sirtm@msn.com

*Country Accents Collectibles,
   Flea Market Finds*
Goodman Media Group, Inc
419 Park Avenue South
New York, NY 10016
(800) 955-3870

NATIONAL NEWSPAPERS

The Antique Trader Weekly
PO Box 1050
Dubuque, IA 52004-1050
(800) 334-7165
fax: (800) 531-0880
web: www.collect.com
e-mail: rojemannb@krause.com

*Antique Week (Central and
   Eastern Editions)*
27 North Jefferson Street
PO Box 90
Knightstown, IN 46148
(800) 876-5133
fax: (800) 695-8153
web: www.antiqueweek.com
e-mail: antiquewk@aol.com

Antiques and the Arts Weekly
The Bee Publishing Company
PO Box 5503
5 Church Hill Road
Newtown, CT 06470-5503
(203) 426-8036
fax: (203) 426-1394
web: www.thebee.com
e-mail: info@thebee.com

Collectors News
506 Second Street
PO Box 306
Grundy Center, IA 50638
(800) 352-8039
fax: (319) 824-3414
web: collectors-news.com
e-mail: collectors@collectors-news.com

Maine Antique Digest
911 Main Street
PO Box 1429
Waldoboro, ME 04572
(207) 832-4888
fax: (207) 832-7341
web: www.maineantiquedigest.com
e-mail: mad@maine.com

Warman's Today's Collector
Krause Publications
700 East State Street
Iola, WI 54990
(800) 258-0929
fax: (715) 445-4087
web: www.krause.com
e-mail: todays_collector@krause.com

REGIONAL NEWSPAPERS

New England

Cape Cod Antiques Monthly
PO Box 546
Farmington, NH 03835
(603) 755-4568

The Fine Arts Trader
PO Box 1273
Randolph, MA 02368
(800) 332-5055
fax: (781) 961-9044
web: www.fineartstrader.com

MassBay Antiques
254 Second Avenue
Needham, MA 02494
(800) 982-4023
e-mail: mbantiques@cnc.com

New England Antiques Journal
4 Church Street
PO Box 120
Ware, MA 01082
(800) 432-3505
fax: (413) 967-6009
web: www.antiquesjournal.com
e-mail: visit@antiquesjournal.com

*New Hampshire Antiques
   Monthly*
PO Box 546
Farmington, NH 03835-0546
(603) 755-4568

Treasure Chest
564 Eddy Street
Suite 326
Providence, RI 02903
(800) 557-9662
fax: (401) 272-9422

Unravel the Gavel
14 Hurricane Road, #1
Belmont, NH 03220
(603) 524-4281
fax: (603) 528-3565
web: www.thegavel.net
e mail: gavel96@worldpath.net

The Vermont Antique Times
2434 Depot Street
PO Box 1880
Manchester Center, VT 05255
(800) 542-4224
e-mail: antique@vermontel.net

Middle Atlantic States

Antiques & Auction News
Route 230 West
PO Box 500
Mount Joy, PA 17552
(717) 492-2541
fax: (717) 653-6165

Antiques Tattler (Adamstown)
PO Box 938
Adamstown, PA 19501

New York City's Antique News
PO Box 2054
New York, NY 10159-5054
(212) 725-0344
fax: (212) 532-7294

New York-Pennsylvania Collector
73 Buffalo Street
Canandaigua, NY 14424-1001
(800) 836-1868
fax: (716) 394-7725

Northeast Journal of Antiques & Art
364 Warren Street
PO Box 37
Hudson, NY 12534
(518) 828-1616
(800) 836-4069
fax: (518) 828-3870
web: www.northeast journal.com
e-mail: nejourl@mhonline.net

Renninger's Antique Guide
2 Cypress Place
PO Box 495
Lafayette Hill, PA 19444
(610) 828-4614
fax: (610) 834-1599
web: www.renningers.com

South

Antique Gazette
PO Box 1050
Dubuque, IA 52004-1050
(615) 352-0941
fax: (615) 352-0941

The Antique Shoppe
PO Box 2175
Keystone Heights, FL 32656
(352) 475-1679
fax: (352) 475-5326
web: www.antiquenet.com/
  antiqueshoppe
e-mail: EDSOPER@aol.com

*The Antique Shoppe of the
  Carolinas*
PO Box 640
Lancaster, SC 29721
(800) 210-7253
fax: (803) 283-8969
e-mail: lanenewsadv@infave.net

Carolina Antique News
PO Box 241114
Charlotte, NC 28224
(704) 553-2865
fax: (704) 643-3960
e-mail: publishr@concentric.net
web: www.antiquestoday.com

Cotton & Quail Antique Trail
205 East Washington Street
PO Box 326
Monticello, FL 32345
(800) 757-7755
fax: (850) 997-3090
e-mail: cottonq@worldnet.att.net

MidAtlantic Antiques Magazine
500 West Jefferson Street
PO Box 5040
Monroe, NC 28111
(704) 289-1541
fax: (704) 289-2929
e-mail: MAAntiques@TheEJ.com

*The Old News Is Good News
  Antiques Gazette*
41429 West I-55 Service Road
PO Box 305
Hammond, LA 70404
(504) 429-0575
fax: (504) 429-0576
e mail: gazette@i–55.com

*Southeastern Antiquing and
  Collecting Magazine*
PO Box 510
Acworth, GA 30301
(770) 974-6495 or
(888) 388-7827
web: www.go-star.com
e-mail: antiquing@go-star.com

Southern Antiques
PO Drawer 1107
Decatur, GA 30031
(404) 289-0054
fax: (404) 286-9727
web: www.kaleden.com
e-mail: southernantiques@msn.com

The Vintage Times
PO Box 7567
Macon, GA 31209
(888) 757-4755
web: www.mylink.met\~antiques
e-mail: antiques@mylink.net

Midwest

The American Antiquities Journal
126 East High Street
Springfield, OH 45502
(937) 322-6281
fax: (937) 322-0294
web: www.americanantiquities.com
e-mail: MAIL@americanantiquities.com

*The Antique Collector and
  Auction Guide*
Weekly Section of *Farm and
  Dairy*
185-205 East State Street
Box 38
Salem, OH 44460
(330) 337-3419
fax: (330) 337-9550
web: farmanddairy.com

Antique Review
12 East Stafford Street
PO Box 538
Worthington, OH 43085
(614) 885-9757 or
(800) 992-9757
fax: (614) 885-9762
web: www.antiquereviewohio.com
e-mail: editor@antiquereviewohio.com

Auction Action Antique News
1404½ East Green Bay Street
Shawano, WI 54166
(715) 524-3076
fax: (800) 580-4568
web: www.auctionactionnews.com
e-mail: auction@auctionaction
  news.com

The Auction Exchange
929 Industrial Parkway
PO Box 57
Plainwell, MI 49080-0057
(616) 685-1343
fax: (616) 685-8840

Auction World
101 12th Street South
Box 227
Benson, MN 56215
(800) 750-0166
fax: (320) 843-3246
web: www.finfolink.morris.mn.us/
  ~jfield
e-mail: jfield@infolink.morris.mn.us

The Collector
PO Box 148
Heyworth, IL 61745
(309) 473-2466
fax: (309) 473-3610
e-mail: collinc@davesworld.net

Collectors Journal
1800 West D Street
PO Box 601
Vinton, IA 52349
(800) 472-4006
fax: (319) 474-3117
web: www.collectorsjournal.com
e-mail: antiquescj@aol.com

Discover Mid-America
400 Grand, Suite B
Kansas City, MO 64106
(800) 899-9730
fax: (816) 474-1427
web: discoverypub.com
e-mail: discopub@aol.com

Great Lakes Trader
132 South Putnam Street
Williamston, MI 48895
(800) 785-6367
fax: (517) 655-5380
web: GLTrader@aol.com

*Indiana Antique Buyer's News,
  Inc*
PO Box 213
Silver Lake, IN 46982
(219) 893-4200 or
(888) 834-2263
fax: (219) 893-4251
e-mail: iabn@hoosierlink.net

Ohio Collectors' Magazine
PO Box 1522
Piqua, OH 45356
(937) 773-6063
fax: (937) 773-6063
e-mail: ocm@wesnet.com

The Old Times
63 Birch Avenue South
PO Box 340
Maple Lake, MN 55358
(800) 539-1810
fax: (320) 963-6499
web: www.theoldtimes.com
e mail: oldtimes@lkdllink.net

Yesteryear
PO Box 2
Princeton, WI 54968
(920) 787-4808
fax: (920) 787-7381
e-mail: yesteryear@vbe.com

Southwest

*The Antique Register & Country
  Register, Inc.*
PO Box 84345
Phoenix, AZ 85071
(602) 942-8950
fax: (602) 866-3136
web: www.countryregister.com

The Antique Traveler
109 East Broad Street
PO Box 656
Mineola, TX 75773
(800) 446-3588
fax: (903) 569-9080
web: www.antiquetraveler.com
e-mail: antique@lakecountry.net

Arizona Antique News
PO Box 26536
Phoenix, AZ 85068
(602) 943-9137

Auction Weekly
PO Box 61104
Phoenix, AZ 85082
(480) 994-4512
fax: (800) 525-1407
web: www.auctionadvisory.com

West Coast

Antique & Collectables
500 Fensler, Suite 205
PO Box 12589
El Cajon, CA 92022
(619) 593-2925
fax: (619) 447-7187
web: www.collect.com/
  antiquesandcollectables
e-mail: antiquenews@aol.com

*Antique Journal for California
   and Nevada*
2329 Santa Clara Avenue, #207
Alameda, CA 94501
(800) 791-8592
fax: (510) 523-5262
web: www.collect.com/antiquejournal
e-mail: antiquesjrl@aol.com

*Antique Journal For the
   Northwest*
3439 North East Sandy Blvd
Suite 275
Portland, OR 97232
(888) 845-3200 or
(888) 523-5262
fax: (503) 284-6043
web: www.collect.com

Antiques Plus
PO Box 5467
Salem, OR 97304
(503) 391-7618
fax: (503) 391-2695
web: www.AntiquesPlus.com
e-mail: editor@antiquesplus.com

Collector
436 West 4th Street, Suite 222
Pomona, CA 91766
(909) 620-9014
fax: (909) 622-8152
web: www.collectorsconference.com
e-mail: lcollect@aol.com

Mountain States Collector
PO Box 2525
Evergreen, CO 80439
(303) 987-3994
fax: (303) 674-1253

Old Stuff
VBM Printers, Inc.
336 North Davis
PO Box 1084
McMinnville, OR 97128
(503) 434-5386
fax: (503) 435-0990
web: www.oldstuffnews.com
e-mail: millers@oldstuffnews.com

The Oregon Vintage Times
856 Lincoln #2
Eugene, OR 97401
(541) 484-0049
web: www.efn.org/~venus/antique/
   antique.html
e-mail: venus@efn.org

West Coast Peddler
PO Box 5134
Whittier, CA 90607
(562) 698-1718
fax: (562) 698-1500
web: www.WestCoastPeddler.com
e-mail: antiques@WestCoastPeddler.com

INTERNATIONAL NEWSPAPERS

Australia

Carter's Antiques & Collectables
Carter's Promotions Pty. Ltd.
Locked Bag 3
Terrey Hills, NSW 2084
Australia
(02) 9450 0011
fax: (02) 9450 2532
web: www.carters.com.au
e-mail: info@carters.com.au

Canada

Antique and Collectibles Trader
PO Box 38095
550 Eglinton Avenue West
Toronto, Ontario
Canada M5N 3A8
(416) 410-7620
fax: (416) 784-9796

Antique Showcase
Trajan Publishing Corp
103 Lakeshore Road, Suite 202
St. Catherines, Ontario
Canada L2N 2T6
(905) 646-7744
fax: (905) 646-0995
web: www.trajan.com
e-mail: office@trajan.com

Thompsons' Antiques Gazette
#50 - 39026 Range Road 275
Red Deer County, Alberta
Canada T4S 2A9
(403) 346-8791
fax: (403) 343-0242
web: www.antiquesalberta.com/
   thompsonantiques
e-mail: mthompso@agt.net

The Upper Canadian
PO Box 653
Smiths Falls, Ontario
Canada K7A 4T6
(613) 283-1168
fax: (613) 283-1345
web: www.uppercanadian.com
e-mail: uppercanadian@recorder.ca

England

Antiques Trade Gazette
Circulation Department
17 Whitcomb Street
London WC2H 7PL
(0171) 930 4957
fax: (0171) 930 6391
web: www.atg-online.com
e-mail: info@antiquestradegazette.com

Antiques & Art Independent
PO Box 1945
Comely Bank
Edinburgh, EH4 1AB
07000 765 263
fax: 07000 268 408
e-mail: antiquesnews@hotmail.com

Finland

Keräilyn Maailma
Vuorikatu 22 B 65
00100 Helsinki
(09) 170090

France

France Antiquités
Château de Boisrigaud
63490 Usson
(04) 73 71 00 04
e-mail: France.Antiquites@wanadoo.fr

La Vie du Collectionneur
B. P. 77
77302 Fontainbleau Cedex
(01) 60 71 55 55

Germany

Antiquitäten Zeitung
Nymphenburger Str. 84
D-80636 München
(089) 12 69 90-0

Sammler Journal
Journal-Verlag Schwend GmbH
Schmollerstrasse 31
D-74523 Schwäbisch Hall
(0791) 404-500
e-mail: info.sj@t-online.de

Sammler Markt
Der Heisse Draht
   Verlagsgesellschaft mbH & Co.
Drostestr. 14-16
D-30161 Hannover
(0511) 390 91-0
web: www.dhd.de/sammlermarkt/

Spielzeug Antik
Verlag Christian Gärtner
Ubierring 4
D-50678 Köln
(0221) 9322266

Tin Toy Magazin
Verlag, Redaktion, Anzeigen,
   Vertrieb
Mannheimer Str. 5
D-68309 Mannheim
(0621) 739687

Trödler & Sammeln
Gemi Verlags GmbH
Pfaffenhofener Strasse 3
D-85293 Reichertshausen
(08441) 4022-0
web: www.vpm.de/troedler

AUCTION HOUSES

The following companies generously supply Rinker Enterprises, Inc., with copies of their auction/sales lists, press releases, catalogs and illustrations, and prices realized. In addition, the auction houses in **bold** typeface graciously provide Rinker Enterprises, Inc. with photographs, digital images, and/or permission to scan images from their catalogs.

Sanford Alderfer Auction Co., Inc.
501 Fairgrounds Road
Hatfield, PA 19440
(215) 393-3000
fax: (215) 368-9055
web: www.alderfercompany.com
e-mail: auction@alderfercompany.com

American Social History and
    Social Movements
4025 Saline Street
Pittsburgh, PA 15217
(412) 421-5230
fax: (412) 421-0903

Arthur Auctioneering
563 Reed Road
Hughesville, PA 17737
(800) ARTHUR-3

Auction Team Köln
Breker – The Specialists
Postfach 50 11 19
D-50971 Köln, Germany
Tel: -/49/221/38 70 49
fax: -/49/221/37 48 78
web: www.breker.com
e-mail: auction@breker.com
Jane Herz, USA Representative
(941) 925-0385
fax: (941) 925-0487

Aumann Auctions, Inc.
20114 Illinois Route 16
Nokomis, IL 62075-1782
(888) AUCTN-4U
fax: (217) 563-2111
e-mail: aumannauctions.com

Bill Bertoia Auctions
1881 Spring Road
Vineland, NJ 08361
(609) 692-1881
fax: (609) 692-8697
web: bba.ccc.nj.net
e-mail: bba@ccnj.net

Butterfield's Auctioneers
220 San Bruno Avenue
San Francisco, CA 94103
(415) 861-7500
fax: (415) 861-8951
web: www.butterfields.com
e-mail: info@butterfields.com

Butterfield & Dunning
441 West Huron Street
Chicago, IL 60610
(312) 377-7500
fax: (312) 377-7501
web: www.butterfields.com
e-mail: info@butterfields.com

Cerebro
PO Box 327
East Prospect, PA 17317
(800) 69-LABEL
fax: (717) 252-3685
web: www.cerebro.com
e-mail: cerebro@cerebro.com

Christie's East
219 East 67th Street
New York, NY 10021
(212) 606-0430
fax: (212) 452-2063
web: www.christies.com

Christie's Inc.
502 Park Avenue
New York, NY 10022
(212) 546-1000
fax: (212) 980-8163
web: www.christies.com

Christmas Morning
1806 Royal Lane
Dallas, TX 75229-3126
(972) 506-8362
fax: (972) 506-7821

Cobb's Doll Auctions
1909 Harrison Road
Johnstown, OH 43031-9539
(740) 964-0444
fax: (740) 927-7701

Collectors Auction Services
RR 2, Box 431 Oakwood Road
Oil City, PA 16301
(814) 677-6070
fax: (814) 677-6166
web: www.caswel.com
e-mail: director@caswel.com

Collector's Sales and Services
PO Box 6
Pomfret Center, CT 06259
(860) 974-7008
fax: (860) 974-7010
web: www.antiquechina.com
web: www.antiqueglass.com
e-mail: collectors@antiquechina.com

Copake Auction, Inc.
226 Route 7A, PO Box H
Copake, NY 12516
(518) 329-1142
fax: (518) 329-3369
web: www.usi-ny.com/copakeauction
e-mail: copakeauction@netstep.net

Robert Coup
PO Box 348
Leola, PA 17540
(717) 656-7780
fax: (717) 656-8233
e-mail: polbandwgn@aol.com

Dawson's
128 American Road
Morris Plains, NJ 07950
(973) 984-6900
fax: (973) 984-6956
web: www.dawsonsauction.com
e-mail: dawson1@idt.net

William Doyle Galleries
175 East 87th Street
New York, NY 10128
(212) 427-2730
fax: (212) 369-0892
web: www.doylenewyork.com
e-mail: info@doylegalleries.com

Dunbar's Gallery
76 Haven Street
Milford, MA 01757
(508) 634-8697
fax: (508) 634-8698
e-mail: Dunbar2bid@aol.com

Early American History Auctions,
    Inc.
PO Box 3341
La Jolla, CA 92038
(619) 459-4159
fax: (619) 459-4373
web: www.earlyamerican.com
e-mail: auctions@earlyamerican.com

Early Auction Co.
Roger and Steve Early
123 Main Street
Milford, OH 45150
(513) 831-4833
fax: (513) 831-1441

Ken Farmer Auctions &
    Appraisals
105 Harrison Street
Radford, VA 24141
(540) 639-0939
fax: (540) 639-1759
web: www.kenfarmer.com
e-mail: auction@usit.net

Fink's Off the Wall Auction
108 East 7th Street
Lansdale, PA 19446-2622
(215) 855-9732
fax: (215) 855-6325
web: www.finksauctions.com
e-mail: lansbeer@finksauctions.com

Flomaton Antique Auction
320 Palafox Street
Flomaton, AL 36441
(334) 296-3059

Freeman\Fine Arts of
    Philadelphia, Inc.
1808 Chestnut Street
Philadelphia, PA 19103
(215) 563-9275
fax: (215) 563-8236
werb: www.auctions-on-line.com/
    Freeman

Garth's Auction, Inc.
2690 Stratford Road
PO Box 369
Delaware, OH 43015
(740) 362-4771
fax: (740) 363-0164
web: www.garths.com
e-mail: info@garths.com

Lynn Geyer's Advertising
    Auctions
300 Trail Ridge
Silver City, NM 88061
(505) 538-2341
fax: (505) 388-9000

Glass-Works Auctions
PO Box 180
120 Jefferson Street
East Greenville, PA 18041
(215) 679-5849
fax: (215) 679-3068
web: www.glswrk–auction.com
e-mail: glswrk@enter.net

Greenberg Auctions
7566 Main Street, Suite 101
Sykesville, MD 21784
(410) 795-7447
fax: (410) 549-2553
e-mail:
    bwimperis@greenbergshows.com

Green Valley Auctions, Inc.
Route 2, Box 434-A
Mount Crawford, VA 22841
(540) 434-4260
fax: (540) 434-4532
web: www.greenvalleyauctions.com
e-mail: gvai@shentel.net

GVL Enterprises
21764 Congress Hall Lane
Saratoga, CA 95070
(408) 872-1006
fax: (408) 872-1007
e-mail: jlally@kpcb.com

Gypsyfoot Enterprises, Inc.
PO Box 5833
Helena, MT 59604
(406) 449-8076
fax: (406) 443-8514
e-mail: Gypsyfoot@aol.com

Hake's Americana and
    Collectibles
PO Box 1444
York, PA 17405-1444
(717) 848-1333
fax: (717) 852-0344
e-mail: hake@hakes.com

**Gene Harris Antique Auction
    Center, Inc.**
203 South 18th Avenue
PO Box 476
Marshalltown, IA 50158
(515) 752-0600
fax: (515) 753-0226
web: www.geneharrisauctions.com
e-mail: ghaac@marshallnet.com

Norman C. Heckler & Co.
Bradford Corner Road
Woodstock Valley, CT 06282
(860) 974-1634
fax: (860) 974-2003

Horst Auction Center
50 Durlach Road
Ephrata, PA 17522
(717) 859-1331
fax: (717) 738-2132

**Michael Ivankovich Antiques,
    Inc.**
PO Box 1536
Doylestown, PA 18901
(215) 345-6094
fax: (215) 345-6692
web: www.wnutting.com
e-mail: mike@wnutting.com

**Jackson's Auctioneers &
    Appraisers**
2229 Lincoln Street
Cedar Falls, IA 50613
(319) 277-2256
fax: (319) 277-1252
web: jacksonsauction.com

S. H. Jemik
PO Box 753
Bowie, MD 20715
(301) 262-1864
fax: (410) 721-6494
e-mail: Shjemik@aol.com

James D. Julia, Inc.
PO Box 830
Route 201, Skowhegan Road
Fairfield, ME 04937
(207) 453-7125
fax: (207) 453-2502
web: www.juliaauctions.com
e-mail: bgage@juliaauctions.com

Gary Kirsner Auctions
PO Box 8807
Coral Springs, FL 33075
(954) 344-9856
fax: (954) 344-4421

Charles E. Kirtley
PO Box 2273
Elizabeth City, NC 27906
(252) 335-1262
fax: (252) 335-4441
e-mail: ckirtley@coastalnet.com

Kruse International
PO Box 190
5540 County Road 11-A
Auburn, IN 46706
(800) 968-4444
fax: (219) 925-5467
web: www.kruseinternational.com

Henry Kurtz, Ltd.
163 Amsterdam Avenue
Suite 136
New York, NY 10023
(212) 642-5904
fax: (212) 874-6018

Lang's Sporting Collectables, Inc.
14 Fishermans Lane
Raymond, ME 04071
(207) 655-4265
fax: (207) 655-4265

Leland's
36 East 22nd Street, 7th Floor
New York, NY 10010
(212) 545-0800
fax: (212) 545-0713

Los Angeles Modern Auctions
PO Box 462006
Los Angeles, CA 90046
(213) 845-9456
fax: (213) 845-9601
web: www.lamodern.com
e-mail: peter@lamodern.com

Howard Lowery
3812 West Magnolia Boulevard
Burbank, CA 91505
(818) 972-9080
fax: (818) 972-3910

Majolica Auctions
Michael G. Strawser
200 North Main
PO Box 332
Wolcottville, IN 46795
(219) 854-2859
fax: (219) 854-3979
web: www.majolicaauctions.com

Manion's International Auction
    House, Inc.
PO Box 12214
Kansas City, KS 66112
(913) 299-6692
fax: (913) 299-6792
web: www.manions.com
e-mail: collecting@manions.com

Mastro Fine Sports Auctions
1515 West 22nd Street, Suite 125
Oak Brook, IL 60523
(630) 472-9551
fax: (630) 472-1201
web: www.mastrofinesports.com

Mastro West Auctions
PMB #278
16200 SW Pacific Highway
Suite H
Tigard, OR 97224
(503) 579-9477
fax: (503) 579-0887
web: www.mastrowest.com

Ted Maurer, Auctioneer
1003 Brookwood Drive
Pottstown, PA 19464
(610) 323-1573
web: www.maurerail.com

Mechantiques
26 Barton Hill
East Hampton, CT 06424
(860) 267-8682
fax: (860) 267-1120
web: www.Mechantiques.com
e-mail: mroenigk@aol.com

Wm Morford
RD 2
Cazenovia, NY 13035
(315) 662-7625
fax: (315) 662-3570
e-mail: morf2bid@aol.com

Ray Morykan Auctions
1368 Spring Valley Road
Bethlehem, PA 18015
(610) 838-6634

**Gary Metz's Muddy River
    Trading Co.**
PO Box 1430
251 Wildwood Road
Salem, VA 24153
(540) 387-5070
fax: (540) 387-3233

New England Auction Gallery
PO Box 2273
West Peabody, MA 01960
(978) 535-3140
fax: (978) 535-7522
web: www.old-toys.com
e-mail: dlkrim@star.net

North Country Antiques and
 Ephemera
Joe and Laureen Millard
PO Box 404
Northport, MI 49670
(231) 386-5351

Norton Auctioneers
Pearl at Monroe
Coldwater, MI 49036-1967
(517) 279-9063
fax: (517) 279-9191
web: www.nortonauctioneers.com
e-mail: nortonsold@cbpu.com

Nostalgia Publications, Inc.
21 South Lake Drive
Hackensack, NJ 07601
(201) 488-4536

Ingrid O'Neil
PO Box 60310
Colorado Springs, CO 80960
(719) 473-1538
fax: (719) 477-0768
e-mail: auction@ioneil.com

Richard Opfer Auctioneers, Inc.
1919 Greenspring Drive
Timonium, MD 21093
(410) 252-5035
fax: (410) 252-5863

Ron Oser Enterprises
PO Box 101
Huntingdon Valley, PA 19006
(215) 947-6575
fax: (215) 938-7348
web: members.aol.com/RonOserEnt
e-mail: RonOserEnt@aol.com

Pacific Book Auction Galleries
133 Kearney Street, 4th Floor
San Francisco, CA 94108
(415) 989-2665
fax: (415) 989-1664
web: www.nbn.com/pba

Past Tyme Pleasures
PMB #204
2491 San Ramon Valley Blvd #1
San Ramon, CA 94583-1601
(925) 484-6442
fax: (925) 484-2551
e-mail: pasttyme1@aol.com

Pettigrew Auction Co.
1645 South Tejon Street
Colorado Springs, CO 80906
(719) 633-7963
fax: (719(633-5035

Phillips New York
406 East 79th Street
New York, NY 10021
(212) 570-4830
fax: (212) 570-2207
web: www.phillips-auctions.com

Postcards International
60-C Skiff Street, Suite 116
Hamden, CT 06517
(203) 248-6621
fax: (203) 281248-0387
web: www.vintagepostcards.com
e-mail: quality@vintagepostcards.com

Poster Mail Auction Co.
1015 King Street
Alexandria, VA 22314
(703) 684-4535
fax: (703) 684-3656

Provenance
PO Box 3487
Wallington, NJ 07057
(973) 779-8785
fax: (212) 741-8756

David Rago Auctions, Inc.
333 North Main Street
Lambertville, NJ 08530
(609) 397-9374
fax: (609) 397-9377
web: www.ragoarts.com

Lloyd Ralston Gallery
109 Glover Avenue
Norwalk, CT 06850
(203) 845-0033
fax: (203) 845-0366

Red Baron's Antiques
6450 Roswell Road
Atlanta, GA 30328
(404) 252-3770
fax: (404) 257-0268
web: www.redbaronsantiques.com
e-mail: rbaron@onramp.net

L. H. Selman Ltd.
123 Locust Street
Santa Cruz, CA 95060
(800) 538-0766
fax: (831) 427-0111
web: www.pwauction.com
e-mail: selman@paperweight.com

Skinner, Inc.
Boston Gallery
The Heritage on the Garden
63 Park Plaza
Boston, MA 02116
(617) 350-5400
fax: (617) 350-5429
web: www.skinnerinc.com

Sloan's Washington DC Gallery
4920 Wyaconda Road
North Bethesda, MD 20852
(800) 649-5066
fax: (301) 468-9182
web: www.sloansauction.com

Smith & Jones, Inc. Auctions
12 Clark Lane
Sudbury, MA 01776
(978) 443-5517
fax: (978) 443-2796
web: smithandjonesauctions.com
e-mail: smthjnes@gis.net

R. M. Smythe & Co., Inc.
26 Broadway, Suite 271
New York, NY 10004-1701
(800) 622-1880
fax: (212) 908-4047
web: www.rm-smythe.com

SoldUSA, Inc.
6407 Idlewild Road
Building 2, Suite 207
Charlotte, NC 28212
(877) SoldUSA
fax: (704) 364-2322
web: www.soldusa.com

Sotheby's London
34-35 New Bond Street
London W1A 2AA
(20) 7293-5000
fax: 0 (171) 293-5074
web: www.sothebys.com

Sotheby's New York
1334 York Avenue
New York, NY 10021
(212) 606-7000
web: www.sothebys.com

Stanton's Auctioneers
144 South Main Street
PO Box 146
Vermontville, MI 49096
(517) 726-0181
fax: (517) 726-0060

Steffen's Historical Militaria
PO Box 280
Newport, KY 41072
(606) 431-4499
fax: (606) 431-3113

Strawser Auctions
200 North Main Street
Wolcottville, IN 46795
(219) 854-2859
fax: (219) 854-3979

Susanin's
Gallery 228, Merchandise Mart
Chicago, IL 60654
(312) 832-9800
fax: (312) 832-9311
web: www.theauction.com

Swann Galleries, Inc.
104 East 25th Street
New York, NY 10010
(212) 254-4710
fax: (212) 979-1017
web: www.swanngalleries.com

Theriault's
PO Box 151
Annapolis, MD 21404
fax: (410) 224-2515

Tool Shop Auctions
Tony Murland
78 High Street
Needham Market
Suffolk, 1P6 8AW England
Tel: (01449) 722992
fax: (01449) 722683
web: www.toolshop.demon.co.uk
e-mail: tony@toolshop.demon.co.uk

Toy Scouts, Inc.
137 Casterton Avenue
Akron, OH 44303
(330) 836-0668
fax: (330) 869-8668
e-mail: toyscout@akron.infi.net

Tradewinds Antiques
PO Box 249
24 Magnolia Avenue
Manchester-by-the-Sea, MA
 01944-0249
(978) 768-3327
fax: (978) 526-3088
web: www.tradewindsantiques.com
e-mail: taron@tiac.net

TV Toyland
223 Wall Street
Huntington, NY 11743
(516) 385-1306
fax: (516) 385-1307
e-mail: itsonlyrocknroll@erols.com

Victorian Images
PO Box 284
Marlton, NJ 08053
(609) 953-7711
fax: (609) 953-7768
web: www.tradecards.com/vi
e-mail: rmascieri@aol.com

York Town Auction Inc.
1625 Haviland Road
York, PA 17404
(717) 751-0211
fax: (717) 767-7729
e-mail: yorktownauction@cyberia.com

CATALOG SALES

Robert F. Batchelder
1 West Butler Avenue
Ambler, PA 19002
(215) 643-1430

Wayland Bunnell
199 Tarrytown Road
Manchester, NH 03103
(603) 668-5466
e-mail: wtarrytown@aol.com

J. M. Cohen, Rare Books
2 Karin Court
New Paltz, NY 12561
(914) 883-9720
fax: (914) 883-9142
web:jmcohenrarebooks.com
e-mail: jmcrb@jmcohenrarebooks.com

Early Industry & Life
Harold R. Nestler
13 Pennington Avenue
Waldwick, NJ 07463
(201) 444-7413

Joel Markowitz
Box 10
Old Bethpage, NY 11804
(516) 249-9405
web: www.sheetmusiccenter.com
e-mail: smctr@sheetmusiccenter.com

Charles F. Miller
708 Westover Drive
Lancaster, PA 17601
(717) 285-2255
fax: (717) 285-2255

Miscellaneous Man
Box 1776
New Freedom, PA 17349-0191
(717) 235-4766
fax: (717) 235-2853

The Old Paperphiles
PO Box 135
Tiverton, RI 02878-0135
(401) 624-9420
fax: (401) 624-4204
e-mail: old_paperphiles@edgenet.net

Cordelia and Tom Platt
2805 E. Oakland Park Blvd #380
Fort Lauderdale, FL 33306
(954) 564-2002
fax: (954) 564-2002
web: www.ctplatt.com
e-mail ctplatt@ctplatt.com

Ken Prag
PO Box 14817
San Francisco, CA 94114
(415) 586-9386
e-mail: Kprag@planeteria.net

Ken Schneringer
271 Sabrina Ct.
Woodstock, GA 30188
(770) 926-9383
web: old-paper.com
e-mail: trademan68@aol.com

Toy Soldiers Etcetera
732 Aspen Lane
Lebanon, PA 17042-9073
(717) 228-2361
fax: (717) 228-2362

If you are an auctioneer, auction company, or antiques and collectibles dealer and would like your name and address to appear on this list in subsequent editions, you can achieve this by sending copies of your auction lists, dealer sales lists, press releases, catalogs and illustrations, prices realized, and/or photographs or digital images to: **Rinker Enterprises, Inc., 5093 Vera Cruz Road, Emmaus, PA 18049.**

ABINGDON POTTERY

The Abingdon Sanitary Manufacturing Company began manufacturing bathroom fixtures in 1908 in Abingdon, Illinois. The company's art pottery line was introduced in 1938 and eventually consisted of over 1,000 shapes and forms decorated in nearly 150 different colors. In 1945 the company changed its name to Abingdon Potteries, Inc. The art pottery line remained in production until 1950, when fire destroyed the art pottery kiln. After the fire, the company focused once again on plumbing fixtures. Eventually, Abingdon Potteries became Briggs Manufacturing Company, a firm noted for its sanitary fixtures.

Reference: Joe Paradis, *Abingdon Pottery Artware: 1934–1950,* Schiffer Publishing, 1997.

Collectors' Club: Abingdon Pottery Club, 210 Knox Hwy 5, Abingdon, IL 61410.

Bookends, pr, #363, reclining colt, 6" h	**$375.00**
Bowl, #361, triform, 8 x 14½"	**65.00**
Bowl, #399, daisy, 6½" d	**45.00**
Bowl, #536, Regency, 9" l	**15.00**
Candleholder, #360, Quatrain	**25.00**
Candleholder, #404, Triple Chain, 3 x 8½"	**25.00**
Candleholder, #427, Fern Leaf, 5½" h	**25.00**
Cookie Jar, #471, Little Ol' Lady	**200.00**
Cookie Jar, #549, hippo, 8" h	**250.00**
Cookie Jar, #561, baby finial, 11" h	**600.00**
Double Cornucopia, #482, 11" l	**25.00**
Figurine, #388, pouter pigeon, 4¼" h	**45.00**
Figurine, #416, peacock, 7" h	**55.00**
Figurine, #562, seagull	**75.00**
Figurine, #571, seated goose, 5" h	**35.00**
Floor Vase, #603, Grecian, 15" h	**150.00**
Flowerpot, #347, Egg & Dart, 7¼" d	**15.00**
Jar, cov, #364, Elite, 4½" h	**50.00**
Planter, #655D, Dutch Shoe, 5" l	**45.00**
Planter, #671, ram, 4" h	**40.00**
Planter, #672, fawn, 5" h	**45.00**
Plate, #344, Wild Rose, 10 x 12"	**125.00**

Vase, Classic shape, blue, embossed leaf band, paper label, ink stamped "Abingdon, U.S.A.," 9⅞" h, $25.00.

Plate, #415, Apple Blossom, 11½" d	**50.00**
Salt and Pepper Shakers, pr, #680, Daisy, 4" h	**25.00**
String Holder, #702D, Chinese face, 7½" h	**175.00**
Vase, #179, Ming white, 10" h	**65.00**
Vase, #373, Manhattan, 12½" h	**115.00**
Vase, #389, Geranium, 7" h	**55.00**
Vase, #463, Star, 7½" h	**25.00**
Vase, #466, wheel handle, 8" h	**45.00**
Vase, #469, Dutch Boy, 8" h	**75.00**
Vase, #496D, Hollyhock, 7" h	**45.00**
Vase, #515, Abbey, 7" h	**25.00**
Wall Pocket, #379, daisy, 7¾" d	**70.00**
Wall Pocket, #590D, Ivy, 7" h	**65.00**
Window Box, #447, Sunburst, 9" l	**25.00**

ACTION FIGURES

Early action figures depicted popular television western heroes from the 1950s and were produced by Hartland. Louis Marx also included action figures in several of its playsets from the late 1950s.

Hassenfield Bros. triggered the modern action figure craze with its introduction of G.I. Joe in 1964. The following year Gilbert produced James Bond 007, The Man From U.N.C.L.E., and Honey West figures. Bonanza and Captain Action figures arrived in 1966.

In 1972 Mego introduced the first six superheroes in a series of thirty-four. Mego also established the link between action figures and the movies with its issue of Planet of the Apes and Star Trek: The Motion Picture figures.

The success of the Star Wars figures set introduced by Kenner in 1977 prompted other toy companies to follow suit, resulting in a flooded market. However, unlike many collecting categories, scarcity does not necessarily equate to high value.

References: John Bonavita, *Mego Action Figure Toys, 2nd Edition,* Schiffer Publishing, 2000; Tom Heaton, *The Encyclopedia of Marx Action Figures,* Krause Publications, 1999; John Marshall, *Action Figures of the 1960s,* Schiffer Publishing, 1998; John Marshall, *Action Figures of the 1980s,* Schiffer Publishing, 1998; Stuart W. Wells III and Jim Main, *The Official Price Guide to Action Figures, Second Edition,* House of Collectibles, 1999.

Periodicals: *Lee's Action Figure News & Toy Review,* 556 Monroe Turnpike, Monroe, CT 06468; *Tomart's Action Figure Digest,* Tomart Publications, 3300 Encrete Ln, Dayton, OH 45439.

Note: All figures are complete and in mint condition in original packaging. For additional listings see G.I. Joe, Star Trek, and Star Wars.

Action Boy, Ideal, 1967	**$500.00**
Action Jackson Frogman Set, Mego	**10.00**
Action Jackson Navy Set, Mego	**10.00**
Addams Family, Playmates, Gomez	**10.00**
Addams Family, Playmates, Lurch	**10.00**
Addams Family, Playmates, Morticia	**22.00**
Addams Family, Playmates, Uncle Fester	**10.00**
Aliens, Kenner, Bishop	**10.00**
Aliens, Kenner, Drake	**10.00**
Aliens, Kenner, Lt Ripley	**10.00**
Aliens, Kenner, Queen Face Hugger Alien	**4.00**
Aliens, Kenner, Scorpion Alien	**4.00**

Batman Forever, Kenner, Night Hunter Batman, 4³/₄" h **8.00**
Batman Forever, Kenner, Sonar Sensor Batman, 4³/₄" h **8.00**
Batman Forever, Kenner, Street Biker Robin, 4³/₄" h **8.00**
Batman Forever, Kenner, Transforming Dick Grayson, 4³/₄" h **8.00**
Batman Forever, Kenner, Wing Blast Batman, 4³/₄" h **6.00**
Batman Returns, Kenner, Air Attack Batman, 4³/₄" h **15.00**
Batman Returns, Kenner, Deep Dive Batman, with torpedo launching scuba gear, 4³/₄" h **10.00**
Batman Returns, Kenner, Laser Batman, 4³/₄" h **10.00**
Batman Returns, Kenner, Penguin, with blast-off umbrella launcher, 4³/₄" h **30.00**
Batman Returns II, Kenner, Hydro Charge Batman, 4³/₄" h **8.00**
Batman Returns II, Kenner, Jungle Tracker Batman, 4³/₄" h **8.00**
Batman Returns II, Kenner, Night Climber Batman, 4³/₄" h **8.00**
Batman, The Animated Series, Kenner, Catwoman, 4³/₄" h **25.00**
Batman, The Animated Series, Kenner, Combat Belt Batman, 4³/₄" h **35.00**
Batman, The Animated Series, Kenner, Robin, with turbo glider and drop missiles, 4³/₄" h **20.00**
Batman, The Animated Series, Kenner, The Riddler, 4³/₄" h **38.00**
Batman, The Animated Series, Kenner, Two-Face, 4³/₄" h **32.00**
Batman, The Dark Knight, Kenner, Crime Attack Batman, 4³/₄" h **20.00**
Batman, The Dark Knight, Kenner, Knock-Out Joker, 4³/₄" h **60.00**
Batman, The Dark Knight, Kenner, Tec-Shield Batman, 4³/₄" h **20.00**
Batman, The Dark Knight, Kenner, Wall Scaler Batman, 4³/₄" h **20.00**
Battle Beasts, Hasbro, Ram **6.00**
Battle Beasts, Hasbro, Reindeer **6.00**
Battlestar Galactica, Mattel, Baltar **185.00**
Battlestar Galactica, Mattel, Colonial Scarab **85.00**
Battlestar Galactica, Mattel, Commander Adama **55.00**
Battlestar Galactica, Mattel, Cylon, gold. **175.00**
Battlestar Galactica, Mattel, Cylon, silver **85.00**
Battlestar Galactica, Mattel, Cylon Raider. **115.00**
Battlestar Galactica, Mattel, Daggit, tan **45.00**
Battlestar Galactica, Mattel, Imperious Leader **35.00**
Battlestar Galactica, Mattel, Lucifer **165.00**
Battlestar Galactica, Mattel, Ovion. **35.00**
Battlestar Galactica, Mattel, Starbuck **60.00**
Beetlejuice, Kenner, Exploding Beetlejuice, 6" h **10.00**
Beetlejuice, Kenner, Harry the Haunted Hunter, 6" h **10.00**
Beetlejuice, Kenner, Shish Kebab Beetlejuice, 6" h **8.00**
Beetlejuice, Kenner, Talking Beetlejuice **35.00**
Big Jim, Mattel, Big Jim Gold Medal Boxer. **20.00**
Big Jim, Mattel, Big Josh **30.00**
Big Jim, Mattel, Professor Obb **22.00**
Black Hole, Mego, Dr Hans Reinhardt **50.00**
Black Hole, Mego, Laserscope Fighter with Captain Holland **175.00**
Black Hole, Mego, Maximillian **95.00**
Black Hole, Mego, Old Bob. **425.00**
Black Hole, Mego, Pizer **60.00**
Blackstar, Galoob, Battle Wagon **75.00**
Blackstar, Galoob, Ice Castle **225.00**
Blackstar, Galoob, Mara **135.00**
Blackstar, Galoob, Neptul **45.00**
Blackstar, Galoob, Trobbit Wind Machine. **60.00**

Broadway Joe Namath, Mego, 1970, 12" h, $18.00

Blackstar, Galoob, Vizir **25.00**
Blackstar, Galoob, Warlock **125.00**
Blackstar, Galoob, White Knight **28.00**
Bonanza, American Character, Ben Cartwright **140.00**
Bonanza, American Character, Hoss. **140.00**
Bonanza, American Character, Little Joe, with pinto **200.00**
Captain Action, Ideal, Captain Action, first issue, 12" h **475.00**
Captain Action, Ideal, Captain Action, second issue, 12" h **600.00**
Captain Action, Ideal, Dr Evil, The Sinister of Earth, 12" h **800.00**
Coneheads, Playmates, Agent Seedling. **8.00**
Coneheads, Playmates, Beldar **8.00**
He-Man: Masters of the Universe, Mattel, Battle Armor Skeletor **50.00**
He-Man: Masters of the Universe, Mattel, Battle Bones **25.00**
He-Man: Masters of the Universe, Mattel, Battle Cat **95.00**
He-Man: Masters of the Universe, Mattel, Beastman **60.00**
He-Man: Masters of the Universe, Mattel, Blade **50.00**
He-Man: Masters of the Universe, Mattel, Blast-Attack **75.00**
He-Man: Masters of the Universe, Mattel, Buzz Saw Hordak **75.00**
He-Man: Masters of the Universe, Mattel, Dragon Blaster Skeletor **65.00**
He-Man: Masters of the Universe, Mattel, Zoar. **40.00**
He-Man: Masters of the Universe, Mattel, Zodac **50.00**
Lord of the Rings, Knickerbocker, Aragorn **300.00**
Lord of the Rings, Knickerbocker, Frodo **375.00**
Lord of the Rings, Knickerbocker, Gollum. **275.00**
Lost In Space, Judy Robinson, 9" h **10.00**
Lost In Space, Will Robinson, 9" h **32.00**
MAD Alfred E. Neuman, DC Direct **10.00**
Man From U.N.C.L.E., Gilbert, Illya Kuryakin, 1965 . . . . **60.00**
Mars Attacks, Talking Martian Spy Girl **30.00**
Micronauts, Mego, Baron Karza. **115.00**
Micronauts, Mego, Betatron. **35.00**
Micronauts, Mego, Cosmo Man **40.00**
Micronauts, Mego, Crater Cruncher **65.00**
Micronauts, Mego, Force Commander **95.00**
Micronauts, Mego, Lantaurion **175.00**
Micronauts, Mego, Lord Meto **175.00**

Micronauts, Mego, Megas **195.00**
Micronauts, Mego, Oberon **85.00**
Micronauts, Mego, Time Traveler **40.00**
OJ Simpson/Super Pro, Shindana Toys, 9½" h **75.00**
Our Gang, Mego, Spanky, 6" h **50.00**
Planet of the Apes, Mego, Verdon **85.00**
Police Academy, Kingpin **10.00**
Police Academy, Zed, with police skateboard **10.00**
Power Lords, Revell, Arkus **45.00**
Power Lords, Revell, Raygoth **35.00**
Power Lords, Revell, Spyzor **30.00**
Power Lords, Revell, Sydot **40.00**
Power Lords, Revell, Tork **45.00**
Princess of Power, Mattel, Arrow **60.00**
Princess of Power, Mattel, Catra **30.00**
Princess of Power, Mattel, Clawdeen **40.00**
Princess of Power, Mattel, Crystal Falls **125.00**
Princess of Power, Mattel, Enchantra **85.00**
Princess of Power, Mattel, Frosta **30.00**
Puppet Master, Jester **12.00**
Puppet Master, Torch **10.00**
Real Ghostbusters, Kenner, Bad-to-the-Bone Ghost **28.00**
Real Ghostbusters, Kenner, Bug-Eye Ghost **20.00**
Real Ghostbusters, Kenner, Ray Stantz and Jail Jaw Ghost **18.00**
Real Ghostbusters, Kenner, Stay-Puff Marshmallow Man,
    6" h **35.00**
Robin Hood Official Super Merry Men, Mego, Robin
    Hood, 8" h **100.00**
Robotech, Armoured Zentraedi **30.00**
Robotech, Bioroid Terminator **15.00**
Robotech, Corg **28.00**
Robotech, Lisa Hayes **22.00**
Robotech, Max Sterling **30.00**
Sir Gordon the Golden Knight, ©1968 Marx, 11½" h **50.00**
Spawn, Red Angela **32.00**
The Waltons, Mego, Pop, 1974, 8" h **50.00**
Thundercats, Bengali **325.00**
Thundercats, Captain Cracker **50.00**
Thundercats, Cheetara **90.00**
Thundercats, Driller **95.00**
Thundercats, Hachiman **40.00**
Thundercats, Jaga **325.00**
Thundercats, Lynx-O **115.00**
Thundercats, Panthro **90.00**
Universal Monsters Frankenstein, 1990 . . . . **12.00**
Welcome Back Kotter, Mattel, Vinnie Barbarino, 8¾" h **50.00**
WWF Dusty Rhodes, Hasbro **85.00**
Xena **10.00**

ACTION FIGURE ACCESSORIES

Batman Forever, Kenner, Electronic Batmobile **$20.00**
Batman Forever, Kenner, Robin Cycle **12.00**
Batman Forever, Kenner, Wayne Manor/Batcave Center **65.00**
Batman Returns, Kenner, Batcave Command Center **75.00**
Batman Returns II, Kenner, Camo Attack Batmobile, with
    Batman figure **25.00**
Batman, The Animated Series, Kenner, Batcycle **18.00**
Batman, The Animated Series, Kenner, Bruce Wayne
    Street Jet **25.00**
Batman, The Animated Series, Kenner, Hydro Bat **15.00**
Batman, The Animated Series, Kenner, Jokermobile **18.00**
Batman, The Dark Knight, Kenner, Batjet **50.00**
Batman, The Dark Knight, Kenner, Joker Cycle **18.00**

Batman, The Dark Knight, Kenner, Turbojet Batwing **65.00**
Beetlejuice, Kenner, Creepy Cruiser **18.00**
Beetlejuice, Kenner, Phantom Flyer **10.00**
Beetlejuice, Kenner, Vanishing Vault **10.00**
Big Jim, Mattel, Arctic Explorer **10.00**
Big Jim, Mattel, Fishing Trip Playset **65.00**
Big Jim, Mattel, Sailing Outfit **25.00**
Bonanza, American Character, Stallion **60.00**
Captain Action, Ideal, Sgt Fury Uniform and Equipment,
    1966 . . . . **350.00**
Captain Action, Ideal, Steve Canyon Uniform and
    Equipment, 1966 . . . . **225.00**
Captain Action, Ideal, The Lone Ranger Uniform and
    Equipment, blue shirt and ring, re-issue, 1967 . . . . **450.00**
Captain Action, Ideal, The Lone Ranger Uniform and
    Equipment, red shirt, 1966 . . . . **350.00**
Captain Action, Ideal, The Phantom Uniform and
    Equipment, 1966 . . . . **300.00**
Dr Evil the Sinister Invader of Earth, Ideal, Gift Set, 1967 . . **1,250.00**
Masters of the Universe, Mattel, Night Stalker Battle
    Steed, 1984 . . . . **45.00**
Real Ghostbusters, Kenner, Air Sickness Plane and Pilot **10.00**
Real Ghostbusters, Kenner, Fire House Headquarters **60.00**
Real Ghostbusters, Kenner, Wicked Wheelie Cycle and
    Driver **10.00**

ADVERTISING

Advertising premiums such as calendars and thermometers arrived on the scene by the 1880s. Diecut point-of-purchase displays, wall clocks, and signs were eagerly displayed. The advertising character was developed in the early 1900s. By the 1950s the star endorser was firmly established. Advertising became a big business as specialized firms, many headquartered in New York City, developed to meet manufacturers' needs. Today television programs frequently command well over one hundred thousand dollars a minute for commercial air time.

Many factors affect the price of an advertising collectible—the product and its manufacturer, the objects or persons used in the advertisement, the period and aesthetics of design, the designer and/or illustrator, and the form the advertisement takes. Almost every advertising item is sought by a specialized collector in one or more collectibles areas.

References: Michael Bruner, *Advertising Clocks,* Schiffer Publishing, 1995; Michael Bruner, *Encyclopedia of Porcelain Enamel Advertising, 2nd Edition,* Schiffer Publishing, 1999; Michael Bruner, *More Porcelain Enamel Advertising,* Schiffer Publishing, 1997; Douglas Congdon-Martin, *Tobacco Tins,* Schiffer Publishing, 1992; Fred Dodge, *Antique Tins* (1995, 1999 value update), *Book II* (1998), *Book III* (1999), Collector Books; Ted Hake, *Hake's Guide to Advertising Collectibles,* Wallace-Homestead, 1992.

Sharon and Bob Huxford, *Huxford's Collectible Advertising, Third Edition* (1997), *Fourth Edition* (1998), Collector Books; Ralph and Terry Kovel, *The Label Made Me Buy It,* Crown, 1998; *Letter Openers: Advertising & Figural,* L-W Book Sales, 1996; Linda McPherson, *Modern Collectible Tins,* Collector Books, 1998; David J. Moncrief, *Got a Drop of Oil? An Introduction & Price Guide to Small Oilers,* L-W Book Sales, 1998; Robert Reed, *Paper Advertising Collectibles,* Antique Trader Books, 1998; B. J. Summers, *Value Guide to Advertising Memorabilia, Second*

Edition, Collector Books, 1999; David Zimmerman, *The Encyclopedia of Advertising Tins, Vol. I* (1994) and *Vol. II* (1999), Collector Books.

Periodicals: *Paper Collectors' Marketplace* (PCM), PO Box 128, Scandinavia, WI 54977; *The Paper & Advertising Collector* (PAC), PO Box 500, Mount Joy, PA 17552.

Collectors' Clubs: Advertising Cup and Mug Collectors of America, PO Box 680, Solon, IA 52333; Antique Advertising Assoc of America, PO Box 1121, Morton Grove, IL 60053; The Ephemera Society of America, PO Box 95, Cazenovia, NY 13035; Inner Seal Club (Nabisco), 6609 Billtown Rd, Louisville, KY 40299; Porcelain Advertising Collectors Club, PO Box 381, Marshfield Hills, MA 02051; Tin Container Collectors Assoc, PO Box 440101, Aurora, CO 80044.

REPRODUCTION ALERT

Alarm Clock, Nestle Cookie Mix, brown enamel painted metal, chocolate chip cookie depicted on face **$50.00**

Ashtray, Globe Ticket Co, glass bottom, metal tire top with lift-out spokes, 1¹/₂" h, 6" d **225.00**

Ashtray, Mokaine, litho on metal, "Made in France; IMPS Metaux Alfred Riom Nantes," 5" l **60.00**

Ashtray, Orkin, cast metal tray and figure, copper-bronze finish, 1950s, 5 x 5 x 5" **175.00**

Bag, Old Plantation Coffee, 1930s, 4 x 8" **10.00**

Blotter, Amoco Oil, "Looks Good for '48," 5¹/₂ x 2³/₄" **10.00**

Blotter, Northwestern Mutual Life Insurance, 1940, 9¹/₄ x 4". **10.00**

Blotter, Walsh Refractories Corp, "Easy Does It," Elvgren illus, 1957, 9 x 4" **10.00**

Booklet, Hires Household Extract, 12 pp, 1920s, 3¹/₂ x 5". . . . **15.00**

Booklet, *Nestles Mother Book,* Nestles Milk, 1923, 4³/₄ x 5¹/₂" **25.00**

Bottle, Bromo-Cedin For Headaches, cobalt, emb, soda bottle shape, 1930s, 3¹/₂" h, 1³/₄" d **5.00**

Box, Blue River Butter, cows on sides, blue, green, and yellow **2.50**

Box, Borden Cheese, vinyl over cardboard, dark olive green ext with gold emb Elsie head image at lid center, inscribed "Borden's/Van Wert, Ohio/The World's Largest Cheese Factory," 1950s, 9¹/₂ x 12 x 3¹/₂" **75.00**

Box, Hill Country Butter, yellow, black, and white, stylized floral border, ¹/₂ lb **1.00**

Box, Shamrock Rolled Oats, cardboard, 9¹/₂ x 5³/₈", 3 lb **225.00**

Bridge Tallies and Sheet, Angelus-Campfire, punch-out sheet holding 4 scoring cards, 1930s, 7 x 9¹/₄" **50.00**

Calendar, August Wichman Work Clothes & Hosiery, 1931, Wear-U-Well Shoes, Seymour, IL, full pad, 10¹/₄ x 16³/₄" **10.00**

Calendar, Hercules Powder Co, 1940, NC Wyeth artwork. **150.00**

Calendar, Newport Culvert Co, 1942, DeVorss illus, full pad, 16 x 33" **75.00**

Calendar Card, Swift's Premium Ham, celluloid, vest pocket, Jack Sprat nursery rhyme illus by Maxfield Parrish, 1³/₄ x 3¹/₂" **100.00**

Can, Donald Duck Coffee, litho tin, key wind, 3⁵/₈ x 5", 1 lb. **675.00**

Catalog, General Electric Refrigerator, 1939, 8¹/₂ x 11" **15.00**

Catalog, Spencer Fireworks, 1940s. **25.00**

Blotter, Blue Sunoco, c1938, $150.00. Photo courtesy Collectors Auction Services.

Charm, Canada Dry Ginger Ale, plastic, figural miniature bottle with paper wrapper, 1950s **5.00**

Charm, Rheingold Beer, plastic, yellow, 1950s **5.00**

Charm Bracelet, Howard Johnson's, silver link bracelet holding mkd sterling silver charm featuring silhouette trademark on black enamel ground, late 1930s. **50.00**

Clicker, Great Lakes Mutual Life Insurance Co **8.00**

Clicker, Gunther's Beer, "The Beer That Clicks!," red lettering on white ground, Kirchof **25.00**

Clicker, Hershey's **60.00**

Clicker, Osh Kosh **8.00**

Clicker, Purity Salt. **15.00**

Clicker, Quaker City Life Insurance Co. **15.00**

Clock, Evervess Sparkling Water, light-up, c1940-50s, 15" d **575.00**

Clock, Exide, light-up, plastic, blue, white, and yellow logo, stylized clock face **50.00**

Clock, Folger's Coffee, light-up, reverse glass, neon, octagonal, c1940s **225.00**

Clock, Masury Paint, light-up, round, 1950s **225.00**

Clock, Philco, light-up, plastic, "Look Ahead...and you'll choose Philco," 1960s **150.00**

Clock, Red Goose Shoes, light-up, fiberboard case, 1940-50s **475.00**

Clock, Thorogood Shoes, light-up, plastic, "Job-Fitted Work Shoes," 1960s, 16" d **125.00**

Coin, Mister Softee, plastic, gold, ice cream cone head figure on front, "Worth 5¢ Towards the Purchase of Mister Softee" on back, 1960s **15.00**

Cookie Jar, Tony the Tiger, painted hard vinyl, ©1969, Kellogg Co, 6¹/₂ x 7¹/₂" **75.00**

Cuff Links, pr, Kodak, brass, top porcelain enamel square depicting red Kodak symbol on yellow ground, 1930-40s **10.00**

Cup and Saucer, Dobb's Hat Maker, white china, charcoal matte perimeter with glossy black top hat, "Dobbs" on underside of cup, 1930s, 2" h cup, 4¹/₄" d saucer. **20.00**

Desk Set, Dutch Boy Paints, painted cast metal Dutch Boy figure on marble base, brass housing center holds calendar paper reel, plastic pen holder and ballpoint pen, c1950s, 3¹/₂ x 9¹/₂" base, 3¹/₂" h figure **100.00**

Display, Brer Rabbit Molasses, diecut cardboard, full color image of chef carrying platter of gingerbread slices, c1930s, 4¹/₂ x 8³/₄" **50.00**

Display, Fixt-Focus Spotlight, Bond Brand Flashlights, cardboard, orig shipping carton, complete with 3 copper finish flashlights, c1930s, 11¹/₂ x 9¹/₂ x 6" **450.00**

Display, Heinz Rice Flakes, cardboard, easel back, full color Col Roscoe Turner illus, wings pin premium offer, 20 x 22" **150.00**

Display, McGregor Happy Foot, figural sock with emb face on foot, base reads "McGregor Happy Foot"...... **1,000.00**

Display, Off 'N' On Tire Chains, cardboard, stand-up, "Off Without Tools/On Without Effort," c1920s, 12¹/₂ x 22" **450.00**

Display, Seagram's Crown Blended Whiskies, painted hollow plaster, simulated fabric crown, c1950s, 8¹/₂" h ... **100.00**

Display, Squirrel Brand Peanut Taffy, litho tin, 24 x 7³/₄ x 7³/₈" **750.00**

Doll, Genie Gas Stove, cloth, plush, stuffed, molded soft vinyl face, c1960s, 19" h **50.00**

Doll, Nestle, Little Hans, cloth, stuffed fabric, Bavarian-style yellow cap, matching shirt under black bib overalls, red stockings, black and white sneaker-type shoes, fleshtone body parts accented in red with black facial markings, Nestle copyright on rear of foot, 1970, 13" h. **50.00**

Doll, Play-Doh Boy, cloth, ©1969 Rainbow Crafts, 16" h **25.00**

Door Pull, Dandee Enriched Bread, metal, yellow, "Keep Dandee Handy!," 13³/₄" h. **40.00**

Door Push, Bunny Bread, metal, "Everybody Loves Bunny Enriched Bread" bunny head illus, ©American Bakers Cooperative, Inc, 3 x 28".................. **225.00**

Door Push, Popsicles, emb tin, "Popsicles 5¢/Push Here," c1930-40s, 3 x 9¹/₂". **400.00**

Door Push, Rex Tobacco, porcelain, c1920s, 4 x 6¹/₂" **100.00**

Door Push, Salada Tea, porcelain, 2-sided, "Thank You–Call Again" on back, 3¹/₄ x 32". **70.00**

Door Push, Sweet Heart Products, porcelain, heart shaped, white lettering on red ground, c1940s **225.00**

Drinking Glass, Heinz, tapered, clear glass, white print, tomato head character above specific tomato juice title, Heinz juice keystone symbol and other various fruit juices on reverse, 5¹/₄" h, 2¹/₂" d. **25.00**

Fan, Hillcrest Dress Shop, flapper illus, 1925 .... **15.00**

Fan, San Marto Coffee, diecut cardboard, full color image of smiling imp in red cap with white trim, black and white text on reverse, 8 x 9" **75.00**

Fan, Tip-Top Bread, diecut cardboard, full color art depicting shooting star beside red, white, and blue loaf of bread, 1930s, 7¹/₄ x 9¹/₄" **20.00**

Figure, Heinz 57, rubber, red and green tomato head figure on black base, c1940s, 2¹/₂ x 2¹/₂ x 5³/₄" **200.00**

Figure, Lamb Knit Sweaters, figural lamb, papier-mâché, "100% Pure Wool," c1920s, 15" h **600.00**

Figure, Mr Hygrade's Hot Dogs, figural hot dog, 1940-50s, 36" h. **350.00**

Finger Puppets, Pillsbury, set of 4, soft hollow vinyl, Poppin' Fresh, Uncle, Biscuit, and Flapjack, ©1974 Pillsbury **50.00**

Flange Sign, Free Land Overalls, "Union Made Guaranteed," red and white lettering on blue ground, c1930s, 10 x 30" **275.00**

Flange Sign, Kern's Bread, metal, 1950-60s **85.00**

Flange Sign, Maxwell House Coffee, tin, coffee cup illus, "The Sign of Good Coffee—We Serve Maxwell House/Good to the Last Drop," c1950s, 14 x 27" **1,000.00**

Fan, Hudson Gasoline adv, cardboard, 2-sided, 13¹/₂" h, 8" w, $175.00. Photo courtesy Collectors Auction Services.

Flange Sign, Mrs Baird's Sliced Bread, porcelain, red, white, blue, and yellow, 1940-50s, 9 x 19"........... **150.00**

Flange Sign, Western Union, porcelain, "Telegraph Here /Western Union," 1940s, 17 x 25" **150.00**

Fruit Crate Label, apple, Plen Tee Color, smiling Indian girl with red apple, blue ground....................... **3.00**

Fruit Crate Label, citrus, Mountain's Pride, 3 different citrus fruits, leaves, and blossoms, Florida .... **.75**

Fruit Crate Label, grapes, Black Bear, comical black bear operating wine press, blue ground **1.50**

Fruit Crate Label, lemon, Parade, drum major leading drummers, Saticoy. **2.00**

Fruit Crate Label, pear, Yuba Orchard, yellow pears, blue ground .... **.50**

Hand Puppet, Dutch Boy, fabric body, painted soft vinyl head, 1960s, 12" h **75.00**

Key Chain Charm, Calvert Reserve Blended Whiskey, brown, bottle image with paper label, 1940s **15.00**

Key Chain Fob, metal, antique gold luster finish, raised tiger head image and Esso logo under "Put A Tiger In Your Tank!," reverse with engraved serial number of "Happy Motoring Key Club" member plus return information, 1950-60s.......................... **5.00**

Key Holder, Veedol, brown cowhide leather, inscribed "Veedol 150 Hour Tractor Oil/100% Pennsylvania," c1930s **8.00**

Kick Plate, Dragon Portland Cement, porcelain, "In Use Since 1889/Sold By MH Sherman," red and blue on white ground, c1930s, 12 x 32" **250.00**

Label, Lady Marion Toilet Water, 3¹/₂ x 1¹/₂" **1.50**

Lapel Insert, Hershey's Cocoa, multicolored, celluloid, center image of youngster at kitchen table holding product packages above inscription "Bittersweets," mounted on wire extension **50.00**

Lapel Stud, Dodge Brothers, brass, blue enamel, 6-point star logo, c1920-30s **25.00**

Letter Opener, De Laval, brass, inscribed "1878–De Laval–1928," 9¹/₂" l. **25.00**

Lighter, Kent, chrome luster finish metal, enameled wrapper depicting gold castle symbol on each side, made in Japan, 1960s **8.00**

Lighter, Minute Maid Orange Juice, chrome luster finish metal, made in Japan, 1960-70s.................... **50.00**

Lighter, Seagram's Seven Crown, chromed metal, made in Japan, orig box, c1950s **25.00**

Left: Jigsaw Puzzle, Cocomalt adv, diecut cardboard, "The Flying Family," Colonel Hutchinson and family, 1933, 6½ x 9⅞", $25.00; **Right: Thermometer, Orange Crush, tin, 16" h, 6" w, $100.00.** Photo courtesy Collectors Auction Services.

Lighter, Vick's Vapor Rub, chrome luster finish metal accented by raised gold luster metal domed replica of miniature product jar, inscription "Vaporizing Ointment/Relieves Distress of Colds," engraved initials "G.A.S." beneath jar image, Park Lighter, Murfreesborn, TN, c1950s, 1¼ x 2¼" **20.00**

Lighter, "Ziemer's Sausage Since 1888," slim style, polished finish, black and red enamel painted engraved logo, Zippo, 1963 .... **25.00**

Matchbook, Carstairs White Seal Blended Whiskey, blue, gold, and red printing, seal balancing ball on nose, seal illus on matches, c1940, 3½ x 4½" **10.00**

Memo Booklet, *Libby's Food Products*, celluloid cov, color view of Chicago factories and 6 products, Whitehead & Hoag Co, 2½ x 4½" **50.00**

Memo Tablet, Frigidaire, celluloid front cover framed in tin, cover art and inscriptions **25.00**

Menu, Hurricane Cove, Catalina Island, CA, 10 pp, 1950s, 10 x 12" **20.00**

Pamphlet, Rosenthal Steel 40 & Steel 80 Corn Husker Shredders, 12 pp, 1936, 8 x 9" **12.00**

Paperweight, Westinghouse, figural Tuff Guy, plaster, gold finish, c1952, 2½ x 3 x 5" **50.00**

Pencil, Thomas Barber Supply, celluloid and silvered tin, bullet shaped, removable nose holding lead, red and white striped design with blue lettering, c1930s, 4" l **20.00**

Pencil Clip, Orange-Crush, celluloid, orange, white lettering on dark blue ground **8.00**

Pencil Sharpener, Sunbeam Bread, plastic, red and white, 1950s **5.00**

Pinback Button, Birds Eye Frosted Foods, red symbol and "We Did It!" on white ground, blue rim, c1930s **15.00**

Pinback Button, Genest's Bread, black, white, and red, identical bakers demonstrating "Twin Pack" double loaf packaging, 1930s **20.00**

Pinback Button, New Orleans Steamboat Bread, multicolored bread loaf, c1930s **20.00**

Pinback Button, Old Dutch Cleanser, multicolored litho on yellow ground, inscribed "Clean-Up Week/Chases Dirt/The Symbol Of Healthful Cleanliness," 1930s **20.00**

Pinback Button, Oscar Meyer's Meat Products, red seal "Approved" symbol on yellow triangle against dark blue ground, c1920s **25.00**

Pinback Button, Purina Chicken Chowder, red and white checkered feed sack on blue ground, white lettering, "If Chicken Chowder Won't Make Your Hens Lay They Must Be Roosters," 1920s **15.00**

Pinback Button, Save At Sears, white lettering on purple ground, 1930s **15.00**

Pinback Button, Snoboy, snowman figure on blue ground, black rim, 1940-50s, 3" d **40.00**

Pinback Button, Standby Tomato Juice, can illus on blue ground, black rim, 1940-50s, 3" d **150.00**

Pinback Button, T&T Bread, black, white, and red, image of plaid toy dog, "Tag" in black lettering, 1930s **20.00**

Pinback Button, Wesley's Bread, 1930s **15.00**

Pinback Button, White Rose Tea, white lettering on purple ground, 1930s **8.00**

Pocket Mirror, "Cesspools and Toilets Cleaned by Gas Engine/Cesspools Built," c1920s **35.00**

Postcard, American Legion Convention, Boston, Oct 6-9, 1930, 2 soldiers shaking hands in front of monument and "Welcome Comrade," multicolored **100.00**

Postcard, Uncle John's Golden Tree Syrup, New England Maple Syrup Co, Boston, MA, "The Real Flavor from the Maple Grove," multicolored **35.00**

Record Brush, Liberty State Bank, celluloid, center blue-tone image of bank building surrounded by dark blue inscriptions on white ground, "Our New Home" building, Wilkes Barre, PA, patent date 1924 by Parisian Novelty Co Chicago on rim curl, 4" d **15.00**

Shoe Button Hook, Miller's Cocoa, multicolored, celluloid Dutch windmill mounted on wire extension hook **25.00**

Shoehorn, Brown's 5-Star Shoes, litho metal, yellow upper side, red printing including red and white trademark symbol for Brown Shoe Co, St Louis, Chas W Shonk Co, Chicago, c1920s, 4½" l **25.00**

Shoe Horn, Queen Quality Shoes, ivory white celluloid, full color portrait illus of young and regal lady, reverse with personalized name plus text offering additional shoe horns from TG Plant Co, Boston, c1920s, 6" l **25.00**

Sign, Angelus Marshmallows, cardboard, "One Taste Invites Another," 8¾ x 11½" **150.00**

Sign, Delicious Monogram Tea, porcelain, 1920-30s, 12 x 36" **175.00**

Sign, Dutch Boy Paint, diecut cardboard, stand-up, Dutch Boy on motorcycle, c1930, 14 x 8½" **475.00**

Sign, Dutch Masters Cigars, litho tin, red and white lettering outlined in black, c1940-50s, 9 x 11" **100.00**

Sign, Everpure Safe Water, porcelain, blue silhouette of spring and nude on white ground, 2-sided, 9 x 12" **100.00**

Sign, Holsum Bread, diecut tin, figural bread loaf over heavy wooden frame, 1950-60s, 25 x 68" **175.00**

Sign, Jaeger's Butter-Nut Bread, porcelain, 1940-50s, 12 x 29" **90.00**

Sign, King Quality Shoes For Men, litho tin, diecut shield, center emb royal crown, 9½ x 12" **100.00**

Sign, Lowe Brothers Paint, electric, neon, metal and glass, 11" h **275.00**

Sign, Nation-Wide Food Stores, diecut porcelain, 2-sided, 1940-50s, 32 x 36" **150.00**

Sign, Peter Pan Fresh Bread, metal, 2-sided, blue, orange, and black lettering, blue ground, 20 x 30" **45.00**

Sign, Pillsbury Cake Mixes, full color Art Linkletter illus, 1950s, 11½ x 22" **20.00**

Sign, Purina Poultry Chows, "Fresh Eggs For Sale," 1947, 26 x 19" **75.00**

Sign, Rhinelander Butter, tin over cardboard, "We Sell A Lot Of Rhinelander Butter," 9 x 13" **175.00**

Sign, Savage Tires, silk screen painted on heavy cardboard, Indian boy waving to man in car, 25¾ x 18¾" **325.00**

Sign, Snow King Baking Powder, cardboard, c1930, 12 x 26" **40.00**

Sign, Sunbeam Bread, tin, emb loaf of bread illus, "Reach For Sunbeam/It's Batter-Whipped," red ground, 1959 .... **600.00**

Sign, Weather-Bird Shoes, diecut cardboard, countertop, crowing black rooster image, yellow beak and legs, red comb, 1940s, 6 x 8" **50.00**

Sign, Westinghouse Mazda Lamps, diecut cardboard, easel back, Jackie Cooper holding sign "Buy 'Em Here!," 1930s, 30 x 40" **325.00**

Spinner Top, Fox Typewriter, celluloid, center color image of fox head centered by wooden spinner dowel, light blue outer rim with white lettering outlined in black, 1930s **75.00**

Spinner Top, Monarch Paint, litho tin, 1930s **15.00**

Squeeze Toy, Charlie the Tuna, soft vinyl, ©1973 Star-Kist Foods, 7½" h **50.00**

String Holder, Sunbeam Bread, painted tin, 2-sided, 16" h, 13" w **100.00**

Tab, Aunt Jemima Breakfast Club, litho tin, color portrait, c1950s **15.00**

Tape Measure, Dixie Lye, Pennsylvania Salt Mfg Co, blue and white celluloid canister, product can illus on front, can of Old Hickory food additive on back, 1920s **25.00**

Thermometer, Dri-Power, curved glass over metal, 12" d **175.00**

Thermometer, Hills Bros Coffee, porcelain, 1-sided, man drinking coffee, 20½" h **450.00**

Thermometer, Mail Pouch Tobacco, porcelain, "Chew Mail Pouch Tobacco/Treat Yourself To The Best," 1920-30s, 19 x 74" **525.00**

Thermometer, Ramon's Pills, wood, red and blue illus on yellow ground, 1930-40s, 9 x 21" **175.00**

Thermometer, Stephenson Union Suits, porcelain, 39 x 8¾" **525.00**

Thermometer, Sunbeam Bread, "Reach For Sunbeam Bread," 12" d **825.00**

Thermometer, Ward's Vitovim Bread, porcelain, c1920s, 9 x 21" **625.00**

Tin, Aero Brand Coffee, flying bi-wing airplane image, 5⅝ x 4⅛", 1 lb **350.00**

Tin, Festival Pop Corn, tin top and bottom, cardboard sides, circus performers illus, 5¼ x 2⅝" **300.00**

Tin, Frigidtest Anti-Freeze, 5½ x 4", 1 qt **125.00**

Tin, Romeos Condoms, ¼ x 1¾ x 2⅛" **275.00**

Tin, Seal-Tite Condoms, Allied Latex Sales Division **75.00**

Tin, Silver-Tex Condoms, Killian Mfg Co. **75.00**

Tin, Teddy Bear Peas, paper label, 4½ x 3¼" **175.00**

Tin, Velvet Coffee, factory image on front, steaming cup of coffee on reverse, 8½ x 8¼" **200.00**

Toy Truck, A&P, litho tin, plastic wheels, opening back door, 27½" l **125.00**

Toy Truck, Heinz 57, pressed steel, battery operated, decals, Metalcraft, 13½" l **300.00**

Tray, Tally-Ho Beer, litho tin, English stagecoach image on white ground, red lettering and rim, City Brewing Corp, NY, c1930-40s, 4¼" d **75.00**

Trolley Card, Heinz Rice Flakes, 21 x 11" **50.00**

Tumbler, Yoo-Hoo, plastic, white, dark blue Yogi Berra image on 1 side, light blue product name on other side, 1950s, 5¼" h **75.00**

Watch Fob, Euclid Machinery, metal, different product depicted on each side, "Euclid Earth Moving Equipment," 1950s **8.00**

Watch Fob, Old Dutch Cleanser, brass, porcelain enamel symbol figure on yellow ground, reverse mkd "Old Dutch Cleaner Chases Dirt," Cudahy Packing Co, 1930s **60.00**

Whistle, Cap'n Crunch Bo'sun Whistle, plastic, 2-tone, 3" l **10.00**

Whistle, Citibank, plastic, red, black lettering with sponsor name and "Blow Whistle On Crime/41st Precinct," c1950s **5.00**

Whistle, Culligan Soft Water, plastic, train shaped, "Whistle For Culligan Soft Water," 3¼ x ¾" **15.00**

Whistle, Good & Plenty, plastic, 2-tone, "Good & Plenty, Choo Choo Charlie," 2⅝ x ⅞ x 3/16" **3.00**

Whistle, Poll-Parrot Shoes, litho tin, red, yellow, and green, double-barrel, keychain hole on left end, made in USA, c1930s **20.00**

Whistle, Purity Dairy Products, plastic, train shaped, "I'm Whistling For Purity Dairy Products," 3¼ x ¾" **15.00**

Whistle, Skeezix Shoes, litho tin, red and blue Skeezix image, girlfriend, and dog's head on white ground, "Outgrown Before Outworn," German, 1930s **15.00**

Whistle, Tastykake, litho tin, blue on white, double-barrel, keychain hole on left end, Kirchhof, c1930-40s **15.00**

Yo-Yo, Buster Brown, litho tin, full color Buster and Tige image on yellow, black lettering "Tread Straight" and red arrow symbol, c1930s, 1⅞" d **100.00**

Tin, Ox-Heart Peanut Butter, Oswego Candy Works, 1 lb, 3¾" h, $275.00. Photo courtesy Past Tyme Pleasures.

ADVERTISING CHARACTERS

Many companies created advertising characters as a means of guaranteeing product recognition by the buying public. Consumers are more apt to purchase an item with which they are familiar and advertising characters were a surefire method of developing familiarity.

The early development of advertising characters also enabled immigrants who could not read to identify products by the colorful figures found on the packaging.

Trademarks and advertising characters are found on product labels, in magazines, as premiums, and on other types of advertising. Character subjects may be based on a real person such as Nancy Green, the original "Aunt Jemima." However, more often than not, they are comical figures, often derived from popular contemporary cartoons. Other advertising characters were designed especially to promote a specific product, like Mr. Peanut and the Campbell Kids.

References: Patsy Clevenger, *The Collector's World of M&M's,* Schiffer Publishing, 1998; Pamela Duvall Curran and George W. Curran, *Collectible California Raisins,* Schiffer Publishing, 1998; Warren Dotz, *Advertising Character Collectibles,* Collector Books, 1993, 1997 value update; Joan Stryker Grubaugh, *A Collector's Guide to the Gerber Baby,* published by author, 1996; Ted Hake, *Hake's Guide to Advertising Collectibles,* Wallace-Homestead, 1992; Mary Jane Lamphier, *Zany Characters of the Ad World,* Collector Books, 1995; Myra Yellin Outwater, *Advertising Dolls,* Schiffer Publishing, 1997; Robert Reed, *Bears & Dolls in Advertising,* Antique Trader Books, 1998; David and Micki Young, *Campbell's Soup Collectibles,* Krause Publications, 1998.

Collectors' Clubs: Campbell Soup Collectors Club, 414 Country Lane Ct, Wauconda, IL 60084; Sorry Charlie...No Fan Club For You, 7812 NW Hampton Rd, Kansas City, MO 64152.

Note: See also Planter's Peanuts.

REPRODUCTION ALERT

Aunt Jemima, pancake mold, aluminum, wooden handle, 4 animal shapes **$100.00**

Aunt Jemima, pinback button, cardboard, litho paper full color portrait on red ground, yellow lettering "Pancake Days Are Happy Days, Try Aunt Jemimas Today!" in black lettering, 1940-50s, 4" d **50.00**

Big Boy, bobbing head, c1950s, 7½" h **200.00**

California Raisins, coloring book, "Sports Crazy," Marvel Books, Canada, ©Calrab, Applause, 1988, 8 x 11" **20.00**

California Raisins, game, The California Raisins Board Game, orig 18¾ x 9½" box **15.00**

Campbell's Kids, menu board, tin, "Campbell's Soups M'm! M'm! Good!/Ready In A Jiffy," lists different types of soups, red, yellow, and white, 1950–60s, 11 x 17" **225.00**

Charlie the Tuna, bank, ceramic, figural Charlie standing on can surrounded by coins, 1988, 9½" h **35.00**

Charlie the Tuna, lamp, painted plaster, figural Charlie Tuna wearing orange cap with "Charlie" on bill, black eyebrows and eyeglasses, lavender eyes dotted in black, red opened mouth with pink tongue, earthtone pedestal base, ©1970 Star-Kist Foods, 10" h **50.00**

Borden's Elsie and Elmer, salt and pepper shakers, Japan, c1930s, $85.00. Photo courtesy Collectors Auction Services.

Charlie the Tuna, pin, gold luster metal, small blue rhinestone accents, ©Star-Kist Foods, c1960s **25.00**

Ernie Keebler, squeeze toy, molded vinyl, 1974, 7" h **15.00**

Hamm's Beer Bear, bank, figural, name on chest, rubber trap, made in Japan, orig 5 x 5 x 12" box, c1980s, 11" h **100.00**

Little Green Sprout, Green Giant Co, transistor radio, figural, plastic, 1980s, 8½" h **30.00**

Miss Curity, display, 20" h hard plastic white painted figure on 3½ x 6½" wooden base with stepped outer edges, c1950s **100.00**

Otto Orkin, figure, plastic, red, inscribed on reverse "Call Otto," 1950-60s **25.00**

Pillsbury Dough Boy, salt and pepper shakers, pr, ceramic, c1980s, 3½" h **30.00**

RCA Victor "Nipper," salt and pepper shakers, pr, white china, figural, base inscribed "RCA Victor/His Master's Voice," black eye dots, nose and ears, thin gold collar, c1930s, 3" h **50.00**

Reddy Kilowatt, cuff links, pr, gold luster metal, domed plastic over portrait in gold, red tongue accent, 1940-50s **60.00**

Reddy Kilowatt, light bulb, clear glass, threaded brass contact fitting, inner diecut filament figure of 1½" h Reddy, c1950s, 4" h, 2½" d **200.00**

Reddy Kilowatt, pinback button, blue and white, red figure image, "Reddy Kilowatt/Your Electric Servant," c1950s **15.00**

Reddy Kilowatt, sign, porcelain, 2-sided, Reddy holding shield, "Warning Gas Pipeline," 1950-60s, 8 x 11" **200.00**

Smokey Bear, mug, ceramic, white, figural Smokey Bear handle, Smokey Bear depiction on 1 side, "I Like Milk/F is for forests–keep fire away!," mkd "WC Kay," 3¼" h, 2¾" d **30.00**

Speedy Alka-Seltzer, bank, figural, soft hollow rubber, coin slot in top side of tablet-like hat inscribed "Alka-Seltzer Bank," red accent, 1960s, 5½" h **200.00**

Speedy Alka-Seltzer, thermometer, glass and aluminum, 12" d **375.00**

Willie the Penguin, Kool Cigarettes, lighter, figural, hard plastic, black and white, yellow beak and webbed foot, decal on chest, late 1930s, 3 x 3½ x 9" **100.00**

Willie the Penguin, Kool Cigarettes, pinback button, multicolored Willie between political donkey and elephant, 1930-40s **25.00**

Willie Wirehand, coin, aluminum, 2-sided, inscription for 25th anniversary, 1960 . . . . **15.00**

Willie Wirehand, pinback button, "The Farmers' Friend,"
red and white, 1960s **45.00**
Woodsy Owl, bank, "Give A Hoot...Don't Pollute" on
base, c1970s, 8½" h **75.00**

Marbleized,
cigarette holder,
blue and white
8-sided, 2³/₄" h,
$15.00. Photo
courtesy Ray
Morykan Auctions.

AUCTION PRICES – BUDDY LEE DOLLS

Gary Metz's Muddy River Trading Co., 9th Annual Fall Antique
Advertising Auction, October 29-30, 1999. Prices include a
10% buyer's premium.

Composition, cowboy, overalls, shirt, cowboy hat,
and red scarf **$121.00**
Composition, dark blue denim coveralls, medium
blue shirt, Lee hat **176.00**
Composition, engineer, wearing dark blue cover-
alls, white shirt, red scarf, and engineer's cap,
few marks and small cracks **187.00**
Plastic, cowboy, overalls, red plaid shirt, black cow-
boy hat with marked band **187.00**
Plastic, engineer, dark blue coveralls, shirt, and hat,
red scarf **198.00**
Plastic, engineer, dark blue coveralls, shirt, hat, and
scarf **242.00**
Plastic, Lee coveralls, denim shirt, Lee hat **165.00**
Plastic, overalls, red and white plaid shirt **77.00**
Plastic, solid denim overalls, shirt, and hat, red scarf . . **154.00**
Plastic, striped coveralls, striped denim shirt **55.00**
Plastic, striped coveralls and shirt, red scarf **165.00**

AKRO AGATE

The Akro Agate Company was founded in Ohio in 1911 primarily
to manufacture agate marbles. In 1914 the firm opened a large factory in Clarksburg, West Virginia.

Increasing competition in the marble industry in the 1930s
prompted Akro Agate to expand. In 1936, following a major fire at
the Westite factory, Akro Agate purchased many of Westite's
molds. Akro Agate now boasted a large line of children's dishes,
floral wares, and household accessories. The company also produced specialty glass containers for cosmetic firms, including the
Mexicali cigarette jar (originally filled with Pick Wick bath salts)
and a special line made for the Jean Vivaudou Company, Inc.

The Clarksburg Glass Company bought the factory in 1951.

Akro Agate glass has survived the test of time because of its
durability. Most pieces are marked "Made in USA" and often
include a mold number. Some pieces have a small crow in the
mark. Early pieces of Akro made from Westite molds may be
unmarked but were produced only in typical Akro colors and color
combinations.

Reference: Roger and Claudia Hardy, *The Complete Line of Akro
Agate: Marbles, General Line, and Children's Dishes,* published by
authors, 1992.

Collectors' Club: Akro Agate Collector's Club, 97 Milford St,
Clarksburg, WV 26301.

Note: See Children's Dishes and Marbles for additional listings.

REPRODUCTION ALERT: Reproduction pieces are unmarked.

Chiquita, child's creamer, baked on cobalt **$10.00**
Chiquita, child's cup, opaque green **6.00**
Chiquita, child's cup, transparent cobalt **14.00**
Chiquita, child's dinner plate, opaque green **8.00**
Chiquita, child's saucer, opaque yellow **12.00**
Chiquita, child's teapot lid, light blue **40.00**
Concentric Rib, child's plate, opaque green **4.00**
Concentric Rib, child's teapot, open, light blue **8.00**
Concentric Rib, child's teapot, open, opaque green **8.00**
Graduated Dart, planter, dark blue, oval, scalloped, 8½" **30.00**
Interior Panel, child's creamer, opaque blue **45.00**
Interior Panel, child's plate, opaque green **8.00**
Interior Panel, child's teapot, cov, opaque green **50.00**
Marbelized, ashtray, blue, 2⁷/₈" sq **8.00**
Marbelized, ashtray, orange shell **7.00**
Octagonal, saucer, beige, closed handle, large **4.00**
Octagonal, set, 17 pcs, green plates and cups, white
saucers **165.00**
Octagonal, sugar lid, beige **12.00**
Stacked Disc, tumbler, opaque beige **12.00**
Stacked Disc, tumbler, white **12.00**
Stacked Disc, water pitcher, opaque green, small **10.00**
Stippled Band, cup, green, large **20.00**
Stippled Band, cup and saucer, cobalt, large **35.00**
Stippled Band, set, 3 pcs, plate, cup and saucer, green **30.00**

ALADDIN LAMPS

Victor Samuel Johnson founded the Western Lighting Company in
Kansas City, Missouri, in 1907. In 1908 the company became the
Mantle Lamp Company of America. In 1909, Johnson introduced
the Aladdin lamp. Although the company has diversified and
become as well known for its lunch boxes and vacuum bottles as
its lamps, Aladdin lamps are still being manufactured today.

References: J. W. Courter, *Aladdin Collectors Manual & Price
Guide #19: Kerosene Mantle Lamps,* published by author, 2000; J.
W. Courter, *Aladdin Electric Lamps: Collectors Manual & Price
Guide #3,* published by author, 1997; J. W. Courter, *Aladdin: The
Magic Name in Lamps, Revised Edition,* published by author,
1997.

Collectors' Club: Aladdin Knights of the Mystic Light, 3935 Kelley Rd, Kevil, KY 42053.

REPRODUCTION ALERT: Tall Lincoln Drape, Short Lincoln Drape, glass and paper shades.

Note: All kerosene lamps priced with complete burners.

ELECTRIC

G-2, table, marble-like glass	$350.00
G-141, table, moonstone	80.00
G-190, opalique	125.00
G-215, blue crystal bowl	300.00
G-294D, alacite, colonial scene	60.00
G-349, planter lamp with planter, alacite	150.00
M-1, table, metal, bronze	150.00
M-93, Whip-O-Lite shade	225.00
M-238, desk, plastic shade	75.00
M-350, pin-up lamp, cast white metal, plated	75.00
M-476, abacus lamp	60.00
P-408, planter lamp	100.00
TV-426, metal, foil shade	25.00

KEROSENE

102, Model A, table, Venetian, peach	$250.00
107, Model B, table, Cathedral, clear crystal	150.00
1240, Model 12, table, crystal vase, variegated verge	250.00
B-30, Model B, table, Simplicity, white	175.00
B-51, Model B, table, Washington Drape, green crystal, filigree stem	175.00
B-60, Model B, table, alacite	600.00
B-86, Model B, table, Quilt, green moonstone	350.00
B-106, Model B, Corinthian, clear font, amber foot	175.00
B-122, Model B, table, Majestic, green moonstone	450.00
B-131, Model B, table, Orientale, green	200.00
B-139, Model C, table, aluminum font	50.00
B-140, Model 21C, low boy, with base, aluminum, font	50.00
B-293, Model B, floor, antique ivory lacquer	225.00
B-294, Model B, floor, bronze and gold lacquer	250.00
Model 12, 4-post, with parchment shade	350.00
Model 23, hanging, aluminum hanger and font, with white paper shade	75.00

ALUMINUM WARE

The mass production of hand-wrought aluminum decorative accessories is indebted to the inventiveness of Charles M. Hall and Paul T. Heroult. Hall of the United States and Heroult in France, working independently, simultaneously discovered an inexpensive electrolytic reduction process in 1886. Soon after, the price of aluminum dropped from $545 per pound to 57¢ per pound.

Aluminum ware's popularity thrived throughout the lean Depression years and into the first years of World War II, when aluminum shortages caused many factories to close. Some resumed production after the war; however, most pieces no longer originated with the artistic craftsman—the Machine Age had arrived. By the late 1960s, decorative aluminum was no longer in fashion.

References: Dannie Woodard and Billie Wood, *Hammered Aluminum: Hand-Wrought Collectibles*, published by authors, 1983, 1990 value update; Dannie A. Woodard, *Hammered*

Aluminum Hand-Wrought Collectibles, Book Two, Aluminum Collectors' Books, 1993.

Collectors' Clubs: Hammered Aluminum Collectors Assoc, PO Box 1346, Weatherford, TX 76086; Wendell August Collectors Guild, PO Box 107, Grove City, PA 16127.

Arthur Armour, relish tray, flying geese, 16 x 5"	$75.00
Arthur Armour, tray, butterfly	25.00
Arthur Armour, tray, wild horses	125.00
Continental, bowl, chrysanthemum, fluted edge, 5½" d	15.00
Continental, bread tray, chrysanthemum, scalloped edge with 2 applied leaves, 11 x 8"	25.00
Continental, candelabra, 3-lite, #833	12.00
Continental, coffee urn, stylized flowers, cone shaped double wire curlicue stem, 8 x 5"	15.00
Continental, ice bucket, chrysanthemum, mushroom and leaf finial on lid, 8 x 9"	40.00
Continental, ice bucket, open, acorn and leaf, cone shaped handles, 7 x 3"	25.00
Continental, serving tray, rose, applied handle with emb roses, 18 x 13"	35.00
Continental, silent butler, wild roses, 8" d	30.00
Continental, tray, chrysanthemum, chopped corners	35.00
Continental, tray, paisley pattern, #1003	45.00
Continental, tray, round, handled, pansies	55.00
Continental, tumbler, ftd, chrysanthemum	35.00
Everlast, ashtray, 3 rests, head of hunting dog superimposed over shotgun with 2 flying ducks in background, 6" d	45.00
Everlast, basket, palms, square handle with round finials, 10 x 5"	30.00
Everlast, casserole, bamboo, no handles, bamboo finial, 7" d	15.00
Everlast, coaster, daisies	35.00
Everlast, crumb brush and tray, grapevine, lucite brush handle with plastic bristles	20.00
Palmer Smith, nut dish, ivy	25.00
Rodney Kent, basket, tulip, hexagon shaped, cutout dogwood floral design on handle, 7 x 4"	30.00
Rodney Kent, casserole, hammered, tulip finial with ribbons, 8 x 6"	20.00

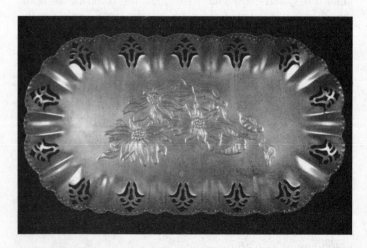

Farber, bread tray, poinsettia-type flower dec, reticulated ruffled sides, marked "Farber & Schlein Inc. Hand Wrought, 1718," 7" w, 12½" l, $20.00.

Wendell August, double server, apple blossom, La
Miranda inserts **350.00**
Wendell August, match box, shotgun with flying ducks **50.00**
Wendell August, mint dish, dogwood, glass insert, 12" d **45.00**
Wendell August, napkin holder, dogwood, 4 x 3 x 4½" **30.00**
Wendell August, plate, dogwood, 9" d **30.00**
Wendell August, plate, jumping trout in water, crimped
edge, 8½" d **50.00**
World, pitcher and 6 plain tumblers, applied flower,
hand forged **100.00**

AMERICAN BISQUE

The American Bisque Company, founded in Williamstown, West
Virginia in 1919, was originally established for the manufacture of
china head dolls. The company soon began producing novelties
such as cookie jars, ashtrays, serving dishes, and ceramic giftware.

B. E. Allen, founder of the Sterling China Company, invested
heavily in the company and eventually purchased the remaining
stock. In 1982 the company operated briefly under the name
American China Company. The plant ceased operations in 1983.

American Bisque items have various markings. The trademark
"Sequoia Ware" is often found on items sold in gift shops. The
Berkeley trademark was used on pieces sold through chain stores.
The most common mark found consists of three stacked baby
blocks with the letters A, B, and C.

Reference: Mary Jane Giacomini, *American Bisque,* Schiffer
Publishing, 1994.

Bank, Figaro, 6¾" h **$75.00**
Bank, Little Audrey, 8¼" h **750.00**
Bank, Sweet Pea, 8¼" h **800.00**
Cookie Jar, basket of cookies, 11¼" h **100.00**
Cookie Jar, cat, standing, hands in pocket, chartreuse,
11½" h **100.00**
Cookie Jar, cat, tail finial, 10¼" h **125.00**
Cookie Jar, cat on quilt, 13" h **100.00**
Cookie Jar, collegiate owl, 11½" h **75.00**
Cookie Jar, cookie barrel, 9½" h **25.00**
Cookie Jar, cowboy boots, 12½" h **175.00**
Cookie Jar, deer, log finial, 9" h **125.00**
Cookie Jar, dog with toothache, 13½" h **650.00**
Cookie Jar, elephant, standing, hands in pocket, 10½" h **150.00**
Cookie Jar, gift box, 9½" h **100.00**
Cookie Jar, igloo, seal finial, 11" h **250.00**
Cookie Jar, kitten on beehive **50.00**
Cookie Jar, Liberty Bell, 9¾" h **100.00**
Cookie Jar, majorette, 11¼" h **225.00**
Cookie Jar, moon rocket, "Cookies Out Of This World,"
12¼" h **250.00**
Cookie Jar, peasant girl, 10½" h **450.00**
Cookie Jar, pig in a poke, 12½" h **75.00**
Cookie Jar, poodle, bow finial, 10¼" h **125.00**
Cookie Jar, saddle, 12" h **250.00**
Cookie Jar, sad iron, 11½" h **125.00**
Cookie Jar, Santa Claus, 9¾" h **375.00**
Cookie Jar, spool of thread, thimble finial, 10¾" h **125.00**
Cookie Jar, SS Kookie, 11¾" h **150.00**
Cookie Jar, strawberry, 8¾" h **30.00**
Cookie Jar, treasure chest, 8" h **175.00**
Cream Pitcher, chick, standing, 7¾" h **20.00**
Planter, bear with beehive, 5¾" h **15.00**

Cookie Jar, churn, marked "USA," $25.00.

Planter, bird with blossom, gold trim, 4" h **30.00**
Planter, cocker spaniel with basket, 6¼" h **20.00**
Planter, donkey pulling cart, 6½" h **10.00**
Planter, elephant in basket, 3¾" h **8.00**
Planter, farmer pig with ear of corn, 6½" h **8.00**
Planter, kitten and shoe, mkd "USA," 3½" h **15.00**
Planter, kitten with fish bowl, 6" h **20.00**
Planter, paddle boat, 4¼" h, 9½" l **20.00**
Planter, rabbit in log, 5¾" h **25.00**
Planter, sailfish, 8 x 10" **45.00**
Planter, wailing kitten, mkd "USA" **20.00**
Range Shakers, pr, strawberry, 5" h **20.00**
Salt and Pepper Shakers, pr, chef, 5" h **25.00**
Salt and Pepper Shakers, pr, chick, 3½" h **12.00**
Salt and Pepper Shakers, pr, clown, 3½" h **15.00**
Salt and Pepper Shakers, pr, lamb, 3½" h **12.00**
Wall Pocket, birdhouse, gold trim, 5½" h **30.00**
Wall Pocket, heart and flowers, gold trim, 6" h **25.00**

AMERICAN INDIAN

Post-1920 American Indian, a.k.a. Native American, objects divide
into two basic groups: (1) objects made for use within the tribe and
(2) objects made for the tourist trade. Tribal pieces are subdivided
into ceremonial and utilitarian objects. Tourist items subdivide into
pre-1940 objects which are highly desirable and post-1945
objects which have only modest collector interest at the moment.

As with all American Indian material, it is extremely important
to identify the tribe of the maker. Identification with a specific
maker, especially if featured in a museum collection or major reference book, also is a value added factor.

Individuals, from school teachers to missionaries, who worked
on Indian reservations often received handmade artifacts as gifts.
Carefully check the authenticity of such an attribution before paying a premium price for an object.

References: Lar Hothem, *North American Indian Artifacts, 6th
Edition,* Krause Publications, 1998; Marian Rodee, *Weaving of the
Southwest,* Schiffer Publishing, 1987; John A. Shuman III,
Warman's Native American Collectibles, Krause Publications,
1998.

Periodicals: *American Indian Art Magazine,* 7314 E Osborn Dr, Scottsdale, AZ 85251; *The Indian Trader,* PO Box 1421, Gallup, NM 87305.

REPRODUCTION ALERT: Watch out for American Indian jewelry imported from the Philippines. Several villages changed their names to correspond to the names of Native American tribes, e.g., Zuni. The Filipinos have plenty of company in the faking of American Indian crafts. Brazilians, Nigerians, and Pakistanis weave copies of Apache, Navajo, and Pima baskets. Mexicans weave imitation Navajo blankets. Chinese carve animal fetishes. Thai workers make imitation jewelry. The Filipinos are branching out. Their latest fakes include Hopi kachina dolls.

Kachina Doll, possibly Poli, polychrome decorated, missing toes, mid-20th C, 11" h, $450.00. Photo courtesy Skinner, Inc., Boston, MA.

Bag, Plateau, beaded cloth and hide, front beaded with US flags, bald eagle, and clouds, on bright orange field, 11½" l **$525.00**

Basket, Apache, burden-style, 2 rows of tin cone danglers, inverted cone at base, early 20th C, 11" h **350.00**

Bolo Tie, Navajo, stamped and relief motifs including bison head set with turquoise and coral, sgd "KD" on back **75.00**

Bowl, Apache, shallow oval, checkerboard zigzags, 4 sets of paired dogs, c1920, 15" l **1,150.00**

Bowl, Santo Domingo Pueblo, wide band of repeating geometric motifs at lip, sgd "Anna Marie, T. Lovate," 8½" d **225.00**

Bowl, Southwest, polychrome, black and red geometric devices on cream ground, applied snake at rim, mid-20th C, 5" h **125.00**

Bowl, Zuni, red, cream, and brown slip designs, geometric band depicting deer with heart lines and flora motif at neck, c1920s, 4¾" d **350.00**

Bracelet, Navajo, stamped and twisted silver with round and elliptical turquoise stones, c1930s, ¾" w **575.00**

Bracelet, Navajo, stamped design with turquoise square stones and applied silver beading, c1920, ½" w **400.00**

Doll, Hopi, Kachina doll, priest in felt kilt and tunic, articulated arms, c1960, 10" h **325.00**

Dough Bowl, Acoma Pueblo, black and orange stepped geometric devices on cream ground, int band of elliptical devices, deeply patinated, c1920, 11½" d **575.00**

Drum, Southwest, probably Tarahumara, hide cov, painted with brick red cross and multipointed star, c1940, 25" d **500.00**

Jar, Santa Clara Pueblo, highly polished gunmetal surface, deeply carved water serpent figure, sgd "Clara Swazo" at base, 4½" h **150.00**

Miniature Pipe and Stem, Central Plains, possibly Lakota, black stone pipe, T-shaped bowl, carved red ash stem with 4 carved turtles, 9" l **375.00**

Moccasins, Cheyenne, beaded white field with powder blue, black, and opaque red geometric and keyhole designs, c1920, 10½" l **375.00**

Necklace, Pueblo, double-strand with carved disk clamshell and turquoise with nugget turquoise, c1920s, 13½" l **150.00**

Olla, Acoma Pueblo, geometric stepped and elliptical devices, black and light orange hatching on white ground, indented base, c1920, 7¾" h **750.00**

Photograph, silvertone, warrior on horseback carrying spear, back labeled "Chief Black Bird, Reed," 10 x 7¾" **750.00**

Pipe Bag, Blackfeet, buckskin, edge beading at top and sides, beaded panel with hourglass and Maltese cross devices, multicolored faceted beads on blue ground, large beads strung singly on fringe, 20" l **425.00**

Saddle Blanket, Navajo, dyed and natural homespun wool, banded style, 51 x 29" **200.00**

Seed Jar, Hopi, ear of corn at base, square opening, intricate geometric design on shoulder and body, sgd "Dextra," 5½" h **925.00**

Seed Jar, Hopi, red and brown slip on creamy ground, stylized bear paw motif, 20th C, 6¼" d **225.00**

Shirt, child's, Navajo, velvet, burnt orange, silver button dec at cuffs, elbow, shoulders, collar, and plaque, c1930s, 22" l **250.00**

Weaving, Navajo, homespun wool, variegated golden browns and gray banded design including Maltese crosses, 50 x 67" **300.00**

AUCTION PRICES – NAVAJO WEAVINGS

Butterfield's Auctioneers, Native American, Pre-Columbian, Spanish Colonial and Tribal Works of Art, November 17, 1999. Prices include a 15% buyer's premium.

Blanket, Transitional Moki, borderless, pair of large interlinked stepped diamonds over finely banded ground, varicolored fire-like tips at corners, red, orange, navy, blue-black, dark brown, and gray-white, approx. 7'7" x 4'10" **$3,163.00**

Rug, Red Mesa, allover pattern of complementary and concentric diamonds in straight-sided and outlined terraced style, single thin banded border, tan, dark brown, orange, red, white, and gray, approx. 6'2" x 4' **920.00**

Saddle Blanket, Germantown, complementary serrated diamonds in contrasting style and color, enclosed by T-form and banded borders, green, gold, orange, maroon, black, white, purple, and red, approx. 2'10" x 2'3" **805.00**

Weaving, Manta design, central horizontal band of stepped diamonds split by narrow zigzag stripe, reciprocal panels above and below, white, red, and variegated dark brown, approx. 4'11" x 3'7" . . **2,300.00**

ANCHOR HOCKING

The Hocking Glass Company was founded in Lancaster, Ohio in 1905. Although the company originally produced handmade items, by the 1920s the firm was manufacturing a wide variety of wares including chimneys and lantern globes, tableware, tumblers, and novelties. Hocking introduced its first line of pressed glass dinnerware in 1928. Molded etched tableware was released shortly thereafter.

Following the acquisition of several glass houses in the 1920s, Hocking began producing new glass containers. In 1937 Hocking merged with the Anchor Cap and Closure Corporation, resulting in a name change in 1939 to Anchor Hocking Glass Corporation. In 1969 the company became Anchor Hocking Corporation.

References: Gene Florence, *Anchor Hocking's Fire-King & More,* Collector Books, 1998; Philip Hopper, *Anchor Hocking Commemorative Bottles and Other Collectibles,* Schiffer Publishing, 2000; Philip Hopper, *Forest Green Glass,* Schiffer Publishing, 2000; Philip Hopper, *Royal Ruby,* Schiffer Publishing, 1998.

Note: See Depression Glass and Fire-King for additional listings.

Berry Bowl, Bubble, 4" d, crystal iridescent	$4.00
Bowl, Early American Prescut, #726, 4¼" d	7.00
Bowl, Royal Ruby, flared, 11½" d	40.00
Butter, cov, Sandwich, crystal	45.00
Candlesticks, pr, Bubble, forest green	40.00
Cereal Bowl, Queen Mary, pink	25.00
Creamer, Sandwich, forest green	30.00
Creamer, Shell, jade-ite	18.00
Cup, Queen Mary, pink	7.00
Cup and Saucer, Meadow Green	3.00
Dessert Bowl, Harvest	5.00
Dinner Plate, Queen Mary, pink	60.00
Dinner Plate, Wheat, 10" d	5.00
Juice Pitcher, Royal Ruby	40.00
Juice Tumbler, Queen Mary, pink	9.00
Mug, Game Birds, 8 oz	8.00
Plate, Queen Mary, 6" d, pink	7.00
Punch Set, Royal Ruby, 14 pcs	125.00
Salad Plate, Royal Ruby, 7¾" d	6.00
Sherbet, Queen Mary, ftd, pink	9.00
Snack Plate, Early American Prescut, #780, 10" d	10.00
Vegetable, Shell, 8½" l, jade-ite	125.00
Water Tumbler, Fleurette, 9½ oz, 4⅛" h	50.00
Water Tumbler, Queen Mary, flat, pink	12.00

Candle Holders, pr, Moonstone, 1941-46, $18.00. Photo courtesy Ray Morykan Auctions.

ANIMAL COLLECTIBLES

The hobby of collecting objects depicting one's favorite animal has thrived for years. The more common species have enjoyed long lives of popularity. Cats, dogs, cows, horses, and pigs are examples of animals whose collectibility is well established. Their markets are so stable, in fact, that they merit separate listings of their own.

The desirability of other animals changes with the times. Many remain fashionable for only a limited period of time, or their popularity cycles, often due to marketing crazes linked to advertising.

References: Alan J. Brainard, *Turtle Collectibles,* Schiffer Publishing, 2000; Lee Garmon and Dick Spencer, *Glass Animals of the Depression Era,* Collector Books, 1993, out of print; Everett Grist, *Covered Animal Dishes,* Collector Books, 1988, 2000 value update.

Newsletter: *The Glass Animal Bulletin,* PO Box 143, North Liberty, IA 52317.

Collectors' Clubs: The Frog Pond, PO Box 193, Beech Grove, IN 46107; International Owl Collectors Club, 54 Triverton Rd, Edgware, Middlesex HA8 6BE U.K.

Note: See Beswick, Breyer Horses, Cat Collectibles, Cow Collectibles, Dog Collectibles, Elephant Collectibles, Figural Planters & Vases, Figurines, Grindley Pottery, Horse Collectibles, Pig Collectibles, Royal Doulton, and other manufacturer categories for additional listings.

Bear, sticker, Texaco adv, diecut paper, brown cub balancing on Texaco logo, "Don't Hibernate–Insulate! Easy Riding With Marfak," c1937, 2 x 4"	$40.00
Bear, wall plaque, brown, black, and white shiny glaze, made in Japan, 5½" w	15.00
Camel, bank, cast iron, painted gold, red trimmed blanket, 4¾" h	150.00
Cocker Spaniel, doorstop, mkd "VA Metalcrafters, Waynebora VA Dream Boy 18-7 1949," 9 x 7"	175.00
Dachshund, bookends, pr, Bradley & Hubbard, mkd "9780," 4½ x 8"	25.00
Deer, figure, amber, blue, and silver foil encased in crystal, red label "Made in Murano, Italy," probably Seguso, 9" h	100.00
Deer, figure, pearlized Winter Rose pattern, Fenton, 5¼" h	20.00
Donkey, toothbrush holder, "If tail is dry–fine. If tail is wet–rain. If tail moves–windy. If tail cannot be seen–fog. If tail is frozen–cold. If tail falls out-earthquake," multicolored shiny glazes, made in Japan, 8½" l	30.00
Dove, figure, white sommerso with silver powdered emerald back encased in clear crystal, applied white and black eyes, probably Seguso, 8½" h	30.00
Duck, bottle, duck form stopper, swirl ribbed black bottle, emerald green shading to amber stopper, mkd "Made in Murano (Italy) for Luxardo, 1969," 12½" h	70.00
Duck, creamer and sugar, orange and yellow shiny glazes, made in Japan, 3¼" h	55.00
Duck, flower frog, brown, blue and gray glaze, Fulper, ink racetrack mark, 3½ x 3¼"	70.00
Duck, patch, "Protect Our Wildlife," quilt style stitched fabric, diecut overlay fabric pair of ducks, white stitched lettering, c1950s, 6 x 7½"	20.00

Owl, pitcher, Kanawha Glass, Vintage color (yellow-red), 5" h, $12.00.

Flamingo, planter, raised wing, Maddux, 6" h **35.00**
Frog, ashtray, multicolored semi-matte glazes, made in
Japan, 5" w **20.00**
Frog, doorstop, cast iron, 1³/₄" h **50.00**
Frog, garden sculpture/fountain, matte green glaze,
Wheatley, unmkd, 7³/₄ x 8¹/₄" **925.00**
Heron, label, Blue Heron Citrus, blue heron stalking
through cattails and reeds, 9" sq. **2.00**
Jaguar, car mascot, chrome plated, 1956-64 . . . . **55.00**
Large Mouth Bass, doorstop, bronze tone finish, 5¹/₂ x
13" **425.00**
Lion, paperweight, Tiger Brand Quarry Products, sil-
vered cast iron, figural cement sack with tiger head,
"Tiger Brand White Rock Finish/Manufactured By The
Keilly Island Lime & Transport Co., Cleveland, Ohio,"
product name repeated on top and bottom of sack,
c1920-30s, 2 x 3 x ³/₄" **65.00**
Lion, pinback button, Lion Coffee **10.00**
Lion, ring holder/soap dish, multicolored shiny glaze,
made in Japan, 2³/₄" h **25.00**
Monkey, pocket mirror, 2 monkeys and inscription "You
Want To See The Third Like Him Just Turn Over," insert
mirror on reverse, Germany, c1930s, 1¹/₈" d **10.00**
Otter, figure, white, Haeger, 5" h **25.00**
Owl, advertising stand-up, diecut cardboard, litho, Wise
Potato Chips owl beside bag of chips, 29¹/₂" h, 20" w **725.00**
Owl, label, Snow Owl Pears, orchard scene, snowy
peak, farmhouse framed by forest trees **1.00**
Owl, pinback button, Owl-Musty Ale, multicolored owl
head on black ground, white lettering, AG Van
Nostrand, Bunker Hill Breweries, Charlestown, MA **40.00**
Parrot, flower frog, multicolored shiny glaze, made in
Japan, 7¹/₂" h **40.00**
Rabbit, seated, bank, cast iron, painted white, 4⁵/₈ x 4³/₈" **275.00**
Seal, bank, cast iron, 4¹/₄ x 5¹/₄" **50.00**
Spider, paperweight, brass, ³/₄" h, 4 x 5" w **40.00**
Squirrel, figure, carnival chalkware, hp features, 3¹/₄ x 3" **10.00**
Squirrel, nutcracker, cast iron, 4¹/₄ x 5⁷/₈" **35.00**
Stork, figure, hp features, 12" h **35.00**
Swan, flower frog, circle of swans, white, orange beaks,
shiny glaze, made in Japan, 4¹/₄" h **40.00**
Zebra, figurine, emb details in glossy white glaze,
Waylande Gregory script signature, 11¹/₂ x 10³/₄" **400.00**

ANIMATION ART

To understand animation art, one must understand its terminology. The vocabulary involving animation cels is very specific. The difference between a master, key production, printed or publication, production, and studio background can mean thousands of dollars in value.

A "cel" is an animation drawing on celluloid. One second of film requires over twenty animation cels. Multiply the length of a cartoon in minutes times sixty times twenty-four in order to approximate the number of cels used in a single cartoon strip. The vast quantities of individual cels produced are mind-boggling. While Walt Disney animation cels are indisputably the most sought after, the real bargains in the field exist elsewhere. Avoid limited edition serigraphs. A serigraph is a color print made by the silk-screen process. Although it appears to be an animation cel, it is not.

References: Jeff Lotman, *Animation Art: The Early Years, 1911–1954,* Schiffer Publishing, 1995; Jeff Lotman, *Animation Art: The Later Years, 1954–1993,* Schiffer Publishing, 1996, out of print.

Periodical: *Animation Magazine,* 30101 Agoura Court, Ste 110, Agoura Hills, CA 91301.

Collectors' Club: Animation Art Guild, Ltd, 330 W 45th St, Ste 9D, New York, NY 10036.

Drawing, colored pencil on animation sheets, MGM
Studio, *Push Button Kitty,* 33 orig black and white
background layout drawings from Tom and Jerry cartoon in which Mammy Two Shoes introduces
Mechano "the cat of tomorrow," color pencil highlights depicting detailed scenes, studio stamps and
notes, unframed, 1952, size ranges: 9 x 12"–9 x 24" . . . **$1,250.00**
Drawing, pencil on animation sheet, MGM Studio, *Tom
and Jerry at the Hollywood Bowl,* Tom and Jerry playing the Hollywood Bowl as rival conductors of all-
feline orchestra, 4 layout drawings showing main
entrance, 2 views of park-like area leading to Bowl,
and view of audience from podium, studio notes and
stamps, unframed, 1950, size ranges: 9 x 18"–9 x 24" **500.00**
Drawing, red and black pencil on animation sheet,
MGM Studio, *The Cat and the Mermouse,* in watery
depths Tom is eyeball-to-eyeball with Jerry the mermouse, studio notes and stamp, matted, 1949, 8 x
11¹/₂" **375.00**
Drawing, red and black pencil on animation sheet,
MGM Studio, *The Peachy Cobbler,* 2 layout drawings
for consecutive scenes of Tex Avery's cartoon depicting 1 of the elves as he unleashes a termite on block
of wood which is transformed into wooden shoe, studio stamp and notes, unframed, 1950, 8¹/₂ x 12", and
6¹/₂ x 9" **500.00**
Drawing, red, black, and blue pencil on animation
sheet, Ub Iwerks Studio, *Movie Mad,* orig drawing of
Flip the Frog, matted, 1931, 7 x 5¹/₂" **450.00**
Drawing, red, green, blue, and black pencil on anima-
tion sheets, MGM Studio, *Texas Tom,* 3 background
layout drawings for 8 scenes depicting dude ranch
scene of Tom and Jerry with cute girl kitten, unframed,
1950, size ranges: 8¹/₂ x 12"–9 x 20" **450.00**

Gouache on Celluloid, De Patie Freleng Studio, *Dr Seuss' The Grinch Grinches the Cat in the Hat,* portrait cel of Grinch wearing sly smile, framed, with 1985 First Day Cover envelope for "Help Fight Hunger" stamp sgd "–Dr. Seuss," untrimmed, framed, 1982, 6½ x 6½" **575.00**

Gouache on Celluloid, Hanna-Barbera Studio, *The Jetsons,* 2 cels from animated TV series, George at controls flying family car as Elroy exits for day at school, trimmed, framed, 1962, 6¼ x 8½" **875.00**

Gouache on Celluloid, tempera on background sheet, Warner Bros Studio, *Yosemite Sam,* Yosemite Sam wearing dressy duds, set over western theme master background from cartoon of another studio, untrimmed, framed, c1980, 8 x 10" overall **375.00**

Gouache on Celluloid, Walt Disney Studio, *The Rescuers,* portrait cel of Madame Medusa, laminated, with Disney seal and certificate of authenticity, untrimmed, matted, 1977, 8 x 10¼" **500.00**

Gouache on Celluloid, Warner Bros Studio, *A Touch of Poison Ivy,* limited edition, hp cel, scene from "Pretty Poison" episode of "Batman the Animated Series," set over color print ground, #206 of 500, with WB seal and certificate of authenticity, framed, 1994, 13 x 15½" **300.00**

Gouache on Celluloid, Warner Bros Studio, *Bugs Bunny's Busting Out All Over,* full figure cel of Bugs Bunny, production #CJ-53 on bottom edge, untrimmed, matted, 1980, 6¼ x 6" **350.00**

Gouache on Celluloid, Warner Bros Studio, *Foghorn Leghorn,* sgd by Friz Freleng, with WB copyright and seal, untrimmed, framed, 1983, 7 x 7½" **625.00**

APPLIANCES

The turn of the century saw the popularity of electric kitchen appliances increase to the point where most metropolitan households sported at least one of these modern conveniences. By the 1920s, innovations and improvements were occurring at a rapid pace. The variations designed for small appliances were limitless.

Some "firsts" in electrical appliances include:

1882   Patent for electric iron (H. W. Seeley [Hotpoint])
1903   Detachable cord (G. E. Iron)
1905   Toaster (Westinghouse Toaster Stove)
1909   Travel iron (G. E.)
1911   Electric frying pan (Westinghouse)
1912   Electric waffle iron (Westinghouse)
1917   Table Stove (Armstrong)
1918   Toaster/Percolator (Armstrong "Perc-O-Toaster")
1920   Heat indicator on waffle iron (Armstrong)
1920   Flip-flop toasters (all manufacturers)
1920   Mixer on permanent base (Hobart Kitchen Aid)
1920   Electric egg cooker (Hankscraft)
1923   Portable mixer (Air-O-Mix "Whip-All")
1924   Automatic iron (Westinghouse)
1924   Home malt mixer (Hamilton Beach #1)
1926   Automatic pop-up toaster (Toastmaster #1h-A-A)
1926   Steam iron (Eldec)
1937   Home coffee mill (Hobart Kitchen Aid)
1937   Automatic coffee maker (Farberware "Coffee Robot")
1937   Conveyance device toaster ("Toast-O-Lator")

References: E. Townsend Artman, *Toasters,* Schiffer Publishing, 1996; Helen Greguire, *Collector's Guide to Toasters & Accessories,* Collector Books, 1997; *Toasters and Small Kitchen Appliances,* L-W Book Sales, 1995.

Collectors' Clubs: Old Appliance Club, PO Box 65, Ventura, CA 93002; Upper Crust: The Toaster Collectors Assoc, PO Box 529, Temecula, CA 92593.

Note: For additional listings see Fans, Electric and Porcelier Porcelain.

Baby Bottle Warmer, Sunbeam, Model B-2, rocketship shape, aluminum and Bakelite, 1956 .... **$75.00**
Blender, Kenmore, Model 116-82421, 2-speed, 1951 .... **55.00**
Coffeepot, Cory, Model DEA, chrome, Bakelite handle, 1937. .... **25.00**
Coffeepot, Electro-Brew, Model 70, Coleman Lamp & Stove Co, Model #70, Pyrex pot, Bakelite and stainless steel lid, 1934. . ... **60.00**
Coffeepot, Farberware, Model 10, chrome and glass, painted wood handles, c1930s **75.00**
Coffeepot, Hotpoint Dorchester, General Electric Co, chrome and glass, Bakelite handles, 1938. .... **65.00**
Coffeepot, Manning Bowman, chrome, Bakelite feet **100.00**
Coffeepot, Silex, Model LE-82, glass, Bakelite handles, 1935. .... **55.00**
Deep Fryer, Handypot, Chicago Electric Mfg Co, aluminum, plastic handles **25.00**
Egg Cooker, Sunbeam, Model E-2, aluminum, Bakelite handles and feet **25.00**
Grill, White Cross, Model 228, chrome, Bakelite handles **25.00**
Hair Jet, Oster Airjet, polished chrome finish, black plastic base stand, insulated electric cord, metal nameplate. **20.00**
Mixer, Hamilton Beach, combination food mixer and extractor, Model B, 1934 .... **55.00**
Mixer, Handywhip, Handyhot, 9½" h. **40.00**
Mixer, Moderne Mixer, Knapp-Monarch Co, 1933 .... **25.00**
Mixer/Coffee Grinder Combination, Sunbeam, 1946 .... **80.00**
Popcorn Popper, Knapp-Monarch Co, aluminum, Bakelite handles **30.00**

Milk Shake Mixer, Hamilton Beach, Model No. 18, stainless steel and porcelain body, stainless steel mixing cup, 2 speeds, 18" h, $175.00. Photo courtesy Collectors Auction Services.

Popcorn Popper, Tel-O-Matic, 1940s **30.00**
Popcorn Popper, US Mfg Corp, 1947, 9" h **40.00**
Spee-Dee Mixer, glass bowl, electric motor, 1940–50s **20.00**
Toaster, General Electric Hotpoint, chrome, single slice,
   Art Deco–style deer design on sides, black Bakelite
   handles and base, black rubber cord, 8 x 5½ x 7" **30.00**
Toaster, Speed-O-Matic, Son Chief Electric Inc, Series
   612, 2-slice, chrome, Bakelite handles **30.00**
Toaster, Sunbeam, Model T-20B, chromed metal, 2-slice,
   Art Deco design on side panels, Bakelite handles, fab-
   ric cord **20.00**
Toaster, Toastmaster, Model 1-B-12, automatic pop-up,
   1941 . . . . **15.00**
Toaster, Westbend Co, Model 3232-E, chrome, Bakelite
   handles **15.00**
Waffle Iron, Modern-Mode Sandwich Queen, Dominion
   Electrical Mfg Co, Model 510, chromed metal,
   Bakelite handles, 1931 . . . . **25.00**
Waffle Iron, Sears Roebuck, Model 307-6604, chromed
   metal, wood handles **20.00**
Waffle Iron, Star-Rite, 1930s **35.00**
Waffle Iron, Universal, Landers, Frary, & Clark, Model
   7424-B, chrome, red jewel light, Bakelite handles **25.00**
Washing Machine, Bendix & Philco Bendix, Duomatic,
   1956 . . . . **200.00**
Washing Machine, Frigidaire, Model WK-60 . . . . **500.00**
Washing Machine, General Electric, combination wash-
   er/dryer, 1964 . . . . **50.00**
Washing Machine, Maytag, Model AMP, 1948-52 . . . . **100.00**
Washing Machine, Montgomery Ward/Wardomatic,
   front loading, 1957-64 . . . . **150.00**
Whipper, Grand Sheet Metal Products Co, chrome top,
   plastic handle, 9" h **25.00**

ART DECO

The famous 1925 Paris "Exposition Internationale des Arts Décoratifs Industriels Modernes" marked the culmination, not the beginning of the Art Deco movement. All the elements of the design style were in place by 1920.

The essential design elements are bold, simplistic geometric shapes based on traditional forms. Ornamentation is greatly simplified, surfaces are smooth, angles are crisp, and curves, when used, are highly controlled. Colors were bold and basic, often used in sharp contrast to one another. Themes were borrowed from ancient cultures such as Aztec, Egyptian, Japanese, Mayan, and sub-Saharan Africa.

Art Deco has a strong feminine quality, stressing luxury and refinement. It found a ready home in the bedroom (boudoir) and living room (parlor). Its American influence was strongest in architecture, jewelry, and Hollywood movies.

Many individuals use Art Deco to describe a wide range of design trends occurring between 1910 and 1940. This is a major mistake. Art Deco is at the periphery of the main evolutionary design style of the period, Modernism. It is modernism, particularly streamlined modern, that continued and expanded upon the design style advances of the Arts and Crafts movement.

References: Donald Brian-Johnson and Leslie Piña, *Chase Complete: Deco Specialties of the Chase Brass & Copper Co.,* Schiffer Publishing, 1999; Mary Frank Gaston, *Collector's Guide to Art Deco, 2nd Edition,* Collector Books, 1997, 2000 value update;

Hutchinson and Johnson, *Affordable Art Deco,* Collector Books, 1999; James R. Linz, *Art Deco Chrome,* Schiffer Publishing, 1999; Leslie Piña and Paula Ockner, *Depression Art Deco Glass,* Schiffer Publishing, 1999.

Collectors' Club: Chase Collectors Society, 2149 West Jibsail Loop, Mesa, AZ 85202.

Note: Many larger cities have Art Deco societies. Consult *Maloney's Antiques & Collectibles Resource Directory* by David J. Maloney, Jr., for more information.

Architectural Grilles, geometric design, painted silver,
   attributed to Cartier Building facade, 73" h, 17½" w,
   ½" d **$1,850.00**
Armchair, chrome tubing with black upholstery, 31" h,
   24" w, 31" d **350.00**
Bookends, pr, cast silvered metal, bird with upright tail
   and outstretched wings on black marble base, 8" h **400.00**
Bookends, pr, chrome colored female head on black
   wood base, 6¼" h, 6¼" w, 30" d **3,675.00**
Boudoir Lamp, chromed metal, cylindrical base with
   shaped shade depicting head of woman, imp linear
   facial features, c1930, 10¼" h **225.00**
Brass Bed, stylized sunburst design on headboard, foot-
   board, and side rails, headboard 42½" h, 48¾" w **500.00**
Chairs, light burgundy colored upholstery with wood
   trim, 30½" h, 26" w, 30" d, price for pair **3,675.00**
Chandelier, 3 arms and posts with floral filigree and gold
   highlighting, each with 3 frosted colorless globes,
   European sockets, missing 1 globe, 32" h, 19½" w **850.00**
Chandelier, 5 frosted colorless glass globes, European
   sockets, 31" h, 21" w **1,150.00**
China Cabinet, burl walnut, 2 doors, glass shelves, elec-
   trified, 50" h, 44½" w, 11¼" d **550.00**
Cigar Box, cloisonné dec, stylized Aztec designs in light
   yellow, blue, and red on black ground with brass
   banding, unsgd, 2⅜" h, 8⅞" l, 6¼" w **900.00**
Clock, Bakelite, amber color, mkd "Lackner, Neon-Glo
   Clock, Cincinnati," 6½" h, 64" w, 3" d **350.00**
Corner Cabinet, exotic veneers on mahogany case, 3 int
   shelves, 71½" h, 71¼" w, 34" d, center 23" d **2,500.00**

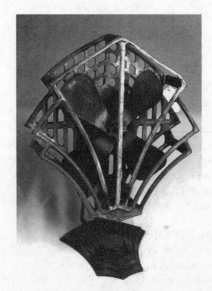

Electric Fan, Robbins & Myers, cast aluminum with tin motor and pressed blade, 1920-30s, $150.00

Dining Set, table and 6 chairs, light burl walnut veneer with inlaid light walnut, chairs recovered with light mocha-colored fabric, table 30½" h, 62¼" w, 33" d, chairs 34¾" h, 18¾" w, 17" d, price for set **925.00**

Hall Rack, chromed metal framework, long hat shelf over center mirror and shelf, flanked by disk-shaped coat hooks over side storage racks, 72" h, 42¾" w, 6¾" deep **3,750.00**

Lamp, bronze, geometric perched bird, unsgd, 23½" h, 5½" w **375.00**

Lamp, figural airplane, chrome rect base with scrolled ends, narrow chrome band supports frosted cobalt blue glass airplane body with chrome wings, propeller, and tail **250.00**

Perfume Bottle, glass, tapered square form, molded geometric pattern in transparent smoky amethyst glass, gilt-metal screw cap, American, 4⁷⁄₈" h **175.00**

Pillow Vase, probably Cleveland School, molded with musicians, instruments, and notes under mottled semi-matte bottle-green glaze, imp artist's mark, 11½ x 8½" **225.00**

Rug, circular, dark mauve center with mocha trim and alternating blue and mocha geometric pattern, 72" d **400.00**

Screen, 3-panel, blue and silver, 63" h, 70½" w, 1" d **175.00**

Screen, 4-panel, muted colors of green, red, and black, sgd, 84" h, 116" w, 1" d **1,725.00**

Sculpture, "Head of Woman," glossy white glaze, Waylande Gregory, script signature, title, and stamped "WG," 10 x 5¼" **650.00**

Serving Carts, burl walnut veneer, 25½" h, 21" w, 19¾" d, price for pair **225.00**

Sideboard, rosewood, black marble top, int with 2 maple drawers and oak shelving, 38" h, 78½" w, 20" d . . **3,250.00**

Statue, metal geometric figure on black wood and metal base, unsgd, 16½" h, 5¾" deep **400.00**

Tea Cart, oval chromed metal curvilinear framework with oblong smoky glass top and shelf, 25¾" h, 31½" l, 18½" w **800.00**

Vase, oviform body with extended rim, deep incised outlines of Egyptian hunters and animals in semi-gloss brown, ocher, green, and cream glazes, unsgd, 7¾" h **350.00**

Wall Sconces, semicircular chrome form over frosted colorless shade, 20½" h, 14" w, 7½" d **1,725.00**

ART POTTERY

Art pottery production was at an all-time high during the late 19th and early 20th centuries. At this time over one hundred companies and artisans were producing individually designed and often decorated pottery which served both utilitarian and aesthetic purposes. Artists often moved from company to company, some forming their own firms.

Condition, quality of design, beauty in glazes, and maker are the keys in buying art pottery. This category covers companies not found elsewhere in the guide.

References: Susan and Al Bagdade, *Warman's American Pottery and Porcelain,* Wallace-Homestead, Krause Publications, 1994; Paul Evans, *Art Pottery of the United States, Second Edition,* Feingold & Lewis Publishing, 1987; Jon Fans and Mark Eckelman, *Collector's Encyclopedia of Muncie Pottery,* Collector Books, 1999; Ralph and Terry Kovel, *Kovels' American Art Pottery: Collector's Guide to Makers, Marks and Factory Histories,* Crown

Publishers, 1993; Nick and Marilyn Nicholson, *Kenton Hills Porcelains Inc.: 1939–1944,* published by authors, 1998; David Rago, *American Art Pottery,* Knickerbocker Press, 1997; Dick Sigafoose, *American Art Pottery: A Collection of Pottery, Tiles and Memorabilia, 1800–1950,* Collector Books, 1997.

Newsletter: *Pottery Lovers Newsletter,* 4969 Hudson Dr, Stow, OH 44224.

Collectors' Club: American Art Pottery Assoc, PO Box 834, Westport, MA 02790.

Note: See California Faience, Clewell, Cowan, Fulper, Hagen-Renaker, Lea Halpern, Marblehead, Moorcroft, Natzler, Newcomb, Niloak, North Dakota School of Mines, Potteries: Regional, Rookwood, Roseville, Teco, Van Briggle, Weller, and Zane for additional listings.

Brouwer, cabinet vase, bulbous, flame-painted, ivory, yellow, and umber glazes, imp whalebone mark, 3¾ x 3" **$500.00**

Brouwer, cabinet vase, molded leaves under frothy amber and gold flame-painted glaze, incised "Brouwer" with whalebone mark, 3 x 3" **2,250.00**

Brouwer, vase, classical, flame-painted in amber and green, whalebone mark, 7 x 6" **1,000.00**

Brouwer, vase, straight rim, green and purple flame-painted glaze, incised flame, 8½ x 5¼" **1,750.00**

Brouwer, vessel, bulbous, lustered purple and black glaze, incised flame, 5½ x 5¼" **875.00**

Brouwer, vessel, squat, closed-in rim, flame-painted in gold, green, brown, and magenta, incised "Brouwer" with wishbone mark, 4 x 5" **1,500.00**

Brouwer, vessel, squat, flame-painted, yellow, amber, and green iridescent glaze, incised flame 3 x 4¼" **300.00**

Chelsea Keramic Art Works, experimental vase, Hugh Robertson, frothy oxblood glaze, stamped "CKAW," 8¾ x 4" **1,750.00**

Chelsea Keramic Art Works, lamp base, squat, applied horse chestnuts and leaves under mustard satin matte glaze, stamp mark, 4½ x 8½" **1,000.00**

Chelsea Keramic Art Works, Pilgrim flask, Hugh Robertson, incised on 1 side with morning glories, other side incised with bird under mottled green glaze, die-stamped mark, incised "HCR," 9 x 7" **775.00**

Chelsea Keramic Art Works, vase, bottle shaped, oxblood orange peel semi-matte glaze, unmkd, 8¼ x 3½" **1,750.00**

Chicago Crucible, bud vase, 4-sided neck, lobed vase, leathery apple green and turquoise glaze, stamped mark, 8 x 4¼" **325.00**

Gouda, planter, Yssel pattern, 4" h, 12" l, $250.00

Hampshire, vase, green matte glaze, imp "Hampshire" and circled "M," 11" h, $770.00. Photo courtesy Smith & Jones, Inc. Auctions

Chicago Crucible, vase, emb leaves under frothy pea green semi-matte glaze, 7 x 5".................550.00

Gregory, Waylande, fish, ceramic, gilded seahorse dec on bright orange ground, sgd in gold glaze, 8¼ x 12"....475.00

Hampshire, ewer, oval body, corseted neck, trefoil-shaped spout, flowing green matte glaze, imp mark, 9¾ x 9 x 6¼".................450.00

Hampshire, inkwell, cylindrical, matte green glaze, with old liner, imp mark, 3½ x 4".................375.00

Hampshire, vase, bulbous, scroll dec, smooth matte green glaze, imp mark, 9 x 9½".................850.00

Hampshire, vase, ovoid, closed-in rim emb with broad leaves, green and blue glaze, incised "Hampshire Pottery," 6¾ x 3¾".................825.00

Jugtown, bowl, flat rim, Chinese blue glaze, circular stamp, 4½ x 7¼".................825.00

Jugtown, cabinet vase, Chinese blue glaze, circular stamp, 4 x 3".................825.00

Jugtown, vase, ovoid, closed-in rim, dripping white semi-matte glaze over brown clay body, circular stamp mark, 6½ x 4¼".................500.00

Merrimac, chamberstick, feathered matte green glaze, paper label and stamped mark, 9 x 5½".................600.00

Merrimac, jar, cov, glossy speckled brown glaze, paper label, 5¼ x 3¼".................500.00

Merrimac, vase, bulbous base, cylindrical neck, green and mirrored black mottled glaze, unmkd, 10 x 5".....1,650.00

Merrimac, vessel, squat, matte green glaze, imp mark, 4 x 9".................1,325.00

Overbeck, cabinet vase, Japanese style dec, 3 panels depicting lady, matte pastel shades, mkd "OBK/E/F," 3 x 2¾".................1,200.00

Paul Revere, bowls, set of 4, brown, green, and ocher semi-matte glaze, largest 3 x 7½".................325.00

Paul Revere, porridger and bowl, E Brown, medallion design of stylized landscape in cuerda seca, in polychrome on deep blue ground, factory mark, 6 x 4".....1,000.00

Paul Revere, vase, bulbous, painted landscape in cuerda seca, in polychrome on deep blue ground, factory mark, 5¾ x 4½".................1,500.00

Paul Revere, vase, classically shaped, medium blue semi-matte glaze, die-stamped mark and ink mkd "GM/7.25," 10 x 5¼".................325.00

Pewabic, cabinet vase, celadon and oxblood lustered glaze, stamped mark, 2½ x 2".................375.00

Pewabic, cabinet vase, iridescent cobalt glaze, imp mark, 3¾ x 2½".................400.00

Pewabic, cabinet vase, Persian blue crackled glaze, circular stamp and "40B," 2 x 2½".................250.00

Pewabic, plate, painted dragonflies in blue slip on white crackled ground, stamped "Pewabic," 10¾" d........1,100.00

Pewabic, vase, bulbous, lustered celadon and purple glaze, stamped cylindrical mark, 4¾ x 4".................550.00

Pewabic, vase, bulbous, mirrored gold glaze dripping over glossy blue ground, circular stamp, 4¾ x 4".....1,200.00

Pewabic, vase, dripping turquoise and purple lustered glaze, stamped circular mark, 3¾ x 3¾".................650.00

Pewabic, vase, emb leaves , flowing matte green glaze, imp "Pewabic," 8 x 6".................6,250.00

Pisgah Forest, vase, bottle shaped, white glaze with white crystals, raised potter's mark and date, 1941, 8 x 5¼".................725.00

Pisgah Forest, vase, classical, amber glaze with tightly packed white and blue crystals, raised potter's mark and date, 1940, 6½ x 4".................650.00

Ruskin, vase, bulbous, stove-pipe neck covered in crystalline sang-de-boeuf glaze, stamped "Ruskin/1922/England," 9 x 4".................1,000.00

Saturday Evening Girls, cabinet vase, cuerda seca dec with brown and blue Greek Key pattern on green ground, inked "S.E.G./E.G./4-1," 4½ x 2¼".................825.00

Saturday Evening Girls, cereal bowl, cuerda seca dec with blue stylized trees on ivory sky, blue-green ground, paper label, incised "S.E.G./R.H./83-2-11," 2¼ x 5".................1,100.00

Saturday Evening Girls, inkwell, square, trees in landscape in green and blues, ink mark and "Bowl Shop" paper label, 2 x 2½".................925.00

Saturday Evening Girls, low bowl, stylized landscape in cuerda seca, green, blue and gray glazes, inked "SEG/7-20/BVC," 8¼" d.................1,650.00

Volkmar, vase, bulbous, mottled and frothy purple glaze, incised "Volkmar," 1929, 6½ x 4".................450.00

Volkmar, vessel, spherical, mottled robin's-egg blue vellum glaze, incised "Volkmar" and dated, 5½ x 5¾".....700.00

Walrath, sculpture, figural kneeling nude picking rose, sheer matte green glaze with yellow details, incised "Walrath," 4 x 6".................325.00

Walrath, vase, bell shaped, painted landscape of cypress trees in ocher and red on blue-gray ground, incised "Walrath Pottery," 5¼ x 3¾".................5,500.00

Walrath, vase, painted stylized dark green trees on olive green ground, incised "Walrath Pottery," 6¼ x 4½"....3,000.00

Walrath, vase, painted stylized purple and dark green flowers on light gray-green ground, incised "Walrath Pottery," 6¼ x 4".................4,500.00

Wheatley, bulbous base, cylindrical neck and 4 buttressed handles, frothy dripping matte green glaze, imp "WP" and "615," 14½ x 10".................3,000.00

Wheatley, bust sculpture of poet Dante, frothy matte green glaze, unmkd, 11½ x 15".................1,000.00

Wheatley, jardiniere, tapering rim, frothy matte green glaze, unmkd, 6 x 8½".................825.00

Wheatley, pitcher, corseted, emb grape clusters and
vines, frothy matte green glaze, imp "WP," 8 x 7³/₄" **775.00**

Wheatley, urn, bulbous, collar rim, frothy matte green
glaze, unmkd, 11 x 11" **400.00**

Wheatley, vase, bulbous, frothy matte green glaze,
unmkd, 10 x 7¹/₂". **550.00**

Wheatley, vase, bulbous, tapering rim, frothy matte
green glaze, imp "WP," 8¹/₄ x 5¹/₂" **500.00**

Wheatley, vase, tapering ribbed rim, frothy matte green
glaze, unmkd, 9³/₄ x 6". **500.00**

ASHTRAYS

Ashtrays can be found made from every material and in any form
imaginable. A popular subcategory with collectors is advertising
ashtrays. Others include figural ashtrays or those produced by a
particular manufacturer. It is still possible to amass an extensive
collection on a limited budget. As more people quit smoking, look
for ashtrays to steadily rise in price.

Reference: Nancy Wanvig, *Collector's Guide to Ashtrays, Second
Edition,* Collector Books, 1999.

Advertising, B-1 Lemon Lime Soda, clear glass, red logo **$10.00**

Advertising, Howard Johnson Ice Cream Shops &
Restaurants, clear glass, red Simple Simon logo and
lettering on white ground, 1930s, 4¹/₈" sq **35.00**

Advertising, Imperial Whiskey by Hiram Walker, white
milk glass, black letters around rim, 5¹/₄" d **5.00**

Advertising, Kentucky Fried Chicken, stamped steel, gray
finish **20.00**

Advertising, Kraft Foods, "Golden Anniversary
1903–1953," 4⁵/₈" l **15.00**

Advertising, Marlboro, plastic, red, white lettering, 3³/₄" d **12.00**

Advertising, Pepsi, plastic, black, Pepsi Cola Memphis
Bottling Co, Memphis, MO logo and "Pepsi's Got Your
Taste For Life" **20.00**

Advertising, Pizza Hut, clear glass, Pizza Hut Pete logo
and red lettering on white ground, "Quality Reigns
Supreme," 1960s, 4" sq **15.00**

**Advertising,
Mr. Bibendum
Michelin man
seated on tray,
plastic, mkd
"Made in USA,"
4¹/₂" h, 5¹/₂" w,
$110.00.**

Advertising, Quaker State, ceramic, red logo and green
lettering on cream ground, 6³/₄" d. **25.00**

Advertising, Wade's Restaurant, logo on tinted glass **5.00**

Aluminum, hand-wrought, flowers in relief center,
3 rests, Trade Continental, c1950s **12.00**

Brass, 1936 Berlin Olympics, athletic figures in relief in
round top, 4⁵/₈" d. **70.00**

Brass, birds and animals on rim, 5¹/₂" d **15.00**

Cast Iron, cowboy hat, tan, painted, 5" l **10.00**

Ceramic, *Queen Elizabeth II* under ship illus **15.00**

Chrome, Chase, center brass whale rest, 4¹/₄" d. **15.00**

Glass, Heisey, military officer's hat, insignia on crown in
front, 1 rest, 4" l **35.00**

Plastic, yellow, 1 rest, chrome plate rim, Japan, 2⁷/₈" d **7.00**

Souvenir, Riverview Park, metal, yellow, center pin-up
girl, blue "Souvenir of Riverview Park," 4³/₄" l **15.00**

Souvenir, Sea World, clear glass, center penguin in
black, yellow, and white, name in black, 1985, 4¹/₈" l **8.00**

Souvenir, Walt Disney World, ceramic, white, center
castle logo **20.00**

Sterling Silver, horseshoe, 2⁷/₈" l. **15.00**

AUTO & DRAG RACING

The earliest automobile racing occurred in Europe at the end of the
19th century. By 1910, the sport was popular in America as well.
The Indianapolis 500, first held in 1911, has been run every year
except for a brief interruption caused by World War II. Collectors
search for both Formula 1 and NASCAR items, with pre-1945
materials the most desirable.

References: Mark Allen Baker, *Auto Racing: Memorabilia and
Price Guide,* Krause Publications, 1996; James Beckett and Eddie
Kelley (eds.), *Beckett Racing Price Guide and Alphabetical
Checklist, Number 2,* Beckett Publications, 1997; David
Fetherston, *Hot Rod Memorabilia & Collectibles,* Motorbooks
International, 1996; Jack MacKenzie, *Indy 500 Buyer's Guide,*
published by author, 1996.

Periodical: *TRACE Magazine,* PO Box 716, Kannapolis, NC
28082.

Newsletter: *Quarter Milestones,* 53 Milligan Ln, Abbeville, MS
38601.

Collectors' Club: National Indy 500 Collectors Club, 10505 N
Delaware St, Indianapolis, IN 46280.

REPRODUCTION ALERT

Autograph, Bobby Allison, PS **$15.00**

Autograph, Cale Yarborough, PS. **15.00**

Autograph, Mario Andretti, PS **20.00**

Comic Book, Hot Rods & Racing Cars, Motormag/
Charlton, #2, Nov 1951. . . . . **65.00**

Game, Flip It: Auto Race and Transcontinental Tour, De
Luxe Game Corp, lid serves as second gameboard,
metal cars, c1920s, 11³/₈ x 9³/₈ x 1" **45.00**

Game, Race-O-Rama, Built Rite, 1960s **20.00**

Model, 1973 Chevy Malibu #12, Bobby Allison, AMT,
1/25 scale. **125.00**

Model, 1989 Pontiac #42, Kyle Petty, Monogram, 1/24
scale. **35.00**

Pennant, felt, white "Speedway, Ind" on green ground,
race car scene, 8½" h, 25" w **100.00**
Pinback Button, Indianapolis Motor Speedway, cellu-
loid, gray aerial view, red lettering, attached thin
white metal charm of racing car with faded red, white,
and blue fabric ribbon, c1940s, 1¾" d **75.00**
Pit Badge, bronze, Indianapolis 500, 1981 . . . . **40.00**
Program, Indianapolis 500, May 30, 1953 . . . . **20.00**
Program, Indianapolis 500, May 29, 1971 . . . . **20.00**
Ticket, United States Auto Club races, Trenton, NJ
Speedway, Sun, Apr 27, 1969, 2½ x 5¾", price for pr **10.00**
Trading Card, Hot Rods, 66 cards, c1965 . . . . **10.00**

AUTOGRAPHS

Early autograph collectors focused on signature only, often discarding the document from which it was cut. Today's collectors
know that the context of the letter or document can significantly
increase the autograph's value.

Standard abbreviations denoting type and size include:

ADS   Autograph Document Signed
ALS   Autograph Letter Signed
AP   Album Page Signed
AQS   Autograph Quotation Signed
CS   Card Signed
DS   Document Signed
FDC   First Day Cover
LS   Letter Signed
PS   Photograph Signed
TLS   Typed Letter Signed

References: Mark Allen Baker, *The Standard Guide to Collecting
Autographs,* Krause Publications, 1999; Kevin Martin, *Signatures
of the Stars: A Guide for Autograph Collectors, Dealers, and
Enthusiasts,* Antique Trader Books, 1998; George Sanders, Helen
Sanders, and Ralph Roberts, *The Sanders Price Guide to
Autographs, 4th Edition,* Alexander Books, 1997; George Sanders,
Helen Sanders and Ralph Roberts, *The Sanders Price Guide to
Sports Autographs, 2nd Edition,* Alexander Books, 1997.

Periodicals: *Autograph Collector,* 510-A S Corona Mall, Corona,
CA 92879; *Autograph Times,* 1125 Baseline Rd, #2-153-M, Mesa,
AZ 85210.

Newsletter: *The Autograph Review,* 305 Carlton Rd, Syracuse, NY
13207.

Collectors' Clubs: The Manuscript Society, 350 N Niagara St,
Burbank, CA 91505; Universal Autograph Collectors Club, PO Box
6181, Washington, DC 20044.

REPRODUCTION ALERT: Forgeries abound. Signatures of many
political figures, movie stars, and sports heroes are machine- or
secretary-signed. Photographic reproduction can also produce a
signature resembling an original. Check all signatures using a good
magnifying glass or microscope.

Aldrin, Buzz, book, *Encounter with Tiber,* co-authored
with John Barnes, 1st printing, bold blue felt tip-pen
signature on second title page "We Came In
Peace/Buzz Aldrin," 1996, dj **$250.00**

Milwaukee Brewers
players Baldwin,
Brabender, Ermer,
Hegan, and Smith,
1970 Baltimore Orioles
Official Scorebook, sgd
back cov 8½ x 11",
$20.00

Angelou, Maya, PS, black and white, smiling portrait
pose, 8 x 10" **60.00**
Ashe, Arthur, PS, black and white, portrait pose, 5 x 7" **125.00**
Ball, Lucille, DS, bank check, sgd "Lucille Ball Arnaz,"
dated 1954 . . . . **400.00**
Benny, Jack, CS, "To Olive/all good wishes," 3 x 3" **125.00**
Bok, Edward, AQS, "Thoroughness first: then speed/
Edward W. Bok/1926," 5 x 4" **75.00**
Chaney, Dick, TLS, on official stationery, 4 paragraph
invitation to ceremony commemorating 50th anniver-
sary of amphibious landing on Guadalcanal, Aug 7,
1992, dated Jul 2, 1992 . . . . **60.00**
Cline, Patsy, PS, sepia, publicity photo, close-up smiling
portrait pose, large purple ink signature, 8 x 10" **2,500.00**
Clinton, Hillary Rodham, PS, color, smiling and waving
¾ pose in checked suit, 8 x 10" **250.00**
Cobb, Tyrus, DS, bank check, filled in and sgd for
$23.96, 1944 . . . . **950.00**
Crabbe, Buster, CS, black and white, smiling portrait
pose in business suit, 8 x 10" **100.00**
Curley, James M, TLS, on official stationery as Mayor of
Boston, to aviation executive HF Pitcairn asking him
to participate in New England States Century of
Progress Exposition, 7 x 10" **90.00**
Eastman, Kevin, orig black India ink sketch, smiling face
and upper chest of Ninja Turtle, full signature on
lower blank of 7 x 10" white card **150.00**
Ferrer, Jose, ALS, on personal stationery, profile carica-
ture of his face near huge signature, 1957 . . . . **125.00**
Gotti, John, *People* magazine, serious portrait, titled
"Public Enemy No. 1, The Real Godfather," large blue
ball-point signature on lapel of gray suit, Mar 27, 1989 . . . **750.00**
Karloff, Boris, PS, sepia, formal portrait pose wearing
2-pc suit with tie, matted under glass, 12 x 15" **850.00**
Kelly, Walt, ADS, bank check, filled in, sgd with green
ink, 1956 . . . . **300.00**
Kennedy, Rose Fitzgerald, CS, printed funeral card for
JFK, "Best Wishes Rose Fitzgerald Kennedy" penned
on lower blank, Nov 22, 1963, 3 x 5" **950.00**
Lamour, Dorothy, DS, photo ID, War Department, US
Army Air Forces **650.00**
Lee, Brandon, CS, ink signature, 5 x 3" **575.00**
Lord, Jack, ALS, on both sides of Regency Hotel station-
ery, 1985 . . . . **100.00**

Mack, Connie, ALS, on "The Athletics" stationery, content explaining his schedule, hand-addressed matching envelope, 1954 . . . . **350.00**

Mancini, Henry, FDC, black signature on upper left First Day Cover honoring Jerome Kern, several notes of music from *Peter Gunn* penned on lower blank area, cancelled NYC, 1985 . . . . **250.00**

McCarthy, Joe, LS, United States Senate, Jan 15, 1954, letter from him thanking student for interest in anticommunist fight **45.00**

McQueen, Steve, DS, bank check, filled in and sgd, Sep 25, 1975. . . . . **850.00**

Peck, Gregory, paperback book, *The Films of Gregory Peck,* image on cov, black felt-tip signature on title page, 8 x 11". **75.00**

Petty, Richard, FDC, honoring 1917 Electric Car, large blue ink signature, 1981 . . . . **30.00**

Presley, Priscilla, PS, color, seated with Elvis on their wedding day, 8 x 10". **55.00**

Quayle, Marilyn, TLS, "The Vice President's House" stationery, thank you for birthday card, full signature, with envelope, Sep 6, 1990 . . . . **50.00**

Reed, Donna, PS, relaxing on set for western movie, inscription wishing recipients happy 50th wedding anniversary, 1954, 8 x 10" **200.00**

Rodman, Dennis, magazine, *Beckett Basketball Monthly,* cover image of Rodman in uniform **75.00**

Ruby, Jack, ADS, bank check drawn on Vegas Club, Dallas, filled in, sgd, and dated Oct 29, 1962 . . . . **850.00**

Sirica, John J, TLS, on stationery as US District Judge, routine thank you, 1976, 8 x 10" **35.00**

Tracy, Spencer, PS, with Claudette Colbert in film *Boom Town,* black fountain pen ink signature, added date "'57," 10 x 8" **500.00**

Updike, John, AQS, typed, 3 lines, from work titled "Rabbit, Run," 8 x 10" **50.00**

Warhol, Andy, magazine, *Interview,* close-up of Rex Smith on cov, large vertical black felt-tip pen signature on cov, 11 x 17" **200.00**

Wells, Orson, ALS, to Marlene Dietrich **3,000.00**

Wood, Natalie, PS, black and white, smiling full pose in checked playsuit, 8 x 10" **550.00**

AUTOMOBILES

The Antique Automobile Club of America instituted a policy whereby any motor vehicle (car, bus, motorcycle, etc.) manufactured prior to 1930 be classified as "antique." The Classic Car Club of America expanded the list, focusing on luxury models made between 1925 and 1948. The Milestone Car Society developed a similar list for cars produced between 1948 and 1964.

Some states, such as Pennsylvania, have devised a dual registration system for classifying older cars—antique and classic. Depending upon their intended use, models from the 1960s and 1970s, especially convertibles and limited production models, fall into the "classic" designation.

Reference: James T. Lenzke and Ken Buttolph (eds.), *2000 Standard Guide to Cars & Prices: Prices For Collector Vehicles 1901–1992, Twelfth Edition,* Krause Publications, 1999.

Periodicals: *Car Collector & Car Classics,* 5211 S Washington Ave, Titusville, FL 32780; *Hemmings Motor News,* PO Box 100, Rt 9W,

Bennington, VT 05201; *Old Cars Price Guide,* 700 E State St, Iola, WI 54990.

Collectors' Clubs: Antique Automobile Club of America, 501 W Governor Rd, PO Box 417, Hershey, PA 17033; Classic Car Club of America, 1645 Des Plaines River Rd, Ste 7, Des Plaines, IL 60018; Milestone Car Society, PO Box 24612, Indianapolis, IN 46224; Veteran Motor Car Club of America, PO Box 360788, Strongsville, OH 44136.

Note: Prices are for cars in good condition.

Ashley, 1961, Sportiva, coupe **$2,000.00**
Aston Martin, 1979, Vantage, coupe, V-8 . . . . **25,000.00**
Cadillac, 1953, Fleetwood, sedan, V-8 . . . . **10,000.00**
Cadillac, 1959, Eldorado, Brougham, V-8 . . . . **13,000.00**
Cadillac, 1962, 62 Park Avenue, short sedan, V-8 . . . . **5,000.00**
Chevrolet, 1967, Impala, station wagon, 8 cyl **3,000.00**
Chevrolet, 1970, Chevelle, coupe, 8 cyl **3,000.00**
Chevrolet, 1975, Corvette, T-Top, V-8 . . . . **6,500.00**
Chrysler, 1937, Imperial Airflow, sedan, 8 cyl **7,500.00**
Chrysler, 1948, New Yorker, sedan, 8 cyl **3,000.00**
Chrysler, 1956, Windsor, sedan, V-8 . . . . **3,000.00**
Chrysler, 1959, Town & Country, station wagon, 8 cyl **2,500.00**
Chrysler, 1965, Imperial Crown, convertible, V-8 . . . . **7,000.00**
Crosley, 1950, Hot Shot, doorless sport, 4 cyl **4,000.00**
Datsun, 1972, 240-Z, coupe, 6 cyl **2,250.00**
DeSoto, 1956, Fireflite, 4-door sedan, V-8, 4.8 litre **3,400.00**
DeSoto, 1958, Firesweep, sedan, 8 cyl **2,500.00**
Dodge, 1930, stake truck, ³/₄ ton, 6 cyl **2,000.00**
Dodge, 1962, Dart 440, station wagon, 8 cyl **2,000.00**
Dodge, 1963, Polara, 2-door hardtop, V-8 . . . . **1,200.00**
Dodge, 1968, Monaco, sedan, 8 cyl **2,200.00**
Dodge, 1971, van, ¹/₂ ton, V-8 . . . . **2,000.00**
Dodge, 1973, Challenge, Rally, 8 cyl **5,000.00**
Ford, 1952, Customline, station wagon, V-8 . . . . **2,800.00**
Ford, 1953, pickup, 1¹/₂ ton, 6 cyl **3,000.00**
Ford, 1955, Fairlane, Town Sedan, V-8 . . . . **3,000.00**
Ford, 1957, pickup, short bed, V-8 . . . . **3,500.00**
Ford, 1960, Galaxie, Town Victoria, V-8 . . . . **4,000.00**
Ford, 1968, Torino, hardtop, V-8 . . . . **2,500.00**
Ford, 1971, LTD, convertible, V-8 . . . . **3,500.00**
Frazer Nash, 1954, Sebring, Sport, 2 litre **3,500.00**
International Harvester, 1967, pickup, ¹/₂ ton, 6 cyl **3,500.00**
Jaguar, 1950, Mark V, Saloon, 6 cyl **7,000.00**
Jeep, 1971, Jeepster, convertible, 4 cyl **2,250.00**
Kaiser, 1955, Manhattan, sedan, 6 cyl **5,000.00**

Cadillac, 1962, Fleetwood 75, Series 6700, $20,000.00. Photo courtesy Auction Team Köln.

Mercedes-Benz, 1959, Model 219, sedan, 4 cyl. **5,000.00**
Mercury, 1962, Comet, station wagon, 6 cyl **2,000.00**
Mercury, 1967, Cougar XR7 289, coupe, V-8 . . . . **5,000.00**
MG, 1974, MGB, Roadster, 4 cyl **3,500.00**
Nash, 1935, Ambassador, sedan, 8 cyl **3,200.00**
Oldsmobile, 1948, Dynamic, sedan, 8 cyl. **4,000.00**
Oldsmobile, 1971, Delta 88, sedan, 8 cyl **1,500.00**
Oldsmobile, 1974, Delta Royale, convertible, V-8 . . . . . . **6,000.00**
Packard, Clipper, 1957, station wagon, V-8 . . . . **4,000.00**
Peugeot, 1970, Model 504, sedan, 1.8 litre **2,000.00**
Plymouth, 1942, Deluxe, sedan, 6 cyl. **3,000.00**
Plymouth, 1964, Barracuda, coupe, V-8 273 . . . . **7,000.00**
Pontiac, 1947, Torpedo, sedan, 8 cyl. **2,500.00**
Pontiac, 1971, Ventura, sedan, 6 cyl **2,000.00**
Studebaker, 1962, Champ, pickup truck, V-8 . . . . **5,000.00**
Studebaker, 1963, pickup, ½ ton, V-8 . . . . **3,000.00**
Triumph, 1964, Spitfire II, Roadster **3,500.00**
Volkswagen, 1953, Micro Bus, station wagon, 4 cyl. **4,000.00**
Volkswagen, 1979, Super Bug, convertible, 1979 . . . . **6,000.00**

AUCTION PRICES – AUTOMOBILES

Kruse International, Bluffton, SC Auction, July 9-11, 1999.
Prices include a 5% buyer's premium.

Austin Chummy, 1928, 4 cyl $7,088.00
Bentley S2, 4-door saloon, 1962, black 15,225.00
Cadillac 62 Series Convertible, 1954, V-8, yellow,
   power steering, power brakes, power windows,
   power top, wander bar radio 17,325.00
Chevrolet Bel Air, 1957, 4-door, 6 cyl, blue 5,670.00
Chevrolet Bel Air Convertible, 1957, V-8 283, red,
   automatic, dual exhaust, restored 31,500.00
Lincoln Mark V, 1960, 4-door hardtop, V-8, black,
   5200 lb 3,780.00
MG TF Roadster, 1954, 4 cyl, red, orig engine, all
   weather equipment, side curtains, tonneau cover,
   owner's handbook and workshop manual 17,850.00
Nash Metro, 1957 . . . . 2,940.00
Oldsmobile, 1950, 2-door, V-8, black, all orig,
   30,000 miles 18,375.00
Porsche 912 Coupe, 1969, 4 cyl, red, tartan leather
   int, completely restored 9,135.00
Triumph TR6 Convertible, 1976, 6 cyl, blue 7,140.00

AUTOMOBILIA

Automobilia can be broken down into three major collecting categories—parts used for restoring cars, advertising and promotional items relating to a specific make or model of car, and decorative accessories in the shape of or with an image of an automobile. Numerous subcategories also exist. Spark plugs and license plates are two examples of automobilia with reference books, collectors clubs, and periodicals dealing specifically with these fields.

References: David K. Bausch, *The Official Price Guide to Automobilia,* House of Collectibles, 1996; Steve Butler, *Promotionals 1934–1983: Dealership Vehicles in Miniature,* L-W Book Sales, 1997; Lee Dunbar, *Automobilia,* Schiffer Publishing, 1998; David Fetherson, *Hot Rod Memorabilia and Collectibles,* Motorbooks International, 1996; Ron Kowalke and Ken Buttolph, *Car Memorabilia Price Guide, 2nd Edition,* Krause Publications, 1998.

Periodicals: *Hemmings Motor News,* PO Box 100, Rt 9W, Bennington, VT 05201; *Mobilia,* PO Box 575, Middlebury, VT 05753; *PL8S: The License Plate Collector's Magazine,* PO Box 222, East Texas, PA 18046.

Collectors' Clubs: Automobile License Plate Collectors Assoc, Inc, PO Box 77, Horner, WV 26372; Automobile Objects D'Art Club, 252 N 7th St, Allentown, PA 18102; Hubcap Collectors Club, PO Box 54, Buckley, MI 49620; Spark Plug Collectors of America, 9 Heritage Lane, Simsbury, CT 06070.

Ashtray, Fish, rubber tire with glass insert, Fish Glider
   600/16, 6½" d $200.00
Ashtray, Phillips 66, metal, set of 4, Suggestion Award
   1964, orig box, 3½" sq 20.00
Ashtray, United States Tire, glass bottom, metal tire top
   with lift-out spokes, 1½" h, 6" d 325.00
Book, *Think Small,* Volkswagen giveaway, 80 pp, ©1967
   Volkswagen of America, 6¾ x 8¼" 25.00
Brochure, 1959 Cadillac, 8 pp, full color folio, 5 inner
   photos of different models, production line of 12
   models on back cov, 12 x 12" 20.00
Cigarette Lighter, Dodge Trucks, hard plastic, removable
   metal cap, dark red hard plastic figural oil drum with
   black lettering "Switch To Dodge Trucks And Save
   Money! Owners Report Savings Up To $95 A Year On
   Gas Alone," black plastic removable disk base, matching red sticker on reverse for local dealership, late
   1930s, 3" h, 1¼" d 75.00
Cigarette Lighter, Jaguar XK-E, desk type, ceramic with
   chrome luster metal cigarette lighter insert in hood,
   underside of base has 1965 copyright by "Amico" and
   "Japan," 2 x 2 x 5" 75.00
Cigarette Lighter, Phillips 66, plain case with orange,
   black, and white enamel painted logo, Zippo, 1966 . . . . . . 35.00
Cigarette Lighter, Pontiac auto emblem, brushed finish,
   black enamel painted, engraved "Louis Frahm Pontiac
   Inc...Downey, Calif.," white and gold box, Zippo,
   1962 . . . . 90.00
Coloring Book, Sinclair, 32 pp, art and captions related
   to history and development of petroleum, center pp
   with aerial perspective view of Sinclair Dinoland of
   1964-65 New York World's Fair, unused, 8 x 10¾" 20.00
Flange Sign, Raybestos Brake Service, tin, 1920-30s,
   14 x 18" 350.00

Salt and Pepper Shakers, pr, Japan, 3-pc set, c1930s, $85.00.

License Plate, Alaska, Bicentennial, red numbers, white ground, mountain scene and grizzly bear, 1976 . . . . **30.00**

License Plate, Arkansas, emb aluminum, black numbers, natural ground **30.00**

License Plate, commemorative, Presidential Inaugural, 1789 Bicentennial 1989 . . . . **10.00**

License Plate, Connecticut, Commercial, 1975 . . . . **10.00**

License Plate, Illinois, trailer, fiberboard, 1947 . . . . **25.00**

License Plate, Iowa, The Corn State, 1953, 5½ x 11⅞" **20.00**

License Plate, Salisbury, North Carolina, Historic, 1979 . . . . . **10.00**

License Plate Attachment, Farm Bureau Insurance, diecut tin, red, white and blue litho emblem for insurance provided by Mutual Automobile Insurance Co, Columbus, OH, c1940s, 3 x 4¼" **20.00**

Pinback Button, attached ribbon mkd "Golden Jubilee Red Crown, 1880-1930," celebrating Standard Oil's 50th birthday, gold, red, and white, 2¼" **45.00**

Pinback Button, Maverick Grabber, litho tin, orange, black, and white, c1970, 3" d **15.00**

Pocket Mirror, Good Year Tires, litho metal, earth surrounded by tire with "Goodyear Balloon," yellow moon and lettering on blue ground, 2¼" d **225.00**

Road Map, American Oil, Ohio, 1973 . . . . **3.00**

Road Map, Chevron, California, 1973 . . . . **3.00**

Road Map, Conoco, Illinois, 1970 . . . . **3.00**

Road Map, Esso, New England, 1936 . . . . **15.00**

Road Map, Esso, New York World's Fair, 1964-65 . . . . **12.00**

Road Map, Esso, War Map II (Europe), 1942-43 . . . . **15.00**

Road Map, Standard Oil Co of California, Gousha "M" code, 1930 . . . . **12.00**

Road Map, Standard Oil Co of California, Seattle/Tacoma and Vicinity, Gousha "CC" code, 1955 . . . . . **6.00**

Road Map, Tydol, Trails Through New Hampshire and Vermont, 1930s **12.00**

Road Map, Tydol, Trails Through New Jersey, 1930s **12.00**

Sign, Mother Penn Motor Oil, porcelain, 2-sided, c1930s, 8½ x 6" **475.00**

Spinning Top, Fisk Red-Top Tires, celluloid, multicolored, wooden dowel spinner inserted through center, 1920-30s **75.00**

Stock Certificate, General Motors Corp, brown and white, 1950 . . . . **20.00**

Stock Certificate, Studebaker-Packard Corp, American Banknote Co, green, silver, and white, 1957 . . . . **12.00**

AUTUMN LEAF

Autumn Leaf dinnerware was manufactured by Hall China Company and issued as a premium by the Jewel Tea Company. The pattern was originally produced between 1933 and 1978. Many other companies produced matching kitchen accessories.

References: C. L. Miller, *The Jewel Tea Company: Its History and Products,* Schiffer Publishing, 1994; Margaret and Kenn Whitmyer, *The Collector's Encyclopedia of Hall China, Second Edition,* Collector Books, 1994, 1997 value update.

Collectors' Club: National Autumn Leaf Collectors Club, PO Box 162961, Fort Worth, TX 76161.

Note: Pieces are in good condition with only minor wear to gold trim unless noted otherwise.

Baker, open, 6½" d, price for 3 . . . . **$100.00**

Bean Pot, cov, 1 handle **475.00**

Bean Pot, cov, 2 handles **200.00**

Bowl, Radiance, 6" d **10.00**

Bowl, Radiance, 7½" d **15.00**

Bowl, Radiance, 9" d **25.00**

Bread and Butter Plate **2.00**

Butter Dish, regular, ¼ lb **165.00**

Cake Safe, tin, 1935 . . . . **15.00**

Cake Server **175.00**

Candlesticks, pr **30.00**

Candy Tin **15.00**

Canister, button lid, 6" h **25.00**

Canister, copper lid, flour and sugar, 7" h, price for 2 . . . . **12.00**

Cereal/Fruit Bowl **6.00**

Coasters, price for 10 . . . . **40.00**

Coffee Dispenser **75.00**

Coffeepot, rayed, 8 cup, no drip **25.00**

Coffeepot, rayed, 8 cup, with drip **55.00**

Coffeepot Lid **10.00**

Condiment Bowl and Underplate **25.00**

Conic Mug **40.00**

Cookbook, *Mary Dunbar Jewel Tea* **10.00**

Cookie Jar, cov, Zeisel **100.00**

Creamer, rayed **10.00**

Cream Soup **15.00**

Cup **2.00**

Cup and Saucer, St Denis **15.00**

Custard, Radiance **3.00**

Drip Jar, cov, 5" h **12.00**

Dutch Oven, 5 qt **25.00**

Fondue Set **45.00**

French Baker, 4⅛" d **12.00**

Gravy Boat, no underplate **20.00**

Hotpad, round, tin back, 7¼" d **12.00**

Irish Coffee Mug **65.00**

Jug, rayed, 2½ pt **25.00**

Luncheon Plate, 8" d **5.00**

Marmalade **45.00**

Mustard **35.00**

Norris Jug, cov, 1991 . . . . **75.00**

Ball Jug, $30.00. Photo courtesy Ray Morykan Auctions.

Pie Baker, spotted, 9" d **50.00**
Platter, oval, 11½" l **30.00**
Platter, oval, 14" l **16.00**
Salad Bowl, 2 qt **12.00**
Salad Plate **3.00**
Soup Bowl **12.00**
Sugar, cov, rayed **12.00**
Sugar, cov, ruffled **12.00**
Tablecloth, sailcloth, 54 x 62" **80.00**
Teapot, Aladdin **30.00**
Teapot, Newport **125.00**
Tea Towel, 16 x 33" **20.00**
Tidbit, 2-tier **75.00**
Toaster Cover **20.00**
Tray, oval, 8¾" l **35.00**
Tumbler, frosted, 5½" h **10.00**
Tumbler, frosted sides, clear base, 5½" h **12.00**
Vegetable, open, 10" l **35.00**

AVIATION COLLECTIBLES

Most collections relating to the field of aviation focus on one of four categories—commercial airlines, dirigibles, famous aviators, or generic images of aircraft.

Early American airlines depended on government subsidies for carrying mail. By 1930, five international and thirty-eight domestic airlines were operating in the United States. A typical passenger load was ten. After World War II, four-engine planes with a capacity of 100 or more passengers were introduced.

The jet age was launched in the 1950s. In 1955 Capitol Airlines used British-made turboprop airliners in domestic service. In 1958 National Airlines began domestic jet passenger service. The giant Boeing 747 went into operation in 1970 as part of the Pan American fleet.

Reference: Richard R. Wallin, *Commercial Aviation Collectibles: An Illustrated Price Guide,* Wallace-Homestead, 1990, out of print.

Collectors' Clubs: Aeronautica and Air Label Collectors Club, PO Box 1239, Elgin, IL 60121; CAL/NX211 Collectors Society (Charles Lindbergh), 727 Youn Kin Pkwy S, Columbus, OH 43207; World Airline Historical Society, 13739 Picarsa Dr, Jacksonville, FL 32225.

Ashtray, center image of single engine passenger aircraft
    on 4½" d aluminum tray with emb rim inscription "Fly
    Piper Planes," c1950s **$15.00**
Baggage Tag, red plastic with white "TWA Press," clear
    reverse has insert for identification, attached plastic
    strap, unused, 1960s **20.00**
Catalog, Aeronca Aircraft Corp Parts and Prices, Jul 1,
    1947, 80 pp **20.00**
Cup, American Airlines, silver plated, black wood han-
    dle, raised relief "AA" eagle emblem, 1930s, 2¼" h **45.00**
Gravy Server, TWA, silver plated, Oneida **25.00**
Lighter, chrome luster finished metal, hinged, 1 side with
    blue Pan Am global logo, orig box, made in Japan for
    "Penguin" distribution, c1960s **15.00**
Luggage Label, American Airlines, red, white, and blue **12.00**
Luggage Label, Via Tac Transamerican Airlines Corp,
    orange and black **20.00**
Magazine, *Model Airplane News,* set of 3, Jul–Sept,
    1941, full color front cover art by Kotula, 8½ x 11½" **20.00**

Sign, Good Year Tires, diecut blimp, 17½" h, 39" w, $3,750.00. Photo courtesy Collectors Auction Services.

Manual, Jeppesen Airway, brown leatherette cover with
    metal binder rings, 1967 . . . . **20.00**
Postcard, American Airlines, "This is my trip on
    American Airlines" mkd in pencil, black and white,
    white border, 1935 . . . . **12.00**
Scarf, Trans-Canada Airlines, sheer pink, early airplanes
    around edge with center large DC-8, "TCA DC-8
    Jetliner Service," blue, gray, green, black, red, and yel-
    low, 1960s, 29" sq **20.00**
Schedule, Piedmont Airlines, flights by Fairchild F27
    Pacemaker aircraft, logo on front, 1958 . . . . **20.00**
Stock Certificate, Pan American World Airways, 100
    shares, dated 1968 . . . . **20.00**
Timetable, Trans-Canada Airlines, effective Apr 28, 4 x 9" **8.00**
Travel Bag, Pan Am, white vinyl body, blue trim, large
    loop handles, logo on each side, attached tag,
    unused, 1960s, 13" sq **25.00**
Travel Bag, Freedomland/Braniff International Airways,
    blue fabric zipper bag, souvenir of Braniff's Space
    Ship, c1960s, 10½ x 16½" **100.00**

AVON

David H. McConnell founded the California Perfume Company in 1886. Saleswomen used a door-to-door approach for selling their wares. The first product was "Little Dot," a set of five perfumes. Following the acquisition of a new factory in Suffern, New York, in 1895, the company underwent several name changes. The trade name Avon, adopted in 1929, was derived from the similarity the Suffern landscape shared with that of Avon, England.

Reference: Bud Hastin, *Bud Hastin's Avon & C.P.C. Collector's Encyclopedia, 15th Edition,* Collector Books, 1998.

Newsletter: *Avon Times,* PO Box 9868, Kansas City, MO 64134.

Collectors' Club: National Assoc of Avon Collectors, Inc, PO Box 7006, Kansas City, MO 64113.

Autumn Aster, Topaz or Sun Blossoms cologne, clear
  glass, gold cap, 1978-80 . . . . **$2.00**
Bubba Lee Bunny, bubble bath or non-tear shampoo,
  white plastic rabbit, yellow cap, 1982-83 . . . . **3.00**
Captain's Lantern, Wild Country or Oland After Shave,
  black glass, black plastic cap, gold ring, 1976-77 . . . . **8.00**
Country Creamery Milk Can, hand lotion, white painted
  over clear glass, 1978-79 . . . . **6.00**
Country Talc Shaker, Sweet Honesty or Charisma per-
  fumed talc, gray and blue speckled metal can, shaker
  top, 1977-79 . . . . **3.00**
Gingerbread Soap Twins, 2 blue plastic gingerbread
  cookie cutters with 2 yellow bars of gingerbread soap,
  orig pink, white, and brown box, 1965 . . . . **30.00**
Kitten's Hideaway, Field Flowers, Bird of Paradise, or
  Charisma Cream Sachet, amber basket, white plastic
  kitten cap, 1974-76 . . . . **6.00**
Lil Tom Turtle Soap, figural green turtle with white hat,
  orig box, 1962-63 . . . . **35.00**
Monkey Shines, Sonnet or Moonwind cologne, clear
  glass painted light gray, brown eyes and ears, red cap
  and neck strap, 1979-80 . . . . **5.00**
Open Golf Cart, Wild Country or Windjammer After
  Shave, green glass bottle, green plastic front end, red
  plastic golf bags, 1972-75, 5½" l **10.00**
Pipe, Tai Winds or Spicy After Shave, light green glass,
  brown plastic stem, 1972-74 . . . . **4.00**
Plate, "A Child's Christmas," white bisque porcelain,
  1985, 7¾" d **10.00**
Plate, "Cherished Moments," Mother's Day, porcelain,
  with stand, dated 1981, 5" d **10.00**
Queen of Scots, Sweet Honesty, Unforgettable,
  Somewhere, Cotillion, or Here's My Heart cologne,
  white milk glass, white plastic head, 1973-76 . . . . **6.00**
Rockabye Pony Decanter, Clearly Gentle Baby Lotion,
  yellow plastic, 1975-76 . . . . **3.00**
Spongaroo Soap and Sponge, brown kangaroo sponge,
  white kangaroo soap in pouch, 1966-67 . . . . **15.00**
Sunny Bunny Candleholder, ceramic, dated 1981, 5½" h **15.00**
Sweet Pickles Zany Zebra Hair Brush, plastic, white,
  black, pink, and green, 1978-79 . . . . **1.00**
Treasure Turtle, Sweet Honesty or Charisma cologne,
  clear glass figural turtle, gold cap, 1977 . . . . **4.00**
Yankee Doodle Shower Soap, figural white drum,
  attached rope, 1969-70 . . . . **15.00**

BANKS

The earliest still banks were made from wood, pottery, gourds, and later, cast iron. Lithographed tin banks advertising various products and services reached their height in popularity between 1930 and 1955. The majority of these banks were miniature replicas of the products' packaging.

Ceramic figural banks were popular novelties during the 1960s and 1970s. The most recent variation of still banks are molded vinyl banks resembling favorite cartoon and movie characters.

References: Don Duer, *Penny Banks Around the World,* Schiffer Publishing, 1997; Beverly and Jim Mangus, *Collector's Guide to Banks,* Collector Books, 1998; Andy and Susan Moore, *Penny Bank Book: Collecting Still Banks,* Schiffer Publishing, 1984, 1997 value update; Tom and Loretta Stoddard, *Ceramic Coin Banks,* Collector Books, 1997; Vickie Stulb, *Modern Banks,* L-W Book Sales, 1997.

Newsletters: *Glass Bank Collector,* PO Box 155, Poland, NY 13431; *Heuser's Quarterly Collectible Diecast Newsletter,* 508 Clapson Rd, PO Box 300, West Winfield, NY 13491.

Collectors' Club: Still Bank Collectors Club of America, 4175 Millersville Rd, Indianapolis, IN 46205.

Note: All banks listed are still banks unless noted otherwise.

Apollo Rocket on Moon, cast iron, antique gold luster
  finish, each side of spacecraft mkd "Apollo," nose
  cone mkd "USA," c1969, 4½" h, 3½" d **$75.00**
Barnaby Bee, ceramic, yellow bee-striped figure, clutch-
  ing gold coins to chest under initials "INB," 1960s,
  6½" h, 2 x 2½" base **75.00**
Esso, figural oil drop, plastic, 1950s, 6½" h, 3" d base **100.00**
Frigidaire, figural refrigerator, metal, white, orig box,
  c1930s **75.00**
Frog on Rock, mechanical, cast iron, designed by
  Elizabeth Cook, "push lever and frog opens his
  mouth, insert a coin in his mouth & release the lever,"
  Kilgore Mfg Co, Westerville, OH, c1920s **600.00**

Log Cabin, litho tin, illus of black man playing banjo and young black girl dancing, Chein, 1930s, 3 x 3¼ x 3", $75.00. Photo courtesy Collectors Auction Services.

Hawaiian Pineapple Face, mechanical, cast iron, painted, commemorates Hawaii becoming 50th state, coin
placed in hand, lever draws it to mouth, USA, 9" h **450.00**

Keene National Bank, dime bank, 1920s, 2½" d **25.00**

Mailbox, cast metal, dark green, raised text "US
Mail/Letters" in gold, 1930s, 1½ x 2 x 3¾" **50.00**

Majestic Radio, figural, cast iron, dark bronze finish,
raised "Majestic" on front, c1920s, 1¾ x 3 x 4½" **100.00**

Mr Magoo, vinyl, dressed as Uncle Sam sitting on patri-
otic soapbox, inscribed "Mr. Magoo First National
Bank of Magoo" below, ©1960 UPA Pictures Inc,
AC Renz Corp, MA, 16" h, 6¼" d **50.00**

My Penny Bank, book type, cardboard, red simulated
leather, comic character Penny carrying umbrella,
wearing raincoat, 1950s, 5¾ x 7¾ x 2" **50.00**

Mystery Bank, windup, litho tin, Nomura Toys, Japan,
1960s, 2½ x 6 x 3½" **25.00**

Peppermint Patty, composition, full figure, smiling, wearing baseball outfit, holding orange bat, Korea gold foil
sticker on underside, ©1977 United Features Syndi-
cate Inc, Determined Products Inc, 7" h **25.00**

Rabbits in Cabbage, mechanical, cast iron, press coin in
slot and ears rise and flop back down, Kilgore Mfg Co,
c1925 . . . . **725.00**

Raggedy Andy, vinyl, smiling seated Andy wearing red,
white, and blue sailor outfit on red base, My Toy Co,
©1972 The Bobbs Merrill Co, 10½" h, 5" d base **25.00**

Rockefeller, tin, 2-sided, bluetone photo on 1 side, red,
white and blue lettering "Rockefeller For Governor"
on other side, 2¼" d **15.00**

Rudolph the Red-Nosed Reindeer, plastic, brown and
tan, kneeling, green antlers, red light-up nose, 1940s,
2⅛ x 5½ x 5" **25.00**

Santa Bank, battery and coin operated, jolly Santa seated on small home, Noel Decorations, Inc, Japan, orig
box **250.00**

Sinclair Power-X, figural gas pump, litho tin, 1950s, 1½
x 2¼ x 4" **75.00**

BARBERSHOP, BEAUTY SHOP & SHAVING

The neighborhood barber shop was an important social and cultural institution in the first half of the 20th century. Men and boys
gathered to gossip, exchange business news, and check current
fashions. With the emergence of *unisex* shops in the 1960s, the
number of barber shops dropped by half in the United States.
Today, most men and women patronize the same shops for services ranging from haircuts to perms to coloring.

References: Ronald S. Barlow, *The Vanishing American Barber
Shop*, Windmill Publishing, 1993; Lester Dequaine, *Razor Blade
Banks*, published by author, 1998; Christian R. Jones, *Barbershop:
History and Antiques*, Schiffer Publishing, 1999; Roy Ritchie and
Ron Stewart, *Standard Guide to Razors, Second Edition*, Collector
Books, 1998; Jim Sargent, *American Premium Guide to Knives &
Razors*, Krause Publications, 1999.

Collectors' Clubs: National Shaving Mug Collectors' Assoc, 320 S
Glenwood St, Allentown, PA 18104; Safety Razor Collectors
Guild, PO Box 885, Crescent City, CA 95531.

Barber Bottle, cobalt blue, vertical rib pattern, white,
orange, and yellow enamel floral dec, 7⅛" h **$125.00**

**Barber Bottle, hp milk
glass, 9" h, $700.00.**
Photo courtesy Collectors
Auction Services.

Barber Bottle, Toilet Water, milk glass, lavender blue,
green, yellow, and brown enamel floral dec, gold let-
tering, 8⅞" h **725.00**

Barber Bottle, West Point Hair Tonic, paper label mkd
"©1935 West Point Laboratories New York," 8¼" h **30.00**

Clock, Brylcreem Your Hair, reverse painted glass, Mains
Time Co, Ltd, London, 14" h, 11" w **100.00**

Clock, Oster Electric Scalp Massage, electric, plastic,
metal hands, 16" sq **75.00**

Curb Sign, Haircut 25¢, metal, 24½" h, 18" w **125.00**

Display Rack, Gillette razor blades, tin, 2-sided, "Buy
Gillette Blades" on front, "Buy your Gillette blades
Here" on back, holds 8 sets of wire hooks, 11" h,
19" w **30.00**

Door Push, tin, "You're Next/Use Zepp's For The Hair,"
Stout Sign Co, St Louis, 10" h, 3¾" w **450.00**

Flange Sign, Ladies & Childrens Hair Bobbing Our
Specialty, porcelain, 2-sided, 12" h, 24" w **350.00**

Pole, glass with red and white stripes, porcelain hexagonal end caps, metal wall mount, light-up style, 23" h,
5½" w **175.00**

Pole, white milk glass panels with red, black, and white
diagonal stripes in tapering rect metal frame, black
painted porcelain top and bottom, wall mounted,
35" h, 12½" deep **875.00**

Pole, wooden top with turned finial, hp red, white, and
blue stripes, 42" h, 2½" d **100.00**

Razor, Collins Safety Razors, silver plated, with spare
blades and instructions, orig box, 3" h **275.00**

Shaving Mug, emblem for Knights of the Golden Eagle
and "A. J. Hendrickson," stamped "C.F.H. G.D.M." on
base, 3¾" h **100.00**

Shaving Mug, man hanging wallpaper scene and "E.F.
Kennedy," stamped "East St. Louis Barber Supply East
St. Louis, MO" on base, 4" h **475.00**

Sign, Bill Alger's Barber Shop, painted metal, 2-sided,
16½" d **125.00**

Sign, Dickinson's Witch Hazel, cardboard, 1-sided,
countertop stand-up, ©1923 EE Dickinson Co, 27½" h . . . **150.00**

Sign, HC Carpenter Barber Shop, Hamlin, NY, 2 girls
feeding horse scene, metal edges, ©1922, printed in
USA, 16¼" h, 12¼" w **75.00**

Sign, Jeris Hair Tonic, diecut cardboard, 1-sided, countertop stand-up, 24¹/₂" h, 18" w **70.00**

Sign, Stephan's Dandruff Remover, diecut cardboard, 1-sided, countertop stand-up, Doris Day and Rock Hudson photo, 24¹/₂" h, 17" w **100.00**

Traveling Barbers Kit, leather covered box with purple velvet lining, holding 12 razors with celluloid, plastic, and wood handles, 7⁵/₈" h, 3¹/₂" w, 3" d **250.00**

BARBIE

The first Barbie fashion dolls, patented by Mattel in 1958, arrived on toy store shelves in 1959. By 1960, Barbie was a marketing success. The development of Barbie's boyfriend, Ken, began in 1960. Many other friends followed. Clothing, vehicles, doll houses, and other accessories became an integral part of the line.

From September 1961 through July 1972 Mattel published a Barbie magazine. At its peak, the Barbie Fan Club was the second largest girls' organization, next to the Girl Scouts, in the nation.

Barbie sales are approaching the 100 million mark. Annual sales exceed five million units. Barbie is one of the most successful dolls in history.

References: Fashion and Accessories: Joe Blitman, *Barbie Doll and Her Mod, Mod, Mod, Mod World of Fashion,* Hobby House Press, 1996; Joe Blitman, *Francie and Her Mod, Mod, Mod, Mod World of Fashion,* Hobby House Press, 1996; Sarah Sink Eames, *Barbie Doll Fashion, Vol. I: 1959–1967* (1990, 1998 value update), *Vol II: 1968–1974* (1997), Collector Books; Connie Craig Kaplan, *Collector's Guide to Barbie Doll Vinyl Cases,* Collector Books, 1999; Patricia Long, *Barbie's Closet: Price Guide for Barbie & Friends Fashions and Accessories: 1959–1973,* Krause Publications, 1999; Rebecca Ann Rupp, *Treasury of Barbie Doll Accessories: 1961–1995,* Hobby House Press, 1996.

General: Scott Arend, Karla Holzerland and Trina Kent, *Skipper: Barbie's Little Sister,* Collector Books, 1998; J. Michael Augustyniak, *The Barbie Doll Boom,* Collector Books, 1996; J. Michael Augustyniak, *Collector's Encyclopedia of Barbie Doll Exclusives and More, Second Edition,* Collector Books, 1999; Sibyl DeWein and Joan Ashabraner, *The Collectors Encyclopedia of Barbie Dolls and Collectibles,* Collector Books, 1977, 1996 value update; Robert Gardner, *Fashion Dolls Exclusively International: ID and Price Guide to World-Wide Fashion Dolls,* Hobby House Press, 1997; A. Glenn Mandeville, *Doll Fashion Anthology and Price Guide, 6th Edition,* Hobby House Press, 1998; Maria Martinez-Esguerra, *Collector's Guide to 1990s Barbie Dolls,* Collector Books, 1999; Marcie Melillo, *The Ultimate Barbie Doll Book,* Krause Publications, 1996; Lorraine Mieszala, *Collector's Guide to Barbie Doll Paper Dolls,* Collector Books, 1997.

Patrick C. Olds and Myrazona R. Olds, *The Barbie Doll Years: 1959–1996, Third Edition,* Collector Books, 1999; Margo Rana, *Barbie Doll Exclusively for Timeless Creations: 1986–1996, Book III,* Hobby House Press, 1997; Margo Rana, *Barbie Exclusives, Book II,* Collector Books, 1996; Margo Rana, *Collector's Guide to Barbie Exclusives,* Collector Books, 1995; Jane Sarasohn-Kahn, *Contemporary Barbie: Barbie Dolls 1980 and Beyond, 1998 Edition,* Antique Trader Books, 1997; Beth Summers, *A Decade of Barbie Dolls and Collectibles, 1981–1991,* Collector Books, 1996; Kitturah B. Westenhouser, *The Story of Barbie, Second Edition,* Collector Books, 1999.

Periodicals: *Barbie Bazaar,* 5617 6th Ave, Kenosha, WI 53140; *Miller's Barbie Collector,* West One Sumner, #1, Spokane, WA 99204.

Collectors' Club: Barbie Doll Collectors Club International, PO Box 586, White Plains, NY 10603.

Note: Prices listed for dolls in MIB condition.

ACCESSORIES

Barbie Carrying Case, vinyl, black, round, 1961 . . . . **$75.00**
Barbie, Francie, Casey & Tutti Doll Trunk, #5037, metal **75.00**
Coloring Book, Barbie & Skipper Sport Stars, Golden **5.00**
Fashion Queen Wig Wardrobe, #871, 1963, MIB **250.00**
Francie & Casey Hair Ornaments, 1966, MIP **100.00**
Hair Fair, #4042, 1966 . . . . **150.00**
Make Me Pretty Barbie **20.00**
Malibu Barbie Beach Party Case, white vinyl, hot pink and orange designs, 1979 . . . . **150.00**
Paper Dolls, Tutti, #1991, Whitman, 1968 . . . . **35.00**
Pretty Pet Parlor. **10.00**
Suzy Goose Barbie Vanity, plastic, 1963, MIP. **75.00**

CLOTHING

Barbie and Stacey, Accessory Pak, shoes and boots **$50.00**
Busy Morning, #956 . . . . **50.00**
Campus Sweetheart, #1616. . . . . **200.00**
Cotton Casual, #912 . . . . **30.00**
Country Fair, #1603 . . . . **40.00**
Evening Splendour, #961 . . . . **75.00**
Floral Petticoat, #921 . . . . **50.00**
Francie and Casey, Snappy Snoozers, #1238 . . . . **50.00**
Golf Gear Action Pak, 1970-71 . . . . **25.00**
Golfing Greats, #3413. . . . . **75.00**
Graduation, #368 . . . . **35.00**
Hooray For Leather, #1477 . . . . **50.00**
Icebreaker, #942. . . . . **45.00**
Ken and Brad Sea Scene, #1449 . . . . **50.00**

Barbie Dictionary, glossy red vinyl cover, Webster's Dictionary Concise Edition, Standard Products, 380 pp, ©1963 Mattell, Inc., $45.00.

Ken In Switzerland, #1404 . . . . **100.00**
Long On Looks, #1227 . . . . **75.00**
Party Date, #958 . . . . **75.00**
Peachy Fleecy Coat, #915 . . . . **40.00**
Perfectly Plaid Gift Set, #1193 . . . . **350.00**
Registered Nurse, #991 . . . . **75.00**
Shift Into Knit, #1478 . . . . **50.00**
Sorority Meeting, #937 . . . . **50.00**
Striped Types, #1243 . . . . **50.00**
Tangerine Scene, #1451 . . . . **50.00**

DOLLS, BARBIE

American Girl, #1070, 1965 . . . . **$975.00**
American Stories Series Pioneer, #12680, 1994 . . . . **25.00**
Barbie Ponytail, #3, blonde, 1959 . . . . **700.00**
Barbie Ponytail, #4, blonde, 1960 . . . . **450.00**
Barbie Ponytail, #5, brunette, 1961 . . . . **400.00**
Beautiful Bride, #9599, 1976 . . . . **250.00**
Busy Talking Barbie, #1195, 1971 . . . . **250.00**
Camp Fun Barbie, #11074, 1993 . . . . **10.00**
Children's Collector Series Rapunzel, #13016, 1994 . . . . **40.00**
Color Magic, #1150, blonde, 1967 . . . . **2,500.00**
Dance Club Barbie, #3509, 1989 . . . . **50.00**
Deluxe Quick Curl Barbie, #9217, 1975 . . . . **75.00**
Dolls of the World Canadian, #4928, 1987 . . . . **80.00**
Fashion Photo Barbie, #2210, 1977 . . . . **80.00**
Fashion Queen Barbie, #870, 1962 . . . . **500.00**
Free Moving Barbie, #7270, 1974 . . . . **65.00**
Growin' Pretty Hair, #1144, 1970 . . . . **275.00**
Hollywood Legends Scarlett, #12815, 1994 . . . . **75.00**
Lights & Lace Barbie, #9725, 1990 . . . . **35.00**
Live Action Barbie, #1155, 1970 . . . . **150.00**
Living Barbie, #1116, 1970 . . . . **250.00**
Mackie Empress Bride, #4247, 1992 . . . . **850.00**
Malibu Barbie, #1067, 1975 . . . . **70.00**
Miss Barbie, #1060, 1964 . . . . **750.00**
Newport Barbie, #7807, 1973 . . . . **175.00**
Now Look Ken, #9342, 1975 . . . . **80.00**
Pretty Changes, #2598, 1978 . . . . **40.00**
Rocker Barbie, #1140, 1985 . . . . **35.00**
Ski Fun Barbie, #7511, 1991 . . . . **25.00**
Sport & Shave Ken, #1294, 1979 . . . . **40.00**
Standard Barbie, #1190, 1969 . . . . **300.00**
Sun Set Malibu Barbie, #1067, 1971 . . . . **75.00**
Supersize Barbie, #9828, 1976 . . . . **200.00**
Supersize Barbie Bridal, #9975, 1977 . . . . **200.00**
Talking Barbie, #1115, side ponytail, 1968 . . . . **300.00**
Twist 'N Turn Barbie, #1160, 1966 . . . . **450.00**
Walk Lively Barbie, #1182, 1971 . . . . **150.00**

DOLLS, BARBIE'S FRIENDS

Allan, #1010, bendable leg, 1965 . . . . **$125.00**
Brad, #1142, 1969 . . . . **125.00**
Busy Talking Ken, #1196, 1971 . . . . **175.00**
California Dream Midge, #4442, 1987 . . . . **40.00**
Casey, #1180, 1966 . . . . **450.00**
Day-to-Night Ken, #1088, 1983 . . . . **25.00**
Fashion Photo PJ, #2323, 1977 . . . . **85.00**
Flight Time Ken, #9600, 1989 . . . . **20.00**
Francie, #1100, first version, 1965 . . . . **1,500.00**
Great Shapes Skipper, #7417, 1983 . . . . **15.00**
Growing Up Ginger, #9222, 1975 . . . . **85.00**

Living Fluff, #1143, 1970 . . . . **125.00**
Living Skipper, #1117, 1970 . . . . **150.00**
Midge, #1080, bendable leg, 1964 . . . . **650.00**
PJ, #1118, twist & turn, 1969 . . . . **275.00**
Quick Curl Francie, #4222, 1972 . . . . **175.00**
Skipper, #1030, bendable leg, 1964 . . . . **350.00**
Skipper, #1105, twist & turn, 1969 . . . . **275.00**
Skipper, #1147, trade-in, 1970 . . . . **200.00**
Skooter, #1120, bendable leg, 1966 . . . . **350.00**
Stacey, #1165, twist & turn, red swimsuit, 1967 . . . . **400.00**
Sun Valley Ken, #7809, 1973 . . . . **100.00**
Talking Stacey, #1125, 1969 . . . . **500.00**
Todd, #3590, 1965 . . . . **175.00**
Tutti Me 'N My Dog, #3554, 1965 . . . . **500.00**

PLAYSETS

Barbie Kitchen and Dinette **$250.00**
Barbie Townhouse **65.00**
Francie House **100.00**
Jamie's Penthouse **125.00**
Lively Livin' House **125.00**
Skipper Dream Room **250.00**

VEHICLES

Baywatch Rescue Station **$20.00**
Camp Barbie Sun Cruiser **15.00**
Classy Corvette **175.00**
Country Camper **30.00**
Sports Cruiser **10.00**

BARWARE

During the late 1960s and early 1970s it became fashionable for homeowners to convert basements into family rec rooms, often equipped with bars. Most were well stocked with both utilitarian items (shot glasses and ice crushers) and decorative accessories. Objects with advertising are usually more valuable than their generic counterparts.

References: Donald A. Bull, *The Ultimate Corkscrew Book*, Schiffer Publishing, 1999; Mark Pickvet, *The Encyclopedia of Shot Glasses,* Glass Press, 1998; Stephen Visakay, *Vintage Bar Ware*, Collector Books, 1997.

Collectors' Club: International Swizzle Stick Collectors Assoc, PO Box 1117, Bellingham, WA 98227.

Note: See also Breweriana, Cocktail Shakers, and Whiskey Bottles.

Bar Set, Soda King, chrome spritzer and 6 glasses **$125.00**
Coaster, anodized aluminum, 3¼" d, price for set of 4 . . . . . . **15.00**
Cocktail Set, The Magic Hour, pitcher, stirrer, 2 glasses,
    amethyst moroccan, Hazel Atlas **50.00**
Cocktail Shaker, chrome, turned maple top, bowling pin
    shape, 56 oz, 1930s **50.00**
Drink Mixer, Spoonomat, stainless steel **15.00**
Ice Bucket, aluminum, Bakelite handles **15.00**
Ice Crusher, Ice-O-Matic **30.00**
Mixer, Mix-All Mixer, "The Electric Bartender,"
    Chronmaster Electric Corp, NY-Chicago, c1930s **50.00**
Set, liquor bottle and shot glasses, crockery-style bottle
    with crossed bones at neck and skull stopper, "Name

Your Poison" across face of bottle, 2 matching brown
glaze skull shot glasses, paper label on bottle base
mkd "Hand painted - Tilso - Japan," 10" h. **25.00**

Shot Glass, "Bottoms Up," 2 blue monkeys hanging from
yellow branch **7.00**

Shot Glass, "Down The Hatch," mother bird bringing
baby red worm, gold rim, 1940s **8.00**

Shot Glass, "Enjoy yourself...it's later than you think,"
woman holding glass, 1940s **8.00**

Shot Glass, "I Say Jolly What!," dapper English gent,
1940s, 2¼" h **7.00**

Shot Glass, "Phooey On A Chaser!," lion chasing giraffe,
1950s **7.00**

Swizzle Stick, Catalin, black, figural leaf **5.00**

Swizzle Stick, glass, plain, red base, price for set of 6 . . . . . . **10.00**

Swizzle Stick, plastic, Seagram's Sea Breeze . . . . **.20**

BASEBALL CARDS

Baseball cards were originally issued by tobacco companies in the
late 19th century. The first big producers of gum cards were
Goudey Gum Company of Boston (1933–41) and Gum, Inc.
(1939). After World War II, Gum, Inc.'s successor, Bowman, was
the leading manufacturer. Topps, Inc. of Brooklyn, New York, followed. Topps bought Bowman in 1956 and monopolized the field
until 1981 when Fleer of Philadelphia and Donruss of Memphis
challenged the market.

References: James Beckett, *The Official 2001 Price Guide to
Baseball Cards, 20th Edition,* House of Collectibles, 2000; Bob
Lemke (ed.), *2000 Standard Catalog of Baseball Cards, 9th Edition,*
Krause Publications, 1999; Sports Collectors Digest, *1999 Baseball
Card Price Guide, 13th Edition,* Krause Publications, 1999; Sports
Collectors Digest, *Baseball's Top 500,* Krause Publications, 1999.

Periodicals: *Beckett Baseball Card Monthly,* 15850 Dallas Pkwy,
Dallas, TX 75248; *Card Trade,* 700 E State St, Iola, WI 54990; *Tuff
Stuff,* PO Box 569, Dubuque, IA 52004.

Note: Prices listed for cards in near mint condition.

Bazooka, 1959, #1, Hank Aaron **$550.00**
Bazooka, 1960, #8, Yogi Berra. **75.00**
Bazooka, 1961, #2, Mickey Mantle. **275.00**
Bazooka, 1962, #7, Orlando Cepeda. **20.00**
Bazooka, 1963, #17, Don Drysdale. **35.00**
Bazooka, 1964, #22, Jim Fregosi. **10.00**
Bowman, 1948, common card (1-36). **20.00**
Bowman, 1949, common card (1-144). **15.00**
Bowman, 1950, #11, Phil Rizzuto. **225.00**
Bowman, 1951, #80, Pee Wee Reese. **125.00**
Bowman, 1952, #27, Joe Garagiola. **50.00**
Bowman, 1953, #46, Roy Campanella **275.00**
Bowman, 1954, #62, Enos Slaughter **40.00**
Burger King, 1986, complete set (20), All-Pro. **2.50**
Burger King, 1987, #1, Wade Boggs, All-Pro . . . . **.15**
Donruss, 1981, complete set (605). **20.00**
Donruss, 1982, complete set (660). **35.00**
Donruss, 1983, complete set (660). **40.00**
Donruss, 1984, complete set (660). **225.00**
Donruss, 1985, complete set (8), Hall of Fame Heroes **7.00**
Donruss, 1986, #19, Mitch Williams, Rookies . . . . **.10**
Donruss, 1986, complete set (4), All Star Box **1.00**

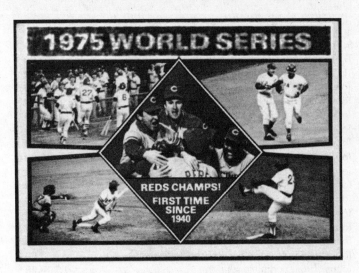

Topps, 1975, #462, World Series, $.50.

Donruss, 1986, complete set (18), Pop-Ups **2.00**
Donruss, 1988, #61, Nolan Ryan. . . . . **.75**
Donruss, 1989, #5, Cal Ripken **1.00**
Donruss, 1992, complete set (27), Diamond Kings **10.00**
Donruss, 1994, complete set (20), Dominators **20.00**
Drake's Cakes, 1983, complete set (33) **3.50**
Drake's Cookies, 1950, #8, Whitey Lockman **35.00**
Fleer, 1960, #14, Ty Cobb **50.00**
Fleer, 1963, #5, Willie Mays **200.00**
Fleer, 1982, #82, Tom Seaver. . . . . **.35**
Fleer, 1984, #34, Willie Hernandez. . . . . **.20**
Fleer, 1986, complete set (6), Future Hall of Famers **8.00**
Fleer, 1986, complete set (660) **30.00**
Fleer, 1988, #4, Barry Bonds, Superstars . . . . **.45**
Fleer, 1988, #19, Don Mattingly, Team Leaders . . . . **.45**
Fleer, 1989, complete set (44), Exciting Stars **2.00**
Goudey, 1933, common card (1-40) **60.00**
Goudey, 1933, common card (53-240) **45.00**
Goudey, 1934, #6, Dizzy Dean **275.00**
Goudey, 1934, common card (1-48) **25.00**
Hostess, 1975, complete set (150) **110.00**
Kahn's Wieners, 1956, complete set (15) **750.00**
Kahn's Wieners, 1962, complete set (41) **500.00**
Kellogg's, 1975, complete set (57) **70.00**
Kellogg's, 1977, complete set (57) **25.00**
Leaf, 1960, complete set (145). **800.00**
Leaf, 1990, complete set (528). **90.00**
O-Pee-Chee, 1965, #57, Cardinals. **3.50**
O-Pee-Chee, 1966, #50, Mickey Mantle. **130.00**
O-Pee-Chee, 1967, #102, Phillies **3.00**
O-Pee-Chee, 1968, #445, Tom Seaver **40.00**
O-Pee-Chee, 1969, #50, Roberto Clemente **35.00**
O-Pee-Chee, 1970, #26, Tug McGraw **1.50**
O-Pee-Chee, 1971, #100, Pete Rose **15.00**
O-Pee-Chee, 1976, complete set (660). **200.00**
O-Pee-Chee, 1986, complete set (396). **7.00**
Pinnacle, 1992, complete set (620) **20.00**
Pinnacle, 1993, #45, Len Dykstra . . . . **.10**
Pinnacle, 1993, complete set (30), Team 2001 . . . . **20.00**
Pinnacle, 1996, complete set (400) **14.00**
Score, 1988, #16, Mike Schmidt . . . . **.10**
Score, 1989, #1, Jose Canseco . . . . **.10**

Score, 1990, complete set (42), Young Superstars **2.00**
Score, 1991, complete set (7), Mickey Mantle **110.00**
Tip Top Bread, 1947, #57, Phil Rizzuto **70.00**
Tip Top Bread, 1947, common card (1-164) **10.00**
Topps, 1952, #37, Duke Snider **100.00**
Topps, 1953, #41, Enos Slaughter **35.00**
Topps, 1954, #45, Richie Ashburn **30.00**
Topps, 1955, complete set (206) **3,000.00**
Topps, 1956, #79, Sandy Koufax **150.00**
Topps, 1957, #10, Willie Mays **100.00**
Topps, 1959, complete set (572) **2,000.00**
Topps, 1960, #18, Dodgers **10.00**
Topps, 1961, #2, Roger Maris **60.00**
Topps, 1962, complete set (598) **2,000.00**
Topps, 1963, #13, Phillies **3.00**
Topps, 1964, #27, New York Mets **3.50**
Topps, 1965, #49, Orioles Rookies **2.00**
Topps, 1965, complete set (598) **1,500.00**
Topps, 1966, #5, Jim Fregosi **1.00**
Topps, 1968, #80, Rod Carew **20.00**
Topps, 1970, ##44, Roberto Pena . . . . **.50**
Topps, 1971, #615, Mel Stottlemyre **2.00**
Topps, 1978, #60, Thurmon Munson **1.25**
Topps, 1979, #321, Gaylord Perry . . . . **.50**
Upper Deck, 1989, complete set (800) **50.00**
Upper Deck, 1990, #17, Sammy Sosa . . . . **.50**
Upper Deck, 1991, #157, Matt Williams . . . . **.05**
Upper Deck, 1992, #124, Andre Dawson . . . . **.10**
Wheaties, 1951, common card (1-6) **60.00**

BASEBALL MEMORABILIA

Baseball traces its beginnings to the mid-19th century. By the turn of the century it had become America's national pastime.

The superstar has always been the key element in the game. Baseball greats were popular visitors at banquets, parades, and more recently at baseball autograph shows. Autographed items, especially those used in an actual game, command premium prices. The bigger the star, the bigger the price tag.

References: David Bushing, *Sports Equipment Price Guide,* Krause Publications, 1995; David Bushing and Joe Phillips, *Vintage Baseball Glove 1997 Pocket Price Guide, Vol. 1, No. 5,* published by authors, 1997; Douglas Congdon-Martin and John Kashmanian, *Baseball Treasures: Memorabilia From the National Pastime,* Schiffer Publishing, 1993; Kevin Keating and Mike Kolleth, *The Negro League Autograph Guide,* Antique Trader Books, 1998; Mark Larson, Rick Hines, and Dave Platta (eds.), *Mickey Mantle Memorabilia,* Krause Publications, 1993; Tom Mortenson (ed.), *2000 Standard Catalog of Sports Memorabilia,* Krause Publications, 1999; Don Raycraft, R. C. Raycraft and Michael Raycraft, *Collectibles 101: Baseball,* Schiffer Publishing, 1999; Tuff Stuff (eds.), *Baseball Memorabilia Price Guide,* Antique Trader Books, 1998; Jim Warren II, *Tuff Stuff's Complete Guide to Starting Lineup: A Pictorial History of Kenner Starting Lineup Figures,* Antique Trader Books, 1997.

Periodicals: *Beckett Sports Collectibles & Autographs,* 15850 Dallas Pkwy, Dallas, TX 75248; *Sports Collectors Digest,* 700 E State St, Iola, WI 54990; *Tuff Stuff,* PO Box 569, Dubuque, IA 52004.

Collectors' Clubs: Society for American Baseball Research, 812 Huron Rd E, #719, Cleveland, OH 44115; The Glove Collector, 14057 Rolling Hills Ln, Dallas, TX 54240.

Note: See Hartland Figures for additional listings.

Ashtray, New York Yankees, porcelain, off-white, inner gold ring and logo, blue lettering, 8" sq **$20.00**
Bobbing Head, Cincinnati Reds, ceramic, on green base with white bottom, 7¾" h **25.00**
Book, *1969 World Series All American League Series Facts for Press–Radio–TV,* 16 pp, Baltimore Orioles publicity, biography of each player **20.00**
Game Ball, Brooklyn Dodgers, "Ten Win Start," given by Roy Campanella to winning pitcher Joe Black after tenth game of the season, inscribed "April 26, 1955, winning pitcher Black, losing pitcher Roberts, Brooklyn 14 – Phillies 4," faded lettering, with letter of authenticity from Joe Black, 1955 . . . . **1,150.00**
Game Ball, Nolan Ryan, 300th win, autographed by Ryan, notated "Game ball – 300th win – 7/31/90" by umpire Al Clark, with letter of authenticity **1,200.00**
Glove, Nokona G13, Dick Williams model, brown leather, left handed, facsimile Dick Williams signature on little finger, button closure on back **20.00**
Glove, Rawlings, Stan Musial model, brown leather, left handed, facsimile Stan Musial signature on palm, c1950–60s **50.00**
Hat, Oakland Athletics Mark McGwire, #25 in marker under bill, heavy sweat marks on band, autographed on yellow bill, game worn **1,225.00**
Miniature Bat, wooden, black, silver printed logo and Rod Carew signature, 16" l **20.00**
Pass, 1934 All-American Tour of Japan, sgd by tour manager Connie Mack, 4 x 3" **750.00**
Pennant, New York Yankees, blue felt, Uncle Sam image, 1950-60s, 28" l **20.00**
Pin, Kansas City Royals, 1985 World Series, gilt, colored enamel logo in center, "Second World Series" on top and "Royals" below, with plastic case, 1985, 1 x 1¼" **40.00**
Pinback Button, black and white Mickey Mantle photo, c1950s **45.00**
Program, 1949 World Series, Ebbets Field, 50 pp, Dodgers vs Yankees **50.00**

Baseball, autographed by Satchel Paige, with letter of authenticity, $550.00. Photo courtesy Collectors Auction Services.

Road Jersey, Oriole's Cal Ripken Jr, 1991 season,
Rawlings label inside left tail, size 48, game-worn,
with letter of aunthenticity from Grey Flannel **3,250.00**

Shirt, Cardinals, wool, light gray, button front, black and
red piping trim, "80" sewn on back, size 42, Coane of
Philadelphia, 1940s **35.00**

Ticket, 1952 World Series, game 7, Dodgers hosting
Yankees at Ebbets Field **850.00**

AUCTION PRICES – BASEBALL MEMORABILIA

Mastro Fine Sports Auctions, Sports Memorabilia Auction, April 30, 1999. Prices include a 15% buyer's premium.

Cobb, Ty, photographic portrait, wearing cuffed
3-pc suit, stiff collar, watch fob chain, and stickpin, holding cigar butt, c1910, 4¾ x 6½" **$510.00**

Jackson, Reggie, NY Yankees road jersey, autographed front and back, game-worn, 1977 . . . . . . **6,562.00**

Mack, Connie, 1934 All-American Tour of Japan
pass, sgd by tour manager Connie Mack, 4 x 3" **746.00**

Maris, Roger, NY Yankees Old-Timers cap, auto-
graphed in black, with letter of authenticity **2,443.00**

Negro League, set of 6 pennants, felt, NY Cubans,
Baltimore Elite Giants, Homestead Grays,
Newark Eagles, NY Black Yankees, and
Philadelphia Stars, 1930s-40s **3,704.00**

Ruth, Babe, notched home run bat, Louisville
Slugger with 8 carved notches, mid- to late
1920s, 35" l **64,287.00**

World Series Ticket, 1952, game 7, Dodgers hosting
Yankees at Ebbets Field, excellent condition **843.00**

BASKETBALL CARDS

Muriad cigarettes issued the first true basketball trading cards in 1911. In 1933 Goudey issued the first basketball cards found in gum packs. The era of modern hoop basketball trading cards dates from 1948 when Bowman created the first set devoted exclusively to the sport. By the 1950s Topps, Exhibit Supply Company, Kellogg's, Wheaties, and other food manufacturers joined with Bowman in creating basketball trading cards. Collectors regard the 1957–58 Topps set as the second true modern basketball set.

Today basketball trading card sets are issued by a wide variety of manufacturers. Collectors also must contend with draft card series, special rookie cards, insert or chase cards and super premium card sets. Keeping up with contemporary issues is time consuming and expensive. As a result, many collectors focus only on pre-1990 issued cards.

References: James Beckett, *The Official 2000 Price Guide to Basketball Cards, 9th Edition,* House of Collectibles, 1999; Sports Collectors Digest, *2000 Standard Catalog of Basketball Cards, 3rd Edition,* Krause Publications, 1999; Tuff Stuff (eds.), *Tuff Stuff's Complete Basketball Card Price Guide & Checklist,* Antique Trader Books, 1998.

Periodicals: *Beckett Basketball Card Magazine,* 15850 Dallas Pkwy, Dallas, TX 75248; *Sports Cards,* 700 E State St, Iola, WI 54990.

Note: Prices listed for cards in mint condition.

McDonald's, NBA Fantasy Pack, premium, foil package, $3.00.

Fleer, 1986-87, #1, Kareem Abdul-Jabbar **$12.00**
Fleer, 1987-88, #11, Larry Bird **30.00**
Fleer, 1988-89, complete set with stickers (143) **175.00**
Fleer, 1992-93, complete set (108), Tony's Pizza **85.00**
Fleer, 1993-94, complete set (400) **20.00**
Globetrotters 84, 1971-72, complete set (85) **200.00**
Globetrotters Wonder Bread, 1974, complete set (6) **40.00**
Hawks, 1986-87, complete set (18), Pizza Hut **30.00**
Hoops 100 Superstars, #12, Michael Jordan **12.00**
Hoops All-Star Panels, 1990-91, compete set (4) **15.00**
Hoops Announcers, 1990-91, #16, Bob Costas **75.00**
Kahn's, 1957-58, common card (1-11) **100.00**
Kahn's, 1959-60, complete set (10) **600.00**
Nabisco Sugar Daddy, 1974, complete set (25) **160.00**
Royal Crown Desserts, common card (1-8) **250.00**
Star, 1983-84, #1, Julius Erving **70.00**
Star, 1983-84, complete set (10), All Star Rookies **40.00**
Star, 1984-85, #1, Larry Bird **175.00**
Supersonics Sunbeam Bread, 1970-71, complete set (11) . . . **125.00**
Topps, 1968-69, #12, Earl Monroe **400.00**
Topps, 1970-71, #7, Bill Bradley **40.00**
Topps, 1973-74, complete set (264) **325.00**
Topps, 1974-75, #19, Lucius Allen **1.00**
Topps, 1975-76, complete set (330) **450.00**
Topps, 1976-77, #1, Julius Erving **70.00**
Topps, 1979-80, complete set (132) **70.00**
Ultra, 1995-96, complete set (350) **50.00**
Ultra Power, 1995-96, complete set (10) **8.00**
Upper Deck, 1991-92, #44, Michael Jordan **3.00**
Upper Deck, 1993-94, complete set (510) **30.00**

BASKETBALL MEMORABILIA

The first basketball game was played on a regulation 94 x 50' court in 1891. James Naismith, physical director of the Y.M.C.A. College, Springfield, Massachusetts, originated the game. Early basketball collectibles relate to high school and college teams.

Professional basketball was played prior to World War II. However, it was not until 1949 and the founding of the United States National Basketball Association that the sport achieved national status. Competing leagues, franchise changes, and Olympic teams compete for collector loyalty.

References: Oscar Garcia, *Collecting Michael Jordan Memorabilia,* Krause Publications, 1998; Tom Mortenson (ed.), *2000 Standard Catalog of Sports Memorabilia,* Krause Publications, 1999.

Autograph, Charles Barkley, PS, 8 x 10" **$20.00**
Autograph, Patrick Ewing, PS, 8 x 10". **40.00**
Basketball, Spalding, sgd by Larry Bird in silver paint
   pen, with Victor Reichman certificate of authenticity **75.00**
Cereal Box, Kellogg's Frosted Mini Wheats, Chris Mullin,
   Team USA, 1992 . . . . **20.00**
Figure, Moses Malone, Kenner Starting Lineup, 1988 . . . . **45.00**
Figure, Patrick Ewing, Kenner Starting Lineup, 1988 . . . . **15.00**
Game, Basket Ball, Russell Mfg Co, #217, 1929 . . . . **85.00**
Game, NBA Bas-Ket, Cadaco, 1983 . . . . **10.00**
Game, Real-Life Basketball, Gamecraft, 1974 . . . . **10.00**
Magazine, *Basketball Digest,* Mar 1975 . . . . **6.00**
Magazine, *Basketball Forecast,* 1965-86 . . . . **10.00**
Magazine, *Basketball Forecast,* 1988-89 . . . . **8.00**
Magazine, *Hoop,* May 1989 . . . . **4.00**
Media Guide, Lakers, 1963-65 . . . . **10.00**
Poster, Willis Reed, *Sports Illustrated,* 1968-71 . . . . **20.00**
Program, NCAA Division I Final Four, 1958 . . . . **100.00**
Sticker, #7, Nate Thurmond, Topps, 1971-72 . . . . **4.00**
Ticket Stub, NBA All-Star Game, Boston, 1964 . . . . **20.00**
Yearbook, Nets, 1975-76 . . . . **25.00**

BAUER POTTERY

John Bauer founded the Paducah Pottery in Paducah, Kentucky, in 1885. John Andrew Bauer assumed leadership of the pottery in 1898 following the death of John Bauer. In 1909 the pottery moved its operations to Los Angeles, California.

The company's award winning artware line was introduced in 1913. Molded stoneware vases were marketed shortly thereafter.

In 1931 Bauer Pottery began production of its most popular line—Ring ware. Decorated in brightly colored glazes, it included over a hundred different shapes and sizes in table and kitchen lines. Ring ware proved to be Bauer's most popular and profitable pattern. Other successful lines include Monterey (1936–45), La Linda (1939–59), and Brusche Contempo and Monterey Moderne (1948–61). Increasing competition at home and abroad and a bitter strike in 1961 forced Bauer to close its doors in 1962.

References: Jack Chipman, *Collector's Encyclopedia of Bauer Pottery,* Collector Books, 1998; Jeffrey B. Snyder, *Beautiful Bauer,* Schiffer Publishing, 2000; Mitch Tuchman, *Bauer: Classic American Pottery,* Chronicle Books, 1995.

Periodical: *Bauer Quarterly,* PO Box 2524, Berkeley, CA 94702.

Brusche Al Fresco, cereal bowl, 5½" deep **$15.00**
Brusche Al Fresco, creamer, green **15.00**
Brusche Al Fresco, dinner plate, lime, 11½" d **12.00**
Brusche Al Fresco, fruit bowl, pink, 5" d **12.00**
Brusche Al Fresco, pitcher, misty gray, 2 pt **40.00**
Brusche Al Fresco, sugar, cov, hemlock green **18.00**
Brusche Al Fresco, vegetable, divided, hemlock green,
   9¼" d **30.00**
Brusche Al Fresco, vegetable, round, yellow, 9½" d **30.00**
Brusche Contempo, bread and butter plate, green, 6" d **6.00**
Brusche Contempo, cereal bowl, pumpkin, 5¼" h **15.00**
Brusche Contempo, mug, pumpkin, 8 oz **30.00**
Brusche Contempo, pitcher, Indio brown, 1 pt **30.00**
Gloss Pastel Kitchenware, batter bowl, yellow, 2 qt **50.00**
Gloss Pastel Kitchenware, casserole, olive green, 1 qt **40.00**
Gloss Pastel Kitchenware, custard cup, pink **8.00**
Gloss Pastel Kitchenware, mixing bowl, #12, green **35.00**

Gloss Pastel Kitchenware, mixing bowl, #36, yellow **12.00**
Gloss Pastel Kitchenware, pitcher, yellow, 2 qt **50.00**
La Linda, bread and butter plate, ivory, 6" d **7.00**
La Linda, cup, blue **18.00**
La Linda, dinner plate, green **15.00**
La Linda, fruit bowl, blue, 5" d **18.00**
La Linda, platter, oval, blue, 10" l **22.00**
La Linda, salad plate, brown, 7½" d **8.00**
La Linda, saucer, yellow **6.00**
La Linda, shaker, brown **6.00**
La Linda, tumbler, ivory **20.00**
Mission Moderne, bread and butter plate, 6" d **10.00**
Mission Moderne, buffet plate **20.00**
Mission Moderne, gravy bowl **35.00**
Mission Moderne, sugar, cov **30.00**
Monterey Moderne, beater pitcher, burgundy, 1 qt **40.00**
Monterey Moderne, butter, cov, pink **65.00**
Monterey Moderne, casserole, individual, chartreuse **25.00**
Monterey Moderne, chop plate, chartreuse. **40.00**
Monterey Moderne, dinner plate, pink, 10½" d **25.00**
Monterey Moderne, pitcher, brown, 1 qt **50.00**
Monterey Moderne, serving bowl, chartreuse, 7" d **25.00**
Monterey Moderne, soup bowl, black, 5¼" d **35.00**
Ring, batter bowl, 2 qt. **85.00**
Ring, bud vase, 5" h **200.00**
Ring, butter, cov, ¼ lb **200.00**
Ring, candleholder, 2½" h **50.00**
Ring, casserole, 8½" d **100.00**
Ring, casserole, individual, 5½" d **200.00**
Ring, creamer **25.00**
Ring, demitasse cup and saucer **150.00**
Ring, eggcup. **175.00**
Ring, mixing bowl, #18 . . . . **50.00**
Ring, mustard, cov **275.00**
Ring, nappy, #5 . . . . **35.00**
Ring, nappy, #8 . . . . **55.00**
Ring, pitcher, 3 qt **125.00**
Ring, platter, oval, 9" l **35.00**
Ring, salad bowl, 12" d **125.00**
Ring, sugar, cov **50.00**
Ring, sugar shaker **200.00**
Ring, syrup pitcher **90.00**
Ring, teapot, 6 cup **125.00**

La Linda, creamer, green, $12.00. Photo courtesy Ray Morykan Auctions.

BEANIE BABIES

The market is flooded with Beanie Baby price guides. Consider carefully how accurately they reflect the secondary retail market. A few years from now, their only value will be the ability to look nostalgically back on the craze and think "if I had only sold then."

These values are highly conservative and far more realistic than those found in many Beanie Baby price guides. They reflect the market. They **DO NOT** prop the market. With a few exceptions, e.g., the very first Beanie Babies, most are selling at one-half to one-third of book—the more recent the example, the greater the discount. The Beanie Baby market collapse is at hand. A year from now, sellers will thank their lucky stars if they can get these prices.

References: Sharon Brecka, *Bean Family Pocket Guide,* Antique Trader Books, 1999; Les and Sue Fox, *The Beanie Baby Handbook,* West Highland Publishing, 1997; Rosie Wells, *Rosie's Price Guide for Ty's Beanie Babies,* Rosie Wells Enterprises, 1997.

Periodicals: *Beans & Bears Magazine,* PO Box 1050, Dubuque, IA 52004; *Mary Beth's Bean Bag World Monthly,* 2121 Waukegan Rd, Ste 120, Bannockburn, IL 60015.

Note: All items are priced each. Dates preceded by an R are retirement dates. Beanie Babies without tags have little or no value.

Chip the Calico Cat, new tag with star, $5.00.

Ants Anteater, R 12/98	**$7.00**
Baldy Eagle, 4th or 5th generation tag, R 5/98	**15.00**
Bessie Cow, 4th generation tag, R 1997	**55.00**
Blackie the Bear, 1st generation tag, R 9/98	**350.00**
Bongo the Monkey, 3rd generation tag, R 12/98	**110.00**
Bruno the Terrier, R 9/98	**8.00**
Bubbles the Fish, 3rd generation tag, R 1997	**145.00**
Bucky the Beaver, 3rd generation tag, R 1/98	**75.00**
Chocolate the Moose, 1st generation tag, R 12/98	**450.00**
Chops the Lamb, 4th generation tag, R 1997	**125.00**
Congo the Gorilla, 4th or 5th generation tag, R 12/98	**10.00**
Coral the Fish, 4th generation tag, R 1996	**135.00**
Cubbie the Bear, 1st generation tag, R 1/98	**450.00**
Curly the Bear, 4th or 5th generation tag, R 12/98	**15.00**
Daisy the Cow, 1st generation tag, R 9/98	**275.00**
Digger the Crab, 1st generation tag, R 1995	**825.00**
Dotty the Dalmatian, 4th or 5th generation tag, R 12/98	**10.00**
Echo the Dolphin, 4th or 5th generation tag, R 5/98	**14.00**
Flip the Cat, 4th generation tag, R 1997	**35.00**
Freckles the Leopard, 4th or 5th generation tag, R 12/98	**10.00**
Gobbles the Turkey, 4th or 5th generation tag, R3/31/99	**8.00**
Goldie the Fish, 1st generation tag, R 1/98	**325.00**
Gracie the Swan, 4th or 5th generation tag, R 5/98	**12.00**
Happy Hippopotamus, 3rd generation tag, R 5/98	**125.00**
Humphrey the Camel, 3rd generation tag, R 1994	**1,500.00**
Jolly the Walrus, 4th or 5th generation tag, R 5/98	**12.00**
Lizzy the Lizard, 3rd generation tag, R 1/98	**175.00**
Magic the Dragon, 3rd generation tag, R 1/98	**110.00**
Manny the Manatee, 3rd generation tag, R 1997	**175.00**
McDonald's Teenie Beanie Baby, Antsy, 1998	**5.00**
McDonald's Teenie Beanie Baby, Chops the Lamb, 1997	**25.00**
McDonald's Teenie Beanie Baby, Peanut, 1998	**6.00**
McDonald's Teenie Beanie Baby, Seamore the Seal, 1997	**15.00**
Mystic the Unicorn, 4th generation tag, coarse mane, tan horn, R 3/31/99	**30.00**
Nanook the Husky, 4th or 5th generation tag, R 3/31/99	**10.00**
Patti the Platypus, 3rd generation tag, maroon, R 9/98	**400.00**
Peanut the Elephant, 3rd generation tag, R 5/98	**525.00**
Pinchers the Lobster, 1st generation tag, R 5/98	**850.00**
Pinky the Flamingo, 3rd generation tag, R 12/98	**90.00**
Radar the Bat, 3rd generation tag, R 1997	**160.00**
Ringo the Raccoon, 3rd generation tag, R 9/98	**60.00**
Scottie the Terrier, 4th or 5th generation tag, R 5/98	**15.00**
Seaweed the Otter, 3rd generation tag, R 9/98	**70.00**
Snip the Siamese Cat, 4th or 5th generation tag, R 12/98	**12.00**
Snort the Bull, 4th or 5th generation tag, R 9/98	**10.00**
Speedy the Turtle, 1st generation tag, R 1997	**550.00**
Splash the Whale, 1st generation tag, R 1997	**550.00**
Squealer the Pig, 1st generation tag, R 5/98	**600.00**
Stinky the Skunk, 3rd generation tag, R 9/98	**60.00**
Tusk the Walrus, 3rd generation tag, R 1996	**150.00**
Twigs the Giraffe, 3rd generation tag, R 5/98	**85.00**
Velvet the Panther, 3rd generation tag, R 1997	**85.00**
Waddle the Penguin, 3rd generation tag, R 5/98	**70.00**
Web the Spider, 3rd generation tag, R 1994	**900.00**
Ziggy the Zebra, 3rd generation tag, R 5/98	**80.00**

BEATLES

Beatlemania took the country by storm in 1964, the year the Beatles appeared on "The Ed Sullivan Show." Members of the Fab Four included George Harrison, John Lennon, Paul McCartney, and Ringo Starr (who replaced original drummer Pete Best in 1962). The most desirable items were produced between 1964 and 1968 and are marked "NEMS."

The group disbanded in 1970 and individual members pursued their own musical careers. John Lennon's tragic murder in New York City in 1980 invoked a new wave of interest in the group and its memorabilia.

References: Jeff Augsburger, Marty Eck, and Rick Rann, *The Beatles Memorabilia Price Guide, Third Edition,* Antique Trader Books, 1997; Perry Cox, *The Official Price Guide to the Beatles, Second Edition,* House of Collectibles, 1999; Barbara Crawford and Michael Stern, *The Beatles, Second Edition,* Collector Books, 1998; Courtney McWilliams, *The Beatles: Yesterday and Tomorrow,* Schiffer Publishing, 1999.

Periodicals: *Beatlefan,* PO Box 33515, Decatur, GA 30033; *Good Day Sunshine,* PO Box 661008, Los Angeles, CA 90066; *Strawberry Fields Forever,* PO Box 880981, San Diego, CA 92168.

Collectors' Clubs: Beatles Connection, PO Box 1066, Miami, FL 33780; Working Class Hero Beatles Club, 3311 Niagara St, Pittsburgh, PA 15213.

REPRODUCTION ALERT: Records, picture sleeves, and album jackets have been counterfeited. Sound quality may be inferior. Printing on labels and picture jackets usually is inferior to the original. Many pieces of memorabilia also have been reproduced, often with some change in size, color, design, etc.

Book, *The Big Beatles Beat Drum Book,* Hanson
  Publications, ©1965 Beatles Ltd, 24 pp, 8½ x 11"...... **$35.00**
Book, *True Story of the Beatles,* Bantam Books, 224 pp..... **10.00**
Costume, fabric, 1-pc, blue rayon, flannel chest with "B"
  and Beatles portraits, Ben Cooper, c1964, 40" l......... **75.00**
Doll, vinyl, inflatable, White Lux Beauty Soap premium,
  cartoon images wearing purple suits and holding
  instruments, ©1966 NEMS Enterprises Ltd, 15" h,
  price for set of 4.............................. **150.00**
Drumsticks, pr, wooden, mkd "13A Ringo Starr Model
  by Ludwig, U.S.A.," MIP....................... **300.00**
Flicker Button, black and white text and photo on yellow
  ground, Vari-Vue, c1964, 2½" d, price for set of 6....... **75.00**
Headband, blue stretch nylon, reversible, red "Love the
  Beatles" on band with heart and music note designs,
  Better Wear, Inc, c1964, MIP..................... **75.00**
Lunch Box, metal, emb, Aladdin Industries, Inc, ©1965
  NEMS Enterprises, Ltd, 7 x 8 x 4"................... **300.00**
Magazine, *Beatles Film,* Sun Printers Ltd, 48 pp, 9 x 11¾".... **50.00**
Magazine, *Teen Talk,* full color cover photo, Saber
  Publishing, NY, 1964, 32 pp..................... **65.00**
Necklace, metal link with gold luster, holds 1" d pendant
  with gold luster metal frame and inset black and white
  cello covered disk with band photo, raised "Yeh, Yeh,
  Yeh" and NEMS copyright on reverse, c1964, 8" l....... **50.00**
Pencil Case, red vinyl, zippered top, front sepia photo of
  band with black facsimile signatures, Standard Plastic
  Products, ©Ramat & Co, Ltd, c1964, 3½ x 8"......... **150.00**
Pin, metal, brass luster frame surrounding 1¼" black and
  white celluloid insert group photo, bar pin with diecut
  metal center area with facsimile autographs of first
  names, ©NEMS, c1964..................... **75.00**
Pinback Button, "I Love the Beatles," red, white, and
  blue, 3½" d............................... **35.00**
Pinback Button, "I'm A Beatles Booster"................. **20.00**
Pinback Button, "John Lennon/In Memory of a Rock
  Superstar," black and white photo on red and white
  ground, includes dates of birth and death............. **15.00**
Poster, group photo with facsimile signatures at lower
  right, 1960s, 39 x 53½"....................... **150.00**
Record, *I Am The Walrus/Hello Goodbye,* 45 rpm,
  orange and yellow swirl label, Capitol, in paper sleeve
  with color photo........................... **75.00**
Rug, fabric, design including Beatles portraits, guitar,
  snare drum, and musical notes, 22 x 34"............ **250.00**
Song Folio, "Beatles Magical Mystery Tour," Hansen
  Publications, Inc, ©1967 Northern Songs Ltd, 40 pp,
  8½ x 11"................................ **35.00**

Soaky Bottle, Paul McCartney, Colgate-Palmolive, ©1965 NEMS Enterprises, Ltd, 9½" h, $100.00.

Tablet, full color glossy photo cover with facsimile sig-
  natures, Lewis F Dow Co, ©NEMS Ltd London, 1967,
  7¾ x 10"............................... **50.00**
Ticket, paper, Beatles Film Festival, New Mexico State
  University Corbett Center, May 22, 1976, group photo
  and text "3½ Captivating Heart Warming Hours With
  The Beatles On Film," complete with stub, 2¼ x 5½".... **60.00**
Ticket, paper, Shea Stadium, NY, Aug 23, 1966, missing
  stub, 1½ x 3½"........................... **150.00**
Ticket, paper, yellow, Suffolk Downs, East Boston, MA,
  Aug 18, 1966, center "Frank Connelly Productions
  Presents The Beatles," with letter of authenticity, com-
  plete and unused, 1½ x 4"..................... **75.00**
Wallet, vinyl, browntone photo on 1 side, black facsim-
  ile signatures on other side, Standard Plastics
  Products, ©1964 Ramat & Co Ltd, 3½ x 4½"......... **100.00**

AUCTION PRICES – BEATLES MEMORABILIA

Sotheby's New York, Collectors' Carrousel Sale #7333, June 12, 1999. Prices include a 15% buyer's premium.

Animation Cels, pair, from *Yellow Submarine,* King
  Features, Ringo and the Nowhere Man and "Sea
  of Time" sequence with one of the Beatles in silhouette, 1968, 3¾" h Ringo image............ **$690.00**
Autographs, group, sgd in blue ballpoint pen on
  pink paper, matted with color tinted photograph
  of the group, c1963, 21¾ x 17¾"............ **2,588.00**
Bicycle, Huffy Yellow Submarine, 3-speed, yellow-
  painted lady's frame, seat decorated with printed
  design featuring the submarine, late 1960s...... **2,588.00**
Spectacles, John Lennon's, wire-rimmed, prescrip-
  tion frames, matted in shadow box with color
  machine print photo of Lennon wearing similar
  pair, accompanied by letter concerning provenance, 11½ x 16½"..................... **25,875.00**

BELLEEK, AMERICAN

The American Belleek era spanned from the early 1880s until 1930. Several American firms manufactured porcelain wares resembling Irish Belleek. The first was Ott and Brewer Company of Trenton, New Jersey, from 1884 until 1893. Companies operating between 1920 and 1930 include Cook Pottery (1894–1929), Coxon Belleek Pottery (1926–1930), Lenox, Inc. (1906–1930), Morgan Belleek China Company (1924–1929), and Perlee, Inc. (1920s–c1930).

Reference: Mary Frank Gaston, *American Belleek*, Collector Books, 1984, out of print.

Chocolate Pot, individual, sterling silver overlay, Lenox
  1906-24, 5¼" h **$150.00**
Coffeepot, cov, applied silver with pink floral garlands
  and thin horizontal yellow enamelled lines, Lenox,
  1906-24, 11" h **550.00**
Demitasse Cup, gold rim, ivory int, sterling silver holder,
  Willets, brown mark **45.00**
Dinner Plate, blue and pink enamelled floral inserts on
  wide maroon border, Morgan Belleek China Co,
  c1924-29, 11" d **200.00**
Mug, hp grapes and leaves, Lenox, 1906-24, 4½" h **75.00**
Pitcher, dec with floral band, silver overlay, Lenox #1038 . . . **150.00**
Salt, individual, 3 ftd, hp leaf dec, gold trim, Cook Pottery . **125.00**
Salt, individual, sterling silver holder with gold band
  border, Lenox, 1906-30, 1½" h **40.00**
Talcum Shaker, hp rose garland with blue bow, light blue
  ground, gilded top, artist sgd, Lenox, 1906-24, 6" h **100.00**
Tea Set, 3 pcs, peacock dec, teapot 5½" h, covered sugar
  4" h, creamer 3¾" h, Perlee Inc, c1920-30 . . . . **350.00**
Tea Set, 7 pcs, blue and pink floral transfer, yellow bor-
  der, gold trim, consisting of teapot, creamer, covered
  sugar, bread and butter plate, and cup and saucer,
  Coxon, 6½" h teapot **1,500.00**
Tea Strainer, hp floral design, artist sgd Lenox, 1906-24,
  6" l **250.00**
Vase, Art Deco, hp peacocks, Lenox, 1906-24, 13" h **325.00**

BELLEEK, IRISH

Belleek is a thin, ivory-colored, almost iridescent-type porcelain. It was first made in 1857 in county Fermanagh, Ireland. Production continued until World War I, was discontinued for a period of time, and then resumed.

Shamrock is the most commonly found pattern, but many patterns were made, including Limpet, Tridacna, and Grasses. Pieces made after 1891 have the word "Ireland" or "Eire" in their mark. Some are marked "Belleek Co., Fermanagh."

The following abbreviations have been used to identify marks:

1BM	=	1st Black Mark (1863–1890)
2BM	=	2nd Black Mark (1891–1926)
3BM	=	3rd Black Mark (1926–1946)
4GM	=	4th Green Mark (1946–1955)
5GM	=	5th Green Mark (1955–1965)
6GM	=	6th Green Mark (1965–c1980)
7B/GM	=	7th Brown/Gold Mark (1980–1992)
8BM	=	8th Blue Mark (1993–present)

References: Susan and Al Bagdade, *Warman's English & Continental Pottery & Porcelain, 3rd Edition*, Krause Publications, 1998; Richard K. Degenhardt, *Belleek: The Complete Collector's Guide and Illustrated Reference, Second Edition*, Wallace-Homestead, 1993.

Collectors' Club: The Belleek Collectors' International Society, 9893 Georgetown Pike, Ste 525, Great Falls, VA 22066.

Coffeepot, Limpet pattern, gilt dec handle, finial, and
  trim, 3BM, 7" h **$250.00**
Creamer, molded satyr head, 1BM, 4⅞" h **125.00**
Cup and Saucer, Limpet pattern, black mark **50.00**
Cup and Saucer, Limpet pattern, green mark **30.00**
Cup and Saucer, Shamrock pattern, harp handle, 3BM . . . **100.00**
Cup and Saucer, Shell pattern, 3BM **100.00**
Cup and Shell, Snail pattern, 3BM **125.00**
Ewer, Aberdeen pattern, green mark, 6" h **120.00**
Figure, Irish greyhound, 3BM, 14" h **625.00**
Figure, leprechaun on mushroom, 3BM, 5½" h **300.00**
Mug, Shamrock pattern, 3BM, 6" h **100.00**
Plate, Limpet pattern, black mark, 8¼" d **35.00**
Plate, Shamrock pattern, basketweave ground, 3BM,
  7" d **60.00**
Plate, Shamrock pattern, basketweave ground, 3BM,
  8¼" d **80.00**
Tea Set, Limpet pattern, black mark, 6¼" h teapot,
  creamer, and open sugar, price for 3-pc set **350.00**
Tea Set, Neptune pattern, 13 pcs, 4¾" h teapot, creamer
  and sugar, 5 cups and saucers, black mark **500.00**
Vase, Dolphin, molded shells with luster, green mark,
  6⅛" h **100.00**
Vase, Lily of the Valley, black mark **125.00**

BESWICK

James Wright Beswick and his son, John Beswick, are well known for their ceramic figures of horses, cats, dogs, birds, and other wildlife. Produced since the 1890s, figures representing specific animal characters from children's stories, such as Winnie the Pooh and Peter Rabbit, have also been modeled. In 1969 the company was bought by Royal Doulton Tableware, Ltd.

References: Diana Callow et al., *The Charlton Standard Catalogue of Beswick Animals, Third Edition*, Charlton Press, 1998; Diana and John Callow, *The Charlton Standard Catalogue of Beswick Pottery*, Charlton Press, 1997; Jean Dale, *The Charlton Standard Catalogue of Royal Doulton Beswick Jugs, 5th Edition*, Charlton Press, 1999.

Newsletter: *Beswick Quarterly*, 10 Holmes Ct, Sayville, NY 11782.

Note: See Royal Doulton for further information.

Ashtray, dachshund, #1932, 1962-69, 8 x 3" **$150.00**
Ashtray, dog, #1918, light brown, 1963-71, 11 x 8" **125.00**
Ashtray, pheasant, #754, 1939-70, 3½" h **50.00**
Ashtray, Piccadilly, #2052, 1965-70, 8⅛" **40.00**
Ashtray, woodbine, #1625, 1959-60 . . . . **40.00**
Bank, fox, #1761, Fun Models series, 1961-67, 8½" h **125.00**
Bank, pig, #1760, Fun Models series, 1961-67, 8½" h **150.00**
Bookends, pr, rabbits, #455, white, 1937-54, 3¼" h **125.00**

Bookends, pr, Scottie standing on chair, #87, white, 7" h. . . . **150.00**
Candleholder, piglet, #2294, brown, 1970-72, 11 x 3½". . . . **100.00**
Figure, clown and dog, #1086, on base, 1947-58, 7¼" h . . . **300.00**
Figure, dachshund, standing, #361, 1936-54, 5½" h **125.00**
Figure, duck on skis, #762, 1939-69, 3¼" h **50.00**
Figure, foxhound, #944, 1941-69, 2¾" h **50.00**
Figure, galloping horse, #1374, brown, 7½" h **175.00**
Figure, Highland Cow, #1740, 1961-90, 5¼" h. **175.00**
Figure, Hiker Boy, #1093, 1947-54, 6" h **300.00**
Figure, horse and jockey, #1862, brown, 1963-84, 8" h . . . **350.00**
Figure, Indian on horse, #1391, 8½" h **450.00**
Figure, monkey drummer, #1255, 1952-62, 2⅝" h **200.00**
Figure, panda, #711, black and white, 1939-54, 4½" h **175.00**
Figure, rabbit, #825, blue, 1940-71, 1½" h. **20.00**
Figure, seal, #383, cream, 1936-54, 10" h **200.00**
Figure, sheep, #935, 1941-71, 3½" h. **50.00**
Figure, spaniel, running, #1057, 1946-67, 3¾" h **175.00**
Figure, Yorkshire Terrier, #2102, laughing, 1967-72, 3" h. . . . **125.00**
Figure, zebra, #845B, discontinued 1969, 7¼" h. **275.00**
Figure, Zodiac Cat, #1560, 1958-67, 11" h. **275.00**
Jug, A Midsummer Night's Dream, #1366, Shakespeare
    series, 1955-73, 8" h **150.00**
Money Box, cat on postbox, #2805, Fun Models series,
    1983-86, 6¼" h. **100.00**
Mug, Queen Elizabeth II Coronation, #1250, 1952-54 . . . . . **25.00**
Plate, Christmas in America, #2598, 1978, 8" sq **60.00**
Salt and Pepper Shakers, pr, cat on chimney pot, #2761,
    Fun Models series, 4" h **150.00**
Tankard, Ghost of Christmas Past, #2523, 1975 . . . . **60.00**
Toothbrush Holder, dog, #624, 1938-54, 4" h. **300.00**
Toothbrush Holder, elephant, #663, 1938-54, 4½" h. **325.00**
Wall Plaque, Lovers, #710, 1939-40, 8" h **200.00**
Wall Plaque, palomino head, #1384, 1955-69, 4" sq **125.00**
Wall Plaque, The Gleaners, #507, 1937-40, 11" h. **250.00**
Whiskey Flask, deer, #2206, 1968-75, 3½" h **20.00**
Whiskey Flask, golf ball, #2318, 1970-86, 1⅝" d **20.00**
Whiskey Flask, otter, #2686, 1981-86, 2¼" h **20.00**

BICYCLES & RELATED

The bicycle was introduced in America at the 1876 Centennial. Early bicycles were high wheelers with heavy iron frames and disproportionately sized wooden wheels. By 1892 wooden wheels were replaced by pneumatic air-filled tires, which were later replaced with standard rubber tires with inner tubes. The coaster brake was introduced in 1898.

Early high wheelers and safety bikes made into the 1920s and 1930s are classified as antique bicycles. Highly stylized bicycles from the 1930s and 1940s represent the transitional step to the classic period, beginning in the late 1940s and running through the end of the balloon tire era.

References: Jim Hurd, *Bicycle Blue Book,* Memory Lane Classics, 1997; Jay Pridmore and Jim Hurd, *The American Bicycle,* Motorbooks International, 1995; Jay Pridmore and Jim Hurd, *Schwinn Bicycles,* Motorbooks International, 1996; Neil S. Wood, *Evolution of the Bicycle, Volume 1* (1991, 1994 value update), *Volume 2* (1994), L-W Book Sales.

Periodical: *The Bicycle Trader,* 858 Stanyan St, San Francisco, CA 94117.

Newsletter: *Classic Bike News,* 5046 E Wilson Rd, Clio, MI 48420.

Collectors' Clubs: Classic Bicycle and Whizzer Club, 35769 Simon Dr, Clinton Twp, MI 48035; Vintage Bicycle Club of America, 325 W Hornbeam Dr, Longwood, FL 32779.

BICYCLES

Colson Packard, girl's, streamlined, orig saddle, snap-in
    "3 rib" tank, headlight, and droop rack, c1939 . . . . **$450.00**
Firestone Pilot, boy's, orig red and white paint, basket,
    and chrome carrier, 26" h **175.00**
Garton, tricycle, 1937, 21½" l, 12" w, restored **400.00**
Garton, tricycle, model #156, 1956 . . . . **400.00**
Huffman Indian, 1948 . . . . **1,000.00**
Inland, Pinky Lee Sports Trike, 1955, orig condition **400.00**
Monark, Silver King, girl's, stepped stainless steel fend-
    ers, lobdell saddle, EA headlight, 1936. . . . . **300.00**
Schwinn, Majestic, boy's, tool box in cross bar, battery
    case attached to cross bar for headlight, 6 jewel
    reflectors, orig paint, tires replaced, 42" h, 72" l **1,000.00**
Schwinn, Manta-Ray, boy's, 5 speed, yellow, c1969,
    24" h **225.00**
Schwinn, Sting Ray "Lil Chik," girl's, 1970s **150.00**
Schwinn, Tiger, 1959. . . . . **350.00**
Schwinn, Town and Country, tandem, green, with child's
    carrier, 1952 . . . . **500.00**
Schwinn, Whizzer, maroon, Stewart-Warner speedo-
    meter, orig steering lock and key, 1948 . . . . **6,500.00**
Shelby Traveler, shock ease internal spring fork, new
    spring seat, tires, and pedals, professionally restored,
    27½" h, 62" l **375.00**
Silver King Wing Bar, model M137, Bailey seat, 1937 . . . . **2,750.00**
Swiss Army, 2 parcel bags, rear wheel and lock key,
    leather tool pouch with tools, air pump, bell, genera-
    tor, and license plate, 1943. **1,250.00**
Western Flyer, reflector and chrome light on front, lug-
    gage rack, streamers in handle bars, "Western Flyer
    Westfield, Mass. Circa 1950" decal on front, 38" h,
    72" l **600.00**

Monark, Gene Autry Silver King, rodeo brown, pony's head on front, jewel studded fenders and chain guard, attached Gene Autry cap pistol in leather holster, with orig guarantee, 29" h, 58" l, $2,500.00. Photo courtesy Collectors Auction Services.

RELATED

Bicycle Rack, cast iron and wood, emb "Ride Sterns
    Bicycles" on both sides, 45" h, 26" w **$200.00**
Catalog, Mead Cycle Co, Chicago, IL, Bargain List #24,
    24 pp, 1924, 8¼ x 10" **25.00**
Light, Schwinn Phantom, chrome, battery operated **70.00**
Pinback Button, Corbin Brake, black and white depic-
    tion of brake unit within red "C" on yellow ground,
    c1920s **10.00**
Pinback Button, Cycle Trades Safety League, multicolor
    litho of yellow bicycle, c1930s **10.00**
Pinback Button, Ride A Fairy Bike, red, white, and green,
    youngster on tricycle made by Colson Co, Elyria, OH,
    c1920s **40.00**
Poster, New Departure Coaster Brake, paper, black and
    white photo of Joan and Jean Corbett/Gene Nelson
    Hollywood models, "Biking with New Departure is
    Twice the Fun!," bicycle coaster brake product at
    lower right, c1940s, 14 x 20½" **20.00**
Ribbon, Star Bicycle Club, maroon fabric, bright gold
    inscription with "Detroit-Mich.," 2 x 6½" **40.00**

BIG LITTLE BOOKS

Big Little Books is a trademark of the Whitman Publishing
Company. In the 1920s Whitman issued a series of books among
which were Fairy Tales, Forest Friends, and Boy Adventure. These
series set the stage for Big Little Books.

The year 1933 marked Big Little Books' first appearance.
Whitman experimented with ten different page lengths and eight
different sizes prior to the 1940s. Many Big Little Books were
remarketed as advertising premiums for companies such as
Cocomalt, Kool Aid, Macy's, and others. Whitman also published
a number of similar series, e.g., Big Big Books, Famous Comics,
Nickel Books, Penny Books, and Wee Little Books.

In an effort to keep the line alive, Whitman introduced television
characters in the Big Little Book format in the 1950s. Success was
limited. Eventually, Mattel-owned Western Publishing absorbed
Whitman Publishing.

References: Lawrence F. Lowery, *Lowery's: The Collector's Guide
to Big Little Books & Similar Books,* Educational Research and
Applications Corp, 1981, out of print; *Price Guide to Big Little
Books & Better Little, Jumbo, Tiny Tales, A Fast-Action Story, Etc.,*
L-W Books Sales, 1995.

Collectors' Club: Big Little Book Collectors Club of America, PO
Box 1242, Danville, CA 94526.

#748, *Little Orphan Annie and Chizzler* **$35.00**
#755, *Men of the Mounted* **25.00**
#772, *Erik Noble and the Forty Niners* **20.00**
#779, *World War in Photographs* **20.00**
#1120, *Little Miss Muffet* **20.00**
#1132, *Last Days of Pompeii, The* **40.00**
#1134, *Moon Mullins and the Plushbottom Twins* **30.00**
#1138, *Jungle Jim* **40.00**
#1139, *Jungle Jim and the Vampire Woman* **35.00**
#1142, *Radio Patrol* **20.00**
#1144, *Secret Agent X-9* **30.00**
#1145, *Hap Lee's Selection of Movie Gags* **50.00**
#1148, *International Spy, Dr Doom Faces Death at Dawn* **15.00**

#1173, *Radio
Patrol, Trailing the
Safeblowers,*
$20.00.

#1150, *Little Men* **20.00**
#1155, *The Silver Streak* **35.00**
#1164, *Freckles and the Diamond Mine* **20.00**
#1176, *Powder Smoke Range* **25.00**
#1180, *Kayo in the Land of Sunshine* **25.00**
#1192, *Arizona Kid, The* **10.00**
#1402, *Chester Gump in the Pole to Pole Flight* **25.00**
#1409, *Thumper and the Seven Dwarfs* **45.00**
#1418, *Mandrake the Magician and the Flame Pearls* **35.00**
#1420, *Tom Beatty Ace of the Service* **30.00**
#1425, *Brad Turner in TransAtlantic Flight* **10.00**
#1426, *Guns in the Roaring West* **15.00**
#1430, *Blondie, Count Cookie in Too* **20.00**
#1433, *Gangbusters Step In* **10.00**
#1435, *Bugs Bunny, All Pictures Comics* **40.00**
#1441, *Andy Panda in the City of Ice* **20.00**
#1443, *Big Chief Wahoo and the Lost Pioneers* **20.00**
#1461, *Uncle Sam's Sky Defenders* **20.00**
#1466, *Pilot Pete Dive Bomber* **15.00**
#1478, *Charlie Chan* **35.00**
#1484, *Donald Duck Is Here Again* **40.00**
#1495, *Dick Tracy Returns* **25.00**
#1496, *Green Hornet Returns* **75.00**

BIG LITTLE BOOK TYPES

Today, Big Little Books is often used as a generic term that
describes a host of look-alike titles from publishers such as Dell,
Engel-Van Wiseman, Lynn, and Saalfield.

References: Lawrence F. Lowery, *Lowery's: The Collector's Guide
to Big Little Books and Similar Books,* Educational Research and
Applications Corp, 1981, out of print; *Price Guide to Big Little
Books & Better Little, Jumbo, Tiny Tales, A Fast-Action Story, Etc.,*
L-W Book Sales, 1995.

Big Big Book, *Tom Mix and the Scourge of Paradise
    Valley,* #4068, ©1937 . . . . **$75.00**
Blue Ribbon Pop-Up, *Dick Tracy, Capture of Boris Arson,*
    3 pop-ups, 1935 . . . . **225.00**
Blue Ribbon Pop-Up, *Little Red Ridinghood,* 1 pop-up,
    1933 . . . . **90.00**

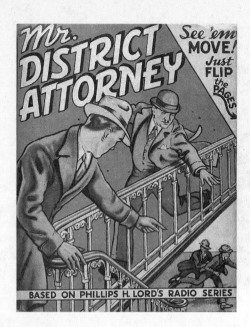

Better Little Book, *Mr. District Attorney,* **#1408, ©1941, $20.00.**

Dell Fast-Action Story, *Captain Marvel, the Return of the Scorpion* **150.00**
Dell Fast-Action Story, *Donald Duck Out of Luck* **125.00**
Engle Van-Wiseman Five Star Library, *Great Expectations*, #8, ©1934 . . . . **15.00**
Feature Movie Book, *The Three Musketeers*, #1311, ©1935 . . . . **50.00**
Golden Press, *Walt Disney's Sleeping Beauty and Cinderella*, #6072, ©1967 . . . . **10.00**
Lynn Book, *O'Shaughnessy's Boy*, #L17, ©1935 . . . . **20.00**
Saalfield, *Corley of the Wilderness Trails*, #1607, paperback, ©1937 . . . . **20.00**
Saalfield, *Last Man Out*, #1128, ©1937 . . . . **20.00**
Samuel Lowe, *Flint Adams and the Stage Coach*, ©1949 . . . . . . **5.00**
Samuel Lowe, *Nevada Jones, Trouble Shooter*, ©1949 . . . . **5.00**
Tiny Tales, *Plush*, #2952, ©1956 . . . . **10.00**
Tiny Tales, *Telling Time*, #2952, ©1959 . . . . **10.00**
Top Line Comic, *Sappo*, ©1935 . . . . **35.00**
Whitman 710 Series, *Cinderella and the Magic Wand*, #711-10 . . . . **15.00**
Whitman 710 Series, *Tarzan and the Journey of Terror*, 709-10 . . . . **20.00**

BING & GRØNDAHL

Frederick Grøndahl and brothers Meyer and Jacob Bing founded Bing & Grøndahl in 1853 to create replicas of the work of the famed Danish sculptor Thorvaldsen. The company's initial success led to an expansion of its products that included elegant dinnerware, coffee services, and other tabletop products.

In 1895 Harald Bing decided to test the idea of a plate designed specifically for sale during the Christmas season. F. A. Hallin, a Danish artist, created "Behind the Frozen Window" which appeared on a limited edition of 400 plates with the words "Jule Aften" (Christmas Eve) scrolled across the bottom and decorated in the company's signature blue and white motif. While Bing & Grondahl's annual Christmas plate is its most recognized and collected product, collectors have expanded their focus to include the company's figurines, dinnerware, and other desirables.

References: Pat Owen, *Bing & Grøndahl Christmas Plates: The First 100 Years*, Landfall Press, 1995, distributed by Viking Import House; Rinker Enterprises, *The Official Price Guide to Collector Plates, Seventh Edition*, House of Collectibles, 1999.

Figurine, cat, white, #2527 . . . . **$50.00**
Figurine, girl kissing boy, 7" h **125.00**
Figurine, girl with milk can, #2181, 8¾" h **375.00**
Ornament, 1985, Christmas Eve at the Farmhouse, E Jensen artist **20.00**
Ornament, 1986, Silent Night, Holy Night, E Jensen artist. **30.00**
Ornament, 1988, Christmas Eve at Rockefeller Center, Christmas in America series, J Woodson artist **20.00**
Ornament, 1989, Santa's Workshop **50.00**
Plate, 1930, The Old Organist, Jubilee Five-Year Christmas series, C Ersgaard artist **200.00**
Plate, 1934, Church Bell in Tower, Christmas series, Immanuel Tjerne artist **100.00**
Plate, 1944, Sorgenfri Castle, Christmas series, Ove Larsen artist **125.00**
Plate, 1976, E Pluribus Unum, Bicentennial series **50.00**
Plate, 1976, Montreal, Canada, Olympic Games series **55.00**
Plate, 1985, Christmas Eve in New England, Christmas in America series, Jack Woodson artist **55.00**
Plate, 1985, Elizabeth and David, Gentle Love series, Adeline Heesen Cooper artist **45.00**
Plate, 1986, Azalea, Carl Larsson Miniature series, Carl Larsson artist **15.00**
Plate, 1986, Elephant with Calf, Mother's Day series, Henry Thelander artist **50.00**
Plate, 1987, Manx and Kittens, Cat Portraits series, L Alice Hanbey artist **40.00**

BLACK GLASS

The modern origin of black colored glass dates back to the mid-17th century when the English adopted it for wine bottles. The black color is achieved by adding manganese to the glass batch. In the last quarter of the 19th century, English manufacturers such as Sowerby and Company made pressed black glass novelties and tableware.

Although a few examples of 19th century American black glass are known, collectors use "black glass" as a generic term to refer to black glass pieces made between 1915 and the present. Black glass divides into two distinct periods: (1) pre-1940 examples by companies such as Cambridge, Fenton, Fostoria, New Martinsville, Paden City, and Westmoreland and (2) post-1945 examples by companies such as Cambridge, Fostoria, Indiana Glass Division of Lancaster Colony, Viking, and Westmoreland. During the first period, black glass enjoyed its greatest popularity in the early 1930s. During the second period, dinnerware production had all but ceased by the early 1960s. A revival focusing on figurines and small novelties occurred in the 1980s.

Reference: Marlena Toohey, *A Collector's Guide to Black Glass* (1988, 1998 value update), *Book 2* (1999), Glass Press.

Avon, bottle, seated poodle, plastic lid, 1973, 5¼" h **$7.00**
Boyd Crystal Art Glass, figurine, kitten on pillow, c1978-83, 3½" h **15.00**
Boyd Crystal Art Glass, open salt, Star Drop pattern, 1989-93, 3⅛" d **15.00**
Cambridge, ashtray, #151, 1922, 3½" sq **20.00**

Fenton, candleholders, pr, #848, 1933, 4¹/₂" d, $10.00. Photo courtesy Ray Morykan Auctions.

Cambridge, cigarette box, cov, #607, intaglio dog on lid, 1920-30s, 5" l **55.00**

Czechoslovakia, salt and pepper shakers, pr, 1¹/₂" h **45.00**

Diamond Glassware, candlesticks, pr, hp gold and floral dec, 1925-32, 9" h **45.00**

Diamond Glassware, plate, #99, c1930, 8" sq **10.00**

Fenton, basket, Peachcrest handle and petticoat, 1986, 4" h **20.00**

Fenton, bell, 1986-87, 6³/₄" h **25.00**

Fenton, figurine, mouse, #5148, 1986, 3" h **20.00**

Fenton, hat, Daisy & Button, c1980s, 2¹/₂" h **30.00**

Fostoria, cup and saucer, Mayfair pattern, 1930s, 5" d **20.00**

Fostoria, plate, Mayfair pattern, c1930s, 8¹/₄" d **20.00**

Fostoria, vase, #2430, Diadem pattern, 1929-33, 8" h **45.00**

Hazel Atlas, plate, Cloverleaf pattern, 1930-36, 8" d **20.00**

Imperial, candy dish, #320, ftd, hp Maytime dec, c1930s, 6" h **40.00**

Indiana, candleholder, c1980-90s, 2¹/₂" h **5.00**

LE Smith, ashtray, duck, 6¹/₂" l **15.00**

LE Smith, console bowl, #1022/4, 3-ftd, c1930s, 9" w **45.00**

LE Smith, figurine, lamb, c1930s, 2¹/₄" l **20.00**

LE Smith, sandwich tray, handled, c1930s, 10" d **35.00**

Made in Taiwan, swizzle stick, figural top hat, c1980s, 6" l **30.00**

McKee, console bowl, Autumn pattern, 1934, 5¹/₂" h, 12" w **60.00**

McKee, pepper shaker, c1930s, 8 oz **25.00**

Mosser, covered animal dish, hen, milk glass head, c1980s, 6¹/₂" w **30.00**

Mosser, figurine, owl, black satin, glass eyes, 1981-83, 4" h **40.00**

Murano, decanter, cased black glass and silver, c1990s, 12¹/₄" h **65.00**

New Martinsville, cigarette box, cov, c1930s, 7" l **65.00**

Paden City, sandwich tray, etched Lela Bird dec, 1929, 10" l **75.00**

Pilgrim Glass, figurine, snail, 1987, 4" h, 4" l **25.00**

Tiffin, candlestick, #63, black satin, 1924-34, 7¹/₂" h **35.00**

Unknown Maker, bottle, figural poodle, 15³/₄" h **35.00**

Viking Glass, salt and pepper shakers, pr, #13, c1980s, 3³/₄" h **45.00**

Westmoreland, bowl, Doric pattern, c1980s, 12" d **70.00**

Westmoreland, compote, #1921, Lotus pattern, c1970s, 4¹/₂" h **25.00**

Westmoreland, goblet, #700, opaque black, c1930s, 8 oz **25.00**

BLACK MEMORABILIA

Black memorabilia is a generic term covering a wide range of materials from advertising to toys made in the image of a black person or featuring an image of a black person in its artwork. The category also includes materials from the era of slavery, artistic and literary contributions by black people, Civil Rights memorabilia, and material relating to the black experience in America.

Much of the material in this category is derogatory in nature, especially pre-1960s material. Despite this, it is eagerly sought by both white and black collectors.

Interest in Civil Rights memorabilia has increased significantly in the past decade.

References: Douglas Congdon-Martin, *Images in Black: 150 Years of Black Collectibles, 2nd Edition,* Schiffer Publishing, 1999; Patiki Gibbs, *Black Collectibles Sold in America,* Collector Books, 1987, 1996 value update; Jan Lindenberger, *More Black Memorabilia, 2nd Edition,* Schiffer Publishing, 1999; J. L. Mashburn, *Black Postcard Price Guide, Second Edition,* Colonial House, 1999; J. P. Thompson, *Collecting Black Memorabilia,* L-W Book Sales, 1996.

Newsletter: *Blackin',* 559 22nd Ave, Rock Island, IL 61201.

Collectors' Club: Black Memorabilia Collector's Assoc, 2482 Devoe Terrace, Bronx, NY 10468.

Ashtray, painted plaster, black boy eating watermelon, removable glass insert, c1930s, 4" h **$75.00**

Baby's Rattle, celluloid, well-dressed black gentleman with flowers in hand, "Made in Japan" on back, 8" h, 2¹/₂" w **45.00**

Banner, cloth, "Here Today! Aunt Jemima In Person Serving Her Famous Pancakes," Aunt Jemima and plate of pancakes in corner, 34" h, 58" w **550.00**

Bobbing Head/Thermometer, painted plaster, black native girl, wearing red skirt and gold metal loop earrings, sitting atop pr of oversized bananas, small thermometer attached to arm, 1960s, 3 x 6¹/₄ x 7" **40.00**

Bottle Cap, Amos 'N Andy Nemo Ginger Beer, metal, dark red, cream lettering, 1930s, 1¹/₄" d **40.00**

Box, Aunt Jemima Pancake Flour, cardboard, "The Quaker Oats Company Successor Address Chicago, U.S.A.," holds 24 pkgs, 13³/₄" h, 13" l, 9" w **100.00**

Box, Coon-Chicken Inn, cardboard carry-out box, unused, c1950s, 8 x 13" **40.00**

Cigar Box Label, Booker T, Perfecto Cigars, black and white Booker T Washington portrait, red and shades of blue border dotted by white stars, c1930s, 6¹/₄ x 10" **20.00**

Doll, Cream of Wheat chef, stuffed cloth, c1930, 18" h **65.00**

Feather Duster Holder/Bank, painted plaster, native boy wearing blue trousers and gold metal loop earring, standing next to oversized pineapple, mkd "Japan," 1960s, 3 x 4¹/₂ x 8" **40.00**

Figure, ceramic, black boy with bare feet seated on stump, wearing red hat with matching shirt and yellow trousers, red lips, white eyes dotted in black, mkd "Moyer Ceramics ©H. P. Moyer," c1950s, 14¹/₄" h **100.00**

Game, The Game of Poor Jenny, Alderman-Fairchild, 1927 . . . . **65.00**

Game, Watch On De Rind, Alderman-Fairchild, 1930 . . . . . . **250.00**

Hot Pad Holder, painted chalk plaster, black child in raised relief, 1950s, 5 x 7" **75.00**

Pattern, fabric, Aunt Jemima doll, 17 x 17" front and back panels, uncut, in orig 5 x 10" brown paper mailing envelope, ©1929 Quaker Oats Co, assembles to 16½" h **175.00**

Pin, carved wood, mammy, wearing white painted bandanna and apron, red blouse with white trim, red dotted skirt, c1940s, 3" h, 2¼" w **50.00**

Pin, emb tin, figural golliwog, black simulated hair, painted red and blue outfit, red dot mouth, recessed white eyes, c1930s, 1½" h **40.00**

Pinback Button, Aunt Jemima Breakfast Club, litho tin, multicolored portrait on red ground, "Eat A Better Breakfast," 1940s, 3" d **20.00**

Pinback Button, Fight For Negro Rights, litho tin, issued for National Negro Congress, black lettering on cream ground, 1930s **20.00**

Pinback Button, "Golden Shred," golliwog in center, blue, yellow, and red outfit, blue ground, 1960s, 1" d **10.00**

Postcard, National Pacific Railway, black waiter serving dinner tray, double-fold, opens to welcome message to passenger, c1930 . . . . **250.00**

Postcard, "Twelve Merit Certificate Winners in National Negro Insurance Week Contest," The Dunbar Mutual Insurance Society, Cleveland, black and white, c1935 . . . . **125.00**

Salt and Pepper Shakers, pr, black chefs, china, "Smokquee" on chef hats, bases inscribed "The Royal/Boise, Idaho," Japan, c1950s, 3¾" h **350.00**

Scale, metal, Aunt Jemima Breakfast Club, cardboard face, glass front, "Old Kentucky Home Belknap How & Mfg Co Louisville, KY" label, 8" h, 6¼" w, 8¼" d **375.00**

String Holder, ceramic, mammy, holding floral bouquet, wearing pink bandanna, white apron over white dress with brown and green dots, 1930s, 6½" h **175.00**

Thermometer, wood, child peeking from behind thermometer, Multi-Products, Inc, 1949, 5½" h **30.00**

Timer, china, black chef holding turning glass timer, 1930s, 1½ x 1½ x 3" **75.00**

Wall Hanger, diecut cardboard, "Shopping List," smiling mammy in polka dot bandanna and red dress with white collar, unused, Japan, 1930s, 4 x 8¾" **75.00**

Windup, Dancing Sam, litho tin, S&E, Japan, orig box, 1950s, 8¼" h, 3" d **100.00**

BLUE RIDGE POTTERY

The Carolina Clinchfield and Ohio Railroad established a pottery in Erwin, Tennessee, in 1917. J. E. Owens purchased the pottery in 1920 and changed the name to Southern Potteries. The company changed hands again within a few years, falling under the ownership of Charles W. Foreman.

By 1938 Southern Potteries was producing its famous Blue Ridge dinnerware featuring hand-painted decoration. Lena Watts, an Erwin native, designed many of the patterns. In addition, Blue Ridge made limited production patterns for a number of leading department stores.

The company experienced a highly successful period during the 1940s and early 1950s, the Golden Age of Blue Ridge. However, cheap Japanese imports and the increased use of plastic dinnerware in the mid-1950s sapped the company's market strength. Operations ceased on January 31, 1957.

References: Betty and Bill Newbound, *Collector's Encyclopedia of Blue Ridge Dinnerware* (1994), *Vol. II* (1998), Collector Books; Frances and John Ruffin, *Blue Ridge China Today*, Schiffer Publishing, 1997; Frances and John Ruffin, *Blue Ridge China Traditions*, Schiffer Publishing, 1999.

Periodical: *Blue Ridge Beacon Magazine*, PO Box 629, Mountain City, GA 30562.

Newsletter: *National Blue Ridge Newsletter*, 144 Highland Dr, Blountville, TN 37617.

Collectors' Club: Blue Ridge Collectors Club, 208 Harris St, Erwin, TN 37650.

Annette's Wild Rose, pitcher, antique shape, 5" h **$75.00**
Bluebell Bouquet, bread and butter plate, 6" d **4.00**
Briar Patch, plate, 10½" d **8.00**
Brittany, demitasse cup and saucer **30.00**
Buttercup, fruit bowl, 6" d **10.00**
Carnival, plate, 9" d **10.00**
Cassandra, pie plate, maroon border **25.00**
Cherries, soup bowl **5.00**
Chick, jug **100.00**
Chintz, cake plate, maple leaf shape **50.00**
Chintz, celery **20.00**
Chintz, creamer, pedestal **25.00**
Christmas Tree, plate, 10" d **70.00**
Crab Apple, cup and saucer **12.00**
Crab Apple, dinner plate **12.00**
Daffodil, sugar **12.00**
Fairmede Fruit, pitcher, Alice shape, earthenware, 6¼" h **85.00**
French Peasant, cake plate, maple leaf shape **50.00**
French Peasant, chocolate pot **300.00**
French Peasant, relish, shell shape **165.00**
French Peasant, salad bowl **125.00**
French Peasant, sugar **75.00**
French Peasant, teapot, leaf shape **125.00**
French Peasant, vase, handled **70.00**
Fruit Fantasy, butter pat **15.00**
Gumdrop, demitasse sugar **35.00**
Jigsaw, child's feeding dish **90.00**
Mardi Gras, creamer **10.00**
Mardi Gras, gravy boat, matching underplate **20.00**
Mardi Gras, pie baker **25.00**
Nocturne, plate, square **12.00**

Red and Blue Flowers, cup and saucer, $5.00.

Nove Rose, celery, leaf shape	40.00
Quaker Apple, dinner service for 4	150.00
Rebecca, pitcher	195.00
Red Barn, plate, 9" d	20.00
Ribbon Plaid, cereal bowl	10.00
Rise & Shine, ashtray	25.00
Rooster, cigarette set, covered box and 4 ashtrays	180.00
Rooster, platter	100.00
Rooster, salt and pepper shakers, pr, toe flake	90.00
Rustic Plaid, sugar	8.00
Spiderweb, bread and butter plate	4.00
Spiderweb, cereal bowl	8.00
Spiderweb, cup and saucer	12.00
Spiderweb, dinner plate	10.00
Spiderweb, fruit bowl	6.00
Spiderweb, vegetable bowl, oval	18.00
Spray, cup and saucer	8.00
Strawberry Sundae, cup and saucer	5.00
Sungold #2, eggcup	15.00
Verna, cake plate, maple leaf shape	60.00
Yellow Nocturne, teapot	15.00

BOEHM PORCELAIN

Edward and Helen Boehm founded The Boehm Studio in 1950. It quickly became famous for its superb hand-painted, highly detailed sculptures of animals, birds, and flowers. Boehm also licensed his artwork to manufacturers of collector plates.

Boehm porcelains are included in the collections of over 130 museums and institutions throughout the world. Many U.S. presidents used Boehm porcelains as gifts for visiting Heads of States.

Reference: Reese Palley, *The Porcelain Art of Edward Marshall Boehm,* Harrison House, 1988, out of print.

Collectors' Club: Boehm Porcelain Society, 25 Princess Diana Ln, Trenton, NJ 08638.

Figurine, Celeste, #67002, 1986	$875.00
Figurine, Debutante Camellia, #3008, 1974	850.00
Figurine, Devina, #67000, 1986	875.00
Figurine, Dogwood, #30045, 1981	950.00
Figurine, Gentians, #3009, 1974	725.00
Figurine, Globe of Light Peony, #10372, 1986	500.00
Figurine, Goldcrest, #1004, 1972	1,200.00
Figurine, Honeysuckle, #300-34, 1979	1,000.00
Figurine, Kirtland's Warble, #40169, 1980	900.00
Figurine, Mattina, #67004, 1986	875.00
Figurine, Pelican, #40259, 1984	1,225.00
Figurine, Poinsettia, #30055, 1981	1,200.00
Figurine, Queen of the Night Cactus, #300-14, 1976	900.00
Figurine, Red-Breasted Nuthatch, #40118, 1979	925.00
Figurine, Rose, Nancy Reagan, #35027, 1981	920.00
Plate, Barn Owl, Owl Collection series, 1980	45.00
Plate, Boehm Orchid, Favorite Florals series, 1979	55.00
Plate, Brandy, Roses of Excellence series, 1983	60.00
Plate, Calliope, Hummingbird Collection series, 1980	80.00
Plate, Jezabels, Butterfly series, 1975	450.00
Plate, Nutcracker, Tribute to Ballet series, 1982	60.00
Plate, Orange Spider Conch, Seashells series, 1976	450.00
Plate, Passion Flowers, Flower series, 1975	500.00
Plate, Puppy Love, Miniature Roses series, 1982	45.00
Plate, Tree Sparrow, European Birds series, 1973	50.00

BOOKENDS

Theme is the most important consideration when placing a value on bookends. In most cases, the manufacturer is unknown, either because the bookends are unmarked or research information about the mark is unavailable. Be alert to basement workshop examples. Collectors prefer mass-produced examples.

References: Louis Kuritzky, *Collector's Guide to Bookends,* Collector Books, 1997; Gerald P. McBride, *A Collector's Guide to Cast Metal Bookends,* Schiffer Publishing, 1997; Robert Seecof, Donna Lee Seecof and Louis Kuritsky, *Bookend Revue,* Schiffer Publishing, 1996.

Collectors' Club: Bookend Collector Club, 4510 NW 17th Pl, Gainesville, FL 32605.

Note: All bookends are priced as pairs.

Abraham Lincoln, seated, gray metal, Nuart, 1924, 6½" h	$110.00
Bishop's Cathedral, iron, c1929, 5½" h	45.00
Bronco Rider, gray metal, Dodge, c1947, 5" h	75.00
Butterfly Girl, gray metal, c1927, 7" h	325.00
Cocker Spaniel, gray metal, c1930, 5" h	100.00
Dancing Ladies with Drape, bronze, c1928, 6½" h	225.00
Doe, gray metal, Frankart, c1934, 5¼" h	125.00
Dogwood, gray metal, PM Craftsman, c1965, 5¼" h	40.00
Egyptian Camel, iron, Connecticut Foundry, 1928, 6" h	100.00
End of the Trail, gray metal, Ronson, c1930, 6" h	110.00
Field and Riley, iron, Bradley & Hubbard, c1925, 5½" h	100.00
Flower Basket, iron, Hubley, c1925, 5¾" h	175.00
Galahad in Archway, iron, c1925, 6" h	50.00
German Shepherd, iron, Hubley, c1925, 5" h	150.00
Kissing Fish, iron, Littco, c1925, 6" h	100.00
Kneeling Nude, gray metal, c1933, 5" h	150.00
Knights of Columbus, gray metal, Ronson, 1922, 3¼" h	85.00
Lamp of Knowledge, iron, Judd, c1925, 4¾" h	100.00
Lily Pad, gray metal, Dodge, 1945, 4½" h	65.00
Lyre, glass, Fostoria, 7" h	150.00
Miniature Pony, gray metal, K&O, c1935, 5½" h	150.00
Patriotic Eagle, coated chalk, c1970, 5" h	20.00
Perched Peacock, iron, Bradley & Hubbard, c1925, 6½" h	125.00
Pirate Booty, iron, Hubley, c1925, 4¾" h	65.00
Sailboat, iron, Littco, c1929, 7½" h	100.00
Scottie on Fence, bronze, c1928, 6" h	175.00
Spanish Galleon, gray metal, Ronson, c1925, 4½" h	50.00
The Thinker, gray metal, Ronson, 5½" h	125.00

Coca-Cola Bottles, bronze, 1963, $275.00. Photo courtesy Gene Harris Antique Auction Center, Inc.

BOOKS

Given the millions of books available, what does a collector do? The answer is specialize. Each edition of this price guide will focus on one or more specialized collecting categories. This edition focuses on books on art and architecture.

References: Allen and Patricia Ahearn, *Book Collecting 2000*, F. P. Putnam's Sons, 2000; *American Book Prices Current*, Bancroft-Parkman, published annually; Ron Barlow and Ray Reynolds, *The Insider's Guide to Old Books, Magazines, Newspapers, Trade Catalogs*, Windmill Publishing, 1995; Ian C. Ellis, *Book Finds: How to Find, Buy and Sell Used and Rare Books*, Berkley Publishing, 1996; *Huxford's Old Book Value Guide, Twelfth Edition*, Collector Books, 2000; Marie Tedford and Pat Goudey, *The Official Price Guide to Old Books, Third Edition*, House of Collectibles, 1999.

Periodicals: *AB Bookman's Weekly*, PO Box AB, Clifton, NJ 07015; *Firsts: The Book Collector's Magazine*, PO Box 65166, Tucson, AZ 85728; *Book Source Monthly*, 2007 Syosett Dr, PO Box 567, Cazenovia, NY 13035.

Newsletter: *Rare Book Bulletin*, PO Box 201, Peoria, IL 61650.

Collectors' Club: Antiquarian Booksellers Assoc of America, 20 West 44th St, 4th Flr, New York, NY 10036.

Abbey, John R, *Life in England in Aquatint and Lithography 1770-1860,* Curwen Press, London, 1953, 4to, 32 collotype plates and 50 text illus, cloth, dj **$400.00**

Blake, William, *Illustrations to the Bible,* Trianon Press, London, 1957, folio, catalogue compiled by Geoffrey Keynes, 9 color plates including litho frontispiece, publisher's ¼ morocco. **400.00**

Bloch, Georges, *Picasso: Catalogue of the Printed Graphic Work: 1904-1967,* Berne, 1968, Vol 1, cloth, dj **175.00**

Bridaham, Lester Burbank, *Gargoyles, Chimeres, and the Grotesque in French Gothic Sculpture,* Architectural Book Publishing, New York, 1930, 4to, introduction by Ralph Adams Cram, photographic plates, gilt-pictorial cloth, dj. **225.00**

Campbell, Bruce, *Bird Paintings of Henry Jones, The,* London, 1976, oblong folio, foreword by the Duke of Edinburgh, 24 color plates, ¼ polished green calf, slipcase. **200.00**

Chagall, Marc, *Ceiling of the Paris Opera, The,* New York, 1966, 4to, color frontispiece, reproductions, folding plate at rear, cloth, dj **300.00**

Cole, Timothy, *Timothy Cole Wood-Engraver,* New York, 1935, 4to, 19 reproductions, blue cloth gilt, bookplate of Mr and Mrs John D Rockefeller, Jr, sgd **100.00**

Cooper, Douglas, *Picasso Theatre,* New York, 1968, 4to, color and black and white plates, pictorial cloth, mylar dj printed in red. **250.00**

Creswell, KAC, *Early Muslim Architecture,* Oxford, 1969, second ed, Vol 1, part 2, folio, 140 plates, green cloth gilt, dj **625.00**

Dali, Salvador, *Diary of a Genius,* Garden City, 1965, 8vo, plates and reproductions, gilt-lettered cloth, first American edition, sgd and dated 1966 .... **150.00**

De Kooning, Willem, *Drawings,* New York, 1967, square 4to, 24 plates reproducing his charcoal drawings, sgd, dj **550.00**

Hind, Arthur H, *An Introduction to a History of the Woodcut,* Boston & New York, 1935, frontispiece and 483 illus, 2 volumes, cloth, slipcase **225.00**

Jones, Dan Burne, *The Prints of Rockwell Kent: A Catalogue Raisonné,* Chicago, 1974, folio, foreword by Carl Zigrosser, illus, cloth, dj **200.00**

Lassaigne, Jacques, *Marc Chagall: Drawings and Water Colors for the Ballet,* New York, 1969, color litho, profusion of color reproductions, folio, cloth, dj **325.00**

Masereel, Frans, *My Book of Hours,* printed by author, 1922, 8vo, foreword by Romain Rolland, 167 wood-engraved illus, blue cloth with paper title and spine labels, sgd, dj **450.00**

Meyer, Franz, *Marc Chagall: His Graphic Work,* Abrams, New York, 1957, 4to, 6 color and 148 black and white plates accompanied by biography and catalogue of etchings, pictorial cloth, dj. **75.00**

Siren, Osvald, *Early Chinese Paintings from the A. W. Bahr Collection,* Chiswick Press, London, 1938, folio, 25 color mounted plates, black cloth gilt **325.00**

Sorlier, Charles, *Ceramics and Sculptures of Chagall, The,* Monaco, 1972, 4to, litho frontispiece, photographic plates and reproductions, cloth, dj **250.00**

Targ, William, *Making of the Bruce Rogers World Bible, The,* Cleveland & New York, 1949, 4to, photographic plates and illus, red cloth gilt **100.00**

Wofsy, Alan, *Georges Rouault: The Graphic Work,* San Francisco, 1976, 4to, 366 reproductions with catalogue entries, cloth, dj. **75.00**

Wright, Frank Lloyd, *Buildings, Plans, and Designs,* Horizon Press, New York, 1963, folio, 100 plates, text booklet and plates loose in paper sleeve in ¼ cloth portfolio **925.00**

Wright, Frank Lloyd, *Future of Architecture, The,* Horizon Press, New York, 1953, 4to, photographic plates, cloth, sgd, dj **1,850.00**

BOOKS, CHILDREN'S

Although children's books date as early as the 15th century, it was the appearance of lithographed books from firms such as McLoughlin Brothers and series books for boys and girls at the turn of the 20th century that popularized the concept. The Bobbsey Twins, Nancy Drew, the Hardy Boys, and Tom Swift delighted numerous generations of readers.

The first Newberry Medal for the most distinguished children's book was issued in 1922. In 1938 the Caldecott Medal was introduced to honor the children's picture book.

Most children's book collectors specialize. Award-winning books, ethnic books, first editions, mechanical books, and rag books are just a few of the specialized categories.

Each edition of this price guide will concentrate on one or more specialized collecting categories. This listing focuses on children's books published by P. F. Volland Publishers, a company well known for its high-quality, fully illustrated hardcover books.

References: E. Lee Baumgarten (comp.), *Price Guide and Bibliographic Checklist for Children's & Illustrated Books for the Years 1880–1960, 1996 Edition,* published by author, 1995; David and Virginia Brown, *Whitman Juvenile Books,* Collector Books, 1997, 1999 value update; E. Christian Mattson and Thomas B. Davis, *A Collector's Guide to Hardcover Boys' Series Books,* published by authors, 1996; Diane McClure Jones and Rosemary Jones, *Collector's Guide to Children's Books, 1850 to 1950* (1997), *Vol. Two* (1999), *Vol. Three: 1950–1975* (2000), Collector Books.

Periodicals: *Book Source Monthly,* 2007 Syosssett Dr, PO Box 467, Cazenovia, NY 13035; *Mystery & Adventure Series Review,* PO Box 3488, Tucson, AZ 85722; *Yellowback Library,* PO Box 36172, Des Moines, IA 50315.

Newsletter: *Martha's KidLit Newsletter,* PO Box 1488, Ames, IA 50010.

Collectors' Club: Movable Book Society, PO Box 11645, New Brunswick, NJ 08906. There are numerous collectors' clubs for individual authors. Consult the *Encyclopedia of Associations* at your local library for further information.

Note: The books listed are all first editions, with color illustrations and illustrated boards. For additional children's book listings see Big Little Books, Big Little Book Types, Little Golden Books, and Little Golden Book Types.

Bemelmans, Ludwig, *Madeline,* New York, 1939, 4to, illus by author, pictorial boards, dj **$300.00**

Best, Herbert, *Bright Hunter of the Skies,* Macmillan, 1961, Bernarda Bryson illus, 164 pp **25.00**

Browning, Robert, *Pied Piper of Hamelin, The,* London, 1934, 8vo, 4 color plates, orig pictorial stiff wrappers, bookplate, dj. **375.00**

Cooper, James Fenimore, *Deerslayer, The,* New York, 1925, 4to, color plates by NC Wyeth, cloth with pictorial onlay **150.00**

Cullen, Countee, and Cat, Christopher, *Lost Zoo, The,* New York, 1940, 8vo, illus by Charles Sebree, yellow cloth, dj **90.00**

De Brunhoff, Jean, *Babar and His Children,* New York, 1938, 4to, pictorial boards. **150.00**

Gag, Wanda, *ABC Bunny Book, The,* New York, 1933, 4to, 28 litho plates, pictorial boards, dj **1,725.00**

Gruelle, Johnny, *Magical Land of Noom, The,* PF Volland, New York, 1922, 4to, illus by author, cloth backed pictorial boards **200.00**

Lanes, Selma G, *Art of Maurice Sendak, The,* Abrams, New York, 1980, oblong 4to, color plates, includes pop-up, pictorial cloth, sgd, dj **125.00**

May, Robert L, *Rudolph the Red-Nosed Reindeer,* 1939, 4to, illus by Denver Gillen, first edition written for Montgomery Ward. **400.00**

Meigs, Cornelia, *The Scarlet Oak,* Elizabeth Orton Jones illus, Macmillan, 1938. . . . . **25.00**

Milne, AA, *Now We Are Six,* London, 1927, 8vo, illus by Ernest H Shepard, gilt pictorial red cloth, owner's signature on half title. **125.00**

Muir, Percy, *English Children's Books 1600-1900,* London, 1954, 4to, cloth, dj **90.00**

Selden, George, *The Dog That Could Swim Under Water,* Viking, 1956, Morgan Denis illus, 126 pp **25.00**

Seuss, Dr (Theodore Geisel), *Cat in the Hat, The,* New York, 1957, 8vo, illus by author, pictorial boards, dj **3,750.00**

Seuss, Dr (Theodore Geisel), *Cat in the Hat Comes Back, The,* New York, 1958, 8vo, illus by author, pictorial boards, dj **525.00**

Thompson, Ruth Plumly, *Grampa in Oz,* Reilly & Lee, Chicago, 1924, 4to, 12 color plates by John R Neill, red cloth, color pictorial label **80.00**

Thompson, Ruth Plumly, *Kabumpo in Oz,* Reilly & Lee, Chicago, 1922, 4to, 12 color plates by John R Neill, blue cloth, color pictorial label **125.00**

Tice, Clara, *ABC Dogs,* New York, 1940, 4to, color plates after etchings, cloth backed pictorial boards **125.00**

Twain, Mark, *Concerning Cats: Two Tales by Mark Twain,* Book Club of California, San Francisco, 1959, 4to, introduction by Frederick Anderson, cloth backed pictorial boards, dj **200.00**

Walt Disney Studios, *Adventures of Mickey Mouse, The,* Book 1, Philadelphia, 1931, David McKay, 8vo, first edition after cloth issue, cloth backed pictorial stiff wrappers. **175.00**

White, EB, *Charlotte's Web,* New York, 1952, 8vo, illus by Garth Williams, pictorial cloth, dj **1,850.00**

BOTTLE OPENERS

In an age of pull-tab and twist-off tops, many young individuals have never used a bottle opener. Figural openers, primarily those made of cast iron, are the most commonly collected type. They were extremely popular between the late 1940s and early 1960s.

Church keys, a bottle opener with a slightly down-turned "V" shaped end, have a strong following, especially when the opener has some form of advertising. Wall-mounted units, especially examples with soda pop advertising, also are popular.

Reference: Don Bull and John Stanley, *Just for Openers,* Schiffer Publishing, 1999.

Collectors' Clubs: Figural Bottle Opener Collectors Club, 9697 Gwynn Park Dr, Ellicott City, MD 21042; Just For Openers, PO Box 64, Durham, NC 27514.

ADVERTISING

Beck's Beer, metal, wood handle, 1940s. **$4.00**
Burgermeister Beer, 2-sided, 1946 Shrine Victory Convention on back **15.00**
Edelweiss Beer, slide-out, 1930s **35.00**
Fort Pitt and Old Shay Beer, plastic handle, 1940s **4.00**
Gallagher & Burton Whiskey, bottle opener/corkscrew, metal, 2³⁄₄" h **15.00**
Gay-Ola Soda, figural high-heel-shoed lady's leg, square and round holes, 3" h **15.00**
Pabst Blue Ribbon Brew, bottle shaped, 1930s **10.00**

Advertising, Dr Pepper, lion's head shape, Crown T&D Co, Chicago, IL, 3" l, $95.00. Photo courtesy Collectors Auction Services.

Pepsi-Cola, metal, raised lettering, wall mount, Starr X
  Brown Co, 3¹/₄" h, 2³/₄" h **50.00**
Piel Brothers Beer, pull-out, 1930s **65.00**
Royal Crown Cola, metal, gray, red raised lettering, wall
  mount, 3¹/₄" h, 2³/₄" w **65.00**
Schreiber Brewing Co, wooden handle, 1930s **10.00**

FIGURAL

Billy Goat, cast iron, 4¹/₂ x 2¹/₂" **$50.00**
Black Golf Caddy, 6 x 1³/₄" **500.00**
Clown, cast iron, wall mount, 4¹/₂ x 4" **50.00**
Donkey, cast iron, open mouth, 3¹/₄ x 3" **50.00**
Elephant, cast iron, trunk up, flat, 3 x 2" **700.00**
Four-Eyed Woman, cast iron, wall mount, 4 x 3³/₄" **150.00**
Palm Tree, cast iron, green, yellow, and red, 4¹/₂ x 2³/₄" **100.00**
Parrot on Stand, cast iron **50.00**
Seagull, cast iron, 3¹/₄ x 2¹/₂" **50.00**
Shark, aluminum, 7" l **20.00**
Squirrel, cast iron, 3 x 4" **50.00**

BOTTLES

This is a catchall category. Its role is twofold—to list a few specialized bottle collecting areas not strong enough to have their
own category and provide the logical place to find information
about bottle references, collectors' clubs, and periodicals.

References: Ralph and Terry Kovel, *The Kovels' Bottles Price List,
Eleventh Edition,* Three Rivers Press, 1999; Jim Megura, *The
Official Identification and Price Guide to Bottles, Twelfth Edition,*
House of Collectibles, 1997; Michael Polak, *Bottles, Second
Edition,* Avon Books, 1997; Carlo and Dorothy Sellari, *The
Standard Old Bottle Price Guide,* Collector Books, 1989, 1997
value update.

Periodical: *Antique Bottle and Glass Collector,* PO Box 180, East
Greenville, PA 18041.

Collectors' Club: Federation of Historical Bottle Collectors, PO
Box 1558, Southampton, PA 18966.

Note: Consult *Maloney's Antiques & Collectibles Resource
Directory* by David J. Maloney, Jr., at your local library for additional information on regional bottle clubs.

**Mobiloil, baked-on label,
1950s, 1 pt, 10³/₄" h, 2³/₄" d,
$120.00.** Photo courtesy
Collectors Auction Services.

Hoffman, "Danny Boy," Mr Shoe Cobbler with music
  box, Occupational series **$15.00**
Hoffman, Flathead Squaw, CM Russell series **15.00**
Hoffman, Generation Gap, "100 Years of Progress,"
  Bicentennial series. **30.00**
Japan, Playboy **8.00**
Japan, Red Lion Man **30.00**
Japan, Sake God, porcelain, 10" h **15.00**
Luxardo, calypso girl, colorful floral headdress, 1962 . . . . . . **12.00**
Luxardo, Sir Lancelot, tan, gray, and gold, 1962, 12" h **8.00**
Miniature, Fox Head 400 Beer, Fox Head Brewing,
  Waukesha, WI, 1940s, 4¹/₄" h **20.00**
Soda, Dad's Root Beer, amber, man's head, yellow, blue
  and red, 10 oz **6.00**
Soda, Frost King, clear, snowman, blue and white, 7 oz **5.00**
Soda, Sargon General Tonic, orig box, 1940s, 8 oz **20.00**
Soda, Worley's Root Beer, amber, globe, orange and
  white, 10 oz **5.00**

BOYD CRYSTAL ART GLASS

Boyd Crystal Art Glass, Cambridge, Ohio, traces its heritage back
to Bernard C. Boyd and Zackery Thomas Boyd, two glass makers
who worked for a number of companies in the Cambridge area. In
1964 Elizabeth Degenhart asked Zack Boyd to assume the management of Degenhart Glass. When Zack died in 1968, Bernard
assumed leadership of the company.

In 1978, Bernard C. Boyd and his son, Bernard F., purchased
Degenhart Glass. Initially working with the fifty molds acquired
from Degenhart, the Boyds began making pieces in a host of new
colors. Eventually, John Bernard, son of Bernard F., joined the
company. Today Boyd Crystal Art Glass has over 200 molds available for its use including a number of molds purchased from other
glass companies such as Imperial.

Reference: *Boyd's Crystal Art Glass: The Tradition Continues,*
Boyd's Crystal Art Glass, n.d.

Newsletter: *Jody & Darrell's Glass Collectibles Newsletter,* PO Box
180833, Arlington, TX 76096.

Bell, Santa, olde lyme **$15.00**
Card Holder, grape, classic black slag **8.00**
Card Holder, grape, primrose. **8.00**
Figurine, airplane, vaseline **6.00**
Figurine, Angel **6.00**
Figurine, Bernie the Eagle, banana cream. **4.00**
Figurine, Bingo Deer, Indian orange. **10.00**
Figurine, bulldog head, ice green. **12.00**
Figurine, Chuckles the Clown, baby blue **10.00**
Figurine, Debbie Duck, snow **8.00**
Figurine, Fuzzy the Bear, country red **10.00**
Figurine, owl, teal swirl **15.00**
Figurine, Pete the Pelican, vaseline **4.00**
Figurine, pooch, confetti **20.00**
Figurine, Rex the Dinosaur, vaseline **8.00**
Figurine, Sammy the Squirrel, cashmere pink **8.00**
Plate, Statue of Liberty, ruby **4.00**
Master Salt, swan, lilac **15.00**
Master Salt, swan, spinnaker blue **15.00**
Ring Holder, nile green **4.00**
Salt, cov, lamb, mirage **4.00**
Salt, open, swan, vaseline **4.00**

BOY SCOUTS

William D. Boyce is the father of Boy Scouting in America. Boyce was instrumental in transferring the principles of Baden-Powell's English scouting movement to the United States, merging other American organizations into the Scouting movement, and securing a charter from Congress for the Boy Scouts of America in 1916.

Scouting quickly spread nationwide. Manufacturers developed products to supply the movement. Department stores vied for the rights to sell Scouting equipment.

The first national jamboree in America was held in Washington, D.C., in 1937. Patch trading and collecting began in the early 1950s. The Order of the Arrow, national Scouting centers, e.g., Philmont, and local council activities continually generate new collectible materials.

Reference: George Cuhaj, *Standard Price Guide to U.S. Scouting Collectibles*, Krause Publications, 1998.

Periodical: *Fleur-de-Lis*, 5 Dawes Ct, Novato, CA 94947.

Collectors' Clubs: American Scouting Traders Assoc, PO Box 210013, San Francisco, CA 94121; National Scouting Collectors Society, 806 E Scott St, Tuscola, IL 61953.

Blotter, cardboard, full color art and black lettering inscription "Cavalcade Of Scouting," name of hosting junior high school Feb 26–28, 1948, 3½ x 8" **$15.00**
Campaign Hat, brown pressed felt with chinstrap, size 6⅞" **40.00**
Flashlight, chromed metal, seamless, green band around body with red, white, and blue stripes, red plastic ring around neck, Boy Scout emblem on side **20.00**
Hat Badge, Junior Assistant Scoutmaster, first class badge on 3 green painted bars, 1940s **25.00**
Hat Badge, Senior Patrol Leader, green enameled bars, gilt first class emblem, 1940s, 2½" d **25.00**
Medal, Ranger Award, circle with center powder horn, green enamel painted compass points around rim, attached green, cream, and green ribbon, 1946-51, 3" d **500.00**

Poster, litho paper with archival backing, ©1942, sgd "Remington Schuyler," 29½ x 19¾", $150.00. Photo courtesy Collectors Auction Services.

Membership Card, with envelope, 3-part fold-out, 1938 . . . . . **10.00**
Patch, white twill, red, blue, black, brown, and white embroidery, red border with blue outer ring lettering "National Jamboree Valley Forge 1957 BSA," red "Onward For God And My Country," kneeling and praying George Washington image, 3" d **20.00**
Pillow, Boy Scouts of America, National Jamboree, Colorado Springs, 50-year anniversary commemorative, silk, acetate, white back, blue fringe, illus of Will Rogers Shrine, Mt of the Holy Cross, Royal Gorge, Air Force Academy, and Columbine state flower **30.00**
Pillow Cover, cream colored satin, yellow fringe, blue and red printed depictions of scenes at Valley Forge, Jamboree patch depicted at center with "BSA National Jamboree Valley Forge 1957," 18" sq **20.00**
Record, *Scouting Along with Burl Ives*, LP, Columbia, CSP-347, with song sheet, 1963 . . . . **20.00**
Shirt, long sleeve, khaki, removable metal BSA buttons, Hyena patrol patch on red felt, Alton community strip, Patrol Leader fabric bars and bugler badge sewn to left sleeve, size 14, 1940s **25.00**

BRASTOFF, SASCHA

In 1948, Sascha Brastoff established a small pottery on Speulveda Boulevard in West Los Angeles. Brastoff's focus was that of designer. Skilled technicians and decorators gave life to his designs.

Brastoff was at the cutting edge of modern design. Figurines were introduced in the early 1950s to a line that included ashtrays, bowls, and vases. In 1953 a new studio was opened at 11520 West Olympic Boulevard. In 1954 production began on the first of ten fine china dinnerware lines.

Although Brastoff left the studio in 1963, the company survived another decade thanks to the inspired leadership of plant manager Gerold Schwartz.

Reference: Steve Conti, A. Dewayne Bethany and Bill Seay, *Collector's Encyclopedia of Sascha Brastoff*, Collector Books, 1995, out of print.

Abstract, candy dish, cov, 096, 10" d **$130.00**
Abstract, dish, C3, freeform, 7" d **45.00**
Alaska, bowl, 190, 10" d **50.00**
Alaska, eggcup, 044A, 7" h **75.00**
Alaska, mug, 077 . . . . **25.00**
Alaska, pitcher, 181A **30.00**
Alaska, plate, 8" d **25.00**
Americana, dish, F42, freeform, 10" d **45.00**
Americana, tiles, unsgd, price for pr **100.00**
Aztec, chop plate, 053, 17" l **175.00**
Aztec, lighter, L6, 6" h **35.00**
Ballet, vase, 5" h **75.00**
Chi Chi Birds, ashtray, 07, 10" l **80.00**
Chi Chi Birds, vase, F20, 5" h **85.00**
Citrus, ashtray, 08, 12" l **35.00**
Citrus, dish, F42, freeform, 10" d **45.00**
Jewel Bird, chop plate, 052, 15" d **150.00**
Jewel Bird, nut dish, 01, 2½" d **20.00**
Merbaby, chop plate, 053, 17" d **150.00**
Merbaby, plate, 9" d **45.00**
Minos, ashtray, 08, 12" l **85.00**
Minos, bowl, ftd, C4, 9" d **75.00**
Misty Blue, bowl, ftd, C4, 9" d **55.00**

Misty Blue, vase, L4, 6" h **40.00**
Mosaic, vase, M73, 10" h **150.00**
Pagoda, bowl, F26, 8" d. **135.00**
Pagoda, vase, 047, 8" h **100.00**
Poodle, ashtray, H6, mkd "Sascha B," 7" l. **75.00**
Provincial Rooster, ashtray, F6A, 10" w. **90.00**
Rooftops, box, cov, 021, 8" l **85.00**
Rooftops, dish, 06, 8" sq **50.00**
Rooftops, tiles, unsgd, price for set of 3 . . . . **150.00**
Smoke Tree, coffee cup **15.00**
Smoke Tree, platter, 14" l **35.00**
Star Steed, ashtray, 05, 7" l **40.00**
Star Steed, bowl, ftd, C14, 10" d **75.00**

BRAYTON LAGUNA CERAMICS

Durline E. Brayton founded Brayton Laguna, located in South Laguna Beach, California, in 1927. Hand-crafted earthenware dinnerwares were initially produced. The line soon expanded to include figurines, flowerpots, tea tiles, vases, and wall plates.

In 1938 Brayton Laguna was licensed to produce Disney figurines. Webb, Durlin's second wife, played an active role in design and management. A period of prosperity followed.

By the end of World War II, Brayton Laguna ceramics were being sold across the United States and abroad. In the early and mid-1960s the company fell on hard times, the result of cheap foreign imports and lack of inspired leadership. The pottery closed in 1968.

Reference: Jack Chipman, *Collector's Encyclopedia of California Pottery, Second Edition,* Collector Books, 1999.

Cookie Jar, hen, stamped mark, 10" h. **$350.00**
Figurine, abstract female torso, white crackle glaze. **200.00**
Figurine, Chinese boy **100.00**
Figurine, cow and calf, price for pr **250.00**
Figurine, elephant, woodtone and white crackle finish,
  13½" h **225.00**
Figurine, fighting pirates, c1956, 9" h, price for pr **650.00**
Figurine, lady with wolfhounds **65.00**
Figurine, Mexican man, 9" h **250.00**
Figurine, mule, 7¼ x 10" **250.00**
Figurine, opera singer, 8½" h **150.00**
Figurine, Pedro, 6½" h **200.00**
Figurine, Rosita, 5½" h **100.00**
Planter, Sally, pink. **30.00**
Tile, black cats on multicolored roof, incised mark,
  4½" sq **300.00**

BREWERIANA

Breweriana is a generic term used to describe any object, from advertising to giveaway premiums, from bar paraphernalia to beer cans, associated with the brewing industry. Objects are divided into pre- and post-Prohibition material.

Breweries were one of the first industries established by early American settlers. Until Prohibition, the market was dominated by small to medium size local breweries. When Prohibition ended, a number of brands, e.g., Budweiser, established themselves nationwide. Advertising, distribution, and production costs plus mergers resulted in the demise of most regional breweries by the 1970s.

Imported beers arrived in America in the 1960s, often contract-ing with American breweries to produce their product. In the 1980s and 1990s America experienced a brewing renaissance as the number of micro-breweries continues to increase.

Collectors tend to be regional and brand loyal. Because of a strong circuit of regional Breweriana shows and national and regional clubs, objects move quickly from the general marketplace into the specialized Breweriana market.

References: Donna Baker, *Vintage Anheuser Busch: An Unofficial Collector's Guide,* Schiffer Publishing, 1999; *Beer Cans: 1932–1975,* L-W Book Sales, 1976, 1995 value update; Herb and Helen Haydock, *The World of Beer Memorabilia,* Collector Books, 1997; Gary Straub, *Collectible Beer Trays With Value Guide,* Schiffer Publishing, 1995; Dale P. Van Wieren, *American Breweries II,* East Coast Breweriana Assoc, 1995.

Periodicals: *All About Beer,* 1627 Marion Ave, Durham, NC 27705; *Suds 'n' Stuff,* 4765 Galacia Way, Oceanside, CA 92056.

Collectors' Clubs: American Breweriana Assoc, Inc, PO Box 11157, Pueblo, CO 81001; Beer Can Collectors of America, 747 Merus Ct, Fenton, MO 63026; National Assoc of Breweriana Advertising, 2343 Met-To-Wee Ln, Milwaukee, WI 53226.

Ashtray, Gunther's Beer, Gunther Brewing, Baltimore,
  MD, metal, glass inlay, 1930s. **$25.00**
Ashtray, Lancer's Beer, Phoenix Brewing, Phoenix, AZ,
  ceramic, 1950s. **6.00**
Ashtray, Lemp Beer, Wm J Lemp Brewing, St Louis, MO,
  metal, 1930s. **50.00**
Back Bar Statue, Miller High Life, Ballantine Brewing,
  Newark, NJ, plaster, 1940s, 6" h **150.00**
Ballknob Insert, Silver Label Lager Beer, Lancaster
  Brewing, Lancaster, PA, 1930s **35.00**
Bank, Standard Erin Brew Beer, chalkware, barrel
  shaped, 8 x 6". **20.00**
Banner, Rainier Old Stock Ale, Rainier Brewing, Seattle,
  WA, vinyl, "Brewed To The Nation's Taste/Fully Aged,"
  1940s, 28 x 66". **25.00**
Belt Buckle, Stat Beer, Stag Brewing, Belleville, IL, brass,
  1960s **12.00**
Blotter, Blatz Old Heidelberg Beer, Old Reading
  Brewing, Reading, PA, 1930s. **20.00**
Bottle, Burgermeister, Hamm Brewing, Los Angeles, CA,
  ceramic, painted label, 1960s, 9 oz **4.00**
Bottle Opener, Tech Beer, Pittsburgh Brewing,
  Pittsburgh, PA, wooden, bottle shaped, 1930s. **10.00**
Calendar Pad, Rheingold Lager Beer, molded plastic,
  1968, 9¾ x 18¼" **12.00**
Can, Buckeye Beer, Buckeye Brewing, Toledo, OH,
  conetop, 1950s **90.00**
Can, Krueger Cream Ale, Krueger Brewing, Newark, NJ,
  conetop, 1930s, 1 qt **175.00**
Can, Old Dutch Beer, Eagle Brewing, Catasauqua, PA,
  conetop, 1930s, 1 qt **125.00**
Can, Old Milwaukee, Schlitz Brewing, Milwaukee, WI,
  flattop, 1960s, 24 oz **35.00**
Clock, Ballantine Beer & Ale, plastic, light-up, 1960s,
  24 x 10" **10.00**
Coaster, Hoosier Beer, South Bend Beverage, South
  Bend, IN, 1930s, 4" d **15.00**
Cookbook, Hyde Park Beer, St Louis, MO, *Sportsman's
  Way Cookbook,* 100 pp, 1940s **25.00**

Coaster, Sunshine Brewing Company, multicolor, 3¹/₂" d, 1950s, $4.00.

Decanter, Hamm's, figural bear, ceramic, 1973, 10" h **45.00**

Figurine, Miller High Life, painted hard plastic, standing lady holding beer can, gold finish, mkd "Form No. 70" with names of Miller Brewing Co and Thomas A Schultz Co, Chicago, c1950s, 6¹/₄" h **75.00**

Foam Scraper, Daeufers Beer, Daeufer Brewing, Allentown, PA, 1-sided, 1940s **30.00**

Foam Scraper, Standard Beer, Standard Brewing, Scranton, PA, 2-sided, 1930s **60.00**

Foam Scraper Holder, Schmidts Beer & Ale, Schmidts Brewing, Philadelphia, PA, cast metal, 4 x 8" **8.00**

Glass, Blue Bonnett Extra Pale Beer, Dallas Brewing, Dallas, TX, 1940s, 4" h **50.00**

Glass, Edelweiss Beer, Schoenhoffen Brewing, Chicago, IL, etched dec, 3¹/₂" h. **25.00**

Glass, Ye Olde Colonial Beer, Weinhard Brewing, Portland, OR, light blue enamel dec, 1930s, 4" h **12.00**

Goblet, Lion Brewery Export, emb lettering, 1930s, 5¹/₂" h **30.00**

Letterhead, Victor Brewing Co, Jeannette, PA, used, 1939 . . . . . **6.00**

Light, Schlitz, wall mount, globe shaped, gold finish band around equator, hangs from white plastic mount attached to woodgrain plastic plaque, lighted and motorized, 9" d **35.00**

Lighter, Budweiser, polished finish with red, white, and blue enamel painted label logo, collector tin, Anheuser-Busch "Official Product" sleeve, Zippo **50.00**

Lighter, Miller High Life, "1954 Chicago I. S. and C. A. Miller High Life the Champagne of Bottle Beer," and woman sitting on moon, brushed finish with enameled logo, with box, Zippo, 1954 . . . . **125.00**

Litter Bag, National Bohemian Beer, National Brewing, Baltimore, MD, cloth, 1950s **10.00**

Menu Board, Daeufers Beer, Daeufer Brewing, Allentown, PA, cardboard, 1930s, 13¹/₂ x 23" **15.00**

Mirror, Carlings Black Label, Carling Brewing, Cleveland, OH, reverse glass, 1940s, 12 x 6" **35.00**

Mirror, Gold Label Beer, Cooper Brewing, Philadelphia, PA, 1940s, 10 x 14". **25.00**

Pilsener Glass, Budweiser, Anheuser-Busch Inc, St Louis, MO, red and black enamel dec, 1950s, 8¹/₂" h **4.00**

Pilsener Glass, Piels, Piel Bros Inc, Brooklyn, NY, etched dec, 1930s, 7" h **4.00**

Pinback Button, Fort Pitt Beer, litho tin, blue and silver lettering on white ground, silver rim, 1930s **15.00**

Playing Cards, Yuengling Brewing, Pottsville, PA, gold foil backs **10.00**

Postcard, Regal Pale, Regal Pale Brewing, San Francisco, CA, unused, 1950s **10.00**

Poster, Schlitz Circus Parade, Jul 4, 1973, 21¹/₂ x 18³/₄" **5.00**

Recipe Book, *The Storz Cook Book*, 195 pp, black and white and color photos, dated 1949 . . . . **20.00**

Sign, Budweiser, "Pick a Pair...A Smart Buy!," diecut cardboard, woman holding 2 six-packs of Budweiser Beer, c1960s, 26 x 15¹/₂" **30.00**

Sign, Kaiser's Draught and Bottles, Mahanoy City, PA, shows 3 example beer, ale, and porter products, name and "Union Made Est. 1862" in red dimensional lettering style under clear celluloid, c1940s, 8¹/₂ x 6" **50.00**

Sign, Miller High Life, light-up, hard plastic, "Miller High Life The Champagne of Beers," 16³/₄ x 7¹/₂ x 4" **25.00**

Sign, Storz, light-up, hard molded plastic, "Storz Beer Light...Dry...Smooth," mounts to edge of shelf, Plasti-Ad, 8 x 6³/₄ x 3¹/₂" **35.00**

Sign, Student Prince Ale, tin on cardboard, 1950s, 6 x 14" **100.00**

Tap Knob, Budweiser, figural Bud Man, molded plastic, 1991, 9¹/₂" h **25.00**

Tap Knob, West Virginia Beer, Fesenmeier Brewing, Huntington, WV, 2-sided, 1940s. **45.00**

Tip Tray, Grain Belt Beers, Grain Belt Brewing, Minneapolis, MN, 1930s **40.00**

Tip Tray, Old India Pale Ale, Commerical Brewing, Boston, MA, 1930s **65.00**

Tray, Genesee Beer, Genessee Brewing, Rochester, NY, 1940s, 12" d **20.00**

Tray, Iroquois Beer & Ale, Iroquois Beverage, Buffalo, NY, 1960s, 12" d. **25.00**

Tray, Portsmouth Ale, Elderedge Brewing, Portsmouth, NH, 1930s, 12" d **65.00**

Tray, Stegmaier Beer, Stegmaier Brewing, Wilkes Barre, PA, 1940s, 12" d **45.00**

Tray, Stroh's Lager Beer, Stroh Brewing, Detroit, MI, porcelain, 12" d **80.00**

Tray, Walter's Beer, Walter Brewing, Eau Claire, WI, 1930s, 13¹/₄ x 10¹/₂". **250.00**

Tray, Yuengling, Yuengling Brewing, Pottsville, PA, 1950s, 12" d **100.00**

BREYER HORSES

When founded in 1943, the Breyer Molding Company of Chicago manufactured custom designed thermoset plastics. After WWII, the company shifted production to injection molded radio and television housings. As a sideline, Breyer also produced a few plastic animals based on designs sculpted by Christian Hess.

By 1958 the Breyer line contained a barnyard full of animals — cats, cows, dogs, and horses. In 1959 the company introduced its woodgrain finish. By the end of the 1970s the sale of horses accounted for most of the company's business.

Reeves International, a distributor of European collectibles such as Britains and Corgi, acquired Breyer in 1984. Manufacturing was moved to a state-of-the-art plant in New Jersey.

References: Felicia Browell, *Breyer Animal Collector's Guide, Second Edition,* Collector Books, 1999; Nancy Atkinson Young, *Breyer Molds and Models: Horses, Riders and Animals, 5th Edition,* Schiffer Publishing, 1998.

Periodicals: *The Hobby Horse News,* 2053 Dryehaven Dr, Tallahassee, FL 32311; *Just About Horses* (company-sponsored), 14 Industrial Rd, Pequannock, NJ 07440.

Newsletter: *The Model Horse Trader,* 34428 Yucaipa Blvd, #E119, Yucaipa, CA 92399.

Collectors' Club: North American Model Horse Show Assoc, PO Box 50508, Denton, TX 76206.

CLASSIC SCALE

Bucking Bronco, #190, matte gray, 1961-67	**$100.00**
Polo Pony, #626, matte bay, 1976-82	**45.00**
Rearing Stallion, #180, matte bay, 1965-80	**20.00**
Silky Sullivan, #603, matte brown, 1975-90	**18.00**
Swaps, #604, matte chestnut, 1975-90	**18.00**

LITTLE BITS SCALE

Arabian Stallion, #1001, matte bay, 1984-88	**$10.00**
Clydesdale, #1025, matte chestnut, 1984-88	**12.00**
Morgan Stallion, #1005, matte bay, 1984-88	**10.00**
Quarter Horse Stallion, #1015, matte black appaloosa, 1985-88	**10.00**

STABLEMATE SCALE

Arabian Mare, #5011, matte dapple gray, 1975-76	**$20.00**
Citation, #5020, matte bay, 1975-90	**8.00**
Quarter Horse Stallion, #5045, matte/semi-gloss chestnut, 1976	**30.00**
Saddlebred, #5001, matte dapple gray, 1975-76	**25.00**
Seabiscuit, #5024, matte bay, 1976-90	**8.00**
Swaps, #5021, matte chestnut, 1976-94	**8.00**

TRADITIONAL SCALE

Adios Rough 'n Ready Quarter Horse, #885, matte red, 1993	**$25.00**

Traditional Scale, Western Horse, #59, alabaster, $50.00.

Black Stallion, #401, semi-gloss black, 1981-88	**30.00**
Clydesdale Foal, #84, matte chestnut, 1969-89	**12.00**
Friesian, #485, matte black, 1992-95	**25.00**
Jumping Horse, #300, matte bay, 1965-88	**35.00**
Lady Phase, #40, matte chestnut, 1976-85	**35.00**
Morgan, #948, matte woodgrain, 1963-65	**475.00**
Pacer, #46, dark bay, 1967-87	**30.00**
Proud Arabian Mare, #215, glossy alabaster, 1956-60	**55.00**
Running Foal, #130, glossy copenhagen, 1963-65	**550.00**
Shire, #95, matte dapple gray, 1972-76	**75.00**
Western Prancing Horse, #110, glossy black pinto, 1961-66	**65.00**

BRIARD, GEORGES

Georges Briard, born Jascha Brojdo, was an industrial designer who worked in a wide range of materials—ceramics, glass, enameled metals, paper, plastic, textiles, and wood. Brojdo emigrated from Poland in 1937. He earned a joint Master of Fine Arts degree from the University of Chicago and the Art Institute of Chicago. In 1947 Brojdo moved to New York where he chose the name Georges Briard as his designer pseudonym.

Columbian Enamel, Glass Guild (The Bent Glass Company), Hyalyn Porcelain, and Woodland were among the early clients of Georges Briard Designs. In the early 1960s Briard designed Pfaltzgraff's Heritage pattern. In 1965 he created sixteen patterns for melamine plastic dinnerware in Allied Chemical's Artisan line, marketed under the Stetson brand name.

Briard continued to create innovative designs for the houseware market through the end of the 1980s. Responding to changing market trends, many of Briard's later products were made overseas.

Reference: Leslie Piña, *'50s & '60s Glass, Ceramics, & Enamel Wares Designed & Signed by Georges Briard, Sascha B., Bellaire, Higgins…,* Schiffer Publishing, 1996.

REPRODUCTION ALERT: Do not confuse Briard knockoffs, many made in Japan, with licensed Briard products. A high level of quality and the distinctive Briard signature are the mark of a Briard piece.

Ambrosia, cheese board, wood, 6" ceramic tile insert, 16 x 7½" board	**$35.00**
Ambrosia, coffee percolator, white porcelainite, polychrome dec, 9¾" h	**35.00**
Ambrosia, tray, white porcelainite, 13 x 19"	**25.00**
Coq D'or, tray, white porcelainite, 23" l	**25.00**
Forbidden Fruit, relish tray, 3-part	**10.00**
Forbidden Fruit, serving tray, white opal glass, brass handle, 12½" d	**35.00**
Golden Celeste, chip 'n dip bowl, 10" d	**25.00**
Green Garden, casserole, cov, white porcelainite, 5⅜" h, 7" d	**35.00**
Heaven Can Wait, cocktail napkins, orig box, price for set of 6	**40.00**
Melange, dinner plate, white porcelainite, 6" d	**5.00**
Paradise, snack bowl, wood and brass center post handle, 8" h, 7" w	**15.00**
Persian Garden, plate, clear aura glass, Glass Guild signature, 6" sq	**8.00**
Royal Chess, ashtray, 5¼ x 9½"	**20.00**
Seascape, serving plate, white opal glass, 11¾" sq	**35.00**
Town & Country, tumbler	**8.00**

BRITISH ROYALTY COMMEMORATIVES

British royalty commemoratives fall into two distinct groups: (1) souvenir pieces purchased during a monarch's reign and (2) pieces associated with specific events such as births, coronations, investitures, jubilees, marriages, or memorials. Items associated with reigning monarchs are the most popular.

Only five monarchs have reigned since 1920 — King George V (May 6, 1910 to January 20, 1936), King Edward VIII (January 20, 1936, abdicated December 10, 1936), King George VI (December 10, 1936 to February 6, 1952), and Queen Elizabeth II (February 6, 1952 to the present).

References: Susan and Al Bagdade, *Warman's English & Continental Pottery & Porcelain, Third Edition,* Wallace-Homestead, Krause Publications, 1998; Douglas H. Flynn and Alan H. Bolton, *British Royalty Commemoratives, 2nd Edition,* Schiffer Publishing, 1999.

Collectors' Club: Commemorative Collector's Society, Lumless House, Gainsborough Rd, Winthrope Near Newark, Nottinghamshire, NG24 2NR U.K.

Beaker, child's, Queen Elizabeth II Coronation, 1953, white, gold rim, multicolored print, Wade England **$75.00**
Beaker, Queen Victoria 1897 Jubilee, Royal Doulton. **300.00**
Coloring Book, Coronation of Queen Elizabeth II, Saalfield, 1953, unused, 36 pp. **25.00**
Cup and Saucer, King Edward VIII Coronation **125.00**
Decanter, Prince Andrew and Sarah Ferguson Wedding, 1986, white, gold bands, multicolored print, black transfer print "Wade–Commemorative Porcelain Decanter from Bell's Scotch Whiskey Perth Scotland–75cl product of Scotland 43% GL" **100.00**
Decanter, Princess Beatrice's Birth, church bell shape, white, gold, red, and blue bands, blue, gold, and brown print, black transfer print "Genuine Wade Porcelain–Commemorative Porcelain Decanter From Bells Scotch Whiskey Perth Scotland–50cl Product of Scotland 40% vol" **75.00**
Drinking Glass, Prince of Wales Stakes, Second Jewel of Canada's Triple Crown, 1984 . . . . **10.00**

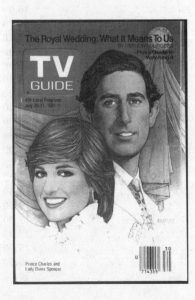

TV Guide, Charles and Diana's Royal Wedding cover story, July 25-31, 1981, $15.00.

Eggcup, Charles and Diana's Royal Wedding, color and sepia portraits and bells, 2³/₄" h **25.00**
Flicker Charm, Queen Elizabeth II and Prince Philip, reverse mkd "Coronation of H. M. Queen Elizabeth II June 2nd 1953" **30.00**
Handkerchief, King Edward VIII Coronation, rayon, center black and white portrait against red, white and blue flag, 5¹/₂ x 3¹/₄" **20.00**
Jug, Edward VIII Coronation, 1937, cream, orange and blue bands, multicolored print, long loop handle, Wadeheath Ware England **100.00**
Loving Cup, Queen Elizabeth II Coronation, 1953 . . . . **450.00**
Loving Cup, Queen Elizabeth and King George VI USA Visit, Royal Crown Derby, 1939 . . . . **600.00**
Mug, Princess Anne and Captain Mark Phillips' Wedding, J&J, May, 1973. . . . . **75.00**
Playing Cards, Prince Andrew and Sarah Ferguson, double deck, Waddington's **30.00**
Stein, Queen Elizabeth II Silver Jubilee, 1977, dark gray, gold crest, Wade England. **100.00**
Thermos, Queen Elizabeth II Coronation, black and white portrait on red, white, blue, and gold ground, 1953, 9³/₄" h **50.00**
Tin, Duke and Duchess of York Wedding, 1923 . . . . **125.00**

BRUSH POTTERY

The J. W. McCoy Pottery and Brush Pottery joined forces in 1911, resulting in the formation of the Brush-McCoy Pottery. The company produced a wide range of ceramic wares, including art ware, cookie jars, garden wares, kitchen wares, novelty planters, and vases. During the 1930s Brush pottery was sold and distributed by The Carson Crockery Company as "Coronado Art Pottery."

References: Sharon and Bob Huxford, *The Collector's Encyclopedia of Brush-McCoy Pottery,* Collector Books, 1978, 1996 value update; Martha and Steve Sanford, *The Guide to Brush-McCoy Pottery,* published by authors, 1992; Martha and Steve Sanford, *Sanfords Guide to Brush-McCoy Pottery, Book 2,* published by authors, 1996.

REPRODUCTION ALERT: Many reproduction cookie jars are unmarked.

Bowl, Jewell, #055, 2¹/₂" d **$250.00**
Bowl, Onyx, #055, 5 x 2¹/₂" **55.00**
Bud Vase, #75, 1940s **25.00**
Bud Vase, Bronze Line, 7¹/₂" h **20.00**
Cookie Jar, Cinderella's pumpkin, W32, 1962. . . . . **175.00**
Cookie Jar, Cloverleaf, K13, 9" h **100.00**
Cookie Jar, Little Angel, W17, 1956 . . . . **800.00**
Cookie Jar, squirrel on log, W26, 1965. . . . . **75.00**
Cornucopia, Bittersweet, 4" h **40.00**
Creamer, #23F, 1940s, 5" h **15.00**
Ewer, floral dec, mkd "Brush USA," 7" h **20.00**
Jardiniere, #292, mkd "Brush USA," 1941, 6¹/₂" h **25.00**
Jardiniere, Jetwood, 7¹/₄" h **350.00**
Lamp, wise bird, 1927, 8" h **175.00**
Match Holder, Kolorkraft, 1932, 6" h **40.00**
Mug, #327, 1928 . . . . **35.00**
Pitcher, #561, mkd "Brush USA," 6" h **20.00**
Pitcher, wise bird, 1927, 10" h **250.00**
Pitcher Vase, yellow, black and gold paper label, 8" h **20.00**

Planter, boat, green, 8" l, $18.00. Photo courtesy Ray Morykan Auctions.

Planter, baby carriage, 1956 . . . . 15.00
Planter, bird, #246, 1957. . . . . 20.00
Planter, double swans, #681, mkd "Brush USA," 1956 . . . . . . 30.00
Planter, elephant, 1939 . . . . 25.00
Planter, gazelle motif, W5, 1950s, 13½" l 20.00
Planter, girl with hobby horse, 1950s 15.00
Planter, girl with hoop skirt, 1941 . . . . 25.00
Planter, kitten with shoe, 1958. . . . . 15.00
Planter, raccoon on log, 1957 . . . . 30.00
Planter, turtle, 7" l 30.00
Salt and Pepper Shakers, pr, Cloverleaf, 1955 . . . . 45.00
Teapot, cov, mirror black, 1920s, 6" h 55.00
Vase, Southern Belle, #218 . . . . 50.00
Vase, wheat motif, 1939, 10" h 50.00
Wall Pocket, fish, 1958 . . . . 65.00
Wall Pocket, horse, #545, 1956. . . . . 75.00

BUSINESS & OFFICE MACHINES

Europeans, especially the Germans, are the leading collectors of business and office equipment. In the United States, decorators buy most examples to use as decorative conversation pieces. It is for this reason that adding machines, check writers, dictating machines, and stock tickers machines are the most eagerly sought after types. Novelty and/or functionality are more important value keys than age.

Collectors' Club: Historical Computer Society, 1 Oakleigh Ct, Richmond, VA 23233.

Note: See Calculators and Typewriters for additional listings.

Apple, computer, Apple III, 6502A, 1.4 Mhz, 96K RAM
  expandable to 128K, 12" monitor displaying 24 lines
  of 40 or 80 characters each, keyboard with numeric
  keypad, built-in 5.25" floppy drive, c1980 . . . . $75.00
Casio, computer, FX-9000P, Intel 8080A processor, 8K
  RAM, built-in 5" monitor displaying 16 lines of 32
  characters each, cassette data storage, c1980 . . . . 25.00
Hewlett-Packard, computer, 86B, 8-bit HP Processor,
  128K RAM expandable to 640K, keyboard, c1985 . . . . 50.00
Instant Checkwriter 20.00
MCM Computers System 700, laptop computer, Model
  782 APL, 8K RAM, integrated plasma alphanumeric
  display, 46-key keyboard, 200K RAM on 2 cassette
  drives, c1977 . . . . 100.00

Paymaster, check protector 25.00
Remington Model 12, bookkeeping machine 350.00
S&P, checkwriter 100.00
Silonics Quietype, printer, ink jet, 180 cps, RS-232 seri-
  al interface, c1978 . . . . 50.00
Star, adding machine. 20.00
Tandy/Radio Shack, printer, TRS-80 Line Printer II, dot
  matrix, 50 cps, c1979 . . . . 50.00
Underwood, bookkeeping machine 400.00
Xerox, printer, Diablo 1260, daisywheel, c1979 . . . . 50.00

CALCULATORS

The first affordable electronic integrated circuit calculator appeared in the early 1970s. Early pocket calculators cost hundreds of dollars. By the early 1980s the price of a basic pocket caluator was $10 or less. Manufacturers such as HP and Texas Instruments made dozens of different models. First models tend to be the most valuable.

References: Guy Ball and Bruce Flamm, *Collector's Guide to Pocket Calculators,* Wilson/Barnett Publishing, 1997; W.A.C. Mier-Jadrzejowica, *A Guide to HP Handheld Calculators and Computers, Second Edition,* Wilson/Barnett Publishing, 1996.

Collectors' Club: International Assoc of Calculator Collectors, 14561 Livingston St, Tustin, CA 92780.

Adler 121C. $45.00
APF Electronics Mark 42 . . . . 30.00
Berkey 4030 . . . . 45.00
Brother 863 . . . . 25.00
Canon Palmtronic LD-84 . . . . 25.00
Casio CM-605, miniature 15.00
Commodore F4146R 35.00
Commodore M55 . . . . 65.00
Craig 4509B 35.00
Hewlett-Packard 27, financial and scientific, red LED 100.00
JC Penney 5000 . . . . 45.00
Keystone SC-652. . . . . 50.00
Lloyd's 502, 4-function, red LED 30.00
Melcor 392. . . . . 45.00
Montgomery Ward P330 . . . . 30.00
Novus 950 . . . . 30.00
Olympia CD-45 . . . . 35.00
Panasonic JE-8220U 25.00
Panasonic Panac SD-1 . . . . 40.00
Radio Shack EC-241 . . . . 30.00
Ricoh RC-8F 25.00
Rockwell 31R 15.00
Sanyo CZ-8101, scientific 45.00
Sears Micro PD12 . . . . 35.00
Sharp PC-1802 . . . . 40.00
Texas Instruments SR-40, scientific 20.00
Toshiba BC-8016 . . . . 25.00
Toshiba SC-6100, scientific 65.00
Toy, Fun 'N Numbers, Radio Shack EC-2029 . . . . 20.00
Toy, Hello Kitty 10.00
Toy, keychain, flip-open type 15.00
Toy, Lego 25.00
Toy, Math to Go 25.00
Toy, Phone Directory. 25.00
Toy, Winnie the Pooh 20.00

CALENDARS

The 19th-century printing revolution made calendars accessible to everyone. As the century ended, calendars were a popular form of advertising giveaway and remained so through much of the 20th century. Cheesecake calendars enjoyed a Golden Age between 1930 and the mid-1960s.

In the 1980s, the "art" or special theme calendar arrived on the scene. Moderately expensive when purchased new, they are ignored by most calendar collectors.

Today, calendars are collected because of the appeal of their subject matter, the artwork created by a famous illustrator, or because the year matches the birth year of the purchaser. If the monthly pages remain attached value increases 10% to 20%.

Reference: Norman E. Martinus and Harry L. Rinker, *Warman's Paper,* Wallace-Homestead, 1994.

Collectors' Club: Calendar Collector Society, 18222 Flower Hill Way #299, Gaithersburg, MD 20879.

REPRODUCTION ALERT

1920, Watkins Products, woman golfer **$20.00**
1923, Round Oak Stove, Indian and squaw, 10½ x 21". **150.00**
1925, Peters Cartridge Co, flying mallards above water,
    18 x 33" **350.00**
1927, Chero-Cola, woman sitting on lifeboat at beach **250.00**
1927, Commercial State Bank, lesson on thrift **75.00**
1928, Edison-Mazda, "Reveries," Maxfield Parrish **575.00**
1930, Peter's Cartridge. **250.00**
1932, American Stores, children with 13-star flag **50.00**
1932, Dr Miles Weather Calendar, with envelope and
    booklet, folded, 7 x 10" **15.00**
1933, Gold Dust Washing Powder **35.00**
1936, Burnham Boilers, man on rocker by furnace **35.00**
1936, Christener Trucking **150.00**
1936, Oliver Tractor **75.00**
1936, Tucson Saddle Shop, Russel print **100.00**
1937, Chevrolet, "The Complete Car–Completely New,"
    6 x 8½". **30.00**

1949, Fisk Tires, full pad, 33½" h, $325.00. Photo courtesy Collectors Auction Services.

SALEM TIRE SERVICE
546 Marion St.   Phone 3412
SALEM, OREGON

JANUARY 1949

FISK TIRES

1937, Hi-Plane Tobacco, Indiana and airplane **475.00**
1937, "Twilight," Maxfield Parrish, Brown & Bigelow **275.00**
1938, Red Goose Shoes, 10 x 17" **35.00**
1938, Richfield Motor Oil, compartments for bills, 14½
    x 10½" **75.00**
1939, Sunshine Cookies **20.00**
1939, The Lone Ranger **75.00**
1940, Keen Kutter **60.00**
1941, Alka-Seltzer. **35.00**
1941, "Yankee Doodle," 3 children with flags in parade,
    add-on pad, 8 x 15". **15.00**
1942, Gilmore Gasoline, San Diego, CA, dog in field, 14
    x 7" **30.00**
1943, Texaco Gasoline **55.00**
1944, Super Jumbos, American flag and plane below
    "Dominate Your Market!," salesman's sample, sgd "J
    Rozen," 44" h, 30" w **50.00**
1945, How Nong Chinese Herb Co, Oakland, CA, 10 x
    16" **12.00**
1947, Collier Body & Paint Co, Chambersburg, PA, 6 x
    3½" **35.00**
1947, "The Special Esquire Girl Calendar," no envelope,
    8½ x 12". **25.00**
1949, Speedway Oil **8.00**
1950, TWA **20.00**
1951, Arkansas Cotton Oil Co **25.00**
1953, Nesbitt's **50.00**
1957, Meadow Gold **8.00**
1959, Girl Scouts **20.00**
1960, Playboy Playmate Calendar, orig envelope, 8½ x
    13". **20.00**
1963, Pasadena Tournament of Roses **15.00**

CALIFORNIA FAIENCE

William Bradgon and Chauncey Thomas first manufactured art pottery and tiles in 1916. In 1924 they named their products California Faience.

Most art pottery pieces are characterized by cast molding and a monochrome matte glaze. Some pieces had a high gloss glaze. Plaster molds were used to make the polychrome decorated tiles. California Faience also produced a commercial floral line and made master molds for other California potteries.

The company was hard hit by the Depresssion. Bradgon bought out Thomas in the late 1930s. He sold the pottery in the early 1950s, working with the new owners until he died in 1959.

Candlesticks, pr, turquoise glaze, imp "California
    Faience," 4½" h **$200.00**
Flowerholder, figural, 2 pelicans, turquoise glaze, 6" h **125.00**
Lamp Base, bulbous, matte speckled ocher and green
    glaze, imp "California Porcelain," 8¾ x 7½" **450.00**
Potpourri Jar, Oriental shape, yellow matte, incised
    mark, 4½" h **225.00**
Trivet, cuenca, polychrome basket of flowers on
    turquoise ground, mounted in Dirk Van Erp ham-
    mered copper casing, stamped "Dirk Van Erp/San
    Francisco," 5¼" d **1,250.00**
Trivet, cuenca, stylized blue flowers on white ground,
    imp "California Faience," 5 x 5¼" **250.00**
Trivet, cuenca, stylized peacock, matte and glossy blue,
    yellow, and turquoise glaze, stamped "California
    Faience," 5¼" d **325.00**

Vase, bulbous, yellow semi-matte glaze, imp "California
Faience," 5 x 5¼" **225.00**
Vase, ovoid, medium blue matte glaze, turquoise int,
incised mark, 8" h............................. **100.00**
Vessel, squat, white semi-matte glaze, imp "California
Pottery," 5" h................................. **175.00**

CAMARK POTTERY

Samuel Jack Carnes founded Camark Pottery, Camden, Arkansas,
in 1926. The company made art pottery, earthenware, and decorative accessories. John Lessell, previously employed at Weller, and
his wife were among the leading art potters working at Camark.

After Carnes sold the plant in 1966, it was run primarily as a
retail operation by Mary Daniels. In January 1986 Gary and Mark
Ashcraft purchased the Camark Pottery building in hopes of re-
establishing a pottery at the site. At the time of the purchase, they
stated they did not intend to reissue pieces using the company's
old molds.

References: David Edwin Gifford, *Collector's Guide to Camark
Pottery,* (1997), *Book II* (1999), Collector Books; Letitia Landers,
Camark Pottery, Vol. 1 (1994), *Vol. 2* (1996), Colony Publishing.

Collectors' Club: National Society of Arkansas Pottery Collectors,
2006 Beckenhame Cove, Little Rock, AR 72212.

Basket, emerald green, mkd "USA, Camark, N-34," 8" h.... **$15.00**
Basket, yellow, hp iris, mkd "805R, USA," 9½" h **100.00**
Bowl, cream mottled, 9½ x 4¾" **175.00**
Box, rose pink, mkd "847R, USA," 5¼ x 3 x 4" **125.00**
Candlesticks, pr, blue and white, hp roses, 5¼" h......... **25.00**
Candlesticks, pr, yellow, mkd "269, USA," 5¼" h **25.00**
Dealer Sign, emerald green, unmkd, 6" h **200.00**
Figure, cat, arched back, white, mkd "USA," 12" l **250.00**
Figure, climbing cat, emerald green, mkd "Camark," 16" l ... **60.00**
Figure, lion, "Lions Club, Camden, Ark.," 3½ x 2¼" **15.00**
Figure, reclining deer, burgundy, 8½ x 4½" **60.00**
Flower Frog, fish, #413, 3½" h...................... **40.00**
Jug, "Arkansas Pure Corn, USA," black Arkansas ink
stamp, 5" h.................................. **60.00**

Vase, orange and green overflow matte glaze, 4½" h, $70.00.

Lily Vase, #537, 3½" h **30.00**
Lily Vase, matte green, 6¼" h....................... **15.00**
Piggy Bank, mirror black, 3¾" h **40.00**
Pitcher, pink and light blue overspray, mkd "513, USA,"
10¼" h..................................... **80.00**
Tulip Vase, emerald green, mkd "USA, Camark, N-19,"
5½" h...................................... **10.00**
Urn, rose pink, hp roses, unmkd, 8¼" h............... **70.00**
Vase, gray and blue mottled, 11¾" h **300.00**
Vase, hp majolica, mkd "Camark 810K, USA," 10½" h **125.00**
Vase, mirror black, #345, 6" h...................... **150.00**
Vase, orange crackle matte, handled, gold Arkansas ink
stamp, 8¼" h................................ **300.00**
Vase, royal blue, brown Arkansas sticker, 8½" h **20.00**
Vase, yellow, mkd "802, USA," 6¼" h **100.00**
Vase, yellow, mkd "846R, USA," 7" h................. **100.00**

CAMBRIDGE GLASS

Cambridge Glass, Cambridge, Ohio, was founded in 1901. The
company manufactured a wide variety of glass tablewares. After
experiencing financial difficulties in 1907, Arthur J. Bennett, previously with the National Glass Company, helped reorganize the
company. By the 1930s, the company had over 5,000 glass molds
in inventory.

Although five different identification marks are known, not
every piece of Cambridge Glass was permanently marked. Paper
labels were used between 1935 and 1954.

Cambridge Glass ceased operations in 1954. Its molds were
sold. Imperial Glass Company purchased some, a few wound up
in private hands.

References: Gene Florence, *Elegant Glassware of the Depression
Era, Eighth Edition,* Collector Books, 1999; National Cambridge
Collectors, Inc., *The Cambridge Glass Co., Cambridge, Ohio*
(reprint of 1930 catalog and supplements through 1934), Collector
Books, 1976, 2000 value update; National Cambridge Collectors,
Inc., *The Cambridge Glass Co., Cambridge Ohio, 1949 Thru 1953*
(catalog reprint), Collector Books, 1976, 1999 value update;
National Cambridge Collectors, Inc., *Colors in Cambridge Glass,*
Collector Books, 1984, 1999 value update.

Periodical: *The Daze,* PO Box 57, Otisville, MI 48463.

Collectors' Club: National Cambridge Collectors, Inc, PO Box
416, Cambridge, OH 43725.

Ashtray, Caprice, blue **$32.00**
Ashtray, Caprice, 214, pink, 3" d **50.00**
Ball Jug, Portia, gold **250.00**
Bitters Bottle, Elaine, 1212........................ **300.00**
Bonbon, Caprice, crystal **12.00**
Bowl, Apple Blossom, 3400/1185, 2 handles, gold trim,
yellow..................................... **100.00**
Bowl, Apple Blossom, 3400/1240, 4-toed, oval, crystal...... **80.00**
Bowl, Caprice, 4-ftd, oval, pink **125.00**
Bowl, Caprice, ftd, pink, 10" d **100.00**
Bread and Butter Plate, Apple Blossom, 3400/60, amber..... **10.00**
Bread and Butter Plate, Rose Point, 3400/60, 6" d **20.00**
Bud Vase, Diane, 274, 10" h **65.00**
Butter, cov, Rose Point, 506 .... **250.00**
Butter, cov, Wildflower, 506........................ **200.00**

Creamer and Open Sugar, Caprice, blue, $35.00.

Cake Plate, Elaine, 170 . . . . 200.00
Cake Plate, Rose Point. 55.00
Cake Salver, Caprice, 31, 2-pc, crystal 200.00
Candleholder, Apple Blossom, 627, amber. 40.00
Candleholder, Caprice, 74, 3-lite, crystal 25.00
Candy Dish, cov, Caprice, 165, crystal. 45.00
Candy Dish, cov, Roselyn 75.00
Card Holder, Caprice, crystal. 10.00
Celery, Caprice, 103, moonlight blue, 11" d 225.00
Celery, Diane, 3500/652, 11" d 50.00
Celery, Rose Point, 3400/6, 5-part 90.00
Champagne, Apple Blossom, 3130, yellow. 30.00
Champagne, Rose Point, 3121. . . . . 30.00
Cheese and Cracker, Portia, 3400/6 . . . . 85.00
Cigarette Box, Caprice, 207, moonlight blue 45.00
Cigarette Box, Elaine, 615 . . . . 165.00
Claret, Caprice, 300, crystal 60.00
Coaster, Caprice, 13, pink. 55.00
Cocktail, Caprice, crystal. 20.00
Cocktail, Chantilly, P101, 32 oz. 200.00
Cocktail, Farber, 6018, amber 20.00
Cocktail, Rose Point, 3121. . . . . 25.00
Cocktail Shaker, Portia, 32 oz 150.00
Cocktail Shaker, Rose Point 200.00
Comport, Diane, 3400/13, 4-toed, amber. 85.00
Comport, Rose Point, 3400/14, tall. 150.00
Cordial, Blossom Time, 3675 . . . . 75.00
Cordial Bottle, Diane, 3400/119, 6 oz 225.00
Corn Dish, Wildflowers, 477, 9½" d 55.00
Creamer, Caprice, crystal. 10.00
Creamer, Rose Point, 3500/15, individual. 25.00
Creamer and Sugar, Caprice, 38, mocha 45.00
Creamer and Sugar, Wildflower, 3900/40, individual 45.00
Cruet, Wildflower, 3900/100 . . . . 85.00
Cup and Saucer, Rose Point, 3400 . . . . 45.00
Cup and Saucer, Wildflower, 3400. . . . . 50.00
Decanter, Portia, 28 oz 300.00
Dinner Bell, Wildflower, 3650. . . . . 175.00
Dinner Plate, Caprice, crystal 45.00
Dinner Plate, Diane, 3400/1177, pink, 10½" sq 225.00
Finger Bowl, Apple Blossom, 3130, yellow. 100.00
French Dressing Bottle, Rosalie, green 250.00
Hat, Blossom Time, 6" h 300.00
Hurricane Lamp Base, Rose Point, 1604. . . . . 55.00

Ice Tub, Mt Vernon, crystal 75.00
Juice, Caprice, 310, 5 oz, moonlight blue. 125.00
Juice, Caprice, ftd, crystal 20.00
Luncheon Set, Caprice, 4 cups and saucers, four 8½" d
   plates, creamer and sugar, and 12" d ftd plate, amber 350.00
Martini Jug, Apple Blossom, 1408, 60 oz 950.00
Martini Jug, Chantilly, P100, sterling base. 175.00
Mayonnaise, Rose Point, 1532, with liner and ladle 60.00
Nut Dish, Caprice, 93, individual, moonlight blue 60.00
Nut Dish, Elaine, 3400/71. . . . . 65.00
Old Fashion, Caprice, 310, moonlight blue 125.00
Oyster Cocktail, Caprice, pink. 85.00
Oyster Cocktail, Rose Point, 3121 . . . . 65.00
Parfait, Rose Point, 3121 . . . . 95.00
Pickle, Rose Point, 477, 9" l. 65.00
Pitcher, Chantilly, sterling base, 20 oz 300.00
Pitcher, Gloria, 935, ebony 950.00
Pitcher, Rose Point, 1561, 86 oz 650.00
Plate, Elaine, 3400/176, 7½" d 25.00
Relish, Apple Blossom, 3400/862, 4-part, center handle,
   amber. 100.00
Relish, Caprice, 120, 2-part, moonlight blue, 6¾" l. 35.00
Relish, Elaine, 3500/71, 3-part, center handle. 125.00
Relish, Portia, 862, 4-part, center handle 100.00
Relish, Rose Point, 3400/88, 2-part, 8¾" l 75.00
Relish, Rose Point, 3500/61, 3-part, ring handle 60.00
Relish, Wildflower, 3400/88, 2-part, 8¾" l 55.00
Relish, Wildflower, 5-part, round 75.00
Salad Dressing Set, Caprice, 112, with blue spoons,
   moonlight blue 400.00
Salt and Pepper Shakers, pr, Elaine, 3900/1177. . . . . 45.00
Sauceboat, Portia, 1402, 7" l 15.00
Server, Rose Point, center handle. 150.00
Shakers, pr, Caprice, screw base, crystal. 80.00
Sherbet, Caprice, crystal 15.00
Sherbet, Portia, 3122, low 20.00
Sherbet, Portia, 3124, low, forest green 65.00
Sherry, Portia, 7966, 2 oz 50.00
Sugar, Rose Point, P253, individual 25.00
Toothpick Holder, Chantilly. 45.00
Torte Plate, Caprice, 33, 14" d, moonlight blue. 100.00
Tray, Caprice, oval, 9" l, moonlight blue. 50.00
Tray, Farber. 45.00
Tray, Portia, 3400/10, center handle. 75.00
Tumbler, Caprice, 184, 12 oz, pistachio. 150.00
Tumbler, Caprice, ftd, 5 oz, moonlight blue 45.00
Tumbler, Caprice, ftd, 3 oz, moonlight blue 100.00
Tumbler, Diane, 498, flat, 12 oz 55.00
Tumbler, Elaine, 1402/96, 7 oz 35.00
Tumbler, Rose Point, 3121, 9 oz 40.00
Tumbler, Rose Point, 3500/1, 10 oz 30.00
Vase, Caprice, 345, plain top, amethyst 150.00
Vase, Gloria, 1242, 10" h, crystal. 250.00
Vase, Wildflower, 1620, 7" h 275.00
Water Goblet, Apple Blossom, 3130, 9 oz, amber 25.00
Water Goblet, Caprice, 300, 9 oz, crystal. 15.00
Water Goblet, Diane, 3122, 9 oz, yellow. 75.00
Water Goblet, Rondo, crystal. 20.00
Whiskey, Apple Blossom, ftd, 2 oz, green. 85.00
Whiskey, Apple Blossom, ftd, 2 oz, yellow. 65.00
Wine Goblet, Diane, 3122, 3½ oz, 6¾" h 45.00
Wine Goblet, Farber, 6093, amethyst. 30.00

CAMERAS & ACCESSORIES

The development of the camera was truly international. Johann Zahn, a German monk, created the first fully portable wood box camera with a movable lens, adjustable aperture, and mirror to project the image in the early 1800s. Joseph Niepce and Louise Daguere perfected the photographic plate. Peter Von Voigtlander, an Austrian, contributed the quality lens. An industry was born.

By the late 19th century, England, France, and Germany all played major roles in the development of camera technology. America's contributions came in the area of film development and marketing.

In 1888 George Eastman introduced the Kodak No. 1, a simple box camera that revolutionized the industry. Model No. 4 was the first folding camera. The Brownie was introduced in 1900.

After World War II, the Japanese made a strong commitment to dominating the camera market. By the 1970s, they had achieved their goal.

Reference: Jim and Joan McKeown (eds.), *Price Guide to Antique and Classic Cameras, 1997-1998, 10th Edition,* Centennial Photo Service, 1996.

Collectors' Clubs: American Photographic Historical Society, Inc, 1150 Avenue of the Americas, New York, NY 10036; American Society of Camera Collectors, 7952 Genesta Ave, Van Nuys, CA 91406; International Kodak Historical Society, PO Box 21, Paoli, PA 19301; Leica Historical Society of America, 7611 Dornoch Ln, Dallas, TX 75248; Nikon Historical Society, PO Box 3213, Hammond, IN 46321; The Movie Machine Society, 903 Maryland Dr, Austin, TX 78758; Zeiss Historical Society, 300 Waxwing Dr, Cranbury, NJ 08512.

CAMERAS

AGFA, Optima Reflex, c1962-66	$175.00
AGFA, Readyset Traveler, c1931	55.00
AGFA, Trolita, folding bed, c1938-40	200.00
Ansco, Arrow, c1925	20.00
Ansco, Titan, c1949	30.00
Argus C3 Matchmatic, 2-tone finish, 1958-66	20.00
Bell & Howell, Stereo Colorist II, 1957-61	200.00
Brownie, Six-16, black leatherette covered box with leather impressed strap handle, silvertone Art Deco design metal frontplate, top and side view prism optics for viewer, 1930s, 3½ x 5 x 6"	20.00
Canon, Snappy '84, 1984 Summer Olympics logo on front	40.00
Canon 7, dual mounting flange, 1961-64	300.00
Fuji, Futura-P, c1953-55	75.00
Fuji, Prince Peerless, folding body, c1934	300.00
Galter, Sunbeam 120, black Bakelite body	10.00
Houghton, Ensign Double-8, strut-folding, c1930-40	75.00
Kodak Deux, black hard molded plastic and gray metal, braided neck cord, 4¾ x 3½ x 2¾"	25.00
Kodak Instamatic Reflex, Xenon 50mm lens, black leatherette case with brushed finish top and bottom, 1968-74, 5 x 4 x 4"	20.00
Kodak Petite Vest Pocket, model B, green, green leatherette case, 1929-33	50.00
Kodak Rainbow Hawk-Eye #2, model C, folding, rose colored case, orig box with brochure, 1930s, 6½ x 3¼ x 1" folded size	100.00

Brownie, Mickey Mouse Target Six 16, c1946, 5¼" h, $2,650.00. Photo courtesy Collectors Auction Services.

Minolta, Electro Shot, 35mm, 1965	50.00
Minolta, SR-1S, 1964	75.00
Olympic, Super-Olympic, 35mm, Bakelite body, c1935	200.00
Olympus, Flex B-1, 1952	200.00
Toy, Irwin, Grand Camera, black plastic	5.00
Toy, Sesame Street Big Bird's 3-D Camera, 1978	15.00
Yashica, Flash-O-Set, 35mm, 1961	25.00
Yashica, Pentamatic, 35mm, 1960-64	75.00

CAMERA ACCESSORIES

Book, *Guide to Kodak Retina, Retina Reflex, Signet and Pony,* Kenneth S Tydings, soft cov, 128 pp, 1952	$10.00
Camera Bag, Silver Lens, soft plastic, 35mm camera shaped, c1987	5.00
Darkroom Timer, red and chrome finished metal, white face, black hands, Arabic numerals	20.00
Exposure Meter, Canon, auxiliary CdS, 1965-67	15.00
Exposure Meter, Votar, electric, orig box	20.00
Sign, Kodak Film, diecut porcelain, 2-sided, "Kodak /Kodak Film," 1930s, 20 x 17"	500.00
Timer, Luxor Photo Timer, Burke & James, c1930s	10.00

CANDLEWICK

Imperial Glass Corporation introduced its No. 400 pattern, Candlewick, in 1936. Over 650 different forms and sets are known. Although produced primarily in cyrstal (clear), other colors exist. The pattern proved extremely popular and remained in production until Imperial closed in 1982.

After a brief period of ownership by the Lancaster-Colony Corporation and Consolidated Stores, Imperial's assets, including its molds, were sold. Various companies, groups, and individuals bought Imperial's Candlewick molds. Mirror Images of Lansing, Michigan, bought more than 200. Boyd Crystal Art Glass, Cambridge, Ohio, bought 18.

References: Mary M. Wetzel-Tomalka, *Candlewick: The Jewel of Imperial, Book II,* published by author, 1995; Mary M. Wetzel-Tomalka, *Candlewick: The Jewel of Imperial, Price Guide '99 and More,* published by author, 1998.

Collectors' Club: The National Candlewick Collector's Club, 6534 South Ave, Holland, OH 43528.

Baked Apple, 400/53X, blue	**$85.00**
Berry Bowl, 1F, 5" d	**12.00**
Bonbon, 51H, heart handle, 6" d	**30.00**
Bowl, 74SC, crimped, 4-toed	**70.00**
Bowl, 131B, oval, 14" l	**325.00**
Bowl, 400/21F, 5" d, blue	**45.00**
Bowl, 400/74B	**100.00**
Bowl, 400/125, divided, oval, 11" l	**575.00**
Bud Vase, 400/186, 7" h	**450.00**
Cake Knife, glass	**550.00**
Candy Dish, 51C, crimped handle, 6" d	**35.00**
Candy Dish, cov, 59	**50.00**
Cheese and Cracker, 88, 2-pc	**50.00**
Cocktail, 3400	**15.00**
Compote, 400/45	**25.00**
Creamer and Sugar	**12.00**
Cream Soup Bowl, with liner	**60.00**
Cruet, 400/279, handled, 6 oz	**75.00**
Cup and Saucer	**10.00**
Fork and Spoon, 400/75	**30.00**
Fruit Tray, 400/68F	**300.00**
Iced Tea, 3400, 12 oz	**17.00**
Iced Tea, ftd	**20.00**
Ice Tub, 63	**125.00**
Ice Tub, 168, handled, 7" d	**225.00**
Juice Pitcher, 19	**200.00**
Mayonnaise, 3-pc	**40.00**
Mustard, cov, 400/156	**25.00**
Nappy, 206, 3-toed	**65.00**
Oil Cruet, 274, 4 oz	**50.00**
Pitcher, 24, 80 oz	**200.00**
Plate, 72C, crimp handle	**40.00**
Platter, 400/131D, 16" l	**275.00**
Puff Box, cov	**200.00**
Relish, 400/52, divided, 6" l	**25.00**
Relish, 400/102, 5-part, 13" l	**100.00**
Relish, 400/213, 3-part, 10" l	**75.00**
Relish, 400/234, divided, sq	**150.00**
Salad Fork and Spoon	**5.00**
Salad Plate, oval, 9" l	**45.00**
Seafood Cocktail, 190, 6-ftd	**90.00**
Sherbet, 190, 5 oz	**25.00**

Snack Jar Lid, 139	**100.00**
Torte Plate, 2 handles, 14" d	**40.00**
Tray, 400/171, 3-part, 8" d	**50.00**
Tumbler, 400/19, 12 oz	**10.00**

CANDY & GUM COLLECTIBLES

Collecting interest in candy and gum collectibles has reached a level where it deserves its own category. Actually, candy and gum collectibles have figured prominently in several key collecting categories, e.g., advertising and coin-operated, for decades. Several recent publications, ranging from a history of chocolate to one about the Hershey and Mars families, has heightened collector interest.

This category is bigger than chocolate, although chocolate related collectibles certainly sweeten the pot. Candy boxes and candy wrappers are two subcategories gaining in popularity.

Here is something to chew on. Several years ago, a single stick of Coca-Cola gum brought over $3,300 at auction.

Reference: *Candy Containers,* L-W Book Sales, 1996.

Newsletter: *Chewing Gum Times,* PO Box 8296, Spokane, WA 99203.

Collectors' Clubs: Bubble Gum Charm Collectors, 24 Seafoam St, Staten Island, NY 10306; Candy Container Collectors of America, PO Box 352, Chelmsford, MA 01824.

Calendar, 1927, Wrigley's Double Mint Gum, 3½ x 6"	**$30.00**
Candy Container, monkey lamp, pressed glass, "See, Speak or Hear No Evil" emb on back of monkey, "A Spec-Tor-product, Made in USA" emb inside shade, TH Stough Co, 1950s, 1¼ x 1¼ x 2⅞"	**225.00**
Candy Container, mule pulling 2-wheeled barrel with man on cart, pressed glass, "Jeannette PA USA," "Victory Glass Co," and "oz Avor" emb on bottom, 1930s, 4½ x 1¼ x 2¾"	**100.00**
Candy Container, nursing bottle, molded glass, "Lynne Doll Nurser" emb on 1 side, "sugar starch corn syrup–US certified colors ¼ oz–TH Stough Co Jeannette, Pa" emb on other, 1950s, 1¼ x 3½"	**60.00**
Candy Container, Peter Rabbit, pressed glass, "Mfg by JH Millstein Co–Jeannette PA–Pat App For" emb on edges of base, c1940-50s, 4¼ x 1¾ x 6½"	**35.00**
Countertop Display, Blony Gum, cardboard, truck shaped, bed holds gum, wood wheels, 8" h, 13½" w	**375.00**
Pinback Button, Nuss's Candies, multicolored image of baby chick emerged from broken eggshell, and 2 colored Easter eggs	**20.00**
Pocket Mirror, Mirror Candies, brass twined handle extending to brass rim holding insert, "Like Lovely Psyche, Good And Pure," mythological lady admiring herself in reflective waters mkd "Mirror Candies"	**75.00**
Sign, Beech-Nut Gum, cardboard, "Beech-Nut Gum presents radio's most interesting program–Chandu The Magician–WJAX 815 Every Tues, Wed, Fri, Sat Night," c1932, 11 x 21"	**200.00**
Sign, Beech-Nut Gum, cardboard, "It costs you no more to enjoy Beech-Nut...the Quality Gum," orig wood frame, 22½ x 46½"	**100.00**
Sign, Oh Boy Gum, tin, matted and framed under glass, c1930s, 7 x 15"	**175.00**

Crescent Salad, $45.00.

Vending Machine, Model 45A, Columbus Vending Machine Co., 1946, 14¹/₂" h, $300.00. Photo courtesy Collectors Auction Services.

Sign, Schrafft's Candy Bars, tin, cartoon figure holding sign "Schrafft's Chocolate Covered Bars Are Mighty Good," framed under glass, 1920-30s, 12 x 18" **825.00**

Sign, Teaberry Gum, tin, "A Happy Thought!/That Mountain Tea Flavor," 1930-40s, 9 x 12". **450.00**

Thermometer, Clark Bar, wood, c1930s, 5 x 19" **150.00**

Tin, Adams Pepsin Gum, litho tin, "American Chiclet Co.,–NY Cleveland Chicago Kansas City San Francisco," 6 x 6¹/₂ x 4³/₄". **500.00**

Tin, Chew Yucatan Gum, litho tin, "American Chiclet Co–NY Cleveland Chicago Kansas City San Francisco," 6 x 6¹/₂ x 4³/₄". **475.00**

Tin, Robin Hood Sweets, litho tin, Federal Tin Co, Baltimore, 6 x 6 x 2" **40.00**

Tin, Whitman's Salmagundi, litho tin, Art Nouveau style, flowing hair portrait of woman on center lid, ©SFW&S Inc, 1920s, 4¹/₄ x 7¹/₂ x 2". **20.00**

Vending Machine, Chiclets, metal marquee, glass globe, metal body, 16" h **80.00**

Vending Machine, Hit the Target Bubble Gum, metal and glass front, with key, B&O, c1950s **200.00**

Vending Machine, U-Select-It, 5¢ candy bar, metal and glass, red and silver plates, with key, "Coan-Sletteland Co, Inc Madison, Wis," 36" h, 8¹/₂" w, 10" d **100.00**

CAP GUNS

The first toy cap gun was introduced in 1870. Cap guns experienced two Golden Ages: (1) the era of the cast iron cap gun from 1870 through 1900 and (2) the era of the diecast metal and plastic cap guns.

Hubley, Kilgore, Mattel, and Nichols are among the leading manufacturers of diecast pistols. Many diecast and plastic pistols were sold as part of holster sets. A large number were associated with television cowboy and detective heroes. The presence of the original box, holster, and other accessories adds as much as 100% to the value of the gun.

References: Rudy D'Angelo, *Cowboy Hero Cap Pistols*, Antique Trader Books, 1997; James L. Dundas, *Cap Guns*, Schiffer Publishing, 1996; Jerrell Little, *Price Guide to Cowboy Cap Guns and Guitars*, L-W Book Sales, 1996; Jim Schleyer, *Backyard*

Buckaroos: Collecting Western Toy Guns, Books Americana, Krause Publications, 1996.

Collectors' Club: Toy Gun Collectors of America, 3009 Oleander Ave, San Marcos, CA 92069.

49-er, Stevens, 1940, 9" l	**$175.00**
101 Ranch, Hubley, 1930, 11¹/₂" l	150.00
Army, Hubley, automatic, 1940, 7" l	60.00
Army, Hubley, single shot, 1940, 7" l	125.00
Bang, Stevens, 1940, 7¹/₂" l	80.00
Bat, Kenton, single shot, 1926, 5" l	40.00
Big Chief, Kilgore, single shot, 1935, 6" l	30.00
Big Scout, Stevens, single shot, 9³/₈" l	40.00
Billy the Kid, Stevens, 1938, 6³/₄" l	100.00
Black Jack, Kenton, single shot, 11" l	100.00
Buc-A-Roo, Kilgore, single shot, 8¹/₄" l	60.00
Buddy, Dent, single shot, 1930, 4¹/₂" l	50.00
Buffalo Bill, Hubley, automatic, 9" l	40.00
Buffalo Bill, Stevens, single shot, 11³/₈" l	175.00
Bulls Eye, Kilgore, 1940, 6¹/₂" l	80.00
Cal, Stevens, single shot, 1925, 5¹/₂" l	50.00
Champ, Hubley, 1940, 5" l	60.00
Clip, Hubley, single shot, 6¹/₄" l	30.00
Cowboy, Stevens, single shot, 1930, 12" l	275.00
Cowpoke Jr, Lone Star, 8¹/₄" l	40.00
Daisy, Hubley, single shot, 1925, 4¹/₈" l	30.00
Dandy, Hubley, 1937, 5³/₄" l	60.00
Dixie, Kenton, 1937, 7" l	75.00
Eagle, Hubley, 1935, 8¹/₂" l	125.00
Fanner 50, Mattel, 11¹/₂" l	60.00
Gem, Stevens, single shot, 1924, 3³/₄" l	35.00
Gene Autry, Kilgore, 8¹/₄" l	125.00
Gene Autry, Stevens, 1940, 7³/₄" l	150.00
Hero, Stevens, 1937, 5¹/₄" l	30.00
Hi-Ho, Kilgore, 1940, 6¹/₂" l	55.00
Kent, Kenton, 1932, 5³/₄" l	30.00
Kido, Kenton, 1937, 5³/₈" l	50.00
Kit Carson, Kenton, 1931, 9" l	125.00
Law Maker, Kenton, 1941, 8³/₈" l	125.00
Lone Ranger, Kilgore, 1938, 8¹/₂" l	150.00
Mohawk, Hubley, 1930, 8⁷/₈" l	60.00
Oh Boy, Kilgore, 1933, 4¹/₈" l	125.00
Old Ironsides, National, 1922, 10¹/₂" l	160.00
Paladin, Leslie Henry, 9³/₄" l	60.00
Pet, Stevens, 1924, 4¹/₈" l	30.00
Rex, Kilgore, 1939, 3⁷/₈" l	50.00

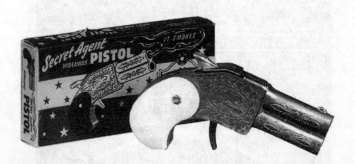

Secret Agent Hideaway, Hamilton, automatic, nickel-plated, diecast, 5³/₄" l, $30.00. Photo courtesy Collectors Auction Services.

Scout, Stevens, 1935, 6³/₄" l	**50.00**
Sure Shot, Hubley, 1940, 4¹/₄" l	**30.00**
Texan Jr, Hubley, 10" l	**40.00**
Texas Kid, Hubley, 10¹/₄" l	**30.00**
Tiger, Hubley, 1935, 6⁷/₈" l	**40.00**
Whoopie, Kenton, 1932, 5¹/₂" l	**50.00**
Zip, Hubley, 1935, 5" l	**40.00**

CARLTON WARE

Wiltshow and Robinson produced Staffordshire earthenware and porcelains at the Carlton Works, Stoke-on-Trent, beginning in the 1890s. In 1957 the company's name was changed to Carlton Ware, Ltd.

Black was the background color most often used on the company's wares. During the 1920s the line included pieces decorated with Art Deco designs in brightly enameled and gilt flowers and porcelain vases featuring luster decoration in oriental motifs. Walking Ware, introduced in the 1970s, was Carlton's most popular line of novelty footed breakfast dishes and serving pieces recognizable by its brightly decorated socks and Mary Janes.

References: Helen Cunningham, *Clarice Cliff and Her Contemporaries: Susie Cooper, Keith Murray, Charlotte Rhead and the Carlton Ware Designers,* Schiffer Publishing, 1999; David Serpell, *Collecting Carlton Ware,* Francis Joseph, 1998.

Collectors' Club: Carlton Ware Collectors International, PO Box 161, Sevenoaks, Kent TN15 6GA UK.

Biscuit Jar, multicolored flowers, cobalt trim, 9¹/₂" h	**$100.00**
Bowl, phoenix bird in flight, multicolored, oriental swirled motif, matte pink ground, 9¹/₄" d	**225.00**
Bowl, stylized black tree with orange flowers on yellow ground, 7" d	**275.00**
Charger, Art Deco girl with hoop skirt and parasol, 15¹/₂" d	**1,500.00**
Dish, figural leaf, yellow, 5" l	**25.00**
Dish, green molded cabbage on lettuce ground, hp red tomatoes, 10¹/₂" l	**55.00**
Jar, cov, ducks in flight, white, blue, and red, multicolored marsh flowers and reeds on base, iridescent cobalt ground, gold rims, molded Foo dog finial, 20" h	**200.00**
Mustard, cov, drum shaped, cream with orange base and top, black lines and drum sticks on cov, 1¹/₄" h	**200.00**
Pitcher, squat, bands of green, blue-green, orange, gray, purple, and black, black handle, 3³/₄" h	**125.00**
Salad Bowl, red tomatoes and molded leaf green border, 3 lobster claw feet, 4" h, 10¹/₂" d	**100.00**
Sugar Shaker, yellow, green, and gold sheaves of wheat, orange and green top, 5" h	**40.00**
Vase, bulbous, stacked enameled hollyhocks with butterflies, cobalt ground, 6" h	**200.00**
Walking Ware, coffeepot, black and blue vertical striped socks, green shoes, 9³/₄" h	**85.00**
Walking Ware, eggcup, chicken, 2-pc, chicken finial, egg with green sash and dots, yellow shoes, 6" h	**20.00**
Walking Ware, plate, blue polka-dot socks, yellow shoes, 4¹/₂" h	**100.00**
Walking Ware, soup bowl, purple polka-dot socks, gray shoes, 3¹/₂" h	**125.00**
Walking Ware, teapot, black and blue vertical striped socks, yellow shoes, 7" h	**75.00**

CARNIVAL CHALKWARE

Inexpensive plaster of Paris figurines made from the 1920s through the 1960s are collected under the generic classification of carnival chalkware because they most frequently were given away as prizes at games of chance. Doll and novelty companies produced them in quantity. Cost was as low as a dollar a dozen. While some pieces are marked and dated, most are not.

References: Thomas G. Morris, *The Carnival Chalk Prize I* (1985), *II* (1994), Prize Publishers, 1998 value update; *Price Guide to Carnival Chalkware, Giveaways and Games,* L-W Book Sales, 1995.

Air Raid Warden, c1940, 14" h	**$100.00**
Bathing Beauty, 1928, 16" h	**150.00**
Black Kewpie, c1935-45, 12" h	**100.00**
Charlie McCarthy, c1938, 16" h	**60.00**
China Boy, incised "C. 1948, J.Y. Jenkins," 13" h	**125.00**
Clown, bank, c1950, 13" h	**40.00**
Dead End Kid, c1930-40, 15" h	**100.00**
Donald Duck, c1934, 13" h	**85.00**
Ferdinand the Bull, bank, c1940-50, 9" h	**50.00**
Fish Bowl Stand, with nude figure posed to peer over bowl, c1930, 15" h	**100.00**
Girl with Banjo, c1940s, 13¹/₄" h	**50.00**
Hula Girl, c1947, 15" h	**150.00**
Jackie Coogan, 17" h	**175.00**
Junior Pig, bank, c1940-50, 9¹/₂" h	**35.00**
King Kong, c1930-40, 12¹/₂" h	**60.00**
Miss America, c1940-50, 15³/₄" h	**55.00**
Pinocchio, c1940, 15" h	**75.00**
Pluto, c1930-40, 6" h	**30.00**
Sailor Boy, c1934, 9" h	**25.00**
Scottish Lass, c1940-50, 15" h	**35.00**
Sea Hag, c1930-40, 8" h	**85.00**
Shirley Temple, c1935-45, 10" h	**65.00**
Snow White, c1937, 14¹/₂" h	**25.00**
Snuffy Smith, c1934-45, 9¹/₄" h	**85.00**
Tom Boy, c1940, 15" h	**40.00**
Tom Boy, c1950, 15" h	**20.00**
Toy Soldier, c1935, 15¹/₂" h	**40.00**
Uncle Sam, c1935, 15" h	**100.00**

Popeye, c1940, 9¹/₂" h, $45.00.

CARNIVAL GLASS

Carnival glass is iridized pressed glass. When collectors refer to "classic" carnival glass, they are talking about patterns manufactured between 1905 (or 1907—scholars do not agree on the exact date when carnival was first introduced) and 1930. Glass manufacturers in Australia, Czechoslovakia, England, Finland, France, Germany, Sweden, and the United States produced carnival glass. Leading American manufacturers include Dugan, Fenton, Imperial, Millersburg, and Northwood.

Carnival glass has been made continuously since its introduction. American manufacturers of carnival glass in the post-1945 period include Boyd, Fenton, Imperial, Mosser, and L. G. Wright. The Jain Glass Works in India made carnival glass from 1935 until 1986.

Period molds survive and are occasionally used to create reproductions. New patterns abound. David Doty notes: "My personal opinion is that there have been far more patterns made in contemporary carnival glass than there were in the classic era."

References: Carl O. Burns, *Imperial Carnival Glass,* Collector Books, 1996, 1998 value update; David Doty, *A Field Guide to Carnival Glass,* Glass Press, 1998; Bill Edwards and Mike Carwile, *Standard Encyclopedia of Carnival Glass, 7th Edition,* Collector Books, 2000; Fenton Art Glass Collectors of America (comp.), *Fenton Glass: The Third Twenty-Five Years Comprehensive Price Guide, 1998,* Glass Press, 1998; William Heacock, *Fenton Glass, The Third Twenty-Five Years, 1956-1980,* O-Val Advertising [Antique Publications], 1989; William Heacock, James Measell and Berry Wiggins, *Dugan Diamond: The Story of Indiana, Pennsylvania, Glass,* Antique Publications, 1993; James Measell and W. C. Roetteis, *The L. G. Wright Glass Company,* Glass Press, 1997; Margaret Whitmyer and Kenn Whitmyer, *Fenton Art Glass: 1907-1939,* Collector Books, 1996, 1999 value update.

Collectors' Clubs: American Carnival Glass Assoc, 9621 Springwater Ln, Miamisburg, OH 45342; Collectible Carnival Glass Assoc (post-1960), 2100 S Fairways Dr, Joplin, MO 64804; International Carnival Glass Assoc, PO Box 306, Mentone, IN 46539.

Fenton, Captive Rose, bowl, amethyst, 9" d, $45.00. Photo courtesy Ray Morykan Auctions.

Dugan, Beaded Shell, mug, amethyst	$75.00
Dugan, Beaded Shell, tumbler, blue	45.00
Dugan, Double Stem Rose, bowl, marigold, ftd, dome, 8¼" d	30.00
Dugan, Fishscales & Beads, bowl, marigold, 6" d	25.00
Dugan, Four Flowers, bowl, marigold, 8¾" d	40.00
Dugan, Grapevine Lattice, plate, marigold, 7" d	100.00
Dugan, Maple Leaf, berry set, amethyst, 6 pcs, stemmed	90.00
Dugan, Maple Leaf, spooner, amethyst	40.00
Dugan, Maple Leaf, sugar, cov, amethyst	35.00
Dugan, Persian Garden, bowl, amethyst, 10¾" d	325.00
Dugan, Puzzle, nappy, white, handled, stemmed	75.00
Dugan, Question Marks nappy, handled, ftd, 3¾" h, 7" w	25.00
Dugan, Round-Up, bowl, white, flat, 9" d	150.00
Dugan, Six Petals, bowl, white, 7½" d	25.00
Dugan, Ski Star, bowl, peach opalescent, tri-fold, dome face, 8" d	45.00
Dugan, Stork and Rushes, tumbler, blue	35.00
Dugan, Wreath of Roses, rose bowl, marigold	30.00
Fenton, Acorn, bowl, red, 7½" d	300.00
Fenton, Autumn Acorns, bowl, green, 9" d	55.00
Fenton, Birds and Cherries, compote, blue, 5¼" h	55.00
Fenton, Blackberry, compote, amethyst, 5½" h	45.00
Fenton, Blackberry, hat face, marigold, banded	16.00
Fenton, Blackberry Bramble, compote, amethyst, 4¾" h	30.00
Fenton, Butterflies, nappy, marigold, handled	30.00
Fenton, Carnival Thistle, bowl, amethyst, 9" d	80.00
Fenton, Chrysanthemum, bowl, blue, ftd, 10¾" d	80.00
Fenton, Coin Dot, bowl, olive, 6¾" d	25.00
Fenton, Dragon and Lotus, bowl, blue, flat, 9" d	40.00
Fenton, Feathered Serpent, bowl, marigold, 9½" d	50.00
Fenton, Heart and Vine, bowl, green, 9" d	65.00
Fenton, Holly, bowl, blue, flat, 9½" d	80.00
Fenton, Knotted Beads, vase, green, 10½" h	10.00
Fenton, Leaf Chain, bowl, white, 8¾" d	65.00
Fenton, Little Flowers, bowl, amethyst, 10" d	65.00
Fenton, Orange Tree, bowl, blue, flat, 8" d	70.00
Fenton, Orange Tree, loving cup, green, 5¾" h	225.00
Fenton, Peacock & Grape, bowl, marigold, flat, 9" d	40.00
Fenton, Persian Medallion, bowl, blue, 5" d	30.00
Fenton, Persian Medallion, nappy, blue, handled	75.00
Fenton, Persian Medallion, rose bowl, marigold	50.00
Fenton, Pond Lily, nappy, blue, handled	45.00
Fenton, Stag & Holly, bowl, blue, spatula foot, 8" d	165.00
Fenton, Stippled Rays, bowl, marigold, flat, 9¼" d	10.00
Fenton, Vintage, fernery, green	25.00
Fenton, Vintage Leaf, plate, green, 7¾" d	100.00
Fenton, Windmill, milk pitcher, marigold	30.00
Imperial, Beaded Bull's Eye, vase, marigold, 11½" h	16.00
Imperial, Frosted Block, bowl, white, 6½" d	15.00
Imperial, Frosted Block, rose bowl, white, 5" d	25.00
Imperial, Grape, berry dishes, amethyst, set of 6	50.00
Imperial, Grape, bowl, amethyst, 6¾" d	30.00
Imperial, Grape, bowl, marigold, 9" d	15.00
Imperial, Grape, tumbler, amethyst	40.00
Imperial, Grape, wine, amethyst	20.00
Imperial, Open Rose, plate, green, 9" d	10.00
Imperial, Ripple, vase, green, 6¾" h	25.00
Imperial, Three-In-One, toothpick holder, green	40.00
Imperial, Tree Bark, water pitcher, marigold	40.00
Jeannette, Iris and Herringbone, bowl, marigold, 12" d	20.00
LG Wright, Banded Grape, tumbler, c1978	35.00
LG Wright, Carnival God and Home, tumbler, purple	45.00
LG Wright, Grape and Daisy, tumbler, purple, c1977	35.00

LG Wright, Grapevine Lattice, tumbler, purple **35.00**
LG Wright, Pony, bowl, crimped, marigold **150.00**
LG Wright, Pony, bowl, crimped, purple, c1976 . . . . **150.00**
LG Wright, Rambler Rose, tumbler, purple, c1977 . . . . **35.00**
LG Wright, Stork and Rushes, bowl, blue opaque **50.00**
LG Wright, Stork and Rushes, creamer, marigold **50.00**
Westmoreland, Louisa, rose bowl, amethyst **50.00**
Westmoreland, Strutting Peacock, covered sugar and
  creamer, amethyst **50.00**

AUCTION PRICES – CARNIVAL GLASS

Gene Harris Antique Auction Center, Carnival Glass, Depression Glass and Art Pottery Auction, October, 30, 1999. Prices include a 10% buyer's premium.

Berry Set, Maple Leaf, Dugan-Diamond, amethyst,
  ftd, 6-pc set **$88.00**
Bowl, Autumn Acorns, Fenton, green 9" d **55.00**
Bowl, Carnival Thistle, Fenton, amethyst, 9" d **77.00**
Bowl, Heart and Vine, Fenton, green, 9" d **66.00**
Bowl, Iris and Herringbone, Jeannette, marigold,
  12" d **17.00**
Bowl, Petal and Fan, Dugan, peach opalescent, 10" d . . **154.00**
Compote, Birds and Cherries, Fenton, blue, 5¼" h **55.00**
Fernery, Vintage, Fenton, green **25.00**
Hat Vase, Blackberry Spray, Fenton, marigold, 3¾" h . . **14.00**
Milk Pitcher, Windmill, Fenton, marigold **28.00**
Nappy, Question Marks, Dugan, ftd, 3¾" h, 7" w **25.00**
Nut Bowl, Grape Delight, Dugan, blue **55.00**
Plate, Apple Blossom Twigs, Dugan-Diamond,
  marigold, 8½" d **66.00**
Powder Jar, Orange Tree, Fenton, blue **55.00**
Rose Bowl, Frosted Block, Imperial, white, 5" d **25.00**
Rose Bowl, Louisa, Westmoreland, amethyst **50.00**
Tumbler, Beaded Shell, Dugan-Diamond, blue **44.00**

CARTOON CHARACTERS

The comic strip was an American institution by the 1920s. Its Golden Age dates from the mid-1930s through the late 1950s. The movie cartoon came of age in the late 1930s and early 1940s as a result of the pioneers at the Disney and Warner Brothers studios. The Saturday morning television cartoon matured through the creative energies of Bill Hanna, Joe Barbera, and Jay Ward.

A successful cartoon character generates hundreds of licensed products. Most collectors focus on a single character or family of characters, e.g., Popeye, Mickey Mouse, or the Flintstones.

References: Bill Bruegman, *Cartoon Friends of the Baby Boom Era*, Cap'n Penny Productions, 1993; Andrea Campbell, *Unauthorized Guide to Ziggy Collectibles*, Schiffer Publishing, 1999; *Cartoon & Character Toys of the 50s, 60s, & 70s: Plastic & Vinyl*, L-W Book Sales, 1995; Ted Hake, *Hake's Guide to Comic Character Collectibles*, Wallace-Homestead, 1993; Jan Lindenberger, *Collecting Garfield*, Schiffer Publishing, 2000; David Longest, *Cartoon Toys & Collectibles*, Collector Books, 1999; Joyce and Terry Losonsky, *The Unauthorized Guide to Smurfs Around the World*, Schiffer Publishing, 1999; Maxine A. Pinsky, *Marx Toys: Robots, Space, Comic, Disney & TV Characters*, Schiffer

Publishing, 1996; Jameson Scott and Jim Rash, *Cartoon Figural Toys*, Schiffer Publishing, 1999; Stuart W. Wells III and Alex G. Malloy, *Comics Collectibles and Their Values*, Wallace-Homestead, Krause Publications, 1996.

Newsletter: *Frostbite Falls Far-Flung Flier* (Rocky & Bullwinkle), PO Box 39, Macedonia, OH 44056.

Collectors' Clubs: The Garfield Connection, 2 Lyons Rd, Armonk, NY 10504; Official Popeye Fan Club, 1001 State St, Chester, IL 62233.

Note: For additional listings see Disneyana, Hanna-Barbera, Peanuts, and Warner Bros.

Alley Oop, tab, litho tin, "See You At The National
  Orange Show & In The Sun Telegram," c1950s, 2" d **$25.00**
Andy Gump, ashtray, brass, relief profile image of smiling Andy yelling "Oh Min!," sgd by Sidney Smith at
  lower right, c1920s, 3¾ x 3¾ x ½" **50.00**
Andy Gump, sheet music, *Andy Gump Fox Trot*, Harold Dixon, 8 pp, cover shows Andy Gump smoking cigars and blowing smoke rings, wearing suit with diamond-studded horseshoe tie, cast of characters at bottom,
  ©1923, 9⅛ x 12¼" **20.00**
Barney Google, game, Barney Google An' Snuffy Smith,
  Milton Bradley, #4416, ©1963 King Features Syndicate, Inc **50.00**
Barney Google, sheet music, *Come On Spark Plug*, Billy Rose and Con Conrad, ©1923 King Features
  Syndicate, Inc, 9¼ x 12" **20.00**
Beany & Cecil, colorforms, ©1962 Colorforms #230 Bob
  Clampett, 8 x 13 x 1" box **75.00**
Beany & Cecil, doll, Talking Beany, vinyl head, hands,
  and feet, orig box, ©1961 Mattel **200.00**
Beany & Cecil, lunch box, vinyl, tan, image of Beany and Cecil having picnic at shoreline, side panel image of Dishonest John and Capt Huffenpuff, Thermos,
  ©1961 Robert E Clampett, 4 x 7 x 3¾" **200.00**
Beany & Cecil, record player, 4-speed, cover lid art of Beany and friends making music on ship as Cecil sings in the ocean, ©1961 Robert E Clampett, 12¼ x
  14 x 5¼" **100.00**
Beetle Bailey, game, Beetle Bailey's Hilarious New Army
  Game, Jaymar, #930, c1950s, 8½ x 16½ x 1¼" box **75.00**
Beetle Bailey, squeaker toy, vinyl, wearing green uniform
  and brown boots, Farmi, ©1978 KFS, 8¾" h **50.00**
Betty Boop, charm, celluloid, Ko-Ko the Clown, wearing bright yellow and red outfit, light green hat and loop,
  c1930s, 1⅛" h **25.00**
Betty Boop, figure, bisque, wearing blue coat, purple and gold belt, red cap and shoes, Fleisher Studios and
  name incised on reverse, 3⅝" h **100.00**
Betty Boop, jointed figure, wood, wearing red dress and
  shoes, black accent hair and face, c1930s, 4¼" h **100.00**
Betty Boop, ring, diecut full color portrait with clear
  acrylic covering on adjustable brass band **10.00**
Blondie, dexterity puzzle, red litho tin frame, colorful image of Blondie, Dagwood, Alexander, and Daisy with bulls-eye center, ©1941 King Features Syndicate,
  Inc, 3½ x 5½" **75.00**
Bullwinkle, squeeze toy, vinyl, figural, Hungerford,
  ©1961 Pat Ward Productions, 12¾" h, 7½" w **200.00**

Calvin & The Colonel, coloring book, #1669, 64 pp, Artcraft, ©1962 Kayro, Inc, 8¼ x 10¾"............... **20.00**

Casper the Friendly Ghost, doll, stuffed, white terrycloth fabric, plastic head, black and red accents, pull-string talker, ©1962 Harvey Famous Cartoons, 16" h **100.00**

Casper the Friendly Ghost, lunch box, vinyl, front scene of Casper and Wendy greeting 3 ghosts flying from haunted house, side panels with various Harvey Cartoons characters, King-Seeley, 7 x 9¼ x 4"......... **175.00**

Dennis the Menace, cup, plastic, figural, Dennis as cowboy in red hat and kerchief, Kellogg's premium, F&F Mold, 3½" h, 2½" d.................. **20.00**

Dennis the Menace, water pistol, plastic, figural, Real Action Toy, ©1954 Hank Ketcham, 5¼" l gun, 2½ x 3⅜ x 6" box **50.00**

Dick Tracy, badge, brass, Dick Tracy Detective Club, c1930s, 1½" h.................... **50.00**

Dick Tracy, booklet, Dick Tracy's Crimefighter's Notebook, redemption coupons from Proctor & Gamble, 2 inside illus of Tracy, 1962 .... **40.00**

Dick Tracy, game, Dick Tracy Detective Game, Famous Artists Syndicate, Chicago, 1937, 6½ x 13" box **55.00**

Dick Tracy, hand puppet, painted soft vinyl head, fabric body, ©1961 Chicago Tribune and New York Daily News Syndicate, 10" h.................. **75.00**

Dick Tracy, Junior Detective Kit Punch-Out Book, Golden Press, ©1962, 7½ x 13"................ **50.00**

Dudley Do-Right, coloring book, #1081, cover shows Dudley on horseback carrying Snidely Whiplash on back tied by rope, unused, 1972 .... **20.00**

Dudley Do-Right, frame tray puzzle, Dudley running in door of Mountie station after rescuing Nell, paddy wagon driving away in background with Snidely Whiplash, Whitman, ©1975 PAT Ward, 8¼ x 11"....... **25.00**

Felix the Cat, cup, ceramic, white, gold accent rim and handle, color image of smiling Felix holding rifle on nervous dog and "Please Felix Don't Shoot" with white cat looking on at center, reverse shows 1" h Felix walking, c1930s, 3" h, 3" d **200.00**

Felix the Cat, figure, wooden, jointed, 1925............ **125.00**

Felix the Cat, license plate, enameled, "Excuse My Dust" with 2 illus of Felix, 5 x 11½" **450.00**

Felix the Cat, pincushion, metal, figural, diecast opening in back contains dark green felt pincushion, c1920s, 3¾" h **200.00**

Felix the Cat, ruler, wooden, 5 different pictures of Felix, American Pencil Co, 7" l **50.00**

Felix the Cat, sheet music, *Felix Kept On Walking*, 8 pp, ©1923 Lawrence Wright Music Co, London, 9¾ x 12⅛" **50.00**

Henry, squeeze toy, rubber, wearing red shirt and socks, black shorts and shoes, stamped "Irwin" on back of head, 1950s, 8½" h.......................... **100.00**

Li'l Abner, birthday card, girl Schmoo with hearts and "Ah' Always Knew Your' An Old Schmoo," inside text "But Not That Old! Happy Birf'day," orig envelope, Superior Greeting Co, Inc, Boston, MA, ©UFS, c1950s, 4 x 8"............................. **5.00**

Little Lulu, Alvin, and Tubby, Cartoon-A-Kit, complete, ©1948 Marjorie H Buell, 10¼ x 13¾ x 1¼" box....... **100.00**

Little Lulu, Colorforms Dress-Up, #589, box shows photo of little girl holding cartoon image of smiling and waving Lulu, complete, orig box, ©1974 Western Publishing Co, Inc.................. **25.00**

Little Lulu, drinking glass, clear glass, red and black image of smiling Lulu jumping rope, reverse image of smiling Baldy the elephant, ©MH Buell, 1940s, 4¾" h, 2⅝" d.................. **75.00**

Little Lulu, jigsaw puzzle, Whitman, #4404, Series 301, cover shows Lulu and Tubby playing tic-tac-toe with tubes of icing on cake, 63 pcs, c1950s, 6¾ x 9 x 2" box.......................... **20.00**

Mammy Yocum, doll, vinyl head and body, corncob pipe in mouth, wearing green felt jacket with yellow trim, brass accent buttons, yellow and black plaid felt skirt, pink leggings, brown vinyl shoes, orig Baby Barry cloth label attached to right sleeve, Missouri Meerschaum foil label on underside of pipe, c1950s, 13½" h **75.00**

Mighty Mouse, game, Mighty Mouse Presents the Game of Hide 'N Seek Rescue Dinky Duck, cover shows Mighty Mouse and various Terrytoons characters, Transogram, ©1961 Terrytoons, 9 x 17½ x 1¾" box **75.00**

Mighty Mouse, game, Mighty Mouse With His Pals Heckle and Jeckle, Milton Bradley, #4701, ©1957 CBS TV Film Sales, Inc, 12 x 12 x 1" box **75.00**

Mighty Mouse, squeaker toy, vinyl, wearing red felt cape with red ribbon attached at neck, ©Terrytoons, 1940s, 9" h **75.00**

Mister Magoo, coloring book, #1137, cover shows Mr Magoo dressed as Shakespearean actor on telephone trying to dial number on cuckoo clock, Whitman, ©1965 UPA Pictures, 8 x 10¾" **15.00**

Mister Magoo, game, Mister Magoo Visits the Zoo, Lowell, ©1961 UPA Pictures, Inc, 9 x 17¾ x 1¾" box.... **100.00**

Moon Mullins, figure, bisque, movable head, wearing black jacket, orange vest, blue pants, yellow bowler and tie, orig wood cigar, name incised on reverse, Germany, c1930s, 3⅝" h **75.00**

Left: Bullwinkle, soaky bottle, Colgate-Palmolive, 1966, $45.00. Right: Popeye, fountain pen, plastic, mkd "King Feature Syndicate Inc. Epenco," 5" h, $75.00. Photo courtesy Collectors Auction Services.

Olive Oyl, birthday card, mechanical, diecut paper, ©1934 King Features, 3½ x 6½"......................**50.00**

Olive Oyl, figure, #2671, vinyl, movable legs, arms, and head, Dakin, c1960s, 9" h.....................**50.00**

Pink Panther, cookie cutter, Hallmark, 1978, 4" h..........**5.00**

Pink Panther, doll, cloth, stuffed, pink, wearing gray silk-like fabric bathrobe with black belt sash, orig paper tag and plastic disk in left ear, Touch of Velvet series, Special Effects, Perth Amboy, NJ, ©1980 United Artists, 15½" h.................................**20.00**

Pink Panther, DS, proposed TV cartoon series contract, sgd by Blake Edwards and Phil DePatie in black ink, onion-skin paper, dated March 30, 1964, to Mirisch Television Inc, 8½ x 11".......................**100.00**

Pogo, badge, litho tin, "I Go Pogo 1956," orange, black and white center image of smiling Pogo, 4" d.........**75.00**

Pogo, jointed figure, vinyl, gray, smiling, full figure, wearing orange shirt with black stripes, holding white felt floral bouquet, white simulated fur shorts, orange accent toes, ©1968 Walt Kelly Poyneter Products, Inc, Japan, 5¼" h................................**100.00**

Popeye, activity book, "Big Popeye Book," 1937, 9¾ x 14¾"......................................**125.00**

Popeye, comic book, #1301, 80 pp, color cov, Saalfield, 1934, 3½ x 8"..............................**20.00**

Popeye, eggcup, china, iridescent glaze, image of Popeye and Olive Oyl skipping in outdoor area, underside mkd "Japan 50," 2¼" h, 1¾" d...........**100.00**

Popeye, key chain/flashlight, hard plastic, red and white, color paper label of Popeye holding can of spinach while eating another, 1950s, 3" l..................**20.00**

Popeye, mug, ceramic, "Eat Spinach" with color image of Popeye and school boy eating spinach, ©King Features, 1940s, 2¾" h......................**75.00**

Popeye, pinback button, "Popeye Is In The News Bee," dark blue and cream Popeye image, 1¼" d.............**75.00**

Popeye, Popeye Bubble Set, contains 2 tin mini tubs, 2 bubble pipes, and bar of figural Popeye head bubble soap, 1936................................**70.00**

Popeye, Popeye Playing Card Game, King Features Syndicate, 1937, orig 5 x 6½" box.................**35.00**

Popeye, pop-up book, *Popeye with the Hag of the Seven Seas,* Blue Ribbon Press, ©1935 Pleasure Books, Chicago, 8 x 9¼"..........................**175.00**

Popeye, View-Master reels, set of 3, "Paint Ahoy, Missile Muscle, and Swee'pea's Edjamacation," orig envelope, ©1962............................**20.00**

Rocky and Bullwinkle, Bullwinkle's Construction Set, soft vinyl tools, nuts, bolts, and wheels to assemble car, Larami, ©1969 PAT Ward, MOC..............**20.00**

Rocky and Bullwinkle, coloring book, Rocky the Flying Squirrel, cover shows Bullwinkle on bucking bronco, Artcraft, #5357, ©1970 PAT Ward, 8 x 10⅝"..........**20.00**

Rocky and Bullwinkle, wallet, brown vinyl, white laced sides, color printed cartoon characters and lettering on front, printed blank ID card and small snap/coin pouch inside, mkd "P.A.T. Ward," 3 x 3½"...........**20.00**

Schmoo, bank, plastic, figural, blue, black face accents, diecut store card at neck with Li'l Abner image and "Al Capp's Li'l Abner Schmoo Bank/Li'l Abner Says– Woo The Schmoo With Lucky Money–Make Your Future Bright And Sunny," ©1948 UP Features Inc, WI Gould & Co, USA, 7" h.......................**75.00**

Schmoo, pencil sharpener, figural, plastic, yellow, black accent design of smiling Schmoo wearing bowtie, center pulls apart to reveal green plastic pencil sharpener inside, c1940s, 1⅛" d....................**100.00**

Smurfs, bank, figural, hard molded plastic, mkd "#25," ©1980 Peyo, 10" h..........................**20.00**

Smurfs, lunch box, with thermos, light blue plastic, color sticker depiction, Thermos, 9 x 7½ x 4"..............**20.00**

Spark Plug, candy container, figural, clear glass, wearing orange blanket, orig red litho tin cov, c1925, 1½ x 4¼ x 3".....................................**50.00**

Spark Plug, hand puppet, soft vinyl head, cloth body, Gund, ©King Features Syndicate, c1950s, 8½ x 10½".....**75.00**

Underdog, coloring book, cover shows Underdog flying to rescue of Sweet Polly, Whitman, #1010, ©1972 TTV & Leonardo Television Productions, 8 x 11"........**20.00**

Underdog, comic book, Underdog March of Comics, #438, 16 pp, ©1978 Leonardo–TTV, 5 x 6¾"..........**15.00**

Underdog, jointed figure, painted hard vinyl head, arms, and legs, foam-type body, Dakin, mkd "©1970 Product of Hong Kong," 6" h...................**100.00**

Wally Walrus, figure, ceramic, full figure, smiling, wearing white shirt, green vest, yellow suspenders with red accent, and brown shoes, foil sticker mkd "copyright Lantz Collection Don Roberto, Los Angeles," c1940s, 5" h....................................**50.00**

Wimpy, figure, wood composition, wearing dark red necktie and black jacket, name on front of base, ©1944 King Features, 4½" h...................**100.00**

Woody Woodpecker, alarm clock, metal, dark blue, brass accent metal bells, full figure smiling Woody image on clock face against white ground, black hands and numbers, ©1972 Walter Lantz Productions, Inc, West Germany, 4¼" h, 3" d..........**50.00**

Woody Woodpecker, cap, cloth, figural, red celluloid diecut rooster comb on top, ©Walter Lantz, c1950s, 8 x 11 x 8"................................**75.00**

Woody Woodpecker, handkerchief, white cloth, various Woody images, #9939, ©Walter Lantz Productions, 1950s, 10¼ x 10¼".........................**20.00**

Woody Woodpecker, toothbrush holder, ceramic, figural, 1940s, 2¾ x 3¾ x 3¾"......................**75.00**

AUCTION PRICES – POPEYE TOYS

Christmas Morning, Mail & Phone Auction #13, November 5, 1999.

Bluto Dippy Dumper, windup, litho tin, c1930s, 9¼" l..**$813.00**

Popeye Figure, jointed wood, flexible arms and legs, c1930s, 11½" h.........................**495.00**

Popeye Floor Puncher, windup, litho tin, Chein, c1930s, 7⅝" h..............................**675.00**

Popeye Heavy Hitter, windup, litho tin, Chein, c1920s-30s, 11⅝" h.......................**3,800.00**

Popeye in a Barrel, windup, litho tin, Chein, c1930s, 7" h...............................**550.00**

Popeye/Olive Oyl Jigger, windup, litho tin, Marx, c1930s, 6½" h............................**797.00**

Popeye Overhead Puncher, windup, litho tin, Chein, c1920s-30s, 9½" h.......................**4,900.00**

Popeye the Pilot, windup, litho tin, Marx, c1930s, 8" wing span............................**700.00**

CATALINA POTTERY

The Catalina Pottery, located on Santa Catalina Island, California, was founded in 1927 for the purpose of making clay building products. Decorative and functional pottery was added to the company's line in the early 1930s. A full line of color-glazed dishes was made between 1931 and 1937.

Gladding, McBean and Company bought Catalina Pottery in 1937, moved production to the mainland, and closed the island pottery. Gladding, McBean continued to use the Catalina trademark until 1947.

References: Jack Chipman, *Collector's Encyclopedia of California Pottery, Second Edition,* Collector Books, 1999; Steve and Aisha Hoefs, *Catalina Island Pottery,* published by authors, 1993.

Ashtray, bear, 3¼ x 5½".............................	**$450.00**
Ashtray, sombrero, Toyon red, 2½ x 4".................	**450.00**
Bookends, pr, seated monk with book, green, c1932, 5" h.............................	**1,000.00**
Candleholder, eggcup shape, Manchu yellow, 4½" h.......	**75.00**
Charger, green, yellow, and blue painted banjo player, ivory ground, red clay body, 12½" d.............	**450.00**
Coffee Mug, Catalina blue......................	**20.00**
Creamer, hexagonal	**150.00**
Creamer and Covered Sugar, powder blue matte glaze, rope handle, c1936......................	**90.00**
Cream Pitcher, turquoise.....................	**225.00**
Cup and Saucer, matte green....................	**35.00**
Cup and Saucer, powder blue....................	**85.00**
Decanter, bulbous, yellow glossy glaze, 7½" h.........	**60.00**
Dessert Bowl, red........................	**15.00**
Dish, shell shape, scalloped edge, white, 14" d.........	**150.00**
Plate, kissing parrots, multicolored, black ground, 10½" d............................	**850.00**
Plate, Moorish design, turquoise, white, orange, and black, c1932......................	**350.00**
Platter, turquoise, 13" d.....................	**75.00**
Punch Cup, Toyon red.......................	**50.00**
Salt and Pepper Shakers, pr, gourd shape, green...........	**70.00**
Teapot, cov, powder blue matte glaze, rope handle.......	**200.00**
Tumbler, orange, 4" h......................	**20.00**
Vase, #325, turquoise, 5" h....................	**300.00**
Vase, #385, Polynesian, 6¾" h..................	**250.00**
Vase, Mandarin yellow, 5½" h..................	**135.00**

CATALOGS

There are three basic types of catalogs: (1) manufacturers' catalogs that are supplied primarily to distributors, (2) trade catalogs supplied to the merchant community and general public, and (3) mail-order catalogs designed for selling directly to the consumer. Montgomery Ward issued its first mail-order catalog in 1872. Sears Roebuck's came out in 1886.

A catalog revolution occurred in the 1980s with the arrival of specialized catalogs and select zip code mailing niche marketing. In the 1990s catalogs began appearing on the Internet. Many predict this will make the printed catalog obsolete by the mid-21st century.

References: Ron Barlow and Ray Reynolds, *The Insider's Guide to Old Books, Magazines, Newspapers and Trade Catalogs,* Windmill Publishing, 1995; Norman E. Martinus and Harry L. Rinker, *Warman's Paper,* Wallace-Homestead, 1994.

1922, Kirsch Mfg Co, Sturgis, MI, 20 pp, rod and window draping book, 1922, 6 x 9"....................	**$20.00**
1923, Charles Williams Stores, NY, #39, 740 pp, spring and summer, 8¼ x 11".............................	**45.00**
1925, Larkin Co Inc, Buffalo, NY, #93, 204 pp, spring and summer, cleaning supplies, housewares, furniture, 8 x 11".............................	**40.00**
1926, Buick Motor Co, Flint, MI, 62 pp, "The Story of the Greatest Buick Ever Built," 7½ x 10¼"................	**65.00**
1928, MW Savage Co, Minneapolis, MN, #53, 512 pp, fall and winter, 8¼ x 11"......................	**50.00**
1928, WW Kimball Co, Chicago, IL, 8 pp, phonographs, sepia illus, 6 x 8½"........................	**25.00**
1929, Strohber Piano Co, Chicago, IL, 32 pp, 6¼ x 9".....	**30.00**
1929, Union Cutlery Co, Olean, NY, 13 pp, 6 x 9"........	**45.00**
1930, American Fashion Co, New York, NY, 64 pp, 10 x 13½"..........................	**12.00**
1930, American Steel Products, Macomb, IL, 32 pp, Macomb poultry raising equipment, 6 x 9".............	**20.00**
1931-32, Taprell Loomis & Co, Eastman Kodak Co, 64 pp, fall, photo mounts and frames, 7½ x 10½"........	**20.00**
1932, Butler Brothers, NY, #2936, 272 pp, home goods, Halloween goods, dolls, and toys, 9¼ x 13¼"...........	**75.00**
1932, Montgomery Ward, Baltimore, MD, #116, 598 pp, 60th anniversary issue, spring and summer, 9½ x 13¼"....	**65.00**
1934, Dent Hardware, Fullerton, PA, 4 pp, cap pistols, 8½ x 11"........................	**25.00**
1935, A Peters, Holland, MI, 32 pp, art needle work and sewing, 8 x 10¼"........................	**15.00**
1938, Elwood Pattern Works, Indianapolis, IN, 72 pp, photographic equipment, 3½ x 6"....................	**25.00**
1938, Fulton Bag & Cotton Mills, Atlanta, GA, #38, 18 pp, canvas goods, 8½ x 11"......................	**15.00**
1938, Olson Rug Co, Chicago, IL, 58 pp, 7¼ x 8½"........	**25.00**
1948, American Mask Mfg Co, Findlay, OH, 23 pp, 6 x 9"............................	**30.00**

1932-33, Lincoln Chair and Novelty Co., sepia photo illus, 9 x 12", $45.00.

1948, Dave Cook Sporting Goods, Denver, CO, 4 pp,
70th anniversary, 8½ x 11" **30.00**
1949, Promotional Publishing Co, New York, NY, 24 pp,
"A Christmas Dream," toys and games, comic book
format, 7 x 10¼" **15.00**
1954, Boy Scouts of America, Altoona, PA, 24 pp, scout-
ing supplies, 6 x 9" **35.00**
1957, Becker-Hazleton Co, Dubuque, IA, 180 pp, gifts,
glassware, and housewares, 8½ x 11". **25.00**
1957, Sears, Roebuck & Co, Boston, MA, 1516 pp, fall
and winter, 8 x 11" **40.00**
1958, Premium Sales Co, Racine, WI, #53, 78 pp, mid-
year general merchandise, 8½ x 11". **20.00**
1959, Montgomery Ward, Albany, NY, 972 pp, spring
and summer, 9¼ x 13¼" **40.00**
1960-61, E&J Cigar Co, 136 pp, gifts, cigars, jewelry,
housewares, etc, special bound, 8½ x 11" **25.00**
1963, Albert Constantine & Son, New York, NY, 128 pp,
woodworking tools, hardware, 7 x 10" **20.00**
1968, Herter's Inc, Waseca, MN, #78, 598 pp, sporting
goods, 8½ x 10¾". **30.00**

CAT COLLECTIBLES

Unlike dog collectors who tend to collect objects portraying a single breed, cat collectors collect anything and everything with a cat
image or in the shape of a cat. It makes no difference if an object
is old or new, realistic or abstract. Cat collectors love it all.

The popularity of cats as pets increased significantly in the
1980s. Many contemporary 1980s cat collectibles, e.g., Kliban's
cats and Lowell Davis porcelains featuring cats, are experiencing
strong secondary markets. Remember, this market is highly speculative. Serious cat collectors stick to vintage (pre-1965) cat collectibles that have withstood the test of time.

References: Marbena Jean Fyke, *Collectible Cats, Book II,*
Collector Books, 1996; J. L. Lynnlee, *Purrrfection: The Cat,* Schiffer
Publishing, 1990.

Collectors' Club: Cat Collectors, PO Box 150784, Nashville, TN
37215-0784.

Bank, cheshire cat shaped, ceramic, made in Japan, 6¼
x 3¼" h. **$20.00**
Bookends, ceramic, weighted, tan, black cat with white
paws on 1 side, gray mouse with mallet on other side,
dated 1983, 5¾" h. **25.00**
Candleholder, figural cat, black metal, MSR Imports
label, 1986, 10½" h. **12.00**
Creamer, Kliban Cat, facsimile Kliban signature on bot-
tom, Sigma, 8" l. **25.00**
Dish, figural Siamese cat face, porcelain, incised
"Porcelain Wade England," 3" w. **50.00**
Figurine, Siamese, Norcrest, 11½" h. **25.00**
Figurine, white Persian with gray specks, plastic eyes,
from "Sparklers" line, incised "Roselane USA,"
1950s, 3½" h, price for pr **75.00**
Grow Chart, Dr Seuss Cat in the Hat, 1978, MIP **40.00**
Invitation, Purina Christmas Get Together, Santa with
basket, basket filled with Purina products, red and
black, 1927. . . . . **20.00**
Pinback Button, Cat's Paw Shoe Heels, yellow, black,
and white, Foster Rubber Co **15.00**

Figure, celluloid, 5¼" l, $8.00. Photo courtesy Ray Morykan
Auctions.

Pinback Button, sepia Morris the Cat image on orange
ground, brown lettering "Purr-sonal Friend of Morris
the 9-Lives Cat," c1970-80s **10.00**
Trinket Box, porcelain, brown base, crackle light and
dark gray cat on lid, "Takahashi Japan" paper label,
3½" h **10.00**

CD'S

CD technology was first introduced in 1982. Although the technology is recent and many compact discs are still available commercially, a dedicated group of CD collectors has emerged.

Collectors focus on three main categories: (1) promotional
issues, including CD singles and radio programs on compact discs,
(2) limited edition discs, especially those with creative or innovative packaging, and (3) out-of-print discs. At the moment,
American collectors are focused almost exclusively on American
manufactured CDs.

As in other emerging collecting categories, prices can vary dramatically. Comparison shopping is advised. Bootleg discs have little to no value. Blues, rock, and pop titles dominate the secondary
collecting market. Country and jazz titles follow. Few collectors
seek classical titles.

References: Gregory Cooper, *Collectible Compact Disc: Price
Guide 2,* Collector Books, 1998; Fred Heggeness, *Goldmine's
Promo Record & CD Price Guide, 2nd Edition,* Krause
Publications, 1998.

Periodicals: *DISCoveries Magazine,* PO Box 1050, Dubuque, IA
52004; *Goldmine,* 700 E State St, Iola, WI 54990; *ICE Magazine,*
PO Box 3043, Santa Monica, CA 90408.

Allman Brothers Band, *It Ain't Over Yet,* Epic 2258, promotional, 1990 . . . . **$5.00**
Axton, Hoyt, *Heartbreak Hotel,* DPI 5001, promotional,
1990. . . . . **5.00**
Bananarama, *Tripping on Your Love,* London 568, pro-
motional, silkscreened, picture sleeve, 1991 . . . . **8.00**
Costello, Elvis, *The Other Side of Summer,* WB4781,
promotional, 1991 . . . . **4.00**
Crosby, Stills, Nash & Young, *American Dream,* Atlantic
2497, promotional, silkscreened picture, 1988 . . . . **10.00**

Foreigner, *Only Heaven Knows,* Atlantic 4242, promotional, silkscreened, rear insert, 1991 . . . . **4.00**

Guns N Roses, *Welcome to the Jungle,* Geffen 2668, promotional, picture sleeve **12.00**

Heart, *Secret,* Capitol 79468, promotional, picture sleeve, 1990 . . . . **8.00**

Jett, Joan, *Love Hurts,* Epic 2013, promotional, silkscreened, rear insert, 1989 . . . . **6.00**

Judas Priest, *I Am a Rocker,* Columbia 3030, promotional, silkscreened **8.00**

Lennon, Julian, *You're the One,* Atlantic 2741, promotional, picture sleeve, 1989 . . . . **5.00**

Meatloaf, *Bat Out of Hell II: Back Into Hell,* MCA 10699, promotional, logo on black, custom sticker **10.00**

Midler, Bette, *Under the Boardwalk,* Atlantic 2772, promotional, rear insert, 1988 . . . . **5.00**

Moody Blues, *I Know You're Out There Somewhere,* Threshold 15, promotional, picture sleeve, 1988 . . . . **8.00**

Nelson, Willie, *A Horse Called Music,* Columbia 45046, promotional, silkscreened, rear insert, special dj version, 1989. . . . . **15.00**

Warner Bros Symphony Orchestra, *Bugs Bunny on Broadway,* WB 26494, promotional, silkscreened, picture sleeve, 1991 . . . . **15.00**

CERAMIC ARTS STUDIO

Lawrence Rabbett and Ruben Sand founded the Ceramic Arts Studio, Madison, Wisconsin, in January 1941 for the purpose of making wheel-thrown ceramics. During World War II the company began production on a line of high-end molded figurines that were sold in jewelry stores and large department stores. The flood of cheap imported ceramics in the early 1950s led to the demise of the studio in 1955.

Reference: Mike Schneider, *Ceramic Arts Studio,* Schiffer Publishing, 1994.

Collectors' Club: Ceramic Arts Studio Collectors Assoc, PO Box 46, Madison, WI 53701.

Ashtray, hippopotamus, open mouth, 3¼ x 4¼" **$35.00**
Figure, Bedtime Boy and Girl, 4½" h **35.00**
Figure, bride and groom, 4¾" bride, 4⅞" groom **110.00**
Figure, Bruce and Beth, chartreuse. **60.00**
Figure, cowboy and cowgirl **75.00**
Figure, Hans and Katrinka, yellow **65.00**
Figure, Hansel and Gretel, 4¼" h **35.00**
Figure, harem girl, reclining, 3½ x 6¼" **45.00**
Figure, Lilibelle, brown hair. **65.00**
Figure, Polish boy and girl **50.00**
Figure, Rhumba Dancers, green and maroon **100.00**
Figure, Sambo, 3¼" h **300.00**
Figure, scratching kitten, white, 1⅞" h **15.00**
Figure, Wee Swedish Boy, 3⅛" h **15.00**
Head Vase, Becky, 5⅛" h **75.00**
Head Vase, Manchu, 7½" h **50.00**
Head Vase, Sven, 6⅜" h **75.00**
Planter, Loreli, "Betty Harrington/Ceramic Arts Studio" inkstamp mark, 6½ x 6". **75.00**
Salt and Pepper Shakers, pr, boy and girl kneeling on chairs **90.00**
Salt and Pepper Shakers, pr, horse heads, 3⅜" h **30.00**

Salt and Pepper Shakers, pr, Thai and Thai-Thai **45.00**
Shelf Sitter, Collie dog, 5⅛" h **35.00**
Shelf Sitter, Maurice and Michelle **50.00**
Wall Plaques, pr, Harlequin and Columbine. **110.00**
Wall Plaques, pr, Zor and Zorina, 9" l **50.00**

CEREAL BOXES

Ready-to-eat breakfast cereal appeared around 1900. Until the 1930s, most advertising and packaging was targeted toward mothers. The popularity of children's radio programs and their sponsorship by cereal manufacturers shifted the focus to youngsters.

By the 1950s cereal premiums inside the box and cutouts on cereal box backs were a standard feature. Cereal boxes also were used to promote television shows and the personalities and characters that appeared on them. By the early 1970s, cereal manufacturers issued special promotional boxes, many of which featured local and national sports heroes.

As the 21st century begins, cereal box prices are highly speculative. Market manipulators are at work. Crossover collectors are paying premium prices for character and personality boxes whose long-term collectibility is uncertain.

References: Scott Bruce, *Cereal Box Bonanza: The 1950's,* Collector Books, 1995; Scott Bruce, *Cereal Boxes & Prizes; 1960s,* Flake World Publishing, 1998; Scott Bruce and Bill Crawford, *Cerealizing America: The Unsweetened Story of American Breakfast Cereals,* Faber and Faber, 1995.

Collectors' Club: Sugar-Charged Cereal Collectors, 5400 Cheshire Meadows Way, Fairfax, VA 22032.

Note: All boxes are in good condition.

Cheerios, General Mills, Wyatt Earp pistol and target game on back, 1955, 8½" h **$125.00**
Corn-Fetti, Post/General Mills, Captain Jolly comic book offer, 1954, 9½" h **150.00**
Corn Flakes, Kellogg's, Dragnet whistle inside, 1955, 9½" h **100.00**

Corn Flakes, Kellogg's, Terry Labonte, 1995, 10" h, $5.00.

Corn Flakes, Kellogg's, Jet-Drive Whistle brochure, 1950, 14" h **50.00**

Corn Flakes, Kellogg's, Superman belt offer, 1955-56, 9½" h **250.00**

Frosted Flakes, Kellogg's, Superman stereo-pix on back, 1954, 9½" h **300.00**

Mother Oats Oatmeal, Quaker, Gabby Hayes comic book offer, 1951, 10" h **75.00**

Muffets Shredded Wheat, Quaker, Sgt Preston trail kit offer, 1956, 8" h **125.00**

Puffed Rice, Quaker, Gabby Hayes cannon ring offer, 1951, 9" h **350.00**

Puffed Rice, Quaker, Sgt Preston ore detector offer, 1952, 9" h **125.00**

Puffed Wheat, Quaker, Gabby Hayes western wagons offer, 1952, 9" h **200.00**

Rice Krispies, Kellogg's, Annie Oakley doll offer, 1955, 10¼" h **100.00**

Rice Krispies, Kellogg's, Howdy Doody inflatable doll offer, 1953, 8" h **300.00**

Sugar Frosted Flakes, Kellogg's, sample box, 1952, 4" h **50.00**

Sugar Jets, General Mills, Mickey Mouse ring inside, 1956, 8½" h **300.00**

Sugar Rice Krinkles, Post/General Foods, flip-top inside, 1955, 9" h **45.00**

Wheat Chex, Ralston Purina, Space Patrol magic space picture and space binoculars offer, 1953, 9" h **350.00**

Wheaties, General Mills, Lone Ranger Moon Flower mask on back, 1954, 8½" h **150.00**

CHILDREN'S DISHES

Children's dish sets date back to the Victorian era. In the 1920s and 1930s American glass companies manufactured sets of children's dishes in their most popular patterns. Inexpensive ceramic sets came from Germany and Japan. Injection molded plastic sets first appeared in the late 1940s. By the 1950s, miniature melamine plastic sets mimicked the family's everyday plastic service.

Most children's dish sets were designed to be used by their owners for tea and doll parties. At the moment, collecting emphasis remains on pre-war sets.

References: Maureen Batkin, *Gifts for Good Children Part II: The History of Children's China 1890-1990*, Richard Dennis Publications, n.d., distributed by Antique Collectors' Club; Lorraine Punchard, *Playtime Pottery and Porcelain From Europe and Asia*, Schiffer Publishing, 1996; Lorraine Punchard, *Playtime Pottery and Porcelain From The United Kingdom and The United States*, Schiffer Publishing, 1996.

Collectors' Club: Toy Dish Collectors Club, PO Box 159, Bethlehem, CT 06751.

CHINA

Blue Willow, bowl, 3½" d **$35.00**
Blue Willow, casserole, 5" d **40.00**
Blue Willow, gravy boat **25.00**
Blue Willow, grill plate, 4¼" d **35.00**
Blue Willow, plate, 5" d **15.00**
Blue Willow, sugar, cov, 2¾" h **12.00**
Blue Willow, teapot, cov, 3¾" h **45.00**

Edwin Knowles China, creamer and sugar, Dutch figures **15.00**
Homer Laughlin, plate, Eggshell, pink rose **8.00**
Japan, casserole, Phoenix Bird **30.00**
Japan, creamer and sugar, Chinaman **60.00**
Japan, Little Hostess Tea Set, 6 pcs **100.00**
Japan, plate, Sunset **4.00**
Japan, platter, Embossed Leaf, burgundy **4.00**
Japan, salt and pepper shakers, pr, Moss Rose, 1⅝" h **20.00**
Japan, sugar, cov, Sunset, 3⅛" h **8.00**
Japan, teapot, cov, Floral Medallion **15.00**
Nippon, plate, floral print, 5" d **4.00**
Noritake, casserole, cov, Bluebird **35.00**
Noritake, cocoa pot, cov, Otter **125.00**
Noritake, cup and saucer, Silhouette **20.00**
Occupied Japan, cup and saucer, floral, white ground **8.00**
Salem China, cup and saucer, Victory **6.00**
Salem China, teapot, cov, Godey Prints **30.00**
Shenango China, mug, Little Bo Peep **20.00**

GLASS

Akro Agate, Concentric Rib, set, 8 pcs, opaque green and white **$30.00**
Akro Agate, Concentric Rib, teapot, cov, opaque white **12.00**
Akro Agate, Concentric Ring, cereal bowl, blue marbleized **40.00**
Akro Agate, Concentric Ring, sugar, cov, opaque blue **20.00**
Akro Agate, Concentric Ring, teapot, cov, opaque blue **40.00**
Akro Agate, Interior Panel, creamer, pink **25.00**
Akro Agate, Interior Panel, plate, azure blue **8.00**
Akro Agate, Interior Panel, set, 16 pcs, azure blue **250.00**
Akro Agate, J Pressman, demitasse cup, pink **25.00**
Akro Agate, J Pressman, demitasse cup and saucer, green . . . **20.00**
Akro Agate, Raised Daisy, plate, blue **10.00**
Akro Agate, Raised Daisy, tumbler, beige **25.00**
Akro Agate, Stacked, creamer and sugar **25.00**
Akro Agate, Stacked, cup and saucer **20.00**
Akro Agate, Stacked, plate **12.00**
Akro Agate, Stacked, teapot lid **25.00**
Fry Glass, Kidibake Set, grill plate, blue **25.00**
Fry Glass, Kidibake Set, pie plate, clear opal **25.00**
Hazel Atlas, 20th Century, cup and saucer, fired-on red **7.00**
Hazel Atlas, 20th Century, cup and saucer, white, cobalt stripe **6.00**
Hazel Atlas, Moderntone, creamer and sugar, rust **20.00**
Hazel Atlas, Moderntone, cup, pink **10.00**
Hazel Atlas, Moderntone, cup, rust **8.00**
Hazel Atlas, Mother Goose, tumbler, cobalt **30.00**
Hazel Atlas, Three Little Pigs, bowl, white milk glass, 5¾" d **12.00**
Hocking, Howdy Wrangler, tumbler, ruby **20.00**
Jeannette, Cherry Blossom, creamer and sugar, pink **45.00**
Jeannette, Cherry Blossom, set, 14 pcs, delphite **325.00**
Jeannette, Doric & Pansy, saucer, pink **7.00**
Jeannette, Doric & Pansy, set, 14 pcs, pink **225.00**
Jeannette, Homespun, plate, crystal **4.00**
Jeannette, Homespun, teapot, cov, pink **100.00**
McKee, Betty Jane Set, Glasbake, 6 pcs, crystal **75.00**
McKee, Laurel, creamer, jade green **25.00**
McKee, Laurel, cup and saucer, Scottie decal **55.00**
Pyrex, custard **1.00**
Pyrex, set, 6 pcs **125.00**
US Glass, Nursery Rhyme, punch set, 7 pcs, crystal **225.00**

CHILDREN'S TEA SETS

Chein, Disneyland, 7 pcs, 1950s $125.00
Ohio Art, Bluebird and Blossoms, 5 pcs, 1920s 95.00
Ohio Art, Fairies, 13 pcs, 1930s 225.00
Ohio Art, King of Tarts, 16 pcs, BK Benjain, 1940s 160.00
Ohio Art, pink floral, 7 pcs, 1950s 35.00
Ohio Art, Queen of Hearts, 9 pcs, 1960s 45.00
Ohio Art, "She Loves Me Not," 8 pcs, Elaine Ends
 Hileman, 1949 . . . . 100.00
Ohio Art, Swiss Miss, 13 pcs, 1967 . . . . 125.00

CHINTZ CHINA

Chintz patterned goods owe their origin to Indian chintes, fabrics decorated with richly hued flowers and brightly plumed mythical birds that were imported to England from India in the 17th century. Although English Staffordshire potters produced chintz pattern ceramics as early as the 1820s, the golden age of chintz decorated ceramics dates from 1920 through 1940. Although dozens of post–World War II patterns were made, collectors prefer pre-war examples.

References: Jo Anne Peterson Welsh, *Chintz Ceramics, 3rd Edition,* Schiffer Publishing, 2000; Susan Scott, *The Charlton Standard Catalogue of Chintz, 3rd Edition,* Charlton Press, 1999.

Collectors' Clubs: Chintz Connection, PO Box 222, Riverdale, MD 20738; Chintz World International, PO Box 50888, Pasadena, CA 91115.

Note: See Royal Winton for additional listings.

Biscuit Barrel, Brama/Springtime, chrome lid, Midwinter . . . $500.00
Bonbon, Coral, Midwinter 50.00
Bonbon, Marigold, Lord Nelson 45.00
Bowl, Rosalynde, James Kent, 9" d 125.00
Bread and Butter Plate, Brama, Midwinter, 6" d 75.00
Bread and Butter Plate, Rose Chintz, Johnson Bros, 6½" d . . . 25.00
Breakfast Set, Apple Blossom, James Kent 1,200.00
Bud Vase, Marigold, trumpet shape, black int, 5½" h 225.00
Bud Vase, Marina, Elijah Cotton, Lord Nelson 165.00
Bud Vase, Primula, James Kent 150.00
Bud Vase, Rosalynde, James Kent, 2½" h 175.00
Butter Dish, Spring Blossom, square, Crown Ducal 325.00
Cake Plate, Chintz, maple leaf shape, Blue Ridge 50.00
Cake Plate, Primula, James Kent, 11" sq 175.00
Cake Stand, 3-tier, Heather, Lord Nelson 150.00
Candlestick, Beaumont, straight stick on round base,
 8½" h 100.00
Celery, Chintz, Blue Ridge 20.00
Center Bowl, Ivory Chintz, Iris shape, black int with pink
 roses border, chintz bottom and ext, 8" d, 3" h 500.00
Coffeepot, Ascot, Crown Ducal, 3 cup 550.00
Coffeepot, Du Barry, James Kent 750.00
Coffeepot, Rosalynde, James Kent 750.00
Compote, Purple Chintz, yellow border, octagonal,
 Crown Ducal 500.00
Compote, Tapestry, ftd, James Kent 120.00
Creamer, Chintz, Blue Ridge, pedestal foot 25.00
Creamer and Sugar, Green Tulip, Lord Nelson 150.00
Creamer and Sugar, Rose Chintz, Johnson Bros 75.00
Cup and Saucer, Briar Rose, Elijah Cotton, Lord Nelson 125.00

Cup and Saucer, Du Barry, James Kent 100.00
Cup and Saucer, Rosalynde, James Kent 85.00
Cup and Saucer, Rosetime, Lord Nelson 80.00
Jam Pot, Lorna Doone/Bird Chintz, chrome lid, round,
 Midwinter 100.00
Jam Pot, Tapestry, James Kent 135.00
Jug, Apple Blossom, James Kent 325.00
Jug, Blue Chintz, Crown Ducal, 6½" h 650.00
Jug, Du Barry, James Kent, 5¾" h 400.00
Jug, Primula, Crown Ducal, 3¾" h 250.00
Jug, Silverdale, Dutch shape, James Kent, 3¾" h 200.00
Nut Dish, Apple Blossom, James Kent 55.00
Nut Dish, Du Barry, James Kent 55.00
Plate, Country Lane, Lord Nelson, 8½" d 100.00
Plate, Du Barry, James Kent, 11" d 150.00
Plate, Marigold, James Kent, 7¾" h 150.00
Plates, Blue Chintz, black trim, 8" d, price for set of 6 . . . . . 850.00
Platter, Florida Chintz, octagonal, black trim, 15¼ x 12" . . 2,200.00
Relish Dish, Country Lane, Lord Nelson 125.00
Salt and Pepper Shakers, pr, Apple Blossom, James Kent 120.00
Salt and Pepper Shakers, pr, Black Beauty, Lord Nelson 125.00
Salt and Pepper Shakers, pr, Silverdale, James Kent 65.00
Sandwich Tray, Lorna Doone, Midwinter 135.00
Saucer Boat and Stand, Rosetime, Elijah Cotton, Lord
 Nelson 180.00
Sugar Bowl, Hydrangea, octagonal, James Kent 85.00
Sugar Shaker, Brama, metal top, Midwinter 375.00
Stacking Teapot, Flow Blue Chintz, Lord Nelson 475.00
Stacking Teapot, Marina, Lord Nelson 800.00
Teacup and Saucer, Coral, Midwinter 100.00
Teacup and Saucer, Marigold, Lord Nelson 85.00
Teapot, Du Barry, James Kent, 3 cup 600.00
Tea Set, Blue Chintz, includes 4-cup covered teapot,
 covered sugar, and creamer, white handles and finials
 with black trim 1,500.00
Tray, Hydrangea, James Kent, 5 x 8" 75.00
Vase, Purple Chintz, 6-sided with high shoulders and
 trumpet-top opening, narrowing to base, 9½" h 625.00

CHRISTMAS COLLECTIBLES

The tradition of a month-long Christmas season beginning the day after Thanksgiving was deeply entrenched by the end of the first World War. By the 1930s retailers from small town merchants to large department stores saw Christmas season sales account for 25% and more of their annual sales volume.

Beginning in the 1960s the length of the Christmas season was extended. By the mid-1990s Christmas decorations appeared in many stores and malls the day after Halloween. Today, some Christmas catalogs arrive in mail boxes as early as September.

References: Robert Brenner, *Christmas Past, 3rd Edition,* Schiffer Publishing, 1996; Robert Brenner, *Christmas Revisited, 2nd Edition,* Schiffer Publishing, 1999; Robert Brenner, *Christmas Through the Decades Revised,* Schiffer Publishing, 2000; Beth Dees, *Santa's Price Guide to Contemporary Christmas Collectibles,* Krause Publications, 1997; Jill Gallina, *Christmas Pins Past and Present,* Collector Books, 1996; George Johnson, *Christmas Ornaments, Lights & Decorations* (1987, 1998 value update), *Vol. II* (1997), *Vol. III* (1997), Collector Books; Polly and Pam Judd, *Santa Dolls & Figurines Price Guide: Antique to Contemporary, Revised,* Hobby House Press, 1994; Chris Kirk, *The Joy of*

Christmas Collecting, L-W Book Sales, 1994, 1998 value update; Mary Morrison, *Snow Babies, Santas and Elves: Collecting Christmas Bisque Figures,* Schiffer Publishing, 1993; Tim Neely, *Goldmine Christmas Record Price Guide,* Krause Publications, 1997.

Newsletter: *Creche Herald,* 117 Crosshill Rd, Wynnewood, PA 19096.

Collectors' Clubs: Golden Glow of Christmas Past, 6401 Winsdale St, Minneapolis, MN 55427; Silver Ornament Society, PO Box 903, Laramie, WY 82073.

Note: See Hallmark for additional listings.

Activity Book,*The Night Before Christmas,* 6 pp, punch-out pcs for assembly of Christmas Eve scene, Whitman, ©1960, unused, 10 x 14" **$50.00**

Badge, celluloid, "Merry Christmas," wreath with holly leaves and berries border, 1950s, 3½" d **15.00**

Bank, painted plaster, Mrs Claus seated on chair while knitting stocking, c1940-50s, 6 x 8 x 13" **50.00**

Banner, paper, Reddy Kilowatt portrait as Santa, Christmas motif and "Merry Christmas" in white on red ground, orig cardboard mailer tube, complete with Reddy mailing label from Detroit Edison Co, postmarked Dec 20, 1962 . . . . **100.00**

Blotter, cardboard under celluloid cover, Santa placing wreath on doorway as sleigh and reindeer await, c1920s, 2¾ x 7½" **20.00**

Book, *Visions of St Nick in Action,* Philips Publishers, Inc, 1950 . . . . **10.00**

Box, Whitman's Candy, diecut cardboard, Santa in open sleigh being pulled by single reindeer, Dolly Toy Co, 1950s, 3½ x 11 x 7" **50.00**

Cake Pan, aluminum, tree, Mirro, 9" h **15.00**

Calendar, 1965, "Things Go Better With Coke," Santa on ladder by tree, children with toys **50.00**

Calendar Card, 1943, celluloid, Santa on snowy rooftop, International Hod Carriers' Building and Common Laborers' Union of America, 2¼ x 3¾" **15.00**

Candy Container, boot, red and gold chenille, holly sprig on side, Japan, 6" h **80.00**

Candy Container, mandolin, cardboard, tinsel neck cords and trim, removable back, Butler Brothers adv, USA, 1920s, 5" l **60.00**

Candy Container, papier-mâché, Santa, white with red and black trim, mesh bag. **45.00**

Candy Container, Santa in boot, silver foil boot, chenille trim, plaster Santa face, Japan, post-1920, 6" h **75.00**

Candy Container, sled, Santa with sack, mica coated cardboard, Japan, 1920-30s, 4" h **50.00**

Catalog, Santa's Playthings 1955-56, 32 pp, 8 x 10¼" **50.00**

Catalog, Sears 1959 Christmas Book, 496 pp, 8 x 11" **20.00**

Child's Spoon, holly berry and leaf markings on handle front topped by small brick chimney with Santa from waist up holding doll house and Christmas tree gifts, bowl inscribed "Merry Christmas," reverse handle tip mkd "Sterling," c1930s, 3½" l **20.00**

Cookie Jar, winking Santa, American Bisque. **75.00**

Creche, figure, Baby Jesus, Hummel, 1951, 2" h **60.00**

Creche, figure, stable animal, plaster, Germany, 1950s **5.00**

Creche, set, 16 pcs, ceramic, painted, 1950s, 5" h **45.00**

Blotter, 1940s, 6 x 3", $5.00.

Cup and Saucer, Santa decal, Universal Pottery, c1940-50s **8.00**

Decoration, star, tinsel and wire, 1950s **10.00**

Figure, Santa, painted bisque, 1930s, 3" h **50.00**

Figure, Santa climbing down chimney, plaster, 1940s, 11" h **50.00**

Figure, Santa holding gift, plastic face, white satin suit, cotton beard, 1940-50s, 28" h **200.00**

Figure, Santa holding lamb, clay face, cotton flannel suit, Japan, 1930-40s, 6" h **75.00**

Figure, Santa on skis, metal, 1930s, 2¼" h **50.00**

Game, Hi-Ho Santa Claus Game, Whitman, 1962 . . . . **8.00**

Greeting Card, LG Kelly–Miller Bros Circus, 4 pp, early 1940s, 5 x 7". **10.00**

Greeting Card, Santa decorating tree, girl behind, 3-part fold-out, printed color, 1920s, 4½". **25.00**

Lamp, Santa holding Bubble Light candle, plastic, 1950s, 8" h **25.00**

Lantern, battery operated, silvered metal and painted glass, glass Santa head, British Crown Colony, Hong Kong, 1950s, 4½" h. **50.00**

Light Bulb, cuckoo clock. **20.00**

Light Bulb, flower, milk glass, Japan, 1930-50s **30.00**

Light Bulb, peacock **50.00**

Lighter, Santa and sled pulled by reindeer, polished finish with multicolor design, "94" at lower right corner, green and gold gift box, Zippo, 1994 . . . . **55.00**

Light Set, Krystal Star Lamps, glass, star shaped, set of 10, Japan, 2½" d **5.00**

Light Set, Noma Mazda Candle Lighting Outfit, luminous candles, 1940s **40.00**

Light Set, Zelco Decorative Lighting Outfit, 1920s **100.00**

Mug, hard plastic, red accent Santa portrait with flicker eyes on white ground, 1950s, 4" h, 3" d **10.00**

Mugs, set of 6, ceramic, Santa face, in 2 x 6 x 7" cellophane pkg with header card, Japan, 1960s **25.00**

Ornament, bird in ring, celluloid, Japan, 6" h **40.00**

Ornament, bird on clip, pearly white with orange crest, black eyes and beak, green wings, and red stripe, spun glass tail, German blown glass, c1920, 3¼" l, 5" l with tail **25.00**

Ornament, clown head, glass, 1930s, 3" h **40.00**

Ornament, cornucopia with raised flowers, pearly pink cornucopia with red and green flowers, pebbly back, German blown glass, c1920, 2" h **35.00**

Ornament, elf, glass, 1920s, 2¾" h **25.00**

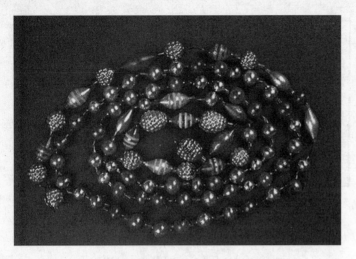

Tree Garland, glass beads, 1920s-30s, $35.00.

Ornament, flapper head, pearly white hat, blue brim,
light gold hair, matte flesh face, German blown glass,
c1920, 2½" h **225.00**
Ornament, Foxy Grandpa head on stylized body, pearly
white, gold, white frosting, silver, and pink, c1920,
5¼" h **100.00**
Ornament, Goldilocks, glass, 1930s, 3½" h **75.00**
Ornament, icicle, glass, 1950s, 14" h **20.00**
Ornament, jester bell, pearly pink and white, pearly
white face, German blown glass, c1920, 3" h **100.00**
Ornament, lamp, glass, 1920-30s **15.00**
Ornament, pig with clover on tummy, pearly white, red
ears, mouth, black eyes, pale gold clover, German
blown glass, c1920, 3¾" h **200.00**
Ornament, sun face, 2-sided, pearly white with green
shading, German blown glass, c1920, 2½" h **190.00**
Ornament, Zeppelin DLZ-127, blown glass, high lus-
ter silver finish, c1920-30s, 4" l, 1" d **200.00**
Palm Puzzle, paper Santa portrait beneath clear plexi-
glass, cardboard rim, 1950s **20.00**
Pinback Button, "Grand Rapids The Christmas Store,"
multicolored Santa portrait on light blue ground,
c1940s **75.00**
Pinback Button, Santa checking list above
"Goodfellows," c1940s **75.00**
Pinback Button, Santa portrait beside "A Gift From
Killian's Means More," 1930-40s **75.00**
Pinback Button, "Wyckoff's For Toys," red, green, and
fleshtone Santa portrait on white ground, red lettering,
c1930s **45.00**
Planter, ceramic, Santa on sleigh, waving, Napco,
1960s, 6 x 5" **15.00**
Postcard, real photo, family gathered around Christmas
tree, German **65.00**
Poster, cardboard, "Buy Christmas Seals," ©1924
National Tuberculosis Assoc, 11 x 13¾" **75.00**
Poster, paper, "Interwoven Socks for Christmas," illus by
Rudolph Zirm, ©Interwoven Stocking Co, Sweeney
Litho Co, Belleville, NJ, 17¼" h, 49½" w **100.00**
Topper, Santa, nylon beard, National Tinsel Mfg,
Manitowoc, WI, 1970s **15.00**
Topper, Star, plastic, clear, white, 5 points, red center
with red beams, Noma, 1950s **25.00**

Topper, Star of Bethlehem, Noma, 1950s, 9" h **50.00**
Toy, battery operated, Happy Santa, plastic face, tin
body, red cotton flannel suit, Cragston, 1950s, 12" h **75.00**
Toy, windup, Mechanical Santa Claus, vinyl head, felt
outfit, black vinyl belt, holding metal bell in 1 hand,
pipe cleaner candy cane in other, built-in key, orig
box, 1960s, Alps, Japan **75.00**
Toy, windup, Santa Claus, litho tin, Chein, 1920-30s,
5½" h **85.00**
Tree, aluminum, 1960s, 18" h **15.00**
Tree, goose feather composition, red berry limb tips,
round wood base, mkd "Made In Germany," 1920-
30s, 26" h **150.00**
Tree, Plastic Art Toy Corp, Carlstadt, NJ, 1950s, 8½" h **80.00**
Tree Stand, light-up, Noma, 1920s **100.00**
Tree Stand, musical, 1920s **175.00**
Wall Decoration, Santa Claus, Glo-lite Corp, Chicago,
IL, 1950s **50.00**

CIGAR COLLECTIBLES

Cigars and cigarettes are not synonymous. Cigars have always had
an aloofness about them. They were appreciated by a select group
of smokers, not the masses. Cigar connoisseurs are as fanatical as
wine aficionados concerning the objects of their affection.

The cigar renaissance of the early 1990s has renewed collector
interest in cigar collectibles. The primary focus is advertising.
Prices remain stable for traditional cigar collectibles such as cutters, molds, and cigar store figures.

References: Tony Hyman, *Tobacciana Price Guide,* Treasure Hunt
Publications, 2000; Jerry Terranova and Douglas Congdon-Martin,
Great Cigar Stuff for Collectors, Schiffer Publishing, 1997.

Newsletter: *The Cigar Label Gazette,* PO Box 3, Lake Forest, CA
92630.

Collectors' Clubs: Cigar Label Collectors International, PO Box
66, Sharon Center, OH 44274; International Seal, Label and Cigar
Band Society, 8915 E Bellevue St, Tucson, AZ 85715.

Cigar Box, American Navy, Perfecto Cigars, US warships
illus **$40.00**
Cigar Box, Square Deal, Perfecto Cigars, full color Teddy
Roosevelt illus, 1920s, 5¼ x 8½ x 2½" **20.00**
Cigar Box/Bottle Opener, Lord Stirling Cigars, Detroit,
MI, metal **50.00**
Counter Change Dish, glass, Red Dot Cigars label under
glass, 1930s, 2 x 6 x 7" **60.00**
Inner Lid Label, Aim Hi, bust of Jefferson, 1924 . . . . **75.00**
Inner Lid Label, Arthur Donaldson, man at desk smoking
cigar, 1926 . . . . **12.00**
Inner Lid Label, Black Hawk, Indian chief, 1938 . . . . **90.00**
Inner Lid Label, Mint Perfecto, government building,
1935 . . . . **75.00**
Inner Lid Label, Uncle Jake's Nickel Seegar, cartoon
character and cat, 1925 . . . . **10.00**
Invoice, Charles Green Cigar Mfg, Ithaca, NY **8.00**
Matchbook Holder, Muriel Cigars, metal, red Muriel
lady insert, 1920s **10.00**
Matchcover, King Edward Cigars, "100 Years Better" on
saddle, "100 Years Better, King Edward Cigars" on
back **4.00**

Cigar/Cigarette Box, copper flashed over chalkware, Richfield Oil Co adv, 1920s-30s, 10" l, $700.00. Photo courtesy Past Tyme Pleasures.

Matchcover, "Perfecto Garcia Finest Havana Cigars, Made in Tampa Florida" on front, blank saddle, Perfecto label on back **6.00**

Outer Box Label, Don Nieto, image of 17th-century scholar, 1923 . . . . **10.00**

Outer Box Label, La Boda, bride and groom at wedding reception, 1924. . . . . **3.00**

Outer Box Label, La Vera, woman wearing red cap, 1921 . . . . . **7.00**

Outer Box Label, Snap Shot, woman's smiling face, 1925 . . . . **10.00**

Pocket Cigar Holder, nickel plated brass, for 3 cigars, engraved "Edwin Cigar Co., New York" on each side, 5 1/2 x 2 1/2" **15.00**

Pocket Pouch, Killeen's High Grade Cigars, leather **40.00**

Punchboard, Y-B Cigars, 1930s **10.00**

Sign, Bank Note Cigars, cardboard, 1930, 21 x 14" **80.00**

Sign, Crüwekk-Tabak, cardboard, German, 1930s, 15 x 9 1/2" **20.00**

Sign, Cyclone Twister, "Five Cents," cardboard, ML Richards Co, Dallas, TX, 1928, 11 x 9" **40.00**

Sign, John Adams, "A Cigar that Makes Friends," 3D cardboard, 1920s, 16 x 18" **150.00**

Tin, North Star Tobacco, litho tin, pocket, image of woman and cherubs, 3 3/4 x 2 3/8 x 5/8" **550.00**

Murray Cards International Ltd. (comp.), *Cigarette Card Values: 1999 Catalogue of Cigarette and Other Trade Cards,* Murray Cards International, 1999; Fernando Righini and Marco Papazzoni, *The International Collector's Book of Cigarette Packs,* Schiffer Publishing, 1998; Neil Wood, *Smoking Collectibles,* L-W Book Sales, 1994.

Collectors' Club: Cigarette Pack Collectors Assoc, 61 Searle St, Georgetown, MA 01833.

Ashtray, Fatima Turkish Cigarettes, ceramic, rect, central cigarette-pack-shaped match holder, "Cameron & Cameron Co. Richmond, VA Liggett & Myers Tobacco Co. Successor," 3" h, 4" l **$175.00**

Banner, oilcloth, "Chesterfield Cigarettes," oversized cigarette-pack image opened from bottom, c1930-40s, 29 1/2 x 62" **75.00**

Booklet, *Magician's Cigarette Tricks,* cover shows magician in tuxedo holding pack of Camel cigarettes, cards and coins in background, 36 pp, illus, Prince Albert adv on back cover, RJ Reynolds, 1933 . . . . **20.00**

Cigarette Box, aluminum, white hard molded plastic divided inserts, 3" l brass plate affixed to top reads "White Sulphur Springs, West Virginia Oldsmobile Dealer Jamboree March 31-April 1, 1941," 5 x 3 x 2" **40.00**

Door Push, Chesterfield Cigarettes, porcelain, 1930-40s, 4 x 9" **250.00**

Matchcover, Chesterfield, unopened pack on front and back, blank saddle, "They Satisfy!" on back **4.00**

Matchcover, Kool, "Filter Kings" on front and back, "Kool" on saddle, "Come up to The ..." on inside **3.00**

Matchcover, L&M, "Reach for flavor...Reach for..." on front, blank saddle, "The Miracle Tip L&M, Pack or Box" on back **3.00**

Pack, Chesterfield, unopened, 1940s **25.00**

Pinback Button, "Vote For Philip Morris," 1940s **20.00**

Playing Cards, Vantage, round, logo on backs, with plastic storage case, 3" d **20.00**

Rolling Papers, Big Ben **30.00**

Rolling Papers, Country Gentleman **10.00**

Rolling Papers, Lorillard's 1760 5 Cent Size **5.00**

CIGARETTE COLLECTIBLES

The number of cigarette smokers grew steadily throughout the 19th century and first two decades of the 20th century. By the 1940s the cigarette was the dominant tobacco product sold in America. In the 1950s cigarette manufacturers were major periodical and television advertisers.

The Surgeon General's Report changed everything. Despite limitations on advertising and repeated non-smoking bans, the cigarette industry has proven highly resourceful in creating public exposure for its product—just watch any televised NASCAR race.

Surprisingly, as the anti-smoking crusade has become stronger, the interest in cigarette collectibles has increased. Cigarette memorabilia, especially advertising dating between 1945 and 1960, is one of the hot collectibles of the 1990s.

References: Douglas Congdon-Martin, *Camel Cigarette Collectibles: The Early Years, 1913-1963,* Schiffer Publishing, 1996; Douglas Congdon-Martin, *Camel Cigarette Collectibles, 1964-1995,* Schiffer Publishing, 1997; Joe Giesenhagen, *The Collector's Guide to Vintage Cigarette Packs,* Schiffer Publishing, 1999;

Advertising Display, Lucky Strike Cigarettes, diecut cardboard, 3D effect, pop-out figures, orig box, 1920s-30s, 34" h, 24" w, $475.00. Photo courtesy Collectors Auction Services.

Rolling Papers, Old North State **5.00**
Rolling Papers, Show Boat, blue. **30.00**
Rolling Papers, Tam Tam **5.00**
Rolling Papers, Target, "It's Blended" **8.00**
Sign, Camel, diecut cardboard, easel back, "Camel's So
    Mild–and they taste so good!," 1950, 20 x 30" **90.00**
Sign, Chesterfield, rigid cardboard, full color litho, por-
    trait of young naval cadet and older naval officer on
    gray ground, opened cigarette pack to right, blue and
    red lettering, c1930-40s, 11 x 21" **50.00**
Sign, "New Wings are Kings/Cost Less–Last Longer,"
    cardboard, 12" h, 18" w **30.00**
Sign, Old Gold Cigarettes, porcelain, 1-sided, "Not a
    Cough in a Carload," 12" h, 36" w **325.00**
Sign, Virginia Cigarettes, woman on beach holding large
    pack of cigarettes, emb tin, 1940s **60.00**
Thermometer, Chesterfield, tin, cigarette pack and "They
    Satisfy!," 13" h. **125.00**
Thermometer, Winston, tin, cigarette pack and "Winston
    tastes good...Like a cigarette should!," 13" h. **50.00**

CIRCUS MEMORABILIA

The 1920s through the 1940s marked the golden age of the tent circus. The circus trains for Ringling and Barnum and Bailey often exceeded 100 cars. The advent of television marked the beginning of the tent circus' decline. Mergers occurred. Most small circuses simply vanished. Today, the majority of circus performances occur at civic and institution auditoriums, not under the Big Top.

Most circus collectors are individuals who remember attending a circus under canvas. When this generation dies, what will be the fate of circus collectibles? Categories with crossover potential, e.g., lithographed posters, will hold collector interest. Others will vanish just as did the great circuses they document.

Reference: Norman E. Martinus and Harry L. Rinker, *Warman's Paper,* Wallace-Homestead, 1994.

Collectors' Clubs: Circus Fans Assoc of America, PO Box 59710, Potomac, MD 20859; Circus Historical Society, 4102 Idaho Ave, Nashville, TN 37209.

Activity Book, Ringling Bros and Barnum & Bailey
    Punch-Out Circus, Lever Bros premium, 35 diecut stiff
    paper pcs of circus performers, animal cages,
    sideshow performer banner panels, and large circus
    tent, orig 1948, 11½ x 11½" envelope **$50.00**
Book, *Emmett Kelly in Willie the Clown,* Elf, 1957 . . . . **12.00**
Book, *How the Clown Got His Smile,* Wonder, 1951 . . . . **5.00**
Book, *The Wonder Book of Clowns,* 1955 . . . . **6.00**
Doll, Willie the Clown, Baby Barry Toy Co, 1950–60,
    24" h **100.00**
Drinking Glass, Big Top Circus, depicts juggling clown
    with circus in background, 5½" h. **25.00**
Figure, clown, metal ball-jointed body, composition
    head and limbs, Bucherer, 1921, 7" h. **400.00**
Game, The Merry Circus Game, Milton Bradley, 1960 . . . . . . **12.00**
Lunch Box, Ringling Bros and Barnum & Bailey Circus,
    vinyl, full color front and back panels, black and
    orange tiger stripe design band, King-Seeley Thermos
    Co, c1970, 7 x 9 x 4" **175.00**
Pinback Button, Tom Mix Sells Floto Circus, c1929,
    1¾" d **75.00**

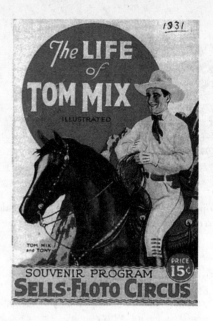

Program, Sells-Floto Circus, *The Life of Tom Mix*, c1931, 10¼ x 6¾", $150.00. Photo courtesy Collectors Auction Services.

Poster, Bentley Bros Circus, Springfield Ozark Empire
    Fairgrounds Arena, tiger with mouth open, 21" h,
    28" w **80.00**
Poster, King Bros & Cristiani, 3 laughing clowns, 1945,
    28 x 41" **175.00**
Poster, Lions Circus, Bellflower High School Stadium,
    Sun Jun 2, flying trapeze act, "Presenting the Best to
    the West," 42" h, 28" w **80.00**
Poster, Ringling Bros and Barnum & Bailey Combined
    Shows, Gargantua the Great, "Litho in USA, P-113,"
    17" h, 24½" w **60.00**
Poster, Rudy Bros Circus, paper, Elks Circus, high-wire
    act, 35" h, 14" w **80.00**
Program, Ringling Bros and Barnum & Bailey Circus,
    72 pp, photos and descriptions of circus performers,
    historic features, sponsorship ads, 1939, 8½ x 11" **5.00**
Window Card, Big Strong Circus, paper, clown and ele-
    phant, "Free Circus at Central City Mall," 28" h, 14" w . . . **100.00**
Window Card, Kelly Miller Bros Circus, paper, Harrison
    Fairgrounds, 2 elephants, sgd "Ray Dirgo," 17" h,
    11" w **100.00**
Window Card, Las Vegas International Circus, card-
    board, 6 photos of various circus acts and pictures of
    showgirls, 28" h, 22" w **100.00**

CLEWELL POTTERY

Charles Walter Clewell of Canton, Ohio, began his ceramic experiments in 1899. He opened his studio in 1906. His "Clewell Ware" pieces were produced in limited quantities between 1902 and 1955. When Clewell died in 1965, his daughter sold off his remaining stock.

Clewell's emphasis was on decorative techniques which ranged from shaped metal over a ceramic lining to glazes based on historic prototypes, the most famous of which was a blue patina on bronze. He bought his blanks from a variety of potteries including Cambridge, Knowles, Taylor and Knowles, Owens, Rookwood, Roseville, and Weller.

Clewell marks include: (1) impressed mark of "CLEWELL / CAN-TON O" inside two circles; (2) impressed mark of small "w" inside a large "C"; (3) impressed three-line mark "Clewell / Metal Art / Canton, O." inside circle; and (4) incised mark "CLEWELL / CANTON O."

Reference: Ralph and Terry Kovel, *Kovel's American Art Pottery,* Crown, 1993.

Jardiniere, copper-clad with verdigris and bronze patina, incised "Clewell 418-2-9," 5¼ x 6½" **$1,000.00**
Vase, bulbous, copper-clad with verdigris and bronze patina, incised "Clewell/250-29," 7½ x 4¼" **600.00**
Vase, classically shaped, copper-clad with brown to verdigris patina, incised "Clewell/463-26," 8½ x 7" **1,975.00**
Vase, classically shaped, copper-clad with verdigris patina, incised "Clewell 323-6," 8¾ x 7" **1,200.00**
Vase, copper-clad with cupped rim, verdigris and bronze patina, incised "Clewell/485-215," 11¼ x 8" . . . **1,650.00**
Vase, copper-clad with flat shoulder, verdigris patina, unmkd, 10 x 5" **1,100.00**
Vase, faceted, copper-clad with verdigris and bronze patina, incised "Clewell 439-2-6," 10 x 3½" **2,650.00**
Vase, organic form, copper-clad with 2 handles, verdigris and bronze patina, incised "Clewell/408-2-6," 6 x 7" **1,500.00**
Vase, ovoid, copper-clad, 3-ftd, verdigris and bronze patina, incised "Clewell/411-2-6," 5¼ x 4¼" **600.00**
Vase, ovoid, copper-clad with verdigris and bronze patina, incised "Clewell/321-4-2," 6½ x 4" **725.00**
Vase, ovoid, copper-clad with verdigris patina, incised "Clewell 331-6," 6 x 3" **525.00**
Vase, spherical, copper-clad with verdigris and bronze patina, incised "Clewell/300-25," 5 x 4¼" **1,200.00**
Vessel, bulbous, ftd, copper-clad with bronzed and verdigris patina, incised "Clewell 417-2-G," 4½ x 5¼" . . . **500.00**

CLICKERS

These noisemakers were extremely popular from the early 1930s through the late 1950s. Many were distributed to adults and children as advertising premiums. Those touting a particular beer, hotel, political, or household product were meant for adults. Children delighted in receiving clickers when buying Buster Brown or Red Goose shoes. The Halloween season was responsible for more clickers than any other holiday season.

Bathing Beauty, litho tin, multicolored **$15.00**
Butter-Nut Bread, litho tin, yellow, 1930s **15.00**
Cadillac, litho tin, red and black on white ground, c1957 . . . . **15.00**
Castles Ice Cream, litho tin, "I'm Chirping For Castle's Ice Cream" **30.00**
Forbes Quality Brand Coffee, litho tin, red, white, and blue **40.00**
Girl, litho tin, printed image of young girl standing in frilled dress holding unopened parasol, underside mkd "T. Cohn, Brooklyn," 1930s **20.00**
"Had Your Toddy Today–A Meal In A Glass," litho tin, yellow, red, and white **45.00**
Little Sergeant Shoes, litho tin, orange, black, and white **30.00**
Peters Weatherbird Shoes, litho tin, full color image of Weatherbird symbol, c1930-40s **25.00**
Poll-Parrot Shoes, litho tin, yellow, red, and green, Japan, late 1930s **20.00**

Fort Pitt Brewing Co, litho tin, red, green, and yellow, $16.00.

Purity Salt, litho tin, "Sundial Shoes Are All Leather," 2½" l **30.00**
Real-Kill, litho tin, black and blue lettering on orange, "Mama get Real-Kill Bug Killer," Kirchhof, 1930s **15.00**
Red Goose Shoes, litho tin, red and yellow, made in Japan, c1930s **20.00**
Robin Hood Shoes, litho tin, tinted color portrait with light blue rim, pictorial logo for "Central Shoes" with silhouette telephone operator, 1930s **50.00**
State Insurance, Harrisburg, litho tin, "Assets Over A Million Dollars," red, white, and blue. **30.00**
Steelco Stainless Steel, Chicago, litho tin **25.00**
Sundial Shoes, airplane, multicolored, 2½" l **30.00**
Tom McAn, Nashua, NH, celluloid, green and white **115.00**
Young Person on Bicycle, Japan, 2⅛" l **20.00**

CLIFF, CLARICE

Clarice Cliff (1899-1972) joined A. J. Wilkinson's Royal Staffordshire Pottery at Burslem, England, in the early 1910s. In 1930 she became the company's art director.

Cliff is one of England's foremost 20th-century ceramic designers. Her influence covered a broad range of shapes, forms, and patterns. Her shape lines include Athens, Biarritz, Chelsea, Conical, Iris, Lynton, and Stamford. Applique, Bizarre, Crocus, Fantasque, and Ravel are among the most popular patterns.

In addition to designer shape and pattern lines, Cliff's signature also appears on a number of inexpensive dinnerware lines manufactured under the Royal Staffordshire label.

References: Susan and Al Bagdade, *Warman's English & Continental Pottery & Porcelain, 3rd Edition,* Krause Publications, 1998; Helen Cunningham, *Clarice Cliff and Her Contemporaries: Susie Cooper, Keith Murray, Charlotte Rhead and the Carlton Designers,* Schiffer Publishing, 1999; Leonard R. Griffin, *Clarice Cliff,* Trafalgar Square, 1999.

Collectors' Club: Clarice Cliff Collector's Club, 1 Foxdell Way, Chellaston, Derby, Derbyshire DE73 1PU UK.

REPRODUCTION ALERT: Lotus vases.

Bowl, Orange Chintz pattern, recessed, raised edges, orange and brown floral with yellow stamen, red and black accents, gold stamped "Lawleys Glass," mkd "32-Hand Painted Bizarre by Clarice Cliff Newport Pottery England," 2" h, 6¾" d **$400.00**

Box, Umbrella pattern, Wilkinson shape, square recessed body, dome cov, ftd pedestal, blue, orange, and green floral with brown accents, honey glaze ground, unmkd, 3" h, 3½" d **500.00**

Candlesticks, pr, Melon pattern, band of overlapping fruit in orange, with yellow, blue, and green, brown outline, stamped on base in black ink "Hand Painted Fantasque by Clarice Cliff Wilkinson Ltd. England," c1930, 3¼" h **1,375.00**

Cup, Chintz pattern, orange, brown, and black glaze, base stamped "Hand Painted Bizarre by Clarice Cliff, Newport Pottery, England" with gilt Lawley's stamp, 3⅝" h **450.00**

Jam Pot, cov, Melon pattern, band of overlapping fruit, orange, with yellow, blue, and green, brown outline, c1930, 4" h **700.00**

Luncheon Plate, Farmhouse pattern, orange, stamped "Hand Painted Bizarre by Clarice Cliff Newport Pottery England," c1930, 9" d **1,500.00**

Pitcher, Alpine Trees and House pattern, 8-sided, orange and black borders, stamped in black on base "Hand Painted Fantasque by Clarice Cliff Wilkinson, England," 6⅜" d **1,725.00**

Pitcher, Autumn Balloon Trees pattern, square base, flattened spherical sides, blue, yellow, green, orange, black, and purple, base stamped "Registration Applied For Fantasque Hand Painted Bizarre by Clarice Cliff Newport Pottery England," 5⅛" h **925.00**

Plate, Autumn Crocus pattern, trio of crocus finished in bright orange, blue, and violet, green blade-like leaves extending outward, swirled brown band center, sun yellow outer band, honey glaze ground, mkd "Crocus Hand Painted Bizarre by Clarice Cliff Newport Pottery England," 7¾" d **600.00**

Shaker, Alpine Trees and House pattern, conical shaped, orange and black borders and trees, green rooftop and grass, base stamped "Hand Painted Bizarre by Clarice Cliff Newport Pottery England," 5¾" h **1,375.00**

Teapot, cov, Geometric pattern, triangular designs in sage green alternating with cobalt blue diamonds, orange-red glaze, honey ground, orange hand script signature on base, incised "H/Bizarre/Hand Painted Newport Pottery," 5¼ x 5½" d **470.00**

Teapot, cov, inverted conical form, angled handle and spout, shades of orange, yellow, and black, base stamped "Hand Painted Bizarre by Clarice Cliff Newport Pottery England," 4½" h **2,250.00**

Tea Stand, Autumn Crocus pattern, raised, narrow green border with recessed center, trio of crocus finished in orange, blue, and violet with brown circular band, sun yellow outer border, mkd "31-Crocus Hand Painted Bizarre by Clarice Cliff Newport Pottery England," 6½" d **350.00**

AUCTION PRICES – CLARICE CLIFF

Smith & Jones, Inc. Auctions, American and European Art Pottery Sale, October 14, 1999. Prices include a 10% buyer's premium.

Cup and Saucer, Green Cowslip pattern, conical, mkd "33-Hand Painted Bizarre by Clarice Cliff Newport Pottery England Made In England," 2¼" h, 5" d **$385.00**

Plate, Autumn Balloon Trees pattern, mkd "4-20-Fantasque Hand Painted Bizarre by Clarice Cliff Hand Painted England," 2 small rim chips on back, 8¾" d **660.00**

Teapot, cov, Autumn Crocus pattern, bulbous body, mkd "Crocus Hand Painted Bizarre by Clarice Cliff Newport Pottery England," nick at spout, 5¼" h **550.00**

Vase, Blue Chintz pattern, Shape No. 358, Fantasque form with flared mouth and 3 protruding rings around neck, mkd "Fantasque Hand Painted Bizarre by Clarice Cliff Newport Pottery England 358," 8" h **3,300.00**

Turkey Platter, blue transfer with hp accents, mkd "Clarice Cliff Made In England," 18" l, $330.00. Photo courtesy Smith & Jones, Inc Auctions.

CLOCKS

This collecting category is heavily dominated by character alarm clocks, especially those dating from the 1940s and 50s. Strong collector interest also exists for electric and key wind novelty clocks and clocks featuring advertising.

Generic clocks such as mass-produced Big Ben alarm clocks have little or no collector interest. 1920s' and '30s' wood-cased mantel clocks, banjo-style wall clocks, and period 1950s' wall clocks prove the exception.

References: Hy Brown, *Comic Character Timepieces: Seven Decades of Memories,* Schiffer Publishing, 1992; Michael Bruner, *Advertising Clocks: America's Timeless Heritage,* Schiffer Publishing, 1995.

Collectors' Club: National Assoc of Watch and Clock Collectors, Inc, 514 Poplar St, Columbia, PA 17512.

Advertising, Ashland Bottled Gas Service, plastic body, glass lens, 17" d **$150.00**

Advertising, Authorized Evinrude Parts & Service, double bubble light-up, electric, metal, glass face and front, orig box, 15" d 1,000.00
Advertising, Ballantine Beer, 12" d 100.00
Advertising, Champion, diecut steering wheel, clock in center, plastic, glass front, Champion trademark and spark plug illus, 11½" d 375.00
Advertising, Cloverdale Ginger Ale, 12" sq 275.00
Advertising, GMC Trucks, electric, neon, tin, octagon shaped face with glass cov, "Sales GMC Trucks Service" 875.00
Advertising, Hastings Piston Rings, red lettering 200.00
Advertising, Mobil, light-up, red Pegasus horse and numbers 375.00
Advertising, Mobil, tire shaped, gold painted metal back, made in Germany, 4" d 225.00
Advertising, Proctor Appliances 150.00
Advertising, Seagrams VO, plastic and glass, dial at top, 12" d 150.00
Advertising, Super Chevrolet Service, metal, blue logo in center, black hands, white ground, Crystal Mfg Co, Chicago, IL, 15⅛" sq 350.00
Advertising, Willard Batteries, light-up, metal, glass face and front, 15" d 225.00
Alarm, Art Deco, circular brushed aluminum case on 2 ball feet, off-center crystal face, mkd "Gilbert," 5¾" d 350.00
Alarm, chrome, circular face, black enameled hands and number markers, designed by Gilbert Rhode for Herman Miller, 6½ x 6" 400.00
Character, Bugs Bunny, "Let's Tell Time," complete with 12-pp full color booklet, ©1962 Warner Bros Pictures, Sea-Wide Industries, PA 20.00
Character, Mickey Mouse, alarm, animated, Bradley Time, 1983 .... 25.00
Character, Three Little Pigs, alarm, animated, bright red dial, Ingersoll, 1934 .... 600.00

Character, Woody Woodpecker, alarm, animated, Columbia Time, 1950 .... 150.00
Commemorative, electric, plastic case, "First Orbit/Feb 20, 1962/Col. John H. Glenn," 4 x 4½ x 8" 100.00
Desk, semi-spherical, cream enameled wood case with inlaid wood face, Howard Miller foil label, 7" h, 5" d ... 2,750.00
Dresser, marbleized green celluloid, Lux Clock Mfg Co 30.00
Kitchen, battery operated, plastic, figural milk can, brushed pewter finish, Seth Thomas, 11" h, 7¾" w 10.00
Kitchen, electric, stamped tin, figural frying pan, Sessions, Forrestville, CT, 1920s 35.00
Table, electric, Art Deco, silver and gray radiating face in chrome case, Paul Frankl for Telechron, 8 x 5 x 3½" 650.00
Table, TV-Tymeter Clock, hard plastic, figural television, maroon and black marbleized body, clear plastic cover over off-white screen, gold accent around screen and knobs, rotating numerals, orig box, Pennwood Numechron Co, 1959, 3½ x 5½ x 5" 75.00
Wall, electric, walnut veneer case, white enameled numeral marks and hands, brushed aluminum face plate, designed by George Nelson for Howard Miller foil label, 31 x 22" 550.00
Wall, triangular, black enameled face, 3 fine brass struts, enameled hands and markers, designed by George Nelson for Howard Miller paper label, 20" d 1,600.00
Wall, weight driven, circular enameled white composition board face inset with plexiglass face and brass hour markers, with 2 brass weights, chrome and brass pendulum, and chimes, Howard Miller paper label, 21" d 100.00

CLOTHES SPRINKLERS

Although steam irons have made it unnecessary, many individuals still sprinkle clothing before ironing. In many cases, the sprinkling bottle is merely a soda bottle with an adaptive cap. However, in the middle decades of the 20th century, ceramic and glass bottles designed specifically for sprinkling were made. Many were figural, a primary reason why they have attracted collector interest.

Reference: Ellen Bercovici, Bobbie Zucker Bryson and Deborah Gillham, *Collectibles for the Kitchen, Bath & Beyond*, Antique Trader Books, 1998.

Cat, ceramic, black face and paws $150.00
Cat, white, glass marble eyes, mkd "Cardinal," 7½" h 150.00
Chinaman, Cleminson's 45.00
Chinaman, green and yellow 45.00
Chinaman, Sprinkle Plenty, holding sad iron 150.00
Clothespin, plastic 65.00
Dachshund, green coat tied at neck, red bow, unmkd 300.00
Dearie Is Weary, yellow dress, holding iron, head is sprinkler 350.00
Dutch Boy 240.00
Dutch Girl, blue and white 150.00
Elephant, trunk up, gray and pink, black accents, American Bisque, 6¼" h 350.00
Elephant, trunk up, gray and pink, Cardinal China, 7" h 55.00
Flatiron, farm couple, Tilso, Japan 175.00
Flatiron, green ivy, Cardinal China, 5¼" h 50.00
Flatiron, rooster, VG Japan 100.00
Frigidaire Alligator, plastic 115.00
Glass Lady, figural 35.00

Advertising, Buckwheat Pancakes, Aunt Jemima image, electric, plastic frame, cardboard face, ©1956, 7" h, $550.00. Photo courtesy Collectors Auction Services.

Rooster, ceramic, metal and cork stopper, $75.00.

Kitchen Prayer Lady, Enesco	500.00
Lady, red, plastic	35.00
Laundry Sprinkler, plastic, pink, 6³/₈" h	15.00
Mammy, white dress with red trim, 8" h	225.00
Mary Poppins, clear glass, holding umbrella and purse	100.00
Mr Sprinkler, plastic, pink and white	35.00
Poodle, sitting on hind legs, white, black accents, Cardinal USA, c1956, 8¹/₄" h	175.00
Rooster, long neck, plastic cap, 10" h	175.00
Rooster, Sierra Vista, 9" h	150.00
Rose Vase, plastic, Minerware	25.00
Siamese Cat, incised "Cardinal USA"	175.00
Turquoise, clear middle, plastic	25.00
Watering Can, ceramic, 6" h	175.00
Yellow, red base, plastic	35.00

CLOTHING & ACCESSORIES

Victorian-era clothing is passé. Clothing of the flapper era has lost much of its appeal. Forget pre-1945 entirely. Today's collectors want post-1945 clothing.

1960s' psychedelic-era clothing is challenging 1950s' clothing for front position on sellers' racks. No matter what the era, a major key to clothing's value is a design which screams a specific period. Further, collectors want clothing that is ready to wear. Older collectors still love to play "dress up."

Hollywood-, television-, and movie-personality-related and high-style fashion designer clothing is now steady fare at almost every major American auction house. Prices continue to rise. Many buyers are foreign. Paris may be center stage for the contemporary clothing market, but the American collectibles marketplace is the focus of vintage clothing sales.

References: Joanne Dubbs Ball and Dorothy Hehl Torem, *The Art of Fashion Accessories*, Schiffer Publishing, 1993; Maryanne Dolan, *Vintage Clothing: 1880-1980, 3rd Edition*, Books Americana, 1995; Kate E. Dooner, *Plastic Handbags, 2nd Edition*, Schiffer Publishing, 1998; Ray Ellsworth, *Platform Shoes*, Schiffer Publishing, 1998; Roseann Ettinger, *20th Century Neckties: Pre-1955*, Schiffer Publishing, 1999; Roseann Ettinger, *Fifties Forever! Popular Fashions for Men, Women, Boys & Girls*, Schiffer Publishing, 1999; Roseann Ettinger, *Handbags, 3rd Edition*,

Schiffer Publishing, 1999; Roseann Ettinger, *Popular and Collectible Neckties: 1955 to Present*, Schiffer Publishing, 1998; Kristina Harris, *Vintage Fashions for Women: 1920s-1940s*, Schiffer Publishing, 1996; Kristina Harris, *Vintage Fashions for Women: The 1950s & 60s*, Schiffer Publishing, 1997.

Ellie Laubner, *Collectible Fashions of the Turbulent 1930s*, Schiffer Publishing, 2000; Ellie Laubner, *Fashions of the Roaring '20s*, Schiffer Publishing, 1996; Jan Lindenberger, *Clothing & Accessories From the '40s, '50s & '60s*, Schiffer Publishing, 1996; Sally C. Luscomb, *The Collector's Encyclopedia of Buttons, 3rd Edition*, Schiffer Publishing, 1999; J. J. Murphy, *Children's Handkerchiefs*, Schiffer Publishing, 1998; Peggy Anne Osborne, *Button, Button, 2nd Edition*, Schiffer Publishing, 1997; Mary Brooks Picken, *A Dictionary of Costume and Fashion: Historic and Modern*, Dover, 1999; Joe Poltorak, *Fashions in the Groove*, Schiffer Publishing, 1998; Maureen Reilly and Mary Beth Detrich, *Women's Hats of the 20th Century for Designers and Collectors*, Schiffer Publishing, 1997; Trina Robbins, *Tomorrow's Heirlooms: Fashions of the 60s & 70s*, Schiffer Publishing, 1997; Nancy M. Schiffer, *Tropical Shirts & Clothing*, Schiffer Publishing, 1998; Desire Smith, *Vintage Style: 1920-1960*, Schiffer Publishing, 1997; Sheila Steinberg and Kate E. Dooner, *Fabulous Fifties: Designs for Modern Living, 2nd Edition*, Schiffer Publishing, 1999; Joe Tonelli and Marc Luers, *Bowling Shirts*, Schiffer Publishing, 1998; Debra J. Wisniewski, *Antique & Collectible Buttons*, Collector Books, 1997.

Newsletter: *The Vintage Connection*, 904 N 65th St, Springfield, OR 97478.

Collectors' Clubs: Collectors of Nasty Old Ties (K.N.O.T.), 1860 Greentree Dr, Plover, WI 54467; The Costume Society of America, 55 Edgewater Dr, PO Box 73, Earleville, MD 21919; National Button Society, 2733 Juno Pl, Apt 4, Akron, OH 44313.

Blouse, rayon crepe, yellow, Peter Pan collar, floral appliqués studded with rhinestones, no label	$20.00
Cap, baby's, wool knit, solid color, Chubby Boy, 1950s	8.00
Cape, fox, white, horizontal bands with tails sewn at bottom edge, Oscar de la Renta	350.00
Cape, velvet, black, large fold-over square collar, shoulder yoke and hem inset with ribbed gold horizontal bands, probably French, 1920s	300.00
Cardigan, boy's, wool, 2-toned, center geometric design, Bluebird, 1950s	20.00
Cardigan, girl's, wool, embroidered dec, 1950s	8.00
Cardigan, lady's, lambs wool, angora, and nylon, applied milk glass beads in palm tree design, Boutique International, 1950s	50.00
Chemise, chiffon, beige, sleeveless and straight, silver metallic ovoid paillettes in swag and vine pattern, rhinestone accents, separate silver lamé slip, size 16, French, early 1920s	700.00
Chemise, chiffon, black, randomly spaced large bead flowers in red, yellow, green, and orange, peacock blue satin underslip, size 14, 1920s	350.00
Christening Gown, white lawn with lace collar and trim, lace insertion, c1920	45.00
Clutch Bag, silver lamé studded allover with large gem set rhinestones, rect, Nettie Rosenstein, 1960s	250.00
Coat, cashmere, charcoal, fabric draped from side pleats at waist seam, side pockets, with dolman sleeves, turned-back lapels, separate self tie belt, Ben Reig, New York, 1950s, size 8	400.00

Coat, mink, broadtail, double-breasted, black jeweled buttons, slightly fitted at waist and flaring outward, bottom horizontal black mink bands, flat mink collar, Donald Brooks, 1960s, size 8. 575.00

Coat, velvet, notched shawl collar, patch pockets, wide separate belt, tie-dyed shades of marigold, forest green, and sable brown, Halston, 1970s, size 6-8 . . . . . 1,375.00

Coat, wool, brown and black small check, fitted wide integral band at torso, flared skirt, large round cape collar, wide lapels, full cut-in-one bishop sleeves gathered at wrist with band cuff, fleur-de-lis buttons, labeled "claire mc cardell clothes/by townley," c1950, size 6 . . . . 350.00

Coat, wool knit, acid green, double-breasted, small fold-over collar, slanted besom pockets, curved shoulder yoke, angular sleeve seams, Givenchy, handwritten tape label "39826," 1960s 525.00

Cocktail Dress, satin, black, woven dots of shiny black tinsel, overblouse bodice with high ruffled neck and ruffled bottom, leather backed satin belt, straight skirt with weighted hem, labeled "Christian Dior/Paris/Made In France, no. 16067," 1960s, size 2 . . . . 225.00

Cocktail Dress, satin, ivory, with black velvet dots, 2-pc, surplice bodice with short sleeves ending at mid torso, straight skirt with strapless boned understructure, labeled "Christian Dior/Paris/Automne-Hiver 1955, no. 7855," 1955, size 4 . . . . 450.00

Cocktail Dress, satin, ivory, with printed chiné flowers and woven bright yellow velvet iris with taupe accent, high waisted, bateau neck, long sleeves, back bared to waist, flat skirt in front, gathered full and slightly longer at back, Galanos, 1950s, size 6 . . . . 375.00

Day Dress, silk, printed large brown disks on black ground, short sleeves, draped cowl neck, wide banded waist, Adrian Original, 1940s, size 8 . . . . 175.00

Dinner Jacket, midnight blue, sewn allover with small sequins in vermiculate pattern, fitted at waist, with pointed lapels, ivory satin lining revealed at neck and turned back cuffs, Chanel, made in France, 1930s. 925.00

Dress, blush satin, woven fawn and brown velvet roses, bodice with jewel neck, slit at center to waist, dolman sleeves and wide gathered cummerbund, full skirt pleated into waist, with pockets, Traina Norell/New York, 1955 . . . . 225.00

Dress, chiffon, black, low waisted chemise, embroidered from top to thigh with grid pattern worked in gilt-metal threads, deep long dolman sleeves similarly worked on outside, box pleated skirt below embroidery, size 8, 1920s. 425.00

Dress, girl's, printed organdy with black velvet waist ribbon, Fruit of the Loom Sister Sue Frock, 1950s 15.00

Dress, ivory tulle with embroidery and lace insertions, lace trim, c1920 . . . . 125.00

Dress, satin, black, A-line, long cut-in-one sleeves, high fold-over neckline, left arm and side each sewn entire length with large gilt-metal zippers and rings at ends, labeled Rudi Gernreich, c1968, size 8 . . . . 175.00

Dress, satin, black, strapless, knee-length sheath with standaway boned bodice notched low at center, fan pleated from center of high curved waistband, separate pink-lined panel draped in bustle effect attached at back, Yaga, 1960s, size 6 . . . . 225.00

Evening Gown, beaded wool, strapless sweetheart bodice, embellished allover with scrollwork, vinery, and fleurs-de-lis in black velvet appliqué and black beads, separate shoulder cape, Balenciaga, 1960s, $2,500.00. Photo courtesy William Doyle Galleries.

Dress, wool knit, blue, floor-length sheath, short sleeves, appliquéd psychedelic bull's-eyes and large daisy heads, marigold and pink band sleeve and neck trim, Rudi Gernreich Design for Harmon Knitwear, c1973, size 6 . . . . 1,250.00

Dungarees, boy's, Little Fellers, vat-dyed denim, HD Lee Co, 1950s 75.00

Evening Bag, petit point, worked in polychrome yarns, 1 side with strolling musicians under balcony, other side with townspeople engaged in daily activities, made in France, 1950s 300.00

Evening Bag, satin, black, embroidered on each side with bright pink carnations in basket, gilt-metal frame, marbled green stone clasp and ornament, green damask lining, probably French, 1930s. 250.00

Evening Coat, woman's, velvet, black, clutch closure, white fur shawl collar, tight sleeves ending with wide trumpet cuff, flared skirt, white silk lining, attributed to Madeleine Vionnet, c1929 . . . . 175.00

Evening Dress, velvet, coral, sleeveless, body-hugging, low V-neck trimmed with beaded trompe l'oeil tie, 2 long sashes cut-in-one with bodice wrapping at waist and attaching at back left with large beaded trompe l'oeil bow, flared skirt at bottom, attributed to Madeleine Vionnet, c1929, size 6 . . . . 325.00

Evening Gown, 2-pc, brown crepe, peplum bodice with high neck, cut-in-one cap sleeves extending into long looped streamers attached at back edge of peplum, straight skirt with slight flair, front slit, Adrian Original, 1940s, size 10 . . . . 1,500.00

Evening Jacket, chiffon, cream, cardigan style, embroidered allover with pearls and gold beads in large swirling pattern, Halston, 1970s, size medium 425.00

Evening Jacket, wool, purple, swing style, circular hem descending from front to back, round shoulders, 3/4 sleeves, set allover with paired small and large rhinestones, Trigère/New York, 1950s, size 8 . . . . 325.00

Gloves, pr, child's, wool knit, embroidered dec 4.00

Gloves, pr, lady's, cotton, brown, double woven, English, 1950s. 8.00

Gown, black lace with fur-trimmed jacket, c1930......... **175.00**

Gown, cut velvet chiffon, red, floral pattern, nude lining, wrap front, self-ties attached at waist, 1930s......... **375.00**

Hand Bag, alligator, burgundy, double handles, opening at center on hinges, key sheath, Trussardi, 1970s....... **450.00**

Hand Bag, Art Deco, glass beads worked in triangle and diamond pattern, shades of turquoise, green, claret, and tobacco, silver metal frame, chain link shoulder strap, 1920s................ **575.00**

Hand Bag, Art Deco, wrought steel body in gold and silver pattern, knotted bead fringe, black enamel and gilt-metal frame with concentric circular pattern, snake link chain handle, French, 1920s............. **200.00**

Hand Bag, crocodile, beige, cutout flap, top handle, ring clasp, Gucci, 1960s................ **175.00**

Handkerchief, cotton, white, printed scene of teenagers talking on telephone on edges with pink embroidery...... **4.00**

Hat, boy's, corduroy, with brim and folding ear flap, 1950s................ **15.00**

Hat, lady's, felt, pill box, ribbon trim and netting, 1950s..... **15.00**

Hat, lady's, wool, curved brim with net, 1950s......... **35.00**

Jacket, lady's, fur, yellow and brown spotted, below hip length, wide black mink stand collar, single button at throat, Schiaparelli/Paris, 1950s................ **750.00**

Jacket, lady's, satin, beige, short bolero style, worked allover with gold metal paillettes and large smoke gray jewel clusters, sable cuffs, Christian Dior/Paris, 1960s, size 4................ **700.00**

Jacket, lady's, snakeskin, beige and brown, boxy hip length jacket with wide pointed collar, low patch pockets, large self buttons, 1970s, size 6............ **750.00**

Jacket, man's, gabardine, brown, zip front, rounded collar, cinch waist, 2 flap pockets, A Bruce Creation....... **80.00**

Maxi Coat, brown, broadtail, double-breasted, open lapels and collar, faux flap pockets, labeled "Alixandre Furs/New York," 1970s, size 10........... **800.00**

Mini Dress, wool tweed, black and white, long sleeves, ribbed patent leather hem, neck, and center front patch pocket, Pierre Cardin/Paris/New York, c1970, size 6................ **550.00**

Necktie, polyester, striped design, 1960s................ **8.00**

Pants, bell bottom, knit, tan and gold with black spots, labeled "BIBA," c1968, size 8.................... **450.00**

Party Dress, velveteen, forest green, wide square neck, puffed sleeves, skirt gathered at waist, with back inverted pleat, side button and loop detail, side pockets, edges outlined in double topstitching, c1947, no label, size 6.................................... **300.00**

Pocket Mirror, plastic, ivorene, swing opening, gold Art Deco flapper girl profile with rhinestone dec on lid, 3³/₄ x 2"................ **30.00**

Purse, carpet material, box style, 1960s................ **10.00**

Purse, patent leather, 1960s................ **10.00**

Robe, boy's, cotton flannel, printed cowboy design, Kaynee Wee Men, 1950s................ **35.00**

Romper, baby's, 1-pc, combed cotton, hp design, Tubby Togs, NY, 1950s................ **15.00**

Scarf, silk, olive green and gold paisley design, orig tag reads "Scarves by Vera/designed & handscreened in U.S.A."................ **15.00**

Scarf, silk and cashmere, printed game birds and hare, natural shades on rust ground, brown border, sgd "Hermès Paris," 1970s................ **225.00**

Shawl, chiffon, black, woven with lamé diaper pattern border, printed in shades of pink and rose, gold, black, and peach attached fringe, 1920s, 44" sq........ **400.00**

Shawl, chiffon, purple, woven velvet floral pattern in mottled pastel blue, peach, and green, knotted fringe, French, 1920s................ **375.00**

Shirt, man's, rayon, printed Hawaiian scene, Terrace Club Sportswear, 1950s................ **85.00**

Shoes, pr, child's, PF Flyers, canvas, with orig Adventure Book, 1950s................ **20.00**

Shoes, pr, lady's, leather, beige, pumps, pearl and rhinestone shoe clips, 1960s................ **10.00**

Shoes, pr, lady's, leather, platform, ankle strap, hand-tooled design, 1940s................ **50.00**

Ski Suit, ribbed wool/nylon with side zipper closure, front V-yoke, high side-buttoning collar, cuffed sleeves, back belt, labeled "Designed by Ernst Engel," 1940s, size 8................ **225.00**

Slip, silk, pink, lace bodice, thin straps, 1960s........... **10.00**

Slipper Socks, pr, child's, wool knit, embroidered and appliqué dec, 1950s................ **5.00**

Stole, triangular, mink, dark brown, bordered with double row of silver fox, labeled "Adolfo," 1960s........ **1,000.00**

Suit, lady's, gray flannel, fitted double-breasted jacket, small round collar opening to lapels, slit pockets, with wrap skirt, labeled "Jean Dessès/17. Avenue Matignon. Paris," 1950s................ **350.00**

Suit, lady's, pink and wine narrow stripes, hip-length fitted jacket with crossed inset bands, 1 band forming collar, slit pockets at shoulders, flared skirt, Adrian Original, 1940s, size 10................ **625.00**

Suit, lady's, wool, black, hip-length jacket fitted at waist, signature ties at throat and waist, sleeves sewn with extra flaps creating geometric pattern, Adrian Original and Janny/Cincinnati, Ohio, 1940s, size 10........... **700.00**

Sundress, cotton, sleeveless, multicolored stripes, Fruit of the Loom, 1950s................ **20.00**

Tank Top, polyester, white daisies on yellow ground, orig "Vera" tag................ **80.00**

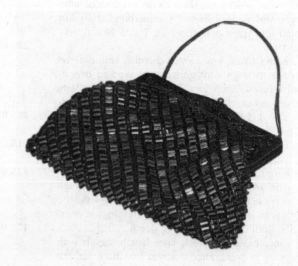

Purse, mesh metal with black cloth int, labeled "Whiting and Davis Mesh Bags," 6³/₄" w, $90.00. Photo courtesy Collectors Auction Services.

COALPORT FIGURINES

After completing an apprenticeship at Caughley, Robert Rose established a pottery at Coalport, located in Shropshire's Severn Gorge, England, in 1796. The pottery remained in the Rose family until acquired by the Bruff family in 1853.

In 1923 Cauldon Potteries, located in Stoke-on-Trent, Staffordshire, bought Coalport. In 1926 operations were moved from the Shropshire plant to Staffordshire. In 1936 the Crescent potteries of George Jones & Sons acquired Cauldon/Coalport. In 1958 E. Brian and Company, whose Foley China Works were established in 1850, purchased Coalport, maintaining its identity as a separate company. Coalport became part of the Wedgwood Group in 1967.

Although known primarily for its dinnerware, Coalport produced a line of porcelain figurines between 1890 and the present that rival those of Royal Doulton and Lladro. Each figure has a distinctive name. Many are found in multiple variations. Backstamps play a role in value with examples bearing the earliest backstamp having the highest value. As with Royal Doulton, the figurine's designer also impacts on value.

Reference: Tom Power, *The Charlton Standard Catalogue of Coalport Figurines*, Charlton Press, 1997.

Collectors' Club: Coalport Collector Society, PO Box 99, Sudbury CO10 6SN, England.

Afternoon Matinee, Age of Elegance series, turquoise
  and lilac, 1991-92, 8¼" h **$300.00**
Alice, Ladies of Fashion series, red and white, 1975-80,
  8½" h **325.00**
Amelia, Somerset Collection, burgundy velvet coat, hat,
  and fur-trimmed muff, 1985-88, 9¾" h **425.00**
Anne Boleyn, Royal Collection, peach, orange, and gray,
  1979-92, 8" h **550.00**
Barbara, Ladies of Fashion series, lilac dress, c1949-72,
  5" h **400.00**
Best Man, The Bridal Party series, black coat and shoes,
  blue waistcoat and tie, tan trousers, white shirt and
  socks, red hair, c1920, 5" h **375.00**
Bridesmaid, The Bridal Party series, blue dress and hat,
  yellow and red bouquet, c1920, 5" h **375.00**
Claudette, Debutante Collection, green dress, 1982-85,
  5" h **150.00**
Harlequin, multicolored, limited edition of 100, 1983,
  9½" h **775.00**
House of Norman, History of Costume series, beige
  dress, blue cape, white headdress, limited edition of
  500, 1979, 10" h **700.00**
Joan, Miniature Crinoline Lady series, blue dress, blue
  hat with pink ribbon, c1949-72, 5" h **400.00**
Michele, Ladies of Fashion series, green dress, 1976-79,
  8½" h **325.00**
Phyllis, Miniature Crinoline Lady series, brown and
  beige dress, brown hat, c1949-72, 3" h **325.00**
Saturday's Child, Children of the Week series, light blue
  and beige, 1989-91, 5½" h **250.00**
Silversmith, Craft Figures series, 1974-80, 7¾" h **300.00**
Stable Girl, Children Studies series, 1979, 8½" h **275.00**
Strawberry Fayre, rose-pink dress, purple bodice, white
  apron, purple hat, brown basket of flowers, c1949-72,
  6¾" h **550.00**

COCA-COLA

John Pemberton, a pharmacist from Atlanta, Georgia, developed the formula for Coca-Cola. However, credit for making Coca-Cola the world's leading beverage belongs to Asa G. Candler. Candler improved the formula and marketed his product aggressively.

The use of "Coke" in advertising first occurred in 1941. Foreign collectors prefer American Coca-Cola items over those issued in their own countries.

Reproduction and copycat items have plagued Coca-Cola collecting for the past three decades. The problem is compounded by Coca-Cola's licensing the reproduction of many of its classic products. Finally, the number of new products licensed by Coca-Cola appears to increase each year. Their sales represent a significant monetary drain of monies previously spent in the vintage market.

References: *B. J. Summers' Guide to Coca-Cola, Second Edition,* Collector Books, 1998; Gael de Courtivron, *Collectible Coca-Cola Toy Trucks,* Collector Books, 1995; Steve Ebner, *Vintage Coca-Cola Machines, Vol. II, 1959-1968,* published by author, 1996; Bob and Debra Henrich, *Coca-Cola Commemorative Bottles,* Collector Books, 1998; Deborah Goldstein Hill, *Price Guide to Vintage Coca-Cola Collectibles; 1896-1965,* Krause Publications, 1999; Allan Petretti, *Petretti's Coca-Cola Collectibles Price Guide, 10th Edition,* Antique Trader Books, 1997; Allan Petretti and Chris Beyer, *Classic Coca-Cola Calendars,* Antique Trader Books, 1999; Allan Petretti and Chris Beyer, *Classic Coca-Cola Serving Trays,* Antique Trader Books, 1998; Al and Helen Wilson, *Wilsons' Coca-Cola Price Guide, 3rd Edition,* Schiffer Publishing, 2000.

Collectors' Clubs: The Coca-Cola Club, PO Box 392, York, PA 17405; Coca-Cola Collectors Club, PO Box 49166, Atlanta, GA 30359.

REPRODUCTION ALERT: Coca-Cola trays.

Blotter, "Cold Refreshment," 1937, 3½" h, 7¾" w **$15.00**
Bookends, pr, bronze, bottle shaped, 1963 . . . . **275.00**
Calendar, 1923, pretty woman wearing shawl and hold-
  ing Coke bottle, matted and framed under glass, Sept
  page only **375.00**
Calendar, 1928, distributor's calendar, lounging woman
  with spit-curl hairdo and long gold dress, matted and
  framed under glass, Nov page only, 7½ x 13½" **850.00**
Calendar, 1932, barefoot boy sitting on well wall next to
  begging dog, matted and framed under glass, Jul page
  only **350.00**
Calendar, 1938, smiling girl wearing wide-brimmed hat
  and white summer dress, framed under glass, pad
  missing cover sheet **175.00**
Calendar, 1939, smiling girl pouring soda from bottle
  into glass, full pad, metal strip and hanger **525.00**
Calendar, 1943, pretty nurse holding Coke bottle,
  framed under glass, complete. **200.00**
Calendar, 1945, blonde girl wearing white scarf, red
  plaid jacket, and red gloves, snowy background,
  framed under glass **175.00**
Calendar Holder, metal, red "Drink Coca-Cola" button
  with "Have a Coke" and gold line border below, par-
  tial 1976 calendar pad, 19" h, 8" w **450.00**
Can, bottle in diamond, 1960s, 12 oz **150.00**
Carrier, aluminum, 6 bottle, emb, 1940s **65.00**

Blotter, 3¹/₂ x 7³/₄", $165.00. Photo courtesy Collectors Auction Services.

Carrier, cardboard, 6 bottle, collapsible, holly berry motif, 1940s **120.00**

Carrier, wood, 6 bottle, divider mkd "new consumer case," 1940s **225.00**

Clicker, metal, 1930s **135.00**

Clock, light-up, fluorescent, 1960s, 13 x 16" . . **350.00**

Cooler, Cavalier Carry Cooler Senior, orig box, 1950s, 13 x 18 x 18" **450.00**

Disk, celluloid, "Coca-Cola" with bottle, orig envelope, unused, 1950s, 9" d **450.00**

Display, folding wire rack, for 6-pack storage, c1940, 56" h **415.00**

Door Push, porcelain, "Thanks Call Again for a Coca-Cola," 3¹/₂ x 13¹/₂" **575.00**

Door Push, tin, "Come in! Have a Coca-Cola," 1940s, 4 x 11¹/₂" **250.00**

Drinking Glass, 1976 Olympics **3.00**

Dry Server Holder, metal, complete with 12 dry server envelopes, 1930s **165.00**

Festoon, 5 pcs, 8 men drinking soda, woman holding fan and glass, 1953 . . . . **2,975.00**

Flange Sign, tin, "Drink Coca-Cola Ice Cold" with bottle, 1953, 18 x 22" **475.00**

Fly Swatter, plastic, 1960s **10.00**

Greeting Card, "Happy Birthday," free drink offer from Coca-Cola Bottling Co, 1950s **20.00**

Lapel Pin, driver's, sterling silver, 1930s **100.00**

Menu, "Welcome," 2-sided, 1950s, folds to 10 x 6" . . . **5.00**

Panel, light-up, plastic, "Refreshing" with cup, 1960s, 24 x 20 x 4" **375.00**

Pencils, box of 36, orig sleeve, unused, 1940s **200.00**

Pinback Button, "Buy someone you love a Coke," 1970s . . . **3.00**

Pinback Button, "Member of Coca-Cola Bottle Club," hand holding bottle **65.00**

Poster, paper, "Keeps you rolling!," man and woman seated at counter by dispenser, 1950-60s, 20 x 53" . . **200.00**

Ruler, plastic, "It's the real thing Coke," 1970s **3.00**

Serving Tray, 2 golfers **1,000.00**

Serving Tray, man and woman wearing bathing suits, 1934 . . . . **150.00**

Serving Tray, woman drinking from bottle, 1928 . . . . **110.00**

Serving Tray, woman holding red and white striped umbrella, 1957 . . . . **300.00**

Serving Tray, woman wearing wide-brimmed hat holding glass, 1922 . . . . **225.00**

Sheet Music, *Rum and Coca-Cola,* The Andrews Sisters, 1940s **20.00**

Sidewalk Sign, porcelain, "Drink Coca-Cola" with dispenser, 2-sided, 1939, 25 x 26" **775.00**

Sign, cardboard, "Entertain your thirst," woman holding bottle singing into microphone, 1941 . . . . **500.00**

Sign, cardboard, "Get this Kit Carson Kerchief," easel back, 1953, 16 x 24" **200.00**

Sign, cardboard, "Tingling refreshment," seated woman holding bottle, 1931, 21 x 38" **55.00**

Sign, diecut cardboard, "Coca-Cola/For Santa," easel back, 1950, 14" h **415.00**

Sign, light-up, neon, "Have A Coke," 1940-50s, 23 x 14" . . . **925.00**

Sign, masonite, "Take a case home Today!/$1.00 Plus Deposit/Coca-Cola," 1950s, 12 x 14" **225.00**

Sign, porcelain, "Drink Coca-Cola/Fountain Service," dual taps, 1941, 14 x 27" **1,875.00**

Sign, porcelain, "Drink Coca-Cola/Pause Refresh/Lunch," 2-sided, 1933, 26 x 28" **3,850.00**

Sign, tin, diecut Coke bottle, 1956, 17" h **90.00**

Sign, tin, "Drink Coca-Cola" with bottle, diamond shaped, 1948, 42 x 42" **325.00**

Sign, tin, emb Christmas bottle at each end, 1930s, 18 x 54" **125.00**

Sign, tin, emb diecut 6 pack, 1960, 30 x 36" **675.00**

Sign, tin, "Pick up 6 For Home Refreshment," 1954, 16 x 50" **1,150.00**

Sign, tin, "Take home a carton Big Ben Size" with 6 pack, 1961 . . . . **1,375.00**

Syrup Keg, wood, paper label, 10 gal, c1940, 21" h . . . **275.00**

Thermometer, round, "Drink Coca-Cola/Sign of Good Taste," glass front, 1957, 12" d **200.00**

Thermometer, tin, coke bottle, 1930s, 16" h **150.00**

Thermometer, tin, double coke bottle, 1941 . . . . . . **450.00**

Thermometer, tin, silhouette of woman drinking from bottle, 1939, 6¹/₂ x 16" **325.00**

Ticket, Coney Island, Cincinnati, Coca-Cola Day, Wed Aug 7, 1968 . . . . **5.00**

Toy Truck, Buddy L, metal, with 8 cases and 2 hand trucks, 1960, 15" l **200.00**

Toy Truck, Marx, plastic, with 3 plastic cases, 1950-54, 11" l **250.00**

Toy Truck, Metalcraft, rubber wheels, working headlights, 1933, 11" l **775.00**

Whistle, tin, "Drink Coca-Cola In Bottles/Pure as Sunlight," 1920s **125.00**

COCKTAIL SHAKERS

The modern cocktail shaker dates from the 1920s, a result of the martini craze. As a form, it inspired designers in glass, ceramics, and metals.

Neither the Depression nor World War II hindered the sale of cocktail shakers. The 1950s was the era of the home bar and outdoor patio. The cocktail shaker played a major role in each. The arrival of the electric blender and the shift in public taste from liquor to wine in the 1960s ended the cocktail shaker's reign.

Reference: Stephen Visakay, *Vintage Bar Ware,* Collector Books, 1997.

Aluminum, Buenilum, straight sides, hand-wrought, grooved Modernistic top, clear plastic knob lid **$20.00**

Aluminum, The Konga, plastic knobs, 1930s, 11¹/₄" h **150.00**

Aluminum, World's Fair souvenir, black letters and building illus around top border, 1933 . . . . **90.00**

Chrome, bowling pin shape, turned maple top, 1930s,
   56 oz **50.00**
Chrome, coffee boiler shape, yellow Catalin handle and
   knobs, black incised bands on handle, Krome Kraft,
   Farber Bros, c1930s, 12" h. **30.00**
Chrome, cylindrical, black enameled bands, Bakelite
   finial, Chase Brass & Copper Co, c1930, 11½" h **55.00**
Chrome, electric, maroon enameled cast-iron base,
   Stevens Electric Co, 1933, 13" h. **200.00**
Chrome, Holiday Cocktail Set, "Gaiety" shaker, tray, and
   4 cups, Chase Brass & Copper Co, 1930s **150.00**
Chrome, teapot shape, red Catalin handle, 1930s. **30.00**
Chrome, Tipper Tumbler, red plastic top, "Tipple Tips"
   booklet, West Bend Aluminum Co, ©1934 . . . . **45.00**
Glass, litho recipes, battery operated, Swank, 1950s. **25.00**
Glass, tapered cylinder, clear with pink elephants dec **45.00**
Glass, tapered cylinder, red, Spun pattern, chrome top,
   Imperial Glass, c1955, 14" h **50.00**
Glass, white sailboats and seagulls, Hazel Atlas, 1930s. **75.00**
Nickeled Brass, bell shape, turned wood handle, 11" h. **65.00**
Stainless Steel, schoolmarm's bell shape, turned wooden
   handle, 11" h **40.00**

COINS & CURRENCY

Chances are you have some old coins and currency around the house. Many individuals deposit their pocket change in a large bank or bottle on a daily basis. People who travel return home with foreign change. Most currency exchanges will not convert coinage. Millions of Americans put aside brand new one-dollar silver certificate bills when America went off the silver standard.

Condition plays a critical role in determining the value of any coin or piece of currency. If your coins and currency show signs of heavy use, chances are they are worth little more than face value, even if they date prior to World War II. Circulated American silver dimes, quarters, half dollars, and dollars from before the age of sandwich coins do have a melt value ranging from two-and-one-half to three times face value. In some foreign countries, once a coin or currency has been withdrawn from service, it cannot be redeemed, even for face value.

The first step in valuing your coins and currency is to honestly grade them. Information about how to grade is found in the opening chapters of most reference books. Be a very tough grader. Individuals who are not serious collectors tend to overgrade.

Remember, values found in price guides are retail. Because coin and currency dealers must maintain large inventories, they pay premium prices only for extremely scarce examples.

Coins are far easier to deal with than currency, due to the fact that there are fewer variations. When researching any coin or piece of currency, the reference must match the object being researched on every point.

Allen G. Berman's *Warman's Coins & Paper Money* (Krause Publications, 1999) is a good general reference. It includes the most commonly found material. However, when detailed research is required, use one of the following:

References: American Coins: Coin World (eds.), *The Comprehensive Catalog and Encyclopedia of U.S. Coins, 2nd Edition,* Avon Books, 1998; David Harper (ed.), *2000 North American Coins & Prices, 9th Edition,* Krause Publications, 1999; Marc Hudgeons and Tom Hudgeons, *The Official 2001 Blackbook Price Guide of U.S. Coins, 39th Edition,* House of Collectibles,

2000; Scott A. Travers (ed.), *The Official Guide to Coin Grading and Counterfeit Detection,* House of Collectibles, 1997.

American Currency: Thomas Hudgeons, Jr. (ed.), *The Official 2000 Blackbook Price Guide to U.S. Paper Money, 31st Edition,* House of Collectibles, 1999; Chester L. Krause, Robert F. Lemke and Robert Wilhite, *Standard Catalog of United States Paper Money, 18th Edition,* Krause Publications, 1999.

Foreign Coins: Marc Hudgeons and Tom Hudgeons, *The Official 2000 Blackbook Price Guide to World Coins, 4th Edition,* House of Collectibles, 2000; Chester L. Krause and Clifford Mishler, *2000 Standard Catalog of World Coins, 1901-Present, 27th Edition,* Krause Publications, 1999; Chester L. Krause, Clifford Mishler and Colin R. Bruce II, *Collecting World Coins, 8th Edition,* Krause Publications, 1999.

Foreign Currency: Colin R. Bruce II and Neil Schafer (eds.), *1998 Standard Catalog of World Paper Money: Modern Issues (1961 to Present), Volume III, 4th Edition,* Krause Publications, 1998; Colin R. Bruce II and Neil Shafer (eds.), *Standard Catalog of World Paper Money, Specialized Issues, 8th Edition,* Krause Publications, 1998; Albert Pick, *Standard Catalog of World Paper Money: General Issues, Volume II, 8th Edition,* Krause Publications, 1997.

Periodicals: *Coin World,* PO Box 150, Sidney, OH 45365; *Coin Prices, Coins, Numismatic News,* and *World Coin News* are all publications from Krause Publications, 700 E State St, Iola, WI 54990.

Collectors' Club: American Numismatic Assoc, 818 N Cascade Ave, Colorado Springs, CO 80903.

COLORING BOOKS

Coloring books emerged as an independent collecting category in the early 1990s, due largely to the publication of several specialized price guides on the subject and the inclusion of the category in general price guides.

The McLoughlin Brothers were one of the first American publishers of coloring books. The Little Folks Painting Books was copyrighted in 1885. Although Binney and Smith introduced crayons in 1903, it was not until the 1930s that coloring books were crayoned rather than painted.

When Saalfield introduced its Shirley Temple coloring book in 1934, it changed a market that traditionally focused on animal, fairy tale, and military themes to one based on characters and personalities. It is for this reason that crossover collectors strongly influence the value for some titles.

Beginning in the 1970s, the number of licensed coloring books began a steady decline. If it were not for Barbie, Disney, and G.I. Joe, today's coloring book rack would consist only of generic titles, primarily because the market focuses on a younger consumer. Further, many of today's coloring books are actually activity books.

Reference: Dian Zillner, *Collectible Coloring Books,* Schiffer Publishing, 1992.

Note: Coloring books are in unused condition unless noted otherwise.

Adventures of Rin Tin Tin, Whitman #1257, 1955 . . . . **$25.00**
Andy Griffith Show, Saalfield, 1963 . . . . **50.00**
Around the World in 80 Days, Saalfield, 1957 . . . . **40.00**

Dick Tracy, Golden #3313-16, 1990, $5.00.

Baby Huey the Baby Giant Coloring Book, Saalfield
  #4536, 1959 . . . . **30.00**
Betsy McCall, Whitman #1069, 1971 . . . . **15.00**
Betty Hutton and Her Girls, Whitman #113415, 1951 . . . . . . **40.00**
Chiquita Banana in a Read and Color Book, Saalfield,
  1967 . . . . **25.00**
Christmas in Kewpieville, Saalfield #9546, 1966 . . . . **40.00**
Circus Boy, Whitman #1198, 1957 . . . . **20.00**
Cisco Kid, Saalfield #2428, 1954 . . . . **25.00**
Debbie Reynolds, Whitman #1133, 1953 . . . . **40.00**
Dick Van Dyke A Coloring Book, Saalfield, 1963 . . . . **40.00**
Doris Day Coloring Book, Whitman, 1955 . . . . **45.00**
Dudley Do-Right Comes to the Rescue, Saalfield #9571,
  1969 . . . . **10.00**
Fame Coloring & Activity Book, Playmore Publishing,
  1983 . . . . **15.00**
Fritzi Ritz to Color, Abbott Publishing #3335, 1940s **35.00**
Gene Autry Coloring Book, Whitman, ©1950 . . . . **50.00**
GI Joe Action Coloring Book, Whitman #1156, 1965 . . . . . . **20.00**
Gilligan's Island, Whitman #1135, 1965 . . . . **35.00**
Hee Haw, Saalfield #4538, 1970 . . . . **15.00**
Jimmy Durante Cut-Out Coloring Book, Pocket Books,
  1952 . . . . **45.00**
Jimmy's Coloring Book, Manor Books, Inc, Jimmy Carter
  face on front with stars and stripes ground, 1976 . . . . **25.00**
Jolly Santa, Whitman #1073, 1965 . . . . **10.00**
Juliet Jones, Saalfield #953, 1954 . . . . **30.00**
June Allyson, Whitman #1135, 1952 . . . . **45.00**
Laurel and Hardy, Saalfield #3883, 1972 . . . . **15.00**
Liddle Kiddles, Western Publishing #1868-B, 1967 . . . . **15.00**
Little Orphan Annie, Saalfield #4689, 1974 . . . . **35.00**
Marge's Little Lulu, Whitman #1186, 1950s **45.00**
Mister Magoo Cut-Out Coloring Book, Golden Press,
  1961 . . . . **30.00**
Mother Goose Paint and Crayon Book, Whitman, black
  and white and colored pages, rhymes and stories,
  1929 . . . . **25.00**
Mutual of Omaha's Wild Kingdom, Whitman, 1976 . . . . . . **15.00**
My First Scissor Book/Pictures Without Paste, Samuel
  Gabriel Sons & Co, illus by Winifred B. Pleninger **15.00**
My Toys to Trace & Color, Samuel Gabriel Sons & Co,
  1950s **10.00**

Our Gang, Saalfield #966, 1933 . . . . **25.00**
Patience and Prudence, Samuel Lowe #2532, 1957 . . . . **40.00**
Peanuts Pictures to Color, Saalfield #5331, 1960 . . . . **35.00**
Pebbles & Bamm-Bamm Play's the Thing, Modern
  Promotions, ©1978 Hanna-Barbera Productions **10.00**
Prince and Princess Paper Dolls with Pictures to Color,
  Saalfield #4464, 1957 . . . . **35.00**
Roy Rogers' Trigger & Bullet, Whitman, 1956 . . . . **35.00**
Shari Lewis and Her Puppets, Saalfield #5335, 1961 . . . . **15.00**
Shirley Temple Coloring Book, Saalfield, 1937 . . . . **65.00**
Sunshine Color Book, McLoughlin Bros, 1928, 9½ x
  12¾" **30.00**
The 3 Stooges Funny Coloring Book, Samuel Lowe
  #2855, 1960 . . . . **45.00**
The Flintstones Coloring Book, Charlton Publications,
  1971 . . . . **15.00**
The Night Before Christmas, Whitman #1126, 1963 . . . . **10.00**
The Road Runner Paint and Color Book, Whitman
  #1133, 1967 . . . . **15.00**
Thunderbirds, Whitman #1115, 1968 . . . . **20.00**
Tweety Coloring Book, Whitman, 1955 . . . . **25.00**
Walter Lantz Flying High with Woody and His Friends,
  Artcraft, 1970s **15.00**
William Boyd Star of Hopalong Cassidy, Lowe #1231,
  1950 . . . . **55.00**
Yogi Bear and the Great Green Giant, Modern
  Promotions, ©1976 Hanna-Barbera **15.00**
Young America Coloring Book, Platt & Munk, 1928 . . . . **20.00**

COMIC BOOKS

The modern comic book arrived on the scene in the late 1930s. Led by superheroes such as Batman and Superman, comics quickly became an integral part of growing up. Collectors classifiy comics from 1938 to the mid-1940s as "Golden Age" comics and comics from the mid-1950s through the the 1960s as "Silver Age" comics. The Modern Age begins in 1980 and runs to the present.

Comics experienced a renaissance in the 1960s with the introduction of the Fantastic Four and Spider-Man. A second revival occurred in the 1980s with the arrival of the independent comic. The number of comic stores nationwide doubled. Speculation in comics as investments abounded. A period of consolidation and a bitter distribution rights fight among publishers weakened the market in the mid-1990s and burst the speculative bubble. The comic book market is in recovery as the 21st century begins.

References: Grant Geissman, *Collectibly MAD: The MAD and EC Collectibles Guide,* EC Publications, 1995; Dick Lupoff and Don Thompson (eds.), *All in Color for a Dime,* Krause Publications, 1997; Alex G. Malloy, *Comics Values Annual, 2000 Edition,* Antique Trader Books, 1999; Robert M. Overstreet, *The Overstreet Comic Book Price Guide, 29th Edition,* Avon Books, Gemstone Publishing, 1999; Robert M. Overstreet and Gary M. Carter, *The Overstreet Comic Book Grading Guide,* Avon Books, 1992; Maggie Thompson and Brent Frankenhoff, *Comic Buyer's Guide 2000 Comic Book Checklist and Price Guide: 1961 to Present,* Sixth Edition, Krause Publications, 1998.

Periodicals: *Comic Book Marketplace,* Gemstone Publishing (West), PO Box 180900, Cornado, CA 92178; *Comics Buyer's Guide,* 700 E State St, Iola, WI 54990.

REPRODUCTION ALERT: Publishers often reprint popular stories. Check the fine print at the bottom of the inside cover or first page for correct titles. Also, do not confuse 10 x 13" treasury-sized "Famous First Edition" comics printed in the mid-1970s with original comic book titles.

Note: All comics listed are in near mint condition.

Addams Family, Gold Key, #3, Apr 1975 . . . . $50.00
Alice In Wonderland, Dell, #24, 1940 . . . . 300.00
All Humor Comics, Quality Comics Group, #17, Dec 1949. . . . . 25.00
Amazing Spider-Man, Marvel, #262. . . . . 5.00
Andy Devine Western, Fawcett, #2, 1951. . . . . 300.00
Angel, Dell, #16, 1958-59. . . . . 12.00
Animal Fair, Fawcett Publications, #11, Feb 1947 . . . . 40.00
Archie Giant Series Magazine, Archie Publications, #2, Archie's Christmas Stocking, 1955 . . . . 550.00
Archie's Mechanics, Archie Publications, #3, 1955 . . . . 300.00
Archie's Pal Jughead, Archie Publications, #100 . . . . 18.00
Archie's TV Laugh-Out, Archie Publications, #1, Dec 1969. . . . . 60.00
Audrey & Melvin, Harvey Publications, #62, Sep 1974. . . . . . 7.00
Awful Oscar, Marvel, #11, Jun 1949 . . . . 50.00
Babe Ruth Sports Comics, Harvey Publications, #11, Feb 1951. . . . . 150.00
Baby Huey Duckland, Harvey Publications, #1, Nov 1962. . . . . 115.00
Badge of Justice, Charlton Comics, #22, Jan 1955. . . . . 60.00
Baloo & Little Britches, Gold Key, #1, Apr 1968 . . . . 25.00
Banana Splits, The, Gold Key, #1, Jun 1969 . . . . 100.00
Barney and Betty Rubble, Charlton Comics, #1, Jan 1973. . . . . 30.00
Barney Google and Snuffy Smith, Charlton Comics, #6, Jan 1971. . . . . 12.00
Batman: The Dark Knight Returns, DC, #4, 1986 . . . . 7.00
Battle Beasts, Blackthorne Publishing, #1, Feb 1988 . . . . 1.50
Battle Heroes, Stanley Publications, #2, Nov 1966 . . . . 8.00
Battle Squadron, Stanmor Publications, #1, Apr 1955 . . . . . . 40.00
Beany and Cecil, Dell, #5, Sep 1963 . . . . 115.00
Best of Bugs Bunny, The, Gold Key, #1, Oct 1966. . . . . 45.00
Betty and Me, Archie Publications, #1, Aug 1965 . . . . 90.00
Beyond the Grave, Charlton Comics, #6, Jun 1976 . . . . 8.00
Bible Tales For Young Folks, Atlas Comics, #5, Mar 1954. . . . . 85.00
Bill Battle, The One Man Army, Fawcett, #4, Apr 1953 . . . . . . 30.00
Bingo, The Monkey Doodle Boy, St John Publishing, #1, Oct 1953 . . . . 25.00
Black Goliath, Marvel, #5, Nov 1976. . . . . 4.00
Black Panther, The, Marvel, #1, Jan 1977 . . . . 15.00
Blazing Combat, Warren Publishing Co, #4, Jul 1966 . . . . . . 25.00
Bob Swift Boy Sportsman, Fawcett, #5, Jan 1952 . . . . 30.00
Boris Karloff Tales of Mystery, Gold Key, #3, Apr 1963 . . . . . 25.00
Boy Detective, Avon Periodicals, #4, May 1952 . . . . 95.00
Bozo the Clown, Dell, #3, 1963 . . . . 50.00
Brady Bunch, The, Dell, #2, May 1970. . . . . 65.00
Brenda Starr, Charlton Comics, #15, Oct 1955 . . . . 250.00
Buck Duck, Atlas Comics, #4, Dec 1953 . . . . 35.00
Bugaloos, Charlton Comics, #4, Feb 1972 . . . . 15.00
Bullwinkle, Charlton Comics, #7, Jul 1971. . . . . 35.00
Buz Sawyer, Standard Comics, #1, Jun 1948. . . . . 150.00
Captain Hook & Peter Pan, Dell, #446, Jan 1953 . . . . 90.00
Casey–Crime Photographer, Marvel, #1, Aug 1949 . . . . 150.00
Casper and Nightmare, Harvey Publications, #6, Nov 1964. . . . . 35.00

Casper the Friendly Ghost, Harvey Publications, #7, Dec 1952. . . . . 300.00
Challenge of the Unknown, Ace Magazines, #6, Sep 1950. . . . . 175.00
Charlie Chan, Dell, #1, 1965. . . . . 35.00
Clint & Mac, Dell, #889, Mar 1958 . . . . 135.00
Cody of the Pony Express, Charlton Comics, #8, Oct 1955. . . . . 40.00
Colossal Show, The, Gold Key, #1, Oct 1969 . . . . 40.00
Comedy Comics, Marvel, #1, May 1948 . . . . 225.00
Comic Album, Dell, #2, Bugs Bunny 40.00
Comic Comics, Fawcett Publications, #1, Apr 1946 . . . . 80.00
Conan the Barbarian, Marvel, #1, Oct 1970 . . . . 200.00
Confessions Illustrated, EC Comics, #2, Spring 1956 . . . . 90.00
Corky & White Shadow, Dell, #707, May 1956 . . . . 70.00
Cosmo the Merry Martian, Archie Publications, #6, Oct 1959. . . . . 65.00
Cougar, The, Seaboard Periodicals, #1, Apr 1975 . . . . 3.00
Count of Monte Crisco, The, Dell, #749, May 1957 . . . . 90.00
Courtship of Eddie's Father, The, Dell, #1, Jan 1970 . . . . 30.00
Covered Wagons, HO, Dell, #814, Jun 1957 . . . . 50.00
Cow Puncher, Avon Periodicals, #2, Sep 1947 . . . . 225.00
Crack Comics, Quality Comics Group, #62, Sep 1949 . . . . . . 95.00
Crazy, Atlas Comics, #7, Jul 1954 . . . . 100.00
Crime on the Waterfront, Realistic Publications, #4, May 1952. . . . . 190.00
Cryin' Lion Comics, William H Wise Co, #1, Fall 1944. . . . . . 95.00
Cupid, Marvel Comics, #2, Betty Page, Mar 1950 . . . . 190.00
Daffy Tunes Comics, Four-Star Publications, #12, Aug 1947. . . . . 35.00
Dagwood, Harvey Publications, #1, Sep 1950 . . . . 100.00
Dale Evans Comics, National Periodical Publications, #1, 1948. . . . . 750.00
Daniel Boone, Gold Key, #1, Jan 1965. . . . . 85.00
Danny Thomas Show, The, Dell, #1180, 1961 . . . . 160.00
Daring Confessions, Youthful Magazines, #4, Nov 1952 . . . . . 80.00
Date With Danger, Standard Comics, #5, Dec 1952 . . . . 45.00
Dazey's Diary, Dell, Jun-Aug 1962. . . . . 30.00
Dead End Crime Stories, Kirby Publishing Co, Apr 1949 . . . . 375.00
Death Valley, Comic Media, #6, Aug 1954. . . . . 30.00
Dennis the Menace and His Dog Ruff, Hallden/Fawcett, Summer 1961 . . . . 40.00
Dennis the Menace Fun Book, Fawcett Publications, Spring 1969 . . . . 35.00
Deputy Dawg Presents Dinky Duck and Hashimoto-San, Gold Key, Aug 1965 . . . . 100.00
Detective Eye, Centaur Publications, #1, Nov 1940 . . . . . 1,600.00
Devil-Dog Dugan, Atlas Comics, #3, Nov 1956 . . . . 30.00
Dexter Comics, Dearfield Publications, Summer 1948 . . . . . . 50.00
Dick Tracy, Harvey Publications, #25, Mar 1950. . . . . 165.00
Dime Comics, Newsbook Publications Corp, 1951. . . . . 20.00
Dino, Charlton Publications, Aug 1973 . . . . 22.00
Dizzy Duck, Standard Comics, #32, Nov 1950 . . . . 55.00
Dr Kildare, Dell, #1, 1962. . . . . 90.00
Don't Give Up the Ship, Dell, #1049, Aug 1959. . . . . 70.00
Dotty Dripple and Taffy, Dell, Sep 1955 . . . . 30.00
Down With Crime, Fawcett Publications, #1, Nov 1952 . . . . . 200.00
Dracula, Dell, #2, Nov 1966 . . . . 25.00
Dragoon Wells Massacre, Dell, #815, Jun 1957 . . . . 80.00
Dudley Do-Right, Charlton Comics, Aug 1970 . . . . 85.00
Duke of the K-9 Patrol, Gold Key, Apr 1963 . . . . 30.00
Ellery Queen, Superior Comics, #4, Nov 1949 . . . . 250.00
Elsie the Cow, DS Publishing, #3, 1950 . . . . 125.00
Emergency, Charlton Comics, Jun 1976 . . . . 10.00

Enchanting Love, Kirby Publishing Co, Oct 1949 . . . . **80.00**
Famous Fairy Tales, KK Publishing Co, 1942 . . . . **300.00**
Famous Indian Tribes, Dell, 1962 . . . . **10.00**
Fantastic Voyages of Sinbad, The, Gold Key, Oct 1965 . . . . . . **45.00**
Fear, Marvel, Nov 1970 . . . . **25.00**
Flipper, Gold Key, #3, Apr 1966 . . . . **35.00**
Fractured Fairy Tales, Gold Key, Oct 1962 . . . . **110.00**
Frenzy, Picture Magazine, Apr 1958 . . . . **55.00**
From Here to Insanity, Charlton Comics, #8, Feb 1955 . . . . . **100.00**
Fugitives From Justice, St John Publishing Co, Feb 1952 . . . . **130.00**
Funland Comics, Croyden Publishers, 1945 . . . . **100.00**
Gabby Hayes Adventure Comics, Toby Press, Dec 1953 . . . . **100.00**
Gene Autry Comics, #11, 1943 . . . . **575.00**
Gentle Ben, Dell, #1, Feb 1968 . . . . **30.00**
Get Smart, Dell, Jun 1966 . . . . **100.00**
Ginger, Archie Publications, #10, Summer 1954 . . . . **60.00**
Girls In Love, Fawcett Publications, May 1950 . . . . **60.00**
Golden Love Stories, Kirby Publishing Co, #4, Apr 1950 . . . . . **95.00**
Golden West Love, Kirby Publishing Co, #3, Feb 1950 . . . . . **90.00**
Hand of Fate, Ace Magazines, #8, Dec 1951 . . . . **250.00**
Hawaiian Eye, Gold Key, Jul 1963 . . . . **45.00**
Heart and Soul, Mikeross Publications, #1, 1954 . . . . **35.00**
Hee Haw, Charlton Press, Jul 1970 . . . . **25.00**
Here's Howie, National Periodical Publications, #18,
   1954 . . . . **30.00**
Hi and Lois, Dell, Nov 1969 . . . . **20.00**
Hillbilly Comics, Charlton Comics, #1, Aug 1955 . . . . **45.00**
Hogan's Heroes, Dell, Jun 1966 . . . . **75.00**
Hot Wheels, National Periodical Publications, #1, 1970 . . . . **80.00**
Howard the Duck, Marvel Comics Group, #9, Mar 1981 . . . . . **4.00**
Huck & Yogi Winter Sports, Dell, #1310, Mar 1962 . . . . **85.00**
Huckleberry Finn, Dell, #1114, Jul 1960 . . . . **50.00**
Intimate Secrets of Romance, Star Publications, Sep 1953 . . . **100.00**
I Spy, Gold Key, #1, Aug 1966 . . . . **250.00**
Jackie Gleason and The Honeymooners, National
   Periodical Publications, #1, 1956 . . . . **650.00**
Jane Arden, St John Publishing Co, #2, Jun 1948 . . . . **75.00**
Jeep Comics, RB Leffingwell & Co, #3, 1948 . . . . **275.00**
Jiggs & Maggie, Dell, #18, 1941 . . . . **400.00**
John Carter of Mars, Dell, #488, 1953 . . . . **150.00**

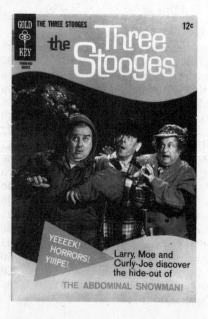

**Three Stooges,
Gold Key No. 38,
March 1968,
$18.00.**

Jonny Quest, Gold Key, Dec 1964 . . . . **350.00**
Ken Maynard Western, Fawcett, #1, Sep 1950 . . . . **450.00**
Kewpies, Will Eisner Publications, Spring 1949 . . . . **325.00**
Kid Montana, Charlton Comics, Nov 1957 . . . . **40.00**
Kitty, St John Publishing Co, Oct 1948 . . . . **40.00**
Knights of the Round Table, Dell, #540, Mar 1954 . . . . **70.00**
Kookie, Dell, #1, 1962 . . . . **70.00**
Laffy-Daffy Comics, Rural Home Publishing Co, Feb
   1945 . . . . **50.00**
Laramie, Dell, Jul 1962 . . . . **60.00**
Laredo, Gold Key, Jun 1966 . . . . **30.00**
Lash Larue Western, Charlton Comics, #47, 1954 . . . . **125.00**
Last Train From Gun Hill, Dell, #1012, Jul 1959 . . . . **90.00**
Laurel and Hardy, Dell, Oct 1962 . . . . **45.00**
Leave It to Beaver, Dell, #912, Jun 1958 . . . . **200.00**
Legend of Jesse James, The, Gold Key, Feb 1966 . . . . **20.00**
Lidsville, Gold Key, #5, Oct 1973 . . . . **18.00**
Life of Riley, The, Dell, #917, Jul 1958 . . . . **120.00**
Linda Lark, Dell, #8, 1963 . . . . **12.00**
Little Ambrose, Archie Publications, Sep 1958 . . . . **100.00**
Little Audrey & Melvin, Harvey Publications, #1, May
   1962 . . . . **75.00**
Little Dot Dotland, Harvey Publications, Jul 1962 . . . . **85.00**
Little King, Dell, Aug 1953 . . . . **100.00**
Little Max Comics, Harvey Publications, #3 . . . . **40.00**
Living Bible, The, Living Bible Corp, Fall 1945 . . . . **275.00**
Lucy Show, The, Gold Key, Jun 1963 . . . . **125.00**
Lucy the Real Gone Gal, St John Publishing Co, Jun
   1953 . . . . **70.00**
Mad About Millie, Marvel Comics Group, Apr 1969 . . . . . . **50.00**
Many Loves of Dobie Gillis, National Periodical
   Publications, May-June, 1960 . . . . **225.00**
Marine War Heroes, Charlton Comics, Jan 1964 . . . . **20.00**
Mars & Beyond, Dell, #866, Dec 1957 . . . . **90.00**
Marvel Tales, Marvel/Atlas Comics, #93, Aug 1949 . . . . . **1,000.00**
Maverick Marshal, Charlton Comics, #1, Nov 1958 . . . . **30.00**
Men Into Space, Dell, #1083, 1960 . . . . **50.00**
Merry Mouse, Avon Periodicals, Jun 1953 . . . . **50.00**
Midnight Mystery, American Comics Group, Jan-Feb
   1961 . . . . **75.00**
Miss Peach, Dell, Oct-Dec 1963 . . . . **70.00**
Mitzi's Boyfriend, Marvel, #2, Jun 1948 . . . . **65.00**
Moon Pilot, Dell, #133, 1962 . . . . **70.00**
Mr District Attorney, #1, 1948 . . . . **775.00**
My Secret Marriage, Superior Comics, #1, May 1953 . . . . . . **65.00**
Nature of Things, Dell, #727, Sep 1956 . . . . **50.00**
New Adventures of Pinocchio, Dell, #3, 1963 . . . . **60.00**
Night Nurse, Marvel Comics Group, #1, Nov 1972 . . . . **90.00**
Oh Susanna, Dell, #1105, 1960 . . . . **125.00**
Old Yeller, Dell, #869, Jan 1958 . . . . **50.00**
On the Double, Dell, #1232, 1961 . . . . **40.00**
Our Love Story, Marvel Comics Group, #1, Oct 1969 . . . . . . **30.00**
Outer Limits, The, Dell, #1, 1964 . . . . **100.00**
Out of This World, Charlton Comics, #1, Aug 1956 . . . . **150.00**
Owl, The, Gold Key, #1, Apr 1967 . . . . **35.00**
Partridge Family, The, Charlton Comics, #1, Mar 1971 . . . . . **45.00**
Patsy & Her Pals, Atlas Comics, #1, May 1953 . . . . **110.00**
Peter Panda, National Periodicals Publications, #1, Aug
   Sep 1953 . . . . **275.00**
Peter Potamus, Gold Key, #1, Jan 1965 . . . . **85.00**
Pink Panther, The, Gold Key, #1, Apr 1971 . . . . **40.00**
Pudgy Pig, Charlton Comics, #1, Sep 1958 . . . . **20.00**
Raggedy Ann and Andy, Dell, #5, 1942 . . . . **500.00**
Rangeland Love, Atlas Comics, #1, Dec 1949 . . . . **100.00**

Rat Patrol, The, Dell, #1, Mar 1967 . . . . **60.00**
Richie Rich, Harvey Publications, #1, Nov 1960 . . . . **1,400.00**
Richie Rich and Dot, Harvey Publications, Oct 1974 . . . . **15.00**
Richie Rich Diamonds, Harvey Publications, Aug 1972 . . . . . . **45.00**
Richie Rich Vault of Mystery, Harvey Publications, #1,
     Nov 1974 . . . . **25.00**
Roman Holidays, The, Gold Key, #1, Feb 1973 . . . . **30.00**
Sabrina the Teenage Witch, Archie Publications, #5,
     1971-83 . . . . **7.00**
Sad Sack Laugh Special, Harvey Publications, Winter
     1958-59 . . . . **100.00**
Sad Sack's Army Life, Harvey Publications, Oct 1963 . . . . **55.00**
Scarlet O'Hara In Hollywood, Standard Comics, Dec
     1948 . . . . **125.00**
Sea Hunt, Dell, #928, 1958 . . . . **125.00**
Secrets of Young Brides, Charlton Comics, #5, Sep 1957 . . . . . **35.00**
Sgt Bilko's Pvt Doberman, National Periodical
     Publications, #1, 1958 . . . . **325.00**
Shadows From Beyond, Charlton Comics, Oct 1966 . . . . **20.00**
Sheriff of Tombstone, Charlton Comics, Nov 1958 . . . . **60.00**
Six Million Dollar Man, The, Charlton Comics, Jul 1976 . . . . . **12.00**
Smitty, Dell, #11, 1940 . . . . **375.00**
Spine-Tingling Tales, Gold Key, #4, Jan 1976 . . . . **5.00**
Star Trek, Marvel Comics Group, Apr 1980 . . . . **6.00**
Stoney Burke, Dell, 1963 . . . . **15.00**
Stumbo Tinytown, Harvey Publications, #1, Oct 1963 . . . . . **130.00**
Sugarfoot, Dell, #907, May 1958 . . . . **135.00**
Super Comics, Dell, #121, 1949 . . . . **40.00**
Swamp Thing, DC, #57, 1972 . . . . **2.50**
Sweetie Pie, Dell, #1185, 1961 . . . . **30.00**
Swiss Family Robinson, Dell, #1156, Dec 1960 . . . . **70.00**
Tailspin, Spotlight Publishers, Nov 1944 . . . . **170.00**
Tales From the Crypt, Dell, Oct 1962 . . . . **175.00**
Tales From the Crypt, EC Comics, #20, 1950 . . . . **950.00**
Tales of the Green Beret, Dell, #5, Oct 1969 . . . . **15.00**
Terry Bears Comics, St John Publishing Co, #3, Mar 1953 . . . . **30.00**
Texas Rangers In Action, Charlton Comics, #5, Jul 1956 . . . . . **45.00**
Time Machine, The, Dell, #1085, Mar 1960 . . . . **160.00**
Tower of Shadows, Marvel Comics Group, #1, Sep 1969 . . . . **40.00**
TV Casper and Company, Harvey Publications, #1, Aug
     1963 . . . . **100.00**
Tweety and Sylvester, Dell, #406, Jun 1952 . . . . **80.00**
Two-Fisted Tales, EC Comics, #18, 1950 . . . . **725.00**
Uncle Wiggly, Dell, #543, Mar 1954 . . . . **40.00**
Underworld Crime, Fawcett Publications, #1, Jun 1952 . . . . . **190.00**
US Tank Commandos, Avon Periodicals, #1, Jun 1952 . . . . . . **50.00**
Valor, EC Comics, #1, 1955 . . . . **225.00**
Vicky, Ace Magazine, #5, Jun 1949 . . . . **25.00**
Vigilantes, The, Dell, #839, Sep 1957 . . . . **70.00**
Wally, Gold Key, #1, Dec 1962 . . . . **25.00**
Wanted: Dead or Alive, Dell, #1102, 1960 . . . . **125.00**
War Battles, Harvey Publications, #9, Dec 1953 . . . . **40.00**
War Heroes, Ace Magazines, #1, May 1952 . . . . **60.00**
Wartime Romances, St John Publishing Co, #1, Jul 1951 . . . . **200.00**
Wedding Bells, Quality Comics Group, #1, Feb 1954 . . . . **90.00**
Weird Science-Fantasy, EC Comics, #23, Mar 1954 . . . . **225.00**
Weird Tales of the Macabre, Atlas/Seaboard Publishing,
     #1, Jan 1975 . . . . **12.00**
Wild, Wild West, The, Gold Key, #1, Jun 1966 . . . . **125.00**
Willow, Marvel, #1, Aug 1988 . . . . **1.00**
Worlds Unknown, Marvel Comics Group, #8, Aug 1974 . . . . . **8.00**
Yogi Bear, Charlton Comics, #35, Jan 1976 . . . . **12.00**
Zoo Animals, Star Publications, #8, 1954 . . . . **25.00**
Zoo Parade, Dell, #662, 1955 . . . . **45.00**

COMPACTS

Cosmetic use increased significantly in the 1920s as women started playing a major role in the business world. Compacts enabled a woman to freshen her makeup on the run.

Although compacts are still made today, they experienced a Golden Age from the mid-1930s through the late 1950s. Collectors designate compacts manufactured prior to 1960 as "vintage."

Compacts are found in thousands of shapes, styles, and decorative motifs in materials ranging from precious metals to injection-molded plastic. Decorative theme, construction material, manufacturer, and novelty are four major collecting themes.

References: Roseann Ettinger, *Compacts and Smoking Accessories, Second Edition,* Schiffer Publishing, 1999; Roselyn Gerson, *Vintage Ladies' Compacts,* Collector Books, 1996, out of print; Roselyn Gerson, *Vintage Vanity Bags and Purses,* Collector Books, 1994; Laura M. Mueller, *Collector's Encyclopedia of Compacts, Carryalls & Face Powder Boxes* (1994, 1999 value update) *Vol. II* (1997), Collector Books; Lynell Schwartz, *Vintage Compacts & Beauty Accessories,* Schiffer Publishing, 1997.

Collectors' Club: Compact Collectors, PO Box 40, Lynbrook, NY 11563.

Amani, vanity case, white metal, loose powder, domed
     case, geometric pattern on lid, pop-up hinged framed
     mirror, case sgd, 2" d **$65.00**
Cara Noma Langlois, vanity case, goldtone, flower bas-
     ket center on incised web lid dec, int reveals mirror,
     powder and rouge compartments, 3¼" d **70.00**
Charles of the Ritz, vanity case, white metal, pressed
     powder glove triple vanity, Art Deco stylized femme
     lid logo, puffs with logo, bottom hinged metallic mir-
     rors, 2" l **100.00**
Coty, vanity case, goldtone, wishbone and star set with
     rhinestone lid dec, int reveals rouge and powder com-
     partments, 3¾ x 2¼" **80.00**
Elgin, compact, goldtone, loose powder, black enam-
     eled case, raised ivory pearl dec on lid, puff with logo,
     case glued mirror, 3" d **45.00**

Flato, goldtone, etched cat with cabochon stone eyes, lipstick sleeve, maroon velvet case, 1950s, $325.00.

Elizabeth Arden, compact, goldtone, loose powder, flapjack, domed case, faux sapphires and rhinestones on lid, framed mirror, case sgd, 3⅞" d **150.00**

Evans, compact, goldtone, loose powder, black enameled case, shooting star motif on lid, prong mounted baguette rhinestones, puff with logo, case glued beveled mirror, 2½" d **150.00**

Evans, vanity case, sterling silver, loose powder, cloisonné domed case, baroque engraved lid inset, link wrist chain, "Tap-Sift" int, side hinged double metallic mirrors, case sgd, 2¼" sq **250.00**

Hampden, compact, spun aluminum, loose powder, Art Deco floral motif, case glued beveled mirror, 3" d **50.00**

Helena Rubinstein, vanity case, goldtone, loose powder, coved case, ivory enameled lid, center cartouche, emb logo on rouge and puffs, case sgd, 2½" l **65.00**

Marhill, compact with matching pill box, mother-of-pearl enhanced with goldtone bands and raised painted flowers, 2¾ x 2½" compact, 1¼" sq pill box **55.00**

Max Factor, vanity case, goldtone, loose powder, Art Deco log motif on stepped lid, fleece puffs, slide powder dispenser, case sgd, 2¾" l **100.00**

Revlon, compact, plastic, pressed powder, flapjack, aqua case, coin purse closures, mermaid motif on lid, silver lurex aqua damask puff, case glued mirror, case sgd, 4" d **65.00**

Rho-Jan, compact, plastic, loose powder, flapjack, gray domed case, hp roses on lid, floral puff with logo, case glued mirror, 5" d **225.00**

Tiffany & Co, compact, sterling silver, int mirror and powder well, case sgd, 2¼" l **125.00**

Tussy, compact, goldtone, loose powder, ribbed, banded and circle lid motif, flanged case, puff with logo, framed mirror, case sgd on reverse, 3¼" d **50.00**

Yardley, compact, goldtone, pressed powder, bee and honeycomb motif, tinted white circles, emb feathers on powder, foam rubber puff, framed mirror, case sgd, 3½" d **35.00**

CONSOLIDATED GLASS COMPANY

The Consolidated Glass Company was founded in 1893, the result of a merger between the Wallace and McAfee Company and the Fostoria Shade & Lamp Company. In the mid-1890s, the company built a new factory in Corapolis, Pennsylvania, and quickly became one of the largest lamp, globe, and shade manufacturers in the United States.

The Consolidated Glass Company began making giftware in the mid-1930s. Most collectors focus on the company's late 1920s and early 1930s product lines, e.g., Florentine, Martelé, and Ruba Rombic.

Consolidated closed its operations in 1932, reopening in 1936. In 1962 Dietz Brothers acquired the company. A disastrous fire in 1963 during a labor dispute heralded the end of the company. The last glass was made in 1964.

Reference: Jack D. Wilson, *Phoenix & Consolidated Art Glass: 1926-1980,* Antique Publications, 1989, out of print.

Collectors' Club: Phoenix & Consolidated Glass Collectors' Club, 41 River View Dr, Essex Junction, VT 05452.

REPRODUCTION ALERT

Cigarette Jar, *Santa Maria* finial, 1931, 6¼" h, $175.00. Photo courtesy Gene Harris Antique Auction Center, Inc.

Ashtray, Ruba Rombic, lavender opalescent **$325.00**
Bonbon, Ruba Rombic, 3-part, smoky topaz, 8" w **250.00**
Bread and Butter Plate, Catalonian, russet, 6" d **100.00**
Bread and Butter Plate, Dancing Nymph, French crystal, 6" d **35.00**
Candleholder, Ruba Rombic, lavender **65.00**
Candlestick, Catalonian, yellow **35.00**
Cigarette Box, Con-Cora, roses dec **45.00**
Cigarette Box, Ruba Rombic, silver **350.00**
Cookie Jar, Con-Cora, milk glass, violets dec, 6½" h **85.00**
Creamer, Ruba Rombic, lavender **75.00**
Fan Vase, Catalonian, ftd, amethyst **25.00**
Finger Bowl, Ruba Rombic, jade **45.00**
Flower Bowl, Catalonian, yellow **85.00**
Goblet, Dancing Nymph, frosted pink **125.00**
Iced Tea Tumbler, Catalonian, emerald green, 12 oz **20.00**
Juice Tumbler, Ruba Rombic, smokey topaz **65.00**
Plate, Dancing Nymph, frosted pink, 10" d **175.00**
Salad Bowl, Catalonian, straight sided, amethyst **40.00**
Sherbet, Dancing Nymph, frosted pink **55.00**
Tumbler, Ruba Rombic, silver-gray, faceted and ftd, 10 oz **250.00**
Vase, Catalonian, flared, yellow, ftd **40.00**
Vase, Ruba Rombic, silver gray, 6½" h **625.00**
Whiskey Jug, Catalonian, amethyst **85.00**

CONSTRUCTION TOYS

Childen love to build things. Modern construction toys trace their origin to the Anchor building block sets of the late 19th and early 20th centuries. A construction toy Hall of Fame includes A. C. Gilbert's Erector Set, Lego, Lincoln Logs, and Tinker Toys.

A construction set must have all its parts, instruction book(s), and period packaging to be considered complete. Collectors pay a premium for sets designed to make a specific object, e.g., a dirigible or locomotive.

References: William M. Bean, *Greenberg's Guide to Gilbert Erector Sets, Vol. One: 1913-1932,* Greenberg Books, Kalmbach, 1993; William M. Bean, *Greenberg's Guide to Gilbert Erector Sets,*

Vol. Two: 1933-1962, Kalmbach, 1998; Craig Strange, *Collector's Guide to Tinker Toys,* Collector Books, 1996.

Collectors' Club: A. C. Gilbert Heritage Society, 1440 Whalley, Ste 252, New Haven, CT 06515.

AC Gilbert, #1, Erector Brik, 1944 . . . . **$160.00**
AC Gilbert, #1, Erector Set, 1926 . . . . **150.00**
AC Gilbert, #2½, Erector Set, 1956 . . . . **150.00**
AC Gilbert, #4, Junior Erector, 1949 . . . . **225.00**
AC Gilbert, #7½, Erector Set, 1951 . . . . **275.00**
AC Gilbert, #7½, White Truck Erector Set, 1931 . . . . **950.00**
AC Gilbert, #8, Erector Zeppelin Set, 1929 . . . . **2,500.00**
AC Gilbert, #8½, Erector Ferris Wheel Set, "First Set with the Whistle," 1942 . . . . **400.00**
AC Gilbert, #8½, Erector Ferris Wheel Set, 1952 . . . . **350.00**
AC Gilbert, #10021, Erector Young Builder's Set, 1960 . . . . . . **90.00**
AC Gilbert, #10057, Electric Engine Erector, 1960 . . . . **150.00**
AC Gilbert, #10092, Master Builder Set, 1958 . . . . **1,850.00**
AC Gilbert, #10171, Engineer's Set, 1962 . . . . **75.00**
AC Gilbert, #10201, Rocket Launcher Set, 1962 . . . . **175.00**
AC Gilbert, #10611, Military Vehicles Set, 1964 . . . . **250.00**
AC Gilbert, #10621, Erector Constructor 5 In 1, 1964 . . . . . **250.00**
AC Gilbert, #18000, Space Age Erector, 1959 . . . . **450.00**
AC Gilbert, #18030, Space Age Erector, 1960 . . . . **150.00**
Gabriel, #30010, Tinkertoy, complete **5.00**
Märklin, #1014 . . . . **475.00**
Meccano, #2, Aeroplane Constructor Outfit, 1940 . . . . . . **2,000.00**
Meccano, #3, blue/gold, 1946 . . . . **500.00**
Meccano, #4, Meccano Set, 1946 . . . . **175.00**
Meccano, Junior Set B, 1985, MIB **75.00**
Noveltoy Corp, Block-Stix, 50 wooden block pcs, orig box, 1930s **35.00**
Questor, #146, Super Transit Tinkertoy, 180 pcs, complete **10.00**
Spalding, Big Boy Tinkertoy, 1957 . . . . **30.00**
Spalding, #747, Circus Tinker Zoo, 222 pcs, complete **20.00**
Spalding, #640, Tinkertoy Curtain Wall Builder, 317 pcs, complete **50.00**
Stokys, K-1 Bridge Set **150.00**

COOKBOOKS

The cookbook was firmly entrentched as a basic kitchen utensil by the beginning of the 20th century. *Fannie Farmer's Cookbook* dominated during the first half of the century; *The Joy of Cooking* was the cookbook of choice of the post-1945 generations.

Cookbooks with printings in the hundreds of thousands and millions, e.g., the *White House Cookbook,* generally have little value except for the earliest editions.

Although some cookbooks are purchased by individuals who plan to use the recipes they contain, most are collected because of their subject matter, cover image, and use as advertising premiums. Do not hesitate to shop around for the best price and condition. The survival rate for cookbooks is exceptionally high.

References: Bob Allen, *A Guide to Collecting Cookbooks and Advertising Cookbooks,* Collector Books, 1990, 1998 value update; Mary Barile, *Cookbooks Worth Collecting,* Wallace-Homestead, 1994; Linda J. Dickinson, *A Price Guide to Cookbooks and Recipe Leaflets,* Collector Books, 1990, 1997 value update; Sandra J. Norman and Karrie K. Andes, *Vintage Cookbooks and Advertising Leaflets,* Schiffer Publishing, 1998.

Collectors' Club: Cook Book Collectors Club of America, PO Box 56, St James, MO 65559.

Adventures In Cooking, R Alsaker, 1927 . . . . **$20.00**
American Home Cookbook, Grace Denison, 537 pp, NY, 1932 . . . . **18.00**
Baker's Best Chocolate Recipes, Walter Baker & Co, Dorchester, MA, 60 pp, 1932 . . . . **10.00**
Betty Crocker Picture Cookbook, 1st ed, 465 pp, 1956 . . . . . **45.00**
Breakfasts, Luncheons, & Dinners, Mary Chambers, Boston Cooking School, May County, Boston, 151 pp, 1928 . . . . **25.00**
Clever Cooks, Lucy G Allen, 1st ed, hardback, Boston, 1924 . . . . **85.00**
Continental Cookbook, The, Josephine Bonne, 425 pp, NY, 1928 . . . . **22.00**
Cookbook of the US Navy, US Government Printing Office, 1927 . . . . **25.00**
Cooking As Men Like It, JG Frederick, 1st ed, 280 pp, NY, 1930 . . . . **30.00**
Fit For a King, Isabell Armitage, 1st ed, NY, 1939 . . . . **40.00**
Fowl & Game Cookery, James Beard, NY, 1944 . . . . **25.00**
French Dishes For English Tables, Claire DePratz, McKay Publishing, c1930 . . . . **12.00**
Glorious Art of Home Cooking, Hannah Dutaud, 284 pp, Chicago, 1935 . . . . **25.00**
Good Housekeeping Continental Cookery, London, 1962 . . . . **10.00**
Hungarian Cookery, Lilla Deeley, 88 pp, London, 1938 . . . . . **20.00**
Little Book of Cheese, Osbert Burdett, 1st ed, 98 pp, London, 1935 . . . . **30.00**
Little Kitchen Garden, Dorothy Giles, 1st ed, 98 pp, Boston, 1929 . . . . **45.00**
Modern Swedish Cookbook, Anna Coombs, 196 pp, 1947 . . . . **15.00**
New York World's Fair Cookbook, Crosby Gaige, 1st ed, 309 pp, The American Kitchen, 1939 . . . . **30.00**
Recipes of All Nations, Countess Morphy, 821 pp, NY, 1947 . . . . **25.00**
Sunset All-Western Cookbook, Gene Callahan, 216 pp, CA, 1933 . . . . **35.00**
Wine In the Kitchen, Elizabeth Craig, 1st ed, blue cloth, 140 pp, London, 1934 . . . . **30.00**

Enjoy Good Eating Every Day The Easy Spry Way, Aunt Jenny, ©1949, Lever Bros., Cambridge, MA, 48 pp, 6 x 8¼", $7.00.

COOKIE JARS

Although cookie jars existed as a form prior to 1945, the cookie jar's Golden Age began in the late 1940s and ended in the early 1960s. Virtually every American ceramics manufacturer from Abingdon to Twin Winton produced a line of cookie jars. Foreign imports were abundant.

There was a major cookie jar collecting craze in the 1980s and early 1990s that included a great deal of speculative pricing and some market manipulation. The speculative bubble is in the process of collapsing in many areas. Reproductions and high-priced contemporary jars, especially those featuring images of famous personalities such as Marilyn Monroe, also have contributed to market uncertainty. This major market shakeout is expected to continue for several more years.

References: Fred Roerig and Joyce Herndon Roerig, *Collector's Encyclopedia of Cookie Jars, Book I* (1991, 1997 value update), *Book II* (1994, 1999 value update), *Book III* (1998), Collector Books; Mike Schneider, *The Complete Cookie Jar Book, 2nd Edition,* Schiffer Publishing, 1999; Mark and Ellen Supnick, *The Wonderful World of Cookie Jars,* L-W Book Sales, (1995, 1998 value update); Ermagene Westfall, *An Illustrated Value Guide to Cookie Jars* (1983, 1997 value update), *Book II* (1993, 2000 value update), Collector Books.

Newsletter: *Cookie Jarrin',* 1501 Maple Ridge Rd, Walterboro, SC 29488.

Collectors' Club: American Cookie Jar Assoc, 1600 Navajo Rd, Noman, OK 73026.

Saturday Bath, Rick Wisecarver, No. 58-91, 11" h, $215.00. Photo courtesy Collectors Auction Services.

Aladdin, Treasure Craft	**$75.00**
Apple and Pear, Puritan	**65.00**
Bananas, turquoise, Red Wing	**170.00**
Barrel of Apples, Metlox	**125.00**
Basketball, Treasure Craft	**30.00**
Basket of Eggs, McCoy	**75.00**
Basket of Potatoes, McCoy	**45.00**
Batman, Warner Bros	**175.00**
Bear in Fire Engine, Twin Winton	**90.00**
Bear with Cookie, bisque, Metlox	**40.00**
Bear with Roller Skates, Metlox	**100.00**
Betsy Ross, Enesco	**150.00**
Betty Boop, Vandor	**500.00**
Black Scotty Dog, Metlox	**100.00**
Blue Daisy, Abingdon	**60.00**
Boy on Football, McCoy	**200.00**
Bridal Bouquet, Metlox	**75.00**
Broccoli, Metlox	**160.00**
Brown Badger, Doranne	**55.00**
Brown Dripped "Cookies," Hull	**15.00**
Brown Peasant, Red Wing	**70.00**
Calico Cat, Metlox	**200.00**
Cat, mouse finial, Treasure Craft	**35.00**
Cat in Basket, American Bisque	**45.00**
Chef Pierre Mouse, McCoy	**65.00**
Children on Drum, Metlox	**75.00**
Choo Choo Train, Abingdon	**180.00**
Cinderella, Applause	**60.00**
Cinderella, Napco	**175.00**
Circus Horse, McCoy	**125.00**
Clown Carousel, Napco	**65.00**

Coffee Grinder, California Originals	**25.00**
Coffee Mug, McCoy	**40.00**
Coffeepot, Treasure Craft	**15.00**
Coke Can, McCoy	**80.00**
Cookie Bag, McCoy	**35.00**
Cookie Cop, Pfaltzgraff	**800.00**
Cookie Time Clock, American Bisque	**90.00**
Cookie Truck, American Bisque	**55.00**
Cottage, Shawnee	**1,500.00**
Covered Wagon, Brush	**475.00**
Cowboy Boots, American Bisque	**175.00**
Cruisin' Dog, Treasure Craft	**85.00**
Crying Clown, Cardinal Pottery	**90.00**
Derby Dan, Pfaltzgraff	**350.00**
Dinosaur, Japan	**35.00**
Dog Biscuit, Japan	**40.00**
Donkey and Cart, American Bisque	**75.00**
Dutch Boy, American Bisque	**60.00**
Dutch Boy, Pottery Guild	**60.00**
Egg Basket, Metlox	**95.00**
Farmer Fox, Treasure Craft	**75.00**
Feedbag, American Bisque	**130.00**
Firetruck, California Originals	**250.00**
Fish, Brush	**350.00**
Fish, Doranne	**45.00**
Fred Flintstone, Vandor	**145.00**
Frog on Lily Pad, Enesco	**20.00**
Genie, Treasure Craft	**75.00**
Gingerbread House, Treasure Craft	**35.00**
Grapefruit, Metlox	**175.00**
Harvest Farm Pig, Fitz & Floyd	**130.00**
Hen on Nest, Brush	**100.00**
Hershel Hippo, Fitz & Floyd	**65.00**
Hey Diddle Diddle, Brush	**200.00**
Hippo, Fitz & Floyd	**90.00**
Honey Bear, McCoy	**85.00**
Hound Dog, Doranne	**22.00**
Humpty Dumpty, Abingdon	**200.00**
Ice Cream Cone, McCoy	**35.00**
Ice Cream Freezer, American Bisque	**350.00**
Jukebox, Treasure Craft	**75.00**
Keebler Tree House	**75.00**
Kitten on Beehive, American Bisque	**55.00**
Kitten with Fish Bowl, Treasure Craft	**45.00**
Kliban in Top Hat, Sigma	**425.00**
Lamb with Suspenders, American Bisque	**65.00**

Lion, California Originals	175.00
Little Bo Peep, Napco	225.00
Little Boy Blue, Brush	625.00
Lucy Goose, Metlox	90.00
Majorette, American Bisque	450.00
Mammy, McCoy	175.00
Mickey Mouse with Santa Hat, Enesco	100.00
Miss Priss, Lefton	100.00
Money Sack, Abingdon	60.00
Monk, Treasure Craft	25.00
Monkey Eating Banana, Japan	30.00
Mother Goose, Metlox	250.00
Mousemobile, Metlox	150.00
Mushroom House, Metlox	225.00
Nighttime Bear, Fitz & Floyd	25.00
Noah's Ark, Treasure Craft	70.00
Old Fashioned Touring Car, McCoy	90.00
Old Shoe, Brush	100.00
Old Woman In Shoe, Pfaltzgraff	450.00
Panda, blue and white, Brush	450.00
Panda, Metlox	75.00
Peek-A-Boo, Regal China	1,400.00
Peter Pan, Brush	350.00
Pinocchio, Metlox	350.00
Polka Dot Bear, American Bisque	80.00
Poodle, bone finial, American Bisque	200.00
Pot Belly Stove, Treasure Craft	25.00
Pumpkin, Brush	125.00
Pumpkin Coach, Twin Winton	125.00
Quail, Red Wing	60.00
Quaker Oats, Regal China	100.00
Raccoon, Metlox	250.00
Raggedy Andy, Metlox	150.00
Raggedy Andy on Drum, Maddux	125.00
Raggedy Ann, Maddux	90.00
Ranger Bear, Twin Winton	30.00
Red Sweater Bear, Avon	25.00
Rooster, American Bisque	45.00
Rose, Metlox	300.00
Saddle, American Bisque	125.00
Seal, Doranne	22.00
Sheriff Pig, red hat, Robinson-Ransbottom	70.00
Shoe, Twin Winton	70.00
Sir Francis Drake, Metlox	95.00
Snoopy on Doghouse, McCoy	175.00
Snowman, California Originals	300.00
Sombrero Bear, Metlox	85.00
Squirrel, Sierra Vista	225.00
Squirrel on Pinecone, Metlox	55.00
Stagecoach, Treasure Craft	60.00
Strawberry, McCoy	40.00
Three Kittens, Fitz & Floyd	65.00
Traffic Light, McCoy	60.00
Treasure Chest, Brush	150.00
Vanilla Cupcake with Chocolate Icing, Doranne	18.00
Victrola, California Originals	375.00
VonDrake Duck, Metlox	30.00
Walrus, Doranne	30.00
White Cookstove, McCoy	20.00
Wilbur Cat, Japan	50.00
Winking Owl, Shawnee	200.00
Winnie the Pooh, California Originals	115.00
World War II Soldier, Robinson Ransbottom	200.00
Yogi Bear, American Bisque	550.00

COOPER, SUSIE

After a brief stint as a designer at A. E. Gray & Co., Hanley Staffordshire, England, Cooper founded the Susie Cooper Pottery in Burslem in 1932. There she designed ceramics that were functional in shape and decorated with bright floral and abstract designs. Cooper introduced the straight-sided "can" shape for coffeepots. Later she was employed by the Wedgwood Group where she developed several lines of bone china tableware.

References: Helen Cunningham, *Clarice Cliff and Her Contemporaries: Susie Cooper, Keith Murray, Charlotte Rhead and the Carlton Ware Designers*, Schiffer Publishing, 1999; Francis Salmon, *Collecting Susie Cooper*, Francis Joseph, 1994.

Collectors' Club: Susie Cooper Collectors Group, PO Box 7436, London N12 7QF UK.

Biscuit Barrel, Moon and Mountain, red, blue, green, yellow, and black, Gray's Pottery, 6⅝" h	$450.00
Bowl, Kestral shape, Gardenia, 6½" d	25.00
Bread and Butter Plate, Wild Strawberry, c1970, 4" d	15.00
Coffeepot, cov, Kestral shape, Tyrol, 7½" h	285.00
Cup and Saucer, Venetia, c1965	15.00
Demitasse Cup and Saucer, pink and green tiger lilies	18.00
Dinner Plate, Wild Strawberry, c1953, 8½" d	10.00
Gravy Boat, Kestral shape, Gardenia	40.00
Jug, Parrot Tulip dec, c1950, 5" h	80.00
Jug, Quail shape, Glen Mist, c1960, 4½" h	25.00
Lemonade Jug, Cubist, black, red, blue, yellow, and green, red handle, Gray's Pottery, 7½" h	550.00
Plate, Kestral shape, Gardenia, 8" d	15.00
Soup Bowl, Kestral shape, red and gray bands, 8" d	30.00
Sugar Bowl, painted blue, green, purple, and black flowerheads on cream ground, red rim, c1925, 2¼" h	150.00
Teapot, cov, Quail shape, Whispering Grass, c1955, 5½" h	65.00
Teapot, cov, Rex shape, Dresden Spray, c1939, 5½" h	170.00

COORS POTTERY

After J. J. Herold went to work for the Western Pottery Company in Denver in 1912, Adolph Coors and the other investors in the Herold China and Pottery Company, Golden, Colorado, kept the factory open and renamed it the Golden Pottery. In 1920 the name was changed to Coors Porcelain Company.

In the 1930s Coors introduced six dinnerware lines: Coorado, Golden Ivory, Golden Rainbow, Mello-Tone, Rock-Mount, and Rosebud Cook-N-Serve. Dinnerware production ceased in 1941. Although the company produced some utilitarian ware such as ashtrays, ovenware, and teapots after the war, it never resumed its dinnerware production.

Reference: Robert H. Schneider, *Coors Rosebud Pottery*, published by author, 1984, 1996 value update.

Newsletter: *Coors Pottery Newsletter*, 3808 Carr Place N, Seattle, WA 98103.

Coorado, gravy boat, attached underplate	$110.00
Coorado, salt and pepper shakers, pr	65.00
Coorado, teapot, cov	175.00
Floree, cake plate	55.00

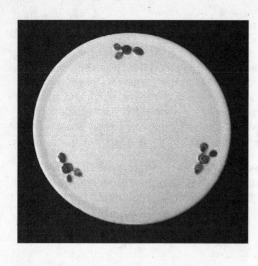

Rosebud, cake plate, 11" d, $35.00.

Floree, casserole, cov, medium **90.00**
Floree, pudding, large **95.00**
Mello-Tone, baker, 8" d **20.00**
Mello-Tone, bread and butter plate, 6¼" d **4.00**
Mello-Tone, cereal bowl, 6¼" d **8.00**
Mello-Tone, gravy boat **45.00**
Mello-Tone, teapot, cov, 6 cup **55.00**
Open Window, cake plate **90.00**
Open Window, coffee percolator, large **200.00**
Open Window, French casserole **100.00**
Open Window, pitcher, cov, small **100.00**
Open Window, pudding, cov **90.00**
Open Window, sugar shaker **65.00**
Open Window, teapot, cov **150.00**
Rosebud, bean pot, small **55.00**
Rosebud, casserole, straight sided, 8" d **65.00**
Rosebud, creamer **30.00**
Rosebud, cream soup **30.00**
Rosebud, cup and saucer **35.00**
Rosebud, Dutch casserole, small **65.00**
Rosebud, honey pot, with spoon **250.00**
Rosebud, platter **35.00**
Rosebud, pudding bowl, 7 pt. **80.00**
Rosebud, tumbler, handled **90.00**
Rosebud, utility jar **85.00**
Rosebud, vegetable dish, deep **35.00**
Tulip, coffee percolator **150.00**
Tulip, waffle pitcher, small **100.00**

COUNTER CULTURE

Counter cultural collectibles are the artifacts left behind by the Beatnik and Hippie culture of the 1960s. These range from concert posters to a wealth of pinback "social cause" buttons.

Some collectors prefer to designate this material as psychedelic collectibles. However, the psychedelic movement was only one aspect of the much broader Counter Culture environment.

Reference: William A. Sievert, *All For the Cause: Campaign Buttons for Social Change, 1960s-1990s,* For Splash, 1997.

Book, *Rebellion in Neward,* Tom Hayden, Random
   House, NY, 1967 . . . . **$75.00**
Booklet, *Beat Talk,* Studio Press, Tulsa, OK, 1960, 30 pp **100.00**

Comic Book, underground, El Perfecto Comics, Print
   Mint, Berkeley, CA, benefit comic for Timothy Leary
   Defense Fund, 1973 . . . . **125.00**
Handbill, Human Be-In, A Gathering of the Tribes,
   Stanley Mouse, Alton Kelley and Michael Bowen
   artists, The Bindweed Press, San Francisco, Jan 14,
   1967, 8½ x 11" **500.00**
Handbill, March Against the War, Los Angeles, Apr 22,
   1970, Student Mobilization Committee, San
   Francisco, 8½ x 11" **125.00**
Handbill, poetry reading, Kenneth Rexroth, Ginsberg,
   Ferlinghetti, Kandel, University of California at Santa
   Barbara gym, April 18, 1970 . . . . **450.00**
Lunch Box, vinyl, 6 hippie children painting wall with
   "Peace/Love" and images of flowers and birds, boy
   wearing hat with peace symbol, Aladdin Industries,
   c1972, 7 x 9 x 3½" **100.00**
Magazine, *Fruitcup,* Beach Books Texts and Documents,
   San Francisco, 1969 . . . . **90.00**
Magazine, *Life,* "Tragedy at Kent State," May 25, 1970 . . . . . **40.00**
Magazine, *The Second Coming,* William Borrough's
   chapter from *Nova Express,* Mar 1962 . . . . **150.00**
Pinback Button, "Free Tom Mooney," black lettering on
   cream ground with photo **20.00**
Pinback Button, "Give Peace A Chance," depicts John
   Lennon and Yoko Ono with person holding sign "War
   Is Over!" in background, 3" d **75.00**
Pinback Button, "Make Love Not War," sepia, white rim
   curl reads "War No More...Give Peace A
   Chance...From The Romance And Sex Investigative
   Intelligence Division Of The Peace Party...POB
   231...Macon, Georgia...31202," 3" d **50.00**
Pinback Button, "Old Enough To Fight, Old Enough To
   Vote," black and white, Greenwich Village under-
   ground store address on rim curl **15.00**
Pinback Button, "We Shall Overcome," blue lettering on
   white ground with red circle, c1963, 3½" d **20.00**
Poster, "Dick Gregory for President, Mark Lane for VP,"
   Peace & Freedom Party, with photos, 1968 . . . . **500.00**
Record, *Poetry for the Beat Generation,* Jack Kerouac,
   monaural LP, Hanover Records, Kerouac reading
   poetry accompanied by Steve Allen on piano **450.00**
Record, *Wake Up America,* Abbie Hoffman, Big Toe
   Records, limited to 1,000 copies, 1969 . . . . **300.00**
Ticket, Woodstock Music and Art Fair, Globe Ticket Co,
   Aug 1969 . . . . **100.00**

COUNTRY WESTERN

This category is primarily record driven—mainly due to the lack of products licensed by members of the Country Western community. There is not a great deal to collect.

Country Western autographed material, other paper ephemera, and costumes have attracted some collectors. Although fan clubs exist for every major singer, few stress the collecting of personal memorabilia.

Reference: Fred Heggeness, *Goldmine Country Western Record & CD Price Guide,* Krause Publications, 1996.

Autograph, Hoyt Axton, PS, promo photo with dog on
   lap, black and white, 8 x 10" **$7.00**
Autograph, Mel Tillis, PS, inscribed, color, 8 x 10" **4.00**

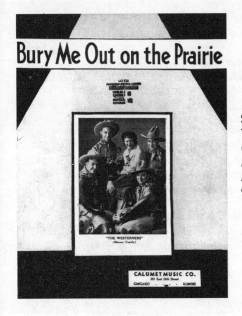

Sheet Music, The Westerners (The Massey Family), *Bury Me Out on the Prairie,* 1935, 9 x 12", $6.00.

Autograph, Patsy Cline, ALS, on 6 x 8" personal stationery, dated Apr 10, 1956 "To Harry," matted with black and white photo **1,850.00**

Autograph, Roseanne Cash, PS, inscribed, black and white, 8 x 10" **4.00**

Autograph, Roy Clark, PS, inscribed, black and white, 8 x 10" **4.00**

Autograph, Roy Orbison, PS, wearing sunglasses, color, 8 x 10" **250.00**

Magazine, *Ernest Tubb's Opry House Songs,* 12 pp, Eddie Arnold cover, 1940s, 8¼ x 10¾" **25.00**

Membership Card, Tex Ritter Fan Club **15.00**

Record, Barbara Mandrell, *Treat Him Right,* LP, Columbia 30967, 1971 . . . . **12.00**

Record, Bill Monroe, *Bill Monroe & His Bluegrass Boys,* EP, Columbia 1709, 1952 . . . . **40.00**

Record, Carter Family, *Can the Circle Be Unbroken,* 78 rpm, Banner 33465, 1935 . . . . **15.00**

Record, Dolly Parton, *Puppy Love,* 45 rpm, Goldband 1086, 1959 . . . . **50.00**

Record, Glen Campbell, *By the Time I Get to Phoenix,* LP, Capitol 2851, 1967 . . . . **15.00**

Record, Hank Williams, *Ramblin' Man,* EP, black label, MGM 1649, 1960 . . . . **50.00**

Record, Johnny Cash, *Don't Take Your Guns to Town,* 45 rpm, Columbia 41313, 1960 . . . . **10.00**

Record, Marty Robbins, *Long Tall Sally,* 45 rpm, Columbia 40679, 1957 . . . . **50.00**

Record, Patsy Cline, *Crazy,* 45 rpm, Decca 31317, 1961 . . . . . **10.00**

Record, Roger Miller, *The Country Side of Roger Miller,* LP, Camden 851, 1964 . . . . **18.00**

Record, Tennessee Ernie Ford, *Ballad of Davy Crockett,* 45 rpm, Capitol 3058, 1954 . . . . **25.00**

Record, Tex Ritter, *Daddy's Last Letter,* 78 rpm, Capitol 1267, 1950 . . . . **10.00**

Shirt, Eddie Rabbit, silk, white, long sleeves, sgd **60.00**

Shoes, pr, Johnny Cash, alligator, black **125.00**

Souvenir Album, Roy Acuff, green, browntone photo of smiling Acuff on front, photos and biographical text, WSM Grand Ole Opry, softcover, c1940s, 8½ x 11" **18.00**

COWAN POTTERY

R. Guy Cowan's first pottery, operating between 1912 and 1917, was located on Nicholson Avenue in Lakewood, Ohio, a Cleveland suburb. When he experienced problems with his gas supply, he moved his operations to Rocky River. The move also resulted in a production switch from a red clay ceramic body to a high-fired porcelain one.

By the mid-1920s Cowan manufactured a number of commercial products including dinnerware, desk sets, and planters. In addition, he made art pottery. In 1931, just a year after establishing an artists' colony, Cowan ceased operations, one of the many victims of the Great Depression.

Reference: Mark Bassett and Victoria Naumann, *Cowan Pottery and the Cleveland School,* Schiffer Publishing, 1997.

Bookends, pr, boy and girl, ivory glaze, 6¼ x 4" **$375.00**

Bookends, pr, elephant, semi-matte green glaze, 7½ x 5" . . . **775.00**

Bowl, ftd, faceted base, semi-matte pink glaze, ivory ext, 8" d **15.00**

Bowl, ftd, seahorse base, semi-matte pink glaze, ivory ext, 6" d **15.00**

Centerbowl, lavender glaze, 17" l **25.00**

Centerbowl, semi-matte mint green glaze, 10½" l **25.00**

Compote, classical shape base, mint green glaze, ivory ext, 3¼" d **25.00**

Console Set, semi-matte green glaze, 3½ x 12½" **30.00**

Flower Frog, "Awakening," ivory glaze, 9 x 3" **325.00**

Flower Frog, "Debutante," ivory glaze, 10¼ x 4¼" **925.00**

Flower Frog, "Duet," ivory glaze, 7¾ x 6¼" **500.00**

Flower Frog, "Grace," ivory glaze, 6½ x 4¼" **575.00**

Flower Frog, "Heavenward," ivory glaze, 7¾ x 4¼" **200.00**

Flower Frog, "Laurel," ivory glaze, 10" h **350.00**

Flower Frog, "Loveliness," ivory glaze, incised "B," 11¾ x 5¼" **500.00**

Flower Frog, "Pan," ivory glaze, 10 x 5¼" **275.00**

Flower Frog, "Pavlova, ivory glaze, 6" h **125.00**

Flower Frog, "Repose," ivory glaze, 6½ x 3" **200.00**

Bookends, pr, flying fish, antique green glaze, 8½" h, $550.00. Photo courtesy David Rago Auctions, Inc.

Flower Frog, "Scarf Dancer," ivory glaze, 7½" h **150.00**
Flower Frog, "Swirl Dancer," ivory glaze, 10¾ x 3¾" **675.00**
Lamp Base, bulbous, Oriental red glaze, 11½ x 9½" **325.00**
Lamp Base, spherical, ridged semi-matte mottled gray
  and orange glaze, 8" sq **90.00**
Low Bowl, lustered blue glaze, 7" d **20.00**
Paperweight, elephant, dark blue and emerald green
  glaze, 4¾" h **300.00**
Paperweight, elephant, ivory glaze, 4½ x 3¼" **325.00**
Vase, spherical, ribbed, feathery vermillion glaze, 10" h **150.00**

COWBOY HEROES

Cowboy Heroes are divided into eight major categories: (1) silent movie cowboys, (2) "B" movie cowboys, (3) "A" movie cowboys, (4) 1950s' and 60s' TV cowboy heroes, (5) Gene Autry, (6) Hopalong Cassidy, (7) The Lone Ranger, and (8) Roy Rogers.

Silent movie cowboys are in the final stages of the last memory roundup. "B" movie cowboys, comprising individuals such as Buck Jones, Ken Maynard, and Tim McCoy, are just down the trail. Reruns of the old "B" westerns have all but disappeared from television—out of sight, out of mind. "A" movie cowboys such as Clint Eastwood and John Wayne have cult followers, but never achieved the popularity of Gene, Hoppy, or Roy.

Currently the market is strong for 1950s' and '60s' television cowboy heroes. The generations that watched the initial runs of *Bonanza, Gunsmoke, Paladin, Rawhide, The Rifleman,* and *Wagon Train* are at their peak earning capacities and willing to pay top dollar to buy back their childhood. Prices for common 1950s' material have been stable for the past few years.

Gene, Hoppy, The Lone Ranger, and Roy are in a class by themselves. Currently, Hoppy collectibles are the hottest of the four with Roy close behind. Gene and The Lone Ranger are starting to eat dust. Look for a major collecting shift involving the collectibles of these four individuals in the next ten years.

References: Joseph J. Caro, *Hopalong Cassidy Collectibles,* Cowboy Collector Publications, 1997; P. Allan Coyle, *Roy Rogers and Dale Evans Toys & Memorabilia,* Collector Books, 2000; Lee Felbinger, *Collector's Reference & Value Guide to the Lone Ranger,* Collector Books, 1998; Ted Hake, *Hake's Guide to Cowboy Character Collectibles,* Wallace-Homestead, 1994; Robert W. Philips, *Roy Rogers,* McFarland & Co, 1995; Harry L. Rinker, *Hopalong Cassidy: King of the Cowboy Merchandisers,* Schiffer Publishing, 1995.

Newsletter: *Cowboy Collector Network,* PO Box 7486, Long Beach, CA 90807.

Collectors' Club: Westerns & Serials Fan Club, 527 S Front St, Mankato, MN 56001.

Note: For information on fan clubs for individual cowboy heroes, refer to *Maloney's Antiques & Collectibles Resource Directory* by David J. Maloney, Jr., published by Antique Trader Books.

Annie Oakley, flip badge, diecut stiff paper, red and yellow, black and white photo image of smiling Annie Oakley in center on 1 side, Wonder Bread loaf image on other, 1930s **$25.00**

Bobby Benson H Bar O Ranger, drinking glass, Bobby on bucking bronco above name, HO-Oats cereal premium, c1935, 4⅞" h **20.00**
Cisco Kid & Pancho, photo, horseback, facsimile signature, Tip Top Bread adv on reverse, c1950, 3½ x 5½" **25.00**
Dale Evans, sheet music, *Jeannie with the Light Brown Hair,* Dale Evans above "W.B.B.M.–Chicago/ Columbia Broadcasting System," ©1939 Calumet Music Co, Chicago, 9½ x 12" **20.00**
Davy Crockett, bank, Frontier Dime Bank, litho tin, 1950s, 2½ x 2½ x ⅝" **175.00**
Davy Crockett, card game, Ed-U-Cards Mfg Corp, NY, 1955, 2½ x 3½ x ½" box **25.00**
Davy Crockett, cereal bowl, milk glass, red image and "Davy Crockett Indian Fighter 1786-1836," 1950s, 4¾" d **20.00**
Davy Crockett, figure, with rifle, plastic, yellow, Peco, c1955, 3½" h **12.00**
Davy Crockett, handkerchief, red, image of young boys dressed as cowboy, soldier, and frontiersman, young girl Indian on horseback, tepees in background, lower right corner image of Crockett standing in front of Alamo with books labeled "Congress/Davy Crockett," military and frontier symbols around edges, 10¾ x 11½" **40.00**
Davy Crockett, pocketknife, 2 blades, clear plastic grip on 1 side with brown Crockett image holding up rifle with fort in background, reverse dark brown grip, 3½" l **35.00**
Davy Crockett, wallet, vinyl, tan, dark brown image of Crockett getting off horse holding rifle, 1950s, 3 x 8" **35.00**
Gabby Hayes, fan card, real photo, sepiatone image of Gabby holding hat, name in white text at bottom, 1940s, 3¼ x 5¼" **25.00**
Gene Autry, lobby card, *Boots and Saddles,* full color, Republic Pictures, 1937, 11 x 14" **22.00**
Gene Autry, photograph, smiling Gene Autry waving from back of rearing Champion, facsimile signature at bottom, 1940s, 8 x 10" **20.00**
Gene Autry, pinback button, black and white Autry with Champion image on shaded black ground, c1940s, 1½" d **50.00**

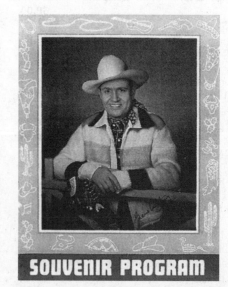

Gene Autry, souvenir program, "The Gene Autry Show," 18 pp, ©1949, 11 x 8½", **$35.00.** Photo courtesy Collectors Auction Services.

Gene Autry, pop gun, diecut cardboard, red accent ground, Gene Autry Show adv, 1954, 4⅝ x 8¾" **40.00**

Gene Autry, View-Master reel, #950, "Gene Autry and His Wonderful Horse, Champion," Sawyers, 1950. . . . . . . **12.00**

Hopalong Cassidy, badge, tab, litho tin, Hoppy image, Post Raisin Bran premium, 2" h **35.00**

Hopalong Cassidy, charm, pink plastic frame with inset glossy black and white photo, c1950, 1" h **15.00**

Hopalong Cassidy, cup, ceramic, white, blue Hoppy image with guns drawn, name in rope lasso design, reverse image of cowboy about to lasso steer in desert, c1950, 3" h, 2¾" d **50.00**

Hopalong Cassidy, membership card, Hoppy Fellow Member, and 3" d pinback button with center Hoppy illus and "Ask Me About The Hopalong Cassidy Savings Club" **35.00**

Hopalong Cassidy, milk bottle cap, white waxed stiff paper, red image of smiling Hoppy, name in red, Superior Dairies, Statesville, NC, 4" d **45.00**

Hopalong Cassidy, party plate, paper, white, colorful image of Hoppy on back of Topper riding down hillside, hat and boot designs in roped border with red accent, 1950s, 8½ x 8¾" **25.00**

Hopalong Cassidy, pencil, wooden, orange, white stripes, Hoppy name in silver, 1950s, 7" l **15.00**

Hopalong Cassidy, pillow, cloth, brown, gold fringe, yellow and red illus in corners showing Hoppy on Topper surrounded by lasso forming name, c1950, 9¼ x 13 x 3" **50.00**

Hopalong Cassidy, pinback button, "I Read Hopalong Cassidy in the Toronto Star," 1¼" d **100.00**

Hopalong Cassidy, View-Master reel, #955, Sawyers, 1950. . . . . **12.00**

Lone Ranger, Blackout Kit, with Lone Ranger Volunteers patch, orig mailing envelope, 1942 . . . . **145.00**

Lone Ranger, boots, child's, The Lone Ranger and Tonto, size 10 . . . . **110.00**

Lone Ranger, certificate, paper, "Lone Ranger Safety Club Charter Certificate," yellow, red, and black text overlaying image of Lone Ranger on rearing Silver, emb gold paper "Official Seal/Lone Ranger Safety Club" in lower left corner, Merlita Bread and Cakes premium, 1939 , 7 x 11" **75.00**

Lone Ranger, coloring book, Whitman, #1117-15, ©1951 The Lone Ranger Inc, 64 pp, 8½ x 10¾" **25.00**

Lone Ranger, fan card, full color painted image of smiling Lone Ranger twirling lasso on back of rearing Silver, Tonto in background against blue sky, bottom right facsimile signature, Silvercup Bread premium, ©1938 The Lone Ranger Inc, 4 x 6½" **30.00**

Lone Ranger, The Lone Ranger Hi-Yo Silver Brush, cloth, blonde wood, black and brown bristles, blue, white, and red Lone Ranger decal, 4½" l **35.00**

Lone Ranger, pinback button, "Cobakco Safety Club–The Lone Ranger," metal, blue and gold, 1" d **55.00**

Lone Ranger, pinback button, "Lone Ranger, Sun Herald and Examiner," litho tin, 1⅛" d **60.00**

Lone Ranger, pinback button, "Trigger," litho tin, multicolored, 1" d **20.00**

Lone Ranger, View-Master reel set, "Mystery Rustler," 1956. . . . . **20.00**

Rin Tin Tin, book, *Rin Tin Tin's Rinty,* Whitman, #1542, 284 pp, ©1954 . . . . **20.00**

Lone Ranger, guitar, wooden body, stamped "Supertone Warranted High Quality Musical Instruments, 2183," 35½" l, $70.00. Photo courtesy Collectors Auction Services.

Rin Tin Tin, comic book, Rin Tin Tin and Rusty, #19, Jun-Jul 1957 . . . . **15.00**

Rin Tin Tin, mask, Sgt O'Hara, stiff paper, smiling image with eyes cut out, Honey Comb cereal premium, 1950s, 6⅛ x 8¼" **20.00**

Roy Rogers, book, *Roy Rogers and the Dwarf Cattle Ranch,* Whitman Better Little Book, #1421, ©1947 . . . . . . **30.00**

Roy Rogers, harmonica, metal and plastic, detailed image of Smiling Roy in good luck horseshoe on both sides, 1⅛ x 4⅛" **40.00**

Roy Rogers, microscope ring, initials "RR" on 1 side, Trigger image on reverse, brass frame with 2-pc red plastic magnifier, Quaker Cereals premium, 1949 . . . . **75.00**

Roy Rogers, napkin, paper, tan, brown accent corner illus of Roy on back of rearing Trigger using rope to spell his name, rope accent design border, 1950s, 6¾" sq **12.00**

Roy Rogers, pencil case, red, black, and white, "Roy Rogers" and image on front, "First to Sears then to School" on back, 4¼ x 8¼" **65.00**

Roy Rogers, pinback button, "Mary Jane Bread," red and black, 1¼" d **50.00**

Roy Rogers, Range Rhythm Guitar, fiberboard, wooden neck, plastic fretboard, red and white Roy and Trigger graphics **175.00**

Roy Rogers, sheet music, *Oh Dem Golden Slippers,* Calumet Music Co, Chicago, ©1935, 9¼ x 12" **20.00**

Roy Rogers, tab, litho tin, with Roy Rogers Riders Club membership card **60.00**

Roy Rogers, tablet, lined, front color photo of smiling Roy wearing red cowboy shirt and blue pants on back of Trigger, facsimile signature "Many Happy Trails Roy Rogers & Trigger" at upper left, Copyright Frontiers Inc, Penworthy Litho in USA, 1950s, 7⅞ x 9⅞" **35.00**

Straight Arrow, bandanna, cotton, National Biscuit Co, 1949, 18½" sq. **45.00**

Tex Ritter, record, *Songs for Children,* 78 rpm **50.00**

Tom Mix, badge, "Straight Shooter," gold colored **100.00**

Tom Mix, cigarette card, Strollers #192, 1⅜ x 2½" **25.00**

Tom Mix, comic book, Tom Mix Western, Vol. 2, #7, Jul 1948, Fawcett **75.00**

Tom Mix, Dixie lid, waxed cardboard, inscribed "Playing In Miracle Rider–A Mascot Picture," c1935, 2¾" d **20.00**

Ken Maynard, banner, paper, 9" h, 42" w, $55.00. Photo courtesy Collectors Auction Services.

Tom Mix, Invisible Ink and Developer, Ralston, orig box with instruction sheet, writing manual, and 1938 premium catalog **250.00**

Tom Mix, Magnet Compass Gun and Whistle, plastic, glow-in-the-dark **150.00**

Tom Mix, pistol, wood with revolving chamber, orig mailing box **250.00**

Tom Mix, RCA Victor TV, 3 different film strips, plastic, brown **50.00**

Tom Mix, ring, brass, adjustable bands, eagle and shield design on sides, target on top accented in black circles, c1937 . . . . **200.00**

Tom Mix, Straight Shooters Signal Arrowhead, clear plastic **40.00**

Wild Bill Hickok, badge, white metal star, silver luster, clear plastic cover at center over black and white photo of Wild Bill and Jingles, c1955, 2⅛" h **75.00**

Wyatt Earp, coloring book, Saalfield, #1131, 1957, 11 x 14" **40.00**

Wyatt Earp, record, *The Legend of Wyatt Earp,* Shorty Long and the Happy Fellows, 45 rpm, RCA Victor Children's Bluebird label, 1950s **20.00**

Wyatt Earp, tumbler, clear glass, painted black and white action scene, red accents, 1960s, 5" h **25.00**

COW COLLECTIBLES

Cow collectors came in from the pasture in the late 1980s, the result of a shift in decorating motif preferences from ducks to cows in Country magazines.

The category is completely image driven. Few collect only a specific breed. Contemporary items are just as popular and desirable as are vintage examples.

Collectors' Club: Cow Observers Worldwide, 240 Wahl Ave, Evans City, PA 16033.

Activity Book, *Elsie's Funbook,* 20 pp, 1950s, 7 x 10¼" **$20.00**

Barbecue Apron and Tablecloth, Elsie, matching fabric picturing cookout picnic scene with Elsie, Elmer, Beulah, and Beauregard in brown, blue, red, and yellow, repeated small black and white images of barbeque cooking tools, salt and pepper shakers, cooler jug, etc, picnic scenes accented by string of printed yellow daisies across bottom edge, tablecloth opens to 36 x 54" with picnic scene repeated on longer edges, 1960s **75.00**

Book, *Elsie and the Looking Club,* 64 pp, hardcover, American Crayon Co, 1946, 5½ x 7½" **50.00**

Calendar, 1942, Borden's, color, Elsie and family members, Beauregard in baby crib with "Greetings for a Happy and Successful Moo Year" on back cov, 8 x 14" **75.00**

Card, "Elsie, The Borden Cow," mechanical, diecut, reverse assembly instructions and adv for RKO movie *Little Men,* c1940s, 2 x 3½" **75.00**

Pin, plastic, diecut daisy centered by relief brass luster metal Elsie portrait, Borden Co, 1940-50s **15.00**

Pinback Button, Daisy Deerfoot, brown cartoon image calf wearing daisy necklace, black lettering, white ground, 1930s **10.00**

Pinback Button, Hoard's Dairyman-Juniors, black and white cow head on gold ground, white rim, blue lettering, c1920s **10.00**

Pinback Button, Hood & Sons Milk, multicolored cow, white rim, red lettering, black accent circle, 1920s **20.00**

Pinback Button, Two Standards/Alderney Butter, multicolored scene of cow standing by US flag **25.00**

Pocket Mirror, Hyatt Mfg Co, celluloid, multicolored cartoon image of cow and calf with red, white, and blue sack of feed, blue inscription "Happy cow–what makes you laugh? Sucrene Feed and a little calf," American Milling Co, Philadelphia **100.00**

Salt and Pepper Shakers, pr, Elmer & Elsie, ceramic, mkd "C Borden," 4" h, 2⅜" w **85.00**

Sign, emb tin, Elsie image above "Borden's Ice Cream and Tony's Mkt," ©Elsie Borden Co, 56" h, 51" w **750.00**

CRACKER JACK

Cracker Jack arrived on the scene at the 1893 World's Columbian Exposition in Chicago when F. W. Rueckhaim, a pop store owner, introduced his world famous mixture of popcorn, peanuts, and molasses. The mix was not called "Cracker Jack" until three years later. The 1908 song, *Take Me Out to the Ball Game,* created national recognition for Cracker Jack.

The first prize in the box appeared in 1912. In the past 85 years plus, over 10,000 different prizes have made an appearance. New examples are being discovered every year. Today's prizes, with the exception of the magnifying glass, are made primarily from paper. The Borden Company, owner of Cracker Jack, buys prizes in lots of 25 million and keeps several hundred in circulation at one time.

References: Ravi Piña, *Cracker Jack Collectibles,* Schiffer Publishing, 1995; Larry White, *Cracker Jack,* Schiffer Publishing, 1999.

Collectors' Club: Cracker Jack Collector's Assoc, PO Box 16033, Philadelphia, PA 19114.

Toy Truck, tin, red with black hood, 1³⁄₈" l, $60.00.

Ambulance, litho tin, black, white, and red, 1930s $75.00
Booklet, "Cracker Jack Riddle Book," 2¾ x 5" 50.00
Clicker, litho tin, yellow, stamped name on top side 15.00
Drawing Book, 2½ x 3½" 40.00
Eyeglasses, diecut cardboard, grommet center, rose-colored transparency disk, inscription "Cracker Jack Wherever You Look" 50.00
Figure, Chester Gump, diecut litho tin, multicolored image, 1930s 75.00
Goat Wagon, diecut litho tin, red, white, and blue, "Shotwell's Checkers," 1920s 75.00
Hickory Dickory Pinball, mkd "Cracker Jack Division, Borden Foods," 1960s 10.00
Paint Book, paper folder opening to 4 panels, blue Cracker Jack art cover with adjoining panel "How To Paint" text instructions, ©APT Litho Co, 1920s, 1¼ x ½" closed size 50.00
Pinback Button, "I'm A Cracker Jack Prize," celluloid, red lettering on ivory white ground, c1950s 50.00
Play School Magic Speller, ©1946 C Carey Cloud 50.00
Railroad Car, Cracker Jack Line, litho tin, engine and coal tender, inscribed "512" on each side 100.00
Railroad Car, Lone Eagle Flyer, litho tin, passenger car 75.00
Ring, expandable white plastic, raised red hippo image under caption "Think Big," c1960-70s 15.00
Service Cap, paper, red lettering, blue trim on white both sides, inner headband has "Ad-Cap" by Union Bag & Paper Corp, NY, and patent number, c1933, 5½ x 11½" 75.00
Sign, cardboard, tri-fold, Cracker Jack and Angeles Marshmallows adv, c1920s, 20 x 27" 250.00
Spinner, diecut cardboard, Cracker Jack Golf, red, white, and blue 100.00
Stand-Up, The Flag of Freedom, diecut litho tin, base inscribed "It's Freedom Forever, Hurrah, Boys, Hurrah, Down with The Shackles And Up With The Star" 15.00
Three Little Pigs Pinball, 1960s 10.00
Whistle, tin, single barrel, c1930s 15.00
Wishbone Puzzle, with brown paper envelope holding wire puzzle, #4 from series of 15, 1930s 20.00

CRACKLE GLASS

Crackle glass, a glass-making technique that results in a multiple-fractured surface appearance, dates back to the 16th century. Martin Bach of Durand Glass is credited with reintroducing the concept in the late 1920s.

Crackle glass achieved widespread popularity in the late 1930s and was produced into the 1970s. Over 500 glass companies made crackle glass. Bischoff Glass, Blenko Glass, Hamon Glass, Kanawha Glass, Pilgrim Glass, Rainbow Art Glass, and Vogelsong Glass are just a few.

References: Judy Alford, *Collecting Crackle Glass*, Schiffer Publishing, 1997; Stan and Arlene Weitman, *Crackle Glass* (1996, 2000 value update), *Book II* (1998), Collector Books.

Collectors' Club: Collectors of Crackle Glass, PO Box 1186, Massapequa, NY 11758.

Candy Dish, tangerine, Pilgrim, 5½" h $100.00
Cruet, ruby, pulled back handle, Pilgrim, 6½" h 45.00
Decanter, crystal, olive green top, Blenko, 10½" h 60.00

Liqueur Glass, orange with applied clear handle, Pilgrim Glass Co, 1949-69, 4" h, $45.00. Photo courtesy Ray Morykan Auctions.

Decanter, lemon lime, Pilgrim, 6" h 100.00
Decanter, topaz, Rainbow, 8½" h 75.00
Drinking Glass, ruby, pinched, Hamon, 6" h 60.00
Fruit, apple, ruby, Boenio, 3½" h 50.00
Fruit, pear, pale sea green, Blenko, 5" h 50.00
Hat, olive green, Pilgrim, 3" h 35.00
Miniature Jug, blue, drop over handle, Pilgrim, 4" h 30.00
Miniature Jug, teal green, drop over handle, Pilgrim, 4" h 30.00
Miniature Pinched Vase, sea green, Blenko, 3¾" h 50.00
Miniature Pitcher, amberina, pulled back handle, Rainbow, 5" h 50.00
Miniature Pitcher, dark amber, drop over handle, Pilgrim, 4" h 25.00
Miniature Pitcher, green, pulled back handle, Kanawha/ Hamon, 3¼" h 35.00
Miniature Pitcher, olive green, drop over handle, Pilgrim, 3¼" h 30.00
Miniature Pitcher, tangerine, drop over handle, Pilgrim, 3½" h 30.00
Miniature Pitcher, topaz, pulled back handle, Hamon, 3¼" h 25.00
Pitcher, green, pulled back handle, Williamsburg Glass Co, 4¾" h 55.00
Punch Bowl, crystal, Blenko, 11¾ x 7" 200.00
Syrup Pitcher, blue, pulled back handle, 6" h 50.00
Vase, blue, Pilgrim, 6½" h 50.00
Vase, ruby, Pilgrim, 12¼" h 125.00
Vase, ruby, Rainbow, 5¼" h 50.00
Vase, sea green, drop over handle, Blenko, 7½" h 75.00

CREDIT CARDS & TOKENS

The charge coin, the forerunner of the credit card, first appeared in the 1890s. Each coin had a different identification number. Charge coins were made in a variety of materials from celluoid to German silver and came in two basic shapes, geometric and diecut. The form survived until the late 1950s.

Metal charge plates, similar to a G.I.'s dog tag, were issued from the 1930s through the 1950s. Paper charge cards also were used. Lamination of the cards to prolong use began in the 1940s.

The plastic credit card arrived on the scene in the late 1950s.

In the 1980s pictorial credit cards became popular. Individuals applied for credit just to get the card. The inclusion of holograms on the card for security purposes also was introduced during the 1980s. Today institutions from airlines to universities issue credit cards, many of which feature a bonus program. Little wonder America has such a heavy credit card debt.

Reference: Lin Overholt, *The First International Credit Card Catalog, 3rd Edition,* published by author, 1995.

Newsletter: *Credit Cards & Phone Cards News,* PO Box 8481, St Petersburg, FL 33738.

Collectors' Clubs: American Credit Card Collectors Society, PO Box 2465, Midland, MI 48640; Token & Medal Society, Inc, 9230 SW 59th St, Miami, FL 33173.

CARDS

ATS, telephone card, Hammermill Paper, 20 minutes	**$12.00**
Diners Club, Citicorp	**15.00**
Fina, 1970s	**5.00**
GTE Hawaii, telephone card, Lanai, 30 minutes	**30.00**
Hilton Hotels, paper, 1955	**35.00**
Husky, plastic, Canadian, 1960s, 1³/₄ x 3¹/₂"	**25.00**
Montgomery Ward, national charge-all card, yellow and white	**8.00**
Pacific Bell, telephone card, Santa & Phone, $5 value	**40.00**
Texaco, paper, Canadian, 1950s, 2³/₈ x 3¹/₂"	**30.00**
Vickers Refining Co, lifetime courtesy card, crown over "V" logo	**20.00**

TOKENS

Brody's Pharmacy, The Rexall Store, bronze, round	**$8.00**
Clark's Rexall Drug Store, "…Citizens Black or White Are Good People," no denomination, bronze, round, 1975	**5.00**
Cross' Cut-Rate Drugs, aluminum, round	**5.00**
Fifield Pharmacy, Hammond, IN, gilt aluminum keytag	**3.00**
Kansas Pharmacists Assoc, 1980 Hundredth Anniversary, no denomination, gilt bronze, round	**2.00**

White Rose Charg-O-Plate, plastic, with brochure, Canadian, $38.00. Photo courtesy Collectors Auction Services.

Massachusetts College of Pharmacy, 1973 Sesqui, no denomination, bronze, round	**2.00**
Red Cross Pharmacy, bronze, round	**5.00**
Wheeler & Stuckey Prescription Shops, Oklahoma City, OK, 1957 Sooners football schedule, aluminum, round	**10.00**
Woody's Pharmacy, "Worth 50¢ On Any New Prescription," aluminum, round	**15.00**

CROOKSVILLE POTTERY

Founded in 1912, the Crooksville Pottery, Crooksville, Ohio, made semi-porcelain dinnerwares and utilitarian household pottery. Their decal decorated "Pantry Bak-In" line was extremely popular in the 1930s and 40s.

The company's semi-porcelain dinnerware line was marketed as Stinhal China. Most pieces are not marked with a pattern name. Check the reference books. The company ceased operations in 1959, a victim of cheap foreign imports and the popularity of melamine plastic dinnerware.

References: Harvey Duke, *The Official Price Guide to Pottery and Porcelain, Eighth Edition,* House of Collectibles, 1995; Lois Lehner, *Lehner's Encyclopedia of U.S. Marks on Pottery, Porcelain & Clay,* Collector Books, 1988.

Apple Blossom, Pantry Bak-In, casserole, cov	**$20.00**
Apple Blossom, Pantry Bak-In, pie baker	**15.00**
Dartmouth, creamer and sugar	**25.00**
Dartmouth, gravy boat	**15.00**
Dartmouth, syrup jug	**30.00**
Dartmouth, teapot, cov	**55.00**
Dawn, bread and butter plate, 6" d	**2.00**
Dawn, casserole	**20.00**
Dawn, gravy boat	**15.00**
Euclid, casserole, 8" d	**25.00**
Euclid, coffeepot, cov	**45.00**
Euclid, creamer and sugar	**15.00**
Euclid, pie baker, 10" d	**15.00**
Harmony, casserole	**25.00**
Harmony, cup and saucer	**8.00**
Ivora, bread and butter plate, 6" d	**2.00**
Ivora, dinner plate, 9¹/₄" d	**8.00**
Ivora, soup bowl, 8¹/₄" d	**10.00**
Pantry Bak-In, batter jug, bulbous	**30.00**
Pantry Bak-In, casserole, 8" d	**25.00**
Pantry Bak-In, custard	**5.00**
Pantry Bak-In, syrup jug, bulbous	**25.00**
Provincial Ware, bread and butter plate, 6" d	**2.00**
Provincial Ware, gravy boat	**15.00**
Provincial Ware, platter, 11¹/₂" l	**12.00**
Quadro, casserole	**25.00**
Quadro, creamer and sugar	**18.00**
Quadro, platter	**12.00**
Silhouette, batter jug, bulbous	**40.00**
Silhouette, casserole, 6" d	**45.00**
Silhouette, mixing bowl, 9³/₄" d	**25.00**
Silhouette, rice canister	**50.00**
Silhouette, soup bowl, 7¹/₄" d	**18.00**
Silhouette, syrup jug, bulbous	**30.00**
Silhouette, tea canister	**50.00**

CUT GLASS

Glass is cut through a grinding process. Metal wheels containing abrasives or stone wheels are used to cut the decoration. Normally, "cut glass" describes glass with deeply cut decorative motifs. "Engraved glass" refers to pieces with lightly cut decorative motifs.

American cut and engraved glass divides into five basic periods: (1) 1740 to 1815; (2) 1815-1880; (3) Brilliant period, 1880 to 1915; (4) 1920 to the end of the 1950s, a period during which many pieces featured a combination of pressed and cut designs; and, (5) Contemporary, 1960s to present.

American tastes changed considerably following World War I. While cut glass continued to be a poplar anniversary, birthday, and bridal gift, buyers preferred lightly engraved patterns over the deep cut patterns of the American Brilliant period. Many established cutting firms experienced hard times. J. Hoare ceased operations in 1920, Egginton in 1918, Sinclair in 1929, and H. C. Fry in 1934. The post–World War I cut glass era effectively ended with the closing of A. H. Heisey & Company in 1958.

Most cut glass sold in the United States today is imported. A few American cut glass studio artisans produce commissioned pieces.

Collectors' Club: American Cut Glass Assoc, PO Box 482, Ramona, CA 92065.

Note: For additional listings see Fry, Heisey, and Stemware.

Bowl, Lyton pattern, Fry Glass, 8" d **$225.00**
Cordial, Harvest, #17724, Tiffin, 6⁵/₁₆" h 40.00
Ice Cream Tray, Daisy pattern, cut leaves, American
     Floral Period, 14" l, 7³/₄" w 80.00
Jug, Omar pattern, Fry Glass, 4 pt 300.00
Nappy, double handled, Wilhelm pattern, Fry Glass 250.00
Pitcher, handled, cut cosmos flower and band of
     Harvard, double notched handle and 6-step spout,
     10¹/₂" h, 6" d 110.00
Relish Dish, Prince pattern, Fry Glass 150.00
Table Lamp, mushroom shape shade with 6 large cos-
     mos and leaves, matching base with 3 cosmos,
     American Floral Period, 20" h lamp, 10¹/₂" d shade 350.00
Tankard Pitcher, 5-cut daisy pattern, cut leaves and
     stems, triple notched handle, large daisy cut flower on
     base, American Floral Period, 11¹/₂" h, 6" d 125.00
Vase, Ivy pattern, Fry Glass, 4 x 6" 325.00
Water Set, 6 pcs, 10³/₄" h pitcher and four 4" h tumblers,
     Daisy pattern, American Floral Period. 60.00

CYBIS

Boleslaw Cybis, a professor at the Academy of Fine Art in Warsaw, Poland, and his wife, Marja, came to the United States in 1939 to paint murals in the Hall of Honor at the New York's World Fair. Unable to return to Poland after war broke out, the couple remained in the United States and opened an artists' studio to create porcelain sculpture.

After a brief stint in New York, the studio moved to Trenton, New Jersey. Sculptures were produced in a variety of themes ranging from the world of nature to elegant historical figures.

American Bullfrog, Animal Kingdom series, 1971 . . . . **$600.00**
Blue Headed Virio Building Nest, Birds & Flowers series,
     1960 . . . . 1,100.00

Christmas Rose, Birds & Flowers series, 1965 . . . . **750.00**
Clematis, Birds & Flowers series, 1977 . . . . 325.00
Cybele, Fantasia series, 1974 . . . . 800.00
Eskimo Mother, North American Indian series, 1973 . . . . . 2,650.00
Folk Singer, Portraits in Porcelain series, 1967 . . . . 850.00
Jason, Children of the World series, 1978 . . . . 375.00
Maxine Dormouse, Animal Kingdom series, 1978 . . . . 225.00
Nativity Camel, Biblical series, 1984 . . . . 825.00
Nativity Joseph, Biblical series, 1984 . . . . 325.00
Pierre the Performing Poodle, Carousel Circus series,
     1986 . . . . 275.00
Queen Esther, Portraits in Porcelain, 1974 . . . . 1,800.00
Sparrow on Log, Birds & Flowers series, 1962 . . . . 450.00
Stallion, Animal Kingdom series, 1968 . . . . 850.00
St Peter, Biblical series, 1964 . . . . 1,250.00
Tabitha Kitten, Animal Kingdom series, 1975 . . . . 150.00
Tiffin, Land of Chemeric series, 1977 . . . . 550.00
Tiger, Carousel Circus series, 1974 . . . . 1,500.00
Tinkerbell, Children to Cherish series, 1959 . . . . 1,500.00
Yankee Doodle Dandy, Children to Cherish series, 1975 . . . . 325.00

CZECHOSLOVAKIAN WARES

The country of Czechoslovakia was created in 1918 from the Czech and Solvak regions of the old Austro-Hungarian Empire. Both regions were actively involved in the manufacture of ceramics and glass.

Czechoslovakian ceramics and glassware were imported into the United States in large numbers from the 1920s through the 1950s. Most are stamped "Made in Czechoslovakia." Pieces mirrored the styles of the day. Czechoslovakian Art Deco glass is stylish, colorful, and bright. Canister sets are one of the most popular ceramic forms.

By 1939, Czechoslovakia had fallen under the control of Germany. The country came under communist influence in 1948. Communist domination ended in 1989. On January 1, 1993, Czechoslovakia split into two independent states, the Czech Republic and the Slovak Republic.

References: Dale and Diane Barta and Helen M. Rose, *Czechoslovakian Glass & Collectibles*, Book II, Collector Books, 1997; Sharon Bowers, Sue Closser and Kathy Ellis, *Czechoslovakian Pottery*, Glass Press, 1999; Ruth A. Forsythe, *Made in Czechoslovakia*, Richardson Printing Corp, 1982, 2000 value update; Ruth A. Forsythe, *Made in Czechoslovakia, Book 2*, Antique Publications, 1993, 2000 value update; Robert and Deborah Truitt, *Collectible Bohemian Glass: 1880-1940* (1995), *Vol II: 1915-1945* (1998), published by authors.

Collectors' Club: Czechoslovakian Collectors Guild International, PO Box 901395, Kansas City, MO 64190.

Basket, white, blue trim, floral transfer dec, 5" h, 4⁵/₈" w **$30.00**
Boudoir Lamp, splatter glass, mushroom shape, yellow,
     blue, aqua, and green, matching glass base with
     chased metal 3-arm mount, c1930, 13¹/₄" h 450.00
Bowl, cased glass, opaque white, iridescent finish over
     geometric angles, 5¹/₂" h 100.00
Casserole, figural crab, 3" h, 7¹/₂" w 125.00
Coffee Canister, blue windmill on white ground, 7³/₄" h 45.00
Console Bowl, ftd, majolica, lilac and purple, green int,
     hp floral dec, 4¹/₈" h, 6³/₄" l 125.00

Sweetmeat Dish, porcelain, pink flowers, blue rim, Pirkenhammer, 3" h, $45.00.

Cow Pitcher, gold luster, emb flower, 3½" h, 6½" l **75.00**
Creamer, yellow, white trim, 3" h **20.00**
Dinner Plate, divided, Cross Eye pattern, yellow, orange, and blue, 10¹³⁄₁₆" d **90.00**
Figural Planter, rooster, white, 12¼" h **100.00**
Figurine, dragon ship, orange and white, 4" h, 8½" l **55.00**
Figurine, ram's head, white, 6" h **70.00**
Figurine, reclining horse, black, 2½" h, 4" l **35.00**
Figurine, seated couple, lilac, pink, and brown, 3⅝" h **45.00**
Gravy Boat, pink floral dec on white ground, 3¼" h **20.00**
Hors d'oeuvre Plate, floral transfer dec, basketweave border, 10" d **55.00**
Oil Cruet, white pastoral scene border, 8½" h. **45.00**
Planter, hp forest scene, 3" h **40.00**
Plate, Niagara Falls transfer dec, orange and white, 8½" d. . . . **20.00**
Playing Card Box, white, cobalt blue trim, "Bridge" transfer dec, 2¾" h, 4½" l, 3¼" w **20.00**
Salt and Pepper Shakers, pr, hen, hp, white, red yellow, and black accents, 1¾" h. **40.00**
Salt and Pepper Shakers, pr, rooster, glass, ceramic top, 3" h **50.00**
Sugar, cov, figural strawberry, 4¼" h **35.00**
Vase, cased glass, attributed to Kralik, globular form, furnace dec, orange glass with aubergine windings, base stamped "Czechoslovakia," 6" h **85.00**
Wall Pocket, bird on wishing well, orange and yellow, 5¾" h **60.00**

DAIRY COLLECTIBLES

The mid-20th century was the Golden Age of the American dairy industry. Thousands of small dairies and creameries were located throughout the United States, most serving only a regional market.

Dairy cooperatives, many of which were created in the 1920s and 30s, served a broader market. Borden pursued a national marketing program. Elsie, The Borden Cow, is one of the most widely recognized advertising characters from the 1940s and 50s.

Reference: Dana G. Morykan, *The Official Price Guide to Country Antiques and Collectibles, Fourth Edition,* House of Collectibles, 1999.

Newsletter: *Creamers,* PO Box 11, Lake Villa, IL 60046.

Collectors' Clubs: Dairy & Cream Collectors Assoc, Rte 3, Box 189, Arcadia, WI 54612; National Assoc of Milk Bottle Collectors, Inc, 4 Ox Bow Rd, Westport, CT 06880.

Drinking Glass, Baby Beulah, image and name in brown, red accent stripe around top, brown stripe around bottom, "And here's Baby Beulah, all comfy and cool; She'll soon be attending a smart Borden's School," 1940s, 3½" h, 2¼" d **$50.00**
Folder, Fairfield Western Maryland Dairy, adv for All-Star Parade Walt Disney Glasses, fold-out, Mickey Mouse illus, ©1939 Walt Disney Productions, 3¼ x 6¼" **55.00**
Game, Merry Milkman Exciting Game and Toy, complete with 3 milk trucks, milk, cheese, dairy, home, and spinner, Hasbro, 1950s **40.00**
Milk Bottle, Sykes Farms, Canton, NY, "A Bottle of Health," maroon inscription and baseball batter image **75.00**
Milk Bottle Cap Opener, Blewett Dairy, Lodi, CA, "Dial 9-3519" **8.00**
Paperweight, glass, Dairymen's Supply Co adv, green "Bestov" shamrock trade symbol, 1920s, 2½ x 4½ x ¾" **50.00**
Pencil Clip, "Drink Milk, Allentown Dairy, Co, Inc," green and white **25.00**
Pinback Button, Arden Milk, delivery boy portrait, red, white, and blue, c1940s, 2¼" d **20.00**
Pinback Button, Borden's Vitamin D Milk, orange and maroon on white ground, 1930s **25.00**
Pinback Button, Cloverlake Milk, litho tin, center Hopalong Cassidy photo, "Hoppy's Favorite Cloverlake Milk," 1⅜" d. **50.00**
Pinback Button, Del Monte Creamery, "A Quart A Day For Every Child," blue and white, sponsored by National Dairy and Food Bureau, Chicago, 1930s. **15.00**
Pinback Button, Golden Guernsey Milk, multicolored cow head accented by blue award ribbon fastened to halter, yellow rim with brown lettering, back paper has black and white image of "Golden Guernsey Products" milk dispenser plus sponsor American Guernsey Cattle Club, c1920-30s. **15.00**

Box, Greer's "Moo Girl" Creamery Butter, cardboard, ©1925, 1 lb, $3.00.

Pinback Button, "I Drink Ayshire Milk," maroon graphic
on white featuring child in Scottish tam and kilt skirt,
©1938 Ayshire Breeders Assoc. **20.00**

Pinback Button, Lincoln Dairy Co, "Safe Clean Milk,"
multicolored Abe Lincoln portrait on gold ground. **15.00**

Pinback Button, Vara Pals, cartoon scene of boy with
milk bottle, orange, white, and brown, 1930s **25.00**

Sign, Carnation Milk, diecut porcelain, milk bottle with
"Carnation Fresh Milk," 1940-50s, 14 x 15" **275.00**

Sign, Shamrock Dairy, porcelain, leprechaun illus,
"America's Table Milk," 1940-50s, 22 x 66" **350.00**

Squeaker Toy, Elsie, figural, soft rubber, Oak Rubber Co,
1950s, ©Borden Co, 2½ x 2½ x 5¼" **175.00**

Thermometer, St Lawrence Milk, celluloid over cardboard, rear wire hanger loop, multicolored scene of
stork delivering baby with milk bottle behind thermometer stem, lower text "Baby's Guardian," Parisian
Novelty Co, Chicago, 1920s, 2 x 6¼" **20.00**

DAVID WINTER COTTAGES

David Winter, born in Caterick, Yorkshire, England, is the son of
Faith Winter, an internationally recognized sculptor. Working from
his garden studio located at his home in Guildford, England,
Winter created his first miniature cottage in 1979.

David Winter Cottages received the "Collectible of the Year"
award from the National Association of Limited Edition Dealers in
1987 and 1988 and was named NALED "Artist of the Year" in
1991. In 1997 Enesco signed an agreement with David Winter to
manufacture David Winter Cottages and operate the David Winter
Cottages Collectors' Guild.

The secondary market for David Winter miniature cottages is as
strong (perhaps stronger) in England. Be cautious of English price
guides that provide a straight conversion from pounds to dollars in
their price listings. Taste and emphasis among collectors differs
between England and the United States.

References: *Collectors' Information Bureau Market Guide & Price
Index, Seventeenth Edition,* Collectors' Information Bureau, 1999,
distributed by Krause Publications; Mary Sieber (ed.), *2000
Collector's Mart Magazine Price Guide to Limited Edition
Collectibles,* Krause Publications, 1999.

Collectors' Club: Enesco David Winter Cottages Collectors Guild
(company-sponsored), 225 Windsor Dr, Itasca, IL 60143.

Ann Hathaway's Cottage, Tiny series, John Hine Studios,
1980. . . . . **$600.00**

Barley Malt Kiln, Cameos Collection, John Hine
Studios, 1992 . . . . **50.00**

Blackfriars Grange, Heart of England Collection, John
Hine Studios, 1985 . . . . **80.00**

Brookside Hamlet, In the Country series, John Hine
Studios, 1982 . . . . **85.00**

Castle Gate, Landowners Collection, John Hine Studios,
1984. . . . . **250.00**

Cat & Pipe Inn, English Village Collection, Enesco, 1997. . . . . **75.00**

Cinderella Castle, Disneyana series, John Hine Studios,
1992 . . . . **1,500.00**

Cooper's Cottage, Centre of the Village Collection, John
Hine Studios, 1985 . . . . **90.00**

The Dingle, Pilgrim's Way Collection, Enesco, 1997 . . . . **50.00**

Friar Tuck's Sanctum, Sherwood Forest Collection,
Enesco, 1997 . . . . **65.00**

House of Usher, Haunted House Collection, Enesco,
1998. . . . . **175.00**

Kent Cottage, Regions Collection, John Hine Studios,
1985. . . . . **125.00**

Lych Gate, Cameos Collection, John Hine Studios, 1992. . . . . **55.00**

Orchard Cottage, West Country Collection, John Hine
Studios, 1987 . . . . **110.00**

Post Office, English Village Collection, Enesco, 1997 . . . . **70.00**

Poultry Ark, Cameos Collection, John Hine Studios,
1992. . . . . **30.00**

Snow Cottage, In the Country Collection, John Hine
Studios, 1984 . . . . **125.00**

Spencer Hall Gardens, Heart of England series, John
Hine Studios, 1995 . . . . **350.00**

St George's Church, Heart of England Collection, John
Hine Studios, 1985 . . . . **75.00**

Stork Cottage/Boy, Celebration Cottages Collection, John
Hine Studios, 1995 . . . . **110.00**

Sunday School, South Downs Collection, Enesco, 1997 . . . . . **75.00**

Tamar Cottage, West Country Collection, John Hine
Studios, 1986 . . . . **90.00**

Welsh Pig Pen, Cameos Collection, John Hines Studios,
1992. . . . . **30.00**

Yeoman's Farmhouse, Heart of England Collection, John
Hine Studios, 1985 . . . . **75.00**

DEDHAM POTTERY

In 1891 a group of influential Bostonians formed Chelsea Pottery,
U.S., and hired Hugh C. Robertson, assisted by his son William, to
perfect a crackle glaze that he had discovered five years earlier.
Crackleware was produced by quickly cooling pieces after they
were taken from the glost kiln. The cracking was then rubbed by
hand with Cobot's lamp black powder to produce the famous spider-web effect.

The company moved to Dedham in 1895, changing its name to
reflect its new location. Although some hand-thrown vases with a
high-fired glaze on a high-fired base were made, cracqule ware
was the company's principal product. Joseph Lindon Smith and
Alice Morse designed the famous Dedham rabbit pattern. Over
fifty different patterns of tableware were produced.

World War I caused a temporary halt in Dedham's growth.
Prosperity returned in the 1920s and 30s. In 1943 J. Milton
Robertson, a Commander in the Navy, closed the pottery because
of a shortage of skilled workers and increasing costs. Gimbels
bought the remaining stock and offered it for sale in its New York
store in September 1943.

In the late 1980s The Potting Shed of Concord, Massachusetts,
created a series of Dedham reproductions including the 10" dinner plate, 8½" salad plate, and 7½" bread and butter plate in the
blue rabbit border motif. Several other companies have also produced reproductions.

Newsletter: *Dedham Pottery Collectors Newsletter,* 248 Highland
St, Dedham, MA 02026.

Note: All items listed are marked "Dedham Pottery Registered."

Ashtray, Rabbit pattern border, flat style rim, 6¾" d **$220.00**

Bread and Butter Plate, Azalea pattern, 6¹⁄₂" d, $125.00.

Bowl, Rabbit pattern border, scalloped edge, 9" d **1,000.00**
Butter Pat, Floral pattern, Wild Rose design int, pansy
    style floral ext, 3¹⁄₂" d **400.00**
Child's Plate, Elephant & Baby pattern border, circular
    elephant motif in center, 7¹⁄₂" d **1,650.00**
Coaster, Rabbit motif, outlined in circular blue line, 4" d. . . . **400.00**
Cup and Saucer, Polar Bear pattern border, 2¹⁄₈" h cup,
    6" d saucer **375.00**
Flower Holder, figural turtle, detailed accents, dome
    shaped shell with hollow opening in repeat, 3¹⁄₂" d **500.00**
Nappy, #2, open, Elephant & Baby pattern border,
    10³⁄₄" d **950.00**
Pitcher, cov, #2, Rabbit pattern border, bulbous, loop
    handle, 5¹⁄₂" h **450.00**
Plate, Butterfly pattern border, alternating floral design,
    2 imp rabbits, 9³⁄₄" d **950.00**
Plate, Chick pattern border, 8¹⁄₂" d **1,200.00**
Plate, Crab motif, multishades of blue, encompassing
    medium to light blue waves, 2 imp rabbits, 1931,
    7¹⁄₂" d **360.00**
Plate, Elephant and Baby pattern border, large border,
    2 imp rabbits, 8¹⁄₂" d **775.00**
Plate, Scottie Dog Pair in center, 8¹⁄₂" d **1,650.00**

DEGENHART GLASS

John and Elizabeth Degenhart directed the operation of Crystal Art Glass, Cambridge, Ohio, from 1947 until 1978. Pressed glass novelties, such as animal covered dishes, salts, toothpicks, and paperweights were the company's principal products.

Boyd Crystal Art Glass, Cambridge, Ohio, purchased many of the company's molds when operations ceased. Boyd continues to manufacture pieces from these molds in colors different from those used by Degenhart. Most are marked with a "B" in a diamond.

Reference: Gene Florence, *Degenhart Glass & Paperweights, Degenhart Paperweight & Glass Museum, 2nd Edition,* 1991, available from the Degenhart Paperweight & Glass Museum.

Collectors' Club: Friends of Degenhart, Degenhart Paperweight and Glass Museum, Inc, 65323 Highland Hills Rd, PO Box 186, Cambridge, OH 43725.

REPRODUCTION ALERT: Although most Degenhart molds were reproductions themselves, many contemporary pieces made by Kanawha, L. G. Wright, and others are nearly identical.

Animal Dish, cov, chicken, aqua **$25.00**
Animal Dish, cov, chicken, blue marble slag **40.00**
Animal Dish, cov, chicken, forest green **25.00**
Animal Dish, cov, hen, aqua **65.00**
Animal Dish, cov, hen, cobalt **50.00**
Animal Dish, cov, hen, emerald green **50.00**
Animal Dish, cov, lamb, canary **35.00**
Animal Dish, cov, turkey, apple green **65.00**
Animal Dish, cov, turkey, bluebell **65.00**
Animal Dish, cov, turkey, crystal **35.00**
Baby Shoe, lemon custard **25.00**
Boot, Rose Marie **25.00**
Coaster, pearl gray **15.00**
Creamer and Sugar, Daisy and Button, sapphire **75.00**
Creamer and Sugar, Texas, vaseline **50.00**
Cup Plate, Heart & Lyre, champagne **8.00**
Cup Plate, Seal of Ohio, honey amber **10.00**
Mug, Stork & Peacock, ruby **35.00**
Owl, light ivory **40.00**
Owl, periwinkle **45.00**
Owl, spice brown **50.00**
Priscilla, smokey blue **95.00**
Salt, Bird, amethyst **15.00**
Salt, Daisy & Button, opalescent **15.00**
Salt, Pottie, cobalt **8.00**
Salt, Star & Dewdrop, topaz **20.00**
Salt and Pepper Shakers, pr, bird, bluebell **30.00**
Slipper, Bow, bittersweet slag **40.00**
Slipper, Kat, Bloody Mary **50.00**
Toothpick Holder, basket, vaseline **15.00**
Toothpick Holder, bird, teal **15.00**
Toothpick Holder, Colonial Drape, cobalt **20.00**
Toothpick Holder, elephant head, Smokey Heather **35.00**
Toothpick Holder, Forget-Me-Not, custard **20.00**
Toothpick Holder, Forget-Me-Not, jade **30.00**
Toothpick Holder, Forget-Me-Not, mint green **15.00**

DELEE ART

While teaching art at Los Angeles' Belmont High School in the 1930s, Jimmie Lee Adair Kohl started a small ceramic figurines business. By the start of 1939, Jimmie Lee had produced over 3,500 salable pieces.

When a shortage of ceramic supplies occurred during World War II, Jimmie Lee borrowed money and moved some production to Cuernavaca, Mexico. Her Los Angeles operations continued on a limited basis. By 1994, Jimmie Lee closed her Mexican facility.

The period from the mid-1940s until the end of the 1950s was deLee's golden age. The company produced high quality, giftware figurines. In 1949 a representative from Barnes & Noble asked her to write a ceramic "how to" book. *Ceramics for All,* part of the Everyday Handbook series, was published in 1950.

The arrival of cheap imported reproductions from Japan and elsewhere at the end of the 1950s spelled doom for deLee. The factory closed in 1958.

Reference: Joanne Fulton Schafer, *deLee Art: The Pictorial Story of a California Artist and Her Company, 1937-1958,* published by author, 1997.

Bank, Peanuts, elephant holding drum, 7" h **$65.00**
Bank, Stinkie, skunk with crossed arms, 7" h **50.00**
Cookie Jar, Cookie Girl, painted words on apron, 12" h **250.00**

Planter, Nina, #43, 7" h, $25.00.

Figure, baby, open blue eyes, 3½" h. **50.00**
Figure, boy and dog, molded base with floral dec. **55.00**
Figure, Bubbles, lamb with closed eyes, 3" h **25.00**
Figure, cat, open arms, wide eyed, 4½" h. **20.00**
Figure, Chesty, squirrel with floral dec, 3½" h. **22.00**
Figure, Freddie, deer with floral dec on base **25.00**
Figure, girl, holding starfish, 7" h **55.00**
Figure, girl, praying, 3" h. **50.00**
Figure, Olga, ballerina, 3½" h **55.00**
Figure, Precious, 3½" h **55.00**
Figure, Rags, English sheepdog, unmkd, 4" h **25.00**
Figure, Sally, holding chick, 1938, 6½" h. **25.00**
Figure, Siamese cat, lying down, painted eyes, 6" h **75.00**
Planter, Annie, carrying basket, 1940, 10" h. **55.00**
Planter, Audrey, 1940, 7" h **30.00**
Planter, Daisy, 8" h **25.00**
Planter, Kitty and Kenny, 1947, 7" h. **75.00**
Planter, Peanuts, elephant holding drum, 1948, 7" h. **65.00**
Planter, Sally, holding chick, 1938, 6½" h **25.00**
Planter, Sonny, 8" h. **50.00**
Salt and Pepper Shakers, pr, Salty and Peppy, chicks
    wearing chef hats, 1940s, 5" h. **35.00**
Salt and Pepper Shakers, pr, Sniffy and Snuffy, skunks
    with floral dec, 4" h. **25.00**
Wall Pocket, "P" and "U," 5" h **50.00**

DEPRESSION GLASS

Depression Glass is a generic term used to describe glassware patterns introduced and manufactured between 1920 and the early 1950s. Most of this glassware was inexpensive and machine made.

In its narrow sense, the term describes a select group of patterns identified by a group of late 1940s and early 1950s collectors as "Depression Glass." Many price guides dealing with the subject have preserved this narrow approach.

Many manufacturers did not name their patterns. The same group of individuals who determined what patterns should and should not be included in this category also assigned names to previously unidentified patterns. Disputes occurred. Hence, some patterns have more than one name.

References: Robert Brenner, *Depression Glass for Collectors,* Schiffer Publishing, 1998; Gene Florence, *Collectible Glassware From the 40s, 50s & 60s...,* Fifth Edition, Collector Books, 1999; Gene Florence, *Collector's Encyclopedia of Depression Glass, Fourteenth Edition,* Collector Books, 1999; Gene Florence, *Elegant Glassware of the Depression Era, Eighth Edition,* Collector Books, 1999; Gene Florence, *Glass Candlesticks of the Depression Era,* Collector Books, 1999; Gene Florence, *Kitchen Glassware of the Depression Years, Fifth Edition,* Collector Books, 1995, 1999 value update; Gene Florence, *Very Rare Glassware of the Depression Years,* Third Series (1993, 1995 value update), *Fifth Series* (1997), and *Sixth Series* (1999), Collector Books; James Jeasell and Berry Wiggins, *Great American Glass of the Roaring 20s & Depression Era,* Glass Press, 1998; Ralph and Terry Kovel, *Kovel's Depression Glass & American Dinnerware Price List, Sixth Edition,* Crown, 1998; Carl F. Luckey, *An Identification & Value Guide to Depression Era Glassware, Third Edition,* Books Americana, 1994; Barbara and Jim Mauzy, *Mauzy's Comprehensive Handbook of Depression Glass Prices, 2nd Edition,* Schiffer Publishing, 2000; Barbara and Jim Mauzy, *Mauzy's Photographic Reference of Depression Glass,* Schiffer Publishing, 1999; Ellen T. Schroy, *Warman's Depression Glass,* Krause Publications, 1997; Hazel Marie Weatherman, *Colored Glassware of the Depression Era, Book 2,* published by author, 1974, available in reprint.

Periodical: *The Daze,* PO Box 57, Otisville, MI 48463.

Collectors' Clubs: 20-30-40's Society Inc, PO Box 856, La Grange, IL 60525; Canadian Depression Glass Assoc, 119 Wexford Rd, Brampton, Ontario, Canada L6Z 2T5; National Depression Glass Assoc, PO Box 8264, Wichita, KS 67208.

REPRODUCTION ALERT: Reproductions (exact copies) of several patterns are known. In other cases, fantasy pieces have been made from period molds in non-period colors. Few of these reproductions and fantasy pieces are marked.

The Daze distributes a list of these reproductions and fantasy items. Send a self-addressed, stamped business envelope along with a request for a copy.

Cameo, Hocking, butter, cov, green **$250.00**
Cameo, Hocking, candy dish, 4" h, low, green **100.00**
Cameo, Hocking, cereal bowl, 5½" d, green **35.00**
Cameo, Hocking, console bowl, 3-ftd, green **75.00**
Cameo, Hocking, creamer, 4¼" h, yellow **20.00**
Cameo, Hocking, cream soup, green **200.00**
Cameo, Hocking, decanter and stopper, green **200.00**
Cameo, Hocking, grill plate, 10½" d, yellow **6.00**
Cameo, Hocking, juice tumbler, ftd, green **135.00**
Cameo, Hocking, sandwich plate, 10" d, pink **40.00**
Cameo, Hocking, sauce bowl, 4¼" d, green. **130.00**
Cameo, Hocking, sherbet, 4⁷⁄₈" h, green. **40.00**
Cameo, Hocking, soup bowl, 9" d, green. **75.00**
Cameo, Hocking, tumbler, flat, 5" h, orig label, green. **40.00**
Cameo, Hocking, vegetable, oval, 10" l, green **35.00**
Cameo, Hocking, water tumbler, 9 oz, 4" h, pink **80.00**
Cameo, Hocking, wine goblet, 4" h, green **120.00**
Dogwood, Mac-Beth Evans, berry bowl, 8½" d, green. **120.00**
Dogwood, Mac-Beth Evans, berry bowl, 8½" d, pink **60.00**
Dogwood, Mac-Beth Evans, cereal bowl, green **40.00**
Dogwood, Mac-Beth Evans, cereal bowl, pink **35.00**
Dogwood, Mac-Beth Evans, cup and saucer, pink. **25.00**
Dogwood, Mac-Beth Evans, dinner plate, 9¼" d, green. **35.00**

Dogwood, Mac-Beth Evans, tumbler, 5" h, pink, $35.00.

Floragold, Jeannette, tray, 13½" d, $22.00. Photo courtesy Ray Morykan Auctions.

Dogwood, Mac-Beth Evans, dinner plate, 9¼" d, pink **40.00**
Dogwood, Mac-Beth Evans, luncheon plate, 8" d, pink **9.00**
Dogwood, Mac-Beth Evans, sherbet, pink **40.00**
Dogwood, Mac-Beth Evans, sugar, ftd, pink **20.00**
Floragold, Jeannette, ashtray, 4" d **5.00**
Floragold, Jeannette, berry bowl, 4½" d **5.00**
Floragold, Jeannette, bowl, 4½" sq. **5.00**
Floragold, Jeannette, bowl, 8½" sq. **15.00**
Floragold, Jeannette, bread and butter plate, 6" d **12.00**
Floragold, Jeannette, butter, cov, ¼ lb **25.00**
Floragold, Jeannette, butter, cov, 1 lb **45.00**
Floragold, Jeannette, candlesticks, pr **50.00**
Floragold, Jeannette, candy dish, 4-ftd **5.00**
Floragold, Jeannette, candy jar, cov **45.00**
Floragold, Jeannette, cereal bowl, 5½" d **40.00**
Floragold, Jeannette, creamer **8.00**
Floragold, Jeannette, creamer and sugar, cov **25.00**
Floragold, Jeannette, cup. **5.00**
Floragold, Jeannette, cup and saucer **15.00**
Floragold, Jeannette, dinner plate, 8½" d **35.00**
Floragold, Jeannette, pitcher, 64 oz **30.00**
Floragold, Jeannette, platter, 11¼" d. **25.00**
Floragold, Jeannette, salt and pepper shakers, pr. **45.00**
Floragold, Jeannette, sherbet, ftd **12.00**
Floragold, Jeannette, sugar, cov **15.00**
Floragold, Jeannette, tumbler, flat, 10 oz **15.00**
Floragold, Jeannette, tumbler, ftd, 11 oz **18.00**
Floragold, Jeannette, tumbler, ftd, 15 oz **100.00**
Florentine No. 2, Hazel Atlas, berry bowl, 4½" d, yellow **25.00**
Florentine No. 2, Hazel Atlas, berry bowl, 8" d, yellow. **35.00**
Florentine No. 2, Hazel Atlas, butter, cov, crystal **110.00**
Florentine No. 2, Hazel Atlas, butter, cov, yellow **150.00**
Florentine No. 2, Hazel Atlas, candlesticks, pr, 2¾" d, yellow **55.00**
Florentine No. 2, Hazel Atlas, candy dish, cov, crystal **120.00**
Florentine No. 2, Hazel Atlas, candy dish, cov, green **135.00**
Florentine No. 2, Hazel Atlas, candy dish, cov, pink **155.00**
Florentine No. 2, Hazel Atlas, cereal bowl, 6" d, yellow **30.00**
Florentine No. 2, Hazel Atlas, creamer and sugar, open, yellow **15.00**

Florentine No. 2, Hazel Atlas, cream soup bowl, 4¾" d, crystal. **15.00**
Florentine No. 2, Hazel Atlas, cream soup bowl, 4¾" d, green **12.00**
Florentine No. 2, Hazel Atlas, cream soup bowl, 4¾" d, yellow **20.00**
Florentine No. 2, Hazel Atlas, cup, crystal **10.00**
Florentine No. 2, Hazel Atlas, cup and saucer, pink **18.00**
Florentine No. 2, Hazel Atlas, cup and saucer, yellow **12.00**
Florentine No. 2, Hazel Atlas, custard cup, yellow **125.00**
Florentine No. 2, Hazel Atlas, dinner plate, 10" d, green. . . . **10.00**
Florentine No. 2, Hazel Atlas, dinner plate, 10" d, pink **35.00**
Florentine No. 2, Hazel Atlas, gravy boat, yellow **35.00**
Florentine No. 2, Hazel Atlas, gravy boat and under plate, yellow. **90.00**
Florentine No. 2, Hazel Atlas, parfait, 6" h, crystal **35.00**
Florentine No. 2, Hazel Atlas, parfait, 6" h, yellow **60.00**
Florentine No. 2, Hazel Atlas, pitcher, cone ftd, 28 oz, 7¼" h, yellow **20.00**
Florentine No. 2, Hazel Atlas, pitcher, flat, 48 oz, with ice lip, 7½" h, pink **135.00**
Florentine No. 2, Hazel Atlas, pitcher, flat, 48 oz, without ice lip, 7½" h, green **125.00**
Florentine No. 2, Hazel Atlas, pitcher, flat, 76 oz, 8¼" h, crystal. **120.00**
Florentine No. 2, Hazel Atlas, platter, 11" l, yellow. **12.00**
Florentine No. 2, Hazel Atlas, salad plate, 8¼" d, yellow **8.00**
Florentine No. 2, Hazel Atlas, salt and pepper shakers, pr, green **40.00**
Florentine No. 2, Hazel Atlas, salt and pepper shakers, pr, yellow **55.00**
Florentine No. 2, Hazel Atlas, saucer, yellow **5.00**
Florentine No. 2, Hazel Atlas, sherbet, ftd, crystal, price for set of 4 . . . . **15.00**
Florentine No. 2, Hazel Atlas, sherbet, ftd, pink **10.00**
Florentine No. 2, Hazel Atlas, sherbet, ftd, yellow **5.00**
Florentine No. 2, Hazel Atlas, sherbet plate, 6" d, green, price for set of 8 . . . . **25.00**
Florentine No. 2, Hazel Atlas, sherbet plate, 6" d, pink **15.00**
Florentine No. 2, Hazel Atlas, sherbet plate, 6" d, yellow **5.00**

Florentine No. 2, Hazel Atlas, comport, 3¹/₂" h, pink, $15.00.

Newport, Hazel Atlas, cup and saucer, amethyst, $18.00.

Florentine No. 2, Hazel Atlas, tumbler, flat, 5 oz, 3¹/₄" h,
yellow **18.00**

Florentine No. 2, Hazel Atlas, tumbler, flat, 9 oz, 4" h,
yellow **20.00**

Florentine No. 2, Hazel Atlas, tumbler, flat, 12 oz, 5" h,
yellow **45.00**

Florentine No. 2, Hazel Atlas, tumbler, ftd, 5 oz, 4" h,
yellow **12.00**

Florentine No. 2, Hazel Atlas, tumbler, ftd, 9 oz, 4¹/₂" h,
green **30.00**

Jubilee, Lancaster, bowl, 13" d, yellow **250.00**

Jubilee, Lancaster, candy jar, cov, 3-ftd, pink. **325.00**

Jubilee, Lancaster, creamer and sugar, yellow **35.00**

Jubilee, Lancaster, cup and saucer, yellow **15.00**

Jubilee, Lancaster, fruit bowl, 3-ftd, 5¹/₈" h, yellow **200.00**

Jubilee, Lancaster, juice tumbler, ftd, 6 oz, 5" h, yellow. . . . **90.00**

Jubilee, Lancaster, luncheon plate, 8³/₄" d, yellow **12.00**

Jubilee, Lancaster, salad plate, 7" d, pink **25.00**

Jubilee, Lancaster, sandwich plate, handled, 13¹/₂" d,
pink **85.00**

Jubilee, Lancaster, sherbet, 8 oz, 3" h, yellow **70.00**

Jubilee, Lancaster, tray, handled, yellow **45.00**

Jubilee, Lancaster, tumbler, 10 oz, 6" h, yellow **35.00**

Mayfair, Hocking, bowl, handled, 10" d, pink. **35.00**

Mayfair, Hocking, bread and butter plate, 6¹/₂" d, pink **12.00**

Mayfair, Hocking, butter, cov, pink. **75.00**

Mayfair, Hocking, cake plate, crystal **25.00**

Mayfair, Hocking, candy jar, cov, crystal. **60.00**

Mayfair, Hocking, celery dish, divided, pink. **275.00**

Mayfair, Hocking, cereal bowl, pink. **30.00**

Mayfair, Hocking, cocktail, pink. **115.00**

Mayfair, Hocking, cookie jar, cov, pink. **65.00**

Mayfair, Hocking, creamer, pink **30.00**

Mayfair, Hocking, cream soup bowl, pink **55.00**

Mayfair, Hocking, cup, pink **20.00**

Mayfair, Hocking, decanter with stopper, pink **215.00**

Mayfair, Hocking, dinner plate, 10¹/₄" d, crystal **15.00**

Mayfair, Hocking, fruit bowl, deep, pink **75.00**

Mayfair, Hocking, grill plate, crystal. **12.00**

Mayfair, Hocking, grill plate, pink **40.00**

Mayfair, Hocking, iced tea tumbler, ftd, pink. **50.00**

Mayfair, Hocking, pitcher, 60 oz, pink **85.00**

Mayfair, Hocking, platter, pink. **30.00**

Mayfair, Hocking, salt and pepper shakers, pr, crystal **30.00**

Mayfair, Hocking, sherbet plate, 5³/₄" d, pink **12.00**

Mayfair, Hocking, sugar, pink **30.00**

Mayfair, Hocking, vegetable, oval, 10" l, crystal **15.00**

Mayfair, Hocking, water goblet, 5³/₄" h, pink. **80.00**

Mayfair, Hocking, wine goblet, 3 oz, pink **125.00**

Miss America, Hocking, candy dish, pink. **180.00**

Miss America, Hocking, celery dish, pink. **30.00**

Miss America, Hocking, cereal bowl, 6¹/₄" d, crystal **12.00**

Miss America, Hocking, cereal bowl, 6¹/₄" d, pink. **30.00**

Miss America, Hocking, coaster, crystal **16.00**

Miss America, Hocking, coaster, pink. **35.00**

Miss America, Hocking, comport, pink. **25.00**

Miss America, Hocking, cup, pink. **30.00**

Miss America, Hocking, cup and saucer, crystal **15.00**

Miss America, Hocking, cup and saucer, pink. **35.00**

Miss America, Hocking, dinner plate, 10¹/₄" d, pink **45.00**

Miss America, Hocking, goblet, 5 oz, pink **100.00**

Miss America, Hocking, goblet, 10 oz, 5¹/₂" h, pink **75.00**

Miss America, Hocking, grill plate, 10¹/₄" d, pink **30.00**

Miss America, Hocking, juice tumbler, 4³/₄" h, crystal **30.00**

Miss America, Hocking, platter, 12¹/₄" l, pink **40.00**

Miss America, Hocking, relish, 4 part, pink **25.00**

Miss America, Hocking, salad plate, 8¹/₂" d, pink **40.00**

Miss America, Hocking, salt and pepper shakers, pr,
crystal. **35.00**

Miss America, Hocking, salt and pepper shakers, pr, pink **70.00**

Miss America, Hocking, shaker, crystal. **18.00**

Miss America, Hocking, sherbet plate, 5³/₄" d, pink **15.00**

Miss America, Hocking, tumbler, 5 oz, pink **60.00**

Miss America, Hocking, tumbler, 10 oz, pink **40.00**

Miss America, Hocking, vegetable, oval, 10" l, pink **40.00**

Miss America, Hocking, water goblet, 5¹/₂" h, crystal. **20.00**

Miss America, Hocking, water goblet, 5¹/₂" h, pink **55.00**

Miss America, Hocking, wine goblet, 3³/₄" h, crystal **25.00**

Newport, Hazel Atlas, berry bowl, blue **25.00**

Newport, Hazel Atlas, bowl, 4³/₄" d, pink. **10.00**

Newport, Hazel Atlas, bread and butter plate, 6" d,
cobalt. **10.00**

Newport, Hazel Atlas, cereal bowl, cobalt **45.00**
Newport, Hazel Atlas, creamer and sugar, amethyst **35.00**
Newport, Hazel Atlas, creamer and sugar, cobalt **35.00**
Newport, Hazel Atlas, cream soup bowl, amethyst **18.00**
Newport, Hazel Atlas, cream soup bowl, cobalt **25.00**
Newport, Hazel Atlas, cup and saucer, cobalt **20.00**
Newport, Hazel Atlas, dinner plate, amethyst **30.00**
Newport, Hazel Atlas, luncheon plate, amethyst **15.00**
Newport, Hazel Atlas, luncheon plate, cobalt **18.00**
Newport, Hazel Atlas, platter, cobalt **55.00**
Newport, Hazel Atlas, salt and pepper shakers, pr,
    amethyst **40.00**
Newport, Hazel Atlas, sherbet, amethyst **4.00**
Newport, Hazel Atlas, sherbet, cobalt **20.00**
Newport, Hazel Atlas, sugar, amethyst **15.00**
Newport, Hazel Atlas, sugar, cobalt **15.00**
Newport, Hazel Atlas, tumbler, 9 oz, 4½" h, cobalt **40.00**
Patrician, Federal, bread and butter plate, 6" d, amber **10.00**
Patrician, Federal, bread and butter plate, 6" d, green **8.00**
Patrician, Federal, bread and butter plate, 6" d, pink **10.00**
Patrician, Federal, butter, cov, amber **85.00**
Patrician, Federal, butter, cov, crystal **100.00**
Patrician, Federal, butter, cov, green **110.00**
Patrician, Federal, cereal bowl, 6" d, amber **25.00**
Patrician, Federal, cereal bowl, 6" d, crystal **25.00**
Patrician, Federal, creamer, ftd, amber **8.00**
Patrician, Federal, creamer, ftd, crystal **10.00**
Patrician, Federal, creamer, ftd, green **12.00**
Patrician, Federal, creamer, ftd, pink **19.00**
Patrician, Federal, creamer and sugar, green **20.00**
Patrician, Federal, cream soup bowl, 4¾" d, amber **15.00**
Patrician, Federal, cup, crystal **8.00**
Patrician, Federal, cup and saucer, amber **18.00**
Patrician, Federal, cup and saucer, green **15.00**
Patrician, Federal, dinner plate, 10½" d, green **40.00**
Patrician, Federal, dinner plate, 10½" d, pink **50.00**
Patrician, Federal, grill plate, 10½" d, amber **15.00**
Patrician, Federal, grill plate, 10½" d, crystal **12.00**
Patrician, Federal, grill plate, 10½" d, green **15.00**

Princess, Hocking, candy dish, pink, $70.00

Patrician, Federal, dinner plate, 10½" d, amber, $6.50.

Patrician, Federal, iced tea pitcher, flat, 5" h, amber **45.00**
Patrician, Federal, individual berry bowl, 5" d, amber **12.00**
Patrician, Federal, juice tumbler, flat, 5 oz, 4" h, amber **30.00**
Patrician, Federal, luncheon plate, 9" d, amber **12.00**
Patrician, Federal, luncheon plate, 9" d, green **12.00**
Patrician, Federal, master berry bowl, 8½" d, amber **40.00**
Patrician, Federal, master berry bowl, 8½" d, crystal **35.00**
Patrician, Federal, master berry bowl, 8½" d, pink **35.00**
Patrician, Federal, pitcher, crystal, molded handle. **100.00**
Patrician, Federal, platter, 11½" l, amber **30.00**
Patrician, Federal, platter, 11½" l, crystal **25.00**
Patrician, Federal, platter, 11½" l, green **25.00**
Patrician, Federal, platter, 11½" l, pink **25.00**
Patrician, Federal, salad plate, 7½" d, amber **12.00**
Patrician, Federal, salt and pepper shakers, pr, amber **50.00**
Patrician, Federal, salt and pepper shakers, pr, green **60.00**
Patrician, Federal, salt and pepper shakers, pr, pink **90.00**
Patrician, Federal, saucer, pink **10.00**
Patrician, Federal, sherbet, ftd, amber **8.00**
Patrician, Federal, sherbet, ftd, green **8.00**
Patrician, Federal, sherbet, ftd, pink **15.00**
Patrician, Federal, sugar, cov, pink **75.00**
Patrician, Federal, sugar, open, amber **6.00**
Patrician, Federal, sugar, open, green **6.00**
Patrician, Federal, tumbler, flat, 9 oz, 4¼" h, amber **25.00**
Patrician, Federal, tumbler, flat, 9 oz, 4¼" h, crystal **30.00**
Patrician, Federal, tumbler, flat, 14 oz, 5½" h, amber **40.00**
Patrician, Federal, tumbler, flat, 14 oz, 5½" h, green **45.00**
Patrician, Federal, tumbler, flat, 14 oz, 5½" h, pink **46.00**
Patrician, Federal, tumbler, ftd, 8 oz, 5¼" h, amber **40.00**
Patrician, Federal, tumbler, ftd, 8 oz, 5¼" h, green **55.00**
Patrician, Federal, vegetable, oval, 10" l, green **35.00**
Princess, Hocking, bread and butter plate, 6" d, green **10.00**
Princess, Hocking, butter, cov, green **100.00**
Princess, Hocking, cake plate, pink **50.00**
Princess, Hocking, candy dish, green **75.00**
Princess, Hocking, cereal bowl, 5" d, green **40.00**
Princess, Hocking, cereal bowl, 5" d, pink **40.00**
Princess, Hocking, cup, green **11.00**
Princess, Hocking, cup, pink **15.00**
Princess, Hocking, cup and saucer, green **25.00**

Princess, Hocking, cup and saucer, pink. **25.00**
Princess, Hocking, dinner plate, 9¹/₂" d, green. **30.00**
Princess, Hocking, dinner plate, 9¹/₂" d, pink **25.00**
Princess, Hocking, iced tea tumbler, ftd, 6¹/₂" h, pink **85.00**
Princess, Hocking, juice pitcher, pink. **55.00**
Princess, Hocking, juice tumbler, flat, 5 oz, 3" h, yellow. . . . **30.00**
Princess, Hocking, pitcher, 60 oz, 8" h, pink **85.00**
Princess, Hocking, platter, green **30.00**
Princess, Hocking, platter, pink **55.00**
Princess, Hocking, salad plate, 8" d, green **18.00**
Princess, Hocking, salad plate, 8" d, pink. **15.00**
Princess, Hocking, salt and pepper shakers, pr, yellow **90.00**
Princess, Hocking, sandwich plate, handled, 10¹/₄" d, pink . . **165.00**
Princess, Hocking, sherbet, green. **25.00**
Princess, Hocking, sherbet, pink **20.00**
Princess, Hocking, sugar, cov, green. **40.00**
Princess, Hocking, sugar, cov, pink **60.00**
Princess, Hocking, tumbler, flat, 9 oz, 4" h, green. **30.00**
Princess, Hocking, tumbler, flat, 13 oz, 5¹/₄" h, yellow **35.00**
Princess, Hocking, tumbler, ftd, 9 oz, 4³/₄" h, pink **70.00**
Princess, Hocking, tumbler, ftd, 10 oz, 5¹/₄" h, green. **35.00**
Princess, Hocking, tumbler, ftd, 10 oz, 5¹/₄" h, pink. **30.00**
Princess, Hocking, vase, orig label, pink. **65.00**
Princess, Hocking, vegetable, oval, green. **45.00**
Princess, Hocking, vegetable, oval, pink. **60.00**

DINNERWARE

This is a catchall category. There are hundreds of American and European dinnerware manufacturers. Several dozen have their own separate listing in this book. It is not fair to ignore the rest.

This category provides a sampling of the patterns and forms from these manufacturers. It is designed to demonstrate the wide variety of material available in the market, especially today when individuals are buying dinnerware primarily for reuse.

References: Susan and Al Bagdade, *Warman's American Pottery and Porcelain,* Wallace-Homestead, Krause Publications, 1994; *China Identification Guide, Kit #1* (1996), *Kit #2* (1996), *Kit #3* (1997), *Kit #4* (1998), Replacements, Ltd; Jo Cunningham, *The Best of Collectible Dinnerware, 2nd Edition,* Schiffer Publishing, 1999; Jo Cunningham, *The Collector's Encyclopedia of American Dinnerware,* Collector Books, 1982, 1998 value update; Harvey Duke, *The Official Price Guide to Pottery and Porcelain, Eighth Edition,* House of Collectibles, 1995; Joanne Jasper, *Turn of the Century American Dinnerware: 1880s to 1920s,* Collector Books, 1996; Lois Lehner, *Lehner's Encyclopedia of U.S. Marks on Pottery, Porcelain & Clay,* Collector Books, 1988; Raymonde Limoges, *American Limoges,* Collector Books, 1996; Harry L. Rinker, *Dinnerware of the 20th Century: The Top 500 Patterns,* House of Collectibles, 1997.

Periodical: *The Daze,* PO Box 57, Otisville, MI 48463.

Castleton China, Caprice, bread and butter plate, 6¹/₄" d **$8.00**
Castleton China, Caprice, creamer, 3" h **20.00**
Castleton China, Caprice, cream soup and saucer. **20.00**
Castleton China, Caprice, cup and saucer, ftd. **18.00**
Castleton China, Caprice, dinner plate, 10³/₄" d **15.00**
Castleton China, Caprice, fruit bowl, 5¹/₂" d **12.00**
Castleton China, Caprice, gravy boat, attached under-
plate. **50.00**

Castleton China, Caprice, platter, 13¹/₄" l **65.00**
Castleton China, Caprice, salad plate, 8³/₈" d **8.00**
Castleton China, Caprice, teapot, cov. **100.00**
Castleton China, Caprice, vegetable, oval, 10¹/₈" l. **40.00**
Castleton China, Gloria, bread and butter plate, 6¹/₂" d **8.00**
Castleton China, Gloria, creamer, 2⁷/₈" h **25.00**
Castleton China, Gloria, cream soup and saucer. **20.00**
Castleton China, Gloria, cup and saucer, ftd. **18.00**
Castleton China, Gloria, dinner plate, 10³/₄" d **12.00**
Castleton China, Gloria, fruit bowl, 5³/₄" d **10.00**
Castleton China, Gloria, gravy boat, attached underplate **50.00**
Castleton China, Gloria, luncheon plate, 9³/₈" d **10.00**
Castleton China, Gloria, sugar, cov **25.00**
Castleton China, Severn, bread and butter plate, 6¹/₄" d. **8.00**
Castleton China, Severn, chop plate, 13¹/₄" d **60.00**
Castleton China, Severn, coffeepot, cov **110.00**
Castleton China, Severn, dinner plate, 10³/₄" d **18.00**
Castleton China, Severn, luncheon plate **15.00**
Castleton China, Severn, platter, 13¹/₄" l **60.00**
Castleton China, Severn, salad plate, 8¹/₂" d **10.00**
Castleton China, Severn, sugar, cov **30.00**
Castleton China, Severn, teapot, cov **110.00**
Castleton China, Severn, vegetable, oval, 10" l **50.00**
Denby Pottery, Camelot, baker, 11¹/₄" l **25.00**
Denby Pottery, Camelot, bread and butter plate, 6³/₈" d **5.00**
Denby Pottery, Camelot, butter, cov, ¹/₄ lb. **18.00**
Denby Pottery, Camelot, cereal bowl, coupe, 6⁵/₈" d **8.00**
Denby Pottery, Camelot, coffeepot, cov **30.00**
Denby Pottery, Camelot, creamer, 2¹/₄" h **8.00**
Denby Pottery, Camelot, dinner plate, 10¹/₈" d **8.00**
Denby Pottery, Camelot, fruit bowl, 5⁷/₈" d **5.00**
Denby Pottery, Camelot, gravy boat **20.00**
Denby Pottery, Camelot, salad plate, 8³/₄" d **5.00**
Denby Pottery, Camelot, salt and pepper shakers, pr **15.00**
Denby Pottery, Castile, bread and butter plate **6.00**
Denby Pottery, Castile, creamer, 3¹/₈" h **12.00**
Denby Pottery, Castile, cup and saucer, ftd. **8.00**
Denby Pottery, Castile, dinner plate, 10³/₄" d. **8.00**
Denby Pottery, Castile, salad plate, 9¹/₈" d **8.00**
Denby Pottery, Castile, sugar, open **12.00**
International China Co, Heartland, butter, cov, ¹/₄ lb **5.00**
International China Co, Heartland, coffee canister, 6" h **8.00**
International China Co, Heartland, cup and saucer, flat **3.00**
International China Co, Heartland, dinner plate, 11" d **3.00**
International China Co, Heartland, salad plate, 7³/₄" d **2.00**
International China Co, Heartland, salt and pepper shak-
ers, pr. **3.00**
International China Co, Heartland, tureen, cov, with
ladle. **20.00**
International China Co, Heartland, vegetable, cov,
round **10.00**
International China Co, Terrace Blossoms, butter lid, ¹/₄ lb. **6.00**
International China Co, Terrace Blossoms, cereal bowl,
flat, 7" d **2.00**
International China Co, Terrace Blossoms, cup and
saucer, flat **2.00**
International China Co, Terrace Blossoms, dinner plate,
10⁷/₈" d. **2.00**
International China Co, Terrace Blossoms, gravy boat
underplate **2.00**
International China Co, Terrace Blossoms, salad plate,
7⁵/₈" d. **1.50**
International China Co, Terrace Blossoms, salt and pep-
per shakers, pr, 2⁷/₈" h **4.00**

International China Co, Terrace Blossoms, sugar, cov **4.00**
International China Co, Terrace Blossoms, tea canister, 4¼" h **5.00**
International China Co, Terrace Blossoms, vegetable, round, 9¼" d **5.00**
Mikasa, Black Tie, bread and butter plate **8.00**
Mikasa, Black Tie, chop plate, 12³⁄₈" d **40.00**
Mikasa, Black Tie, cup and saucer, ftd **18.00**
Mikasa, Black Tie, dinner plate, 10³⁄₄" d **15.00**
Mikasa, Black Tie, fruit bowl, 6¼" d **8.00**
Mikasa, Black Tie, salad plate, 8³⁄₈" d **8.00**
Mikasa, Black Tie, sugar, cov **35.00**
Mikasa, Blue Daisies, bread and butter plate **4.00**
Mikasa, Blue Daisies, chop plate, 12½" d **12.00**
Mikasa, Blue Daisies, dinner plate **8.00**
Mikasa, Blue Daisies, salad plate, 8" d **4.00**
Mikasa, Blue Daisies, sugar, cov **10.00**
Mikasa, Blue Daisies, vegetable, round, 9³⁄₄" d **12.00**
Mikasa, Just Flowers, bread and butter plate, 6⁵⁄₈" d **4.00**
Mikasa, Just Flowers, coffeepot, cov, 8" h **70.00**
Mikasa, Just Flowers, cream soup and saucer **18.00**
Mikasa, Just Flowers, cup and saucer, flat **8.00**
Mikasa, Just Flowers, dinner plate, 10⁵⁄₈" d **8.00**
Mikasa, Just Flowers, fruit bowl, 5" d **4.00**
Mikasa, Just Flowers, luncheon plate, 9¹⁄₈" d **8.00**
Mikasa, Just Flowers, platter, oval, 13" l **40.00**
Mikasa, Just Flowers, salad plate, 7⁵⁄₈" d **5.00**
Mikasa, Just Flowers, salt and pepper shakers, pr **12.00**
Mikasa, Just Flowers, sugar, cov **20.00**
Mikasa, Just Flowers, teapot, cov, 2⁷⁄₈" h **40.00**
Mikasa, May Dreams, bread and butter plate **3.00**
Mikasa, May Dreams, coffee canister **12.00**
Mikasa, May Dreams, cup and saucer, flat **6.00**
Mikasa, May Dreams, dinner plate, 10³⁄₄" d **8.00**
Mikasa, May Dreams, salad plate, 8" d **4.00**
Mikasa, May Dreams, tureen, cov **50.00**
Royal Worcester, Astley, bread and butter plate **5.00**
Royal Worcester, Astley, casserole, cov, oval, 9" l **50.00**
Royal Worcester, Astley, coffeepot, cov **30.00**
Royal Worcester, Astley, cup and saucer, flat **12.00**
Royal Worcester, Astley, dinner plate **12.00**
Royal Worcester, Astley, fruit bowl, 5½" d **8.00**
Royal Worcester, Astley, salad plate **8.00**
Royal Worcester, Astley, sugar, cov **25.00**
Royal Worcester, Evesham Gold, baker, oval, 9⁵⁄₈" l **18.00**
Royal Worcester, Evesham Gold, bread and butter plate, 6½" d **12.00**
Royal Worcester, Evesham Gold, butter, cov, ¼ lb **15.00**
Royal Worcester, Evesham Gold, casserole, cov, oval, 8³⁄₄" l **25.00**
Royal Worcester, Evesham Gold, cereal bowl, coupe, 6³⁄₄" d **6.00**
Royal Worcester, Evesham Gold, cream soup and saucer **15.00**
Royal Worcester, Evesham Gold, dinner plate **6.00**
Royal Worcester, Evesham Gold, fruit bowl, 5⁵⁄₈" d **5.00**
Royal Worcester, Evesham Gold, luncheon plate, 9¹⁄₈" d **5.00**
Royal Worcester, Evesham Gold, platter, oval, 15" l **25.00**
Royal Worcester, Evesham Gold, salad plate, 8¼" d **4.00**
Royal Worcester, Evesham Gold, vegetable, cov, round **20.00**
Spode, Cowslip, bread and butter plate, 6½" d **8.00**
Spode, Cowslip, chop plate, 12⁷⁄₈" d **40.00**
Spode, Cowslip, cranberry bowl 5⁵⁄₈" d **20.00**
Spode, Cowslip, cream soup and saucer **25.00**
Spode, Cowslip, dinner plate, 10½" d **12.00**

Spode, Cowslip, cup and saucer, Chelsea wicker shape, S713, 5¹⁄₂" d saucer, $22.00. Photo courtesy Ray Morykan Auctions.

Spode, Cowslip, fruit bowl, 5¼" d **10.00**
Spode, Cowslip, luncheon plate, 8⁷⁄₈" d **10.00**
Spode, Cowslip, salad plate, 7⁷⁄₈" d **8.00**
Spode, Cowslip, sugar, cov **25.00**
Spode, Cowslip, vegetable, oval, 10¼" l **35.00**
Spode, Rosalie, bread and butter plate, 6⁵⁄₈" d **8.00**
Spode, Rosalie, chop plate, 12⁷⁄₈" d **55.00**
Spode, Rosalie, cranberry bowl **30.00**
Spode, Rosalie, cream soup bowl **20.00**
Spode, Rosalie, demitasse cup and saucer **15.00**
Spode, Rosalie, dinner plate, 10½" d **12.00**
Spode, Rosalie, fruit bowl, 5³⁄₈" d **10.00**
Spode, Rosalie, luncheon plate, 8⁷⁄₈" d **10.00**
Spode, Rosalie, platter, oval, 13" l **40.00**
Spode, Rosalie, salad plate, 7⁷⁄₈" d **10.00**
Spode, Rosalie, sugar, cov **30.00**
Spode, Rosalie, vegetable, oval, 9" l **35.00**

DIONNE QUINTUPLETS

Annette, Cecile, Emilie, Marie, and Yvonne Dionne were born on May 28, 1934, in rural Canada between the towns of Corbeil and Callander, Ontario. Dr. Dafoe and two midwives delivered the five girls. An agreement to exhibit the babies at the Chicago World's Fair led to the passage of "An Act for the Protection of the Dionne Quintuplets" by the Canadian government.

The Dafoe Hospital, which served as visitor viewing center for thousands of people who traveled to Canada to see the Quints, was built across the street from the family home. The Quints craze lasted into the early 1940s. Hundreds of souvenir and licensed products were manufactured during that period. Emile died in August 1954 and Marie on February 27, 1970. In 1998 the surviving sisters accepted a settlement for financial compensation from the Ontario government.

Reference: John Axe, *The Collectible Dionne Quintuplets,* Hobby House Press, 1977, out of print.

Collectors' Club: Dionne Quint Collectors, PO Box 2527, Woburn, MA 01888.

Advertising Tear Sheet, *Ladies Home Journal,* May 1941, Baby Ruth Candy Bars, half page **$2.00**

Advertisement, paper, Quaker Mother's Oats, framed, ©1935, 17³/₄" h, 35" w, $100.00. Photo courtesy Collectors Auction Services.

Advertising Tear Sheet, *Look Magazine,* Apr 26, 1938,
    Karo Syrup adv **5.00**
Book, *Dionne Quintuplets Going on Three,* Dell. **35.00**
Book, *The Dionne Quintuplets, We're Two Years Old,*
    black and white photos, 1936 . . . . **30.00**
Cereal Bowl, chrome plated metal, late 1935, Quaker
    Oats premium, 5⁷/₈" d **25.00**
Fan, cardboard, "Sweethearts of the World," 1936, 8¼ x
    8³/₄" **20.00**
Game, Line Up the Quinties, The Embossing Co, Albany,
    NY, complete with illus instruction leaflet, small
    wooden black tiles with baby or flower images, mid-
    1930s, orig ½ x 3¼ x 5¼" box. **50.00**
Photograph, tinted color, first year, 7¼ x 9" photo, 10 x
    12" glass frame with cardboard easel **25.00**
Plaque, plaster, raised image of Quint heads, "Souvenir
    From Quintland Callander, Canada," inked inscription
    "Souvenir de Oliva Dionne Aug 6/37," 4¼" d **75.00**
Postcard, quints having second birthday party, ©NEA,
    1936. . . . . **8.00**

DISNEYANA

The Disney era began when *Steamboat Willie,* Walt Disney's first animated cartoon, appeared on theater screens in 1928. The success of Walt Disney and his studio are attributed to two major factors: (1) development of a host of cartoon characters, feature-length cartoons, and feature movies enjoyed throughout the world, and (2) an aggressive marketing and licensing program.

European Disney and Disney theme park collectibles are two strong growth areas within Disneyana. Be especially price conscious when buying post-1975 Disneyana. Large amounts have been hoarded. The number of licensed products increased significantly. Disney shopping mall stores and mail-order catalog sales have significantly increased the amount of new material available. In fact, products have been created to be sold exclusively through these channels. It is for this reason that many Disneyana collectors concentrate on Disney collectibles licensed before 1965.

References: Bill Cotter, *The Wonderful World of Disney Television: A Complete History,* Hyperion, 1997; Robert Heide and John Gilman, *Disneyana: Classic Collectibles 1928-1958,* Hyperion,

1994; Robert Heide and John Gilman, *The Mickey Mouse Watch: From the Beginning of Time,* Hyperion, 1997; David Longest and Michael Stern, *The Collector's Encyclopedia of Disneyana,* Collector Books (1992, 2000 value update); R. Michael Murray, *The Golden Age of Walt Disney Records: 1933-1988,* Antique Trader Books, 1997; Maxine A. Pinsky, *Marx Toys: Robots, Space, Comic, Disney & TV Characters,* Schiffer Publishing, 1996; Margo Rana, *Disney Dolls,* Hobby House Press, 1999; Dave Smith, *Disney A to Z: The Official Encyclopedia,* Hyperion, 1996; Michael Stern, *Stern's Guide to Disney Collectibles, First Series* (1989, 1992 value update), *Second Series* (1990, 1995 value update), *Third Series* (1995), Collector Books; Tom Tumbusch, *Tomart's Illustrated Disneyana Catalog and Price Guide, Condensed Edition,* Wallace-Homestead, 1990, out of print.

Periodical: *Tomart's Disneyana Digest,* 3300 Encrete Ln, Dayton, OH 45439.

Collectors' Clubs: National Fantasy Club For Disneyana Collectors & Enthusiasts, PO Box 19212, Irvine, CA 92713; The Mouse Club, 2056 Cirone Way, San Jose, CA 95124.

Alice in Wonderland, Sticker Fun Stencil and Coloring
    Book, Whitman, 1951, 10¼ x 12" **$75.00**
Bambi, figurine, ceramic, brown and yellow body, pink
    inner ears and accents on nose and mouth, 1940s,
    1½ x 3 x 4³/₄" **50.00**
Bambi, planter, china, Bambi lying on ground looking
    back at 2 bluebirds seated on tree branch, Napco,
    1950s, 3 x 4 x 3½" **75.00**
Brer Rabbit, figurine, ceramic, seated, arms and legs
    raised in air, pink shirt, blue pants, dark red nose,
    Japan, 1970s, 2½ x 3½ x 3½" **20.00**
Davy Crockett, Tennessee Colonel Clip-On Bow Tie,
    brown velour-type bow tie with depiction of Davy
    Crockett and his rifle, Best Clip, 4" w, MOC **25.00**
Davy Crockett, wash mitt/hand puppet, white terrycloth
    with green trim, brown and green silkscreened Davy
    Crockett image with crossed flintlock guns, c1955,
    8 x 8½" **50.00**
Disneyland, ashtray, china, white, "Disneyland" with
    castle and Tinker bell, 1970s, 5" d **10.00**
Disneyland, book, *A Visit to Disneyland,* Whitman Big-
    Tell-A-Tale Book, 28 pp, color illus and photos, cover
    shows Mickey Mouse as bandleader with castle in
    background, 1965, 6 x 8½" **20.00**
Disneyland, booklet, *Walt Disney's Disneyland Pictorial
    Souvenir,* 32 pp, full color illus and photos, "Bear
    Country" on back cov, 1973, 8³/₄ x 11½" **20.00**
Disneyland, booklet, *Walt Disney's Guide to
    Disneyland,* 28 pp, full color illus and photos, 1962,
    8 x 11½" **20.00**
Disneyland, coin purse, tan leather, snap closure on
    front, "Souvenir From Disneyland," ©1955, 2¼ x 2³/₄". **20.00**
Disneyland, game, Disneyland Electric Quiz, battery
    operated, Jacmar Mfg Co, c1955, 8 x 10 x 2" box. **50.00**
Disneyland, pin, brass, needlepost and clutch reverse,
    "Disneyland Hotel July 4, 1966," 1³/₈" h **25.00**
Disneyland, souvenir spoon, silvered metal, red and
    white enameled shield-shaped attachment at top
    depicting Disneyland castle, small metal figural castle
    charm with gold luster attached below, state of
    California emb on bowl, 1960s, 4½" l **20.00**

Rug, Bambi and Thumper, brown, blue, red, yellow, pink and green, new old stock, 22" h, 40" w, $82.00. Photo courtesy Collectors Auction Services.

Disneyland, souvenir tray, aluminum, "Swift & Co In Disneyland," photo of Main Street store int, old-time scene of butcher shop filled with Swift products, packaging, and large sign in background, c1950s, 11" d **20.00**

Disneyland, thermos, metal, Mark Twain Steamboat illus, red cup, Aladdin Industries, c1957, 6½" h **50.00**

Disneyland, toy, ferris wheel, clockwork motor, bell, and 6 gondolas, litho Disney characters and fairground scenes, Chein, 16¾" h **350.00**

Donald Duck, bank, ceramic, Donald with hand in air holding coin, black, red, yellow, and blue, Leeds China Co, c1947, 4 x 4 x 6" **75.00**

Donald Duck, book, *Donald and the Wishing Star,* Whitman, Cozy Corner series, 24 pp, ©1952, 7¼ x 8¼" **50.00**

Donald Duck, costume, vinyl, 1-pc, molded plastic mask, Ben Cooper, 1974, 8¼ x 11 x 3½" box.......... **20.00**

Donald Duck, figurine, bisque, green paint, 3½" h **65.00**

Donald Duck, napkin, textured paper, scalloped edges, front color image of Donald holding glass in 1 hand and milk bottle in other, 1950s, 6½" sq **20.00**

Donald Duck, pencil sharpener, plastic, yellow-tan, full color Donald decal in center, 1930s, 1¼" h **75.00**

Donald Duck, ramp walker, hard plastic, Donald pushing wheelbarrow, painted features, 1950s, Marx, 3" h **50.00**

Dumbo, doll, painted composition, movable head and trunk, black and white google eyes, fabric collar, large felt ears, back mkd "Cameo Doll Prod.," 1941, 3½ x 4 x 3¼"....................................... **200.00**

Dumbo, mask, painted starched linen, "Dumbo" ink stamped on brim, 1940s, 13 x 18" **20.00**

Dumbo, salt and pepper shakers, pr, ceramic, white, red, black, and blue accents, cork stoppers, Leeds China Co, c1947, 3¼" h **50.00**

Figaro, figurine, ceramic, paw raised in air, painted and glazed, black and white, pink inner ears, black, yellow, and dark pink facial accents, mkd "Geppetto Pottery," Brayton Laguna, c1940, 2½ x 4¼ x 3¾" **75.00**

Goofy, charm, sterling silver, full figured Goofy leaning over with hands on knees, ¾" h **20.00**

Grumpy, lamp, painted composition, mkd "Grumpy" on base, ©1938 Walt Disney Enterprises, 9¾" h **225.00**

Horace Horsecollar, figure, bisque, red bib overalls and hat with orange collar, yellow bow tie and hands, 1930s, 3½" h.................................. **100.00**

Jiminy Cricket, valentine, mechanical, stiff paper, movable arm holding "Love" heart with "Jiminy Cricket, Yes That's Me, My Valentine I Wish You'd Be," 1939, 3 x 5¼".................................... **20.00**

Jungle Book, card game, complete deck of 36 cards with instructions, Edu-Cards, ©1966, 2 x 3 x ½" box **10.00**

Jungle Book, figures, set of 6, "Jungle Pals," Mowgli, Bagheera, Baloo, Buzzy, Kaa, and King Louie, Nabisco Wheat Honnies premium, 1967 .... **75.00**

Lady and the Tramp, wallet, vinyl, recessed images on front, c1955, 3¼ x 4¼" **50.00**

Mary Poppins, dish set, 3 pcs, hard plastic, 3¾" h cup, 5" d bowl, 7¼" d plate...................... **20.00**

Mary Poppins, hand puppet, cloth body, soft vinyl head, bow at neck, felt hands, separate apron section stitched to front, Mary Poppins logo in umbrella design, Gund, c1964, 11" h........................ **75.00**

Mary Poppins, lunch box, vinyl, plastic thermos, Aladdin Industries, 1970s, 7 x 9 x 4"........................ **75.00**

Mickey Mouse, bank, painted composition, wearing bright yellow shirt, red pants, and shoes, gold foil sticker mkd "Made In Japan," c1960s, 3 x 4 x 6"........ **50.00**

Mickey Mouse, box, cardboard, Mickey Mouse Cookies, Mickey and Minnie on lid, wrap-around design on sides depicting Mickey running with box of cookies and being chased by Donald, Pluto, Elmer, Goofy, Horace, Clarabell, Tortoise and Hare, and Clara Cluck, complete with fabric carrying strap and closure flap on lid, National Biscuit Co, ©1937, 2 x 5 x 3"...... **100.00**

Mickey Mouse, candy box, waxed cardboard, Mickey Mouse Chocolate Bar, large Mickey image on top and bottom panels, sides show Mickey, Minnie, Pluto, Horace, and Clarabell, orig held Caramel Nougat Chocolate Bar by William Patterson Ltd, 1930s, 1½ x 4 x 1¼" **200.00**

Mickey Mouse, cigarette case, blue enameled metal case, spring-loaded opening mechanism with push button on side, unmkd, 1930s, 2½ x 3¼ x ½"......... **200.00**

Mickey Mouse, clock, electric, square green metal case, Mickey figure dial strip contains Mickey, Minnie, and friends, Ingersoll, c1933, 4½" h **350.00**

Mickey Mouse, coloring book, Mickey & Minnie Mouse, 28 pp, Saalfield, ©1933, 10¾ x 15½"................. **75.00**

Mickey Mouse, cookie cutter, heart shaped, Hallmark **15.00**

Mickey Mouse, doll, molded plastic, pull-string talker, mkd "WDP," ©1976 Mattel, 6¾" h.................. **45.00**

Mickey Mouse, earrings, pr, clip-on, brass luster, small loop holds ⅞" h Mickey figure with black, white, and red accents, reverse has Productions copyright, c1960s **20.00**

Mickey Mouse, flip book, *Mickey Mouse In Actual Motion Pictures (Series A),* ©Moviescope Corp, 1930s, 1¾ x 2½".................................. **100.00**

Mickey Mouse, greeting card, "For Your Eleventh Birthday!," parachuting Mickey holding birthday cake..... **25.00**

Mickey Mouse, napkin ring, silver plated, 4 different images of Mickey on outside ring, International Silver Co, c1934, 1½" d, ¾" w **75.00**

Mickey Mouse, patch, fabric, Mickey image on white ground, red rim, 1960s, 2" **15.00**

Mickey Mouse, pinback button, "Mickey Mouse Undies," "©1928-1930 W. E. Disney," ³/₄" d **55.00**

Mickey Mouse, place setting, includes silver plated dinner plate with spoon and fork rests, silver plated spoon, fork, and napkin ring holder, emb images and wording **225.00**

Mickey Mouse, pull-toy xylophone, #748, paper on wood, Fisher-Price, 9" l **350.00**

Mickey Mouse, sign, cardboard, adv for Mickey Mouse Watch and Tarzan School Tablets for 1935-36 school season, Birmingham Paper Co, 11 x 13³/₄" **75.00**

Mickey Mouse, soap, figural, white castile, carved in shape of standing Mickey Mouse with black and red vegetable coloring details, Lightfoot Schultz Co, Walt Disney Enterprises, 4" h **85.00**

Mickey Mouse, thermometer, metal case, painted green, Mickey standing on Pluto's house with stick in hand pointing to temperature reading, Walt Disney Enterprises, 3¹/₄" h, 3¹/₄" w **90.00**

Mickey Mouse Club, Magic Multiplier, Jacmar, battery operated, complete with question and answer sheet, Walt Disney Productions **35.00**

Mickey Mouse Club, soaky bottle, girl mouseketeer, wearing red and white outfit, orange bow in hair, 1960s **45.00**

Minnie Mouse, toothbrush holder, bisque, mkd "Made In Japan," 1930s, 2¹/₂ x 2³/₄ x 5" **200.00**

Peter Pan, book, *Walt Disney's Peter Pan,* 247 pp, black and white and color illus, mkd "WDP," ©1967, Golden Star Book **35.00**

Peter Pan, coloring book, Whitman, used, 128 pp, 1952, 8 x 10³/₄" **20.00**

Peter Pan, doll, stuffed plush body, soft vinyl head, green body with yellow feet, bow around neck, felt buttons on chest, fleshtone head with brown hair, green hat with red feather, Gund, 1950s, 11" h **50.00**

Peter Pan, game, Walt Disney's Peter Pan: A Game of Adventure, Transogram, 1953 . . . . **30.00**

Pinocchio, coloring book, "Walt Disney's Pinocchio," Whitman, 1939, unused **30.00**

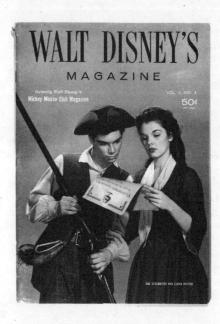

Mickey Mouse Club, magazine, *Walt Disney's Magazine,* Jun 1957, Vol. 11, 8th issue, color photo cover of Hal Stalmaster and Luana Patten, $20.00.

Pinocchio, doll, painted composition, jointed, movable arms, Crown, 1940, 4 x 4 x 9¹/₄" **100.00**

Pinocchio, ice cream cup lid, Fudgee Cup, Pinocchio portrait, issued by Erie County Milk Assoc, c1939, 2³/₄" d **20.00**

Practical Pig, bobbing head, painted composition, blue bib overalls, green hat, red base, sticker mkd "Japan," 5¹/₂" h, 2¹/₂" d base **100.00**

Sleeping Beauty, drinking glasses, "Sampson/Prince Philip's Horse," black, orange, purple, and green, 1958, price for set of 6 . . . . **20.00**

Sleeping Beauty, lunch pail, litho tin container, hinged lid, attached carrying handles, Briar Rose and Prince Philip on lid, castle, forest animals, and good fairies illus on sides, General Steel Wares, c1959, 4¹/₂ x 7 x 4¹/₂" **100.00**

Sneezy, drinking glass, 1942 . . . . **20.00**

Sneezy, figure, soft molded rubber, "Sneezy" on front, mkd "WDP," c1950s, 8¹/₄" h **35.00**

Snow White, bank, ceramic, blue and yellow dress, pink accents, Leeds China Co, c1949, 3 x 4 x 6¹/₂" **75.00**

Snow White, bank, ceramic, painted and glazed, Snow White standing next to well, gold text on roof "Wishing And Saving Will Make It So," Enesco, 1960s, 2¹/₂ x 4¹/₂ x 5" **75.00**

Snow White, game, Walt Disney's Snow White Game, Tek Toothbrush premium, orig paper sleeve, ©1937 Walt Disney Enterprises **90.00**

Snow White, greeting card, "Do You Mind If Us Dwarfs Come In," inside picture of Dwarfs and Snow White, White & Wyckoff, Walt Disney Enterprises, 1938 . . . . **30.00**

Snow White and the Seven Dwarfs, playing cards, red and white backs, Snow White and Dwarfs on fronts, ©Walt Disney Enterprises, orig 1³/₄ x 2¹/₂" box **50.00**

Three Little Pigs, book, *Three Little Pigs,* 64 pp, color and black and white drawings, story from Walt Disney Silly Symphony, written and illus by Walt Disney Studio, ©1933 . . . . **50.00**

Three Little Pigs and Wolf, figure, bisque, hp, Japan, ©Walt Disney, 3¹/₄" h **165.00**

Mickey, Minnie, and Pluto, toy drum, litho tin, Ohio Art, 7" d, $165.00. Photo courtesy Collectors Auction Services.

Thumper, salt and pepper shakers, pr, ceramic, white, black, pink, and red, Leeds China Co, c1947, 3¼" h **25.00**

Tinker Bell, lunch box, vinyl, Aladdin Industries, c1969, 7 x 9 x 4" **75.00**

Tinker Bell, pin, brass luster, bow holding full figure Tinker Bell with green enamel paint on dress and 3 green rhinestones on wing tip, other wing with single rhinestone, Disney copyright on reverse, c1950s, 1½" h **20.00**

Walt Disney, activity book, Walt Disney's Sketch A Graph Paint Book, "Another Creation By The Ohio Art Company," Whitman Publishing Co, 1955, 8 x 10¾" **50.00**

Walt Disney, sign, "Walt Disney's Happiest Songs," cardboard, 2-sided, depicts Peter Pan, Mary Poppins, White Rabbit, and Jiminy Cricket gathered around large banner at center, Gulf Oil premium, c1967, 12 x 17" **50.00**

Winnie the Pooh, ceiling light shade, glass, 4 different images of Pooh, with Piglet, Rabbit, Eeyore, and Tigger, 1960s, 13½ x 13½ x 2½" **75.00**

AUCTION PRICES – DISNEY TOYS AND LUNCH BOXES

Skinner, Inc., Boston, MA auction of the Stephen & Victoria Montifiore Collection, March 2, 2000. Prices include a 15% buyer's premium.

Lunch Kit, metal, oval with pie tray and folding handles, Handy, 1935 Mickey Mouse **$1,265.00**

Lunch Boxes, pr, metal, Adco 1954 Mickey Mouse and Aladdin 1961 Ludwig Von Drake in Disneyland **149.50**

Lunch Boxes, pr, metal, Aladdin, 1957 Disneyland with thermos and 1960 Disneyland **1,035.00**

Lunch Boxes, pr, metal, dome top, Aladdin, 1969 Fire Fighters with thermos and 1961 School Bus . . . **172.50**

Toy, Happy Pluto, Linemar, clockwork mechanism causes head to bob, tail to spin, and body to move, 5½" l **172.50**

Toy, Jumping Donald Duck, Linemar, litho tin with palm-operated coil cable, 7" h **316.25**

Toy, Pluto with Cart, Linemar, friction-powered, with incomplete orig box, 9" l **488.75**

DOG COLLECTIBLES

There are over 100 breeds of dogs divided into seven classes: herding, hounds, non-sporting, sporting, terriers, toy breeds, and working dogs. The first modern dog show was held in Newcastle, England, in 1859. The recording of bloodlines soon followed.

Unlike other animal collectors, dog collectors are breed specific. A Scottie collector is highly unlikely to own a Boxer collectible. In most cases, these collections mate with the breed of dog owned by the collector. Finally, dog collectors demand that the collectibles they buy closely resemble their pet. The fact that the collectible portrays a German Shepherd is not enough. It must remind them specifically of their pooch.

References: Edith Butler, *Poodle Collectibles of the 50's & 60's,* L-W Book Sales, 1995; Candace Sten Davis and Patricia Baugh, *A Treasury of Scottie Dog Collectibles* (1998), *Vol. II* (1999),

Collector Books; Wanda Gessner, *Spaghetti Art Ware: Poodles and Other Collectible Ceramics,* Schiffer Publishing, 1998; Patricia Robak, *Dog Antiques and Collectibles,* Schiffer Publishing, 1999.

Newsletter: *Colliectively Speaking!,* 331 Regal Dr, Abingdon, MD 21009.

Collectors' Clubs: Canine Collectors Club, 10290 Hill Rd, Erie, IL 61250; Wee Scots, PO Box 450, Danielson, CT 06239.

Bookends, pr, terrier, standing, cast iron, mkd "294," Hubley, 5 x 5¾" **$110.00**

Cabinet, Sergeant's Dog Medicines, litho tin, German Shepherd and boy, "Ask For Free Dog Book," c1930-40s, 7 x 12 x 14" **625.00**

Calendar, 1956, DuPont Explosives Department, hunting dog in field, ©1955 El DuPont De Nemours and Co Inc, 23½" h, 16½" w **100.00**

Doorstop, Great Dane, standing, cast iron, mkd "Great Dane Trailers, Savannah, Georgia," 8 x 8½" **300.00**

Figurine, borzoi, brown and white, Pfeffer Porcelain Co, c1945, 4" h **50.00**

Figurine, dachshund, sgd "Kuspert," Rosenthal, c1936, 4" h **150.00**

Figurine, dachshund, Stanford Pottery, 1950s, 15" l **15.00**

Figurine, terrier, green luster glaze, Zsolnay, 4" h **75.00**

Figurine, terrier puppies in basket, Royal Doulton, HN2588, c1941-85, 3" h **125.00**

Game, Dog Race, Toy Creations, #1213, "New Racing Game Sensation," 1937 . . . . **30.00**

Paperweight, bulldog, metal, black luster finish, each side inscribed "Never Loses Its Grip On The Seam," with British Empire motto and "What We Have We Hold," Whitehead & Hoag, Montreal, 2½" h, 4" l, 3½" d base **75.00**

Planter, bulldog, Morton Pottery, 3½" h **6.00**

Planter, collie with basket, 4¾" h **8.00**

Planter, hound dog, Shawnee, 7" l **8.00**

Planter, poodle with bow, 5½" h **8.00**

Plate, Boxer, Stuart Bruce, Syracuse China, c1950s **20.00**

Calendar, 1938, Gilmore Gasoline adv, pin-up picture of girl with Scottie dogs tangled around her legs, sgd "Elvgren," 15¼" h, 7" w, $30.00. Photo courtesy Collectors Auction Services.

DOLL HOUSES & FURNISHINGS

Handmade doll house furniture falls into the realm of miniatures. Miniatures are exact copies of their larger counterparts. Depending on the accuracy of detail, material used, and recognition of the maker, these miniatures can quickly jump into the hundreds of dollars. Miniature collectors tend to look down on machine-made material.

Petite Prince, Plastic Art Toy Corporation, Tootsietoy, and Renwal are just four of hundreds of major manufacturers of machine-made doll house furniture. Materials range from wood to injection-molded plastic. This furniture was meant to be used, and most surviving examples were. The period packaging and its supporting literature can double the value of a set.

References: Charles Donovan, Jr., *Renwal–World's Finest Toys: Doll House Furniture,* L-W Book Sales, 1999; Jean Mahan, *Doll Furniture: 1950s-1980s,* Hobby House Press, 1997; Dian Zillner, *American Dollhouses and Furniture From the 20th Century,* Schiffer Publishing, 1995; Dian Zillner and Patty Cooper, *Antique and Collectible Dollhouses and Their Furnishings,* Schiffer Publishing, 1998.

Periodicals: *Doll Castle News,* PO Box 247, Washington, NJ 07882; *Dollhouse Miniatures,* PO Box 1612, Waukesha, WI 53187; *Miniature Collector,* 30595 Eight Mile, Livonia, MI 48152.

Collectors' Clubs: Dollhouse & Miniature Collectors, PO Box 16, Bellaire, MI 49615; National Assoc of Miniature Enthusiasts, PO Box 69, Carmel, IN 46032.

DOLL HOUSES

2-Story, Schoenhut, "Daggle," #50/50, wood and fiberboard, emb faux gray stone siding and tile roof, off-white window and door trim, wooden front steps and chimney, 8 rooms plus attic, rooms finished in litho paper representing woodwork, doors, and fancy wallpapers, complete with 53 pcs Tootsietoy furniture, 1923, 27⁵/₈ x 25¹/₂ x 23⁵/₈" **$2,400.00**
2-Story, T Cohn, Spanish, litho tin, 1948 . . . . **150.00**
Bungalow, Rich, white, red roof, 4 windows, 2 chimneys, Arts & Crafts style, 1930s **200.00**
Bungalow, Schoenhut, painted wood and board, blue building, cream and orange trim, red roof, orig wall covering on wall, 1920s, 11 x 12¹/₄ x 12¹³/₁₆" **300.00**
Cape Cod, Meritoy, litho tin, clapboard and gray stone, red roof, 3 dormers, 1 chimney, 5 windows, 1949, 21 x 15" **200.00**
Miniature, Ohio Art, #95, litho tin, complete with 28 pcs of plastic furniture, 3 x 8¹/₂ x 5¹/₄" **75.00**
Suburban, Marx, litho tin, 1950s **110.00**

FURNISHINGS

Baby, Renwal **$12.00**
Baby Bath, Renwal **20.00**
Baby Swing, Acme/Thomas, 3¹/₂" h **25.00**
Bed, Superior, 2¹/₂" l **5.00**
Brother, Renwal **30.00**
Chair, Plasco, 2³/₄" h **10.00**
Chair, Renwal **8.00**
Chair, Superior, 2" h **5.00**
Chest of Drawers, Jaydon, drawers open, 2¹/₄" h **10.00**
Chest of Drawers, Superior, 3¹/₂" h **8.00**
Club Chair, Ideal, 2¹/₄" h **15.00**
Dining Room Chair, Jaydon **3.00**
Father, Renwal **30.00**
Highboy, Plasco, 4 drawers, 4¹/₂" h **10.00**
Ironing Board, with iron, Renwal **25.00**
Kitchen Chair, Ideal **5.00**
Kitchen Chair, Renwal **5.00**
Kitchen Table, Ideal **8.00**
Lamp Table, Renwal **10.00**
Lawn Chair, Marx **8.00**
Living Room Suite, Renwal, 13 pcs, box opens to reveal stage with grand piano, fireplace, and period floor radio, MIB **175.00**
Mother, Renwal **30.00**
Nightstand, Renwal **5.00**
Playpen, Renwal **18.00**
Potty Chair, Ideal, removable potty **10.00**
Potty Chair, Renwal **15.00**
Pump Sink, Allied Molding, with 4 dishes, MIB **45.00**
Refrigerator, Ideal, 3¹/₂" h **15.00**
Refrigerator/Freezer, Ideal, Princess Patti, 2 opening doors, pull-out vegetable bins, rotating shelves, with ice tray, turkey, and Jell-O mold, MIB **150.00**
Seesaw, Acme/Thomas **18.00**
Sewing Machine, Ideal **20.00**
Sewing Machine, Renwal, 2" h **15.00**
Sewing Machine and Cabinet, Renwal **35.00**
Sink, Ideal, 2¹/₂" h **15.00**
Swing, Acme/Thomas **3.00**
Table Lamp, Renwal **10.00**
Television, Renwal **25.00**
TV/Radio/Record Player Console, Ideal, Mighty Mouse picture glued to TV screen, early 1950s **40.00**
Umbrella Table, Marx **18.00**
Vanity, Superior, 2" h **8.00**
Vanity and Bench, Plasco **10.00**
Vanity and Bench, Superior **10.00**

DOLLS

The middle decades of the 20th century witnessed a number of major changes in doll manufacture. New materials (plastic), technology (injection molding), and manufacturing location (the Far East) all played a major role in revolutionizing the industry by the mid-1960s.

Hard, then soft plastic dolls dominated the market by the mid-1950s. Barbie arrived on the scene in 1959. The Cabbage Patch doll was the marketing sensation of the 1970s.

Doll manufacturers are quick to copy any successful doll. Horsman's Dorothy looked surprisingly like Effanbee's Patsy doll. Cosmopolitan's Ginger could easily be mistaken for Vogue's Ginny. Even with a single manufacturer, the same parts were used to make a variety of dolls. Barbie and her friends borrowed body parts from each other.

While condition has always played a major role in doll collecting, it became an obsession in the 1980s, particularly among collectors of contemporary dolls. MIB, mint-in-box, gave way to NRFB, never-removed-from-box.

More and more collectors, especially those under the age of forty-five, are focusing on 1950s and 60s dolls. Many values have doubled in the past five years.

References: J. Michael Augustyniak, *Thirty Years of Mattel Fashion Dolls,* Collector Books, 1998; Kim Avery, *The World of Raggedy Ann Collectibles,* Collector Books, 1997; John Axe, *Effanbee: A Collector's Encyclopedia, 1949-Present, Revised Edition,* Hobby House Press, 1999; Carolyn Cook, *Gene,* Hobby House Press, 1999; Carla Marie Cross, *Crissy Family Encyclopedia,* Hobby House Press, 1998; Carla Marie Cross, *Modern Doll Rarities,* Antique Trader Books, 1997; Linda Crowsey, *Madame Alexander: Collector's Dolls Price Guide #25,* Collector Books, 2000; Linda Crowsey, *Madame Alexander Store Exclusives & Limited Editions,* Collector Books, 2000; Maryanne Dolan, *The World of Dolls,* Krause Publications, 1998; Stephanie Finnegan, *Madame Alexander Dolls,* Portfolio Press, 1999; Jan Foulke, *14th Blue Book Dolls & Values,* Hobby House Press, 1999; Susan Ann Garrison, *The Raggedy Ann & Andy Family Album, 3rd Edition,* Schiffer Publishing, 2000; Cynthia Gaskill, *More American Dolls from the Post War Era: 1945-1965,* Gold Horse Publishing, 1996; Beth C. Gunther, *Crissy & Friends: Collector's Guide to Ideal's Girls,* Antique Trader Books, 1998; Beth Gunther, *Crissy Doll and Her Friends,* Antique Trader Books, 1998.

Patricia Hall, *Raggedy Ann and More: Johnny Gruelle's Dolls and Merchandise,* Pelican Publishing, 1999; Dawn Herlocher, *200 Years of Dolls,* Antique Trader Books, 1996; Dawn Herlocher, *Doll Makers & Marks,* Antique Trader Books, 1999; Judith Izen, *Collector's Guide to Ideal Dolls, Second Edition,* Collector Books, 1998; Judith Izen and Carol Stover, *Collector's Guide to Vogue Dolls,* Collector Books, 1998; Polly Judd, *Cloth Dolls of the 1920s and 1930s,* Hobby House Press, 1990; Polly and Pam Judd, *Composition Dolls: 1909-1928, Volume II,* Hobby House Press, 1994; Polly and Pam Judd, *Composition Dolls: 1928-1955,* Hobby House Press, 1991; Polly and Pam Judd, *European Costumed Dolls,* Hobby House Press, 1994; Polly and Pam Judd, *Glamour Dolls of the 1950s & 1960s, Revised Edition,* Hobby House Press, 1993; Polly and Pam Judd, *Hard Plastic Dolls I, Third Revised Edition,* Hobby House Press, 1993; Polly and Pam Judd, *Hard Plastic Dolls II, Revised,* Hobby House Press, 1994.

Michele Karl, *Composition & Wood Dolls and Toys,* Antique Trader Books, 1998; Sean Kettelkamp, *Chatty Cathy and Her Talking Friends,* Schiffer Publishing, 1998; Kathy and Don Lewis, *Chatty Cathy Dolls,* Collector Books, 1994, 1998 value update; Kathy and Don Lewis, *Talking Toys of the 20th Century,* Collector Books, 1999; A. Glenn Mandeville, *Madame Alexander Dolls Collector's Price Guide, 3rd Edition,* Hobby House Press, 2000; A. Glenn Mandeville, *Ginny,* Hobby House Press, 1998; A. Glenn Mandeville, *Sensational '60s Doll Album,* Hobby House Press, 1996; Ursula R. Metz, *Collector's Encyclopedia of American Composition Dolls: 1900-1950,* Collector Books, 1999; Marjorie A. Miller, *Nancy Ann Storybook Dolls,* Hobby House Press, 1980, available in reprint; Patsy Moyer, *Doll Values: Antique to Modern, Fourth Edition,* Collector Books, 2000; Patsy Moyer, *Modern Collectible Dolls, Vol. II* (1998), *Vol. III* (1999), *Vol. IV* (2000), Collector Books; Dorisanne Osborn, *Sasha Dolls Throughout the Years,* Gold Horse Publishing, 1999.

Susan Nettleingham Roberts and Dorothy Bunker, *The Ginny Doll Encyclopedia,* Hobby House Press, 1994; Cindy Sabulis, *Collector's Guide to Dolls of the 1960s and 1970s,* Collector Books, 2000; Cindy Sabulis and Susan Weglewski, *Collector's Guide to Tammy,* Collector Books, 1997; Nancy N. Schiffer, *Indian Dolls,* Schiffer Publishing, 1997; Patricia N. Schoonmaker, *Patsy Doll Family Encyclopedia: Vol. II,* Hobby House Press, 1998; Patricia R. Smith, *Collector's Encyclopedia of Madame Alexander Dolls, 1965-1990,* Collector Books, 1991, 1997 value update; Evelyn Robson Strahlendorf, *The Charlton Standard Catalogue of Canadian Dolls, 3rd Edition,* Charlton Press, 1997; Marci Van Ausdall, *Betsy McCall,* Hobby House Press, 1999; Dian Zillner, *Dolls and Accessories of the 1950s,* Schiffer Publishing, 1998.

Periodicals: *The Cloth Doll Magazine,* PO Box 2167, Lake Oswego, OR 97035; *Doll Reader,* 741 Miller Dr SE, Ste D2, Harrisburg, PA 20175; *Dolls—The Collector's Magazine,* 170 Fifth Ave, 12th Floor, New York, NY 10010; *Doll World,* 306 E Parr Rd, Berne, IN 46711.

Newsletters: *Betsy's (McCall) Fan Club,* PO Box 946, Quincy, CA 95971; *The Cabbage Line,* 8500 CR 21, Clyde, OH 43410; *Doll-E-Gram* (Black Dolls), PO Box 1212, Bellevue, WA 98009; *Patsy & Friends,* PO Box 311, Deming, NM 88031; *Rags,* PO Box 823, Atlanta, GA 30301.

Collectors' Clubs: Chatty Cathy Collectors Club, PO Box 4426, Seminole, FL 33775; Ginny Doll Club (company-sponsored), PO Box 338, Oakdale, CA 95361; Ideal Toy Co Collector's Club, PO Box 623, Lexington, MA 02173; International Golliwogg Collectors Club, PO Box 612, Woodstock, NY 12498; Liddle Kiddles Klub, 3639 Fourth Ave, La Crescenta, CA 91214; Madame Alexander Doll Club (company sponsored), PO Box 330, Mundelein, IL 60060; Peggy Nisbet International Collectors' Society, PO Box 325, Orrville, OH 44667; United Federation of Doll Clubs, 10920 N Ambassador Dr, Ste 130, Kansas City, MO 64153.

Note: For additional listings see Barbie, Kewpies, and Limited Edition Collectibles. Prices listed are for dolls in excellent condition, unless otherwise noted.

Advertising, Allergic Annie, cloth, stuffed, Honeywell Co . . . **$35.00**

Advertising, Bubble Yum, battery operated, rooted hair, painted eyes, mkd "Lifesavers, Inc. 1988," 13" h **15.00**

Advertising, Buddy Lee, plastic, cowboy, overalls, red and black shirt, red scarf, black cowboy hat with marked band **150.00**

Alexander Doll Co, Cissy, hard plastic, jointed elbows and knees, high heel feet, farm girl outfit and shoes, c1950s, 20" h **350.00**

Alexander Doll Co, Cissy Queen, hard plastic, jointed elbows and knees, high heel feet, orig outfit, c1955, 20" h **600.00**

Alexander Doll Co, Little Genius, hard plastic head and body, vinyl limbs, orig outfit, 1960s **275.00**

Alexander Doll Co, Pussy Cat, cloth and vinyl, brown sleep eyes, closed mouth, cry voice, c1965, 20" h **100.00**

Alexander Doll Co, Sonja Henie, composition, sleep eyes, open mouth, 18" h **1,000.00**

American Character, Cricket, vinyl, bendable legs, orig box, mkd "Amer Char/1964," 9" h **75.00**

American Character, Eloise, cloth, yellow yarn hair, orig outfit, c1955, 21" h **400.00**

American Character, Pouty Pixie, vinyl head, foam body and limbs, rooted hair, freckles, mkd "Amer. Char. Inc./1968," 14" h **25.00**

American Character, Sweet Sue, hard plastic, vinyl arms, jointed knees and elbows, inset wig, flat feet, walker, felt skirt, cap, and purse, cotton blouse, 18" h **400.00**

American Character, Sweet Sue Cotillion, hard plastic, walker, 30" h **450.00**

American Character, Sweet Sue Dream Bride, hard plastic, rooted hair, 17" h **275.00**

American Character, Tiny Tears, hard plastic head, rubber body, blue sleep eyes, drink/wet, 1950s, 14" h **65.00**

American Character, Toodles, vinyl, jointed, rooted saran hair, open nurser mouth, cry voice, c1960, 29" h **225.00**

American Character, Whimsie, vinyl, rooted blonde hair, painted eyes and freckles, closed mouth, 1960s, 20" h **75.00**

Applause, Dick Tracy, vinyl head, cloth body, lower arms, and legs, painted features, molded hat, orig outfit, 9" h **20.00**

Applause, Pippi Longstocking, cloth, yarn hair, painted features, 1988 . . . . **35.00**

Armand Marseille, character doll, composition toddler body, jointed at shoulders and hips, blue glass sleep eyes, closed mouth, imp "AM 323," 1920s, 8" h **850.00**

Armand Marseille, dream baby, bisque head, cloth body, brown glass fixed open eyes, closed mouth, composition hands, 1920s, 16" h **350.00**

Armand Marseille, Just Me, bisque head, composition body, jointed at shoulders and hips, blue glass sleep eyes, 1920s, 10³/₄" h **975.00**

Arranbee, Debú Teen, composition, human hair wig, orig outfit with tag, 1940s, 17" h **225.00**

Arranbee, Kewty, composition, bent arm, side-glancing painted eyes, painted molded hair, mkd "Kewty" on back, 1930s, 13¹/₂" h **225.00**

Arranbee, Little Angel, cloth body, composition head and limbs, glued-on wig, sleep eyes, mkd "R&B," 1940s, 22" h **150.00**

Arranbee, Little Imp, vinyl head, hard plastic body, rooted hair, green sleep eyes, molded lashes, orig outfit, 10" h **80.00**

Arranbee, Littlest Angel, hard plastic, sleep eyes, molded and painted lashes, mkd "R&B," 10" h **45.00**

Arranbee, Miss Coty, vinyl, jointed waist, rooted hair, sleep eyes, 10¹/₂" h **150.00**

Arranbee, Nancy Lee, composition, mohair braided hair, sleep eyes, orig outfit, 14" h **250.00**

Arranbee, Nanette Bride, hard plastic, satin wedding gown, hooped petticoat, long veil, 14" h **275.00**

Arranbee, Sweet Pea, vinyl, rooted saran hair, drink/wet, c1950s, MIB **125.00**

Christel Florchinger, Rosel, vinyl, human hair, inset eyes with lashes, cloth outfit, Germany, 1991, 24" h **700.00**

Cosmopolitan, Little Miss Ginger, vinyl, jointed waist, high heel feet, rooted hair, sleep eyes, 10¹/₂" h **100.00**

Dam, Troll, blue hair, blue felt off-the-shoulder outfit, mkd "Made in Denmark Thomas Dam" on back, 7" h **35.00**

Debby Doll Mfg, Scotch Girl, hard plastic, c1950s, 7¹/₂" h, MIB **25.00**

Eegee, Bubbles, composition, stuffed body, sleep eyes, open mouth, dimples, 24" h **500.00**

Eegee, Sniffles, plastic and vinyl, rooted hair, painted eyes, head mkd "#7" and "Eegee/18 U-2," 17" h **20.00**

Eegee, Softina, plastic and vinyl, painted eyes, open nurser mouth, mkd "Eegee/16VS," 1967, 14" h **10.00**

Effanbee, Baby Dainty, composition arms, legs, and shoulder plate, stuffed cloth body and upper legs, molded hair, painted features, disc jointed arms, c1920s, 15" h **250.00**

Effanbee, Babyette, cloth body, arms, and legs, composition hands, painted molded hair, sleep eyes, orig outfit, 13" h **500.00**

Effanbee, Billy Bum, plastic and vinyl, rooted hair, sleep eyes, mkd "Effanbee 1979/Faith Wick" on head, 17" h **75.00**

Effanbee, Cuddle Up, vinyl head and limbs, oil cloth body, molded hair, sleep eyes, open/close mouth with 2 lower teeth, orig outfit and box, 1954, 24" h **150.00**

Effanbee, Dy-Dee Baby, hard plastic head, rubber body and ears, 18" h **180.00**

Effanbee, Dy-Dee Ellen, hard plastic, rubber ears, sleep eyes, drink/wet, orig outfit, c1956, 11" h **125.00**

Effanbee, Fall, plastic and vinyl, sleep eyes, Four Season's Collection, 1983, 14¹/₂" h **60.00**

Effanbee, Gum Drop, vinyl, rooted hair, sleep eyes, orig outfit, 16" h **50.00**

Effanbee, Heartbeat Baby, composition and cloth, clockwork mechanism, 17" h **150.00**

Effanbee, Honey Walker, hard plastic, sleep eyes, closed mouth, orig outfit, mkd "Effanbee" on head and body, 19" h **400.00**

Effanbee, Lamkins, composition, fully jointed, painted hair, sleep eyes, open mouth, 18" h **500.00**

Effanbee, Little Lady, composition, human hair wig, mkd "Effanbee/Anne Shirley," c1939-40s, 15" h **300.00**

Effanbee, Mary Jane, vinyl head, rooted hair, freckles, 31" h **250.00**

Effanbee, Patsy Joan, composition, mohair wig, sleep eyes, closed mouth, c1930s, 16" h **400.00**

Effanbee, Patsykins, black composition, glassine eyes, closed mouth, c1931, 11" h **600.00**

Effanbee, Rosemary, composition, human hair wig, blue tin eyes, orig outfit, c1925, 25" h **450.00**

Effanbee, Suzanne, composition, human hair wig, orig outfit, c1940, 14" h **300.00**

Elite, Vicki Ballerina, hard plastic, sleep eyes with molded lashes, 8" h **65.00**

Engel-Puppen, Alex, vinyl, sleep eyes with lashes, cloth outfit, Germany, 1988, 19" h **130.00**

Galoob, Happy Baby Hanna, vinyl, sleep eyes, 14" h **25.00**

Galoob, Sad Baby Brooke, vinyl, sleep eyes, 1992, 14" h **30.00**

Effanbee, Suzette, composition, 1930s, 11¹/₂" h, $275.00.

Horsman, molded plastic head and hands, painted features, rooted curly hair, bean bag body, mkd "Horsman Dolls Inc.," 11" h, $6.00.

Georgene Novelties, Raggedy Ann, cloth, c1950s, 18" h **100.00**

German, Shebee, Charles Twelve Trees character, bisque, molded and painted features, jointed at shoulders and hips, white undershirt and pink booties, imp "Germany" at back lower edge of undershirt, paper label on chest, orig paper bib, 1923, 8½" h **425.00**

Gladdie, character doll, bisque head, cloth body, composition hands, molded blonde hair, brown glass sleep eyes, open mouth with teeth and tongue, imp "Gladdie Copyright By Helen W. Jensen," 1929, 11" h . . **1,500.00**

Hasbro, Love A Bye Baby, vinyl, fully jointed, rooted hair, painted features, mkd "Hasbro 1987," 5" h **8.00**

Heidi Ott, Sylvie, vinyl face, cloth body, orig outfit, c1989, 18" h **300.00**

Horsman, Baby Precious, vinyl, orig outfit and box, c1960-70s, 14" h **65.00**

Horsman, Dimples, composition, painted molded hair, tin sleep eyes, open mouth, c1927, 20½" h **250.00**

Horsman, Lil Charmer, vinyl, rooted hair, sleep eyes, 1968, 14" h **20.00**

Horsman, Poor Pitiful Pearl, vinyl, rooted saran hair, orig outfit, 12" h **85.00**

Horsman, Rosebud, composition head, cloth body, human hair wig, sleep eyes, orig outfit, c1930s, 17½" h **275.00**

Horsman, Softee Kid, cloth, stuffed, vinyl face, rooted hair, 1991 . . . . **15.00**

Ideal, Betsy Wetsy, composition head, rubber body **150.00**

Ideal, Bibsy, vinyl, rooted hair, mouth closes when squeezed, produces squeak sound, mkd "Ideal Toy Corp/D-20-1" on head, and "Ideal Toy Corp/D/23" on back, 1969, 23" h **55.00**

Ideal, Blessed Event, vinyl head and lower limbs, oil cloth body and upper limbs, molded tongue, painted eyes, c1950. . . . . **170.00**

Ideal, Bye-Bye Baby, vinyl, jointed, painted molded hair, c1960, 25" h **225.00**

Ideal, Carol Brent, vinyl head and limbs, plastic body, painted side-glancing eyes, high heel feet, orig outfit, mkd "Ideal Toy Corp/M-15-L" on head, and "Ideal Toy Corp/M-15" on body, 1961, 15" h **75.00**

Ideal, Cinnamon, vinyl, rooted growing hair, painted eyes, c1972-74, 13½" h **40.00**

Ideal, Cream Puff, vinyl, sleep eyes, closed mouth, orig outfit, mkd "Ideal/OB-19-2" on head, and "Ideal Toy Corp/19/1961" on back, 1959, 18" h **50.00**

Ideal, Crissy, vinyl, swivel waist, orig outfit and box, c1969, 18" h **50.00**

Ideal, Flexy Sunny Sam, composition, painted molded hair, wire arms and legs, wooden torso and feet, orig outfit, c1930s, 13" h **175.00**

Ideal, Little Miss Revlon, vinyl, swivel waist, rooted hair, sleep eyes, pierced ears, c1958-60, 10½" h **125.00**

Ideal, Patty Playpal, vinyl, battery operated, talker, princess outfit, mkd "Ideal Doll/1987," 26" h **160.00**

Ideal, Snoozie, cloth body, vinyl arms and legs, blonde rooted saran hair, sleep eyes, crier, open and close mouth, c1964, 20" h **55.00**

Ideal, Thumbelina, vinyl face, cloth body, orig outfit, c1983-85, 18" h **45.00**

Ideal, Tickletoes, cloth body, rubber arms and legs, composition face, flange neck, open mouth, orig outfit, c1928-39, 14" h **200.00**

Kathe Kruse, Kathkin, vinyl and cloth, human hair wig, painted features, 1984, 10" h **275.00**

Kenner, Chocolate Strawberry Shortcake, vinyl face, cloth body, rooted hair, painted features and freckles, scented, orig outfit, mkd "American Greeting/Corp/1982/Made in Hong Kong," 19" h **40.00**

Kenner, Darci, vinyl, jointed hands, rooted auburn hair, c1978, 12½" h **45.00**

Kerr & Hinz, Miss Auburn, bisque, jointed shoulders, Peg O' My Heart series, 1947, 7" h **100.00**

Knickerbocker, Bedtime Raggedy Ann, cloth, red yarn hair, painted features, red and white checkered outfit with printed "I Love You" on bib, 1980s, 16" h **85.00**

Lenci, flapper girl, felt, painted features, side-glancing eyes, orig outfit, mkd "K&H/USA," c1920s, 9" h **200.00**

Lenci, golfer, felt, blonde mohair wig, patchwork outfit, wool stockings, leather shoes, 1920s, 16½" h **1,800.00**

Lenci, smoking boy, felt, hard cardboard-like face, cotton outfit, c1940s, 12" h **500.00**

Libby Dolls, Happy Baby, composition and cloth, tin sleep eyes, open mouth with 2 upper and 2 lower teeth, orig outfit and wrist tag, 1935, 26" h **250.00**

Madame Alexander, Abigail Fillmore, #1514, First Ladies Series, 3rd set, 1982-84 . . . . **55.00**

Madame Alexander, Amy, #411, Little Women series, 1974-86, 8" h **25.00**

Madame Alexander, Bliss, Betty Taylor, #1512, First Ladies Series, 2nd set, 1979-81 . . . . **55.00**

Madame Alexander, Chin, #572, Internationals Series, 1973-88, 8" h **20.00**

Madame Alexander, Cleopatra, #1315, Portraits of History Series, 1980-85, 12" h **45.00**

Madame Alexander, Elise, #1655, 19" h **40.00**

Madame Alexander, Napoleon, #1330, Portraits of History Series, 1980-86, 12" h **20.00**

Madame Alexander, Princess Elizabeth, composition, sleep eyes, taffeta floral print dress with black ribbon around waist, black velvet ribbon crown with rhinestone trim, c1937-41, 15" h **550.00**

Madame Alexander, Romeo, #1370, Portrait Children Series, 1978-87, 12" h **30.00**

Madame Alexander, Scarlett, hard plastic, green taffeta outfit with black braid trim, orig box, c1968, 10" h **425.00**

Madame Alexander, Sleeping Beauty, #1595, Classic Series, 1971-85, 14" h **35.00**

Madame Alexander, Southern Belle, hard plastic, white nylon dress with lace and green ribbon trim, matching hat with red flowers, c1971-73, 10" h **160.00**

Mattel, Baby Love Light, vinyl head and hands, cloth body and limbs, battery operated light-up eyes, mkd "1970 Mattel Inc/Mexico" **25.00**

Mattel, Baby Say 'n' See, vinyl, talker, c1960s, 17" h **35.00**

Mattel, Baby Skates, vinyl, painted features, 16" h **40.00**

Mattel, Charmin' Chatty, soft vinyl face, hard vinyl body, long rooted hair, c1963-64, 24" h **225.00**

Mattel, Drowsy, cloth body, vinyl face, rooted hair, painted eyes, pull-string talker, 15½" h **10.00**

Mattel, Hot Looks, stockinette body, vinyl face, rooted synthetic hair, decal eyes, c1986, 18" h **10.00**

Mattel, Lil' Bit Country, cloth body, vinyl head and limbs, rooted hair, sleep eyes, 1992, 14" h **25.00**

Mattel, Mrs Beasley, vinyl face, stuffed cloth body, pull-string talker, 22" h **225.00**

Mattel, Sister Belle, vinyl face, cloth body, yellow yarn hair, pull-string talker, c1960s, 16" h **175.00**

Merrythought, child, cloth, mask face, glass eyes, velvet and fur outfit, mkd "Merrythought/Hygenic Toys/Made in England/Regd Design #809372," c1930s, 11" h **425.00**

Mollye, Shara Lou, hard plastic, mohair wig, sleep eyes, molded eyelids, 14" h **250.00**

Nancy Ann Storybook, Muffie, #811, walker, painted eyebrows, 1954. . . . . **175.00**

Nancy Ann Storybook, Thursday's Child Has Far to Go, #183, bisque, painted features, c1940s, 5" h **75.00**

Nancy Ann Storybook, To Market, To Market, #120, bisque, painted features, orig outfit, c1940s, 5" h **75.00**

Old Cottage Toys, Pearlie, composition face, felt body, black dress with pearl buttons and sequins, c1948, 7½" h **140.00**

Personality Doll Co, Buddy Palooka, stuffed soft vinyl body, molded hair, painted eyes, orig outfit, 1953, 16" h, MIB **600.00**

PM Sales, Honey Tears, vinyl, rooted hair, sleep eyes with lashes, orig outfit, 12" h **35.00**

Robin Woods, Beth, vinyl, sleep eyes, orig outfit, Little Women series, 1986, 14" h **360.00**

Robin Woods, Heidi, vinyl, painted eyes, orig outfit, 14" h **275.00**

Roddy, Walking Princess, plastic, sleep eyes, open mouth, orig outfit, England, 10" h **85.00**

Royal House of Dolls, Susie, vinyl, rooted hair, sleep eyes with lashes, orig outfit, 1989, 16" h **50.00**

Schoenhut, character, wooden head, spring-jointed wooden body, carved hair with comb marks, intaglio eyes, closed mouth, orig outfit. **2,000.00**

Schoenhut, Mama, wooden head and hands, cloth body, 1920s. **1,200.00**

Suzanne Gibson, Rain, Rain, Go Away, vinyl, rooted hair, sleep eyes with lashes, 1988, 9" h **55.00**

Tyco, Twinkling Thumbelina, vinyl, rooted blonde hair, glass eyes, battery operated, orig outfit, c1991, 16½" h **40.00**

Uneeda, Baby Glee, vinyl head, cloth body, open/close mouth, molded tongue, mkd "Uneeda Doll Co, Inc," 1978, 22" h **35.00**

Uneeda, Dollikin, vinyl, jointed arms, legs, feet, and waist, mkd "Uneeda Doll Co Inc/MCMLX/Made in Hong Kong," c1960, 11" h **50.00**

Uneeda, Double-Nik Troll, short green and yellow hair, red, black, and white plaid outfit, red tinged amber eyes, mkd "Uneeda 19©65" on head, 4" h **45.00**

Uneeda, I Love You Dolly, vinyl face, cloth body, inset eyes with lashes, 1989, 14" h **15.00**

Uneeda, Sally Starr, vinyl, rooted hair, sleep eyes, felt outfit and hat, plastic boots, printed name on skirt, 10½" h **85.00**

Virga, Lucy, hard plastic, walker, head turns, sleep eyes with molded lashes, majorette outfit. **75.00**

Vogue, Brikette, vinyl, ball jointed swivel waist, orange hair, sleep eyes, c1959-61, 22" h **65.00**

Vogue, Fairy Godmother, hard plastic, painted eyes, orig outfit, 1950s, 8" h **325.00**

Vogue, Ginnette, vinyl, jointed, open mouth, c1956, 8" h, MIB **200.00**

Vogue, Ginny Baby, vinyl, sleep eyes, open nurser mouth, 16" h **30.00**

Vogue, Jill, hard plastic, bent-knee walker, saran wig, sleep eyes, red and white outfit, c1958, 10½" h **175.00**

Vogue, Toodles, composition, mohair wig, painted eyes, orig outfit, c1937-48, 7½" h **200.00**

DOORSTOPS

Prior to the 1920s, the three-dimensional, cast-metal figural doorstop reigned supreme. After 1920, the flat-back, cast-metal doorstop gained in popularity. By the late 1930s, it was the dominant form being manufactured. Basement workshop doorstops, made primarily from wood, were prevalent from the 1930s through the mid-1950s. By the 1960s the doorstop more often than not was a simple plastic wedge.

Crossover collectors have a major influence on value. Amount of surviving period paint also plays a critical role in determining value.

References: Jeanne Bertoia, *Doorstops*, Collector Books, 1985, 1999 value update; Douglas Congdon-Martin, *Figurative Cast Iron*, Schiffer Publishing, 1994.

Collectors' Club: Doorstop Collectors of America, 2413 Madison Ave, Vineland, NJ 08630.

REPRODUCTION ALERT: Beware of restrikes. Many period molds, especially those from Hubley, have survived. Manufacturers are making modern copies of period examples.

Note: All doorstops listed are cast iron unless otherwise noted.

Cairn Terrier, Bradley & Hubbard, rubber knob on back, 9 x 6" **$450.00**

Clipper Ship, Kleistone Rubber Specialties, mkd "Old Ironsides," rubber, 11 x 8" **160.00**

Cocker Spaniel, Hubley, full figure, black and white, 6¾ x 11" **250.00**

Colonial Lawyer, Waverly Studios, mkd "Pat Applied For," 9⅝ x 5¼" **450.00**

Cottage In the Woods, National Foundry, 4⅝ x 10" **325.00**

Daisy Bowl, 7 x 5¾" **200.00**

Mrs. Sloper, English, repainted, c1920-40, $150.00.

Dog and Bone, "Imp" on base, mkd "GHR ©1921, #142," 5¼ x 8¼"..................................... 350.00
Fireplace, Eastern Specialty Co, colonial theme, 6¼ x 8"... 275.00
Flower Basket, Bradley & Hubbard, mkd "B&H," 8⅝ x 5"... 450.00
French Basket, Hubley, mkd "69," orig sticker, 11 x 6½".... 350.00
German Shepherd, Hubley, full figure, 9¾ x 13"............ 375.00
Gladiolus, Hubley, mkd "489," 10 x 8"................... 275.00
House, Judd Co, mkd "cjo 1288," 8⅛ x 4½"............... 275.00
Jonquils, Hubley, 7½ x 8"............................ 325.00
Little Boy Blue, holding bear, Albany Foundry, full figure,
    5¼ x 3½"...................................... 925.00
Little Red Riding Hood and Wolf, National Foundry,
    7¼ x 5⅜"...................................... 450.00
Malamute, Creation Co, mkd "Copr 1930, C Co," 7½ x6"... 650.00
Minuet Girl, Judd Co, mkd "1278," 8½ x 5"............. 240.00
Pansy Bowl, Hubley, 7 x 6½"........................ 500.00
Peacock, full spread, 6½ x 6½"..................... 350.00
Rabbit By Fence, mkd "Kleistone Rubber Specialties,
    Warren, RI," rubber, 6 x 6¾"...................... 380.00
Scottie, mkd "Wilton Products Inc, Wrightsville PA,"
    7¾ x 4½"...................................... 200.00
Squirrel on Stump, 9 x 6"........................... 425.00
Turtle, Wilton, full figure, 7½ x 9".................... 720.00
Woman with Curtsy, Judd Co, mkd "1279," 8½ x 4½"..... 130.00
Yawning Pup, full figure, 7 x 5"...................... 600.00

DRINKING GLASSES, PROMOTIONAL

The first promotional drinking glasses date from 1937 when Walt Disney licensed Libbey to manufacture a set of safety edge tumblers featuring characters from *Snow White and the Seven Dwarfs*. The set was sold in stores and used by food manufacturers for promotional product packaging. In the early 1950s Welch's sold its jelly in jars featuring Howdy Doody and his friends.

The first fast-food promotional glasses appeared in the late 1960s. Gasoline stations also found this premium concept a good trade stimulator. The plastic drinking cup arrived on the scene in the late 1980s. A decade later, they have become collectible.

A never-out-of-the-box appearance is the key value component for any promotional drinking glass, whether made from glass or plastic. Regional collecting preferences affect value. Beware of hoarding. Far more examples survive in excellent to mint condition than most realize.

References: Mark Chase and Michael Kelly, *Collectible Drinking Glasses, Second Edition,* Collector Books, 1999; John Hervey, *Collector's Guide to Cartoon & Promotional Drinking Glasses,* L-W Book Sales, 1990, 1995 value update; Barbara E. Mauzy, *Peanut Butter Glasses,* Schiffer Publishing, 1997.

Periodical: *Collector Glass News,* PO Box 308, Slippery Rock, PA 16057.

Collectors' Club: Promotional Glass Collectors Assoc, 2654 SE 23rd, Albany, OR 97321.

'57 Thunderbird, Round Table Pizza, car series............ $8.00
Al Capp, Sneaky Pete's Hot Dog, Li'l Abner, mid-1970s 75.00
Batman, "Zok, Whack, Craack," gray and blue, 5" h......... 9.00
Bloomsburg Fair Blue Ribbon Birch Beer, blue logo,
    5¼" h....................................... 9.00
Breeder's Crown, "Rosecroft 1985," etched, 5⅜" h.......... 4.00
Care Bears, Pizza Hut, Good Luck Bear................. 16.00
Colonel Sanders, Kentucky Fried Chicken, balloon rac-
    ing team, Forest Park, 1978, Brockway, 16 oz.......... 10.00
Flintstones, Welch's, Fred goes hunting, orange, 1964....... 12.00
Ford, "Safety Kick Off," football shaped, 5" h............. 3.00
Gasoline Alley, Sunday Funnies...................... 6.00
Goosebumps, "Curly the Master of Scaremonies," 5¾" h 4.00
Gulf, "The World War I Years," 6¼" h.................. 4.00
He-Man, Masters of the Universe, 5½" h 3.00
Howdy Doody, Welch's, "Hits the Spot," Mr Bluster, red,
    1953....................................... 10.00
Hulkmania, WWF, Swarts Peanut Butter................. 5.00
International Harvester, "Louisville Works, Safety
    Millionaires Club"............................ 5.00
Keebler Cookies, "Ernest, Soft Batch reminds me...,"
    1984...................................... 4.00
Margo Bonded Root Beer, red, with syrup line, 4⅜" h....... 16.00
Mutant, Universal Monsters, 1980 .... 160.00

Toughy, Disney's Lady and the Tramp, 1960s, $100.00. Photo courtesy *Collector Glass News.*

National Flag Foundation, Series 1, Grand Union, pedestal, 6½" h **3.00**

New York Islanders, Jack in the Box, orange and blue, 5⅛" h **3.00**

New York World's Fair 1964-65, Schaefer Beer, Schaefer Center, 6⅛" h **10.00**

Old Mother Hubbard, Nursery Rhymes, orange, 4⅝" h **9.00**

Pappy Parker, "Pappy Parker Fried Chicken, Fish, Hamburgers," Brockway, 16 oz **10.00**

Popeye, Popeye's Fried Chicken, 1978 Sports Series **8.00**

Porky Pig, Nutella, Warner Bros, 1992 . . . . **9.00**

Reymer's Blend Soda, frosted, 5" h **5.00**

Sigmund, Taco Villa, 1977 . . . . **3.00**

Snow White and the Seven Dwarfs, Disney All Star Parade, 1939 . . . . **50.00**

Sweet Polly, Pepsi, Leonardo TTV, black lettering, 6" h **17.00**

Twinkie the Kid, Hostess Twinkies **4.00**

University of Alabama, bowl appearances through 1963, red and white, 3½" h **3.00**

World Series 1962, Babe Ruth League, Bridgeton Recreation Center **3.00**

Ziggy, Pizza Inn, "Be Nice To Little Things" **4.00**

DRUGSTORE COLLECTIBLES

Product type (e.g., laxative), manufacturer (such as Burma Shave), and advertising display value are three standard approaches to drugstore collectibles. Unlike country store collectors, whose desire it is to display their collections in a country store environment, few drugstore collectors recreate a pharmacy in their home or garage.

Emphasis is primarily on products from the first two-thirds of the 20th century. Few individuals collect contemporary chain drugstore, e.g., CVS, memorabilia. Dental and shaving items are two subcategories within drugstore collectibles that are currently seeing value increases.

References: G. K. Elliott, George Goehring and Dennis O'Brien, *Remember Your Rubbers: Collectible Condom Containers,* Schiffer Publishing, 1998; Patricia McDaniel, *Drugstore Collectibles,* Wallace-Homestead, 1994.

Alka-Seltzer, display, litho tin, mkd "loaned for better merchandising by Miles Laboratories, Inc, Elkhart, Indiana, USA," tape dispenser on back, 9¾" h, 7" w, 12" l **$100.00**

Allen Sanitary Fountain, galvanized metal, without attachments or box, 4 qts **50.00**

Bayer Aspirin, sign, litho cardboard, tri-fold, standup, "Genuine Aspirin/Does Not Depress The Heart," woman holding box, 33¾" h, 42⅝" w **650.00**

Clairol Hair Coloring, flicker, "Will She Or Won't She?," full color facial image and blonde hair, "Clairol Says She Will!," 1960s **50.00**

De-Luxe Blue Ribbon Condoms, tin, American Hygienic Co, Baltimore, MD, German shepherd **350.00**

Dr Caldwell's Syrup Pepsin, tape measure, celluloid, yellow, white, and blue, 1920s **50.00**

Dr Scholl's Foot Balm, tin, 1½" d **10.00**

Ex-Lax, thermometer, porcelain, 1930-40s **275.00**

Fleet's Chap Stick, tin, 1" d **10.00**

Gillette Safety Razor, pocket mirror **110.00**

Hygienic Baby Talc, tin, 4¾" h **20.00**

Kantlek Enema, Rexall, combination water bottle and fountain syringe, red, with attachments **8.00**

St Joseph's Aspirin, clock, light-up, metal body, glass front, Pam Clock Co, NY, stamped "Sep 1954," 14½" d **250.00**

Tampax, sign, celluloid over cardboard, "Go where you want...do what you wish...," woman in car in field, 14⅛" h, 10⅛" w **80.00**

Three Knights Condoms, tin, Goodwill Rubber Co, NY, knights on horseback **150.00**

Trojans Condoms, sign, litho tin, different products and prices listed on back, "Buy 25 Gross...Get 8 Gross Free," 10½ x 8⅛" **125.00**

Vicks Vaporub, door push, porcelain, 4 x 6½" **375.00**

EASTER COLLECTIBLES

Easter collectibles are the weak sister when it comes to holiday collectibles. The number of collectors is a far cry from those of Valentine, Halloween, or Christmas memorabilia.

Focus is primarily on objects related to the secular side of this important religious holiday. Rabbit (Easter Bunny), chicken, decorated eggs, and Easter baskets head the list of desired objects. While plenty of two-dimensional material exists, most collectors focus primarily on three-dimensional objects.

References: Lissa Bryan-Smith and Richard Smith, *Holiday Collectibles,* Krause Publications, 1998; Pauline and Dan Campanelli, *Holiday Collectibles,* L-W Books, 1997; H. N. Schiffer, *Collectible Rabbits,* Schiffer Publishing, 1990.

Basket, metal, floral dec, 1940s **$15.00**

Basket, reed, multicolored, made in Japan **10.00**

Book, *The Tale of Peter Rabbit,* Edna M Aldredge and Jessie F McKee, Harter Publishing Co, 1931 . . . . **20.00**

Candy Box, cardboard, egg shaped, chick emerging from egg, yellow, purple flowers, 1940s **20.00**

Candy Container, egg, papier-mâché, hen and chick dec, rooster standing on dirigible flying overhead, 1920s, 5⅜" h **200.00**

Candy Container, rabbit, cardboard, Germany **50.00**

Candy Container, rabbit, composition, brown flocked, glass eyes, Germany, 10" h **85.00**

Candy Container, rabbit, glass, JH Millstein Co, 1940s **50.00**

Candy Container, rabbit holding basket, plastic, 4" h **10.00**

Cookie Cutter, rabbit, plastic **1.00**

Decoration, honeycomb, rabbit and egg **3.00**

Figure, rabbit and cart, wood, 1940s **60.00**

Figure, seated rabbit, celluloid, floppy ears, radish in mouth, Japan, 3" h **30.00**

Pinback Button, "Patterson Park Egg Rolling–East End Impr Assn PAL," yellow, blue, and white, c1930s **20.00**

Postcard, "Easter Greetings," boy and girl carrying flowers, emb, early 20th C **5.00**

Pull Toy, rabbit, papier-mâché, on wooden platform with wheels, 1940s **150.00**

Stuffed Toy, rabbit, plush, Gund, 1940-50s **35.00**

Toy, friction, Easter Bunny on bicycle, hard plastic, Creative Creations, 1970s, 4" h **15.00**

Toy, musical, egg shaped, rabbit dec, side crank handle, Mattel, 1950s **25.00**

Toy, wind-up, celluloid rabbit, wearing red shirt, pulling painted tin carrot-shaped cart, attached silvered metal bell, Occupied Japan, 1940s, 2 x 7 x 3½" **100.00**

EDWIN KNOWLES

In 1900 Edwin M. Knowles founded the Edwin M. Knowles China Company. The company's offices were located in East Liverpool, Ohio, the plant in Chester, West Virginia. Products included dinnerware, kitchenware, specialties, and toilet wares.

In 1913 the company opened a plant in Newell, West Virginia. Harker Pottery purchased the Chester plant in 1931. Knowles continued production at the Newell plant until 1963.

Collectors focus primarily on the company's dinnerware. Three of its popular patterns are: Deanna (introduced 1938); Esquire (1956-1962); and Yorktown (introduced in 1936).

In the 1970s the Bradford Exchange bought the rights to the Knowles name and uses it for marketing purposes as a backstamp on some limited edition collector plates. These plates are manufactured offshore, not in America.

References: Susan and Al Bagdade, *Warman's American Pottery and Porcelain,* Wallace-Homestead, Krause Publications, 1994; Harvey Duke, *The Official Identification and Price Guide to Pottery and Porcelain, Eighth Edition,* House of Collectibles, 1995; Lois Lehner, *Lehner's Encyclopedia of U.S. Marks on Pottery, Porcelain & Clay,* Collector Books, 1988.

Note: See Limited Edition Collectibles for collector plate listings.

Alice Ann, bowl, oval, 9" l	$10.00
Alice Ann, butter, cov	20.00
Alice Ann, creamer	4.00
Alice Ann, cream soup cup	15.00
Alice Ann, gravy boat	12.00
Alice Ann, plate, 5½" d	2.00
Alice Ann, platter, 13" l	12.00
Alice Ann, soup bowl, 7½" d	10.00
Arcadia, bread and butter plate, 6" d	2.00
Arcadia, casserole	20.00

Tia Juana, bowl, 9¼" d, $15.00. Photo courtesy Ray Morykan Auctions.

Arcadia, creamer	5.00
Arcadia, platter, 11" l	10.00
Beverly, bowl, 9½" d	15.00
Beverly, bowl, 36s	8.00
Beverly, casserole	20.00
Beverly, cream soup cup	15.00
Beverly, gravy boat	12.00
Beverly, plate, 8½" d	5.00
Beverly, sherbet	8.00
Deanna, bowl, 36s	8.00
Deanna, casserole	20.00
Deanna, cup	4.00
Deanna, eggcup, double	10.00
Deanna, gravy boat	12.00
Deanna, plate, 8" d	5.00
Deanna, platter, 11½" l	10.00
Deanna, teapot, cov	30.00
Diana, creamer	4.00
Diana, plate, 6" d	3.00
Diana, plate, 9" d	8.00
Diana, platter, 13" l	12.00
Diana, sugar, cov	8.00
Esquire, fruit dish, ftd, 12½" w, 7½" h	6.00
Esquire, gravy boat	35.00
Esquire, jug, 2 qt	85.00
Esquire, plate, 10¼" d	10.00
Esquire, platter, 16" l	65.00
Esquire, sugar, cov	30.00
Hostess, casserole	20.00
Hostess, cup	4.00
Hostess, plate, 9¼" d	8.00
Hostess, sugar, cov	8.00
Marion, plate, 5¼" d	2.00
Marion, plate, 7" d	4.00
Marion, sugar, cov	8.00
Potomac, bowl, oval, 9½" l	10.00
Potomac, bowl, round, 9" d	15.00
Potomac, butter, open	15.00
Potomac, creamer	4.00
Potomac, cream soup cup	12.00
Potomac, plate, 8¼" d	5.00
Potomac, platter, 8½" l	8.00
Potomac, sugar, cov	8.00
Roslyn, plate, 5½" d	2.00
Roslyn, plate, 9⅛" d	8.00
Roslyn, sugar, cov	8.00
Tia Juana, dinner plate	18.00
Tia Juana, fruit dish	6.00
Tia Juana, salad plate	12.00
Utility Ware, cake server	12.00
Utility Ware, casserole, 7½" d	20.00
Utility Ware, leftover, 4" d	6.00
Utility Ware, mixing bowl, 6" d	6.00
Utility Ware, pie baker, 9½" d	10.00
Utility Ware, salad bowl, 9" d	15.00
Williamsburg, creamer	4.00
Williamsburg, plate, 6" d	1.00
Williamsburg, plate, 9¾" d	8.00
Williamsburg, sugar, cov	8.00
Yorktown, bowl, 8" d	15.00
Yorktown, casserole	25.00
Yorktown, creamer	6.00
Yorktown, gravy liner	8.00

EGGBEATERS

Kitchen collecting is becoming specialized. A new collecting category often evolves as the result of the publication of a book or formation of a collectors' club. In this instance, eggbeaters became a separate category as the result of the publication of a checklist book on the subject.

Learn to differentiate between commonly found examples and those eggbeaters that are scarce. Novelty and multipurpose beaters are desired. American collectors are expanding their collecting horizons by seeking out beaters from Canada and Europe.

Reference: Don Thornton, *The Eggbeater Chronicles, Second Edition,* published by author, 1999.

A&J, metal, Bingo No. 72, 10³/₄" l **$15.00**
A&J, metal, Lady Bingo No. 72, 10³/₄" l **15.00**
A&J, Super Speed Spinnit Cream and Egg Whip, 11¹/₂" l **40.00**
Alexander & Littlefield Co, metal, wood handle, Biltrite,
   9³/₄" l **45.00**
Alexander & Littlefield Co, Whipwell, 11" l **20.00**
Androck, Bakelite handle, 11" l **20.00**
Aurelius, Favorite, 11³/₄" l **35.00**
EKCO, Deluxe Egg Beater, orig box, 12" l **35.00**
EKCO, Maid of Honor, orig box, 11¹/₂" l **35.00**
Frederick Benson, Benson Beater, 12" l **200.00**
Henderson Corp, The Minute Maid, heart shaped dash-
   ers, 11¹/₂" l **300.00**
Ladd, #5, Ladd Ball Bearing Beater, 11¹/₂" l **20.00**
Louis Ullman, aluminum, Instant Whip Premium Beater,
   10¹/₂" l **35.00**
Maynard Mfg Co, Maynard Super No. 111, plastic han-
   dle, 7" l **40.00**
Metal Goods Mfg, Delight Egg-Beater and Cream-Whip,
   7¹/₂" l **140.00**
Minatajo Sydney, Sydney Egg Beater, 12" l **200.00**
Roos Mfg, Wonder Beater, 11³/₄" l **75.00**
Stuber & Kuck, Biltrite, apron, wavy dashers, 9³/₄" l **110.00**
Thomas J White Plastics Co, Whip-R-Well, 10³/₄" l **120.00**
Turner & Seymour, metal, Blue Whirl, 10¹/₂" l **75.00**

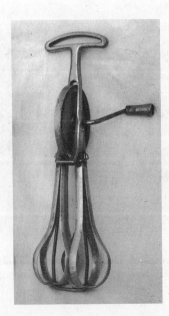

**Rotary, aluminum,
c1920, 10¹/₂" l, $15.00.**

Turner & Seymour, metal, Dainty, 12" l **80.00**
Turner & Seymour, metal, Merry Whirl, 11¹/₂" l **15.00**
Wallace Bros, wooden T-handle, 11" l **10.00**
Yoder Mfg, Yoder Food Mixer, 3 attachments, 11³/₄" l **75.00**

ELEPHANTS

In 1882 when P. T. Barnum bought Jumbo, a 13,000-pound African elephant, from the London Zoo where he resided for seventeen years and brought him to America, the country was swept with elephant mania. When Jumbo was struck by a railway locomotive and died on September 15, 1885, the nation mourned.

America's fascination with the pompous pachyderm dates back to the colonial period. Because of his size, the elephant was considered an exotic creature. Early owners exhibited their elephants in barns and other buildings, moving them at night so that few received a "free" look.

By the first part of the 20th century, most zoological parks featured one or more elephants. The tent circus further increased the pachyderm's visibility. Articles about elephants appeared regularly in periodicals such as *National Geographic*. Hunters donated record specimens to museums.

By the mid-20th century, the mysticism surrounding the elephant disappeared. Elephants were commonplace. The elephant remains in the news today, largely due to the controversy over the excessive killing of elephants for their ivory tusks.

Newsletter: *Jumbo Jargon,* 1002 West 25th St, Erie, PA 16502.

Collectors' Club: The National Elephant Collectors Society, 380 Medford St, Somerville, MA 02145.

Ashtray, glass, green, 5 rests, 2⁵/₈" h **$10.00**
Bank, cast iron, elephant howdah pull tail, white, place
   coin in end of elephant's trunk, pull his tail and trunk
   swings over head and deposits coin in front of how-
   dah, Hubley Mfg Co, c1930 . . . . **300.00**
Bank, glass, Lucky Jumbo **50.00**
Book, *Little Orphan Annie and Jumbo, the Circus
   Elephant,* pop-up,1935, 8 x 9¹/₄" **125.00**
Chambersticks, pr, green glaze, Rookwood, 4" h **275.00**
Chocolate Mold, tin, 3 cavities **75.00**
Cigarette Dispenser, cast iron, tail turns and cigarette
   rolls from elephants tummy, 5¹/₂" h, 4" w, 8¹/₄" l **125.00**
Clothes Sprinkler, trunk curled up for handle, happy
   face, fat and squatty **275.00**
Cookie Jar, mkd "826 USA," California Originals **85.00**
Cookie Jar, raised trunk, mkd "California," Doranne **125.00**
Doorstop, cast iron, elephant seated on barrel, mkd
   "No. 2C, 1930 Taylor Cook," 8¹/₂ x 6¹/₂" **1,500.00**
Figure, cast iron, gray, white trunk, red blanket with
   "Landon Roosevelt 1936" in raised gold lettering, 2 x
   5 x 3" **375.00**
Figure, porcelain, trunk down, 3 x 4" **20.00**
Planter, ceramic, raised trunk, 7³/₄" h **20.00**
Planter, resin, elephant sitting by tree stump, 4³/₄" h **8.00**
Sign, Brown's Jumbo Bread, diecut tin, 1940-50s, 15 x
   13" **550.00**
Toy, wind-up, litho tin, Flying Elephant, gyro attached to
   trunk, orig box, Yone, 1950s, 6" l **100.00**
Toy, wind-up, litho tin, Jumbo, mkd "Made In US Zone
   Germany," 1950s, 2 x 4¹/₂ x 3³/₄" **100.00**

ENESCO

Enesco Corporation is a producer and distributor of fine gifts, collectibles, and home decor accessories. Enesco was founded in 1958 as a division of N. Shure Company. Following N. Shure's sale, the import division reorganized as Enesco, formed from the phonic spelling of the prior parent company's initials–N.S.Co. Originally based in Chicago, Enesco relocated it corporate offices to Elk Grove Village in 1975 and to Itasca in 1995. The company's international showroom, warehouse, and distribution facility remains in Elk Grove Village.

The Enesco product line includes more than 12,000 gift, collectible, and home accent items. Enesco markets licensed gifts and collectibles from well-known artists such as Sam Butcher (Precious Moments), Priscilla Hillman (Cherished Teddies and Calico Kittens), David Tate and Ray Day (Lilliput Lane), and David Winter (David Winter Cottages).

In 1983 Enesco became a wholly owned subsidiary of Westfield, Massachusetts-based Stanhome, Inc., a multinational corporation. In 1997 The Bradford Group entered into a long-term licensing agreement to market the product lines of Stanhome's subsidiary, Enesco Giftware Group. In 1998 Stanhome, Inc., changed its name to Enesco Group, Inc. Today, Enesco products are distributed in more than thirty countries.

Note: For additional listings see David Winter Cottages, Limited Edition Collectibles, Music Boxes, Prayer Ladies, and Precious Moments.

KITCHEN AND GIFT WARES

Candlesticks, pr, swans, black, blue or yellow tipped, redware base	**$25.00**
Card Holder, Granny, winking	**25.00**
Cookie Jar, Snappy the Snail, 9½" h	**125.00**
Cutting Board, Dutch Boy and Girl, "Kissin' Don't Last, Cookin' Do"	**50.00**
Recipe Holder, George Washington holding scroll "We the people of the United States," 5¾" h	**20.00**
Salt and Pepper Shakers, pr, Betsy Ross salt, George Washington pepper, George holding scroll "Bill of Rights," 4½" h	**22.00**
Salt and Pepper Shakers, pr, Dutch Boy and Girl	**12.00**
Salt and Pepper Shakers, pr, Snappy the Snail, 3½" h	**15.00**
Tea Bag Holder, Snappy the Snail, 3½" h	**6.00**

LIMITED EDITION COLLECTIBLES

Cherished Teddies, figurine, Beth, P Hillman, 1992	**$40.00**
Cherished Teddies, ornament, Baby Angel On Cloud, P Hillman, 1995	**14.00**
Cherished Teddies, plate, Some Bunny Loves You, P Hillman, 1996	**35.00**
David Winter, plate, Little Mill, M Fisher, 1992	**30.00**
Kinka Bells, bell, Easter…Filled With Hope & Blessings, 1989	**25.00**
Mary's Moo Moos, plate, It's Butter To Give Than To Receive, M Rhyner-Nadig, 1997	**35.00**
Mary's Moo Moos Cowabungas, ornament, I Love Moo, M Rhyner-Nadig, 1996	**8.00**
Memories of Yesterday, bell, Here Comes the Bride/God Bless Her, M Attwell, 1990	**25.00**
Memories of Yesterday, doll, Hilary, M Attwell, 1990, 11" h	**100.00**
Memories of Yesterday, figurine, What Will I Grow Up To Be?, M Attwell, 1988	**45.00**
Memories of Yesterday, ornament, Baby's First Christmas, M Attwell, 1988	**50.00**
Memories of Yesterday, plate, Join Me For A Little Song, M Attwell, 1995	**50.00**

ERTL

Fred Ertl, Sr., founded Ertl, the world's largest manufacturer of toy farm equipment, in 1945. The company has licenses from most major manufacturers. Located in Dyersville, Iowa, Ertl also manufactures a line of promotional banks, promotional trucks, and toys ranging from airplanes to trucks.

Ertl makes many of its toys in a variety of scales. It also has a line of limited edition, highly detailed models designed for direct sale to the adult collector market. When researching an Ertl toy be certain you are looking in the right scale and quality categories.

Collectors' Club: Ertl Collectors Club, PO Box 500, Dyersville, IA 52040.

Note: All toys listed are in very good condition. Banks are in mint condition. See Farm Toys for additional listings.

BANKS

Amoco, 1913 Model T Van, #9150, 1987	**$150.00**
Ben Franklin, 1918 Runabout, #1319, 1989	**25.00**
Dairy Queen, 1932 Ford Panel, #9034, 1989	**100.00**
Edy's Ice Cream, 1905 Ford Delivery Van, #9644, 1989	**30.00**
Holly Cliff Farms, 1926 Mack Tanker, #9477, 1987	**50.00**
JC Penney, Horse & Carriage, #9232, 1985	**65.00**
Lipton Tea, 1913 Model T Van, #7505, 1989	**75.00**
Old Country, Step Van, #9478, 1987	**100.00**
Red Rose Tea, 1913 Model T Van, #2130, 1984	**40.00**
Texaco, 1930 Diamond T Tanker, #9330VO, 1990	**75.00**
US Mail, 1937 Ford Tractor Trailer, #9727, 1988	**40.00**

Bank, Pep Boys, 1923 Chevrolet Delivery Van, "1921-1996, 75 Years" on side, 3½" h, 6¾" l, $10.00. Photo courtesy Collectors Auction Services.

TRUCKS

Ford 7500 Backhoe	$55.00
Ford 8N Utility Tractor, 7" l	35.00
Hydraulic Dump Truck, #1645	30.00
Iron Horse Van	50.00
John Deere Tilt Bed	180.00
John Deere Turbo Combine, 16" l	15.00
Loadstar Tilt Bed	125.00
Mary Kay Cosmetics Trailer Truck	150.00
Mobile Tanker	60.00
Moran's Ground Beef Semi, 23" l, MIB	20.00
Oklahoma Crude Semi, 23" l, MIB	20.00
Plantation Thoroughbreds, 22" l	20.00
Shopko Semi, 23" l	15.00
Transtar Texaco Tanker	90.00

FANS, ELECTRIC

While hundreds of companies made electric fans, the market was mostly dominated by Emerson Electric, General Electric, and Westinghouse Electric. Other collectible manufacturers include Berstead Manufacturing, Hunter-Century Gilbert, Menominee, Peerless, Robbins & Meyers, and StarRite/Eskimo.

Montgomery Ward, Sears, Singer, and Western Electric never manufactured electric fans. They put their brand names on fans made by others. Polar Cub electric fans were made for the five-and-dime store trade.

Electric fan collecting came of age in the 1990s. Currently, the focus is primarily on desk fans made prior to 1960. The market for large ceiling fans, with the exception of those of unusual design, is still primarily reuse.

Reference: John M. Witt, *Collector's Guide to Electric Fans,* Collector Books, 1997, 1999 value update.

Collectors' Club: American Fan Collectors Assoc, PO Box 5473, Sarasota, FL 34277.

REPRODUCTION ALERT: Beware of assembled fakes. Unscrupulous individuals assemble fictitious fans by using parts from several different fans. Buy only from sellers willing to provide a money-back, no-questions-asked guarantee.

Note: All fans listed are in excellent condition.

Art Deco Style, Bakelite motor housing, 7½" blades	$300.00
Century, #J-10, model 55, 10" blades	3.00
Century, #K-3, model 56, oscillator, 10" blades	8.00
Century, #P-7, model 611, oscillator, 12" brass blades	3.00
Colonial Fan and Motor Co, style P16, 8" blades	475.00
Domestic Electric Co, #S2660, 30" h, 14¾" blades	110.00
Emerson, type 6250-H, 10" blades	10.00
Emerson, type 6850-M, 10" blades	3.00
Emerson, type 11646, #118187, 12½" blades	200.00
Emerson, type 19646, #135795, oscillator, 12⅜" blades	75.00
Emerson, type 21546, #291125, oscillator, 12½" blades	65.00
Emerson, type 27646, #A19253, oscillator, 12½" brass blades	35.00
General Electric, #363587, 16" blades	8.00
General Electric, type AAU, #1223535, oscillator, 12" brass blades	30.00
Gilbert, oscillator, 8¾" blades	6.00

Barcol (Barber/Coleman), Bakelite base and motor housing, aluminum guard and airplane-style blade, off-center motor, 1920-30s, $30.00.

Handy Breeze, catalog #3909, 8" blades	6.00
Hunter, style #V45780, type 10, oscillator, repainted 10" blades	25.00
Luminaire, floor model	550.00
Polar Cub, 8¾" blades	6.00
Robbins & Myers, list #2410, oscillator, 11¾" brass blades	15.00
Robbins & Myers, list #3500, 8" blades	10.00
Robbins & Myers, list #5224, oscillator, 11¾" blades	8.00
Signal, type 150A, oscillator, 9¾" blades	6.00
Westinghouse, style #16, 12" brass blades	10.00
Westinghouse, style #177109D, 16⅛" brass blades	110.00
Westinghouse, style #1013812, 12" brass blades	100.00

FARM TOYS

Although there are pre–World War I lithograph tin toys with a farm theme, the cast-iron farm toys of the 1920s and 1930s are considered the first "farm toys." Arcade, Hubley, Vindex, and Wilkens are among the earliest manufacturers. Many of these early toys were horse-drawn.

Collecting farm toys became popular in the 1950s and 60s when miniatures by Brubaker, Peterson, and White became available and collectors turned their attention to real tractors. In the late 1950s and 60s, Ertl issued farm toys based upon brand name products such as Allis-Chalmers, Case, John Deere, International, Minneapolis-Moline, Massey-Ferguson, and Oliver.

Claire Scheibe founded the National Farm Toy Show in 1978 in Dyersville, Iowa, home of Ertl and Scale Models. Annual attendance now exceeds 15,000. In addition, over 100 regional farm toy shows are held each year throughout America, with a heavy concentration in the Midwest and Plains states.

Collectors differentiate between industrial models, i.e., highly detailed display models, and toys, objects made specifically for play. Both are collected but the primary emphasis is on toys.

Recently, several manufacturers introduced collector model series. These are often as fully detailed as industrial models, and are meant to be displayed. The collector model secondary market is highly speculative at this time.

References: Richard Sonneck, *Dick's Farm Toy Price Guide & Check List,* published by author, 1990; Bill Vossler, *Toy Farm Tractors,* Voyageur Press, 1998.

Periodicals: *Tractor Classics CTM,* PO Box 489, Rocanville, Saskatchewan, S0A 3L0 Canada; *Toy Farmer,* 7496 106th Ave SE, Lamoure, ND 58458; *The Toy Tractor Times,* PO Box 156, Osage, IA 50461.

Collectors' Club: Antique Engine, Tractor & Toy Club, 5731 Paradise Rd, Slatington, PA 18080.

Note: All toys are in mint condition in their original box. See Ertl, Matchbox, and Tonka for additional listings.

MINIATURES

Allis-Chalmers Tractor and Dump Trailer, Arcade, #2657, 1937, 12¾" l	**$450.00**
Brute Road Grader, Buddy L, 1970, 6½" l	**100.00**
Bulldozer, Doepke, #2012, 15" l	**550.00**
Caterpillar Tractor, Arcade, #267X, 1931, 3" l	**50.00**
Caterpillar Tractor, Tootsietoy, 1931	**50.00**
Caterpillar Tractor and Trailer, Structo, #46	**450.00**
Concrete Mixer, Buddy L, 1949, 9⅝" l	**200.00**
Corn Harvester, Arcade, #4180, 5" l	**300.00**
Crawler, Arcade, 1930, 3⅞" l	**300.00**
Crawler, Marx, 1950, 1/25 scale	**150.00**
Dredge, Buddy L, 1924, 19" l	**1,500.00**
Earthmover, Auburn Rubber, red and yellow	**30.00**
Fordson Tractor, Arcade, 1923, 5¾" l	**275.00**
Fordson Tractor, Barclay, #203, 2⅛" l	**25.00**
Garden Roller, Dinky, #105A	**35.00**
Husky Tractor, Buddy L, 1966, 13" l	**100.00**
International Harvester A Tractor, Arcade, cast iron, 1941, 1/12 scale	**850.00**
International Harvester Crawler, Arcade, cast iron, 1936, 1/16 scale	**3,000.00**
John Deere Tractor, Auburn Rubber, 1/20 scale	**50.00**
Massey-Ferguson Tractor, Tootsietoy, #1011	**400.00**
McCormick-Deering Farmall Tractor, Arcade, cast iron, 1936, 6¼" l	**550.00**
McCormick-Deering Thresher, Arcade, 1927, 12" l	**1,000.00**
Minneapolis Moline Tractor, Auburn Rubber, red, 1950, 1/16 scale	**50.00**
Oliver Plow, Arcade, red, 1926, 6½" l	**450.00**
Oliver Tractor, Arcade, #3560, 1940s, 7½" l	**175.00**
Power Grader, Marx, 17½" l	**125.00**
Road Grader, Corgi, #963, 1970s	**70.00**
Road Grader, Nylint, 1955, 19¼" l	**225.00**
Road Scraper, Hubley, plastic, 1950s	**60.00**
Sand Loader, Buddy L, 1931, 21" l	**350.00**
Scoop and Loader, Buddy L, 1956, 18" l	**110.00**
Stake Truck, Structo, 1930s, 21" l	**400.00**
Stake Truck, Tonka, #404	**120.00**
Stake Truck, Wyandotte, 20" l	**175.00**
Threshing Machine, Arcade, cast iron, 10" l	**325.00**
Tipping Farm Trailer, Corgi, 4¼" l	**25.00**
Tournatractor, Nylint, 1955, 14¾" l	**200.00**

Schoenhut Farmer Set, jointed wood figures, includes farmer, wife, cow and pig with glass eyes, donkey with painted eyes, and new accessories, $1,325.00. Photo courtesy Gene Harris Antique Auction Center, Inc.

Tractor, Marx, wind-up, litho tin, 1940s, 5½" l	**275.00**
Wooldrige Earth Hauler, #2000, 25" l	**350.00**

PEDAL TRACTORS

AMF Western Flyer Tractor, 1970s	**$300.00**
International Harvester Farmall, #400, red, 1955	**900.00**
John Deere Tractor, #30, green and yellow, 1973	**600.00**
John Deere Tractor and Trailer, Series 10, 1961	**325.00**
Kubota Pedal Tractor, Model M6950, 1980s	**250.00**
Murray Diesel Tractor and Trailer, red and white, 1965	**600.00**

FAST-FOOD COLLECTIBLES

McDonald's dominates the field. In fact, it has become so important that it has its own category. If you have a McDonald's fast-food collectible, look under "M."

Each year dozens of new fast-food franchises are launched. Each year dozens of fast-food franchises fail. Collectors focus primarily on collectibles from those which have achieved national success. National fast-food chains do regional promotions. Collectors' club newsletters are the best way to keep up with these and the premiums that result.

All the major fast-food franchises have gone international. Collectors also are hopping aboard the international bandwagon. Many American collections now contain examples from abroad.

References: Joyce and Terry Losonsky, *The Encyclopedia of Fast Food Toys, 2 Vols.,* Schiffer Publishing, 1999; Gail Pope and Keith Hammond, *Fast Food Toys, 3rd Edition,* Schiffer Publishing, 1999; Robert J. Sodaro and Alex G. Malloy, *Kiddie Meal Collectibles,* Antique Trader Books, 1998; Elizabeth A. Stephan (ed.), *Ultimate Price Guide to Fast Food Collectibles,* Krause Publications, 1999.

Arby's, jigsaw puzzle book, *Cousin Arthur's New Camera,* 1990	**$2.00**
Arby's, jigsaw puzzle book, *Mr Men and Little Miss,* cardboard, 1986, 4" sq	**4.00**
Arby's, mini frisbee, Yogi & Friends, 1993	**1.00**
Arby's, ornament, Bugs Bunny as Santa Claus, 1989	**3.00**
Arby's, water squirter, Babar's World Tour, rubber, 1992	**2.00**
Arby's, wristpack, Babar, green and purple strap, 1992	**2.00**

Big Boy, box, You Name the Sports **3.00**
Big Boy, time capsule, 1993 . . . . **1.00**
Burger Chef, box, Blueburger's Pirate Crew, 1973 . . . . **15.00**
Burger Chef, box, Land Speeder, Star Wars series, 1978 . . . . . **20.00**
Burger King, activity book, Crayola Coloring Mystery
    series, 1990, 8½ x 7" **1.00**
Burger King, badge, Teenage Mutant Ninja Turtles Rad
    Badge, 1990 . . . . **2.00**
Burger King, bicycle license plate, Chipmunk Adventure
    series, 1987 . . . . **3.00**
Burger King, book, *The Circus Train*, Trak-Pak series,
    1988, 6½ x 7¼" **4.00**
Burger King, book, *The Wild West*, cardboard, 1985, 6 x
    12" **4.00**
Burger King, book and cassette, *Jack and the Beanstalk*,
    Fairy Tales series, 1989 . . . . **4.00**
Burger King, figure, Aladdin & Magic Carpet, 1992 . . . . **2.00**
Burger King, figure, Belle, Beauty and the Beast series,
    1991 . . . . **3.00**
Burger King, figure, Capitol Critters series, 1992 . . . . **1.00**
Burger King, figure, Dino Crawlers series, 1994 . . . . **1.00**
Burger King, figure, hamburger, Food Miniatures series,
    1983 . . . . **3.00**
Burger King, figure, IQ on dolphin, Water Mates series,
    1991 . . . . **1.00**
Burger King, figure, Kid Vid, 1991 . . . . **2.00**
Burger King, figure, Life Savers Freaky Fellas series, 1992 . . . . . **1.00**
Burger King, figure, Troll, glow-in-the-dark, 1993 . . . . **2.00**
Burger King, flip-top car, Purrtenders series, 1988 . . . . **2.00**
Burger King, mask, Meal-Bots series, 1986 . . . . **3.00**
Burger King, model, T-Rex, Bone Age series, 1989 . . . . **3.00**
Burger King, rubber ball, Nerfuls series, 1989 . . . . **1.00**
Burger King, secret message ring, Thundercats series,
    1986 . . . . **3.00**
Burger King, stuffed toy, plush, Theodore, Chipmunk
    Adventure series, 1987 . . . . **4.00**
Carl's Jr, book, *Just Me and My Dad*, Mercer Mayer,
    Western Publishing, 1986, 8" sq. **3.00**
Carl's Jr, book, *Meet My Pet Monster*, My Pet Monster
    series, 1986 . . . . **3.00**
Carl's Jr, Dino-Pour Bottle Topper, 1992, 3½ x 3" **3.00**
Carl's Jr, figure, Monster Days series, rubber, 1988 . . . . **2.00**

Carl's Jr, flying disc, Beach Creatures series, 1990 . . . . **2.00**
Carl's Jr, magnet, Happy Star series, 1988 . . . . **3.00**
Carl's Jr, paper clip holder, brown bear, Animal Office
    Supplies series, 1987 . . . . **4.00**
Carl's Jr, spinner thrower, Camp California series, 1992 . . . . . . **2.00**
Carl's Jr, stamper, Addams Family series, 1993 . . . . **2.00**
Chick-Fil-A, book, *Last Great Adventure of Summer*,
    Adventures In Odyssey series, 1991, 4 x 5" **2.00**
Chick-Fil-A, cup, Doodles Kid's series **2.00**
Chick-Fil-A, sand mold, Hilda Hippo, The Busy World of
    Richard Scarry series, 1993 . . . . **3.00**
Dairy Queen, activity book, Underwater Fun series, 1994 . . . **1.00**
Dairy Queen, case, heart shaped, plastic, 1994 . . . . **1.00**
Dairy Queen, Dinocardz Collector Cards, #1-26 . . . . **1.00**
Dairy Queen, figure, cowboy, bendable, DQKids series **10.00**
Dairy Queen, figure, Edmond the Cat, Rock-A-Doodle
    series, 1992 . . . . **3.00**
Dairy Queen, figure, Radio Flyer Wagon, plastic, 1991,
    4" l **4.00**
Dairy Queen, figure, Santa, Holiday Bendies series,
    1993, 3½" h **2.00**
Dairy Queen, funbunch flyer **2.00**
Dairy Queen, Krazy Fork, Knife, and Spoon Set, molded
    plastic, 1993 . . . . **1.00**
Dairy Queen, paint set, translucent teddy bear, plastic,
    1993, 5" l **3.00**
Dairy Queen, stuffed toy, plush, Kangachew, 1990 . . . . **5.00**
Denny's, ornament, Jetsons Puzzle Ornaments series,
    1992 . . . . **1.00**
Denny's, secret spy decoder, The Mysterious Madame X,
    Adventure Seekers series, 1993 . . . . **1.00**
Denny's, stuffed toy, plush, miniature, Flintstones Mini
    Plush Toys series, 1989, 3½" h **4.00**
Denny's, water squirter, Flintstones Fun Squirters series,
    1991 . . . . **1.00**
Domino's Pizza, ornament, clear plastic, silkscreen
    Noid looking through holly wreath, 1988 . . . . **3.00**
Hardee's, activity book, *Dinosaur Activity Fun*, 1992,
    4 x 6" **2.00**
Hardee's, book, *Little Red Riding Hood*, Little Little
    Golden Books series, 1987 . . . . **2.00**
Hardee's, box, Crazy Stuff!, Donald Duck Presents series **5.00**
Hardee's, box, Ectomobile, Ghostbusters II series, 1989 . . . . . **5.00**
Hardee's, candy, Gummi Bears, ½ oz bag, 1992 . . . . **2.00**
Hardee's, cup, skeleton with pumpkin, Halloween
    Glow-Cups series, 1993, 4¼" h **1.00**
Hardee's, figure, California Raisins, 1987 . . . . **3.00**
Hardee's, Fold 'n Solve Travel Pictures, Waldo's Travel
    Adventure series, 1992 . . . . **1.00**
Hardee's, Marvel Super Heroes Vehicle, 1990 . . . . **2.00**
Hardee's, noise maker, Ghostbusters II series, 1989 . . . . **8.00**
Jack-In-The-Box, activity book, *Earth Day*, 1992 . . . . **2.00**
Jack-In-The-Box, book and record, *Why a House Makes
    Noise, Vol 1*, Adventures of Jack-In-the-Box series,
    1980s **10.00**
Jack-In-The-Box, yo-yo, Ollie O Ring, 1992, 1" d **2.00**
Kentucky Fried Chicken, bank, Colonel Sanders, white
    hard molded plastic, painted details, 12¼" h **35.00**
Little Caesars, crayon holder, 1993-94 . . . . **3.00**
Little Caesars, license plate, 1993-94 . . . . **3.00**
Long John Silver's, book, *The Biggest Dinosaurs*, Michael
    Berenstain, Golden Look Look Book, I Love Dinosaurs
    series, 1993 . . . . **2.00**
Long John Silver's, car, fish shaped, plastic, 1986 . . . . **2.00**

Burger King, baseball card, Topps, Burger King Phillies, #1, Dallas Green, 1980, $.40. Photo courtesy Ray Morykan Auctions.

Domino's Pizza, promotional drinking glass, Dick Tracy, $185.00. Photo courtesy *Collector Glass News.*

Long John Silver's, car, metal, Racing Champions series, 1989. . . . . **3.00**

Long John Silver's, pencil topper, Treasure Trolls series, 1993. . . . . **1.00**

Long John Silver's, Sea'Watcher Telescope, 1990 . . . . **2.00**

Pizza Hut, box, Dinosaurs series, 1993 . . . . **2.00**

Pizza Hut, box, Ferngully–The Last Rainforest, 1992. . . . . **2.00**

Pizza Hut, cup, plastic, Fievel Goes West series, 1991 . . . . **3.00**

Pizza Hut, seed packet, Ferngully series, 1992 . . . . **3.00**

Popeye's Famous Fried Chicken, figure, Olive Oyl **1.00**

Roy Rogers, Bag-A-Wag series. **2.00**

Roy Rogers, cup critter, 1994. . . . . **1.00**

Roy Rogers, figure, dinosaur, glow-in-the-dark, 1993 . . . . **1.00**

Roy Rogers, figure, Hide 'n' Keep Dinos series, 1988 . . . . **4.00**

Roy Rogers, magnet, Be a Sport series, 1989 . . . . **4.00**

Subway, Doodletop Jr, 1994 . . . . **2.00**

Subway, hackeysack ball, 1993 . . . . **1.00**

Taco Bell, book, *My Fair Lioness,* Zoobilee Zoo Coloring Storybooks series, 1984 . . . . **4.00**

Taco Bell, Cave of Wonders Paint with Water Set, Aladdin series, 1993 . . . . **3.00**

Taco Bell, finger puppet, Lowly Worm, Busy World of Richard Scarry series, 1993 . . . . **4.00**

Taco Bell, inflatable ball, Adventures of Rocky and Bullwinkle series, 1993 . . . . **5.00**

Taco Bell, pop-up card, *Free Willy* series, 1993 . . . . **1.00**

Taco Bell, sand mold, star, Sand City series, 1993. . . . . **1.00**

Taco Bell, stickers, Dinosaur Days series, 1993. . . . . **1.00**

Taco Bell, stuffed toy, plush, Hugga Bunch series, 1984 . . . . . . **8.00**

Wendy's, ball, rubber, Baseballasaurus, Saurus Sport Balls series, 1991 . . . . **1.00**

Wendy's, box, Nockmaar Castle, *Willow* series, 1988 . . . . **2.00**

Wendy's, calligraphy stencil, 1983. . . . . **3.00**

Wendy's, card game, Crazy Eight, Endangered Animals series, 1993 . . . . **1.00**

Wendy's, cup, plastic, *Follow That Bird,* Sesame Street series, 1985 . . . . **4.00**

Wendy's, Cybercycle, 1994, 3¹⁄₂" l **2.00**

Wendy's, figure, Charlie, *All Dogs Go to Heaven* series, 1989. . . . . **2.00**

Wendy's, figure, Moodie, 1984, 2¹⁄₂" h **2.00**

Wendy's, figure, Sir Scallop, Potato Head Kids series, 1987 . . . . **2.00**

Wendy's, figure, Teddy Ruxpin, 1987 . . . . **4.00**

Wendy's, iron-on patch, printed scene, Gobots series, 1986, 5 x 4" **4.00**

Wendy's, puffy stickers, "Where's The Beef?," 1984, 9 x 3³⁄₄" sheet **5.00**

Wendy's, reflector wrist band, Gear Up series, 1992 . . . . **1.00**

Wendy's, stuffed toy, plush, Furskins Bears series, 1986, 7" h **6.00**

Wendy's, Tom Thumb Plant Starter Kit, 1987 . . . . **4.00**

White Castle, bucket, plastic, Beach Buddies series, 1988. . . . . **3.00**

White Castle, cup, plastic, Castle Creature series, 1992, 4" h **3.00**

White Castle, figure, King Wooly & Queen Winnevere, Castle Meal Friends series, 1992-93 . . . . **4.00**

White Castle, sand pail and shovel, Marvel Superheroes series, 1989 . . . . **4.00**

White Castle, Shape & Shout Color Dough, 1989 . . . . **3.00**

White Castle, sunglasses, Fabulous Funshades series, 1988. . . . . **3.00**

White Castle, water bottle, Camp White Castle series, 1990. . . . . **2.00**

FENTON GLASS

The Fenton Art Glass Company, founded by Frank L. Fenton in 1905 in Martins Ferry, Ohio, originally offered decorating services to other manufacturers. By 1907 the company had relocated to Williamstown, West Virginia, and was making its own glass.

The company's first products included carnival, chocolate, custard, and opalescent glass. Art glass and stretch glass products were introduced in the 1920s. Production of slag glass began in the 1930s. Decorating techniques ranged from acid etching to hand painting.

Through the 1970s, Fenton marked its products with a variety of paper labels. The company adopted an oval raised trademark in 1970. Recently a date code has been added to the mark.

References: Robert E. Eaton, Jr. (comp.), *Fenton Glass: The First Twenty-Five Years Comprehensive Price Guide 1998,* Glass Press, 1998; Robert E. Eaton, Jr. (comp.), *Fenton Glass: The Second Twenty-Five Years Comprehensive Price Guide 1998,* Glass Press, 1998; Fenton Art Glass Collectors of America (comp.), *Fenton Glass: The Third Twenty-Five Years Comprehensive Price Guide 1998,* Glass Press, 1998; William Heacock, *Fenton Glass: The First Twenty-Five Years,* O-Val Advertising Corp. (Antique Publications), 1978; William Heacock, *Fenton Glass: The Second Twenty-Five Years,* O-Val Advertising Corp. (Antique Publications), 1980; William Heacock, *Fenton Glass: The Third Twenty-Five Years,* O-Val Advertising Corp. (Antique Publications), 1989; James Measell (ed.), *Fenton Glass: The 1980s Decade,* Glass Press, 1996; Margaret and Kenn Whitmeyer, *Fenton Art Glass: 1907-1939* (1996, 1999 value update), *1939-1980* (1999), Collector Books.

Newsletter: *Butterfly Net,* 302 Pheasant Run, Kaukauna, WI 54130.

Collectors' Clubs: Fenton Art Glass Collectors of America, Inc, PO Box 384, Williamstown, WV 26187; National Fenton Glass Society, PO Box 4008, Marietta, OH 45750.

Colonial Amber, basket, Daisy and Button, #1936, "Olde Virginia Glass Handmade 1936 CA" paper label, c1970, 8" h, $25.00. Photo courtesy Ray Morykan Auctions.

Colonial Blue, ashtray, round, Hobnail $10.00
Colonial Blue, bonbon, handled, Hobnail 12.00
Colonial Blue, toothpick holder, Hobnail 10.00
Cranberry Opalescent, barber bottle, Coin Dot 400.00
Cranberry Opalescent, decanter, Coin Dot, #894 . . . . 700.00
Cranberry Opalescent, pitcher, Coin Dot, #1353 . . . . 375.00
Cranberry Opalescent, salt and pepper shakers pr,
   Hobnail 95.00
Cranberry Opalescent, salt and pepper shakers, pr, Rib
   Optic, #1605, 4" h 190.00
Cranberry Opalescent, tumbler, Coin Dot, #1353, 10 oz 60.00
Cranberry Opalescent, water pitcher, Coin Dot 300.00
Cranberry Opalescent, wine bottle, Rib Optic, #1667,
   13" h 225.00
Custard, vase, ruffled, Hobnail, #3956, 5½" h 10.00
Emerald Crest, relish set, 2 bowls, frame, and spoon 100.00
French Opalescent, creamer and sugar, Hobnail, #3900 . . . . 12.00
French Opalescent, jug, Hobnail, 4½" h 15.00
French Opalescent, salt and pepper shakers, pr, Hobnail 25.00
French Opalescent, sugar, Hobnail, #3901 . . . . 5.00
French Opalescent, top hat, optic, 6½ x 10" 200.00
French Opalescent, vase, Hobnail, #389, 4" h 7.00
French Opalescent, wine goblet, Hobnail 15.00
Green Opalescent, creamer, Hobnail 25.00
Green Opalescent, rose bowl, Hobnail 50.00
Green Opalescent, tumbler, Hobnail, 9 oz 40.00
Green Opalescent, vase, black foot 250.00
Lincoln Inn, wine, cobalt 30.00
Orchid Opalescent, basket, handled, Hobnail, 7½" h 85.00
Orchid Opalescent, vase, Hobnail, 6" h 60.00
Peach Crest, basket, 7" h 40.00
Peach Crest, candleholder 35.00
Peach Crest, shell bowl, #9020, 10" d 75.00
Plum Opalescent, basket, oval, Hobnail, 12" l 525.00
Plum Opalescent, bowl, Hobnail, 9" d 75.00
Plum Opalescent, candy jar, ftd, Hobnail 150.00
Plum Opalescent, syrup jug, Hobnail, 12 oz 60.00
Rose Crest, basket, #36, handled, 4½" h 45.00
Rose Crest, bowl, #205, 8½" d 40.00
Rose Crest, cup and saucer, #680 . . . . 35.00

Rose Pastel, basket, Hobnail 25.00
Rose Pastel, creamer and sugar 25.00
Rose Pastel, epergne set, Hobnail, #3801 . . . . 85.00
Rose Pastel, hurricane lamp, Hobnail 65.00
Silver Crest, basket, handled, #7336, 6½" h 40.00
Silver Crest, bowl, #7223/DC, 13½" d 75.00
Silver Crest, bowl, shallow, #7321/DC, 12" d 50.00
Silver Crest, cake plate, ftd, #7213, 13" h 55.00
Silver Crest, compote, ftd, #7429/DC 30.00
Silver Crest, compote, ftd, low, #7228 . . . . 30.00
Silver Crest, cup and saucer 30.00
Silver Crest, float bowl, 13" d 40.00
Silver Crest, lazy susan, 3-tier, 6", 8", and 13" d 45.00
Silver Crest, mayonnaise set, liner and spoon, #7203 . . . . . . 45.00
Silver Crest, relish, heart shaped handle, #7333 . . . . 25.00
Silver Crest, salad plate, #60, 8½" d 30.00
Silver Crest, server, center handle, 12½" d 40.00
Silver Crest, tidbit tray, 2-tier, ruffled bowl, #7394 . . . . 70.00
Silver Crest, vase, #7258, ruffled top, 8" h 20.00
Silver Crest, vase, #7451/DC, 6" h 25.00
Silver Crest, vase, #7453/SC, 8" h 40.00
Spanish Lace, compote, pink 75.00
Topaz Opalescent, basket, Hobnail, sgd, 8" h 75.00
Topaz Opalescent, candleholder, Hobnail 35.00
Topaz Opalescent, candy jar, Hobnail 75.00
Topaz Opalescent, creamer and sugar, Hobnail, #3901 . . . . . 40.00
Topaz Opalescent, syrup jug, Hobnail 30.00
White Milk Glass, apothecary jar, cov, Hobnail, 11" h 100.00
White Milk Glass, candy dish, cov, Hobnail, 6½ x 6½" 40.00
White Milk Glass, jug, squat, Hobnail, #3965 . . . . 35.00
White Milk Glass, mayonnaise liner, Hobnail, #3803 . . . . . . 10.00
White Milk Glass, salt and pepper shakers, pr, Hobnail,
   #3806 . . . . 15.00
White Milk Glass, shakers, pr, Hobnail 25.00
White Milk Glass, tumbler, Hobnail, #3945, 5 oz 10.00

FIESTA

Homer Laughlin began production of its Fiesta line in 1936. Frederick Rhead was the designer. Concentric bands of rings were the only decorative motif besides color. Dark blue, light green, ivory, red, and yellow were the first five colors. Turquoise followed a year later.

Fiesta was restyled in 1969. Antique gold, turf green, and mango red (really the old red retitled) were introduced. These changes were not enough to save Fiesta. Production ceased in 1973.

Wishing to capitalize on the tremendous secondary market interest in Fiesta, Homer Laughlin reintroduced Fiesta in 1986. Several new colors made their appearance at that time.

References: Sharon and Bob Huxford, *Collector's Encyclopedia of Fiesta: Plus Harlequin, Riviera, and Kitchen Kraft, Eighth Edition*, Collector Books, 1998; Ronald E. Kay, *1999 FCOA Fiesta Price Guide, Bk. III*, Fiesta Club of America, 1999; Jeffrey B. Snyder, *Fiesta, 2nd Edition*, Schiffer Publishing, 1999.

Collectors' Club: Fiesta Club of America, PO Box 15383, Loves Park, IL 61115.

Chartreuse, after dinner cup and saucer $625.00
Chartreuse, coffeepot 575.00
Chartreuse, cream soup 90.00
Chartreuse, demitasse cup and saucer 525.00

Chartreuse, dessert dish, 6" d. 50.00
Chartreuse, mug 90.00
Chartreuse, plate, 7" d. 15.00
Cobalt, after dinner cup and saucer 95.00
Cobalt, carafe 500.00
Cobalt, casserole lid, individual, Kitchen Kraft 75.00
Cobalt, coffeepot. 350.00
Cobalt, creamer, stick handled. 70.00
Cobalt, cup. 35.00
Cobalt, deep plate. 70.00
Cobalt, demitasse cup and saucer 90.00
Cobalt, eggcup 75.00
Cobalt, jar, cov, Kitchen Kraft. 500.00
Cobalt, jug pitcher, 2 pt. 125.00
Cobalt, juice tumbler 40.00
Cobalt, mixing bowl, #2 . . . . 200.00
Cobalt, mixing bowl, Kitchen Kraft, 6" d. 250.00
Cobalt, mug 85.00
Cobalt, salt and pepper shakers, pr 30.00
Cobalt, spoon, Kitchen Kraft 200.00
Cobalt, teapot lid, medium 125.00
Cobalt, vase, 12" h 1,100.00
Cobalt, water pitcher, disk 125.00
Cobalt, water tumbler 90.00
Gray, after dinner cup and saucer 875.00
Gray, casserole, cov 375.00
Gray, coffeepot 750.00
Gray, eggcup 175.00
Gray, juice tumbler, 5 oz 200.00
Gray, mug 95.00
Green, after dinner cup and saucer 85.00
Green, bud vase 85.00
Green, carafe 300.00
Green, cup and saucer 45.00
Green, fork, Kitchen Kraft 125.00
Green, juice tumbler 40.00
Green, mixing bowl, #1 . . . . 225.00
Green, mixing bowl, #3 . . . . 225.00
Green, mixing bowl, #4 . . . . 200.00
Green, mixing bowl, #5 . . . . 225.00
Green, mixing bowl, #7 . . . . 475.00
Green, mustard 250.00
Green, onion soup, cov 850.00
Green, plate, 6" d 15.00
Green, plate, 10" d 30.00
Green, salad bowl, ftd 475.00
Green, teapot, large 225.00
Green, water tumbler 65.00
Ivory, after dinner cup and saucer 150.00
Ivory, carafe 650.00
Ivory, casserole 150.00
Ivory, coffeepot 390.00
Ivory, mixing bowl, #1 . . . . 375.00
Ivory, mixing bowl, #3 . . . . 165.00
Ivory, mixing bowl, #5 . . . . 275.00
Ivory, mixing bowl, #7 . . . . 575.00
Ivory, mixing bowl lid, #4 . . . . 1,400.00
Ivory, nested mixing bowl, #4 . . . . 175.00
Ivory, onion soup, cov 950.00
Ivory, plate, 10" d 40.00
Ivory, relish tray 175.00
Ivory, syrup 600.00
Ivory, teapot, cov, medium. 375.00
Ivory, turkey plate, 9" d 115.00

Light Green, chop plate, 15" d 40.00
Light Green, nested mixing bowl, #4 . . . . 100.00
Light Green, platter, oval, 12" l 30.00
Medium Green, creamer 110.00
Medium Green, cup and saucer, with rings 50.00
Medium Green, fruit bowl, 4³/₄" d 425.00
Medium Green, fruit bowl, 5¹/₂" d 65.00
Medium Green, plate, 6" d 35.00
Medium Green, plate, 10" d 200.00
Red, after dinner coffeepot 725.00
Red, bud vase 110.00
Red, carafe 475.00
Red, creamer, individual 375.00
Red, creamer, stick handle 85.00
Red, cream soup 65.00
Red, cup and saucer 40.00
Red, juice pitcher 750.00
Red, juice tumbler 40.00
Red, mug 110.00
Red, mustard base 125.00
Red, plate, 7" d 10.00
Red, plate, 10¹/₄" d 40.00
Red, salad bowl, ftd 650.00
Red, sauceboat 60.00
Red, spoon, Kitchen Kraft 200.00
Red, syrup 725.00
Red, teapot, medium 275.00
Rose, bowl, 4³/₄" d 40.00
Rose, bowl, 5³/₄" d 40.00
Rose, coffeepot 850.00
Rose, cream soup 90.00
Rose, juice tumbler 65.00
Rose, mug 100.00
Rose, plate, 7" d 14.00
Rose, water pitcher, disk 190.00
Turquoise, after dinner cup and saucer 110.00
Turquoise, carafe. 225.00
Turquoise, coffeepot 250.00

Nested Mixing Bowls, red #2 (6" d), yellow #3 (7" d), green #4 (8" d), and red #5 (9" d), 1936-43, price for set of 4, $500.00.

Turquoise, creamer, stick handle **125.00**
Turquoise, cup and saucer. **30.00**
Turquoise, ice pitcher **200.00**
Turquoise, juice tumbler **55.00**
Turquoise, mug. **55.00**
Turquoise, mustard **275.00**
Turquoise, nappy, $5^1/_2$". **25.00**
Turquoise, nested mixing bowl, #1. . . . . **240.00**
Turquoise, nested mixing bowl, #5. . . . . **90.00**
Turquoise, nested mixing bowl, #7. . . . . **60.00**
Turquoise, plate, 6" d **8.00**
Turquoise, plate, 7" d **8.00**
Turquoise, plate, 10" d **30.00**
Turquoise, relish tray **300.00**
Turquoise, salt and pepper shakers, pr **135.00**
Turquoise, sugar, cov. **40.00**
Turquoise, teapot, medium **150.00**
Turquoise, vase, 10" h **900.00**
Turquoise, water tumbler, 10" h **50.00**
Yellow, after dinner cup and saucer **95.00**
Yellow, candleholders, pr, bulb **75.00**
Yellow, candleholders, pr, tripod **400.00**
Yellow, compartment plate **95.00**
Yellow, disk pitcher. **100.00**
Yellow, juice tumbler. **250.00**
Yellow, mixing bowl, #1 . . . . **325.00**
Yellow, mixing bowl, #2 . . . . **140.00**
Yellow, mixing bowl, #4 . . . . **145.00**
Yellow, mug **90.00**
Yellow, plate, 6" d. **5.00**
Yellow, plate, 10" d. **30.00**
Yellow, salad bowl, ftd, 12" d. **110.00**

FIGURAL PLANTERS & VASES

Initially collected as a form by individuals collecting products of a specific maker, figural planters evolved as a collecting category unto itself in the mid-1990s. Figural baby planters are a major subcategory. Lady head vases command their own category.

Most generic examples and pieces whose design and shape do not speak to a specific time period have little value. Crossover collectors, especially those seeking animal, black, and vehicle images, skew value.

References: Kathleen Deel, *Figural Planters,* Schiffer Publishing, 1996; Betty and Bill Newbound, *Collector's Encyclopedia of Figural Planter & Vases,* Collector Books, 1997.

Note: Refer to specific manufacturers for additional listings.

PLANTERS

Baby Ballerina, Haeger, $5^1/_2$" h. **$8.00**
Baby Cradle, pink, Monmouth Pottery, $7^1/_2$" l **8.00**
Baby Wearing Bonnet, Brush, USA #219, $6^1/_8$" h. **15.00**
Balinese Woman, Royal Copley, $8^1/_4$" h. **25.00**
Barking Seal, unmkd, $5^1/_4$" h **10.00**
Barn Dance Couple, light blue, unmkd, $4^3/_4$" h **8.00**
Bassett Hound, C7087, Napco, $6^1/_4$" h **20.00**
Bird on Fence, Japan, $3^3/_4$" h **6.00**
Boxing Gloves, McCoy, $5^1/_2$" h. **18.00**
Calico Cat, Napco, C7116, 7" h. **15.00**
Colonial Man, Royal Copley, 8" h **35.00**

Planter, Twin Geese, Hull, #95, 1951, $7^1/_4$" h, $40.00. Photo courtesy Ray Morykan Auctions.

Country Peddler, unmkd $8^3/_4$" l. **18.00**
Dachshund, brown, Napco, C6717, $4^1/_2$" h. **15.00**
Elf Pushing Wheelbarrow, Shawnee, $3^3/_4$" h. **12.00**
Girl Drummer, unmkd, $6^3/_4$" h **8.00**
Girl Feeding Duck, unmkd, $4^1/_2$" h **8.00**
Girl Holding Basket, Shawnee, $6^1/_2$" h **12.00**
Girl Leaning on Barrel, Royal Copley, $6^1/_4$" h. **15.00**
Hat and Pipe, Lefton, H5959, $3^3/_4$ x $7^1/_2$". **15.00**
Humpty Dumpty on Wall, McCoy, $4^1/_2$" h. **12.00**
Kewpie Seated by Tree Stump, unmkd, $5^1/_2$" h. **6.00**
Lady Godiva on Horse, Japan, 7" l **18.00**
Mammy Seated on Scoop, McCoy, 7" l. **25.00**
Mortar and Pestle, black, gold trim, unmkd, $6^1/_2$" h **8.00**
Mother Cat and Kitten, Napco, C8857, 5" h **20.00**
Santa on Boot, Napco, 1CX-5396/A, 1962, $4^1/_2$" h **18.00**
St Francis, Inarco, Japan, 12" h. **12.00**
Tugboat, American Bisque, $9^1/_2$" l **20.00**
Valentine Girl, Relpo, A918, $6^3/_4$" h **18.00**
Wishing Well, USA, #200, 8" h **10.00**
Woman Holding Hat, Lefton, #5658, Japan, $7^1/_2$" h. **20.00**

VASES

Cat, blue and white specks, black highlights, Napco, $8^1/_4$" h **$8.00**
Cat and Dog, Japan, $3^3/_4$" h **6.00**
Cat on Book with Pot, black, redware, Occupied Japan. **12.00**
Elephant with Ball, Royal Copley, $7^1/_2$" h. **25.00**
Flamingo, unmkd, $8^1/_2$" h. **8.00**
Giraffe with Leaves, Hull, $8^1/_4$" h **50.00**
Long-Tailed Bird, Czechoslovakia, 5" h. **40.00**
Ostrich, white, Brush, $5^3/_4$" h **18.00**
Owl, Irish Belleek, green mark, 8" h. **200.00**
Pouter Pigeon, McCoy, 9" h **12.00**
Ram Head, McCoy, $9^1/_2$" h. **45.00**
Row Home, unmkd, $7^1/_2$" h **10.00**
Squirrel on Tree, white, gold trim, incised "430," 8" h. **12.00**
Unicorn, Hull, 10" h **50.00**
Watering Can with Pot, Robinson-Ransbottom, #1302, 4 x $5^3/_4$". **10.00**

FIGURINES

Figurines played a major role in the household decorating decor between the late 1930s and the early 1960s. Those with deep pockets bought Boehm, Lladro, and Royal Doulton. The average consumer was content with generic fare, much of it inexpensive imports, or examples from a host of California figurine manufacturers such as Kay Finch and Florence Ceramics.

Animals were the most popular theme. Human forms came next. Subject matter and the ability of a piece to speak the decorative motifs of a specific time period are as important as manufacturer in determining value.

Reference: Kathleen Deel, *Napco*, Schiffer Publishing, 1999.

Note: Refer to Limited Edition Collectibles and specific manufacturer and animal categories for additional listings.

CERAMIC

American Art Clay Co, Art Deco style bust of woman,
  glossy caramel glaze, ink stamp mark, 8" h **$120.00**
Arnart, lamb, white, pink and gold accents, 3 pink roses
  on left ear, gray paws, spaghetti dec, 5½" h **25.00**
Bauer, Scottie, matte glaze, Cal-Art line **300.00**
Billy Ray Hussey, black man eating watermelon, incised
  "BH" on bottom with inscription "Always Keep a
  Smile Along with You," 8" h **200.00**
Billy Ray Hussey, dog with basket in mouth, glossy green
  and ivory glaze, incised "BH," 6½" h **325.00**
Boehm, Cygnus Olor, stamped mark, 6" l **50.00**
Boehm, horse and jockey, jockey with blue and yellow
  jersey, thoroughbred horse wearing #1, oval base,
  sgd, "Boehm," 10¼" h, 10½" l **600.00**
Boehm, kitten, high-glaze, white and gray, orig stamp
  mark, 3½" h, 6½" l **90.00**
Brayton Laguna, jazz musicians, set of 4, polychrome
  glaze, 7" h **550.00**
Brayton Laguna, stylized bird, frosted orange and brown
  glaze, stamped mark, 7¾ x 9½" **40.00**
Cordey, colonial lady holding bouquet, roses in hair,
  stamp mark, 9 1/4" h **75.00**
Cybis, Little Red Riding Hood, wearing white cape and
  red gloves, mkd, 6½" h **140.00**
Frankoma, woman, glossy orange glaze, imp mark,
  10" h **110.00**
Fulper, dog, butterscotch and blue flambé glaze, unmkd,
  8" h **340.00**
Herend, canary, yellow and white, 4" l **140.00**
Herend, fox, green and white, 7" h **350.00**
Herend, giraffes, pr, green and white, 8¼" h **925.00**
Herend, jaguar, black and white, 6½" l **375.00**
Herend, penguin, black and white, 5" h **175.00**
Herend, ram, blue and white, 4½" l **175.00**
Herend, sea otter, green and white, 7½" l **425.00**
Herend, unicorn, black and white, 5" h **200.00**
Japan, stallion, green, spaghetti art dec on mane, tail,
  and hoofs, 4½ x 5¾" **35.00**
Keramous, young maiden, wearing bonnet and holding
  floral bouquet, polychrome glazes, ink stamp, 8" h **40.00**
Lamberton, Art Deco kneeling woman holding bouquet
  of flowers, white glossy glaze, stamped "Lamberton
  Scammell/Sculptured by Geza De Vegh," 8" h **200.00**
LaMiranda, deer, turquoise crackle glaze, 5" h **12.00**

Ceramic, Cybis, circus seal, stamped mark, 5¼" h, $140.00. Photo courtesy David Rago Auctions, Inc.

Lefton, poodle, #KB8055P, silver rhinestone-studded
  black bow tie, 4 green leaf roses and gold dots on top
  of bonnet, gold highlights on spaghetti art fur, 5 x 3" **30.00**
Lena Tomalo, pigeons, brown, blue, and white enameled
  details on tan ground, mkd, 7½" h, price for pr **20.00**
Mike Hanning, "Ride Um Rooster," black man on back
  of rooster, polychrome glazes, incised signature, date
  on bottom, titled around base,1994, 8½" h **50.00**
Napco, "April Showers," AH1D, 5" h **15.00**
Napco, ballerina, S1250, 5" h **18.00**
Napco, boy bowling, C3202C, 1958, 5" h **20.00**
Napco, Calendar Cutie, 5¼" h **25.00**
Napco, Christmas girl, X-8387, 3¾" h **18.00**
Napco, girl and boy praying, "–and God Bless Mommy
  & Daddy," C1861A, 1956, 5" h **18.00**
Napco, girl playing accordion, C4012C, 1959, 3" h **18.00**
Napco, "Home Stretch," A2715/6, 4½" h **25.00**
Napco, kitten, #1G4306, pink, gold dec, 4¾" h **15.00**
Napco, schnauzer, #9854, 7½" h **35.00**
Pennsbury, roosters, 1 brown and ivory glaze, other
  polychrome on white ground, 12" h, price for pr **325.00**
Ram Pottery, black woman laundering clothes with
  washboard, brown, yellow, and ivory glazes, incised
  signatures, Nan Dean and Sally Langford, dated
  "8/23/95," 9" h **110.00**
Ram Pottery, pig, mottled blue and green glaze, incised
  mark, Claude Miller, 1994, 5" h **30.00**
Royal Doulton, elephant with raised trunk, flambé glaze,
  ink stamp, 5½" h **180.00**
Royal Doulton, "Fragrance," ink stamp, 7½" h **130.00**
Stangl, bird of paradise, stamped mark "3626," 15" h **1,525.00**
Stangl, penguin, stamped mark "3274," 5" h **200.00**
Waylande Gregory, doves, gilded details on white glossy
  ground, script signature, 4½ x 7½", price for pr **60.00**
Waylande Gregory, rooster, silver leaf details on glossy
  white ground, script signature, 14 x 13½" **225.00**
Weller, frog, Coppertone, incised "Weller Pottery," 2¼" l . . . **250.00**
Weller, "Pop-eye" dog, black and brown features on
  white ground, incised mark, 3¾" h **400.00**
Weller, turtle, Coppertone, incised "Weller Pottery,"
  5½" l **300.00**

Ceramic, Goldscheider, woman, green dress with rose ribbon, mkd "F. G. Wien," Austria, 9" h, $35.00.

GLASS

Baccarat, shark, crystal	$110.00
Baccarat, wild boar, crystal	150.00
Boyd Crystal Art Glass, kitten on pillow, black, 3½" h	15.00
Boyd Crystal Art Glass, Pooch the Dog, black, 3" h	20.00
Boyd Crystal Art Glass, Tucker Car, black, 3¾" l	15.00
Boyd Crystal Art Glass, Willy Mouse, black, 2" h	15.00
Cambridge, bridge hound, ebony, 1¾" h	30.00
Cambridge, draped lady, light emerald, 8½" h	100.00
Cambridge, frog, crystal satin	20.00
Degenhart, Priscilla, ivory, 1976	65.00
Duncan & Miller, donkey and peasant, crystal	425.00
Duncan & Miller, fat goose, crystal	275.00
Fenton, alley cat, velva rose, 11" h	75.00
Fenton, fawn, Burmese	35.00
Fenton, fish, pink	15.00
Fenton, unicorn, ruby iridized	20.00
Fostoria, chanticleer, #2629, crystal, 10¾" h	175.00
Fostoria, doe, blue, 4½" h	35.00
Fostoria, mermaid, #2634, crystal, 11½" h	100.00
Fostoria, standing deer, #2589, blue, 4⅜" h	35.00
Heisey, airedale, crystal, 5¾" h, 6½" l	400.00
Heisey, baby elephant, crystal, 4½" h, 5" l	175.00
Heisey, duck, crystal, 2½" h	125.00
Heisey, German shepherd, crystal, 5" h	60.00
Heisey, giraffe, crystal, 10¾" h, 3" l	175.00
Heisey, mama elephant, crystal, 4" h, 6½" l	350.00
Heisey, piglet, crystal, ⅞" h, 1½" l	75.00
Heisey, ringneck pheasant, crystal, 5" h, 12" l	110.00
Heisey, sparrow, crystal	150.00
Heisey, tropical fish, crystal, 12" h, 6½" l	1,500.00
KR Haley, jumping horse, crystal, 7½" h, 9½" l	45.00
Imperial, bull, black, 3¾" h, 7¾" l	1,000.00
Imperial, owl, glossy jade green slag	85.00
Imperial, pig, black, 3" h, 5" l	300.00
Imperial, terrier, amethyst carnival, 3½" h	40.00
Imperial, tiger, black, 2½" h, 8" l	150.00
LE Smith, reclining horse, green, 9" l	100.00
New Martinsville, baby bear, sun colored	35.00
New Martinsville, baby seal with ball, ruby, 4½" h	40.00

New Martinsville, eagle, 8" h	65.00
New Martinsville, hen	75.00
New Martinsville, leaping gazelle, crystal, frosted base, 8¼" h	45.00
New Martinsville, polar bear	50.00
New Martinsville, squirrel, eating nut	35.00
New Martinsville, starfish, crystal, 7¾" h	65.00
Venetian, birds, burgundy opaque sommerso overlaid in silver and encased in clear, 1 with "Vetro Artistico Veneziano, Made in Murano, Italy" label, 9" h, price for pr	100.00
Venetian, clown, spherical red body, blue collar and buttons, and comical face, "Made in Murano, Italy" round paper label in gold on black, 6½" h	55.00
Venetian, rooster, internal dec in emerald green with silver foil and patches of white, crimson, and purple, encased in clear, free-form clear base, "Crown Venetian Co/Made in Italy" paper label, 13½" h	35.00
Venetian, sailfish, blue and white layered sommerso with bullicante and large clear applied fins, rising from twisted free-form base with bullicante, 17" h	85.00
Venetian, Siamese cat, internal dec in magenta aventurine and encased in white opalescent with controlled bubbles, ground and polished base, possibly Barovier & Toso, 7½" h	115.00
Viking, baby bear, #487, black, 3¼" h, 5" l	75.00
Viking, cat, #8252, black, 2½" h	20.00
Viking, teddy bear, black, 2½" h	20.00
Westmoreland, bulldog, #75, black, faceted eyes, mkd "WG," 2½" h	25.00

AUCTION PRICES – CERAMIC FIGURINES

David Rago Auctions, Inc., Collector Auction On-Line, November 1999. Prices include a 10% buyer's premium.

American Encaustic Tile Co, colt, blue flambé glaze, stamped "12-201," 10½" h	$160.00
Billy Ray Hussey, panting bear, metallic charcoal volcanic glaze, incised "BH," 5" h, 6" l	140.00
Boehm, rabbits, pr, glossy white with pink details, green stamp mark, 2¼" h	120.00
Cybis, Wendy, young girl in nightgown holding doll, sgd, 6½" h	120.00
Fulper, dog, butterscotch and blue flambé glaze, unmkd, grinding chips to base, 8" h	340.00
General Ceramics, elephants, pr, glossy lemon yellow glaze, ink stamp mark, Volly Wieselthier, 5¼" h	190.00
Nan Dean, Woman with Bowl, black woman kneading dough, polychrome glazes, incised mark and date "1995," nicks at base, 7" h	50.00
Overbeck, colonial woman wearing pink and blue striped dress, incised "OBK," 5" h	310.00
Royal Doulton, Autumn Breezes, young girl in flowing dress with bonnet and muff, polychrome glazes, ink stamp, 7¾" h	130.00
WA Flowers, Pickin' Frog, frog strumming banjo, mottled glossy green glaze, incised mark, titled around base, 10½" h	60.00
Zsolnay, peasant girl carrying platter, lustered green and yellow glazes, medallion mark, 8½" h	110.00

FINCH, KAY

After over a decade of ceramic studies, Kay Finch, assisted by her husband Braden, opened her commercial studio in 1939. A whimsical series of pig figurines and hand-decorated banks were the company's first successful products.

An expanded studio and showroom located on the Pacific Coast Highway in Corona del Mar opened on December 7,1941. The business soon had forty employees as it produced a wide variety of novelty items. A line of dog figurines and themed items were introduced in the 1940s. Christmas plates were made from 1950 until 1962.

When Braden died in 1963, Kay Finch ceased operations. Freeman-McFarlin Potteries purchased the molds in the mid-1970s and commissioned Finch to model a new series of dog figurines. Production of these continued through the late 1970s.

References: Devin Frick, Jean Frick and Richard Martinez, *Collectible Kay Finch,* Collector Books, 1997; Mike Nickel and Cindy Horvath, *Kay Finch,* Schiffer Publishing, 1997; Frances Finch Webb and Jack R. Webb, *The New Kay Finch Identification Guide,* published by authors, 1996.

Ashtray, dog face, stamped mark $60.00
Ashtray, Song of the Sea, 5 x 7" 35.00
Bank, English Village, 1944, 5½" h. 300.00
Canister, emb raspberries, turquoise, #5108 . . . . 30.00
Cup, "Missouri Mule," "Southern Comfort" on reverse,
   paper label inside, c1949. 250.00
Dish, fan, silver and white, #4960 . . . . 65.00
Figure, angel, #140A 125.00
Figure, cat, "Hannibal," 10¼" h 750.00
Figure, cat, "Jezebel," 6 x 9" 375.00
Figure, chanticleer, 10¾" h 500.00
Figure, dog, airedale, 5" h 450.00
Figure, dog, cocker spaniel, "Vicki," 11" h 1,200.00
Figure, dog, dachshund, 5" l 500.00
Figure, dog, westie, 4" l 400.00
Figure, fish, 3¼ x 7" 100.00
Figure, girl, blue dress, yellow hair, 5¼" h 75.00
Figure, monkey, "Happy," 11" h 1,000.00

Figure, monkey, "Jocko," c1948, 4" h 400.00
Figure, owl, "Toot," 6" h 65.00
Figure, pig, "Sassy" 125.00
Figure, poodle, "Doggie with Silver Bell," 7½" h. 750.00
Figure, prancing lamb, 10½" h 1,200.00
Figure, rabbit, "Cottontail," 2½" h 100.00
Figure, skunk, 5" h 250.00
Figure, turkey, 5" h 75.00
Flower Bowl, low, seashell, 2 x 12¾" 50.00
Salt and Pepper Shakers, pr, "Pup and Puss," 6½" h 800.00
Toby Mug, Santa Claus, 4¼" h 75.00

FIREARMS & ACCESSORIES

Many Americans own firearms, whether a .22 plunking rifle or pistol or a 12-gauge shotgun for hunting. The vast majority were inexpensive when purchased, bought for use and not investment, and have only minor secondary value in today's market. Many firearms sold on the secondary market are purchased for reuse purposes.

Recent federal statutes have placed restrictions on the buying and selling of certain handguns and rifles on the secondary market. Check with your local police department to make certain you are in compliance with state and federal laws before attempting to sell any weapon.

Collector interest in firearm advertising, prints, ammunition boxes, and other firearm accessories has increased significantly in the last decade. Auctioneers such as Dixie Sporting Collectibles (1206 Rama Rd, Charlotte, NC 28211) and Langs (31R Turtle Cove, Raymond, ME 04071) hold several specialized catalog sales each year in this field.

References: David D. Kowalski (ed.), *Standard Catalog of Winchester,* Krause Publications, 2000; John Ogle, *Colt Memorabilia Price Guide,* Krause Publications, 1998; Russell and Steve Quetermous, *Modern Guns, Twelfth Edition,* Collector Books, 1999; Ned Schwing, *2000 Standard Catalog of Firearms, 10th Edition,* Krause Publications, 2000; John Walter, *Rifles of the World,* Krause Publications, 1998; R. L. Wilson, *The Official Price Guide to Gun Collecting, 2nd Edition,* House of Collectibles, 1999.

Periodicals: *Gun List,* 700 E State St, Iola, WI 54990; *Military Trader,* PO Box 1050, Dubuque, IA 52004; *The Gun Report,* PO Box 38, Aledo, IL 61231.

Collectors' Clubs: Colt Collectors Association, PO Box 2241, Los Gatos, CA 95031; The Winchester Arms Collectors Assoc, PO Box 6754, Great Falls, MT 59406.

Note: Prices are for firearms in very good condition.

FIREARMS

BB Gun, Daisy Model 1000, wood stock and forearm,
   painted metal finish. $25.00
BB Gun, Daisy Model 1201, lever action, gold metal
   finish, light colored plastic stock 20.00
Handgun, Charter Arms Undercover, 38 Special, single
   and double action, 5-shot cylinder, blued or nickel
   finish, plain or hand-checkered walnut grips. 150.00
Handgun, Hartford Repeating Pistol, 22 caliber, manual
   operation, 10-shot clip, 6¾" l barrel, blued finish,
   black rubber grips 350.00

Figure, dove, gold on white ground, #5102, 5¼" h, $125.00.
Photo courtesy Ray Morykan Auctions.

Handgun, Mauser Model HSC Pocket Pistol, 32 ACP caliber, semi-automatic, double action, exposed hammer, 8-shot clip, 3³/₈" l barrel, blued or nickel finish, checkered wood grips, 6¹/₄" l **300.00**

Handgun, Smith & Wesson Model 439, 9mm Luger, semi-automatic, double action, exposed hammer, thumb safety, 8-shot clip, 4" l barrel, blued or nickel finish, checkered walnut grips with monogram **300.00**

Rifle, Browning 22 Semi-Automatic Grade I, 22 caliber, hammerless, blued barrel, hand checkered walnut pistol grip stock and forearm **250.00**

Rifle, Daisy Model 2203, 22 caliber, clip fed automatic, plastic stock and forearm, Ted Williams 4 power scope **25.00**

Rifle, Marlin Model 122 Target Rifle, 22 caliber, bolt action, single shot, 22" l barrel, wood Monte Carlo pistol grip stock and forearm **80.00**

Rifle, Universal 440 Vulcan, 44 magnum, slide action, hammerless, repeating action, 5-shot clip, 18¹/₄" l barrel, walnut semi-pistol grip stock and slide handle **200.00**

Shotgun, Beretta Silver Pigeon, 12 gauge, slide action, hammerless, 5-shot tubular magazine, 26 to 32" l barrel, blued finish, engraved and inlaid with silver pigeon, checkered walnut pistol grip stock and slide handle **300.00**

Shotgun, Browning B-80 Buck Special, 24" l slug barrel, rifle sights **350.00**

Shotgun, Davidson Model 63B Magnum, 10, 12, or 20 gauge **275.00**

Shotgun, Marlin Model 28, 12 gauge, slide action, 30" l barrel **125.00**

Shotgun, Remington Model 1900, 12 or 16 gauge, side-by-side double barrel, checkered walnut pistol grip stock **475.00**

Shotgun, Smith & Wesson Model 916, 12 gauge, slide action, hammerless, blued finish, satin finish receiver, walnut semi-pistol grip stock, grooved slide handle **150.00**

Shotgun, Winchester Model 42, 410 gauge, slide action, hammerless, 26" l barrel, blued finish, plain walnut pistol grip stock, grooved slide handle **650.00**

ACCESSORIES

Ammunition Box, Peters HV, 12 gauge, multicolored flying mallard scene, empty **$25.00**

Ammunition Box, Ward's Red Head, 20 gauge, black goose flying across yellow moon on red ground, full **30.00**

Book, *Pageant of the Gun*, Harold Peterson, 300 pp, 200 illus, 1967, hard cov, dj **6.00**

Book, *The Book of Pistols and Revolvers*, WHB Smith, updated by Kent Bellah, 752 pp, 1965, dj **20.00**

Calendar, 1978, Remington, 12 multicolor wildlife scenes, Oscar Robbins Co, Pittsburgh, PA **7.00**

Catalog, Colt's The Arm of Law and Order, 40 pp, 1931, 10 x 7¹/₂" **30.00**

Catalog, Winchester Shells and Cartridges, red, black, and yellow cov, 44 pp, 1938 . . . . **200.00**

Cleaning Rod, Winchester, 22 caliber, brass, from Jr Rifle kit, 23¹/₂" l **45.00**

Coasters, Remington "First in the Field," set of 6, round, "Upland Game Birds," England **20.00**

Counter Display, Remington Keanbore .22's, metal, glass front, battery operated bell rings when box is removed, green, yellow, red, and white, 13" h, 12" w **500.00**

Pinback Button, "Ducks Unlimited/1950," celluloid, flying duck scene **50.00**

Pinback Button, Remington, multicolored quail on fence, black border, white lettering, 1¹/₂" d **60.00**

Pinback Button, "Shoot Peters Shells," white, black, red, and gold, shot shell in center **80.00**

Pinback Button, Winchester, "Always Shoot Winchester Cartridges," white, black, and red, red "W" in center bull's-eye **125.00**

Playing Cards, Remington "First in Field–Outdoorsmen's Playing Cards," double deck, Lynn Bogue Hunt images of ducks, hinged lid tin case **30.00**

Poster, Smith & Wesson, paper, multicolored scenes of different models, 1980s, 39 x 23¹/₂" **12.00**

Poster, Western Super-X Wildfowl Load, paper, red, white, black, and yellow, 15¹/₂ x 8¹/₄" **115.00**

Rifle Cleaning Kit, Marble's, #834, 3-pc, cleaning rod, tips, patches, gun blue, 3 oz gun oil, in orange tin case with orig sleeve **75.00**

Shipping Crate, Winchester Leader, wood, nail construction, 16 gauge **20.00**

Sign, tin, "Winchester-Western Sportsman's Game Guide," multicolored scenes of game animals and Super-X cartridges, self-framed, 28 x 23" **60.00**

Tin, Dead Shot, American Powder Mills, square, green stenciled label, duck on front and back, brass screw cap, 1 lb **175.00**

Tin, Revelation Gun Oil, Western Auto Supply, red, black, white, and yellow, with cap, 3 oz **50.00**

FIRE-KING

Fire-King is an Anchor Hocking product. Anchor Hocking resulted from the 1937 merger of the Anchor Cap Company and Hocking Glass Corporation, each of which had been involved in several previous mergers.

Oven-proof Fire-King glass was made between 1942 and 1976 in a variety of patterns including Alice, Fleurette, Game Bird, Honeysuckle, Laurel, Swirl, and Wheat, and body colors such as azurite, forest green, jadeite, peach luster, ruby red, and white. Non-decorated utilitarian pieces also were made.

Housewives liked Fire-King because the line included matching dinnerware and ovenware. Anchor Hocking's marketing strategy included the aggressive sale of starter sets.

Anchor Hocking used two methods to mark Fire-King—a mark molded directly on the piece and an oval foil paper label.

References: Monica Lynn Clements and Patricia Rosser Clements, *An Unauthorized Guide to Fire-King Glassware,* Schiffer Publishing, 1999; Gene Florence, *Anchor Hocking's Fire-King & More, Second Edition,* Collector Books, 2000; Gary Kilgo et al., *A Collectors Guide to Anchor Hocking's Fire-King Glassware, 2nd Edition,* published by authors, 1997.

Collectors' Club: The Fire-King Collectors Club, 1406 E 14th St, Des Moines, IA 50316.

Alice, creamer and sugar, blue trim **$15.00**
Alice, creamer and sugar, vitrock **15.00**
Alice, cup and saucer, blue trim **15.00**
Alice, cup and saucer, jadeite **10.00**
Alice, dinner plate, blue trim, 9¹/₂" d **35.00**
Alice, dinner plate, jadeite, 9¹/₂" d **45.00**

Alice, saucer, jadeite, $2.00. Photo courtesy Ray Morykan Auctions.

Alice, dinner plate, vitrock, 9½" d	25.00
Charm, berry bowl, jadeite, 4¾" d	18.00
Charm, saucer, azurite, with label	2.00
Charm, saucer, jadeite	2.00
Charm, sugar, jadeite	20.00
Jane Ray, bowl, jadeite, 4½" d	25.00
Jane Ray, bowl, jadeite, 8¼" d	30.00
Jane Ray, butter, cov, jadeite, ¼ lb, orig label	130.00
Jane Ray, cereal bowl, jadeite, 6" d	25.00
Jane Ray, creamer, jadeite	15.00
Jane Ray, creamer and covered sugar, jadeite	40.00
Jane Ray, cup	6.00
Jane Ray, demitasse cup and saucer, jadeite	90.00
Jane Ray, dinner plate	10.00
Jane Ray, flat soup bowl, jadeite	25.00
Jane Ray, fruit bowl, jadeite	15.00
Jane Ray, luncheon plate	12.00
Jane Ray, platter, oval, jadeite	30.00
Jane Ray, salad plate, jadeite, 7½" d	15.00
Jane Ray, saucer, jadeite	3.00
Jane Ray, soup bowl, 7¾" d	30.00
Jane Ray, sugar, cov, jadeite	30.00
Jane Ray, sugar lid	12.00
Laurel, berry bowl, small	9.00
Laurel, plate, gray, 11" d	20.00
Laurel, sugar, gray	10.00
Leaf and Blossom, bowl, blue, small	12.00
Ovenware, baker lid, 4½" d	5.00
Ovenware, baker lid, 7¼" d	7.00
Ovenware, cereal bowl, 5½" d	20.00
Ovenware, nurser, 4 oz	15.00
Ovenware, refrigerator dish lid, 4½ x 5"	8.00
Philbe, luncheon plate, blue, 8" d	125.00
Philbe, tumbler, blue, 5¼" h	135.00
Plain Jane, mug, blue	10.00
Plain Jane, relish, blue, 3-part	12.00
Restaurant Ware, ball pitcher, jadeite, 80 oz	900.00
Restaurant Ware, bowl, G-300, jadeite, 15 oz	75.00
Restaurant Ware, bowl, G-305, jadeite, 8 oz	20.00
Restaurant Ware, bowl, G-309, jadeite, 10 oz	55.00
Restaurant Ware, bread and butter plate, G-315, jadeite	15.00
Restaurant Ware, butter, cov, jadeite	100.00
Restaurant Ware, plate, G-311, 5-part, jadeite	30.00
Shell, berry bowl, jadeite, 4½" d	15.00
Shell, cereal bowl, jadeite	25.00
Shell, creamer and covered sugar, jadeite	125.00
Shell, cup and saucer, jadeite	15.00
Shell, dinner plate, jadeite	25.00
Shell, platter, oval, jadeite	90.00
Shell, salad plate, jadeite	18.00
Stripes, grease jar, cov	35.00
Swirl Orange, demitasse cup	10.00
Swirl Orange, demitasse saucer	5.00
Turquoise, cereal bowl, 4½" d	15.00
Turquoise, creamer and sugar	16.00
Turquoise, cup and saucer	8.00
Turquoise, mug	15.00
Turquoise, plate, 5" d	25.00
Turquoise, plate, 7" d	20.00
Turquoise, plate, 9" d	20.00
Turquoise, salad bowl, 8" d	40.00
Wheat, creamer and covered sugar	20.00

FISHER-PRICE

Irving L. Price, a retired F. W. Woolworth executive, Herman G. Fisher, previously with Alderman-Fairchild Toy Company, and Helen M. Schelle, a former toy store owner, founded Fisher-Price Toys in 1930. The company was headquartered in East Aurora, New York. Margaret Evans Price, a writer and illustrator of children's books and wife of Irving Price, was the company's first artist and designer.

Toys made prior to 1962 are marked with a black and white rectangular logo. Plastic was introduced for the first time in 1949.

The company remained in private hands until acquired by the Quaker Oats Company in 1969.

Reference: Brad Cassity, *Fisher-Price Toys*, Collector Books, 2000.

Collectors' Club: Fisher-Price Collectors Club, 1442 N Ogden, Mesa, AZ 85205.

Note: Prices listed are for toys in excellent condition.

Air Lift Copter, #635	$5.00
Barky Buddy, #150	600.00
Bizzy Bunny Cart, #306	40.00
Bonny Bunny Wagon, #318	40.00
Bossy Bell, #656	60.00
Buddy Bronc, #430	350.00
Buddy Bullfrog, #728	75.00
Bunny Cart, #5	75.00
Bunny Push Cart, #303	75.00
Bunny Truck, #12	75.00
Butch the Pup, #333	75.00
Chatter Telephone, #747	30.00
Cookie Pig, #476	50.00
Corn Popper, #788	10.00
Creative Block Wagon, #161	75.00
Creative Coaster, #987	50.00
Crib Rattle, #787	15.00

Cry Baby Bear, #711 . . . . **30.00**
Cuddly Cub, #719 . . . . **5.00**
Dizzy Dino, #407 . . . . **50.00**
Doctor Doodle, #477 . . . . **225.00**
Doggy Racer, #7 . . . . **200.00**
Ducky Cart, #16 . . . . **75.00**
Ducky Daddles, #148 . . . . **225.00**
Farmer-In-Dell Music Box, #763 . . . . **20.00**
Farmer In the Dell TV-Radio, #166 . . . . **20.00**
Fuzzy Fido, #444 . . . . **225.00**
Golden Gulch Express, #191 . . . . **100.00**
Happy Hippo, #151 . . . . **85.00**
Hot Dog Wagon, #445 . . . . **250.00**
Huffy Puffy Train, #999 . . . . **80.00**
Humpty Dumpty Truck, #145 . . . . **40.00**
Jingle Giraffe, #472 . . . . **225.00**
Johnny Jumbo, #712 . . . . **550.00**
Jumbo Jitterbug, #422 . . . . **225.00**
Lady Bug, #695 . . . . **5.00**
Lift & Load Railroad, #943 . . . . **50.00**
Little People Jetliner, #2360 . . . . **10.00**
Lofty Lizzy, #405 . . . . **225.00**
Looky Chug-Chug, #220 . . . . **85.00**
Lop Ear Looie, #415 . . . . **225.00**
Mickey Mouse Choo-Choo, #485 . . . . **100.00**
Mickey Mouse Xylo, #714 . . . . **275.00**
Moo-oo Cow, #155 . . . . **85.00**
Musical Elephant, #145 . . . . **225.00**
Musical Mutt, #725 . . . . **350.00**
Musical Tick-Tock Clock, #997 . . . . **40.00**
Music Box Lacing Shoe, #991 . . . . **60.00**
Music Box Movie Camera, #919 . . . . **40.00**
Music Box Sweeper, #131 . . . . **85.00**
Nosey Pup, #445 . . . . **75.00**
Picnic Basket, #677 . . . . **30.00**
Play Family Camper, #994 . . . . **75.00**
Play Family Castle, #993 . . . . **100.00**
Play Family Nursery Set, #761 . . . . **30.00**
Playland Express, #192 . . . . **100.00**
Pocket Camera, #464 . . . . **5.00**
Pound and Saw Bench, #728 . . . . **25.00**
Pull-A-Tune Xylophone, #870 . . . . **35.00**
Queen Buzzy Bee, #444 . . . . **40.00**
Racing Ponies, #760 . . . . **350.00**
Rainbow Stack, #446 . . . . **15.00**
Roller Chime, #123 . . . . **50.00**
Shaggy Zilo, #738 . . . . **75.00**
Snap-Quack, #141 . . . . **225.00**
Snoopy Sniffer, #181 . . . . **35.00**
Snorky Fire Engine, #169 . . . . **100.00**
Stoopy Storky, #410 . . . . **225.00**
Sunny Fish, #420 . . . . **225.00**
Super Jet, #415 . . . . **225.00**
Suzie Seal, #694 . . . . **15.00**
Tailspin Tabby, #400 . . . . **250.00**
Teddy Station Wagon, #480 . . . . **225.00**
Tiny Tim, #496 . . . . **40.00**
Tool Box Work Bench, #935 . . . . **25.00**
Tote-A-Tune Radio, #793 . . . . **10.00**
Tow Truck, #615 . . . . **75.00**
Tuggy Turtle, #139 . . . . **100.00**
Uncle Timmy Turtle, #125 . . . . **100.00**
Winky Blinky Fire Truck, #200 . . . . **100.00**
Woofy Wagger, #447 . . . . **85.00**

FISHING

The modern fishing lure (plug) evolved at the end of the 19th century. Wood was used primarily for the body until replaced by plastic in the mid-1930s. Hundreds of lures, many with dozens of variations, are known to exist.

As lures became more sophisticated so did reels and rods. Improvement occurred in two areas—material and mechanism. Each improvement led to demand for more improvement. Drags and multiplying gears were added to reels. The split bamboo rod was eventually challenged by the modern graphite rod.

Serious collectors only buy examples in virtually unused condition and with their period packaging when possible. The high end of the market has become very investment focused. Many collectors are turning to licenses, paper ephemera, and secondary equipment in an effort to find affordable items within the category.

References: Carl F. Luckey, *Old Fishing Lures and Tackle, 5th Edition,* Krause Publications, 1999; Dudley Murphy and Rick Edmisten, *Fishing Lure Collectibles: An Identification and Value Guide to the Most Collectible Antique Fishing Lures,* Collector Books, 1995; Donald J. Peterson, *Folk Art Fish Decoys,* Schiffer Publishing, 1997; Harold E. Smith, *Collector's Guide to Creek Chub Lures & Collectibles,* Collector Books, 1997; R. L. Streater, *The Fishing Lure Collector's Bible,* Collector Books, 1999; Donna Tonelli, *Top of the Line Fishing Collectibles,* Schiffer Publishing, 1997; Karl T. White, *Fishing Tackle Antiques and Collectibles,* Holli Enterprises, 1995.

Periodical: *Fishing Collectibles Magazine,* 2005 Tree House Ln, Plano, TX 75023.

Newsletter: *The Fisherman's Trader,* PO Box 203, Gillette, NJ 07933.

Collectors' Clubs: American Fish Decoy Assoc, 624 Merritt St, Fife Lake, MI 49633; National Fishing Lure Collectors Club, HC#33, Box 4012, Reeds Spring, MO 65737; Old Reel Collectors Assoc, 160 Shoreline Walk, Alpharetta, GA 30022.

Angler's Bag, Hardy Bros Ltd, Alnwick, England, canvas, full flap cov, 2 int pockets, catch-all net bag on front, shoulder strap, c1930, 13 x 13" **$200.00**
Bait, crab wiggler, Heddon, #1800, glass eyes, U-shaped collar, L-rig hardware, green scale finish, 4" l **25.00**
Bait, Crazy Crawler, Heddon, #2100, 2-pc hardware, glow-worm finish **225.00**
Bait, Deep-O-Diver, glass eyes, L-rig hardware, "O" collar and pin on back, shiny green scale finish **400.00**
Bait, Meadow Mouse, Heddon, L-rig hardware, black bead eyes, leather ears and tail **55.00**
Bait, underwater minnow, Heddon, #150, white and red glass eyes, L-rig hardware, mkd props, 3 hp gill marks, 3³⁄₄" l **70.00**
Book, *Bait Casting,* Wm C Vogt, 1st ed, 1928, 104 pp **15.00**
Book, *Matching the Hatch,* Ernest G Schwiebert, Jr, Macmillan, NY, 1955, 1st printing, 221 pp, inscription by author, dj **325.00**
Book, *Tales of Swordfish and Tuna,* Harper, NY, 1927, 203 pp, 90 illus, gilt blue cloth covers **140.00**
Bootjack, fish shaped, open foot-shaped slot for boot **75.00**
Catalog, Hardy's Anglers Guide, 419 pp, 20 color plates of flies and lures, 1937 . . . . **55.00**

Booklet, *Where to fish in Western Michigan*, published by the *Grand Rapids Herald*, 64 pp, 1932, 6 x 9", $8.00.

Catalog, Marine Hardware–Fisherman's Supplies Etc, Sunde & d'Evers Co, Seattle, 468 pp, color paint chart and flags, 1931 . . . . **10.00**

Catalog, Pflueger, No. 145, 116 pp, full color, with order blank and cover letter intact, 1926 . . . . **115.00**

Creel, reversed birch, brown painted figures of rabbits and ducks on side, lid attached with leather laces, painted fish on lid, leather shoulder strap attached to sides **525.00**

Creel, splint construction, off-center hole, simple notched wood peg lid latch, 7 x 11 x 9" **275.00**

Creel, split willow, large off-center hole, strap, and buckle lid latch, replaced leather hanging strap, old leather harness, green painted finish, 7½ x 13½" **325.00**

Creel, split willow, off-center hole, orig leather hinges, belt, and buckle lid latch, canvas and leather harness, 6 x 11" **150.00**

Creel, wicker, off-center hole, leather hanging strap, 9" ruler printed on lid trim, strap and buckle lid latch **80.00**

Creel, willow, bulbous, center hole, orig twisted reed hinges, small reed hanging loop on back, old plywood lid, replaced leather thong lid latch, 5 x 8½" **55.00**

Creel, woven twig, football shaped, built-in handle and opening at top, 15" l, 13" d **200.00**

Decoy, sucker, Bud Stewart, ice spearing, folk art style, early paint pattern, metal fins, painted tack eyes, unsgd, c1930s, 6½" l **55.00**

Flask, silver plated, teardrop shaped, engraved scene of fisherman and hunter shooting bird, screw-off metal cap, removable cup at bottom, engraved initials "JRC" on reverse, mkd "Derby Silver Co" **200.00**

Fly Box, cedar lined, 2 locking hasps, carved trout on lid, 12 x 17 x 5½" **65.00**

Ice Skimmer, solid copper, hand forged, randomly punched holes in scoop, hole at end of handle with leather thong, 16" l handle **70.00**

License, 1935, Maryland, full color state seal, pale blue center band and rim accent, black lettering for resident use **45.00**

License, 1940, Canada, black, white, and blue, issued by province of New Brunswick for 7-day tourist use restricted to salmon and trout fishing **75.00**

Minnow Bucket, galvanized cylinder, torpedo shaped, sliding lid, irong rings on ends, orig dark green paint, 5 x 28" **140.00**

Net, aluminum, triangular, folding, mkd "Brit Pat 623933," collapsible 29" l handle and belt clip **50.00**

Net, collapsible boat net, 47" l cane handle, brass fittings, Wm Mills & Sons **115.00**

Poster, cardboard, South Bend Bait Co adv, illus of colorful leaping rainbow trout, reels, lines, and lures, 1950, 16 x 26", in 20 x 29" frame **225.00**

Poster, "Ninth Canadian Fly Fishing Forum," Toronto, Apr 7-8, 1984, large feather illus, lists workshops, exhibits, and prizes, anodized metal frame, 12 x 28" **30.00**

Rack, wood, 20 slots, 21 x 26" **200.00**

Reel, "Dragonfly," Sierra Angling Corp, Reno, NV, aluminum with black finish, combination spinning and fly casting reel, c1950 . . . . **115.00**

Reel, "Fin-Nor No. 2 Since 1933," anti-reverse salmon or salt water reel, gold and iodized reel, orig box with case, paper, spare parts and ST-9-F line, 3⅛" d **325.00**

Reel, Gayle, Simplicity #0, side-mount reel, sheet metal, riveted construction, wood knobs painted black, sgd, c1930 . . . . **50.00**

Reel, Sellers, Fly Casting "Bas-Kit Reel," chrome plated brass, side-mount, adjustable click, agatine line guide, fixed walnut knob, c1935 . . . . **950.00**

Reel, unknown maker, aluminum frame and spool painted black, side-mount, dual white plastic knobs, adjustable drag, old silky fly line, c1935 . . . . **30.00**

Rod, Hardy, "Palakona," trout rod, 7'2" l, 2-pc, 1 tip, 5-wt line, 3-oz rod, slide band downlocking over cork reel seat, red wraps tipped black, agate stripper guide, orig labeled canvas bag with hanging tag and tube **450.00**

Rod, Orvis, Superlight Spinning Rod, 6' l, 2-pc, 1 tip, 2¾ oz rod for ¹/₁₆-oz to ¼-oz lures, stainless steel guides, 2 slide band over cork handle reel seat, orig bag and labeled tube, sgd by Atwood on slideband **350.00**

Rod, Orvis, Model 99, trout rod, 7' l, 2-pc, 1 tip, screw up-locking over walnut reel seat, bag and tube with "Charles F Orvis Co" paper label, sgd by Atwood on reel seat **500.00**

Rod, Payne, salmon rod, 9½' l, 3-pc, 2 mids, 2 tips, 9-wt line, short mid-sections, screw up-locking reel seat, orig bag and tube, sgd by Atwood on reel seat **225.00**

Rod, Phillipson, "Premium," trout rod, 8' l, 3-pc, 3 tips, 4¼ oz, HDH line, 1" invisible wrap on 1 tip, flat sided "Hammer" handle, screw down-locking reel seat and black wraps tipped black-white, orig bag and square tube, sgd by Atwood on reel seat **380.00**

Sign, "Sebago Lake Maine–Salmon and Trout Fishing," bird's-eye maple, painted red, yellow, and white lettering, 17 x 54" **275.00**

Tackle Box, cedar, tongue-and-groove strips construction, shallow lift-out tray, brass nails, molded folding handle, brass plated hasp, stamped "George C Brown & Co Greensboro, NC," 7 x 16 x 7½" **140.00**

Tackle Box, metal, 2 cantilevered trays, folding metal handle, "Heddon-Outing" decal on int, 6½ x 12 x 7" **10.00**

Tackle Box, wood, 2 lift-out divided trays, folding wood handle, contains fly book, small metal fly box, and assorted flies and tackle, 6 x 18 x 7" **80.00**

FLASHLIGHTS

The flashlight owes its origin to the search for a suitable bicycle light. The Acme Electric Lamp Company, New York, NY, manufactured the first bicycle light in 1896. Development was rapid. In 1899 Conrad Hubert filed a patent for a tubular hand-held flashlight. Two years later, Hubert had sales offices in Berlin, Chicago, London, Montreal, Paris, and Sydney.

Conrad Hubert's American Eveready company has dominated the flashlight field for the past century. National Carbon purchased the balance of the company in 1914, having bought a half-interest in it in 1906. Aurora, Chase, Franco, and Ray-O-Vac are other collectible companies.

Collectors focus on flashlights from brand name companies, novelty flashlights, and character licensed flashlights.

References: L-W Book Sales, *Flashlights Price Guide,* L-W Book Sales, 1995; Stuart Schneider, *Collecting Flashlights,* Schiffer Publishing, 1997.

Collectors' Club: *Flashlight Collectors of America,* PO Box 4095, Tustin, CA 92781.

Advertising, Captain Ray-O-Vac, "Leader of Light," 1955, 7½" l	$35.00
Advertising, Maxwell House Coffee, with whistle and keychain, 1940, 4" l	10.00
Advertising, Schlitz Beer, plastic bottle, 1968, 10" h	15.00
Burgess, pen light, 1961, 5⅛" l	5.00
Burgess, Snaplight, Art Deco, 1930s	45.00
Burgess, Twin-Six Lantern, 1935, 9¼" h	25.00
Character, Davy Crockett, pocket, 1960, 3⅛" l	10.00
Character, Roy Rogers Lantern Light, Ohio Art, 1956, 8" h	75.00
Character, Zorro, Bantam Lite, pocket, 1946, 3¼" l	10.00
Dura-Lux, lighter and flashlight, 1950, 1⅞" x 2½"	35.00
Eveready, Masterlight Tablelight, chrome, black, 1936	18.00
Eveready, tubular light, nickel plated, 1930s	18.00
Figural, gun, aluminum, 1937, 5⅜" l	30.00
Hipco, aluminum, 1948, 6" l	10.00
Kwik-Lite, nickel plated, opens in center, 1920s	40.00
Sol-Ray, aluminum, bull's-eye lens, 1929, 6½" l	35.00
USA Army, Model MX944/U, olive drab green plastic	30.00
USA-Lite, Silly Symphonies, 1936	350.00
Winchester, copper, 1940, 6½" l	30.00
Winchester, hammered nickel, 1923, 7" l	45.00

FLATWARE

Flatware refers to forks, knives, serving pieces, and spoons. There are four basic types of flatware: (1) sterling silver, (2) silver plated, (3) stainless, and (4) Dirilyte.

Sterling silver flatware has a silver content of 925 parts silver per thousand. Knives have a steel or stainless steel blade. Silver plating refers to the electroplating of a thin coating of pure silver, 1,000 parts silver per thousand, on a base metal such as brass, copper, or nickel silver. While steel only requires the addition of 13% chromium to be classified stainless, most stainless steel flatware is made from an 18/8 formula, i.e., 18% chromium for strength and stain resistance and 8% nickel for a high luster and long-lasting finish. Dirilyte is an extremely hard, solid bronze alloy developed in Sweden in the early 1900s. Although gold in color, it has no gold in it.

Most flatware is purchased by individuals seeking to replace a damaged piece or to expand an existing pattern. Prices vary widely, depending on what the seller had to pay and how he views the importance of the pattern. Prices listed below represent what a modern replacement service quotes a customer.

Abbreviations used in the listings include:

FH	Flat Handle	SP	Silver Plated
HH	Hollow Handle	SS	Sterling Silver
		ST	Stainless Steel

References: Frances M. Bones and Lee Roy Fisher, *Standard Encyclopedia of American Silverplate and Hollow Ware,* Collector Books, 1998, 2000 value update; Maryanne Dolan, *American Sterling Silver Flatware, 1830's-1990's,* Books Americana, 1993; Tere Hagan, *Silverplated Flatware, Revised Fourth Edition,* Collector Books, 1990, 1999 value update; Tere Hagan, *Sterling Flatware, Revised Second Edition,* L-W Book Sales, 1999; Richard Osterberg, *Sterling Silver Flatware for Dining Elegance,* 2nd Edition, Schiffer Publishing, 1999; Dorothy T. Rainwater, *Encyclopedia of American Silver Manufacturers, Fourth Edition,* Schiffer Publishing, 1998; Replacements, Ltd., *Stainless Steel Flatware Identification Guide,* Replacements, Ltd., n.d.; Harry L. Rinker, *Silverware of the 20th Century: The Top 250 Patterns,* House of Collectibles, 1997.

Dansk, Thistle, ST, fork	$25.00
Dansk, Thistle, ST, iced tea spoon	25.00
Dansk, Thistle, ST, knife	25.00
Dansk, Thistle, ST, salad fork	20.00
Dansk, Thistle, ST, serving spoon	50.00
Dansk, Thistle, ST, soup spoon, oval bowl, 7⅞" l	15.00
Dansk, Thistle, ST, teaspoon	20.00
Gorham, Andante, SS, butter knife, HH, 7" l	40.00
Gorham, Andante, SS, cocktail fork, 5¾" l	35.00
Gorham, Andante, SS, fork, 7⅛" l	55.00
Gorham, Andante, SS, gravy ladle, 6⅜" l	100.00
Gorham, Andante, SS, knife, HH, modern blade, 9" l	40.00
Gorham, Andante, SS, soup spoon, oval bowl, 6½" l	65.00
Gorham, Andante, SS, sugar spoon, 5⅞" l	45.00
Gorham, Andante, SS, teaspoon, 6" l	30.00
Gorham, Chapel Bells, SS, butter spreader, FH, 5¾" l	20.00
Gorham, Chapel Bells, SS, carving knife, ST blade, 10⅜" l	65.00
Gorham, Chapel Bells, SS, fork, 7¼" l	45.00
Gorham, Chapel Bells, SS, gravy ladle, 5¾" l	80.00
Gorham, Chapel Bells, SS, iced tea spoon, 7½" l	40.00
Gorham, Chapel Bells, SS, knife, HH, modern blade, 8⅞" l	30.00
Gorham, Chapel Bells, SS, salad fork, 6½" l	40.00
Gorham, Chapel Bells, SS, sugar tongs, 4" l	60.00
Gorham, Chapel Bells, SS, tablespoon, 8½" l	80.00
Gorham, Chapel Bells, SS, teaspoon, 6" l	25.00
Gorham, Hacienda, ST, butter spreader, FH, 6⅜" l	25.00
Gorham, Hacienda, ST, fork, 7⅜" l	25.00
Gorham, Hacienda, ST, iced tea spoon, 7¾" l	25.00
Gorham, Hacienda, ST, knife, HH, modern blade, 8½" l	30.00
Gorham, Hacienda, ST, salad fork, 6⅞" l	25.00
Gorham, Hacienda, ST, sugar spoon, 6" l	25.00
Gorham, Hacienda, ST, tablespoon, 8¾" l	35.00
Gorham, Hacienda, ST, teaspoon, 6⅛" l	20.00
Gorham, Nouveau, ST, butter knife, HH, 7" l	25.00
Gorham, Nouveau, ST, gravy ladle, 7⅛" l	45.00

International, Today, ST.

Gorham, Nouveau, ST, knife **30.00**
Gorham, Nouveau, ST, salad fork **25.00**
Gorham, Nouveau, ST, sugar spoon, 6¹/₈" l **20.00**
Gorham, Nouveau, ST, tablespoon, 8⁵/₈" l **45.00**
Gorham, Nouveau, ST, teaspoon **25.00**
International, Frontenac, SS, baby spoon, straight han-
    dle, 4¹/₄" l **45.00**
International, Frontenac, SS, carving knife, ST blade, 10" l **70.00**
International, Frontenac, SS, dessert fork, 6¹/₈" l **50.00**
International, Frontenac, SS, fork, 7¹/₈" l **55.00**
International, Frontenac, SS, grapefruit spoon, round
    bowl, 6⁷/₈" l **60.00**
International, Frontenac, SS, knife **45.00**
International, Frontenac, SS, punch ladle, ST bowl, 12¹/₂" l . . . **100.00**
International, Frontenac, SS, salad fork **70.00**
International, Frontenac, SS, soup ladle, 10³/₄" l **100.00**
International, Frontenac, SS, teaspoon **30.00**
International, Reflection, SP, butter spreader, FH, 6¹/₈" l **12.00**
International, Reflection, SP, cocktail fork, 5¹/₂" l **12.00**
International, Reflection, SP, fruit spoon, 6" l **15.00**
International, Reflection, SP, gravy ladle, 6¹/₈" l **30.00**
International, Reflection, SP, sugar spoon, shell-shaped
    bowl, 6" l **12.00**
International, Reflection, SP, tablespoon, 8¹/₂" l **20.00**
International, Reflection, SP, teaspoon, 6¹/₈" l **10.00**
International, Today, ST, butter spreader, FH, 6¹/₈" l **30.00**
International, Today, ST, dessert spoon, 6⁷/₈" l **25.00**
International, Today, ST, fork **25.00**
International, Today, ST, gravy ladle, 6³/₈" l **45.00**
International, Today, ST, iced tea spoon, 7³/₄" l **30.00**
International, Today, ST, knife **20.00**
International, Today, ST, salad fork, 6³/₄" l **25.00**
International, Today, ST, soup spoon, oval bowl, 7³/₈" l **25.00**
International, Today, ST, teaspoon **25.00**
Kirk Stieff, Rose, SS, butter spreader, FH, 5³/₈" l **35.00**
Kirk Stieff, Rose, SS, cream soup spoon, round bowl, 6" l **70.00**
Kirk Stieff, Rose, SS, fork, 7³/₈" l **60.00**
Kirk Stieff, Rose, SS, gravy ladle, 7¹/₄" l **115.00**
Kirk Stieff, Rose, SS, iced tea spoon, 7⁵/₈" l **45.00**
Kirk Stieff, Rose, SS, salad fork, 6³/₈" l **60.00**
Kirk Stieff, Rose, SS, tablespoon, 8³/₈" l **100.00**
Kirk Stieff, Rose, SS, teaspoon, 6" l **35.00**
Oneida, Classic Shell, ST, butter spreader, HH, paddled
    blade, 6³/₄" l **12.00**
Oneida, Classic Shell, ST, cocktail fork, 5⁷/₈" l **10.00**
Oneida, Classic Shell, ST, fork, 7⁵/₈" l **10.00**
Oneida, Classic Shell, ST, iced tea spoon, 7⁵/₈" l **10.00**
Oneida, Classic Shell, ST, knife, HH, modern blade, 9¹/₂" l **12.00**
Oneida, Classic Shell, ST, salad fork, 6³/₄" l **10.00**
Oneida, Classic Shell, ST, teaspoon, 6" l **10.00**
Oneida, Frostfire, ST, cocktail fork, 6" l **10.00**
Oneida, Frostfire, ST, grapefruit spoon, round bowl, 6⁷/₈" l **12.00**

Oneida, Frostfire, ST, gravy ladle, 7¹/₄" l **20.00**
Oneida, Frostfire, ST, iced tea spoon, 7¹/₂" l **12.00**
Oneida, Frostfire, ST, knife, HH, modern blade, 9¹/₈" l **15.00**
Oneida, Frostfire, ST, salad fork, 6¹/₂" l **12.00**
Oneida, Frostfire, ST, soup spoon, oval bowl, 6³/₄" l **10.00**
Oneida, Frostfire, ST, sugar spoon, 6" l **15.00**
Oneida, Frostfire, ST, teaspoon, 6¹/₈" l **12.00**
Oneida, Twin Star, ST, butter spreader, FH, 6³/₈" l **12.00**
Oneida, Twin Star, ST, cocktail fork, 6¹/₈" l **10.00**
Oneida, Twin Star, ST, fork, 7¹/₂" l **15.00**
Oneida, Twin Star, ST, fruit spoon, 5⁷/₈" l **8.00**
Oneida, Twin Star, ST, pie server, 9⁵/₈" l **20.00**
Oneida, Twin Star, ST, salad fork, 6¹/₄" l **10.00**
Oneida, Twin Star, ST, soup spoon, oval bowl, 6⁷/₈" l **12.00**
Oneida, Twin Star, ST, sugar spoon, 6" l **12.00**
Oneida, Twin Star, ST, teaspoon, 6" l **12.00**
Oneida, Will 'O' Wisp, ST, carving fork, 9¹/₈" l **40.00**
Oneida, Will 'O' Wisp, ST, cocktail fork, 6¹/₈" l **20.00**
Oneida, Will 'O' Wisp, ST, fork, 7¹/₂" l **20.00**
Oneida, Will 'O' Wisp, ST, fruit spoon, 6¹/₈" l **20.00**
Oneida, Will 'O' Wisp, ST, gravy ladle, 6⁵/₈" l **30.00**
Oneida, Will 'O' Wisp, ST, iced tea spoon, 7¹/₂" l **20.00**
Oneida, Will 'O' Wisp, ST, soup spoon, oval bowl, 6⁷/₈" l **15.00**
Oneida, Will 'O' Wisp, ST, sugar spoon, 6¹/₈" l **20.00**
Oneida, Will 'O' Wisp, ST, teaspoon, 6¹/₈" l **20.00**
Reed & Barton, Classic Rose, SS, baby fork, 4¹/₂" l **45.00**
Reed & Barton, Classic Rose, SS, butter knife, HH, 6⁷/₈" l **40.00**
Reed & Barton, Classic Rose, SS, fork, 7¹/₂" l **60.00**
Reed & Barton, Classic Rose, SS, gravy ladle, 6⁷/₈" l **95.00**
Reed & Barton, Classic Rose, SS, jelly spoon, 6³/₈" l **40.00**
Reed & Barton, Classic Rose, SS, knife, HH, modern
    blade, 9¹/₈" l **40.00**
Reed & Barton, Classic Rose, SS, salad fork, 6⁵/₈" l **50.00**
Reed & Barton, Classic Rose, SS, sugar spoon, 6" l **40.00**
Reed & Barton, Classic Rose, SS, teaspoon **25.00**
Reed & Barton, Modern Provincial, ST, butter knife, FH,
    7¹/₄" l **30.00**
Reed & Barton, Modern Provincial, ST, fork **30.00**
Reed & Barton, Modern Provincial, ST, gravy ladle, 6⁵/₈" l **65.00**
Reed & Barton, Modern Provincial, ST, knife, HH, mod-
    ern blade, 8⁷/₈" l **30.00**
Reed & Barton, Modern Provincial, ST, salad fork **25.00**
Reed & Barton, Modern Provincial, ST, soup spoon, oval
    bowl, 6⁵/₈" l **30.00**
Reed & Barton, Modern Provincial, ST, sugar spoon, 6" l **30.00**
Reed & Barton, Modern Provincial, ST, teaspoon **25.00**
Royal Crest, Castle Rose, SS, butter knife, FH, 6⁷/₈" l **27.00**
Royal Crest, Castle Rose, SS, butter spreader, FH, 5⁷/₈" l **20.00**
Royal Crest, Castle Rose, SS, cocktail fork, 5³/₈" l **20.00**
Royal Crest, Castle Rose, SS, cream soup spoon, round
    bowl, 6¹/₄" l **27.00**
Royal Crest, Castle Rose, SS, fork, 7¹/₄" l **35.00**
Royal Crest, Castle Rose, SS, gravy ladle, 6¹/₄" l **70.00**
Royal Crest, Castle Rose, SS, knife **27.00**
Royal Crest, Castle Rose, SS, salad fork, 6³/₈" l **30.00**
Royal Crest, Castle Rose, SS, sugar spoon, 6¹/₈" l **30.00**
Royal Crest, Castle Rose, SS, tablespoon, 8¹/₈" l **65.00**
Royal Crest, Castle Rose, SS, teaspoon, 6¹/₈" l **17.00**
Wallace, Romance of the Sea, SS, butter knife, HH, 6⁵/₈" l **30.00**
Wallace, Romance of the Sea, SS, carving fork, ST tines,
    9⁷/₈" l **50.00**
Wallace, Romance of the Sea, SS, cheese knife, ST
    blade, 7" l **40.00**
Wallace, Romance of the Sea, SS, cocktail fork, 5⁵/₈" l **25.00**

Wallace, Romance of the Sea, SS.

FLORENCE CERAMICS

Florence Ward of Pasadena, California, began making ceramic objects as a form of therapy in dealing with the loss of a young son. The products she produced and sold from her garage workshop provided pin money during the Second World War.

With the support of Clifford, her husband, and Clifford, Jr., their son, Florence Ward moved her ceramics business to a plant on the east side of Pasadena in 1946. Business boomed after Ward exhibited at several Los Angeles gift shows. In 1949 a state-of-the-art plant was built at 74 South San Gabriel Boulevard, Pasadena.

Florence Ceramics is best known for its figural pieces, often costumed in Colonial and Godey fashions. The company also produced birds, busts, candleholders, lamps, smoking sets, and wall pockets. Betty Davenport Ford joined the company in 1956, designing a line of bisque animal figures. Production ended after two years.

Scripto Corporation bought Florence Ceramics in 1964 following the death of Clifford Ward. Production was shifted to advertising specialty ware. Operations ceased in 1977.

Reference: Doug Fouland, *The Florence Collectibles,* Schiffer Publishing, 1995.

Collectors' Club: Florence Collector's Club, PO Box 122, Richland, WA 99352.

Wallace, Romance of the Sea, SS, cold meat fork, 8" l	90.00
Wallace, Romance of the Sea, SS, fork, 7³/₈" l	40.00
Wallace, Romance of the Sea, SS, gravy ladle, 6¹/₄" l	95.00
Wallace, Romance of the Sea, SS, iced tea spoon, 7³/₄" l	40.00
Wallace, Romance of the Sea, SS, salad fork	35.00
Wallace, Romance of the Sea, SS, soup spoon, oval bowl, 7" l	45.00
Wallace, Romance of the Sea, SS, sugar spoon, 6" l	30.00
Wallace, Romance of the Sea, SS, tablespoon, 8¹/₂" l	90.00
Wallace, Romance of the Sea, SS, teaspoon, 6" l	25.00
Wallace, Shenandoah, SS, butter knife, HH, 6⁵/₈" l	30.00
Wallace, Shenandoah, SS, carving fork, ST tines, 9⁷/₈" l	55.00
Wallace, Shenandoah, SS, cheese knife, ST blade, 7" l	40.00
Wallace, Shenandoah, SS, cocktail fork, 5⁵/₈" l	25.00
Wallace, Shenandoah, SS, cold meat fork, 8" l	90.00
Wallace, Shenandoah, SS, fork, 7³/₈" l	40.00
Wallace, Shenandoah, SS, gravy ladle, 6¹/₄" l	95.00
Wallace, Shenandoah, SS, iced tea spoon, 7³/₄" l	40.00
Wallace, Shenandoah, SS, salad fork	35.00
Wallace, Shenandoah, SS, soup spoon, oval bowl, 7" l	45.00
Wallace, Shenandoah, SS, sugar spoon, 6" l	30.00
Wallace, Shenandoah, SS, tablespoon, 8¹/₂" l	90.00
Wallace, Shenandoah, SS, teaspoon, 6" l	25.00
Westmorland, George & Martha Washington, SS, butter spreader, FH, 6¹/₈" l	25.00
Westmorland, George & Martha Washington, SS, carving fork, ST tines, 9¹/₈" l	55.00
Westmorland, George & Martha Washington, SS, cocktail fork, 5⁵/₈" l	30.00
Westmorland, George & Martha Washington, SS, fork, 7¹/₈" l	40.00
Westmorland, George & Martha Washington, SS, fruit spoon, round bowl, 6" l	30.00
Westmorland, George & Martha Washington, SS, gravy ladle, 7" l	80.00
Westmorland, George & Martha Washington, SS, iced tea spoon, 7¹/₂" l	35.00
Westmorland, George & Martha Washington, SS, salad fork, 6" l	40.00
Westmorland, George & Martha Washington, SS, soup spoon, oval bowl, 7¹/₈" l	40.00
Westmorland, George & Martha Washington, SS, tablespoon, 8¹/₄" l	70.00

Figurine, Ann, 6" h	$125.00
Figurine, Barbara, 8¹/₂" h	200.00
Figurine, Birthday Girl	125.00
Figurine, Blondi & Sandy, 7¹/₂" h	180.00
Figurine, Carol, 7¹/₂" h	375.00
Figurine, Clarissa	100.00
Figurine, Cleopatra, 12" h	375.00
Figurine, Darlene	200.00
Figurine, Delia, 7¹/₄" h	150.00
Figurine, Georgette, 10¹/₄" h	275.00
Figurine, Halloween Child, 4" h	110.00
Figurine, Irene, 6" h	55.00
Figurine, Jim, 5¹/₂" h	75.00
Figurine, Kay, 7" h	35.00
Figurine, Lavon, 8¹/₂" h	225.00
Figurine, Marc Antony, 13¹/₂" h	375.00
Figurine, Margaret	325.00
Figurine, Misha & Haru, price for pr	575.00
Figurine, Musette, 8³/₄" h	150.00
Figurine, Nita, 8" h	100.00
Figurine, Pamela, 7¹/₄" h	125.00
Figurine, Reggie, 7¹/₂" h	150.00
Figurine, Scarlet, 8³/₄" h	150.00
Figurine, Sue, 6" h	50.00
Figurine, Summer Child, 6¹/₄" h	85.00
Figurine, Wynkin, 5¹/₂" h	225.00
Flower Holder, Bee	35.00
Flower Holder, Belle	70.00
Flower Holder, Emily	35.00
Flower Holder, Lea	50.00
Flower Holder, Lyn	50.00
Flower Holder, Molly	35.00
Lamp, Charles	250.00
Lamp, Marie Antionette	400.00
Planter, swan	250.00
Vase, cornucopia, pink	50.00

FOLK ART

The definition of folk art is fluid, defined by what subcategories contemporary collectors decide are in or out at any given moment. Simply put, folk art is trendy. Edie Clark's "What Really Is Folk Art?" in the December 1986 issue of *Yankee* continues to be one of the most insightful pieces yet written on the subject.

The folk art craze struck with a vengeance in the early 1970s. Auction houses hyped folk art ranging from quilts to weathervanes as great long-term investments. Several market manipulators cornered then touted the work of contemporary artists. The speculative bubble burst in the late 1980s when the market was flooded and excellent reproductions fooled many novice buyers.

References: Chuck and Jan Rosenak, *Contemporary American Folk Art: A Collector's Guide,* Abbeville Press, 1996; Clifford A. Wallach and Michael Cornish, *Tramp Art,* Wallach-Irons Publishing, 1998.

Newsletter: *Folk Art Finder,* 117 North Main St, Essex, CT 06426.

Collectors' Club: Folk Art Society of America, PO Box 17041, Richmond, VA 23226.

Decoy, Bluebill Drake, Dave Hodgman, Niles, MI, carved wing detail, orig paint, glass eyes, 14" l **$55.00**
Decoy, seagull, Nantucket, MA, carved wing and eye detail, orig paint, c1930 . . . . 350.00
Figure, bathing beauty, Clarence Stringfield, carved and painted wood, 18½" h 925.00
Figure, caveman, Russell Gillespie, carved and stained pine roots, pine knots, lichen, and moss, 1975, 23 x 18½" 675.00
Figure, eagle, stylized, standing erect with head up, wings out to sides, and tail down, carved feather detail, green glass eyes, painted black, white, and yellow, standing on shaped brown base, initialed "S.P.," Reading, PA, 20th C, 15½" h 625.00
Figure, gooney bird, carved pine, stylized, chip-carved wings, long legs, painted black with orange, blue, and yellow details, standing on rect base, PA, 20th C, 6⅜" h 525.00
Figure, horse, carved wood, worn polychrome, replaced fiber tail, 16" h 200.00
Figure, Indian, carved wood, green, yellow, red, brown, black, and blue paint, "Smokem" on pipe, 14" h 135.00
Figure, leopard, Miles Carpenter, carved wood, tan, red, and black accents on yellow, sgd "Miles Carpenter, 1978" on stomach, 4¼ x 11" 925.00
Figure, Madonna and Child, carved pine, natural patina, 15" h 20.00
Figure, man on turtle, carved wood, black painted suit, white skin, brass tack buttons, and yellow shoes, red and black wrought iron turtle, 23½" h 1,300.00
Garden Stake, wood cutout, painted, black boy fishing, c1950, 28" h 60.00
Painting, oil on canvas, Eugene Schroeder, landscape with Indian, sgd, dated, and titled on back "His Sunset, orig. comp. By G. Eugene Schroeder, 1923," 22½" h, 18" w, gilt frame 28¼" h, 24" w 875.00
Painting, watercolor on paper, hunting scene, sgd "M.L. O'Kelley 1972," 9¼ x 12¼" 800.00
Sewer Tile Art, lion battling serpent, realistically modeled, rect base, 11" l, 8" h 225.00

Sewer Tile Art, squirrel eating nut, yellow slip eye, incised "CM1980," 6¾" h 25.00
Theorem, stylized tulips with other flowers and foliage, painted on velvet, red, black, green, and yellow, inscribed on back edge "To Cora Lee from David Elliger," framed, 16¾" h, 13½" w 200.00
Tramp Art, lamp, 3-tier, labeled "Made by Chas. Baeumel, Dec. 22, 1951," 15" h plus socket 175.00
Wall Plaque, eagle flying with head down and turned to right, clutching shield with stars and stripes in 1 talon, arrows in other, traces of paint, varnished, in the style of Bellamy, 20th C, 44" w 925.00
Whirligig, kicking mule, wood, polychrome paint, 20th C, 48" l 275.00
Whirligig, man wearing black jacket and blue trousers, painted dec, sheet metal paddles, 12" h 1,375.00

AUCTION PRICES – LESTER BREININGER REDWARE

Alderfer Auction Company, The Tamar Bair Collection, May 19-20, 1999. Prices include a 10% buyer's premium.

Bank, standing eagle, 1976 . . . . **$193.00**
Center Bowl, daisy motif, 1975, 14 x 10" 72.00
Chamber Set, double-handled basin with insert pocket (soap dish) with applied birds and scroll design, pitcher with applied birds, 1979 . . . . 413.00
Charger, #1, tulip design, octagonal, 1977 . . . . 94.00
Charger, German saying "Good Luck...," tulip tree design, scalloped rim, 1977 . . . . 72.00
Jar, cov, floral dec, 1975 . . . . 116.00
Jelly Mold, figural fish, 1978 . . . . 61.00
Plate, #18, bicentennial eagle design, painted yellow and green, 1975 . . . . 275.00
Plate, "Cherry Pie," slip dec, 1978 . . . . 33.00
Platter, #15, green and yellow comb dec, 1973, 15 x 11" 94.00
Wall Hanging, angel, 1977 . . . . 121.00

FOOD MOLDS

The earliest food molds were ceramic and cast-iron molds used for baking. Today most collectors think of food molds in terms of the cast-iron candy molds, tin chocolate molds, and pewter ice cream molds used in factories, candy shops, and drugstores throughout the first half of the 19th century. Many of these chocolate and pewter molds were imported from Germany and Holland.

A substantial collection of Jell-O and post-1960 metal and plastic molds can be assembled with a minimum of effort and expenditure. Collector interest in these items is minimal.

Beware of reproduction chocolate molds. They are old enough to have developed a patina that matches some period molds.

Butter, cast aluminum, star, ½ lb, R Hall, Burlington, NC, 3½" d **$15.00**
Cake, cast aluminum, rabbit, 10" h 40.00
Cake, cast iron, rabbit, 2 halves, #862 and #863, Griswold, 11" h 250.00
Cake, stamped aluminum, lamb, lying down, 2-pc, 8" h 6.00

Candy, metal, top hats, 10 on flat tray, 14½" l, 1¼" w **25.00**
Candy, nickel alloy, pair of hands, flat **35.00**
Chocolate, cast aluminum, rabbit pulling cart, hinged **35.00**
Chocolate, cast metal, chocolate bars, tray type, Wilbur
    Candy Co **20.00**
Chocolate, nickel silver, stamped tin, pretzel, 1½ x 2" **8.00**
Chocolate, stamped alloy, champagne bucket and bot-
    tle, Eppelsheimer #4580 . . . . **85.00**
Chocolate, tinned metal, rabbit, basket on back, hinged,
    9" h, 4" w **125.00**
Ice Cream, pewter, American flag **40.00**
Ice Cream, pewter, baby shoe **25.00**
Jelly, aluminum, stamped heart shape, mkd "Jell-O" **10.00**
Jelly, salt-glazed stoneware, basket of flowers, German **30.00**
Jelly, tin, strawberry, cherry, apple, pear, grapes, and
    plum, 2-part, strap handle, Kreamer **25.00**
Maple Sugar, stamped tin, fluted shallow pan **5.00**
Pudding, ceramic, relief apple, fluted sides, spouted,
    3¾ x 4¾" **25.00**

FOOTBALL CARDS

Although football cards originated in the 1890s, the 1948 Bowman and Leaf Gum sets mark the birth of the modern football card. Leaf only produced cards for two seasons. The last Bowman set dates from 1955.

Topps entered the field in 1950 with a college stars set. It produced a National Football League set each year between 1956 and 1963. Topps lost its National Football League license to the Philadelphia Gum Company for the 1964 season. Topps produced only American Football League cards between 1964 and 1967. Topps recovered the ball in 1968 when it once again was licensed to produce National Football League cards. It has remained undefeated ever since.

Football cards remain a weaker sister when compared to baseball cards. Many felt the collapse of the baseball market in the mid-1990s would open the door for a strong surge in the collectibility of football cards. This has not happened.

References: James Beckett, *The Official 2000 Price Guide to Football Cards, 19th Edition,* House of Collectibles, 1999; James Beckett and Dan Hitt (eds.), *Beckett Football Price Guide, No. 16,* Beckett Publications, 1999; Sports Collectors Digest, *2000 Standard Catalog of Football Cards, 3rd Edition,* Krause Publications, 1999.

Periodicals: *Beckett Football Card Magazine,* 15850 Dallas Pkwy, Dallas, TX 75248; *Sports Cards,* 700 E State St, Iola, WI 54990; *Tuff Stuff,* PO Box 569, Dubuque, IA 52004.

Note: Prices listed are for cards in near mint condition.

Bowman, 1948, #25, Pat McHugh **$18.00**
Bowman, 1950, #26, John Lujack **80.00**
Bowman, 1951, #27, Thurman McGraw **18.00**
Bowman, 1952, #23, Gino Marchetti **175.00**
Bowman, 1953, #30, Buddy Young **25.00**
Bowman, 1954, #57, Chuck Bednarik **30.00**
Bowman, 1955, #19, Leon Hart **7.00**
Bowman, 1991, complete set (561) **5.00**
Finest, 1992, common card (1-44) . . . . **.14**
Finest, 1994, complete set (220) **60.00**
Fleer, 1962, #59, Don Maynard **45.00**

Fleer, 1963, #5, Gino Cappelletti **10.00**
Fleer, 1974, complete set (50), Hall of Fame **45.00**
Fleer, 1975, complete set (84), Hall of Fame **55.00**
Fleer, 1976, complete set (66), Team Action **450.00**
Fleer, 1977, complete set (67), Team Action **75.00**
Fleer, 1978, complete set (68), Team Action **40.00**
Fleer, 1979, #14, Dallas Cowboys, "The Right Place at
    the Right Time," Team Action . . . . **.75**
Fleer, 1980, #44, Pittsburgh Steelers, "All Systems Go,"
    Team Action . . . . **.25**
Fleer, 1981, #24, Kansas City Chiefs, "Seeing Red," Team
    Action . . . . **.14**
Fleer, 1982, complete set (88), Team Action **23.00**
Fleer, 1983, complete set (88), Team Action **10.00**
Fleer, 1984, complete set (88), Team Action **9.00**
Kahn's, 1959, #19, Walt Michaels **18.00**
Kahn's, 1960, #32, Billy Ray Smith **13.00**
Kahn's, 1961, #36, Jim Wooten **9.00**
Kahn's, 1963, #23, Frank Gifford **35.00**
Kahn's, 1964, #21, Alex Karras **13.00**
Leaf, 1948, #40, John Nolan **10.00**
Leaf, 1948, complete set (98) **2,700.00**
Leaf, 1949, #16, Charlie Trippi **25.00**
Leaf, 1949, complete set (49) **900.00**
Pacific, 1991, #1, Steve Young, Flash Cards . . . . **.23**
Pacific, 1991, #27, Andre Reed . . . . **.07**
Pacific, 1992, #22, Thurman Thomas . . . . **.11**
Pacific, 1992, complete set (25), Pick the Pros **18.00**
Pacific, 1994, complete set (36), Marquee Prisms **15.00**
Philadelphia, 1964, #12, John Unitas . . . . **.16**
Philadelphia, 1965, #15, Chicago Bears **1.50**
Philadelphia, 1966, #32, Mike Ditka **12.00**
Philadelphia, 1967, #35, Gale Sayers **32.00**
Pinnacle, 1991, #6, Troy Aikman **2.00**
Pinnacle, 1992, #1, Reggie White . . . . **.10**
Pinnacle, 1993, #15, Dan Marino, Men of Autumn **2.00**
Pinnacle, 1994, #30, Alvin Harper . . . . **.05**
Playoff, 1992, #11, Michael Ervin . . . . **.90**
Playoff, 1993, #82, Nick Lowery . . . . **.10**
Playoff, 1994, complete set (6), Playoff Club **12.00**
Playoff, 1994, complete set (6), Rookie Contenders **80.00**

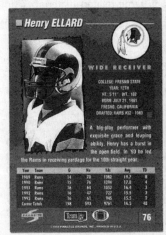

Score, 1994, #76, Henry Ellard, $.05. Photo courtesy Ray Morykan Auctions.

Playoff, 1995, complete set (30), Die Cut Helmets **350.00**
Playoff, 1995, complete set (50), Absolute Quad **1,100.00**
Proline, 1991, complete set (7), Portraits Wives . . . . **.35**
Proline, 1992, #15, Rodney Peete, Profiles . . . . **.02**
Proline, 1992, #28, Thurmon Thomas, Prototypes . . . . **.35**
Score, 1989, #3, Boomer Esiason . . . . **.18**
Score, 1990, #34, Jim Kelly, 100 Hottest . . . . **.14**
Score, 1991, #20, Barry Sanders . . . . **.45**
Score, 1992, #104, Keith Jackson . . . . **.05**
Score, 1994, #1, Barry Sanders . . . . **.45**
Score, 1995, #9, Deion Sanders . . . . **.25**
SkyBox, 1992, complete set (6), Impact Holograms **8.00**
SkyBox, 1992, complete set (350), Impact **5.50**
SkyBox, 1992, complete set (360), Primetime **14.00**
Topps, 1955, complete set (100), All-American **1,500.00**
Topps, 1956, #101, Roosevelt Grier **15.00**
Topps, 1957, #14, Pat Summerall **7.00**
Topps, 1958, #27, Washington Redskins **3.50**
Topps, 1959, #23, Bart Starr **20.00**
Topps, 1960, complete set (132) **300.00**
Topps, 1961, #67, checklist card **4.00**
Topps, 1962, #39, Don Meredith **35.00**
Topps, 1963, #44, Deacon Jones **20.00**
Topps, 1964, #34, Ken Rice **3.50**
Topps, 1965, #122, Joe Namath **700.00**
Topps, 1966, complete set (132) **650.00**
Ultra, 1991, #4, Randall Cunningham, All-Stars . . . . . . **.45**
Ultra, 1991, #75, Marcus Allen . . . . **.07**
Ultra, 1992, #87, Jay Novacek . . . . **.05**
Ultra, 1993, #13, Chris Miller . . . . **.18**
Ultra, 1993, complete set (10), All-Rookies **35.00**
Upper Deck, 1991, complete set (9), Game Breaker
    Holograms **4.50**
Upper Deck, 1992, common card (1-620) . . . . **.02**

FOOTBALL MEMORABILIA

Football memorabilia divides into two distinct groups, professional and collegiate, and two distinct categories, equipment and paper ephemera. Collectors of professional football memorabilia far outnumber collectors of collegiate memorabilia. Equipment collectors exceed the number of collectors of paper ephemera.

The category is heavily post-1970 driven, due to availability, and regional in nature. Collectors want game-related material. Team logo material licensed for sale in sports shops has minimal to no appeal.

References: Tom Mortenson (ed.), *2000 Standard Catalog of Sports Memorabilia*, Krause Publications, 1999; Jim Warren II, *Tuff Stuff's Complete Guide to Starting Lineup*, Antique Trader Books, 1997.

Periodical: *Sports Collectors Digest*, 700 E State St, Iola, WI 54990.

Autograph, Bradshaw, Terry, PS, 8 x 10" **$25.00**
Autograph, Butkus, Dick, cut signature **8.00**
Autograph, Csonka, Larry, cut signature **6.00**
Autograph, Gifford, Frank, CS, 3 x 5" **3.00**
Autograph, Sayers, Gale, PS, 8 x 10" **20.00**
Book, *Great Pass Receivers of the NFL*, Dave Anderson **20.00**
Book, *New York Giants*, Al Derogatis **25.00**
Bookends, pr, cast iron, Knute Rockne, raised portrait,
    incised "The Rock Of Notre Dame," early 1930s **150.00**

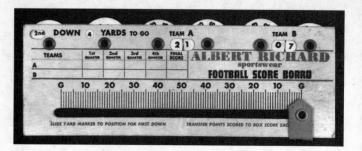

Score Keeper, Albert Richard Sportswear adv, heavy cardboard, 6 movable score wheels, 1948, 6¹⁄₂" l, $22.00.

Cigarette Lighter, San Francisco 49ers Super Bowl XVI,
    silvered metal and plastic **25.00**
Coin, Johnny Unitas, Salada Tea premium **100.00**
Figure, Herschel Walker, Kenner's Starting Lineup, 1988 . . . . . **35.00**
Figure, Irving Fryar, Kenner's Starting Lineup, 1995 . . . . **15.00**
Figure, Marcus Allen, Kenner's Starting Lineup, 1989 . . . . **40.00**
Football, Spalding, white, sgd by New York Giants team,
    1960 . . . . **200.00**
Football, Wilson, sgd by Cleveland Browns team, 1962 . . . . **350.00**
Game, All-Pro Football, Ideal, 1967 . . . . **25.00**
Game, Pro Football, Milton Bradley, 1964 . . . . **20.00**
Helmet, leather, tan, black, and russet, wool felt lining,
    black elastic chin strap, c1930s **45.00**
Limited Edition Plate, Emmitt Smith, 3054-02, Sports
    Impressions, 1996, 4¹⁄₄" d **10.00**
Magazine, *Football Digest*, Bart Starr, Apr 1968 . . . . **30.00**
Magazine, *NFL Report*, Franco Harris, 1976 . . . . **15.00**
Magazine, *Pro Football Weekly*, OJ Simpson, Feb 13,
    1969 . . . . **12.00**
Magazine, *Sporting News Football Register*, Roman
    Gabriel, 1970 . . . . **30.00**
Pennant, Los Angeles Rams, white, blue, and gold,
    1970s, 12 x 30" **20.00**
Pennant, Philadelphia Eagles, green felt, inked in white
    with white felt trim strip and streamers at end, depic-
    tion of eagle in light green and white, c1960s, 5 x 12" **15.00**
Pinback Button, Baltimore Colts, blue lettering on silver
    ground, 1960s **10.00**
Pinback Button, Barnstable High School, football
    shaped, center black and white team photo, c1930s **20.00**
Pinback Button, Coe College, Cedar Rapids, IA, "Go
    Coe" and "C" with football player image, Minneapolis
    button maker on rim curl, 1940s **15.00**
Pinback Button, "Penn State Numero Uno," cartoon
    Nittany Lion mascot, blue lettering on white ground,
    c1980s **10.00**
Pinback Button, Super Bowl XIX, "Crush Dolphins," dark
    red lettering, blue dolphin, 1965 . . . . **10.00**
Program, 1934 Rose Bowl, Columbia vs Stanford **500.00**
Program, 1945 Orange Bowl, Georgia Tech vs Tulsa **200.00**
Program, 1948, Cotton Bowl, Penn State vs SMU **150.00**
Ticket Stub, Super Bowl IV, Sun Jan 11, 1970, Tulane
    Stadium, New Orleans **450.00**
Yearbook, 1965, Buffalo Bills, Bills vs Chiefs **35.00**
Yearbook, 1972, Roger Staubach **30.00**
Yearbook, 1979, Pittsburgh Steelers, Bradshaw and
    Greene **10.00**

FOSTORIA

The Fostoria Glass Company broke ground for a glass factory in Fostoria, Ohio, on January 1, 1888. Within six months the factory was producing a line of glass bottles, shakers, and utilitarian wares. By 1891 Fostoria relocated to Moundsville, West Virginia.

Fostoria's stemware and tableware included a wide variety of products in crystal and colors designed to compete actively against Cambridge, Heisey, and Westmoreland. Fostoria changed with the times. When pressed and needle-etched glass fell from favor, the company turned to plate and master etchings. The role of color was increased. When teas and luncheons were replaced by brunches and cocktail parties, Fostoria added new patterns, shapes, and forms. Fostoria marketed aggressively, especially to the post-1945 bridal market.

Fostoria purchased Morgantown Glass in 1965, moving its operations to Moundsville in 1971. In 1983 Lancaster Colony Corporation purchased Fostoria. The Moundsville factory closed in 1986.

References: Frances Bones, *Fostoria Glassware: 1887-1982*, Collector Books, 1999; Ann Kerr, *Fostoria* (1994, 1997 value update), *Vol. II* (1997), Collector Books; Milbra Long and Emily Seate, *Fostoria Stemware* (1995), *Fostoria Tableware: 1924-1943* (1999), *Fostoria Tableware: 1944-1986* (1999), *Fostoria: Useful and Ornamental* (2000), Collector Books; Leslie Piña, *Fostoria Designer George Sakier*, Schiffer Publishing, 1996; Leslie Piña, *Fostoria: Serving the American Table 1887-1986*, Schiffer Publishing, 1995.

Periodical: *The Daze*, PO Box 57, Otisville, MI 48463.

Collectors' Clubs: Fostoria Glass Collectors, Inc, PO Box 1625, Orange, CA 92856; Fostoria Glass Society of America, PO Box 826, Moundsville, WV 26041.

Note: See Stemware for additional listings.

American, crystal, appetizer, 7-pc $250.00
American, crystal, basket, reed handle 90.00
American, crystal, bowl, cupped, 7" d 55.00
American, crystal, bread and butter plate, 6" d 12.00
American, crystal, butter, cov. 120.00
American, crystal, butter lid, dome 90.00
American, crystal, candle lamp chimney 70.00
American, crystal, candy dish, cov, 3-part 85.00
American, crystal, cheese and cracker set. 65.00
American, crystal, compote, cov, 9" d 50.00
American, crystal, cordial decanter 90.00
American, crystal, creamer and covered sugar, handled 35.00
American, crystal, creamer and sugar, miniature. 20.00
American, crystal, cup and saucer 10.00
American, crystal, dinner plate 25.00
American, crystal, flat pitcher, ½ gal 85.00
American, crystal, hurricane lamp base 60.00
American, crystal, ice tub, large. 95.00
American, crystal, jelly compote, cov. 35.00
American, crystal, ketchup, with stopper 135.00
American, crystal, lemon dish 35.00
American, crystal, mayonnaise, flat, with ladle 40.00
American, crystal, milk pitcher, 1 pt. 25.00
American, crystal, nappy, cov, 5" d 30.00
American, crystal, plate, 7½" d 10.00

American, crystal, platter, oval, 12" l 55.00
American, crystal, punch bowl, with base, 14" d 275.00
American, crystal, punch bowl, with base, 18" d 350.00
American, crystal, punch cup, flared 10.00
American, crystal, service tray, 9½" d. 30.00
American, crystal, sherbet, handled 150.00
American, crystal, sweet pea vase 70.00
American, crystal, tea creamer and sugar 20.00
American, crystal, toothpick holder 20.00
American, crystal, torte plate, 20" d 130.00
American, crystal, whiskey decanter 100.00
American Lady, sherbet, crystal, 4" h 90.00
Century, bowl, ftd 15.00
Century, bowl, handled, 8" d 25.00
Century, creamer and sugar 25.00
Century, creamer and sugar tray, individual 30.00
Century, cup and saucer 15.00
Century, mayonnaise set, 3-pc 40.00
Century, pitcher, 7" h. 75.00
Century, salt and pepper shakers, pr 20.00
Colony, cake plate, 2 handles, 10" d 25.00
Colony, cake salver 125.00
Colony, celery dish, oval, 11½" l 30.00
Colony, cocktail goblet 12.00
Colony, cup and saucer. 10.00
Colony, fruit bowl, ftd, 10" d 125.00
Colony, lunch tray, center handle. 35.00
Colony, muffin tray 30.00
Colony, plate, 8" d 15.00
Colony, plate, 15" d 70.00
Colony, shakers, pr, 3⅝" h. 20.00
Colony, water goblet. 18.00
Colony, wine goblet 25.00
Fairfax, cocktail, pink, 3 oz 23.00
Fairfax, creamer and covered sugar, blue 56.00
Heather, cake plate, 2 handles. 32.00
Heather, candy jar, ftd. 55.00
Heather, creamer and sugar, individual 35.00
Heather, mayonnaise, ftd, 3-pc, 2-part 45.00
Heather, relish, 2-part, 7" l 20.00
Heather, shakers, pr 45.00
Navarre, claret, blue, 6½" h. 50.00
Navarre, dinner plate, 2375, 9½" d 40.00
Navarre, high ball, 064 . . . . 60.00
Versailles, baker, yellow, oval 55.00

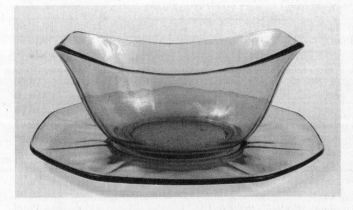

Fairfax, sauce boat and underplate, green, $100.00.

Versailles, berry bowl, yellow, small. 25.00
Versailles, bowl, scroll center, yellow, 10" d 70.00
Versailles, bread and butter plate, yellow 4.00
Versailles, dinner plate, yellow 40.00
Versailles, salad plate, yellow, 7" d 9.00
Versailles, sherbet, crystal 15.00
Versailles, sherbet, yellow, tall 20.00
Versailles, single shaker, yellow 50.00
Versailles, soup bowl, yellow. 70.00
Wakefield, crystal, cocktail 12.00
Wakefield, crystal, cordial 18.00
Wakefield, crystal, sherbet/champagne. 12.00
Wakefield, crystal, water goblet 18.00
Wakefield, crystal, wine goblet 15.00
Willowmere, crystal, cake plate, handled. 35.00
Willowmere, crystal, creamer and sugar. 38.00
Willowmere, crystal, cup and saucer 28.00
Willowmere, crystal, mayonnaise, 3-pc 45.00
Willowmere, crystal, plate, 7" d. 18.00
Willowmere, crystal, relish, 3-part, 10" d 35.00
Willowmere, crystal, sherbet/champagne 18.00
Willowmere, crystal, torte plate, 14" d 45.00
Willowmere, crystal, tumbler, ftd, 5 oz. 12.00
Willowmere, crystal, tumbler, ftd, 9 oz. 20.00

FRANCISCAN

Gladding, McBean and Company, Los Angeles, developed and
produced the Franciscan dinnerware line in 1934. The line
includes a variety of shapes, forms, and patterns. Coronado, El
Patio, Metropolitan, Montecito, Padua, and Rancho are solid color
dinnerware lines.

The Franciscan hand-painted, embossed patterns of Apple,
Desert Rose, and Ivy dominated the secondary collecting market
in the 1980s and early 1990s. Today collectors are seeking out
some of the more modern Franciscan decaled patterns such as
Oasis and Starburst.

References: Delleen Enge, *Franciscan: Embossed Handpainted,*
published by author, 1992; Delleen Enge, *Plain and Fancy
Franciscan Made in California,* published by author, 1996; Harry L.
Rinker, *Dinnerware of the 20th Century: The Top 500 Patterns,*
House of Collectibles, 1997; Jeffrey B. Snyder, *Franciscan Dining
Services,* Schiffer Publishing, 1997.

Collectors' Club: Franciscan Collectors Club, 8412 5th Ave NE,
Seattle, WA 98115.

Apple, baker, 1½ qt, 14 x 9" $150.00
Apple, batter bowl 250.00
Apple, coaster, 3¾" d 20.00
Apple, compote 75.00
Apple, eggcup 18.00
Apple, grill plate, 11" d. 50.00
Apple, jam jar, apple shaped 110.00
Apple, milk pitcher, 6¼" h. 115.00
Apple, mixing bowl, 9" d. 150.00
Apple, mug, 7 oz 15.00
Apple, platter, 12¾" l 50.00
Apple, snack plate, 8" sq 90.00
Apple, tureen, ftd 25.00
Apple, vegetable, divided, 10¾" l 35.00
Coronado, butter, cov, ¼ lb 30.00

Coronado, casserole, 10½" d 45.00
Coronado, chop plate, 12½" d 20.00
Coronado, cream soup cup 20.00
Coronado, plate, 7¼" d 6.00
Coronado, plate, 10½" d 10.00
Coronado, platter, 13" l 20.00
Coronado, salad plate 15.00
Coronado, soup bowl, 8" d. 12.00
Coronado, sugar, cov 18.00
Coronado, teapot, ftd, 6 cup 100.00
Desert Rose, bouillon bowl, cov, rosebud finial 150.00
Desert Rose, butter, cov. 45.00
Desert Rose, cereal bowl. 15.00
Desert Rose, compote. 75.00
Desert Rose, cup and saucer 18.00
Desert Rose, grill plate, 11" d 50.00
Desert Rose, jam jar 80.00
Desert Rose, mixing bowl, small, H354, 4" h, 6" d 95.00
Desert Rose, platter, 12¾" l 45.00
Desert Rose, salt and pepper shakers, pr 65.00
Desert Rose, soup bowl, flat, 8½" d 15.00
Desert Rose, tumbler, 10 oz. 20.00
El Patio, candleholders, pr, matte turquoise. 45.00
El Patio, creamer and sugar, yellow 45.00
El Patio, cream soup, turquoise 20.00
El Patio, cup and saucer, turquoise. 15.00
El Patio, eggcup, turquoise. 25.00
El Patio, gravy boat, with liner, turquoise 65.00
El Patio, onion soup, lug handle, turquoise. 20.00
El Patio, ramekin, turquoise 20.00
El Patio, salt and pepper shakers, pr, turquoise 35.00
El Patio, sherbet, yellow. 20.00
El Patio, teapot, satin ivory. 90.00
El Patio, teapot, turquoise 95.00
Fresh Fruit, platter, oval, 14½" l 80.00
Fresh Fruit, salad plate. 25.00
Ivy, bread and butter plate, 6½" d 9.00
Ivy, cake plate. 175.00
Ivy, chop plate, 12" d 100.00
Ivy, coffeepot, 8 cup 175.00

El Patio, carafe, turquoise, 7¾" h, $50.00.

Ivy, creamer 30.00
Ivy, gravy boat, with liner 75.00
Ivy, mug, 12 oz. 50.00
Ivy, plate, 8½" d 18.00
Ivy, plate, 10½" d 25.00
Ivy, platter, 13" l 100.00
Ivy, tidbit tray, 2-tier 100.00
Metropolitan, berry bowl. 15.00
Metropolitan, cake plate 35.00
Metropolitan, coffeepot, 6 cup. 75.00
Metropolitan, demitasse cup and saucer, ivory 70.00
Metropolitan, plate, 8" d 6.00
Metropolitan, sugar, cov 18.00
Metropolitan, tumbler 20.00
Montecito, fruit dish, matte ivory 20.00
Montecito, salt and pepper shakers, pr, matte ivory 35.00
Rancho, bread and butter plate 8.00
Rancho, cereal bowl, fluted. 25.00
Rancho, chop plate. 35.00
Rancho, dessert plate 10.00
Rancho, dinner plate 20.00
Rancho, fruit dish 20.00
Rancho, utility bowl 18.00
Tiempo, bread and butter plate, 6" d 5.00
Tiempo, butter, cov, ¼ lb. 35.00
Tiempo, creamer and sugar 25.00
Tiempo, platter, 14" l 25.00
Tiempo, salad bowl. 30.00
Tiempo, tumbler 20.00
Tiempo, vegetable, divided 20.00
Wild Flower, casserole, 1½ qt 250.00
Wild Flower, chop plate, 12" d 150.00
Wild Flower, dish, 6" d 45.00
Wild Flower, sherbet, 10 oz. 250.00

FRANKOMA

John Frank, a ceramics instructor at Oklahoma University, established Frankoma in 1933. In 1938 he moved his commercial production from Norman to Sapulpa. When a fire destroyed the plant in 1939, he rebuilt immediately.

A honey-tan colored clay from Ada was used to make Frankoma pieces prior to 1954. After that date, the company switched to a red brick clay from Sapulpa. Today some clay is brought into the plant from other areas.

Fire again struck the Sapulpa plant in September 1983. By July 1984 a new plant was opened. Since the early molds were lost in the fire, new molds were designed and made.

References: Phyllis and Tom Bess, *Frankoma and Other Oklahoma Potteries, 3rd Edition,* Schiffer Publishing, 1999; Gary V. Schaum, *Collector's Guide to Frankoma Pottery 1933 Through 1990,* L-W Book Sales, 1997.

Collectors' Club: Frankoma Family Collectors Assoc, PO Box 32571, Oklahoma City, OK 73123.

Ashtray, Westwind, #458, red **$15.00**
Baker, Wagon Wheel, #94W, desert gold, 3 qt 40.00
Bean Bowl, Plainsman, #5W, prairie green, 3 qt 15.00
Candleholders, pr, Wagon Wheel, #454, desert gold. 25.00
Cereal Bowl, Lazybones, #4X, brown satin. 5.00
Creamer and Covered Sugar, Aztec, #7A/7B, prairie green 40.00

Leaf Dish, Gracetone, #226, 12¼" l, $15.00.

Creamer and Sugar, Wagon Wheel, #94A and 94B, desert gold 25.00
Cup, Plainsman, #5C, desert gold, 7 oz 6.00
Cup, Westwind, #6C, prairie green 5.00
Gravy, Westwind, #6S, blue and brown 12.00
Lazy Susan, Plainsman, #818, with base 75.00
Luncheon Plate, Wagon Wheel, #94F, desert gold. 8.00
Mug, elephant, 1972. . . . . 20.00
Plate, Wagon Wheel, #94F, desert gold, 9" d 15.00
Plate, Wagon Wheel, #94G, desert gold, 7" d. 8.00
Platter, Wagon Wheel, #94Q, prairie green, 13" l 16.00
Rice Bowl, #F34, desert gold, 8" d. 6.00
Salad Plate, Wagon Wheel, #94G, desert gold 10.00
Salt and Pepper Shakers, pr, Lazybones, #4H 10.00
Salt and Pepper Shakers, pr, Wagon Wheel, #94H, prairie green 15.00
Sauce Boat, Plainsman, #5S, prairie green 25.00
Saucer, Wagon Wheel, #94E, desert gold 7.00
Serving Dish, Wagon Wheel, #94N, desert gold 15.00
Soup Cup, Lazybones, #4SC, brown satin 7.00
Sugar, individual, Wagon Wheel, #10, prairie green 10.00
Teacup, Plainsman, #5C, desert gold, 5 oz. 8.00
Trivet, "Liberty Bell 1776-1976," white sand. 15.00
Trivet, Shriner's 1981, prairie green 20.00
Vase, ftd, black, #55 . . . . 20.00
Vegetable, Lazybones, #4N, prairie green. 10.00

FRATERNAL & SERVICE ORGANIZATIONS

Benevolent and fraternal societies from the Odd Fellows to the Knights of Columbus continued to play a major role in American life through the first two-thirds of the 20th century. Local service clubs such as the Lions and Rotary established themselves as a major force in community life in the 1920s and 30s. Their golden age spanned the 1950s and 60s. Increasing workplace and family demands have cut heavily into membership. Membership has stabilized at best in most clubs. In many cases, the average age of club members is well above fifty.

Brotherhood of Locomotive, Fireman, and Enginemen, medal, ship in harbor design with Detroit in background, double chain hangers with "Detroit" bar, mkd "Abel/Union," 1925. . . . . **$30.00**
Brotherhood of Teamsters, pinback button, "Oakland Local 70s," red, white, and blue, dues button for third quarter of 1923, union logo in center with pr of horse heads 10.00
Knights of Pythias, pin, 25-year membership, "Pythian Veteran," blue, yellow, and red enameled shield. 20.00

Masonic, ashtray, brown and cream, raised Masonic
symbol on bottom center, 6¼ x 5¾" **20.00**

Masonic, Bible, 1,200 pp, leather binding, illus, 22k
gold stamping, c1931, 9½ x 11½ x 2½" **65.00**

Masonic, book, *Revised Encyclopedia of Freemasonry*,
1,217 pp, 2 vol, illus, 1929 . . . . **55.00**

Odd Fellows, medal, triangular shaped pendant with
seal and motto of Grand Lodge to obverse, ring and
staff to reverse, on braided red and purple cord, 1934 . . . . . **20.00**

Order of the Moose, badge, brass with white enamel,
shield shaped, inlaid moose head and "IOF LBC" in
smaller shield, knight's head and bird mounted to top
with attached ring, etched castle scene on reverse **150.00**

Shriners, bobbing head, man wearing tuxedo and
Shriner's cap, hp, Dee Bee Co Imports, Japan, 7" h **45.00**

Shriners, letter opener, 32nd emblem, c1920 . . . . **20.00**

FRISBEES

In 1915 Joseph P. Frisbie built a new bakery in Bridgeport, Connecticut, to produce Frisbie pie. During lunch hour, company employees played catch with the company's pie pans. In the 1920s Yale students picked up the sport. By the 1930s the craze spread to Princeton and the University of Michigan.

In 1937 the Buck Roger's Flying Saucer, the first throw and catch flying disk, appeared for sale. In 1948 Walter (Fred) Morrison and Warren Franscioni created the first plastic flying disc. In the same year, Arthur "Spud" Melin and Rich Knerr started Wham-O to market wooden sling shots. Numerous Frisbee prototypes appeared.

In the mid-1950s Fred Morrison designed the Pluto Platter Flying Saucer, teaming up with Wham-O in 1956 to market the product. The first of over 300 million Wham-O Frisbees was produced on January 23, 1957. By the end of the 1950s, Frisbee mania swept across America.

Wham-O introduced its professional model Frisbee in 1964 and founded the International Frisbee Association in 1967. Membership quickly exceeded 100,000.

In 1982 Kransco, a large toy company, bought Wham-O and its Frisbee trademark. Mattel bought the Frisbee trademark from Kransco in 1994. In 1997 Mattel sold the Frisbee trademark to Charterhouse Group International, a group of New York City investors.

Reference: Victor A. Malafronte, *The Complete Book of Frisbee: The History of the Sport & the First Official Price Guide,* American Trends Publishing, 1998.

Note: Prices listed are for frisbees in very good condition.

All American Frisbee, Wham-O, 1971 . . . . **$15.00**
AMF Vector, Destiny, 1981 . . . . **50.00**
AMF Voit Sport, AMF, 1982 . . . . **45.00**
CPI Giant Saucer Tosser, Continental Promotions, 1972 . . . . . **40.00**
Freestyle, Positive Pyramids, 1970s **15.00**
Future Flight, Polaris Mfg Co, 1970s. **30.00**
Harlem Globetrotters World Frisbee Champions,
Wham-O, 1974. . . . . **40.00**
High Flyers, Wham-O, 1980s **50.00**
Li'l Abner's Flyin' Saucer, Pipco Products, 1950 . . . . **350.00**
Magna HDR, Wham-O, 1984 . . . . **30.00**
Moon Saucer, Reliable Toy Co, 1970s **30.00**
Pluto Platter, Wham-O, 1959-60 . . . . **125.00**

Speedy Flying-Saucer, Wham-O, 1956-66 . . . . **225.00**
Sky Pie, Hall Mfg Co, 1949 . . . . **400.00**
Skyro, Parker Bros, 1970s **35.00**
Sky Saucer, Copar, 1959 . . . . **150.00**
Space Saucer, Bill Robes, 1950s. **175.00**
Super Frisbee 14-G, Wham-O, 1980s **5.00**
Wham-O Master, Wham-O, 1967 . . . . **30.00**
Wham-O Mini, Wham-O, 1968. . . . . **35.00**
Wham-O Moonlighter Mini Frisbee, Wham-O, 1968 . . . . **75.00**
Whistle-Disc, Joyful Toy Co, 1970s **30.00**

FRUIT JARS

The canning of fruits and vegetables played a major role in the American household until the late 1950s. Canning jars were recycled year after year. Jars utilizing zinc lids and rubber-sealed metal lids are extremely common. These jars usually sell for about 50¢.

Do not assume the date on a jar indicates the year the jar was made. In almost every case, it is a patent date or the founding date of the company that made the jar.

References: Douglas M. Leybourne, Jr., *The Collector's Guide to Old Fruit Jars, Red Book No. 8,* published by author, 1997; Jerry McCann, *The Guide to Collecting Fruit Jars: Fruit Jar Annual, Vol. 3–1998,* Phoenix Press, 1997; Bill Schroeder, *1000 Fruit Jars: Priced and Illustrated, 5th Edition,* Collector Books, 1987, 1996 value update.

Collectors' Clubs: Ball Collectors Club, 497 Fox Dr, Monroe, MI 48161; Federation of Historical Bottle Collectors, Inc, PO Box 1558, Southampton, PA 18966; Midwest Antique Fruit Jar & Bottle Club, PO Box 38, Flat Rock, IN 47234.

Atlas, Good Luck, 4-leaf clover, clear, glass lid, wire bail,
½ pt, c1920 . . . . **$5.00**
Atlas Junior Mason, clear, metal lid, c1950, ¾ pt **10.00**
Atlas Wholefruit, clear, wide mouth glass lid, wire
bail, c1935 . . . . **3.00**
Ball Eclipse, clear, glass lid, wire bail, c1920 . . . . **3.00**
Ball Wide Mouth, clear, c1960 . . . . **1.00**
Bernardin Mason, clear, c1940 . . . . **3.00**
Bosco Double Seal, glass lid, wire bail, c1920 . . . . **25.00**
Canadian Sure Seal, clear, c1930. . . . . **2.00**
Corona Jar, clear, glass insert, Corona/zinc screw band **2.00**
Crystal Mason, clear, Mason zinc cap, c1920. . . . . **10.00**
Harvest Mason, clear, glass lid, Harvest/gold lacquered
metal screw band, c1930. . . . . **10.00**
Jeannette Mason Home Packer, clear, glass insert,
Jeannette Mason/gold lacquered metal band, c1940 . . . . **5.00**
Lewis's Liverpool, light green, glass cap, tinned iron
band, c1920 . . . . **100.00**
L'Ideale, aqua, glass or porcelain lid, hinged wire clamp. **35.00**
McDonald New Perfect Seal, Ball blue, glass lid, wire
bail, c1920. . . . . **5.00**
Metro Easi-Pak Mason, clear, glass insert, c1940. . . . . **5.00**
Mid West, clear, glass insert, zinc screw band, c1930. . . . . **3.00**
Mom's Mason Jar, clear, 2-pc Mason cap, c1975 . . . . **3.00**
National Super Mason, clear, 2-pc Mason cap, c1935,
½ gal **15.00**
Ohio Quality Mason, clear, 2-pc Mason cap, c1925. . . . . **5.00**
Perfect Seal, clear, glass lid, wire bail. **5.00**
Pine Deluxe Jar, clear, glass lid, wire bail, c1925 . . . . **10.00**
Pine Mason, clear, Mason zinc cap, c1925, ½ pt **75.00**

Presto Glass Top, clear, glass lid, wire bail, c1930 . . . . **3.00**
Quong Hop & Co, clear, glass lid, wire bail, pt. **10.00**
Robinson, clear, glass lid, metal clamp, c1942 . . . . **5.00**
Safe Seal, Ball blue, glass lid, wire bail **5.00**
Safety Seal, clear, glass lid, wire bail, c1920. . . . . **5.00**
Sang Yuen Co, clear, glass lid, wire bail, c1940, pt **10.00**
Sanijar, aqua, glass lid, c1932 . . . . **5.00**
Sierra Mason Jar, clear, Mason zinc cap, c1920 . . . . **35.00**
Signal, clear, Mason aluminum wide mouth cap. **25.00**
Solidor, green, glass lid, hinged wire clamp, c1930 . . . . **50.00**
Stark Jar, clear, glass lid, metal clamp and spring, c1928. . . . . **50.00**
Texas Mason, clear, 2-pc Mason cap, c1950. . . . . **20.00**
Wan-Eta Cocoa Boston, Ball blue, tinned iron cap,
    c1920. . . . . **10.00**
Wing Wah Sing & Co Bean Cake, clear, glass lid, wire
    bail, c1940, pt. **10.00**

FRY GLASS

H. C. Fry Glass, Rochester, Pennsylvania, operated between 1901 and 1933. After an initial production period making Brilliant cut glass, the company turned to manufacturing glass tableware.

Pearl Oven Glass, a heat-resistant opalescent colored glass, was patented in 1922. Most pieces are marked with "Fry" and a model number. For a two-year period, 1926-27, H. C. Fry produced Foval, an art glass line. Its pieces are identified by their pearly opalescent body with an applied trim of jade green or Delft blue. Silver overlay pieces are marked "Rockwell."

Reference: The H. C. Fry Glass Society, *The Collector's Encyclopedia of Fry Glassware,* Collector Books, 1990, 1998 value update.

Collectors' Club: H. C. Fry Glass Society, PO Box 41, Beaver, PA 15009.

REPRODUCTION ALERT: Italian reproductions of Foval, produced in the 1970s, have a teal blue transparent trim.

After Dinner Cup and Saucer, Foval, #2003, Delft blue
    handle **$85.00**
Baker, Oven Ware, #1919, clear, round, 6" d **20.00**

Bowl, Pershing pattern, 3¹⁄₂" h, 8" d, $275.00.

Bean Pot, Oven Ware, #1924, clear, orange trim **75.00**
Berry Bowl, Foval, #2503, Delft foot, sgd Rockwell silver
    overlay in Pineapple design, 8" d **300.00**
Bowl, ftd, crystal connector, royal blue. **200.00**
Cake Plate, emerald, Sunnybrook pattern **50.00**
Candleholders, pr, amber, gold trim, paper label. **65.00**
Casserole, cov, Oven Ware, #1954, etched lid, silver
    holder. **55.00**
Comport, crystal, gold threading, controlled bubbles
    and teardrop stem **130.00**
Creamer, fuchsia **50.00**
Creamer and Open Sugar, rose **75.00**
Custard Cup, Oven Ware, #1927, leaf design **20.00**
Dinnerware Set, plate, goblet, cup and saucer, fuchsia **65.00**
Dinnerware Set, plate, goblet, cup and saucer, royal blue **90.00**
Meatloaf Pan, cov, Oven Ware, #1928, clear, emb grape,
    9" l **40.00**
Reamer, ruffled edges, canary **225.00**
Relish Dish, rose. **35.00**
Salad Plate, Pearl, #2504, Delft edge, 8¹⁄₂" d **75.00**
Snack Set, royal blue. **65.00**
Spice Tray, rose **75.00**
Teacup and Saucer, Pearl, #9003, tall. **80.00**
Tea Set, covered teapot, cup, and saucer, Foval, #2000,
    blue enamel trim. **400.00**

FULPER

Fulper Art Pottery was made by the American Pottery Company, Flemington, New Jersey, beginning around 1910 and ending in 1930. All pieces were molded. Pieces from the 1920s tend to be of higher quality due to less production pressures.

Pieces exhibit a strong Arts and Crafts and/or oriental influence. Glazes differed tremendously as Fulper experimented throughout its production period.

References: John Hibel et al., *The Fulper Book,* published by authors, n.d.; Ralph and Terry Kovel, *Kovel's American Art Pottery: The Collector's Guide to Makers, Marks and Factory Histories,* Crown Publishers, 1993.

Collectors' Club: Stangl/Fulper Collectors Club, PO Box 538, Flemington, NJ 08822.

REPRODUCTION ALERT

Basket, flaring, split handle, Flemington green over rose
    flambé glaze, rect ink mark, 6¹⁄₂ x 9" **$100.00**
Centerpiece Bowl, low, Chinese blue crystalline flambé
    glaze, ink racetrack mark, 2¹⁄₂ x 14³⁄₄". **325.00**
Chinese Urn, mirrored black glaze, raised racetrack
    mark, 9 x 8" **775.00**
Effigy Bowl, gargoyles under bowl, cafe-au-lait and yel-
    low crystalline glaze int and gargoyles, mustard matte
    ext, rect ink mark, 7¹⁄₂ x 10". **550.00**
Floor Vase, mottled brown, green and ivory flambé mir-
    ror glaze, raised racetrack mark, 17 x 9". **500.00**
Flower Frog, turtle, mottled brown matte glaze, ink race-
    track mark, 2 x 4" **70.00**
Jug, cov, mahogany, green, and ivory flambé glaze, rect
    ink mark, 10¹⁄₂ x 5¹⁄₂". **525.00**
Low Bowl, emb fish and waves, butterscotch flambé and
    leopard skin crystalline glaze, rect ink mark, 11¹⁄₂". **1,200.00**

Low Bowl, roped border, matte blue glaze, Chinese blue
flambé glaze int, ink racetrack mark, 3 x 13" **325.00**
Pillow Vase, curled handles, Flemington green to cat's
eye flambé mirror glaze, rect ink mark, 10 x 7½" **550.00**
Urn, 2 scrolled handles, mirrored black and copper dust
crystalline flambé glaze, ink racetrack mark, 14½ x 7" . . . **650.00**
Urn, classical, mirror black glaze, incised racetrack
mark, 13 x 8" **475.00**
Vase, baluster, butterscotch flambé glaze, incised race-
track mark, 12 x 4½" **450.00**
Vase, bulbous, ribbed body and flaring rim, ivory,
mahogany, mirrored black, and blue flambé glaze,
rect ink mark, 12¼ x 7½" **825.00**
Vase, classical, bright Chinese blue to Flemington green
flambé glaze, incised racetrack mark, 13¼ x 5¾" **775.00**
Vase, corseted, buttressed handles, copperdust crystalline to Flemington green flambé glaze, incised
racetrack mark, 9½ x 7" **500.00**
Vase, faceted, blue, mahogany, and ivory flambé glaze,
incised racetrack mark, 10 x 5¼" **525.00**
Vase, octagonal, collar rim, textured ivory to blue and
green flambé glaze, incised racetrack mark, 8 x 6¾" **775.00**
Vase, spherical, leopard skin crystalline glaze, rect ink
mark, 6 x 7" **725.00**
Vessel, buttressed, Chinese blue to cat's-eye flambé
glaze, unmkd, 13 x 10½" **3,575.00**
Vessel, corseted, oriental form, angular handles, copper
dust crystalline glaze, incised racetrack mark, 4½ x
5¾" **450.00**
Vessel, spherical, scalloped, 2-handled, mirrored black
glaze, horizontal stamped mark, 6½ x 9¼" **200.00**
Vessel, squat, 2-handled, mottled cucumber matte
glaze, ink racetrack mark, 6¼ x 7¾" **550.00**
Vessel, squat, oriental form, collar rim, frothy Chinese
blue glaze, incised racetrack mark, 4½ x 6½" **225.00**

FURNITURE

The furniture industry experienced tremendous growth immediately following World Wars I and II as America's population bal-
looned and wartime advances in materials and technology were
applied to furniture. Furniture was made in a variety of grades,
making the latest styles available to virtually every income level.

Beginning in the 1920s, the American popular taste tended to go
in two directions, Colonial Revival and upholstered furniture.
Colonial Revival furniture divides into two distinct groups: (1)
high-style pieces that closely mirrored their historic counterparts,
and (2) generic forms that combined design elements from many
different styles in a single piece. Large numbers of upholstered
pieces utilized frames that drew their inspiration from English and
European revival styles. Buyers with a modern bent fell in love
with the Art Deco and Streamlined Modern styles.

While leading designers such as Charles Eames experimented
with new materials and forms prior to World War II, it was after the
war that modern furniture reached the mass market. Colonial
Revival gave way to Early American; upholstered furniture veered
off in a sectional direction. Many trendy styles, e.g., tubular,
Mediterranean, and Scandinavian, survived less than a decade.

In the post-1945 period designers shifted their focus from household furniture to office and institutional furniture. Design became
truly international as English and European design studios
replaced America as the major influence for style change.

American tastes became traditional and conservative again in
the mid-1970s. Colonial Revival styles made a strong comeback.
Modernism was out, except among a select few in large metropolitan areas. Today, many people desiring a modern look are buying
pieces manufactured from the mid-1940s through the early 1960s.

Collectors pay a premium for furniture made by major manufacturers based on designs by internationally recognized furniture
designers. Name counts heavily, even in mass-produced furniture.

Style Chronology:

Craft Revival 1900-1940
Colonial Revival (High Style and Generic) 1915-1940
International 1920s
Art Deco 1925-1935
Streamlined Modern .1930s/early 1940s
Contemporary/Post-War Modernism . . . .late 1940s/early 1960s
Early American 1950s-1960s
Neo-Modernism and Pop 1960s
Craft Revival 1970s-present
Colonial Revival 1970s-present
Memphis 1980s

References: *American Manufactured Furniture, Furniture Dealers'
Reference Book,* reprint by Schiffer Publishing, 1988, 1996 value
update; Richard and Eileen Dubrow, *Styles of American Furniture:
1860-1960,* Schiffer Publishing, 1997; *Fine Furniture Reproductions:
18th-Century Revivals of the 1930s and 1940s From Baker Furniture,*
Schiffer Publishing, 1996; Oscar Fitzgerald, *Four Centuries of
American Furniture,* Wallace-Homestead, 1995; Philippe Garner,
Twentieth-Century Furniture, Van Nostrand Reinhold, 1980, out of
print; Cara Greenberg, *Mid-Century Modern: Furniture of the
1950s,* Crown Publishers, 1995; *Indiana Cabinets With Prices,* L-
W Book Sales, 1997; Emyl Jenkin, *Emyl Jenkin's Reproduction
Furniture: Antiques for the Next Generation,* Crown Publishers,
1995; David P. Lindquist and Caroline C. Warren, *Colonial Revival
Furniture With Prices,* Wallace-Homestead, 1993; Karl Mang,
History of Modern Furniture, Translation, Harry N. Abrams, 1979,
out of print.

Leslie Piña, *Classic Herman Miller,* Schiffer Publishing, 1998;
Leslie Piña, *Fifties Furniture, 2nd Edition,* Schiffer Publishing,
1999; Harry L. Rinker, *Warman's Furniture,* Wallace-Homestead,
1993, out of print; Steven and Linda Rouland, *Knoll Furniture:
1938-1960,* Schiffer Publishing, 1999; Steve Rouland and Roger
W. Rouland, *Heywood-Wakefield Modern Furniture,* Collector
Books, 1995, 1999 value update; Harvey Schwarz, *Rattan
Furniture,* Schiffer Publishing, 1999; Klaus-Jurgen Sembach,
Modern Furniture Designs: 1950-1980s, Schiffer Publishing, 1997;
Penny Sparke, *Furniture: Twentieth-Century Design,* E. P. Dutton,
1986, out of print; Robert W. and Harriett Swedberg, *Collector's
Encyclopedia of American Furniture, Vol. 2,* Collector Books, 1992,
1999 value update; Robert W. and Harriett Swedberg, *Furniture of
the Depression Era,* Collector Books, 1987, 1999 value update.

Art Deco, club chair, burlwood, plank sides, fluted feet,
orig blue and white brocade-upholstered cushions,
30" h, 27½" w, 34" d **$1,200.00**
Art Deco, coffee table, Watkins Brothers, mahogany,
circular top, bentwood legs, metal tag, 19" h, 28¼" d **250.00**
Art Deco, desk, Stanley Matthews, black and brown
Bakelite with aluminum details and open cubby hole,
sgd in pencil, 1938, 31" h, 42½" w, 22½" d **1,750.00**

Art Deco, desk, walnut top, 7 burlwood veneer drawer fronts with wood and brass pulls, matching wall mirror, desk size 25½" h, 54" w, 18" d, mirror size 38" h, 28" w **250.00**

Art Deco, dining table, Hastings, Walter Dorwin Teague designer, rect top with lift sides in bookmatched figured walnut veneer, black lacquer and faux painted wood base with aluminum supports, unmkd, 1930s, 54" w, 28" d, 30" h **250.00**

Art Deco, end table, 2-tier construction, shaped walnut top and base shelf, chrome U-shaped support and lamp arm, refinished, 20" w, 14" d, 43" h **110.00**

Art Deco, serving cart, cube form, chrome plated steel frame, sliding glass doors and sides, 30" w, 17" d, 30" h **1,000.00**

Art Deco, side table, in the style of Ruhlmann, single drawer cabinet, bird's-eye maple veneer with marquetry banding and ivory-like inlay on fluted legs, Bakelite feet and drawer pull, unmkd, 15" w, 16" d, 29" h **350.00**

Art Deco, vanity and stool, burlwood, stepped and inlaid detail, skyscraper mirror, needlework seatcover and footrest on stool, vanity size 30¼" h, 38¼" w, 17¼" d **350.00**

Colonial Revival, Pre-War, armchair, Chippendale style, Martha Washington, mahogany frame, worn finish, gold striped upholstery, 38" h. **250.00**

Colonial Revival, Pre-War, bed, Regency style, inlaid rosewood upholstered headboard, conforming footboard, shaped framework, brass inlay and mounts, double mattress size, 56" h **500.00**

Colonial Revival, Pre-War, cabinet, generic, figured walnut veneer panels and drawer front, solid walnut back rail, 3 curly maple overlay shield designs, hardwood frame, bulbous turned front legs, H-stretcher base, 1920s, 38 x 14 x 65" **300.00**

Colonial Revival, Pre-War, card table, Hepplewhite style, mahogany, inlaid, D-shaped top, drop leaves, minor wear, 19" w, opens to 38" w, 38" d, 31" h **500.00**

Art Deco, desk, The Umphrey Mfg Co, madrone burl walnut, macassar ebony and matched oriental walnut panels, natural finish, 1929, 40" w, $550.00.

Colonial Revival, Pre-War, chest of drawers, Hepplewhite style, solid mahogany, inlay on drawers and back rail, 2 small drawers over 2 long drawers, eagle brasses, 1920s, 42 x 19 x 38". **500.00**

Colonial Revival, Pre-War, chifferobe, generic, burl walnut, burl mahogany, bird's-eye maple, and Macassar striped ebony veneers, shaped scalloped pediment over 2 shaped doors over 2 drawers, molded cornice, int with 3 small drawers over 3 long drawers, ring-turned bulbous feet, 59" h **300.00**

Colonial Revival, Pre-War, china cabinet, Chippendale style, walnut veneer breakfront, scrolled broken pediment, center urn finial, pair of glazed doors and panels, long drawer over 2 cupboard doors, 44 x 15 x 76" . . . **850.00**

Colonial Revival, Pre-War, desk, Chippendale style, block front, solid walnut case, walnut veneered slant front lid, fitted int, paw feet, 32 x 18 x 42" **750.00**

Colonial Revival, Pre-War, desk, Governor Winthrop style, mahogany veneer, solid mahogany slant front, fitted int with 2 document drawers, shell-carved center door, serpentine front, 4 long drawers, brass pulls and escutcheons, 1920s. **600.00**

Colonial Revival, Pre-War, desk, Jacobean style, carved oak, 9 dovetailed drawers, applied foliage scrolls and lion's heads, pullout writing surface, worn blue felt covering, rope carved legs, old soft legs, 51 x 28½ x 40¾". **750.00**

Colonial Revival, Pre-War, desk, Spinet style, solid mahogany, hinged front, fitted int with drawers and pigeonholes, cylindrical reeded legs, 33 x 21 x 39". **450.00**

Colonial Revival, Pre-War, dining chairs, generic, set of 6, mahogany, Cupid's bow crest, pierced splat, slip seat, cabriole legs joined by box stretcher. **750.00**

Colonial Revival, Pre-War, dining table, Queen Anne style, mahogany, console table shape, pullout frame, 2 shaped leaves, worn finish, 39 x 30½", 66" l extended. **750.00**

Colonial Revival, Pre-War, drop leaf table, Charak, Tommi Parzinger designer, Hepplewhite style, mahogany with inlaid design of concentric squares in birch, refinished, label, closed size 20" w, 36" d, 29" h, open size 66" w **1,500.00**

Colonial Revival, Pre-War, drop leaf table, Duncan Phyfe style, mahogany stained and veneered, 16" w D-shaped leaves, brass casters on outswept reeded legs, 41 x 24 x 30" **350.00**

Colonial Revival, Pre-War, night stand, generic, walnut veneer, drawer over blind cupboard door, applied beaded molding around drawer, reeded trumpet legs, 15" sq top **75.00**

Colonial Revival, Pre-War, Pembroke table, Hepplewhite style, Grand Rapids, plain cut mahogany veneer top and drop leaves, figured mahogany drawer front, solid base, medallion inlay, square tapering legs, 17 x 15 x 22" **300.00**

Colonial Revival, Pre-War, rocker, Windsor style, Colonial Furniture Co, Grand Rapids, MI, comb back, birch, mahogany finish, turned legs, 21 x 17 x 27½" h from seat to top of back **250.00**

Colonial Revival, Pre-War, secretary/bookcase, Governor Winthrop, bookcase with broken pediment, center urn finial, molded cornice, pair of glazed doors, shelved and fitted int with slant front, 3 graduated drawers, oval brasses, ball and claw feet, 33" w, 80" h . . **1,000.00**

Colonial Revival, Pre-War, settee, William and Mary style, loose cushions, turned baluster legs and stretcher, 48" l............................... **800.00**

Colonial Revival, Pre War, sewing stand, generic, Priscilla type, painted red, dark trim, floral decal, turned rod-type handle, 13 x 11 x 25".............. **85.00**

Colonial Revival, Pre-War, sewing stand, Martha Washington style, solid mahogany, 3 drawers, shaped ends, ring-turned legs, 28 x 14 x 29".............. **350.00**

Colonial Revival, Pre-War, sideboard, Chippendale style, mahogany, central bow front of 2-drawer frieze over 2 deep drawers, flanked by wine drawer, central section flanked by drawers over curved cupboard, whole raised on cabriole legs ending in ball and claw feet, 46 x 18 x 40½".......................... **1,500.00**

Colonial Revival, Pre-War, sideboard, Federal style, Landstrom Furniture Co, mahogany, serpentine front, molded top edge, 2 drawers flanked by doors, square tapering legs, 116 x 22 x 37"................... **750.00**

Colonial Revival, Pre-War, side chair, Queen Anne style, walnut veneer, vase splat, slip upholstered seat, modified cabriole legs, 1920s...................... **125.00**

Colonial Revival, Pre-War, side chair, Queen Anne style, walnut veneer slat, walnut stained hardwood frame, pressed cane seat, French legs, 1920s, 27" h............ **85.00**

Colonial Revival, Pre-War, smoking stand, generic, straight cut walnut veneer, rect top, figured walnut veneered door, painted William and Mary–style base, 18 x 11 x 30"................................. **150.00**

Colonial Revival, Pre-War, vanity, generic, walnut, Chippendale-style swing mirror, reeded mirror supports, mahogany veneered front, central drawer flanked by sections with small drawer over blind cupboard door, reeded trumpet feet, casters, 48" w, 20" d.... **250.00**

Colonial Revival, Pre-War, wing chair, Queen Anne style, Kittinger, Williamsburg reproduction, pink striped silk upholstery, 49" h.................... **2,500.00**

Contemporary, armchair, Herman Miller, George Nelson designer, swag leg, white fiberglass seat and back, black enameled metal base with 4 legs, label, 29" w, 19" d, 31" h................................. **750.00**

Contemporary, armchair, Widdicomb, TH Robsjohn-Gibbings, walnut, black wool upholstery, arched crest and legs, 27" w, 29" d, 33" h, price for pr............ **925.00**

Contemporary, bedroom suite, Heywood-Wakefield, Riviera, 4-drawer chest with hanging mirror, 2 end tables, 2 twin bed headboards, champagne finish, branded mark, 50" w chest...................... **950.00**

Contemporary, bench, George Nelson for Herman Miller, Primavera, slatted top, angular ebonized legs, unmkd, 14" h, 48" l........................... **500.00**

Contemporary, "C" chair, Artek, Alvar Aalto designer, wide molded wood arms in natural walnut, seat and back reupholstered in textured white fabric, c1950s, 30" w, 31" d, 27" h............................. **2,500.00**

Contemporary, chest of drawers, James Mont designer, rect, plinth base, 3 drawers, green lacquer with sandblasted and pickled oak front, c1946, 46" w, 20" d, 34" h.................................... **3,200.00**

Contemporary, coffee table, Johnson Furniture Co, Paul Frankl, rect cork top in cream lacquer, dark mahogany Greek key shaped base, top refinished, 1940s, 84" w, 21" d, 12" h.............................. **1,500.00**

Colonial Revival, occasional table, The Umphrey Mfg Co, William and Mary–style, 4-way matched stump walnut, walnut veneered top, 1929, 28" w, $275.00.

Contemporary, daybed, George Nelson for Herman Miller, birch with single horizontal plank back on tubular chrome supports, tapering dowel legs, orig white woven fabric seat and back cushions, unmkd, 23½" h, 75" w, 34" d......................... **1,250.00**

Contemporary, desk, Marcel Breuer, bank of 4 drawers and bentwood legs flanking open cubby hole, 29¼" h, 50" w, 24¾" d.................................. **2,250.00**

Contemporary, desk, Singer & Sons, Geo Ponti designer, rect walnut top on 4 square tapering legs with brass caps, suspended medial section with 4 drawers and bookshelf in back, refinished, 51" w, 26" d, 29" h...... **4,000.00**

Contemporary, dinette table, Knoll, Isamu Noguchi designer, circular black laminated top, chrome wire struts, plastic coated metal base, label, 36" d, 29" h.... **1,200.00**

Contemporary, dining chairs, pr, Nathan Lerner designer, plywood construction, plaid fabric upholstery, Chicago Bauhouse design, c1940, 16" w, 19" d, 30" h... **500.00**

Contemporary, dining chairs, set of 6, Dunbar, Edward Wormley designer, 2 armchairs and 4 side chairs, dark mahogany frames, caned back and arm supports, seats reupholstered in off-white patterned fabric, 25" w, 18" d, 33" h............................. **650.00**

Contemporary, dining chairs, set of 6, Plycraft, Norman Cherner designer, 2 armchairs and 4 side chairs, molded walnut plywood, label, 25" w, 22" d, 31" h armchair, 17" w, 22" d, 31" h side chair............. **3,200.00**

Contemporary, dining table, Dunbar, Edward Wormley designer, rect maple veneer top set in bleached mahogany frame, square legs with carved feet, 2 leaves, 66" w, 44" d, 29" h...................... **275.00**

Contemporary, dining table, Herman Miller, Charles Eames designer, rect white laminated plywood top, folding chrome legs, 54" w, 34" d, 29" h............. **650.00**

Contemporary, dining table, Widdicomb, TH Robsjohn-Gibbings designer, circular patterned walnut veneer top, dowel legs with U-shaped stretchers and 2 leaves, refinished, 48" d, 29" h.......................... **1,750.00**

Contemporary, folding screen, Herman Miller, Charles Eames designer, 6 molded ash plywood sections, canvas hinges, 72" w, 68" h 3,000.00

Contemporary, hutch, Frank Lloyd Wright for Henredon, mahogany, No. 2006 China Deck top with glass-enclosed cabinet flanked by 2 sections of 4 open shelves, No. 200 Triple Dresser Base with 8 drawers and 2 doors, Taliesin pattern, branded mark, 84½" h, 66" w, 20" d 3,000.00

Contemporary, LCM chair, Herman Miller, Charles Eames designer, molded birch plywood seat and back, chrome frame, 22" w, 24" d, 27" h 450.00

Contemporary, magazine stand, Dunbar, Edward Wormley designer, ebonized wood, 5 shelves increasing in size from top to base, trestle feet, label, 28" w, 15" d, 24" h 1,500.00

Contemporary, occasional table, Johnson Furniture Co, Paul T Frankl designer, 2-tier, rect cork top, dark mahogany Greek key base, 36" w, 33" d, 24" h 350.00

Contemporary, serving cart, Calvin, Paul McCobb designer, rect terrazzo top, brass frame with 2 doors and shelves in bleached mahogany, label, 36" w, 19" d, 29" h 825.00

Contemporary, settee, Knoll, Warren Platner designer, wire frame, wrap-around upholstered seat and back in charcoal wool, 68" w, 29" d, 32" h 1,325.00

Contemporary, shelving unit, Herman Miller, Charles Eames designer, ESU 400, primary color masonite panels in zinc angle iron frame with white fiberglass sliding doors and black laminated drawers, c1952, 47" w, 17" d, 58" h 13,000.00

Contemporary, sideboard, George Nakashima for Widdicomb, walnut veneer, beveled trapezoidal top, 2 sliding doors with spindled panels, int drawers and shelves, plank feet with cross-stretcher, Widdicomb label, 32" h, 83¾" w, 22½" d 2,500.00

Contemporary, sofa, Dunbar, Edward Wormley designer, dark mahogany frame, tufted seat and back, reupholstered in black and white pattern fabric, 39" w, 28" d, 28" h 1,200.00

Contemporary, stool, Calvin, Paul McCobb designer, square white vinyl cushion, brass base with 4 legs and X-form stretcher, 20" sq top, 16" h, price for pr 450.00

Contemporary, Surfboard table, Herman Miller, Charles Eames designer, elliptical laminated plywood top, black wire cage base, top relaminated, base repainted, label, 89" w, 30" d, 12" h 1,500.00

Contemporary, tub chair, Heywood-Wakefield, sculptural form, reupholstered turquoise wool fabric, blond wood frame, 20" w, 30" d, 30" h 150.00

Contemporary, vanity and stool, Herman Miller, George Nelson designer, leather-wrapped cabinet with attached mirror and central lighted surface flanked by 2 lift-top compartments, birch legs, stool with cream upholstered seat and splayed birch legs, 48" w, 20" d, 57" h vanity, 22" w, 16" d, 17" h stool. 700.00

Craftsman, coffee table, George Nakashima, free-form burlwood top, cantilevered base, unmkd, 13¼" h, 52" l, 24" w 5,000.00

Craftsman, music stand, Wendell Castle, carved from block-laminated walnut, floral free-form, carved "W.C.'72," 1972, 41½" h, 23" w, 22" d 7,250.00

Craftsman, stool, George Nakashima, 3-sided slab on 3 spindled flaring legs, unmkd, 12½" h, 21" w, 14" d . . . 1,000.00

Modern, womb chair and ottoman, Eero Saarinen for Knoll, reupholstered in taupe boucle fabric on bright chrome legs, unmkd, chair size 35½" h, $1,750.00. Photo courtesy David Rago Auctions, Inc.

Early American, commode (table), solid maple, autumn brown finish, rect top, single drawer, false front with 2 drawers over 2 drawers, shaped skirt, slightly splayed baluster-turned legs, 26 x 21 x 23" 40.00

Early American, rocker, Beacon Hill, maple frame, finished in Salem (light maple), removable cushions padded with cotton liners, mint green oval motif cotton print cover, ruffled skirt, 25 x 24 x 34" 65.00

Early American, sofa, Chippendale style, Harmony House, upholstered in medium gold tweed fabric, 2 back Serofoam plastic foam cushions with shaped tops, 2 reversible cushions on seat, padded arms and wing sides, pleated skirt, 85 x 37 x 36" 100.00

International Modern, coffee table, Richard Schultz for Knoll, 8-petal redwood top, pedestal base with 8 legs, 15½" h, 42" d 575.00

International Modern, daybed and armchair, Poul Kjaerholm, leather-upholstered, loose brown cushions on angular steel frames, die-stamped "Denmark," 22" h, 30" w, 28½" d chair, 11½" h, 76" l, 34" w daybed, price for 2-pc set 4,000.00

International Modern, executive desk, Edward Wormley for Dunbar, ebonzied walnut top with rosewood veneer tambour roll-tops flanking flat writing surface, gallery back, 3 shallow frieze drawers, ebonized legs with leather padded footrest, gold D metal tag, 35" h, 74¾" w, 24" d 2,500.00

International Modern, occasional table, Knoll, square walnut veneer top on chrome frame, Knoll Associates label, 17" h, 27" sq top 150.00

International Modern, sofa, Royal Metal Corp, 3-seat, chartreuse vinyl upholstery, chrome frame, seats can be arranged in different configurations, metal tag, cloth label, 31½" h, 26½" w, 21" d 400.00

Memphis, dining table, circular top with abstract design, attached shelving on chrome and metal legs 1,250.00

Modern, armchair, TH Robsjohn-Gibbings for Widdicomb, green tweed upholstery, flaring dowel legs, 33¼" h, 27¼" w, 33" d **750.00**

Modern, desk, ash, rectilinear frame with bank of 3 drawers and offset pulls, 29¼" h, 38" w, 19" d **475.00**

Modern, stool, Stendig, tubular chrome frame with contoured beige velour seat cushion, paper label, 29" h, 18½" w, 25½" d **30.00**

Neo-Modern, credenza, Paul Evans, polished stainless steel, cubic design with 4 drawers and 2 doors with grooved recessed pulls, rect pedestal base, unmkd, 29¼" h, 72" w, 20¾" d **3,500.00**

1940s, dining room suite, Edward Wormley for Dunbar, No. 4576, walnut veneer, extension dining table with 2 drop-leaves, 5 additional 14" leaves, and trestle base with 2 extendable supports, 4 dining side chairs with upholstered contoured seats, unmkd, closed table size 29" h, 28" w, 42" d, price for 5-pc suite **2,000.00**

1950s, buffet, Paul McCobb for Winchendon, china hutch with 2 sliding glass doors above base with 2 sliding doors covered in linen-textured yellow vinyl, flaring dowel legs, orig pamphlet, branded mark, 1955, 57¾" h, 60" w, 18¼" d **2,250.00**

1950s, chest of drawers, Tommy Parzinger for Charak, mahogany, 12 drawers, 4 narrow center drawers with conical bronze pulls flanked on either side by 4 wide drawers with bronze ring pulls, Chinese-style broad base with bracket feet, paper label inside drawer "This piece was handmade in the workshops of Charak Furniture Company, Boston, Mass. No. 104, made 1-20-53," 33¼" h, 66" w, 18" d **2,750.00**

1950s, desk and chair, generic, ranch style, oak, rect top, 3 dovetailed drawers to left, drawer beneath writing surface, block and ring legs to right, ox yoke hardware, chair with bowed back slats, plank seat, turned splayed front legs, double stretchers on sides, single stretcher in front, 44 x 16 x 32", price for 2 pcs **100.00**

1950s, dining suite, Paul McCobb for Winchendon, extension dining table on flaring dowel legs, 2 additional leaves, 4 side chairs and 2 armchairs with spindled backs, saddle seats, and flaring dowel legs, 1955, 29" h, 54" w, 36" d table, 31" h, 22" w, 21" d armchair, price for 7-pc suite **2,500.00**

1950s, end table, generic, stepped, walnut finished hardwood frame and legs, rect top, splayed round tapered legs, stepped-back shelf raised on 2 spindles on each end, 16 x 24 x 21" **50.00**

1950s, patio chair, Hoffer, "Spider-web," red elasticized webbing in circular folding 3-legged black metal frame, unmkd, 24" h, 33" w **250.00**

1950s, sofa, generic, Harmony House (Sears), rectilinear form, hardwood frame, walnut finished legs, orange plastic cover, spring seat base, cotton felt padded button back, welt trim, 68 x 27 x 30" **150.00**

1950s, telephone stand, generic, wrought metal, 2 wire grill shelves, pinched paper clip–style side supports, bronze lacquer finish, 12½ x 12 x 17" **15.00**

1960s, dinette set, generic, table and 6 chairs, table with 2 leaves and high pressure plastic top in wood-grain pattern, tapered black antique finished frame and legs, pillow-back chairs with vinyl plastic covers in abstract tree motif on block grid ground **150.00**

1960s, dinette table, ebonized wood popsicle stick shaped base, circular glass top, 48" d, 29" h **775.00**

1960s, dining table, generic, high pressure plastic top in wood-grain pattern, bronze plated metal tapered block legs, 2 leaves, 42 x 84" **150.00**

1960s, stereo chair and ottoman, white fiberglass, egg shaped chair with black and white wool fabric int and loose black vinyl cushion, matching fiberglass footstool with black vinyl cushion, 36" w, 30" d, 50" h chair, 19" w, 16" d, 11" h footstool **750.00**

Scandinavian, coffee table, Hvidt & Molgaard for France & Son, teak, circular top, caned lower shelf, tapering dowel legs, orig catalog reference, 16" h, 38½" d **350.00**

Scandinavian, dining armchairs, Johannes Hansen, Hans Wegner designer, teak, brown and blue woven fabric seat cushions, branded mark, 25" w, 19½" d, 30" h, price for set of 6 . . . . **2,500.00**

Scandinavian, dining chairs, Finsven, Sweden, Alvar Aalto designer, stacking design, birch plywood seat and back on birch frame, stamped, c1940s, 19" w, 19" d, 31" h, price for set of 6 . . . . **1,750.00**

Scandinavian, occasional table, Gjerlov & Lind for France & Son, "Moduline," teak, L-shaped, mitered grain top, notched corners, plank legs, France metal tag and orig catalog reference, 20½" h, 37½" sq **450.00**

Scandinavian, teacart, L Pontoppidan designer, teak, drop leaves, inset black laminate top, single draw above 2 lower shelves, on casters, 28" h, 27" w, 21" d . . . **250.00**

Streamlined Modern, armchair, Russel Wright designer, bent maple frame, fabric upholstered seat and back cushions, refinished, 27" w, 34" d, 30" h **850.00**

Streamlined Modern, breakfront, Heritage Henredon, Frank Lloyd Wright designer, mahogany, upper section with 8 open shelves flanking cabinet door with 4 glass panels, base with 10 drawers in varying sizes with recessed handles, Taliesin design to edges, script signature, 65" w, 20" d, 83" h **2,750.00**

Streamlined Modern, coffee table, Quigley & Co, Samuel Marx designer, arched form, covered in patterned parchment, c1941, 24" w, 16" d, 16" h **8,250.00**

Scandinavian, lounge chair and ottoman, designed by Jørn Utzon for Fritz Hansen, Denmark, molded plywood and chrome-plated steel, dark red upholstery, undulating form, sticker label, 1969, $460.00. Photo courtesy William Doyle Galleries.

Streamlined Modern, end table, Herman Miller, Gilbert
  Rohde designer, amoeba shaped ³/₄" glass top, 3 cylindrical lucite legs with brass caps, 29" w, 18" d,
  18" h, price for pr **2,500.00**
Streamlined Modern, Morris chair, H Wakefield, Gilbert
  Rohde designer, walnut, adjustable back, drop-in seat
  cushion, 1930s, 27" w, 34" d, 28" h **300.00**
Streamlined Modern, sling sofa, Troy Sunshade, Gilbert
  Rohde designer, tubular and flat band chrome construction, rocking seat, channeled back, needs
  reupholstering, 1930s, 48" w, 39" d, 31" h **7,000.00**

GAMBLING COLLECTIBLES

Gambling collectibles divide into two basic groups, those associated with gambling casinos and saloons, and gaming materials
designed for private "back room" use. Casino material further sub-
divides into actual material and equipment used on the gambling
floors and advertising giveaways and premiums.

Gambling supply houses located throughout the country sold
gambling paraphernalia to casinos, saloons, and private individuals through catalogs. Many of the items were "gaffed," meaning
fixed in favor of the owner. Obviously, the general public was not
meant to see these catalogs.

Gaming tables and punchboards dominated the 1980s collecting market. Gambling chips are today's hot collectible.

References: Leonard Schneir, *Gambling Collectibles,* Schiffer
Publishing, 1994; Dale Seymour, *Antique Gambling Chips,
Revised,* Past Pleasures, 1998.

Periodical: *Gaming Times,* 4089 Spring Mountain Rd, Las Vegas,
NV 89102.

Collectors' Club: Casino Chips & Gaming Tokens Collectors Club,
PO Box 340345, Columbus, OH 43234.

Note: See Punchboards and Slot Machines for additional listings.

Ashtray, Kings Inn Casino, Reno, NV, glass, amber, black
  lettering on yellow ground, 4¹/₈" d **$8.00**
Ashtray, Las Vegas Hilton, glass, black, gold ext lettering
  around edge, 4⁵/₁₆" d **2.00**
Ashtray, Lucky Pierre's Gambling Hall and Saloon, glass,
  black amethyst, white lettering, 3¹/₂" d **3.00**
Card Press, dovetailed, holds 10 decks, handle, 9¹/₂ x 4¹/₂
  x 3" **150.00**
Game, Dollar Bill Poker, ES Lowe, 1974. . . . . **10.00**
Game, Jimmy the Greek Odds Maker Poker-Dice,
  Aurora, 1974. . . . . **12.00**
Gaming Wheel, red, green, and yellow, shaped spoked
  center forming curvilinear design, bars and stars dec
  on spokes, 42" d **800.00**
Gaming Wheel, white, black numbers with red accents,
  yellow clowns on center spokes, 24" d **700.00**
Poker Chip, Colonial Club, Augusta, GA, 1930-40s,
  1¹/₂" d **5.00**
Poker Chip, owl on moon, engraved, 1¹/₂" d **5.00**
Poker Chip, ram's head, engraved, 1¹/₂" d **15.00**
Poker Chip Rack, wood, revolving, holds 4 decks of
  cards and 400 chips **35.00**
Roulette Wheel, wood, inlaid dec, F Denzler, Denver,
  31¹/₂" d **75.00**

GAMES

This category deals primarily with boxed board games. The board
game achieved widespread popularity in the period from 1890 to
1910. After modest sales in the 1920s, board games increased in
popularity in the 1930s and experienced a second golden age
from the late 1940s through the mid-1960s. Television and movie
licensing played a major role in board game development. As a
result, crossover collectors frequently skew market values.

Generic board games such as Monopoly have little value except
for the earliest editions. The same holds true for games geared to
children aged 4 to 8, e.g., Candyland, Go to the Head of the Class,
etc. Generic board games dominate toy store shelves in the 1990s.
Disney and a few mega-movie licensed games are the exceptions.

References: *Board Games of the 50's, 60's, and 70's With Prices,*
L-W Book Sales, 1994; Mark Cooper, *Baseball Games,* Schiffer
Publishing, 1995; Alex G. Malloy, *American Games,* Antique
Trader Books, 1998; Harry L. Rinker, *Antique Trader's Guide to
Games & Puzzles,* Antique Trader Books, 1997; Desi Scarpone,
Board Games, Schiffer Publishing, 1995.

Periodicals: *Toy Shop,* 700 E State St, Iola, WI 54990; *Toy Trader,*
PO Box 1050, Dubuque, IA 52004.

Collectors' Clubs: Association of Game and Puzzle Collectors,
PMB 321, 197M Boston Post Rd West, Marlborough, MA 01752;
Gamers Alliance, PO Box 197, East Meadow, NY 11554.

Note: Prices listed are for complete games in mint condition
unless otherwise noted.

4 Cyte, Milton Bradley, 1967 . . . . **$12.00**
Acquire, 3M, 1968 . . . . **15.00**
Addiction, Createk, 1968 . . . . **5.00**
Adventures of Tom Sawyer and Huck Finn, Stoll &
  Edwards Co, 1925 . . . . **75.00**
Aeroplane Race, No. 60 "Mac" Whirling, McDowell
  Mfg Co, c1930s **85.00**
Allan Sherman's Camp Granada Game, Milton Bradley,
  1965 . . . . **30.00**

**Fess Parker Wilderness Trail Card Game, Transogram, 1964,
$30.00.**

All in the Family, Milton Bradley, 1972 . . . . **15.00**
American Boy Game, Milton Bradley, c1924-26 . . . . **150.00**
Animal Game, Saalfield Publishing Co, c1920s **50.00**
Animal Talk Game, Mattel, 1963 . . . . **25.00**
Ant Farm Game, Uncle Milton's Industries, 1969 . . . . **20.00**
Anti-Monopoly, Ralph Anspach, 1973 . . . . **40.00**
Arbitrage, HC Jacoby Inc, 1986 . . . . **10.00**
Balance the Budget, Elten Game Corp, 1938 . . . . **20.00**
Bang Box Game, Ideal, 1969 . . . . **18.00**
Bat Masterson, Lowell, 1958 . . . . **65.00**
Battle Line Game, Ideal, 1964 . . . . **40.00**
Battle Stations, John E Burleson, 1952 . . . . **30.00**
Betsy Ross and the Flag Game, Transogram, 1961 . . . . **30.00**
Bid It Right, Milton Bradley, 1964 . . . . **25.00**
Big Board, Eskay Co, 1975 . . . . **15.00**
Bild-A-Word, Educational Card & Game Corp, 1929 . . . . . . **15.00**
Billy Blastoff Space Game, Danlee, 1969 . . . . **30.00**
Billy Whiskers, Saalfield, #280, c1923-26 . . . . **50.00**
Bionic Crisis, Parker Bros, 1975 . . . . **20.00**
Black Beauty, The Game of, Transogram, 1958 . . . . **35.00**
Blacks and Whites, Psychology Today, 1970-71 . . . . **20.00**
Blockade, Corey Games, 1941 . . . . **50.00**
Boy Scouts Progress Game, The, Parker Bros, 1924-26 . . . . **250.00**
Branded Game, Milton Bradley, 1966 . . . . **50.00**
Break the Bank, Bettye-B, 1955 . . . . **40.00**
Breakthru, 3M, 1965 . . . . **20.00**
Bridge Keno, Milton Bradley, 1930 . . . . **15.00**
Bruce Force and the Treasure of Shark Island, Ideal, 1963 . . . . **30.00**
Bulls and Bears, Parker Bros, 1936 . . . . **100.00**
Bunny Rabbit, or Cottontail & Peter, The Game of, Parker
   Bros, c1928-29 . . . . **150.00**
Burke's Law Target Game, Transogram, 1964 . . . . **30.00**
Call My Bluff, Milton Bradley, 1965 . . . . **30.00**
Camelot, Parker Bros, 1932 . . . . **40.00**
Camp Runamuck Game, Ideal, 1965 . . . . **45.00**
Caper, Parker Bros, 1970 . . . . **35.00**
Captain Kidd Junior, Parker Bros, 1926 . . . . **75.00**
Cargo For Victory, All-Fair, 1943 . . . . **45.00**
Casey Jones Game Box, Saalfield, 1959 . . . . **50.00**
Checkline, Crestline Mfg & Supply Co, 1960s **90.00**
Cherry Ames' Nursing Game, Parker Bros, 1959 . . . . **50.00**
Choo Choo Charlie Game, Milton Bradley, 1969 . . . . **40.00**
Chubby Checker's Limbo Game, Wham-O, 1961 . . . . **50.00**
Columbo Detective Game, Milton Bradley, 1973 . . . . **12.00**
Comical Game of Whip, The, Russell Mfg Co, 1930-32 . . . . **20.00**
Cones and Corns, Parker Bros, 1924 . . . . **40.00**
Controlling Interest, American Greetings, 1972 . . . . **20.00**
Courtroom, W Roy Tribble, 1970s **15.00**
Cowboy Roundup, Parker Bros, 1952 . . . . **35.00**
Crow Hunt, Parker Bros, 1940s **45.00**
Deduction, Ideal, 1976 . . . . **7.00**
Dig, Parker Bros, 1968 . . . . **10.00**
Diner's Club Credit Card Game, The, Ideal, 1961 . . . . **45.00**
Doctor Dolittle, Mattel, 1967 . . . . **45.00**
Dodging Donkey, The, Parker Bros, c1924 . . . . **65.00**
Dolly and Daniel Whale, Milton Bradley, 1964 . . . . **40.00**
Dracula Mystery Game, Hasbro, 1963 . . . . **115.00**
Dude Ranch Game, Gene Autry's, Built Rite, 1956 . . . . **50.00**
Eddie Cantor's Automobile Game "Tell It to the Judge,"
   Parker Bros, 1930s **30.00**
Eliot Ness and the Untouchables Game, Transogram,
   1961 . . . . **60.00**
Espionage, Transogram, 1963 . . . . **40.00**
Fame and Fortune, Whitman, 1962 . . . . **18.00**

Get the Message, Milton Bradley, 1964, $12.00.

Fan-Tel, O Schoenhut Inc, 1937 . . . . **18.00**
Farmer Electric Maps, JM Farmer, 1938 . . . . **45.00**
Feeley Meeley, Milton Bradley, 1967 . . . . **15.00**
Flagship Airfreight, Milton Bradley, 1946 . . . . **55.00**
Flight Round the World, A, Spears, 1928 . . . . **45.00**
Flip For Fun, Parker Bros, 1966 . . . . **15.00**
Flying the Beam, Parker Bros, 1941 . . . . **75.00**
Fu Manchu's Hidden Hoard, Ideal, 1967 . . . . **45.00**
Geo-Graphy, World Wide, Cadaco, 1958 . . . . **15.00**
George of the Jungle, Parker Bros, 1968 . . . . **50.00**
Get That License, Selchow & Righter, 1955 . . . . **30.00**
Giant Barrel of Monkeys, Lakeside, 1969 . . . . **15.00**
Giant Wheel Cowboys 'N Indians, Remco, 1958 . . . . **40.00**
Going Hollywood, Hollywood Game Co, 1943 . . . . **35.00**
Great Escape, The, Ideal, 1967 . . . . **18.00**
Guided Missile Navy Game, Milton Bradley, 1964 . . . . **15.00**
Happy Little Train Game, The, Milton Bradley, 1957 . . . . . **10.00**
Harpoon, Gabriel, 1955 . . . . **25.00**
Heidi Elevator Game, Remco, 1965 . . . . **20.00**
Hendrik Van Loon's Wide World Game, Parker Bros,
   1933 . . . . **45.00**
Heroes of America, Paul Educational Games, 1920s **25.00**
Hickety Pickety, Parker Bros, 1924 . . . . **40.00**
Hippety-Hop, Corey Games, 1940 . . . . **30.00**
Holly Hobbie Wishing Well Game, Parker Bros, 1976 . . . . . **12.00**
Honey West, Ideal, 1965 . . . . **65.00**
Hot Spot, 1-2-3 Game!, Parker Bros, 1961 . . . . **18.00**
Huggin' the Rail, Selchow & Righter, 1948 . . . . **50.00**
India, Whitman, 1950s **10.00**
India Bombay, Cutler & Saleeby Co, #4023, c1920 . . . . **30.00**
Interpretation of Dreams, 3M, 1969 . . . . **15.00**
Jack and Jill Jacks Game, Hasbro, 1966 . . . . **15.00**
Jack and the Beanstalk, Transogram, 1957 . . . . **35.00**
Jig Race, Game Makers, 1940s **30.00**
Johnny On the Pony, Remco, 1959 . . . . **32.00**
Jollytime Dominoes, Milton Bradley, 1955 . . . . **12.00**
Journey to the Unknown Game, Remco, 1968 . . . . **100.00**
Jungle Skittles, American Toy Works, 1950s **45.00**
Keeping Up With the Joneses, The Game of, Phillips
   Co, 1921 . . . . **85.00**
Kewpie Doll Game, Parker Bros, 1963 . . . . **30.00**
Kimbo, Parker Bros, 1960 . . . . **15.00**
King Kong Game, Milton Bradley, 1966 . . . . **15.00**
King of the Cheese, Milton Bradley, 1959 . . . . **30.00**

Krull, Parker Bros, 1983. . . . . **10.00**
Lazy Pool, Dashound, 1965. . . . . **5.00**
Leaping Lena, Parker Bros, 1920s. **100.00**
Let's Face It, Hasbro, 1955. **50.00**
Life, The Game of, Milton Bradley, 1960s. **12.00**
Little Black Sambo, Cadaco, 1951 . . . . **90.00**
Little Noddy's Taxi Game, Parker Bros, 1956. . . . . **90.00**
Little Orphan Annie Game, Milton Bradley, #4359, 1927 . . . . **130.00**
Little Rascals Clubhouse Bingo, The Original, Gabriel,
 1958. . . . . **20.00**
Lobby, Milton Bradley, 1949 . . . . **20.00**
Lost Gold, Parker Bros, 1975. . . . . **15.00**
Lucan Game, Milton Bradley. **10.00**
Lucky Star Gum Ball Game, Ideal, 1961. . . . . **30.00**
Magic! Magic! Magic! Game, Remco, 1975. . . . . **20.00**
Magnetic Fish Pond, Milton Bradley, 1942 . . . . **10.00**
Magnificent Race, The, Parker Bros, 1975. . . . . **15.00**
Mah-Jongg "Junior," Mah-Jongg Sales of America, 1923 . . . . . **25.00**
Management, Avalon Hill, 1960 . . . . **30.00**
Mandinka, ES Lowe, 1978. . . . . **10.00**
Margie, The Game of Whoopee!, Milton Bradley, 1961. . . . . . **35.00**
Marlin Perkins' Zoo Parade, Cadaco-Ellis, 1955 . . . . . . **15.00**
Mary Hartman Mary Hartman, Reiss, 1976-77 . . . . . . **25.00**
M*A*S*H Game, Milton Bradley, 1981 . . . . **25.00**
Mask, Parker Bros, 1985 . . . . **5.00**
Masterpiece, Parker Bros, 1970 . . . . **15.00**
McDonald's Game, The, Milton Bradley, 1975 . . . . **18.00**
Meet the Presidents, Selchow & Righter, 1950 . . . . **20.00**
Melvin the Moon Man, Remco, 1959-60 . . . . **70.00**
Men Into Space, Milton Bradley, 1960 . . . . **50.00**
Men of Destiny, Milton Bradley, 1956 . . . . **20.00**
Merry Circus Game, The, Milton Bradley, 1960 . . . . . . **12.00**
Mexican Pete, Parker Bros, 1940s **30.00**
Miami Vice The Game, Pepperlane Industries, 1984 . . . . . . **20.00**
Mighty Hercules, Hasbro, 1963 . . . . **150.00**
Mind Over Matter, Ideal, 1967 . . . . **15.00**
Miss America Pageant Game, The, Parker Bros, 1974 . . . . . . **15.00**
Miss Popularity Game, Transogram, 1961. . . . . **30.00**
Mob Strategy, Hasbro, 1969 . . . . **15.00**
Money! Money! Money!, Whitman, 1957 . . . . **15.00**
Moneypower, Sherman Games, 1980. . . . . **10.00**
Monkeys and Coconuts, Schaper, 1965 . . . . **12.00**
Monopoly, Parker Bros, 1957. . . . . **15.00**
Moon Blast Off, Schaper, 1970 . . . . **20.00**
Mother Hen Target Game, TST, 1970 . . . . **25.00**
Mother's Helper, Milton Bradley, 1969. . . . . **20.00**
Mouse Trap Game, Ideal, 1963 . . . . **35.00**
Movie Land Keeno, Wilder Mfg, 1929 . . . . **100.00**
Mr Machine Game, Ideal, 1961. . . . . **55.00**
Murder on the Orient Express, Ideal, 1967 . . . . **30.00**
Murder, She Wrote, Warren, 1985 . . . . **8.00**
Mystery Date Game, Milton Bradley, 1965. . . . . **50.00**
Mystic Skull, Ideal, 1964. . . . . **40.00**
Name That Tune Game, Milton Bradley, 1957. . . . . **25.00**
Nancy Drew Mystery Game, The, Parker Bros, 1957. . . . . . . **45.00**
National Velvet Game, Transogram, 1961. . . . . **35.00**
Naval Maneuvers, McLoughlin Bros, c1920 . . . . **400.00**
Nemo, Creston Industries, 1969. . . . . **15.00**
Newlywed Game, The, Chuck Barris Productions, 1979 . . . . . **10.00**
Noah's Ark, Cadaco, 1961. . . . . **15.00**
Notch, Remco, 1960. . . . . **12.00**
No Time For Sergeants, Ideal, 1964 . . . . **35.00**
Nurses Game, The, Ideal, 1963 . . . . **20.00**
Oil, J&L Randall, 1960s. **25.00**

**Radar Search,
Ideal, 1960s,
$15.00.**

Organized Crime, Koplow Games, 1974 . . . . **12.00**
Parcheesi, Selchow & Righter, 1940s **30.00**
Pathfinder, Milton Bradley, 1954 . . . . **12.00**
Perils of Pauline, Marx, 1964. . . . . **45.00**
Phalanx, Whitman, 1964. . . . . **20.00**
Pinky Lee & The Runaway Frankfurters, Whiting, 1954 . . . . . . **55.00**
Pirate and Traveler, Milton Bradley, 1953 . . . . **25.00**
Play and Defend Bridge, Charles Goren's, Milton
 Bradley, 1965 . . . . **15.00**
Playful Trails Game, Lakeside, 1968. . . . . **35.00**
Play Your Hunch, Transogram, 1970. . . . . **20.00**
Point of Law, 3M, 1972. . . . . **10.00**
Police Patrol, Hasbro, 1955-57 . . . . **60.00**
Pollyanna, Parker Bros, 1950s **18.00**
Pollyanna Dixie, Parker Bros, 1952 . . . . **20.00**
Polly Pickles: The Great Movie Game: A Burlesque,
 Parker Bros, 1921 . . . . **75.00**
Pony Express, Game of, Polygon Corp, 1947 . . . . **20.00**
Poppin' Hoppies, Ideal, 1968 . . . . **25.00**
Prediction Rod, Parker Bros, 1970 . . . . **15.00**
Prince Valiant, Transogram, 1955 . . . . **35.00**
Project CIA, Waddington, 1973 . . . . **10.00**
PT Boat 109, Ideal, 1963. . . . . **30.00**
Race Trap, Multiple Toymakers, 1960s **35.00**
Radio Game, Milton Bradley, 1920s. **75.00**
Radio Game, Wilder Mfg, #27, 1927 . . . . **70.00**
Ranger Commandos, Parker Bros, 1942 . . . . **35.00**
Rebel, The, Ideal, 1961 . . . . **20.00**
Recall, Milton Bradley, 1967 . . . . **20.00**
Red Skelton's "I Dood It!," Zondine Game Co, 1947. . . . . . . **70.00**
Revlon's $64,000 Question Quiz Game, Lowell, 1955 . . . . . . **25.00**
Rex Morgan, MD, Ideal, 1972 . . . . **25.00**
Rich Uncle Stock Market Game, Parker Bros, 1959. . . . . . . **20.00**
Risk, Parker Bros, 1968 . . . . **10.00**
Rodeo, The Wild West Game, Whitman, 1957 . . . . **30.00**
Roman X, Selchow & Righter, 1964 . . . . **15.00**
Rrib-Bit, Genesis Enterprises, 1973. . . . . **15.00**
Ruff and Reddy Circus Game, Transogram, 1962 . . . . . . **30.00**
Safari, Selchow & Righter, 1950. . . . . **30.00**
Scoop, The Game, Parker Bros, 1956 . . . . **30.00**
Secrecy, Universal Games, 1965 . . . . **25.00**

Seven Keys, Ideal, 1961	**20.00**
Show-Biz, Lowell, 1956	**40.00**
Sinking of the Titanic, The, Ideal, 1976	**30.00**
Skirmish, American Heritage, Milton Bradley, 1975	**20.00**
Skudo, Parker Bros, 1949	**15.00**
Smokey Bear Game, Milton Bradley, 1973	**30.00**
Soldier On Fort, The, Joseph Borzellino & Son, 1931	**25.00**
Son Of Hercules Game, The, Milton Bradley, 1966	**30.00**
Speed Circuit, 3M, 1971	**15.00**
Speedy Boat Race, Milton Bradley, #4506, 1930s	**45.00**
Spot, Game of, Milton Bradley, c1925	**40.00**
Spots, Milton Bradley, 1959	**25.00**
Square Mile, Milton Bradley, 1962	**25.00**
State Capitals, Game of, Parker Bros, 1952	**15.00**
Stop, Look and Listen, Game of, Milton Bradley, c1926	**35.00**
Stratego, Milton Bradley, 1961	**20.00**
Strategy, Corey Games, 1938	**40.00**
Sub Attack Game, Milton Bradley, 1965	**25.00**
Sugar Bowl, Transogram, c1950	**35.00**
Super Market, Selchow & Righter, 1953	**20.00**
Surfside 6, Lowell, 1962	**45.00**
Swords and Shields, Milton Bradley, 1970	**20.00**
Taffy's Baubles & Bangles Game, Transogram, 1966	**12.00**
Talk to Cecil, Mattel, 1961	**40.00**
Tank Battle Game, Milton Bradley, 1975	**18.00**
Tell Bell, The, Knapp Electric Inc, 1928	**30.00**
Tom and Jerry Game, Milton Bradley, 1968	**20.00**
Tootsie Roll Train Game, Hasbro, 1964	**25.00**
Transaction, John R Tusson, 1962	**12.00**
Traps and Bunkers–A Game of Golf, Milton Bradley, #4091, c1930	**110.00**
Triple Play, National Games Inc, #D3902, c1930s	**10.00**
Video Village, Milton Bradley, 1960	**25.00**
Voyage Round the World, Game of, Milton Bradley, #4189, c1930s	**125.00**
White Glove Girl, American Publishing Corp, 1966	**15.00**
Whodunit?, Cadaco-Ellis, 1959	**20.00**
World of Wall Street, The, Hasbro, 1969	**15.00**
Wow Pillow Fight Game for Girls, Milton Bradley, 1964	**20.00**
Yertle, The Game of, Revell, 1960	**50.00**
Zaxxon, Milton Bradley, 1982	**10.00**

Truth or Consequences, Gabriel, 1955, $30.00.

GAS STATION COLLECTIBLES

Many of today's drivers no longer remember the independently owned full-service gas station where attendants pumped your gas, checked your oil, and cleaned your windshield. Fortunately, collectors do. Many are recreating golden age (1930s through the 1960s) versions of the independent gas station in their basements and garages.

While pump globes and oil cans remain the principal collecting focus, gasoline station advertising, uniforms, and paper ephemera are other hot collecting subcategories in the 2000s. Road maps, especially those issued prior to the Interstate system, double in value every few years.

References: Mark Anderton, *Encyclopedia of Petroliana*, Krause Publications, 1999; Mark Anderton and Sherry Mullen, *Gas Station Collectibles*, Krause Publications, 1994; Robert W. D. Ball, *Texaco Collectibles*, Schiffer Publishing, 1994; Rob Bender and Tammy Cannoy-Bender, *An Unauthorized Guide to Mobil Collectibles*, Schiffer Publishing, 1999; Scott Benjamin and Wayne Henderson, *Gas Globes*, Schiffer Publishing, 1999; Scott Benjamin and Wayne Henderson, *Sinclair Collectibles*, Schiffer Publishing, 1997; Mike Bruner, *Gasoline Treasures*, Schiffer Publishing, 1996; Todd P. Helms, *The Conoco Collector's Bible*, Schiffer Publishing, 1995; J. Sam McIntyre, *The Esso Collectibles Handbook*, Schiffer Publishing, 1998; Rick Pease, *Service Station Collectibles*, Schiffer Publishing, 1996; Sonya Stenzler and Rick Pease, *Gas Station Collectibles*, Schiffer Publishing, 1993; B. J. Summers and Wayne Priddy, *Value Guide to Gas Station Memorabilia*, Collector Books, 1995, 2000 value update; Charles Whitworth, *Gulf Oil Collectibles*, Schiffer Publishing, 1998.

Periodical: *Check the Oil!*, 30 W Olentangy St, Powell, OH 43065.

Newsletter: *Petroleum Collectibles Monthly*, PO Box 556, La Grange, OH 44050.

Collectors' Clubs: Oil Can Collectors Club, 4213 Derby Ln, Evansville, IN 47715; Road Map Collectors of America, 5832 NW 62nd Terrace, Oklahoma City, OK 73122.

Badge, Esso Service, employee's, silvered metal, oval logo, red enamel "Esso," and blue enamel "Service," rect opening for insertion of attendants name paper from rear, back bar pin fastener, c1930s	**$75.00**
Bank, Shell Oil, hard plastic, raised Shell name on each side, coin slot in top, mkd "Made In U.S.A.," c1950s, 2 x 4 x 4"	**100.00**
Banner, Esso, canvas, fluorescent, "World's First Choice," Esso man with oil drip, 83" h, 36" w	**125.00**
Beverage Carrier, Esso, metal over insulated glass with wire carrying handle, red plastic threaded cup lid, perimeter has full color litho cartoon travel map of US with 2 smaller inset map scenes, images of Happy Oil Drop symbol character, Skotch Kooler, c1960s, 7½" h, 6" d	**75.00**
Blotter, Barney Oldfield, "If Barney Trusts Them You Can/The Most Trustworthy Tires Built," Boedeker Brothers, Higinsville, MO, 6" l, 3¼" w	**110.00**
Blotter, Pan-Am, airplane flying over countryside illus, "Keep Pace With Pan-Am Gasoline," 3" h, 6¼" w	**175.00**

Calendar, 1931, Bloboline Motor Oil, cardboard, black and white lettering on red ground, "Cylinder, Engine, Automobile, Tractor, Special Oils and Greases," complete 12-month tablet, 3¼ x 6¼" **20.00**

Calendar, 1937, Richfield/Richlube dealer, cardboard, upper overlay panel centered by 3 x 7¼" delivery truck, complete 12-month tablet plus spring clip pencil holder, 10½ x 14" **45.00**

Candy Container, glass, figural gas pump, emb "Gas 23¢ To-Day," 4¼" h, 2" w **140.00**

Cufflinks, pr, Oilzum, metal, oval, molded head of Oilzum man with racing goggles and hat, ¾" l **200.00**

Game, Shell Oil, "Stop and Go," 10 x 10½" stiff paper playing sheet, complete with 25 paper playing pcs separated from orig perforation sheet, missing spinner and instructions, late 1930s **20.00**

Gas Globe, Fleet-Wing, 1-pc wide milk glass body, glass lens, blue lettering, red flying bird silhouette, white ground, red and blue rim stripes, 14" d **350.00**

Gas Globe, Red Crown Gas, 1-pc white milk glass crown-shaped globe with red trim and metal base, 16½" h, 16" w **450.00**

Gas Globe, Sinclair Dino Supreme, newer white capcolite plastic body, 2 glass lenses, red lettering, green dinosaur and rim stripe, "Registered Sinclair Logo and Dino Registered," 13½" d **200.00**

Hot Pad, Texaco, quilted white fabric, inscribed "Victory Villa" on 1 side in blue lettering with red and white striping and hanger loop, 6" sq. **25.00**

Mechanical Pencil, Cities Service Gas Station, cream and brown, vial of oil affixed to end, green and black logo and adv for "JE Cox...Hot Springs, Ark," 5½" l **20.00**

Mechanical Pencil, Pure Oil Co, "Tiolene Motor Oil/Made from Cabin Creek Crude/Jerry's Pure Oil Station, Park River, North Dakota," oil samples in plastic base, 5⅞" l **100.00**

Pen and Pencil Set, Amoco logo on diecut metal pocket clasp, Cross, 5⅜" l **30.00**

Photograph, Gulf Gas station, full color, matted and framed, 22¾" h, 41" w **160.00**

Pinback Button, Orange American Gas, red, white, and blue litho, late 1930s, 3" d **20.00**

Playing Cards, Flying A Service, complete deck, black and white basset hound next to black, white, and red logo with "When it comes to your car...Ooooh, do we worry!," c1950s, ⅝ x 2¼ x 3½", MIP **20.00**

Poster, Shell, paper, litho, "Join the Share-the Road Club here," 33⅜" h, 57½" w **75.00**

Salt and Pepper Shakers, pr, Conoco, plastic, figural gas pump, "Doyle M Bostick Service Station, Temple TX," 2¾" h, 1" w **170.00**

Salt and Pepper Shakers, pr, Sunoco, plastic, blue, detailed graphics, 2¾" h, 1" w **225.00**

Sign, Amoco, porcelain, 2-sided, "American Amoco Gas/Courtesy Cards Honored Here," 15" h, 24" w **100.00**

Sign, Shell Oil, metal, 2-sided, shell shaped, red and yellow enamel painted, 40¼" x 41¾" **300.00**

Sign, Sunoco, tin, 1-sided, self-framed, "Need Gas?/Sunoco/1 mi Ahead–Rest Rooms," 45" h, 93" w **225.00**

Sign, Texaco Sky Chief Gasoline, "Super-Charged with Petrox," 12 x 22" **55.00**

Thermometer, Prestone Antifreeze, porcelain, "You're Set Safe Sure," 36" h, 9" w **175.00**

Visor, Texaco Fire Chief, diecut cardboard, elastic string, top printed in red and black on white with Texaco logo and fire helmet image, "Compliments of Texaco Exhibit/Atlantic City," 1937, 3¼ x 9½" **25.00**

GEISHA GIRL

Geisha Girl is a generic term used to describe Japanese export ceramics made between the 1880s and the present whose decoration incorporates one or more kimono-clad Japanese ladies. Most collectors focus on pre-1940 ware. Geisha Girl ceramics made after 1945 are referred to as "modern" Geisha Girl.

Reference: Elyce Litts, *The Collector's Encyclopedia of Geisha Girl Porcelain,* Collector Books, 1988, out of print.

REPRODUCTION ALERT: Be alert for late 1970s' and early 1980s' Geisha Girl reproductions in forms ranging from ginger jars to sake sets. These contemporary pieces have red borders. Other telltale characteristics include lack of detail, very bright gold highlights, and a white porcelain body.

Czechoslovakian ceramic manufacturers also copied this ware in the 1920s. Some are marked "Czechoslovakia" or have a false Chinese mark. Many are unmarked. Decal decoration was used extensively. However, the real clue is in the faces. The faces on Czechoslovakian Geisha do not have a strong oriental look.

Berry Set, Porch, master and 5 individuals, scalloped edge, red and gold, price for 6-pc set **$40.00**

Bowl, Bamboo Trellis, 7½" d **40.00**

Bread and Butter Plate, Bamboo Tree, 6" d **10.00**

Candleholder, ring handle **40.00**

Candlesticks, pr, Parasol D, red **110.00**

Child's Pitcher, Garden Bench, red, Variant N, 2½" h **20.00**

Chocolate Pot, cov **60.00**

Creamer, Meeting B **25.00**

Creamer and Sugar, River's Edge **70.00**

Cup and Saucer, Bird Cage **15.00**

Gas Globe, Frontier, red and black on white milk glass, 13½" d, $900.00. Photo courtesy Collectors Auction Services.

Hair Receiver, Long-Stemmed Peony **35.00**
Hatpin Holder, 4" h. **45.00**
Ice Cream Set, Fan A, red, 6 pcs **100.00**
Mug, Bamboo Trellis **20.00**
Plate, Child Reaching For Butterfly, red, Variation A, 7" d **15.00**
Sake Cup, Meeting B. **15.00**
Salt and Pepper Shakers, pr, squat, gold trim **30.00**
Teacup and Saucer, Bamboo, Torii, Japan **10.00**
Teacup and Saucer, Porch, cobalt blue, 2 streams of gold
    lacing, gold striped handle, red-orange, modern **12.00**

G.I. JOE

Hasbro introduced G.I. Joe at the February 1964 American International Toy Fair in New York. Initially, this 12-inch poseable figure was produced in only four versions, one for each branch of the military.

A black G.I. Joe joined the line in 1965, followed by a talking G.I. Joe and female nurse in 1967. The G.I. Joe Adventure Team introduced this all-American hero to civilian pursuits such as hunting and deep sea diving. The 1976 Arab oil embargo forced Hasbro to reduce G.I. Joe's size from 12 to 8 inches. Production stopped in 1977.

Hasbro reintroduced G.I. Joe in 1982 in a 3¼-inch format. In 1994 Hasbro resumed production of the 12-inch figure, targeted primarily toward the adult collector market. Action Man, G.I. Joe's British equivalent, was marketed in the United States during the 1996 holiday season.

Collectors concentrate on pre-1977 action figures. Collecting interest in accessories, especially those with period boxes, continues to grow.

References: John Marshall, *GI Joe and Other Backyard Heroes,* Schiffer Publishing, 1997; Vincent Santelmo, *The Complete Encyclopedia to GI Joe, 2nd Edition,* Krause Publications, 1997; Vincent Santelmo, *GI Joe, 1964-1999,* Krause Publications, 1999.

Periodical: *GI Joe Patrol,* PO Box 2362, Hot Springs, AR 71914.

Collectors' Club: GI Joe Collectors Club, 225 Cattle Baron Parc Dr, Fort Worth, TX 76108.

ACCESSORIES

81mm Mortar Shell, with chain and pin **$35.00**
Action Team Indian Tent and Headdress, MIB **150.00**
Adventure Team Campfire **30.00**
Adventure Team Jump Suit **35.00**
Adventure Team Solar Communicator. **25.00**
Ammunition Can **25.00**
Billy Club **15.00**
Canteen and Mess Set **30.00**
Carbine Rifle, 30 caliber **30.00**
Deep Sea Diver Helmet. **40.00**
Deluxe Pup Tent, with stakes **50.00**
Flak Vest. **45.00**
Flare Pistol **15.00**
Frogman Face Mask **15.00**
Frogman Scuba Tanks **30.00**
Frogman Swim Fins, pr **15.00**
Japanese Soldier Nambu Pistol **30.00**
M-60 Machine Gun Bullets **30.00**

Market Buoy. **15.00**
Medic Crutch **20.00**
Medic Splint. **5.00**
Sailor Cap. **20.00**
Sailor Life Jacket **30.00**
Ski Patrol Cartridge Belt. **35.00**
Ski Patrol Sun Goggles. **30.00**
Snowshoes, white **30.00**
White Shore Patrol Helmet **55.00**

ACTION FIGURES

Adventure Team Fantastic Freefall, MIP. **$375.00**
Adventure Team Sea Adventurer, orig box. **150.00**
Battle of the Bulge Soldier, orig box, 1996, 12" h **75.00**
Black Adventurer, 1970 . . . . **150.00**
Dress Marine, orig box, 1966, 12" h **75.00**
F-15E Pilot, made by Hasbro for FAO Schwarz, orig box,
    1996, 12" h. **200.00**
Land Adventurer, 1970 . . . . **75.00**
Man of Action, 1970 . . . . **75.00**
Sea Adventurer, 1970 . . . . **75.00**
Talking Action Pilot, complete **700.00**
Talking Action Sailor, complete **600.00**
Talking Adventure Team Commander, 1970 . . . . **125.00**
Talking GI Joe Action Marine, with instruction sheet, and
    "Marine Manual," orig box, 1964, 12" h. **225.00**
Talking Man of Action, 1970 . . . . **125.00**

CLOTHING

Action Team Sheriff Outfit, MIB **$175.00**
Adventure Team Black Jacket **20.00**
Adventure Team Blue Flight Suit. **30.00**
Adventure Team Desert Explorer Shirt and Belt **20.00**
Adventure Team Light Blue Shirt **20.00**
Adventure Team Tan Shirt **15.00**
Astronaut Suit, with helmet, boots, gloves, and chest
    pack **100.00**
Combat Fatigue Shirt. **25.00**
Combat Field Jacket **35.00**
Desert Explorer Shirt and Belt **20.00**
Secret Agent, MIP **175.00**
White Tiger Hunt, 1970 . . . . **125.00**
Winter Rescue, MIP. **150.00**

PLAYSETS

Adventure Team Headquarters, 1972, MIB **$200.00**
Capture of the Pygmy Gorilla, 1970, MIB. **325.00**
Mystery of the Boiling Lagoon, Sears, 1973 . . . . **200.00**

VEHICLES

Action Man Jeep, complete with box **$450.00**
Action Man Power-Hog ATV, complete with box. **425.00**
Action Team Escape Car, complete with box. **50.00**
Action Team Lifeline Catapult, complete with box **50.00**
Action Team Turbo Copter, complete with box **50.00**
Adventure Team Helicopter, complete with box **500.00**
Desert Patrol Adventure, JC Penney, complete with box. . . . **800.00**
Motorcycle and Sidecar, complete with box **600.00**
Official Adventure Team Vehicle, complete with box. **600.00**
Sea Wolf, complete with box. **500.00**

GIRL SCOUTS

Juliette Gordon Low of Savannah, Georgia, began the Girl Scout movement in 1912. It grew rapidly. The 1928 Girl Scout manual suggested selling cookies to raise money. Today the annual Girl Scout cookie drive supports local troops and councils.

Girl Scout collectibles enjoy limited collector interest. There is a ready market for flashlights and pocketknives, primarily because they cross over into other collecting fields.

Blanket, green, woven Girl Scout logo, c1930s. **$150.00**
Book, *Girl Scouts Good Turn*, Edith Lavell, Burt, 1922-25 . . . . **12.00**
Book, *Lady From Savannah, The Life of Juliette Low,*
    Schultz & Lawrence, Lippincott, 1st ed, 1958 . . . . **15.00**
Calendar, 1953, full-color photo, full pad. **25.00**
Camera, Official Girl Scout, folding, Kodak, c1929. . . . . **65.00**
Catalog, Brownie Equipment, 16 pp, 1950 . . . . **10.00**
Comic Book, Daisy Lowe of the Girl Scouts, 16 pp, full
    color, history text, ©1954 . . . . **20.00**
First Aid Kit, Johnson & Johnson, complete with contents
    and cloth belt pouch, 1930s **35.00**
Handbook, *Girl Scout Handbook,* 1st printing **12.00**
Handbook, *Scouting For Girls,* 3rd printing, 1922. . . . . **20.00**
Lunch Box, metal, brown, illus on sides, complete with
    cover insert, 1920s, 7½ x 5 x 4". **90.00**
Magazine, *The American Girl,* Jun 1934, 52 pp **8.00**
Manual, Scouting for Girls, 1920, 557 pp. **20.00**
Patch, First Class, bright green with crimped edges, 1950s . . . **10.00**
Pin, Challenge Pin, Community Action, 1963-80 . . . . **8.00**
Pin, Golden Eaglet, 1st type, gold plated, 1919-30 . . . . **500.00**
Pin, Second Trefoil, c1918-23 . . . . **50.00**
Pinback Button, New Bedford Girl Scouts Silver
    Anniversary, 1913-38, silver and dark green **15.00**
Pocketknife, Kutmaster, clear plastic over red handle,
    locking blade **25.00**
Ring, Brownie, sterling, rect face, adjustable, 1950s **15.00**
Sewing Kit, Brownies, red case, c1940. . . . . **15.00**
Thermos, metal, red, green, and white, logos and stripes,
    white plastic cup, Aladdin, c1960 . . . . **40.00**
Uniform, khaki, complete with 10 khaki badges on
    sleeves, brimmed hat, web belt, c1915-28 . . . . **250.00**

GLASS SHOES

Glass shoe is a generic term for any figural shoe (or slipper, boot, ice skate, etc.) made of glass, ceramic, or metal. Some examples are utilitarian in nature, e.g., the Atterbury shoe night lamp or the ruby glass cocktail shaker in the shape of a leg and foot wearing a metal sandal. Most were made for purely decorative purposes.

Shoes were extremely popular during the Victorian era, when household bric-a-brac from toothpick holders to pincushions to salt cellars were made in the form of footwear. Once the glass shoe entered the form vocabulary, it never went out of production. There was a lull during the Depression, when few families had money for non-essential items.

Several contemporary glass companies including Boyd, Degenhart, Fenton, and Moser have reproduced early designs and introduced new ones. Thanks to several new books on the subject, glass shoes are enjoying a collecting renaissance.

References: Earlene Wheatley, *Collectible Glass Shoes: Including Metal, Pottery Figural & Porcelain Shoes,* Collector Books, 1996, 1998 value update; Libby Yalom, *Shoes of Glass, 2,* Antique Publications, 1998.

Collectors Club: Miniature Shoe Collectors Club, PO Box 2390, Apple Valley, CA 92308.

Baby Bootee, Fenton Art Glass, aquamarine, #1994,
    1938-39 . . . . **$40.00**
Baby Bootee, frosted, hollow sole, c1930, 3⅛ x 2⅛" **35.00**
Baby Bootee, Waterford, paperweight, c1986, 4⅛ x 2¼" **85.00**
Boot, Czechoslovakian, green, black painted heel, brass
    colored metal band around top edge, mkd
    "Czechoslovakia," 7¼ x 10". **150.00**
Boot, Fenton, Hobnail, white, with logo. **15.00**
Boot, ruby cut back to crystal, c1980, 5½ x 7¾". **130.00**
Boot, yellow, 4¼ x 6½". **10.00**
Cat Slipper, Degenhart, Bermuda slag **15.00**
High-Heeled Shoe, Czechoslovakian, teal, crystal orna-
    ment at front opening, 8½ x 4⅝" **300.00**
High-Heeled Shoe, pressed glass, blue, Diamond pat-
    tern sole, c1980s, 6½ x 3". **60.00**

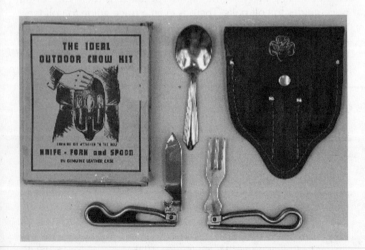

Chow Kit, green leather case with stamped emblem, silver plated folding knife, folding fork, and spoon, orig box, **$30.00.**

Kitten Slipper, Fenton, Daisy & Button pattern, opalescent glass, 1970, 3½" h, **$15.00.**

High-Heeled Shoe, Tiffin, crystal, "Tiffin" gold sticker,
    c1942-57, 3¼ x 2⅜" **45.00**
Santa Boot, amethyst, turned toe, 2½ x 2¾" **30.00**
Santa Boot, cobalt blue, c1930, 2½ x 2¾" **15.00**
Shoe, Guernsey Glass Co, Cambridge, OH, Daisy &
    Button, lavender **10.00**
Shoe, LE Smith, Daisy & Button, amber, c1969 . . . . **15.00**
Shoe, Venetian Glass, frosted red, white, and blue mille-
    fiore on orange ground, 6 x 2¼" **80.00**
Slipper, crystal, gold bow dec, c1984, 5 x 2¼" **25.00**
Slipper, Georgian Crystal Tutbury LTD, crystal, paper
    label **25.00**
Slipper, green, scalloped border, double lines on vamp,
    hollow sole, solid heel, c1920, 4½ x 2½" **55.00**
Slipper, pale blue, spun glass, yellow glass band around
    top forming bow, c1920, 2 x ¾" **45.00**

GOEBEL

Franz and William Goebel, father and son, founded the F. D. & W.
Goebel Porcelain Works near Coburg, Germany, in 1879. Initially,
the firm made dinnerware, utilitarian ware, and beer steins. Marx-
Louis, William's son, became president in 1912. He introduced
many new porcelain figurine designs and added a pottery figurine
line. Franz Goebel, son of Marx-Louis, and Dr. Eugene Stocke, his
uncle, assumed control of the company in 1929.

Franz Goebel is responsible for making arrangements to pro-
duce the company's famous Hummel figurines. During World War
II, Goebel concentrated on the production of dinnerware.
Following the war, the company exported large quantities of
Hummels and other figurines. Today Goebel manufactures high
quality dinnerware, limited edition collectibles, the popular
Hummel figurines, and figurine series ranging from Disney char-
acters to Friar Tuck monks.

Collectors' Club: Friar Tuck Collectors Club, PO Box 262,
Oswego, NY 13827.

Note: This category consists of Goebel's non-Hummel production.
See Limited Editions and Hummel Figurines for additional listings.

Figurine, Alice in the Garden, Miniatures–Alice In
    Wonderland, R Olszewski, 1982 . . . . **$500.00**
Figurine, Carousel Ride, Miniatures–Americana Series,
    R Olszewski, 1986 . . . . **50.00**
Figurine, Fore, Charlot Byj Redheads, C Byj, 1975 . . . . **130.00**
Figurine, House in the Woods, Miniatures–Snow White,
    Disney, 1988 . . . . **125.00**
Figurine, Jiminy Cricket, Miniatures–Pinocchio, Disney,
    1990 . . . . **110.00**
Figurine, kitten, paper label **40.00**
Figurine, Love Bugs, Charlot Byj Blondes, C Byj, 1972 . . . . . **150.00**
Figurine, Mike the Jam Maker, Co-Boy, G Skrobek, 1971 . . . . **80.00**
Figurine, Robby the Vegetarian, Co-Boys Culinary,
    Welling/Skrobek, 1994 . . . . **30.00**
Figurine, Roses, Miniature–Women's Series, R Olszewski,
    1984 . . . . **70.00**
Figurine, She Loves Me, N Rockwell, 1963 . . . . **250.00**
Figurine, Stable Donkey, Miniatures–Nativity Collection,
    R Olszewski, 1991 . . . . **125.00**
Figurine, Summer Days, Miniatures–Children's Series,
    R Olszewski, 1981 . . . . **150.00**

Figurine, Schnauzer, imp #30110 and #41, 4⅞" h, $50.00. Photo courtesy Ray Morykan Auctions.

Figurine, Toni the Skier, Co-Boys Sports, Welling/
    Skrobek, 1994 . . . . **30.00**
Jug, figural cardinal, stylized bee mark, 4" h **175.00**
Lemon Reamer, 2 pc, green and yellow body, cream top,
    brown handle, crackle finish, imp mark, 1927, 4½" h **145.00**
Mustard Pot, Friar Tuck, stylized bee mark, 3¾" h **75.00**
Planter, swan, 1969 . . . . **135.00**
Salt and Pepper Shakers, pr, Friars, SB153/1, 2¾" h **30.00**

GOLF COLLECTIBLES

Golf roots rest in 15th-century Scotland. Initially a game played
primarily by the aristocracy and gentry, by the mid-19th century
the game was accessible to everyone. By 1900, golf courses were
located throughout Great Britain and the United States.

Golf collectibles divide into four basic groups: (1) golf books, (2)
golf equipment, (3) items associated with a famous golfer, and (4)
golf ephemera ranging from tournament programs to golf prints.
Golf collecting has become highly specialized. There are several
price guides to golf balls. There is even a price guide to golf tees.

References: Chuck Furjanic, *Antique Golf Collectibles, 2nd
Edition,* Krause Publications, 2000; John F. Hotchkiss, *500 Years of
Golf Balls,* Antique Trader Books, 1997; John M. Olman and
Morton W. Olman, *Golf Antiques & Other Treasures of the Game,
Expanded Edition,* Market Street Press, 1993; Beverly Robb,
Collectible Golfing Novelties, Schiffer Publishing, 1992.

Newsletter: *Golfingly Yours,* 5407 Pennock Point Rd, Jupiter, FL
33458.

Collectors' Clubs: Golf Collectors Society, PO Box 241042,
Cleveland, OH 44124, World Logo Ball Assoc, PO Box 91989,
Long Beach, CA 90809.

Advertising Tear Sheet, Elgin, "Correctly Timed," sgd by
    Glenna Collett, *Ladies Home Journal,* 1925 . . . . **$300.00**
Autograph, Ben Hogan, PS, *Sports Illustrated* photo,
    1955 . . . . **200.00**

Matchcover, The Olympic Club, golfing scene across matches, $12.00. Photo courtesy Ray Morykan Auctions.

operations were moved to Zanesville. Hurt by the flood of cheap foreign imports, Gonder sold his business in 1975 to the Allied Tile Company.

Many Gonder pieces have a double glaze and a pink interior. Most pieces are marked GONDER or GONDER USA in a variety of ways and are numbered. Some pieces were marked with a paper label.

Reference: Ron Hoopes, *The Collector's Guide and History of Gonder Pottery,* L-W Books, 1992, out of print.

Collectors' Club: Gonder Collectors Club, 917 Hurl Dr, Pittsburgh, PA 15236.

Console, #500, 17 x 9" **$100.00**
Cookie Jar, pirate, 12" h. **600.00**
Creamer and Sugar, La Gonda, 4" h. **35.00**
Ewer, #606, 10" h **75.00**
Figurine, Chinese girl, #763, 13" h. **50.00**
Figurine, coolie, kneeling, #547, 6" h. **25.00**
Figurine, game hen, 7" h **100.00**
Figurine, horse head, #545, 10" h **100.00**
Figurine, panther, #210, 19" l **250.00**
Lamp Base, driftwood, 13" h **80.00**
Lamp Base, gazelles, 15" h **150.00**
Lamp Base, horse, 11" h **125.00**
Lamp Base, leaf and acorns, 9" h. **65.00**
Lamp Base, sailing ship, green and ocher, 13¼" h. **250.00**
Planter, #752, 10" l **15.00**
Relish Dish, #871, 18 x 11". **50.00**
Salt and Pepper Shakers, pr, La Gonda. **10.00**
Teapot, #914, La Gonda, 7½" h. **75.00**
Tumbler, #909, volcanic glaze, 5" h. **8.00**
TV Lamp, black panther, 18" l **100.00**
Vase, #514, seagull, 12" h **200.00**
Vase, #519, Comedy and Tragedy Mask **50.00**
Vase, #748, white crackle glaze, 7" h **75.00**
Vase, H-73, 8" h **45.00**
Vase, H-78, 9" h **30.00**
Vase, H-81, 9" h **30.00**
Vase, M-8, 12" h **75.00**

Book, *Bob MacDonald's Golf at a Glance The Pocket "Pro,"* 1931 . . . . **120.00**
Book, *Gene Sarazen's Common Sense Golf Tips,* 1924 . . . . . . **35.00**
Book, *Golf For Young Players,* 1st ed, Glenna Collett, Little, Brown & Co, 1926. . . . . **65.00**
Bottle Opener, metal, golf ball in center, leather back, 4" l **30.00**
Club, Super Stick, Highlander brand, tubular nickel finish, black rubber grip, extends from 24 to 38" l, 1950-60s **25.00**
Golf Balls, Sam Snead, boxed set of 12 "Wilson 100" golf balls, 1950s, MIB **100.00**
Greeting Card, Valentine's Day, pop-up type, little golfer wearing knickers **45.00**
Magazine, *Golfing,* 1950s **8.00**
Magazine, *Golf World,* Jan 17, 1951 . . . . **8.00**
Magazine, *Professional Golfer,* May 1947 . . . . **10.00**
Mug, pewter, lists US Open Championship winners, Sheffield, England, 1938 . . . . **150.00**
Program, Bob Hope Desert Classic, 1967 . . . . **15.00**
Salt and Pepper Shakers, pr, ceramic, 2" d grass mound centered by brown pedestal tee serving as shaker, and dimpled white ceramic golf ball rests on top of tee as other shaker, c1950s **10.00**
Shot Glass, figural pewter golfer on handle, 2" h **15.00**
Sign, Beech-Nut Gum, cardboard, "Finest Peppermint Flavor," 2 lady golfers illus, c1930s, 9 x 16" **175.00**
Tee, plastic, figural tools **2.00**
Tee, rubber, combination. **10.00**

GONDER POTTERY

After a distinguished ceramic career working for American Encaustic Tiling, Cherry Art Tile, Florence Pottery, and Ohio Pottery, Lawton Gonder purchased the Zane Pottery, Zanesville, Ohio, in 1940 and renamed it Gonder Ceramic Arts. The company concentrated on art pottery and decorative accessories. Gonder hired top designers and sculptors to create his products. Gonder's glazes were innovative.

In 1946 Gonder expanded his Zanesville plant and purchased the Elgee Pottery to produce lamp bases. Elgee burned in 1954;

GRANITEWARE

Graniteware is a generic term used to describe enamel-coated iron or steel kitchenware. Originating in Germany, the first American graniteware was manufactured in the 1860s. American manufacturers received a major market boost when World War I curtailed German imports.

Graniteware is still being manufactured today. Older examples tend to be heavier. Cast-iron handles date between 1870 and 1890; wood handles between 1900 and 1910.

This market experienced a major price run in the early 1990s as dealers raised their prices to agree with those published by Helen Greguire. At the moment, the category as a whole appears to be greatly overvalued.

References: Helen Greguire, *The Collector's Encyclopedia of Graniteware: Colors, Shapes & Values* (1990, 1994 value update), *Book 2* (1993, 1997 value update), Collector Books; Dana G. Morykan, *The Official Price Guide to Country Antiques & Collectibles, Fourth Edition,* House of Collectibles, 1999; David T.

Pikul and Ellen M. Plante, *Collectible Enameled Ware: American & European,* Schiffer Publishing, 1998.

Collectors' Club: National Graniteware Society, PO Box 10013, Cedar Rapids, IA 52410.

Angel Food Pan, lava	$175.00
Baking Pan, Chrysolite	150.00
Berry Bucket, cov, blue swirl, granite lid	325.00
Berry Bucket, cov, brown swirl, granite lid	275.00
Berry Bucket, cov, cobalt swirl, granite lid	925.00
Berry Bucket, cov, emerald swirl, tin lid	200.00
Biscuit Cutter, gray	400.00
Bucket, gray, miniature	300.00
Bundt Pan Carrier, gray swirl	60.00
Butter Dish, gray, pewter trim, with insert	350.00
Coffeepot, emerald swirl, 8" h	600.00
Coffeepot, gray, miniature, straight spout	850.00
Coffee Roaster, onyx	140.00
Colander, gray, salesman's sample	550.00
Cream Can, cov, blue swirl, granite lid	350.00
Cup, emerald swirl	850.00
Dish Pan, emerald swirl	200.00
Egg Pan, emerald swirl, 2 handles	400.00
Funnel, cobalt swirl, 5" d	400.00
Liquid Measure, blue swirl, stacked, iron rack, 11 1/8" h	45.00
Liquid Measure, gray, round	225.00
Muffin Pan, cobalt swirl, 8 cavities	200.00
Roaster, iris swirl, with insert	80.00
Salt Box, hanging, gray	950.00
Soap Dish, emerald swirl, granite insert	200.00
Spittoon, emerald swirl, 2-pc	170.00
Spooner, brown swirl	325.00
Sugar Bowl, cov, gray, tin top	1,000.00
Teapot, cov, gooseneck, emerald swirl, 10" h	1,800.00
Teapot, cov, gooseneck, gray, granite biggin and lid	700.00
Teapot, cov, gooseneck, iris swirl, granite lid with knob finial	750.00

Pitcher, cov, red "Campbell's Tomato Juice" on both sides, 9" h, $100.00. Photo courtesy Collectors Auction Services.

Teapot, cov, gooseneck, onyx, 5" h	125.00
Tea Steeper, cov, lava, granite lid	225.00
Wash Basin, blue swirl, salesman's sample	125.00
Water Pitcher, Chrysolite	600.00
Water Pitcher, light blue swirl	275.00

GREETING CARDS

The modern greeting card originated in the middle of the 15th century in the Rhine Valley of medieval Germany. Printed New Year greetings gained in popularity during the 17th and 18th centuries. Queen Victoria's interest in holiday and special occasion cards helped establish the sending of greeting cards as a regular event.

Louis Prang, a color lithography printer, was one of the first American manufacturers of greeting cards. The post-1945 era witnessed the growth of a number of card manufacturers who eventually would dominate the industry. The Hall Brothers (Joyce C., Rollie, and William), Kansas City postcard distributors and publishers, began printing greeting cards in 1910. Fred Winslow Rust established Rust Craft Company. Cincinnati's Gibson Art Co. entered the greeting card field. Arthur D. and Jane Norcross formed a mutual partnership in 1915.

Although greeting cards are collected primarily by event or occasion, a growing number of collectors seek specialized type cards, e.g., diecut or mechanical. Holiday and specialized collectors represent the principal buyers of greeting cards in the 1990s.

Reference: Ellen Stern, *The Very Best From Hallmark: Greeting Cards Through the Years,* Harry N. Abrams, 1988, out of print.

Note: See Valentines for additional listings.

Advertising, Breyer Ice Cream, Christmas scene, c1920	$20.00
Birthday, front shows Mickey walking Pluto who has wish bone in mouth with "Somebody's Wishing You...," inside "A Happy Birthday and I Don't Mean Mickey!," inside fold-out, Hall Bros, Disney Enterprises	35.00
Birthday, "I'm Happy on Your Birthday," Happy from *Snow White* on front, inside Doc giving Dopey birthday paddling, White & Wyckoff, dated 1938	30.00
Chanukah, emb paper, gilt dec	15.00
Christmas, Bugs Bunny, Dell Comics	40.00
Christmas, Lon Chaney Jr, CS, "With All Best Wishes For A Merry Christmas And A Happy New Year," sgd, Mexican theme design on front and inside, ink signature, 4 1/2 x 5 1/2"	100.00
Christmas, Santa in sleigh on moonlit night being pulled by Hanna-Barbera characters, full color, ©1967, 3 3/8 x 8 1/2"	50.00
Christmas, "Season's Greetings/Philadelphia Athletics," Santa waving pennant at elephant climbing ladder, c1950s, 5 x 7"	75.00
Christmas, mechanical, "The Yule Log," from *Ladies Home Journal,* 2 doors open, hauling log to castle, printed color, Curtis Publishing Co, 1924, 5 x 8 1/4"	20.00
Get Well, Lady and The Tramp, stiff paper, orig envelope, Gibson, 1950s	20.00
Mother's Day, Cracker Jack, diecut, puppy, c1940	45.00
Thanksgiving, family seated at table	5.00
Thanksgiving, feather tail, 1930s	10.00
Thanksgiving, "Happy Thanksgiving," turkey illus	8.00

Christmas, activity card, full color, bi-fold, Sunshine Card, 1960s, $1.00.

Valentine, Blondie and Dagwood, "A Valentine For My Husband In The Service," full color, Hallmark, ©1943, 5 x 5³/₄" **20.00**

Valentine, fold-out, girl's head in heart, flowers with white lace, 1940 . . . . **20.00**

Valentine, mechanical, winter scene, boy on skis **30.00**

GRINDLEY POTTERY

Arthur Grindley and his son, Arthur Grindley, Jr., established the Grindley Artware Manufacturing Co. in Sebring, Ohio, in 1933. The pottery produced novelty items such as banks and figurines, usually in animal form. A fire destroyed the plant in 1947. Although the plant was rebuilt, economic factors prevented the firm from attaining its earlier level of production. The pottery closed its doors in 1952.

Reference: Mike Schneider, *Grindley Pottery*, Schiffer Publishing, 1996.

Figurine, bear, green, 4" h **$15.00**

Figurine, camel, 5³/₈" h **10.00**

Figurine, colt, white with gold highlights, 2¹/₂" h **5.00**

Figurine, cow, 2⁷/₈ x 4¹/₂" **15.00**

Figurine, dog, cobalt blue with gold highlights, 4¹/₂" h **35.00**

Figurine, dog, white with brown spots, 3¹/₂" h **10.00**

Figurine, dog and pup, pink with gold highlights, 1³/₄ x 3¹/₄" **15.00**

Figurine, donkey, Art Deco, blue with gold highlights, 5" h **30.00**

Figurine, Egyptian cat, Art Deco, blue with gold highlights, 6³/₄" h **35.00**

Figurine, giraffe, white with gold highlights, 5³/₈" h **15.00**

Figurine, goat, white with gold highlights, 4¹/₂ x 6" **15.00**

Figurine, grazing horse, 5¹/₂" h **60.00**

Figurine, ox, pink with gold highlights, 2 x 4¹/₄" **10.00**

Figurine, scratching horse, 5¹/₄ x 7" **75.00**

Figurine, work horse, white with gold highlights, 7¹/₂" h **20.00**

Salt and Pepper Shakers, pr, birds, yellow with gold highlights **10.00**

Salt and Pepper Shakers, pr, German shepherds, gold, 3" h **15.00**

Salt and Pepper Shakers, pr, monkeys, blue with gold highlights, 2³/₄" h **10.00**

GRISWOLD

Griswold Manufacturing was founded in the mid-1860s by Matthew Griswold and John and Samuel Selden. Originally the Selden & Griswold Manufacturing Co., Griswold bought out the Selden family interests in 1884. Since then the company has changed hands several times, including being bought by its major competitor, Wagner Manufacturing Co., in 1957. In August 1969, the General Housewares Corp. acquired all rights to Griswold and Wagner. Cast cookware is still being made.

References: *Griswold Cast Iron, Vol. 1* (1993, 2000 value update), *Vol. 2* (1995, 1998 value update), L-W Book Sales; John B. Haussler, *Griswold Muffin Pans,* Schiffer Publishing, 1997; David G. Smith and Charles Wafford, *The Book of Griswold & Wagner: Favorite Piqua, Sidney Hollow Ware, Wapak, 2nd Edition,* Schiffer Publishing, 1999.

Newsletter: *Kettles 'n' Cookware,* PO Box 247, Perrysburg, NY 14129.

Collectors' Club: Griswold & Cast-Iron Cookware Assoc, PO Box 243, Perrysburg, NY 14129.

Apple Cake Pan, #32 . . . . **$40.00**

Bundt Pan **775.00**

Chuckwagon Dutch Oven, #10 . . . . **200.00**

Corn Stick Pan, #262 . . . . **50.00**

Crispy Corn Stick Pan, #273, pattern 930 . . . . **35.00**

Deep Patty Bowl, #72 . . . . **60.00**

Deep Skillet, #8, cov, pattern 777A **120.00**

Dutch Oven, #6, plain cov, black porcelain lining **250.00**

Fat Fryer and Basket, #103 . . . . **75.00**

Fish Baking Dish, #82, oval, red and cream porcelain **125.00**

Fish Skillet, #15, oval **275.00**

Food Chopper, #2 . . . . **20.00**

French Roll Pan, #11, wide band **50.00**

French Waffle Paddles, pr, orig wood handles **125.00**

Gem Pan, #50, Hearts & Star **1,800.00**

Gem Pan, #A802, Hearts & Star **450.00**

Golfball Pan, #9, 10 cup **250.00**

Griddle, #0, handled **900.00**

Griddle, #7, diamond logo **125.00**

Griddle, #8, aluminum, wood handle **15.00**

Grinder with Sausage Stuffer, #3 . . . . **45.00**

Muffin Pan, #8, wide band **45.00**

Muffin Pan, #10 . . . . **40.00**

Popover, #18, 6 cup **40.00**

Skillet, #3 . . . . **20.00**

Skillet, #6 . . . . **45.00**

Skillet, #8 . . . . **20.00**

Skillet, cov, #15, oval **1,000.00**

Skillet Lid, #7, high dome **65.00**

Turk Head Pan, #20, pattern #953 . . . . **225.00**

Vienna Roll Pan, #4 . . . . **125.00**

Vienna Roll Pan, #6, full writing inside cups **135.00**

Waffle Iron, #0 . . . . **2,900.00**

Wheat Stick Pan, #28 . . . . **225.00**

GUNDERSON

Robert Gunderson purchased the Pairpoint Corporation, Boston, Massachusetts, in the late 1930s and operated it as the Gunderson Glass Works until his death in 1952. Operating as Gunderson-Pairpoint, the company continued for only five more years.

In the 1950s, the Gunderson Glass Company produced a wide range of reproduction glassware. Its peachblow-type art glass shades from an opaque faint pink tint to a deep rose.

Robert Bryden attempted a revival of the firm in 1970. He moved the manufacturing operations from the old Mount Washington plant in Boston back to New Bedford.

Pitcher, pink floral dec, mkd "Royal Haeger," 14" h, $12.00.

Compote, Camelia Swirl, bubble ball connector, clear base, bell tone flint, 6" h	$475.00
Compote, Morning Glory, acid finish, 5" h	375.00
Cordial, amberina, set of 10	350.00
Goblet, flared, deep rose stem, 7¼" h	175.00
Hat, Diamond Quilted pattern, satin finish, 3¼" h	150.00
Jug, bulbous, applied white loop handle, acid finish, 4½" h	450.00
Mug, Peachblow, dec, orig paper label, c1970	125.00
Syrup Pitcher, cased, offset handle, 2¾" h	165.00
Tumbler, matte finish, 3¾" h	175.00
Vase, Peachblow, satin, applied ribbon and acorn at neck, 5½" h	250.00

HAEGER POTTERIES

Haeger Potteries was founded by David H. Haeger in Dundee, Illinois in 1871. The first Haeger Art Pottery was produced in 1914. In 1938, Royal Arden Hickman joined the firm and introduced the Royal Haeger line. The following year the Buckeye Pottery Building in Macomb was purchased for the production of florist trade items. That year also saw the formation of the Royal Haeger Lamp Co.

Many Haeger pieces can be identified by molded model numbers. The first Royal Haeger item was assigned the number R01, with subsequent numbers ascending in chronological order.

Numbers found on giftware from the Studio Haeger line, designed by Helen Conover in 1947-48, are preceded by the letter "S." The Royal Garden Flower-ware line, produced from 1954 until 1963, is numbered RG-1 through RG-198, with the lowest numbers found on the earliest examples.

References: David D. Dilley, *Haeger Potteries*, L-W Book Sales, 1997; Joe and Joyce Paradis, *The House of Haeger: 1914-1944*, Schiffer Publishing, 1999.

Collectors' Club: Haeger Pottery Collectors of America, 5021 Toyon Way, Antioch, CA 94509.

Ashtray, #1030, 1950s, 9⅛ x 5½ x 1"	$8.00
Ashtray, #2124, c1970s, 7 x 7 x 2"	50.00
Ashtray, #2145, green leaf with acorns, 1976, 9¾" sq	15.00
Bank, winking dog, #8034, white, 8½" h, 7½" l	85.00
Bookends, pr, R-475, calla lily, amber, 6⅛" h, 4½" l	60.00
Bookends, pr, R-1144, water lily, green with white flowers, c1952, 5 x 5 x 7½"	60.00
Bowl, R-557, chartreuse and silver spray, 15¾" l	30.00
Candleholders, pr, #3004, blue crackle, 5¾ x 3¼ x 1⅜"	25.00
Candleholders, pr, R-1285, lily, 5½ x 3¼ x 5"	15.00

Candy Dish, cov, R-431, lily, chartreuse and yellow, 7½" d	65.00
Cookie Jar, R-188, shell design at top and bottom, rose and blue mottled, 10½" h, 7¼" d	225.00
Creamer, R1582-S, turquoise, c1957, 4¾" h	20.00
Figurine, 502-H, bullfighter, red, 13" h	125.00
Figurine, R-451, mare and foal, c1943, 11" h, 13" l	150.00
Figurine, elephant, chartreuse and honey, 6" h, 8¼" l	40.00
Figurine, fawn, green, c1960, 5½" h, 4½" l	35.00
Figurine, mermaid, gold tweed, 12½" h	65.00
Flower Frog, R-838, figural frog, chartreuse, 3¾" h, 4½" l	75.00
Lamp, #5205, girl on turtle, turquoise, 19" h base	250.00
Lamp, fishing on crest of wave, yellow, 10½" h base	125.00
Lighter, #8054, figural boot, 9¼" h	35.00
Planter, #617, fawn, yellow, c1939, 6½" h, 4¼" d	15.00
Planter, #4200, glossy brown and matte with tan, 5½" h	15.00
Planter, #8008-H, bird, blue crackle, 7¾" h	15.00
Planter, giraffe, ebony cascade, 15¾" h	175.00
Vase, #3220, rooster, white, 14" h	75.00
Vase, #3225, feather plume, blue, 6¼" h	15.00
Vase, #4131, peasant olive, 7" h	10.00
Vase, #4165, peasant orange, black int, 11⅜" h	40.00

HAGEN-RENAKER

John and Maxine Renaker founded the ceramic firm of Hagen-Renaker in Monrovia, California, in 1946. The name Hagen is in honor of Maxine's father, Ole Hagen, who owned the land on which the ceramic factory was built.

Hagen-Renaker was one of dozens of California ceramic manufacturers in the late 1940s and 1950s who specialized in molded porcelain figures, knickknacks, and household accessories. In addition to John and Maxine, company designers included Nell Bortells, Maureen Love Calvert, Helen Perrin Farnlund, Joe Griffith, Tom Masterson, Bill Mintzer, and Bill Nicely.

The "Holy Cow" figurine was the company's first success. A Disney license was acquired in 1955. In 1958 the Little Horribles line was introduced.

After closing for a year between 1960-61 because of Japanese competition, Hagen-Renaker retrenched. In 1962, the company built a new pottery in San Dimas, California. The company's miniature line flourished. In 1997 the company produced two million pieces. Susan Nikas, John and Maxine's daughter, heads the company.

References: Nancy Kelly, *Hagen-Renaker Pottery,* Schiffer Publishing, 2000; Gayle Roller, *The Charlton Standard Catalogue of Hagen-Renaker, 2nd Edition,* Charlton Press, 1999.

Collectors' Club: The Hagen-Renaker Collector's Club, 3651 Polish Line Rd, Cheboygan, MI 49721.

Ballerina, A-403, left leg up, blonde hair, black leotard, gold base, 2½" h	$50.00
Basset Hound Puppy, A-953, running, white, brown, and black, ¾" h	5.00
Camel Baby, A-282, light brown with red fez, Circus Collection, ⅞" h	20.00
Chickadee Baby, A-287, blue, ⅝" h	5.00
Cinderella, #5048, Walt Disney Productions, 2⅝" h	275.00
Crow's Nest, A-393, brown, ⅝" h	10.00
Dachshund Puppy, A-348, seated, red-brown, ⅞" h	5.00
Dodo Bird, #5, black bisque, bright blue-green enamel, 3¼" h	45.00
Heidi's Goat, white, floral dec, 4½" h	45.00
Leghorn Rooster, A-3159, black and white with red comb, 1½" h	5.00
Persian Cat, B-676, lying down, white, green eyes, salmon nose, 5 x 9¾"	100.00
Ribbon Clerk, D-430, Little Horribles, blue, 1¼" h	55.00
Shih-Tzu "Mandy," A-2076, white and black with light blue bow, 1½" h	5.00
Shoe, H-1509A, brown, ½" h	25.00
Siamese Kitten, A-181, on hind legs, 1½" h	15.00
Three-Armed Pete, Little Horribles, green and blue, pink face with black accents, 1⅛" h	55.00
Wise Old Owl, A-883, brown and white with yellow eyes, 1¾" h	8.00

HALL CHINA

In 1903 Robert Hall founded the Hall China Company in East Liverpool, Ohio. Taggert Hall, his son, became president following Robert's death in 1904. The company initially made jugs, toilet sets, and utilitarian whiteware. Robert T. Hall's major contribution to the firm's growth was the development of an economical, single-fire process for lead-free glazed ware.

Hall acquired a new plant in 1930. In 1933 the Autumn Leaf pattern was introduced as a premium for the Jewel Tea Company. Other premium patterns include Blue Bonnett (Standard Coffee Company), Orange Poppy (Great American Tea Company), and Red Poppy (Grand Union Tea Company).

The company launched a decal-decorated dinnerware line in 1933. Hall's refrigerator ware was marketed to the general public along with specific patterns and shapes manufactured for General Electric, Hotpoint, Montgomery Ward, Sears, and Westinghouse.

Hall made a full range of products, from dinnerware to utilitarian kitchenware. Its figural teapots in the shape of Aladdin lamps, automobiles, etc., are eagerly sought by collectors.

Reference: Margaret and Kenn Whitmyer, *The Collector's Encyclopedia of Hall China, Second Edition,* Collector Books, 1994, 1997 value update.

Collectors' Club: Hall Collector's Club, PO Box 360488, Cleveland, OH 44136.

Note: See Autumn Leaf for additional listings.

Blue Blossom, ball jug, #1	$250.00
Blue Blossom casserole, round, #76	40.00
Blue Blossom, jug, Five Band, 1½ pt	50.00
Blue Bouquet, ball jug, #3	80.00
Blue Bouquet, cereal bowl, D-style, 6" d	12.00
Blue Bouquet, creamer, Boston	10.00
Blue Bouquet, custard, thick rim	12.00
Blue Bouquet, leftover, rect	60.00
Blue Bouquet, plate, D-style, 9" d	15.00
Blue Bouquet, sugar, cov, Boston	18.00
Blue Garden, casserole	55.00
Brown Eyed Susan, baker, ftd	20.00
Cameo Rose, creamer	8.00
Cameo Rose, flat soup, 8" d	10.00
Cameo Rose, platter, oval, 11¼" l	15.00
Cameo Rose, tidbit tray, 3-tier	35.00
Carrot, casserole, Radiance	60.00
Century Fern, gravy	12.00
Coffeepot, Amtrak, solid	45.00
Coffeepot, Hollywood, Monterey, green	60.00
Coffeepot, New York, marine blue, 12 cup	40.00
Coffeepot, Orange Poppy, S lid	50.00
Coffeepot, pheasant decal, electric	125.00
Coffeepot, Red Poppy, Daniel	50.00
Coffeepot, Red Poppy, New York	110.00
Coffeepot, Washington, cadet blue, 10 cup	65.00
Crest, minuet coffee server	45.00
Crocus, ball jug	190.00
Crocus, bean pot, New England, #4	100.00
Crocus, cake plate	30.00
Crocus, casserole, cov	60.00
Crocus, cup, St Denis	35.00
Crocus, cup and saucer	18.00
Crocus, French baker, fluted	20.00
Crocus, gravy boat	35.00
Crocus, mixing bowl	50.00
Crocus, plate, 8¼" d	10.00
Crocus, plate, 9" d	12.00
Crocus, plate, 10" d	35.00
Crocus, pretzel jar	200.00
Crocus, soup tureen	425.00
Fantasy, ball jug, #2	100.00
Fantasy, casserole, rayed	45.00
Fantasy, creamer and sugar	75.00
Five Band, casserole, red, 8" d	30.00
Five Band, jug, ivory, 5" h	18.00
Game Bird, casserole, #78, 10" d	40.00
Game Bird, coffee mug	15.00
Game Bird, fruit bowl, 5½" d	8.00
Game Bird, Irish coffee	25.00
Gold Dot, nesting bowls, set of 3	40.00
Golden Glo, bean pot, #4	90.00
Golden Glo, creamer and sugar	50.00
Golden Glo, teapot, sugar, and creamer	125.00

Heather Rose, bowl, 6" d 8.00
Heather Rose, cup and saucer 8.00
Heather Rose, pie baker 20.00
Heather Rose, plate, 9" d 10.00
Heather Rose, tureen, cov 18.00
Homewood, bowl, Radiance, 6" d 12.00
Homewood, salt and pepper shakers, pr, handled. 20.00
Meadow Flowers, casserole, ivory 50.00
Monticello, fruit bowl 8.00
Monticello, platter, oval, 15½" l 18.00
Monticello, vegetable, cov. 25.00
Mount Vernon, cereal bowl, E-style, 6¼" d 6.00
Mount Vernon, sugar, cov, E-style 10.00
Mulberry, berry bowl, 5¾" d 8.00
Mulberry, cereal bowl, 6" d 18.00
Mulberry, salt and pepper shakers, pr. 25.00
Mulberry, vegetable bowl, open, 9" sq 25.00
Mums, cereal bowl, D-style, 6" d 8.00
Mums, cup, D-style. 25.00
Mums, drip jar, open, Kitchenware, #1188 . . . . 35.00
Mums, jug, Kitchenware, Simplicity 30.00
Mums, saucer, D-style. 2.00
New England #4, bean pot, ivory 45.00
No. 488, creamer, New York 18.00
No. 488, drip jar, cov, Radiance 22.00
No. 488, French baker, Kitchenware 20.00
No. 488, leftover, square 70.00
No. 488, shaker, Teardrop 15.00
Orange Poppy, bean pot 115.00
Orange Poppy, bowl, Radiance, 6" d 10.00
Orange Poppy, cake plate 20.00
Orange Poppy, canister, Radiance 275.00
Orange Poppy, casserole, oval, handled 60.00
Orange Poppy, cup, C-style 15.00
Orange Poppy, leftover 75.00
Orange Poppy, plate, 6" d 6.00
Orange Poppy, plate, 9" d 15.00
Orange Poppy, platter, oval, 13" l 20.00
Orange Poppy, salt and pepper shakers, pr 65.00
Orange Poppy, sugar, cov 25.00
Pastel Morning Glory, ball jug, #3 . . . . 75.00
Pastel Morning Glory, bean pot, handled 165.00
Pastel Morning Glory, bowl, oval 40.00
Pastel Morning Glory, cereal bowl, D-style, 6" d 12.00
Pastel Morning Glory, creamer and sugar, D-style 60.00
Pastel Morning Glory, drip jar, cov, Radiance 20.00
Pastel Morning Glory, flat soup 25.00
Pastel Morning Glory, pie baker 25.00
Pastel Morning Glory, plate, 6" d 8.00
Pastel Morning Glory, plate, 7" d 18.00
Pink Rose, teapot, sugar, and creamer 50.00
Primrose, creamer. 7.00
Primrose, jug, Rayed 25.00
Primrose, sugar, cov 15.00
Red Dot, baker, individual, handled. 35.00
Red Dot, bowl, 8¾" d 30.00
Red Dot, cereal bowl, 6" d 20.00
Red Dot, custard. 20.00
Red Poppy, cup and saucer, outside decal 5.00
Red Poppy, platter, large 18.00
Red Poppy, salt and pepper shakers, pr, handled. 18.00
Red Poppy, tumbler. 5.00
Red Poppy, tumbler, frosted 10.00
Red Poppy, vegetable, round 18.00

Rose, casserole, white 35.00
Rose Parade, bean pot, cov 75.00
Rose Parade, casserole, cov 40.00
Rose Parade, drip jar 25.00
Rose Parade, sugar 15.00
Serenade, berry bowl, 5½" d 8.00
Serenade, bowl, Radiance, 7½" d 15.00
Serenade, cup and saucer 15.00
Serenade, fruit bowl, D-style 5.00
Serenade, plate, 9" d 15.00
Serenade, salad bowl, 9" d 25.00
Silhouette, ball jug, #3 . . . . 90.00
Silhouette, bowl, oval, D-style 25.00
Silhouette, mug. 35.00
Silhouette, saucer, St Denis 10.00
Teapot, Airflo, canary yellow, gold trim, 6 cup 85.00
Teapot, Airflo, cobalt, gold trim, 6 cup. 90.00
Teapot, Airflo, orange, gold trim, 6 cup 250.00
Teapot, Albany, cobalt, gold trim, 6 cup 100.00
Teapot, Albany, mahogany, gold trim, 6 cup 65.00
Teapot, Amtrak, solid. 45.00
Teapot, Automobile, turquoise, platinum trim, 6 cup. . . . 650.00
Teapot, Bird Cage, canary yellow. 35.00
Teapot, Boston, canary yellow, 2 cup. 60.00
Teapot, Boston, silver luster, solid. 125.00
Teapot, Boston, yellow, 2 cup 60.00
Teapot, Cleveland, emerald green 70.00
Teapot, Cleveland, yellow 60.00
Teapot, Danielle, light blue, 6 cup 350.00
Teapot, Globe, emerald green 80.00
Teapot, Lipton, black, 6 cup 100.00
Teapot, Los Angeles, canary yellow, 4 cup 50.00
Teapot, Moderne, ivory, gold trim 35.00
Teapot, Murphy, blue, 6 cup 60.00
Teapot, Nautilus, canary yellow, gold trim 110.00
Teapot, New York, black, 2 cup 55.00
Teapot, New York, canary yellow, 2 cup. 65.00
Teapot, Parade, yellow, gold trim, 6 cup. 35.00
Teapot, Philadelphia, black, 6 cup 60.00
Teapot, Philadelphia, pink, 6 cup. 75.00
Teapot, Star, cobalt, gold trim, 6 cup 125.00
Teapot, Star, cobalt, no gold, 6 cup 165.00

Teapot, Connie, green, $60.00.

Wildfire, gravy boat, Ruffled-D shape, #85, 9" l, $25.00. Photo courtesy Ray Morykan Auctions.

Teapot, Star, turquoise, 6 cup	85.00
Teapot, Streamline, blue blossom, 6 cup	550.00
Teapot, Streamline, red	170.00
Teapot, Surfside, cadet blue, 6 cup	275.00
Teapot, Surfside, canary yellow, 6 cup	225.00
Teapot, Windshield, Gold Dot	60.00
Teapot, Windshield, gold trim, 6 cup	65.00
Teapot, Windshield, ivory, gold trim	45.00
Teapot, Windshield, turquoise, gold trim	65.00
Thorley, casserole, grape	25.00
Tri Tone, bean pot	160.00
Tulip, creamer and covered sugar	35.00
Tulip, cup and saucer	15.00
Tulip, fruit bowl, 5½" d	10.00
Tulip, nesting bowls, set of 3	60.00
Tulip, platter, oval, 13¼" l	42.00
Waverly, dripolator, jonquil	35.00
Wildfire, bowl, 5½" d	12.00
Wildfire, bread and butter plate, 6½" d	6.00
Wildfire, coffee server	70.00
Wildfire, creamer and sugar, cov	50.00
Wildfire, cup and saucer	12.00
Wildfire, dessert bowl, small	12.00
Wildfire, French baker	25.00
Wildfire, luncheon plate, 7¼" d	10.00
Wildfire, shaker, teardrop	30.00

HALLMARK

In 1913 brothers Joyce and Rollie Hall launched a firm to sell Christmas cards. The line soon expanded to all types of holiday cards. In January 1913, a fire destroyed their entire stock of valentines. Undaunted, the Halls purchased a Kansas City engraving firm a year later and began printing and marketing Hallmark cards. Within two years, Hallmark cards were sold nationwide.

Following World War II, Hallmark launched a major expansion. In 1948 Norman Rockwell became the first "name" artist to appear on Hallmark cards. Hallmark's Plans-A-Party line was introduced in 1960. Playing cards appeared a year later. Hallmark introduced a Cookie Cutter line in the early 1960s, its Keepsake Christmas Ornament line in 1973, and its Merry Miniature line in 1974.

Hallmark is a leader in preserving its company's heritage. The Hallmark Historical Collection is one of the finest company archives in America.

Reference: *Hallmark Keepsake Ornaments: Secondary Market Price Guide and Collector Handbook, 3rd Edition,* Checker Bee Publishing, 1999.

Periodical: *Twelve Months of Christmas,* PO Box 97172, Pittsburgh, PA 15229.

Note: Prices listed are for ornaments MIB; see Greeting Cards for additional Hallmark listings.

Bell, Mr Ashbourne, #5056, Dickens Caroler Bells series, 1990	$30.00
Cookie Cutter, Goofy head, 1979, 3½" h	8.00
Cookie Cutter, Joan Walsh Anglund, mkd "Wolfpit Enterprises, Inc," 4½" h	10.00
Cookie Cutter, Kermit the Frog, painted dec, Valentine line, 1981	15.00
Figurine, 1938 Lincoln Zephyr, QHG9038, Garton Sidewalk Cruisers series, retired 12/97	95.00
Figurine, 1956 Dragnet Police Car, QHG9016, Garton Kiddie Car Classics, 1994-97	90.00
Figurine, 1958 Atomic Missile, QHG9018, Murray Kiddie Car Classics	100.00
Figurine, 1961 Casey Jones Locomotive, QHG9010, Garton Kiddie Car Classics, 1995-96	90.00
Ornament, 1957 Corvette, #4319, Classic American Cars series, 1991	125.00
Ornament, A Kiss From Santa, #4821, 1988	25.00
Ornament, Bob Cratchit, #4997, A Christmas Carol Collection, 1991	20.00
Ornament, Bright Blazing Colors, #4264, Crayola Crayon series, 1992	25.00
Ornament, Caught Napping, #3411, Cameo series, 1984	20.00
Ornament, Christmas 1973, #1102, Betsy Clark Ball Ornaments series	125.00
Ornament, Christmas Carousel, #1467, Carousel series, 1979	150.00
Ornament, Christmas Time Mime, #4429, 1987	35.00
Ornament, Coca-Cola Ball, #2796, 1986	16.00
Ornament, Dancer Ice Skating, #4809, Reindeer Champs series, 1987	30.00

Ornament, Santa, #500QX1821, Yesteryear Collection, $100.00.

Ornament, Eskimo and Seal, #4409, Frosty Friends
   series, 1987 . . . . **40.00**
Ornament, George Washington Bicentennial, #3862,
   George Washington series, 1989 . . . . **15.00**
Ornament, Heavenly Trumpeter, #4052, 1985 . . . . **60.00**
Ornament, Magical Unicorn, #4293, 1986. . . . . **75.00**
Ornament, Palomino, #4016, Rocking Horse series,
   1986. . . . . **60.00**
Ornament, Santa's Motor Car, #1559, Here Comes Santa
   series, 1979. . . . . **550.00**
Ornament, Snoopy & Woodstock, #4391, 1984 . . . . **90.00**
Ornament, Victorian Doll House, #4481, Nostalgia
   Houses and Shops series, 1984 . . . . **175.00**

HALLOWEEN

Halloween collectors divide material into pre- and post-1945
objects. Country of origin—Germany, Japan, or the United
States—appears to make little difference. Image is everything. The
survival rate of Halloween collectibles is extremely high.
Currently, Halloween is second only to Christmas in respect to
popularity among holiday collectors.

References: Pamela E. Apkarian-Russell, *Collectible Halloween*
(1997), *More Halloween Collectibles* (1998), *Halloween:
Collectible Decorations and Games* (2000), Schiffer Publishing;
Dan and Pauline Campanelli, *Halloween Collectibles,* L-W Books,
1995; Charlene Pinkerton, *Halloween Favorites in Plastic,* Schiffer
Publishing, 1998; Stuart Schneider, *Halloween in America,* Schiffer
Publishing, 1995.

Newsletters: *Boo News,* PO Box 143, Brookfield, IL 60513; *Trick
or Treat Trader,* PO Box 499, Winchester, NH 03470.

Blotter, Whitinsville Savings Bank, MA, "In the night
   time all cats are black," 1926. . . . . **$15.00**
Candy Container, jack-o-lantern, hard plastic, Rosbro,
   2½" d **35.00**
Candy Container, witch in rocket, Kokomold,1950s, 4 x
   5½" **375.00**
Costume, mummy, vinyl, 1-pc, molded plastic mask,
   Ben Cooper, 8¼ x 11 x 3" orig box **20.00**
Costume, Shari Lewis' Charlie Horse, rayon, 1-pc, mold-
   ed plastic mask, size medium, Halco, ©1961 Tarcher
   Productions, Inc, 9 x 11 x 3½" orig box **20.00**
Decoration, skeleton playing guitar, Beistle, 14" h. **20.00**
Decoration, witch on flying saucer, cardboard and tissue
   paper, orange, black, and white repeated image on
   each side, opens to 360 degrees to form honeycomb
   flying saucer, 1950s, 10 x 11" **75.00**
Figure, bisque, hollow, painted, orange pumpkin head,
   red smile, unfinished white bisque eyeballs dotted in
   black, black top hat and shoe tips, green suit, c1930s,
   3" h **25.00**
Figure, black cat, celluloid, hollow, arched back design,
   vintage orange fabric ribbon on neck, 1930s, 1 x 2½
   x 4" **45.00**
Figure, cat holding pumpkin, orange and black, Rosbro,
   1950s, 5" h. **90.00**
Glasses, bat shaped, Foster Grant, 1950s **90.00**
Hanger Card, emb diecut cardboard, 2 mice on crescent
   moon face with frightened cat, c1930-40s, 8 x 10" **45.00**

**Hanger Card,
emb cardboard,
black, orange,
and white, 1930s,
6 x 6½", $18.00**

Lantern, clown, papier-mâché, inset paper eyes and
   mouth, wire handle, early 20th C, 2¾" h **750.00**
Lantern, devil's head, papier-mâché, early 20th C, 2½" h . . . **450.00**
Lantern, owl, painted tin, c1935, 5½" h **40.00**
Lantern, pumpkin head, wire bail handle,
   Union Products, early 1950s, 4" d **50.00**
Noisemaker, cymbals, litho tin, black witch, owl, and
   cat on orange ground, 1940s, 5½" d. **35.00**
Nut Cup, basket, witch on handle, Best Plastics **10.00**
Pinback Button, "Bradley's Pumpkin Pie," orange and
   black jack-o-lantern, 1930s **50.00**
Postcard, real photo, children dressed in costumes **175.00**
Sucker Holder, black cat, 1950s, 3½" h **35.00**
Toy, Halloween Jumping Jack, E Rosen, 1961, 5¾" h. **100.00**
Wall Decoration, owl in moon, emb paperboard,
   German, 18" h **35.00**
Whistle, witch on wheels, Tico Toys/Rosbro, early 1950s. **75.00**

HALPERN, LEA

Lea Halpern studied ceramics in Amsterdam, Germany, and
Vienna in the 1920s. During the 1930s she exhibited in Holland
and London. In 1939 she came to New York to exhibit at the
Rockefeller Plaza. When World War II broke out, she remained in
the United States and eventually settled here.

Halpern's work is distinguished by its simple forms and com-
plexity of glazing. Major retrospectives of her work were held in
1974 at the Frans Halzmuseum in Haarlem, Holland and in 1975
at the Baltimore Museum of Art. Her work is in the collections of
museums ranging from the Metropolitan Museum of Art to the
Victoria and Albert Museum.

In June 1999, William Doyle Galleries offered at auction a large
block of Halpern's ceramics.

Vase, "Autumn," tapering cylindrical form, iridescent
   gray glaze, sgd, numbered "940," paper labels, 5¼" h. . . **$800.00**
Vase, "Firmament," spherical, streaked gray and tan
   glaze, sgd, titled, paper labels, 8½" h **4,500.00**
Vase, "Gobi Desert," swollen cylindrical form, orange
   and brown glaze, sgd, titled, paper labels, 8½" h **3,400.00**
Vase, "Mediterranean," cylindrical, turquoise glaze, sgd,
   paper labels, 11" h **1,100.00**

Vase, "Solitude," matte gray craquelé glaze, sgd, paper labels, 11¹/₂" h, $3,565.00. Photo courtesy William Doyle Galleries.

Vase, "Rock of Ages," ovoid, dark brown glaze, paper labels, 5³/₄" h **925.00**

Vase, "Sea Nymph," cylindrical, light green craquelé glaze, sgd, titled, paper labels, 7¹/₂" h **3,325.00**

Vase, Untitled, cylindrical, bright blue glaze, sgd, paper labels, 4¹/₄" h **850.00**

Vase, Untitled, globular with flaring rim, mottled yellow and brown glaze, sgd, paper labels, 5" h **225.00**

Vase, Untitled, ovoid, gray craquelé glaze, sgd, paper labels, 9" h **1,725.00**

Vase, Untitled, ovoid with flaring rim, gray-green glaze, sgd, paper labels, 8¹/₄" h **1,100.00**

Vase, Untitled, shaped cylindrical form, brown and white craquelé glaze, sgd, paper labels, 6¹/₂" h **700.00**

Vase, Untitled, spherical, white and light green volcanic glaze, sgd, 12¹/₂" h **3,150.00**

Vase, "Wings of Crete," flaring cylindrical form, triangular buttress handles, green volcanic glaze, sgd, titled, paper labels, 9¹/₂" h **1,150.00**

Vase, "Woodbine," ovoid with flaring neck, sang de boeuf and aventurine glaze, sgd, numbered "704," paper labels, 8³/₄" h **800.00**

HANNA-BARBERA

William Denby Hanna was born on July 14, 1910, in Melrose, New Mexico. A talent for drawing landed him a job at the Harman-Ising animation studio in 1930. Hanna worked there for seven years.

Joseph Roland Barbera was born in New York City in 1911. After a brief stint as a magazine cartoonist, Barbera joined the Van Beuren studio in 1932 where he helped animate and script Tom and Jerry.

In 1938 Hanna and Barbera were teamed together. Their first project was Gallopin' Gals. By 1939 the two were permanently paired, devoting much of their energy to Tom and Jerry shorts.

Twenty years after joining MGM, Hanna and Barbera struck out on their own. Their goal was to develop cartoons for television as well as theatrical release. The success of Huckleberry Hound and

Yogi Bear paved the way for The Flintstones, one of the most successful television shows of the 1960s.

In 1966 Taft Communications purchased Hanna-Barbera Productions for a reported 26 million dollars. Hanna and Barbera continued to head the company.

Hanna-Barbera Productions produced over 100 cartoon series and specials. In several cases, a single series produced a host of well-loved cartoon characters. Some of the most popular include Atom Ant, Auggie Doggie and Doggie Daddy, The Flintstones, Huckleberry Hound, The Jetsons, Jonny Quest, Magilla Gorilla, Peter Potamus, Penelope Pitstop, Quick Draw McGraw, Ricochet Rabbit, Ruff and Reddy, Space Ghost, Top Cat, and Yogi Bear.

References: Joseph Barbera, *My Life in 'Toons: From Flatbush to Bedrock in Under a Century,* Turner Publishing, 1994; Debra S. Braun, *The Flintstones Collectibles,* Schiffer Publishing, 2000; Bill Hanna, *A Cast of Friends,* Taylor Publishing, 1996; David Longest, *Cartoon Toys & Collectibles,* Collector Books, 1999.

Atom Ant, comic book, Gold Key #1, 1965 . . . . **$50.00**

Flintstones, ashtray, ceramic, Fred and Wilma dancing, Fred's name at upper right, Wilma's name at middle right, 4 rests, Arrow Houseware Products, Chicago, IL, ©1961 Hanna-Barbera Prod, 5¹/₂ x 8¹/₄ x 1" **45.00**

Flintstones, badge, color image of smiling Fred, black text "Yabba-Dabba-Doo Kelowna B.C. Bedrock City," 3¹/₂" d **10.00**

Flintstones, bank, ceramic, Fred and Wilma holding hands against cave wall background, "Fred Loves Wilma" incised in heart on reverse, 1960s, 4³/₄ x 6 x 8¹/₄" **175.00**

Flintstones, dinnerware set, white melmac, 5¹/₄" d bowl, 7³/₄" plate, and 3⁵/₈" h cup, 1960s **20.00**

Flintstones, doll, Bamm Bamm, orig box, Ideal, 1962 . . . . **75.00**

Flintstones, Drive Log Car, friction, plastic, Fred at wheel, Marx, #5333, ©1977 Hanna-Barbera, 3⁵/₈ x 3⁵/₈ x 5³/₈" orig box **75.00**

Flintstones, figures, TV-Tinykins, set of 8, hp plastic, Marx, ©1961 Hanna-Barbera Prod, each in orig 1 x 1³/₈ x 2¹/₄" box **75.00**

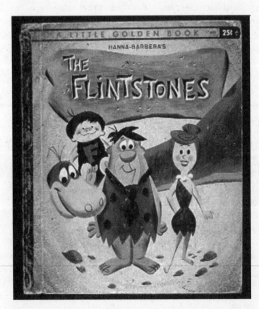

Flintstones, Little Golden Book, *The Flintstones,* #450, 1961, $15.00.

Yogi Bear, soaky bottle, Purex, 1960s, $25.00.

Flintstones, Fuzzy Felt Stick-On Fabric Set, Standard Toykraft #221, ©1961 Hanna-Barbera Prod, 8³/₈ x 13¹/₄ x 1¹/₄" orig box. **75.00**

Flintstones, game, The Flintstones Hoppy the Hopparoo, Transogram, 1965 . . . . **60.00**

Flintstones, game, The Flintstones Stone Age Game, Transogram #3843, 1961, 9 x 17¹/₂ x 1³/₄" orig box **40.00**

Flintstones, hassock, stuffed, plush fabric top, vinyl bottom, Knickerbocker, ©1961 Hanna-Barbera Prod, 11¹/₂" h, 12" d **75.00**

Flintstones, lamp, hard vinyl, figural Fred against simulated rocks standing on litho tin base, 9¹/₂" h **75.00**

Flintstones, paper dolls, Pebbles and Bamm-Bamm, Whitman, #1983, 10 x 13" **50.00**

Flintstones, pinback button, Fred in black, gray, and red, light orange facial accents, yellow ground, red lettering "Fred Flintstone Yabadabadoo," 1960s, 1" d **25.00**

Flintstones, playset, hard molded plastic, complete with character figures and accessories, "Another great Magic Marxie Toy," Marx, #4672 . . . . **400.00**

Flintstones, push puppet, Wilma, red hair, wearing white skirt, on blue base, silver foil sticker #3991, Kohner Bros, c1960s, 3⁷/₈" h **75.00**

Flintstones, salt and pepper shakers, pr, bisque, Bamm-Bamm salt and Pebbles pepper, dark green base, Dino attached at center, foil sticker "Flintstones Bedrock City, Custer, South Dakota," 2 x 5¹/₄ x 4¹/₂" **100.00**

Grape Ape, drawing slate, Super Slate Fun With Grape Ape, Rand McNally, #H5102, ©1972 Hanna-Barbera Prod, 8¹/₄ x 11" **15.00**

Grape Ape, game, The Great Grape Ape, Milton Bradley #4607, 1975, 8 x 15¹/₂ x 1¹/₄" orig box **20.00**

Huckleberry Hound, game, Huckleberry Hound Western Game, Milton Bradley, #4017, 1959, 8¹/₂ x 16¹/₂ x 1¹/₈" orig box. **50.00**

Huckleberry Hound, gloves, red cotton/acetate, smiling Huck in center, attached silver accent plastic ring with black top and gold image of smiling Mr Jinx, Boss, #853, ©1959 Hanna-Barbera Prod, MOC. **45.00**

Quick Draw McGraw, game, Quick Draw McGraw Private Eye Game, Milton Bradley, 1960-61 . . . . **25.00**

Quick Draw McGraw, jigsaw puzzle, Whitman Jr, #301, ©1960 Hanna-Barbera Prod, 6³/₄ x 9¹/₄ x 1³/₄" orig box **20.00**

Scooby Doo, cookie cutter, Hallmark, 1978. . . . . **5.00**

Scooby Doo, drawing slate, Super Slate Fun With Scooby Doo, Rand McNally, #H5101, ©1972 Hanna-Barbera Prod, 8¹/₄ x 11". **15.00**

Secret Squirrel, frame tray puzzle, Whitman, #4559, ©1967 Hanna-Barbera Prod, 11¹/₄ x 14¹/₂" orig box **20.00**

Squiddly Diddly, soaky, Squiddly Diddly Bubble Club, vinyl, full figure, arms folded, wearing white hat, orange vest, name incised on base, Purex, 1960s, 6³/₄" h **75.00**

Top Cat, costume, Ben Cooper, #848, c1970, 8¹/₂ x 11 x 2¹/₂" orig box. **50.00**

Yogi Bear, activity book, *Boo Boo Bear Featuring Yogi Bear*, with cut-out sticker pictures, Golden Funtime Stickum Book, Golden Press, 1961, 7¹/₄ x 13". **50.00**

Yogi Bear, book, *Yogi Bear A Christmas Visit*, Big Golden Book #10357, 1st edition, 24 color pp, illus by Sylvia and Burnett Mattinson, 1961, 9¹/₄ x 12¹/₂" **20.00**

Yogi Bear, cereal box, OKs Cereal, image of Yogi making muscles with photo of cereal bowl in foreground, ©1963 Kellogg Co, 2¹/₂ x 7 x 9³/₄". **200.00**

Yogi Bear, cookie jar, ceramic, smiling full figure Yogi, name incised on front of hat, "Better Than Average Cookies" incised on front of sign on simulated tree stump, American Bisque, 1961, 5 x 6¹/₂ x 13¹/₂". **175.00**

Yogi Bear, costume, vinyl, molded vinyl mask, size medium, Ben Cooper, ©1974 Hanna-Barbera Prod, 8¹/₄ x 11 x 2⁵/₈" orig box. **20.00**

Yogi Bear, doll, stuffed, plush body, soft vinyl face, felt hat and tie, Kellogg's cereal premium, ©1959, 17¹/₂" h **75.00**

Yogi Bear, pinback button, red, black, and yellow on yellow ground, "Hey There, It's Yogi Bear," Hanna-Barbera copyright on rim curl, c1960, 1" d **25.00**

Yogi Bear, squeeze toy, vinyl, Dell, #81005, 1960s, MOC. . . . **20.00**

HARKER POTTERY

Harker Pottery Co., founded as Harker, Taylor and Co. in 1840, manufactured a wide range of products, beginning with doorknobs, toys, and ceramic hearth and table top tiles. Production soon included Rockingham and yellow wares. In 1879, the company began manufacturing white ironstone toilet wares, tea sets, and dinnerware. A shift to semi-porcelain ware was made in 1890.

By 1931 vitreous hotel ware, toilet sets, advertising novelties, and kitchen and dinnerware lines were produced. Notable patterns include Amy, Cameo Ware, Red Apple, White Clover (designed by Russel Wright), and White Rose.

The Jeannette Glass Company purchased Harker Pottery in 1969. It made reproduction Rebekah-at-the-Well teapots and Toby jugs. Harker ceased operations in 1972.

References: Susan and Al Bagdade, *Warman's American Pottery and Porcelain*, Wallace-Homestead, 1994; Harvey Duke, *The Official Price Guide to Pottery and Porcelain, Eighth Edition*, House of Collectibles, 1995.

Newsletter: *The Harker Arrow*, 69565 Crescent Rd, St Clairsville, OH 43950.

Amy, bread and butter plate, 6" d.	$3.00
Amy, cake lifter	10.00
Amy, casserole, cov.	25.00
Amy, dinner plate	10.00
Amy, serving spoon	10.00
Cactus, pie baker	15.00
Cactus, rolling pin	10.00
Cactus, utility plate, Virginia	15.00
Ivy Wreath, creamer and sugar	20.00
Ivy Wreath, dinner plate	10.00
Ivy Wreath, platter	15.00
Mallow, creamer, cov, paneled sides	10.00
Mallow, custard cup	5.00
Mallow, mixing bowl	25.00
Modern Tulip, custard cup, Zephyr	5.00
Modern Tulip, pie baker, Modern Age	15.00
Modern Tulip, utility cup, Zephyr	8.00
Monterey, casserole	25.00
Monterey, coffeepot, cov	50.00
Monterey, luncheon plate	6.00
Red Apple I, batter jug	20.00
Red Apple I, bowl, Zephyr	6.00
Red Apple I, mixing bowl	20.00
Red Apple I, utility bowl, Zephyr	6.00
Red Apple I, utility plate, Virginia	25.00
Red Apple II, salt and pepper shakers, pr, Modern Age	20.00
Red Apple II, teapot, cov, Zephyr	30.00
Red Apple II, utility plate, Virginia	25.00
Rosemere, bread and butter plate, 6¼" d	2.00
Rosemere, casserole	20.00
Rosemere, cup and saucer	5.00
Rosemere, plate, 9" d	8.00
Rosemere, platter, 11" l	10.00
Royal Gadroon, bread and butter plate, 6¼" d	2.00
Royal Gadroon, casserole	20.00
Royal Gadroon, creamer and sugar	12.00
Royal Gadroon, onion soup bowl	8.00
Royal Gadroon, plate, 8¼" sq	6.00
Royal Gadroon, salad bowl, 10½" d	15.00
Royal Gadroon, soup bowl, 8½" d	10.00
Royal Gadroon, tidbit tray, 3-tier	15.00

Royal Gadroon, vegetable, oval, 9" l	10.00
Vine Lace, bread and butter plate, 6" d	5.00
Vine Lace, cup and saucer	10.00
Vine Lace, dinner plate	10.00
Vine Lace, luncheon plate	8.00
Vine Lace, vegetable, divided	5.00
White Clover, bread and butter plate, 6" d	5.00
White Clover, casserole, cov, 2 qt	45.00
White Clover, cereal bowl, 5" d	6.00
White Clover, chop plate, 10" d	12.00
White Clover, fruit dish	4.00
White Clover, jug, cov, 2 qt	50.00
White Clover, plate, 10" d	10.00
White Clover, platter, 13¼" l	20.00
White Clover, sugar, cov	15.00
White Clover, vegetable, 7¼" d	20.00
Wood Song, bread and butter plate, 6¼" d	2.00
Wood Song, butter, ¼ lb	20.00
Wood Song, creamer	5.00
Wood Song, cup and saucer	5.00
Wood Song, plate, 9" d	8.00
Wood Song, sugar, cov	8.00
Wood Song, teapot, cov	25.00
Zephyr, au gratin	20.00
Zephyr, bowl, 7" d	10.00
Zephyr, casserole, 1½ qt	20.00
Zephyr, cheese tray, round	12.00
Zephyr, coffeepot, 6 cup	30.00
Zephyr, teapot, cov, white, cottage by sea decal	35.00

HARTLAND FIGURES

Hartland Plastics, located in southern Wisconsin, produced a series of sport and western figures between 1953 and the early 1960s. These painted acetate plastic figures came with removable accessories.

Western figures ranged from generic figures, e.g., Western Champ, to licensed figures, e.g., The Lone Ranger and Wyatt Earp. Hartland occasionally used the same mold for more than one character, e.g., #804 for St. Preston and Sgt. Lance O'Rourke and #817 for Jim Bowie and Davy Crockett. A different paint scheme, accessories, and packaging distinguished one from the other.

The sports series contains thirty different football players (a generic offensive and defensive player for each of the fourteen NFL teams at the time plus two personality figures) and eighteen baseball players (eighteen personality figures and a bat boy).

In 1989 Hartland reissued all nineteen baseball figures in a twenty-fifth anniversary edition. They are identified by a "25" in a circle located on their back just below the belt.

References: Gail Fitch, *Hartland Horsemen*, Schiffer Publishing, 1999; Elizabeth Stephan (ed.), *O'Brien's Collecting Toys, 9th Edition*, Krause Publications, 1999.

Note: Unless noted otherwise, prices are for mint condition figures with original mint conditon tag and/or box.

Annie Oakley, #823	$525.00
Babe Ruth, #911	400.00
Bat Masterson, #769	900.00
Bill Longley, #827	1,400.00
Bret Maverick, #762	475.00
Buffalo Bill Cody, #819	850.00

Colonial Lady, mixing bowl with pour spout, $25.00.

Cactus Pete, #612 . . . . **500.00**
Chief Brave Eagle, #812 . . . . **575.00**
Chief Thunderbird, #813, on semi-rearing horse **700.00**
Chris Colt, #761 . . . . **525.00**
Clay Hollister, #763 . . . . **600.00**
Cleveland Browns, lineman **450.00**
Colonel Randal MacKenzie, #829 . . . . **1,750.00**
Dale Evans, #802, green outfit **475.00**
Dallas Cowboys, lineman **400.00**
Dan Troop, #767 . . . . **875.00**
Davy Crockett, #817 . . . . **825.00**
Dizzy Dean **320.00**
Duke Snider, #921 . . . . **1,275.00**
Eddie Mathews, #913 . . . . **475.00**
General Custer, #814 . . . . **400.00**
George Washington, #815 . . . . **750.00**
Gil Favor, #831, on semi-rearing horse **1,325.00**
Hoby Gilman, #825 . . . . **575.00**
Jim Bowie, #817 . . . . **625.00**
Jim Hardie, #764 . . . . **550.00**
Johnny McKay, #768 . . . . **1,400.00**
Johnny Unitas **725.00**
Josh Randall, #828 . . . . **1,550.00**
Kid Commanche, #613 . . . . **500.00**
Lance O'Rourke, #804 . . . . **825.00**
Lone Ranger and Silver, #801, with chaps **500.00**
Lou Gehrig **325.00**
Lucas McCain, #826 . . . . **700.00**
Matt Dillon, #822 . . . . **550.00**
Mickey Mantle, #910 . . . . **875.00**
Minnesota Vikings, lineman **425.00**
Paladin, #766 . . . . **900.00**
Philadelphia Eagles, running back **475.00**
Rebel, #832 . . . . **1,425.00**
Rin Tin Tin, #700 . . . . **125.00**
Robert E Lee, #808 . . . . **400.00**
Roy Rogers, #806, on rearing horse **1,050.00**
Sgt Preston, #804 . . . . **1,375.00**
Tom Jeffords, #821 . . . . **425.00**
Ty Cobb **1,100.00**
Vint Bonner, #765 . . . . **1,350.00**
Whitey Ford **150.00**
Willie Mays, #918 . . . . **750.00**
Wyatt Earp, #709 . . . . **600.00**
Yogi Berra, #917 . . . . **500.00**

HAVILAND CHINA

There are several Haviland companies. It takes a detailed family tree to understand the complex family relationships that led to their creations.

David and Daniel Haviland, two brothers, were New York china importers. While on a buying trip to France in the early 1840s, David Haviland decided to remain in that country. He brought his family to Limoges where he supervised the purchase, design, and decoration of pieces sent to America. In 1852, Charles Field Haviland, David's nephew, arrived in France to learn the family business. Charles married into the Alluaud family, owner of the Casseaux works in Limoges. Charles Edward and Theodore Haviland, David's sons, entered the firm in 1864. A difference of opinion in 1891 led to the liquidation of the old firm and the establishment of several independent new ones. [Editor's note: I told you it was complicated.]

Today, Haviland generally means ceramics made at the main Casseaux works in Limoges. Charles Edward produced china under the name Haviland et Cie between 1891 and the early 1920s. Theodore Haviland's La Porcelaine Theodore Haviland was made from 1891 until 1952.

References: Harry L. Rinker, *Dinnerware of the 20th Century: The Top 500 Patterns,* House of Collectibles, 1997; Arlene Schleiger, *Two Hundred Patterns of Haviland China, Books I-VI,* now published by Dona L. Schleiger; Nora Travis, *Haviland China,* Schiffer Publishing, 1997, 1998 value update.

Collectors' Club: Haviland Collectors Internationale Foundation, PO Box 802462, Santa Clarita, CA 91380.

Autumn Leaf, bread and butter plate, 6³/₈" d **$18.00**
Autumn Leaf, cup and saucer, ftd, 2" h **35.00**
Autumn Leaf, dinner plate, 11¹/₄" d **30.00**
Autumn Leaf, fruit bowl, 5" d **20.00**
Autumn Leaf, gravy boat, attached underplate **135.00**
Autumn Leaf, luncheon plate, 8⁵/₈" d **25.00**
Autumn Leaf, platter, oval, 16" l **135.00**
Autumn Leaf, salad plate, 7¹/₂" d **20.00**
Autumn Leaf, soup bowl, flat, 7⁷/₈" d **25.00**
Autumn Leaf, sugar, cov **75.00**
Autumn Leaf, vegetable, cov, oval, 9¹/₂" l **80.00**
Delaware, bread and butter plate, 6³/₈" d **15.00**
Delaware, cream soup and saucer **45.00**
Delaware, cup and saucer, flat, 2¹/₈" h **35.00**
Delaware, demitasse cup and saucer **30.00**
Delaware, fruit bowl, 5¹/₈" d **18.00**
Delaware, gravy boat, attached underplate **125.00**
Delaware, luncheon plate, 8³/₄" d **25.00**
Delaware, platter, oval, 11⁵/₈" l **75.00**
Delaware, salad plate, 7¹/₂" d **20.00**
Delaware, sugar, cov **60.00**
Delaware, vegetable, oval, 9⁵/₈" l **75.00**

Delaware, dinner plate, $30.00

Montmery, bouillon cup and saucer	**40.00**
Montmery, bread and butter plate, 6³/₈" d	**20.00**
Montmery, butter, cov, round	**100.00**
Montmery, cereal bowl, 6¹/₄" d	**25.00**
Montmery, cream soup and saucer	**60.00**
Montmery, dinner plate	**35.00**
Montmery, fruit bowl, 5" d	**25.00**
Montmery, gravy boat, attached underplate	**175.00**
Montmery, platter, oval, 11¹/₄" l	**95.00**
Montmery, salad plate, 7¹/₂" d	**25.00**
Montmery, soup bowl, coupe, 7¹/₂" d	**30.00**
Montmery, sugar, cov	**80.00**
Montmery, vegetable, cov, oval	**250.00**
Pasadena, bread and butter plate, 6¹/₂" d	**15.00**
Pasadena, coffeepot, cov	**185.00**
Pasadena, cream soup and saucer	**45.00**
Pasadena, cup and saucer, ftd, 2¹/₄" h	**37.00**
Pasadena, demitasse cup and saucer	**30.00**
Pasadena, dinner plate	**27.00**
Pasadena, fruit bowl, 5" d	**20.00**
Pasadena, gravy boat, attached underplate	**135.00**
Pasadena, platter, oval, 11⁵/₈" l	**80.00**
Pasadena, salad plate, 7⁵/₈" d	**20.00**
Pasadena, soup bowl, flat, 7⁷/₈" d	**30.00**
Pasadena, sugar, cov	**75.00**
Pasadena, vegetable, cov, round	**200.00**
Princess, bouillon cup and saucer	**40.00**
Princess, bread and butter plate, 6¹/₄" d	**18.00**
Princess, butter, round, no lid	**75.00**
Princess, cranberry bowl, 5⁵/₈" d	**75.00**
Princess, cup and saucer, flat, 2¹/₈" d	**35.00**
Princess, demitasse cup and saucer, 2¹/₄" h	**35.00**
Princess, dinner plate, 9³/₄" d	**35.00**
Princess, fruit bowl, flat, 5¹/₈" d	**18.00**
Princess, gravy boat, attached underplate	**135.00**
Princess, luncheon plate, 8⁵/₈" d	**20.00**
Princess, nut dish, 5³/₄" d	**30.00**
Princess, platter, oval, 12¹/₈" l	**100.00**
Princess, salad plate, 7¹/₂" d	**20.00**
Princess, soup bowl, flat, 7¹/₂" d	**30.00**
Princess, sugar, cov, 3¹/₈" d	**80.00**
Princess, vegetable, cov, round	**20.00**
Rosalinde, France, bread and butter plate, 6¹/₂" d	**20.00**
Rosalinde, France, coffeepot, cov	**200.00**
Rosalinde, France, cup and saucer, flat, 2" h	**20.00**
Rosalinde, France, demitasse cup	**40.00**
Rosalinde, France, dinner plate, 10¹/₂" d	**40.00**
Rosalinde, France, fruit bowl, 5" d	**30.00**
Rosalinde, France, gravy boat, attached underplate	**200.00**
Rosalinde, France, platter, oval, 13³/₄" l	**135.00**
Rosalinde, France, salad plate, 7⁵/₈" d	**25.00**
Rosalinde, France, soup bowl, coupe, 7¹/₂" d	**35.00**
Rosalinde, France, sugar, cov	**80.00**
Rosalinde, France, vegetable, oval, 9¹/₂" l	**100.00**
Varenne, bread and butter plate, 6¹/₂" d	**18.00**
Varenne, chop plate, 12³/₄" d	**135.00**
Varenne, cream soup and saucer	**50.00**
Varenne, cup and saucer, flat, 2¹/₈" h	**35.00**
Varenne, demitasse cup and saucer	**35.00**
Varenne, dinner plate, 9³/₄" d	**30.00**
Varenne, fruit bowl, 5¹/₈" d	**20.00**
Varenne, gravy boat, attached underplate	**135.00**
Varenne, luncheon plate, 8³/₄" d	**25.00**
Varenne, platter, oval, 11⁵/₈" l	**100.00**

Varenne, soup bowl, coupe, 7¹/₂" d	**35.00**
Varenne, sugar, cov	**75.00**
Varenne, vegetable, round, 10" d	**100.00**

HAZEL ATLAS GLASSWARE

Hazel Atlas resulted from the 1902 merger of the Hazel Glass Company and the Atlas Glass and Metal Company, each located in Washington, Pennsylvania. The company's main offices were located in Wheeling, West Virginia.

The company was a pioneer in automated glassware manufacture. A factory in Clarksburg, West Virginia, specialized in pressed glassware and achieved a reputation in the late 1920s as the "World's Largest Tumbler Factory." Two factories in Zanesville, Ohio, made containers, thin-blown tumblers, and other blown ware. Washington and Wheeling plants made containers and tableware, the latter including many of the Depression-era patterns for which the company is best known among collectors.

Continental Can purchased Hazel-Atlas in 1956. Brockway Glass Company purchased the company in 1964.

References: Gene Florence, *Collectible Glassware From the 40s, 50s, 60s...*, *Fifth Edition*, Collector Books, 2000; Gene Florence, *Kitchen Glassware of the Depression Years, Fifth Edition*, Collector Books, 1995, 1999 value update.

Note: See Depression Glass for additional listings.

Cloverleaf, creamer and sugar, black	**$18.00**
Cloverleaf, cup and saucer, black	**25.00**
Cloverleaf, sherbet, green	**10.00**
Criss Cross, bowl, cov, 5¹/₄" d, crystal	**150.00**
Criss Cross, butter, ¼ lb, blue	**150.00**
Criss Cross, creamer, crystal	**40.00**
Criss Cross, lemon reamer, pink	**325.00**
Criss Cross, orange reamer, blue	**300.00**

Criss Cross, refrigerator dish, cov, 4" sq, crystal, $10.00. Photo courtesy Ray Morykan Auctions.

Dots, tumblers, 3⁵/₈" h and 3" h, Capri blue, price each, $7.00. Photo courtesy Ray Morykan Auctions.

Criss Cross, orange reamer, pink 250.00
Criss Cross, refrigerator dish, 3¹/₂ x 5³/₄", blue 175.00
Criss Cross, refrigerator dish, 4" sq, blue. 65.00
Dots, bowl, 4⁷/₈" d, Capri blue. 8.00
Dots, bowl, 6" d, Capri blue 8.00
Dots, candy, cov, Capri blue 30.00
Dots, cup and saucer, Capri blue. 8.00
Dots, sherbet, Capri blue. 5.00
Dots, tumbler, 4" h, Capri blue 6.00
Dots, tumbler, 5¹/₄" h, Capri blue 7.00
Dots, tumbler, 6" h, Capri blue 8.00
Dots, vase, 8" h, Capri blue 25.00
Florentine #1, ashtray, 5³/₄" h, green 30.00
Florentine #1, creamer, green 15.00
Florentine #1, cup and saucer, green 18.00
Florentine #1, dinner plate, 9³/₄" d, green 25.00
Florentine #1, grill plate, 9³/₄" d, green 18.00
Florentine #1, luncheon plate, 8" d, green 14.00
Florentine #1, nappy, 9" d, green 35.00
Florentine #1, nut bowl, ruffled handle, pink 25.00
Florentine #1, pitcher, ftd, 36 oz, 6¹/₂" h, green. 45.00
Florentine #1, pitcher, straight sided, 48 oz, 7" h, green 85.00
Florentine #1, platter, 11¹/₂" l, green 25.00
Florentine #1, shaker, green. 42.00
Florentine #1, sherbet plate, 6" d, green 12.00
Florentine #1, sugar, cov, green 40.00
Florentine #1, tumbler, ftd, 5 oz, 3³/₄" h, green 20.00
Florentine #1, vegetable, oval, 9¹/₂" l, green 30.00
Fruits, cup, green 10.00
Hobnails, cup, round 5.00
Hobnails, dinner plate, 9⁷/₈" d 10.00
Hobnails, salad bowl, 5³/₈" d 8.00
Hobnails, salad plate, 7¹/₄" d 6.00
Hobnails, saucer, 6" d 2.00
Moderntone, berry bowl, 5" d, Platonite on pink 3.00
Moderntone, cereal bowl, deep, 5" d, Platonite on pink 8.00
Moderntone, creamer, maroon. 8.00
Moderntone, creamer, Platonite on yellow 3.00
Moderntone, creamer and sugar, cobalt 20.00
Moderntone, creamer and sugar, turquoise, white int 15.00
Moderntone, cream soup bowl, cobalt 25.00
Moderntone, cream soup bowl, handled, amethyst. 20.00
Moderntone, cup, maroon. 8.00

Moderntone, cup and saucer, cobalt 18.00
Moderntone, cup and saucer, Platonite on blue 4.00
Moderntone, dinner plate, 9" d, cobalt. 25.00
Moderntone, dinner plate, 9" d, dark green 10.00
Moderntone, dinner plate, 9" d, Platonite on pink. 5.00
Moderntone, ice bowl and bail, cobalt. 35.00
Moderntone, luncheon plate, 8" d, cobalt. 15.00
Moderntone, nappy, 5" d, amethyst 25.00
Moderntone, nappy, 5" d, cobalt 25.00
Moderntone, nappy, 9" d, cobalt 60.00
Moderntone, platter, oval, Platonite on yellow 6.00
Moderntone, salad plate, 7" d, cobalt. 15.00
Moderntone, salad plate, 7" d, orange 7.00
Moderntone, salad plate, 7" d, Platonite on pink 5.00
Moderntone, salt and pepper shakers, pr, Platonite on
  blue 25.00
Moderntone, sherbet, cobalt 15.00
Moderntone, sherbet, gold. 8.00
Moderntone, sherbet, Platonite on green 3.00
Moderntone, sugar, Platonite on green. 2.00
Moderntone, tumbler, 9 oz, cobalt. 45.00
Moderntone, whiskey tumbler, 1¹/₂ oz, cobalt. 50.00
Royal Lace, bowl, rolled edge, 10" d, pink 45.00
Royal Lace, bowl, ruffled edge, 10" d, pink 100.00
Royal Lace, butter, cov, crystal 75.00
Royal Lace, cookie jar, blue, metal lid 90.00
Royal Lace, cream soup bowl, blue 45.00
Royal Lace, cream soup bowl, cobalt 45.00
Royal Lace, cream soup bowl, green 30.00
Royal Lace, cup and saucer, green 30.00
Royal Lace, juice tumbler, flat, pink 45.00
Royal Lace, pitcher, crystal 65.00
Royal Lace, platter, pink 55.00
Royal Lace, salt and pepper shakers, pr, cobalt. 390.00
Royal Lace, salt and pepper shakers, pr, green 135.00
Royal Lace, sherbet, ftd, green. 26.00
Royal Lace, sugar, cov, crystal 25.00
Royal Lace, tumbler, 9 oz, green 30.00
Royal Lace, water tumbler, pink. 30.00

Royal Lace, cup, pink, $15.00. Photo courtesy Ray Morykan Auctions.

HEAD VASES

The lady head vase craze began in the early 1940s and extended through the early 1960s. They were just one of hundreds of inexpensive ceramic novelties made by American and foreign manufacturers, primarily Japanese, in the period immediately following World War II.

References: Kathleen Cole, *The Encyclopedia of Head Vases*, Schiffer Publishing, 1996; Mike Posgay and Ian Warner, *The World of Head Vase Planters*, Antique Publications, 1992, 1996 value update; Mary Zavada, *Lady Head Vases*, Schiffer Publishing, 1988, 1996 value update.

Collectors' Club: Head Vase Society, PO Box 83H, Scarsdale, NY 10583.

Ceramic Arts Studio, Bonnie, open eyes, brown hair, yellow hat and dress, earrings, 7¼" h **$40.00**

Enesco, Elegant Miss, open eyes, light brown hair with flowers, pearl necklace, 5¼" h **45.00**

Enesco, light brown hair, pink dress with gold clasp, pearl earrings and necklace, 4½" h **32.00**

Enesco, nurse, blonde hair, white cap, hand, 5½" h **60.00**

Enesco, open eyes, black hair with yellow bow, blue dress with daisy, 5¼" h **40.00**

Inarco, E190/L, lashes, hand on chin, blonde hair, black hat with flowers, black dress, pearl necklace and earrings, 7" h **50.00**

Inarco, E193/M, 1961 transfer, lashes, hand, blonde hair with pink rose, light pink dress, pearl necklace, 5¾" h **40.00**

Inarco, E621, short brown hair, purple dress and hat, yellow bow on hat, bisque finish, 6⅝" h **50.00**

Lefton, 2359, lashes, hand on chin, blonde hair, white hat with flower, black dress with white collar and flower, 6¼" h **45.00**

Lefton, 2666, lashes, white hat, white dress with rose, 6½" h **35.00**

Lefton, 3278, closed eyes, 2 hands, hand on ear, yellow hat and dress, gold and red necklace, 5½" h **35.00**

Relpo, purple bow and dress, pearl necklace and earrings, 5½" h, $45.00

Napco, C2532B, 1956 transfer, lashes, hand on bonnet, brown hair, white hat with black trim, pearl earrings and bracelet, 7" h **55.00**

Napco, C3282A, 1950 transfer, lashes, hand, white hat, black dress, pearl earrings and bracelet, 5¼" h **35.00**

Napco, C4553D, 1960 transfer, brown hair, white hat, pink dress, black and white bow, 5¾" h **40.00**

Relpo, K1662, open eyes, flowers in hair, green dress, pearl earrings, 5¾" h **45.00**

Shafford, made in Japan, nun, black and white, gold trim, 5¾" h **12.00**

HEISEY GLASS

In April 1896, Augustus H. Heisey opened a sixteen-pot glass furnace in Newark, Ohio. Eventually the plant expanded to three furnaces and employed over 700 people.

Early production was limited to pressed ware and bar and hotel ware. In the late 1890s, Colonial patterns with flutes, scallops, and panels were introduced.

George Duncan Heisey, a son of Augustus H., designed the famous "Diamond H" trademark in 1900. The company registered it in 1901. In 1914 blown ware was first manufactured. Not content with traditional pulled stemware, the company introduced fancy pressed stemware patterns in the late 1910s.

Edgar Wilson, another son of Augustus H., became president in 1922 following Augustus' death. He was responsible for most of the colored Heisey glass. While some colored glass was made earlier, the first pastel colors and later deeper colors, e.g., cobalt and tangerine, were manufactured in quantity in the 1920s and 30s. By the time of Edgar Wilson's death in 1942, colored glassware had virtually disappeared from the market.

T. Clarence Heisey, another son of Augustus, assumed the presidency of the company. Shortages of manpower and supplies during World War II curtailed production. Many animal figures were introduced in the 1940s. An attempt was made to resurrect colored glass in the 1950s. Increasing production costs and foreign competition eventually resulted in the closing of the Heisey factory in December 1957.

The Imperial Glass Corporation of Bellaire, Ohio, bought the Heisey molds in 1958. Only a small number were kept in production, primarily those of patterns Heisey had in production when it ceased operations. Some pieces still carried the Heisey mark. In January 1968, Imperial announced it would no longer use the Heisey mark.

References: Neila Bredehoft, *The Collector's Encyclopedia of Heisey Glass, 1925-1938*, Collector Books, 1986, 1999 value update; Frank L. Hahn and Paul Kikeli, *Collector's Guide to Heisey and Heisey By Imperial Glass Animals*, Golden Era Publications, 1991, 1998 value update; Harry L. Rinker, *Stemware of the 20th Century: The Top 200 Patterns*, House of Collectibles, 1997.

Collectors' Club: Heisey Collectors of America, Inc, 169 W Church St, Newark, OH 43055.

Animal, gazelle **$1,500.00**
Animal, goose, wings up **125.00**
Animal, plug horse **115.00**
Animal, standing pony **100.00**
Carcassonne, cocktail, 3 oz, sahara **35.00**
Carcassonne, goblet, 11 oz, sahara **50.00**

Carcassonne, goblet, short stem, 11 oz, sahara **45.00**
Carcassonne, juice tumbler, ftd, 5 oz, sahara **40.00**
Carcassonne, sherbet, 6 oz, sahara. **40.00**
Chintz, cordial, #3389, 1 oz, crystal **120.00**
Crystolite, cocktail, low. **20.00**
Crystolite, cup and saucer **25.00**
Crystolite, goblet, #5003 . . . . **30.00**
Crystolite, ice jug, ½ gal **125.00**
Crystolite, mayonnaise with underplate **60.00**
Crystolite, plate, 8½" d **20.00**
Crystolite, plate, 2-handled, 7" d **20.00**
Crystolite, salad plate, 7" d **15.00**
Crystolite, sherbet, #5003 . . . . **15.00**
Danish Princess, sherbet, tall **15.00**
Diamond Optic, water goblet, flamingo pink **30.00**
Empress, plate, 7½" d, alexandrite **90.00**
Empress, bowl, 6" d, sahara. **35.00**
Empress, creamer and sugar, sahara **70.00**
Empress, plate, 8" sq, sahara **20.00**
Greek Key, punch bowl base, crystal **80.00**
Greek Key, tumbler, flat, 10 oz. **100.00**
Lariat, basket, ftd, 10" **225.00**
Lariat, celery and olive dish. **55.00**
Lariat, cheese dish, cov, crystal **50.00**
Lariat, cocktail, moonglow cut. **25.00**
Lariat, dinner plate, crystal **115.00**
Lariat, goblet, blown, 10 oz. **20.00**
Lariat, iced tea tumbler, ftd, moonglow cut. **30.00**
Lariat, punch set, 14 pcs **350.00**
Lariat, sherbet, blown, 5 oz **15.00**
Lariat, sherbet, moonglow cut **20.00**
Lariat, sugar, crystal. **20.00**
Lariat, vase, crystal, 7" h **25.00**
Lariat, vase, ftd, 7" h **45.00**
Lariat, water goblet, moonglow cut **25.00**
Mahabar, ashtray, 3" sq **12.00**
Minuet, champagne, #5010, tall **25.00**
Minuet, goblet, #5010. . . . . **35.00**
Minuet, iced tea, #5010 . . . . **65.00**
Minuet, plate, 8" d **20.00**
Minuet, sandwich plate, 15" d **70.00**
Old Colony, creamer, topaz **20.00**
Old Colony, cup and saucer, topaz **40.00**
Old Colony, plate, 8" sq, topaz **20.00**
Old Colony, sherbet, topaz **15.00**
Old Colony, soda tumbler, 10 oz, topaz **20.00**
Old Sandwich, cup, pink. **60.00**
Orchid, cigarette holder, ftd. **165.00**
Orchid, cocktail icer with insert. **275.00**
Orchid, compote, ftd, low **50.00**
Orchid, cruet, ftd, with stopper, 3 oz **200.00**
Orchid, French dressing bottle with #80 stopper. **225.00**
Orchid, pitcher **535.00**
Orchid, platter **225.00**
Orchid, sherry decanter. **300.00**
Orchid, sugar **40.00**
Orchid, tumbler, ftd, 12 oz, 7¾" h **60.00**
Orchid, water goblet, 10 oz. **50.00**
Plantation, candy dish, cov **190.00**
Plantation, jelly, flared. **65.00**
Plantation, pitcher. **500.00**
Plantation, relish, 3-part, 11¼" l **90.00**
Plantation, relish, 4-part, 8" l **70.00**
Pleat and Panel, cruet, pink **125.00**

Queen Ann, jug, 3 pt, Olympiad etch **125.00**
Ridgeleigh, creamer **30.00**
Ridgeleigh, creamer, individual **20.00**
Rococo, bowl, 8" d **85.00**
Rosalie, cocktail, 3 oz **10.00**
Rose, cake plate **300.00**
Rose, candlesticks, pr, 3-lite. **300.00**
Rose, celery, oval **100.00**
Rose, champagne **25.00**
Rose, cordial. **150.00**
Rose, creamer and sugar **65.00**
Rose, cruet **225.00**
Rose, dinner plate **400.00**
Rose, goblet, 9 oz, crystal **40.00**
Rose, pitcher. **625.00**
Rose, plate, 8½" d. **20.00**
Rose, relish, 3-part, 11" l **80.00**
Rose, sandwich plate, center handle **225.00**
Rose, sherbet, low. **20.00**
Rose, torte plate, 14" d **65.00**
Rose, vase, 6½" h **175.00**
Rose, water pitcher, #4164, 73 oz **625.00**
Rose, wine goblet, 3 oz **100.00**
Thumbprint, tumbler, ftd, 4 oz, crystal **4.00**
Twentieth Century Dawn, iced tea tumbler. **60.00**
Victorian, sherbet, 2-ball stem **15.00**
Warwick, vase, 7" h, sahara. **95.00**
Waverly, cup and saucer **20.00**
Yeoman, parfait, crystal **10.00**

HESS TRUCKS

Hess Oil and Chemical Corporation of Perth Amboy, New Jersey, introduced its first toy truck in 1964. The Hess Tank Trailer, with operating headlights and taillights and a fillable cargo tank with drainer hose, sold for $1.29, batteries included. It was reissued, unchanged, in 1965.

These promotions were so well received that vehicles have been distributed annually ever since. Available for initial purchase only at Hess service stations, these limited edition plastic toys are known for their quality construction. Each was issued complete with batteries and instructions in a sturdy cardboard box with superb graphics.

Reference: *Toy Truck Collector Official 1999 Price Guide*, F.S.B.O., 1999.

Note: Prices listed are for Hess Trucks MIB.

1964, Model B Mack Tanker Truck, with funnel **$2,200.00**
1965, Model B Mack Tanker Truck, with funnel **2,200.00**
1966, Voyager Tanker Ship, with stand. **2,500.00**
1967, Split Window Tanker Truck, with red velvet base
　box **2,400.00**
1968, Split Window Tanker Truck, without red velvet
　base, Perth Amboy, NJ **600.00**
1969, Amerada Hess Split Window Tanker Truck **2,300.00**
1969, Split Window Tanker Truck, Woodbridge, NJ on
　box. **650.00**
1970, Red Pumper Fire Truck. **800.00**
1971, Red Pumper Fire Truck, in Season's Greetings box . . **2,000.00**
1972, Split Window Tanker Truck. **350.00**
1974, Split Window Tanker Truck. **350.00**

1970, Red Pumper Fire Truck, $800.00. Photo courtesy Collectors Auction Services.

1975, Box Trailer, with 3 unlabled oil drums, 1-pc cab,
  Hong Kong **300.00**
1976, Box Trailer, with 3 labeled oil drums, 2-pc cab,
  Hong Kong **300.00**
1977, Tanker Truck, with large rear label **175.00**
1978, Tanker Truck, smaller label than 1977 version **150.00**
1980, GMC Training Van **300.00**
1982, '33 Chevy, "The First Hess Truck," red switch **80.00**
1983, '33 Chevy, "The First Hess Truck," bank **80.00**
1984, Hess Tanker Truck Bank, similar to 1977 truck **75.00**
1985, '33 Chevy, "The First Hess Truck," bank, reissue of
  1983 truck **85.00**
1985, Hess Tanker Truck Bank, reissue of 1984 truck **80.00**
1986, Aerial Ladder Fire Truck, red **100.00**
1987, White Box Trailer, with 3 labeled oil drums. **70.00**
1988, Car Transporter with Race Car **75.00**
1989, Aerial Ladder Fire Truck with Siren, white. **45.00**
1990, Semi-Tanker Truck with Horn, white. **40.00**
1991, Car Transporter with Race Car **45.00**
1992, 18-Wheeler Box Truck with Race Car inside **40.00**
1993, Patrol Car, with 2 sirens and flashing lights **25.00**
1993, Premium Diesel Semi-Tanker Truck, not sold
  publicly **1,200.00**
1994, Rescue Truck. **20.00**
1995, Hess Truck and Helicopter **35.00**
1996, Emergency Truck **25.00**
1997, Toy Truck and Racers **25.00**
1998, Hess Miniature Tanker Truck, first miniature **50.00**
1998, Recreation Van with Dune Buggy and Motorcycle. **25.00**
1999, Toy Truck and Space Shuttle with Satellite. **25.00**

HI-FI EQUIPMENT

1950s and 60s Hi-Fi equipment is now collectible. Vacuum tube-type amplifiers, pre-amplifiers, AM-FM tuners, and receivers are sought. Look for examples from Acrosound, Altec, Eico, Fisher, McIntosh, Marantz, and Western Electric. Some American and English record turntables and speakers are also collectible. Garrard and Thorens are two leading brand names.

Prices reflect equipment in working order. If a piece of equipment does not work, it has parts value only, usually $25 or less. Because collectors restore equipment, unused tubes in their period boxes have value, albeit modest.

Amplifier, Acrosound, Model ULII, Ultra Linear, mono,
  60 watts, EL 34 output tubes **$120.00**
Amplifier, Altec, Model 350A, mono, 60 watts, 6550
  output tubes **100.00**
Amplifier, Heathkit, Model W5-M, mono, 25 watts,
  KT 66 output tubes **75.00**
Amplifier, Marantz, Model 8-B, stereo, 70 watts, EL 34
  output tubes **400.00**
Pre-Amplifier, Audio Research, Model SP-7, tube, stereo **100.00**
Pre-Amplifier, Conrad Johnson, Model PV-2, tube, stereo **75.00**
Pre-Amplifier, Marantz, Model 7-C, stereo, tubes, wood
  case, metal knobs **250.00**
Pre-Amplifier, McIntosh, Model MC-75, mono, chrome
  chassis, 75 watts, 6550 tubes **150.00**
Record Player, Westinghouse, model H75AC1, wood
  cover with gray and white material, hard molded plas-
  tic accessories, front speaker with tone and volume
  knobs, 14¹/₂ x 16¹/₂ x 9" **25.00**
Speaker, Altec, Model 605A, coaxial horn, 16 ohms. **50.00**
Speaker, Tannoy, 12 or 15" dual concentric **50.00**
Tuner, Marantz, 10-B, stereo, tubes, AM/FM, oscillo-
  scope display **300.00**
Vacuum Tube, Western Electric, Model 300-B, output
  triode **25.00**

HIGGINS GLASS

Michael Higgins and Frances Stewart Higgins were actively involved in designing and decorating glass in their Chicago studio by the early 1950s. Between 1958 and 1964, the couple worked in a studio provided for them by Dearborn Glass, an industrial glass company located outside Chicago. Pieces were mass produced. A gold signature was screened on the front of each piece before the final firing. During the period with Dearborn, the Higgins developed new colors and enamels for their double-layered pieces and experimented with weaving copper wire into glass, fusing glass chips to create crystalline forms, and overlaying colors onto glass panels.

After leaving Dearborn, the Higgins established a studio at Haeger. In 1966 they re-established their own studio. During the late 1960s and early 1970s, the Higgins manufactured large quantities of glass plaques, often framed in wood. In 1972 they moved their studio to Riverside, Illinois. Pieces made after 1972 have an engraved signature on the back. Michael Higgins passed away on February 13, 1999.

Reference: Donald-Brian Johnson and Leslie Piña, *Higgins: Adventures in Glass*, Schiffer Publishing, 1997.

Note: Unless stated otherwise, all pieces have a gold signature.

Ashtray, blue and yellow ray, inside signature, 10 x 14". **$80.00**
Ashtray, red sawtooth, rolled over edge, 8¹/₂" d **50.00**
Bowl, beige and brown flowers, etched signature, 8" d **115.00**
Bowl, black oriental tree motif on orange ground,
  Dearborn signature, 8¹/₂" d **85.00**
Bowl, blue tones abstract pattern, 12¹/₂" d **150.00**
Bowl, center blue wheel spoke pattern, peacock feather
  motif around rim, etched signature, 8³/₄" d **100.00**
Bowl, center radiating purple and brown triangular
  spokes, Dearborn signature, 12" d **90.00**
Bowl, red and yellow Chinese calligraphy, etched signa-
  ture, 8¹/₂" d **100.00**

Bowl, freeform, green, orange, and blue check with bubbles, gold signature, 9" l, $110.00. Photo courtesy Jackson's Auctioneers & Appraisers.

Bowl, red, orange, and periwinkle blue flowers, etched
  signature, 12³/₄" d 175.00
Bowl, yellow floral motif, octagonal, Dearborn signa-
  ture, 8¹/₄" d 110.00
Charger, fall season, etched signature, 15" d 550.00
Charger, yellow and chartreuse ray, 17" d 160.00
Plate, chartreuse and white stripes, gold seaweed, 8¹/₂" d 55.00
Plate, clear, center radiating black bead on string pat-
  tern, etched signature, 5" d 25.00
Plate, freeform, center radiating yellow and black
  stripes, Dearborn signature 90.00
Plate, orange 6-spoked wheel design, Dearborn signa-
  ture, 8¹/₄" d 55.00
Tray, black and chartreuse, Michael Higgins etched sig-
  nature with Stickman, 7" sq 175.00
Tray, orange, red, and amber curvilinear geometric
  design, 17" d 100.00
Tray, orange, red, and avocado ray, orig label, 14" sq 90.00
Tray, yellow and chartreuse ray, gold spiral dec, 14 x 17" 65.00

HOCKEY CARDS

The first hockey cards were three cigarette sets produced between 1910 and 1913. Four candy card sets and one cigarette set were issued in the 1920s. In the 1930s Canadian chewing gum manufacturers, e.g., World Wide Gum Company, offered hockey cards as a premium.

The modern hockey card dates from the 1950s. Parkhurst issued hockey card sets between 1951 and 1964, the exception being the 1956-57 season. Topps produced its first hockey card set in 1954. Topps sets focused on American teams; Parkhurst on Canadian teams. Starting with the 1964-65 season, Topps issued card sets that included players from all teams in the National Hockey League. O-Pee-Chee, a producer of card sets in the 1930s, re-entered the market in 1968.

There were five major card sets for the 1990-91 season: Bowman, O-Pee-Chee Premier, Pro Set, Score, and Upper Deck. Like trading cards for other sports, current hockey card sets contain special feature cards. This is one collectible that is equally at home in either Canada or the United States.

Reference: James Beckett, *Beckett Hockey Card Price Guide & Alphabetical Checklist No. 7,* Beckett Publications, 1997.

Periodicals: *Beckett Hockey Collector,* 15850 Dallas Pkwy, Dallas, TX 75248; *Sports Cards,* 700 E State St, Iola, WI 54990.

Note: Prices are for cards in good condition.

Bazooka, 1971-72, #4, Bobby Hull $7.50
Bazooka, 1971-72, #36, Bobby Orr 15.00
Bowman, 1990-91, #24, Brett Hull 12
Bowman, 1990-91, #50, Patrick Roy 02
Bowman, 1990-91, #92, Sergei Makarov 04
O-Pee-Chee, 1933-34, #9, Harold Oliver 8.00
O-Pee-Chee, 1933-34, #42, John Sorrell 4.00
O-Pee-Chee, 1934-35, #60, Baldy Northcott 4.50
O-Pee-Chee, 1934-35, #71, Cecil Dillon 4.50
O-Pee-Chee, 1935-36, #81, Marty Barry 9.00
O-Pee-Chee, 1935-36, #84, Nick Metz 5.00
O-Pee-Chee, 1936-37, #116, Cy Wentworth 7.50
O-Pee-Chee, 1937-38, #168, Dave Trottier 4.00
O-Pee-Chee, 1939-40, #2, Walter Broda 6.00
O-Pee-Chee, 1940-41, #105, Johnny Mowers 2.00
O-Pee-Chee, 1968-69, #29, Gordie Howe 7.00
O-Pee-Chee, 1968-69, #143, Peter Mahovlich 30
O-Pee-Chee, 1969-70, #24, Bobby Orr 10.00
O-Pee-Chee, 1969-70, #138, Tony Esposito 9.00
O-Pee-Chee, 1970-71, #78, Bernie Parent 1.20
O-Pee-Chee, 1971-72, #110, Tony Esposito 1.20
O-Pee-Chee, 1972-73, #145, Ken Dryden 3.50
O-Pee-Chee, 1972-73, complete set (22), Player Crests
  series 6.00
O-Pee-Chee, 1974-75, complete set (396), NHL series 30.00
O-Pee-Chee, 1975-76, complete set (132), WHA series 27.00
O-Pee-Chee, 1979-80, complete set (396) 75.00
O-Pee-Chee, 1980-81, #55, Bobby Clarke 15
O-Pee-Chee, 1981-82, #106, Wayne Gretzky 4.00
O-Pee-Chee, 1982-83, #7, Ray Bourque 60
O-Pee-Chee, 1984-85, #129, Pat LaFontaine 2.00
Parkhurst, 1951-52, #14, Boom Boom Geoffrion 18.00
Parkhurst, 1952-53, #10, Dickie Moore 5.50
Parkhurst, 1953-54, #2, Sid Smith 1.00
Parkhurst, 1954-55, #20, Fern Flaman 1.60
Parkhurst, 1955-56, #4, George Armstrong 1.70
Parkhurst, 1957-58, #28, Dick Duff 1.00
Parkhurst, 1958-59, #50, Brian Cullen 1.20
Parkhurst, 1959-60, #5, Ed Chadwick 1.00
Parkhurst, 1960-61, #54, Claude Provost 75
Parkhurst, 1962-63, complete set (54) 100.00
Parkhurst, 1963-64, complete set (99) 125.00
Popsicle, 1975-76, complete set (18) 1.80
Popsicle, 1976-77, complete set (18) 1.80
Score, 1990-91, #2, Mario Lemieux 10
Score, 1990-91, #48, Tony Granato 02
Score, 1990-91, #85, Adam Oates 02
Score, 1990-91, complete set (40), Young Superstars
  series 1.80
Topps, 1954-55, #8, Gordie Howe 100.00

Topps, 1954-55, #45, Tony Leswick **2.00**
Topps, 1957-58, #29, Ron Murphy **1.00**
Topps, 1958-59, #2, Terry Sawchuk **7.50**
Topps, 1959-60, #55, Brian Cullen **75**
Topps, 1961-62, #36, Stan Mikita **10.00**
Topps, 1962-63, #37, Chico Maki **1.25**
Topps, 1963-64, complete set (66) **80.00**
Topps, 1964-65, complete set (110) **400.00**
Topps, 1965-66, complete set (128) **250.00**
Topps, 1967-68, #6, Terry Harpet **60**
Upper Deck, 1990, complete set (2), Promo series **9.00**
Upper Deck, 1990-91, #12, John Cullen **05**
Upper Deck, 1990-91, complete set (150), Extended
    series **4.50**

HOCKEY MEMORABILIA

Hockey memorabilia focuses primarily on professional hockey teams. Although the popularity of college hockey is growing rapidly and Canada's Junior Hockey is deeply entrenched, professional teams have generated almost all licensed collectibles.

Collecting is highly regionalized. Most collectors focus on local teams. Even with today's National Hockey League, there is a distinct dividing line between collectors of material related to American and Canadian teams.

Superstar collecting is heavily post-1980 focused. Endorsement opportunities for early Hockey Hall of Famers were limited. Collectors want game-related material. Logo licensed merchandise for sale in sports shops has minimal or no appeal.

References: *Beckett Hockey Card Price Guide & Alphabetical Checklist, No. 9,* Beckett Publications, 1999; Tom Mortenson (ed.), *2000 Standard Catalog of Sports Memorabilia,* Krause Publications, 1999.

Autograph, Bobby Hull, sgd puck **$25.00**
Autograph, Gordie Roberts, cut signature **18.00**
Autograph, Mario Lemieux, cut signature **5.00**

Advertising Display, Sportsman Cigarettes, diecut cardboard, 35½" h, $70.00. Photo courtesy Collectors Auction Services.

Autograph, Stan Mikita, PS, 8 x 10" **20.00**
Autograph, Tony Esposito, PS, 8 x 10" **20.00**
Book, *Hockey Is My Game,* Bobby Hull, 1967, 212 pp,
    dj **25.00**
Book, *Mr Hockey: The World of Gordie Howe,* 1975,
    197 pp, dj **20.00**
Figure, Eric Lindros, Kenner Starting Lineup, 1993 . . . . **40.00**
Figure, Mario Lemieux, Corinthian Headliners, 1997 . . . . **8.00**
Gloves, Joe Juneau, Boston Bruins, Easton, sgd, 1993,
    game worn **275.00**
Gloves, Kevin Dineen, Philadelphia Flyers, game worn **100.00**
Jersey, Brett Hull, St Louis Blues, game worn, 1989-90 . . . . **2,700.00**
Jersey, Paul Coffey, sgd, 1993 All-Star game, game worn . . **2,000.00**
Limited Edition Plate, Winston Roland, The Puck Stops
    Here, Hockey in Canada series, G McLaughlin, 1988 . . . . . **35.00**
Media Guide, Boston Bruins Bobby Orr, 1967-68 . . . . **60.00**
Media Guide, Los Angeles Kings, 1967-68 . . . . **75.00**
Periodical, *Sporting News,* May 6, 1972, Gary Cheevers **5.00**
Program, NHL All-Star Magazine, Chicago, 1973-74 . . . . **35.00**
Program, Stanley Cup, Montreal vs Boston, 1977-78 . . . . **75.00**
Skates, Eric Lindros, Bauer Supreme, game worn **1,200.00**
Stick, Toronto Maple Leafs, sgd by team, 1992-93 . . . . **100.00**

HOLIDAY COLLECTIBLES

Holiday collectibles can be broken down into three major periods: (1) pre-1940, (2) 1945 to the late 1970s, and (3) contemporary "collector" items. Crossover collectors, e.g., candy container collectors, skew the values on some items.

This is a catchall category for those holiday collectibles that do not have separate category listings. It includes Fourth of July and Thanksgiving collectibles. Look elsewhere for Christmas, Easter, Halloween, and Valentines.

References: Lisa Bryan-Smith and Richard Smith, *Holiday Collectibles,* Krause Publications, 1998; Pauline and Dan Campanelli, *Holiday Collectables,* L-W Book Sales, 1997; Charlene Pinkerton, *Holiday Plastic Novelties,* Schiffer Publishing, 1999.

Newsletter: *St Patrick Notes,* 10802 Greencreek Dr, Ste 703, Houston, TX 77070.

Bicentennial, lighter, polished finish, red, white, and
    blue enamel painted engraved symbols for 200th
    Birthday, white "1776" on lid surrounded by stars,
    Zippo, 1975 . . . . **$40.00**
Birthday, pinback button, "Happy Birthday To You," boys
    and girls seated at table holding cake lighted by 7 can-
    dles, red, white, blue, and yellow, c1930s **10.00**
Children's Day, pinback button, young girl and boy
    holding hands, floral garden background **10.00**
Father's Day, limited edition plate, Little Shaver, Edwin M
    Knowles, Father's Love series, B Bradley, 1985 . . . . **20.00**
Fourth of July, pinback button, "Lodge Park," sponsored
    by "Harper Van Dyke Business Assn," red, white, and
    blue, 1930-40s **10.00**
Fourth of July, pinback button, "Spend the 4th in
    Malden," red, white, and blue, 1930s **15.00**
Halloween, clicker, litho tin, orange and black, witch on
    broomstick with bats flying above under full moon,
    T Cohn, c1940s, 2 x 3" **20.00**

Mother's Day, limited edition plate, Mother's Day, Gorham Collection, Moppets Mother's Day series, 1973. . . . . **30.00**

Mother's Day, pinback button, "God Bless Mother," sepia portrait of hooded mother embracing infant, 1920s. **10.00**

Parent's Day, pinback button, 3 pink roses on green leaves and stem, black lettering inscription at bottom margin, back paper for Westminster Press, Philadelphia, c1920s. **15.00**

St Patrick's Day, candy container, top hat, cardboard, green foil, shamrock and clay pipe on top, made in Germany, 3" h **50.00**

St Patrick's Day, cookie cutter, Kermit the Frog with shamrock, Hallmark, 1982. . . . . **4.00**

St Patrick's Day, decoration, leprechaun riding goat, cardboard, green and white, 1950s, 15" h **15.00**

St Patrick's Day, figure, Irish man, hard plastic, 3¾" h **10.00**

Thanksgiving, candy container, turkey, composition body, metal legs, made in Germany, 5" h **50.00**

Thanksgiving, decoration, turkey, cardboard, green, brown, and red, 1930s, 3" h **8.00**

Thanksgiving, pinback button, "Mill's Annual Turkey Week," turkey image on white ground, black lettering, 1920s. **50.00**

Thanksgiving, place card, cardboard, Pilgrim girl's head, 3" h **2.00**

Valentine's Day, activity book, Valentine Play-Book, 12 pp, Fuld & Co, 1950s, unused, 11 x 16" **15.00**

Valentine's Day, pinback button, "Valentine's Day," black lettering on white ground surrounded by 8 tiny hearts, 1930s. **15.00**

Valentine's Day, stickpin, heart, diecut, celluloid, 1930s **10.00**

HOLT-HOWARD

A. Grant Holt and brothers John and Robert J. Howard formed the Holt-Howard import company in Stamford, Connecticut in 1948. The firm is best known for its novelty ceramics, including the Cat and Christmas lines and the popular Pixieware line of condiment jars. Designed by Robert J. Howard and produced between 1958 and the early 1960s, these ceramic containers proved to be so successful that knock-offs by Davar, Lefton, Lipper & Mann, M-G, Inc., and Norcrest quickly found their way into the market. Kay Dee Designs purchased Holt-Howard in 1990.

Authentic Pixieware is easily identified by its single-color vertical stripes on a white jar, flat pixie-head stopper (with attached spoon when appropriate), and condiment label with slightly skewed black lettering. An exception is three salad dressing cruets which had round heads. All pieces were marked, either with "HH" or "Holt-Howard," a copyright symbol followed by the year "1958" or "1959," and "Japan." Some pieces may be found with a black and silver label.

Reference: Walter Dworkin, *Price Guide to Holt-Howard Collectibles and Related Ceramic Wares of the '50s & '60s,* Krause Publications, 1998.

Bunnies in Basket, salt and pepper shakers, pr **$25.00**
Chattercoons, salt and pepper shakers, pr. **30.00**
Coq Rouge, ashtray. **8.00**
Coq Rouge, cigarette box, wooden **35.00**
Coq Rouge, cookie jar. **100.00**

Winter Green, candy dish, 1959, 13¾" l, $15.00. Photo courtesy Ray Morykan Auctions.

Coq Rouge, creamer and sugar **35.00**
Coq Rouge, napkin holder. **25.00**
Coq Rouge, pitcher, 32 oz. **60.00**
Coq Rouge, recipe box, wooden **65.00**
Coq Rouge, salt and pepper shakers, pr, wooden **12.00**
Coq Rouge, trivet **35.00**
Cozy Kittens, ashtray/match holder **55.00**
Cozy Kittens, bud vase **80.00**
Cozy Kittens, cottage cheese crock **45.00**
Cozy Kittens, kitty catch clip **25.00**
Cozy Kittens, spice set, 4 pcs. **100.00**
Cozy Kittens, sugar shaker. **55.00**
Cozy Kittens, wall caddy **70.00**
Daisy 'Dorable, bud vase **65.00**
Daisy 'Dorable, candleholder **30.00**
Daisy 'Dorable, cigarette holder **55.00**
Daisy 'Dorable, lipstick caddy **65.00**
Daisy 'Dorable, salt and pepper shakers, pr **35.00**
Jeeves, cherries jar. **125.00**
Jeeves, martini shaker set, 5 pcs. **175.00**
Lovebirds, salt and pepper shakers, pr **35.00**
Merry Mouse, cheese crock. **45.00**
Merry Mouse, match holder. **65.00**
Merry Mouse, salt and pepper shakers, pr **35.00**
Naughty Choir Boys, candleholders, pr **20.00**
Peeking Pets in Basket, salt and pepper shakers, pr **30.00**
Pixieware, Berries Server **100.00**
Pixieware, Chili Sauce. **175.00**
Pixieware, Cocktail Onions **65.00**
Pixieware, Cream Crock & Lil' Sugar **75.00**
Pixieware, Mustard Max **100.00**
Pixieware, Party Pixies Hors d'oeuvre Dish. **150.00**
Pixieware, Relish Jar **100.00**
Pixieware, Spoon **50.00**
Pixieware, Sam 'n Sally Salad Cruet Set **125.00**
Pixieware, Stacking Salt and Pepper Set **55.00**
Pixieware, Tartar Tom **100.00**
Santa, candleholder **15.00**
Santa, napkin holder. **20.00**
Santa, Starry-Eyed Santa Pitcher. **25.00**

Santa, Starry-Eyed Santa Salt and Pepper Shakers, pr **25.00**
Santa, Winking Santa Beverage Set, 7 pcs, 32 oz pitcher
    and six 6-ounce mugs, 1960 . . . . **50.00**
Santa, Winking Santa Stackable Creamer and Sugar **30.00**
Wee Three Kings, candleholders, set of 3 . . . . **45.00**

HOMER LAUGHLIN

In 1870 Homer and Shakespeare Laughlin established two pottery kilns in East Liverpool, Ohio. Shakespeare left the company in 1879. The firm made whiteware (ironstone utilitarian products). In 1896 William Wills and a group of Pittsburgh investors, led by Marcus Aaron, purchased the Laughlin firm. The company expanded, building two plants in Laughlin Station, Ohio, and another in Newall, West Virginia. A second plant was built in Newall in 1926.

Cookware, dinnerware, and kitchenware were the company's principal products. Popular dinnerware lines include Fiesta, Harlequin, Rhythm, Riviera, and Virginia Rose.

References: Jo Cunningham, *Homer Laughlin: 1873-1939,* Schiffer Publishing, 1998; Bob and Sharon Huxford, *Collector's Encyclopedia of Fiesta: Plus Harlequin, Riviera, and Kitchen Kraft, Eighth Edition,* Collector Books, 1998; Joanne Jasper, *The Collector's Encyclopedia of Homer Laughlin China,* Collector Books, 1993, 1997 value update; Richard G. Racheter, *Collector's Guide to Homer Laughlin's Virginia Rose,* Collector Books, 1997.

Newsletter: *The Laughlin Eagle,* 1270 63rd Terrace S, St Petersburg, FL 33705.

Collectors' Club: The Homer Laughlin Collector's Club, Inc., PO Box 26021, Crystal City, VA 22215.

Note: See Fiesta for additional listings; see Figurines for Harlequin animals.

Americana, bread and butter plate, 6" d **$4.00**
Americana, eggcup **15.00**
Americana, plate, 10" d **10.00**
Americana, platter, oval, 15" l **15.00**
Americana, teapot **65.00**
Americana, vegetable, oval, 8" l **20.00**
Briar Rose, bowl, 5" d **8.00**
Briar Rose, bread and butter plate, 6¼" d **4.00**
Briar Rose, dinner plate, 9⅝" d **15.00**
Briar Rose, luncheon plate, 8⅝" d **12.00**
Briar Rose, platter, 11" l **25.00**
Briar Rose, platter, 14" l **40.00**
Briar Rose, salad plate, 7" d **9.00**
Briar Rose, soup, flat **12.00**
Brittany, casserole **20.00**
Brittany, chop plate, 12" d **15.00**
Brittany, cup and saucer **5.00**
Brittany, plate, 7¼" d **4.00**
Brittany, plate, 9" d **8.00**
Brittany, vegetable, oval **10.00**
Eggshell Theme, creamer and covered sugar **25.00**
Eggshell Theme, cup and saucer **15.00**
Eggshell Theme, gravy, attached underplate **18.00**
Eggshell Theme, salad plate **8.00**
Harlequin, bowl, green, 5½" d **30.00**
Harlequin, butter base, maroon **85.00**
Harlequin, butter base, turquoise **25.00**

Harlequin, candlesticks, pr, mauve **550.00**
Harlequin, casserole, cov, chartreuse **250.00**
Harlequin, casserole, cov, maroon **200.00**
Harlequin, casserole, cov, spruce **200.00**
Harlequin, cat, spruce **275.00**
Harlequin, creamer, high lip, mauve **175.00**
Harlequin, creamer and sugar, gray **130.00**
Harlequin, deep plate, green **125.00**
Harlequin, donkey, spruce **325.00**
Harlequin, duck, mauve **275.00**
Harlequin, fish, spruce **300.00**
Harlequin, marmalade base, green **250.00**
Harlequin, nut dish, green **110.00**
Harlequin, nut dish, rose **100.00**
Harlequin, penguin, maroon **275.00**
Harlequin, plate, green, 7" d **45.00**
Harlequin, plate, red, 10" d **25.00**
Harlequin, saucer, green **10.00**
Harlequin, sugar, cov, green **225.00**
Harlequin, sugar, cov, mauve **25.00**
Harlequin, syrup, yellow **575.00**
Harlequin, teapot, gray **175.00**
Harlequin, teapot, rose **100.00**
Harlequin, tumbler, rose **85.00**
Oven Serve, cake server **25.00**
Oven Serve, cup and saucer **15.00**
Oven Serve, leftover **6.00**
Oven Serve, pie baker, 9" d **10.00**
Rhythm, bread and butter plate, 6" d **5.00**
Rhythm, casserole **45.00**
Rhythm, cup and saucer **8.00**
Rhythm, plate, 9" d **8.00**
Rhythm, platter, 11½" l **15.00**
Rhythm, tidbit, 3-tier **35.00**
Riviera, after dinner cup and saucer, ivory **110.00**
Riviera, bowl, blue, 5" d **8.00**
Riviera, bowl, red, 5" d **8.00**
Riviera, bowl, yellow, 5" d **8.00**

Eggshell Theme, dinner plate, 10" d, $8.00. Photo courtesy Ray Morykan Auctions.

Riviera, bread and butter plate, blue, 6" d **7.00**
Riviera, bread and butter plate, green, 6" d. **7.00**
Riviera, bread and butter plate, red, 6" d **7.00**
Riviera, butter dish, cov, ½ lb **110.00**
Riviera, casserole, cov, green **100.00**
Riviera, casserole, cov, yellow **120.00**
Riviera, creamer and sugar, green **20.00**
Riviera, cup, blue **8.00**
Riviera, cup and saucer, green **15.00**
Riviera, deep plate, ivory **45.00**
Riviera, oatmeal bowl, green **85.00**
Riviera, plate, green, 9" d **15.00**
Riviera, plate, red, 7"d **15.00**
Riviera, plate, red, 9" d **18.00**
Riviera, platter, green, 11" l **25.00**
Riviera, salt and pepper shakers, pr, yellow **10.00**
Riviera, saucer, ivory **5.00**
Riviera, saucer, yellow **4.00**
Riviera, soup bowl, flat, green **20.00**
Riviera, soup bowl, flat, ivory **20.00**
Riviera, soup bowl, flat, yellow **20.00**
Riviera, sugar, cov, yellow **10.00**
Riviera, syrup lid, red **95.00**
Riviera, teapot, ivory **65.00**
Riviera, tumbler, blue **60.00**
Riviera, vegetable, red **30.00**
Riviera, vegetable, yellow, 8¼" d **30.00**
Virginia Rose, bread and butter plate, 6¼" d **3.00**
Virginia Rose, casserole **75.00**
Virginia Rose, dish, 6" d **5.00**
Virginia Rose, jug, 22 oz **40.00**
Virginia Rose, plate, 8" d **12.00**
Virginia Rose, platter, 11½" l **15.00**

HORSE COLLECTIBLES

Objects shaped like a horse or featuring an image of a horse are everywhere. Most collectors specialize, e.g., collectors of carousel horses. Horse-related toys, especially horse-drawn cast-iron toys, are bought and sold within the toy collecting community.

Reference: Jan Lindenberger, *501 Collectible Horses, 2nd Edition,* Schiffer Publishing, 2000.

Note: For additional listings see Breyer Horses.

Ashtray, reclining horse, ceramic, brown, 2 rests, 3⅞" h **$10.00**
Bank, cast iron, pinto **20.00**
Bookends, pr, rearing horse, glass, LE Smith, 8" h **100.00**
Brush, leather back, soft bristles, 1930s **15.00**
Candy Dish, milk glass, reclining horse **15.00**
Comic Book, Francis the Talking Mule, Dell #4-C-501,
   1953 . . . . **10.00**
Figure, pony, plastic, jointed, with saddle, Empire Toy
   Co, 1979, 4" h **5.00**
Figure, prancing horse, ceramic, white fur mane, bead-
   ed blanket, Japan, 3¾" h **15.00**
Figure, rocking horse, brass, 7¼ x 5½" **25.00**
Figure, standing horse, pot metal **18.00**
Figure, Zara, Hagen-Renaker, 1980s **250.00**
Pocket Mirror, "Be Merciful To Your Horse," Humane
   Horse Collar Co **75.00**

Figure, "Winchester," Buffalo Bill Pony Express Rider, cast bronze, mkd "Artupo Bruni 1966," 7¼" h, 8" l, $185.00. Photo courtesy Collectors Auction Services.

Program, Cheyenne Frontier Days, Cheyenne, Wyoming,
   man riding bucking horse on cov, 1937, 10¾" h **200.00**
Puzzle, Old Dobbin Scroll Puzzle, diecut puzzle, 15 pcs,
   1920s, set of two 7½ x 10¼" puzzles **12.00**
Saddle, leather, tooled floral design, stitched suede cov,
   underside sheep wool lining, wood stirrups wrapped
   in leather, 3½" saddle horn, mkd "Texas Saddlery
   T Bastrop, Texas, 1978" **450.00**
Salt and Pepper Shakers, pr, donkeys, earthenware **6.00**
Spurs, lady's, chrome plated, from Ft Worth, TX, stock
   show, 5½" l **200.00**
Toothpick Holder, horse pulling wagon, ceramic **10.00**

HORSE RACING

Items associated with Hall of Fame horses, e.g., Dan Patch and Man O'War, bring a premium. Paper ephemera, e.g., postcards and programs, and drinking glasses are two strong areas of focus. A program was issued for the first Belmont Stakes in 1867, the first Preakness Stakes in 1873, and the first Kentucky Derby in 1875. Kentucky Derby glasses date back to 1938, Preakness glasses to 1973, Belmont glasses to 1976, and Breeders Cup glasses to 1985. Pins were introduced at the Kentucky Derby in 1973 and at other major stakes races in the 1980s.

References: Bill Friedberg, *Racing into the 21st Century: Glass Collector's Illustrated Price Guide,* published by author, 1999; Roderick A. Malloy, *Malloy's Sports Collectibles Value Guide: Up-to-Date Prices for Noncard Sports Memorabilia,* Attic Books, Wallace-Homestead, 1993.

Brandy Snifter, Maryland Jockey Club, gold logo, 4¾" h **$4.00**
Drinking Glass, 1964 Kentucky Derby **20.00**
Drinking Glass, 1966 Kentucky Derby **25.00**

Drinking Glass, 1971 Kentucky Derby **15.00**

Drinking Glass, 1973-75 Delaware Handicap Winner, Susan's Girl, 3³/₈" h **3.00**

Drinking Glass, 1979 Gulfstream, Home of the Florida Derby, Derby Daquari, frosted with pink, 3¹/₃" h **5.00**

Drinking Glass, 1979 Preakness. **15.00**

Drinking Glass, 1982 Kentucky Derby **4.00**

Drinking Glass, 1982 Preakness. **15.00**

Drinking Glass, 1982 West Virginia Derby, Waterford Park **25.00**

Drinking Glass, 1985 Rosecroft Breeder's Crown, etched with sulky, 5³/₈" h **5.00**

Drinking Glass, 1986 XIX Clasico Marlboro Del Caribe **10.00**

Pin, Belmont Stakes, 1989. . . . . **10.00**

Pin, Breeders Cup, 1985 . . . . **20.00**

Pin, Kentucky Derby, plastic, 1974. . . . . **100.00**

Pin, Preakness, 1991 . . . . **15.00**

Pinback Button, Belmont Stakes Winner 1973, "Secretariat," center brown photo **20.00**

Pinback Button, Suffolk Downs Maintenance, light blue, center black and white photo **15.00**

Pinback Button, "The Lady Is A Champ/Lady's Secret," black and white horse head on red ground, white lettering, Belmont Park, 1968. . . . . **15.00**

Program, Belmont Stakes, 1944 . . . . **300.00**

Program, Breeders Cup, 1985 . . . . **12.00**

Program, Kentucky Derby, 1947. . . . . **125.00**

Program, Preakness Stakes, 1956 . . . . **225.00**

Seat Cushion, white vinyl, brown edge, "Midnight Sun" over horse image, "National Champion 1945–46" on front, list of world champion horses and owners from 1939–74 on back **20.00**

Tag, Mammoth Park Jockey Club, tan and black diecut cardboard disk under thin plastic, metal tab fastener on reverse, dated 1964 . . . . **15.00**

HOT WHEELS

Automobile designer Harry Bradley, Mattel designer Howard Newman, Mattel Chairman Elliot Handler, and R & D chief Jack Ryan were the principal guiding forces in the creation of Hot Wheels. The creative process began in 1966 and culminated with the introduction of a diecast metal 16-car line in 1968. Hot Wheels were an immediate success.

Initially, cars were produced in Hong Kong and the United States. Mattel continually changed styling and paint motifs. Copies of modern cars were supplemented with futuristic models. Since the cars were meant to be raced, Mattel produced a variety of track sets. A Hot Wheels licensing program was instituted, resulting in Hot Wheels comic books, lunch kits, etc. In the 1980s Mattel did a number of Hot Wheels promotions with McDonald's and Kellogg's. In 1993 Mattel introduced a reproduction line focused toward the adult collector market. In 1997 Mattel acquired Tyco, bringing Hot Wheels and Matchbox under one roof.

References: Bob Parker, *The Complete & Unauthorized Book of Hot Wheels, 3rd Edition*, Schiffer Publishing, 1999; Michael Thomas Strauss, *Tomart's Price Guide to Hot Wheels, 3rd Edition*, Tomart Publications, 1998.

Periodical: *Toy Cars & Vehicles*, 700 E State St, Iola, WI 54990.

Newsletter: *Hot Wheels Newsletter*, 26 Madera Ave, San Carlos, CA, 94070.

Note: Prices listed are for cars in mint condition.

ACCESSORIES

24 Car Case, vinyl, #5138 . . . . **$35.00**

72 Car Case, #4978, 1970. . . . . **35.00**

Bridge Pak, #6482. . . . . **15.00**

Bug Bite Set, #5645 . . . . **50.00**

Construction Crew 5-Car Gift Pack, #3871 . . . . **5.00**

Cutoff Canyon, #7672 . . . . **90.00**

Daredevil Loop Pak, #6226 . . . . **15.00**

Double-Dare Race Set, #6280 . . . . **50.00**

Drag 'Chute Stunt Set, #6437 . . . . **45.00**

Dual-Lane Lap Counter, #6476 . . . . **20.00**

Dual-Lane Rod Runner, #6480. . . . . **30.00**

Hazard Hill, #6248. . . . . **50.00**

Hot Ones Patch Pack, #5086 . . . . **30.00**

Hot Strip Track Pak, #6224 . . . . **15.00**

Hot Wheels Factory, #4355 . . . . **150.00**

Jump Ramp Pak, #6283 . . . . **12.00**

Mongoose vs Snake Drag Race Set, #6438 . . . . **350.00**

Pop-Up Speed Shop, #5135. **35.00**

Real Riders Stamper 3-Pack, #9328 . . . . **45.00**

Rod Runner Speedway Set, #6439 . . . . **40.00**

Service Station, #5013. . . . . **60.00**

Stunt Action Set, #6201 . . . . **50.00**

Super Charger, #6294 . . . . **40.00**

Super Charger Grand Prix Race Set, #6292 . . . . **45.00**

Super Charger Rally 'n Freeway, #6430 . . . . **50.00**

Tune-Up Tower, #6481 . . . . **80.00**

CARS

1932 Ford Victoria, #6250, blue. **$25.00**

Cadillac Eldorado Coupe de Ville, metallic blue **35.00**

Cement Mixer, #6452, metallic orange. **25.00**

Custom Corvette, #6215, metallic blue **50.00**

Double Header, #5880, plum **70.00**

Dump Truck, #6453, metallic brown **20.00**

Dune Daddy, #6967, red. **65.00**

Evil Weevil, #6471, metallic red **35.00**

Fire Chief Cruiser, #6469, red **15.00**

Ford Thunderbird, #6207, metallic blue **50.00**

Hairy Hauler, #6458, metallic gold **30.00**

Hiway Robber, #6979, yellow **65.00**

Hot Heap, #6219, metallic magenta **15.00**

Jack Rabbit Special, #6421, white **15.00**

Light My Firebird, #6412, metallic orange **20.00**

Lotus Turbine, #6262, olive **15.00**

Mantis, #6423, metallic yellow **15.00**

Maserati Mistral, #6277, blue **45.00**

Mutt Mobile, #6185, metallic aqua **45.00**

Nitty Gritty Kitty, #6405, metallic blue **40.00**

Odd Job, #6981, lime green **90.00**

Peepin' Bomb, #6419, metallic purple **15.00**

Prowler, #6965, orange **170.00**

Red Baron, #6400, red **20.00**

Rolls Royce Silver Shadow, #6276, red **45.00**

S'Cool'Bus, #6468, yellow. **100.00**

Show Off, #6982, fluorescent pink. **125.00**

Silhouette, #6209, metallic yellow	**10.00**
Snake, #6409, yellow	**75.00**
Strip Teaser, #6188, metallic aqua	**50.00**
Swingin' Wing, #6422, metallic green	**20.00**
Team Trailer, #6019, metallic red	**70.00**
Turbofire, #6259, magenta	**15.00**
Volkswagen Beach Bomb, #6274, brown	**50.00**
Xploder, #6977, dark blue	**90.00**

HULL POTTERY

In 1905 Addis E. Hull purchased the Acme Pottery Company, Crooksville, Ohio, and changed its name to the A. E. Hull Pottery Company. By 1917, Hull's lines included art pottery for gift shops and florists, kitchenware, novelties, and stoneware.

Tile production helped the company weather the economic difficulties of the Depression. Hall's Little Red Riding Hood kitchenware arrived in 1943 and remained in production until 1957.

A 1950 flood and fire destroyed the company's plant. Two years later the company returned as the Hull Pottery Company. It was during this period that Hull added a new line of high-gloss glazed ceramics and developed Floraline and Regal, its product lines for the floral industry. The popularity of the California movement prompted a production shift to kitchen and dinner wares in 1960, with noteable lines including Mirror Brown, Rainbow, Provincial, Heartland, and Blue Belle. The plant closed in 1985.

Hull's early stoneware is marked with an "H." Matte pieces contain pattern numbers. Series numbers identify Open Rose/Camellia pieces (100s), Iris (400s), and Wildflower (W plus a number). Many Hull pieces also are marked with a number indicating their height in inches. Pieces made after 1950, usually featuring the high-gloss glaze, are marked "hull" or "Hull" in a script signature.

References: Barbara Loveless Glick-Burke, *Collector's Guide to Hull Pottery: The Dinnerware Lines,* Collector Books, 1993; Joan Gray Hull, *Hull: The Heavenly Pottery, Sixth Edition,* published by author, 1998; Brenda Roberts, *The Collectors Encyclopedia of Hull Pottery,* Collector Books, 1980, 1999 value update.

Newsletter: *Hull Pottery Newsletter,* 7768 Meadow Dr, Hillsboro, MO 63050.

Collectors' Club: Hull Pottery Assoc, 4 Hilltop Rd, Council Bluffs, IA 51503.

Note: See Little Red Riding Hood for additional listings.

Ashtray, Butterfly, B-3, 7" d	**$30.00**
Basket, Blossom Flite, T-9, 10" h	**135.00**
Basket, Bow-Knot, B-29, 12" h	**1,500.00**
Basket, Ebb Tide, 6¼" h	**100.00**
Basket, Magnolia, glossy, H-14, 10½" h	**325.00**
Basket, Open Rose, 107, 8" h	**260.00**
Basket, Parchment and Pine, S-8, 16½" l	**175.00**
Basket, Poppy, 601, 12" h	**200.00**
Basket, Rosella, R-12, 7" h	**240.00**
Basket, Sunglow, 84, 6½" h	**65.00**
Basket, Water Lily, L-14, 10½" h	**325.00**
Basket, Wildflower, W-16, 10½" h	**300.00**
Basket, Woodland, W-22, 10½" h	**225.00**
Bookends, pr, Orchid, 316, 7" h	**950.00**
Bowl, Calla Lily, 500/32, 10" d	**175.00**

Tulip Vase, Sun Valley Pastels, #162, green, 1956-57, 11½" h, $50.00. Photo courtesy Ray Morykan Auctions.

Bud Vase, Iris, 410, 7½" h	**150.00**
Bud Vase, Orchid, 306, 6¾" h	**150.00**
Bud Vase, Sueno Tulip, 104-33, 6" h	**100.00**
Candleholder, Bow-Knot, B-17, 14" h	**100.00**
Candleholder, Calla Lily, 2¼" h	**75.00**
Candleholder, Open Rose, 117, 6½" h	**130.00**
Candleholder, Water Lily, L-22, 4½" h	**45.00**
Console Bowl, Ebb Tide, E-12, 15¾" l	**130.00**
Console Bowl, Magnolia, matte, 26, 12" l	**45.00**
Console Bowl, Open Rose, 116, 12" l	**300.00**
Console Bowl, Wildflower, 70, 12" l	**350.00**
Creamer, Ebb Tide, E-15, 4" h	**75.00**
Creamer, Open Rose, 111, 5" h	**100.00**
Creamer, Wildflower, 73, 4¾" h	**190.00**
Ewer, Bow-Knot, B-1, 5½" h	**150.00**
Ewer, Dogwood, 520, 4¾" h	**95.00**
Ewer, Iris, 401, 13½" h	**450.00**
Ewer, Magnolia, matte, 14, 4¾" h	**40.00**
Ewer, Open Rose, 128, 4¾" h	**75.00**
Ewer, Orchid, 311, 13" h	**650.00**
Ewer, Poppy, 610, 4¾" h	**115.00**
Ewer, Rosella, R-11, 7" l	**125.00**
Ewer, Sueno Tulip, 109-33, 13" h	**325.00**
Ewer, Sunglow, 90, 5½" h	**35.00**
Ewer, Water Lily, L-17, 13½" h	**400.00**
Ewer, Wildflower, 55, 13½" h	**800.00**
Ewer, Woodland, W-24, 13½" h	**225.00**
Hanging Basket, Open Rose, 132, 7" h	**250.00**
Jardiniere, Bow-Knot, B-18, 5¾" h	**175.00**
Jardiniere, Open Rose, 114, 8¼" h	**275.00**
Jardiniere, Orchid, 310, 6" h	**200.00**
Jardiniere, Sueno Tulip, 115-33, 7" h	**250.00**
Jardiniere, Water Lily, L-23, 5½" h	**90.00**
Jardiniere, Wildflower, 64, 4" h	**100.00**
Pitcher, Sunglow, 52, 24 oz	**35.00**
Planter, Blossom Flite, 10½" l	**85.00**
Planter, Poppy, 602, 6½" h	**190.00**
Rose Bowl, Iris, 412, 7" h	**175.00**
Teapot, Bow-Knot, B-20, 6" h	**400.00**

Teapot, Open Rose, 110, 8½" h 275.00
Teapot, Parchment and Pine, 6" h 90.00
Teapot, Water Lily, L-18, 6" h 175.00
Teapot, Woodland, W-26, 6½" h 130.00
Vase, Calla Lily, 502/33, 6½" h 110.00
Vase, Calla Lily, 520/33, 8" h 110.00
Vase, Dogwood, 517, 4¾" h 70.00
Vase, Iris, 402, 7" h 150.00
Vase, Magnolia, matte, 12, 6¼" h 50.00
Vase, Open Rose, 123, 6½" h 100.00
Vase, Orchid, 304, 10¼" h 350.00
Vase, Pinecone, 55, 6½" h 100.00
Vase, Poppy, 606, 10½" h 375.00
Vase, Rosella, R-2, 5" h 70.00
Vase, Serenade, S-4, 5¼" h 55.00
Vase, Sunglow, 94, 8" h 50.00
Vase, Thistle, 51, 6½" h 115.00
Vase, Water Lily, L-A, 8½" h 190.00
Wall Pocket, Poppy, 609, 9" h 300.00
Window Box, Dogwood, 508, 10½" l 190.00

HUMMEL FIGURINES

Berta Hummel, a German artist, provided the drawings that were the inspiration for W. Goebel's Hummel figurines. Berta Hummel, born in 1909 in Massing, Bavaria, Germany, enrolled at age eighteen in the Academy of Fine Arts in Munich. In 1934 she entered the Convent of Siessen and became Sister Maria Innocentia.

W. Goebel, Rodental, Bavaria, produced its first Hummel figurines in 1935. John Schmid of Schmid Brothers, Randolph, Massachusetts, secured American distribution rights. When Goebel wished to distribute directly to the American market in 1967, the two companies and Berta Hummel's heirs became entangled in a lawsuit. A compromise was reached. Goebel would base its figurines on drawings made by Berta Hummel between 1934 and her death in 1964. Schmid was given the rights to produce pieces based on Hummel's pre-convent drawings.

A Hummel figurine must have the "M. I. Hummel" legend on its base and a Goebel trademark. If either is missing, the figurine is not a Goebel Hummel. Seven different trademarks are used to identify the production period of a figurine:

Trademark 1	Incised Crown Mark	1935-1949
Trademark 2	Full Bee	1950-1959
Trademark 3	Stylized Bee	1957-1972
Trademark 4	Three Line Mark	1964-1972
Trademark 5	Last Bee Mark	1972-1979
Trademark 6	Missing Bee Mark	1979-1991
Trademark 7	Current/New Crown Mark	1991-Present

References: Ken Armke, *Hummel*, Wallace-Homestead, 1995; Carl F. Luckey, *Luckey's Hummel Figurines & Plates, 11th Edition*, Krause Publications, 1997; Robert L. Miller, *The No. 1 Price Guide to M. I. Hummel: Figurines, Plates, More...*, *Eighth Edition*, Portfolio Press, 2000.

Collectors' Clubs: Hummel Collectors Club, 1261 University Dr, Yardley, PA 19067; M. I. Hummel Club, Goebel Plaza, PO Box 11, Pennington, NJ 08534.

Accordion Boy, 185, trademark 3 . . . . $75.00
Angel Serenade, kneeling, 214/D, trademark 2 . . . . 50.00

Harmony in Four Parts, 471, trademark 6, $175.00. Photo courtesy Jackson's Auctioneers & Appraisers.

Artist, The, 304, trademark 5 . . . . 120.00
Barnyard Hero, 195/I, trademark 5 . . . . 130.00
Begging His Share, 9, trademark 5 . . . . 80.00
Be Patient, 197/I, trademark 6 . . . . 110.00
Big House-Cleaning, 363, trademark 6 . . . . 170.00
Bird Duet, 169, trademark 3 . . . . 85.00
Birthday Candle, 440, trademark 6 . . . . 110.00
Blessed Event, 333, trademark 5 . . . . 185.00
Boy with Horse, advent candlestick, 117, trademark 2 . . . . . 50.00
Boy with Toothache, 217, trademark 5 . . . . 125.00
Chimney Sweep, 12, trademark 2 . . . . 95.00
Coffee Break, 409, trademark 6 . . . . 130.00
Cross Roads, 331, trademark 5 . . . . 225.00
Daisies Don't Tell, 380, trademark 6 . . . . 120.00
Doll Bath, 319, trademark 5 . . . . 155.00
Flower Madonna, 10/I, trademark 2 . . . . 210.00
For Father, 87, trademark 5 . . . . 100.00
Friends, 136/I, trademark 5 . . . . 110.00
Girl with Fir Tree, advent candlestick, 116, trademark 2 . . . 35.00
Girl with Nosegay, advent candlestick, 115, trademark 3 . . . 32.00
Good Friends, 182, trademark 3 . . . . 115.00
Goose Girl, 47/3/0, trademark 5 . . . . 60.00
Happy Traveller, 109/0, trademark 3 . . . . 65.00
Heavenly Angel, 21/I, trademark 3 . . . . 100.00
Hello, 124, trademark 2 . . . . 175.00
Home From Market, 198/1, trademark 5 . . . . 100.00
It's Cold, 421, trademark 6 . . . . 125.00
Kiss Me, 311, trademark 4 . . . . 55.00
Little Bookkeeper, 306, trademark 5 . . . . 170.00
Little Drummer, 240, trademark 3 . . . . 90.00
Little Fiddler, 4, trademark 2 . . . . 150.00
Little Music Makers, 741, trademark 6 . . . . 20.00
Little Pharmacist, 322, trademark 5 . . . . 120.00
Mediation, 13/0, trademark 5 . . . . 100.00
Merry Wanderer, 11/0, trademark 5 . . . . 65.00
Morning Concert, 447, trademark 6 . . . . 90.00
Not For You, 317, trademark 5 . . . . 110.00
Puppy Love, 1, trademark 3 . . . . 115.00

Nativity Set, 214, trademark 2, $1,500.00. Photo courtesy Gene Harris Antique Auction Center, Inc.

Sensitive Hunter, 6/I, trademark 5	**60.00**
She Loves Me, She Loves Me Not, 174, trademark 2	**145.00**
Signs of Spring, 203/2/0, trademark 3	**85.00**
Singing Lesson, 63, trademark 2	**60.00**
Street Singer, 131, trademark 3	**70.00**
Strolling Along, 5, trademark 3	**100.00**
Surprise, 94/3/0, trademark 5	**85.00**
Surprise, The, 431, trademark 6	**100.00**
Sweet Music, 186, trademark 3	**90.00**
Trumpet Boy, 97, trademark 3	**70.00**
Valentine Gift, 387, trademark 5	**225.00**
Valentine Joy, 399, trademark 6	**120.00**
Village Boy, 51/0, trademark 5	**70.00**
Wayside Harmony, 111/3/0, trademark 3	**60.00**
Weary Wanderer, 204, trademark 5	**110.00**

HUMMEL LOOK-ALIKES

If imitation is the most sincere form of flattery, Berta Hummel and W. Goebel should feel especially honored. Goebel's Hummel figurines have been stylistically copied by ceramic manufacturers around the world.

A Hummel look-alike is a stylistic copy of a Goebel Hummel figurine or a completely new design done in an artistic style that mimics that of Berta Hummel. It does not require much of an alteration to avoid infringing on a design patent. These copycats come from a host of Japanese firms, Herbert Dubler (House of Ars Sacra), Erich Stauffer (Arnart Imports), Decorative Figures Corporation, Beswick, and Coventry Ware.

Reference: Lawrence L. Wonsch, *Hummel Copycats with Values,* Wallace-Homestead, 1987, 2nd printing by Bumblebee Press.

April Showers, Erich Stauffer, ES8561, 8" h	**$30.00**
Astronaut, Erich Stauffer, 6" h	**20.00**
Band Leader, Dubler, 1943, 5¾" h	**30.00**
Boy with Ducks, Erich Stauffer, #44/137	**24.00**
Boy with Rake, Erich Stauffer, #U8515, 6½" h	**20.00**
Country Boy with Dog, Arnart, 5¼" h	**10.00**
Girl Reading Book with Duck, Erich Stauffer, 5" h	**20.00**

Girl with Bucket and Goose, Erich Stauffer, #8213	**12.00**
Girl with Carrots, Farm Chore, Erich Stauffer, Arnart label, #55/973, 4¼" h	**20.00**
Girl with Flowers, Erich Stauffer, #3262, 7" h	**15.00**
Girl with Rabbit and Geese, Erich Stauffer, Arnart label	**15.00**
Goose Boy, Erich Stauffer, 5" h	**12.00**
Goose Girl, Erich Stauffer, #18394, 5" h	**12.00**
Life on the Farm, boy with axe, Erich Stauffer, Arnart label, #2818, 4¾" h	**15.00**
Little Cobbler, Dubler, #36, 1942	**110.00**
Little Hiker Boy and Girl, pr, Coventry Ware	**25.00**
Luck of the Draw, Arnart, #95769	**55.00**
Open Laces, Erich Stauffer, #8248, 6½" h	**30.00**
Picnic Girl, Erich Stauffer, #55/972, 4" h	**15.00**
Play Time, Erich Stauffer, Arnart label, #441173, 6" h	**12.00**
Sleepy Baby, Dubler, #39, 1942	**25.00**

HUNTING

Hunting came into its own as a major collecting category in the 1980s. The initial focus was on hunting advertising and paper ephemera, e.g., books, calendars, and catalogs. Examples from firms such as DuPont, Peters Cartridge Company, Remington, and Winchester command premium prices.

Collectors also have identified a group of illustrators whose hunting scenes and images have become highly desirable. Look for works by G. Muss Arnolt, Phillip Goodwin, Lynn Bogue Hunt, and Edmund Osthaus. Beware of the limited edition hunting prints issued in the 1970s and 80s. The secondary market is volatile—more will decline than rise in value over the next decade.

Hunting licenses and ammunition boxes currently are two hot subcategories. Even some post-1945 decoys have joined the collectible ranks.

References: Ralf Coykendall, Jr., *Coykendall's Complete Guide to Sporting Collectibles,* Wallace-Homestead, Krause Publications, 1996; Jim and Vivian Karsnitz, *Sporting Collectibles,* Schiffer Publishing, 1992; Carl F. Luckey, *Collecting Antique Bird and Duck Calls, 2nd Edition,* Books Americana, 1992; Donna Tonelli, *Top of the Line Hunting Collectibles,* Schiffer Publishing, 1998.

Periodical: *Sporting Collector's Monthly,* PO Box 305, Camden Wyoming, DE 19934.

Collectors' Clubs: Call & Whistle Collectors Assoc, 2839 E 26th Place, Tulsa, OK 74114; Callmakers & Collectors Assoc of America, 137 Kingswood Dr, Clarksville, TN 37043.

Ammunition, Hunters Red Dog Shells, 12 gauge, yellow, red, and white, empty	**$55.00**
Catalog, Marble's Outing Equipment, #20, 48 pp, 1923	**135.00**
Counter Display, plastic, Winchester, for 8 columns of .22 ammunition boxes, red and white	**130.00**
Decoy, ears of corn, cast iron, painted yellow, 5" l, price for 2	**100.00**
Deer Call Kit, Sport Lore, complete with instructions, MIB	**15.00**
Hunting and Fishing License Button, West Virginia, dark green and black, 1940	**75.00**
Photograph, black and white, 3 hunters with 6 large bucks, 1940s, 8 x 10"	**12.00**
Pinback Button, American Trappers' Association, members button, 1920-30s	**75.00**

Sign, Ithaca Featherlight Repeaters, 2-pc, diecut cardboard, 21" w, $125.00. Photo courtesy Collectors Auction Services.

Pinback Button, Daisy Air Rifle Safety Club, litho tin, blue and white, red "Shoot Safe Buddy," 1940s 20.00

Pinback Button, "Ducks Unlimited," celluloid, multicolored, pintail duck, 1948 . . . . 80.00

Pinback Button, Raccoon Hunters Club, sepia art with dark brown inscription on white ground, 1938 . . . . 20.00

Pocket Compass, brass frame, Marbles 35.00

Poster, diecut, "Get your game with Remington," 2 hunters with Model 11 shotguns, 32½ x 28" 225.00

Sign, molded plastic, "Browning Sporting Arms," gold, brown, and white, self-framed, 13 x 20" 40.00

Sign, tin, "State Game Reserve Hunting," Department of Conservation, Division of Fish and Game, "Penalty Under Acts of 1928," black lettering, yellow ground 50.00

Sign, tin, "Winchester Western Sportsman's Game Guide," multicolored, depicts animals and game birds, Super-X shot shells adv, 28 x 23" 75.00

Thermometer, painted tin, "Winchester Western AA clay target ammunition sold here," red, black, white, and gold, 26½ x 7" 300.00

AUCTION PRICES – GAME CALLS

SoldUSA.com, Fine Sporting Collectibles, game calls, March 31, 1999. Prices include a 10% buyer's premium.

Crow, FA Allen, black-painted metal body, wood stopper, 50% orig paint, well-used, 2¾" l $46.00

Deer, Herter's No 903 Deer Master, walnut barrel, amber colored plastic stopper, orig box, 4" l 26.00

Duck, Cajun, walnut barrel and stopper, plastic reed, ink-stamped name and address, 4½" l 12.00

Duck, NC Hansen "Broadbill," painted dark green, light green mouth, 1930s, 5¼" l 83.00

Goose, Catlett Darnell, maple barrel, walnut stopper, plastic reed, sgd on barrel "Catlett Darnell" in script, 7" l 168.00

Squirrel, Herter's No 99 Famous Squirrel Call, walnut boey, brass strike plate, steel striker, new in box with papers 30.00

Turkey, PS Olt No CT-220, "Crank Turkey Call," walnut/cedar constructed, decal label, 5" 121.00

Turkey, Rebel Yell Jake Talker, striker box type, stamped name on 2 sides, 5½" l 22.00

ICE CREAM COLLECTIBLES

The street ice cream vendor dates from the 1820s. In 1846 Nancy Johnson invented the hand-cranked ice cream freezer, a standard household fixture by the mid-1850s. The urban ice cream garden arrived on the scene in the middle of the 19th century.

The ice cream parlor was superseded by the drugstore soda fountain in the 1920s and 30s. Improvements in the freezer portions of refrigerators, the development of efficient grocery store freezers, and the spread of chain drugstores in the 1950s, 60s, and 70s slowly lessened the role of the local drugstore soda fountain.

Ice cream collectibles fall into two basic groups: (1) material from the dairy industry, and (2) ice cream and soda fountain items. Beware of reproductions, reputed "warehouse" finds, and fantasy items.

Reference: Wayne Smith, *Ice Cream Dippers,* published by author, 1986.

Collectors' Clubs: National Assoc of Soda Jerks, PO Box 115, Omaha, NE 68101; The Ice Screamers, PO Box 465, Warrington, PA 18976.

Clock, Swift's Ice Cream, light-up, plastic with metal case, c1960s, 16" sq **$80.00**

Display, ice cream cone, papier-mâché, "Eat-It-All," hanging or stand-up, c1950s, 17" h 110.00

Door Push, "5¢ Popsicles Sold Here, a Frozen Drink On a Stick," emb tin, rect, orange, yellow, and black, c1930-40s, 3 x 9½" 450.00

Milk Shake Mixer, Hamilton Beach, Model #33, stainless steel mixing cup, stainless steel and porcelain body, 2 speeds 175.00

Pinback Button, Adventurer's Popsicle Club, black, white, and gold litho, c1930s. 20.00

Pinback Button, Breyer's Ice Cream 75th Anniversary, 1866-1941, oval, red and green design and lettering on white ground 20.00

Pinback Button, National Ice Cream Week, blue and white litho of crowned man, ©Ice Cream Review on rim curl, c1930s 25.00

Pinback Button, Piper Rainbow Ice Cream Cones, 1930s 75.00

Pinback Button, Stewart's Ice Cream, blue and white, features baby calf "Perky," c1940s 20.00

Pinback Button, The National Dessert, multicolored, back mkd "National Dairy and Food Bureau, Chicago," 1930s 20.00

Place Mat, Swift Premium's Jack and Jill, glossy rigid cardboard, full color art of nursery rhyme scene, copyright for Sass-Dorne Studios, reverse with simulated wood-grain finish centered by nursery rhyme text above depiction of 2 canned meat baby products by Swift & Co, 1945, 10½ x 16" 25.00

Record Brush, Abbott's Ice Cream, celluloid, "Sixth Anniversary," pale red brick left and right against pale blue sky ground, red lettering by product name, 1920s, 3½" d 50.00

Serving Tray, "Pittsburgh Ice Cream Co," rect, woman serving ice cream to children, 1920-30s 1,200.00

Sign, Carnation Ice Cream, diecut porcelain, shield shaped, 1940-50s, 22 x 23" 1,200.00

Sign, Crown Quality Ice Cream, emb tin, The Scioto Sign Co, Kenton, OH, 24 x 18" 175.00

Sign/Clock, Jane Logan De Luxe Ice Cream, electric, wrought-iron frame, plastic illuminated sign, Ohio Advertising Display Co, 24" h, $200.00.

Sign, "Enjoy Ice Cream," Ice Cream Manufacturers, hanging, diamond shaped, red, black, and white, c1940-50s, 10 x 10" 275.00
Sign, "Everybody Likes Popsicles, Frozen Suckers," emb tin, rect, orange, white, and black, 1930-40s, 10 x 28" ... 325.00
Sign, Ludwig's Ice Cream, porcelain, "We Serve Ludwig's Ice Cream/The Ice Cream Supreme," blue lettering on yellow ground, blue border, 1930-40s, 20 x 14" 100.00
Sign, Pet Ice Cream, tin, red, white, and blue, 1959, 42 x 54" 110.00
Sign, Pevely Super Test Ice Cream, 2-sided, diecut porcelain, red, white, and black, 1930-40s, 17" sq 300.00
Sign, "Sunfreze Ice Cream by Arden," 2-sided, porcelain, red, yellow, and white, c1930-40s, 28 x 32" 825.00

ILLUSTRATORS

The mass-market printing revolution of the late 19th century marked the advent of the professional illustrator. Illustrators provided artwork for books, calendars, magazines, prints, games, jigsaw puzzles, and a host of advertising and promotional products.

Illustrator art breaks down into three major categories: (1) original art, (2) first strike prints sold as art works, and (3) commercially produced art. While the first two categories are limited, the third is not. Often images were produced in the millions.

Magazines, more than any other medium, were responsible for introducing the illustrator to the general public. Norman Rockwell's covers for *Boy's Life* and *The Saturday Evening Post* are classics. Magazine covers remain one of the easiest and most inexpensive means of collecting illustrator art.

References: Clifford P. Catania, *Boudoir Art,* Schiffer Publishing, 1997; Karen Choppa, *Bessie Pease Gutman,* Schiffer Publishing, 1998; Patricia L. Gibson, *R. Atkinson Fox, William M. Thompson,* Collectors Press, 1995; William Holland, Clifford Catania and

Nathan Isen, *Louis Icart: The Complete Etchings, Revised 3rd Edition,* Schiffer Publishing, 1998; Rick and Charlotte Martin, *Vintage Illustration: Discovering America's Calendar Artists, 1900-1960,* Collectors Press, 1997; Rita C. Mortenson, *R. Atkinson Fox,* L-W Book Sales, 1991, 1999 value update; Norman I. Platnick, *Coles Phillips: A Collector's Guide,* published by author, 1997; Sarah Steiner and Donna Braun, *A Bit of [Frances] Brundage,* Schiffer Publishing, 1999; Naomi Welch, *American & European Postcards of Harrison Fisher,* published by author, 1999; Naomi Welch, *The Complete Works of Harrison Fisher,* published by author, 1999.

Newsletters: *Calendar Art Collectors' Newsletter,* 45 Brown's Ln, Old Lyme, CT 06371; *Fern Bisel Peat Newsletter,* 20 S Linden Rd, Apt 112, Mansfield, OH 44906; *The Illustrator Collector's News,* PO Box 1958, Sequim, WA 98382.

Collectors' Clubs: Arthur Szyk Society, 1200 Edgehill Dr, Burlingame, CA 90410; Gutmann Collectors Club, 24A E Roseville Rd, Lancaster, PA 17601; The Harrison Fisher Society, 123 N Glassell, Orange, CA 92666; Hy Hintemeister Collector's Group, 5 Pasture Rd, Whitehouse Station, NJ 08889; R. Atkinson Fox Society, 8141 Main, Kansas City, MO 64114.

Note: For additional listings see Nutting, Wallace; Parrish, Maxfield; Rockwell, Norman; and Children's Books, Kewpies, Pin-Up Art, Postcards and Prints.

Bisel Peat, Fern, magazine cover, *Children's Play Mate,* Apr 1943 .... $5.00
Cappiello, Leonetto, postcard, Job, "Papier A Cigarettes," used, French, 1931 .... 150.00
Christy, Earl, magazine cover, *The American Magazine,* Dec 1923 .... 12.00
Coffin, Haskell, magazine cover, *Modern Priscilla,* Aug 1926, 12 x 9" 10.00
Coffin, Haskell, sheet music, *Land of My Dreams,* c1922 .... 10.00
Crandall, John Bradshaw, portrait, A Mid-Summer Night's Dream, c1932, 8 x 6". 20.00
Crandall, John Bradshaw, portrait, The Lady in Red, c1933, 9 x 7" 25.00
Dali, Salvador, postcard, Tour de France, "Arriving in Paris," black and white, 1959 .... 400.00
Elsley, Arthur, portrait, A Good Old Friend, c1921, 8 x 6".... 50.00
Fox, Robert Atkinson, portrait, The Buffalo Hunt, c1932, 8 x 10" 100.00
Fox, Robert Atkinson, portrait, The Treasure Fleet, c1925, 8 x 11" 85.00
Fukiya, Koji, postcard, Art Deco woman wearing fur, 1928. .... 125.00
Goddard, L, portrait, A Fair Catch, c1927, 8 x 10" 35.00
Goddard, L, portrait, Moonbeams, c1924, 9 x 7" 30.00
Goldberg, YE, jigsaw puzzle, Sailing Off Block Island, wood, hand cut, Glencraft/Glendex, 512 pcs, 1960s, orig box 45.00
Goodwin, Phillip R, portrait, An Early Morning Thrill, c1926, 10 x 8" 30.00
Goodwin, Phillip R, portrait, Taking the Trail, c1926, 8 x 6" 25.00
Hintermeister, Hy, jigsaw puzzle, The Birth of Our Country, Ben Franklin at hearthside, 80 pcs, c1920, 13 x 9" 20.00
Hintermeister, Hy, portrait, Precious Little Fellow, c1932, 10 x 7" 25.00

Maude Fangel, sign, 1920s, 11 x 13", $40.00.

Humphrey, Walter Beach, calendar top, Hercules
Powder Co adv, c1940s **125.00**

Icart, Louis, print, *Coach,* etching and aquatint with
touches of hand-coloring, Rives BFK paper with
M Robbe Fils watermark, sgd, artist's blindstamp, and
"Gravure Garantie Originale" inkstamp, full margins,
1926, 2¼ x 18¼", 35½ x 24¾" sheet **925.00**

Icart, Louis, print, *Mignon,* etching and aquatint with
touches of hand-coloring, wove paper, sgd, artist's
blindstamp, copyrighted and dated in plate, laid
down, with margins, surface abrasions and water
staining in image area, 1928, 20¼ x 13½ x 18" sheet **800.00**

Kenyon, Zula, portrait, Carmel by the Sea, c1924, 13 x
10" **20.00**

Kenyon, Zula, portrait, Nature's Shrine, c1924, 9 x 12" . . . **15.00**

O'Neill Wilson, Rose Cecil, postcard, woman golfing,
"Golf – a mile above sea level in Colorado – has
unusual charms," Rock Island Railroad adv **500.00**

Parrish, Maxfield, postcard, Christmas Life, 2 women
carrying large bread pudding, from Dec 1921 *Life
Magazine* cov **300.00**

Phillips, Cole, magazine tear sheet, Community Plate,
"Flapper Girl," full page, color, 1923 . . . . **10.00**

Thompson, TN, calendar, Studio Sketches, spiral bound,
1952 . . . . **50.00**

Wyeth, NC, calendar top, c1940s **40.00**

IMPERIAL GLASS

In 1901 a group of investors founded the Imperial Glass Company.
Production began on January 13, 1904 and was mass-market
directed, e.g., jelly glasses, tumblers, and tableware. Imperial's
success was guaranteed by one of its first orders, approximately 20
different items to be supplied to almost 500 F. W. Woolworth
stores. McCrory and Kresge were also major customers.

Between 1910 and 1920 Imperial introduced a number of new
glassware lines. "Nuart" iridescent ware was followed by "Nucut"
crystal, a pressed reproduction of English cut glass pieces which
sold well as a premium and was widely distributed by The Grand
Union Tea Company. In the 1950s, "Nucut" was reintroduced as
"Collectors Crystal."

Imperial declared bankruptcy in 1931 but continued to operate
through court-appointed receivers. Imperial Glass Corporation, a
new entity, was formed during July and August of 1931. In 1937
Imperial launched Candlewick, its best selling line.

In 1940 Imperial acquired the Central Glass Works. It proved to
be the first of a number of acquisitions, including A. H. Heisey and
Company in 1958 and the Cambridge Glass Company in 1960.

In 1973, Imperial became a subsidiary of Lenox Glass Corporation. In 1981 Lenox sold the company to Arthur Lorch, a private
investor, who in turn sold it to Robert Stahl, a liquidator, in 1982.
In October 1982 Imperial declared bankruptcy. Consolidated-
Colony, a partnership of Lancaster Colony Corporation and
Consolidated International, purchased Imperial in December
1984. Most of the company's molds were sold. Maroon Enterprises
of Bridgeport, Ohio, purchased the buildings and property in
March 1985.

References: Margaret and Douglas Archer, *Imperial Glass: 1904-
1938 Catalog,* reprint, Collector Books, 1978, 1998 value update;
National Imperial Glass Collectors' Society, *Imperial Glass Ency-
clopedia, Vol I: A - Cane* (1995), *Vol II: Cape Cod - L* (1998), *Vol III:
M - Z* (1999), Glass Press; Harry L. Rinker, *Stemware of the 20th
Century: The Top 200 Patterns,* House of Collectibles, 1997.

Collectors' Club: National Imperial Glass Collectors Society, PO
Box 534, Bellaire, OH 43906.

Note: For additional listings see Candlewick, Carnival Glass, and
Milk Glass,

Beaded Block, bowl, green, 5½" sq **$12.00**
Beaded Block, creamer, pink **18.00**
Beaded Block, plate, pink, 7¾" sq **10.00**
Beaded Block, sugar, green **15.00**
Cape Cod, basket, 160/73/0 . . . . **350.00**
Cape Cod, bowl, 160/67F, ftd, 9" d **90.00**
Cape Cod, bowl, 160/125, divided, oval, 11" l **100.00**
Cape Cod, butter, cov, 160/144, handled **55.00**
Cape Cod, cake plate, pedestal, 10" d **65.00**
Cape Cod, cake stand, 160/103D, 11" d **125.00**
Cape Cod, candleholders, pr, 160/80, 5" h **40.00**
Cape Cod, candy dish, ftd, 160/110 . . . . **85.00**
Cape Cod, celery, 160/189 . . . . **85.00**
Cape Cod, center bowl, 160/75L **65.00**
Cape Cod, claret, 1602 . . . . **15.00**
Cape Cod, coaster, 160/78 . . . . **10.00**
Cape Cod, coaster, amber **15.00**
Cape Cod, compote, cov, 160/140, ftd **85.00**
Cape Cod, cordial, 1602 . . . . **10.00**
Cape Cod, creamer and sugar with tray **40.00**
Cape Cod, cruet, 160/119, 4 oz **20.00**
Cape Cod, cup and saucer **8.00**
Cape Cod, cupped plate, 16" d **50.00**
Cape Cod, decanter, 160/163, 30 oz **75.00**
Cape Cod, decanter, 160/212, 24 oz **65.00**
Cape Cod, dinner plate, 10" d **35.00**
Cape Cod, goblet, 1602, crystal, 11 oz **6.00**
Cape Cod, ice lip jug, 160/19, 40 oz **85.00**
Cape Cod, milk pitcher, 160/240, 16 oz **50.00**
Cape Cod, old fashioned, 160/3, 7 oz **12.00**
Cape Cod, oyster, 1602 . . . . **8.00**
Cape Cod, parfait, 1602 . . . . **10.00**
Cape Cod, pastry tray, yellow **275.00**

Cape Cod, pepper mill, 160/235 . . . . **30.00**
Cape Cod, punch cup, 160/37. . . . . **5.00**
Cape Cod, relish dish, 160/1602, 3-part **150.00**
Cape Cod, salad plate, 8" d **8.00**
Cape Cod, salt shaker, 160/238 . . . . **20.00**
Cape Cod, shakers, pr, green **60.00**
Cape Cod, sherbet, low, 1602 . . . . **5.00**
Cape Cod, sherbet, red **20.00**
Cape Cod, tumbler, 1602, ftd, 10 oz **10.00**
Cape Cod, tumbler, 1602, ftd, 12 oz **10.00**
Cape Cod, water goblet, red **25.00**
Cape Cod, wine, 1602 . . . . **8.00**
Cape Cod, wine, blue, 4 oz. **30.00**
Lace Edge, creamer and sugar, blue opalescent **80.00**
Lace Edge, dinner plate, green opalescent, 10" d **85.00**
Lace Edge, fruit bowl, blue opalescent **30.00**
Lace Edge, luncheon plate, green opalescent, 12" d **80.00**
Lace Edge, platter, blue opalescent, 13" l **175.00**
Lace Edge, vegetable, green opalescent **95.00**
Old Williamsburg, bread and butter plate, 6" d. **8.00**
Old Williamsburg, candy dish, cov, ftd, 10" h. **8.00**
Old Williamsburg, compote. **20.00**
Old Williamsburg, creamer and covered sugar, handled **35.00**
Old Williamsburg, iced tea, ftd **15.00**
Old Williamsburg, juice, ftd **15.00**
Old Williamsburg, mayonnaise, 3 pcs **27.00**
Old Williamsburg, nappy **15.00**
Old Williamsburg, double old fashioned **15.00**
Old Williamsburg, salad bowl, 9" d **45.00**
Old Williamsburg, torte plate, 13" d. **20.00**
Old Williamsburg, tumbler **12.00**
Twist, champagne, 4³/₈" h **15.00**
Twist, cordial, 3⁵/₈" h **15.00**
Twist, iced tea, flat **15.00**
Twist, parfait, 6¹/₄" h **15.00**
Twist, plate, 8³/₈" d **15.00**
Twisted Optic, bowl, blue, 9" d **25.00**
Twisted Optic, bowl, pink, 9" d **15.00**
Twisted Optic, cereal bowl, blue, 5" d **10.00**

Twisted Optic, creamer and sugar, canary yellow **25.00**
Twisted Optic, cream soup bowl, blue **15.00**
Twisted Optic, cream soup bowl, pink **10.00**
Twisted Optic, cup and saucer, blue **15.00**
Twisted Optic, luncheon plate, canary yellow **8.00**
Twisted Optic, salad bowl, blue, 7" d **15.00**
Twisted Optic, sherbet plate, blue, 6"d. **4.00**

INSULATORS

The development of glass and ceramic insulators resulted from a need created by the telegraph. In 1844 Ezra Cornell obtained the first insulator patent. Armstrong (1938-69), Brookfield (1865-1922), California (1912-16), Gayner (1920-22), Hemingray (1871-1919), Lynchburg (1923-25), Maydwell (1935-40), McLaughlin (1923-25), and Whitall Tatum (1920-38) are the leading insulator manufacturers.

The first insulators did not contain threads. L. A. Cauvet patented a threaded insulator in the late 1860s. Drip points were added to insulators to prevent water from accumulating and creating a short. A double skirt kept the peg or pin free of moisture.

Insulators are collected by "CD" (consolidated design) numbers as found in N. R. Woodward's *The Glass Insulator in America*. The numbers are based upon the design style of the insulator. Color, name of maker, or lettering are not factors in assigning numbers. Thus far over 500 different design styles have been identified.

References: Michael Bruner, *The Definitive Guide to Colorful Insulators,* Schiffer Publishing, 2000; John and Carol McDougald, *Insulators: A History and Guide to North American Glass Pintype Insulators, Volume 1* (1990), *Volume 2* (1990), value update (1999), published by authors; Marion and Evelyn Milholland, *Glass Insulator Reference Book, 4th Revision,* published by authors, 1976, available from C. D. Walsh (granddaughter).

Periodical: *Crown Jewels of the Wire,* PO Box 1003, St Charles, IL 60174.

Collectors' Club: National Insulator Assoc, 1315 Old Mill Path, Broadview Heights, OH 44147.

Note: Insulators are in near mint/mint condition unless otherwise noted.

CD 102, "W BPOOKFIELD, NEW YOPK" emb dome,
　misprint, light aqua **$15.00**
CD 106, McLaughlin-9, 7-up emerald green **20.00**
CD 106, OVG Co, teal blue aqua, flat top **12.00**
CD 121, California, sage green **15.00**
CD 121, McLaughlin-16, emerald green **20.00**
CD 121, McLaughlin-16, teal emerald green **30.00**
CD 121, pleated skirt, 1899 on dome, light blue **30.00**
CD 122, McLaughlin-16, apple green **50.00**
CD 122, McLaughlin-16, lime green **20.00**
CD 126, Brookfield Cauvet-1865/1870/1870, light aqua,
　milk glass in skirt. **12.00**
CD 133, California, aqua **15.00**
CD 135, Chicago Diamond, emb, blue **70.00**
CD 141, dome glass, blue aqua. **15.00**
CD 145, Brookfield, 1883/1884 on dome, mint green. **30.00**
CD 145, California, sage green **15.00**
CD 152, California, sage green **8.00**
CD 152, Hemingray-40, blue, amber streaks **18.00**

Lace Edge, compote, #749F, white, 1950-60, 5¹/₄" h, $20.00.

CD 123,
EC&M Co SF,
yellow-green,
$40.00.

CD 154, ESA, CTNE, dark teal green aqua	25.00
CD 154, Lynchburg-44, ginger ale	15.00
CD 154, McLaughlin-40, aqua	12.00
CD 154, McLaughlin-42, smooth base, delft blue	40.00
CD 154, McLaughlin-42, light cornflower blue	35.00
CD 154, McLaughlin-42, lime green	20.00
CD 154, McLaughlin-42, pastel blue aqua	15.00
CD 154, Whitall Tatum-1, dark apple	25.00
CD 161, California, "A" in dome, dark purple rose	25.00
CD 162, California, milk glass in dome, blue aqua	18.00
CD 162, Gayner-190, aqua	5.00
CD 162, grass green with olive wisps, bubbles	20.00
CD 162, Hemingray-19, smooth base, blue	10.00
CD 162, Maydwell-19, bright straw	8.00
CD 162, McLaughlin-19, smooth base, sage green	8.00
CD 164, Maydwell-20, white milk glass	18.00
CD 164, McLaughlin-20, cornflower blue	20.00
CD 164, McLaughlin-20, emerald green	15.00
CD 286, FM Locke Victor NY, 5 dates, light blue	80.00
CD 296, Locke Victor NY, olive green with amber streaks	30.00
CD 297, #16, dark green aqua	18.00
CD 1071, Hemingray-110, "only spool with threads," clear	10.00

IRONS

The modern iron resulted from a series of technological advances that began in the middle of the 19th century. Until the arrival of the electric iron at the beginning of the 20th century, irons were heated by pre-heating a slug put into the iron, burning solid or liquid fuels or by drawing heat from a heated surface such as a stove top.

Pre-electric irons from the late 19th and early 20th centuries are common. Do not overpay. High prices are reserved for novelty irons and irons from lesser known makers.

H. W. Seeley patented the first electric iron in 1882. The first iron, a General Electric with a detachable cord, dates from 1903. Westinghouse introduced the automatic iron in 1924 and Edec the steam iron in 1926. Electric irons are collected more for their body design than their historical importance or age. Check the cord and plug before attempting to use any electric iron.

References: David Irons, *Irons By Irons* (1994), *More Irons By Irons* (1997), *Even More Irons By Irons* (2000), published by author.

Newsletter: *Iron Talk,* PO Box 68, Waelder, TX 78959.

Automatic Cordless, Chicago, IL, electric, double stand, 2 irons, c1930, 6³/₈" l	$150.00
Boston Electric Heating Corp, Whitman, MA, Electric Hat, blue light indicator for use, c1925, 7" h	200.00
Coleman, Instant Lite, Model 609, gasoline, black enamel, plastic handle, c1930, 8³/₈" l	100.00
Coleman, Model 609A, gasoline, black enamel body, black plastic handle, complete with box, pump, can, wrench, papers, and parts list with prices, c1935, 8" l	300.00
Coleman, Model 615, made in Canada, kerosene, black enamel body, blue tank, c1940, 7³/₄" l	300.00
Czechoslovakian, Filakovd, green enamel, cold red handle, iron stand at rear, c1930, 7" l	200.00
Czechoslovakian, Moravia 4, black enamel body, cold handle, release button in handle, c1930, 6³/₄" l	200.00
Czechoslovakian, travel iron, made in Kraupner Roudnice, folding, can also be used as hot plate, perm-hair attachment, 1930, 8¹/₈" l	300.00
Dover Sad Iron #2, cold handle, c1925, 6¹/₂" l	50.00
Edison Electric Appliance Co, Inc, Hot Point, electric, folding box with trivet and curling iron, cloth covered box with instructions for repacking box, draw string to close, c1925, 5¹/₂" l	100.00
Electro-Coo, Calrus, Electric Egg, English, 5 positions to set egg, wood board, c1940, 10¹/₄" h	150.00
European, F Habelt C Tesin, natural gas, EPPA PAT dep 4347, chrome plated, c1930, 11³/₈" l	200.00
European, flat, gray and white enamel, c1920, 6¹/₄" l	100.00
European, Universella, travel, electric, lift-off handle and reverse to change from 110 to 220 volts, red enamel top, c1930, 6⁷/₈" l	100.00
German, Blitzplate, made in Carl Pack, Deutschland, cold handle, unusual latching mechanism, c1935, 7" l	200.00
GLC A Kenrick & Son, natural gas, green enamel body, black handle, pat #426086, English, 6³/₄" l	200.00
Hawking Machine, Cuyahoga Falls, OH, Flaming Feather, polisher/sealer, c1925, 9¹/₂" l	70.00
Imperial, box, Oriental characters, red handle, c1925, 7¹/₄" l	70.00
Keith Blackman, natural gas, blue enamel body, English, c1930, 7" l	200.00
LG Dyson and Co, Brisbane, Australia, The Trump, gas line, c1930, 7" l	150.00
Metro, natural gas, blue enamel body, English, c1930, 7¹/₄" l	200.00
Montgomery Ward & Co, electric, red enamel top and handle, c1930, 6⁷/₈" l	150.00
Oriental, aluminum, tall chimney, with trivet, chimney swivels, c1940, 6⁵/₈" l	100.00
Quality Appliance Co, Riverside, IL, Quality Iron, white enamel, with trivet, c1930, 7¹/₄" l	150.00
SG Shapiro & Son, NY, Curv-A-Curl, fur curler, electric, patented Feb 26, 1948, 5¹/₂" l	30.00
Simplex Ironer, Algonquin, IL, mangle, c1940, 22¹/₄" l	150.00
The Perfection Line, Hatters Iron, cordless, tolliker, c1925, 3⁵/₈" l	150.00
Thomas Mfg Co, Dayton, OH, The Kerosafe, c1930, 7¹/₂" l	200.00

JEANNETTE GLASS

The Jeannette Glass Company, Jeannette, Pennsylvania, was founded in 1898. Its first products were glass jars, headlight lenses, and glass brick, known as sidewalk tile. The company supplied glass candy containers to other firms during the 1920s.

Jeannette introduced pressed table and kitchenware in the 1920s. Popular Depression era patterns include Adam (1932-34), Cherry Blossom (1930-39), Cube (1929-33), Doric (1935-38), Doric and Pansy (1937-38), Hex Optic (1928-32), Homespun (1939-49), Iris and Herringbone (1928-32, 1950s, and 1970s), Swirl (1937-38), and Windsor (1936-46).

The company continued to thrive in the post–World War II era. Anniversary (1947-49, late 1960s to mid-1970s), Floragold (1950s), Harp (1954-1957), Holiday (1947 through mid-1950s), and Shell Pink Milk Glass (1957-1959) were among the most popular patterns. The popularity of Iris was so strong it easily made the transition from pre-war to post-war pattern.

In 1952 Jeannette purchased the McKee Glass Corporation, enabling the company to expand into the production of heat resistant and industrial glass.

The Jeannette Glass Company ceased operations in the mid-1980s.

Note: For additional listings see Depression Glass and Kitchen Glassware.

Windsor, tumbler, 5 oz, 3¹/₄" h, pink, $25.00. Photo courtesy Ray Morykan Auctions.

Adam, butter, cov, pink **$95.00**
Adam, cake plate, 10", pink. **25.00**
Adam, cereal bowl, 5³/₄" d, pink **50.00**
Adam, creamer, pink. **25.00**
Adam, cup, pink **30.00**
Adam, dinner plate, 9" d, pink. **40.00**
Adam, nappy, 4³/₄" d, pink. **20.00**
Adam, platter, 11⁵/₈" l, pink **25.00**
Adam, platter, 13" l, monax **145.00**
Adam, relish, 2-part, pink **20.00**
Adam, salad plate, 7³/₄" d, pink **20.00**
Adam, salt and pepper shakers, pr, pink **100.00**
Adam, sherbet, 6" d, pink **12.00**
Cherry Blossom, bowl, handled, 9" d, pink. **65.00**
Cherry Blossom, coaster, green **15.00**
Cherry Blossom, creamer, pink **20.00**
Cherry Blossom, dinner plate, 9" d, delphite. **25.00**
Cherry Blossom, mug, 7 oz, green **200.00**
Cherry Blossom, pitcher, straight sided, 42 oz, 7" h,
  green **60.00**
Cherry Blossom, platter, 11" l, green **50.00**
Cherry Blossom, platter, 11" l, pink **50.00**
Cherry Blossom, salad plate, 7" d, green **20.00**
Cherry Blossom, salad plate, 7" d, pink **25.00**
Cherry Blossom, sandwich tray, handled, 10¹/₂" d, pink **30.00**
Cherry Blossom, sherbet, 6" d, green. **10.00**
Cherry Blossom, sherbet, 6" d, pink **12.00**
Cherry Blossom, soup bowl, pink. **100.00**
Cherry Blossom, sugar, cov, green **40.00**
Cherry Blossom, sugar, cov, pink **45.00**
Cherry Blossom, sugar, open, pink. **6.00**
Cherry Blossom, tray, 10¹/₂" l, pink. **30.00**
Cherry Blossom, tumbler, 4¹/₂" h, pink **40.00**
Cherry Blossom, tumbler, 4 oz, pink **20.00**
Cherry Blossom, tumbler, 9 oz, pink **20.00**
Doric, bowl, 4¹/₂" d, green. **10.00**

Doric, creamer, green **15.00**
Doric, cup and saucer, green. **15.00**
Doric, platter, green **35.00**
Doric, sherbet, green. **15.00**
Doric, sugar, cov, green. **45.00**
Homespun, bowl, 4¹/₂" d, pink. **12.00**
Homespun, bread and butter plate, 6" d, pink **6.00**
Homespun, dinner plate, 9¹/₄" d, pink. **25.00**
Homespun, platter, 13" l, pink. **25.00**
Homespun, sherbet, pink. **20.00**
Homespun, sugar, pink. **10.00**
Homespun, tumbler, 6³/₈" h, pink. **35.00**
Iris, bowl, ruffled, 11¹/₂" d, iridescent **20.00**
Iris, bowl, scalloped, 11¹/₂" d, crystal **18.00**
Iris, butter, cov, iridescent **55.00**
Iris, candlesticks, pr, crystal **40.00**
Iris, claret, 4 oz, 5³/₄" h, crystal **30.00**
Iris, cup and saucer, crystal **35.00**
Iris, pitcher, 60 oz, 9¹/₂" h, crystal. **40.00**
Iris, service plate, 12" d, crystal **15.00**
Iris, sherbet, low, 2¹/₂" h, iridescent **15.00**
Iris, sherbet/champagne, ftd, 4" h, crystal **20.00**
Iris, tumbler, ftd, 6" h, crystal. **20.00**
Iris, vase, crimped, iridescent. **30.00**
Iris, wine goblet, 3 oz, 4¹/₂" h, crystal. **15.00**
Swirl, berry bowl, small, ultramarine **20.00**
Swirl, bowl, 9" d, ultramarine **30.00**
Swirl, cup and saucer, ultramarine. **25.00**
Swirl, plate, 12¹/₂" d, ultramarine **35.00**
Swirl, tumbler, flat, 9 oz, ultramarine **40.00**
Swirl, vase, slant top, ultramarine **35.00**
Windsor, ashtray, pink. **40.00**
Windsor, berry bowl, pink **25.00**
Windsor, bowl, handled, 9¹/₂" d, pink **30.00**
Windsor, bowl, 12¹/₂" d, pink **150.00**
Windsor, bowl, boat shaped, pink **50.00**
Windsor, bread and butter plate, 6" d, green. **10.00**
Windsor, bread and butter plate, 6" d, pink **5.00**
Windsor, butter, cov, pink **60.00**
Windsor, cake plate, pink **25.00**
Windsor, candlesticks, pr, 3" h, crystal **20.00**

Windsor, cereal bowl, pink **30.00**
Windsor, chop plate, 13⁵/₈" d, pink. **50.00**
Windsor, creamer and covered sugar, pink. **45.00**
Windsor, cream soup bowl, green **30.00**
Windsor, cup, pink **12.00**
Windsor, cup and saucer, crystal **8.00**
Windsor, cup and saucer, pink. **18.00**
Windsor, nappy, 8¹/₂" d, pink **25.00**
Windsor, pitcher, 48 oz, 6¹/₂" h, green **50.00**
Windsor, pitcher, 52 oz, 6³/₄" h, pink **35.00**
Windsor, platter, pink **20.00**
Windsor, relish, divided, 11¹/₂", pink **300.00**
Windsor, salad plate, 7" d, green **30.00**
Windsor, salad plate, 7" d, pink **25.00**
Windsor, salt and pepper shakers, pr, green **55.00**
Windsor, sandwich plate, 13³/₄" d, green **40.00**
Windsor, sandwich plate, 13³/₄" d, pink **45.00**
Windsor, sandwich tray, 10¹/₄", pink **20.00**
Windsor, shaker, green **30.00**
Windsor, sherbet, pink **15.00**
Windsor, sugar, cov, crystal **5.00**
Windsor, sugar, cov, pink. **40.00**
Windsor, tray, 4" sq, no handles, pink. **200.00**
Windsor, tray, 8³/₄" sq, divided, no handles, pink. **210.00**
Windsor, tray, 10" d, crystal. **8.00**
Windsor, tumbler, 9 oz, green **300.00**
Windsor, tumbler, 9 oz, pink **20.00**

JEWELRY

Jewelry divides into two basic groups: precious and non-precious (a.k.a., costume after 1920). This category focuses on precious jewelry. While collected, most precious jewelry is purchased to be worn or studied.

U.S. custom laws define antique jewelry as jewelry over one hundred years old. Estate or Heirloom jewelry is generally assumed to be over twenty-five years old.

Craftsmanship, aesthetic design, scarcity, and current market worth of gemstones and the precious metal are the principal value keys. Antique and period jewelry should be set with the cut of stone prevalent at the time the piece was made. Names (manufacturer, designer, or both) also play a major role in value.

Be extremely cautious when buying jewelry. Reproductions, copycats (stylistic reproductions), fantasies (non-period shapes and forms), and fakes abound. Also be alert for married and divorced pieces.

References: Lillian Baker, *Art Nouveau & Art Deco Jewelry*, Collector Books, 1981, 1997 value update; Howard L. Bell, Jr., *Cuff Jewelry: A Historical Account for Collectors and Antique Dealers*, published by author, 1994; Jeanenne Bell, *Answers to Questions About Old Jewelry, 1840-1950*, 5th Edition, Krause Publications, 1999; Monica Lynn Clements and Patricia Rosser Clements, *Cameos*, Schiffer Publishing, 1999.

Arthur Guy Kaplan, *The Official Identification and Price Guide to Antique Jewelry*, Sixth Edition, House of Collectibles, 1990, reprinted 1994; Penny Chittim Morrill and Carol A. Beck, *Mexican Silver: 20th-Century Handwrought Jewelry and Metalwork, Revised 2nd Edition*, Schiffer Publishing, 1998; Dorothy T. Rainwater, *American Jewelry Manufacturers*, Schiffer Publishing, 1988; Christie Romero, *Warman's Jewelry*, 2nd Edition, Krause Publications, 1998; Nancy N. Schiffer, *Silver Jewelry Treasures*,

Schiffer Publishing, 1993; Sheryl Gross Shatz, *What's It Made Of?: A Jewelry Materials Identification Guide, Third Edition*, published by author, 1996; Doris J. Snell, *Antique Jewelry With Prices, Second Edition*, Krause Publications, 1997.

Periodicals: *Gems & Gemology*, Gemological Inst of America, 5345 Armada Dr, PO Box 9022, Carlsbad, CA 92008; *Jewelers' Circular Keystone/Heritage*, 201 King of Prussia Rd, Radnor, PA 19089.

Newsletter: *Adornment*, PO Box 122, 1333A North Ave, New Rochelle, NY 10804.

Collectors' Clubs: American Society of Jewelry Historians, Box 103, 1333A North Ave, New Rochelle, NY 10804; National Cuff Link Society, PO Box 5700, Vernon Hills, IL 60061.

Bangle Bracelet, 7 graduated oval opals spaced by pairs
of mounted diamonds, 18K yellow gold **$575.00**
Bar Pin, Rene Lalique, molded glass, floral design with
blue background mounted on brass, hallmark for
Rene Lalique and stamped "Lalique" **350.00**
Bracelet, multicolored hexagon shaped gemstones set
within round and oval links, 14K yellow gold,
10.4 dwt, 7¹/₄" l **400.00**
Brooch, Alphonse La Paglia, sterling silver, 2 leaves
attached to scrolling vine with 4 round bead accents,
stamped "USA No. 108," "LP" hallmark **150.00**
Brooch, Anthony Puccio, jade and 14K yellow gold, textured gold coral reef branch with carved nephrite
jade, highlighted by 5 round green stones, mkd, orig
box. **275.00**
Brooch, Arthur King, baroque pearl and diamond,
abstract design with center large South Sea pearl with
4 round white and 5 fancy brownish-yellow diamond
accents, textured 18K gold mount, sgd "King,"
28.7 dwt. **850.00**
Brooch, Cartier, figural flower bud highlighted by 4 cir-
cular cut rubies and 1 circular cut diamond, 18K yel-
low gold, 12.5 dwt **1,150.00**

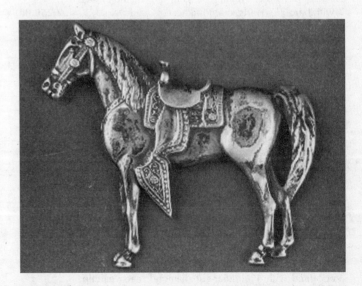

Pin, sterling silver, 2³/₄" l, $75.00. Photo courtesy Ray Morykan Auctions.

Brooch, bowknot, 2-tone 14K gold, sapphires and diamonds, $1,200.00.

Brooch, circular, 20 channel-set sapphires and 20 circular-cut diamonds, 14K white gold mount **750.00**

Brooch, clover shaped with 3 carved emerald leaves, diamond stem, 18K yellow gold mount **510.00**

Brooch, figural turtle, body set with matrix turquoise, diamonds, and sapphires, cabochon garnet eyes, 18k yellow gold mount **275.00**

Brooch, floral design with moonstone petals spaced by sapphires, similar flower bud, 14K yellow gold mount. . . . **700.00**

Brooch, Georg Jensen, sterling silver, open square design depicting 2 dolphins and vine, stamped "925, Georg Jensen, Denmark, No. 251" with English hallmark letter date for 1969 . . . . **250.00**

Brooch, Martine, enamel and gold, figural butterfly, plique-a-jour opaque and translucent enamel flexible wings, gold textured body, circular cut diamond eyes, 18K yellow gold **450.00**

Brooch, Tiffany, figural giraffe, maroon guilloche enamel body with gold wire accents, 18K yellow gold mount, sgd, 7.2 dwt **400.00**

Earclips, pr, openwork fan design with 4 diamond accents, 14K yellow gold mount **625.00**

Earrings, pr, 22 round diamonds suspended within 18k gold ropetwist mount, 1.1 cts **700.00**

Earrings, pr, coral bead-set within 14K yellow gold wire and ropetwist mount suspended from gold floret-capped coral drop, omega earclips **250.00**

Earrings, pr, David Webb, 18K gold and diamond, set with baroque pearls, diamond accents, sgd **2,250.00**

Necklace, barrel shaped coral knotted beads with 14k yellow gold coral bead clasp, 23½" l **250.00**

Necklace, cultured pearls, double strand approx 8.5mm with diamond and pearl cluster clasp, 16½" l **700.00**

Pendant, pear shaped amethyst mounted in 18K gold surmounted by 2 curvilinear forms accented with 15 single-cut bead-set diamonds and 1 brilliant-cut diamond, platinum mount **400.00**

Pin, Georg Jensen, sterling silver, circle form, stylized flowerhead design, stamped "925, Georg Jenson, GI, Denmark, No. 86" **150.00**

Ring, 3 round opals highlighted by 4-diamond melee in scroll motif, 18K yellow gold mount, size 6¼ **525.00**

Ring, Georg Jensen, center cabochon oval amethyst, 18k yellow gold mount, sgd "Georg Jensen No. 1046A" **925.00**

Scarf Pin, Hermes, emb leather insert with Hermes padlock, gilt metal **200.00**

Suite, brooch and earclips, figural sea urchins, brooch accented with 1 circular-cut diamond, each earclip accented with 3 circular-cut rubies and 2 diamonds, 14K yellow gold **1,150.00**

Suite, Tiffany, necklace and earclips, designed by Angela Cummings, 18K yellow gold, sgd "Tiffany," ©1979 . . . . . **3,750.00**

Suite, Tiffany, pin and earclips, figural bee, red stone eyes, 14K yellow gold, 11.0 dwt **800.00**

Wristwatch, Eloga "Incablock," lady's, Art Deco style, 17j movement, white metal dial with Arabic numerals and geometric indicators, bezel flanked by old European-cut diamonds, accented by 42 diamonds, black cord band with gold-filled clasp, 0.9 cts **850.00**

JEWELRY, COSTUME

Prior to World War I, non-precious jewelry consisted of inexpensive copies of precious jewelry. This changed in the 1920s when Coco Chanel advocated the wearing of faux jewelry as an acceptable part of haute couture. High-style fashion jewelry continued to exercise a strong influence on costume jewelry until the middle of the 20th century.

During the 1930s costume jewelry manufacture benefited from developments such as more efficient casting machines and the creation of Bakelite, one of the first entirely synthetic plastics. Material shortages during World War II promoted the increased use of ceramics and wood. Copper, plastic novelty, and rhinestone crazes marked the 1950s and 60s.

Because of this category's breadth, collectors and dealers focus on named manufacturers and designers. A maker's mark is not a guarantee of quality. Examine pieces objectively. This is a very trendy category. What is in today may be out tomorrow. Just ask anyone who collected rhinestone jewelry in the early 1980s.

References: Lillian Baker, *Fifty Years of Collectible Fashion Jewelry: 1925-1975,* Collector Books, 1986, 1997 value update; Lillian Baker, *100 Years of Collectible Jewelry, 1850-1950,* Collector Books, 1978, 1997 value update; Joanne Dubbs Ball, *Costume Jewelers, Second Edition,* Schiffer Publishing, 1997; Dee Battle and Alayne Lesser, *The Best of Bakelite and Other Plastic Jewelry,* Schiffer Publishing, 1996; Vivienne Becker, *Fabulous Costume Jewelry,* Schiffer Publishing, 1993; Jeanenne Bell, *Answers to Questions About Old Jewelry, 1840-1950, 5th Edition,* Krause Publications, 1999; Marcia Brown, *Unsigned Beauties of Costume Jewelry,* Collector Books, 2000; Matthew L. Burkholz and Linda Lictenberg Kaplan, *Copper Art Jewelry,* Schiffer Publishing, 1992.

Deanna Farneti Cera, *Costume Jewelery,* Antique Collectors' Club, 1997; Monica L. Clements and Patricia Rosser Clements, *Avon Collectible Fashion Jewelry and Awards,* Schiffer Publishing, 1998; Monica L. Clements and Patricia Clements, *Sarah Coventry Jewelry,* Schiffer Publishing, 1999; Maryanne Dolan, *Collecting Rhinestone Jewelry, 4th Edition,* Krause Publications, 1998; Roseann Ettinger, *Forties & Fifties Popular Jewelry,* Schiffer Publishing, 1994; Roseann Ettinger, *Popular Jewelry: 1840-1940, Second Edition,* Schiffer Publishing, 1997; Roseann Ettinger, *Popular Jewelry of the '60s, '70s & '80s,* Schiffer Publishing, 1997; Sandy Fichtner and Lynn Ann Russell, *Rainbow of Rhinestone Jewelry,* Schiffer Publishing, 1996.

S. Sylvia Henzel, *Collectible Costume Jewelry, Third Edition,* Krause Publications, 1997; Mary Jo Izard, *Wooden Jewelry and Novelties,* Schiffer Publishing, 1998; Sibylle Jargstorf, *Glass in Jewelry, Revised 2nd Edition,* Schiffer Publishing, 1998; Lyngerda Kelley and Nancy Schiffer, *Costume Jewelry, Revised 3rd Edition,* Schiffer Publishing, 1998; Lyngerda Kelley and Nancy Schiffer, *Plastic Jewelry, Third Edition,* Schiffer Publishing, 1996; J. L.

Lynnlee, *All That Glitters, 3rd Edition,* Schiffer Publishing, 1986, 1999 value update; Harrice Simons Miller, *Costume Jewelry, Second Edition,* Avon Books, 1994; Mary Morrison, *Christmas Jewelry,* Schiffer Publishing, 1999; Fred Rezazadeh, *Costume Jewelry,* Collector Books, 1998.

Christie Romero, *Warman's Jewelry, 2nd Edition,* Krause Publications, 1998; Nancy N. Schiffer, *Costume Jewelry,* Schiffer Publishing, 1988, 1996 value update; Sheryl Gross Shatz, *What's It Made Of?: A Jewelry Materials Identification Guide,* published by author, 1991; Cherri Simonds, *Collectible Costume Jewelry,* Collector Books, 1997; Nicholas D. Snider, *Sweetheart Jewelry and Collectibles,* Schiffer Publishing, 1995; Donna Wassestrom and Leslie Piña, *Bakelite Jewelry,* Schiffer Publishing, 1997; Christianne Weber and Renate Moller, *Fashion and Jewelry: 1920-1970,* Arnoldsche, 1999.

Collectors' Club: Vintage Fashion & Costume Jewelry Club, PO Box 265, Glen Oaks, NY 11004.

Bangle Bracelet, carved with veined leaves, red Bakelite, 1½" w **$500.00**
Bangle Bracelet, geometric, 5-color laminate Bakelite stripe, 1" w **275.00**
Bangle Bracelet, geometric, orange cut through Bakelite with kinetic center black Bakelite ball detail, 1¼" w **375.00**
Bracelet, Ballesteros, geometric hinged, sterling silver with bright green Bakelite inlaid polka dots, stamped, 2¼" inner diameter, 1½" w **1,000.00**
Bracelet, Bent Knudsen, sterling silver, geometric heart shaped links with circular openwork, stamped, 7½" l **225.00**
Bracelet, Schiaparelli, gilt metal, with prong-set purple and white rhinestone detail, stamped, 7" l **200.00**
Bracelet, Weiss, thermoset plastic, imbedded multicolored rhinestones of various sizes and shapes, hinged, 2½" w **325.00**
Brooch, Georg Jensen, figural bird, accented with jade cabochons, stamped, 1½" h **400.00**
Clip, Chanel, carved apple juice Bakelite with set multicolor crystals in gilt metal mount, 2½" w **200.00**
Cuff Bracelet, Fromm, sterling silver, oval stone bezel set on central plaque, stamped, 2¼" inner diameter, .25" w . . . **135.00**
Cufflinks, pr, Antonio, sterling silver flattened circular design embellished with bezel set synthetic purple faceted corundum centers, stamped, 1" h **165.00**
Cufflinks, pr, Sigi, sterling and rosewood, rect design with circular grommet-like openwork, stamped, 1" h. **110.00**
Dress Clip, apple juice Bakelite reverse carved with 2 swimming goldfish accented with seaweed, reverse painted detail **85.00**
Necklace, Arnold Scaasi, amber and pale yellow prong-set rhinestones with pendulous baroque pearl teardrops in assymetrical design, paper label, 15" l **550.00**
Necklace, Coppola Toppo, pink, sepia, and clear faceted crystal beads wired to hand-cut brass plaque in assymetrical bow shaped design, with elaborate clasp, stamped, 17" l **825.00**
Necklace, Fromm, sterling silver, 16 concentric circles, each bezel set with circular blue glass cabochons, 14½" l **400.00**
Necklace, Miriam Haskell, 3 strands of baroque pearls with multicolor rhinestone rondelles and crystal spacers, small gilt metal and rhinestone multicolor clasp, 15" l **375.00**

Charm Bracelet, silver, c1968, $40.00.

Necklace, Miriam Haskell, 4 strands of clear ruby crystals in contoured forms, with baroque pearls and rhinestone montee log elements, stamped, 16½" l **375.00**
Pin, Boucher, figural dangling cherries and leaves, enamel rhodium plated metal with pave rhinestone detail, stamped, 2¼" h **350.00**
Pin, Boucher, floriform, enameled rhodium plated metal, oversized crystal and pave rhinestone flower head, with pave rhinestone and enameled detailed leaves, stamped, 5" h **775.00**
Pin, Coro, figural blowfish, gilt and enameled metal, aqua rhinestone in mouth, pink rhinestone eyes, stamped, 3" h **275.00**
Pin, Coro, figural fuchsia orchid and bud, enameled on rhodium plated metal with pave rhinestone detail, stamped, 4¼" h **350.00**
Pin, Derosa, floral, gilt and enameled metal with emerald-cut fuchsia prong-set crystals, 4" h **275.00**
Pin, figural Bakelite guitar, banjo, and violin drops suspended from horizontal metal treble clef, 2½" l **350.00**
Pin, figural bunch of currants, translucent carved green leaves above cluster of dark butterscotch Bakelite currants attached with individual brass rings, 2¾" h **325.00**
Pin, figural lobster, resin wash overdyed Bakelite, gimp antennae, glass eyes, 3" h **875.00**
Pin, figural parrot, apple juice Bakelite with silver reverse painting and surface painted details, 3¾" h **225.00**
Pin, figural sailor behind ship's wheel, bone Bakelite with painted detail, 2½" h **450.00**
Pin, figural swimsuit-clad blonde under palm tree, translucent green Bakelite with painted detail, 2½" h **600.00**
Pin, Hobe, figural basket, 14K gold and sterling silver with bezel set crystal flowers and gilt metal leaves, 2¾" h **275.00**
Pin, Staret, figural hand and torch of Statue of Liberty, enameled metal with pave rhinestone detail, orig painted detail, 3¾" h **775.00**
Ring, Bent Knudsen, sterling silver, simple band consisting of 7 circular rings, stamped **65.00**
Ring, Ellis Kauppi, Viking ship design, cross-hatched textured surface, tiger-eye quartz ball accent, stamped. **110.00**

JOHNSON BROTHERS

In 1883 three brothers, Alfred, Frederick, and Henry Johnson, purchased the bankrupt J. W. Pankhurst Company, a tableware manufactory in Hanley, Staffordshire, England and established Johnson Brothers. Although begun on a small scale, the company prospered and expanded.

In 1896, Robert, a fourth brother, joined the firm. Robert, who lived and worked in the United States, was assigned the task of expanding the company's position in the American market. By 1914 Johnson Brothers owned and operated five additional factories scattered throughout Hanley, Tunstall, and Burslem.

Johnson Brothers continued to grow throughout the 1960s with acquisitions of tableware manufacturing plants in Hamilton, Ontario, Canada, and Croydon, Australia. Two additional English plants were acquired in 1960 and 1965.

Johnson Brothers became part of the Wedgwood Group in 1968.

References: Mary J. Finegan, *Johnson Brothers Dinnerware: Pattern Directory & Price Guide,* published by author, 1993; Harry L. Rinker, *Dinnerware of the 20th Century: The Top 500 Patterns,* House of Collectibles, 1997.

Coaching Scenes, bread and butter plate, 6¼" d	$6.00
Coaching Scenes, chop plate, 12" d	40.00
Coaching Scenes, creamer and sugar	50.00
Coaching Scenes, dinner plate, 9⅞" d	15.00
Coaching Scenes, gravy boat and underplate	20.00
Coaching Scenes, pitcher, 5¾" h	35.00
Coaching Scenes, platter, 12" l	25.00
English Chippendale, cereal bowl, flat, 6¼" d	15.00
English Chippendale, creamer and sugar	50.00
English Chippendale, dinner plate, 10" d	15.00
English Chippendale, fruit bowl, 5¼" d	10.00
English Chippendale, luncheon plate, 8⅞" d	15.00
English Chippendale, platter, 12" l	20.00
English Chippendale, salad plate, 7½" sq	10.00
Friendly Village, chop plate, 12¼" d	35.00
Friendly Village, cup and saucer, flat, 2⅜" h	10.00
Friendly Village, dessert plate, 7" d	2.00
Friendly Village, gravy boat	30.00
Friendly Village, serving tray, 2-tier	25.00
Friendly Village, spoon holder	15.00
Friendly Village, teapot, cov	40.00
Hearts & Flowers, cup and saucer, flat, 2½" h	15.00
Hearts & Flowers, dinner plate, 10" d	18.00
Hearts & Flowers, platter, 12¼" l	40.00
Hearts & Flowers, salad plate	12.00
Hearts & Flowers, sugar, cov	25.00
Hearts & Flowers, vegetable, cov, no lid, round	80.00
Heritage Hall, bread and butter plate, 6¼" d	7.00
Heritage Hall, cereal bowl, coupe, 6⅛" d	10.00
Heritage Hall, coffeepot, cov	60.00
Heritage Hall, creamer and sugar	45.00
Heritage Hall, dessert plate, 6⅞" d	8.00
Heritage Hall, platter, 11⅞" l	35.00
Heritage Hall, salad plate, 8" d	10.00
Old Britain Castles, butter, cov, blue, ¼ lb	35.00
Old Britain Castles, butter, cov, pink, ¼ lb	20.00
Old Britain Castles, cereal bowl, flat, blue, 6⅛" d	12.00
Old Britain Castles, cereal bowl, flat, pink, 6⅛" d	10.00
Old Britain Castles, cup and saucer, flat, blue, 2¼" h	15.00
Old Britain Castles, cup and saucer, flat, pink, 2¼" h	13.00
Old Britain Castles, dinner plate, blue, 10" d	18.00
Old Britain Castles, dinner plate, pink, 10" d	12.00
Old Britain Castles, fruit bowl, blue, 5⅛" d	10.00
Old Britain Castles, fruit bowl, pink, 5⅛" d	7.00

JOSEF FIGURINES

When Muriel Joseph George could no longer obtain Lucite during World War II for her plastic jewelry, she used clay to fashion ceramic jewelry. George loved to model, making a wide variety of serious and whimsical figures for her own amusement.

In 1946 Muriel and her husband, Tom, made their first commercial ceramic figures in their garage. The printer misspelled Joseph, thus inadvertently creating the company's signature name Josef. Despite the company's quick growth, early 1950s' cheap Japanese imitations severely undercut its market.

In 1959 Muriel, Tom, and George Good established George Imports. Production was moved to the Katayama factory in Japan. Muriel created her designs in America, sent them to Japan with production instructions, and approved samples. Once again, the company enjoyed a period of prosperity.

In 1974 the company became George-Good Corporation. When Muriel retired in 1981, George Good purchased her interest in the company. Muriel continued to do design work until 1984. In 1985 George Good sold the company to Applause, Inc.

References: Dee Harris, Jim and Kaye Whitaker, *Josef Originals, 2nd Edition,* Schiffer Publishing, 1999; Jim and Kaye Whitaker, *Josef Originals: Figurines of Muriel Joseph George,* Schiffer Publishing, 2000.

Newsletter: *Josef Original Newsletter,* PO Box 475, Lynnwood, WA 98046.

Angel, praying, pink dress, 5¼" h	$75.00
Birthday Girl, #8	30.00
Birthstone Doll, April	45.00
Bonnie, playing mandolin, paper label, 6" h	100.00
Bridal Shower, Special Occasions series, 4½" h	70.00

Heritage Hall, dinner plate, 9¾" d, $15.00.

**Birthday Girl, #12,
$30.00.**

JUKEBOXES

A jukebox is an amplified coin-operated phonograph. The 1940s and early 1950s were its golden age, a period when bubble machines ruled every teenage hangout from dance hall to drugstore. Portable radios, television's growth, and "Top 40" radio were responsible for the jukebox's decline in the 1960s.

Pre-1938 jukeboxes were made primarily of wood and resemble a phonograph or radio cabinet. Wurlitzer and Rock-Ola, whose jukeboxes often featured brightly colored plastic and animation units, made the best of the 78 rpm jukeboxes of the 1938-1948 period. The 45 rpm jukebox, popularized by the television show *Happy Days*, arrived on the scene in 1940 and survived until 1960. Seeburg was the principal manufacturer of these machines. Beginning in 1961, manufacturers often hid the record mechanism. These machines lack the collector appeal of their earlier counterparts.

References: Michael Adams, Jürgen Lukas, and Thomas Maschke, *Jukeboxes,* Schiffer Publishing, 1995; *Always Jukin' Official Guide to Collectible Jukeboxes,* Always Jukin', n.d.; Jerry Ayliffe, *American Premium Guide to Jukeboxes and Slot Machines, Gumballs, Trade Stimulators, Arcade, 3rd Edition,* Books Americana, 1991; Stephen K. Loots, *The Official Victory Glass Price Guide to Antique Jukeboxes: Pre-1967,* published by author, 1999.

Periodicals: *Always Jukin',* 1952 1st Ave S, #6, Seattle, WA 98134; *Antique Amusements, Slot Machines & Jukebox Gazette,* 909 26th St NW, Washington, DC 20037; *Gameroom Magazine,* PO Box 41, Keyport, NJ 07735; *Jukebox Collector,* 2545 SE 60th Court, Des Moines, IA 50317.

Cat, seated, white	35.00
Cheese Shaker, penguin	20.00
Elephant, butterfly on trunk	65.00
Elephant, holding flower	45.00
England Girl, International Series	65.00
Frog, with baby turtle, 3" h	30.00
Girl, with basket of flowers, 4¼" h	75.00
Girl, with puppy and ball, 4" h	85.00
Graduation Angel	55.00
Groom Mouse, with tophat	15.00
Hawaiian Girl, International Series, paper label	100.00
Hippo, with nest on head	55.00
Kangaroo and Joey	75.00
Lady on Telephone, 8" h	225.00
Lady with Butterfly, 7" h	165.00
Little Girl, holding puppy	30.00
Little Nun Rosary Holder, 5" h	65.00
Love Is Forever, gold trim, 5½" h	75.00
Mama Elephant, with butterflies	80.00
Marie Antionette, 5½" h	125.00
Milky Way Mouse	10.00
Mouse, in Christmas hat	18.00
Mouse, with bow on tail	8.00
Mouse, with cheese	12.00
Mouse, with ladybug	15.00
Mouse, writing "I Love You," paper label	15.00
Ostrich, pr	140.00
Portugal, International Series	65.00
Proud Mama and Papa Mouse, pr	35.00
Rabbit	25.00
Rooster, brown and cream	75.00
Siamese Cat	35.00
Squirrel	40.00
Sugar Bowl, mouse on mushroom	35.00
Sugar Bowl, Santa	35.00
Sugar 'N Spice, 3½" h	50.00
Sweden Girl, International Series, bisque finish, incised	50.00
Troubles the Mouse	12.00
Turtle, snail on back, 3" h	30.00
Wee Folk, "Don't Cry Over Spilt Milk"	40.00

AMI, Canteen (BMS)	$375.00
AMI, F-80	850.00
AMI, H-200	1,800.00
Concert, 240I	300.00
Festival	300.00
Jupiter 160L Astral	250.00
Mills, Do-Re-Me	500.00
NSM, Consul 120	200.00
Prestige, E160	300.00
Rock-ola, 414	600.00
Rock-ola, 1428, unrestored	4,500.00
Rock-ola, 1438, unrestored	3,500.00
Rock-ola, 1485	1,500.00
Rowe, JBM	300.00
Seeburg, 100B	1,000.00
Seeburg, 100G	1,000.00
Seeburg, 100R, restored	2,300.00
Seeburg, 147	625.00
Seeburg, 148, restored	2,500.00
Seeburg, 201	1,400.00
Seeburg, 222, unrestored	2,500.00
Seeburg, L100	1,200.00
Seeburg, Q160	600.00
Seeburg, V200	3,500.00
Wurlitzer 750E, unrestored	6,000.00
Wurlitzer, 1450	950.00
Wurlitzer, 1800	2,500.00
Wurlitzer, 2100, unrestored	2,200.00
Wurlitzer, 2700	650.00
Wurlitzer, 4008	4,500.00

Wurlitzer 1015, restored, 1946, $8,500.00. Photo courtesy Auction Team Köln.

Wurlitzer, HF 1700, restored 3,300.00
Wurlitzer, P12 . . . . 375.00
Wurlitzer, W1100, unrestored 3,800.00
Wurlitzer, W2000, unrestored 5,500.00

KEMPLE GLASS

In May 1945 John E. and Geraldine Kemple leased two buildings in East Palestine, Ohio, for the purpose of manufacturing tabletop glassware. They acquired many old molds from the 1870-1900 era along with molds from the Mannington Art Glass Company of West Virginia and McKee Glass.

During its twenty-five years of operation (1945-1970), Kemple Glass produced a large number of "Authentic Antique Reproductions." Concerned that purchasers not confuse its products with period pieces, Kemple initially used milk glass for its restrikes from earlier molds. Color was added to the line in 1960, again in shades that make Kemple's products easy to distinguish from earlier examples. Kemple Glass was marked either with a paper sticker or the letter "K," an addition made to earlier molds whenever possible.

Kemple Glass moved to the old Gill Glass Works in Kenova, West Virginia, following a fire at its East Palestine plant in 1956. When John E. Kemple died in 1970, the company was sold and production ended in Kenova. Today, many of the Kemple molds are in the possession of Wheaton Industries, Millville, New Jersey.

Reference: John R. Burkholder and D. Thomas O'Connor, *Kemple Glass: 1945-1970*, Glass Press, 1997.

Ashtray, Star & Tear Drops $30.00
Bowl, Blackberry, 9" d 18.00
Butter, cov, Lace & Dewdrop, flat finial 65.00
Candlesticks, pr, Moon & Star Variant 55.00
Cigar Jar, cov, Scroll Variant 45.00
Compote, cov, Sunburst, 7½" h 35.00
Covered Animal Dish, cat, split rib base, green 55.00
Covered Animal Dish, cow 55.00
Covered Animal Dish, fox 25.00

Cracker Jar, Aztec 45.00
Creamer, Ivy-in-Snow 45.00
Creamer and Sugar, Blackberry 45.00
Cruet, Splatter 45.00
Decanter, with rigaree, crackle glass 45.00
Decanter, Yutec, with rigaree and spout 65.00
Dolphin Dish, blue 85.00
Dolphin Dish, light green 95.00
Dresser Box, Cabbage Rose 20.00
Ewer, ruffled spout, crackle glass 35.00
Figurine, Colonial Lady 65.00
Goblet, Blackberry 45.00
Hat, Lace & Dewdrop 18.00
Mug, Cabbage Rose 65.00
Nappy, Aztec, handled 15.00
Nut Dish, cov, Lace & Dewdrop 18.00
Plate, Angel Head, 8½" d 30.00
Plate, Cabbage Leaf, 7" d 25.00
Plate, Lacey Heart, 6" d 25.00
Plate, Sandwich, 8" d 25.00
Plate, Shell & Club, 7" d 25.00
Salt and Pepper Shakers, pr, Sunburst 12.00
Slipper, Puss-in-Boots, pointed toe 35.00
Spooner, Aztec 80.00
Spooner, Yutec, crimped 20.00
Toothpick Holder, Lincoln hat 25.00
Vase, Ivy-in-Snow, flared, milk glass 40.00
Vase, Jubilee, flared, 8" h 35.00
Wine, Aztec, 3 oz 15.00

KEWPIES

Rose Cecil O'Neill (1876-1944) created the Kewpie doll. This famous nymph made its debut in the December 1909 issue of *Ladies' Home Journal*. The first doll, designed in part by Joseph L. Kallus, was marketed in 1913. Kallus owned the Cameo Doll Company; Geo. Borgfelt Company owned the Kewpie production and distribution rights.

Most early Kewpie items were manufactured in Germany. American and Japanese manufacturers also played a role. Composition Kewpie dolls did not arrive until after World War II.

O'Neill created a wide variety of Kewpie characters. Do not overlook Ho-Ho, Kewpie-Gal, Kewpie-Kin, Ragsy, and Scootles.

Kewpie licensing continues, especially in the limited edition collectibles area.

References: John Axe, *Kewpies: Dolls & Art of Rose O'Neill & Joseph L. Kallus*, Hobby House Press, 1987, out of print; Cynthia Gaskill, *The Kewpie Kompanion: A Kompendium of Kewpie Knowledge*, Gold Horse Publishing, 1994.

Collectors' Club: International Rose O'Neill Club, PO Box 668, Branson, MO 65616.

Creamer, sage and pink, imp "Rose O'Neill Germany,"
   2⅝" h $125.00
Desk Timepiece, sage and pink Jasperware, imp "Rose
   O'Neil Kewpie Germany," 4⅝" h 175.00
Doll, composition, jointed at shoulders and hips, orig
   cotton sunsuit, shoes, and socks, paper label, Cameo,
   1930s, 13" h 150.00
Figure, bisque, farmer, with wooden rake, paper label on
   back, imp "O'Neil" under feet, 5½" h 525.00

Figure, bisque, hugger, imp "O'Neil" under foot, 3½" h **55.00**
Figure, bisque, playing guitar, red and navy cloth ribbons on guitar, paper label on back, 3⅝" h **400.00**
Figure, bisque, sitting in wicker armchair, 3½" h **350.00**
Figure, bisque, sitting with black cat, paper label on back, 3¼" h **575.00**
Figure, bisque, traveler, with valise and umbrella, paper tag on chest, 3½" h **200.00**
Figure, bisque, with broom and dust bin, imp "O'Neil" under feet, 3½" h **225.00**
Jar, cov, Jasperware, blue and white cotton ball jar, finial missing, imp "Rose O'Neil Germany," 3¾" h **125.00**
Letter Opener, pewter, Kewpie finial, 7" l **40.00**
Paper Dolls, Kewpie-Kin, Saalfield, ©1967 . . . . **40.00**
Perfume Vial, china, Kewpie wearing headphones, Goebel of Germany, c1930, 2¼" h **75.00**
Postcard, Victory Ice Cream, full color illus, 1920, 3 x 5½" **25.00**
Teacup, white china, color illus, c1920, 2¼" h **65.00**

KEYS & KEY CHAINS

People collect keys and key chains more for their novelty than any other reason. Because they are made in such quantities, few examples are rare. Most collectors specialize, focusing on a specific subject such as automobile, hotel, presentation keys ("Key to the City"), railroad, etc.

Beware of fantasy keys such as keys to the Tower of London, a *Titanic* cabin, or a Hollywood movie star's dressing room.

Collectors' Club: License Plate Key Chain & Mini License Plate Collectors, 888 Eighth Ave, New York, NY 10019.

KEYS

Cabinet, nickel plated, Art Deco bow, 2½" l **$5.00**
Cabinet, standard bow and bit, 3" l . . . . **.75**
Car, Nash, Ilco #132 . . . . **5.00**
Clock, steel, iron, Waterbury Clock Co, 2¼" l **16.00**
Door, steel, standard bow and bit **3.00**
Jail, bronze, bit-type with cuts, barrel type, 4½" l **30.00**
Railroad, LM RR, Little Miami Railroad **55.00**
Railroad, TT RR, Toledo Terminal Railroad **18.00**

Key Chain, metal, IAM Tool & Die Makers Lodge 688, St Louis, MO, back inscribed "1933 Half Century of Craftsmanship 1983," 3½" d, $7.00.

KEY CHAINS

Acrylic and Metal, 1964 New York World's Fair, domed acrylic over silver and black unisphere title, dates, flat silvered metal back **$15.00**
Enamel, Swift Premium Ham **12.00**
Ivory Plastic, PF Sneakers, animal tooth shape, logo and antelope head dec, built-in siren whistle, sun dial and alphabet code, 1960s, 3" l **25.00**
Metal, Esso, tiger head, 3" l **4.00**
Metal, Packard, attached ring, shades of gold and silver, blue, white, and black enameled convertible titled "Packard Panther," brass Packard logo, 1950s **20.00**
Metal, Texaco, St Christopher medal on reverse, 3" l **4.00**
Plastic, dayglow, Dutch Boy, holding brush behind back, c1940s **30.00**

KITCHEN COLLECTIBLES

Collectors are in love with the kitchen of the 1920s and 30s. A few progressive collectors are focusing on the kitchens of the 50s and 60s. Color and style are the two collecting keys. Bright blue, green, and red enamel handled utensils are in demand, not for use but to display on walls. Everything, from flatware to appliances, in Streamline Modern and Post-War Modern design styles is hot. Do not overlook wall clocks and wall decorations. There are even individuals collecting Tupperware.

References: Ellen Bercovici, Bobbie Zucker Bryson and Deborah Gillham, *Collectibles for the Kitchen, Bath & Beyond,* Antique Trader Books, 1998; Brenda C. Blake, *Egg Cups,* Antique Publications, 1995; Linda Fields, *Four and Twenty Blackbirds (Pie Birds),* published by author, 1998; Linda Campbell Franklin, *300 Years of Housekeeping Collectibles,* Books Americana, 1992; Linda Campbell Franklin, *300 Years of Kitchen Collectibles, Fourth Edition,* Krause Publications, 1997; Michael J. Goldberg, *Collectible Plastic Kitchenware and Dinnerware: 1935-1965,* Schiffer Publishing, 1995; Michael J. Goldberg, *Groovy Kitchen Designs for Collectors: 1935-1965,* Schiffer Publishing, 1996; Jan Lindenberger, *The 50s and 60s Kitchen, 2nd Edition,* Schiffer Publishing, 1999; Jan Lindenberger, *Black Memorabilia for the Kitchen, 2nd Edition,* Schiffer Publishing, 1999; Barbara Mauzy, *Bakelite in the Kitchen,* Schiffer Publishing, 1998; Barbara Mauzy, *The Complete Book of Kitchen Collecting,* Schiffer Publishing, 1997; Dana G. Morykan, *Country Antiques & Collectibles, Fourth Edition,* House of Collectibles, 1999; Don Thornton, *Apple Parers,* Off Beat Books, 1997.

Newsletter: *Cookies,* 9610 Greenview Ln, Manassas, VA 20109.

Collectors' Clubs: Cookie Cutter Collectors Club, 1167 Teal Rd SW, Dellroy, OH 44620; Eggcup Collectors' Corner, 67 Stevens Ave, Old Bridge, NJ 08857; International Society for Apple Parer Enthusiasts, 735 Cedarwood Terrace, Rochester, NY 14609; Jelly Jammers, 6086 W Boggstown Rd, Boggstown, IN 46110; Kollectors of Old Kitchen Stuff, 354 Rte 206 North, Chester, NJ, 07930; Pie Bird Collectors Club, 158 Bagsby Hill Ln, Dover, TN 37058.

Note: See Advertising, Appliances, Cookbooks, Cookie Jars, Egg Beaters, Fire-King, Food Molds, Fruit Jars, Graniteware, Griswold, Kitchen Glassware, Linens, Pyrex, Reamers, Salt & Pepper Shakers,

Wagner Ware, Yellow Ware, and individual glass and pottery categories for additional listings.

Apron, cotton, slip-on, embroidered, deep pockets, 1928. . . . . **$20.00**

Biscuit Cutter, stamped tin, loop handle, mkd "Old Gristmill," 2" d **10.00**

Bottle Opener, cast iron, donkey **30.00**

Bread Board, maple, round, matching knife **45.00**

Cake Pan, tin, with spout and side handle, Vanity Co, 10" d **15.00**

Calendar, 1939, Sunshine Cookies. **18.00**

Can Opener, iron and wood, A&J Miracle, 1930s, 6¼" l **10.00**

Clock, figural teapot, electric, stamped metal, Sessions, 7" h, 8½" w **35.00**

Coffeepot, electric, chrome, football shaped, tan handles and spigot, Edison General Electric Hotpoint **25.00**

Colander, tin and wire frame with wire mesh, wooden handles, Androck, 1930s **12.00**

Cookbook, *Cookies & More Cookies*, L Sumption, 1938 . . . . . . **5.00**

Cookie Cutter, angel, tin, strap brace handle, 5" h. **10.00**

Cookie Cutter, Christmas tree, plastic, 4½" h **1.00**

Cookie Cutter, lion, tin, 3½" l **15.00**

Cookie Cutter, Raggedy Ann and Andy, red and blue, Hallmark, 1972, 4¾" h, price for pr **30.00**

Cookie Jar, cat's head, Metlox **125.00**

Corn Stick Pan, cast aluminum, Wearever No. 22, 13 x 5½" **15.00**

Cream Dipper, stamped tin, dated 1924. . . . . **8.00**

Eggbeater, Ekco, plastic side handle, 11½" h **5.00**

Eggcup, bird, whistle handle, Japan **100.00**

Eggcup, Walking Ware, Carlton Ware, England, 1970s **45.00**

Egg Slicer, cast aluminum, steel wire and spring, German, 5¾" l **15.00**

Egg Timer, black chef. **15.00**

Egg Timer, cat, holding timer in mouth, mkd "Germany" **65.00**

Egg Timer, chef holding egg, wood. **35.00**

Egg Timer, dachshund, "Shorty Timer" label **35.00**

Egg Timer, Humpty Dumpty, mkd "California Cleminson". **50.00**

Egg Timer, Little Black Sambo, wood **85.00**

Egg Timer, white scottie, chalkware **45.00**

Egg Timer, windmill, yellow and green, Cardinal China. **25.00**

Flour Sifter, tin, wood crank knob, 3 cup **5.00**

Knife Sharpener, iron, wooden handle, Eversharp **20.00**

Ladle, enamelware, tan, green trim, 1930s. **10.00**

Measuring Cups, tin, "Mary Ann's Accurate Measure," flared sides, tab handles, set of 4 . . . . **12.00**

Mixing Bowl, yellow ware, triple brown band, mkd "20 Made in USA," 8" d. **25.00**

Napkin Lady, Colonial Girl, blue, 7¾" h. **60.00**

Napkin Lady, holding fan, white and blue dress, 9¾" h. **35.00**

Napkin Lady, holding heart, blue dress, white hair, mkd "Brockmann," 6½" h **65.00**

Napkin Lady, Southern Belle, holding blue hat, gold highlights, 9¾" h **135.00**

Napkin Ring, bisque, cat, mkd "Japan" **20.00**

Napkin Ring, celluloid, figural grapes, emb **12.00**

Napkin Ring, celluloid, figural tiger **35.00**

Napkin Ring, metal, lady holding stick, c1942 . . . . **15.00**

Nutcracker, alligator, brass, 10½" l **25.00**

Pie Bird, blackbird in pie, 4" h. **150.00**

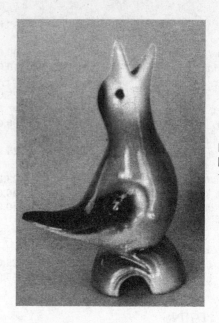

Pie Bird, blue body, black details, 1950s-60s, $20.00.

Pie Bird, black-faced chef, blue, yellow, or green, 1940-60s **100.00**

Pie Bird, long-neck duckling, blue, yellow, or pink, 1950-60s **35.00**

Pie Bird, mammy holding spoon, yellow **125.00**

Pie Bird, rooster, Marion Drake **65.00**

Pie Bird, songbird, blue, pink, or light brown, 1940-60s **50.00**

Pie Bird, walrus, Japan **125.00**

Pie Plate, Pyrex, clear, 8" d **6.00**

Place Mats, set of 8, white cotton, Battenberg, lavish corners and edging, matching napkins, c1940 . . . . **75.00**

Pot Holder, cotton, embroidered house, 1920-30s **10.00**

Pot Holder, crocheted, multicolored, brass ring, 1950s **3.00**

Rolling Pin, milk glass, metal handles, 16" l **75.00**

Rolling Pin, plastic, pink, Ekco, 1960s **10.00**

Rolling Pin, wood, red lacquered handles, 1930s, 17" l **10.00**

Salt and Pepper Shakers, pr, cactus, Arcadia Ceramics **25.00**

Salt and Pepper Shakers, pr, Esso pumps **30.00**

Salt and Pepper Shakers, pr, mermaids, Enesco. **15.00**

Salt and Pepper Shakers, pr, mice and cheese, plastic **12.00**

Spatula, tin, emb handle, "Aurora Ice Cream". **12.00**

Tablecloth, white cotton, colorful appliquéd linen flowers, crocheted edges, 6 matching napkins, c1930, 54 x 56". **35.00**

Teapot, enamelware, green and tan, gooseneck spout, 1930s. **25.00**

Teapot, Stangl, Town & Country, blue. **75.00**

Teapot, Universal Pottery, red, "National Brotherhood of Operative Potteries" stamped on bottom," 5½" h, 7" w **30.00**

Toaster, chrome, black Bakelite, 1-slice, Merit-Made Co, 1940s **25.00**

Trivet, cast iron, Grain Belt Beer adv **25.00**

Waffle Iron, electric, pedestal base, side handle, Universal, Landers, Frary & Clark, 1920s **35.00**

Whistle Cup, boy with cork gun, "Whistle Time" **15.00**

Whistle Cup, Pixie handle, "Always Drink Milk". **35.00**

Whistle Cup, poodle face on front, bird on handle **30.00**

KITCHEN GLASSWARE

Depression Glass is a generic term for glass produced in the United States from the early 1920s through the 1960s. Depression Glass patterns make up only a fraction of the thousands of glass patterns and types produced during this period.

Kitchen Glassware is a catchall category for inexpensive kitchen and table glass produced during this period. Hundreds of companies made it. Hocking, Hazel Atlas, McKee, U.S. Glass, and Westmoreland are a few examples.

Kitchen glassware was used on the table and for storage. It usually has a thick body, designed to withstand heavy and daily use. The category is dominated by storage glass and utilitarian items prior to 1940. Following World War II, tabletop glass prevailed. Kitchen glassware was a favored giveaway premium in the 1950s and early 1960s.

References: Gene Florence, *Kitchen Glassware of the Depression Years, Fifth Edition,* Collector Books, 1995, 1999 value update; Joe Keller and David Ross, *Jadite,* Schiffer Publishing, 1999.

Newsletter: *Knife Rests of Yesterday & Today,* 495 Linden Way, Pleasanton, CA 94566.

Collectors' Club: Jelly Jammers, 110 White Oak Dr, Butler, PA 16001.

Note: For additional listings see Depression Glass, Drinking Glasses, Fire-King, Pyrex, Reamers, and individual glass company categories.

Batter Bowl, Hocking, jadite	**$40.00**
Batter Jug, McKee, red	**175.00**
Beater Bowl, Fire-King, jadite	**75.00**
Bowl, Hazel Atlas, metal holder, 6⅝" d, cobalt	**40.00**
Bowl, Pyrex, 7" d, delphite	**18.00**
Bowl, Pyrex, 10" d, delphite	**24.00**
Butter, Hocking, transparent green	**135.00**
Butter, McKee, Ships, 1 lb, white milk glass	**80.00**
Canister, Hazel Atlas, glass lid, transparent green	**75.00**
Canister, Hocking, glass lid, transparent green	**100.00**

Mixing Bowls, Jeannette, #K-1, nesting set of 3, fired-on colors over clear glass, red 10½" d, green 8¾" d, and yellow 7¼" d, $40.00. Photo courtesy Ray Morykan Auctions.

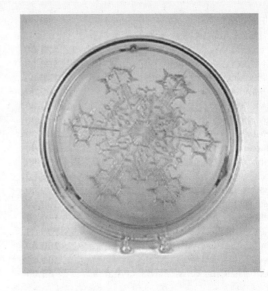

Cake Plate, snowflake pattern, ftd, 12¾" d, pink, $22.00. Photo courtesy Ray Morykan Auctions.

Canister, Hocking, metal screw-on lid, transparent green	**100.00**
Canister, Hocking, Vitrock, red circle with flowers, metal screw-on lid	**55.00**
Canister, Jeannette, jadite	**125.00**
Casserole, cov, Fire-King, Philbe, 2 qt, sapphire blue	**45.00**
Cereal Bowl, Federal, Sharon, 6" d, pink	**25.00**
Cereal Jar, Fire-King, 40 oz, custard	**65.00**
Cruet, Fire-King, green	**65.00**
Flour Shaker, Hocking, jadite	**55.00**
Flour Shaker, McKee, jadite	**90.00**
Grease Jar, Fire-King, black dots	**70.00**
Grease Jar, Fire-King, tulips	**65.00**
Grease Jar, Hocking, Vitrock, red flower pots	**34.00**
Knife, Hazel Atlas, Criss Cross, ¼ lb, blue	**150.00**
Measuring Cup, Fire-King, Philbe, 1 cup, sapphire blue	**25.00**
Measuring Cup, Hazel Atlas, 8 oz, green	**13.00**
Measuring Cup, Hocking, ¼ cup, ultramarine	**70.00**
Measuring Cup, Hocking, ⅓ cup, delphite	**55.00**
Measuring Cup, Hocking, 1 cup, delphite	**125.00**
Measuring Cup, Jeannette, ¼ cup, jadite	**45.00**
Measuring Cup, Jeannette, 1 cup, delphite	**125.00**
Measuring Cup, McKee, 4 cup, custard	**50.00**
Measuring Cups, Hocking, jadite, set of 3	**155.00**
Milk Pitcher, Fire-King, jadite	**75.00**
Mixing Bowl, Federal, 9¾" d, pink	**35.00**
Mixing Bowl, Fire-King, 4 qt	**70.00**
Mixing Bowl, Fire-King, 6½" d, apple	**50.00**
Mixing Bowl, Fire-King, 8½" d, black dots	**50.00**
Mixing Bowl, Fire-King, 9½" d, black dots	**55.00**
Mixing Bowl, Hazel Atlas, 6⅝" d, pink	**25.00**
Mixing Bowl, Hazel Atlas, 7⅝" d, cobalt	**55.00**
Mixing Bowls, Hocking, nesting set of 5, transparent green	**160.00**
Mixing Bowl, McKee, jadite, 6" d	**30.00**
Mixing Bowls, McKee, Ships, nesting set of 4, white milk glass	**50.00**
Nutmeg Canister, Hocking, jadite	**175.00**
Nutmeg Canister, Jeannette, jadite	**175.00**
Pepper Shaker, Hocking, jadite	**55.00**
Pepper Shaker, Hocking, Vitrock, red flower pots	**35.00**
Platter, Fire-King, 9½" l, jadite	**40.00**
Refrigerator Dish, Federal, 5½" d, pink	**15.00**

Refrigerator Dish, Fire-King, Philbe, 4½ x 5", jadeite **60.00**
Refrigerator Dish, Hazel Atlas, Criss Cross, 3½ x 5¾",
 blue **175.00**
Refrigerator Dish, Hocking, 4 x 4", delphite **100.00**
Refrigerator Dish, Hocking, 4 x 8", delphite **130.00**
Refrigerator Dish, Jeannette, 4 x 4", delphite. **100.00**
Refrigerator Dish, McKee, 4 x 5", custard **35.00**
Refrigerator Dish, McKee, 5 x 8", custard **75.00**
Refrigerator Dish, McKee, 5 x 8", seville yellow **200.00**
Salt and Pepper Shakers, pr, Hocking, ultramarine **75.00**
Salt and Pepper Shakers, pr, Jeannette, delphite **155.00**
Spice Jar, Griffiths **8.00**
Straw Jar, milk glass, no insert, short. **250.00**
Straw Jar, milk glass, no insert, tall **500.00**
Sugar Canister, McKee, custard **110.00**
Sugar Shaker, McKee, jadite. **100.00**
Tea Canister, Jeannette, metal screw-on top, jadite **180.00**
Tea Canister, McKee, 48 oz, jadite **200.00**
Water Bottle, Hazel Atlas, Criss Cross, 32 oz, crystal **65.00**

KOREAN WAR

The Korean War began on June 25, 1950, when North Korean troops launched an invasion across the 38th parallel into South Korea. The United Nations ordered an immediate cease-fire and withdrawal of the invading forces. On June 27 President Harry Truman ordered U.S. Forces to South Korea to help repel the North Korean invasion. The United Nations Security Council adopted a resolution for armed intervention.

The first American ground forces arrived in Korea on July 1, 1950. General Douglas MacArthur was named commander of the United Nations forces on July 8, 1950. The landing at Inchon took place on September 15, 1950. U.S. troops reached the Yalu River on the Manchurian border in late November.

On November 29, 1950, Chinese Communist troops counterattacked. Seoul was abandoned on January 4, 1951, only to be recaptured on March 21, 1951. On April 11, 1951, President Truman relieved General MacArthur of his command. General Matthew Ridgway replaced him. By early July a cease-fire had been declared, North Korean troops withdrew above the 38th parallel, and truce talks began. A stalemate was reached.

On November 29, 1952, President-elect Dwight Eisenhower flew to Korea to inspect the United Nations forces. An armistice was signed at Panmunjom by the United Nations, North Korea, and Chinese delegates on July 27, 1953.

References: Richard J. Austin, *The Official Price Guide to Military Collectibles, Sixth Edition,* House of Collectibles, 1998; Ron Manion, *American Military Collectibles Price Guide,* Antique Trader Books, 1995.

Periodical: *Military Trader,* PO Box 1050, Dubuque, IA 52004.

Ammunition Belt, dark olive drab canvas and web with
 metal fittings, Bar 6 pocket, mkd "US," dated 1952 . . . . . . **$25.00**
Badge, South Korea, Air Gunner, silver, stylized wings
 flanking target, jet in center **20.00**
Book, *This Is War!* Duncan, 200 pp, photos, dj, 1980s **30.00**
Dog Tags, USMC, oval, on beaded neckchain. **35.00**
Flight Jacket, dark blue nylon body, real fur cuff trimmed
 built-in hood, zipper and button front, printed USAF
 patch design on left shoulder, size medium. **375.00**

Flight Trousers, dark blue gabardine with woven spec
 label and USAF ink stamp markings, zipper front, size
 large. **50.00**
Helmet, navy aviator's, model H-4, black ext, right side
 boom mike mount, int leather and web head
 restraints, size large **50.00**
Lead Soldiers, set of 18, models of American Army of
 Korean War, 1" h **15.00**
Lighter, brushed silver finish case with flip-top, engraved
 and painted design of Japan and Korea with locations,
 small South Korea, UN, and Japan flag designs, made
 in Korea **20.00**
Parachutist Weapon Case, padded dark olive drab can-
 vas with zipper, mkd "US," dated 1951 . . . . **35.00**
Parka and Liner, olive drab, built-in hood, zipper and
 snap closure front, button-in liner, 1951 dated
 Quartermaster markings. **20.00**
Patch, USAF 335th Fighter Squadron, embroidered, 3¾
 x 4". **400.00**
Plaque, oak, USAF 5th Air Force, center hp emblem
 with "5th Air Force" above "Korea" **55.00**
Scarf, silk, hp map of Korea, border of flags, and verses
 from Korean songs, dated 1953 . . . . **30.00**

KREISS CERAMICS

In 1946 Murray Kreiss founded Murray Kreiss and Company as an importer and distributor of Japanese-made ceramic figurines to the five and dime store and souvenir trade. The company changed its name to Kreiss & Company in 1951.

Kreiss contracted for a wide variety of figures ranging from Christmas Santas to a large variety of animals. Copycat examples mimicked Dr. Seuss and Disney characters. In the late 1950s, Kreiss introduced its Beatnik series followed in 1958 by its Psycho-ceramics series. Ashtrays, mugs, napkin ladies, and planters are Kreiss forms found in addition to figurines.

Norman Kreiss, Murray's son, assumed control of the company as the Sixties ended. He redirected the company's efforts into the sale of fine furniture. While the precise date for the termination of imported figures is unknown, collectors assume it occurred in the early 1970s.

All Kreiss ceramic figurines were made in Japan. Beware of examples stamped on the bottom "West Germany."

Reference: Pat and Larry Aikins, *The World of Kreiss Ceramics,* L-W Book Sales, 1999.

Animal, cat, attached bell at neck, 4⅝" h **$20.00**
Animal, Powder Puff Puppy **18.00**
Animal, Powder Puff Pussy and Kittens. **15.00**
Animal, seal with ball, 3¼" h. **10.00**
Animal, turtle, 2¾" h. **8.00**
Ashtray, "Have a dog gone Merry Christmas," 6" l **12.00**
Ashtray, "I can't give you anything but love," 6¼" l **15.00**
Ashtray, Psycho, "Please finish your cigarette and get off
 my back," 5" l **190.00**
Bank, pig, 6" h **30.00**
Bank, Psycho, "Mad Money," 5⅜" h. **125.00**
Bank, reindeer, 6⅞" h **35.00**
Card Holder, Santa with sleigh, 6 x 8⅜". **30.00**
Cookie Jar, Psycho, "Cookies For My Monster" **250.00**
Decanter, boy skunk, gold top hat with feather, 5½" h **40.00**

Figure, Beatnik, "Dad–I'm waiting for the world to go pfft!," 6¹/₈" h 85.00
Figure, Beatnik Santa. 45.00
Figure, choir boy, 4³/₄" h 12.00
Figure, Elegant Heir, "Cuddle up a little closer," 7³/₈" h 125.00
Figure, Elegant Heir, "My mother thinks I have what it takes, but no one wants it!," 6⁵/₈" h 60.00
Figure, Flapper Girl. 55.00
Figure, King of Clubs, 6⁵/₈" h 20.00
Figure, Lil Rascals, Freckles, 5¹/₂" h. 25.00
Figure, Psycho, Christmas, "Mom said something about being frightened by a dachshund," 4¹/₄ x 4³/₈" 45.00
Figure, Psycho, "My job is sooooo!," 5¹/₄" h 100.00
Figure, Psycho, "Want to lose ten ugly pounds?, Cut off your hair," 4⁷/₈" h 55.00
Mug, Elegant Heir, 3³/₄" h 55.00
Napkin Lady, girl, yellow hat and dress, 8⁷/₈" h 35.00
Planter, Colonial girl, 7¹/₄" h. 25.00
Plate, "Noel," 5⁷/₈" d 18.00
Salt and Pepper Shakers, pr, bears 20.00
Salt and Pepper Shakers, pr, Christmas trees, 3⁵/₈" h 20.00
Salt and Pepper Shakers, pr, "I'm A Little Devil," 4¹/₄" h. 20.00
Salt and Pepper Shakers, pr, mice, 4³/₄" h 18.00
Salt and Pepper Shakers, pr, penguins, 3³/₈" h 20.00
Salt and Pepper Shakers, pr, worms, 2³/₄" h. 25.00
Shelf Sitter, country boy eating apple, 7¹/₈" h. 20.00

K.T. & K. CALIFORNIA

Homer J. Taylor established K.T. & K. California pottery in Burbank, California, in 1937. The son of one of the original founders of the Knowles, Taylor & Knowles pottery in East Liverpool, Ohio, he served as president of that company after his father's death in 1914. Following Knowles, Taylor & Knowles' closing, Homer moved to Burbank and started his own company.

K.T. & K. California produced decorative accessories such as figural planters, vases, and wall pockets. "K.T.K. Calif" was incised on all items. "Hand Made" was sometimes included in the mark.

Bowl, applied bow and ribbon, light red glaze, 5¹/₂" w $40.00
Bowl, twisted rope handles, peach monochrome glaze, 3¹/₄" h, 8¹/₂" w 80.00

Cornucopia Vase, blue, 7¹/₂" h, $85.00.

Candleholder, bowl form scalloped body, mottled glaze 25.00
Candleholders, pr, bow dec, mottled chartreuse brown, 3" h 80.00
Centerpiece Vase, 3 flower holders on pedestal base, mkd "KT&K Cabaña Calif," 5¹/₄" h 50.00
Cornucopia Vase, abstract design on body and base 80.00
Creamer and Open Sugar, applied floral design, 2¹/₂" h 50.00
Creamer and Open Sugar, dimple marks on body, twisted rope handle, peach monochrome glaze. 60.00
Figure, boy with barrel on back 35.00
Figure, lamb, applied bow at neck. 30.00
Match Holder, figural wheelbarrow, 3" h 30.00
Pitcher, rounded body with 3 sections, flared neck, twisted rope handle, sgd "B," 4" h. 45.00
Planter, duck, 4¹/₂" h 50.00
Vase, applied pear and leaf design, 5¹/₂" h 50.00
Vase, incised abstract leaf design, light red glaze, 5¹/₂" sq 40.00
Vase, overlapping abstract lines on body, incised "SS" with mark, 6¹/₄" h 35.00
Wall Pocket, applied floral design, matte blue monochrome glaze 45.00
Wall Pockets, pr, woman with fancy headdress, 7³/₄" l 125.00

LALIQUE

René Lalique (1860-1945) began his career as a designer and jewelry maker. His perfume flacons attracted the attention of M. Francois Coty. Coty contracted with Lalique to design and manufacture perfume bottles for the company. Initially, the bottles were made at Legras & Cie de St. Dennis. In 1909 Lalique opened a glassworks at Combs-la-Ville. Lalique acquired a larger glassworks at Wingen-sur-Moder in Alsace-Lorraine in 1921 and founded Verrerie d'Alsace René Lalique et Cie.

Although René was not involved in the actual production, he designed the majority of the articles manufactured by the firm. Lalique glass is lead glass that is either blown in the mold or pressed. There are also combinations of cutting and casting and some molded designs were treated with acids to produce a frosted, satiny effect. Lalique blown wares were almost all confined to stemware and large bottles. Glass made before 1945 has been found in more than ten colors, including mauve and purple.

Early pieces were of naturalistic design—molded animals, foliage, flowers, or nudes. Later designs became stylized and reflected the angular, geometric characteristics of Art Deco.

Each piece of Lalique glass is marked on the bottom or near the base. It is often marked in several places, in block letters and in script. Marks include: R. LALIQUE FRANCE (engraved and sandblasted block and script); LALIQUE FRANCE (diamond point tool, engraved, sandblasted block and script); and LALIQUE (engraved). The "R" was deleted from the mark following René's death in 1945. Collectors prefer pre-1945 material.

Lalique closed its Combs-la-Ville factory in 1937. The factory at Wingen-sur-Moder was partially destroyed during World War II. Lalique made no glass between 1939 and 1946. Production resumed after the war. In 1965 Lalique made its first limited edition Christmas plate, ending the series in 1976. Marc Lalique and his daughter, Marie-Claude Lalique, have contributed a number of new designs. The company still produces pieces from old molds.

Reference: Robert Prescott-Walker, *Collecting Lalique Glass,* Francis Joseph Publications, 1996, distributed by Krause Publications.

Collectors' Club: Lalique Collectors Society (company-sponsored), 400 Veterans Blvd, Carlstadt, NJ 07072.

REPRODUCTION ALERT: Beware of the Lalique engraved signature and etched mark applied to blanks made in Czechoslovakia, France, and the United States.

Ashtray, Caravelle, clear and frosted glass with molded sailing ship, model introduced 1930, 2½" h, 4" d **$115.00**

Ashtray, Faune, clear and frosted glass with molded satyr, gray stain, model introduced 1931, 3¾" h, 4⅛" d **1,000.00**

Bowl, Dauphins, clear and frosted iridescent glass with molded mermaids, flaring rim, blue stain, model introduced 1932, 9¼" d **1,000.00**

Bowl, Ondines, clear and frosted opalescent glass with molded nude females, model introduced 1921, 8¼" d . . **2,250.00**

Bowl, opalescent, intaglio fish spiraling out from center bubbles, int base mkd "VDA," base inscribed "R Lalique France," 9⅜" d **400.00**

Bracelet, Cerisier, clear and frosted dark blue glass with molded cherries and leaves, model introduced 1928 . . . **2,250.00**

Clock, Marguerites, frosted colorless glass with molded bouquet of daisies, model introduced 1920, 5¾" h **2,500.00**

Figure, Ara, frosted, figural cockatoo, model #11621 . . . . . **1,850.00**

Figure, Pigeon Bruges, clear and frosted colorless glass, model introduced 1931, 10½" l **750.00**

Figure, toad, frosted and polished colorless glass, 3⅛" h **225.00**

Finger Bowl, Thionville, clear and frosted colorless glass with molded abstract fruit design, black enamel detail, model introduced 1931, 4½" d **115.00**

Hood Ornament, Coq Nain, frosted, stamped "Lalique France," mkd "R. Lalique," 8" h **500.00**

Hood Ornament, dragonfly with upright wings, frosted, sgd and inscribed "R Lalique France," 8¼" h, 8" l, price for pr **5,000.00**

Hood Ornament, greyhound, frosted, intaglio form on press-molded ovoid disc, mkd "R Lalique France," 7¾" l **1,725.00**

Necklace Beads, Fleurettes, set of 11, barrel shaped, gray glass with lavender-mauve patina over floral motif, 1¼" l **1,375.00**

Paperweight, Tete de Paon, clear and frosted figural peacock's head on black glass base, model introduced 1928, 7" h **5,750.00**

Pendant, Guêpes, clear and frosted amethyst glass with molded wasps, model introduced 1920, 2⅜" h **1,150.00**

Pendant, Serpents, clear and frosted blue glass with 2 molded snakes, model introduced 1920, 1¾" h **1,850.00**

Perfume Bottle, Dans la Nuit for Worth, clear and frosted, molded stars, dark blue stain, model introduced 1924, 3" h **450.00**

Perfume Bottle, Relief for Forvil, clear, molded beaded spirals, model introduced 1924, 5½" h **800.00**

Perfume Bottle, Sans Adieu for Worth, green, cylindrical form, stopper in form of stacked tapering disks, model introduced 1929, 5½" h **800.00**

Powder Box, clear glass with brown patina, molded figural scene of 2 women in garden, molded mark "R. Lalique," base rim inscribed "France...," 1¾" h, 2¾" d . . . **500.00**

Suite, Dahlias, necklace and bracelet, molded colorless frosted glass with petal motif **1,725.00**

Tray, Galon, clear and frosted glass, model introduced 1936, 15⅝" l **700.00**

Vase, Actinia, clear and frosted opalescent glass with molded stylized wave motif, model introduced 1934, 8⅝" h **2,250.00**

Vase, Champagne, clear and satin colorless glass with molded conical projections, model introduced 1927, 6⅛" h **1,500.00**

Vase, Davos, clear plum brown glass with molded allover different size bubbles in geometric pattern, model introduced 1932, 11" h **5,500.00**

Vase, Deauville, clear and frosted colorless glass with molded leafy vines, green stain, model introduced 1941, 6" h **800.00**

Vase, Domrémy, frosted green glass with molded thistles, white stain, model introduced 1926, 8¼" h **6,000.00**

Vase, Formose, clear and frosted cased white glass with molded fish motif, model introduced 1924, 6⅝" h **2,500.00**

Vase, Grenade, clear and frosted colorless glass with molded stylized flower petal motif, blue stain, model introduced 1930, 4½" h **1,375.00**

LAMPS

Kerosene lamps dominated the 19th century and first quarter of the 20th century. Thomas Edison's invention of the electric light bulb in 1879 marked the beginning of the end of the kerosene lamp era.

The 1930s was the Age of Electricity. By the end of the decade electricity was available throughout America. Manufacturers and designers responded quickly to changing styles and tastes. The arrival of the end table and television as major pieces of living room furniture presented a myriad of new design opportunities.

Most lamps are purchased for reuse, not collecting purposes. Lamps whose design speaks to a specific time period or that blend with modern decor have decorative rather than collecting value. Decorative value is significantly higher than collecting value.

With the broad lamp category, there are several lamp groups that are collected. Aladdin lamps, due primarily to an extremely strong collectors' club, are in a league of their own. Other collecting subcategories include character lamps, figural lamps, novelty, motion or revolving lamps, student lamps, Tiffany and Tiffany-style lamps, and TV lamps.

References: *Electric Lighting of the 20s-30s, Vol. 1* (1994, 1998 value update), *Vol. 2,* (1994, 1998 value update), L-W Book Sales; Donald-Brian Johnson and Leslie Piña, *Moss Lamps*, Schiffer Publishing, 2000; Jan Lindenberger, *Lamps of the 50s & 60s,*

Eagle Head Mascot, molded frosted glass, mkd "Lalique France," 4¼" h, $1,430.00. Photo courtesy Collectors Auction Services.

Schiffer Publishing, 1997; L-W Book Sales (ed.), *Better Electric Lamps of the 20's & 30's*, L-W Book Sales, 1997; L-W Book Sales (ed.), *Quality Electric Lamps*, L-W Book Sales, 1992, 1996 value update; Nadja Maril, *American Lighting: 1840-1940*, Schiffer Publishing, 1995; Leland and Crystal Payton, *Turned On: Decorative Lamps of the 'Fifties*, Abbeville Press, 1989; Jo Ann and Francis Thomas, *Early Twentieth Century Lighting Fixtures: Selections from the R. Williamson Lamp Catalog*, Collector Books, 1999.

Note: For additional listings see Aladdin, Motion Lamps, and Television Lamps.

Character, Mickey Mouse, painted plaster, Mickey in Boy Scout uniform with canteen over shoulder, La Mode Studios, 1938, 7³/₄" h **$375.00**

Character, Popeye, ceramic, spinach can with raised figures, King Features, 1975 . . . . **150.00**

Character, Winnie the Pooh, ceramic, Pooh and Tigger sitting on log and leaning against tree, illus shade, mkd "MR" and "Made In Japan," 11¹/₂" h **175.00**

Desk, ceramic bulbous body, metal half moon trim, 10" h **25.00**

Desk, metal and brass, angular brass shaft, bar-shaped weighted foot, black enameled disk shade, Philips, attributed to Pierre Paulin, 15¹/₄ x 13" **400.00**

Floor, black enameled metal, 3 adjustable tubular arms with flaring fixtures with brass int and enameled white, gray, or black ext, Lightolier, unmkd, c1950, 68 x 24" **500.00**

Floor, chrome, flaring pedestal base, frosted glass mushroom shaped shade, 37 x 13" **300.00**

Floor, enameled black steel frame with 3 mounted bright chrome spherical fixtures, Arteluce, stamped "Italy," c1968, 60 x 11" sq **875.00**

Floor, metal, 2 angled black enameled tubular shafts, conical orange shade, French, c1955, 66 x 20" **925.00**

Floor, Panthella, molded flaring base, hemispheric white plastic shade, Verner Panton for Louis Poulsen, 50 x 20" **325.00**

Floor, torchere style, 3 flaring black enameled rods, orig white glass shade, Lightolier, unmkd, c1940s, 65¹/₂ x 21", price for pr **825.00**

Floor, torchere style, black enameled tubular base with shallow white enameled reflecting shade, unmkd, 72 x 26" **3,850.00**

Floor, torchere style, brushed aluminum, adjustable arm and semi-spherical shade, Nessen, unmkd, 61³/₄ x 17" . . **2,500.00**

Floor, walnut, 3-pronged, complete with white string shade, Vladimir Kagan, 62 x 18¹/₂" **3,000.00**

Floor, white enamel flaring base, frosted white mushroom shaped shade, Laurel, 56 x 12", price for pr **440.00**

Hanging, Bubble lamp, bulbous middle, tapering ends, George Nelson for Howard Miller, 19¹/₂ x 16" **375.00**

Hanging, saucer shaped, white spun fibrous material over thin wire frame, George Nelson for Howard Miller, 9 x 26¹/₂" **400.00**

Table, Akari-Gemini, black wire frame with mulberry paper and bamboo tapering 4-sided shade, Isamu Noguchi, stamped signature, 25 x 12" **350.00**

Table, aluminum, circular base, glass globe **85.00**

Table, black wire legs, pyramidal mulberry paper and bamboo shade, Isamu Noguchi for Akari, 14¹/₄ x 15" sq **250.00**

Table, ceramic, black panther planter base, light green Venetian blind shade, 24" h, $80.00.

Table, brass, spiral shaped body, cardboard shade **25.00**

Table, brass, S-shaped body, double fiberglass shades **100.00**

Table, ceramic, driftwood style body, cloth shade, 26" h **50.00**

Table, ceramic, pagoda style body, fiberglass shade, 26" h **40.00**

Table, Italian glass, squat base, egg shaped globe, 22¹/₂ x 10¹/₂" d **125.00**

Table, sgraffito and enamel, Art Deco maiden on horseback motif on green speckled ground, complete with orig fittings, unmkd, 20 x 13" **325.00**

LEFTON CHINA

George Zoltan Lefton was the driving force behind Lefton China, a china importing and marketing organization. Following World War II, Lefton, a Hungarian immigrant, began importing giftware made in the Orient into the United States. Following Lefton's death in May 1996, the presidency of the company was assumed by Magda Lefton, George's wife. Magda Lefton passed away in August 1998. The company is now jointly controlled by their daughter, Margo Lefton, and grandson, Steven Lefton.

Until the mid-1970s Japanese factories made the vast majority of Lefton China. After that date, China, Malaysia, and Taiwan became the principal supply sources.

Most Lefton pieces are identified by a fired-on trademark or a paper label. Numbers found on pieces are item identification numbers. When letters precede a number, it is a factory code, e.g., "SL" denotes Nippon Art China K.K.

References: Loretta DeLozier, *Collector's Encyclopedia of Lefton China* (1995, 1998 value update), *Bk II* (1997, 1999 value update), and *Bk III* (1999), Collector Books; Ruth McCarthy, *Lefton China* (1998) and *More Lefton China* (2000), Schiffer Publishing, 1998.

Collectors' Club: National Society of Lefton Collectors, 1101 Polk St, Bedford, IA 50833.

Ashtray, puppy **$55.00**
Bank, Hubert the Lion **40.00**

Planter, ivory, rope design, #4519, 9¼" l, $20.00.

Bank, lovebirds	75.00
Bookends, pr, tiger cub, #H663	35.00
Butter Dish, Toodles	145.00
Child's Cup, bluebird	45.00
Child's Cup and Bowl, Toodles	150.00
Condiment Set, island boy and girl	375.00
Cookie Jar, Bambi and Friends, Canadian ink stamp	200.00
Cookie Jar, bluebird	225.00
Cookie Jar, Rustic Daisy	55.00
Cookie Jar, Toodles	155.00
Creamer, Thumbelina	30.00
Creamer and Sugar, Bloomer Girl	100.00
Creamer and Sugar, honey bee	55.00
Creamer and Sugar, Little Lady	85.00
Creamer and Sugar, Miss Priss	40.00
Dish, divided, Little Lady	185.00
Eggcup, bluebird	85.00
Eggcup, Christmas Girl	20.00
Figurine, Bloomer Girl, #KW4833, bisque	65.00
Figurine, boy of the month, March, #2300, 5" h	35.00
Figurine, bride with blonde ponytail, #6363, 8" h	100.00
Figurine, lady with umbrella, #KW1274A, pink, gold trim, sgd	110.00
Figurine, spaghetti poodle, 4¾" h	60.00
Flour Canister, Clover Bud pattern	45.00
Marmalade, Toodles	75.00
Mug, elf	18.00
Planter, Little Lady, holding beach ball	65.00
Planter, Toodles, #2631, pink bow	65.00
Salt and Pepper Shakers, pr, Dutch girl and boy	65.00
Salt and Pepper Shakers, pr, honey bee	30.00
Salt and Pepper Shakers, pr, Miss Priss	20.00
Salt and Pepper Shakers, pr, Poinsettia, #4390	30.00
Salt and Pepper Shakers, pr, Toodles, #3235	35.00
Shelf Sitter, oriental kids, #KW127	70.00
Sugar, Dutch girl	55.00
Sugar, grapes	35.00
Teapot, Dutch girl	185.00
Teapot, honey bee, #1278, no label	50.00
Teapot, Miss Priss	145.00
Tidbit Tray, honey bee, 3-tier	35.00
Tray, Rustic Daisy, rect, divided, center handle	30.00
Wall Pocket, Little Lady	55.00

LENOX

In 1889, Walter Scott Lenox and Jonathan Coxon, Sr., founded the Ceramic Art Company in Trenton, New Jersey. Lenox acquired sole ownership in 1894. In 1906 he formed Lenox, Inc.

Lenox gained national recognition in 1917 when President Woodrow Wilson ordered a 1,700-piece dinner service. Later, Presidents Franklin D. Roosevelt and Harry S. Truman followed Wilson's lead. First Lady Nancy Reagan ordered a 4,732-piece set of gold-embossed bone china from Lenox in 1981. According to Eric Poehner, the Lenox craftsman who did much of the work, each raised golden seal in the center of the Reagan service plates took two-and-one-half to three hours to hand paint.

During the last two decades, Lenox, Inc., has expanded, acquiring Art Carved, Inc., H. Rosenthal Jewelry Corporation, Imperial Glass Corporation, and many other companies. Operating today as Lenox Brands, the company is a multimillion-dollar enterprise producing a broad range of tabletop and giftware.

References: Susan and Al Bagdade, *Warman's American Pottery and Porcelain,* Wallace-Homestead, Krause Publications, 1994; Harry L. Rinker, *Dinnerware of the 20th Century: The Top 500 Patterns,* House of Collectibles, 1997.

Note: For additional listings see Limited Edition Collectibles.

Amethyst, bread and butter plate, 6½" d	**$17.00**
Amethyst, creamer and covered sugar	150.00
Amethyst, cup and saucer, ftd, 3⅛" h	40.00
Amethyst, demitasse cup and saucer	40.00
Amethyst, dinner plate, 10¾" d	35.00
Amethyst, platter, oval, 16" l	150.00
Amethyst, salad plate, 8¼" d	25.00
Amethyst, vegetable, oval, 9½" l	100.00
Blue Breeze, bread and butter plate, 6¼" d	6.00
Blue Breeze, butter, cov, ¼ lb	45.00
Blue Breeze, casserole, open, round, 6⅞" d	60.00

Figurine, American Robin, 1989, 3¾" h, $20.00. Photo courtesy Ray Morykan Auctions.

Blue Breeze, creamer and covered sugar **50.00**
Blue Breeze, cup and saucer, flat, 2³/₄" h **15.00**
Blue Breeze, dinner plate **20.00**
Blue Breeze, salad plate **15.00**
Dewdrops, baker, rect, 15¹/₂" l **100.00**
Dewdrops, bread and butter plate, 6³/₈" d **6.00**
Dewdrops, casserole, cov, round, 6¹/₄" d **60.00**
Dewdrops, creamer and covered sugar **20.00**
Dewdrops, cup and saucer, flat, 2³/₄" h **15.00**
Dewdrops, dinner plate **20.00**
Dewdrops, salad plate **15.00**
Dewdrops, salt and pepper mill **50.00**
Figurine, girl, porcelain, flowing gown covered in glossy
　　ivory glaze, imp "Lenox/ABC '37," 13³/₄ x 5³/₄" **375.00**
Fire Flower, bread and butter plate, 6¹/₂" d **6.00**
Fire Flower, casserole, cov, individual, 4³/₈" d **25.00**
Fire Flower, cereal bowl, coupe, 6¹/₈" d **15.00**
Fire Flower, creamer and covered sugar **20.00**
Fire Flower, cup and saucer, flat, 2³/₄" h **15.00**
Fire Flower, dinner plate, 10¹/₄" d **15.00**
Fire Flower, fruit bowl, 4³/₄" d **15.00**
Fire Flower, gravy boat **50.00**
Fire Flower, salad plate **10.00**
Fire Flower, salt shaker and pepper mill **50.00**
Holiday, ashtray, 4¹/₄" d **30.00**
Holiday, bread and butter plate, 6³/₈" d **10.00**
Holiday, candy dish **35.00**
Holiday, chop plate, 12⁵/₈" d **100.00**
Holiday, demitasse cup and saucer, 2³/₄" h **20.00**
Holiday, dinner plate, 10³/₄" d **20.00**
Holiday, fruit bowl, 5¹/₄" d **25.00**
Holiday, gravy boat, attached underplate **125.00**
Holiday, mint dish **25.00**
Holiday, nut dish, 4¹/₄" d **25.00**
Holiday, pie server, stainless blade, 10" l **20.00**
Holiday, platter, oval, 14" l **100.00**
Holiday, salad bowl, serving, 9¹/₂" d **55.00**
Holiday, salt and pepper shakers, pr, 3³/₄" h **20.00**
Holiday, soup bowl, coupe, 7³/₈" d **35.00**
Holiday, vegetable, round, 9¹/₈" d **45.00**
Lamp, lady, long dress and fan, stamp mark, 1929, 8¹/₂" h **75.00**
Lamp, Leda and the Swan, porcelain, stamp mark, 1929,
　　11" h **175.00**

L. E. SMITH GLASS

L. E. Smith Glass began when Lewis E. Smith, a gourmet cook, needed glass jars for a mustard he planned to market. Rather than buy jars, he bought a glass factory in Mt. Pleasant, Pennsylvania, and made them himself. Smith remained active in the company from 1908 through 1911. He is credited with inventing the glass top for percolators, the modern-style juice reamer, the glass mixing bowl, and numerous other kitchen implements.

Smith sold his interest in L.E. Smith Glass in 1911. The company continued, making automobile lenses, cookware, fruit jars, kitchenware, novelties, and tableware. Black glass was a popular product in the 1920s and 30s. Giftware and tableware products remain the company's principal focus today.

Note: See Black Glass and Milk Glass for additonal listings.

Amy, cookie jar, black **$100.00**
Do-Si-Do, cup and saucer, black **18.00**

No. 81, Bonbon, pink, $10.00. Photo courtesy Ray Morykan Auctions.

Do-Si-Do, cup and saucer, pink, gold trim **6.00**
Do-Si-Do, plate, black, 8" d **12.00**
Figurine, lamb, black, 2¹/₄" l **18.00**
Figurine, rooster, black **15.00**
Figurine, swan, white opaque **15.00**
Greek Key, fern dish, 3 ftd, white opaque **8.00**
Homestead, creamer, pink **5.00**
Kent, sugar, cov **7.00**
Moon 'n Star, compote, cov, amberina **35.00**
Moon 'n Star, cruet, ruby **30.00**
Moon 'n Star, water goblet, amberina **15.00**
Mt Pleasant, cup and saucer, black **18.00**
Mt Pleasant, nut dish, handled, black, #505, 8¹/₄" d **25.00**
Mt Pleasant, plate, black, 8" d **12.00**
Mt Pleasant, salad tray, 2 handles **50.00**
Mt Pleasant, sandwich tray, handled, black, 10" d **25.00**
Romanesque, candlesticks, pr, pink **10.00**
Romanesque, sherbet, black **10.00**
Soda Shop, soda glass **6.00**
Wigwam, candlesticks, pr, black, 3¹/₄" h **20.00**

L. G. WRIGHT GLASS

L. G. Wright Glass reproduced many types of late 19th and early 20th century glass. The company also introduced new forms, shapes, and patterns.

Lawrence Gale Wright (1904 to 1969) began buying and selling glass "seconds" in 1936/37. In 1938 he contracted with Fenton to manufacture a reproduction Hobnail barber bottle in amber and vaseline. As the 1930s ended, Wright was buying glass from Cambridge, Fenton, Morgantown, and Westmoreland. He ordered his first new molds in 1937.

Not all L. G. Wright glass was made from period molds. Although Wright purchased period molds from Northwood and Dugan, the company ordered hundreds of new molds from firms such as Albert Boston's B. Machine & Mould, Island Mould and Machine, National Mould and Machine, and Stiehm & Son.

Wright's early customers included "reproduction" wholesalers such as AA. Sales, Koscherak Brothers, and F. Pavel. The period from 1950 to 1970 was L. G. Wright's golden age. Peachblow was produced between 1955 and 1963. A glass decorating plant opened in early 1968.

Verna Mae Wright, L. G. Wright's wife, directed the company following Wright's death in 1969. She added custard glass to the company's line in 1969, and carnival in 1972. Verna Mae Wright died in 1990. Dorothy Stephen and Phyllis Stephan Buettner, her daughter, inherited the company. In October 1996 the company opened a museum adjacent to its gift shop and plant in New Martinsville, West Virginia.

Reference: James Measell and W. C. "Red" Roetteis, *The L. G. Wright Glass Company,* Glass Press, 1997.

Apothecary Jar, Fern $200.00
Barber Bottle, Honeycomb 135.00
Creamer and Sugar, Thumbprint. 140.00
Cruet, Honeycomb 150.00
Cruet, Rib. 150.00
Finger Bowl, Daisy and Fern 65.00
Finger Bowl, Thumbprint 40.00
Lamp, Beaded Curtain, green cream 75.00
Lily Bowl, Panel Grape, blue opalescent. 100.00
Pickle Jar, Dot. 275.00
Punch Bowl, with ladle, Panel Grape, blue opalescent 170.00
Rose Bowl, Daisy and Fern 75.00
Rose Bowl, Moss Rose, peachblow 140.00
Sugar Shaker, Thumbprint 65.00
Syrup Pitcher, Thumbprint 120.00
Tumbler, Beaded Curtain, peachblow. 75.00
Tumbler, Honeycomb 55.00
Tumbler, Stars and Stripes 60.00
Vase, Beaded Curtain, green overlay 400.00
Water Pitcher, Dot. 250.00
Water Pitcher, Thumbprint, plain handle. 175.00

LIBBEY GLASS

The Libbey Glass Company traces its origins to the New England Glass Company, founded in 1818 in Boston. In 1888 New England Glass moved to Toledo, Ohio, to be nearer a better fuel source. The company became the Libbey Glass Company in 1892, named for the family that managed it for several decades.

Financial difficulties arising from the move ended when Libbey began producing light bulbs. The company also manufactured a brilliant cut glass line. By the 1920s, Libbey introduced an art glass line (amberina, pomona, peachblow, etc.) and a hotel and restaurant line. In 1925 Libbey acquired the Nonik Glassware Corp., a major tumbler manufacturer.

In 1933, under the direction of Douglas Nash, Libbey re-emphasized its fine glass lines. It also acquired the H. C. Fry Company. In 1935 Owen-Illinois Glass Company purchased Libbey Glass, then billed as the "world's largest producers of glass containers." Owen-Illinois established a separate division and continues to manufacture products using the Libbey name.

References: Carl U. Fauster (comp.), *Libbey Glass Since 1818: Pictorial History & Collector's Guide,* Len Beach Press, 1979, out of print; Bob Page and Dale Fredericksen, *A Collection of American Crystal: A Stemware Identification Guide for Glasonbury/Lotus, Libbey/Rock Sharpe & Hawkes,* Page-Fredericksen Publishing, 1995; Kenneth Wilson, *American Glass 1760-1930; The Toledo Museum of Art,* 2 vols., Hudson Hills Press and The Toledo Museum of Art, 1994.

Pitcher, blue and red stripes, late 1950s, 9" h, $12.00. Photo courtesy Ray Morykan Auctions.

Bowl, Filigree $40.00
Candy Dish, ftd, Moire 40.00
Candy Jar, Morning 35.00
Cocktail, Silhouette, clear bowl, black kangaroo silhouette in stem 125.00
Cocktail Set, Morning 100.00
Cordial, 3002 Line, crystal. 15.00
Cordial, American Prestige 40.00
Cordial, Nob Hill, crystal, 3¹⁵/₁₆" h 6.00
Cordial, Rock Sharpe, Buckingham, 1008 Line, 5½" h 30.00
Cordial, Rock Sharpe, Burma, 1017 Line, 4⁷/₁₆" h 30.00
Cordial, Silhouette, Greyhound pattern, black, 4" h 200.00
Cordial, Silver Foliage, 3002 Line, 4³/₁₆" h 5.00
Decanter, Moire, large. 40.00
Decanter, Moire, small 25.00
Drinking Glass, Alice in Wonderland, Libbey Classics. 10.00
Drinking Glass, Moby Dick, Libbey Classics. 10.00
Drinking Glass, Tom Sawyer, Libbey Classics 10.00
Iced Tea, Galway. 18.00
Jug, Moire. 75.00
Luncheon Plate, Galway 18.00
Tumbler, Morning 15.00
Water Goblet, Galway. 18.00

LIBERTY BLUE

In 1973 the Grand Union Company, a retail supermarket chain based in New Jersey, commissioned Liberty Blue dinnerware to be offered as a premium in grocery stores throughout the eastern United States. Ironically, though intended to celebrate America's independence, the dinnerware was produced in Staffordshire, England.

Liberty Blue dinnerware, introduced in 1975, portrayed patriotic scenes in blue on a white background. It combined several elements of traditional Staffordshire dinnerware while remaining unique. The Wild Rose border was reproduced from a design dating back to 1784. Original engravings depicted historic buildings and events from the American Revolutionary period.

Liberty Blue is easy to identify. Most pieces contain the words "Liberty Blue" on the underside and all are marked "Made in England." The back of each dish also contains information about the scene illustrated on it.

Reference: Harry L. Rinker, *Dinnerware of the 20th Century: The Top 500 Patterns,* House of Collectibles, 1997.

Bread and Butter Plate, 6" d.	**$3.00**
Butter, cov	**65.00**
Cereal Bowl	**15.00**
Coasters, set of 4	**35.00**
Creamer	**20.00**
Cup and Saucer, flat, 2⁵⁄₈" h	**10.00**
Dessert Bowl	**6.00**
Dinner Plate, 10" d	**10.00**
Gravy Boat and Liner	**55.00**
Luncheon Plate	**15.00**
Meat Platter, 12" l	**50.00**
Mug	**15.00**
Mugs, boxed set of 4	**60.00**
Nappy, 5" d	**5.00**
Pitcher	**135.00**
Place Setting, 5 pcs	**30.00**
Platter, oval, 11⁷⁄₈" l	**40.00**
Platter, oval, 14" l	**90.00**
Salad Plate, 8½" d	**12.00**
Salt and Pepper Shakers, pr	**35.00**
Soup Bowl	**25.00**
Soup Tureen	**250.00**
Sugar, cov	**30.00**
Teapot, cov	**150.00**
Vegetable, cov	**150.00**
Vegetable, open, oval	**40.00**
Vegetable, open, round	**45.00**

Dinner Plate, 10" d, $10.00. Photo courtesy Ray Morykan Auctions.

LIFE MAGAZINES

The first *Life* magazine appeared in January 1883. Its covers featured artwork by some of America's foremost illustrators between 1898 and 1936. Illustrators include John Held, Jr., F. X. Leyendecker, Maxfield Parrish, Coles Phillips, and Norman Rockwell. Value for these issues is driven more by the cover illustration than the interior content. Covers are often cut from the magazine and sold as tear sheets.

On November 13, 1936, a new oversized *Life* featuring a photographic format cover replaced the old *Life.* Once again, the cover subject matter usually determines value. Interior advertising (especially in full color and personality driven) and key feature stories increase value. Many examples are purchased by crossover collectors, e.g., a Hopalong Cassidy collector seeking the June 12, 1950, issue with William Boyd's picture on the cover.

Collectors want complete issues when purchasing a post-November 1936 magazine. Removal of advertising or featured articles reduces the value by more than half.

Post-November 1936 *Life* magazines survive in extremely high quantities. As a result, only those in fine or better condition command top dollar.

Reference: Denis C. Jackson, *Life Magazines: 1899-1994,* published by author, 1998.

Periodical: *Paper Collectors' Marketplace (PCM),* PO Box 128, Scandinavia, WI 54977.

1936, Nov 30, West Point Cadet	**$80.00**
1937, Jan 11, Japanese Soldiers	**20.00**
1937, Feb 1, Tennis	**12.00**
1937, May 17, Dionne Quintuplets	**35.00**
1938, Jan 24, Alpine Skier	**10.00**
1939, May 1, Joe DiMaggio	**75.00**
1940, Jan 1, Queen Elizabeth	**12.00**
1941, Jul 28, Circus, Joe DiMaggio	**30.00**
1942, Mar 2, Ginger Rogers	**18.00**
1942, Aug 3, Gen MacArthur's Son	**10.00**
1943, Feb 22, Army Air Observer	**10.00**
1944, Sep 11, Nazi War Prisoners	**10.00**
1945, Feb 5, Florida Fashions	**12.00**
1946, Aug 19, Yellowstone Park	**10.00**
1947, Sep 1, Racing Car and Driver	**15.00**
1948, Dec 13, Dwight Eisenhower	**12.00**
1949, Oct 3, Football	**15.00**
1950, Apr 10, Horsewoman, Baseball	**20.00**
1951, Dec 24, Nativity Scene	**10.00**
1952, Dec 29, Marionettes	**10.00**
1953, Dec 14, Richard Nixon	**12.00**
1954, Feb 15, Oceangoing Turtle	**10.00**
1955, May 16, Fashions	**10.00**
1956, Apr 30, Margaret Truman	**10.00**
1957, Mar 4, Queen Elizabeth and Philip	**12.00**
1958, Feb 3, Shirley Temple and Daughter	**15.00**
1959, Sep 14, US Astronauts	**20.00**
1960, Mar 14, Princess Margaret	**18.00**
1961, Mar 31, German Cherub	**10.00**
1962, Sep 28, Don Drysdale	**25.00**
1963, May 10, Bay of Pigs Cuba	**15.00**
1964, Feb 14, Winter Olympics	**7.00**
1965, Jul 2, Vietnam War	**7.00**

1936, Nov 23, Fort Peck Dam, 1st Issue, $110.00.

1966, Mar 25, LSD **10.00**
1967, Oct 20, Vietnam POW. **6.00**
1968, Mar 15, Boris Karloff **10.00**
1969, Nov 21, Johnny Cash. **6.00**
1970, Oct 23, Muhammad Ali. **15.00**
1971, Apr 9, J Edgar Hoover **4.00**
1972, Sep 29, POW Wife **3.00**
1979, May, Three Mile Island. **3.00**
1980, Jun, Folk Art **3.00**
1981, Jun, Stars, Beatles **6.00**
1982, Apr, Firearms and Debate **3.00**
1983, Sep, Best and Worst Autos **4.00**
1984, Apr, Penguins in Arctic **3.00**
1985, Oct, Princess Diana **10.00**
1986, Jul, Statue of Liberty **2.00**
1987, Oct, Gorbachev **2.00**
1988, Nov, Our Planet **2.00**
1989, Spring, Hollywood **4.00**
1990, Nov, Al Pacino **2.00**
1991, Jun, Michael Landon **2.00**
1992, Mar, Afterlife. . . . . **.75**
1993, Nov, Black Child. . . . . **.50**
1994, Oct, Cat and Dog . . . . **.50**

LIGHTERS

By the 1920s the cigarette lighter enjoyed a prominent place in most American homes, even those of non-smokers who kept a lighter handy for guests.

Well-known manufacturers include Bowers, Dunhill, Evans, Marathon, Parker, Ronson, and Zippo. Well over a thousand different manufacturers produced lighters. Although the principal manufacturing centers were Japan and the United States, there was at least one lighter manufacturer in every industrialized country in the 20th century.

Collectors shy away from lighters in less than average condition. It is important that the sparking or lighting mechanism works, whether it be flint, liquid fuel, or gas. Repairing a lighter to working order is accepted among collectors.

References: Larry Clayton, *The Evans Book*, Schiffer Publishing, 1998; James Flanagan, *Collector's Guide to Cigarette Lighters*, (1995, 1998 value update), *Bk. II* (1999), Collector Books; Stuart Schneider and Ira Pilossof, *The Handbook of Vintage Cigarette Lighters*, Schiffer Publishing, 1999; Neil S. Wood, *Collecting Cigarette Lighters* (1994) and *Vol. II* (1995), L-W Book Sales.

Collectors' Clubs: International Lighter Collectors, PO Box 1733, Quitman, TX 75783; Pocket Lighter Preservation Guild & Historical Society, 380 Brooks Dr, Ste 209A, Hazelwood, MO 63042.

Note: See Zippo for additional listings.

Advertising, Adelphia Coffee & Tea Co, chrome finish metal, gold insert panel on side inscribed "Adelphia Coffee & Tea Co, New York, NY/50th Anniversary 1916-1966," mkd "Direct D54/Japan," orig box **$20.00**
Advertising, Bowers, Firestone dealer, Russell, KS, brass colored aluminum, red leatherette strap **20.00**
Advertising, Chesterfield Cigarettes, chrome luster finish metal, high gloss litho paint of replica cigarette pack on each side, Continental, made in Japan, 1960s **10.00**
Advertising, Coca-Cola, figural bottle, hard plastic body, tin bottle cap, 2½" h **20.00**
Advertising, Niblets Corn, silvered metal, plastic wrapper with sponsor, "Now Quick Cooked" on reverse, made in Japan, c1950s, ⅞" h **20.00**
Advertising, Royal Club Whiskey, chrome luster finish metal, white paint wrapper with gold and black logo on 1 side, other side inscribed "Royal Club Canadian MacNaughton Whiskey/Schenley Import Co," CMC/Continental, Japan, c1960s **15.00**
Advertising, Royal Crown Cola, figural bottle, silvered metal, red, yellow, and blue, Kem Inc, Detroit, c1930s **20.00**
Advertising, Salem Cigarettes, chrome finish metal, turquoise and white with gold accent, orig box, Penguin, Japan, 1970s **15.00**
Advertising, School Photographer, chrome luster finish metal, inlay enamel panels on each side, 1 side with "For the finest in school pictures," other side with "School Pictures-Partners Plan," Vulcan, Japan, c1960s **15.00**
Advertising, Winston Cigarettes, chrome finish metal, identical insert panels on each side for "Filter Tipped Winston Cigarettes," red, white, and gold, orig box, Zenith Lighters, c1960s **10.00**

Advertising, Dodge Pickup Trucks, 2³/₈" h, $35.00. Photo courtesy Collectors Auction Services.

Dub-L-Lite, chromium, double wick, c1948, 2¼" h **30.00**
Evans, pocket, brass, leather band, c1934, 1½" h **30.00**
Figural, beer stein, ceramic, Germany, c1958, 3¾" h **25.00**
Figural, cowboy boot, Evans, c1948, 5" h **20.00**
Figural, golf club, gold toned, Ronson-style insert, Japan,
  1961 presentation engraved text on side, 4" l **20.00**
Figural, knight, Occupied Japan, c1948, 3½" h **50.00**
Figural, trophy, table, Evans insert, gold-toned finish,
  raised leaf design around top, 6¾" h **65.00**
Golden Wheel, pocket, chromium lift arm, leather band,
  plate for engraving initials, c1928, 1¾" h **40.00**
Redilite, brass, cylinder shaped, c1928, 2⅞" h **10.00**
Ronson, Touch-Tip, table **75.00**

LIMITED EDITION COLLECTIBLES

In 1895 Bing and Grondahl produced its first Christmas plate. Royal Copenhagen followed in 1908 and Rosenthal in 1910. Limited edition art prints, many copies of Old Masters, were popular in the 1920s and 30s.

In the late 1960s and extending through the early 1980s, Americans eagerly purchased large quantities of limited edition bells, eggs, mugs, ornaments, plates, and prints. Many came with a "Certificate of Authenticity," in reality a meaningless document.

With production runs often exceeding 100,000 units, very few of these issues were truly limited. Many individuals purchased them as investments rather than for display. The speculative limited edition bubble burst in the mid-1980s. Today, the vast majority of limited edition collectibles issued between the late 1960s and the early 1980s sell for less than 50¢ on the dollar.

Limited edition collectibles is a broad category. Not all items are numbered. In some cases, limited means produced for a relatively short period of time.

Currently, prices are stable or slowly rising on a few select pieces—those that collectors have identified as desirable or whose image crosses over into other collecting categories.

References: *Collectibles Price Guide & Directory to Secondary Market Dealers, Tenth Edition,* Collectors' Information Bureau, 2000; Collectors' Information Bureau, *Collectibles Market Guide & Price Index, 16th Edition,* Collectors' Information Bureau, 1998, distributed by Krause Publications; Annette Power, *The Charlton Standard Catalog of Lilliput Lane, Second Edition,* Charlton Press, 1998; Rinker Enterprises, *The Official Price Guide to Collector Plates, Seventh Edition,* House of Collectibles, 1999; Mary Sieber (ed.), *2000 Price Guide to Limited Edition Collectibles, 5th Edition,* Krause Publications, 1999.

Periodicals: *Collector Editions,* 170 Fifth Ave, 12th Floor, New York, NY 10010; *Collectors Mart Magazine,* 700 E State St, Iola, WI 54990; *Collectors News,* PO Box 306, Grundy Center, IA 50638; *Informart,* 204 Playhouse Corner, Southbury, CT 06488.

Collectors' Club: International Plate Collectors Guild, PO Box 487, Artesia, CA 90702.

Note: In addition to company-sponsored collectors' clubs, there are numerous clubs for specific limited edition collectibles. Consult *Maloney's Antiques & Collectibles Resource Directory* by David J. Maloney, Jr., at your local library for further information. For additional listings see individual manufacturers' categories.

Architecture, Dave Grossman Creations, Sand Island
  Light, Lighthouses Series, C Spencer Collins, 1993 . . . . . . **$70.00**
Architecture, Department 56, The Cathedral, Christmas
  in the City Series, 1987 . . . . **325.00**
Architecture, Fitz & Floyd, Great Oak Town Hall,
  Charming Tails Squashville Lighted Village Series,
  D Griff, 1995 . . . . **45.00**
Architecture, Lilliput Lane, Country Church, American
  Collection Series, 1984 . . . . **500.00**
Art Print, Cross Gallery, Rosapina, etching, PA Cross,
  1989 . . . . **1,200.00**
Art Print, Flambro Imports, All Star Circus, Emmett Kelly
  Jr Lithograph Series, B Leighton-Jones, 1995 . . . . **150.00**
Art Print, Gartlan USA, George Brett "The Swing," Litho-
  graph Series, J Martin, 1986 . . . . **200.00**
Art Print, Glynda Turley, Elegance, Print Series, 1988 . . . . **30.00**
Art Print, Glynda Turley, Floral Fancy, Canvas Series,
  1991 . . . . **130.00**
Art Print, Greenwich Workshop, Little Star, J Bama, 1979 . . . **900.00**
Art Print, Greenwich Workshop, Northern Light,
  R Frederick, 1987 . . . . **165.00**
Art Print, Greenwich Workshop, World of White,
  R Frederick, 1988 . . . . **150.00**
Art Print, Hadley House, The Apache, O Franca, 1988 . . . . . **175.00**
Art Print, Hadley House, Silence Unbroken, M Casper,
  1992 . . . . **100.00**
Art Print, Imperial Graphics Ltd, Blue Bird of Paradise,
  HC Lee, 1988 . . . . **35.00**
Art Print, Imperial Graphics, Morning Glories &
  Hummer, L Liu, 1987 . . . . **45.00**
Art Print, Lightpost Publishing, Morning Lane, Kinkade
  Member's Only Collectors' Society Series, T Kinkade,
  1992 . . . . **350.00**
Art Print, Marty Ball, Blush of Spring, England Series,
  M Bell, 1989 . . . . **125.00**
Art Print, Mill Pond Press, Call of the Wild–Bald Eagle,
  R Bateman, 1983 . . . . **200.00**
Art Print, New Impressions, Secret Thoughts, Limited
  Edition Paper Prints Series, A Maley, 1985 . . . . **850.00**

Architecture, David Winter Cottage, St. Anne's Well, British Traditions Collection, 1990, $45.00.

Architecture, George Z Lefton, Alcatraz 1909, Historic American Lighthouse, 1998, $70.00.

Art Print, New Masters Publishing, Nuance, P Bannister, 1982. . . . . **500.00**

Art Print, Pemberton & Oakes, Brotherly Love, Zolan's Children–Lithograph Series, D Zolan, 1989. . . . . **300.00**

Art Print, Roman Inc, Bouquet, F Hook, 1982. . . . . **350.00**

Art Print, VF Fine Arts, First Snow, proof, S Kuck, 1990 . . . . . **150.00**

Bell, Goebel, Sweet Song, MI Hummel Collectibles Annual Bells Series, 1985 . . . . **70.00**

Bell, Kirk Stieff, Santa's Workshop, 1992 . . . . **40.00**

Bell, Lenox Crystal, Angel Bell, 1988. . . . . **45.00**

Bell, Lladró, Christmas Bell, 1991 . . . . **45.00**

Bell, Reed & Barton, Noel Musical Bell, 1981 . . . . **40.00**

Bell, River Shore, Garden Girl, Rockwell Children Series II, N Rockwell, 1978 . . . . **40.00**

Bell, Seymour Mann, Bluebird, Connoisseur Collection Series, Bernini, 1995. . . . . **15.00**

Doll, All God's Children, Skating Anika, Anika Series, M Root, 1997 . . . . **125.00**

Doll, Annalee Mobilitee Dolls, Leprechaun with Sack, A Thorndike, 1974, 10" h. **350.00**

Doll, Annalee Mobilitee Dolls, Martha Cratchet, Doll Society–Log Kids Series, A Thorndike, 1974, 18" h **425.00**

Doll, Annalee Mobilitee Dolls, Robin Hood, Doll Society, Folk Heroes Series, A Thorndike, 1984, 10" h **850.00**

Doll, Annalee Mobilitee Dolls, Rooster, A Thorndike, 1977, 8" h. **350.00**

Doll, Anri, Annie, Sarah Kay Dolls Series, S Kay, 1991, 7" h **300.00**

Doll, Ashton-Drake Galleries, Baby Grace, Little House on the Prairie Series, J Ibarolle, 1995 . . . . **75.00**

Doll, Ashton-Drake Galleries, Diana Berry, Anne of Green Gables Series, J Kovacik, 1996. . . . . **70.00**

Doll, Ashton-Drake Galleries, Now I Lay Me Down, God Hears the Children Series, B Conner, 1995 . . . . **80.00**

Doll, Ashton-Drake Galleries, Patty Cake, As Cute As Can Be Series, D Effner, 1995 . . . . **50.00**

Doll, Attic Babies, Heffy Cheffy, M Maschino-Walker, 1988. . . . . **125.00**

Doll, Daddy Long Legs/KVK Inc, Faith, Collectors Club Members Only Series, K Germany, 1993 . . . . **350.00**

Doll, Dolls by Jerri, Yvonne, J McCloud, 1986 . . . . **500.00**

Doll, Elke's Originals, Aurora, E Hutchens, 1990. . . . . **900.00**

Doll, Goebel, Little Knitter, MI Hummel Collectible Dolls Series, 1964 . . . . **200.00**

Doll, Gorham, Annemarie, Bonnets & Bows Series, B Gerardi, 1988 . . . . **450.00**

Doll, Hamilton Collection, Laura, Dolls by Autumn Berwick Series, A Berwick, 1993 . . . . **135.00**

Doll, Kurt S Adler, Nicholas on Skates, Royal Heritage Collection Series, J Mostrom, 1993 . . . . **125.00**

Doll, Reco International, Bedtime, Precious Memories of Motherhood Series, S Kuck, 1993. . . . . **150.00**

Doll, Roman Inc, Flora, The 1900s Bride, Classic Brides of the Century Series, E Williams, 1991 . . . . **150.00**

Doll, Seymour Mann, Daisy, Connossieur Doll Collection, E Mann, 1990 . . . . **90.00**

Figurine, All God's Children, Toby, M Root, 3½" h **75.00**

Figurine, Anri, Dad's Helper, 1994, 4½" h **400.00**

Figurine, Armani, Clown with Dog, Clown Series, G Armani, 1984 . . . . **100.00**

Figurine, Artists of the World, My First Horse, Goebel Miniatures Series, R Olszewski, 1985. . . . . **90.00**

Figurine, Band Creations, Fishing Friends, Best Friends–First Friends Begin at Childhood Series, Richards/Penfield, 1993. . . . . **18.00**

Figurine, Byers' Choice Ltd, King Gaspar, Nativity Series, J Byers, 1989. . . . . **100.00**

Figurine, Dave Grossman Creations, Young Couple, Norman Rockwell Collection–Select Collection Ltd, Rockwell Inspired, 1982 . . . . **30.00**

Figurine, Department 56, I'll Put Up the Tree, Snowbabies Series, 1991 . . . . **35.00**

Figurine, Fitz & Floyd, Bag of Tricks...Or Treats, Charming Tails Autumn Harvest Series, D Griff, 1996 . . . . . **15.00**

Figurine, Franklin Mint, Dressing Up, Joys of Childhood Series, N Rockwell, 1976. . . . . **175.00**

Figurine, Gorham, Shared Success, Old Buddies Series (Four Seasons), N Rockwell, 1984 . . . . **250.00**

Figurine, Hamilton Collection, Azalea, American Garden Flowers Series, D Fryer, 1987. . . . . **75.00**

Architecture, Lilliput Lane, Coke Country Five & Dime, cold cast, 3¼" h, $100.00.

Bell, Bing & Grøndahl, 1985, 3" h, $45.00.

Figurine, Lowell Davis Farm Club, Chow Time, L Davis, 1988. . . . . **100.00**
Figurine, Lowell Davis Farm Club, Company's Coming, Davis Cat Tales Series, L Davis, 1982 . . . . **200.00**
Figurine, Lowell Davis Farm Club, Sun Worshippers, Davis Friends of Mine Series, L Davis, 1989 . . . . **135.00**
Figurine, Maruri USA, Bobcat with Cactus, Kingdom of Cats Series, 1997. . . . . **70.00**
Figurine, Maruri USA, Loon, North American Waterfowl II Series, W Gaither, 1983 . . . . **250.00**
Figurine, Maruri USA, Sable, African Safari Animals Series, W Gaither, 1983 . . . . **1,200.00**
Figurine, Pemberton & Oakes, Winter Angel, Zolan's Children Series, D Zolan, 1984 . . . . **150.00**
Figurine, Reco International, Sunny, Laughables Series, J Bergsma, 1995 . . . . **15.00**
Figurine, Rick Cain Studios, Wind Horse, Master Series, R Cain, 1986. . . . . **100.00**
Figurine, Roman Inc, Clarinet Player, Jam Session Series, E Rohn, 1985 . . . . **145.00**
Figurine, Sarah's Attic, Alex Bear, Beary Adorables Collection Series, 1987 . . . . **12.00**
Figurine, Sarah's Attic, Angels on Assignment, Angels in the Attic Series, 1996. . . . . **65.00**
Figurine, Tudor Mint, Sir Lancelot, Arthurian Legend Series, M Locker, 1990 . . . . **40.00**
Figurine, United Design Corp, Boy with Basket and Egg, Easter Bunny Family Babies Series, D Kennicutt, 1994. . . . . . **8.00**
Figurine, United Design Corp, Chickadee, Backyard Birds Series, S Bradford, 1988 . . . . **18.00**
Figurine, United Design Corp, Joy to the World, Angels Collection Series, D Newburn, 1992 . . . . **95.00**
Figurine, United Design Corp, Sparrow, Backyard Birds Series, S Bradford, 1988. . . . . **10.00**
Figurine, Walnut Ridge Collectibles, Tiny Cat, Cat Figurines Series, K Bejma, 1991 . . . . **30.00**
Figurine, Wee Forest Folk, Peter's Pumpkin, Mice Series, M Peterson, 1984 . . . . **50.00**
Figurine, Wee Forest Folk, Red Riding Hood, Fairy Tale Series, A Peterson, 1980. . . . . **400.00**
Ornament, Armani, Christmas, G Armani, 1991 . . . . **45.00**
Ornament, Artists of the World, White Dove, DeGrazia Annual Ornaments Series, T DeGrazia, 1987 . . . . **100.00**

Ornament, Band Creations, America, Santa Claus, Kringle Toppers Series, 1996 . . . . **10.00**
Ornament, Band Creations, Baseball Girl, Best Friends– A Star Is Born Series, Richards/Penfield, 1995 . . . . **6.00**
Ornament, Bing & Grøndahl, Christmas Anchorage, Christmas Series, E Jensen, 1989 . . . . **25.00**
Ornament, Bing & Grøndahl, Winter at the Old Mill, Christmas Series, 1996. . . . . **40.00**
Ornament, Brandywine Collectibles, Windmill, Williamsburg Series, M Whiting, 1989 . . . . **10.00**
Ornament, Carlton Cards, O Holy Night, Summit Heirloom Collection Series, 1988. . . . . **10.00**
Ornament, Christina's World, Beaded Airplane, C Mallouk, 1994 . . . . **10.00**
Ornament, Christopher Radko, Alpine Flowers, Holiday Collection Series, C Radko, 1988 . . . . **90.00**
Ornament, David Winter Cottages, Mr Fezziwig's Emporium, Enesco, 1991 . . . . **15.00**
Ornament, Department 56, Shooting Star, bisque, light up, clip-on, 1986 . . . . **22.00**
Ornament, Fitz & Floyd, The Drifters, Charming Tails Deck the Halls Series, D Griff, 1992. . . . . **20.00**
Ornament, Hamilton Collection, Angel of Faith, Christmas Angels Series, 1995 . . . . **20.00**
Ornament, Hand & Hammer, Butterfly, DeMatteo, 1985 . . . . . **55.00**
Ornament, House of Hatten, Elf with Lantern, Enchanted Forest Series, 1989 . . . . **20.00**
Ornament, June McKenna Collectibles, Baby Pig, J McKenna, 1985 . . . . **100.00**
Ornament, Kirk Stieff, Toy Ship, K Stieff, 1990 . . . . **35.00**
Ornament, Kurt S Adler, Rose, Christmas in Chelsea Collection Series, J Mostrom, 1992. . . . . **20.00**
Ornament, Lowell Davis Farm Club, Blossom's Gift, Lowell Davis Glass Ornaments Series, L Davis, 1987 . . . . . **15.00**
Ornament, Roman Inc, Happy Holidaze, Catnippers Series, I Spencer, 1989. . . . . **15.00**
Ornament, United Design Corp, Rose of Sharon, Angels Collection Series, PJ Jonas, 1990 . . . . **20.00**
Ornament, Wallace Silversmiths, Peppermint, Candy Canes Series, 1981 . . . . **150.00**

Doll, Ashton-Drake, Andy, Yesterday's Dreams, M Oldenburg, 1990, $70.00.

Ornament, Walnut Ridge Collectibles, Cat-cicle, K Bejma, 1996 .... **25.00**

Plate, American Greetings, Millions of Stars in the Heavens Above, Holly Hobbie Mother's Day Series, 1975 .... **16.00**

Plate, American Legacy, To Kiss a Winner, Walter Brennan Series, W Brennan, 1984 .... **45.00**

Plate, Anna-Perenna, Clowns and Unicorns, Capricious Clowns Series, M Kane, 1981 .... **100.00**

Plate, Anna-Perenna, Spring's Surprise, Bashful Bunnies Series, M Ellen Wehrli, 1981 .... **60.00**

Plate, Anri, Cliff Gazing, Father's Day Series, 1974 .... **90.00**

Plate, Antique Trader, First Thanksgiving, Thanksgiving Series, 1972 .... **12.00**

Plate, Artaffects, Striped Bass, Angler's Dream Series, J Eggert, 1983 .... **55.00**

Plate, Artaffects, The Wedding, Times of Our Lives Series, R Sauber, 1982, 10¼" d **35.00**

Plate, Artists of the World, We Believe, Sweetheart Series, R Money, 1984 .... **40.00**

Plate, Artists of the World, White Dove, Children Miniature Series, I DeGrazia, 1981 .... **100.00**

Plate, Avondale, Daddy and I, Cameos of Childhood Series, T Williams, 1981 .... **75.00**

Plate, Aynsley, Prince of Wales, Single Issue, 1969 .... **50.00**

Plate, B&J Art Designs, Laurel, Old-Fashioned Country Series, J Hagara, 1985 .... **42.00**

Plate, Bareuther, Black Forest Church, Christmas Series, 1974 .... **20.00**

Plate, Bing & Grøndahl, Christmas Eve at the White House, Christmas in America Series, J Woodson, 1987 .... **35.00**

Plate, Bing & Grøndahl, The Little Gardeners, Children's Day Series, C Roller, 1987 .... **30.00**

Plate, Boehm Studios, Peaches, Hard Fruits Series, (Hamilton/Boehm), 1975 .... **450.00**

Plate, Bomar Studio, Mr Showmanship, Liberace Signature Collection, 1984 .... **100.00**

Plate, Bradford Exchange, A Difference of Opinion, Big League Dreams Series, S Sherwood (Canada), 1994 ...... **35.00**

Ornament, Department 56, Swinging On a Star, 1995, $15.00.

Doll, Lee Middleton, Loving Tribute, 1998, $200.00.

Plate, Braymer Hall, Summer Bounty, American Folk Art Series, 1982 .... **25.00**

Plate, California Porcelain Inc, Snow Leopards, Vanishing Animals Series, G Dieckhoner, 1979 .... **45.00**

Plate, Capo Di Monte, Bells and Holly, Christmas Series 1973 .... **55.00**

Plate, Castleton China, Amelia Earhart, Aviation Series, (American Historical), 1972 .... **40.00**

Plate, Chilmark, Wisemen, Holy Night Series, 1979 ...... **65.00**

Plate, Christian Fantasy Collectibles, Forest of the Unicorn, Realms of Wonder I Series, T Hildebrandt, 1987 .... **50.00**

Plate, Creative World, Girl at the Mirror, Rockwell Series, R Brown, 1979 .... **55.00**

Plate, Danbury Mint, Molly Pitcher, Bicentennial Series, 1978 .... **125.00**

Plate, D'Arceau Limoges, The Magical Window, Les Noels de France Series, J Claude Guidou, 1986 .... **50.00**

Plate, Daum, Mozart, 1971 .... **75.00**

Plate, Dave Grossman Creations, Friday's Child, Children of the Week Series, Barbard, 1980 .... **30.00**

Plate, David Kaplan Studios, Fiddler on the Roof, Fiddler's People Series, R Vig, 1978 .... **60.00**

Plate, David Kaplan Studios, Little Angel, Loveables Series, 1982 .... **40.00**

Plate, Delphi, Indiana Jones and His Dad, Adventures of Indiana Jones: The Last Crusade Series, V Gadino, 1989 .... **25.00**

Plate, Department 56, The Spirit of Christmas Present, A Christmas Carol Series, R Innocenti, 1993 .... **60.00**

Plate, Edna Hibel Studios, Angels' Message, Christmas Annual, E Hibel, 1985 .... **45.00**

Plate, Edwin M Knowles, Earth, Four Ancient Elements Series, G Lambert, 1984 .... **30.00**

Plate, Fontana, Sleighing, Christmas Series, 1973 .... **35.00**

Plate, Franklin Mint, Children With Teddy Bears, Calendar Series, M Murphy, 1984 .... **55.00**

Plate, Franklin Mint, Skating Party, Hometown Memories Series, J Sickbert, 1982 .... **30.00**

Plate, Gartlan USA, Magic Johnson "The Magic Show," Magic Johnson Gold Rim Collection Series, R Winslow, 1987, 10¼" d 350.00

Plate, Gorham Collection, April Fool's Day, April Fool Annual (Ghent Collection), N Rockwell, 1978 .... 50.00

Plate, Hackett American, Spirit of St Louis, Famous Planes of Yesterday Series, R Banks, 1983 .... 40.00

Plate, The Hamilton Collection, Love, Eternal Wishes of Good Fortune, Shuho and Senkin Kage, 1983 .... 70.00

Plate, Haviland, Magic Horse, 1001 Arabian Nights Series, L Tellier, 1979 .... 55.00

Plate, Haviland and Parlon, Brought to the Castle, Tapestry I Series, 1976 .... 50.00

Plate, Heirloom Tradition, Charles Dickens' Christmas Carol, Hollywood's View of Christmas Series, S Edison, 1986 .... 35.00

Plate, Historic Providence Mint, Red and White Queens, Alice in Wonderland Series, G Terp, 1986 .... 30.00

Plate, House of Global Art, Dolly Dingle Visits France, Dolly Dingle World Traveler Series (Goebel/MI Hummel), G Drayton, 1982 .... 30.00

Plate, Imperial, Golden Gate, America the Beautiful Series, 1974 .... 20.00

Plate, Incolay Studios, Anthony and Cleopatra, Great Romances of History Series, 1979 .... 65.00

Plate, International Museum, Portrait of Michelangelo, Letter Writer's Series, 1982 .... 40.00

Plate, John Hine Ltd, Dove Cottage, David Winter Plate Collection Series, Enesco (Viletta China), M Fischer, 1993 .... 30.00

Plate, Kaiser, Tender Moment, Anniversary Series, K Bauer, 1975 .... 25.00

Plate, Kera, Apollo 13, Moon Series, 1970 .... 6.00

Plate, Kern Collectibles, Quarterhorses, Horses of Harland Young Series, H Young, 1980 .... 55.00

Plate, Kirk, Constellation, Bicentennial Series, 1972 .... 75.00

Plate, Lenox, Red Foxes, American Wildlife Series, N Adams, 1983 .... 65.00

Plate, American Heritage, Emmet With a Bang, Sawdust Antics, 1983, $25.00.

Plate, Cavanagh, Good Boys and Girls, Coca-Cola Santa Claus Heritage Collection, 1995, $45.00.

Plate, Lilliput Lane, Autumn/When I Was Your Age..., Coca-Cola Country Four Seasons Series, R Day, 1998 ..... 40.00

Plate, Lowell Davis Farm Club, Cutting the Family Christmas Tree, Davis Christmas Annual Series, L Davis, 1988 .... 75.00

Plate, Lynell, Chief Crowfoot, Great Chiefs of Canada, M Killman, 1981 .... 65.00

Plate, Meissen, Sleeping Beauty, Annual Series, 1974 .... 75.00

Plate, Modern Concepts Limited, David's Dilemma, Special Moments Series, L Raad, 1982 .... 50.00

Plate, Modern Masters, Garden Gathering, Through the Eyes of Love Series, K Schaefers, 1983 .... 55.00

Plate, Modern Masters, Moment's Rest, Babes in the Woods Series, S Miller, 1984 .... 50.00

Plate, Paul Briant and Sons, Fruits of Spirit, Christmas Series, 1971 .... 125.00

Plate, Pemberton & Oakes, Beach Break, Childhood Friendship Series, D Zolan, 1986 .... 55.00

Plate, Pickard, Cleopatra, Let's Pretend Series, I Spencer, 1984 .... 80.00

Plate, Reco International, First Love, Arabelle and Friends Series, C Greunke, 1983 .... 35.00

Plate, Reco International, Jack and Jill, McClelland's Mother Goose Series, J McClelland, 1986 .... 30.00

Plate, Reco International, Joseph's Coat of Many Colors, Great Stories from the Bible Series, G Katz, 1987 .... 30.00

Plate, Reco International, Star Spangled Sky–July, Childhood Almanac Series, S Kuck, 1985 .... 35.00

Plate, Ridgewood, All Hallows Eve, Vasils Series, 1976 ..... 40.00

Plate, Ridgewood, Tenderness, Mother's Day Series, JC Leyendecker, 1977 .... 35.00

Plate, River Shore, Adoration, Della Robbia Annual Series, R Brown, 1979 .... 550.00

Plate, River Shore, A New Leash on Life, Puppy Playtime Series, R Brown, 1981 .... 60.00

Plate, River Shore, Rockwell Museum, Captain January, Shirley Temple Classic Collection Series, W Jacobson, 1983 .... 35.00

Plate, House of Global Art, Dolly Dingle Visits Holland, Dolly Dingle World Traveler, 1982, $15.00.

Plate, Rockwell Society, Somebody's Up There, Christmas Series, N Rockwell, 1979 . . . . **30.00**

Plate, Roman Inc, Christmas Mourning, Catnippers Series, I Spencer, 1986. . . . . **35.00**

Plate, Roman Inc, Lead Us Not, Lord's Prayer Series, A Williams, 1986 . . . . **25.00**

Plate, Rosenthal, Marien Church in Danzig, Christmas Series (Hibel Studios), 1940 . . . . **200.00**

Plate, Royal Bayreuth, Consolation, Mother's Day Series, L Jansen, 1973 . . . . **50.00**

Plate, Royal Copenhagen, Sunshine Over Greenland, Christmas Series, H Henrik Hansen, 1958. . . . . **165.00**

Plate, Royal Cornwall, Jacob's Ladder, Creation Series, Y Koutsis, 1980 . . . . **75.00**

Plate, Royal Doulton, Pennsylvania Pastorale, I Remember America Series, E Sloane, 1977 . . . . **90.00**

Plate, Royal Orleans, Sleigh Ride, Pink Panther Christmas Collection Series, D DePattie, 1982 . . . . **18.00**

Plate, Royalwood, Cornflake Girl, JC Leyendecker, 1978 . . . . . **25.00**

Plate, Royal Worcester, Bunny Chase, Kitten Encounters Series, P Cooper, 1987. . . . . **30.00**

Plate, Royal Worcester, Peacocks, Fabulous Birds Series, 1976. . . . . **65.00**

Plate, Sango, Sweethearts, Living American Artists Series, N Rockwell, 1976. . . . . **60.00**

Plate, Schmid, Starlight Angel, Berta Hummel Christmas Series, 1979 . . . . **40.00**

Plate, Schofield Gallery, Keystone Kop, Clowns, Klowns, Klonz Series, M Schofield, 1986. . . . . **50.00**

Plate, Southern Living Gallery, Wild Turkey, Game Birds of the South Series, A Heritage, 1983 . . . . **40.00**

Plate, Stieff, Betsy Ross, Bicentennial Series, 1974 . . . . **50.00**

Plate, Sterling America, Turtle Doves, Twelve Days of Christmas Series, 1971. . . . . **25.00**

Plate, Towle Silversmiths, Entwined Hearts, Valentines Series, 1973 . . . . **10.00**

Plate, United States Bicentennial Society, Thomas Jefferson, American Revolutionary Patriots, J Trumball, 1974. . . . . **25.00**

Plate, US Historical Society, Spring Flowers, Annual Spring Flowers Series, M Wampler, 1984 . . . . **135.00**

Plate, Viletta China, Last of the Ninth, Children's Series, 1979. . . . . **45.00**

Plate, Wexford Group, Afternoon Tea, Grandmother's World Series, C Knapton, 1983 . . . . **45.00**

Plate, Wildlife Internationale, Barred Owl Family, Owl Family Series, 1983 . . . . **55.00**

Plate, Winston Roland, Lyns in Winter, Brush with Life Series, G Loates, 1988 . . . . **40.00**

Plate, WS George, Precious Embrace, Bonds of Love Series, B Burke, 1989 . . . . **30.00**

Plate, Zanobia, Half Pint, African Violet Miniatures, Zanobia, 1985 . . . . **30.00**

Plate, Zolan Fine Arts/Winston Roland, Heavenly Song, Angel Songs Series, D Zolan, 1997. . . . . **20.00**

Stein, Anheuser-Busch, Air Force, Budweiser Military Giftware Series, M Watts, 1994 . . . . **25.00**

Stein, Hamilton Collection, Thundering Hooves, Warriors of the Plains Series, G Stewart, 1992 . . . . **125.00**

LINENS, LACE, CROCHET WORK & OTHER EMBROIDERED HOUSEHOLD TEXTILES

Linen is now a generic term used for any household covering made from cotton, lace, linen, man-made fibers, or silk. Linens experienced two golden ages, the Victorian era and the 1920s-30s. Victorian ladies prided themselves on their household linen handwork of delicate stitchery, lace insertions, fine tucking, and ruffles.

Lace divides into bobbin, embroidered, needlepoint, and machine made (also includes chemical and imitation lace). Machine-made lace dates to the first quarter of the 19th century. By 1840 technology had reached the point where machines were able to produce an imitation lace that was indistinguishable from most handmade laces.

Inexpensive mass-produced linens arrived at the turn of the century. Women turned to pre-stamped embroidery kits. The popularity of bridge and formal dining in the period following World War I brought with it a renewed interest in linens.

Today the vast majority of linens are manufactured in China, Europe, and the United States. Collectors feel modern examples lack the intricate handwork and freshness of design associated with pre-1945 linens.

References: Maryanne Dolan, *Old Lace & Linens Including Crochet,* Books Americana, 1989; Loretta Smith Fehling, *More Terrific Tablecloths,* Schiffer Publishing, 1999; Frances Johnson, *Collecting Household Linens,* Schiffer Publishing, 1997; Elizabeth Kurella, *The Complete Guide to Vintage Textiles,* Krause Publications, 1999; Elizabeth M. Kurella, *Guide to Lace and Linens,* Antique Trader Books, 1998; Elizabeth Scofield and Peggy Zalamea, *20th-Century Linens and Lace,* Schiffer Publishing, 1995.

Collectors' Club: International Old Lacers, PO Box 554, Flanders, NJ 07836.

Cocktail Napkins, linen, white, top-hatted men embroidered on corner, self-fringed edge, 5 x 8", price for set of 6. . . . . **$10.00**

Doily, muslin, white, embroidered roses in red silk floss and green leaves, scalloped edge in green silk floss, 18" d **6.00**

Dresser Scarf Set, linen, multicolored embroidery, price for 5-pc set, $30.00. Photo courtesy Ray Morykan Auctions.

Fingertip Towel, linen, white, embroidered light gray floral design, scalloped edge, 9 x 14" 8.00

Handkerchief, cotton, red on white, printed bird design 20.00

Handkerchief, white linen, hand-embroidered border of small flowers and vines on sides, scalloped edge, 12 x 12" 25.00

Hand Towel, linen, white, embroidered orange and blue oriental designs, hand-tied fringe on ends, 18 x 24" 10.00

Luncheon Napkins, linen, white, embroidered flower basket in corner, scalloped edge, price for set of 4 . . . . 15.00

Mattress Cover, homespun, blue and white, 1 seam, white homespun backing, 60 x 104" 110.00

Pillow Case, muslin, white, embroidered girl holding parasol surrounded by multicolored flowers, machine-made lace edges, 21 x 29" 15.00

Place Mats, linen, woven red and tan checks, fringe, matching napkins, 12 x 18", price for set of 4 . . . . 20.00

Sheet, cotton homespun, 2-pc, center seam, hand-sewn hem, 77 x 78" 65.00

Tablecloth, cotton, abstract butterfly designs, Vera Salaff Neumann, 48" sq 25.00

Tablecloth, cotton, red, yellow, and blue floral motif, Vera Salaff Neumann, 44 x 48" 30.00

Tablerunner, linen homespun, natural, brown pinstripe, 2-pc, hand-sewn seam, hand hemmed, embroidered initials, 66 x 85" 50.00

LITTLE GOLDEN BOOKS

The first Little Golden Books were published in September 1942. George Duplaix and Lucile Olge of the Artist and Writers Guild, a company formed by Western Printing & Publishing in the 1930s to develop new children's books, and Albert Leventhal and Leon Shimkin of Simon & Shuster developed Little Golden Books.

The key to the success of Little Golden Books was their price, 25¢. Within the first five months, 1.5 million copies were printed. Simon & Shuster published the books, the Artists and Writers Guild produced them, and Western Printing and Lithographing printed them. By the 10th anniversary (1952), over 182 million copies had been sold, 4 million of which came from sales of The Night Before Christmas.

The first Walt Disney title was published in 1944. Many of the titles issued in the 1950s and 60s were direct tie-ins with TV shows, especially westerns and Saturday-morning cartoons. In 1958 Western Printing and Lithographing and Pocket Books purchased the rights to Little Golden Books from Simon & Shuster. A Golden Press imprint was introduced. Eventually Western bought out Pocket Books and created Golden Press, Inc.

Little Golden Books are identified by a complex numbering system that experienced several changes over the years. Many titles have remained in print for decades. Value rests primarily in first printing examples in near mint condition. If the book contained a dust jacket or any other special feature, it must be intact for the book to have any retail market value.

Reference: Steve Santi, *Collecting Little Golden Books, Fourth Edition,* Krause Publications, 2000.

Newsletter: *The Gold Mine Review,* PO Box 209, Hershey, PA 17033.

Note: Prices listed are for books in mint condition.

All Aboard, #152, 1952 . . . . **$14.00**
A Day at the Playground, #119, 1951 . . . . 25.00
Animal Friends, #167, 1953 . . . . 10.00
Animals of Farmer Jones, The, #211, 1942 . . . . 7.00
A Pony For Tony, #220, 1955 . . . . 12.00
A Year in the City, #48, 1948 . . . . 20.00
Baby's Book, #10, 1942 . . . . 75.00
Baby's House, #80, 1950 . . . . 15.00
Bible Stories of Boys and Girls, #174, 1953 . . . . 8.00
Birds, #184, 1973 . . . . 7.00
Bobby and His Airplanes, #69, 1949 . . . . 16.00
Cars, #251, 1956 . . . . 8.00
Chip Chip, #28, 1947 . . . . 25.00

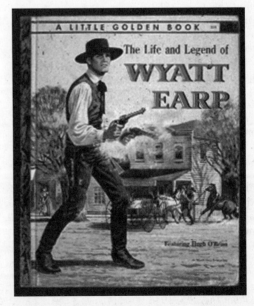

The Life and Legend of Wyatt Earp, #315, 1958, $12.00.

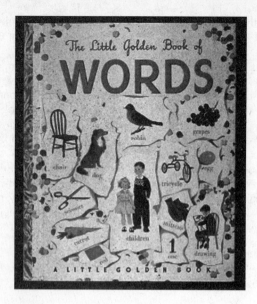

The Little Golden Book of Words, #45, 1948, $8.00.

Christmas Carols, #26, 1946 . . . . 18.00
Circus Time, #31, 1948 . . . . 20.00
Come Play House, #44, 1948 . . . . 25.00
Counting Rhymes, #257, 1947 . . . . 7.00
Five Little Firemen, #64, 1948 . . . . 20.00
Fix It, Please, #32, 1947 . . . . 25.00
Fun with Decals, #139, 1952 . . . . 125.00
Gingerbread Shop, The, #126, 1952 . . . . 15.00
Golden Book of Fairy Tales, The, #9, 1942 . . . . 40.00
Golden Book of Flowers, The, #16, 1943 . . . . 30.00
Golden Goose, The, #200, 1954 . . . . 12.00
Happy Family, The, #216, 1955 . . . . 15.00
Heidi, #258, 1954 . . . . 8.00
Just Watch Me, #104, 1975 . . . . 6.00
Kitten's Surprise, The, #107, 1951 . . . . 12.00
Little Boy with a Big Horn, #100, 1950 . . . . 15.00
Little Eskimos, The, #155, 1952 . . . . 15.00
Little Fat Policeman, The, #91, 1950 . . . . 15.00
Little Golashes, #68, 1949 . . . . 20.00
Little Golden Book of Hymns, The, #34, 1947 . . . . 15.00
Little Gray Donkey, #206, 1954 . . . . 12.00
Little Indian, The, #202, 1954 . . . . 15.00
Little Red Caboose, The, #162, 1953 . . . . 10.00
Magic Compass, The, #146, 1953 . . . . 18.00
Mr Wigg's Birthday Party, #140, 1952 . . . . 18.00
My Christmas Treasury, #144, 1976 . . . . 6.00
My Kitten, #163, 1954 . . . . 15.00
My Little Golden Dictionary, #90, 1949 . . . . 15.00
My Puppy, #233, 1955 . . . . 15.00
My Teddy Bear, #168, 1953 . . . . 25.00
Noises and Mr Fibberty-Jib, #29, 1947 . . . . 35.00
Nursery Tales, #14, 1943 . . . . 25.00
Open Up My Suitcase, #207, 1954 . . . . 20.00
Out of My Window, #245, 1955 . . . . 15.00
Pets For Peter, #82, 1950 . . . . 15.00
Prayers For Children, #205, 1952 . . . . 7.00
Sailor Dog, The, #156, 1953 . . . . 20.00
Shy Little Kitten, The, #23, 1946 . . . . 25.00
Surprise For Sally, #84, 1950 . . . . 20.00

Twins, The, #227, 1955 . . . . 75.00
Up in the Attic, #53, 1948 . . . . 15.00
When You Were a Baby, #70, 1949 . . . . 15.00
Wiggles, #166, 1953 . . . . 30.00

LITTLE GOLDEN BOOK TYPES

Competitors quickly rose to challenge Little Golden Books. Wonder Books, part of a publishing conglomerate that included Random House, arrived on the scene in 1946. Rand McNally published its first Elf Books in September 1947 and a Hanna-Barbera Character Series between 1975 and 1977.

Golden Press also produced variations of its successful Little Golden Book line. Giant Little Golden Books arrived in 1957, followed by the Ding Dong School Book series in 1959.

Reference: Steve Santi, *Collecting Little Golden Books, Fourth Edition,* Krause Publications, 2000.

Newsletter: *The Gold Mine Review,* PO Box 209, Hershey, PA 17033.

Note: Prices are for books in mint condition.

Big Golden Book, *Big and Little,* 1966 . . . . **$4.00**
Big Golden Book, *Caroline at the Ranch,* 1961 . . . . **20.00**
Big Golden Book, *Favorite Fairy Tales,* 1949 . . . . **20.00**
Big Golden Book, *Gergely's Golden Circus,* 1954 . . . . **20.00**
Big Golden Book, *Good Morning Farm,* 1964 . . . . **8.00**
Ding Dong School Book, *Debbie and Her Nap,* #201, 1953 . . . . **10.00**
Ding Dong School Book, *Dolls of Other Lands,* #213, 1954 . . . . **10.00**
Ding Dong School Book, *Growing Things,* #210, 1954 . . . . . **8.00**
Ding Dong School Book, *My Big Brother,* #214, 1954 . . . . . **8.00**
Disney Big Golden Book, *Babes in Toyland,* 1961 . . . . **25.00**
Disney Big Golden Book, *Chicken Little,* 1965 . . . . **4.00**
Disney Big Golden Book, *Dumbo,* 1955 . . . . **15.00**
Eager Reader, *Cat Who Stamped His Feet,* #806, 1974 . . . **5.00**
Eager Reader, *Elephant on Wheels,* #807, 1974 . . . . **5.00**
Eager Reader, *Little Black Puppy, The,* #804, 1974 . . . . **5.00**
Fuzzy Golden Book, *Mouse's House,* 1949 . . . . **15.00**
Fuzzy Golden Book, *Walt Disney's Circus,* 1944 . . . . **25.00**
Giant Golden Book, *Kittens,* #5013, 1958 . . . . **15.00**
Giant Golden Book, *My Christmas Treasury,* #5003, 1957 . . . . **20.00**
Giant Golden Book, *Plants and Animals,* #5017, 1958 . . . . **15.00**
Giant Golden Book, *Quiz Fun,* #5024, 1959 . . . . **15.00**
Giant Golden Book, *Wild Animals,* #5010, 1958 . . . . **16.00**
Golden Classic Library, *Black Beauty,* 1986 . . . . **4.00**
Golden Classic Library, *Little Women,* 1987 . . . . **4.00**
Golden Hours Library, *Heidi,* 1954 . . . . **3.00**
Golden Hours Library, *Little Cottontail,* 1960 . . . . **3.00**
Golden Hours Library, *Littlest Raccoon, The,* 1961 . . . . **3.00**
Golden Tiny Book, *Four Puppies,* 1960 . . . . **2.00**
Golden Tiny Book, *Little Cottontail,* 1960 . . . . **2.00**
Happy Book, *I Am a Bunny,* 1963 . . . . **4.00**
Happy Book, *Numbers,* 1963 . . . . **3.00**
Illustrated Classic, *Heidi,* 1965 . . . . **8.00**
Illustrated Classic, *Sherlock Holmes,* 1965 . . . . **5.00**
Illustrated Classic, *Tales of Edgar Allen Poe,* 1965 . . . . **6.00**
Lift and Look Book, *Baby Brown Bear's Big Bellyache,* 1989 . . . . **3.00**

Giant Little Golden Book, *This World of Ours,* **#5026, 1959, $20.00.**

Lift and Look Book, *Saggy Baggy Elephant and the New Dance,* 1985 . . . . **3.00**
Little Golden Land Series, *Shy Little Kitten's Secret Place,* #GBL372, 1989 . . . . **5.00**
Little Golden Land Series, *Welcome to Little Golden Book Land,* #GBL370, 1989 . . . . **5.00**
Little Little Golden Book, *Little Red Caboose,* 1953 . . . . **2.00**
Little Little Golden Book, *Three Little Kittens,* 1942 . . . . **2.00**
Little Silver Book, *Jerry at School,* 1950 . . . . **2.00**
Little Silver Book, *My Baby Sister,* 1958 . . . . **5.00**
Read-It-Yourself, *Good Friends, The,* 1966 . . . . **2.00**
Read-It-Yourself, *Pickle for a Nickel,* 1961 . . . . **2.00**

LITTLE RED RIDING HOOD

Design Patent #134,889, June 29,1943, for a "Design for a Cookie Jar," was granted to Louise Elizabeth Bauer of Zanesville, Ohio, and assigned to the A. E. Hull Pottery Company. This patent protected the design for Hull's Little Red Riding Hood line, produced between 1943 and 1957.

Hull and the Royal China and Novelty Company, a division of Regal China, made the blanks. Decoration was done almost exclusively at Royal China. Because the pieces were hand painted, many variations in color scheme have been discovered.

Reference: Mark and Ellen Supnick, *Collecting Hull Pottery's Little Red Riding Hood,* L-W Book Sales, 1998.

REPRODUCTION ALERT: Be alert for Little Red Riding Hood cookie jar reproductions. The period piece measures 13" h; the Mexican reproduction is shorter.

Cinnamon Canister, 4³/₄" h **$900.00**
Coffee Canister, sprig flower decal **85.00**
Creamer, poppy decal, ruffled skirt, 5" h **575.00**
Creamer, tab handle, 5" h **375.00**
Creamer and Sugar, poppy decal, tab handle, 5" h **375.00**
Dresser Jar, green bow, 8³/₄" h **900.00**

Flour Canister, poppy decal **850.00**
Grease Jar, wolf finial, yellow, 6¹/₂" h **800.00**
Hot Chocolate Mug **2,500.00**
Match Holder, blue dress, 6" h **1,400.00**
Mug **2,500.00**
Peanuts Canister, poppy decal, 9¹/₂" h **6,000.00**
Salt and Pepper Shakers, pr, blue trim, 3" h **750.00**
Salt and Pepper Shakers, pr, kneeling, 5¹/₄" h **2,000.00**
Salt Canister, poppy decal, 9¹/₄" h **2,250.00**
Spice Jar, allspice **900.00**
String Holder, 9" h **2,500.00**
Teapot, poppy decal **425.00**

LLADRÓ PORCELAINS

In 1951 José, Juan, and Vincente Lladró established a ceramics factory in Almacera, Spain. Each was educated at the Escuela de Artes y Oficios de San Carlos. José and Juan focused on painting and Vincente on sculpting. The Lladró brothers concentrated on the production of ceramic figurines, initially producing diminutive ceramic flowers.

In 1953 the brothers built a kiln that could produce temperatures sufficient to vitrify porcelain. With it, they began to make porcelain pieces in styles duplicating those of Dresden and Sevres. In 1955 they opened a shop in Valencia, and in 1958 began construction of a factory in the neighboring town of Tavernes Blanques.

In 1985 the company organized the Lladró Society, a collectors' club. Rosa Maria Lladró assumed the presidency of the Society in 1995. She, along with her sister Marie Carmen, and her cousins, Rosa and Juan Vicente, represent the second generation of the Lladró family to become involved in the business.

References: Collectors' Information Bureau, *Collectibles Market Guide & Price Index, 17th Edition,* Collectors' Information Bureau, 1999; Glenn S. Johnson, *The Lladró Collection Reference Guide,* Clear Communications, 1996; Mary L. Sieber (ed.), *2000 Price Guide to Limited Edition Collectibles, 5th Edition,* Krause Publications, 1999.

Collectors' Club: Lladró Collectors Society (company sponsored), 1 Lladró Dr, Moonachie, NJ 07074.

Afternoon Tea, #1428, 1982-99, 14¹/₄" h **$100.00**
Aggressive Duck, #1288, 1974-96, 8¹/₂" h **200.00**
Barrow of Blossoms, #1419, 1982, 10" h **300.00**
Boy on Carousel Horse, #1470, 1985, 16" h **425.00**
Bridal Bell, #6200, 1995, 8¹/₂" h **150.00**
Caught in the Act, #6239, 1997, 8¹/₂" h **115.00**
Clown, #4618, 1969, 14" l **350.00**
Daddy's Girl, #5584, 1989-97, 8¹/₂" h **150.00**
Debutante, #1431, 1982-99, 14" h **115.00**
Destination Big Top, #6245, 1996, 8" h **225.00**
Dreams of a Summer Past, #6401, 1997, 9¹/₂" h **150.00**
Fawn and a Friend, 1990-97, 6" h **250.00**
Fishing and Gramps, #5215, with stand, 1983, 15¹/₂" l **500.00**
Flapper, #5175, 1982-96, 13¹/₄" h **140.00**
Flower Harmony, #1418, 1982-96, 8¹/₂" h **130.00**
Flowers of the Season, #1454, 1983, 11" h **1,725.00**
For a Perfect Performance, #7641, 1995, 10¹/₂" h **140.00**
Fragrant Bouquet, #5862, 1992, 8" h **150.00**
From My Garden, #1416, 1982-98, 10" h **175.00**

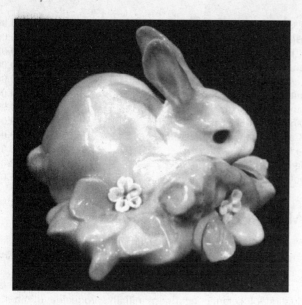

Rabbit, 4¹/₂" l, $100.00.

Gift of Love, #5596, 1989-99, 9³/₄" h **230.00**
Girl on Carousel Horse, #1469, 1985, 16" h. **425.00**
Grand Dame, #1568, 1987, 14" h **200.00**
Guest of Honor, #5877, 1992-97, 8¹/₂" h **80.00**
Harpist, #6312, 1996, 13¹/₂" h **375.00**
Hi There, #5672, 1990-98, 6" h **250.00**
How Do You Do?, #1439, 1983, 4¹/₂" h **110.00**
I Love You Truly, #1528, 1987, 13¹/₂" h. **315.00**
Jesse, #5129, with base, 1982, 12" h **185.00**
My Goodness, #1285, 1974, 9" h **150.00**
Nostalgia, #5071, 1980, 6¹/₂" h **100.00**
Once Upon a Time, #5721, 1990, 10¹/₂" h **300.00**
Pensive Clown, #5130, with base, 1982, 11" h. **185.00**
Recital, #5496, 1988, 6¹/₂" h **100.00**
Spring Flirtation, #6365, 1997, 12¹/₂" h. **150.00**
Tailor Made, #6489, 1997, 7³/₄" h **80.00**
Teruko, #1451, 1983, 10¹/₂" h **225.00**
Windblown Girl, #4922, 1974, 14" h. **150.00**

AUCTION PRICES – LLADRÓ PORCELAINS

Estate Auction, Sloan's Washington DC Gallery, May 21-23,
1999. Prices include a 15% buyer's premium.

Lady of Monaco, #6236, 1995, 14" h **$98.00**
Lady of the East, #1488, with base, 1986-94, 9¹/₂" h . . **633.00**
Little Gardener, #1283, 1974, 9¹/₂" h. **403.00**
Matrimony, #5542, with base, 1989, 12" h **207.00**
Modern Mother, #5873, 1992-97, 11¹/₂" h. **138.00**
My Flowers, #1284, 1974, 9" h **259.00**
Nature's Bounty, #1417, 1982-98, 11" h **230.00**
Over the Clouds, #5697, 1990, 8" h **92.00**
Picking Flowers, #1287, 1974-99, 7" h **345.00**
Quiet Moment, #5673, 1990-98, 5¹/₄" h **259.00**
Refreshing Pause, #6330, 1996, 3" h. **58.00**
Rose Ballet, #5919, 1992, 8" l **109.00**
Socialite of the Twenties, #5283, 1985, 13¹/₂" h. **288.00**
Spring Splendor, #5898, 1992, 11³/₄" h **316.00**
Swan and the Princess, #5705, 1990-95, no box. **184.00**
Teatime, #5470, 1998, 14¹/₄" h **155.00**

LONGABERGER BASKETS

Dave Longaberger (1934-99) began his business career as the owner of Harry's Dairy Bar and an IGA Foodliner in Dresden, Ohio. John Wendell Longaberger, Dave's father, owned the Ohio Ware Company, a firm making ware baskets for the pottery industry. In 1972 Dave asked his father to make sample baskets for sale to the retail department store trade. Successful initial sales led to Dave's opening J. W.'s Handwoven Baskets later that year.

Today The Longaberger Company has 42,000 independent sales consultants located in all 50 states and the District of Columbia. In 1990 the company opened a new modern facility located just outside Dresden. Its home office is located in a replica seven-story Market Basket located in Newark, Ohio. Tami and Rachel Longaberger, his two daughters, assumed control of the company following Dave's death on March 17, 1999.

Although Longaberger stresses a handmade craft ancestry for its baskets, they are mass produced. The company sold 7.7 million baskets in 1997, indicating that scarcity is not a word that will be used to describe a Longaberger basket, even fifty years from now.

Collectors of antique and vintage baskets will tell you that Longaberger baskets are vastly overrated. While not something Longaberger basket collectors want to hear, they will regret not paying attention when the current speculative bubble, fueled by a market manipulative price guide, company hype, a company controlled collectors' club, and Internet auction prices, finally bursts.

Reference: *The Bentley Collection Guide to Longaberger Baskets, Seventh Edition,* J. Phillips, 1999.

Newsletter: *The Basket Collector's Gazette,* PO Box 100, Pitkin, CO 81241.

All American, All-Star Trio Combo, 1993 . . . . **$60.00**
All American, Carry Along Combo, 1996 . . . . **60.00**
All American, Partiot, liner and protector, 1997 . . . . **60.00**
All American, Picnic Pal Combo, protector, 1998 . . . . **50.00**
All American, Pie, liner and protector, 1998 . . . . **135.00**
Bee Basket, Bee, 1993. . . . . **100.00**
Bee Basket, Bee, liner and protector, 1996 . . . . **160.00**
Bee Basket, Bee, liner and protector, 1997 . . . . **130.00**
Bee Basket, Bee, liner and protector, 1998 . . . . **100.00**
Bee Basket, Bee Combo, 1996. . . . . **120.00**
Booking Basket, Ambrosia, liner and protector, 1993 . . . . . . **55.00**
Booking Basket, Ambrosia, liner and protector, 1996 . . . . . . **60.00**
Booking Basket, Thyme, protector, 1998. . . . . **30.00**
Booking Basket, Thyme Combo, Garden Splendor, 1997 . . . . **40.00**
Christmas Collection, Bayberry Combo, 1993. . . . . **80.00**
Christmas Collection, Christmas Cranberry, red, protec-
tor, 1995. . . . . **125.00**
Christmas Collection, Holiday Cheer, liner and protec-
tor, 1996. . . . . **90.00**
Christmas Collection, Jingle Bell, green, 1994 . . . . **100.00**
Christmas Collection, Memory, green, 1989 . . . . **90.00**
Christmas Collection, Mistletoe, red, 1989 . . . . **110.00**
Christmas Collection, Season's Greetings, red, SU plaid
liner, protector, 1992 . . . . **120.00**
Christmas Collection, Snowflake, liner and protector,
1997. . . . . **90.00**
Collector's Club, 25th Anniversary Flag, protector, 1998 . . . **125.00**
Collector's Club, Charter Membership Combo, with box,
1996. . . . . **110.00**
Collector's Club, Harbor, protector, 1998 . . . . **10.00**

Collector's Club, Serving Tray Combo, with box, 1996 . . . . . **250.00**
Collector's Club, Welcome Home, liner, protector, box, and product cards, 1997 . . . . **150.00**
Easter Series, Blue Easter, protector, 1989 . . . . **90.00**
Easter Series, Easter Combo, small, matching fabric lid, 1997 . . . . **45.00**
Feature Basket, Horizon of Hope Combo, Heritage Green, 1996 . . . . **50.00**

Vase, Mandarin Yellow, 1984, $200.00.

INTERNET PRICES – LONGABERGER BASKETS

EBay auction results, February 2000. Prices include shipping and handling charges.

All American Combo Basket, 2 qt, swing handles, red trim around top, red and blue trim around center, with red, white, and blue fabric liner and orig product card, 9³/₄ x 9³/₄ x 5³/₄" **$103.00**
Christmas Basket "Glad Tidings" Combination, red accent weaving, berry red striped stand-up liner and protector, 1998, excellent condition **60.00**
Commemorative Corn Basket, family sgd, leather handles, blue accent weaving, brass tag, 1991, 17" d, 11¹/₂" h **320.00**
Community Basket, Traditions Collection, Tradition's Heritage green top band, ³/₈" accent weave, brass tag reads "Longaberger Traditions Collection Community Basket 1996 Edition," with green and gold fabric liner in orig plastic wrap, protector tray, product card, and orig box, never removed from box **129.20**
Holiday Basket of Thanks, leather handles, red and dark green trim on top band, brass tag, sgd by Judy and Ginny Longaberger, 1993 . . . . **51.00**
Lavender Booking Basket **31.00**
Sweet Basil Booking Basket, never used **38.00**
Sweetheart Combination, heart-shaped basket, regular protector, over-the-edge letters of love liner, woodcrafts lid, red leather weaving, 13¹/₂ x 12¹/₂ x 4¹/₄" basket, retired **115.50**

LOTTON, CHARLES

Charles Gerald Lotton (born October 21, 1935) is a contemporary glass artist. In 1970 Lotton built a small glass studio behind his house in Sauk Village, Illinois. In June 1971 Lotton sold his first glass to C. D. Peacock, a downtown Chicago jeweler.

A chance meeting with Dr. Ed McConnell during a visit to Corning, New York, resulted in a meeting with Lillian Nassau, a leading New York City art glass dealer. Paul Nassau, Lillian's son, and Lotton signed an exclusive five-year contract in 1972. Lotton leased a former lumber yard in Lansing, Illinois, to serve as his studio. In 1975 he built a new studio in Lynwood, Illinois, eventually building a glassworks behind his home in Crete, Illinois, in 1982.

By 1977 Lotton had achieved a national reputation and wanted the freedom to sell glass directly to his own distributors. Lotton glass is sold through a number of select retailers and at antiques shows. The four Lotton children, Daniel, David, John, and Rachel, are all involved with some aspect of glassmaking.

Reference: D. Thomas O'Connor and Charles G. Lotton, *Lotton Art Glass,* Antique Publications, 1990, out of print.

Bud Vase, cylindrical, purple oil spot finish, blue luster King Tut dec, sgd and dated "John Lotton 1991," 3" h . . . **$175.00**
Toothpick, vasiform, cobalt blue iridescent, sgd and dated "Charles Lotton 1981," 2¹/₂" h **200.00**
Vase, classical shape, verre de soie with multicolor floral design in pink, blue, and green, sgd and dated "Charles Lotton 1983 multi flora," 8¹/₂" h **500.00**
Vase, flared rim, bulbous body, opalescent with blue luster leaves, purple int, sgd and dated "David Lotton 1995," 5" h **375.00**
Vase, flared rim and narrow neck above corseted body, black amethyst with blue leaf and vine design, sgd and dated "Lotton 1991," 8" h **275.00**
Vase, narrow flared neck, bulbous body, opalescent with blue pulled drape pattern, sgd and dated "Lotton 1975," 7¹/₂" h **400.00**
Vase, ovoid, iridescent pulled feather design, sgd and dated "Charles Lotton 1983," 7" h **450.00**
Vase, slightly flared rim, bulbous body, mottled pink with pink leaf and green iridescent vine design, sgd and dated "John Lotton 1990," 6" h **450.00**

LUNCH BOXES

A lunch kit is comprised of a lunch box and a thermos. Both must be present for the unit to be complete.

Although lunch kits date back to the 19th century, collectors focus on the lithographed tin lunch kits made between the mid-1930s and the late 1970s. Gender, Paeschke & Frey's 1935 Mickey Mouse lunch kit launched the modern form. The 1950s and early 1960s was the lunch kit's golden age. Hundreds of different kits were made, many featuring cartoon, movie, and television show images. Aladdin Company, Landers, Frary and Clark, Ohio Art, Thermos/King Seeley, and Universal are among the many companies who made lunch kits during the golden age.

This market went through a speculative craze that extended from the late 1970s through the early 1990s at which point the speculative bubble burst. Prices have dropped from their early

1990s high for most examples. Crossover collectors, rather than lunch kit collectors, are keeping the market alive in the late 1990s.

References: Larry Aikins, *Pictorial Price Guide to Metal Lunch Boxes & Thermoses,* L-W Book Sales, 1992, 1996 value update; Larry Aikins, *Pictorial Price Guide to Vinyl & Plastic Lunch Boxes & Thermoses,* L-W Book Sales, 1992, 1999 value update; Allen Woodall and Sean Brickell, *The Illustrated Encyclopedia of Metal Lunch Boxes, 2nd Edition,* Schiffer Publishing, 1999.

Note: Prices listed reflect boxes with thermos, both in near mint condition.

Alf, Thermos, 1987 . . . . **$15.00**
Alvin and the Chipmunks, King-Seeley, vinyl, 1963 . . . . **175.00**
Annie, Aladdin, emb steel, 1981 . . . . **20.00**
Big Jim, King-Seeley, plastic, 1972 . . . . **50.00**
Bionic Woman, Aladdin, metal, c1977 . . . . **25.00**
Bonanza, Aladdin, metal, 1963 . . . . **75.00**
Boston Red Sox, Ardee, vinyl, 1960s **75.00**
Buccaneer, Aladdin, metal, dome, c1957 . . . . **100.00**
Captain Kangaroo, King-Seeley, vinyl, 1964 . . . . **175.00**
Carousel, Aladdin, vinyl, c1962 . . . . **175.00**
Central Station, Thermos, metal, dome, 1959 . . . . **175.00**
Charlie's Angels, Aladdin, metal, 1978 . . . . **25.00**
Cheerleaders, Travel Toy, Prepac, vinyl, 1960s **175.00**
Coca-Cola, Aladdin, vinyl, c1980 . . . . **100.00**
Cowboy and Cowgirl, metal, c1950s **50.00**
Davy Crockett/Kit Carson/Frontierland, Adco Liberty, metal, c1955 . . . . **100.00**
Dawn, Aladdin, vinyl, 1970 . . . . **75.00**
Deputy Dawg, Thermos, vinyl, 1961 . . . . **375.00**
Disneyland, Aladdin, metal, c1957 . . . . **100.00**
El Chapulin Colorado, Aladdin, metal, c1979 . . . . **20.00**
ET, Aladdin, metal, 1982 . . . . **20.00**
Fess Parker From the Daniel Boone TV Show, Aladdin, metal, 1965 . . . . **125.00**

Flags of the United Nations, Universal, metal, c1959 . . . . . . **175.00**
Flintstones, Aladdin, metal, 1964 . . . . **75.00**
Football Scene, Abeama Industries, vinyl, 1960s **75.00**
Fraggle Rock, Thermos, plastic, 1987 . . . . **15.00**
Freihofer's Chocolate Chip Cookies, vinyl, 1960s **100.00**
Fruit, Ohio Art, metal **20.00**
Game Birds, metal, c1950s **100.00**
Globe-Trotter, Aladdin, metal, dome, c1959 . . . . **75.00**
Go-Go, Aladdin, vinyl, c1966 . . . . **100.00**
Guns of Will Sonnett, King-Seeley, metal, 1960s **100.00**
Jack and Jill, Ohio Art, metal, c1982 . . . . **175.00**
Jim Henson's Muppet Movie, King-Seeley, metal, 1979 . . . . . . **20.00**
Jonathan Livingston Seagull, Aladdin, vinyl, 1973 . . . . . . **100.00**
Jungle Safari, Ardee Industries, vinyl, 1960s **75.00**
Junior Miss, Aladdin, metal, c1973 . . . . **20.00**
Kaboodle Kit, Aladdin, vinyl, 1960s **100.00**
Kellogg's Corn Flakes, Taiwan, plastic, 1985 . . . . **25.00**
Knight Rider, King-Seeley, metal, 1983 . . . . **20.00**
Kooky Canooky, Design Motivation Ltd, Canada, plastic, 1970 . . . . **100.00**
Lawman, King-Seeley, metal, 1961 . . . . **100.00**
Legend of the Lone Ranger, Aladdin, emb steel, 1980 . . . . . **20.00**
Life and Times of Grizzly Adams, Aladdin, metal, 1977 . . . . **75.00**
Little Miss Dutch, Universal, metal, c1959 . . . . **20.00**
Looney Tunes Characters, Thermos, metal, Mexican scene, 1959 . . . . **75.00**
Love, Two's Company Inc, metal brunch bag, removable lid, attached metal handle, 1970s **75.00**
Lunch 'N Munch, Thermos, vinyl, pirate scene, 1959 . . . . . **100.00**
Lunch 'N Munch, Thermos, vinyl, space scene, 1959 . . . . . **200.00**
Mam'zelle, Aladdin, vinyl, 1971 . . . . **100.00**
Man From U.N.C.L.E., Thermos, metal, 1966 . . . . **75.00**
Marvel Super Heroes, Aladdin, metal, 1976 . . . . **20.00**
Mickey Mouse, Geuder, Paeschke & Frey Co, litho tin, c1935 . . . . **400.00**
Mini Swinger, Prepac, vinyl, 1960s **25.00**
Monkees, Thermos, vinyl, 1967 . . . . **150.00**
Panda Bears Playing Ping Pong, Travel Toy, Prepac, vinyl, 1972 . . . . **175.00**
Peanuts, King-Seeley, vinyl brunch bag, 1977 . . . . **50.00**
Peter Pan Peanut Butter, Taiwan, plastic, 1984 . . . . **40.00**
Philadelphia Flyers, vinyl, c1960-70s **175.00**
Ponytail East 'N Treats, Thermos, vinyl, 1959 . . . . **100.00**
Ponytail Tid Bid Kit, Thermos, metal, 1959 . . . . **100.00**
Popeye, Aladdin, emb steel, 1980 . . . . **20.00**
Porky's Lunch Wagon, Thermos, metal, dome, 1959 . . . . . **175.00**
Psychedelic, Aladdin, metal, 1969 . . . . **100.00**
Racing Wheels, King-Seeley, metal, 1977 . . . . **50.00**
Red Barn, King-Seeley, metal, dome, 1971 . . . . **50.00**
Ringling Bros and Barnum & Bailey Circus, King-Seeley, vinyl, c1970 . . . . **175.00**
Sleeping Beauty, Aladdin, vinyl, 1970 . . . . **100.00**
Smokey Bear, Thermos, vinyl, 1960s **100.00**
Space Boys, Ardee Industries, vinyl, 1960s **100.00**
Stewardess, Aladdin, vinyl, c1960s **175.00**
Strawberry Shortcake, Aladdin, vinyl, 1980 . . . . **35.00**
Teenage Girl Fashions, Prepac, vinyl, 1963 . . . . **100.00**
US Mail, vinyl, c1960s **175.00**
US Space Shuttle Challenger, Nappe-Babcock, vinyl brunch bag, c1986 . . . . **100.00**
Woody Woodpecker and Buzz Buzzard, leather, 1970s **75.00**
Yellow Submarine, King-Seeley Thermos, metal, 1968 . . . . . **200.00**
Yogi Bear and Friends, Aladdin, metal, 1963 . . . . **100.00**

Star Trek, Aladdin, metal, 1968, $920.00. Photo courtesy Skinner, Inc., Boston, MA.

MADE IN JAPAN

Prior to 1921, objects made in Japan were marked NIPPON or MADE IN NIPPON. After that date, objects were marked JAPAN or MADE IN JAPAN.

Although MADE IN OCCUPIED JAPAN was the primary mark used between August 1945 and April 28, 1952, some objects from this period were marked JAPAN or MADE IN JAPAN.

This is a catchall category for a wide range of ceramic, glass, and metal items made by Japanese manufacturers for export to the United States. Many were distributed by American import companies who designed the products in America, had them manufactured in Japan, and marketed them in the United States.

References: Carol Bess White, *Collector's Guide to Made in Japan Ceramics* (1994, 1999 value update), *Book II* (1996, 1998 value update), *Book III* (1998), Collector Books.

Note: See Figurines and Occupied Japan for additional listings.

Biscuit Barrel, multicolored floral motif on cream and
　pink ground, 6³/₄" h **$50.00**
Biscuit Barrel, multicolored fruit motif on red ground,
　5³/₄" h **50.00**
Bonbon Dish, multicolored 4-leaf clover motif on shiny
　white ground, 5¹/₄" d **15.00**
Bookends, pr, Asian man and woman, multicolored
　shiny glaze, 5¹/₂" h **30.00**
Bookends, pr, train, black, tan, and red shiny glaze,
　5¹/₂" h **20.00**
Bowl, Art Deco, tudor house motif, multicolored shiny
　glaze, 7" d **40.00**
Cache Pot, reclining camel, basket on back, majolica
　style, multicolored shiny glaze, 8" l **45.00**
Creamer and Sugar, figural owls, multicolored shiny
　glaze **35.00**
Figurine, cat, shiny white glaze, 8" h **30.00**
Powder Box, figural rabbit, ivory luster glaze, 4" h **45.00**
Salt and Pepper Shakers, pr, black boy with water-
　melons, 3" h **45.00**

Vase, butterfly and blue and yellow tulips with black stems on rust-red ground, black bands at top and bottom, mkd "Hand Painted Made In Japan" in band around swallow, 10" h, $25.00. Photo courtesy Ray Morykan Auctions.

Toy, Boy on Tricycle, windup, celluloid boy in red outfit
　with yellow bow tie, atop litho tin red, white, blue,
　and yellow tricycle, tiger and duck illus on wheels,
　portrait of dog, monkey, and pig on bell, eagle on
　front handle bars, mkd "Made in Japan," 1960s, 2 x 4
　x 3¹/₂" **25.00**
Wall Pocket, butterfly and floral motif, multicolored
　shiny glaze, 6¹/₄" l **35.00**
Whistle, diecut tin, figural owl, silver luster finish, mkd
　"Japan," 1930s **15.00**

MAGAZINES

In the early 1700s general magazines were a major source of information. Literary magazines such as *Harper's* became popular in the 19th century. By 1900 the first photo-journal magazines appeared. Henry Luce started *Life,* the prime example, in 1932.

Magazines created for women featured "how to" articles about cooking, sewing, decorating, and child care. Many were devoted to fashion and living a fashionable life. Men's magazines were directed at masculine skills of the time, such as hunting, fishing, and woodworking. "Girlie" titles became popular in the 1930s and enjoyed a golden age in the 1950s and 60s.

Popular magazines, such as *Collier's, Life, Look,* and *Saturday Evening Post,* survive in vast quantities. So do pulps. Value is driven primarily by cover image, content, and advertisements.

Many magazines are torn apart and the pages sold individually. The key value component for these "tear sheets" is subject matter. As a result 99% plus are purchased by crossover collectors. Except for illustrator collectors, crossover collectors care little if the tear sheet features a drawing or photograph. The most desirable tear sheets are in full color and show significant design elements.

References: Ron Barlow and Ray Reynolds, *The Insider's Guide to Old Books, Magazines, Newspapers, Trade Catalogs,* Windmill Publishing, 1995; Denis C. Jackson, *Men's "Girlie" Magazines: Newstanders, 4th Edition,* TICN, 1994; Denis C. Jackson, *Old Magazines, 4th Edition,* TICN, 1997; *Old Magazine Price Guide,* L-W Book Sales, 1994, 2000 value update; Frank M. Robinson and Lawrence Davidson, *Pulp Culture: The Art of Fiction Magazines,* Collectors Press, 1998; Lee Server, *Danger Is My Business: An Illustrated History of the Fabulous Pulp Magazines: 1896-1953,* Chronicle Books, 1993.

Periodical: *PCM (Paper Collectors' Marketplace),* PO Box 128, Scandinavia, WI 54977.

Newsletter: *The Illustrator Collector's News,* PO Box 1958, Sequim, WA 9839.

Note: For additional listings see *Life, Playboy* and *TV Guide.*

Action Packed Western, May 1950 . . . . **$5.00**
Air Progress, Nov 1941 . . . . **15.00**
Air Travel News, 1920s **3.00**
Amazing Stories, Mar 1929 . . . . **30.00**
American Artist, 1930-70s **3.00**
American Builder, 1922-26 . . . . **12.00**
American Detective, 1930s **4.00**
American Field, 1930-40s **3.00**
American Furrier, 1920-30s **4.00**
American Glass Review, 1900-50 . . . . **5.00**

American Heritage, 1950-70s 3.00
*American Home,*1920-30s. 5.00
American Magazine of Art, 1934 . . . . 20.00
American Motorcyclist and Bicyclist, 1925-26 . . . . 25.00
American Photography, 1928-41 . . . . 8.00
American Poultry, 1920-30s. 3.00
American Rifleman, 1925-26 . . . . 5.00
American West, 1960s. 3.00
American Woodsman, 1930s 4.00
Architectural Digest, 1930-40 . . . . 4.00
Argosy, Oct 5,1940 . . . . 5.00
Arizona Highways, 1947 annual 45.00
Art Photography, 1950s. 8.00
Astounding Science Fiction, 1955-58 . . . . 4.00
Astronomical Journal, 1930-40s 2.00
Atlantic Sportsman, 1932 . . . . 10.00
Automobile Trade Journal, 1931-40 . . . . 10.00
Aviation, 1925-27 . . . . 6.00
Barber's Journal, 1937-42 . . . . 5.00
Bedtime Story, 1932 . . . . 35.00
Better Homes and Gardens, 1941-50. . . . . 2.00
Beyond Reality, 1972. . . . . 15.00
Billboard, Aug 6,1921 . . . . 20.00
Black Book Detective, 1940s 25.00
Boxing, 1950s 10.00
Boy's Life, 1912-35 . . . . 8.00
Brides Magazine, 1930s 4.00
Broadcasting, 1930s 3.00
Building Age, Mar 1927 . . . . 7.00
Business Week, 1930s 2.00
Car and Driver, 1960-80 . . . . 3.00
Cartoon Humor, Jan 1939 . . . . 20.00
Cashbox, 1950s 6.00
Cinema, 1972-73 . . . . 20.00
Clyde Beatty's Circus, 1940-50s. 10.00
Colliers, Apr 1923, Maxfield Parrish cov 30.00
Comfort, 1931-38 . . . . 3.00
Complete Photographer, 1941-43 . . . . 2.00
Confidential, Dec 1952 . . . . 20.00
Coronet, Feb 1956 . . . . 30.00

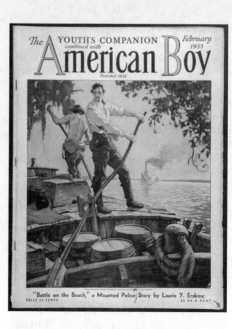

American Boy,
Feb 1933, $10.00.

Cosmopolitan, 1950s. 5.00
Crime Detective, 1940-60s 5.00
Cue Magazine, 1950s 4.00
Daring Detective, 1930-50s 5.00
Detective World, Apr 1948 . . . . 10.00
Dog World, 1930-40s 2.00
Ellery Queen's Mystery Magazine, Jan 1949 . . . . 20.00
Esquire, Jun 1948 . . . . 15.00
Exhibitor Magazine, 1950s 2.00
Eye Magazine, May 1949 . . . . 15.00
Fantastic Novels, 1950s 6.00
Farmer's Wife, Jun 1935. . . . . 15.00
Field and Stream, 1930s 4.00
Flying, 1940-50. . . . . 5.00
Flying Saucers, Aug 1960. . . . . 10.00
Fortune, Nov 1933 . . . . 18.00
Fruit Grower, 1940s. 4.00
Garden and Home Builder, 1920s 5.00
Gentlewoman, 1930-73. . . . . 3.00
Gourmet, 1940-60s. 3.00
Headquarters Detective, May 1940 . . . . 5.00
Hollywood Family Album, Apr 1952 . . . . 10.00
Hollywood Magazine, Mar 1937 . . . . 25.00
House and Garden, Sep 1927 . . . . 12.00
Hunting and Fishing, 1930s 5.00
Infinity Science Fiction, Nov 1955 . . . . 6.00
Inside TV, Dec 1959, Fabian 8.00
Jayne Medical Almanac, 1900-33. . . . . 4.00
Jubilee, Sep 1950 . . . . 20.00
Keyhole Detective Cases, Mar 1942 . . . . 20.00
Kiwanis Magazine, 1937-38. 4.00
Liberty, May 1942, Donald Duck 12.00
Look Magazine, Jul 18, 1939, *Gone With the Wind*. 20.00
Look Magazine, Oct 29, 1946, Basil Rathbone 20.00
Major League Baseball, 1948, Ted Williams 12.00
Mercury Mystery Book, Mar 1956 . . . . 45.00
Mike Shayne Mystery Magazine, 1970-85 . . . . 2.00
Modern Railroad, 1940-50 . . . . 4.00
Modern Romance, 1940-50s 5.00
Modern Screen, Sep 1931, Nancy Carroll. 20.00

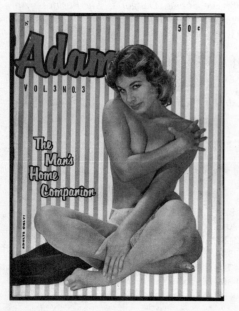

Adam, Vol. 3,
No. 3, 1959,
$8.00.

Motion Picture, Jul 1939 . . . . 20.00
Motion Picture, Sep 1941 . . . . 18.00
Motion Picture Herald, 1940s 10.00
Motor Age, Nov 1955 . . . . 10.00
Movie Fan, Mar 1955 . . . . 12.00
Movie Mirror, May 1935, Ginger Rogers 18.00
Movies, Nov 1944, Lucille Ball 15.00
Movie Show, 1940s 15.00
Movie Story, 1937-42 . . . . 15.00
Mystic Magazine, Nov 1953 . . . . 7.00
Nature Magazine, 1940s 1.00
New Flash Detective, Oct 1946 . . . . 10.00
New Stars, 1940s 8.00
Newsweek Magazine, May 17,1954, Grace Kelly 50.00
Pencil Points, 1920s 3.00
Penthouse, 1980s 20.00
Photoplay Magazine, Feb 1947, Ingrid Bergman 10.00
Photoplay Magazine, Apr 1949, Betty Grable 20.00
Photoplay Magazine, Apr 1951, Esther Williams 12.00
Photoplay Magazine, Jun 1952, June Allison 10.00
Photoplay Magazine, Nov 1935, Ann Harding 18.00
Photoplay Magazine, Nov 1955, Kim Novak 15.00
Photoplay Magazine, 1960s 8.00
Pictorial Review, Jun 1928 . . . . 15.00
Playboy, Mar 1959 . . . . 15.00
Popular Mechanics, 1950s 3.00
Popular Radio, 1920-30s 8.00
Quick Magazine, 1949-59 . . . . 2.00
Radio Dial, 1930s 10.00
Reader's Digest, 1950-70s 1.00
Real Western, Dec 1952 . . . . 5.00
Redbook, 1950-60s 2.00
Rexall Almanac, 1929-76 . . . . 3.00
Rod & Gun, 1950-60s 3.00
Science, 1920-50s 5.00
Science & Invention, 1920s 10.00
Scouting, 1930s 2.00
Screen Play, Jul 1933, Mae West 15.00
Silver Screen, Oct 1939, Greta Garbo 30.00
Song Hits, 1940s 4.00
Southern Bottler, soda pop adv, May 1947 . . . . 25.00

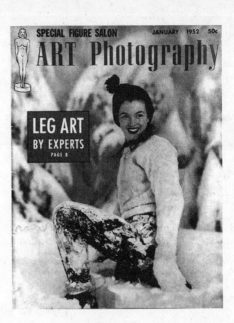

Art Photography,
Jan 1952, Marilyn
Monroe cover,
$40.00.

Sporting Goods Journal, 1930s 6.00
Sporting News, 1960s 8.00
Sports Illustrated, 1970-79 . . . . 10.00
Stage, Apr 1939 . . . . 8.00
Tattler Magazine, 1930s 5.00
Terror Tales, 1934-41 . . . . 40.00
Thrilling Western Stories, Jan 1935 . . . . 6.00
Time Magazine, Apr 1945, General Patton 12.00
Time Magazine, Oct 4, 1948, Joe DiMaggio 15.00
Trail and Timberline, 1920s 2.00
True Story, 1931, Jean Harlow 8.00
US News & World Report, 1940-60 . . . . 2.00
View, 1940s 2.00
Vogue, Apr 1925, George Plank cov 40.00
Weird Tales, Jul 1947 . . . . 30.00
Western Family, 1940-50s 5.00
Western Horsemen, 1950-66 . . . . 4.00
Whirl, 1956-59 . . . . 5.00
Wrestling World, Jul 1954 . . . . 15.00
Youth's Companion, Nov 1925 . . . . 30.00

MARBLEHEAD POTTERY

In 1904 Dr. Herbert J. Hall established the Marblehead Pottery as one of several craft projects for his Deveraux Mansion sanitarium patients. Four years later, Arthur Baggs, one of the instructors, established the pottery as a separate business operation. In 1915 Baggs became the pottery's owner.

The pottery was moved to 111 Front Street, Marblehead. After 1920, the pottery only operated in the summer. During the balance of the year, Baggs first taught at the Cleveland School of Art and eventually at Ohio State University. Production ended in 1936.

Baggs attracted a number of leading artists, designers, and decorators to his pottery among whom were Annie Aldrich, Rachel Grimwell, Arthur Hennessey, Maude Milner, and Mrs. E. D. (Hannah) Tutt. After an initial design period based primarily on geometric forms, conventional animal, bird, floral, fruit, and marine motifs appeared on pieces.

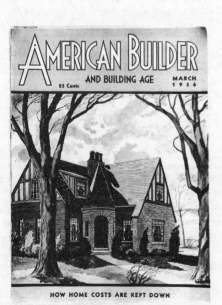

American Builder
and Building Age,
Mar 1936, $10.00.

Many pieces are marked with a ship flanked by the letters "M" and "P."

Reference: Ralph and Terry Kovel, *Kovel's American Art Pottery,* Crown, 1993.

Collectors' Club: American Art Pottery Assoc, PO Box 834, Westport, MA 02790.

Bookends, pr, emb ship in green and orange glaze on
blue ground, ship stamp, 5½ x 5½" **$875.00**
Bowl, flaring, emb lotus pattern, ext in dark blue matte
glaze, int in light blue semi-matte glaze, stamped ship
mark, 3¾ x 8" **350.00**
Chamberstick, rounded handle, smooth dark green
matte glaze, imp ship mark, 8½ x 5" **550.00**
Tile, molded tall ship, matte white glaze on blue ground,
imp ship mark, 9½" sq **1,000.00**
Vase, bulbous, charcoal and oyster gray flying geese on
speckled dove gray ground, imp ship mark and "MP,"
9 x 7" **12,000.00**
Vase, bulbous squat, dark green semi-matte glaze, imp
mark, 3¼ x 5" **500.00**
Vase, cylindrical, lavender-gray matte glaze, imp ship
mark, 9 x 4" **875.00**
Vase, Hannah Tutt, emb repeated pattern of stylized
brown and blue fruit and leaves on speckled gray
ground, imp ship mark and "HT," 5 x 3¾" **1,425.00**
Vase, ovoid, smooth speckled matte green glaze,
stamped ship mark and "MP," 8 x 4¼" **1,100.00**
Vase, ovoid, stylized olive green trees on dark blue
ground, stamped ship mark, 7 x 4" **3,575.00**
Vase, straight sided, imp stylized flowers in red with
green leaves on dark blue ground, ship mark and "M,"
4 x 3¼" **1,975.00**
Vessel, squat, emb stylized rose repeating pattern in
ocher and green on speckled brown ground, imp ship
mark, 3½ x 5" **1,200.00**
Vessel, squat, ribbed body, smooth green and charcoal
matte glaze, incised "winged M" mark, 3 x 4¼" **450.00**

Vase, cylindrical with bulbous base, incised with stylized trees in brown on speckled green ground, imp ship mark and "MT," 1" hairline to rim, 6¼" h, 3¾" d, $3,575.00. Photo courtesy David Rago Auctions, Inc.

MARBLES

Marbles divide into three basic types: (1) machine-made clay, glass, and mineral marbles, (2) handmade glass marbles made for use, and (3) handmade glass marbles made for display. Machine-made marbles usually sell for less than their handmade counterparts, comic strip marbles being one of the few exceptions. Watch for modern reproduction and fantasy comic strip marbles.

The Akro Agate Company, Christensen Agate Company, M. F. Christensen & Son Company, Marble King Company, Master Marble Company, Peltier Glass Company, and Vitro Agate/Gladding-Vitro Company are some of the leading manufacturers of machine-made marbles. Today, collector emphasis is on marble sets in their period packaging.

Handmade marbles are collected by type—Bennington, china (glazed and painted), china (unglazed and painted), clay, end of day, Lutz, mica, sulfide, and swirl—and size. Over a dozen reproduction and fantasy sulfide marbles have appeared during the last decade.

Many contemporary studio glassblowers have made marbles, often imitating earlier styles, for sale to the adult collector market. These marbles show no signs of wear and have not been tested in the secondary resale market. Any value associated with these marbles is highly speculative.

References: Paul Baumann, *Collecting Antique Marbles, 3rd Edition,* Krause Publications, 1999; Robert Block, *Marbles, 3rd Edition,* Schiffer Publishing, 1999; Stanley Block (ed.), *Marble Mania,* Schiffer Publishing, 1998; Everett Grist, *Antique and Collectible Marbles, Third Edition,* Collector Books, 1992, 1998 value update; *Everett Grist's Big Book of Marbles, Second Edition,* Collector Books, 2000; *Everett Grist's Machine Made and Contemporary Marbles, Second Edition,* Collector Books, 1998; Dennis Webb, *Greenberg's Guide to Marbles, Second Edition,* Greenberg Books, 1994.

Collectors' Clubs: Marble Collectors Society of America, PO Box 222, Trumbull, CT 06611; National Marble Club of America, 440 Eaton Rd, Drexel Hill, PA 19026.

Akro Agate, Corkscrew, 2 colors, opaque **$15.00**
Akro Agate, Corkscrew, 3 colors **15.00**
Akro Agate, Cornelian **20.00**
Akro Agate, Lemonade Corkscrew **20.00**
Christensen Agate Co, American Agate, ¾" d **20.00**
Christensen Agate Co, Blue Rays, transparent cobalt blue
base with bright orange swirl, ⅝" d **70.00**
Christensen Agate Co, Diaper Fold, light green and
orange opaque swirls, ¹¹⁄₁₆" d **35.00**
Christensen Agate Co, Flame, yellow and black on gray
base, ¾" d **125.00**
Christensen Agate Co, Guinea, purple base **300.00**
Christensen Agate Co, Red Devil, transparent red base
with yellow patches, ¾" d **100.00**
Christensen Agate Co, Red Slag, ¾" d **10.00**
Christensen Agate Co, Rocket, translucent black and
orange swirl, ¹¹⁄₁₆" d **100.00**
Christensen Agate Co, Slag, green, ¾" d **2.00**
Christensen Agate Co, Slag, yellow, ¾" d **20.00**
Christensen Agate Co, Submarine, semi-translucent
green and yellow, green and orange opaque swirls **150.00**
Marble King, Girl Scout **6.00**

Marble King, Spider-man, blue and red	150.00
Marble King, watermelon	200.00
Peltier Glass Co, Christmas tree	50.00
Peltier Glass Co, patch with adventurine	20.00
Vitro Agate/Gladding-Vitro Co, conqueror	1.00
Vitro Agate/Gladding-Vitro Co, victory	2.00

MATCHBOX

In 1947 Leslie Smith and Rodney Smith, two unrelated Navy friends, founded Lesney (a combination of the first letters in each of their names) in London, England. Joined by John Odell, they established a factory to do die casting.

In 1953, Lesney introduced a miniature toy line packaged in a box that resembled a matchbox. The toys quickly became known as "Matchbox" toys. The earliest Matchbox vehicles had metal wheels. These were eventually replaced with plastic wheels. In 1969 the Superfast plastic wheel was introduced. Slight variations in color and style occurred from the beginning due to paint and parts shortages. In 1956 the Models of Yesteryear series was introduced, followed in 1957 by Major Packs.

Matchbox toys arrived in the United States in 1958 and achieved widespread popularity by the early 1960s. Mattel's Hot Wheels arrived on the scene in 1968, providing Matchbox with a major competitor. Matchbox revamped its models through the 1970s and added the "1-75" numbering system. "Nostalgia" models were introduced in 1992.

In 1982 Universal Group bought Lesney. Production was moved to the Far East. In 1992 Tyco Toys bought Universal Group. In 1997 Mattel, owner of Hot Wheels, acquired Tyco.

References: Dana Johnson, *Matchbox Toys: 1947-1998, Third Edition*, Collector Books, 1999; Charlie Mack, *Lesney's Matchbox Toys: 1969-1982, 2nd Edition*, Schiffer Publishing, 1999; Charlie Mack, *Matchbox Toys: The Universal Years, 1982-1992, 2nd Edition*, Schiffer Publishing, 1999; Charlie Mack, *The Encyclopedia of Matchbox Toys: 1947-1996*, Schiffer Publishing, 1997; Nancy Schiffer, *Matchbox Toys, 5th Edition*, Schiffer Publishing, 2000.

Collectors' Clubs: Matchbox Collectors Club, PO Box 977, Newfield, NJ 08344; Matchbox USA, 62 Saw Mill Rd, Durham, CT 06422; The Matchbox International Collectors Assoc, PO Box 28072, Waterloo, Ontario, Canada N2L 6J8.

Airport Foamite Crash Tender, 63-B	$5.00
Alfa Romeo 155, 3-H	1.00
Army Saracen Personnel Carrier, 54-A	20.00
Aston Martin DB2 Saloon, metallic green, plastic wheels, 53-A	30.00
Audi Quattro, 23-G	2.00
Austin A50 Sedan, 36-A	35.00
Austin Water Truck, 71-A	30.00
Beach Buggy, pink, 30-E	20.00
Bedford Horse Box, metallic green, 40-E	5.00
Bedford Low Loader, dark green cab, tan trailer, 27-A	35.00
Bedford Milk Delivery Van, 29-A	45.00
Bedford Wreck Truck, metal wheels, 13-B	40.00
Caterpillar Tractor, 8-A	80.00
Cement Mixer, dark green, red barrel and handle, yellow wheels, Lesney, 1948, 3⁹/₁₆" l	175.00
Chevy Bel Air, metallic magenta, 4-H	6.00
Chevy Impala, metallic blue, 57-B	30.00

Chop Suey Motorcycle, magenta, red handlebars, 49-C	15.00
Combine Harvester, red, 51-F	5.00
Commer Pickup, 50-A	40.00
Coronation Coach, silver, Lesney, 1953, 4½" l	100.00
Daimler Ambulance, metal wheels, 14-B	35.00
Dodge Caravan, silver, 68-F	6.00
Dodge Cattle Truck, 37-E	12.00
Dodge Challenger Hot Rod, 1-J	3.00
Dodge Dragster, 70-D	15.00
Dragon Wheels, 43-E	15.00
Ferrari F1 Racing Car, 73-B	20.00
Foden Concrete Truck, 21-D	6.00
Ford Atkinson Grit Spreader, 70-C	20.00
Ford Fairlane Police Car, light blue, black plastic wheels, 55-B	30.00
Ford Galaxie Fire Chief Car, 59-C	15.00
Ford Heavy Wreck Truck, 71-D	20.00
Ford Kennel Truck, 50-C	6.00
Ford Pickup, 6-E	15.00
Ford Supervan, 6-I	3.00
Ford Thames Singer Van, light green, 59-A	30.00
Ford Thunderbird, cream and pink, gray plastic wheels, 75-A	50.00
Ford Zodiac Convertible, 39-A	100.00
Formula Racing Car, metallic tan, 28-H	3.00
GMC Refrigerator Truck, red, 44-D	30.00
GMC Tipper Truck, 26-D	15.00
Greyhound Bus, 66-D	15.00
Harley Davidson Motorcycle, 50-G	4.00
Harley Davidson Motorcycle with Sidecar, 66-B	85.00
Horse Drawn Milk Float, orange, Lesney, 1949, 5³/₈" l	700.00
Hot Rod Draguar, 36-E	15.00
Jaguar XJ220, 31-M	3.00
Land Rover Fire Truck, 57-C	180.00
Lincoln Continental, metallic blue, 31-C	8.00
Lincoln Town Car, 43-K	2.00
Lotus Racing Car, 19-E	30.00
Lotus Super Seven, orange, 60-D	15.00
Mack Dump Truck, olive drab, 28-E	30.00
Massey Harris Tractor, 4-B	50.00
Mazda Savannah RX7, light green, 76-A	4.00
Mercedes Benz Ambulance, 3-C	6.00
Mercury Commuter Police Station Wagon, 55-F	12.00
Mercury Cougar Villager Station Wagon, metallic blue, 74-E	5.00
Mercury Sable Wagon, 55-L	2.00
MGA Sports Car, gray plastic wheels, 19-B	80.00

Ford Thunderbird, 75-A, 2-tone flesh and cream, 1960, $45.00.

Massey Harris Tractor, 4-A, with fenders, 1954, $65.00.

Nissan 300ZX Turbo, 24-I **2.00**
Oldsmobile Aerotech, metallic silver, 62-L **3.00**
Peterbilt Tanker, blue and white, 56-G **4.00**
Rhino Rod, 53-J **1.00**
Rolls Royce Phantom, metallic tan, 44-B **80.00**
Saab Sonnet, blue, 65-D **10.00**
Seasprite Helicopter, white, 75-E **3.00**
Site Dumper, yellow, 26-F **3.00**
Slingshot Dragster, pink, 64-D **12.00**
Stoat Armored Truck, olive drab, chrome hubs, 28-F **45.00**
Studebaker Lark Wagonaire, 42-B **12.00**
Sunburner Maserati Bora, 37-H **4.00**
Toyota Celica, 77-A. **4.00**
Trailer Caravan, 23-C **12.00**
TV News Truck, Graffic Traffic series, 68-H. **6.00**
Vantastic, orange, white base, 34-F **4.00**
Volkswagen Beetle, black, metallic brown sides, 46-G **4.00**
Volvo 760, purple, 62-K **3.00**
Weasel Armored Vehicle, metallic green, 73-F **5.00**

MATCHCOVERS

Joshua Pusey, a Philadelphia lawyer who put ten cardboard matches into a plain white board cover, is credited with inventing the matchcover. In 1892 he sold 200 to the Mendelson Opera Company, which hand-printed the cover with its advertisement.

Binghamton Match Company, Binghamton, New York, made the first machine-made matchcover for the Piso Company of Warren, Pennsylvania. Only one example survives, owned by the Diamond Match Company.

Matchcovers dating prior to the early 1930s are scarce. The modern collecting craze dates from the Chicago Century of Progress World's Fair of 1933-34. The matchcover's golden age began in the mid-1940s and extended through the early 1960s.

The introduction of the throw-away lighter in the mid-1960s and rising production costs ended the matchcover era. The per unit cost of diecut matchcovers today falls in the seven to eight cents range. Given this, matchcovers lost their appeal as a free giveaway.

The 1990s saw matchcover prices soar. The $1,000 barrier was broken. Many of these higher prices are being paid by crossover, not matchcover collectors. Trading, usually on a one-for-one basis, remains the principal form of exchange among collectors.

Reference: Bill Retskin, *The Matchcover Collector's Price Guide, 2nd Edition,* Antique Trader Books, 1997.

Collectors' Clubs: Rathkamp Matchcover Society, 432 N Main St, Urbana, OH 43078; The American Matchcover Collecting Club, PO Box 18481, Asheville, NC 28814.

Note: Prices are for matchcovers in mint or near mint condition.

10-Strike, "Courtesy of Central Bakery, Lorain, Ohio" on
    front, "Phone 5648" on saddle, loaf of bread on back **$5.00**
10-Strike, "Daniel Webster Straight Bourbon Whiskey"
    on front, "Tomek Liquor Co" on saddle, "Gibson's
    Restaurant" on back, Universal Match **4.00**
10-Strike, "Wil Wright's Ice Cream" with little boy angel
    on front, blank saddle, "Wil Wright's Ice Cream" with
    red and white stripes on back, Universal Match **4.00**
30-Strike, Labatt's, logo on front, blank saddle, "Labatt's
    Blue" on back. **5.00**
30-Strike, "Mrs Baird's Slice Bread, Always fresh…At
    Your Grocers" with loaf on front, "Stays Fresh Longer"
    on saddle, "leading grocers know…" on back. **5.00**
30-Strike, The President and Mrs Ford, White House, and
    seal on front, back striker. **3.00**
42-Strike, "Greetings from the Massachusetts Turnpike"
    with maps and stops on front, Howard Johnson logo
    and color photos of turnpike on back, Universal
    Match. **4.00**
Advertising, College Candy Kitchen Inc, "Finest Eating
    Place In Amherst" on front, "Over Fifteen Years in
    Business" on saddle, "Home Made Pastry, Ice Cream,
    Candy, Salted Nuts" on back, Diamond Match **4.00**

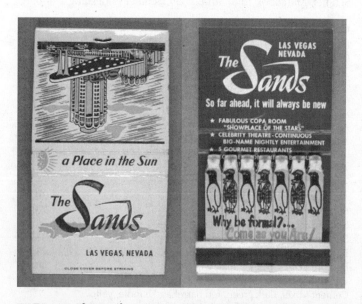

21-Feature, The Sands, Las Vegas, NV, 30 sticks, penguin on each stick, Lion Match, $12.00. Photo courtesy Ray Morykan Auctions.

Military, Bond Bread Navy Plane Set, Wildcat Fighter, Lion Match, 1942, $8.00. Photo courtesy Ray Morykan Auctions.

Advertising, Hamm's Beer, "From the land of sky blue waters" on front, "Hamm's" on saddle, "Hamm's... The smooth" with bear holding sign on back **5.00**

Advertising, Hess Brothers, Allentown, PA, repeated design on front, blank saddle, "One of America's Better Stores" with black child in turban on back **8.00**

Advertising, "Holmes Delicious Ice Cream, Union Springs, Alabama" on front, "It's Better" on saddle, "For The Best Always Ask For Holmes..." on back **3.00**

Advertising, Valvoline Motor Oil, can on front, "Valvoline" on saddle **4.00**

Display, Dick Raymond Finance Company, Bakersfield, California, "Phone 8-8573" on front and back, photo of man with Dick Raymond, address, and services on inside, 30-strike size **4.00**

Features, Andy Won's Chinese Sky Room, San Francisco, front doors with "Thru These Portals..." on back, 3 Chinese dancers across sticks with "The Wongettes," 20-strike size, Lion Match **10.00**

Features, "Chaffee Machine Co" on front, blank saddle, tug boat with "1860 Bay Front, San Diego, Calif..., Phone BElmont 4-3451" on back, pleasure boat across sticks, 20-strike size, Lion Match **12.00**

Features, "Jimbo's Restaurant..., San Bernadino, Calif" on front, restaurant on back, restaurant with name across sticks, 20-strike size, Lion Match **8.00**

Features, "Lou Slicer's Denison Restaurant..., Indianapolis, Indiana" on front, blank saddle, "Choice sea food" with lobster and steaks on back, "Noon Luncheons, Evening Dinners" with chef's head on each match tip, 20-strike size, Lion Match **10.00**

Features, Military Inn, "Bar-Restaurant, Wrightstown, New Jersey" on front, "Military Inn" across sticks, "Fort Dix 9112 9113" on inside, woodgrain, 20-strike size, Lion Match **8.00**

Midget-Type, Cadet Room, majorette on front, "Cadet Room, Dining & Dancing, Hotel Peabody" on back **6.00**

Midget-Type, "Rooney's Restaurant & Grille, Wilkes-Barre, PA" with lobster on front, "25 Years Serving the Best Land & Sea Foods" on saddle, ship with "SS Rooney" on back, name on inside, Lion Match **3.00**

Military, "Join The Navy!, Be A Fighting Bluejacket!..." on front, "Space Contributed by Maryland Match Co" on saddle, "The Navy Offers Men 17 to 50..." on back **6.00**

Military, "Walker Air Force Base, Officer's Club, Roswell, New Mexico" on front, blank saddle, "509th Bomb Wing" with small crest on back **4.00**

Patriotic, "Own a share in American/Minutemen Buy War Bonds" on front, "Step on it! World to crush the Axis!" on back **3.00**

Political, Air Force One, Kennedy Administration, 30-strike size. **5.00**

Transportation, American Airlines, Admirals Club logo on front and back, blank saddle **5.00**

Transportation, Greyhound Union Bus Terminal, Elmira, NY, "Phone 4214" on saddle, "Bus Information, Newsstand" on back **4.00**

MCCOY POTTERY

In 1910 Nelson McCoy, with his father's (J. W. McCoy) support, founded the Nelson McCoy Sanitary Stoneware Company to manufacture crocks, churns, and jugs. Early pieces were marked on the side with a stencil of a clover within a shield with an "M" above. By the mid-1920s, the company also made molded artware in forms ranging from jardinieres to vases.

In 1933 the company became the Nelson McCoy Pottery. Products included cookware, dinnerware, floral industry ware, gardenware, kitchenware, and tableware.

In 1967 Mount Clemens Pottery, owned by David Chase, purchased the company. Some pieces were marked "MCP" on the bottom. In 1974 Chase sold McCoy to Lancaster Colony Corporation, which added its logo to the bottom. Nelson McCoy, Jr., served as president under the Mount Clemens and Lancaster Colony Corporation ownership until 1981. After being sold to Designer Accents in 1985, operations at McCoy ceased in 1990.

References: Bob Hanson, Craig Nissen, and Margaret Hanson, *McCoy Pottery* (1997, 1999 value update), *Vol. II* (1999), Collector Books; Sharon and Bob Huxford, *The Collectors Encyclopedia of McCoy Pottery*, Collector Books, 1980, 1999 value update; Martha and Steve Sanford, *Sanfords Guide to Pottery by McCoy*, Adelmore Press, 1997.

Newsletter: *The NM Express*, 8934 Brecksville Rd, Brecksville, OH 44141.

REPRODUCTION ALERT: Nelson McCoy Pottery Company reproduced many of its original pieces.

Ashtray, hands, gold leaf and berries dec **$65.00**
Ashtray, flower petal with bird **20.00**
Bank, football, brown and white **125.00**
Bean Pot, brown gloss, 2 qt, 6½" h **30.00**
Beverage Server, with stand, Brocade Line **60.00**
Bookends, pr, rearing horse, white, gold trim, 8" h **100.00**
Butter, cov, floral design **18.00**
Candleholder Tray, green, 11½" l **125.00**
Coffee Mug, hammered design **10.00**
Console Bowl, Butterfly Line, 8½ x 6" **50.00**
Flower Holder, pigeon, 4 x 3½" **30.00**
Flower Holder, turtle, 4¼ x 2" **30.00**
Hanging Basket, bird feeder. **40.00**
Hanging Basket, iron, Green Thumb Line, 6½ x 6½". **35.00**
Hanging Basket, Rustic Line **25.00**

Jardiniere, Antique Curio Line, white, 7½" d 45.00
Jardiniere, Wild Rose Line, 6 x 2½ x 6" 40.00
Lamp, hyacinth, 8" h 400.00
Lamp, Model A Truck, sunburst gold, 8 x 4½" 85.00
Lamp, rearing horse 65.00
Lamp, wagon wheel, 8" h 75.00
Lamp, Wild Rose 300.00
Match Holder, blue and white speckled finish, 5¾ x 3¼" 30.00
Pitcher and Bowl Set, ship motif, 11½" x 9½" 60.00
Pitcher Vase, yellow, Garden Club Line, 8" h 20.00
Planter, baby crib, 6½ x 4" 50.00
Planter, baseball glove, 6 x 6" 125.00
Planter, caterpillar, Floraline, 13½" l 35.00
Planter, dog carrying bird in mouth, 12½ x 8½" 175.00
Planter, fish, pink and green, 12 x 7" 400.00
Planter, frog holding umbrella, black and yellow, 6½ x
    7½" 125.00
Planter, lamb, pink or blue cold paint, 8½ x 7¼" 40.00
Planter, lamb with baby block, 5 x 4½" 60.00
Planter, Liberty Bell, ivory and green, cold painted black
    bell 150.00
Planter, Madonna, matte white, Floraline, 7 x 6" 125.00
Planter, poodle, 7½ x 7½" 50.00
Planter, sprinkling can, Antique Rose Line, 7 x 6" 50.00
Planter, turtle, Floraline, 5¼ x 3¼" 12.00
Planter, zebra, 8½ x 6½" 200.00
Reamer, white, 8" l 60.00
Snack Set, turquoise 35.00
Spoonrest, penguin, 7 x 5" 75.00
Tray, hands, 8½" l 100.00
Stretch Animal, butting goat, 5½ x 3¼" 175.00
Stretch Animal, dachshund, 8¼ x 5" 100.00
Stretch Animal, lion, 7½ x 5½" 175.00
Teapot, Brown Antique Rose Line, 36 oz 40.00
Teapot, cat, black and white, red bow, paw is spout 100.00
TV Lamp, mermaid, 9¾ x 6" 200.00
Vase, green diamond design, 9" h 25.00
Vase, hand with glove, Lily Bud Line, 8¼" h 50.00
Vase, Harmony Line, 9¼" h 20.00
Vase, hyacinth, 8" h 100.00

Mammy carrying cauliflower, McCoy, 9¾" h, $325.00. Photo courtesy Collectors Auction Services.

Vase, sunflower, 9" h 40.00
Vase, Uncle Sam, white, yellow, and green, 7½" h 40.00
Vase, Wild Rose Line, 6½ x 4½" 35.00
Wall Pocket, apple, brown leaves 100.00
Wall Pocket, black woman wearing bonnet, dated 1944 . . . . 400.00
Wall Pocket, butterfly, yellow, 7 x 6" 200.00
Wall Pocket, cuckoo clock, 8" h 125.00
Wall Pocket, leaf, sprayed dec, 7 x 5½" 35.00
Wall Pocket, leaves and berries, 7" l 150.00
Wall Pocket, lily bud, 8" l 175.00
Wall Pocket, Mexican, 7½" l 50.00
Wall Pocket, pear, brown leaves 50.00

MCDONALD'S

In 1948 Dick and Mac McDonald opened their first limited menu, self-service McDonald's drive-in restaurant in San Bernadino, California. They began franchising their operation as the Speedee Service System in 1952. In 1955 Ray Kroc became a franchising agent for the McDonald brothers and opened his first McDonald's restaurant in Des Plaines, Illinois.

The 100th McDonald's restaurant opened in 1959 and the 200th in 1960. In 1961 Kroc bought out the McDonald brothers and launched the All American Meal of a hamburger, french fries, and milkshake. The Golden Arches replaced the Speedee logo in 1962. The first "Ronald McDonald," Willard Scott, made his debut in Washington, D.C.'s Cherry Blossom Parade in 1963. The Happy Meal dates from 1977. Toys were introduced in 1982.

By 1983, McDonald's had 7,000 restaurants in the United States and additional restaurants in thirty-one foreign countries. McDonald's has continued to build new restaurants around the world. Promotional tie-ins with movies, television shows, and major toy products have proven highly successful. By 1994, the 15th anniversary of the Happy Meal, McDonald's was serving 25 million customers daily in 70 countries.

References: Gary Henriques and Audre DuVall, *McDonald's Collectibles,* Collector Books, 1997 (1999 value update); Joyce and Terry Losonsky, *McDonald's Happy Meal Toys from the Eighties* (1999) *From the Nineties* (1999), Schiffer Publishing; Joyce and Terry Losonsky, *McDonald's Pre-Happy Meal Toys from the Fifties, Sixties and Seventies,* Schiffer Publishing, 1999; Terry and Joyce Losonsky, *McDonald's Happy Meal Toys Around the World,* Schiffer Publishing, 1995; Terry and Joyce Losonsky, *McDonald's Happy Meal Toys in the U.S.A.,* Schiffer Publishing, 1995; Meredith Williams, *Tomart's Price Guide to McDonald's Happy Meal Collectibles, Revised Edition,* Tomart Publications, 1995.

Newsletter: *Collecting Tips Newsletter,* PO Box 633, Joplin, MO 64802.

Collectors' Club: McDonald's Collectors Club, 1153 S Lee St, Ste 200, Des Plaines, IL 60016.

Activity Book, Workshop of Activities, *Santa Claus the
    Movie,* 1985 . . . . $3.00
Bank, figural wastebasket, yellow and white plastic, logo
    on sides, mkd "McDonald Corp" on bottom, 5¼" h 25.00
Baseball, vinyl, McDonald's logo, Sports Ball, 1990 . . . . 2.00
Beachcomber Happy Pail, 1986 . . . . 15.00
Belt, manager's, brown leather, 1½" sterling belt buckle
    depicting golden arches, size 36, Hickok, 1960s 30.00

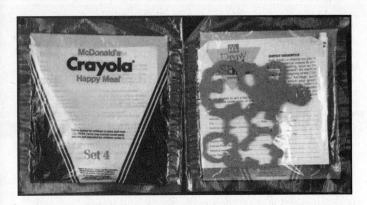

Crayola Stencils, yellow and green, set #3 of 4, 1986, $3.00.

Birdie Seaside Submarine, test, 1989 . . . . **20.00**
Book, *Grimace Goes to School,* Read Along With
    Ronald, 1989 . . . . **10.00**
Book, *Tale of Flopsy Bunnies,* Peter Rabbit, 1988 . . . . **10.00**
Bumper Car Tag Game, Giggles & Games, 1982 . . . . **10.00**
Changeable, McDino Cone, 1991 . . . . **2.00**
Changeable, milk shake, 1987 . . . . **4.00**
Changeable, quarter pounder with cheese, 1987 . . . . **2.00**
Colorforms, Grimace/Beach Sticker Set, 1986 . . . . **2.00**
Connectible, Ronald in soap-box racer, 1991 . . . . **2.00**
Crazy Vehicle, Birdie Airplane, pink **2.00**
Director's Megaphone, Makin' Movies, 1994 . . . . **1.00**
Figure, construction worker, Playmobile, test, 1981 . . . . **40.00**
Figure, Garfield on scooter, 1989 . . . . **1.00**
Figure, Garfield on skateboard, test, 1988 . . . . **25.00**
Figure, Hamburglar Jet Boat, Ship Shape, 1983 . . . . **10.00**
Figure, Mario, pops-up, Super Mario Brothers, 1990 . . . . **1.00**
Figure, Oliver, 1988 . . . . **2.00**
Figure, Snoopy's Hay Hauler, 1990 . . . . **1.00**
Figure, Snow White and the Seven Dwarfs, hard mold-
    ed plastic, complete set, MIP **30.00**
Figure, Transformer, 1985 . . . . **15.00**
Flying Disc, Michael Jordan Fitness Fun Challenge,
    6½" d, MIP **20.00**
French Fry Faller, Circus Series, 1983 . . . . **10.00**
Fry Guy Floater, Sailors, 1988 . . . . **3.00**
Happy Meal Box, Lego, 1985 . . . . **2.00**
Happy Meal Box, Little Engineer, 1987 . . . . **2.00**
Happy Meal Box, lunch box, plastic **10.00**
Happy Meal Box, Magic Show, 1985-86 . . . . **2.00**
Happy Meal Box, Popoids, 1984 . . . . **20.00**
Happy Meal Box, Sailors, 1988 . . . . **2.00**
Happy Meal Box, Star Trek, 1979-80 . . . . **15.00**
Happy Meal Box, Story of Texas, 1986 . . . . **20.00**
Looney Tunes Quack-Up Car, Bugs Bunny Swingin'
    Sedan, 1993 . . . . **1.00**
Magic String Pull, Magic Show, 1985-86 . . . . **4.00**
McBoo Bag, day-glow witch, 1991 . . . . **2.00**
McDonaldland Dough, 1990 . . . . **2.00**
Pail, ghost face, 1989 . . . . **1.00**
Pail, McBunny, 1989 . . . . **4.00**
Pail, McPunky, orange, 1985 . . . . **10.00**
Pencil Sharpener, Ronald McDonald, School Days, 1984 . . . . . **4.00**
Ring, *USS Enterprise,* Star Trek, 1979-80 . . . . **10.00**
Sailboat, inflatable, Super Summer, test, 1987 . . . . **15.00**

Sand Pail with Rake, Super Summer, 1988 . . . . **1.00**
Shovel, Birdie, with marigold seeds, Little Gardener, 1989 . . . . **2.00**
Soap Dish, Grimace, Feeling Good, 1985 . . . . **2.00**
Soccer Ball, McDonald's logo, Sports Ball, 1990 . . . . **2.00**
Sonic Rubber Ball, Sonic 3 the Hedgehog, 1994 . . . . **2.00**
Stencil, Grimace, with crayons, 1991 . . . . **2.00**
Stopwatch, Fitness Fun Challenge, 1992 . . . . **1.00**
Stuffed Toy, Dolly Dolphin, Sea World of Ohio, 1988 . . . . **10.00**
Toothbrush, Ronald McDonald, Feeling Good, 1985 . . . . **3.00**
Trading Card, Dallas Cowboys, 1980 . . . . **15.00**
Trumpet, Fry Kid, McDonaldland Band, 1986 . . . . **2.00**
Undersea Adventure Game, Magic School Bus, 1994 . . . . **1.00**
Wacky Game, Birdie sorting eggs, 1992 . . . . **2.00**
Watch, Polly Pocket, Attack Pack, 1995 . . . . **1.00**

MCKEE GLASS

McKee and Brothers was founded in Pittsburgh, Pennsylvania, in 1853. In 1888 the factory moved to Jeannette, Pennsylvania. The company reorganized in 1903, renaming itself the McKee Glass Company. It manufactured a wide range of household and industrial glassware. McKee introduced its Glasbake line in the 1910s.

The company is best known for its crystal pressed patterns, Depression glass kitchenware, and opaque ware. Tableware lines in color were first made in the early 1920s. Many older clear patterns, e.g., Aztec and Rock Crystal Flower, became available in color. Between 1923 and the late 1930s, new colors were added to the line each year. The popularity of the colorful opaque ware, made between 1930 and 1940, helped the company weather the hard times of the Depression.

In 1951 Thatcher Glass Company purchased McKee, selling it in 1961 to the Jeannette Glass Corporation. Upon purchasing McKee, Jeannette Glass Corporation closed the manufacturing operations at its plant and moved them to the McKee factory.

References: Gene Florence, *Kitchen Glassware of the Depression Years, 5th Edition,* Collector Books, 1995, 1999 value update; Gene Florence, *Very Rare Glassware of the Depression Years, Fifth Series,* Collector Books, 1997.

Note: For additional listings see Kitchen Glassware and Reamers.

Dots, butter, cov, blue and red, 1 lb **$100.00**

Reamer, jadite, emb "SUNKIST," base mkd "Made in U.S.A. Pat. No. 68764," $30.00. Photo courtesy Ray Morykan Auctions.

Dots, eggbeater bowl, black and green. **20.00**
Dots, mixing bowl, 9" d, blue and red **15.00**
Dots, pitcher, blue and red, 2 cup **35.00**
Dots, refrigerator dish, 4 x 5", black and green **15.00**
Glasbake, measuring cup, white, 1 cup **40.00**
Glasbake, tea kettle, crystal **15.00**
Laurel, bowl, 3 ftd, blue **65.00**
Laurel, bowl, 5¾" d, jadite **140.00**
Laurel, bowl, 6" d, French ivory **18.00**
Laurel, bowl, 9" d, French ivory **25.00**
Laurel, candlestick, French ivory **20.00**
Laurel, cereal bowl, French ivory **10.00**
Laurel, champagne **15.00**
Laurel, cheese dish, cov, French ivory **55.00**
Laurel, cocktail goblet. **15.00**
Laurel, creamer. **17.00**
Laurel, grill plate, opal **10.00**
Laurel, platter, 10¾" d, French ivory. **25.00**
Laurel, salad plate, 7¼" d, blue **14.00**
Laurel, salad plate, 7½" d, French ivory **10.00**
Laurel, salt and pepper shakers, pr, French ivory. . . . **45.00**
Laurel, sherbet, low. **15.00**
Laurel, soup bowl, blue. **75.00**
Laurel, tumbler, 9 oz, French ivory. **35.00**
Laurel, water goblet **17.00**
Laurel, wine goblet **15.00**
Red Ships, beater bowl **30.00**
Red Ships, bowl, 3½" d. **35.00**
Red Ships, butter, cov, 1 lb **60.00**
Red Ships, canister, 10 oz **20.00**
Red Ships, canister, 46 oz **35.00**
Red Ships, egg beater bowl **40.00**
Red Ships, mixing bowl, 8" d. **15.00**
Red Ships, refrigerator dish, 4 x 5" **18.00**
Red Ships, refrigerator dish, 5 x 8" **20.00**
Red Ships, salt and pepper shakers, pr, square, red lids. **50.00**
Red Ships, shaker **18.00**
Red Ships, tumbler **20.00**
Rock Crystal, bowl, ftd, 12½" d, crystal **75.00**
Rock Crystal, cake stand, amber **35.00**
Rock Crystal, candy dish, cov, red **325.00**
Rock Crystal, celery tray, 13½" d, crystal **35.00**
Rock Crystal, cheese comport, red. **50.00**
Rock Crystal, cocktail, ftd, crystal **15.00**
Rock Crystal, comport, 4¾" h, ftd, red **85.00**
Rock Crystal, comport, 11½" h, amber. **65.00**
Rock Crystal, cordial, red **80.00**
Rock Crystal, cracker plate, 11" d, amber, gold trim **55.00**
Rock Crystal, creamer and sugar, red **250.00**
Rock Crystal, finger bowl, 5" d, red **85.00**
Rock Crystal, goblet, green **30.00**
Rock Crystal, goblet, red **60.00**
Rock Crystal, nut bowl, center handle, red. **325.00**
Rock Crystal, oyster cocktail, red **85.00**
Rock Crystal, parfait, crystal. **28.00**
Rock Crystal, parfait, red **125.00**
Rock Crystal, pitcher, cov, pink **350.00**
Rock Crystal, plate, 6½" d, red **30.00**
Rock Crystal, plate, 7½" d, red **30.00**
Rock Crystal, plate, 8½" d, red **60.00**
Rock Crystal, plate, 10½" d, red. **85.00**
Rock Crystal, punch bowl, 14" d, crystal **350.00**
Rock Crystal, relish, 5-part, crystal. **20.00**
Rock Crystal, sundae, red **3.00**

Rock Crystal, tumbler, ftd, 7 oz, pink **25.00**
Rock Crystal, vase, 11" h, amber with gold trim **100.00**
Rock Crystal, water pitcher, cov, pink. **350.00**
Rock Crystal, whiskey, red. **90.00**
Rock Crystal, wine, 3 oz, red. **65.00**

MEDICAL ITEMS

Doctors are the primary collectors of medical apparatus and instruments. Most collect material that relates to their medical specialty. Medical apparatus and instruments are sold by specialist dealers or auctions. This is why so little medical material is found at flea markets and antiques malls, shops, and shows.

Office furniture, especially large wooden storage cabinets with unusual drawer configurations, are popular in the general antiques marketplace. The same holds true for wall charts, ranging from the standard eye examination chart to those dealing with anatomy.

Pharmaceutical items divide into two groups: (1) items used by druggists to prepare medicines and (2) packaging associated with over-the-counter and doctor-prescribed medications. There is little added value if the contents are intact. In fact, most collectors prefer that they are not.

Reference: C. Keith Wilbur, *Antique Medical Instruments,* Schiffer Publishing, 1987, 1998 value update.

Collectors' Club: Medical Collectors Assoc, Montefiore Medical Park, 1695A Eastchester Rd, Bronx, NY 10461.

Note: See Drugstore for additional listings.

MEDICAL ITEMS

Bath Thermometer, Dr Forbes style, in floating wooden case, chain for hanging, 1920, 12" l **$20.00**
Beam Scale, brass base, pillar, balance chain, pans, and forceps, Seederer-Kohlbusch, Englewood, NJ, c1920. . . . . **275.00**
Belltone Hearing Aid, Concerto, Mono-Pac Model C, cylindrical plug and wires leading to ear piece, orig case, 1951-54 . . . . **30.00**
Book, *The Cole Library of Early Medicine and Zoology,* Nellie B Eales, 2 vol, 1st vol orig cloth, second in orig wrappers, 4to **100.00**

Cadaver Table, brass with heavy brass table top frame with glass, mechanically tilted with crank, drain at end of table, "T. B. Hennessy Chicago, U.S.A.," base restored, 31" h, 76" l, 24" w, $875.00. Photo courtesy Collectors Auction Services.

Book, *Compact History of the American Red Cross, The*, illus, 308 pp, 1959 . . . . **15.00**

Bottle, WH Bull's Vegetable Worm Syrup, WH Bull Medicine Co, St Louis, MO, orig cardboard box, full syrup bottle **20.00**

Catalog, Becton, Dickinson & Co, illus, syringes and needles, veterinary cases and equipment, stetho-scopes, nurses instrument cases and bags, doctor bags, 145 pp, 1930 . . . . **45.00**

Chemist's Scale, brass and steel, oak box with drawers, glazed top and sides, Becker's Sons, Rotterdam **225.00**

Poster, Dr Caldwell's Syrup Pepsin, cardboard, stand-up, boy standing on stool yelling "Hey Mom! Where'd Grandpa Put The Syrup Pepsin," 37" h, 27" w **140.00**

Quack Heat Massager, disc applicator on black wooden handle, c1940s **10.00**

Rectal Medicine, The Inside Story, Medicone Co, NY, tan, red, full professional sample packet, 1950s **5.00**

MELMAC

Thermosetting plastics, principally melamine resins, were used to make dinnerware. Melamine resins result from the interaction of melamine and formaldehyde. A chemical reaction creating permanent hardness occurs when thermosetting plastics are heated.

Melmac is a trade name of American Cyanamid. Like Kleenex and Xerox, it soon became a generic term describing an entire line of products.

The first plastic dinnerware was used in cafeterias, hospitals, restaurants, and other institutional settings. Melamine dinner-ware's popularity waned in the early 1960s. Repeated washing caused fading and dullness. Edges chipped, knives scratched sur-faces, and foods left stains. Pieces placed too close to heat discol-ored or scarred. Many early 1960s designs were too delicate. Pieces actually broke. The final death blow came from the import of inexpensive Asian and European ceramic dinnerware in the late 1960s and early 1970s.

Reference: Gregory R. Zimmer and Alvin Daigle, Jr., *Melmac Dinnerware*, L-W Book Sales, 1997.

Note: Prices listed are for items in mint condition.

Aztec, cup and saucer **$2.00**
Aztec, creamer and sugar **4.00**
Aztec, dinner plate **2.00**
Aztec, salad bowl **2.00**
Aztec, serving bowl, divided **4.00**
Boonton, bread tray **8.00**
Boonton, butter, cov **10.00**
Boonton, casserole, cov **20.00**
Boonton, cereal bowl **5.00**
Boonton, dinner plate **4.00**
Boonton, jug, cov **20.00**
Boonton, mixing bowl **8.00**
Boonton, sugar **6.00**
Boonton, tidbit tray, 3-tier **15.00**
Boonton, cereal bowl **4.00**
Boonton, cup and saucer **3.00**
Boonton, serving dish, oblong **8.00**
Branchell, butter, cov **10.00**
Branchell, dinner plate **4.00**
Branchell, fruit bowl **3.00**

Branchell, salad plate **4.00**
Branchell, salt and pepper shakers, pr **6.00**
Branchell, soup bowl, cov **5.00**
Branchell, vegetable, divided **8.00**
Branchell Royale, dinner plate **4.00**
Branchell Royale, salt and pepper shakers, pr **6.00**
Branchell Royale, soup bowl, cov **5.00**
Brookpark Arrowhead, dinner plate, divided **4.00**
Brookpark Arrowhead, tidbit tray, 2-tier, Town and Country **12.00**
Debonaire, dinner plate **2.00**
Debonaire, sugar, cov **3.00**
Debonaire, tumbler, 10 oz **6.00**
Flite Lane, dinner plate **2.00**
Flite Lane, tumbler, 6 oz **6.00**
Fostoria, cereal bowl **7.00**
Fostoria, dinner plate **6.00**
Fostoria, serving bowl **15.00**
Fostoria, sugar, cov **12.00**
Harmony House, butter, cov **10.00**
Harmony House, cup and saucer **3.00**
Harmony House, salt and pepper shakers, pr **6.00**
Holiday, cup and saucer **3.00**
Holiday, serving bowl, divided **8.00**
Imperial Ware, creamer **5.00**
Imperial Ware, salad plate **4.00**
Lucent, bread and butter plate **3.00**
Lucent, dinner plate **6.00**
Lucent, platter **12.00**
Lucent, serving bowl, divided, April in Paris **15.00**
Mallo-Ware, butter, cov **5.00**
Mallo-Ware, creamer **1.00**
Mallo-Ware, gravy boat **5.00**
Mallo-Ware, soup bowl **3.00**
Mar-Crest, dinner plate **2.00**
Mar-Crest, soup bowl **3.00**
Mar-Crest, tumbler, 10 oz **7.00**

Lexington, dinner plate, shades of blue and brown on white ground, $2.00.

Monte Carlo, cup and saucer. **2.00**
Monte Carlo, salt and pepper shakers, pr **4.00**
Prolon, dinner plate **4.00**
Prolon, salad plate **4.00**
Prolon, salt and pepper shakers, pr **6.00**
Royalon, bread and butter plate. **1.00**

METLOX

In 1927 T. C. Prouty and Willis, his son, established Metlox Pottery, Manhattan Beach, California, primarily for the purpose of making ceramic outdoor signs. When business declined during the Depression and T. C. died in 1931, Willis converted the plant to the production of ceramic dinnerware. Brightly colored California Pottery was the company's first offering. Between 1934 and the early 1940s, Metlox produced its Poppytrail line of kitchenware and tableware. In 1936 the company adopted the poppy, California's state flower, as its trademark.

Designer Carl Romanelli, who joined Metlox in the late 1930s, created Metlox's miniature line and the Modern Masterpiece line that included bookends, figural vases, figurines, and wall pockets.

The company shifted to war production during the early 1940s. California Ivy, Metlox's first painted dinnerware, was introduced in 1946. That same year, Willis Prouty sold Metlox to Evan Shaw, owner of American Pottery, Los Angeles, a company under contract to Disney for ceramic figurines. Production of Disney figurines continued until 1956. In the 1960s and 70s, Metlox made Colorstax (solid color dinnerware), cookie jars, and Poppet (stoneware flower holders and planters).

In 1958 Metlox purchased Vernon Kiln. The company's Vernon Kiln division made artware in the 1950s and 60s, American Royal Horses, and Nostalgia, a scale model carriage line.

Shaw died in 1980. His family continued the business for another decade, ending operations in 1989.

References: Carl Gibbs, Jr., *Collector's Encyclopedia of Metlox Potteries,* Collector Books, 1995, out of print; Harry L. Rinker, *Dinnerware of the 20th Century: The Top 500 Patterns,* House of Collectibles, 1997.

Antique Grape, coffeepot **$80.00**
Antique Grape, compote. **80.00**
Antique Grape, dinner plate **25.00**
Antique Grape, platter, 12½" l **25.00**
Antique Grape, salt and pepper shakers, pr **30.00**
Antique Grape, tea canister **65.00**
Antique Grape, vegetable, 8½" l **40.00**
California Confetti, fruit bowl **12.00**
California Confetti, place setting **50.00**
California Confetti, soup bowl **20.00**
California Ivy, bowl, 5" d. **10.00**
California Ivy, bowl, 7" d. **15.00**
California Ivy, cereal bowl, 6" d. **11.00**
California Ivy, creamer **22.00**
California Ivy, dinner plate, 10½" d **12.00**
California Ivy, fruit bowl, 5¼" d **12.00**
California Ivy, gravy boat. **35.00**
California Ivy, jam and jelly dish **35.00**
California Ivy, pitcher, 2½ qt **65.00**
California Ivy, salad bowl, 11¼" d **60.00**
California Ivy, salt and pepper shakers, pr **25.00**
California Ivy, sugar, cov **25.00**

California Ivy, tumbler, 13 oz. **25.00**
California Ivy, vegetable, 9" d **12.00**
California Provincial, condiment shakers, pr. **40.00**
California Provincial, flour canister **100.00**
California Provincial, gravy boat **55.00**
California Provincial, luncheon plate, 9" d **20.00**
California Provincial, salt and pepper shakers, pr **30.00**
California Provincial, sugar canister **100.00**
California Strawberry, coffeepot **60.00**
California Strawberry, creamer **20.00**
California Strawberry, dinner plate **6.00**
California Strawberry, pitcher, 4½" h **30.00**
California Strawberry, vegetable, 8" d **30.00**
Colonial Homestead, coffeepot **120.00**
Colonial Homestead, teapot **50.00**
Della Robbia, bowl, 6½" d **9.00**
Della Robbia, bowl, 10½" d **40.00**
Della Robbia, bread and butter plate, 6½" d. **5.00**
Della Robbia, butter, cov. **50.00**
Della Robbia, creamer and covered sugar **45.00**
Della Robbia, cup and saucer **15.00**
Della Robbia, deep bowl, 7" d. **12.00**
Della Robbia, gravy boat. **35.00**
Della Robbia, plate, 7½" d **10.00**
Della Robbia, plate, 10¾" d **15.00**
Della Robbia, platter, oval, 14" l **45.00**
Della Robbia, saucer. **2.00**
Della Robbia, shaker. **10.00**
Della Robbia, sugar, cov **20.00**
Homestead Provincial, butter, cov, blue **50.00**
Homestead Provincial, canister set, 4 pc **375.00**
Homestead Provincial, casserole, cov, hen lid, 9" l, blue. **20.00**
Homestead Provincial, cereal bowl, oatmeal **15.00**
Homestead Provincial, chop plate, oatmeal **55.00**
Homestead Provincial, coffeepot **125.00**
Homestead Provincial, creamer, blue. **25.00**
Homestead Provincial, cup and saucer, blue **15.00**
Homestead Provincial, fruit bowl, blue **12.00**

Della Robbia, dinner plate, $15.00.

Homestead Provincial, gravy boat, blue, 1 pt **20.00**
Homestead Provincial, luncheon plate, blue. **20.00**
Homestead Provincial, oil and vinegar cruets, blue,
   wood tray **100.00**
Homestead Provincial, relish, divided, handle, blue **60.00**
Homestead Provincial, salad bowl, blue, 11" d **60.00**
Homestead Provincial, salt and pepper shakers, pr, blue **25.00**
Homestead Provincial, soup bowl, blue **15.00**
Homestead Provincial, tea kettle **125.00**
Homestead Provincial, turkey platter, blue **250.00**
Homestead Provincial, vegetable **30.00**
La Mancha Gold, dinner plate **12.00**
La Mancha Gold, platter, 11¾" l **25.00**
Nasturtium, bread and butter plate, 6" d **3.00**
Nasturtium, butter, cov, oval **20.00**
Nasturtium, coffeepot, creamer, and sugar **70.00**
Nasturtium, cup and saucer **5.00**
Nasturtium, gravy boat and stand **20.00**
Provincial Blue, bread server, "bread" on side **50.00**
Provincial Blue, casserole, cov, chicken **110.00**
Provincial Blue, chop plate **50.00**
Provincial Blue, coffeepot **100.00**
Provincial Blue, platter **30.00**
Provincial Blue, salad bowl **50.00**
Provincial Blue, vegetable, basket design **30.00**
Red Rooster, casserole, small **75.00**
Red Rooster, cup and saucer **18.00**
Red Rooster, flour canister **75.00**
Rose, coffeepot **70.00**
Rose, cruet set, 5 pcs **150.00**
Rose, ice lip pitcher, large **60.00**
Rose, pitcher, small **35.00**
Rose, vegetable, cov **70.00**
Sculptured Daisy, bowl, handled, 7" d **30.00**
Sculptured Daisy, coffeepot **100.00**
Sculptured Daisy, dinner plate **15.00**
Sculptured Daisy, platter, small **35.00**
Sculptured Daisy, salad plate **55.00**
Sculptured Daisy, sugar, cov **30.00**
Sculptured Daisy, tumbler **40.00**
Sculptured Daisy, vegetable, tab handles, oval **65.00**
Strawberry, casserole, cov **12.00**
Strawberry, cup and saucer **12.00**
Strawberry, dinner plate **12.00**

MILK BOTTLES

Hervey Thatcher is recognized as the father of the glass milk bottle. Patents are one of the best research sources for information about early milk bottles. A. V. Whiteman received a milk bottle patent as early as 1880. Patent recipients leased or sold their patents to manufacturers. The golden age of the glass milk bottle spans from the year 1910 to 1950.

Milk bottles are collected by size: gill (quarter pint), half pint, ten ounces (third of a quart), pint, quart, half gallon (two quarts), and gallon.

Paper cartons first appeared in the early 1920s and 30s and achieved popularity after 1950. The late 1950s witnessed the arrival of plastic bottles. Today, few dairies use glass bottles.

References: John Tutton, *Udderly Beautiful: A Pictorial Guide to the Pyroglazed or Painted Milk Bottle*, published by author, no date; John Tutton, *Udderly Delightful: Collecting Milk Bottles & Related Items*, published by author, 1994.

Newsletter: *The Udder Collectibles,* HC73 Box 1, Smithville Flats, NY 13841

Collectors' Club: National Assoc of Milk Bottle Collectors, Inc, 4 Ox Bow Rd, Westport, CT 06880.

Becky's Milky Way Dairy, Marshfield, MO, "Milky Way
   is Healthy Way," round, red pyroglaze, 1 qt **$40.00**
Ben Jansing Farm Dairy, Licking Pike, Newport, KY,
   image of family on reverse, round, red pyroglaze, 1 qt **40.00**
Brown's Dairy, Buckhannon, WV, square, brown
   pyroglaze **15.00**
Charlotte Dale Dairy Farm, "Reg Guernseys, Visitors
   Always Welcome," round, brown and orange
   pyroglaze, 1 pt **35.00**
Cloverleaf Dairy, Everett, WA, squat, poem on back,
   green pyroglaze, 1 qt **30.00**
Collier Bros Creamery, Martinville, IN, emb, 1 qt **30.00**
Crescent Milk, Reno, NV, orange pyroglaze, ½ pt **15.00**
Deseret LDS Church Welfare Plan, Salt Lake City &
   Ogden, UT, square, orange pyroglaze **20.00**
Elkhorn Farm, Watsonville, elk and "Elkhorn Farm Dairy
   Prod Phone 224, Reg Cal," round, orange pyroglaze,
   ¼ pt **50.00**
Ennes Dairy, H Zupke, Greely, CO, round, black
   pyroglaze, 1 qt **35.00**
George Benedick's Jersey & Guernsey Milk, Mobile, AL,
   emb, 1 pt **25.00**
Katahdin Creamery, Caribou and Fort Fairfield, ME,
   green pyroglaze, 1 qt **30.00**
Kendig Dairy, Millersville, PA, square, green, 1 qt **40.00**
Lake City Farm, Marion, NC, Grade A Milk **12.00**
Lobdell's Dairy Inc, Fairfield, CT, square, yellow
   pyroglaze **15.00**
Maple Leaf Dairy, Gardner, IL, "US Needs Us Strong" on
   reverse, round, maroon pyroglaze, 1 qt **50.00**
McWilliams Pure Milk Co, Sheffield, AL, "Phone 2702" **12.00**

Bangor Sanitary Dairy, Bangor, PA, emb label, ½ pt, $12.00. Photo courtesy Ray Morykan Auctions.

Model Dairy, Pueblo, CO, "Golden Cream" image of barn, round, orange pyroglaze, 1 qt **40.00**

Moons Farm, Catterall, England, red and blue pyroglaze, 1 pt **20.00**

Orchard Farms, Patchogue, LI, calf and "Oh Boy Do I Feel Fine," orange pyroglaze **24.00**

Pine Grove Dairy, Skaneateles, NY pine trees on reverse, round, green and orange pyroglaze, 1 qt **30.00**

Pinewood Dairy, Flagstaff, AZ, round, orange pyroglaze, 1 qt **35.00**

Rosedale Dairy, Silver City, NM, red pyroglaze, 1 pt **20.00**

Sanitary Dairy Co, Waynesburg, PA, squat, orange pyroglaze, 1 qt **25.00**

Smith & Cutbush Dairy, Ballston Spa, NY, red pyroglaze **15.00**

Spurlin Grade A Dairy, Carlsbad, NM, square, orange pyroglaze **20.00**

Superior Dairy, Hagerstown, MD, "Safe For Babies" on back, emb cream top **15.00**

Sykes Farms, Canton, NY, large baseball player, round, red pyroglaze, 1 qt **30.00**

Wauregan Dairy, WT Burns, poem on back, red and black pyroglaze **75.00**

MILK GLASS

Opaque white glass, also known as milk glass, enjoyed its greatest popularity in the period immediately prior to World War I when firms such as Atterbury, Challinor-Taylor, Flaccus, and McKee made a wide range of dinnerware, figural, household, kitchenware, and novelty forms. Despite the decline in popularity of milk glass during the 1920s, several manufacturers continued its production, especially for kitchenware and decorative novelty items.

Milk glass enjoyed a brief renaissance extending from the early 1940s through the early 1960s. Most milk glass offered for sale in today's market dates after 1940 and was produced by Fenton, Imperial, Kemple, and Westmoreland.

References: Frank Chiarenza and James Slater, *The Milk Glass Book,* Schiffer Publishing, 1998; Everett Grist, *Covered Animal Dishes,* Collector Books, 1988, 2000 value update; Betty and Bill Newbound, *Collector's Encyclopedia of Milk Glass,* Collector Books, 1995, 2000 value update.

Collectors' Club: National Milk Glass Collectors Society, 46 Almond Dr, Hershey, PA 17033.

Note: For more information and additional listings see Fenton, Imperial, Kemple, and Westmoreland. All items listed are white unless noted otherwise.

Ashtray, bare foot, 4³/₄" l **$12.00**
Ashtray, grape leaf, Consolidated **8.00**
Bottle, Merry Mouse, Avon, 3¹/₂" h **4.00**
Bowl, cov, Randolph, Fostoria, 9³/₄ x 8¹/₄" **30.00**
Bowl, handled, Daisy Ray, 8 x 4³/₄" **15.00**
Bud Vase, 5³/₄" h **5.00**
Butter, cov, child's, Wild Rose **70.00**
Candlestick, dolphin, 9¹/₄" h. **40.00**
Candlestick, pineapple, Indiana Glass **8.00**
Candlestick, swirl, blue, miniature **10.00**
Compote, Daisy and Button, petticoat edge, 6 x 6" **25.00**
Compote, lacy edge, Imperial, 6¹/₂ x 5¹/₂" **15.00**

Compote, Vinelf pattern, Imperial, 8¹/₂" h **55.00**
Cookie Jar, quilted pattern, 8" h **25.00**
Cookie Jar, tufted pillow, Con-Cora Line, Consolidated, green ivy dec, gold highlights, 8¹/₂" h **65.00**
Covered Animal Dish, fox, diamond basket base, Kemple, 5³/₄" h **100.00**
Covered Animal Dish, Irish Setter, Vallerysthal, 6¹/₂" h **200.00**
Covered Animal Dish, lion, lace edge, Westmoreland **125.00**
Covered Animal Dish, rabbit, split rib base, Kemple **65.00**
Covered Animal Dish, standing rooster on log, Kanawha, blue, 9³/₄" h. **40.00**
Creamer and Sugar, flat diamond, 2¹/₄" h **18.00**
Creamer and Sugar, Hobnail, 2¹/₄" h. **18.00**
Dish, cov, coach, LE Smith, 5 x 4¹/₄" **75.00**
Dish, cov, pie wagon, Imperial, caramel slag, 5" h **165.00**
Dish, lady and fan, Fenton, gold dec, 7" **45.00**
Dresser Box, emb girl and doll on lid, 3⁷/₈" d **15.00**
Figure, Madonna, Fenton, 7" h. **15.00**
Figure, Santa face, flat back, Mosser, red, and black **10.00**
Figure, swan, open, LE Smith, 9" l **35.00**
Fruit Bowl, Monroe, Fostoria, 1960s, 10⁵/₈" d **25.00**
Honey Jar, cov, Jeannette, pink **30.00**
Jar, cov, Santa Claus, Fostoria, red trim, 9¹/₂" h **350.00**
Lamp, dancing couple, 7⁵/₈" h **35.00**
Match Safe, butterfly **25.00**
Match Safe, Indian Chief **60.00**
Mug, child's, bird and wheat **5.00**
Pin Tray, cov, lion, 4³/₄ x 3¹/₂" **10.00**
Pipe, Uncle Sam, Avon **8.00**
Plate, Petalware, MacBeth-Evans, fruits dec **15.00**
Powder Jar, colonial lady, Akro Agate, blue. **40.00**
Relish Dish, apple, Imperial, 9¹/₂ x 9" **25.00**
Salt and Pepper Shakers, pr, bird, handled **75.00**
Salt and Pepper Shakers, pr, owl **300.00**
Shaker, Flower Sprig, 3" h **20.00**
Snack Set, Grape, Indiana **10.00**

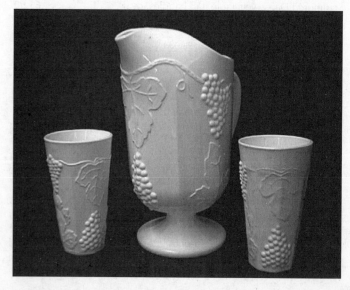

Beverage Set, vintage pattern, 10³/₄" h pitcher and ten 5⁷/₈" h tumblers, white, **$75.00.** Photo courtesy Ray Morykan Auctions.

Vase, Hobnail pattern, #3952, Fenton, white, 1960s, 4" h, $10.00. Photo courtesy Ray Morykan Auctions.

Sugar, cov, Cactus, 6 1/8" h 20.00
Sugar, cov, child's, lamb, Boyd Crystal Art Glass, pink 135.00
Toothpick Holder, 3 swans, Westmoreland, 2 3/8" h 25.00
Toothpick Holder, frog with shell 50.00
Torte Plate, Roses, Imperial, 12" d 25.00
Tumbler, Jenny Lind, Fostoria, 4 1/2" h 20.00
Vase, Grape, oil lamp shape, Imperial, 7 1/4" h 20.00
Wall Pocket, whisk broom, Imperial, 7 1/2" l 35.00

MODEL KITS

Model kits break down into three basic types: (1) wood, (2) plastic, and (3) cast resin. Scratch-built wooden models, whether from magazine plans or model kits, achieved widespread popularity in the 1930s. Airplanes were the most popular form. Because of the skill levels involved, these were built primarily by teenagers.

England's 1/72 Frog Penguin kits of the mid-1930s were the first plastic model kits. After 1945, manufacturers utilized the new plastic injection molding process developed during World War II to produce large quantities of plastic model kits. Automobile model kits quickly replaced airplanes as the market favorite.

Model kits are sold by scale with 1/48, 1/72, and 1/144 among the most common. By the 1960s, some model kit manufacturers introduced snap-together models. The 1970s oil crisis significantly reduced production. However, the market fully recovered by the mid-1980s. While vehicles still dominate model kit sales, monster and other personality kits have gained in popularity.

Resin model kits are designed for the adult market. Gruesome monsters, scantily dressed women, and fantasy creatures abound.

Box art influences the value of a model kit, especially when the cover art is more spectacular than the assembled model. Surprisingly, collectors prefer unassembled models. If the model is assembled, its value declines by 50% or more.

References: Bill Bruegman, *Aurora: History and Price Guide, 3rd Edition,* Cap'n Penny Productions, 1996; Bill Coulter, *Stock Car Model Kit: Encyclopedia and Price Guide,* Krause Publications, 1999; Bill Coulter and Bob Shelton, *The Directory of Old and New Model Car Kits by American Manufacturers 1/24–1/25,* published by authors, 1999; Gordon Dutt, *Collectible Figure Kits of the 50's, 60's & 70's,* Gordy's KitBuilders Magazine, 1995; Thomas Graham, *Greenberg's Guide to Aurora Model Kits,* Kalmbach Books, 1998; Rick Polizzi, *Classic Plastic Model Kits,* Collector Books, 1996.

Periodical: *KitBuilders Magazine,* Box 201, Sharon Center, OH 44274.

Collectors' Club: Kit Collectors International, PO Box 38, Stanton, CA 90680.

1925 Model T Ford, AMT, 3 in 1 . . . . $50.00
Alfa Romeo, Aurora, 1963, NMIB 45.00
American Airlines Boeing 707 Astrop Jet, Aurora, 1965, MISB 55.00
American Astronaut, Aurora, #409-100, 1067, MISB 75.00
B-17 Flying Fortress, Monogram, 1975 . . . . 30.00
B-24 Liberator, Revell, #H218-98, Pre "S," 1954 . . . . 65.00
Babe Ruth, Aurora, #862-198 . . . . 375.00
Baja Beast Street 'N Beach, Monogram, MISB 40.00
Batman, Aurora, comic scenes, MISB 55.00
Big Frankie, Aurora 1,500.00
Black Falcon Pirate Ship, Aurora, 1972, MIB 65.00
Black Fury, Aurora, 1959, MIB 75.00
Blue Jays, Addar, #250, MIB 15.00
Blue Nose Schooner, Aurora, NMIB, 1957 . . . . 40.00
Buck Rogers Marauder, Monogram, MISB 20.00
Camaro SS 396, AMT, #T292-200, 1969 . . . . 40.00
Charlie's Angels Van, Revell, MISB 45.00
Chevy Convertible, AMT, 3 in 1, #77760, 1960 . . . . 100.00
Chinese Mandarin, Aurora, MIB 45.00
Chitty Chitty Bang Bang, Aurora, #838-300, MISB 155.00
Comic Scenes Lone Ranger, Aurora, MIB 50.00
Comic Scenes Tonto, Aurora, MIB 35.00
Creature from the Black Lagoon, Aurora 400.00
Creature from the Black Lagoon, Monogram, #6490, MISB 20.00
Cro-Magnon Man, Aurora, 1971 . . . . 60.00
Cro-Magnon Woman, Aurora, 1971, MISB 60.00
Custom C-Cab Street Rod "Outcast," MPC, 1981, MIB 40.00
Cutty Sark 72, Aurora, MISB 30.00
Dempsey vs Firpo, Aurora, #861 . . . . 50.00
Dick Tracy, Aurora, #818, MISB 125.00
Dick Tracy Space Coupe, Aurora, MISB 225.00
Douglas Skyhawk, Revell, #H719, Famous Artist Series, 1961 . . . . 15.00
Dracula, Aurora 350.00

2 in 1 Dragster "Exterminator," Lindberg, 1964, $250.00.

Robotech 2 in 1, Revell, 1964, $200.00.

Dracula, Monogram **40.00**
Dukes of Hazzard General Lee, MPC, MIB. **25.00**
Ecto 1A Ghostbusters II, AMT, MISB. **30.00**
F-86 Sabre Superkit, Monogram, #T5, 1952 . . . . **40.00**
First Lunar Landing 25th Anniversary Kit, Monogram,
   MIB **20.00**
Flying Saucer, Aurora **150.00**
Gangbusters '32 Chrysler Imperial, MPC, MIB **25.00**
Gemini Astronaut, Revell, large version, 1967, NMIB **90.00**
George Washington, Aurora, 1965, NMIB **125.00**
George Washington Sub, Revell, #H365-198, 1958 . . . . **45.00**
Giant Wooly Mammoth, Monogram, #6075, MISB **20.00**
Glow-in-the-Dark UFO, Lindberg, MIB **20.00**
Godzilla, 1/350 scale, Bandai, 1980s, MIB **20.00**
Green Beret, Aurora, #413-98, 1966 . . . . **150.00**
Hang Out Touchdown, AMT, #T614, 1960s **15.00**
Hunchback Glow, Aurora, 1972 . . . . **75.00**
Hunchback of Notre Dame, Aurora, Anthony Quinn box . . . **275.00**
Invaders Flying Saucer, Aurora. **140.00**
Jaguar XJS, Revell, snap together, 1979. . . . . **25.00**
Jaguar XK120 Roadster, Aurora, 1961. . . . . **35.00**
Jaws, Scenes in a Bottle, Addar, MISB. **100.00**
Jeb Allen's Praying Mantis T/F Dragster, Revell, 1974,
   MISB **90.00**
Jerry West Great Moments in Sports, Aurora, NMIB. **200.00**
John F Kennedy, Aurora, #815-149, 1965. . . . . **150.00**
John Travolta Firebird, Revell, MISB **35.00**
King Kong Glow, Aurora, 1972, MISB. **190.00**
Land of the Giants Snake Scene, Aurora, NMIB **400.00**
Leonardo DaVinci Moveable Crane, AMT, MISB. **35.00**
Lotus Checkered Flag Series, 1/25 scale, AMT, NMIB **55.00**
Madame Tussaud's Chamber of Horrors Guillotine,
   Aurora **650.00**
Mork & Mindy Jeep, Monogram, MISB. **35.00**
Mr Spock with Snake, AMT, #S956, horizontal box,
   1968. . . . . **70.00**
Mummy Glow, Aurora, 1972, MISB **75.00**
Mustang Fastback 65, AMT, NMIB **35.00**
Outlaw Mustang Horse, Addar, #200, 1975, MISB **40.00**
PBM-5 Mariner, Revell, #H258-98, "S" kit, 1957 . . . . **75.00**

Raiders of the Lost Ark Desert Chase, MPC, MIB. **35.00**
Rampaging Scorpion, AMT/Ertl, MISB **15.00**
Ratfink's Mother's Worry 1963 Roadster, Revell, NMIB **115.00**
Red Knight, Aurora, 1963, MIB **60.00**
Return of the Saint Jaguar XI, Revell. **25.00**
Robert E Lee, Revell, #H328-198, "S" kit **50.00**
Robin the Boy Wonder, Aurora, MIB **175.00**
Roman Birena Warship, Aurora, 1967, NMIB **65.00**
Sabre-Tooth, Aurora, pre-historic scene, 1971. . . . . **35.00**
Sea View, Aurora. **450.00**
Sopwith Camel, Revell, large scale, 1965. . . . . **45.00**
Superman, Aurora, #185, 1974, MISB **40.00**
Surf Woody, AMT, NMIB **65.00**
Thunderbirds Secret Base, IMAI, 1980s, MIB **75.00**
Tonto, Aurora, #183, 1974, MISB. **40.00**
Tyrannosaurus Rex, 1/13 scale, Monogram, 1977 . . . . **45.00**
V-156 German U-Boat, Aurora, 1972, NMIB **35.00**
Warlord TransAm, MPC, NMIB **35.00**
Willie Mays, Aurora, #860-98 . . . . **225.00**
WWI Albatross D3 Plane, Aurora, 1956, NMIB **40.00**

MODERNISM

Art Deco is one of the most misused attributions in the current antiques market for both furniture and decorative arts. More than half the Art Deco pieces actually should be attributed to Modernism, a movement little understood by collectors and dealers.

Modernism continued and expanded upon the design style advances of the Arts and Crafts Movement. Perhaps it is easier to understand Modernism by viewing it as Machine Modern, a design period when functionalism and carefully reasoned design were dominant. Architects provided the motivating force for much of the design.

Modernism began in Germany, spreading to the United States in the late 1920s and 30s. Modernist furniture of the 1920s rejected decoration and relied heavily on the use of glass and steel. The 1930s were a decade of eclecticism. Surrealistic furniture enjoyed a brief vogue.

Part of the difficulty involved in understanding Modernism is that the term is used to describe the movement as a whole as well as one of the major components. Establishing a mental decade chronology can help keep the sequence of events straight. International Modernism, the first period, covers the period of conception (1900s through World War I) and the period when the movement was centered in Germany (1920s). Modernism is the period when many of the German designers fled Germany and moved to England and the United States (1930s). After World War II, Modernism reached its zenith in the Contemporary Style (1945 through 1960s) that enjoyed great popularity in the United States. The 1970s Neo-Modernism was a brief attempt to rechannel the movement. Current scholarship continues to refine these basic divisions.

Modernist pieces are listed in their specialized collecting categories. This introduction provides a brief introduction to this important post-1920 design style.

Reference: Marianne Aav, et al., *Finnish Modern Design*, Bard Graduate Center for Studies in the Decorative Arts and Yale University Press, 1998.

Periodicals: *Echoes*, PO Box 155, Cummaquid, MA 02637; *The Modernism Magazine*, 333 N Main St, Lambertville, NJ 08530.

MONROE, MARILYN

Marilyn Monroe was born Norma Jean Mortenson in Los Angeles, California, on June 1, 1926. An illegitimate child, Marilyn spent her early years in a series of foster homes. She was only 16 when she married Jim Doughtery on June 19, 1942. While Jim was in the Merchant Marines, a photographer discovered Marilyn. She soon found work with the Blue Book Modeling Studio.

After a brief flirtation with the movies in 1947-48, Marilyn found herself without a contract. Her life changed dramatically after Tom Kelley's "Golden Dreams" photograph appeared in magazines and calendars across the nation in 1950. By March, Marilyn had signed a seven-year film contract with MGM. In 1953 *How to Marry a Millionaire* and *Gentlemen Prefer Blondes* turned Marilyn into a superstar. *Bus Stop* (1956), *Some Like It Hot!* (1959), and *The Misfits* (1961) are considered among her best films.

Divorced from Doughtery, Marilyn married Joe DiMaggio in January 1951. Divorce followed in October 1954. Her marriage to Arthur Miller in June 1956 ended in 1961 following an affair with Yves Montand. The threat of mental illness and other health problems depressed Marilyn. She died on August 5, 1962, from an overdose of barbiturates.

References: Denis C. Jackson, *The Price & ID Guide to Marilyn Monroe, 3rd Edition*, TICN, 1996; Clark Kidder, *Marilyn Monroe Collectibles*, Avon, 1999; Clark Kidder, *Marilyn Monroe: Cover to Cover*, Krause Publications, 1999; Dian Zillner, *Hollywood Collectibles: The Sequel*, Schiffer Publishing, 1994.

Book, *Marilyn*, Norman Mailer, 270 pp, hard cov, 1973 . . . . **$55.00**
Book, *My Story*, Milton H Greene, Stein & Day, 144 pp **20.00**
Book, *Seven Year Itch*, paperback, 1955 . . . . **30.00**
Calendar, 1954, glossy nude photo **150.00**
Calendar, 1956, full color photos, 8 x 14" **200.00**
Lapel Pin, metal, Monroe in 1-pc red bathing suit, dated
 1953 on back **40.00**
Limited Edition Plate, Forever, Marilyn, Marilyn by
 Milton H Greene: Up Close and Personal Series,
 Bradford Exchange, 1997 . . . . **35.00**

Limited Edition Plate, *How to Marry a Millionaire*, 20th
 Century Fox, Marilyn–An American Classic Series,
 Royal Orleans **35.00**
Limited Edition Plate, *River of No Return*, Marilyn
 Monroe Collection Series, Delphi, 1992 . . . . **65.00**
Lobby Card, *The Seven Year Itch*, #8, 1955 . . . . **40.00**
Magazine, *Focus*, Jun 1954 . . . . **25.00**
Magazine, *Movieland's Annual*, 1954 . . . . **75.00**
Magazine, *Movie Secrets*, Feb 1955 . . . . **25.00**
Magazine, *Movie World*, 1953 . . . . **75.00**
Magazine, *People Today*, Jun 18, 1952 . . . . **40.00**
Magazine, *Photo*, Jun 1954 . . . . **25.00**
Magazine, *Redbook*, Sep 13, 1953 . . . . **75.00**
Magazine, *See*, Nov 1954, 52 pp, 10¼ x 13" **75.00**
Magazine, *Tempo*, Aug 31, 1953, Monroe and
 DiMaggio article **50.00**
Magazine, *That Girl Marilyn*, 1953 . . . . **50.00**
Newspaper, *Chicago Sun Times*, Aug 6, 1962, "Marilyn
 Monroe Dies of Drug Overdose" **80.00**
Photograph, Monroe wearing white bathing suit and
 lying in sand as surf comes in, taken by Sam Shaw,
 black and white, matted, 11¼ x 17" **450.00**
Playing Cards, double deck, nude pose on red drapery
 on backs, orig velveteen finished box, 1950s **100.00**
Postcard, glossy, full color photo of Monroe in white
 robe against green ground, inscription "Marilyn
 Monroe Stars in 20th Century-Fox's Gentlemen Prefer
 Blondes," reverse with repeated inscription and
 stamping for "Midway Theatre," c1953, 3½ x 5½",
 unused **15.00**
Poster, *Facciamo L'Amore*, 20th Century Fox **20.00**
Poster, *River of No Return*, 1954, 22 x 28" **100.00**
Pressbook, *All About Eve*, Fox Studio, 1950 . . . . **75.00**
Pressbook, *Bus Stop*, 1956 . . . . **50.00**
Pressbook, *Some Like It Hot*, United Artists, 1959 . . . . **100.00**
Puzzle, Marilyn Star Puzzle, #82, Alpsco, Adult Leisure
 Products, Locust Valley, NY, 300 pcs, round, metal
 film-type canister **30.00**
Record Jacket, *Some Like It Hot*, Ascot, 1964 . . . . **75.00**
Sheet Music, *My Heart Belongs to Daddy*, 1938 . . . . **30.00**
Sheet Music, *There's No Business Like Show Business* **35.00**

Pocketknife, Colonial Jack Knife, photo under clear plastic handle, $5.00.

MONSTERS

Animal monsters played a major role in the movies from the onset. King Kong is the best known of the pre-1945 genre. The Japanese monster epics of the 1950s introduced Godzilla, a huge reptile monster. Godzilla, his foes, and imitators are all very collectible. The 1950s also saw the introduction of a wide range of animal monsters with human characteristics, e.g., the Creature From the Black Lagoon and numerous werewolf variations.

Early film makers were well aware of the ability of film to horrify. Dracula, Frankenstein, and the Mummy have been the subjects of dozens of films.

The Addams Family and The Munsters introduced a comedic aspect to monsters. This was perpetuated by the portrayal of monsters on Saturday-morning cartoon shows. The chainsaw-wielding mentally deranged villains of the 1960s to the present are a consequence of this demystification of the monster.

After a period of speculation in monster material from the mid-1980s through the early 1990s, market prices now appear to have stabilized.

References: Dana Cain, *Collecting Godzilla Memorabilia,* Antique Trader Books, 1998; Dana Cain, *Collecting Japanese Movie Monsters,* Antique Trader Books, 1998; Dana Cain, *Collecting Monsters of Film and TV,* Krause Publications, 1997; Sean Linkenback, *An Unauthorized Guide to Godzilla Collectibles,* Schiffer Publishing, 1998; John Marshall, *Collecting Monster Toys,* Schiffer Publishing, 1999.

Periodical: *Toy Shop,* 700 E State St, Iola, WI 54990.

Bride of Frankenstein, costume, Collegeville, 1980 . . . . **$40.00**
Bride of Frankenstein, model kit, Mad Lab **15.00**
Bride of Frankenstein, movie poster, *Bride of Frankenstein/ Son of Frankenstein,* 1953 . . . . **200.00**
Creature From the Black Lagoon, charm, red plastic, black image with red accent on lips and claws, bright green ground, 1" h. **10.00**
Creature From the Black Lagoon, costume, Ben Cooper, 1973 . . . . **40.00**
Creature From the Black Lagoon, flicker ring, silver base, 1960s **40.00**
Creature From the Black Lagoon, trading card, Creature Feature wrapper, Topps, 1980. . . . . **1.00**
Dracula, flicker ring, silver base, 1960s **35.00**
Dracula, game, I Van to Bite Your Finger, Hasbro, 1981. . . . . **20.00**
Dracula, magazine, *Dracula Classic,* Eerie Publications, 1976. . . . . **15.00**
Dracula, model kit, glow version, Aurora, 1965 . . . . **250.00**
Dracula, model kit, Luminators, Revell/Monogram, 1991 . . . . **10.00**
Dracula, movie poster, *Dracula,* 1-sheet, re-release, 1951 . . . . **1,000.00**
Dracula, movie poster, *Son of Dracula,* 1-sheet, 1943 . . . . **1,000.00**
Dracula, paint by number set, Hasbro, 1963 . . . . **165.00**
Dracula, pinback button, "Hi Fiend," light green, purple, and red Dracula-like creature with fangs on black ground **10.00**
Frankenstein, action figure, #1, AHI, 1973, 8" h **75.00**
Frankenstein, action figure, plastic, Palmer Plastic, 1963, 3" h. **20.00**
Frankenstein, costume, Ben Cooper, 1963 . . . . **60.00**
Frankenstein, model kit, Big Frankie, Gigantic Frankenstein, Aurora, 1964 . . . . **700.00**
Frankenstein, movie poster, *Ghost of Frankenstein,* 3-sheet, 1942 . . . . **2,000.00**
Frankenstein, pinback button, "Monsters Need Love Too," black and white cartoon Frankenstein image holding flower on orange ground, black bats and spider accents, Norcross Inc, 1970s **10.00**
Frankenstein, windup, litho tin, Marx, 1960, 6" h **150.00**
Godzilla, magazine, *Famous Monsters,* #135 . . . . **10.00**
Godzilla, model kit, Lindberg, 1995 . . . . **4.00**
Godzilla, poster, King Kong vs Godzilla, 1-sheet, Japanese, style B **550.00**
Hunchback of Notre Dame, action figure, removable clothes, Lincoln International, 1975, 8" h **85.00**
Invisible Man, model kit, Dark Horse **100.00**
Invisible Man, movie poster, *The Invisible Man's Revenge,* 1-sheet, 1944 . . . . **200.00**
Mummy, costume, Ben Cooper, 1973 . . . . **15.00**
Mummy, model kit, glow version, Aurora, 1969 . . . . **25.00**
Mummy, model kit, Mummy's Chariot, 1965 . . . . **250.00**
Mummy, movie poster, *The Mummy's Curse,* 1-sheet, 1944. . . . . **800.00**

The Mutant, drinking glass, Universal Monsters, $160.00. Photo courtesy *Collector Glass News.*

Mummy, pinback button, "Meet My Mummy," bright yellow bandages against black coffin design and dark pink ground **10.00**
Phantom of the Opera, game, Phantom of the Opera Mystery Game, Hasbro, 1963 . . . . **175.00**
Phantom of the Opera, magazine, *Famous Monsters,* #3 . . . . **250.00**
Phantom of the Opera, model kit, Horizon, 1988 . . . . **40.00**
Wolfman, flicker ring, blue base, 1960s **35.00**

MOORCROFT POTTERY

After extensive study that included classes at the Wedgwood Institute, Royal College of Art, and British Museum and an initial career at James Macintyre & Company in Burselm, William Moorcroft built a new state-of-the-art pottery, the Washington Works, in Burselm in 1913. Enlargements followed in 1915 and 1919.

Initially, Moorcroft produced pieces that featured simple, bold designs, often incorporating dark colored exotic flowers. In 1928 Moorcroft received a Royal Warrant. A few years later the company introduced its flambe glaze. New decorative motifs, e.g., birds, boats, fish, and fruit, joined the line in the 1930s.

William Moorcroft died in 1945 and was succeeded by his son, Walter. In the 1950s Walter expanded the line by adding Caribbean and marine life motifs and a more dramatic use of color in traditional designs. The use of flambe glaze continued until 1973. Liberty & Co., who helped finance Moorcroft, ended its joint share-ownership in 1961.

In 1984 John, Walter's brother, became managing director and a controlling interest in the first was sold to three Roper brothers. They sold within two years to a consortium of the Dennis and Edwards families. Walter retired in 1987.

Reference: Susan and Al Bagdade, *Warman's English & Continental Pottery & Porcelain, 3rd Edition,* Krause Publications, 1998.

Bowl, squeezebag dec in waving corn pattern on celadon ground, ftd, stamped "Moorcroft" and sgd in ink, 4 x 9" **$700.00**

Box, cov, Anemone pattern, shallow rect form, mauve, blue, and green glossy glaze on green ground, imp "Moorcroft" on base, printed Royal paper label under cover, 2" h, 3½" w, 4⅞" l 150.00

Box, cov, Pansy pattern, round squat form, shades of mauve, purple, and green glossy glaze on cobalt blue ground, imp "Moorcroft" under cover and on base, c1930, 4" h, 6" d 400.00

Box, Pomegranate pattern, circular squat form, mauve, purple, and green glossy glaze on cobalt blue ground, imp facsimile signature, "Potter to H.M. The Queen," and painted initials, 4" h, 6" d 575.00

Compote, Wisteria pattern, circular ftd bowl with flared rim, yellow, green, and purple glossy glaze on cobalt blue ground, imp "Moorcroft" with painted signature on base, c1925, 3⅝" h, 11" d 550.00

Perfume Bottle, lavender and yellow pansies on cobalt ground, hallmarked silver cap, unsgd, 2 x 1¾" 650.00

Table Lamp, elongated tapered oval form, low relief cascading grapes and pomegranates, shades of purple and mauve against cobalt blue ground, 2-socket gilt-metal fixture and base, 20½" h 975.00

Vase, bulbous, extended flared neck, blue-red flowers and light green leaves on green shading to dark blue ground, imp "Moorcroft," paper label, 5¼" h 225.00

Vase, Fish pattern, oval form, flared rim, fish and seaweed dec in shades of yellow, orange, and green against shaded orange and blue flambé ground, imp Moorcroft mark and painted initials, c1930, 7¼" h 3,675.00

Vase, Florian Ware, Poppy pattern, blue flowers and green leaves over white glaze, script signature and McIntyre stamp, 6½ x 3" 50.00

Vase, Florian Ware, Violet pattern in yellow, blue, and celadon glossy glaze, script signature, 9 x 3¾" 875.00

Vase, Orchid pattern, tapered oviform, flared rim, shades of mauve, purple, yellow, and green glossy glaze on cobalt blue ground, imp facsimile signature, painted Walter Moorcroft initials and stamped "Potter to H.M. The Queen," c1947, 6¼" h 525.00

Vase, Wisteria pattern, ruby flambé glaze, stamped "Moorcroft/Made In England" and script signature, 14¼ x 6" 4,675.00

Vase, Wisteria pattern, purple, mauve, and yellow blossoms on cobalt blue ground, imp factory mark, painted signature, mid-20th C, 9¾" h, $4,000.00.

MORGANTOWN GLASS

In 1903 the Morgantown Glass Works (West Virginia), founded in 1899, changed its name to the Economy Tumbler Company which became the Economy Glass Company in 1924. It marketed its products under the "Old Morgantown" label. In 1929 the company reassumed it original name, Morgantown Glass Works.

Morgantown eventually expanded its line to include household and kitchen glass. The company also made blanks for decorating firms. Morgantown is known for several innovative design and manufacturing techniques, e.g., ornamental open stems, iridization, and application of gold, platinum, and silver decoration.

The company became a victim of the Depression, closing in 1937. In 1939 glassworkers and others associated with the company reopened it as the Morgantown Glassware Guild. In 1965 Fostoria purchased the company and continued to produce most of the Morgantown patterns and colors, marketing them under a Morgantown label. Fostoria closed the plant in 1971. In 1972 Bailey Glass Company purchased the factory and used it primarily to make lamp globes.

References: Jerry Gallagher, *A Handbook of Old Morgantown Glass, Vol. I*, published by author, 1995; Jeffrey B. Snyder, *Morgantown Glass From Depression Glass Through the 1960s*, Schiffer Publishing, 1998.

Collectors' Club: Old Morgantown Glass Collectors' Guild, PO Box 894, Morgantown, WV 26507.

Candleholders, pr, Golf Ball, Spanish red and crystal $150.00

Candy Jar, Leora, #7858, Ritz blue, crystal foot and finial, 5½" h 160.00

Champagne, Art Modern, green 50.00

Champagne, Golf Ball, Ritz blue 45.00

Champagne, Plantation, #8445, cobalt 120.00

Cocktail, American Beauty, pink, 3¼ oz 60.00

Cocktail, Chanticleer, crystal 25.00

Cocktail, Golf Ball, red 35.00

Cocktail, Golf Ball, Stiegel green 35.00

Cocktail, Old English, #7678, Stiegel green 30.00

Cordial, Plantation, cobalt 175.00

Dinner Plate, Mexicano Lomax, ice, 9" d 45.00

Finger Bowl, Sunrise Medallion, ftd, crystal 45.00

Goblet, Cynthia, #7659, Sonoma etch, crystal, 10 oz 60.00

Martini Set, Wallace, pitcher and 5 glasses 55.00

Pitcher, Mexicano Lomax, ice 150.00

Plate, Anna Rose, #1500, Bramble Rose etch, 8⅓" d 35.00

Plate, Mexicano Lomax, ice, 7" d 25.00

Sherbet, Golf Ball, red 35.00

Tumbler, American Beauty, crystal, 10 oz, 3¼" 45.00

Vase, Palm Optic, #59, squat, aquamarine, 6" h 135.00

Water Goblet, Adonis, crystal 40.00

Water Goblet, Art Modern, Le Mons, crystal/black 85.00

Water Goblet, Art Modern, star cut, crystal/black 85.00

Water Goblet, Golf Ball, cobalt 45.00

Water Goblet, Golf Ball, red 45.00

Water Goblet, Plantation, cobalt 135.00

Water Set, Melon, #20069, pitcher and six 11 oz tumblers, Ritz blue trim, alabaster 650.00

Wine, Golf Ball, red 45.00

Wine, Old English, #7678, cobalt 65.00

Wine, Plantation, cobalt 165.00

MORTON POTTERIES

Morton, Illinois, was home to several major potteries, all of which trace their origins to six Rapp Brothers who emigrated from Germany in 1877 and established the Morton Pottery Works.

American Art Potteries (1945-1961), Cliftwood Art Potteries (1920-1940), Midwest Potteries, the continuation of Cliftwood (1940-44), Morton Pottery Company (1922-1976), and Morton Pottery Works, also known as Morton Earthenware Company (1877-1917), were all founded and operated by Rapp descendants.

These companies produced a variety of art, household, novelty, and utilitarian pottery. Morton Pottery Company specialized in kitchenwares, novelty items, and steins. In the 1950s they made a variety of TV lamps ranging from animal figures to personality, e.g., Davy Crockett. Under contract to Sears Roebuck, they produced some of the Vincent Price National Treasures reproductions. The American Art Pottery produced a line of wares marketed through floral and gift shops.

Reference: Doris and Burdell Hall, *Morton's Potteries: 99 Years, 1877-1976, Volume II,* L-W Book Sales, 1995.

Midwest Potteries, figurine, crane, 11" h, $30.00.

American Art Potteries, cornucopia vase, feathered dec,
10½" h **$25.00**
American Art Potteries, figurine, wild horse, brown drip,
11½" h **30.00**
American Art Potteries, planter, bunny behind log, 4¾" h **15.00**
American Art Potteries, TV lamp, Afghan hounds, 15" h **45.00**
Cliftwood Art Potteries, candlestick, cobalt blue, 10½" h **25.00**
Cliftwood Art Potteries, dinner plate, apple green, 10" d **20.00**
Cliftwood Art Potteries, figurine, elephant, blue mulberry glaze **50.00**
Cliftwood Art Potteries, grease jar, old rose over white **20.00**
Cliftwood Art Potteries, incense burner, billiken doll, Rockingham brown, 7½" h **55.00**
Cliftwood Art Potteries, lemonade set, pitcher and 6 mugs, Tree Trunk Line, chocolate brown drip **150.00**
Cliftwood Art Potteries, milk jug, chocolate brown drip, small **35.00**
Cliftwood Art Potteries, pretzel jar, barrel shape, cobalt blue **50.00**
Cliftwood Art Potteries, salt and pepper shakers, pr, old rose over pink and white **20.00**
Cliftwood Art Potteries, sweetmeat bowl, green and yellow drip **45.00**
Cliftwood Art Potteries, water pitcher, chocolate brown drip, 7³⁰⁄₄" h **50.00**
Midwest Potteries, cow creamer, 5" h **15.00**
Midwest Potteries, figurine, cockatoo, green and yellow, 8½" h **18.00**
Midwest Potteries, figurine, heron, matte turquoise, 6" h **12.00**
Midwest Potteries, figurine, Irish Setter, natural colors, 4" h, 8" l **30.00**
Midwest Potteries, planter, bird and nest, 6½" h **12.00**
Midwest Potteries, planter, leaping fawn, blue, 8" h **12.00**
Morton Pottery, Amish Pantry Ware, bean pot, 3 qt **45.00**
Morton Pottery, Amish Pantry Ware, jug, blue, 4½ pt **50.00**
Morton Pottery, Amish Pantry Ware, salt and pepper shakers, pr, green, hp dec **25.00**
Morton Pottery, Amish Pantry Ware, water jug **40.00**
Morton Pottery, bank, bulldog **15.00**
Morton Pottery, bank, church **20.00**

Morton Pottery, bookends, pr, parrot, rose, yellow, green, and blue over white **25.00**
Morton Pottery, cookie jar, fruit basket **30.00**
Morton Pottery, cookie jar, turkey **100.00**
Morton Pottery, deviled egg tray, center turkey dec **30.00**
Morton Pottery, figurine, seeing eye dog **18.00**
Morton Pottery, planter, creeping rabbit, 4½" h, 7½" l **12.00**
Morton Pottery, planter, hen **20.00**
Morton Pottery, planter, Scottie dog **10.00**

MOSSER GLASS

The glassmaking art has been passed down through three generation of the Mosser family.

Mosser Glass, Cambridge, Ohio, makes reproductions and copycats of late 19th-and early 20th-centuries glassware as well as figurines and decorative accessories. Daisy and Button, Inverted Thistle, Log Cabin, Rose, Shell, and Thistle are a few of the Mosser reproduction pattern glass patterns.

Bell, Daisy and Button, #145, blue **$5.00**
Bread Plate, Last Supper, #147, cobalt, 5½ x 3½" **6.00**
Butter, cov, Cherry Thumbprint, #141B, crystal **12.00**
Butter, cov, Queen's, #171B, vaseline **12.00**
Creamer, Grape, #151SU, chocolate **15.00**
Creamer and Sugar, Jennifer, #140, apple green **20.00**
Cup Plate, cat, #155, 3½" d **2.00**
Cup Plate, collie, #156, 3½" d **4.00**
Cup Plate, Nursery Rhyme, #136D, set of 4 . . . . **30.00**
Figurine, cat, #194, crystal satin, 2" h, 4" l **6.00**
Figurine, frog, #121, satin **8.00**
Figurine, lion, #184, crystal **8.00**
Figurine, pony, #174, gold krystal **8.00**
Goblet, Rose, #123, cobalt **6.00**
Lamp Holder, Daisy and Button, #183, amethyst **8.00**
Mug, bird, #102, iridescent cobalt, 8 oz **6.00**
Paperweight, Madonna, #195, crystal **8.00**
Pitcher, Inverted Thistle, #179P, red **15.00**

Toothpick, #168, amber, $2.00.

Salt and Pepper Shakers, pr, owl, #154, green 4.00
Salt Dip, Bird, #131, yellow 4.00
Salt Dip, Hen, #112, green opalescent 5.00
Slipper, Rose, #117, iridescent cobalt 6.00
Spoon Holder, Rose, cobalt 8.00
Sugar, Cherry, #132SU, purple carnival 15.00
Sugar Shaker, Inverted Thistle, #179SS, red 20.00
Toothpick, car, #168, green 4.00
Toothpick, stove, #139, green, 2½" h 3.00
Tumbler, Cherry, #132T, purple carnival, 8 oz 8.00
Tumbler, Grape, #151T, iridescent cobalt 8.00
Tumbler, Inverted Thistle, #179D, red 30.00

MOTION LAMPS

A motion lamp is a lamp with animation, usually consisting of a changing scene, which is activitated by the rising heat from the lamp's bulb. There are three basic types: (1) stationary exterior cylinder, revolving interior cylinder; (2) revolving exterior cylinder, stationary interior cylinder; and (3) revolving shade.

Motion lamps first appeared in the 1920s. They disappeared in the early 1960s. Econolite Corporation (Los Angeles, California), L. A. Goodman Manufacturing Company (Chicago, Illinois), Ignition Company (Omaha, Nebraska), Rev-O-Lite (Brunswick, New Jersey), and Scene in Action Company (Chicago, Illinois) were the principal manufacturers.

Reference: Sam and Anna Samuelian, *Collector's Guide to Motion Lamps*, Collector Books, 1998.

Note: All lamps are plastic unless noted otherwise.

1933 Chicago World's Fair, Rev-o-Lite, 1933 . . . . $375.00
1933 Chicago World's Fair, Scene-in-Action, 1933 . . . . 350.00
Advertising, Budweiser Beer, Visual Effects Co, 1970s 75.00
Advertising, Cook's Goldblume Beer, Hal Mfg Co, 1950s 75.00
Advertising, Fireside Toasted Peanuts, 1930s 350.00
Advertising, Phillips 66 Trop-Artic Motor Oil, 1960s 100.00
Autumn, LA Goodman, 1956 . . . . 250.00
Barbershop Pole, LA Goodman, 1950s 200.00
Bayou Boats, Econolite, 1962 . . . . 325.00
Buddha, Scene-in-Action, 1931 . . . . 350.00
Butterfly, Econolite, 1954 . . . . 150.00
Butterflies and Flowers, LA Goodman, 1956 . . . . 200.00
Campfire with Bugler, Gritt, 1920s 275.00

Circus, Econolite, 1958 . . . . 350.00
Dance at Dawn, Rev-o-Lite, 1930s 200.00
Davy Crockett, LA Goodman, 1955 . . . . 400.00
Ducks, Econolite, 1955 . . . . 200.00
Eiffel Tower, Econolite, 1963 . . . . 450.00
Farmhouse, LA Goodman, 1956 . . . . 250.00
Fish in Windows, LA Goodman, 1957 . . . . 175.00
Flames, Scene-in-Action, 1931 . . . . 200.00
Flying Geese, LA Goodman, 1957 . . . . 150.00
Forest Fire, Ignition Co, 1948 . . . . 100.00
Fountains of Rome, Econolite, 1962 . . . . 350.00
Fountains of Versailles, Econolite, 1963 . . . . 350.00
Hawaiian Scene, Econolite, 1959 . . . . 350.00
Indian Chief, Gritt, 1920s 200.00
Indian Maiden, Gritt, 1920s 225.00
Lighthouse, LA Goodman, 1956 . . . . 125.00
Lighthouse at Sunset, National Co, 1930s 300.00
Mallards in Flight, Econolite, 1950s 225.00
Mermaid, Econolite, 1960s 300.00
Miss Liberty, Econolite, 1958 . . . . 350.00
Nature's Splendor, National Co, 1930s 300.00
Niagara Falls, LA Goodman, 1957 . . . . 100.00
Niagara Falls, Scene-in-Action, 1931 . . . . 125.00
Ocean Creatures, LA Goodman, 1955 . . . . 200.00
Oriental Fantasy, LA Goodman, 1957 . . . . 200.00
Oriental Garden, Econolite, 1959 . . . . 350.00
Peacocks, LA Goodman, 1957 . . . . 200.00
Planets, LA Goodman, 1957 . . . . 250.00
Plantation Scene, LA Goodman, 1957 . . . . 200.00
Sailboats, LA Goodman, 1954 . . . . 225.00
Steamboats, Econolite, 1957 . . . . 200.00
Storybook, LA Goodman, 1957 . . . . 250.00
Trains Racing, LA Goodman, 1957 . . . . 150.00
US Leviathan Cruise Ship, Scene-in-Action, 1930s 600.00
Venice Canal, Econolite, 1963 . . . . 350.00
Waterski, Econolite, 1958 . . . . 400.00
White Christmas, Econolite, 1953 . . . . 300.00

Antique Autos, Econolite, $200.00.

MOTORCYCLE COLLECTIBLES

The motorcycle came of age with the dawn of the 20th century. In 1901 Oscar Hedstrom and George Hendee produced the first Indian motorcycles in Springfield, Massachusetts. Indian was quickly challenged by Harley.

The popularizing of the motorcycle followed much the same route as that of the automobile. The Federation of American Motorcyclists was organized in 1903. It became the American Motorcyclist Association in the early 1920s. 1905 to World War I was the golden age of motorcycle racing. Harley and Indian military motorcycles performed yeoman duty in World War I and again in World War II.

Prior to World War I, there were over 300 different motorcycle manufacturers. When Indian ceased production in the early 1950s, Harley-Davidson became the sole remaining American motorcycle manufacturer.

Motorcycle collectibles divide into three basic groups: (1) objects associated with actual motorcycles including sales and promotional material, (2) objects in the shape of motorcycles, e.g., motorcycle toys, and (3) objects featuring the image of a motorcycle. All three groups are heavily collected.

Motorcycle collectibles became a hot ticket item in the mid-1990s. Everything motorcycle, from cast-iron toys to Harley-Davidson showroom signs, experienced price jump multiples. Prices have stabilized, but speculation remains.

References: Michael Dregni, *Harley-Davidson Collectibles,* Town Square Books, Voyageur Books, 1998; Leila Dunbar, *Motorcycle Collectibles* (1996), *More Motorcycle Collectibles* (1997), Schiffer Publishing.

Booklet, *BMW Motorcycle Road Test Report,* 16 pp, inside front cover and 6 pp in English text with black and white photos, remaining pps in German text, back cover with center logo for maker Bayerische Motoren Werke, Munich, 1955, 5³/₄ x 8¹/₄" $25.00

Business Card, Indian Motorcycle dealer, Delavan, WI, 2 x 3³/₄" 25.00

Sign, Harley-Davidson Cycle Oil, porcelain, "Bierman Signs 192 Los Angeles, Chicago, St. Louis" stamped on back, 11" h, 8" w, **$1,750.00.** Photo courtesy Collectors Auction Services.

Catalog, Harley-Davidson Accessories, black and white, 1932, 23 pp, 9" h, 6" w 25.00

Catalog, Spare Parts for Harley-Davidson Motorcycles and Sidecars, 1930 to 1933 models, contains detailed information and photos, 84 pp, 9¹/₄" h, 6¹/₄" w 25.00

Child's Hat, black cloth, white vinyl visor, metal buttons with braid above visor, embroidered Harley-Davidson patch with flying wheel insignia, size 6⁵/₈ 30.00

Hat, black cloth, white plastic visor, metal buttons with braid above visor, embroidered Harley-Davidson winged emblem stitched on front, Harley-Davidson logo screen-printed inside, size 6³/₄ 100.00

Letter Opener, brass, handle mkd "J. Paul Delphey, Harley-Davidson Motorcycles Deluxe Bicycles–Frederick, MD" 50.00

Magazine, *Harley-Davidson Enthusiast,* 1935, black and white photos 25.00

Magazine, *Harley-Davidson Enthusiast,* Jun 1936, 24 pp, black and white photos 25.00

Magazine, *The Enthusiast,* Aug 1957, 24 pp, black and white photos, features Harley-Davidson motorcycles, includes photo of Joe Harley with Joe Leonard and Don Gore 20.00

Oil Can, Harley-Davidson Cycle Oil, Harley-Davidson Motor Co, Milwaukee, WI, unopened, 8 fl oz, 4" h, 2¹/₂" d 150.00

Patch, purple and black twill, "The Rising Sons MC Los Angeles California," embroidered depiction of rising sun and motorcyclist, c1960-70s, 10" d 50.00

Poster, "Cycles Favor Motos, de la belle mécanique!," French, mechanic holding miniature bicycle in 1 hand, motorcycle in other, paper litho with archival backing, sgd "P. Bellenger," 18" h, 27" w 90.00

Record Book, Indian Motorcycle Co, Springfield, MA, vinyl, contains maintenance hints, sidecar pointers, speed table, and other information concerning Indian Motorcycles, 1929, 4¹/₄" h, 2³/₄" w 100.00

Ticket, Tourist Trophy Races, sponsored by Sheboygan Motorcycle Club, May 22, 1938, black on buff, blank reverse, 2¹/₄ x 4" 20.00

Neon Sign, Harley-Davidson Motorcycles, wood, 30" h, 40" w, $950.00. Photo courtesy Collectors Auction Services.

Token, brass, "Indian Motorcycles 1901-1932 World
    Famous," emb Indian, holed at top for key chain,
    reverse shows George Washington with 1932 date **70.00**
Trophy, metal trophy of motorcycle perched on stylized
    eagle wings, mounted on wood base with American
    Motorcycle Association logo on unengraved plate,
    14¹/₂" h, 3¹/₂" w **8.00**

MOVIE MEMORABILIA

This category includes material related to movies and the individuals who starred in them. Movie collectibles divide into two basic groups, silent and sound era. With the exception of posters, material from the silent era is scarce and collected by only a small number of individuals.

Prior to the 1960s movie licensing was limited. Most collectibles are tied to media advertising and theater promotions. This changed with the blockbuster hits of the 1970s and 80s, e.g., the *Star Wars* series. Licensing, especially in the toy sector, became an important method of generating capital for films.

Many collectors focus on a single movie personality. Regional association plays a major role. Many small communities hold annual film festivals honoring local individuals who went on to fame and glory on the silver screen.

Two-dimensional material abounds. Three-dimensional material is scarce. Pizzazz is a value factor—the greater the display potential, the higher the price.

In the 1980s movie studios and stars began selling their memorabilia through New York and West Coast auction houses. Famous props, such as Dorothy's ruby glass slippers from *The Wizard of Oz*, broke the $10,000 barrier.

References: Dana Cain, *Film & TV Animal Star Collectibles*, Antique Trader Books, 1998; Anthony Curtis, *Lyle Film & Rock 'n' Roll Collectibles*, The Berkley Publishing Group, 1996; Ephraim Katz, *The Film Encyclopedia, 2nd Edition*, Harper Collins, 1994; John Kisch (ed.), *Movie Poster Almanac: 1997-98*, Separate Cinema Publications, 1998; David Loehr and Joe Bills, *The James Dean Collectors Guide*, L-W Book Sales, 1999; Robert Osborne, *65 Years of The Oscar: The Official History of The Academy Awards*, Abbeville, 1994; Edward Pardella, *The Judy Garland Collector's Guide*, Schiffer Publishing; Christopher Sausville, *Planet of the Apes*, Schiffer Publishing, 1998; Jay Scarfone and William Stillman, *The Wizard of Oz Collector's Treasury*, Schiffer Publishing, 1992; Moe Wadle, *The Movie Tie-In Book: A Collector's Guide to Paperback Movie Editions*, Nostalgia Books, 1994; Jon R. Warren, *Warren's Movie Poster Price Guide, 4th Edition*, American Collectors Exchange, 1997; Dian Zillner, *Hollywood Collectibles* (1991), *The Sequel* (1994), Schiffer Publishing.

Periodicals: *Big Reel*, PO Box 1050, Dubuque, IA 52004; *Collecting Hollywood Magazine*, PO Box 2512, Chattanooga, TN 37409; *Movie Advertising Collector*, PO Box 28587, Philadelphia, PA 19149; *Movie Collector's World*, 17230 13 Mile Rd, Roseville, MI 48066.

Note: For additional listings see Animation Art, Autographs, Disneyana, Marilyn Monroe, Posters, Shirley Temple, Star Trek, and Star Wars.

Hot Water Bottle, Jayne Mansfield, Poynter Products, 22" h, $250.00. Photo courtesy Collectors Auction Services.

Autograph, Buddy Ebson, DS, receipt from Paramount
    Continental Cafe, blue signature, dated 1953, 3¹/₂ x
    5¹/₂" **$50.00**
Autograph, Dustin Hoffman, PS, black and white, 8 x
    10" **20.00**
Autograph, Spike Lee, TLS, letter to American
    Cinematheque, on Forth Acres and a Mule Filmworks
    letterhead, blue ink signature at bottom, 8¹/₂ x 11" **65.00**
Autograph, Pernell Roberts, DS, Twentieth Century Fox
    contract, green paper, black signature at bottom, 8¹/₂ x
    14" **75.00**
Autograph, Tyrone Power, sgd page from autograph
    book, pink paper, small black and white photo
    attached, center blue ink signature, Walter Huston
    signature on reverse, 6 x 4¹/₄" **55.00**
Book, *Hollywood and the Great Fan Magazines*,
    M Levin, NY, 1st ed, 1970 . . . . **5.00**
Brochure, *Let's Go to the Movies*, #62, Reed Publishing,
    black and white photos, 48 pp, 4 x 6" **12.00**
Certificate, A Loving Tribute to the Memory of Rudolph
    Valentino, multicolored Valentino photo, 1926,
    7 x 11" **15.00**
Cigarette Card, Clark Gable, #46, Park Drive Cigarettes **25.00**
Comic Book, *Dorothy Lamour–Jungle Princess*, #3, Aug
    1950, 36 pp, Hero Books. **25.00**
Cup and Saucer, brown and white 20th Century Fox logo **20.00**
Figure, *Gremlins*, plastic, posable head and arms, Lin
    Toys Ltd, 1984, 6³/₄" h **35.00**
Film, *The King and I*, 16mm, cinemascope, 2 tins with
    shows logo **450.00**
Finger Puppets, The Three Stooges, painted hard plastic
    heads on flexible vinyl finger sleeves, 1950-60s, each
    3³/₄" h **100.00**
Flicker Ring, Three Stooges, "I'm Moe," alternating flicker image on red and yellow ground, mounted on gold
    luster ring base, 1960s. **15.00**
Game, Hollywood Movie-Bingo, Whitman Publishing
    Co, 1937 . . . . **40.00**

Poster, *Dragstrip Girl*, 1957, 41½ x 27", $160.00. Photo courtesy Collectors Auction Services.

Game, James Bond Secret Agent 007, Milton Bradley, 1964 . . . . **25.00**

Game, The Godfather Family, Family Games, 1971 . . . . **45.00**

Game, The Sting Game, Ideal, 1976 . . . . **15.00**

Insert, *Three Little Words,* Fred Astaire, Vera Mills, 1950 . . . . . **25.00**

Lighter, metal, 14K gold plate finish, raised relief caricature image of Bob Hope, Florentine, 1950-60s, 1¼ x 1⅞ x ⅜" **25.00**

Lobby Card, *Cinderfella,* Jerry Lewis Productions Corp, #3, 1960, 11 x 14" **25.00**

Lobby Card, *Miss Tatlock's Millions,* Robert Stack, Dorothy Wood, framed, 1948 . . . . **40.00**

Lobby Card, *Rawhide Rangers,* Universal **15.00**

Lobby Card, *Teenage Monster* **20.00**

Lobby Card, *Yogi Bear,* 1964 . . . . **20.00**

Magazine, *Motion Picture,* Jun 1974 . . . . **8.00**

Magazine, *Movie Play,* Vol 1, #1, Winter 1944 . . . . **20.00**

Magazine, *Screen Secrets,* Aug 1929 . . . . **20.00**

Magazine, *Screen Stories,* Oct 1951 . . . . **12.00**

Magazine, *Story in Pictures,* Frank Sinatra biography, Film Publishing Corp, 1945, 9 x 11¾" **50.00**

Movie Folder, *Son of the Sheik,* Valentino **25.00**

Movie Still, *The Three Stooges in Orbit,* Columbia Pictures, black and white glossy, 1962, 8 x 10", price for set of 6 . . . . **75.00**

Paperback Book, *A Dictionary to the Cinema,* Peter Graham, 1964 . . . . **15.00**

Paperback Book, *Errol and Me,* Signet, 1st ed, 176 pp, Oct 1960, 4¼ x 7" **25.00**

Pin, Lana Turner, diamond, figural angel **675.00**

Pinback Button, "ET Extra-Terrific," white and red, 1¾" d **10.00**

Pinback Button, "Lizabeth Scott A Paramount Star," Quaker Oats Cereal premium, 1940s **15.00**

Pocket Mirror, Elizabeth Taylor, full color photo on green ground surrounded by green celluloid rim, c1950s, 2¼" d **25.00**

Popsicle Coin, aluminum, detailed Johnny Weissmuller portrait on front, reverse with Popsicle name and "MGM Star in *Tarzan and His Mate,*" c1936, ¹⁵⁄₁₆" d **25.00**

Postcard, Jane Wyman, handwritten, sgd, early 1940s **40.00**

Poster, *Angels With Dirty Faces,* Warner Bros, 1-sheet, re-release, 1948, 27 x 41" **50.00**

Poster, *Henry Aldrich–Boy Scout,* Paramount Pictures, 1-sheet, 1944, 27 x 41" **75.00**

Poster, *House on Haunted Hill,* Allied Artists, 1958, 27 x 41" **700.00**

Poster, *Jason and the Argonauts,* Columbia Pictures, 1-sheet, 1963, 27 x 41" **75.00**

Poster, *Let's Go Navy,* Monogram, starring Bowery Boys, full color, 1-sheet, 1951, 27 x 41" **50.00**

Poster, *Old Overland Trail,* Rex Allen, 1952, 27 x 41" **90.00**

Poster, *The Great Rupert,* Pathe Industries, starring Jimmy Durante, Terry Moore, and Tom Drake, 1-sheet, 1950, 27 x 41" **50.00**

Poster, *The Man Who Knew Too Much,* linen, 1956, 41 x 81" **225.00**

Press Book, *Girl Happy,* Elvis Presley, 1965 . . . . **20.00**

Press Book, *Julius Caesar,* Marlon Brando, 16 pp. **15.00**

Program, *My Fair Lady,* Warner Bros, 36 pp, printed in England, 8½ x 11" **25.00**

Salt and Pepper Shakers, pr, Laurel & Hardy, ceramic, separate base, stamped "Beswick/England" **100.00**

Scarf, *Gone With the Wind,* printed fabric, movie title in each corner, c1940 . . . . **175.00**

Sheet Music, *As Time Goes By,* Bogart, Bergman, and Henreid cov, *Casablanca,* 1942 . . . . **100.00**

Sheet Music, *Wait and See,* Judy Garland cov, 1945 . . . . **5.00**

Souvenir Book, *Beau Geste,* 1939, 8 x 11" **20.00**

Souvenir Book, *Funny Girl,* Columbia Pictures, 52 pp, 1968, 8½ x 11" **15.00**

Souvenir Book, *Lawrence of Arabia,* Peter O'Toole **15.00**

Tablet, color cover photo of Elizabeth Taylor as young adult with facsimile signature, 1940s, 5½ x 8¾" **25.00**

Toy, Freddie Fright Squirter, *Nightmare on Elm Street,* Freddie Krueger head as hand puppet with built-in water squirter, Entertech, 1989, MIB **25.00**

Poster, *The Sea of Grass,* Tracy and Hepburn, 1947, 22 x 27½", $50.00. Photo courtesy Collectors Auction Services.

MOXIE

During the height of its popularity, 1920 to 1940, Moxie was distributed in approximately 36 states and even outsold Coca-Cola in many of them. It became so popular that moxie, meaning nervy, became part of the American vocabulary.

Moxie is the oldest continuously produced soft drink in the United States. It celebrated its 100th birthday in 1984. It traces its origin to a Moxie Nerve Food, a concoction developed by Dr. Augustin Thompson of Union, Maine, and first manufactured in Lowell, Massachusetts.

Moxie's fame is due largely to the promotional efforts of Frank Morton Archer, an intrepid entrepreneur endowed with a magnificent imagination. Archer created an advertising campaign as famous as the soda itself. Scarcely an event occurred in the first half of the 20th century that Archer did not exploit. The famous World War I "I Want You For The U.S. Army" Uncle Sam poster has a striking resemblance to the Moxie man pointing at his viewers and commanding them to "Drink Moxie."

Many firms attempted to play upon the Moxie name. Hoxie, Noxie, Proxie, Rixie, and Toxie are just a few. Most of these spurious products were produced in limited quantities, thus making them a prime find for collectors.

Moxie is still produced today, not in New England but Georgia. However, its popularity remains strongest in the Northeast.

Reference: Allan Petretti, *Petretti's Soda Pop Collectibles Price Guide,* Antique Trader Books, 1996.

Collectors' Club: New England Moxie Congress, 445 Wyoming Ave, Millburn, NJ 07041.

Apron, repeated image of man pointing finger above
"Moxie," 1930s **$30.00**
Ashtray, ceramic, man pointing finger and "Drink
Moxie" in center, 1930s. **45.00**
Bottle Bag, waiter holding tray, "Drink Moxie" in circle,
1920s **30.00**
Bottle Carrier, cardboard, 2-bottle, 1940s. **12.00**
Bottle Display, carousel shape, 1950s. **125.00**
Bottle Opener, bowling pin shape, 1930s. **10.00**
Can, aluminum, pull tab, Diet Moxie, Mad About
Moxie, 12 oz **25.00**
Cap, "I've Got Moxie," 1930s **25.00**
Cap, Moxie logo, 1930s **30.00**
Case, wood, 1930s **40.00**
Clock, glass, "Drink Moxie/It's Always A Pleasure…To
Serve You Moxie," 1950s **200.00**
Display Sign, "Half Quart King Size Moxie/2 for 25¢/No
Deposit," 1960s. **25.00**
Display Sign, "Invigorating as an Ocean Breeze 5¢,"
woman wearing cap holding ship's wheel, 1940s **125.00**
Fan, "The Sensible Drink/Drink Moxie," 1925. . . . . **45.00**
Fan, "When the Heat Waves Go Astray/Drink Moxie,"
1950s. **45.00**
Flange Sign, "Drink Moxie," 1940s, 12 x 18" **325.00**
Menu Board, tin, "It's Always A Pleasure… To Serve You
Moxie," 1950s, 20 x 28" **100.00**
Sheet Music, *Moxie Songs,* 1921 . . . . **125.00**
Sign, cardboard, "Ya Gotta Have Moxie," boy wearing
boxing glove holding up bottle, 1960s, 10 x 14" **35.00**
Sign, diecut cardboard, "Drink Moxie," woman pointing
finger, 1920s, 16 x 16". **450.00**

Sign, tin, 1956, 34" h, 44" w, $250.00. Photo courtesy Gary Metz's Muddy River Trading Co.

Sign, diecut cardboard, "Drink Moxie–Distinctively
Different," boy pointing finger, 1930, 15 x 26" **350.00**
Sign, diecut cardboard, "Drink Moxie/Never…Sticky
Sweet," man pointing finger, 1950s, 8¹/₂ x 11". **85.00**
Sign, diecut cardboard, "The Swing is to Moxie," woman
on swing, 1930s, 26 x 40" **500.00**
Sign, diecut cardboard, "He's Got Moxie 5¢," easel
back, smiling boy in baseball uniform holding bottle,
1940s, 8 x 13". **325.00**
Sign, emb tin, "Drink Moxie" above "Distinctively
Different," 20 x 28" **450.00**
Sign, paper, "Drink Moxie," 1930s, 6 x 11" **35.00**
Thermometer, glass, outdoor, "Drink Moxie/It's Always A
Pleasure…To Serve You," 1950s **100.00**
Thermometer, tin, "Drink Moxie/Take home a case
tonight," 1920s **550.00**

MUSICAL INSTRUMENTS

Most older musical instruments have far more reuse than collectible value. Instrument collecting is still largely confined to string and wind instruments dating prior to 1900. Collectors simply do not give a toot about brass instruments. The same holds true for drums unless the drum head art has collectible value.

Celebrity electric guitars is the current hot musical instrument collecting craze. They are standard offering at rock 'n roll auctions held by leading New York and West Coast auction houses. In the 1980s a number of individuals began buying guitars as investments. Prices skyrocketed. Although the market has appeared to stabilize, it should still be considered highly speculative.

From the 1890s through the 1930s, inexpensive student violins marked with a stamp or paper label featuring the name of a famous violin maker—Amati and Stradivarius are just two examples—were sold in quantity. They were sold door to door and by Sears Roebuck. The advertisements claimed that the owner would have a violin nearly equal in quality to one made by the famous makers of the past. The cheap model sold for $2.45, the expensive model for $15. If cared for and played, these student violins have developed a wonderful, mellow tone and have a value in the $150 to $200 range. If damaged, they are $30 to $40 wall hangers.

References: S. P. Fjestad (ed.), *Blue Book of Guitar Values, Third Edition,* Blue Book Publications, 1996; Robert Goudy, *Electric Guitars,* Schiffer Publishing, 1999; Alan Greenwood, *The Official Vintage Guitar Price Guide, 6th Edition,* Vintage Guitar Magazine, 1998; George Gruhn and Walter Carter, *Electric Guitars and Basses: A Photographic History,* Miller Freeman Books, GPI Books, 1994; Paul Trynka (ed.), *The Electric Guitar,* Chronicle Books, 1993.

Periodical: *Vintage Guitar Magazine,* PO Box 7301, Bismarck, ND 58507.

Collectors' Clubs: American Musical Instrument Society, RD 3, Box 205-B, Franklin, PA 16323; Harmonica Collectors International, 741 Cedar Field Ct, Chesterfield, MO 63017.

Banjo, tenor, The Vega Co, Boston, Vegaphone Professional model, nickel plated top tension rim and flange, 28-bracket rim, laminated maple neck with pearl inlay at peghead, bound ebony fingerboard with pearl inlay, maple resonator, dowel stick stamped "Made By The Vega Company Boston Mass USA 85468," laminated pot stamped "85468," with case, c1930, 11" d head. **$525.00**
Cornet, Carl Fisher Cornet, silver, modified shepherd's crook, orig mouthpiece, flat spring missing, no case **100.00**
Cornet, Standar (Vega), Boston, silver, pitch change crook, double split, short lead pipe, mouthpiece. **150.00**
Cornet, Wurlitzer, American, silver, 6 crooks and "C" crook, orig case with accessories **300.00**
Guitar, Fender, Coronado I, semi-hollow body, 1966-70 . . . . **500.00**
Guitar, Gibson, Chet Atkins Classical Electric, rosewood board and single cutaway, 1982-92 . . . . **800.00**
Guitar, Gibson, Les Paul Custom, 2 pickups, 1954-56 . . . . **6,000.00**
Guitar, Gibson, Les Paul Custom, 3 humbuckers, 1957. . . **10,000.00**

Harmonica, Rolomonica, brown Bakelite case, plays music rolls, $150.00.

Guitar, Gibson, Les Paul, The Les Paul, maple top, 2 humbuckers, gold hardware, 1976-78. . . . . **10,000.00**
Guitar, Gibson, Les Paul Standard, cherry, 1963. . . . . **3,500.00**
Guitar, Gibson, Les Paul Studio, mahogany body, 2 humbuckers, 1984-95 . . . . **500.00**
Guitar, Gretsch, Chet Atkins Hollowbody, archtop electric, 1954-55 . . . . **6,500.00**
Guitar, Gretsch, Chet Atkins Nashville, 1964-79 . . . . **1,200.00**
Guitar, Gretsch, Super Chet, 1973-79 . . . . **1,700.00**
Guitar, Martin, D-28, 12-fret neck, 1931-36 . . . . **35,000.00**
Guitar, Martin, D-28, 1971–93 . . . . **1,200.00**
Guitar, Martin, O-18, mahogany backs and sides, 1920-40 . . . . **2,000.00**
Guitar, Martin, OO-42, Brazilian rosewood back and sides, 1929. . . . . **15,000.00**
Guitar, Stratocaster, black or natural, 1981 . . . . **600.00**
Guitar, Stratocaster, walnut, 1978. **700.00**
Guitar, Telecaster, blonde, black pick guard, 1951 . . . **10,000.00**
Harmonica, 1,000,000 $ Baby, Japan, miniature, 4 holes, cardboard box. **20.00**
Harmonica, Echo-Luxe, Hohner, 14 double holes, curved front and back, Art Deco design on cover plates, "Century of Progress" box **125.00**
Harmonica, Harmonetta, Hohner, complete with wind box containing harmonica, trumpet-like mouthpiece, 10 buttons, and 5 brass horns, orig box **350.00**
Harmonica, Philmonet, Christ Kratt Instrument Co, USA, 10 holes, black plastic body, c1950 . . . . **25.00**
Harmonica, Super Scout, Magnus Harmonica Corp, Newark, NJ, 10 holes, cowboy on harmonica and box, c1948 . . . . **25.00**
Mandolin, European, bowl-back, rosewood body, mahogany neck, spruce top, unlabeled, c1920 . . . . **175.00**
Mandolin, Gibson Mandolin Guitar Co, Kalamazoo, MI, 1-pc maple back and sides, bound wide grain top, cedar neck with ebony fingerboard inlaid with pearl eyes, labeled "Gibson Mandolin Style A, Number 551102 Is Hereby Guaranteed," c1920. . . . . **525.00**
Ukulele, American, CF Martin & Co, stamped "CF Martin & Co Nazareth, PA" on back of head, Koa back and top, mahogany sides and neck, rosewood fingerboard with pearl eyes, c1920, 9½" l **1,100.00**
Ukulele, Hawaiian, The Mele Hawaiian Ukulele B&J New York Genuine Koa Wood label, Koa back, monkeypod sides, mahogany neck, inlaid rosette mahogany top, c1920, 9" l. **115.00**
Viola, Loveri Brothers, Naples, irregular light curl 2-pc back and ribs, plain scroll, medium grain top, brown varnish, labeled "Loveri Fratelli, Napoli," with case, 1942, 15-dowel stick stamped "Made By The Vega Company Boston Mass USA 85468," laminated pot stamped "854683," 4" l. **3,450.00**
Viola, Polish, 2-pc back, labeled "Ladislav F. Prokop," 16-dowel stick stamped "Made By The Vega Company Boston Mass USA 85468," laminated pot stamped "85468," 1924, 16⁹⁄₁₆" l **625.00**
Violin, German, Edmund Glaesel, Markneukirchen, 1-pc narrow curl back and ribs, plain scroll, fine grain top, golden varnish, labeled "Edmund Glaesel & Son, Markneukirchen," 1950, 13¹⁵⁄₁₆" l **2,175.00**
Violin, Giovanni Longiaru, New York, 2-pc medium curl back, narrow curl ribs and scroll, medium grain top, yellow varnish, labeled "Giovanni Longiaru Venice New York, AD 1925, No. 24," 1925, 14" l **2,650.00**

MUSIC BOXES

Antoine Favre, a Swiss watchmaker, made the first true music box in 1796. The manufacture of music boxes was largely a cottage industry until Charles Paillard established a factory in Sainte-Croix, Switzerland, in 1875.

The golden age of the music box was from 1880 to 1910. A cylinder or disc music box occupied a place of importance in many Victorian-era parlors. The radio and record player eventually replaced the parlor music box.

Although novelty music boxes date to the Victorian era, they enjoyed increased popularity following World War II. In the case of the novelty box, the musical portion is secondary to the shape of the box itself. This category focuses primarily on these boxes.

References: Collectors' Information Bureau, *Collectibles Market Guide & Price Index, 17th Edition,* Collectors' Information Bureau, 1999; Mary Sieber (ed.), *2000 Price Guide to Limited Edition Collectibles,* Krause Publications, 1999.

Collectors' Club: Musical Box Society International, 700 Walnut Hill Rd, Hockessin, DE 19707.

After the Pageant, Holiday Memories, Ace Product
   Management Group, 1994 . . . . **$50.00**
Baby and Cradle, Lucy & Me, L Rigg, Enesco, 1995 . . . . 30.00
Bear on Rocking Reindeer, Cherished Teddies,
   P Hillman, Enesco, 1992 . . . . 85.00
Blossom & Hickory, Little Cheesers/Cheeserville Picnic,
   Ganz, 1991 . . . . 65.00
Can I Open It Now?, Snowbabies Pewter Miniatures,
   Pierro/Kirchner, Department 56, 1993 . . . . 35.00
Cat in Water Can, Kenji, Seymour Mann, 1989 . . . . 35.00
Charlie Chaplin, composition figure on green cobble-
   stone circle that turns to brick red around perimeter,
   hp black derby, jacket, and shoes, gray necktie and
   trousers, gold cane, ©1979 Bubbles Inc, Japan, 7½" h 50.00
Clown on Ball, Cherished Teddies Under the Big Top,
   P Hillman, Enesco, 1996 . . . . 40.00

Cowardly Lion, Wizard of Oz, Rockwell Inspired, Dave
   Grossman, 1996 . . . . 35.00
Don't Fall Off, Department 56, Snowbabies, 1987 . . . . 35.00
Enchanted Evening, From Barbie With Love, L Rigg,
   Enesco, 1995 . . . . 100.00
I'd Like to Buy the World a Coke, Small World of
   Music, S Butcher, Enesco, 1996 . . . . 250.00
Iris, Rainbow's End Glitterdome, Seraphim Studios,
   Roman Inc, 1997 . . . . 50.00
Moonbeams Waterglobe, Snowbabies, Department 56,
   Pierro/Kirchner, 1998 . . . . 35.00
Reading a Story, Snowbabies, Department 56, miniature,
   1993 . . . . 25.00
Rockwell's Studio, Norman Rockwell Gallery, 1997 . . . . 35.00
Santa With Lantern, Jaimy, Seymour Mann, 1991 . . . . 35.00
Tulips and Ribbons Trinket Box, Pigsville,
   C Thammavongsa, Ganz, 1992 . . . . 30.00
Under the Mistletoe, Holiday Memories, Ace Product
   Management Group, 1994 . . . . 50.00
What Child Is This?, Small World of Music, S Butcher,
   Enesco, 1996 . . . . 30.00

NATZLER ART POTTERY

Gertrude Amon Natzler (1908-1971) and Otto Natzler (1908--) were born and studied in Vienna, Austria. After working as textile designers, they established their first ceramic studio in 1934. Gertrude made the forms. Otto did the glazing, becoming famous for his volcanic or crater glazes. In 1937 they won a Silver Medal at the Paris International Exhibition.

In 1939 they moved to Los Angeles, where they taught ceramics from 1939 to 1942. Otto Natzler introduced his slab constructions at a 1977 exhibit at the Craft and Folk Museum in Los Angeles. Examples of Natzler Art Pottery are found in more than thirty-five museums including The Metropolitan Museum of Art and the Philadelphia Museum of Art.

Bottle, cylindrical, flaring rim above narrow neck, mottled semi-gloss crystalline turquoise glaze, black ink
   "Natzler," paper tag "0257," 8½" h, 4½" d **$2,750.00**
Bottle, Mariposa RG, squat, narrow tapered neck, blue,
   green, and yellow mottled glossy glaze with melt fissures, black ink "Natzler," paper tag "N954," 1967,
   5¼" h, 10" d 5,000.00
Bowl, 4-sided dimple form, glossy hare's fur bright yel-
   low glaze, black ink "Natzler," 3½" h, 5" w 2,750.00
Bowl, flaring sides, ftd, semi-gloss light blue glaze, black
   ink "Natzler," 2½" h, 6¼" d 1,325.00
Bowl, flaring sides, ftd, verdigris and purple volcanic
   glaze, black ink "Natzler," paper tag "M891," 1963,
   3" h, 6½" d 3,575.00
Bowl, semi-spherical, blue and green hare's fur glaze
   with melt fissures, black ink "Natzler," 2 x 5½" 5,500.00
Bowl, semi-spherical, cream and yellow volcanic glaze,
   black ink "Natzler," paper tag "L610," 4½ x 6" 5,500.00
Bowl, semi-spherical, light blue frothy hare's fur glaze,
   black ink "Natzler," paper tag "M994," 4 x 5" 2,500.00
Bowl, shallow, flaring sides, semi-gloss chartreuse glaze,
   black ink "Natzler," 2½" h, 8½" d 3,850.00
Bowl, shallow, flaring sides, thick volcanic verdigris
   glaze, black ink "Natzler," paper tag "F912," 1½" h,
   5½" d 1,750.00

Kitty Cucumber, plays "Happy Birthday To You," Schmid, 5" h, $20.00.

Vessel, glossy hare's fur chartreuse glaze, mkd "Natzler" in black, 6" h, 5¹/₂" d, $2,850.00. Photo courtesy David Rago Auctions, Inc.

Bowl, small compressed form, semi-gloss hare's fur butterscotch glaze, black ink "Natzler," 2³/₄" h, 5¹/₄" d **2,250.00**
Bowl, spherical, light green and brown volcanic glaze, black ink "Natzler," paper tag "N129," 5 x 5" **6,500.00**
Bowl, straight tapering sides, flat bottom, glossy hare's fur cobalt glaze, black ink "Natzler," 3¹/₄" h, 5¹/₄" d **2,300.00**
Cabinet Vase, bulbous, blue, turquoise, and brown flambé crystalline glaze, black ink "Natzler," paper tag "L254," 4 x 3" **5,000.00**
Dish, cov, volcanic turquoise glaze, black ink "Natzler," 5¹/₂" d **1,100.00**
Vessel, bottle shaped, turquoise, blue, and brown flambé crystalline glaze, black ink "Natzler," paper tag "N828," 12¹/₂ x 3³/₄" **8,750.00**
Vessel, straight walls, beige walls with melt fissures black ink "Natzler," paper tag "K986," 4³/₄ x 3³/₄" **2,850.00**
Vessel, straight sides, brown and yellow volcanic glaze, black ink "Natzler," paper tag "M288," 4³/₄ x 6¹/₂" **6,000.00**

NAZI ITEMS

Anton Drexler and Adolf Hitler founded The National Socialist German Workers Party (NSDAP) on February 24, 1920. The party advocated a 25-point plan designed to lift the German economy and government from the depths of the Depression.

When the Beer Hall Putsch failed in 1923, Hitler was sentenced to a five-year prison term. Although serving only a year, he used that time to write *Mein Kampf*, a book that became the NSDAP manifesto.

During the early 1930s the NSDAP grew from a regional party based in Southern Germany to a national party. Hitler became Reich's chancellor in 1933. Following the death of President von Hindenberg in 1934, Hitler assumed that title as well.

Nazi items are political items, not military items. Do not confuse the two. Although the Wehrmacht, the German military, was an independent organization, it was subject to numerous controls from the political sector. Nazi memorabilia were popular war souvenirs. Large quantities of armbands, daggers, flags, and copies of *Mein Kampf* survive in the United States.

References: Richard J. Austin, *The Official Price Guide to Military Collectibles, Sixth Edition,* House of Collectibles, 1998; Bob Evans, *Third Reich Belt Buckles,* Schiffer Publishing, 1999; Gary Kirsner, *German Military Steins: 1914 to 1945, Second Edition,* Glentiques Ltd, 1996; Ron Manion, *German Military Collectibles Price Guide,* Antique Publications, 1995.

Periodical: *Military Trader,* PO Box 1050, Dubuque, IA 52004.

Ashtray, white ceramic, brown-tone profile of Hitler, gilt trim, mkd "CKW Buringia" **$150.00**
Cloth Insignia, cuff title, SS enlisted man's, black ground, 7-strand aluminum borders, gray embroidered Sutterlin script "Adolf Hitler," 13¹/₂" l **500.00**
Cloth Insignia, sleeve eagle, Waffen SS, first type, gray embroidered dipped-wing tip eagle on gray wool **250.00**
Cup and Saucer, white porcelain, gold trim, Hitler portrait and oak leaf band on ftd cup, oak leaf band and center swastika on saucer, mkd "Heil Hitler! 24 April 1932," KPM cobalt blue hallmark and painter's signature **1,750.00**
Fat Saver Scorecard, yellow card with "I Helped To Save His Life Today" at top, calendar bottom with caricatures of Hitler, Mussolini, and Tojo, instructions on back for rendering fat, 5¹/₂ x 8¹/₂" **40.00**
Figurine, figural rat with Hitler face, plaster with gray flocking and painted black facial features, black cord tail, "Adolf" stamped on spine, 3" l **225.00**
Figurine, skunk body with Hitler head, painted plaster, 5" h, 5" l **150.00**
Flag, red cotton ground, black printed swastikas on sewn white circles, 30 x 60" **40.00**
Pincushion, figural Hitler bending over, cushion attached to backside, mkd "Stick a Pin in the Axis" and "Mason Co," 6¹/₂" h **150.00**
Plaque, bronze-finished terra cotta, Hitler profile, mkd "Meissen," 1933, 8¹/₂" h **200.00**
Plaque, silver-plated soldier profile mounted on black painted oak base, Nazi eagle on steel helmet **125.00**
Novelty, boxed "poop," cardboard box with cartoon art showing Hitler with limp wrist being hit in eye with moist object and "Right in der Fuehrer's Eye," contains realistic-looking brown composition imitation "poop" nestled in bed of tissue paper **150.00**

NEWCOMB POTTERY

In 1886 Ellsworth and William Woodward founded the New Orleans Pottery Company. Thirty women from the Ladies Decorative Art League worked at the firm. The company lasted a year. Attempts by the Art League Pottery Club and later the Baronne Street Pottery to keep the pottery tradition alive also met with failure.

In 1895 Ellsworth Woodward convinced Sophie Newcomb College, the women's college of Tulane University, to establish a pottery class and sell its products. Mary G. Sheerer from Cincinnati was hired to teach pottery decoration. Joseph Fortune Meyer became the chief potter in 1896 and remained until 1925. Paul E. Cox, a technician, arrived in 1910.

Sadie Irvine, one of Newcomb's foremost decorators, worked from 1908 to 1952. Kenneth E. Smith and Professor Lota Lee Troy guided the pottery's operations through the 1930s. Robert Field and John Canady succeeded them.

Collectors divide Newcomb College wares into four basic periods: (1) 1895-1899; (2) 1900 to 1910; (3) 1910-1930, the period of the pale blue and green tree dripping with Spanish moss reflected in the moonlight; and, (4) 1930-1945. Commercial production ended in 1939. The Newcomb Guild was organized to sell student's work. It was dissolved when Sadie Irvine retired in 1952.

References: Ralph and Terry Kovel, *Kovel's American Art Pottery*, Crown, 1993; Jessie Poesch, *Newcomb Pottery*, Schiffer Publishing, 1984.

Collectors' Club: American Art Pottery Assoc, PO Box 834, Westport, MA 02790.

Cabinet Vase, Sadie Irvine, matte, Español pattern, mkd "NC/QH65/SI," 1927, 2½ x 2¾" **$1,500.00**
Candlesticks, pr, Gertrude Maes, carved white and yellow flowers on blue and green matte ground, carved "GM," 6½ x 3½" **1,000.00**
Candlesticks, pr, Sadie Irvine, matte, pink spiderwort on blue ground, mkd "NC/JM/SI/NP82" with paper label, 1923, 7¼ x 4¼" **1,875.00**
Milk Pitcher, Sadie Irvine and Aurelia Arbo, matte, stylized green leaves on dark blue ground, stamped "NC/AA/SI/UO1," 4 x 4" **1,325.00**
Toothpick Holder, stylized triangular flowers in ivory and green, mkd "NC/JH/A/TG39," 1931, 2 x 3" **800.00**
Vase, Anna Frances Simpson, corseted, matte, carved with tall white and yellow narcissus and green leaves on pale blue ground, mkd "NC/AFS/223/NT6," 1924, 8½ x 3¼" **3,575.00**
Vase, Anna Frances Simpson, ovoid, tall oaks and Spanish moss in moonlit landscape, mkd "NC/133LE74/AFS," 8½ x 3¾" **5,500.00**
Vase, Henrietta Bailey, spherical, pink flowers and green leaves on cobalt ground, paper label, mkd "NC/HB/PM7/75," 4¼ x 5" **1,550.00**
Vase, Sadie Irvine, bulbous, butterflies and cotton blossoms dec, stamped "NC/100/SI/JM/PE71," 1926, 7 x 6¼" **8,750.00**

Vase, waisted cylinder form, alternating rose buds and leaves around collar, green and blue, mkd, 12¼" h, $2,500.00.

Vase, Sadie Irvine, bulbous, matte, band of stylized blossoms and leaf blades on medium blue ground, mkd "NC/KW45/271/SI," 1926, 4 x 4½" **2,100.00**
Vase, Sadie Irvine, bulbous, matte, carved with oaks and Spanish moss under rising moon, mkd "NC/RA89/SI," 1929, 5 x 3¾" **7,150.00**
Vase, Sadie Irvine, cylindrical, flaring rim, Español pattern, stamped "NC/229/SI/JM/PE95," 1926, 9½ x 4½" . . . **7,150.00**
Vase, Sadie Irvine, light blue and yellow daffodils on blue ground, mkd "NC/JM/121/MQ40," 5 x 5½" **1,700.00**
Vase, Sadie Irvine, squat, matte, landscape of oak trees and Spanish moss, stamped "NC/SI/501/S150," 9 x 3½" **5,000.00**
Vase, Sadie Irvine, squat, matte white daffodils and green leaves on medium blue ground, mkd "NC/271/KW46/S," 1920, 3½ x 5" **1,650.00**
Vessel, Sadie Irvine, spherical, scenic, carved landscape of Spanish moss in front of full moon, imp "NC/SI/KS/UB46," 1932, 3¾ x 5½" **2,000.00**
Vessel, Sadie Irvine, spherical, white gladiola on green stems, blue ground, stamped "NC/JM/SI/75/PK97," 4¼ x 5¼" **2,650.00**

NEW MARTINSVILLE/VIKING GLASS

The New Martinsville Glass Manufacturing Company was founded by Mark Douglass and George Matheny in New Martinsville, West Virginia, in 1901. The company's products included colored and plain dishes, lamps, and tumblers. John Webb, a cousin of the famous English glass maker Thomas Webb, joined the firm in December 1901. Within a brief period of time, New Martinsville was making Muranese, a direct copy of Peachblow.

After being destroyed by a major fire in 1907, the glasshouse was rebuilt and production was resumed in 1908. Harry Barth joined the firm in May 1918. He and Ira Clarke guided the company through the difficult years of the Depression. R. M. Rice and Carl Schultz, two New Englanders, bought New Martinsville Glass in July 1938.

New Martinsville Glass Company was renamed Viking Glass in 1944. Post-1945 product lines included handmade cut and etched giftware, novelties, and tableware. Most pieces were marked with a paper label reading "Viking." In 1951 Viking purchased a number of Paden City and Westmoreland molds.

Viking purchased the Rainbow Art Glass Company, Huntington, West Virginia, in the early 1970s, and continued production of its "Rainbow Art" animal figurines.

Kenneth Dalzell, former head of the Fostoria Glass Company, purchased the Viking Glass Company in mid-1986. After closing the plant for renovations, it was reopened in October 1987. The company's name was changed to Dalzell-Viking Glass. Dalzell-Viking, using models in Viking's inventory, reintroduced animal figurines and other items, often using non-period colors.

Reference: James Measell, *New Martinsville Glass: 1900-1944*, Antique Publications, 1994.

Janice, compote, low, blue **$20.00**
Janice, cruet set, includes 2 cruets and tray, emerald green handles, 9 x 4¼" tray **125.00**
Janice, cup and saucer, blue **36.00**
Janice, fruit bowl, ruffled, blue, 12" d **80.00**
Janice, jam jar, cov, blue, 6" h **40.00**

Janice, mayonnaise, round crystal **10.00**
Janice, mustard, blue. **75.00**
Janice, plate, 8½" d, blue **20.00**
Janice, plate, handled, silver overlay 40th Anniversary
   dec, ruby, 12" w **50.00**
Janice, platter, blue **50.00**
Janice, salad plate, blue. **12.00**
Janice, sherbet, blue **18.00**
Janice, swan bowl, red **225.00**
Janice, swan celery, red **125.00**
Janice, tumbler, ftd, blue **20.00**
Janice, vase, blue, 3½" h **25.00**
Janice, vase, cupped-in, red. **165.00**
Janice, vase, flared, black **150.00**
Moondrops, ashtray, red **35.00**
Moondrops, berry bowl, red, 5" d **30.00**
Moondrops, bowl, 3-part, 3-toed, red, 8½" d **45.00**
Moondrops, bowl, 3-toed, amber, 8" d **22.00**
Moondrops, bowl, oval, cobalt **85.00**
Moondrops, bread and butter plate, amber. **6.00**
Moondrops, bread and butter plate, cobalt. **7.00**
Moondrops, bread and butter plate, red **10.00**
Moondrops, butter, cov, cobalt. **550.00**
Moondrops, butter, no lid, red **75.00**
Moondrops, cordial, blue, 2⅞" h **50.00**
Moondrops, cordial, red, 2⅞" h **50.00**
Moondrops, creamer, red **20.00**
Moondrops, cup and saucer, cobalt **20.00**
Moondrops, cup and saucer, ftd, red **20.00**
Moondrops, dinner plate, cobalt, 9½" d **25.00**
Moondrops, gravy, red. **350.00**
Moondrops, juice tumbler, blue, 3¼" h **20.00**
Moondrops, liqueur, blue, ¾ oz, 2⅞" h **30.00**
Moondrops, mint dish, 3-ftd, red **100.00**
Moondrops, pickle dish, red **35.00**
Moondrops, shot tumbler, amber, 2 oz, 2¾" h **8.00**
Moondrops, shot tumbler, red, 2 oz, 2¾" h **20.00**
Moondrops, sugar, amber **10.00**
Moondrops, tumbler, red, 9 oz, 4⅞" h **20.00**
Moondrops, water goblet, metal stem, red, 9 oz, 6¼" h **25.00**
Powder Jar, Deco, 3-part, ice blue **135.00**
Powder Jar, round, amethyst, 4½" d **50.00**
Powder Jar, round, blue, 4½" d **50.00**
Prelude, oil cruet, with stopper, crystal. **50.00**
Prelude, tumbler, ball, 10 oz **20.00**
Radiance, bonbon, ruffled, metal pedestal, cobalt. **150.00**
Radiance, butter, red **650.00**
Radiance, candy jar lid, red. **100.00**
Radiance, celery, metal pedestal, cobalt. **150.00**
Radiance, cheese stand, amber **35.00**
Radiance, cheese stand, red. **65.00**
Radiance, cordial, red. **30.00**
Radiance, decanter, silver overlay **250.00**
Radiance, honey jar lid, red. **150.00**
Radiance, mayonnaise liner, ice blue **18.00**
Radiance, pitcher, blue **325.00**
Radiance, punch cup, ice blue **12.00**
Radiance, relish, 2-part, red, metal handle **40.00**
Radiance, relish, 3-part, red. **45.00**
Radiance, salt and pepper shakers, pr, blue **110.00**
Radiance, salt and pepper shakers, pr, pink **225.00**
Radiance, vase, crimped, green, 10" **90.00**
Radiance, vase, ruffled, cobalt, 12" **275.00**
Vogue, #4554/401, candleholders, pr, 1-lite, crystal **35.00**

NEWSPAPERS

Newspapers are collected first for their story content and second for their advertising. Volume One, Number One of any newspaper brings a premium because of its crossover value. Beware of assigning too much value to age alone; 18th-century and 19th-century newspapers with weak story content and advertising are frequently framed and used for decorative purposes.

A newspaper must be complete and have a minimal amount of chipping and cracking to be collectible. Newsprint, commonly used after 1880, is made of wood pulp and deteriorates quickly without proper care. Pre-1880 newsprint is made from cotton and/or rag fiber and survives much better. If only the front page of a 20th-century headline newspaper survives, value is reduced by 40% to 50%. Banner headlines, those extending across the full page, are preferred. Add a 10% to 20% premium to headline newspapers from the city where the event occurred.

Two of the most commonly reprinted papers are the January 8, 1880, *Ulster Country Gazette*, announcing the death of George Washington, and the April 15, 1865, issue of the *N.Y. Herald*, announcing Lincoln's death. If you have one of these papers, chances are you have a reprint.

References: Ron Barlow and Ray Reynolds, *The Insider's Guide to Old Books, Magazines, Newspapers, Trade Catalogs,* Windmill Publishing, 1995; Norman E. Martinus and Harry L. Rinker, *Warman's Paper,* Wallace-Homestead, Krause Publications, 1994.

Periodical: *PCM (Paper Collectors' Marketplace),* PO Box 128, Scandinavia, WI 54977.

Collectors' Clubs: Newspaper Collectors Society of America, 6031 Winterset, Lansing, MI 48911; Newspaper Memorabilia Collectors Network, PO Box 797, Watertown, NY 13601.

1920, Prohibition takes effect **$25.00**
1921, Aug 3, *Nashville Tennessean,* Black Sox acquitted
   by jury **28.00**
1923, Aug 3, *San Francisco Journal,* "President Harding
   Dies of Stroke, Executive Passes Without Warning" **50.00**
1924, Coolidge/Davis election. **5.00**
1925, Scopes "Monkey" trial verdict **25.00**
1926, Sep 23, Tunney defeats Dempsey **25.00**
1927, *Galveston Daily News,* Babe Ruth's 60th homerun **85.00**
1929, Feb 14, St Valentine's Day massacre **65.00**
1929, May 17, Capone tax-evasion sentencing. **35.00**
1929, Oct 28, stock market crash **65.00**
1929, Nov 29, Byrd flies to South Pole. **10.00**
1931, Jun 5, *Berkshire Evening News,* Pittsfield, MA,
   aviation news **20.00**
1933, Jan 30, Hitler named Chancellor of Germany **15.00**
1933, Dec 5, Prohibition repealed **25.00**
1934, May 23, Bonnie and Clyde killed **75.00**
1934, Jul 22, Dillinger killed **35.00**
1936, *The Morning Post,* first Hall of Famers **15.00**
1936, Dec 10, King Edward VIII renounces the crown. **18.00**
1937, May 6, *Hindenburg* crashes **40.00**
1937, Jul 7, Earhart vanishes on round-the-world flight **15.00**
1938, Mar 11, Nazis seize Austria **10.00**
1938, Jun 22, *Chicago American,* Chicago, IL,
   Schmeling vs Lewis **20.00**
1939, Jul 3, *Chicago Examiner,* "Chamberlain Warns
   Britain Ready For War!" **7.00**

1939, Sep 4, *Boston Herald*, Boston, MA, British steamer torpedoed 20.00
1941, Dec 8, *Milwaukee Journal*, "1500 Killed In Hawaii Raid; Two US Warships Down – EXTRA!" 35.00
1941, Dec 8, *The Morning Post*, Lou Gehrig's death 32.00
1941, Dec 8, *San Francisco Chronicle*, Pearl Harbor attack 60.00
1943, Sep 8, Italy surrenders 10.00
1944, Jun 5, D-Day. 20.00
1945, Jun 6, *Buffalo Evening News*, Buffalo, NY, war victory news 4.00
1945, Aug 6, atomic bomb dropped on Japan 25.00
1945, Aug 14, Japan surrenders 25.00
1951, Apr 10, Truman relieves MacArthur of command 10.00
1952, Eisenhower/Stevenson elected 8.00
1953, Jul 26, Korean war ends. 12.00
1954, May 17, court bans school segregation. 10.00
1957, Oct 4, Soviets launch *Sputnik* 15.00
1958, Jun 30, Alaska joins The Union 18.00
1959, Mar 12, Hawaii joins The Union 18.00
1962, Feb 20, Glenn orbits Earth 15.00
1963, Nov 22, JFK assassinated 50.00
1968, Apr 5, Martin Luther King assassinated 15.00
1969, Jul 20, man walks on moon 20.00
1973, Vietnam peace pacts signed 10.00
1977, Aug 17, *Commercial Appeal*, Memphis, TN, Elvis' death 30.00
1980, John Lennon's death 4.00
1986, Jan 28, *Challenger* explodes. 5.00

NICODEMUS POTTERY

After attending the Cleveland Art School where he studied under Herman Matzen and Frank Wilcox, Chester Roland Nicodemus served as instructor and head of the sculpture department of the Dayton Art Institute (1925-1930) and then head of the sculpture department and later dean of the Columbus Art School (1930-1943). In 1943 Nicodemus left teaching to establish Ferro-Stone Ceramics.

Between 1943 and 1973 Nicodemus supplied fountain figures, portrait heads, and other sculptural forms to the retail trade. He continued to sell privately after ending his retail business.

Ferro-Stone ceramics were made from an Ohio clay with a high iron content. Fired between 2,000 and 2,500 degrees Fahrenheit, the finish product has a russet brown body and is stone hard. Favorite glaze colors were deep blue, mottled green, antique ivory, pussy willow, turquoise, and dark yellow. Products include specialized advertising pieces, Christmas cards, dinnerware, figurines (especially animals and birds), fountain pieces, medallions, plaques, statues, and vases.

In January 1990 Nicodemus fell and broke his hip. He died in November of the same year.

Nicodemus used a variety of marks including an incised "Nicodemus" and a two-tone paper label reading "NICODEMUS / FERRO-STONE."

Reference: Jim Ribel, *Sanfords Guide to Nicodemus: His Pottery and Art*, Adelmore Press, 1998.

Ashtray, #88, green $18.00
Ashtray, #404 . . . . 50.00
Ashtray, figural pelican, #106. . . . . 125.00

Ashtray, Lake Hope State Park 20.00
Ashtray, Michigan State University, 4½" d. 20.00
Bank, elephant, #37, 4½" l 200.00
Bank, rabbit, #38 . . . . 175.00
Bookends, pr, camels, #122. . . . . 400.00
Christmas Ornament, stocking, 1961 . . . . 50.00
Cigarette Jar, #89 . . . . 45.00
Creamer and Sugar, cov, #281 and #282 . . . . 100.00
Figurine, Dachshund, #36, 6½" l 150.00
Figurine, goldfinch, #592, 4½" h 100.00
Figurine, Great Dane, #12, 14" l 450.00
Figurine, kitten, blue-green, #133 . . . . 70.00
Figurine, Young Robin, plastic, mkd "Young Robin by Nicodemus, copyright 1971 Ebonlite," 3½" h 35.00
Flower Arranger, figural duck, green, 6" h. 200.00
Flower Block, #562, 4½" sq. 80.00
Jug, #85, mustard yellow and brown, 3 pt 75.00
Match Holder, elephant, #102 . . . . 75.00
Monument Souvenir Dish, White Sulphur Springs. 375.00
Pitcher, #205 . . . . 30.00
Planter, swan, #250. . . . . 80.00
Salt and Pepper Shakers, pr, #412, 2¾" h 35.00
Snack Set, plate and cup, #233 and #235. . . . . 75.00
Teapot, #224, 1¼ qt 125.00
Vase, #50 . . . . 125.00
Vase, bulbous, #409 . . . . 135.00
Vase, emb seahorse and fish medallions, #216 . . . . 200.00
Vase, rope handles, brown and green speckled glaze, #75, 8½" h 175.00
Wall Pocket, #71. . . . . 225.00

NILOAK POTTERY

In 1910 Hyten Bros. Pottery, Benton, Arkansas, introduced Mission, a marbleized art pottery line based on a swirl ware developed by Arthur Dovey when he worked at Ouachita Pottery. It was an immediate success.

In 1911 the company name was changed to the Niloak (kaolin spelled backwards) Pottery Company and Dovey left to pursue other interests. Money was raised for a new plant. Niloak produced stoneware and decorated glazed wares in addition to its colored-clay marbleized pieces. Charles D. "Bullet" Hyten bought control of the company in 1918. During the 1920s, production reached an annual high of fifty thousand pieces.

Niloak sales fell during the Depression. The company survived by making hand-thrown and cast wares in high and matte finishes. These pieces are marked "Hywood Art Pottery," "Hywood by Niloak, Benton, Arkansas," "Hywood by Niloak," or simply "Niloak." Heavily mortgaging the pottery, Hyten eventually lost control in the early 1940s. Production was sporadic through 1947, when the plant became the Winburn Tile Company.

References: David Edwin Gifford, *The Collector's Encyclopedia of Niloak*, Collector Books, 1993, out of print; Ralph and Terry Kovel, *Kovel's American Art Pottery*, Crown, 1993.

Collectors' Clubs: American Art Pottery Assoc, PO Box 834, Westport, MA 02790; National Society of Arkansas Pottery Collectors, PO Box 2006, Little Rock, AR 72212.

Cabinet Pitcher, emb woven design, blue, raised "N" mark, 3½" h $12.00

Candlesticks, pr, Mission ware, classical shape with rolled rim and flaring ft, brown, blue, terra cotta, and sand scroddled clays, stamped "Niloak," 8" h, 5" d **325.00**

Cornucopia Vase, gray, raised mark, 4" h **15.00**

Ewer, angled handle, green, 6½" h **28.00**

Planter, figural Dutch shoe **20.00**

Planter, figural elephant, white **20.00**

Planter, figural squirrel, blue **18.00**

Planter, figural swan, burgundy, 7" h **25.00**

Vase, classical shape with flared rim and 2 handles, green, 6" h **30.00**

Vase, long cylindrical neck, short bulbous base, deep burgundy, 6½" h **25.00**

Vase, Mission ware, classical shape, blue, terra cotta, and sand scroddled clays, stamped "Niloak," 8" h, 5" d **200.00**

Vase, Mission ware, corseted cylinder, brown, blue, terra cotta, and purple scroddled clays, stamped "Niloak," 12¼" h, 5½" d **350.00**

Vase, Mission ware, flaring rim, bulbous base, brown, blue, and tan scroddled clays, stamped "Niloak," 8" h, 4" d **200.00**

Vase, Mission ware, pear-shaped with flared rim and ring foot, brown, blue, terra cotta, and sand scroddled clays, stamped "Niloak," 9¾" h, 4¾" d **375.00**

Vase, Mission ware, spherical with closed-in rim, brown, blue, terra cotta, and sand scroddled clays, stamped "Niloak" and paper label, 5¾" h, 7" d **250.00**

Vase, twisted body, bulbous base, yellow, 6½" h **25.00**

Vessel, Mission ware, brown, beige, and terra cotta scroddled clays, stamped "Niloak," 6" h, 8" d **450.00**

NODDERS & BOBBIN' HEADS

A nodder consists of two separate molded parts. A pin is used as the fulcrum to balance one piece on the other. A true nodder works by gravity, a counterbalance weight attached to the fulcrum located in the base piece. Eventually, electrical, frictional, mechanical, and windup mechanisms were used. While bisque nodders are the most common, nodders were made from almost every medium imaginable.

Most nodders are characterizations, often somewhat grotesque. Buddhas, 18th-century courtiers, ethnic and professional types, cartoon figures, and animals are just a few examples. Most collectors specialize, e.g., nodding salt and pepper shakers or holiday theme nodders.

Bobbin' heads have no weight. Their motion comes from a spring or other mechanism inside their head. While most individuals think of bobbin' heads in respect to the Beatles, Peanuts, and Sports Mascot series from the 1960s, papier-mâché cartoon and holiday figures date from the early decades of the 20th century.

References: Tim Hunter, *Bobbing Head Dolls: 1960-2000,* Krause Publications, 2000; Hilma R. Irtz, *Figural Nodders,* Collector Books, 1997.

Collectors' Club: Bobbin' Head National Club, PO Box 9297, Daytona Beach, FL 32120.

Beatnik Fisherman Bank **$100.00**

Beetle Bailey **150.00**

Boston Red Sox, green base **1,000.00**

Brylcreem Kissing Pair **350.00**

Bugs Bunny **350.00**

Campbell's Kids **750.00**

Charlie Weaver **175.00**

Chicago Cubs, bear head, green base **425.00**

Cincinnati Bengals, gold base, Merger series, 1968 . . . . **80.00**

Colonel Sanders, papier-mâché **150.00**

Cowboy and Cowgirl Kissing **50.00**

Dallas Cowboys, square base, blue, 1962 . . . . **200.00**

Davy Crockett **300.00**

Denver Broncos, gold base, 1965 . . . . **650.00**

Dobie Gillis **250.00**

Elmer Fudd **325.00**

Florida Orange **50.00**

Happy Homer **500.00**

Hershey Bears **275.00**

Hoover Housewife **500.00**

Indy 500 Car **450.00**

Joe Cool, 4" h **45.00**

Kansas City A's, green base, dark blue hat **400.00**

Kansas City Royals, gold base **125.00**

Knott's Berry Farm **150.00**

Los Angeles Kings, gold base, 1967 . . . . **425.00**

Lucky Troll **75.00**

Miami Dolphins, gold base, 1965 . . . . **350.00**

Mickey Mantle, white square base, 1962-64 . . . . **750.00**

Minneapolis Twins **450.00**

Mr Peanut **200.00**

NASA Space Boy **100.00**

New York World's Fair, 1964 . . . . **60.00**

Nixon For President, elephant, 1960 . . . . **200.00**

Oakland Raiders, round base, black, 1962 . . . . **400.00**

Old King Cole **175.00**

Paul Bunyan **150.00**

Peter Pan **100.00**

Philadelphia Phillies, white base **225.00**

Phillips 66 . . . . **600.00**

Pig Pen, 6" h **250.00**

Pittsburgh Pirates, 4½" h **425.00**

Pittsburgh Steelers, square base, black, 1962 . . . . **170.00**

Beatles, ceramic, mkd "1964 Car Mascots, Inc.," gold sticker mkd "Made in Japan, Car Mascots, Inc., Los Angeles, 26, Calif. U.S.A.," orig boxes, 8" h, price each, $125.00.

Poll Parrot Shoes	625.00
Raggedy Ann	225.00
Roberto Clemente, white round base, 1962-64	1,500.00
Roger Maris, with box	750.00
Salt Lake City Eagles	800.00
Santa Bank	90.00
Sgt Snorkel	150.00
Six Flags Over St Louis	400.00
Smokey Bear	250.00
Universal Studios Cop	150.00
Washington Redskins, square base, maroon, 1962	200.00
Willie Mays, white round base, dark base	450.00
Woodstock, miniature, 1970s	35.00
Yosemite Sam	350.00

Batman, National Periodical Publications, Penguin Puzzle Cards, #3 "Flying Foes," 1966, $2.00. Photo courtesy Ray Morykan Auctions.

NON-SPORT TRADING CARDS

Tobacco insert cards of the late 19th century are the historical antecedents of the modern trading (bubble gum) card. Over 500 sets, with only 25 devoted to sports, were issued between 1885 and 1894. Tobacco cards lost popularity following World War I.

In 1933 Indian Gum marketed a piece of gum and a card inside a waxed paper package, launching the era of the modern trading card. Goudey Gum and National Chicle controlled the market until the arrival of Gum, Inc., in 1936. In 1948 Bowman entered the picture, followed a year later by Topps. The Bowman-Topps rivalry continued until 1957 when Topps bought Bowman.

Although Topps enjoyed a dominant position in the baseball trading card market, Frank Fleer Company and Philadelphia Chewing Gum provided strong competition in the non-sport trading card sector in the 1960s. Eventually Donruss also became a major player in the non-sport trading card arena.

Non-sport trading cards benefited from the decline of the sport trading card in the early 1990s. Fueled by a strong comic book store market, many companies issued non-sport trading card sets covering a wide range of topics from current hit movies to pin-up girls of the past. Dozens of new issues arrived each month. As the 1990s end, the craze appears to be over. High prices, too many sets, and the introduction of chase and other gimmick cards have had a negative impact. Secondary market value for these post-1990 sets is highly speculative, a situation not likely to change within the next ten to fifteen years.

References: Christopher Benjamin, *The Sport Americana Price Guide to Non-Sports Cards: 1930-1960, No. 2*, Edgewater Books, 1993, out of print; Christopher Benjamin, *The Sport Americana Price Guide to Non-Sports Cards: 1961-1992, No. 4*, Edgewater Books, 1992, out of print; Timothy Brown and Tony Lee, *The Official Price Guide to Collectible Card Games*, House of Collectibles, 1999; Timothy Brown and Tony Lee, *The Official Price Guide to Role Playing Games*, House of Collectibles, 1998.

Periodicals: *Collect!*, PO Box 569, Dubuque, IA 52004; *The Wrapper*, 1811 Moore Ct, St Charles, IL 60174; *Non-Sport Update*, 4019 Green St, PO Box 5858, Harrisburg, PA 17110.

Collectors' Club: United States Cartophilic Society, PO Box 4020, St Augustine, FL 32085.

Action Gum, Goudy, 1938, card	$12.00
Animal Cards, Frostick, 1930s, card	3.00
Astronauts, Topps, 1963, card	5.00

Auto License Plates, Goudey, 1936, card	5.00
Babylon 5, SkyBox, Fleer/SkyBox 1996, 60-card set	8.00
Barbie Fashion Play Cards, River Group, 1993, pack	2.00
Batman, Topps, 1966, unopened pack	75.00
Batman Animated, Topps, 1993, card	.15
Battle, Topps, 1965, card	8.00
Battleship Gum, Newport, 1938, card	12.00
Battlestar Galactica, Topps, 1978, card	.25
Baywatch, Sports Times, 1995, card	.15
Beanie Baby Collector's Cards, Ty, 1998, card	.25
Beat Characters, Kitchen Sink, 1996, boxed set of 36 cards	12.00
Beatles, Topps, 1964, Series 1, 60-card set	150.00
Beautiful People, Fleer, 1978, card	.50
Beauty and the Beast, Mother's Cookies, 1987, 16-card set	15.00
Beetle Bailey, Authentix, 1995, card	.25
Beetlejuice, Dart, 1990, card	.10
Believe It or Not, Fleer, 1970, card	1.50
Bench Warmers, Overtime Concepts, 1992, card	.15
Betty Boop, Krome Prod, 1995, card	.10
Beverly Hillbillies, Topps, 1963, card	4.50
Beverly Hills 90210, Topps, 1991, card	.10
Bikini Open, T&M Enter, 1992, 50-card set	5.00
Choppers and Hot Bikes, Donruss, 1970s, card	1.50
Civil War Heritage, Bon Air, 1991, 20-card set	7.00
Civil War News, Topps, 1962, #88 checklist	50.00
Classic Pulps, Sperry Mfg, 1992, card	.15
Comics Greatest World, Topps, 1994, card	.15
Conan III, All Chromium, Comic Images, 1995, chromium card	.25
Coneheads, Topps, 1993, card	.15
DC Cosmic Teams, SkyBox, 1993, card	.10
Deathwatch 2000, Classic, 1993, 100-card set	12.00
Desert Storm Trading Cards, Spectra Star, 1991, Series 1, 60-card set	8.00
Dinosaurs, Milwaukee Museum, 1986, 4-card set	3.00
Disneyana, Disney, 1992, 5-card promo pack	20.00
Elvis Presley, Donruss, 1978, card	.40
Endless Summer, Portfolio International Inc, 1993, card	.20

Face the Fire, Ikon, 1994, promo **1.00**
Fantasmic, Disney/Kodak, 1992, 6-card set **20.00**
Fem Force III–Fem Force Foes, AC Comics, 1993,
 14-card set **10.00**
Fire Engines, Bon Air Collectibles, 1993, Series 1, card **15**
Firefighters, Bowman, 1953, card **6.00**
Flintstones Movie Cards, Topps, 1994, 88-card set **10.00**
Friendly Dictators, Eclipse, 1990, 36-card set **10.00**
Fright Flicks, Topps, 1988, card **15**
Full Moon Vari-View Cards, Full Moon, 1989, card **5.00**
Gamefish of the World, Impact Productions, 1992,
 promo **1.50**
Garfield, SkyBox, 1992, hologram card **8.00**
Garrison's Gorillas, Leaf, 1967, card **2.00**
Gen 13 Classic, Wildstorm, 1997, card **20**
Generals & Their Flags, WS, 1939, card **10.00**
George of the Jungle, Upper Deck, 1997, card **25**
GI Joe, Hasbro, 1986, 192-card set **50.00**
Gil Elvgren's Calendar Pin-Ups, Comic Images, 1993,
 card **10**
Gong Show, Fleer, 1979, card **25**
Groo, Wildstorm, 1996, 153-card set **30.00**
Hanna-Barbera Classics, Cardz, 1994, card **20**
Happy Days "A," Topps, 1976, card **75**
Heroes of the Sea, WS, 1939, card **10.00**
Hershey's Trading Cards, Dart, 1995, card **15**
Hopalong Cassidy Wild West Trading Cards, Post Cereal,
 1951, card **8.00**
Horror Monsters, Nu-Card, 1961, green card **6.00**
Kennedy, John F, Topps, 1964, card **2.00**
Killer Cards I, Pirahna, 1988, 46-card set **15.00**
Knight Rider, Donruss, 1983, 55-card set **16.00**
Lone Ranger, Gum Inc, 1940, card #48 . . . . **175.00**
Magnum PI, Donruss, 1983, card **15**
Marvel Universe 1994, Fleer, 1994, card **10**
Monkees, Donruss, 1966, sepia card **2.50**
Muscle Cards, Performance Years, 1992, card. **20**
Oddball Comics Cards, Kitchen Sink, 1993, boxed set of
 36 cards **12.00**
Playboy Jumbo Cards, Sports Time, 1997, Barbie Benton
 card **25.00**
Race Toons, Carolina Custom Cars, 1991, promo #1. . . . . . . **5.00**
Razor: Mega Chromium, Krome, 1994, card **50**
Ren and Stimpy, Topps, 1994, 50-card set **20.00**
Return to Oz, Topps, 1985, 44-card set **12.00**
Rock 'n Bubble, Dandy, 1986, card **75**
Sailor Moon, Dart Flipcards, 1997, card. **25**
Scary Monster Parody Cards, Druktenis, 1994, 36-card set **15.00**
Sex Maniacs II, First Amendment, 1993, promo **1.50**
Sgt Pepper's Lonely Hearts Club Band, Donruss, 1978,
 card **15**
Sgt Preston Cards, Quaker Cereal, 1950, card **2.00**
Simpsons, Tempo, 1996, Homer chase card **8.00**
Simpsons, Topps, 1990, card **10**
Soap Star, Jim Warren, 1989, 15-card set **12.00**
Space Shots, Space Ventures, 1990, Series 1, card **25**
Spawn Chromium Cards, WildStorm, 1996, card **25**
Spoofy Tunes, Butthedz Trading Cards, 1993, card **20**
Stargate, Collect-a-Card, 1994, card **15**
Star Trek, Leaf, 1967, card. **20.00**
Star Trek, Topps, 1976, card. **2.50**
Star Wars, Wonder Bread, 1977, card **1.00**
Superman Action Packs, Fleer/SkyBox, 1996, pop-out
 card **30**

Teddy Girls, Jacqueline Smith Designs, 1995, 36-card set **15.00**
Terminator 2, Impel, 1991, card **20**
Tootsie Circus, Sweets Co, 1933, card **25.00**
Toy Story, SkyBox, 1995, card **15**
Twin Peaks, Star Pics, 1991, 76-card set. **20.00**
US Presidents, Topps, 1972, unopened pack. **10.00**
Voyage to the Bottom of the Sea, Donruss, 1964, card **2.00**
Washington DC's Big Budget Circus, Tundra, 1992,
 36-card set **9.00**
Weird-Ohs, Fleer, 1965, card **2.00**
X-Files, Topps, 1995, card. **15**
X-Men Ultra, Fleer, 1994, card **10**
You Slay Me, Imagine, 1992, unopened box **40.00**
Zero Heroes, Donruss, 1984, sticker card. **15**
Zorro, Topps, 1958, card. **3.00**

NORITAKE

Ichizaemon Morimura, one of the founders of Noritake, established Morimura-kumi, a Japanese exporting company located in Tokyo in 1867. An import shop was also founded in New York to sell Japanese traditional goods. In 1904 he founded Nippon Toki Kaisha Ltd., the forerunner of Noritake, in Nagoya, Japan.

The Larkin Company, Buffalo, New York, was one of the principal distributors for Noritake China in the 1920s. The Azalea, Braircliff, Linden, Modjeska, Savory, Sheriden, and Tree in the Meadow patterns were utilized as Larkin premiums.

The factory was heavily damaged during World War II and production was greatly reduced. The company sold its china under the "Rose China" mark between 1946 and 1948 because the quality did not match that of earlier Noritake China. High quality was achieved once again by early 1949.

Noritake Company was established for selling tableware in the United States. Over the next thirty years, companies were created in Australia, Canada, the United Kingdom, Sri Lanka, Guam, the Philippines, and Ireland for the manufacture and distribution of Noritake products.

In 1956 Noritake began an expansion program that eventually resulted in a full line of tabletop products. Crystal glassware joined the line in 1961, earthenware and stoneware dinnerware and accessories in 1971. The company's name was changed to Noritake Company, Ltd. in 1981.

Close to 100 different Noritake marks have been identified. Most pieces are marked with "Noritake," a wreath, "M," "N," or "Nippon."

References: Aimee Neff Alden, *Collector's Encyclopedia of Early Noritake,* Collector Books, 1995; Robin Brewer, *Noritake Dinnerware,* Schiffer Publishing, 1999; Joan Van Patten, *Collector's Encyclopedia of Noritake* (1984, 1997 value update), *Second Series* (1994), Collector Books; Harry L. Rinker, *Dinnerware of the 20th Century: The Top 500 Patterns,* House of Collectibles, 1997; David Spain, *Collecting Noritake A to Z,* Schiffer Publishing, 1999.

Collectors' Club: Noritake Collectors' Society, 145 Andover Pl, West Hempstead, NY 11552.

Note: For additional listings see Noritake Azalea and Noritake Tree in the Meadow.

Asian Song, #7151, Victorian shape, bread and butter
 plate, 6³/₈" d **$5.00**

Asian Song, #7151, Victorian shape, dinner plate, $15.00.

Asian Song, #7151, Victorian shape, creamer **18.00**
Asian Song, #7151, Victorian shape, cup and saucer. **15.00**
Asian Song, #7151, Victorian shape, fruit bowl, 5⅝" d **10.00**
Asian Song, #7151, Victorian shape, gravy boat,
    attached liner **40.00**
Asian Song, #7151, Victorian shape, platter, oval, 11⅝" l **40.00**
Asian Song, #7151, Victorian shape, platter, oval, 13¾" l **45.00**
Asian Song, #7151, Victorian shape, salad plate, 8⅜" d **8.00**
Asian Song, #7151, Victorian shape, soup bowl, coupe. **15.00**
Asian Song, #7151, Victorian shape, sugar, cov **20.00**
Asian Song, #7151, Victorian shape, vegetable, oval,
    10⅛" d **30.00**
Blue Hill, #2482, Commander shape, platinum trim,
    bread and butter plate, 6¼" d **5.00**
Blue Hill, #2482, Commander shape, platinum trim,
    butter, cov, ¼ lb **25.00**
Blue Hill, #2482, Commander shape, platinum trim,
    candlestick, 1-lite **15.00**
Blue Hill, #2482, Commander shape, platinum trim,
    coffeepot, cov **50.00**
Blue Hill, #2482, Commander shape, platinum trim,
    creamer **12.00**
Blue Hill, #2482, Commander shape, platinum trim, cup
    and saucer **12.00**
Blue Hill, #2482, Commander shape, platinum trim,
    demitasse cup and saucer **10.00**
Blue Hill, #2482, Commander shape, platinum trim,
    fruit bowl, 5½" d **5.00**
Blue Hill, #2482, Commander shape, platinum trim,
    napkin ring **5.00**
Blue Hill, #2482, Commander shape, platinum trim,
    platter, oval, 12" l **20.00**
Blue Hill, #2482, Commander shape, platinum trim,
    platter, oval, 14⅛" l **30.00**
Blue Hill, #2482, Commander shape, platinum trim,
    platter, oval, 16⅛" l **40.00**
Blue Hill, #2482, Commander shape, platinum trim,
    salad plate, 8¼" d **12.00**

Blue Hill, #2482, Commander shape, platinum trim, salt
    and pepper shakers, pr **15.00**
Blue Hill, #2482, Commander shape, platinum trim,
    sandwich plate, handled **15.00**
Blue Hill, #2482, Commander shape, platinum trim,
    soup bowl, coupe **8.00**
Blue Hill, #2482, Commander shape, platinum trim,
    sugar, cov **18.00**
Blue Hill, #2482, Commander shape, platinum trim,
    teapot, cov **50.00**
Blue Hill, #2482, Commander shape, platinum trim,
    vegetable, cov, round **40.00**
Blue Hill, #2482, Commander shape, platinum trim,
    vegetable, open, oval, 9¾" l **25.00**
Cervantes, #7261, Remembrance II shape, bread and
    butter plate, 6½" d **5.00**
Cervantes, #7261, Remembrance II shape, cup and
    saucer. **12.00**
Cervantes, #7261, Remembrance II shape, dinner plate,
    10½" d **15.00**
Cervantes, #7261, Remembrance II shape, salad plate,
    8¼" d **10.00**
Cervantes, #7261, Remembrance II shape, sugar, cov **18.00**
Holly, #2228, Commander shape, ashtray **8.00**
Holly, #2228, Commander shape, bread and butter
    plate, 6½" d **8.00**
Holly, #2228, Commander shape, butter pat **8.00**
Holly, #2228, Commander shape, cereal bowl, lug
    handle **20.00**
Holly, #2228, Commander shape, coffeepot, cov **85.00**
Holly, #2228, Commander shape, creamer. **20.00**
Holly, #2228, Commander shape, cup and saucer **20.00**
Holly, #2228, Commander shape, mug **35.00**
Holly, #2228, Commander shape, napkin ring **15.00**
Holly, #2228, Commander shape, platter, oval, 11⅝" l **35.00**
Holly, #2228, Commander shape, platter, oval, 13⅝" l **40.00**
Holly, #2228, Commander shape, salad plate, 8⅜" d **12.00**
Holly, #2228, Commander shape, sugar, cov **25.00**

Holly, #2228, Commander shape, dinner plate, $20.00.

Holly, #2228, Commander shape, tidbit, 3-tier **50.00**
Holly, #2228, Commander shape, vegetable, cov **75.00**
Mayfair, #6109, platinum trim, bread and butter plate,
   6³/₈" d **6.00**
Mayfair, #6109, platinum trim, butter, cov, ¼ lb **30.00**
Mayfair, #6109, platinum trim, cereal bowl, lug handle **10.00**
Mayfair, #6109, platinum trim, creamer **15.00**
Mayfair, #6109, platinum trim, cup and saucer **15.00**
Mayfair, #6109, platinum trim, dinner plate **12.00**
Mayfair, #6109, platinum trim, fruit bowl, 5½" d **6.00**
Mayfair, #6109, platinum trim, gravy boat, attached liner **30.00**
Mayfair, #6109, platinum trim, platter, oval, 13³/₈" l **35.00**
Mayfair, #6109, platinum trim, salad plate, 8¼" d **6.00**
Mayfair, #6109, platinum trim, sugar, cov **18.00**
Mayfair, #6109, platinum trim, vegetable, oval, 10" l **25.00**
Mirano, #6878, bread and butter plate, 6³/₈" d **5.00**
Mirano, #6878, coffeepot, cov **65.00**
Mirano, #6878, creamer **18.00**
Mirano, #6878, cream soup and saucer **45.00**
Mirano, #6878, cup and saucer **15.00**
Mirano, #6878, dinner plate **14.00**
Mirano, #6878, fruit bowl, 5½" d **8.00**
Mirano, #6878, platter, oval, 12" l **30.00**
Mirano, #6878, platter, oval, 14" l **35.00**
Mirano, #6878, salad plate, 8¼" d **6.00**
Mirano, #6878, sugar, cov **20.00**
Mirano, #6878, vegetable, cov, round **60.00**
Mirano, #6878, vegetable, open, oval, 9⅝" l **25.00**
Morning Jewel, #2767, gold trim, bread and butter plate,
   6³/₈" d **8.00**
Morning Jewel, #2767, gold trim, coffeepot, cov **80.00**
Morning Jewel, #2767, gold trim, creamer **20.00**
Morning Jewel, #2767, gold trim, cup and saucer **18.00**
Morning Jewel, #2767, gold trim, demitasse cup and
   saucer **15.00**
Morning Jewel, #2767, gold trim, dinner plate, 10½" d **15.00**
Morning Jewel, #2767, gold trim, fruit bowl, 5½" d **12.00**
Morning Jewel, #2767, gold trim, platter, oval, 13½" l **40.00**
Morning Jewel, #2767, gold trim, relish, 9¼" l **12.00**
Morning Jewel, #2767, gold trim, salad plate, 8¼" d **12.00**
Morning Jewel, #2767, gold trim, salt and pepper
   shakers, pr **25.00**
Morning Jewel, #2767, gold trim, soup bowl, flat, 8⅞" d . . . **15.00**
Morning Jewel, #2767, gold trim, sugar, cov **25.00**
Morning Jewel, #2767, gold trim, teapot, cov **75.00**
Morning Jewel, #2767, gold trim, vegetable, cov, round **75.00**
Morning Jewel, #2767, gold trim, vegetable, open, oval,
   10⅛" l **40.00**
Morning Jewel, #2767, gold trim, vegetable, open,
   round, 9" d **40.00**
Violette, #3054, bread and butter plate, 6³/₈" d **5.00**
Violette, #3054, creamer **15.00**
Violette, #3054, cup and saucer **16.00**
Violette, #3054, dinner plate, 10½" d **14.00**
Violette, #3054, fruit bowl, flat, 5⅝" d **6.00**
Violette, #3054, gravy boat, attached liner **25.00**
Violette, #3054, platter, oval, 11⅞" l **25.00**
Violette, #3054, platter, oval, 13¾" l **30.00**
Violette, #3054, platter, oval, 16³/₈" l **45.00**
Violette, #3054, salad plate, 7⅝" d **8.00**
Violette, #3054, soup bowl, flat, 8¼" d **10.00**
Violette, #3054, sugar, cov **18.00**
Violette, #3054, vegetable, cov, round **55.00**
Violette, #3054, vegetable, open, oval, 10½" l **25.00**

NORITAKE AZALEA

Azalea is a Noritake hand-painted china pattern first produced in the early 1900s. Because the pieces are hand painted, subtle variations are common.

The Larkin Company, Buffalo, New York, used Azalea as one of its "Larkin Plan" premiums. In 1931 Larkin billed it as "Our Most Popular China." Some Azalea accessory pieces appeared in Larkin catalogs for three or four years, others for up to nineteen consecutive years. Azalea decorated glass and other coordinating items were made, but never achieved the popularity of the dinnerware.

Reference: Walter Ayars, *Larkin China, Catalog Reprint*, Echo Publishing, 1990.

Note: All items listed are china, unless otherwise noted. For additional information see Noritake China.

Bonbon, 6¼" **$50.00**
Bowl, divided **200.00**
Breakfast Plate, 8½" d **15.00**
Butter Chip, 3½" d **15.00**
Butter Tub, with insert **35.00**
Casserole, cov **125.00**
Child's Set, 15 pcs **1,500.00**
Coffeepot **450.00**
Condiment Set, 5 pcs **75.00**
Creamer and Sugar **45.00**
Cream Soup, 2-handled, 5½" d **85.00**
Demitasse Cup and Saucer **125.00**
Fan Vase, ftd **120.00**
Grapefruit Bowl, 4½" d **125.00**
Jam Jar Set, 3 pcs **150.00**
Mayonnaise Set, 3 pcs **50.00**
Milk Jug **150.00**
Mustard Jar, handled **50.00**
Nut Dish, shell shape, 7¾" l **250.00**
Oatmeal Bowl, 5½" d **15.00**
Plate, 7⅝" sq **35.00**
Platter, 16" l **450.00**
Refreshment Set, 2 pcs **45.00**

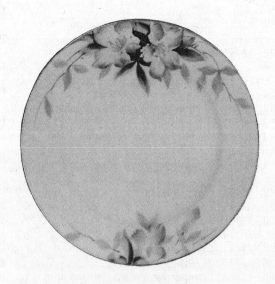

Dinner Plate, 10" d, $15.00.

Relish, 4-part, 10" l	100.00
Relish, oval, 8¼" l	12.00
Salad Bowl, 10" d	50.00
Salt and Pepper Shakers, pr, individual, 2½" h	25.00
Salt and Pepper Shakers, pr, tapered, 3½" h	35.00
Sauce Dish, 5½" d	10.00
Spoon Holder, 8" l	65.00
Syrup Pitcher, with underplate	130.00
Tea Plate, 7½" d	12.00
Teapot, cov, gold finial	450.00
Teapot Tile	40.00
Tobacco Jar, cov	500.00
Vase, bulbous	750.00
Vegetable, oval, 10½" l	50.00

NORITAKE TREE IN THE MEADOW

Tree in the Meadow is another popular hand-painted Noritake pattern. The basic scene includes a meandering stream (usually in the foreground), a peasant cottage, and a large tree. Muted tones of brown and yellow are the principal colors.

Noritake exported the first Tree in the Meadow pieces to the United States in the early 1920s. Several different backstamps were used for marking purposes. The Larkin Company distributed the pattern in the 1920s and 30s.

Reference: Walter Ayars, *Larkin China, Catalog Reprint,* Echo Publishing, 1990.

Berry Set, master bowl and 6 individual bowls	$70.00
Bowl, oval, 7" l	20.00
Bowl, oval, 9¼" l	40.00
Bread and Butter Plate, 6½" d	15.00
Bread Tray	45.00
Celery Dish, 12" l	35.00
Cereal Bowl, 5¾" d	20.00
Coffeepot, cov	175.00
Creamer and Sugar	50.00
Cup and Saucer	18.00
Demitasse Cup and Saucer	35.00
Dinner Plate	18.00

Salt and Pepper Shakers, pr, $30.00.

Dish, pierced handles, blue luster border	40.00
Eggcup	20.00
Fruit Bowl, 5¼" d	12.00
Lemon Dish, center ring handle, 5½" d	15.00
Luncheon Plate, 8½" d	20.00
Mug	100.00
Platter, 11½" l	50.00
Relish, divided	50.00
Salad Plate, 7½" d	15.00
Soup Bowl, 7½" d	30.00
Sugar Shaker	12.00
Toothpick Holder, fan shape, 7" h	75.00

NORTH DAKOTA SCHOOL OF MINES

Earle J. Babcock, a University of North Dakota chemistry instructor, was instrumental in promoting the use of North Dakota clay with the pottery industry. The first experimental pieces produced at the North Dakota School of Mines date from 1904. In 1910 a Ceramics Department was established.

Margaret Kelly Cable, department director from 1910 to 1949, was the driving force behind North Dakota School of Mines pottery. Pottery was exhibited at numerous fairs and expositions. Flora Cable Huckfield, Margaret's sister, arrived in 1924 as a decorator. By 1930 she was in charge of marketing the pottery's wares. Freida Louise Hammers, Julia Edna Mattson, Margaret Davis Pachl are other women who played a prominent role in the success of North Dakota School of Mines Pottery. Pachl succeeded Margaret Cable when she retired in 1949. Commercial production lessened. Pachl retired in 1970.

A cobalt blue university seal was used to mark wares produced between 1913 and 1963. Other early marks include a stamped or hand-printed "UND" or "U.N.D. Grand Forks, N.D." Only student names appear on pieces made after 1963.

Reference: Darlene Hurst Dommel, *Collector's Encyclopedia of the Dakota Potteries,* Collector Books, 1996, out of print.

Collectors' Club: North Dakota Pottery Collectors Society, PO Box 14, Beach, ND 58621.

Bookends, pr, Margaret Cable, wheat shocks, matte maroon glaze, 5½" h	$450.00
Bowl, Flora Huckfield, Prairie Rose, 2½ x 5"	250.00
Ginger Jar, McCosh, sgraffito dec, stylized cherry blossoms in buff clay against cobalt blue glaze, circular ink mark, incised "McCosh," 7 x 6"	1,500.00
Vase, F Cunningham, carved mocha-brown narcissus against dark brown ground, ink stamp, incised "F Cunningham/12/6/50," 9 x 5"	1,100.00
Vase, F Cunningham, excised with brown daffodils on dark brown ground, ink stamp and incised signature, 1950, 8¾ x 5"	1,875.00
Vase, Flora Huckfield, bulbous, emb cowboy scene under matte chocolate brown glaze, circular ink stamp, sgd and titled "ND Rodeo," 7¼ x 5"	1,650.00
Vase, Flora Huckfield, ovoid, "No Dak Wheat" carved sheaths of wheat under purple-brown matte glaze, ink stamp and incised "Huck 30/No Dak Wheat," 10 x 5½"	1,425.00
Vase, Margaret Cable, blue Art Deco sgraffito deer, flowers, and meadow on white ground, sgd and dated "M Cable 1946," 8" h	1,500.00

Vessel, Bentonite, Native American motif with birds, circular stamp, incised "Armstrong/1948," 4¼" h, 4¾" d, $1,000.00. Photo courtesy David Rago Auctions, Inc.

Vase, Mattson, cobalt blue sgraffito coyote on rust
  ground, 3½" h 450.00
Vase, McCosh, carved daffodils under mahogany matte
  glaze, circular ink mark, incised "McCosh '48," 1948,
  8 x 5½" 1,200.00
Vessel, Margaret Cable, carved, repeating frieze of
  bison, matte brown and green glaze, ink stamp, and
  "M Cable," 5 x 6" 5,200.00

NUTCRACKERS

Lever-action cast-iron nutcrackers, often in the shape of animals, appeared in the mid-19th century. Designs mirrored the popular design styles of each era. Art Deco and 1950s-era nutcrackers and sets are eagerly sought by collectors. Beginning in the 1960s, wooden nutcrackers from Germany's Erzgebirger region began flooding the American market. These Erzgebirger-style figures are now being made around the world, especially in the Far East, and from a wide variety of material.

Reference: James Rollband, *American Nutcrackers: A Patent History and Value Guide,* Off Beat Books, 1996.

Collectors' Club: Nutcracker Collectors' Club, 12204 Fox Run Dr, Chesterland, OH 44026.

Aluminum, squirrel $20.00
Brass, alligator 25.00
Brass, cat, nickel plated, 4½" l 45.00
Brass, eagle 30.00
Brass, jester head 75.00
Brass, parrot, 15½" l 15.00
Brass, rooster 30.00
Bronze, running whippet, 3¾" h 75.00
Cast Iron, dog, bronze finish 45.00
Cast Iron, skull and crossbones, 6" l 85.00
Wood, fish 20.00
Wood, ram, glass eyes, 8½" l 65.00

NUTTING, WALLACE

Wallace Nutting was born in 1861 in Rockingham, Massachusetts. He attended Harvard University and the Hartford Theological Seminary and Union Theological Seminary in New York. In 1904 Nutting opened a photography studio in New York. Within a year, he moved to Southby, Connecticut and opened a larger studio. His pictures sold well. In 1907 he opened a branch office in Toronto, Canada. By 1913 Nutting's operation was located in Framingham, Massachusetts. Business boomed. At its peak, Nutting employed over 200 colorists, framers, salesmen, and support staff.

Nutting took all his own pictures. However, printing, coloring, framing, and even signing his name were the work of his employees. Over 10,000 photographs in an assortment of sizes have been identified.

In the 1920s when the sale of pictures declined, Nutting explored a host of other business opportunities. His books, especially the *States Beautiful and Furniture Treasury* series, were the most successful.

Wallace Nutting died on July 19, 1941. His wife continued the business. When Mrs. Nutting died in 1944, she willed the business to Ernest John Donnelly and Esther Svenson. In 1946, Svenson bought out Donnelly. In 1971 Svenson entered a nursing home and ordered the destruction of all of the Nutting glass negatives. A few were not destroyed and are in the hands of private collectors.

References: Michael Ivankovich, *Collector's Guide to Wallace Nutting Pictures,* Collector Books, 1997; Michael Ivankovich, *The Alphabetical & Numerical Index to Wallace Nutting Pictures,* Diamond Press, 1988; Michael Ivankovich, *The Guide to Wallace Nutting Furniture,* Diamond Press, 1990; *Colonial Reproductions* (reprint of 1921 catalog), Diamond Press, 1992; Wallace Nutting (reprint of 1915 catalog), Diamond Press, 1987; Wallace Nutting, *Wallace Nutting General Catalog, Supreme Edition* (reprint of 1930 catalog), Schiffer Publishing, 1977; Wallace Nutting, *Windsors* (reprint of 1918 catalog), Diamond Press, 1992.

Collectors' Club: Wallace Nutting Collector's Club, PO Box 22475, Cleveland, OH 44122.

Book, *Furniture Treasury, Volumes I-II-III, 1st Edition,*
  1928 and 1933 . . . . $225.00
Book, *Maine Beautiful, 2nd Edition* 35.00
Book, *New Hampshire Beautiful, 1st Edition* 45.00
Book, *Virginia Beautiful, 1st Edition* 50.00
Book, *Virginia Beautiful, 2nd Edition,* with dj 45.00
Mirror with Print, 10 x 12" Garden of Larkspur, England,
  picture with narrow path winding through flower gar-
  den to thatch-roofed cottage, sgd lower center, framed
  above mahogany mirror, 12 x 41" 400.00
Print, A Berkshire Brook, miniature ext, shallow rocky
  stream winds between rail fence, blossom tree, and
  curving country road, 4 x 5" 100.00
Print, A Call for More, Haverhill, MA, little girl sits eating at table while mother sews at fireside of Hazen
  Garrison House, 11 x 14" 575.00
Print, A Cluster of Zinnias, close-framed floral with colorful flowers in decorated golden tabletop vase, sgd
  lower right, orig copyright label on back, 8 x 10" 625.00
Print, Affectionately Yours, Saugus, MA, girl writing let-
  ter, sitting in writing-arm Windsor chair near
  Broadhearth fireplace, 17 x 21" 475.00

Print, View From Casino, Funchal, Funchal Harbor, Madeira, 12 x 16", $2,250.00. Photo courtesy Michael Ivankovich Antiques, Inc.

Print, A Formal Call, Danvers, MA, girl in yellow dress sits beside marble fireplace and 3 empty chairs, 11 x 17" 375.00

Print, A Little River, NH, country road runs along rocky rapid-running stream with Mt Washington in background, sgd lower right, copyright lower left, orig copyright label on back, 20 x 30". 400.00

Print, Among October Birches, NH, country road winds past long rows of fall-colored birch trees, original copyright label on back, 16 x 20". 300.00

Print, An October Array, Hartford, CT, fall-colored trees reflecting in calm stream near green grass and stone bridge, 13 x 16" 250.00

Print, An Old Time Romance, Framingham, MA, girl with chin resting in hand reading book while seated at table in Nuttingholme parlor, 16 x 20" 425.00

Print, A Perkiomen October, PA scene with fall-colored trees reflecting in calm Perkiomen Creek, orig copyright label on back, 9 x 11" 325.00

Print, Apple Tree Bend, country road winds along stone wall and orchard's pink blossoms, 14 x 17". 200.00

Print, A Sip of Tea, Southbury, CT, girl reaches for copper teapot hanging over roaring Nuttinghame fire, 12 x 16" 325.00

Print, A Story of Chivalry, Wethersfield, CT, girl reads book while sitting beside Webb House fire near wall with Revolutionary War pictorial wallpaper, 10 x 12" 300.00

Print, A Welcome Task, Wethersfield, CT, girl works at table beside red-brick fireplace in a Webb House parlor, 11 x 14" 325.00

Print, Bonnie Dale, Ireland, blue stream winds past green trees and colorful blue and orange flowers, 13 x 16" 300.00

Print, Cathedral Brook, shallow rocky brook running between fall-colored trees, orig copyright label on back, 16 x 20". 275.00

Print, Dainty China, Framingham, MA, girl arranges china in Nuttingholme parlor corner cupboard, 13 x 16" 350.00

Print, Dell Dale Road, country road winds past fall-colored trees, 16 x 20". 225.00

Print, Easter in Washington, Washington, DC, pink blossoms stand beside blue lake, 13 x 16" 375.00

Print, Honeymoon Drive, white petals on country road beneath arching blossom trees, 11 x 14". 175.00

Print, Joy Path, England, narrow path winds through colorful flower garden, 6 x 8" 125.00

Print, Larkspur, foreign miniature, narrow path leads past girl in flower garden to thatch-roofed cottage, 4 x 5" 100.00

Print, Lined with Petals, Berkshires, MA, country path winds past birch cluster and roadside rocks, 11 x 17" 185.00

Print, Red Eagle Lake, NH, fall-colored trees reflecting in a still blue lake with a distant mountain sitting above the clouds, orig copyright label on back, 13 x 16". 250.00

Print, Terrace of Steps, VA scene with stone steps leading through green Montibello garden to marble statue, 13 x 16" 800.00

Print, The Coming Out of Rosa, MA, little Rosa stands beside Mother on large rose-covered porch, 10 x 13" 350.00

Print, The Dim Old Forest, Ireland, narrow path winding between forest flowers and tall trees, 20 x 24" 425.00

Print, The Maple Sugar Cupboard, Southbury, CT, close-framed int scene with girl reaching into Nuttinghame fireplace mantel cupboard, orig backing and copyright label, 20 x 30". 750.00

Print, The Quilting Party, Portsmouth, NH, 3 girls quilt beside canopied bed in Wentworth-Gardiner House bedroom, orig "Wentworth-Gardiner House Colonial Chain of Picture Houses" label on back, 11 x 14". 375.00

Print, The Rug Maker, MA, girl braids rug while sitting beside Broadhearth fire, Saugus Iron Works, 11 x 14" 300.00

Print, The Way Through the Orchard, MA, country road runs between stone walls and pink blossoms, 11 x 14". . . . 185.00

Print, untitled ext, country road runs through orchard past pink blossom trees, 8 x 10". 110.00

Print, untitled int, girl in bonnet stands by Nuttingholme parlor mirror, 7 x 9". 165.00

Print, Wells from the Palace Pool, England, 2 white swans swim in blue lake near massive stone cathedral and green treeline, 14 x 17". 750.00

Silhouette, girl plays piano near flower vase 40.00

Silhouette, girl stands by armless statue 40.00

The Meeting Place, horse and cows at stream, 13 x 16", $2,000.00. Photo courtesy Michael Ivankovich Antiques, Inc.

NUTTING-LIKE PHOTOGRAPHS

The commercial success of Wallace Nutting's hand-colored, framed photographs spawned a series of imitators. David Davidson (1881-1967), Charles Higgins (1867-1930), Charles Sawyer (born 1904) and his Sawyer Picture Company, and Fred Thompson (1844-1923) are only a few of the dozens of individuals and businesses that attempted to ride Nutting's coattails.

Most of these photographers followed the same procedure as Nutting. They took their own photographs, usually with a glass plate camera. Prints were made on special platinum paper. Substitute paper was used during World War I. Each picture was titled and numbered, usually by the photographer. A model picture was colored. Colorists then finished the remainder of the prints. Finally, the print was matted, titled, signed, and sold.

References: Carol Begley Gray, *The History of the Sawyer Pictures*, published by author, 1995; Michael Ivankovich, *Collector's Value Guide to Early Twentieth Century American Prints*, Collector Books, 1998.

Carlock, Lincoln Memorial, Washington DC, close-framed, memorial standing above pink blossoms and green treeline reflects in the Potomac River, orig Carlock label on back, 5 x 7" $75.00

Carlock, US Capitol Building, Washington DC, close-framed close-up view of Capitol Building, "©Carlock" imp lower left, orig Carlock label on back, 5 x 7" 85.00

Davidson, David, The Birches, cluster of white birches stand beside blue lake, 8 x 12" 85.00

Davidson, David, Her House in Order, closed-framed int with chairs, spinning wheel, and hooked rug beside fire and mantel china, signature and color a little light, 12 x 16" 125.00

Davidson, David, Prize Pewter, close-framed int with large pewter-filled cupboard in parlor beside dining room table, sgd and titled on picture, orig Davidson label on back, 12 x 16" 150.00

Gibson, Waterfall in Autumn, broad waterfall flowing into rippling pool, 10 x 11" 50.00

Harris, Rainbow Falls, Watkins Glen, NY, tall rocky falls flowing past cliffside bridge and walkway, 4 x 8" 65.00

Haynes, Old Faithful geyser blows in Yellowstone National Park, "Haynes" imp in picture and matting lower right, 6 x 13" 110.00

Sawyer, Ammonoosuc Falls, NH, country road runs along rocky, rushing stream, orig "Sawyer Pictures" and "Ammonoosuc Falls" labels, 7 x 14" 160.00

Sawyer, Echo Lake, Franconia Notch, NH, hilltop view of broad Echo Lake and distant Hotel and Franconia Notch, "Echo Lake, Franconia Notch" label on back, 8 x 10" 150.00

Sawyer, Mt Chocorua, NH, close-framed hilltop view of distant Mt Chocorua near white birch cluster and large blue lake, orig backing and Sawyer stamp, 10 x 13" 150.00

Sawyer, Silver Birches, Lake George, NY, white birch cluster stands beside long Lake George, 8 x 10" 160.00

Trott, MA, One Gun Alley, Bermuda scene with narrow alley separating 2 rows of flower-bordered houses, 12 x 15" 100.00

Yates, Paul, Bay of Fundy Prime, Canada, white waves crash against rocky tree-lined Nova Scotia shoreline, 6 x 8" 75.00

Unknown, girl on wall, close-framed, Flapper-type girl in pink hat and fur coat sits on tall stone wall, 8 x 10" 45.00

Unknown, ivy-covered building and cars, close-framed, 2 1930s-era automobiles sit outside a large, ivy-covered red-brick institution, 6 x 10" 60.00

Unknown, locomotive and train, close-framed close-up view of long train winding up steep hill beside rushing stream and tall Rocky Mountain, 7 x 11" 85.00

Sawyer, The Sea, $220.00. Photo courtesy Michael Ivankovich Antiques, Inc.

OCCUPIED JAPAN

America occupied Japan from August 1945 until April 28, 1952. World War II devastated the Japanese economy. The Japanese ceramics industry was one of the first to be revitalized. Thousands of inexpensive figurines and knickknacks were exported to the United States and elsewhere in the late 1940s and 1950s.

Not all products made in Japan between 1946 and April 1952 are marked "Occupied Japan." Some pieces simply were marked "Japan" or "Made in Japan." However, collectors of Occupied Japan material insist that "Occupied" be found in the mark for an item to be considered a true Occupied Japan collectible.

Beware of Occupied Japan reproductions, copycats, fantasy pieces, and fakes. Period marks tend to be underglaze. They will not scratch off. Rubber-stamped fake marks will. The marks on recent reproductions are excellent. Shape, form, color, and aging characteristics are now the primary means of distinguishing period pieces from later examples.

References: Florence Archambault, *Occupied Japan For Collectors*, Schiffer Publishing, 1992; Gene Florence, *The Collector's Encyclopedia of Occupied Japan Collectibles*, First Series (1976), Second Series (1979), Third Series (1987), Fourth Series (1990), Fifth Series (1992), (1999 value update for series I-V), Collector Books; Anthony Marsella, *Toys From Occupied Japan*, Schiffer Publishing, 1995; Lynette Palmer, *Collecting Occupied Japan*, Schiffer Publishing, 1997.

Collectors' Club: The Occupied Japan Club, 29 Freeborn St, Newport, RI 02840.

Ashtray, metal, figural baseball glove $10.00
Ashtray, metal, figural hand 10.00
Ashtray, metal, figural leaf and grapes 3.00
Biscuit Jar, tomato, Maruhonware 60.00
Chocolate Pot, floral dec, 7½" h 20.00
Cigarette Box, blue floral dec, gold trim, Rossetti
  Chicago 10.00
Cigarette Set, plated metal, covered box, with Scottie
  dog, matching lighter. 20.00
Clock, bisque, double feature, colonial dancing couple
  atop floral encrusted case, 10½" h 250.00
Coolie, Chinese boy and girl, 7¾" h 60.00
Cornucopia Vase, pink roses dec, gold trim, mkd
  "Lamore China entirely hand made GZL USA." 30.00
Creamer, cottage, 2⅝" h 15.00
Creamer, honeycomb, 2¾" h 15.00
Creamer, Windmill pattern, figural windmill, 2¾" h 10.00
Creamer and Tray, silver toned white metal creamer with
  emb grapevine designs on sides, swan and "T" logo
  on bottom, mkd "Made in Occupied Japan," with sil-
  ver toned tray mkd "Made in Occupied Japan" 20.00
Crumb Pan, metal, emb New York scenes. 10.00
Cup and Saucer, dragon, blue and white 20.00
Cup and Saucer, ribbed, floral motif, mkd "Merit China
  HP" 15.00
Demitasse Cup and Saucer, floral dec, green, gold, and
  blue, mkd "Ucagco China" 15.00
Demitasse Cup and Saucer, yellow ext, floral motif
  inside cup, Jyoto China 10.00
Demitasse Set, coffeepot, sugar, creamer, and 3 cups
  and saucer, translated script "Black like the devil, hot
  like hell, pure like an angel, sweet like love: Recipe
  of Rareecand" 40.00
Figurine, clown, Ucagco China, 5¼" h. 35.00
Figurine, clown playing saxophone 8.00
Figurine, colonial couple dancing, mkd "LD" in flower
  face emblem, 7¼" h 30.00
Figurine, colonial couple playing mandolin, 4⅜" h 35.00
Figurine, colonial man, red jacket, striped pants,
  Ucagco China. 20.00
Figurine, colonial man with basket on arm. 12.00
Figurine, Dutch girl with flowers, Ucagco China, 10⅛" h 55.00
Figurine, Hawaiian girl playing ukelele 10.00
Figurine, Indian in canoe. 10.00
Figurine, organ grinder 20.00
Figurine, oriental couple with mandolin, 5½" h 25.00
Figurine, oriental man playing violin 8.00
Figurine, reclining elf 10.00
Honey Jar, honeycomb design with ivy dec 18.00
Lamp, bisque, seated colonial couple, Maruyama. 65.00
Lighter, figural horse head, mkd "CMC" 15.00
Lighter, figural swan, table, cast white metal, lighter
  insert in back, mkd "Made in Occupied Japan,"
  3½ x 3". 20.00
Mug, purple grapes on brown ground, 4" h 10.00
Pin, celluloid, Scottie dog 10.00
Pincushion, figural cat with arched back, pink floral dec
  on white ground 6.00
Planter, boy playing guitar, dog at side, 4⅛" h 10.00
Planter, boy standing by cherry tree, 3⅝" h 8.00

Salt and Pepper Shakers, pr, Mammy and Pappy, gold trim, 4¾" h, $40.00. Photo courtesy Ray Morykan Auctions.

Planter, dog standing beside tophat, 3⅝" h 8.00
Planter, flamingo on brown basket. 10.00
Planter, goose, head down, blue, orange, and green on
  white ground 6.00
Planter, lady holding skirt 20.00
Planter, lady's shoe, hp flowers on white ground. 20.00
Planter, shepherd boy with lamb 8.00
Plate, cloverleaf shape, floral dec on brown ground 8.00
Plate, hp scene of lake and shoreline, pine trees and
  rocks, and mountains in background, sgd "S Toka,"
  9" d 35.00
Plate, hp scene of sailboat on water and building on
  shore, mountains in background, sgd "Y Mezutabi,"
  9" d 35.00
Plate, leaf shape, pink floral dec on white ground. 3.00
Plate, reticulated, white, hp roses in center, mkd "ATYO
  China," 8" d 15.00
Reamer, strawberry shape, red with green leaves and
  handle, 3¾" h 65.00
Salt and Pepper Shakers, pr, Aunt Jemima and chef, sou-
  venir from Thousand Islands, NY 45.00
Salt and Pepper Shakers, pr, Dutch girl. 6.00
Salt and Pepper Shakers, pr, Indian with paddle 7.00
Salt and Pepper Shakers, pr, strawberry, with tray 20.00
Sugar, cov, floral motif on white ground, Ucagco China 22.00
Tape Measure, celluloid, pig, blue 45.00
Teapot, emb dragon, mkd "KS" 100.00
Teapot, emb flowers on brown ground. 30.00
Teapot, floral dec, blue trim 30.00
Tea Set, teapot, creamer, and covered sugar, mkd "Sango
  China, Made in Occupied Japan". 30.00
Toby Mug, man with granny glasses. 30.00
Wall Pocket, lady with full skirt, 6" h 35.00
Windup, walking bear, dark brown plush body, white
  muzzle, ears, and paws, glass eyes and nose, walks
  forward as head moves side to side, mkd "Occupied
  Japan," 1940s, orig box 75.00

OCEAN LINER COLLECTIBLES

This category is devoted to collectibles from the era of the diesel-powered ocean liner, whose golden age dates between 1910 and the mid-1950s. It is dominated by legendary companies, e.g., Cunard and Holland-American, and ships, e.g., *Queen Elizabeth* and *Queen Elizabeth II*. Many World War II servicemen and women have fond memories of their voyage overseas on a fabulous ocean liner.

Collectors focus primarily on pre-1960 material. Shipboard stores sold a wide range of souvenirs. Printed menus, daily newspapers, and postcards are popular. The category is very much fame driven—the more famous, the more valuable.

References: Myra Yellin Outwater, *Ocean Liner Collectibles*, Schiffer Publishing, 1998; Karl D. Spence, *How to Identify and Price Ocean Liner Collectibles*, published by author, 1991; Karl D. Spence, *Oceanliner Collectibles* (1992), *Vol. 2* (1996), published by author; James Steele, *Queen Mary*, Phaidon, 1995.

Collectors' Club: Oceanic Navigation Research Society, Inc., PO Box 8005, Universal City, CA 91618.

Accommodations List, *RMS Queen Elizabeth*, Cunard, "Plan of First Class Accommodation," 1950s **$35.00**

Ashtray, Carnival Cruise Lines, glass, rect, ocean liners *Mardi Gras, Carnivale*, and *Festivale* **30.00**

Ashtray, *Queen Elizabeth 2*, white china, ocean liner in center, gold trim, 1970s **30.00**

Baggage Label, *White Star*, Cunard Line, oval **10.00**

Candy Tin, *RMS Queen Mary*, litho tin, octangular, full color lid art of huge ocean liner cutting through choppy waters, colorful perimeter panels with depiction of various wrapped candy pcs produced by Bensons Confectionery Ltd, England, hinged lid opens to bright silver flashing finish int, c1930s, 5 x 8 x 2" **25.00**

Cigarette Case, ocean liner and *"RMMV 'Highland Princess'"* on cover, 1950s **65.00**

Cocktail Shaker, *Liberte*, sterling silver, 1950s **475.00**

Deck Plan, Cunard Lines, *SS Scythia*, fold-up, color coded layout of rooms, black and white photos, dated 1925, 36 x 34" **15.00**

Luggage Tag, United States Lines, ship and "First Class Baggage Room," 1950s **12.00**

Magazine Article, *Life* magazine, "The *'Normandie'* Floats Again," Aug 23, 1943 . . . . **75.00**

Menu, *Andania*, Cunard, 1925 . . . . **20.00**

Matchcover, *Cunard Line*, each panel with black, white, and red steamship image on 1 side, logo ensign flag on opposite side, text for travel service between Europe, US, and Canada, striker panels slightly used, c1920-30s, ¾ x 1½ x 2¼" **25.00**

Menu, "Hamburg Amerika Line, Glass Bottom Dinner, on Board the *SS Resolute*," 3-part fold-out, diecut windows on bottom of boat, clear cellophane, reverse adv for "Amber, The German Gold–If Interested–After Dinner–Meet," 1935 . . . . **25.00**

Menu, *United States*, multicolor ocean liner image, gold party hat and horn background, 1969 . . . . **20.00**

Olive Dish, Italian lines, "Italia" and logo, blue and gold band, 1950s **75.00**

Passenger List, *SS Stuttgart*, North German Lloyd, 1930s **35.00**

Matchcover, French Line, *Normandie*, full length, inside lists 4 ships and their tonnage, Lion Match, $12.00. Photo courtesy Ray Morykan Auctions.

Pen, *RMS Queen Elizabeth*, souvenir, ballpoint, black hard molded plastic and gold toned metal, clear hard molded plastic end holds colorful plastic depiction of ocean liner, orig box with instructions **20.00**

Pen, Royal Caribbean cruise line, plastic, 1990s **3.00**

Playing Cards, Concordia Line, complete deck of 52 cards plus 2 Joker cards, dark blue with black and white design centered by symbol of "H" flag above sponsor title, inscription "Christian Haaland/ Haugesnund, Norway," c1930s, ¾ x 2½ x 3¾" **25.00**

Playing Cards, Cunard Line, complete deck of 52 cards plus 2 Joker cards, black, yellow, and silver design with symbolic crowned lion holding world globe, John Waddington Ltd, Leeds, England, ¾ x 2¼ x 3½" **20.00**

Postcard, *Bremen*, 1920s **10.00**

Postcard, *RMS Aquitania*, Cunard Line, sepia, specs on back, unmailed **10.00**

Postcard, *Vistafjord*, Cunard Line, Cunard logo and ship's name above ocean liner image, 1990s **2.00**

Spoon, *Chandris Lines*, silver plated, flag symbol and title on handle tip, underside of handle mkd "BLS Plate England," c1930s, 5¼" l **20.00**

AUCTION PRICES – OCEAN LINER POSTERS

Swann Galleries, Inc., Vintage Posters, January 27, 2000. Prices include a 15% buyer's premium.

Cunard, view looking up from deck, red and black funnel, white railings, and brown mast, red and light brown lettering "Votre Route pour les Etats-Unis et le Canada," restoration and wrinkles in margins, 40 x 25" **$488.00**

Fred Olsen Lines, couple sitting on red-striped deck chairs beneath towering yellow funnel, dark blue background, Johs Berggren, Officin, Oslo, restoration at edges, 39¾ x 24½" **517.00**

Furness Cruise Ships, *Queen of Bermuda* and *Ocean Monarch*, 2 liners leaving blue mountains and palm trees of Caribbean island port as they set out to sea beneath a light blue sky, Adolph Treidler, screen print, repaired tears, restoration, and scuffing in margins and image, 40⅜ x 61¾" . **1,955.00**

NYK Line, *SS Nitta Maru*, *SS Yawata Maru*, and *SS Kasuga*, allegorical image of 3 young Japanese women representing additions to fleet, R Koisso, Toppan Printing Co, Japan, minor restoration in margins and image, c1941, 42 x 30" **862.00**

OLYMPIC MEMORABILIA

Athens, Greece, was the site of the first modern Olympic games in 1896. Baron Pieree de Coubertin, who created the Olympic rings symbol, is the father of the modern games. The first flag featuring the Olympic rings appeared at the 1914 Paris games. The first torch run, carrying the Olympic flame from Greece to the site of the games, occurred in 1936.

Collectors seek anything and everything associated with the games from athletes' medals to officials' badges. Posters are among the high-end items; contemporary "pins" rank at the bottom.

Reference: Roderick A. Malloy, *Malloy's Sports Collectibles Value Guide: Up-to-Date Prices for Noncard Sports Memorabilia,* Attic Books, Wallace-Homestead, 1993.

Collectors' Club: Olympic Pin Collector's Club, 1836 Fifth St, Schenectady, NY 12303.

1932 Los Angeles, X Summer Games, Hungary, NOC team pin, stud, tombac, cloisonné, round, enameled emblem attached to globe over South America silhouette and "X Olimpiai Jate-Kok Los-Angeles 1932," 25mm. **$225.00**

1932 Los Angeles, X Summer Games, stadium pass, Jeffries Banknote Co, Los Angeles, with orig presentation leather wallet **225.00**

1936 Berlin, XI Summer Games, German, ticket, Leichtathletik, Aug 9, valid upon presentation of press card, used **175.00**

1936 Berlin, XI Summer Games, NOC team pin, Swedish Fencing, with bent wire catch, tombac, cloisonné, Olympic rings shape, 2 crossed swords over Olympic rings on blue ground, 27 x 42mm **175.00**

1948 London, XIV Summer Games, basketball ticket, Jul 30, morning session stub used, printed by Waterlow & Sons, in orig presentation envelope **100.00**

1948 London, XIV Summer Games, Czechoslovakia, NOC team pin, with metal catch, tombac silver, struck, rect, "CS Vybor Olymp" on white ground, Bohemian lion on red ground, "1948" on blue ground, and multicolored Olympic rings, 35 x 25mm **165.00**

1948 London, XIV Summer Games, souvenir spoon, metal, "XIV Olympiad/London 1948" on front, reverse mkd "Reg No. 851108/E.P.O.B./Made In England" **125.00**

1952 Helsinki, XV Summer Games, drinking glass, red stamped "A.S.A.," Olympic torch and rings below. **50.00**

1952 Helsinki, XV Summer Games, official guide, 200 pp, black and white photos and illus, city map **60.00**

1952 Helsinki, XV Summer Games, Olympic rings and blue trim, 8½ x 4½" **50.00**

1956 Melbourne, XVI Summer Games, Czechoslovakia, NOC team pin, metal catch, nickel-copper, struck, disc thrower over Olympic rings, red star with Bohemian lion top right, Olympic flame bottom left, and "CS Olympijaky Vybor 1956," 39 x 27 mm **165.00**

1964 Innsbruck, IX Winter Games, German, season ticket. **90.00**

1968 Grenoble, X Winter Games, official guest badge, tombac gilted, obverse with snowflake and 3 roses, Olympic rings below, symbol of Grenoble and official games emblem, "Arthus Bertrand, Paris" **475.00**

1968 Mexico City, XIX Summer Games, NOC team pin, with metal catch, tombac gilt, cloisonné, shield

shape, Argentinian flag in shield shape, Olympic rings, and "Argentina/Mexico XIX Olimpiada–1968," 19 x 15mm **45.00**

1972 Munich XX Summer Games, Bulgaria, NOC team pin, stick pin, tombac gilt, cloisonné, rect, Olympic rings, Bulgarian lion, and "1972," Bulgarian flag colors with white above, green in center, and red below, 31 x 17mm **50.00**

1976 Montreal, XXI Summer Games, NOC team pin, South Korean wrestling, post with military clutch, tombac gilt, struck, shape of 2 wrestlers over "Korea/Montreal '76," 24 x 21mm **40.00**

1980 Lake Placid, NY, XIII Winter Games, coloring book, 32 pp, unused, 10½ x 14½". **15.00**

1980 Lake Placid, NY, XIII Winter Games, poster, figure skating, "XIII Olympic Winter Games/Lake Placid 1980," designed by LeRoy Neiman, Inc, 39 x 20" **400.00**

1984 Sarajevo, XIV Winter Games, mascot, Voochko, stuffed, plush, orange scarf, attached tag, Wallace Berrie & Co, made in Korea, 8" h **75.00**

1984 Los Angeles, XXIII Summer Games, Guyana, NOC team pin, bent wire catch, paper label on plastic and metal, round, Olympic colors and map of Guyana surrounded by "Guyana Olympic Association XXIII Olympiad," 32mm. **65.00**

1988 Calgary, XV Winter Games, NOC team pin, Jamaican Bobsleigh, post with military clutch, tombac gilt, fine enamel, shield shape, 2-man bobsled over stylized mountain with palm trees at base, "Jamaica/Calgary 1988" above and "Bobsleigh/Team" below, white ground, 19 x 11mm. **45.00**

1988 Seoul, XXIV Summer Games, Bangladesh, NOC team pin, post with military clutch, tombac gilt, epoxy, round, NOC logo and Olympic rings above "Bangladesh/1988/XXIV Olympiad," 18mm **40.00**

PADEN CITY GLASS

The Paden City Glass Manufacturing Company, Paden City, West Virginia, was founded in 1916. David Fisher, formerly president and general manager of the New Martinsville Glass Company, headed the company. When he died in 1933, Sam Fisher, David's son, assumed the presidency.

Initially the company produced pressed lamps, tableware, and vases. Later the company expanded its lines to include hotel and restaurant glassware. The company also acted as a jobber, doing mold work for other glass companies.

Color was one of Paden City's strong points. It offered a wide range of colored glasswares, e.g., amber, blue, cheriglo, dark green, ebony, mulberry, and opal. Thus far over 35 etchings have been identified as being done at Paden City.

In 1949 Paden City purchased the fully automated American Glass Company, continuing production of ashtrays, containers, and novelties. The American Glass acquisition proved disastrous. Paden City Glass ceased operations in 1951.

Reference: Gene Florence, *Very Rare Glassware of the Depression Years, Fifth Series,* Collector Books, 1997.

Ardith, beverage set, pitcher and 6 tumblers, green. **$575.00**
Ardith, bowl, Miss B blank, ftd, yellow, 11" d **55.00**
Ardith, candy, square, green **150.00**
Ardith, cup, yellow **50.00**

Echo, #116, candlesticks, ebony, 10" h, $20.00. Photo courtesy Ray Morykan Auctions.

Ardith, gravy boat, green	80.00
Ardith, plate, 2-handled, pink	135.00
Black Forest, bowl, 2-handled, black, 10" d	100.00
Black Forest, bowl, rolled edge, pink, 11¾" d	250.00
Black Forest, bowl, rolled edge, green, 13¼" d	300.00
Black Forest, compote, pink, 6½" h	100.00
Black Forest, ice tub, 2-handled, pink	150.00
Black Forest, tray, center handle, green	80.00
Black Forest, vase, Regina, black, 10" h	200.00
Cotton Ball Bunny, ears down, blue frosted	300.00
Crows Foot, bowl, flat, cobalt, 8½"	125.00
Crows Foot, candleholders, pr, open center, white	250.00
Crows Foot, compote, cobalt, 6½" h	75.00
Crows Foot, cup and saucer, red	15.00
Crows Foot, cup and saucer, round saucer, forest green	75.00
Crows Foot, cup and saucer, square saucer, light green	45.00
Crows Foot, tumbler, flat, blue	100.00
Crows Foot, vase, cupped-in, black, 8" h	225.00
Cupid, bowl, rolled edge, pink, 11" d	400.00
Cupid, cake plate, pink	175.00
Cupid, cake stand, pink	225.00
Cupid, compote, pink	325.00
Cupid, ice tub, green	325.00
Cupid, ice tub, pink	325.00
Cupid, mayonnaise and liner, green	225.00
Cupid, tray, center handle, green, 10½" d	225.00
Cupid, tray, oval, ftd, pink, 11" l	275.00
Futura, cup, #836, cobalt	10.00
Gadroon, bowl, #881, cobalt, 8" d	85.00
Gadroon, mayonnaise, #881, cobalt	35.00
Gazebo, cake salver, #555, crystal	125.00
Gazebo, candy dish, 3-part, crystal, gold trim	75.00
Gazebo, candy dish, cov, pedestal base, blue	145.00
Gazebo, plate, crystal, 11" d	50.00
Gazebo, tray, center handle, swan head, crystal	100.00
Gothic Arch, server, center handle, yellow	50.00
Hotcha, cup and saucer, ruby	12.00
Hotcha, plate, ruby, 6" d	7.00
Hotcha, plate, ruby, 9" d	25.00
Lela Bird, cheese plate, green	65.00
Lela Bird, tray, center handle, pink	125.00
Nora Bird, candy dish, cov, flat, green	350.00
Nora Bird, candy dish, cov, flat, pink	325.00
Nora Bird, cup and saucer, pink	200.00

Nora Bird, mayonnaise and spoon, green	120.00
Orchid, bowl, oval, 2-handled, red	250.00
Orchid, cake stand, yellow	70.00
Orchid, compote, low, ftd	50.00
Orchid, gardenia bowl, 9" d	60.00
Orchid, mayonnaise, liner, and ladle, yellow	160.00
Orchid, plate, red, 10" sq	85.00
Orchid, sherry, #5025, 2 oz	125.00
Paden City, #210, tumbler, crystal, 5 oz	3.00
Paden City, #555, punch bowl, crystal	75.00
Paden City, #1504, server, center handle, crystal	35.00
Party Line, soda tumbler, green, 7" h	12.00
Peacock and Wild Rose, bowl, ftd, pink, 9" d	175.00
Peacock and Wild Rose, cake plate, low, ftd, green	75.00
Peacock and Wild Rose, cake plate, low, ftd, pink	150.00
Peacock and Wild Rose, candleholders, pr, pink	175.00
Peacock and Wild Rose, console bowl, pink, 11" d	200.00
Peacock and Wild Rose, console bowl, rolled edge, green, 14" d	180.00
Peacock and Wild Rose, vase, black, 10" h	325.00
Peacock and Wild Rose, vase, elliptical, green	375.00
Penny Line, candlesticks, pr, amber	30.00
Penny Line, soda tumbler, green, 7" h	20.00
Penny Line, speakeasy cocktail shaker, with spout, green	100.00
Penny Line, tumbler, green, 5¾" h	10.00
Penny Line, vase, ftd, amber	25.00

PADEN CITY POTTERY

Paden City Pottery, located near Sisterville, West Virginia, was founded in 1914. The company manufactured high quality, semi-porcelain dinnerware. The quality of Paden City's decals was such that their ware often was assumed to be hand painted.

The company's Shenandoah Ware shape line was made with six different applied patterns. Sears Roebuck featured Paden City's Nasturtium pattern in the 1940s. Bak-Serv, a 1930s kitchenware line, was produced in solid colors and with decal patterns. Paden City also made Caliente, a line of single-color glazed ware introduced in 1936. Russel Wright designed the company's Highlight pattern, manufactured in five colors between 1951 and 1952.

Paden City Pottery ceased operation in November 1963.

Reference: Harvey Duke, *The Official Price Guide to Pottery & Porcelain, Eighth Edition,* House of Collectibles, 1995.

Bak-Serv, mixing bowl, 5" d	$6.00
Bak-Serv, plate, Elite shape, 9" d	10.00
Bak-Serv, soup bowl, Elite shape, 7" d	15.00
Blue Willow, chop plate, 12¾" d	15.00
Blue Willow, plate, 9" d	10.00
Blue Willow, saucer	2.00
Caliente, dinner plate, cobalt	10.00
Caliente, pitcher, orange	20.00
Caliente, serving plate, 13" d, tangerine	20.00
Caliente, teapot, blue	30.00
Elite, bread and butter plate, 6½" d	1.00
Elite, chop plate, 12¾" d	15.00
Elite, creamer and sugar	12.00
Elite, soup bowl	10.00
Far East, creamer	5.00
Far East, soup bowl	5.00
Highlight, bread and butter plate	8.00
Highlight, chop plate	40.00

Highlight, cup and saucer **25.00**
Highlight, platter, oval **35.00**
Highlight, vegetable, round **40.00**
Manhattan, casserole **20.00**
Manhattan, gravy boat **12.00**
Manhattan, plate, 7" d **4.00**
Manhattan, platter, 12½" l **12.00**
New Virginia, creamer and sugar **12.00**
New Virginia, dinner plate **10.00**
New Virginia, gravy boat **12.00**
New Virginia, salad bowl **15.00**
New Virginia, salad plate **4.00**
New Virginia, teapot **25.00**
Papoco, casserole **20.00**
Papoco, creamer and sugar **12.00**
Papoco, plate, 8¾" d **4.00**
Papoco, platter, rect, 13½" **12.00**
Regina, creamer and sugar **12.00**
Regina, gravy boat **12.00**
Regina, platter, 11½" l **10.00**
Regina, soup bowl **10.00**
Sally Paden, casserole **20.00**
Sally Paden, plate, 9¼" d **8.00**
Sally Paden, platter, 11½" l **10.00**
Shell Crest, casserole, ftd **30.00**
Shell Crest, cup and saucer **8.00**
Shell Crest, soup bowl **12.00**
Shell Crest, teapot **40.00**
Shenandoah, bread and butter plate, 6¼" d **1.00**
Shenandoah, creamer and sugar **12.00**
Shenandoah, gravy boat **12.00**
Virginia, casserole **20.00**
Virginia, creamer and sugar **12.00**
Virginia, plate, 9" d **8.00**

PAINT BY NUMBER SETS

Paint By Number sets achieved widespread popularity in the early 1950s. They claimed to turn rank amateurs into accomplished painters overnight. Virtually every generic scene, from a winter landscape to horse or clown portraits, was reduced to an outlined canvas with each section having a number that corresponded to one of the paints that came with the set.

Craft House Corporation (Toledo, Ohio), Craft Master (Toledo, Ohio, a division of General Mills), and Standard Toykraft (New York, New York) were among the leading manufacturers. Hassenfeld Brothers (Hasbro) did a number of licensed sets, e.g., Popeye and Superman.

Contemporary licensed paint by number sets, sometimes employing acrylic crayons rather than paint, can be found in today's toy stores. Rose Art Industries makes many of them.

Reference: Dan Robbins, *Whatever Happened to Paint-By-Numbers?*, Possum Hill Press, 1997.

Buck Rogers, Craft Master, 1980s **$10.00**
Combat Oil Paint By Number Set, Hasbro, 1963 . . . . **100.00**
Craftint Big 3 Set **20.00**
Davy Crockett Magic Paint with Water Pictures, Artcraft, 1950s **150.00**
Dennis the Menace Paint Set, crayons, paints, brush, and trays, Pressman, 1954 . . . . **40.00**

Disneyland Oil Painting By Numbers, Hassenfeld Brothers, 5 pictures, oil paints, and brush, unused, orig box, 1960s **25.00**
Flintstones Oil Painting By Numbers Set, Hasbro, 1966 . . . . . . **65.00**
Flipper "Stardust" Paint Set, Hasbro, two 7 x 11" pictures, 6 paint vials, application, and instruction sheet, 1966 . . . . **20.00**
Green Hornet Paint By Number Set, Hasbro, 1966 . . . . **90.00**
Herman & Katnip Deep View Paint Set, Pressman, 3-D picture with painted background, 6 paints, water bowl, and brush, 1961 . . . . **55.00**
Howdy Doody, Art Ward, acrylic, 1976 . . . . **25.00**
Hulk Comics Paint By Number Set, Transogram, 1982 . . . . **15.00**
Land of the Giants, Hasbro, 1969 . . . . **50.00**
Masterpiece Oil Painting Set, Craft Master **35.00**
New Artist Series, Craft Master, #18, 18 oil paints, 2 mounted 16 x 20" panels, 3 brushes, cleaner, and instructions **20.00**
Pann, Craft Master, 22 oil paints, 2 mounted 10 x 14" panels, brush, and instructions **25.00**
Pebbles and Bamm Bamm Paint By Numbers Coloring Set, Transogram, 8 inlaid paint tablets, plastic paint tray, 8 pre-numbered sketches, and brush, 1965 . . . . **55.00**
Popeye Paint By Number Set, Hasbro, 1981 . . . . **10.00**
Rin Tin Tin, Transogram, four 9¼ x 12" sheets, watercolor tablets, orig box, 1956 . . . . **60.00**
Space Traveler Paint-By-Number Set, Standard Toykraft, 1950s **100.00**
Star Trek Paint By Number Set, Craft House, 1980s **20.00**
Tales of Wells Fargo Paint By Number Set, Transogram, 1959 . . . . **45.00**
The Rifleman, Standard Toykraft, 1960 . . . . **70.00**

PAINTINGS

It is impossible to provide a short list that accurately represents the breadth and depth of available 20th-century paintings. Tens, if not hundreds, of thousands of paintings are sold each year at pricing ranging from a few dollars to millions.

Directing users to the best available research information is a goal of *The Official Rinker Price Guide To Collectibles*. This is the purpose of this introduction.

Keep one thing in mind. If you do not find information about the artist or painting you are researching in one of these reference books, it does not mean the artist or painting is rare. "No one cares" is probably a more correct interpretation.

Artist Dictionaries: Emmanuel Benezit, *Dictionnaire Critique et Documentaire des Peintres, Sculpteurs, Dessinateurs et Graveurs, 14 volumes*, Editions Grund, 1999; Peter Hastings Falk (ed.), *Who Was Who in American Art*, Sound View Press, 1999; Mantle Fielding, *Dictionary of American Painters, Sculptors and Engravers, Second Edition*, Reprint Services, 1994; Frances Spalding, *Dictionary of 20th Century Painters and Sculptors*, Antique Collectors' Club, 1991.

Introduction: Alan Bamberger, *Buy Art Smart*, Wallace-Homestead, 1990, out of print; Alan S. Bamberger, *How to Buy Fine Art You Can Afford*, Wallace-Homestead, 1994, out of print.

Price Guide References, Basic: Susan Theran, *Fine Art: Identification and Price Guide, Third Edition*, Avon Books, 1996.

Price Guide References, Advanced: *ADEC: Art Price Annual International and Falk's Art Price Index,* Ehrmann, St. Romain au Mont d'Or, France, annual since 1987; R. J. Davenport, *Davenport's Art Reference & Price Guide, 1999-2000,* Davenport Publishing, 1999; Richard Hislop (ed.), *The Art Sales Index,* Weybridge, Surrey, England, annual; *Mayer International Auction Records: Prints, Drawings, Watercolors, Paintings, Sculpture,* Acatos, annual since 1967, available on CD-ROM.

Museum Directories: *American Art Directory,* National Register Publishing; American Association of Museums, *The Official Museum Directory: United States and Canada,* National Register Publishing, updated periodically.

PAIRPOINT

The Pairpoint Manufacturing Company, a silver plating firm, was founded in New Bedford, Massachusetts, in 1880. In 1894 Pairpoint merged with Mount Washington Glass Company and became Pairpoint Corporation. The company produced a wide range of glass products, often encased in silver-plated holders or frames.

In 1938 the Kenner Salvage Company purchased Pairpoint, selling it in 1939 to Isaac N. Babbitt. Babbitt reorganized the company and named it the Gunderson Glass Works. Robert Gunderson, a master glass blower at Pairpoint, guided the new company.

When Gunderson died in 1952, Edwin V. Babbitt, president of National Pairpoint Company, a manufacturer of aluminum windows, chemical ordinance, glass, and toys, purchased Gunderson Glass Works and renamed it Gunderson-Pairpoint Glass Works. The company made a full line of plain and engraved lead crystal.

In 1957 old equipment and a decline in sales forced a closure. Robert Bryden was assigned the task of moving the plant from New Bedford to Wareham, Massachusetts. The Wareham plant closed in February 1958.

Desiring to fill existing orders, Bryden leased facilities in Spain and moved Pairpoint there. In 1968 Bryden, along with a group of Scottish glassworks, returned to Massachusetts. In 1970 Pairpoint opened a new, two-pot factory in Sagamore, Massachusetts.

When Bryden retired in 1988, Robert Bancroft bought the company. Production of lead crystal continues.

References: Edward and Sheila Malakoff, *Pairpoint Lamps,* Schiffer Publishing, 1990; Leonard E. Padgett, *Pairpoint Glass,* Wallace-Homestead, 1979, out of print; John A. Shumann III, *The Collector's Encyclopedia of American Art Glass,* Collector Books, 1988, 1999 value update.

Boudoir Lamp, domed shade flaring to rim with autumn
  leafed trees amid grass and flowers with butterflies
  dec on frosted glass ground, raised on patinated metal
  base, raised Pairpoint mark "C3064" on base, 14½" h,
  9¾" d shade **$1,250.00**
Boudoir Lamp, Portsmouth shade with reverse painted
  roses on pale yellow and white ground, black enamel
  outline highlights, bronzed metal base, shade mkd
  "The Pairpoint Corp'n," base mkd "Pairpoint," 14" h **2,000.00**
Candle Lamps, pr, flared colorless glass shades with ice
  lip finish, leafy birch trees ext dec on int yellow
  ground, metal mounts and mahogany standards,
  21½" h **800.00**

Candlesticks, pr, amethyst cup and tapered stem raised
  on colorless glass bubble ball connector on amethyst
  disk foot, 9" h **350.00**
Table Lamp, reverse painted ribbed quatrefoil blown-out
  shade with black and gold striped butterflies at each
  corner, blue and pink floral design on white ground,
  stamped "The Pairpoint Corp," raised on gilt-metal 2-
  socket base with relief lapped leaf pattern, imp
  "Pairpoint Mf'g Co C3066" with trademark on base,
  22½" h, 16½" d shade **2,300.00**
Vase, amethyst glass cornucopia supported by colorless
  glass bubble ball connector on disk foot, 8" h **500.00**
Vase, flared form, ruby glass with colorless bubble ball
  connector raised on ruby glass stem and disk foot,
  polished pontil, 11¾" h **225.00**
Vase, flared silver plated vessel mkd "Pairpoint C1553,"
  mounted on colorless bubble ball connector and
  cobalt blue base, 12¼" h **175.00**

PAPERBACK BOOKS

The mass-market paperback arrived on the scene in 1938. Selling for between 15¢ and 25¢, the concept was an instant success. World War II gave paperback book sales a tremendous boost. Hundreds of publishers rushed into the marketplace.

The mid-1940s through the end of the 1950s was the golden age of paperback books.

Price is a key factor in dating paperback books. Collectors focus on titles that sold initially for 75¢ or less. Huge collections still enter the market on a regular basis. Further, many paperbacks were printed on inexpensive pulp paper that has turned brown and brittle over time. Although books in excellent condition are difficult to find, they are available.

Most collections are assembled around one or more unifying themes, e.g., author, cover artist, fictional genre, or publisher.

References: Gary Lovisi, *Collecting Science Fiction and Fantasy,* Alliance Publishing, 1997; Kurt Peer, *TV Tie-Ins: A Bibliography of American TV Tie-In Paperbacks,* Neptune Publishing, 1997; Dawn E. Reno, *Collecting Romance Novels,* Alliance Publishers, 1995; Lee Server, *Over My Dead Body: The Sensational Age of the American Paperback: 1945-1955,* Chronicle Books, 1994; Moe Wadle, *The Movie Tie-In Book: A Collector's Guide to Paperback Movie Editions,* Nostalgia Books, 1994.

Periodical: *Paperback Parade,* PO Box 209, Brooklyn, NY 11228.

Note: Prices listed are for paperback books in fine condition.

Adams, Cleveland F, *What Price Murder,* 1952 . . . . **$4.00**
Anon, *Guide to American Waterfowl,* Collier 419, 1962 . . . . . . **5.00**
Baker, George, *Passion Pirate,* Bedside BB 1228, 1962 . . . . **5.00**
Berger, John, G, Dell 02757, 1st printing, 1973 . . . . **4.00**
Bernstein, Leonard, *Joys of Music,* Signet Q 3215, 1st
  printing, 1967 . . . . **5.00**
Burroughs, Edgar Rice, *Pellucidar,* Ace, 1972 . . . . **4.00**
Burroughs, Edgar Rice, *The Cave Girl,* 1981 . . . . **5.00**
Burroughs, Edgar Rice, *The Monster Men,* Ace **4.00**
Burroughs, Edgar Rice, *The Warlord of Mars,* 1963 . . . . **5.00**
Christie, Agatha, *13 at Dinner,* Dell D 404, 1st printing,
  1961 . . . . **1.00**
Christie, Agatha, *Appointment With Death,* Bestseller B
  58, 1944 . . . . **7.00**

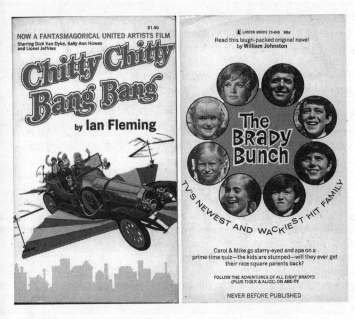

Left: Ian Fleming, *Chitty Chitty Bang Bang*, Scholastic 03428, 1964, $6.00. Right: William Johnston, *The Brady Bunch*, Lancer Books 73-849, 1969, $8.00.

Conklin, Groff, *Twisted*, Belmont B 50-771, 1967 . . . . **4.00**

Duncan, Thomas W, *Gus the Great*, Dell F 50 . . . . **5.00**

Fleming, Ian, *Man With the Golden Gun*, Signet P 2735, 1st printing, 1966 . . . . **3.00**

Gehman, Richard, *Sinatra & His Rat Pack*, Belmont L 514, 1961 . . . . **6.00**

Grey, Zane, *Fugitive Trail*, Cardinal C 441, 1st printing, 1961 . . . . **5.00**

Hitchcock, Alfred, *Hangman's Dozen*, Dell 3428, 1st printing, 1962 . . . . **1.00**

Hitchcock, Alfred, *More Stories My Mother Never Told Me*, Dell 5816, 1st printing, 1965 . . . . **4.00**

Innes, Michael, *Silence Observed*, Berkley F 915, 1st printing, 1964 . . . . **2.00**

Janson, Hank, *Desert Fury*, New Fiction **15.00**

Keats, Charles, *Body of Love*, Berkley G 51, 1957 . . . . **40.00**

Ketcham, Hank, *In This Corner...Dennis the Menace*, Crest 298, 1st printing, 1959 . . . . **6.00**

Key, Ted, *Cat From Outer Space*, Pocket 56054, 5th printing, 1978 . . . . **2.00**

Koontz, Dean, *Beastchild*, Lancer 74-719, 1st printing, 1970 . . . . **15.00**

Koontz, Dean, *Werewolf Among Us*, Ballantine 3055, 1st printing, 1973 . . . . **20.00**

Lee, Gypsy Rose, *Gypsy*, Dell D 307 . . . . **4.00**

Lewis & Martin, *Naked Eye*, Pocket 770 . . . . **7.00**

Melville, David, *Moby Dick*, Pocket PL 28, 1955 . . . . . . **3.00**

Merril, Judith, *Tomorrow People*, Pyramid F 806, 1962 . . . . **4.00**

Meyers, Harold, *Smoking Room Joke Book*, Avon 698, 1956 . . . . **40.00**

Millar, Kenneth, *Trouble Follows Me*, Lion 47, 1st edition, 1950 . . . . **60.00**

Neely, Richard, *Death to My Beloved*, Signet T 4774, 1971 . . . . **4.00**

Niven, Larry, *Shape of Space*, Ballantine, 1st edition, 1969 . . . . **20.00**

Norris, Kathleen, *Secrets of Hillyard House*, PB Library 53-823, 3rd edition, 1965 . . . . **3.00**

Norton, Andre, *Star Born*, Ace M 148, 1966 . . . . **2.00**

Partridge, Bellamy, *Excuse My Dust*, Popular 320, 1951 . . . . . . **6.00**

Purdy, James, *Malcolm*, Avon VS 6, 1965 . . . . **4.00**

Puzo, Mario, *Dark Arena*, Bantam 24860, 1985 . . . . **3.00**

Queen, Ellery, *Kill As Directed*, Pocket 4704, 1963 . . . . **5.00**

Queen, Ellery, *There Was an Old Woman*, Pocket 326, 3rd printing, 1946 . . . . **4.00**

Ross, Sam, *You Belong to Me*, Popular 657, 1st edition, 1955 . . . . **12.00**

Sheckley, Robert, *Untouched By Human Hands*, Ballantine 73, 1954 . . . . **8.00**

Spillane, Mickey, *Bloody Sunrise*, Signet D 2718, 1965 . . . . . . **3.00**

Spillane, Mickey, *Twisted Thing*, Signet D 2949, 1966 . . . . . . **5.00**

Stoker, Bram, *Garden of Evil*, PB Library 53946, 1966 . . . . . . **4.00**

Stoker, Bram, *Lair of the White Worm*, Arrow 585, 1960 . . . . . . **9.00**

Stuart, Matt, *Saddle: Man (Gun Smoke Showdown)*, Bantam 924 . . . . **6.00**

Thayer, Tiffany, *One-Man Show*, Avon 327, 1951 . . . . **6.00**

Thompson, Jim, *Texas by the Tail*, Gold Medal K 1502, 1965 . . . . **60.00**

Vance, Jack, *Space Opera*, Pyramid R 1140, 1965 . . . . **15.00**

Verne, Jules, *City in the Sahara*, Ace H 43, 1968 . . . . **6.00**

Verne, Jules, *Journey to the Center of the Earth*, Ace D 155, 1956 . . . . **7.00**

Vidal, Gore, *Best Television Plays*, Ballantine 160, 1956 . . . . . . **12.00**

Voltaire, *Candide*, Lion 107, 1952 . . . . **50.00**

Wallace, Ian, *Z-Sting*, DAW 308, 1st edition, 1979 . . . . **7.00**

Webb, Jack, *Broken Doll*, Signet 1311, 1956 . . . . **10.00**

Welles, Orson, *Invasion From Mars*, Dell 305, 1st edition, 1949 . . . . **3.00**

Wells, HG, *Candle in the Sun*, Berkley S 2016, 1971 . . . . **4.00**

Wells, HG, *Invisible Man*, Scholastic 540, 1st printing, 1963 . . . . **5.00**

Wilhelm, Kate, *Mile-Long Spaceship*, Berkley F 862, 1st edition, 1963 . . . . **10.00**

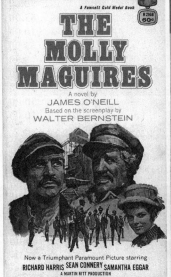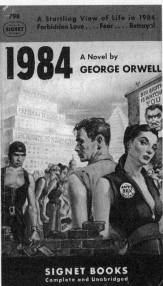

Left: James O'Neill, *The Molly Maguires*, Fawcett Gold Medal Books 02168, 1969, $6.00. Right: George Orwell, *1984*, Signet Book 798, 1st edition, 1950, $2.00.

PAPER DOLLS

Paper dolls were used as advertising and promotional premiums. *Good Housekeeping, Ladies' Home Journal,* and *McCall's* are just a few of the magazines that included paper doll pages as part of their monthly fare. Children's magazines, such as *Jack and Jill,* also featured paper doll pages.

The first paper doll books appeared in the 1920s. Lowe, Merrill, Saalfield, and Whitman were leading publishers. These inexpensive stiffboard covered books became extremely popular. Celebrity paper dolls first appeared in the 1940s. Entertainment personalities from movies, radio, and television were the primary focus.

Most paper dolls are collected in uncut books, sheets, or boxed sets. Cut sets are valued at 50% of the price of an uncut set if all dolls, clothing, and accessories are present.

Many paper doll books have been reprinted. An identical reprint is just slightly lower in value. If the dolls have been redrawn, the price is reduced significantly.

References: Lorraine Mieszala, *Collector's Guide to Barbie Doll Paper Dolls,* Collector Books, 1997; Mary Young, *Tomart's Price Guide to Lowe and Whitman Paper Dolls,* Tomart Publications, 1993.

Newsletter: *Paper Doll News,* PO Box 807, Vivian, LA 71082.

Collectors' Club: Original Paper Doll Artist Guild, PO Box 14, Kingsfield, ME 04947.

Note: Prices listed are for paper doll books and sets in unused condition.

Airline Pilot and Stewardess, Merrill, #1560, 1953 . . . . **$15.00**
American Beauty Paper Dolls, Merrill, #1548, 1951 . . . . **30.00**
Ann Blyth, Merrill, #2550, 1952 . . . . **70.00**
Annette Cut-Out Doll, Whitman, 1960 . . . . **25.00**
Around the Clock with Sue and Dot, Merrill, #1546, 1952 . . . . **10.00**
Baby Ann, Whitman, #943, c1932 . . . . **65.00**
Baby Nancy, Whitman, #938, 1931 . . . . **50.00**
Baby Patsy, Whitman, #980, 1934 . . . . **65.00**
Baby Sister and Baby Brother Dolls, Merrill, #1564, 1950 . . . . **10.00**
Beauty Contest, Lowe, #1026, 1941 . . . . **65.00**
Betty and Her Play Pals, Saalfield, #1335 . . . . **8.00**
Blondie, Whitman, #1174, 1953 . . . . **50.00**
Bobby Socks, Whitman, #988, 1945 . . . . **40.00**
Brenda Lee, Lowe, #2785, 1961 . . . . **50.00**
Bridal Party, Saalfield, #1342, 1963 . . . . **10.00**
Bride and Groom Military Wedding Party, Merrill, #3411, 1941 . . . . **40.00**
Career Girls, Lowe, #1045, 1942 . . . . **50.00**
Carmen Miranda, Whitman, #995, 1942 . . . . **100.00**
Carnation Ice Cream, 1955 . . . . **12.00**
Cathy Goes to Camp, Merrill, #1562, 1954 . . . . **10.00**
Charming, Saalfield, #1357 . . . . **6.00**
Children 'Round the World, Merrill, #2565, 1955 . . . . **20.00**
Cora Sue Collins, Whitman, #1016, 1942 . . . . **60.00**
Daisy Bunny, Whitman, #987, 1938 . . . . **75.00**
Debbie Reynolds, Whitman, 1960 . . . . **25.00**
Dennis the Menace, Golden Funtime Punch-Out Book, #156, 1960 . . . . **50.00**
Dolls From Storyland, Merrill, #1554, 1948 . . . . **20.00**
Dolly Jean, Saalfield, #877 . . . . **25.00**

Double Date, Whitman, #962, 1949 . . . . **35.00**
Down on the Farm, Lowe, #1056 . . . . **20.00**
Dresses Worn by the "First Ladies" of the White House, Saalfield, #2164, 1937 . . . . **75.00**
Dress Me Cut-Out Dolls, Whitman, #970, 1943 . . . . **60.00**
Dress Up For the New York World's Fair, Spertus Publishing Co, 1964-65 . . . . **25.00**
Dude Ranch, Lowe, #1026, 1943 . . . . **20.00**
Esther Williams, Merrill, #2553, 1953 . . . . **70.00**
Gene Autry's Melody Ranch, Whitman, #990, 1950 . . . . **75.00**
Gene Tierney, Whitman, 1947 . . . . **100.00**
Girls in the War, Lowe, 1943 . . . . **20.00**
Goldilocks and the Three Bears, Saalfield, #2245, 1939 . . . . **60.00**
Gulliver's Travels, Saalfield, #1261, 1939 . . . . **75.00**
Harry the Soldier, Lowe, #1074 . . . . **8.00**
Hayley Mills "In Summer Magic," Whitman, 1963 . . . . **50.00**
Hayley Mills "The Moon Spinners," Whitman, 1964 . . . . **50.00**
Heavenly Blue Wedding, Merrill, #2580, 1955 . . . . **15.00**
Heidi, Whitman, #1952, 1966 . . . . **15.00**
Jackie & Caroline Magic Wand Paperdolls Set, 1962-63 . . . . **75.00**
Jeans Jeans, Whitman, #1961, 1975 . . . . **5.00**
Joan Carroll, Saalfield, #2426, 1942 . . . . **50.00**
June Allyson, Whitman, #970, 1950 . . . . **75.00**
Karen Goes to College, Merrill, #1564, 1955 . . . . **10.00**
Kitchen Play, Saalfield, #2183, 1938 . . . . **20.00**
Let's Play with the Baby, Merrill, #1550, 1948 . . . . **12.00**
Little Kitten to Dress, Lowe, 1942 . . . . **12.00**
Little Orphan Annie, Whitman, #938, 1934 . . . . **150.00**
Little Women, Saalfield, #1345, 1963 . . . . **10.00**
Many Things to Do, Saalfield, #881, 1932 . . . . **5.00**
Mary Martin Dolls and Costumes, Saalfield, #2427, 1942 . . . . **80.00**
Mary Poppins, Whitman, 1963 . . . . **25.00**
Matchin' Mods, Whitman, #1968, 1973 . . . . **4.00**
Miss America, Whitman, 1974 . . . . **25.00**
Movie Starlets, Whitman, #960, 1946 . . . . **75.00**
New Toni Hair-Do Dress Up Dolls, Lowe, #1251, 1951 . . . . . **50.00**
Nursery School Dolls, Whitman, #1176, 1953 . . . . **35.00**
Nurses Three, Whitman, #1964, 1964 . . . . **20.00**

Brenda Starr Reporter, Sunday color comics, Dale Messick, 1950, 14 x 9¹/₂", $15.00.

National Velvet Cut-Outs, Whitman, #1948, 1962, $35.00.

Paper Doll Family, Whitman, #985, 1937	85.00
Patience and Prudence, Lowe, #2411, 1957	30.00
Pink Prom Twins, Merrill, #2583, 1956	10.00
Pinocchio Cut-Out Book, Whitman, #974, 1939	200.00
Piper Laurie, Merrill, #2551, 1953	70.00
Playtime Pals, Lowe, #1045, 1946	20.00
Seven and Seventeen, Merrill, #3441, 1945	25.00
Shirley Temple Playhouse, Saalfield, #1739, 1935	100.00
Shrinkin' Violette, Whitman, #1952, 1965	15.00
Square Dance, Lowe, #968, 1950	20.00
Tammy and Pepper, Whitman, #1953, 1966	35.00
Teen Town, Merrill, #3443, 1946	25.00
The Little Princess, Merrill, #3405, 1936	60.00
Tina and Tony, Lowe, #1022, 1940	35.00
Tiny Tot Shop, Whitman, #1965, 1969	35.00
Tiptop Paper Dolls, Saalfield, #2321, 1940	40.00
TV Tap Stars, Lowe, #990, 1952	20.00
Tyrone Power and Linda Darnell, Merrill, #3438, 1941	100.00
Umbrella Girls, Merrill, #2562, 1956	20.00

PAPER EPHEMERA

This is a catchall category. Maurice Richards, author of *Collecting Paper Ephemera,* defines ephemera as the "minor transient documents of everyday life," i.e., material destined for the wastebasket but never quite making it.

Ephemera collecting has a distinguished history, tracing its origins back to English pioneers such as John Bagford (1650-1716), Samuel Pepys (1633-1703), and John Seldon (1584-1654). The Museum of the City of New York and the Wadsworth Athenaeum, Hartford, Connecticut, are two American museums with outstanding ephemera collections. The libraries at Harvard and Yale also have superior collections.

It is wrong to think of ephemera only in terms of paper objects, e.g., billhead, bookplates, documents, tickets, etc. Many three-dimensional items also have a transient quality to them. Advertising tins and pinback buttons are two examples.

References: Norman E. Martinus and Harry L. Rinker, *Warman's Paper,* Wallace-Homestead, 1994; Gordon T. McClelland and Jay T. Last, *Fruit Box Labels,* Hillcrest Press, 1995; Craig A. Tuttle, *An Ounce of Preservation: A Guide to the Care of Papers and Photographs,* Rainbow Books, 1995; Gene Utz, *Collecting Paper,* Books Americana, 1993.

Periodicals: *Bank Note Reporter,* 700 E State St, Iola, WI 54990; *Paper & Advertising Collector (P.A.C.),* PO Box 500, Mount Joy, PA 17552; *PCM (Paper Collectors' Marketplace),* PO Box 128, Scandinavia, WI 54977.

Collectors' Clubs: American Society of Check Collectors, PO Box 577, Garrett Park, MD 20896; Fruit Crate Label Society, Rt 2, Box 695, Chelan, WA 98816; The Citrus Label Society, 131 Miramonte Dr, Fullerton, CA 92365; The Ephemera Society of America, Inc, PO Box 95, Cazenovia, NY 13035.

Note: For additional listings see Advertising, Autographs, Catalogs, Cigar Collectibles, Photographs, Postcards, and Posters.

Blotter, Arm & Hammer Baking Soda, black and white, 1920s, 4 x 9¼"	$10.00
Blotter, Jersey Cream, children illus, 1920s, 4 x 9"	3.00
Blotter, Nash Auto, 1928, 5 x 9"	4.00
Booklet, Facts You Should Know About Furs, Boston Better Business National Association Better Business Bureaus, 12 pp, 1936	5.00
Booklet, Famous Guide to New York, pictorial and tour guide information, 96 pp, 1956	8.00
Booklet, Let's Go to the Movies, Reed Publishing Co, #62, 48 pp, ©1932, 4 x 6"	15.00
Booklet, Making Bread, Northwestern Yeast Co, 1939	12.00
Booklet, Rates For Telegrams/Cables & Money Transfers, Western Union, 12 pp, 1925	10.00
Booklet, The Meat Packing Industry in America, Swift & Co, 108 pp, 1937	5.00
Catalog, Daniel Low & Co, Inc, Salem, MA, 164 pp, 1926, 9½ x 6½"	30.00
Catalog, Decorators Supply Co, Chicago, IL, Illustrated Catalogue of Period Ornaments for Furniture, #117, furniture hardware, 148 pp, 1924	50.00
Certificate, book, Mallott-Hofman Co, Wholesale Grocery Co, 32 unissued certificates, eagle vignettes, 1931-33	16.00

Cigar Label, Franklin D Roosevelt, $10.00.

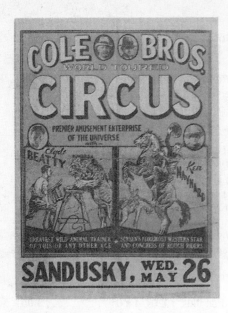

Program, Cole Bros Circus with Ken Maynard Wild West Show, 8 pp, 22³/₄" h, 17" w, $165.00. Photo courtesy Collectors Auction Services.

Certificate, Pupils Reading Circle, printed, butterflies and moth illus, 1933 . . . . **10.00**

Certificate, trust, Guarantee National Trust, 1st United Trust, 1965-66. . . . . **4.00**

Check, Carter's Warehouse, Plains Mercantile Co, sgd by Rosalyn S Carter **20.00**

Check, First National Bank of Nevada, filled in and sgd by Tyrus R Cobb, cancellation mark, 1945 . . . . **100.00**

Directory, Gehrig Hotel Directory & Tourist Guide...US & Canada, 60 pp, black and white road maps, 1927, 256 pp, 1927 . . . . **10.00**

Directory, Sullivan's Chicago Law Directory 1936-37, 696 pp **8.00**

Label, Alpine Kidney Beans, mountain climber, bowl of white kidney beans, NY. . . . . **.50**

Label, Blue Hill White Corn, house by river, conifers **3.00**

Label, Capital Park Pears, California state Capitol buildings and grounds, blue **3.00**

Label, Ellendale Lima Beans, forest, stream, mountains, lima beans in pods, Ellendale, DE **1.00**

Label, Forever First Pears, red holly berries, greens, and plump juicy pears, blue **2.00**

Label, Honest John Yams, smiling man in bib overalls and straw hat holding crate of yams. . . . . **.75**

Label, Jo Sole, grape juice, 2 images of young black boy, "So soul tasty," 1969, 13¹/₂ x 6¹/₂" **2.00**

Label, Little Joe Crowder Peas, whistling black youngster going fishing **2.00**

Label, Mammy Citrus, black lady eating orange, yellow, 3¹/₂ x 8¹/₂" **2.00**

Label, Morning Cheer Lemons, pair of lemons with mountains behind, brown and shaded orange-gold. **2.00**

Label, Og-Na Corn, Indian chief profile, peace pipe, tomahawk, white corn, emb, gilt, 1920s. **1.50**

Label, Old Mill Soda, old mill and pond, silver and black. . . . . . **.25**

Label, Orchard Boy Apples, red headed boy's face with trio of red apples. **2.00**

Label, Perfection Lemons, orchard scene, purple mountains with lemons and leaves, blossoms in lower corner, aqua shading into dark blue border **2.00**

Label, Raspberry Cordial, oval, berries, 3¹/₂ x 2³/₄". . . . . **.50**

Label, Silver Spruce Apples, big pine tree and snowy mountain scene. . . . . **.50**

Label, Sno-Gem Apples, snowcapped "Sno-Gem" on blue ground **2.00**

Label, Tropic Peas, roaring lion's head, fruits, navy blue on white, Philadelphia, PA. **2.00**

Label, Uncle Sam Apples, sad Uncle Sam with hat in hand. **6.00**

Label, Valley Plum Plums, purple plums on aqua ground, 7 x 9". **1.00**

Letter, Office of the Minority Leader, House of Representatives, sgd by Joseph W Martin Jr, Dec 30, 1949. . . . . **10.00**

Letterhead, United States Cigar Co, York, PA, 2-color, 1933. . . . . **8.00**

Letterhead, Winchester Repeating Arms Co, New Haven, CT, non pictorial, black and white, used, 1929 . . . . **10.00**

License, Junior Hunter, waterproof tagboard, blue, black letters and numbers, 1963 . . . . **6.00**

License, trapping, non-resident, white, stamped year in black ink, red letters and numbers, 1951 . . . . **10.00**

Manual, Mechanical Engineers Handbook, Baumeister, McGraw Hill, 6th ed, 1964 . . . . **15.00**

Manual, One Hundred and One Uses For Diamond Crystal Salt, Diamond Crystal Salt Co, St Clair, MI, 20 pp, 1925, 3¹/₂ x 6" **8.00**

Manual, operators, 1947 Ford heavy duty truck **10.00**

Manual, Overland Whippet-Operation and Care, Model 96, 36 pp, 1926 . . . . **50.00**

Map, Alaska, geological map of China River Valley and surrounding areas, 1939, 29 x 53" **15.00**

Map, New York City street map, fold-out, 1922, 8¹/₂ x 17" opened size **10.00**

Menu, Santa Fe, Super Chief, luncheon, folder, 1971 . . . . **4.00**

Menu, Union Pacific, City of Los Angeles, dome liner, breakfast, 1971 . . . . **2.50**

Pamphlet, Food Triumphs with New Minute Tapioca, General Foods, 47 pp, 1934 . . . . **4.00**

Pamphlet, Keep on the Sunny Side of Life, Kellogg's, 32 pp, 1933. . . . . **5.00**

Pamphlet, Knox Gelatin Desserts, Salads, Candies & Frozen Dishes, 75 pp, 1933. **10.00**

Pamphlet, Ladies' Aid Society, Lancaster, NY, 1932-35 . . . . **3.00**

Pamphlet, The Railroad Workers and The War, Wm Z Foster, 15 pp, 1941, 5 x 7". **20.00**

Pamphlet, Things to Do With Plastic Wood, Addison Leslie Co, Canton, MA, 48 pp, 1930 . . . . **6.00**

Program, Bank of California Annual Christmas Dinner, Fairmont Hotel, Dec 15, 1927 . . . . **8.00**

Stock Certificate, Babcock & Wilcox Co, Nuclear Plant Designers, green border, 2 men and logo vignette, 1959-71 . . . . **4.00**

Stock Certificate, Northampton Brewing Corp, orange, engraved, 1934. . . . . **20.00**

Ticket, Sturgeon Bay Transit, 1946 . . . . **5.00**

Ticket, Wasworth Transfer Co, bus fare. **3.00**

Ticket Book, NY World's Fair 1939, combination souvenir tickets, two 25¢ tickets for money off at entrance, 2 removed **10.00**

Toy, Flash Gordon Super-Flyer Kite, orig package, unused, 1950s. **25.00**

Toy, G Man Pop Gun, cardboard, red, black, and gray, Lesher's, Perkasie, PA adv, 7" l **5.00**

PAPERWEIGHTS

The paperweights found in this category divide into three basic types: (1) advertising, (2) souvenir or commemorative, and (3) contemporary glass. Advertising paperweights were popular giveaway premiums between 1920 and the late 1950s. Cast-iron figural paperweights are the most eagerly sought.

Souvenir paperweights are valued highest by regional collectors. Most were cheaply made. Many are nothing more than a plastic disk with information stenciled on the top or a colored photograph applied to the bottom. No wonder collector interest is limited.

Paperweights enjoyed a renaissance in the 1970s and 80s. Baccarat, Perthshire, and Saint Louis are leading contemporary manufacturers. Many studio glassmakers, e.g. Ray and Bob Banford, Paul Stankard, and Victor Trabucco, make paperweights.

References: Peter von Brackel, *Paperweights: Historicism, Art Nouveau, Art Deco, 1842 to Present,* Schiffer Publishing, 2000; Andrew H. Dohan, *Paperweight Signature Canes: Identification and Dating,* Paperweight Press, 1997; Monika Flemming and Peter Pommerencke, *Paperweights of the World, 2nd Edition,* Schiffer Publishing, 1998; Robert G. Hall, *Scottish Paperweights,* Schiffer Publishing, 1999; John D. Hawley, *The Glass Menagerie: A Study of Silhouette Canes in Antique Paperweights,* Paperweight Press, 1995; Paul Hollister, Jr., *The Encyclopedia of Glass Paperweights,* Paperweight Press, 1969; Sibylle Jargstorf, *Paperweights,* Schiffer Publishing, 1991; Lawrence H. Selman, *All About Paperweights,* Paperweight Press, 1992; Colin Terris, *The Charlton Standard Catalogue of Caithness Paperweights,* Charlton Press, 1999.

Collectors' Clubs: Caithness Collectors Club, Bldg 12, 141 Lanza Ave, Gardield, NJ 07026; International Paperweight Society, 761 Chestnut St, Santa Cruz, CA 95060; Paperweight Collectors Assoc, Inc, PO Box 40, Barker, TX 78748.

Advertising, Atlas Portland Cement, glass, black lettering
on white ground, 1920s, 3" d **$15.00**
Advertising, Benson's Wild Animal Farm, cast iron, figural elephant, earthtone orange with blue blanket on
side mkd "Nashau NH," 1930s, 5" l, 5³/₄" h **75.00**
Advertising, Boston Safe Deposit and Trust Co, paperweight/mirror, center sepia picture of office building
at 100 Franklin St, c1920s **25.00**
Advertising, Byers "Bear Cat" Crane, cast iron, 1930s,
3" d **25.00**
Advertising, The Wolf Co, metal, celluloid insert panels depicting "Roller Machine," ivory on white ground,
black lettering, Whitehead & Hoag, c1920, 2³/₄" d **50.00**
Advertising, United States Life Insurance Co, paperweight/mirror, center gold, red, white, and blue patriotic design with spray of pinpoint stars, dark blue border, gold lettering, 1920s, 3¹/₂" d **25.00**
Contemporary, Baccarat, green and yellow snake with
blue flower on dark mottled ground, 1970, 3¹/₈" d **375.00**
Contemporary, Baccarat, spray of small pink and white flowers and 7 white bulbs on mauve ground, limited
155/200, 3" d **375.00**
Contemporary, Deacon, John, butterfly on pink and
white striped latticinio cushion, "JD" cane, 3" d **200.00**
Contemporary, Deacon, John, pink and white flower
bouquet on white swirl, "JD" cane, 2³/₄" d **225.00**
Contemporary, Holmes, Peter, dark purple pansy and
bud on white swirl, "PH" cane, 2⁷/₈" d **250.00**

Advertising, "Use Violet Ray Lens, Safety First," figural baby logo, cornflower-colored glass, 4¹/₄" h, $110.00. Photo courtesy Collectors Auction Services.

Contemporary, Holmes, Peter, faceted miniature snow-drop spray on clear ground, scratch sgd (Selkirk), limited 14/500, 2³/₈" d **100.00**
Contemporary, Hudin, L, Orient & Flume, peacock, signature cane and scratch sgd, 2³/₄" d **175.00**
Contemporary, Manson, William, green and white dragonfly with adventurine on deep wine base, green and
white millefiori outer circle, Scotia, 2⁷/₈" d **150.00**
Contemporary, Manson, William, nesting bluebird with eggs on dark rose flash ground, 2 small birds in flight
in background, slant front facet, 2³/₄" d **125.00**
Contemporary, Manson, William, spray of 3 lavender heather blossoms with green leaves on amber flash
ground, "WM" cane, 1/10 facets **400.00**
Contemporary, Perthshire, barber pole chequer with multicolored complex canes and red and white rods,
limited 350, 1993, 2³/₄" d **275.00**
Contemporary, Perthshire, millefiori on deep blue
ground, signature cane, 1973, 2³/₄" d **125.00**
Contemporary, Rosenfeld, Ken, bouquet of 2 orange and 2 yellow blossoms with buds on blue flash ground,
cane and scratch sgd, 1990 .... **255.00**
Contemporary, Rosenfeld, Ken, carrots, beets, radishes,
and asparagus, cane and scratch sgd, 1986, 2⁷/₈" d **80.00**
Contemporary, Rosenfeld, Ken, fruit on clear ground,
cane and scratch sgd, 1989 .... **550.00**
Contemporary, Rosenfeld, Ken, red, yellow, and aqua blossoms and 2 buds on mauve ground, cane and
scratch sgd, 1988, 3⁵/₈" d **250.00**
Contemporary, St Louis, American eagle sulphide on deep blue ground, red and white double overlay, limited 400, 1976 .... **175.00**
Contemporary, St Louis, Autun cathedral sulphide on purple ground, blue and white millefiori outer ring,
faceted, 1973, 3" d **500.00**
Contemporary, St Louis, blue and orange floral spray, blue and white double overlay, "SL" cane, 1/5
faceting, 1973, 3" d **200.00**
Contemporary, Trabucco, John and David, flowers with blueberries on clear ground, frosted and etched dec
around base, scratch sgd, 1991, 3" d **475.00**

Contemporary, Trabucco, Victor, Chinese red rose with
4 buds and green leaves, cane sgd, 1987, 3" d **415.00**
Contemporary, Whittemore, F, small mushroom spray on
dark blue ground, signature cane in bottom, 2" d **175.00**
Contemporary, Ysart, Paul, 3 circles of millefiori in rose,
green, blue, and white, large center cane, black base,
paper label **725.00**
Contemporary, Ysart, Paul, central cane with millefiori
circles of pink, white, and light green on dark blue
ground **450.00**
Figural, clutching hand, brass, c1920, 3" h on 2 x 2" base
formed in image of sleeve cuff **25.00**
Figural, German shepherd, hollowed white metal, dark
bronze luster, underside mkd "JB," dated 1928, 1½ x
3" h, 7" l **25.00**

PARRISH, MAXFIELD

Maxfield Parrish was born in Philadelphia on July 25, 1870.
Originally named Frederick Parrish, he later adopted his mother's
maiden name, Maxfield, as his middle name.

Parrish received his academic training at Haverford College and
the Pennsylvania Academy of Fine Arts, and spent a brief period as
a pupil of Howard Pyle at Drexel. His first art exhibit was held at
the Philadelphia Art Club in 1893; his first magazine cover illustration appeared on an 1895 issue of *Harper's Bazaar.* He soon
received commissions from *Century Magazine, Collier's, Ladies'
Home Journal, Life,* and *Scribners.* In 1897 Parrish was elected to
the Society of American Artists.

Parrish established a studio, The Oaks, in Cornish, New
Hampshire. He painted a large number of works for advertisements, book illustrations, and calendars. He is best known for the
work he did between 1900 and 1940.

Maxfield Parrish died on March 30, 1966.

Reference: Erwin Flacks, *Maxfield Parrish, 3rd Edition,* Collectors
Press, 1998.

Newsletter: *The Illustrator Collector's News,* PO Box 1958,
Sequim, WA 98382.

Blotter, cardboard, ink splot billboard blocking out
scenic view, 3½ x 6" **$450.00**
Book, *Emerald Storybook,* Duffield, 1924. . . . . **75.00**
Bookplate Print, Aladdin and the Wonderful Lamp, man
in rocky mountains reels in surprise as magic lamp
spews black smoke, 8 x 10" **65.00**
Bookplate Print, Cassim in the Cave of the 40 Thieves,
bearded man sitting in cave with large sword in hand,
8 x 10" **75.00**
Bookplate Print, Shuffle-Shoon and Amber Locks, young
child playing with building blocks at foot of seated old
man, 8 x 10" **65.00**
Bookplate Print, The Landing of the Brazen Boatsman,
lone man in boat with pole in hand, standing before
tall stone steps and massive temple, 8 x 10" **75.00**
Calendar, "Reveries," 1927 Edison Mazda adv, 2 women
in garden sitting next to raised pool, full pad, framed
and matted in modern metal frame, 8½ x 19⅛" **650.00**
Cigar Box Label, Old King Cole Cigars, stone litho emb
image of Old King Cole, c1920s, 6½ x 10" **175.00**
Magazine Cover, *Yankee Magazine,* Dec 1968, 6 x 9" **25.00**

Calendar, "Sunrise," Forbes Lithograph Mfg Co, 1933 full pad, 38½" h, 19⅜" w, 20¼ x 14½" image size, $7,500.00. Photo courtesy Wm Morford.

Magazine Cover, *You and Your Work,* Tranquility,
May 13, 1944 . . . . **45.00**
Matchcover, Old King Cole design on back, adv for King
Cole Bar at St Regis Hotel, NY **120.00**
Pocket Calendar, Jack Spratt, Swift's Premium Ham adv,
1921, 3½ x 1¾" **325.00**
Poster, "Buy Products Not Advertised On Our Roadside,"
1939. . . . . **600.00**
Print, The Manager, Knave of Hearts print with stage
manager dressed in red opening green curtain to
reveal background setting that appears, "Parrish Blue"
lower left, framed, c1905, 8 x 10" **100.00**
Print, The Theater at Villa Gori, Italian Villas and Their
Gardens print with single tall tree rising high above
shorter trees near stone wall and garden, framed,
c1904, 6 x 9" **55.00**
Print, Villa Gori, Italian Villas and Their Gardens print
with long green shrub leading to distant mansion, title
at lower center above "MP," framed, c1904, 6 x 9" **65.00**

PATRIOTIC COLLECTIBLES

Uncle Sam became a national symbol during the Civil War. His
modern day appearance resulted from drawings by Thomas Nast in
Harper's Weekly and portraits by the artist, James Montgomery
Flagg. Uncle Sam played a major role in military recruiting during
World Wars I and II.

Other important symbols of American patriotism include
Columbia and the Goddess of Liberty, the eagle, the flag, the
Liberty Bell, and the Statue of Liberty. Today they are most preva-
lent during national holidays, such as Memorial Day and the
Fourth of July, and centennial celebrations. They often appear sub-
tley in print advertising and television commercials.

Reference: Gerald E. Czulewicz, Sr., *The Foremost Guide to Uncle
Sam Collectibles,* Collector Books, 1995.

Collectors' Club: Statue of Liberty Collectors' Club, 26601
Bernwood Rd, Cleveland, OH 44122.

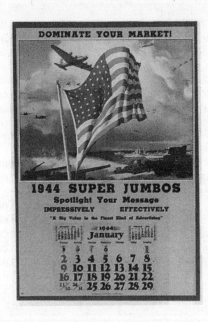

Flag, calendar, salesman's sample, sgd "J. Rozen," 1944, 44" h, 30" w, $55.00. Photo courtesy Collectors Auction Services.

Eagle, chocolate mold, tin, clamps style, wings spread, shield at chest, "Liberty" above, #JAB 10, 4½" h **$55.00**

Eagle, poster, Pledge of the Soldier of Supply, eagle and flag, Zarv, 1943, 34 x 43" **175.00**

Eagle, program, Democratic National Convention, eagle on cov, 1948, 80 pp **45.00**

Flag, bandanna, silk, flag and wreath with 36 stars, 22 x 25" **110.00**

Flag, key chain fob, yellow plastic on brass key chain, red, white, and blue flag with "We Are Proud To Be Americans," "God Bless America" in black on reverse, 1940s, ⅞ x 1¼ x ¼" **25.00**

Flag, name card, "A Token of Affection," hand holding American flag, view of bridge in shield **6.00**

Flag, pin, enamel, gold luster finish, 2 flags, 1 depicting yellow and black Mr Peanut on white, other depicting red, white, and blue flag **15.00**

Flag, pin, metal, red and white striping with 13 tiny crystal rhinestones inserted on star field, on card inscribed "America Forever," reverse with Pledge of Allegiance text, 1940s **15.00**

Flag, pinback button, litho tin, center bluetone Eisenhower photo draped by red, white, and blue flags and "For President Eisenhower" **15.00**

Flag and Shield, paper clip, celluloid, red, white, and blue, steel spring clip, center inscription in shield "The Grand Rapids Furniture Record," 1922 . . . . **10.00**

George Washington, plate, black, white, and gray design pattern with center portrait and years 1732 and 1932, border pictures and names of 6 events related to Washington's life plus bottom inscription "To Commemorate The 200th Anniversary of the Birth of George Washington Feb 22, 1732," underside with "Memorial Plate" design and text plus signature of maker Lamberton-Scammell, 10¾" d **50.00**

George Washington, sheet music, *Father of the Land We Love*, George Washington illus, James Montgomery Flagg artist, ©1931 . . . . **6.00**

Liberty Bell, candy container, pressed glass, amber, emb "Liberty Bell" on center hanger, and "Pat Apld For," Westmoreland Glass Co, 1920s, 2⅝ x 3⅜" **65.00**

Liberty Bell, jar, glass, clear, metal lid with flag and black letters, emb "Liberty Cherries Jar 1776-1976," 6 x 6½" **8.00**

Stars and Stripes, pinback button, red, white, and blue patriotic design with center Coca-Cola bottle image, 3 green stars to right of bottle, 1970s, 2¼" d **15.00**

Stars and Stripes, pinback button, red, white, and blue patriotic design with center "V-J Day," 1945 . . . . **25.00**

Statue of Liberty, watch, commemorative, quartz, orig box and papers, 1986 . . . . **50.00**

Uncle Sam, money clip, metal, coin-like disk depicting Uncle Sam standing before rippling US flag, rim inscription "United We Stand For Democracy, 1945" **25.00**

Uncle Sam, ornament, pressed tin, Uncle Sam Keepsake Ornament, Hallmark, 1984 . . . . **25.00**

Uncle Sam, pinback button, black and white photos of George Bush and Dan Quayle on gold ground with Uncle Sam and "My Boys," oval, dated 1989 . . . . **10.00**

Uncle Sam, pinback button, Uncle Sam flanked by "RCA," red, white, and blue, 1940s **50.00**

Uncle Sam, figure, plastic, wearing red, white, and blue outfit holding banner with text "200 Years," ©1975 All State Management Corp, 3 x 3 x 10¼" **25.00**

PEANUTS

In 1950 Charles M. Schulz launched Peanuts, a comic strip about kids and a beagle named Snoopy. Charlie Brown, Lucy, Linus, and the Peanuts gang have become a national institution. They have been featured in over sixty television specials, translated in over a dozen languages.

Charles M. Schulz Creative Associates and United Features Syndicate have pursued an aggressive licensing program. Almost no aspect of a child's life has escaped the licensing process. Given this, why is the number of Peanuts collectors relatively small? The reason is that the strip's humor is targeted primarily toward adults. Children do not actively follow it during the formative years, i.e., ages seven to fourteen, that influence their adult collecting.

References: Freddi Karin Margolin, *Peanuts: The Home Collection*, Antique Trader Books, 1999; Andrea Podley and Derrick Bang, *Peanuts Collectibles*, Collector Books, 2000.

Collectors' Club: Peanuts Collector Club, 539 Sudden Valley, Bellingham, WA 98226.

Note: See Peanuts—Exclusive Report on page 435 for listings.

PEDAL CARS

Pedal car is a generic term used to describe any pedal-driven toy. Automobiles were only one form. There are also pedal airplanes, fire engines, motorcycles, and tractors.

By the mid-1910s pedal cars resembling their full-sized counterparts were being made. Buick, Dodge, Overland, and Packard are just a few examples. American National, Garton, Gendron, Steelcraft, and Toledo Wheel were the five principal pedal car manufacturers in the 1920s and 30s. Ertl, Garton, and Murray made pedal cars in the post-1945 period. Many mail-order catalogs, e.g., Sears, Roebuck, sold pedal cars. Several television shows issued pedal car licenses during the mid-1950s and 60s.

Pedal car collecting is serious business in the 1990s. The $10,000 barrier has been broken. Many pedal cars are being stripped down and completely restored to look as though they just came off the assembly line. Some feel this emphasis, especially when it destroys surviving paint, goes too far.

References: *Evolution of the Pedal Car, Vol. 1* (1989, 1996 value update), *Vol. 2* (1990, 1997 value update), *Vol. 3* (1992), *Vol. 4* (1993, 1997 value update), *Vol. 5* (1999), L-W Book Sales; Jane Dwyre Garton, *Pedal Cars*, Schiffer Publishing, 1999; Andrew G. Gurka, *Pedal Car Restoration and Price Guide*, Krause Publications, 1996.

Newsletter: *The Wheel Goods Trader*, PO Box 435, Fraser, MI 48026.

Collectors' Club: National Pedal Vehicle Assoc, 1720 Rupert NE, Grand Rapids, MI 49505.

Allis Chalmers, C 190, complete $550.00
Allis Chalmers, 200, complete 850.00
Allis Chalmers, CA, complete 1,600.00
Allis Chalmers, D-14, complete 1,700.00
AMF Custom Coca-Cola Truck, red and white, 1960s 500.00
AMF Dr Pepper Delivery Truck, white, green, and red, 1962 . . . . 400.00
AMF Fire Truck, red and white, plastic, 1980s 100.00
AMF Pacer, blue, 1968 . . . . 300.00
AMF Safari Wagon, 1968 . . . . 500.00
AMF Tow Wrecker, black and white, 1955 . . . . 800.00
BMC Blue Streak, blue, white, trim, 1953 . . . . 400.00
Case 90 Series, replaced steering wheel and rear tires 625.00
Case Agri King, replaced steering shaft and steering wheel 525.00
Case VAC, replaced steering wheel and pedals 3,000.00
Farmall 560, complete 450.00
Farmall Tall M, cast in rear hub, orig 13,500.00
Ford 8000 Tractor, blue, white trim, 1968 . . . . 150.00
Garton Hayseed Racing Car, 1960 . . . . 700.00
Garton Kidillac, 1950s 1,500.00
Garton Race Car, dark blue, yellow trim, 1950s 650.00
Garton Tin Lizzy, green, yellow trim, 1950s 500.00
Hiesler, small 3,400.00
International Harvester, 856, complete 750.00
International Harvester, 1026, complete 600.00
John Deere, #10, 4-Hole, complete 850.00

John Deere, #20, D65, complete 475.00
John Deere, #4020, complete 1,100.00
John Deere, #LGT, complete 1,100.00
Murray Champion Fire Chief, red and white, attached bell on front with rope, 1950s 600.00
Murray Earth Mover, yellow and black, 1960s 1,000.00
Murray Fireball Racer, red and white, 1968 . . . . 300.00
Murray Official Astronauts Car, white, red and blue rocket dec on side, 1965 . . . . 800.00
Murray Police Radar Patrol, blue, red and white trim, 1955 . . . . 600.00
Murray Sand and Gravel Truck, yellow, 1952 . . . . 1,000.00
Murray Sport Crest Race Car, blue, red and white trim, 1962 . . . . 400.00
Oliver 1850, complete 1,200.00
Oliver Super 88, complete 2,000.00
Oliver/White 1855, complete 850.00
Tru-matic Hand Pedal Tractor 475.00

PENNANTS

Felt pennants were popular souvenirs from the 1920s through the end of the 1950s. College sports pennants decorated the walls of dormitory rooms during this period. Pennants graced the radio antenna of hot rods and street rods. A pennant served as a pleasant reminder of a trip to the mountains, shore, or an historic site.

Most commercial pennants were stenciled. Once a pennant's paint cracks and peels, its value is gone. Handmade pennants, some exhibiting talented design and sewing work, are common.

Ali-Frazier Fight, "World's Heavyweight Championship Fight," white felt, red and black lettering and crown, black and white screened photos of Frazier and Ali, 1974, 21" l, 8" h $50.00
Apperson Motor Car, dark blue felt, car name and running rabbit symbol in white, c1920-26, 3 x 7½" 20.00
Army, black felt, yellow-gold lettering and mascot mule symbol, gray felt trim, yellow-gold streamers, 1940-50s, 11½ x 29" 20.00
Canada Alaska Hi-Way, gold felt overlaid by red felt stitched lettering and blue/black designs, 1942, 6 x 14" 20.00
Chicago White Sox, "White Sox, Zeke Bonura," navy blue felt, white lettering, 1934-37, 4¼" l, 2¼" h 20.00
Coney Island, "Souvenir of Coney Island," dark red felt, female sunbather, white lettering, dark blue end strip, 1940s, 11" l, 4½" h 20.00
FDR, "I Was At the 1st Third Term Inauguration, January 20, 1941," red felt, white FDR portrait, Capitol building, and lettering, yellow end strip, 12" l, 4½" h 75.00
Gene Autry, "Back in the Saddle Again, Gene Autry and Champ," purple felt, white image of Autry on rearing Champ, white lettering and end strip, early 1940s, 28" l, 11" h 60.00
Green Hornet, images of Green Hornet, Kato, and Black Beauty, orange felt, green and white lettering, ©1966 Greenway Products Inc, 8½" l, 4½" h 50.00
Humphrey/Muskie, "Vote Democrat," blue felt, black and white jugate photos, 20" l, 9" h 12.00
Indianapolis Speedway, "Indianapolis, Souvenir of Speedway, May 30th, 1939," green felt, cross checkered flags and race car, white lettering, rear end strip, 26½" l, 11½" h 75.00

Mobil Racer, fiberglass body, white with red and blue trim, metal steering wheel mechanism, rubber tires, 19" h, 53" l, $150.00. Photo courtesy Collectors Auction Services.

New York World's Fair, dark purple felt, orange band, white lettering, multicolor images in letters, 1939, 7¹/₂" h, 27" l, $45.00. Photo courtesy Ray Morykan Auctions.

New York World's Fair, "I Was There Closing Day, October 27, 1940, New York World's Fair," corn-colored yellow felt, dark blue ink Trylon, Perisphere, and lettering, 1940, 8¹/₂" l, 3¹/₂" h **40.00**

Ohio State, red felt, gray lettering and tie strings, 1940s, 23" l **20.00**

Philadelphia "Fightin' Phillies," maroon felt, white inscription, art accented in gray and pink on white, yellow-gold trim band and streamers, 1950s, 5¹/₄ x 12". **50.00**

"Remember Pearl Harbor, Let's Go Americans," blue felt, white lettering, image of Uncle Sam flanked by civilian workers on left and military personnel on right, 23" l, 7" h **60.00**

Seattle '62 Expo, "Seattle World's Fair," black felt, white lettering, blue, yellow, lavender, and orange circular Century 21 Exposition design, gold end strip and streamer strips, 27" l, 9" h **15.00**

"Target for 1943 from the Boys Down Under," dark blue felt, white lettering, Australian soldier and US sailor riding kangaroo and holding spear aimed at Japanese flag target on trouser seat of fleeing Japanese soldier, banner attached to spear reads "AUS USA," 24¹/₂" l, 9¹/₂" h **100.00**

TWA/LA Guardia Airport, felt, TWA 4-engine passenger plane, c1940s, 5 x 10¹/₂" **20.00**

Walt Disney World, purple felt, multicolored castle, gold flocked lettering, gold end strip and streamer strips, 24" l, 8³/₄" h **15.00**

PENNSBURY POTTERY

In 1950 Henry Below, a ceramic engineer and mold maker, and Lee Below, a ceramic designer and modeler, founded Pennsbury Pottery. The pottery was located near Morrisville, Pennsylvania, the location of William Penn's estate, Pennsbury.

Henry and Lee Below previously worked for Stangl, explaining why so many forms, manufacturing techniques, and motifs are similar to those used at Stangl. A series of bird figurines were Pennsbury's first products.

Although Pennsbury is best known for its brown wash background, other background colors were used. In addition to Christmas plates (1960-70), commemorative pieces, and special order pieces, Pennsbury made several dinnerware lines, most reflecting the strong German heritage of eastern Pennsylvania.

The company employed local housewives and young ladies as decorators, many of whom initialed their work or added the initials of the designer. At its peak in 1963, Pennsbury had forty-six employees.

Henry Below died on December 21, 1959; Lee Below on December 12, 1968. Attempts to continue operations proved unsuccessful. The company filed for bankruptcy in October 1970 and the property was auctioned in December. The pottery and its supporting buildings were destroyed by fire on May 18, 1971.

References: Harvey Duke, *The Official Price Guide to Pottery and Porcelain, Eighth Edition,* House of Collectibles, 1995; Lucile Henzke, *Pennsbury Pottery,* Schiffer Publishing, 1990; Mike Schneider, *Stangl and Pennsbury Birds,* Schiffer Publishing, 1994.

REPRODUCTION ALERT: Some Pennsbury pieces (many with Pennsbury markings) have been reproduced from original molds purchased by Lewis Brothers Pottery in Trenton, New Jersey. Glen View in Langhorne, Pennsylvania, marketed the 1970s' Angel Christmas plate with Pennsbury markings and continued the Christmas plate line into the 1970s. Lenape Products, a division of Pennington, bought Glen View in 1975 and continued making products with a Pennsbury feel.

Amish, mug, incised Amish couple drinking beer and eating pretzels, 4³/₄" h **$5.00**

Amish, oil and vinegar, 7" h. **65.00**

Amish, plaque, 4¹/₂" h **20.00**

Amish, pretzel bowl, 12 x 8" **45.00**

Barbershop Quartet, mug, 4³/₄" h **5.00**

Bird Over Heart, candy dish, heart shaped **35.00**

Black Rooster, butter, cov **45.00**

Black Rooster, pie pan, 9¹/₂" d **100.00**

Black Rooster, plate, 10" d. **30.00**

Black Rooster, salt and pepper shakers, pr **25.00**

Courting Buggy, plate, 8" d. **70.00**

Dutch Talk, bowl, 9" d. **140.00**

Eagle, pitcher, 4" h **30.00**

Gay Ninety, mug, 5" h. **30.00**

Harvest, pie pan, 9" d **145.00**

Hex, coffeepot, 2 cup, 5¹/₂" h. **50.00**

Hex, coffeepot, 6 cup **65.00**

Hex, pretzel bowl **55.00**

Holly, serving tray **50.00**

Gay Ninety, pretzel bowl, $45.00.

Red Rooster, vegetable dish, divided, 9¹/₂" l, 6" w, $35.00.

Making Pie, cookie jar. **175.00**
Maypole Dance, candlesticks, pr **225.00**
Mother Serving Pie, pie pan, 9" d. **145.00**
Quartet, pretzel bowl, 12 x 8" **35.00**
Red Barn, mug, 5" h **125.00**
Red Barn, plate, 8¹/₂" d **65.00**
Red Barn, pretzel bowl, 12 x 8" **80.00**
Red Rooster, butter, cov. **30.00**
Red Rooster, chip and dip plate, 11" d **100.00**
Red Rooster, creamer, 4" h. **20.00**
Red Rooster, mug, 6" h **60.00**
Red Rooster, pitcher, 2³/₄" h **15.00**
Red Rooster, pitcher, 7¹/₂" h **90.00**
Red Rooster, plate, 13¹/₂" d **80.00**
Red Rooster, salt and pepper shakers, pr. **45.00**
Red Rooster, snack set. **25.00**
Red Rooster, tureen, cov, with ladle, wrought iron base **250.00**
Two Birds Over Heart, plate, 11" d **125.00**

PENS & PENCILS

Fountain pens are far more collectible than mechanical pencils. While a few individuals are beginning to collect ballpoint pens, most are valued by collectors more for their advertising than historical importance. Defects, e.g., dents, mechanical damage, missing parts, or scratches, cause a rapid decline in value. Surprisingly, engraved initials, a monogram, or name has little impact on value.

Lewis Waterman developed the fountain pen in the 1880s. Parker, Sheaffer, and Wahl-Eversharp refined the product. Conklin, Eversharp, Moore, Parker, Sheaffer, Wahl, and Waterman were leading manufacturers. Reynolds' introduction of the ballpoint pen in late 1945 signaled the end for the nib fountain pen.

Sampson Mordan patented the mechanical pencil in 1822. Early mechanical pencils used a slide action mechanism. It was eventually replaced by a spiral mechanism. Wahl-Eversharp developed the automatic "click" mechanism used on pens as well as pencils.

Fountain pen values rose dramatically from the late 1970s through the early 1990s. Many of these values were speculative. The speculative bubble burst in the mid-1990s. Today, prices are extremely stable with common fountain pens a very difficult sell.

References: Paul Erano, *Fountain Pens,* Collector Books, 1999; George Fischler and Stuart Schneider, *Fountain Pens and Pencils, 2nd Edition,* Schiffer Publishing, 1998; Henry Gostony and Stuart Schneider, *The Incredible Ball Point Pen,* Schiffer Publishing, 1998; Regina Martini, *Pens & Pencils, 2nd Edition,* Schiffer Publishing, 1998; Stuart Schneider and George Fischler, *The Illustrated Guide to Antique Writing Instruments, 3rd Edition,* Schiffer Publishing, 2000.

Periodical: *Pen World Magazine,* 3946 Glade Valley Dr, Kingwood, TX 77339.

Newsletter: *Float About* (floaty pens), 1676 Millsboro Rd, Mansfield, OH 44906.

Collectors' Clubs: American Pencil Collectors Society, 7640 Evergreen Dr, Mountain View, WY 82939; Pen Collectors of America, PO Box 821449, Houston, TX 77282.

PENS

Conway Stewart, mkd "Conway Stewart 27, Made in England, 14ct gold," 5" l **$35.00**
Epenco, pen and holder, Art Deco style, black and ivory Bakelite, lever fill **30.00**
Esterbrook, Bakelite, multicolor green pearlescent **25.00**
Eversharp, ballpoint, CA model, black, gold-filled cap, 1946. . . . . **40.00**
Mont Blanc style, mkd "Iridium Point Germany," with felt pouch **20.00**
National Pen Products, green marbleized and gold finish, side plunger, 14K gold tip, stamped "The Lincoln Pen, National Pen Products Co, Chicago, Dan Patch Pens," 5³/₈" l **35.00**
Parker 45 Convertible, gold-colored clip and trim, orig clear plastic-top box and instructions **40.00**
Parker Vacumatic, Bakelite, gold and tan striped on dark brown ground **150.00**
Parker Vacumatic, black, 5¹/₈" l **60.00**
Sheaffer, gold tip, mkd "WA Sheaffer Pen Co, Fort Madison, Iowa, USA, Made in USA, 14K" **35.00**
Sheaffer, pump, plastic, mkd "Sheaffer Made in USA, Sheaffer's 14K USA" **35.00**
Sheaffer 500, brown striped, lever fill, mkd "Sheaffer's Feather Touch Made in USA 5 14K," gold with silver end. **15.00**
Velvet Point 6, black **5.00**
Wahl-Eversharp, pearl and black, roller clip, iridium tip, mkd "Wahl 14K" **150.00**
Waterman, set with fountain pen and ballpoint pen, engraved "Waterman, 18Kt, 750" **125.00**
Waterman's Ideal, gray and brown marbleized, lever fill, 14K **65.00**

PEN AND PENCIL SETS

Esterbrook, gray marbleized, nib mkd "2668," lever fill. **$30.00**
Kreisler, Karat Crown Pen and Viceroy Pencil, 5¹/₄" l gold pen, center band mkd "Kreisler Heavy Gold Electroplate Karat Crown," 5¹/₄" l silver-colored pencil mkd "Kreisler Viceroy" **10.00**
Parker 51, brown with stainless steel caps and mother-of-pearl jeweled tops, feather-type clips, orig case. **80.00**

Mechanical Pencil, Lion Head Motor Oil adv, black and orange on cream ground, calendar on end, 5³/₄" l, $70.00. Photo courtesy Collectors Auction Services.

Sheaffer, pen mkd "WA Sheaffer Pen Co Fort Madison, Iowa, USA Patented in the USA875, 14K," pencil stamped "Shaeffer's, made in USA, Pat's USA 350, 14K" 40.00

PEN/PENCIL COMBINATIONS

Conklin Toledo, 1925 . . . . $140.00
Sheaffer's, 5-30, black, gold-filled trim, lever filled, 1936 . . . 225.00

PEPSI-COLA

Caleb D. Bradham, a pharmacist and drugstore owner in New Bern, North Carolina, developed "Brad's Drink," a soda mix, in the mid-1890s. By 1898, Brad's Drink had become Pepsi-Cola. By 1902 Bradham was promoting Pepsi-Cola on a full-time basis. Two years later he sold his first franchise.

In 1910 the Pepsi-Cola network consisted of 250 bottlers in 24 states. Investing in the sugar market, Pepsi-Cola found itself in deep financial difficulties when the market collapsed immediately following World War I. Roy Megargel, a Wall Street financier, rescued and guided the company out of its difficulties. Pepsi-Cola survived a second bankruptcy in 1931.

In 1933 Pepsi-Cola's fortunes soared when the company doubled its bottle size and held its price to a nickel. Walter Mack (1938 to 1951) provided the leadership that enabled Pepsi to challenge Coca-Cola for the number one spot in the soda market. "Pepsi-Cola Hits The Spot, Twelve Full Ounces That's A Lot" was one of the most popular advertising jingles of the 1950s.

Pepsi Co., a division of Beatrice, enjoys a worldwide reputation, outselling Coca-Cola in a number of foreign countries. This is one reason why many foreign buyers have an interest in Pepsi-Cola memorabilia.

Beware of a wide range of Pepsi-Cola reproductions, copycats, fantasy items, and fakes. The 1970s Pepsi and Pete pillow, a Pepsi double bed quilt, and a 12" high ceramic statute of a woman holding a glass of Pepsi are a few examples.

Collectors place little secondary market value on contemporary licensed products.

References: James C. Ayers, *Pepsi-Cola Bottles Collectors Guide,* RJM Enterprises, 1995 (1999 value update); Everette and Mary Lloyd, *Pepsi-Cola Collectibles,* Schiffer Publishing, 1993; Bill Vehling and Michael Hunt, *Pepsi-Cola Collectibles, Vol. 3* (1993, 1995 value update), L-W Book Sales.

Collectors' Club: Pepsi-Cola Collectors Club, PO Box 817, Claremont, CA 91711.

Ashtray, glass, "Pepsi Beats The Others Cold!," 1960s, 4" sq $25.00
Book, *The Story of Pepsi-Cola,*1950s, 12 x 6" 25.00
Bottle Carrier, metal, 12-pack, 1940s 200.00
Bottle Carrier, wooden, 6-pack, 1930-40s. 95.00
Bottle Opener, celluloid handle, 1930s, 4" l 125.00
Bottle Opener, plastic handle, 1960s, 6" l. 25.00
Cap, tin, 1950s, 28" d 220.00
Clock, light-up, double bubble, "say Pepsi please," "Pepsi-Cola" with bottle cap, 1950s 1,250.00
Clock, light-up, double bubble, "think young–Say 'Pepsi, please!'" 900.00
Drinking Glass, applied color label, 12 oz, 1960s 25.00
Flag, fabric, "Pepsi-Cola," red, white, and blue, 1930-40s, 42 x 70". 100.00
Kick Plate, porcelain, depicts bottle bursting through paper beside cap, 1940s, 14 x 36". 5,700.00
Lighter, metal, bottle cap illus on side, 1950s, 4" l 150.00
Lighter, metal, "Drink Pepsi Today," 1960s, 1½ x 2½". 25.00
Mechanical Pencil, plastic barrel with silvered metal point end and eraser holder, attached pocket clip, inscription "Drink Pepsi-Cola" in red on white ground flanked by blue trimbands, barrel inscribed for Pepsi Cola Bottling Co, Auburn, NY, Scripto, 1950s, 5" l 50.00
Menu, 1 sheet, Pepsi glass and bottle cap, 1940s, 8 x 11". . . . 50.00
Money Clip, plastic, 1950s, 2" d 25.00
Napkin Dispenser, black and white, red, white, and blue bottle cap design on sides, c1940s 350.00
Paperweight, glass, "Delicious Pepsi-Cola," c1940, 3 x 3" 75.00
Pencil Clip, 1940s, 1" d. 75.00
Pinback Button, "Bigger/Pepsi-Cola/Better," red lettering on yellow ground, 1940s 25.00
Program, Pepsi-Cola Evervess Convention, Atlantic City, Nov 1947, 6 x 12". 75.00

Left: Menu Board, painted tin, $275.00. Right: Thermometer, emb metal, 27¹/₄" h, $200.00. Photos courtesy Collectors Auction Services.

Register Sign, diecut cardboard, emb, "Purity...Pepsi-Cola...In The Big, Big Bottle," complete with counterfeit bill spotting instructions on back, 1940s, unused..... **750.00**

Ruler, tin, Pepsi button on each end, "The Light Refreshment," 1950s, 12" l............................ **20.00**

Salt and Pepper Shakers, pr, plastic, 1950s, 3 x 4" **50.00**

Sign, celluloid, "Ice Cold Pepsi-Cola Sold Here," red, white, and blue, complete with orig string hanger and rubber stoppers, 1940s, 9" d **325.00**

Sign, diecut cardboard, "Buy Pepsi-Cola Today!," comical policeman holding club, 1940s, 12 x 13" **200.00**

Sign, diecut cardboard, "Pepsi-Cola Double Size/5¢ Ice Cold," 6½ x 13½" **225.00**

Sign, paper, woman in bathing suit sitting on beach holding bottle, carrier in sand, "Pepsi-Cola" on button beside "Pepsi's Best...Take No Less," 1940s, 36 x 24" **475.00**

Sign, porcelain, bottle cap shape, "Drink Pepsi-Cola," 1950s, 42" d **600.00**

Sign, tin, 2-sided, "Take Home A Carton 12 Full Glasses/Pepsi-Cola/Finer Flavor–Better Value,"1940s, 10 x 15".... **450.00**

Sign, tin, couple in surf on rocks, bottle cap to upper right, 23 x 30"....................................... **275.00**

Sign, tin, emb, "Curb Service/Pepsi-Cola Ice Cold 5¢/Bigger–Better," 1939, 20 x 28" **575.00**

Sign, tin, girl at rail with camera, bottle cap to lower right, 20 x 28" **375.00**

Tape Measure, 1950s, 1¼ x 1¼" **25.00**

Thermometer, wall, tin, center clear plastic convex dome over dial face with red, blue, and black name, 1960s, 9 x 9"... **50.00**

Token, 1950s, 1½" d **25.00**

Transistor Radio, soda fountain cooler shape, complete with orig leather carrying strap, 1930s **375.00**

PERFUME BOTTLES

Perfume manufacturers discovered that packaging is almost as important a selling factor for a perfume as its scent. Coty contracted with Lalique to produce exquisitely designed bottles for many of its perfumes. Many Czechoslovakian perfume bottles manufactured between the 1920s and 1960s are architectural miniatures reflecting the very best in design styles of the period.

A perfume bottle is a bottle with a stopper, often elongated, that serves as an applicator. A cologne bottle is usually larger than a perfume bottle. Its stopper also serves as an applicator. An atomizer is a bottle with a spray mechanism.

After a period of speculation and rapidly escalating prices in the 1980s and early 1990s, perfume bottle prices have stabilized, especially for common and middle range examples. Large countertop display bottles enjoyed a brief speculative price run in the early 1990s. They are tough sells today, largely because most collectors consider them overvalued.

References: Joanne Dubbs Ball and Dorothy Hehl Torem, *Commercial Fragrance Bottles,* Schiffer Publishing, 1993; Glinda Bowman, *Miniature Perfume Bottles,* Schiffer Publishing, 1994; Jacquelyne Jones-North, *Commercial Perfume Bottles, Third Edition,* Schiffer Publishing, 1996; Jacquelyne Y. Jones-North, *Czechoslovakian Perfume Bottles and Boudoir Accessories, Revised,* Glass Press, 1999; Jacquelyne Y. Jones-North, *Perfume, Cologne and Scent Bottles, 3rd Edition,* Schiffer Publishing, 1999; Tirza True Latimer, *The Perfume Atomizer,* Schiffer Publishing, 1991; Jeri Lyn Ringblum, *A Collector's Handbook of Miniature Perfume Bottles,* Schiffer Publishing, 1996.

Collectors' Clubs: International Perfume Bottle Assoc, 3314 Shamrock Rd, Tampa, FL 33629; Miniature Perfume Bottle Collectors, 28227 Paseo El Siena, Laguna Niguel, CA 92677.

Atomizer, blue opalescent, ringed spherical body with flattened sides, 6" h, 2½" d **$60.00**

Atomizer, Czechoslovakian, Art Deco style, blue and white geometric pattern on frosted bottle, collar mkd "Czechoslovakia," 7" h **275.00**

Atomizer, frosted glass with dragonflies, 4½" h........... **30.00**

Cologne, Dana, Tabu, violin shaped bottle, c1930s, 2" h..... **15.00**

Cologne, Nash Glass, chintz, paperweight stopper **225.00**

Cologne, Pairpoint, applied vertical cranberry ribbing, flower form cranberry and clear stopper, 8" h **110.00**

Perfume, blown glass, blue-green with gold trim, 10" h..... **25.00**

Perfume, Cambridge, cobalt blue, 4⅛" h ringed bottle, 3½" l faceted and scalloped stopper, 5" h overall **125.00**

Perfume, Chanel No. 5, rect, faceted stopper, orig boxes, 2¹⁵⁄₁₆" h **100.00**

Perfume, Christian Dior, Diorissimo, amphora shaped, miniature, clear, gold cap, 1½" h **40.00**

Perfume, cranberry flashed with Coin Spot pattern, round faceted stopper, 3" h **18.00**

Perfume, Czechoslovakian, cut glass, yellow base, clear stopper, 5" h including stopper..................... **35.00**

Perfume, Estee Lauder, miniature set with 4 perfumes and gold-colored bag and key chain, orig box **30.00**

Perfume, Forever Yours, heart shaped bottle held by 2 white metal hands on satin-covered cardboard base, glass dome, 4¼" h................................... **100.00**

Perfume, Lalique "L'Air Du Temps," bird stopper, mkd "Nina Ricci, Lalique France," 2" h bottle.............. **25.00**

Perfume, Phoenix glass, Art Deco motif, 3 bottles and tray, sgd "5th Ave NY, DIR," 4¼" h bottles, 10" l tray..... **125.00**

Perfume, Tiffany Eau de Toilette spray, $35.00.

Perfume, red and white ribbon latticinio, metal fittings,
  unmkd, 3½" h, 2⅛" d **35.00**
Perfume, Two's Company, frosted, heart shaped stopper,
  6" h **8.00**
Perfume, Waterford Crystal Marquis, unopened, 6½" h **65.00**

PEZ

Eduard Haas, an Austrian food manufacturer, developed the Pez formula in 1927. He added peppermint (Pffefferminz in German) oil to a candy formula, pressed it into small rectangular pellets, and sold it as an adult breath mint and cigarette substitute.

World War II halted the production of Pez. When it reappeared in the late 1940s it was packaged in a rectangular dispenser. An initial foray into the United States market in 1952 was only modestly successful. Evaluating the situation, Haas added fruit flavors and novelty dispensers, thus enabling Pez to make a major impact on the children's candy market.

Because the company carefully guards its design and production records, information regarding the first appearance of a particular dispenser and dispenser variations is open to interpretation. Pez Candy, Inc., is located in Connecticut. A second, independent company with distribution rights to the rest of the world, including Canada, is located in Linz, Austria. Although the two cooperate, it is common for each company to issue dispensers with different heads or the same dispenser in different packaging.

There are three basic types of dispensers—generic, licensed, and seasonal. New dispensers appear regularly. Further, the company is quite willing to modify an existing design. The Mickey Mouse dispenser has gone through at least a dozen changes.

Pez has been made in Austria (current), Czechoslovakia (closed), Germany (closed), Hungary (current), Mexico (closed), United States (current), and Yugoslavia (current). Plants in Austria, China, Hong Kong, Hungary, and Slovenia make dispensers.

References: Richard Geary, *More PEZ For Collectors, 3rd Edition* (2000), *PEZ Collectibles, 3rd Edition* (1999), Schiffer Publishing; David Welch, *Collecting Pez*, Bubba Scrubba Publications, 1994.

Collectors' Club: Fliptop PEZervation Society, PO Box 124, Sea Cliff, NY 11579.

Note: Prices listed are for Pez containers in mint condition.

Air Spirit, soft head **$250.00**
Angel, removable eyes **125.00**
Angel, with feet **65.00**
Annie **165.00**
Baloo, royal blue **135.00**
Baloo, with feet **25.00**
Bambi **60.00**
Bambi, black nose, with feet **65.00**
Barney Bear **10.00**
Baseball Glove, brown glove, white ball **120.00**
Batgirl, blue mask, black hair **75.00**
Batgirl, soft head, no feet **175.00**
Batman, soft head **240.00**
Batman, with cape, no feet **100.00**
Betsy Ross, red stem, black hair, white bonnet **20.00**
Boy with Cap, no feet **100.00**
Bozo **200.00**
Bubbleman, with feet **8.00**

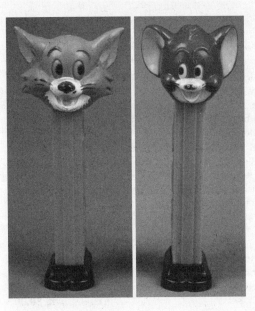

Tom and Jerry,
price each,
$10.00.

Bullwinkle, brown stem **500.00**
Bullwinkle, yellow stem **325.00**
Camel Whistle, with feet **50.00**
Candy Shooter, black **135.00**
Candy Shooter, orange **80.00**
Candy Shooter, red **100.00**
Captain America, black mask **150.00**
Captain Hook, no feet **85.00**
Captain Pez **85.00**
Cat with Derby **100.00**
Charlie Brown, with feet, blue cap **20.00**
Clown with Collar, no feet **65.00**
Coach Whistle **45.00**
Cockatoo, blue, with feet **55.00**
Cockatoo, green **75.00**
Cocoa Marsh, no feet, light blue **250.00**
Cool Cat, with feet **75.00**
Cow, no feet **100.00**
Cowboy, tan hat **295.00**
Creature from the Black Lagoon **500.00**
Crocodile, neon green **150.00**
Dalmatian, with feet **55.00**
Daniel Boone **250.00**
Diabolic, soft head **250.00**
Dino **3.00**
Doctor, no feet **250.00**
Dog Whistle, with feet **25.00**
Dog Whistle, without feet **40.00**
Droopy Dog, with feet **25.00**
Dumbo, with feet **50.00**
Easter Bunny, color variation, entirely in pink, test mold
  bunny, 1990 . . . . **120.00**
Elephant, blue hair **200.00**
Elephant, orange, blue flat hat **100.00**
Elephant, yellow or aqua **125.00**
Elephant, pointed hat **100.00**
Fat Ears Rabbit, pink, no feet **25.00**
Fireman **100.00**
Foghorn Leghorn, with feet **100.00**
Football Player, no feet, red **125.00**

Fozzie Bear 1.00
Frankenstein 145.00
Frog Whistle, with feet. 45.00
Giraffe 250.00
Goofy, removable teeth, no feet 45.00
Gorilla, brown face 115.00
Groom, blank side 600.00
Henry Hawk, with feet 65.00
Icee Bear, purple stem, MOC. 6.00
Icee Bear, with feet, MOC 10.00
Incredible Hulk 5.00
Indian Chief, dark face 175.00
Indian Chief, reddish face 165.00
Indian Chief, rubber headdress 130.00
Indian Squaw 50.00
Jerry, no feet 50.00
Jiminy Crickett 235.00
Johnny Lightning Pez Car. 20.00
Joker, soft head 225.00
King Louie, with feet 25.00
Koala Whistle, with feet. 30.00
Lamb Whistle, white 25.00
Li'l Bad Wolf. 25.00
Li'l Lion 75.00
Little Orphan Annie, red stem, golden brown hair 25.00
Maharajah, no feet 50.00
Mary Poppins 375.00
Merlin, with feet 25.00
Mexican 300.00
Mimic, blue head 50.00
Monkey Sailor 55.00
Monkey Whistle, with feet. 25.00
Moo Moo Cow, Kooky Zoo 20.00
Mowgli, with feet 20.00
Mr Ugly, aqua. 85.00
Mr Ugly, green, MIP 65.00
Mr Ugly, yellow 90.00
Nermal. 3.00
Ninja Turtle. 2.00
Nurse, no feet 200.00
One-Eyed Monster 85.00
Orange 250.00
Panda Whistle A, removable eyes 25.00
Panther 250.00
Papa Smurf, with feet 5.00
Penguin, soft head. 175.00
Peter Pan 200.00
Peter Pez 65.00
Petunia Pig, no feet 45.00
Pez Pal Mariner, with feet 10.00
Pig Whistle, with feet 60.00
Pilot 300.00
Pineapple, Crazy Fruit 200.00
Pinocchio 175.00
Pirate, no feet 60.00
Pluto, no feet 15.00
Policeman 55.00
Pony, orange head, no feet. 100.00
Popeye, red hat with pipe 150.00
Power Pez A 6.00
Practical Pig 25.00
Rhino Whistle, with feet, MOC 5.00
Roar the Lion, no feet 125.00
Robot, blue, c1950 . . . . 75.00

Rooster Whistle, with feet 50.00
Rooster, white, with feet 35.00
Rudolph the Red-Nosed Reindeer 60.00
Sailor, no feet 200.00
Santa, no feet 130.00
Scarewolf, soft head 250.00
Scrooge, with feet 25.00
Sheik, red band. 60.00
Silly Clown. 25.00
Silver Glow. 10.00
Skull, no feet 15.00
Smurf, with feet 5.00
Smurfette, with feet, MOC 10.00
Snoopy 5.00
Snowman, yellow or orange, MOC 20.00
Snow White 60.00
Space Gun, red, 1980s 90.00
Space Gun, silver, 1980s 140.00
Speedy Gonzalez 10.00
Spider-man, no feet 20.00
Spike, painted eyes and feet 30.00
Spook, soft head 250.00
Stewardess 275.00
Sylvester. 2.00
Thumper, with feet 45.00
Tiger Whistle 6.00
Tinker Bell 300.00
Uncle Sam 275.00
Wile Coyote, with feet. 55.00
Winnie the Pooh, yellow head. 125.00
Witch, green hair 325.00
Wounded Soldier, no feet 100.00
Yappy Dog, orange 75.00
Yappy Dog, green, with feet. 60.00
Zombie, soft head 250.00
Zorro 65.00

PFALTZGRAFF

The name Pfaltzgraff is derived from a famous Rhine River castle, still standing today, in the Pfalz region of Germany. In 1811 George Pfaltzgraff, a German immigrant potter, began producing salt-glazed stoneware in York, Pennsylvania.

The Pfaltzgraff Pottery Company initially produced stoneware storage crocks and jugs. When the demand for stoneware diminished, the company shifted its production to animal and poultry feeders and red clay flowerpots. The production focus changed again in the late 1940s and early 1950s as the company produced more and more household products, including its first dinnerware line, and giftwares.

In 1964 the company became The Pfaltzgraff Company. Over the next fifteen years, Pfaltzgraff expanded via construction of a new manufacturing plant and distribution center at Thomasville, North Carolina, the purchase of the Stangl Pottery of Trenton, New Jersey, and the acquisition of factories in Dover, Aspers, and Bendersville, Pennsylvania. Retail stores were opened in York County, Pennsylvania; Flemington, New Jersey; and Fairfax, Virginia.

References: Susan and Al Bagdade, *Warman's American Pottery and Porcelain*, Wallace-Homestead, Krause Publications, 1994; Harvey Duke, *The Official Price Guide to Pottery and Porcelain*,

Eighth Edition, House of Collectibles, 1995; Harry L. Rinker, *Dinnerware of the 20th Century: The Top 500 Patterns,* House of Collectibles, 1997.

Collectors' Club: Pfaltzgraff America Collectors Club, 2536 Quint Ln, Columbia, IL 62236.

America, cup and saucer	**$6.00**
America, dinner plate	**7.00**
America, salad plate	**4.00**
America, salt and pepper shakers, pr	**15.00**
America, sugar, cov	**15.00**
Christmas Heirloom, cup and saucer	**8.00**
Christmas Heirloom, salt and pepper shakers, pr	**12.00**
Gourmet, ashtray	**5.00**
Gourmet, baker, oval, 10" l	**22.00**
Gourmet, casserole, cov, 12 oz, no lid	**30.00**
Gourmet, cup and saucer	**8.00**
Gourmet, gravy boat and underplate	**12.00**
Gourmet, vegetable, oval, divided, 12³⁄₈" l	**12.00**
Village, bread tray, 12¹⁄₂" l	**10.00**
Village, casserole, cov, round, 6³⁄₄" d	**8.00**
Village, creamer	**10.00**
Village, pitcher, 6³⁄₈" h	**15.00**
Village, tureen, cov	**50.00**
Windsong, bread and butter plate	**6.00**
Windsong, dinner plate	**12.00**
Yorktowne, augratin	**12.00**
Yorktowne, baker, individual	**10.00**
Yorktowne, baker, oval, 8" l	**12.00**
Yorktowne, baker, rect, 14¹⁄₄" l	**20.00**
Yorktowne, baker, 9" sq	**25.00**
Yorktowne, boiled corn holder, 8¹⁄₂" l	**6.00**
Yorktowne, butter, cov, ¹⁄₄ lb	**10.00**
Yorktowne, butter tub	**12.00**
Yorktowne, candleholder, 2¹⁄₈" h	**12.00**
Yorktowne, candy dish, 6³⁄₄" h	**15.00**
Yorktowne, casserole, cov, individual, 4¹⁄₄" d	**12.00**

Yorktowne, coffee canister, no lid, 5³⁄₄" h	**12.00**
Yorktowne, cookie jar, 5⁵⁄₈" h	**20.00**
Yorktowne, crock, open, 7⁷⁄₈" h	**65.00**
Yorktowne, cup and saucer, flat, 2¹⁄₂" h	**3.00**
Yorktowne, flour canister, 7¹⁄₄" h	**12.00**
Yorktowne, grill plate, 10" d	**6.00**
Yorktowne, measuring cup	**6.00**
Yorktowne, mixing bowl, 6" d	**6.00**
Yorktowne, mixing bowl, 8" d	**14.00**
Yorktowne, oil cruet	**15.00**
Yorktowne, relish, 7¹⁄₂" l	**8.00**
Yorktowne, salad plate, 6⁷⁄₈" d	**2.00**
Yorktowne, salt and pepper shakers, pr, 4" h	**10.00**
Yorktowne, soup server, open, individual	**3.00**
Yorktowne, sugar canister, 6¹⁄₄" h	**15.00**
Yorktowne, sugar, cov	**10.00**
Yorktowne, teapot, cov	**30.00**
Yorktowne, toothpick	**4.00**
Yorktowne, wine and cheese set, 4 pcs	**20.00**

PHOENIX BIRD CHINA

The Phoenix Bird pattern features a phoenix bird facing back over its left wing, its chest spotted and wings spread upward. Although produced predominantly in blue and white, pieces have been found in celedon (green).

There are a number of Phoenix Bird pattern variations: (1) Firebird with its downward tail, (2) Flying Dragon typified by six Chinese characters and a pinwheel-like design, (3) Flying Turkey with no spots on its chest and one wing only partially visible, (4) Howo with no feet and a peony-like flower, and (5) Twin Phoenix with two birds facing each other. Pieces with a cloud and mountain border are the most common. Pieces with a heart-like border are known as HO-O for identification purposes.

Phoenix Bird china was manufactured by a number of companies and made available in a wide variety of markets. Beginning in the 1970s many new pieces of Phoenix Bird arrived on the market. The shapes are more modern, the blues more brilliant, and most lack an identifying backstamp.

References: Joan Collett Oates, *Phoenix Bird Chinaware, Book 1* (1984), *Book II* (1985), *Book III* (1986), *Book IV* (1989, 1996 value update), published by author.

Collectors' Club: Phoenix Bird Collectors of America, 685 S Washington, Constantine, MI 49042.

Bouillon Cup, 2¹⁄₂" h, 2¹⁄₂" w handle to handle	**$25.00**
Bowl, oval, 7¹⁄₂" l, 1³⁄₄" h	**50.00**
Bowl, round, 7¹⁄₂" d, 2" h	**50.00**
Bowl, scalloped edge, 9¹⁄₂" d, 3" h	**100.00**
Cake Plate, 12¹⁄₄" w	**30.00**
Charger, 10³⁄₄" d	**25.00**
Cocoa Set, consisting of pot and 6 cups and saucers, 9" h pot	**500.00**
Creamer, 3" h	**15.00**
Cup and Saucer	**20.00**
Demitasse Cup and Saucer	**15.00**
Eggcup, single, 3¹⁄₈" h, 2¹⁄₂" d	**15.00**
Fruit Bowl, 5" d	**15.00**
Fruit Bowl, 5¹⁄₂" d	**15.00**
Pitcher, 4" h	**45.00**
Pitcher, 5" h	**125.00**

Yorktowne, cereal bowl, 6" d, $5.00.

Plate, 6¼" d **35.00**
Plate, 7⅜" d **20.00**
Plate, 8½" d **25.00**
Plate, 9" d **50.00**
Plate, 9¾" d **80.00**
Plate, 10" d **100.00**
Ramekin, with liner, 3¾" d, 1½" h **40.00**
Rice Bowl, cov, 3¼" h, 6¼" w handle to handle **275.00**
Rice Bowl, cov, 5" h, 7½" w handle to handle **275.00**
Sauce Boat, 6½" l, 2¼" h **150.00**
Sauce Boat, with underplate, 5½" l, 2¾" h **275.00**
Saucer, 5½" d **10.00**
Sugar, cov, 6" w **30.00**
Trivet, 6⅜" d **40.00**
Vegetable, cov, oval, 12½" l **250.00**
Whipped Cream Pail, cov, rattan handle, 3½" h, 3" d **125.00**

PHOENIX GLASS

In 1880 Andrew Howard founded the Phoenix Glass Company in Phillispburg (later Monaca), Pennsylvania, to manufacture glass tubes for the new electrical wires in houses. Phoenix bought J. A. Bergun, Charles Challinor's decorating business, in 1882. A year later Phoenix signed a contract with Joseph Webb to produce Victorian art glass. Phoenix began producing light bulbs in the early 1890s. In 1893 Phoenix and General Electric collaborated on an exhibit at the Columbian Exposition.

In 1933 the company introduced its Reuben and Sculptured lines. Phoenix acquired the Co-Operative Flint molds in 1937. Using these molds, Phoenix began manufacturing Early American, a pressed milk glass line in 1938.

In 1970 Anchor Hocking acquired Phoenix Glass. The construction of Phoenix's new plant coincided with the company's 100th anniversary in 1980. In 1987 Newell Corporation acquired Anchor Hocking.

Reference: Jack D. Wilson, *Phoenix & Consolidated Art Glass, 1926-1980,* Antique Publications, 1989, out of print.

Collectors' Club: Phoenix & Consolidated Glass Collectors Club, 41 River View Dr, Essex Junction, VT 05452.

Pillow Vase, flying geese, white on brown, 9½" h, 12" w, $180.00.

Bowl, swallows, purple wash **$150.00**
Console Bowl, diving nudes, 3 colors on white ground, 14" d **250.00**
Creamer and Sugar, Catalonia, yellow **50.00**
Dish, lotus blossoms and dragonflies, amber ground, 8½" l **100.00**
Fan Vase, grasshoppers perched on blades of grass, pink satin glass, 8½" h, 8½" w **275.00**
Floor Vase, bushberry, light green, 18" h **450.00**
Pillow Vase, flying geese, blue on white, 1930s, 9½" h, 12" w **200.00**
Pillow Vase, flying geese, green, 9½" h, 12" w **75.00**
Pillow Vase, flying geese, red over white, 9½" h, 12" w . . . **150.00**
Planter, green lion, white ground **50.00**
Plate, cherries, 8½" d **50.00**
Plate, dancing nudes, yellow ground, 8¼" d **70.00**
Vase, blue-gray flowers and green foliage, 10½" h, 4½" d **100.00**
Vase, coral flowers and green foliage, 9½" h, 4" d **60.00**
Vase, hummingbirds, tan, peach, and aqua frosted, 5½" h **85.00**
Vase, spherical, flowers and leaves, dark blue, 7" h **550.00**

PHOTOGRAPHS

In 1830 J. M. Daugerre of France patented a process of covering a copper plate with silver salts, sandwiching the plate between glass for protection, and exposing the plate to light and mercury vapors to imprint an image. The process produced Daguerreotypes. Fox Talbot of Britain patented the method for making paper negatives and prints (calotypes) in 1841. Frederick Scott Archer introduced the wet collodion process in 1851. Dr. Maddox developed dry plates in 1871. When George Eastman produced roll film in 1888, the photographic industry reached maturity.

Cartes de visite (calling card) photographs flourished from 1857 to 1910 and survived into the 1920s. In 1866 the cabinet card first appeared in England. The format quickly spread to the United States. It was the preferred form by the 1890s.

The family photo album was second only to the Bible in importance to late 19th- and early 20th-century families. The principal downfall of family albums is that the vast majority of their photographs are unidentified. Professional photographers produced and sold "art" folios. Two post-1945 developments produced profound changes. The 35mm "slide" camera and home video equipment decreased the importance of the photographic print.

Before discarding family photos, check them carefully. A photograph showing a child playing with a toy or dressed in a costume or an adult at work, in military garb, or shopping in a store has modest value. Collectors prefer black and white over color prints, as the latter deteriorate over time.

References: Norman E. Martinus and Harry L. Rinker, *Warman's Paper,* Wallace-Homestead, 1994; John S. Waldsmith, *Stereo Views: An Illustrated History and Price Guide,* Wallace-Homestead, 1991.

Periodicals: *Art on Paper,* 39 E 78th St, #501, New York, NY 10021; *The Photograph Collector,* 301 Hill Ave, Langhorne, PA 19047.

Collectors' Clubs: American Photographic Historical Society, 1150 Avenue of the Americas, New York, NY 10036; National

Stereoscopic Assoc, PO Box 14801, Columbus, OH 43214; The Photographic Historical Society, PO Box 39563, Rochester, NY 14604.

Note: See Wallace Nutting and Nutting-Like Photographs for additional listings.

Professional Photographer, Alfred Wertheimer, Elvis Presley tongue-kissing fan, silver print, photographer's signature and handstamp, handwritten caption and edition notations in pencil and copyright handstamp on verso, 1979, 6³/₄ x 10" **$700.00**

Professional Photographer, Bernice Abbott, St Luke's Church, Hudson Street, New York City, silver print, photographer's signature in pencil on mount recto, handstamp and title in pencil on mount verso, 1930s, 9¹/₄ x 7¹/₂" **925.00**

Professional Photographer, Dorothea Lange, employment agency, San Francisco, silver print, with FSA handstamp, typewritten caption, and notations on verso, 1930s, 7¹/₂ x 9³/₄" **975.00**

Professional Photographer, Edward Weston, James Cagney, silver print, photographer's inventory notations in ink on verso, 1930s, 9¹/₂ x 7¹/₂" **3,000.00**

Professional Photographer, Elliott Erwitt, Yale's Oldest Living Graduate, silver print, sgd and editioned by photographer in pencil on verso, 1955, 7 x 9¹/₂" **675.00**

Professional Photographer, Germaine Krull, radio control panel, silver print, photographer's backstamp on verso, 1930s, 6¹/₂ x 9" **1,250.00**

Professional Photographer, Weegee, air raid drill, silver print, with photographer's handstamp on verso, 1940s, 13 x 10³/₄" **1,725.00**

Snapshot, 2 black men with liquor bottles, 1920s **8.00**

Snapshot, 2 men with shotguns, 2 hunting dogs, "Compliments of AL Guthrie, Manchester, Ind–The Gang," black and white, 8 x 10" **25.00**

Snapshot, barbershop, interior view, black and white, 8 x 10" **30.00**

Snapshot, boy on tricycle, black and white, 7 x 9" **15.00**

Snapshot, bride and bridesmaid, 1930, 9¹/₂ x 7" **20.00**

Snapshot, Christmas tree, decorated, dolls and toys beneath, 10 x 12" **40.00**

Snapshot, circus wagon pulled by ponies, black and white **8.00**

Snapshot, fire department hose cart, Milwaukee, WI, black and white, 8¹/₂ x 10¹/₂" **75.00**

Snapshot, fisherman with rod and reel, "Is This Large Enough?," black and white, 8 x 10" **20.00**

Snapshot, hardware store int, black and white, 8 x 10" **40.00**

Snapshot, logging camp cooks, 1 holding large horn, black and white **8.00**

Snapshot, man with motorcycle, 1943 . . . . **8.00**

Snapshot, office, int view, 7 x 9" **15.00**

Snapshot, radio studio, int view, close up of equipment, man at mike, and engineer, black and white, 1920s, 11 x 7" **18.00**

Snapshot, seed store, int view with Ferry Seed Co display racks and salespeople, 1920, 5 x 7" **10.00**

Snapshot, silver shop, int view, 6 x 8" **25.00**

Snapshot, supermarket, int view, 1950s, 8 x 10" **15.00**

Snapshot, "The Cadillac Evening News," Cadillac, MI, Jan 18, 1927, newsboys and bags, black and white **20.00**

Snapshot, woman with quadruplets, "Mrs Ormsby, Edith, Willie, John, Theodore, black and white, 5 x 8" **22.00**

PICKARD CHINA

In 1894 Willard Pickard founded Pickard China in Chicago, Illinois. Until 1938, the company was a decorating firm; it did not manufacture the ceramics it decorated. Blanks were bought from foreign manufacturers, primarily French prior to World War I and German after the war.

Most of Pickard's early decorators were trained at Chicago's famed Art Institute. The company's reputation for quality soon attracted top ceramic painters from around the world. Many artists signed their work. Edward S. Challinor, noted for his bird, floral, fruit, and scenic designs, began working at Pickard in 1902 and remained with the company until his death in 1952. By 1908 Pickard offered more than 1,000 shapes and designs. In 1911 the company introduced gold-encrusted and gold-etched china.

In 1938 Pickard opened its own pottery in Antioch, Illinois. Pickard made china for the Navy during World War II. Decal patterns were introduced after the war. The company entered the limited edition bell and plate market in 1970 and introduced its first Christmas plate in 1976. In 1977 the U.S. Department of State selected Pickard to manufacture the official china services used at embassies and diplomatic missions around the world.

References: Susan and Al Bagdade, *Warman's American Pottery and Porcelain,* Wallace-Homestead, 1994; Alan B. Reed, *Collector's Encyclopedia of Pickard China With Additional Section on Other Chicago China Studios,* Collector Books, 1995, 2000 value update.

Collectors' Club: Pickard Collectors Club, 300 E Grove St, Bloomington, IL 61701.

Note: AOG stands for "all over gold."

Professional Photograph, Ad Topperwein, autographed, black and white, $325.00. Photo courtesy Collectors Auction Services.

Cake Plate, scenic with gold rim and handles, sgd "Marker," gold mark, $300.00.

Candlesticks, pr, Poppy, AOG, JH Stouffer Co, 1930-42,
2³/₄" h **$75.00**
Charger, Golden Pheasant, sgd "Challinor," Pickard
China, 1919-22, 12¹/₂" d **400.00**
Creamer and Sugar, flowered festoon with alternate blue
ribbon festoons on white, sgd "Tol," ZS & Co, Bavaria
blank, 1925-38 . . . . **100.00**
Creamer, Sugar, and Tray, Rose and Daisy, AOG, Eamag
UnShonwald, Bavaria blank, 1938-45 . . . . **85.00**
Demitasse Cup and Saucer, scalloped rim, burnished
gold, mkd "Richard * * * Ginori 1-40 Italy, The Sterling
& Welch Co," Cleveland blank, JH Stouffer
Co, 1930-42 . . . . **25.00**
Lemonade Pitcher, orange carp amid seaweed and water
lilies, sgd "Blet," scrolls with "WG & Co, France"
blank, 1914-23, 8" h **350.00**
Limited Edition Plate, Maria, Children of Mexico Series,
J Sanchez, 1981 . . . . **85.00**
Limited Edition Plate, Summer Splendor, Gardens of
Monet Series, 1986 . . . . **85.00**
Mayonnaise and Underplate, Strawberry, AOG, Tolpin
Studios, 1922-30, 7" l **45.00**
Plate, galloping camel in front of pyramids, sgd
"Utwich," White's Art Co, 1914-23, 8" d **180.00**
Plate, Poppy and Forget-Me-Not, AOG, Hutschenreuther
Selb (in circle) lion LHS Bavaria Germany, Sylvia
blank, Osborne Art Studio, 1928-40, 8" d **55.00**
Relish, lavender, pink, and white blossom spray on pale
green, gold banding, oblong, perforated handles, sgd
"Osborne," M&Z eagles, Austria blank, Osborne Art
Studio, 11" l **35.00**
Salt and Pepper Shakers, pr, pink flowers and leaves,
black highlights, sgd "Regina," JH Stouffer Co, 1938-
46, 3¹/₂" h **15.00**
Syrup, cov, oriental bird, sgd "Nichols," Pickard China,
1919-22 . . . . **150.00**

PICTURE FRAMES

Until the early 1990s most picture frames were sold at auction in boxed lots. This is no longer true. Collectors discovered that picture frames are an excellent indication of changing design styles and that the manufacturing quality of many picture frames, whether handmade or mass produced, was quite high.

Tabletop frames are the "hot" portion of the market in the late 1990s. Beware of placing too much credence in the prices on frames associated with a licensed movie or television character. Crossover collectors are the group forcing these values upward.

Collectors' Club: International Institute for Frame Study, 443 I St NW, PO Box 50156, Washington, DC 20091.

Brass, oval, easel back, 3¹/₂" h **$80.00**
Cast Iron, rect, fleur-de-lis design, gold-painted, easel
back, 12 x 9" **75.00**
Ceramic, Florence Ward, pink with applied pink, blue,
and white flowers and green leaves, mkd "Florence
Ward, California, Pat No. 2540951," 5 x 4¹/₂" **125.00**
Crystal, Mikasa, holds 4 pictures, orig box **20.00**
Gesso on Wood, oval, raised acorns and foliage, 15 x 12" . . **125.00**
Glass, Avon, Dad's Pride and Joy, Fostoria, orig box,
1982 . . . . **15.00**
Hammered Aluminum, Palmer Smith, sgd on back
"Palmer Smith," logo, and number "329," 7 x 9" **150.00**
Metal, chrome plated with silver and black printed mat,
easel back, 10 x 12", 7 x 9" opening **20.00**
Plastic, mahogany finish, oval swivel mirror on stand,
emb flowers, 10" h, 5 x 7" opening **18.00**
Resin, Boyds, Rocky All Stars **15.00**
Rosewood, rect, antique style, metal-mounted corners,
7³/₄ x 9³/₄" **20.00**
Silver on Copper, floral design **35.00**

Silver-colored Metal, silver and black cardboard mat, easel back, 7 x 9", $20.00.

PIERCE, HOWARD

After working for William Manker Ceramics in Claremont, California, and doing freelance work for other California potteries such as Key Finch Ceramics, Howard Webster Pierce established his La Verne, California, studio in 1941. His initial efforts focused on the production of pewter and copper finished pins.

Although producing some dinnerware and high gloss planters and vases, Pierce is best known for his bird, human, marine, and wildlife figurines. Numbers of some pieces are limited. Although in production for over fifty years, Pierce remained a small, home-based business.

In 1941 Howard married Ellen Van Voorhis, an art teacher and graduate of the Chicago Art Institute. They worked together as a team. The Pierce children, Janet, Linda, and Jerry, also worked at the pottery. In 1968 the Pierces moved to a new home/studio in Joshua Tree, near Palm Springs.

Reference: Darlene Hurst Dommel, *Collector's Encyclopedia of Howard Pierce Porcelain*, Collector Books, 1998.

Bowl, freeform, speckled blue-black int, black ext **$20.00**
Figurine, bear cub, brown, 5¼" 30.00
Figurine, black cat, 10¼" 65.00
Figurine, deer, brown speckled, 5½" 40.00
Figurine, giraffe, 10" 85.00
Figurine, horse, 8½" 175.00
Figurine, howling coyote, 5¾" 240.00
Figurine, Madonna and Child, white, 7¾" 80.00
Figurine, owl, brown and white, 5" 25.00
Figurine, penguin, 4¼" 40.00
Figurine, penguin, 7" 45.00
Figurine, pigeon, 7¼" 15.00
Figurine, polar bear, 4½" 230.00
Figurine, quail, mottled brown matte glaze, 6" 10.00
Figurine, raccoon, 9" 130.00
Figurines, mother goose and baby, 8½" mother mkd
     "250P," price for pr 45.00
Figurines, penguins, 4½" and 3½", price for pr 100.00
Figurines, quail mother and babies, 6" mother, price for
     3-pc set 35.00
Figurines, rabbits, 4" standing rabbit, 3" kneeling rabbit,
     price for pr 40.00
Figurines, Siamese cat family, 10¼", 5½", 2¼", price for
     3-pc set 130.00
Gondola Bowl, 5" h, 9½" l 50.00
Low Bowl, S-shaped, 13" l 18.00
Planter, rect, green, emb holly leaves, 12" 65.00
Planter, ribbed rect form, ivory with light green jasper
     ware–type panel with raised white leaves, #82P, 9½" 60.00
Planter Bowl, green freeform bowl with white bisque
     doe, 10" 85.00
Vase, cylindrical, 7" 50.00
Vase, dark green, open center with flamingo, #P300,
     9" 200.00
Vase, elongated neck, bulbous base, brown textured ext,
     9¾" 25.00
Vase, green, open center with giraffe and palm tree,
     8¾" 75.00
Vase, owl and foliage motif, glossy mottled glaze, 5" 50.00
Vase, white, giraffe figure, #250P, 7½" 65.00

PIG COLLECTIBLES

Austrian, English, and German bisque and hand-painted glazed ceramic pig figurines and planters were popular souvenirs and fair prizes at the turn of the century. So many early banks were in the shape of a pig that "Piggy Bank" became a generic term for a child's bank in the early 20th century.

As an important food source, the pig was featured prominently in farm advertising. Warner Brothers' Porky Pig and Walt Disney's The Three Little Pigs are among the most recognized cartoon characters of the mid-20th century.

A pig collecting craze swept across America in the late 1970s and early 1980s, eventually displaced by cow mania.

Three German bisque pig figurines have been reproduced—a pig by an outhouse, a pig playing a piano, and a pig poking his head out of a large purse. Their darker green color distinguishes them from period pieces.

Collectors' Club: The Happy Pig Collectors Club, PO Box 17, Oneida, IL 61467.

Note: For additional listings see Shawnee Pottery's Smiley Pig and Winnie Pig kitchen accessories and figural pigs with various decorative motifs.

Ashtray, 2 pigs getting married, mkd "Made in
     Germany," 3½" x 4½" **$125.00**
Bank, figural change purse with pig head on 1 side and
     tail on other, souvenir of Niagara Falls, NY 65.00
Bank, figural pig, hp floral dec, Occupied Japan, 2 x 3" 15.00
Bank, pink pig alongside band, "Saving His Pennies To
     Make Pounds," 3½" h 50.00
Bank, Porky Pig, plastic 25.00
Cookie Jar, Harley-Davidson Hog, McCoy, ©1984 HD 300.00
Figurine, 3 piglets inside egg shaped basin, "Triplets o'
     fancy," mkd "Germany" 65.00
Figurine, black pig jumping over green fence, bisque 5.00
Figurine, pig in cradle 60.00
Figurine, pig inside teacup, unmkd, 3" h 65.00
Figurine, pig sitting by green satchel 50.00
Figurine, pig sitting by windmill, orange roof 80.00
Figurine, pig standing behind opera glasses, unmkd,
     3½" h 65.00

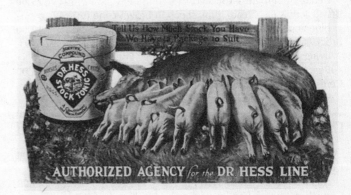

Sign, diecut cardboard, Dr Hess Stock Tonic, 14" h, 27" w, **$500.00.** Photo courtesy Collectors Auction Services.

Figurine, pig standing beside bean pot mkd "Boston Baked Beans," mkd "Made in Germany," 4" h **80.00**

Gravy Boat, porcelain, 2 pigs swinging **45.00**

Jar, pig alongside, orange seal, 2³/₄" h **40.00**

Paperweight, figural, glass, "Best Pig Forceps, compliments J Reimers, Davenport, IA" **100.00**

Pinback Button, "Emmarts Pigs," piglets enjoying ride on mother pig's back, 1920s **100.00**

Pin Dish, Good Luck horseshoe, yellow and green, pink pig, stamped "Made in Germany," 5" w **80.00**

Salt and Pepper Shakers, pr, figural, 1 playing accordion, other playing saxophone, glazed and painted, mkd "Japan," 1930, 4" h **45.00**

Sign, diecut painted cardboard, easel back, standing pig with "Finck's Detroit–Special Overalls/Wear Like a Pig's Nose," 24¹/₂" h, 34³/₄" w **200.00**

Toothpick Holder, souvenir, Watertown, NY, stamped "Made in Germany," 3" w **55.00**

PINBACK BUTTONS

In 1896 Whitehead & Hoag Company, Newark, New Jersey, obtained the first celluloid button patent. The celluloid buttons golden age stretched from 1896 through the early 1920s. Hundreds of manufacturers made thousands of buttons.

J. Lynch Company of Chicago introduced the first lithograph tin pinback buttons during World War I. Although lithograph buttons could be printed in multiple colors, the process did not produce the wide color range found in celluloid buttons. This mattered little. Lithograph tin buttons were much less costly to produce.

The lithograph tin pinback button played a major role in political campaigns from the early 1930s through the 1980s. Advertising buttons increased in size. Social cause buttons were dominant in the 1960s, colorful rock group buttons in the 1970s.

As the cost of lithograph tin pinback buttons rose, their popularity diminished. Today pinback buttons are sold primarily by greeting card manufacturers and retail gift shops.

Reference: William A. Sievert, *All For the Cause: Campaign Buttons For Social Change, 1960s-1990s,* Decoy Magazine/For Splash, 1997.

1933 Chicago World's Fair, shades of gold with "1933–A Century of Progress–Chicago," 1¹/₂" d **$25.00**

Ben & Jerry's Ice Cream, pink scoop in brown cone on blue and yellow ground, 1980-90s **12.00**

Brockway Bottles, black and white terrier dog watching flying bee under inscription "Keep Your Eye On The Bee," 1930s **25.00**

Ceresota Flour, multicolored image of youngster using knife to slice open flour canister, black lettering on white ground **20.00**

Cherry Smash, multicolored portrait of George Washington on dark red and lime green ground, 1920s **14.00**

Cincinatti Reds, red, white, and blue "Red Legs" cartoon character **15.00**

Columbus Mutual Life Insurance Co, black and white Christopher Columbus on white ground **15.00**

Draft Eisenhower For President, red, white, and blue with bluetone photo, 1948 . . . . **20.00**

Drewry's Ale & Lager Beer, black, white, and red Canadian Royal Mountie, 1940s **15.00**

Dutch Java Coffee, multicolored image of Dutch couple kissing with center "Dutch Java And Santos Blend Fancy Roasted Coffee" **50.00**

Ferguson's Honey Bread, multicolored toasted brown plump bread loaf on yellow ground, red and black lettering **15.00**

Fort Bedford Peanuts, black and white image of smiling girl, "Fort Bedford Peanuts Are Better Than Others" **25.00**

Four Roses Whiskey, red roses and green leaves on white ground, black lettering, 1940s **8.00**

Free the Panther 21, black lettering on yellow and black diagonal stripes ground, 1960s **25.00**

General Accident–Philadelphia, Liberty Bell in shades of blue on white, gold lettering **15.00**

George Foreman World Heavyweight Champion, black and white photo, 3" d **25.00**

Hiawatha Tribe Member, Milwaukee Railroad Club member, yellow, black, and white, 1930-40s **4.00**

I Believe in George McGovern, browntone photo and lettering on white ground **8.00**

I Like Calvert, red, white, and blue, rim curl inscription for Calvert Distillers Corp, New York City, 1940s **10.00**

Jet Age Progress, red lettering on white ground, "TRW Harrisburg 1951-1966" **15.00**

Johnny Lawrence Club, "The freshest thing in town!," 1930s, 1³/₈" d **25.00**

Milk Makes Me Happy, smiling child clown, 1950s **5.00**

Moxie, Uncle Sam hat above "What This Country Needs Is Plenty Of Moxie," red, white and blue, 1940s **25.00**

Nabisco, Golden Anniversary, multicolored portrait of youngster in yellow rain hat and jacket on gold ground, red lettering, 1948 . . . . **15.00**

National Air Mail Week, red, white, and blue, wing symbols around perimeter with "Via US Air Mail" emblem at top center, 1930-40s **25.00**

National Tom Mix Festival, center Tom Mix and horse, DuBois, PA, Oct 9-12, 1980, black and beige, 2¹/₈" d **15.00**

Peace Symbol, dark blue symbol on white ground **15.00**

New Chevrolet Six, Queen of the Shows, litho tin, Ceraghty & Co, ⁷/₈" d, $5.00.

Pelham Puppets Pelpup Club, multicolored lettering on bright yellow background with dark blue and red accents, 1960s, 1¼" d 15.00

Pep-O Safety Club, "Always Be Careful," sponsored by Lehigh Valley Motor Club, green lettering on white ground, 1940s. 25.00

Philadelphia Life Insurance Co, multicolored official seal emblem on white ground, black lettering, "Life/Health/Accident" 15.00

Piedmont/Airline of the Year, gold on blue, 1960s. 5.00

Provident Sick Benefit Fund Association, multicolored patriotic eagle centered by US shield on white ground, black and red lettering 15.00

Queen Elizabeth II, black and white photo, 1953 . . . . 15.00

Red White and Blue Coffee, 1930s 15.00

Rin Tin Tin Club, brown on cream, 1930s. 50.00

Souvenir of Circus, white-faced clown wearing bright yellow costume with red and green accents on light blue ground, c1930, 1¾" d 15.00

Souvenir of Rodeo/Let 'er Buck, red, white, and blue, glass mirror on reverse, 1940s, 1¾" d 25.00

Stop Climbing Mountains/Bob Kennedy We Need You In '72, black and white cartoon mountain and real photo 25.00

Studebaker Champion, "Priced with the Lowest," orange and green, 1930s. 25.00

Sunshine Biscuits, red, white, and blue, packaged product with "Takhoma Biscuit," and "Sunshine Biscuits" on blue end paper 20.00

The Rocky Horror Picture Show, red lettering on black ground, 1980s, 1¾" d 10.00

Third World People Unite Against War, black lettering on dark red ground, silhouette of black clenched fist and "April 2-3-4" and "April 24". 20.00

Van Camps Pork and Beans, multicolored canister on white ground, ⅞" d 25.00

Worcester Salt, salt sack over steaming train engine pulling boxcars 20.00

World's Fair South Hi Band Booster, black, white, and orange image of band majorette on white ground, black lettering, 1¾" d 25.00

PINBALL MACHINES

The introduction of Gottlieb's "Baffle Ball" in 1931 marked the beginning of the modern pinball machine era. Pre-1940 pinball machines typically had production runs of 25,000 to 50,000 machines. After 1945 production runs fell within the 500 to 2,000 range with an occasional machine reaching 10,000. Some scholars suggest that over 200 manufacturers made over 10,000 models, a result of a machine's high attrition rate. Several companies released a new model every three weeks during the 1950s.

The first electric machine appeared in 1933. Bumpers were added in 1936. Flippers arrived in 1947, kicking rubbers in 1950, score totalizers in 1950, multiple player machines in 1954, and solid state electronics in 1977. Machines by D. Gottlieb are considered the best of the pinballs, primarily because of their superior play and graphics.

The entire pinball machine was collected through the mid-1980s. More recently, collecting back glasses has become popular. Manufacturers were not concerned with longevity when making these glasses. Flaking paint is a restoration nightmare.

References: Richard M. Bueschel, *Collector's Guide to Vintage Coin Machines, 2nd Edition,* Schiffer Publishing, 1998; Richard M. Bueschel, *Encyclopedia of Pinball: Contact to Bumper, 1934-1936, Vol. 2,* Silverball Amusements, 1997; Heribert Eiden and Jürgen Lukas, *Pinball Machines, 3rd Edition,* Schiffer Publishing, 1999; Jeffrey Lawton, *Bally Bingo Pinball Machines,* Schiffer Publishing; Marco Rossignoli, *The Complete Pinball Book,* Schiffer Publishing, 1999.

Periodicals: *Coin Drop International,* 5815 W 52nd Ave, Denver, CO 80212; *PinGame Journal,* 31937 Olde Franklin Dr, Farmington, MI 48334.

Note: Prices are for machines in near mint to excellent condition.

Barbwire, Gottlieb $1,400.00
Bazaar, Bally, 1966 . . . . 500.00
Big Top, Genco, 1949 . . . . 550.00
Black Hole, Gottlieb 750.00
Blue Bird, Bally, 1936 . . . . 600.00
Buccaneer, Gottlieb. 675.00
Captain Fantastic, Bally, #1062, 1976 . . . . 650.00
Caveman, Gottlieb, 1981 . . . . 500.00
Champion, Bally, 1939 . . . . 900.00
Charlie's Angels, Gottlieb, 1978. . . . . 400.00
Chicago Cubs "Triple Play," Premier, 1985 . . . . 550.00
Contact, Exhibit Supply, 1939 . . . . 450.00
Criss Cross A-Lite, Genco, 1935. . . . . 350.00
Daisy, Peo, 1932 . . . . 250.00
Dracula, Williams, 1993 . . . . 900.00
Genesis Pinball, Gottlieb. 700.00
Golden Wheel, Bally, 1937. . . . . 1,000.00
Hook, Data East, 1991 . . . . 875.00
Hurricane, Williams 1,150.00
Ice Revue, Gottlieb, 1965 . . . . 750.00
Jacks to Open, Gottlieb, electronic, 1983 . . . . 600.00
Keep 'em Flying, Gottlieb, 1942 . . . . 500.00
Life, American Amusement, 1932 . . . . 300.00
Lightning, Exhibit, 1938. . . . . 400.00
Live Power, Dudley Clark 400.00
Magic City, Williams, 1967 . . . . 700.00
Major League, Pacific, 1934 . . . . 750.00
Metro, Genco, 1940 . . . . 500.00
Midget Racer, Bally, 1946 . . . . 300.00
New Improved Rocket, Bally, 1934 . . . . 1,000.00
O'Boy, Novelty Coin, 1939 . . . . 350.00
Prospector, Bally, 1935. . . . . 1,000.00
Rainbow, Williams, 1948. . . . . 450.00
Rancho, Williams, 1977 . . . . 450.00
Repeater, Keeney, 1936. . . . . 600.00
Screwy, Bally, 1932 . . . . 350.00
Shanghai, Chicago Coin, 1948. 400.00
Show Girl, Williams, 1947 . . . . 600.00
Sinbad, Gottlieb, 1978 . . . . 350.00
Sing Along, Gottlieb, 1967 . . . . 700.00
Ski-Doo "23," Amusement Corp, 1932. . . . . 250.00
Special Force, Bally. 500.00
Target, Beverator, 1935 . . . . 375.00
The President, Bally, 1932 . . . . 300.00
Tiny, Western Equipment, 1935 . . . . 550.00
Tit-For-Tat, Chicago Coin, 1935 . . . . 400.00
Totem, Pierce, 1935 . . . . 500.00
Truck Stop, Bally. 700.00

PIN-UP ART

The pin-up beauty owes her origin to 1920s' film magazines such as *Film Fun* and *Real Screen* whose front covers showed women with a fair amount of exposed skin. Artists such as Cardwell Higgins, George Petty, and Charles Sheldon continued to refine the concept through the 1930s. Petty's first gatefold appeared in *Esquire* in 1939.

Pin-up art reached its zenith in the 1940s. Joyce Ballantyne, Billy DeVorss, Gillete Elvgren, Earl Moran, and Alberto Vargas (the "s" was dropped at Esquire's request) were among the leading artists of the period. Their pin-up girls appeared everywhere—blotters, calendars, jigsaw puzzles, matchcovers, magazine covers, posters, punchboards, etc.

The reign of the pin-up girl ended in the early 1960s when the photograph replaced the artist sketch as the preferred illustration for magazines.

References: Max Allen Collins and Drake Elvgren, *Elvgren: His Life & Art,* Collectors Press, 1998; Denis C. Jackson, *The Price & ID Guide to Pin-Ups & Glamour Art,* TICN, 1996; Charles G. Martignette and Louis K. Meisel, *The Great American Pin-Up,* Taschen, 1996.

Newsletters: *Glamour Girls: Then and Now,* PO Box 34501, Washington, DC 20043; *The Illustrator Collector's News,* PO Box 1958, Sequim, WA 98382.

Ballpoint Pen, black plastic, floating image of 2 models wearing black swimsuits, suits disappear when pen is inverted, Denmark, 1960s, 5½" l $20.00

Blotter, cardboard, blonde nude seated at edge of pond, artist sgd "Rolf Armstrong," © 1935 Brown & Bigelow, 3½ x 6" 45.00

Blotter, cardboard, Moran art, Penn Securities, Jul-Sep 1948 calendar, 4 x 9" 15.00

Bumper Sticker, "Vote For Linda Lovelace," paper, red, white, and blue lettering on blue ground, 3¾ x 13½", unused 15.00

Poster, sgd "DeVorss," 24" h, 18" w, $150.00. Photo courtesy Collectors Auction Services.

Sign, Kist Beverages adv, sgd "Elvgren," 17½" h, 13½" w, $225.00. Photo courtesy Collectors Auction Services.

Calendar, "A Good Number," Petty, 1942, 14 x 21½" 100.00
Calendar, Chippendale Revue, 1988 . . . . 10.00
Calendar, "Come On Along," Petty, 1949, 7½ x 16" 75.00
Calendar, "Curly Horse Ranch, cowgirl pin-up, Elvgren, 1969. . . . . 50.00
Calendar, *Esquire* Glamour Gallery, artwork by various artists including Ben-Hur Baz, Fritz Willis, Joe Demers, Al Moore, J Frederick Smith, and Ron Wicks, 1948, 8½ x 12" 50.00
Calendar, *Esquire* Varga Calendar, orig envelope, 1946, 8¾ x 12" 100.00
Calendar, "Irresistible," Rolf Armstrong, Brown & Bigelow copyright, 1950, 11 x 23" 100.00
Calendar, "It's A Date," Rolf Armstrong, Seattle Jeweler's date book, 1946 . . . . 25.00
Calendar, "Ladies of the Harem," *Esquire,* full pad, 1948 . . . . 15.00
Calendar, MacPherson Sketch Book, spiral-bound, artist sgd, missing cover page, 1953, 9½ x 12½" 70.00
Calendar, "Reflection," Earl Moran, 1948, 11x 23" 110.00
Calendar, "Starlight," blonde model, dark green drape, black ground, Earl Moran, 1945 . . . . 50.00
Calendar Print, "Daisy," DeVorss artwork, 22 x 30" 110.00
Calendar Print, "Exclusively Yours," color photo of Diane Webber on beach towel, wearing only straw hat, #5262, ©A Scheer, 12 x 13½" 30.00
Coasters, litho tin, PA firemen's convention rim inscriptions, center image of partially clad model, 1960, 3¼" d, price for set of 5 . . . . 65.00
Desk Calendar, *Esquire,* cardboard, red and white, diecut window for calendar sheets, Al Moore art, 12 pp, 5½ x 6" 35.00
Drink Stirrer, green plastic, figural stylized profile of nude, late 1940s, 6" l 8.00
Illusion Card, "Sally of Hollywood and Vine," cardboard folder, model undresses from nightgown to underwear to nude, 1940s-50s, 1½ x 3¼" 40.00
Letter Opener, plastic, figural nude, ivory, Ace Plastics, 1940s, 11" l 12.00
Matchcover, "Keep Your Distance," color photo of Diane Webber in striped bikini, c1960, 1¾ x 2" 15.00

Print, "Never Too Young To Yearn," Earl Moran, auburn-haired woman wearing burgundy shoulder blouse and matching bikini brief, turquoise ground bordered in gray, ©Brown & Bigelow, c1940-50s, 10 x 12" **50.00**
Playing Cards, "Hats Off," Elvgren, double deck, 1940s **60.00**
Pocket Mirror, brunette wearing low-cut feathered gown, artist sgd "Albert," 1940s, 2 x 3" **25.00**
Poster, model in shorts walking dog, Walt Otto artwork, c1951, 17 x 33" **50.00**
Print, "Adoration," model on bed with scarf, Elvgren, 15 x 19" **60.00**
Sample Calendar, Studio Sketches, Thompson, 1957, 8³/₄ x 13¹/₄" **75.00**
Stationery Kit, WWII, "Thinking of You," cardboard folder with GI sitting on trunk, pin-up model in trunk, complete with 50 sheets of note paper and 20 envelopes, 10 with air mail markings, early 1940s **65.00**
Telephone Memo Card, cardboard, lift-up page with Diane Webber photo, "Prized Possession," Artcraft Calendars, 8⁵/₈ x 10³/₄" **35.00**
Television Viewer, miniature orange plastic television featuring color photos of Marilyn Monroe in 8 poses, including "Golden Dreams," Hong Kong, c1970s, 1 x 1¹/₂ x 2" **75.00**
Television Viewer, miniature plastic television featuring 8 color photos of various models, including 2 Jayne Mansfield and 1 Bettie Page, Hong Kong, c1970s, 1 x 1¹/₂ x 2" **60.00**
Viewer, "Cutie View," clear plastic cocktail glass with pin-up art in stem, blonde on beach, orig box, 1950s **60.00**

PLANTERS PEANUTS

In 1906 Amedeo Obici, known as a peanut specialist, and Mario Peruzzi founded the Planters Nut and Chocolate Company, Wilkes-Barre, Pennsylvania. Initially, the company sold Spanish salted red skins priced at 10¢ a pound.

The Mr. Peanut trademark evolved from a 1916 contest. A young Italian boy submitted a rough sketch of a monocled Peanut figure. Hundreds of Mr. Peanut advertising and promotional items have been issued.

Reference: Jan Lindenberger, *Planters Peanut Collectibles: 1906-1961*, Schiffer Publishing, 1999.

Collectors' Club: Peanut Pals, PO Box 652, St Clairsville, OH 43950.

Bank, Mr Peanut Vender Bank, figural, red plastic, hat holds peanuts which are dispensed through neck area, complete with coin trap in bottom and orig instructions, c1950s, 8³/₄ x 5¹/₂" **$425.00**
Bank, plastic, gold wash finish, figural Mr Peanut, 8¹/₂" h . . **2,750.00**
Bank, plastic with silver wash finish, figural Mr Peanut, "Souvenir of Salem, Mass" decal on hat, 8¹/₂" h **2,650.00**
Bookmark, diecut stiff paper, figural Mr Peanut, 1940s, 7⁷/₈" h **15.00**
Box, cardboard, Planters Roasted Peanuts, white with black and red lettering, 10" h, 6¹/₄" w, 6¹/₄" d **150.00**
Display Box, cardboard, 2-pc, Planter Peanuts, WWII motif with Victory Eagle and "Defend America, Buy US War Bonds and Stamps," red and white on blue peanut background, 1940s, 8³/₄ x 8¹/₂ x 3" **625.00**

Left: Bag, waxed paper, red and blue printing, 1920s, 5¹/₂" h, $18.00. Right: Mug, blue plastic, 3³/₄" h, $5.00.

Display Box, cardboard, Planters Peanuts, standup diecut image of woman eating nuts, peanut background, "Fresh, 5¢," 1940s, 9¹/₂ x 9 x 6³/₈" **450.00**
Drinking Glass, enameled images of Mr Peanut doing circus acts, c1950s, 5 x 2³/₄" **150.00**
Employee's Pin, cloisonné-inlaid 14K gold, commemorates 20 years of service, Mr Peanut standing atop wreathed "20" plaque, 1¹/₂" h, ⁵/₁₆" w **125.00**
Employee's Pin, cloisonné-inlaid 14K gold, commemorates 25 years of service, Mr Peanut standing atop wreathed "25" plaque, 1¹/₂" h, ⁵/₁₆" w **250.00**
Fan, hand-held, cardboard, Mr Peanut driving peanut car, c1940, 5¹/₄" h, 8" w **475.00**
Mug, ceramic, figural squat Mr Peanut with arm handle and rhinestone monocle, 3⁷/₈" h, 3³/₄" w **400.00**
Nut Spoon, brass, figural Mr Peanut handle, 1930s, 5¹/₈" l **18.00**
Nut Tray, brown plastic tray with 3 recessed sections, 3" h figural Mr Peanut center handle, 1960s, 5¹/₄" d **15.00**
Nut Tray, fluorescent see-through pink plastic, 3-section tray, 3" h figural Mr Peanut center handle, 1960s, 5¹/₄" d **350.00**
Peanut Butter Pail, litho tin, Planters High Grade Peanut Butter, white label with red Mr Peanut and black lettering, red ground, bail handle, 5 lbs, 6" h, 6¹/₄" d **3,750.00**
Pop Gun, cardboard, Mr Peanut image both sides, "Bang! For Planters Peanuts" pop-out, c1940, 4¹/₂ x 9" . . . **200.00**
Toy Train Car, red plastic, carrying oversized clear plastic peanut, "Planters" emb on peanut, "Souvenir of Allentown" decal on end, 1950s, 2¹/₂" h, 5¹/₈" l **175.00**
Vending Machine, enameled metal, wall mount, "Planters Salted Peanuts 10¢," large Mr Peanut image, 1940s, 36" h, 7" w, 7¹/₄" d **1,800.00**
Walking Toy, figural Mr Peanut, plastic, windup, black and tan, 1950s, 8¹/₂" h **400.00**
Walking Toy, figural Mr Peanut, plastic, windup, green, 1950s, 8¹/₂" h **450.00**
Wrapper, waxed paper, repeated Mr Peanut images, 1950s, 7¹/₄ x 10" **3.00**

PLASTICS

There are hundreds of different natural, semisynthetic, and synthetic plastics known. Collectors focus on three basic types: celluloid, Bakelite, and melamine. Celluloid, made from cellulose nitrate and camphor, is a thin, tough, flammable material. It was used in the late 1880s and through the first four decades of the 20th century to make a wide range of objects from toilet articles to toys. Celluloid's ability to mimic other materials, e.g., amber, ivory, and tortoise shell, made it extremely popular.

In 1913 L. H. Baekeland invented Bakelite, a synthetic resinous material made from formaldehyde and phenol. It proved to be a viable substitute for celluloid and rubber. Easily dyed and molded, Bakelite found multiple uses from radio cases to jewelry. Often it was a secondary element, e.g., it was commonly used for handles.

Although injection molding was developed prior to World War II, its major impact occurred during and after the war. Many new plastics, e.g., melamine, were developed to take advantage of this new technology. The 1950s through the 1960s was the golden age of plastic. It was found everywhere, from the furniture in which one sat to the dashboard of a car.

This is a catchall category. It includes objects made from plastic that do not quite fit into other collecting categories.

References: Robert Brenner, *Celluloid,* Schiffer Publishing, 1999; Shirley Dunn, *Celluloid Collectibles,* Collector Books, 1996; Michael J. Goldberg, *Collectible Plastic Kitchenware and Dinnerware: 1935-1965,* Schiffer Publishing, 1995; Keith Lauer and Julie Robinson, *Celluloid,* Collector Books, 1999; Jan Lindenberger, *Collecting Plastics, 2nd Edition,* Schiffer Publishing, 1999; Jan Lindenberger, *More Plastics for Collectors,* Schiffer Publishing, 1996; Barbara Mauzy, *Bakelite in the Kitchen,* Schiffer Publishing, 1998; Lyndi Stewart McNulty, *Wallace-Homestead Price Guide to Plastic Collectibles,* Wallace-Homestead, 1987, 1992 value update; Bryan Meccariello, *Plastic Cup Collectibles,* Schiffer Publishing, 1998; Holly Wahlberg, *Everyday Elegance: 1950s Plastic Design, 2nd Edition,* Schiffer Publishing, 1999.

Note: For additional listings see Costume Jewelry, Melmac, and Toys.

Bakelite, chess set, hand-carved bone and black Bakelite
   silhouettes, each on Bakelite plinth base, possibly
   Ben-Hur Corp, from 2-4" h **$1,650.00**
Bakelite, cigarette box, fluted butterscotch body, ovoid
   form with circular ball finial top, 4" h **325.00**
Bakelite, dresser box, butterscotch, leaf carved frieze,
   turned finial knob, 2" h **450.00**
Bakelite, dresser box, fluted butterscotch body, marbleized green base and top, contrasting color finial
   knob, 4" h. **550.00**
Bakelite, lamp base, industrial machine-age style, red
   Bakelite base with ring supports, end-of-day Bakelite
   column with turned segments, skyscraper form at top,
   red machine finial, 23½" h **1,975.00**
Bakelite, napkin rings, pr, Trylon and Perisphere shape,
   for 1939 New York World's Fair, blue and orange **450.00**
Bakelite, powder box, geometric, green and black, circular box form with 2-color top, tilted cube finial,
   cube feet, 5" h. **550.00**
Bakelite, radio, Fada, maroon and cream bullet design,
   orig crystal, dial, and knobs **1,325.00**
Bakelite, ring stand, black and rust, figural hand, 4" h **200.00**

Bakelite, left to right: Mountaineer, $1,500.00; Harpo Marx, $3,200.00; Mexican, $450.00. Photos courtesy David Rago Auctions, Inc.

Celluloid, barrette, oval, translucent amber with rhinestone dec **8.00**
Celluloid, brush and comb set, light pink with roses and
   hp gold trim, 1930s **25.00**
Celluloid, dresser clock, marbleized green, Lux Clock
   Mfg Co **30.00**
Celluloid, guitar pick, tortoise shell **1.00**
Celluloid, hair comb, Art Deco style, butterscotch, green
   rhinestone dec **50.00**
Celluloid, hair comb, tri-fold, metal mounted, made in
   Germany. **25.00**
Celluloid, hand mirror, red and white polka dots, shell
   shaped back, 3¼" l **250.00**
Celluloid, manicure set, white birch wood laminated
   with black celluloid, orig box, 1930s **20.00**
Celluloid, playing card case, laminated amber and
   pearlescent, red and black short-haired woman and
   4 card suits dec, c1930 . . . . **20.00**
Celluloid, rattle, pink, emb swirl design in pink frame
   handle, 7" l **25.00**
Celluloid, rattle, pink, hollow, hp polka dot dec, mkd
   "Made in Japan," 7" l **30.00**
Celluloid, ruler, 6" l **10.00**
Celluloid, salt and pepper shakers, pr, skyscrapers **35.00**
Celluloid, sewing kit, mottled blue, contains needles,
   thread, and scissors, 3¼ x 2" **25.00**
Celluloid, straight razor, bamboo, Camilus Cuttery Co **20.00**
Celluloid, straight razor, black, Torrey Razor Co **30.00**
Celluloid, suite, pendant and earrings, Art Deco feather
   motif with rhinestone dec, red, blue, and topaz enamel paint, c1925 . . . . **125.00**
Celluloid, tape measure, figural strawberry. **200.00**
Celluloid, thermometer plaque, rural windmill and cottage at sunset scene, inset celluloid thermometer,
   back cardboard insert with cord hanger loop and
   diecut easel tab, bottom margin mkd "Compliments of
   Smith & Richards Lumber Co," c1920s, 6" d **20.00**
Celluloid, windup, kitten, cream, bright pink spots,
   jointed limbs, Occupied Japan **55.00**
Plastic, ashtray, red, 3 rests, round **5.00**
Plastic, barrette, alligator, 1970s **5.00**
Plastic, butter dish, yellow, multicolored molded fruit on
   lid **10.00**
Plastic, candy dish, leaf shape, painted flamingo center,
   "Silver Springs, Fla" **10.00**
Plastic, cheese grater, yellow, fluted sides, 1960-70s **5.00**

Celluloid, rattle, black man holding bouquet, Japan, 8" h, $45.00. Photo courtesy Collectors Auction Services.

Plastic, flour sifter, white swirled, rose dec, red plastic
 handle, 5 cup **10.00**
Plastic, hair comb, bow shaped, 1970s **5.00**
Plastic, pin, elephant riding bicycle, Avon, 1975 . . . . **8.00**
Plastic, pin, figural toucan, rhinestone eyes and chest,
 1950s **40.00**
Plastic, pitcher and tray set, marbleized burgundy, black,
 and brown, Viceroy Plastics Co **30.00**
Plastic, purse, tortoise stained acetate, hard-edged geo-
 metric form and brass clasp, Wilardy **275.00**
Plastic, reamer, red, Lustro-Ware, 1950s. **8.00**
Plastic, salt and pepper shakers, pr, cornucopia, ivory,
 1960s **18.00**
Plastic, salt and pepper shakers, pr, red, white lettering,
 Lustro-Ware **12.00**
Plastic, sewing box, round, pink, clear lid, divided int **10.00**

PLAYBOY

Hugh M. Hefner launched the first issue of *Playboy,* featuring the now famous calendar photograph of Marilyn Monroe, in December 1953. There was no cover date. Hefner was not certain the concept would work. *Playboy* grew at a phenomenal rate.

During the 1960s and 70s, Hefner opened a series of Playboy Clubs, launched several foreign editions, operated several gambling casinos, and organized a Hollywood production company. *Playboy* went public in 1971 and was listed on the New York and Pacific stock exchanges. *Oui* was launched in October 1972.

Christie Hefner became president of Playboy Enterprises in 1982. In the mid-1980s more than sixty companies were licensed to market products bearing the Playboy, Playmate, and Rabbit Head trademarks.

Reference: Denis C. Jackson, *The Price & ID Guide to Playboy Magazines, 3rd Edition,* TICN, 1997.

Collectors' Club: Playboy Collectors Assoc, PO Box 653, Phillipsburg, MO 65722.

Cake Pan, Playboy bunny head, aluminum, stock #2105-
 3025, orig paper label, Wilton, 10¹/₄" w, 15" h **$10.00**
Cup and Saucer, "The Playboy Club," repeated title
 around top perimeter in black with Femlin figure,
 white int and underside, Jackson China Co, Falls
 Creek, PA, 1960s, 2¹/₄" h cup, 5¹/₄" d saucer **35.00**
Desk Calendar, 1965 Playboy Playmate, cardboard,
 easel back, gold lettered inscription on green, 6 x 6". **50.00**
Glasses, clear glass, black bunny symbol on 1 side,
 c1960s, 5³/₄" h, 2¹/₄" d, price for set of 4 . . . . **45.00**
Goblet, clear glass, "Playboy" text in black on 2 sides,
 used in Playboy Clubs, c1960, 6" h, 3³/₄" d **30.00**
Jigsaw Puzzle, "Playboy Playmate Puzzle," orig 5¹/₂" h,
 4" d canister, ©1968 . . . . **25.00**
Magazine, 1957 . . . . **5.00**
Magazine, 1966 . . . . **3.00**
Matchcover, Playboy Club, Atlanta. **2.00**

Mug, black glass, gold Femlin logo, 1960s, 6" h, $35.00.

Mug, "Atlantic City Playboy Hotel & Casino," clear glass, black text on front and back, 5 rabbit head symbols at bottom, c1960s, 5½" h, 3" d **30.00**

Plate, "The Playboy Club," repeated title in circular black lettering around Femlin image in black with gray torso lines, Jackson China Co, Falls Creek, PA, 1960s, 9½" d **25.00**

Purse, "Bunny Bag," black and white vinyl, zipper top and vinyl carrying strap, 1960s, 4½ x 6", unused **25.00**

Shot Glass, clear glass, weighted bottom, black art of Femlin on front holding room key with Playboy Club name around rim, used in Playboy Clubs, c1960s, 3" h, 2" d **30.00**

PLAYING CARDS

Playing cards came to America with the colonists. They were European in origin. The first American playing cards did not arrive on the scene until after the American Revolution. Caleb Bartlett (New York), Thomas Crehore (Dorchester, Massachusetts), David Felt (New York), the Ford (Foord) family (Milton, Massachusetts), and Amos and Daniel Whitney printed some of the first playing cards made in America. A. Dougherty, The New York Consolidated Card Company, and the United States Playing Card Company were the leading American manufacturers of playing cards. U.S. Playing Card introduced its Bicycle Brand in 1885. American card manufacturers are credited with introducing the classic joker, slick finish for shuffling, standard size, and upper corner indexes.

Card collectors specialize. Advertising, children's card games, miniature decks, novelty decks, and souvenir decks are just a few examples. Some collectors only collect one type of card, e.g., jokers. Although play is the primary focus of most playing cards, cards also have been used for fortune telling, instruction, e.g., World War II airplane spotting, and aiding travelers, e.g., a language set. These sets also appeal to collectors.

Always count the cards to make certain you are buying complete decks. American poker decks have 52 cards plus one or two jokers, pinochle decks have 48 cards, and Tarot decks 78 cards.

References: Everett Grist, *Advertising Playing Cards,* Collector Books, 1992, out of print; Norman E. Martinus and Harry L. Rinker, *Warman's Paper,* Wallace-Homestead, 1994.

Collectors' Clubs: 52 Plus Joker, 204 Gorham Ave, Hamden, CT 06514; Chicago Playing Card Collectors, 1826 Mallard Lake Dr, Marietta, GA 30068; International Playing Card Society, 3570 Delaware Common, Indianapolis, IN 46220.

52 Selected Views of Ireland, complete deck of 52 cards plus card, with sponsor Irish Tourist Assn, Dublin, and publisher C T Co Ltd, each card with different black and white oval photo of Ireland captioned tourist attraction, identical photos in vertical and horizontal format, card backs with shamrock over musical harp in shades of green with white accents, c1930s, ¾ x 2½ x 3½" **$25.00**

1933 World's Fair **40.00**

Aero Willys 2600, Willys emblem on maroon ground, ornate trophy cup above inscriptions in Spanish, boxed set, 1952 . . . . **25.00**

Boomtown Wild West, red and white. **4.00**

Brown Derby Restaurant, celebrity caricatures, 1946 . . . . **75.00**

California, Bullock's, Orange Grove, 1927 . . . . **50.00**

Cosmopolitan Line, double deck, each deck with 52 cards plus Joker, photo of transport ship with blue or red border, velveteen over cardboard box with gold accent trim, underside of box inscribed "Cosmopolitan Line/ Owners A/S J. Ludwig Mowinckels Rederi/Bergen, Norway" with title of New York City agent, boxed set, 1950s **15.00**

Cuba, flags on back, c1930 . . . . **30.00**

Esquire, blonde with black ground, double deck, 1943 . . . . . . **35.00**

Eureka Vacuum Cleaner Co, eagle, black, gold, and white **3.00**

Greene Line Steamers, double deck, each deck with 52 cards plus Joker, sponsored by Green Line Steamers Inc, Cincinnati, boxed set, 1930-40s **25.00**

Life Savers, 1 panel depicts full color assortment of packaged Life Saver candy, other panel depicts single cherry Life Saver candy, boxed set, 1950s **15.00**

Maislin Bros, double deck, each deck has 52 cards plus Joker, image of transport truck in blue on gold or silver ground, in clear styrene plastic slipcase cover, Guild, 1950-60s **25.00**

Ozark Airlines, 1984 World's Fair, sealed deck **2.00**

Pin-Up, double deck, each with 52 cards plus Joker, blonde model wrapped in bath towel while talking on telephone, velveteen finish over cardboard box with inscription "Play Canasta" on side, 1950s **25.00**

Pin-Up, Quick on the Draw, double deck, each deck with 52 cards plus Joker, cowgirl theme, blonde woodgrain box with maroon lettering and diecut overlay flocked surface cowboy hat, boxed set, 1950s **50.00**

Sea World, blue, black, and white, 1978 . . . . **7.00**

Sells-Floto Circus and Buffalo Bill Himself, full deck, orig box, $300.00. Photo courtesy Collectors Auction Services.

POCKETKNIVES

American manufacturers such as Samuel Mason and C. W. Platts of the Northfield Knife Company began making pocketknives in the 1840s. Numerous design, manufacturing, and marketing advances occurred. Collectors consider the period between the 1880s and 1940 as the pocketknife's golden age. American manufacturers received favorable tariff protection beginning in the 1890s. Before 1940, the best factory knives were handmade in a wide variety of designs and with the best material available.

The period between 1945 and the early 1960s is considered a dark age. Many pre-war manufacturers went out of business. A renaissance occurred in the 1970s as individual knife craftsmen began making pocketknives geared more for collecting and display than use. Bob Hayes, Jess Horn, Ron Lake, Jimmy Lile, Paul Pehlmann, Robert Ogg, and Barry Wood were leaders in the craftsman revival. Recently, collector and limited edition knives have flooded the market.

Pocketknives divide into three main groups: (1) utilitarian and functional knives, (2) advertising, character, and other promotional knives, and (3) craftsman knives. Alcas, Case, Colonial, Ka-Bar, Queen, Remington, Schrade, and Winchester are the best known manufacturers of the first group. Aerial Cutlery, Canton Cutlery, Golden Rule Cutlery, Imperial Knife Company, and Novelty Cutlery made many of the knives in the second group.

References: Jacob N. Jarrett, *Price Guide to Pocket Knives, 1890-1970,* L-W Books, 1993, 1998 value update; Bernard Levine, *Levine's Guide to Knives and Their Values, 4th Edition,* Krause Publications, 1997; C. Houston Price, *The Official Price Guide to Collector Knives, 12th Edition,* House of Collectibles, 1998; Roy Ritchie and Ron Stewart, *The Standard Knife Collector's Guide, 3rd Edition,* Collector Books, 1997, 1999 value update; Jim Sargent, *American Premium Guide to Pocket Knives & Razors,* Krause Publications, 1999; Ron Stewart, *Big Book of Pocket Knives,* Collector Books, 2000; Richard D. White, *Advertising Cutlery,* Schiffer Publishing, 1999.

Periodical: *Blade Magazine,* 700 E State St, Iola, WI 54990.

Note: Prices are for pocketknives in mint condition.

Advertising, Bon Ami, 1 blade, metal case with emb chick and "Bon Ami," blade mkd "The W&H Co, USA Newark NJ". **$125.00**
Advertising, Coca-Cola, 1 blade, scissors, and file, stainless steel, gold-tone Coke emblem, 2⁵/₁₆" l closed size **12.00**
Advertising, Esso "Happy," 1 blade, 2" l closed size **60.00**
Advertising, F Dessandier & Co, Cognac, 1 blade and corkscrew, 5¹/₂" l open size **60.00**
Advertising, Heidseck & Co, 1 blade, corkscrew, and scissors, 4" l open size. **100.00**
Advertising, US Royal Golf Balls, 1 blade and file, blade mkd "Lataka Italy, stainless," 2¹/₂" l closed size. **10.00**
Argyle Cutlery, Germany, 2 blades, metal handle with brown and yellow filler, 2¹/₂" l closed size. **20.00**
Barlow, commemorative, Hopalong Cassidy, 2 blades, multicolor picture handle. **15.00**
Barlow, So-Cal Electric Supply adv, brushed stainless steel with black lettering, 2-blade, black leather case, 2³/₄" l closed size. **15.00**
Blue Grass Cutlery, Winchester Trapper W20 19005, 1 blade, mkd "1st Production Run 1 of 1000" on blade **25.00**

Advertising, De Laval, Miller Bros, Meriden, 3¹/₂" l, $175.00.

Camillus, Kent, swell-end, black composition handles, 1930s-40s. **12.00**
Case XX, 6165 SAB, 5¹/₄" closed size **25.00**
Case XX, Dale Earnhardt, 2 blades, Earnhardt signature on red bone handle, 1 blade etched with picture of #3 car, other etched "1991 Winston Cup Champion," limited edition, wood case with picture of #3 car on inside cover **45.00**
Cattaraugus Cutlery Co, 2 blades and file, Masonic, black enameled design with pyramids, silver camel's head, 2³/₄" l closed size **35.00**
Commemorative, Charles A Lindbergh, 2-blade, mkd "Charles A Lindbergh May, 1927–The Spirit of St Louis–The Lone Eagle," 3¹/₂" l closed size **10.00**
Commemorative, Dale Evans, multicolor picture handle, black back, 3¹/₂" l closed size. **15.00**
Commemorative, John F Kennedy, 2-blade, mkd "John F Kennedy Jan 20, 1961–Nov 22, 1963, 35th President Democratic Party," 3¹/₂" l closed size. **18.00**
Commemorative, POW/MIA, 1 blade, white plastic handle with black lettering, surgical steel blade, mkd "POW/MIA Pocketknife–You Are Not Forgotten!" **10.00**
Cook Bros, 2 blades, pearl handles, 2¹/₄" l closed size. **18.00**
E Bruckmann, corkscrew, 2 drop point blades, mkd "Mann" and "E Bruckmann, Solingen-0" on tangs, black handles with white and olive green swirls, 3¹/₂" closed size **60.00**
EC Simmons, Keen Kutter, tortoiseshell handles, translucent red and black, 2 blades, 3¹/₂" l closed size. **50.00**
EC Simmons, Keen Kutter Whittler, 3 blades, brown bone handles, federal shield, brass liners, nickel silver tip bolsters, 2⁷/₈" l closed size. **85.00**
Franklin Mint, Colt 1877, Colt Legendary Pocketknife Collection, engraved Art Nouveau flowers and vine, orig box and zippered case, 4" l closed size **35.00**
H Hackfield & Co, Ltd, 1 blade, corkscrew, and bottle opener, maker's name on 1 side, "Honolulu, TH" on other, mkd "Germany" on blade, 3¹/₄" l closed size **60.00**
Imperial, 2 blades, brown, white, and silver marbleized handles, pre-1938. . . . . **25.00**
Imperial, stainless steel **15.00**
Keen Kutter, #788, 2 blades, cracked ice handles, 3¹/₄" l closed size **30.00**
Keen Kutter, Lockback #KK505DS, orig felt-lined box **45.00**
Keystone Cutlery, Germany, 3 blades, metal casing with brown and yellow filler, eagle on handle, 3" l closed size. **15.00**

Remington UMC, R10 Farmhand, 2 blades, orig green
box, 6⁷/₈" l open size **20.00**
Remington UMC, R10 Outdoorsman, orig box with
leather case and booklet **30.00**
Schrade, 3 blades, mkd "Old Timer" **10.00**
Souvenir, 1962 Seattle World's Fair, Colonial, orig red
cardboard box. **20.00**

POLITICAL & CAMPAIGN

Collectors prefer three-dimensional items. Material associated with winning candidates is more desirable than that associated with individuals who lost. While there are third party collectors, their number is small.

The period from the late 1890s through the mid-1960s is the golden age of political and campaign material. Today candidates spend most of their money on television advertising. The 1996 presidential election was noteworthy for its lack of political collectibles.

Political and campaign item collectors were one of the first specialty collector groups to organize. As a result, large hoards of post-1970 material exist. This is why most collectors concentrate on material dating prior to the 1970s.

Reference: Ted Hake, *Hake's Guide to Presidential Campaign Collectibles,* Wallace-Homestead, 1992.

Periodical: *The Political Collector,* PO Box 5171, York, PA 17405.

Newsletter: *The Political Bandwagon,* PO Box 348, Leola, PA 17540.

Collectors' Club: American Political Items Collectors, PO Box 340339, San Antonio, TX 78234.

REPRODUCTION ALERT: Campaign buttons have been widely reproduced. Examine the curl for evidence of modern identification marks having been scratched out. The backs of most early buttons were bare or had a paper label. Beware of any button with a painted back. Buttons made prior to 1896 were celluloid. Any lithograph button from an election earlier than 1896 is incorrect. Celluloid buttons need a collar since they are made in a sandwich fashion. Lithograph buttons have a one-piece construction.

Agnew, pen, silvered metal with facsimile signature,
c1972, 5" l, MIP **$12.00**
Agnew, wastebasket, litho tin, red, white, and blue, oval
opening, caricature sides with Agnew playing golf and
tennis, Chein, 1970, 13" h **25.00**
Democratic Convention, badge, pinback, gold toned
brooch and pendant with bust of Thomas Jefferson,
"Democratic National Convention 1932," attached
red, white, and blue ribbon, 4¹/₂" l, MIB **40.00**
Eisenhower, bracelet, brass link chain holding diecut
brass 4-leaf clover with mounted diecut brass letters
forming name **15.00**
Eisenhower, flicker, black and white photo with "Win
With Ike" **18.00**
Eisenhower, key fob, diecut brass, "I Like Ike" **8.00**
Eisenhower, pennant, felt, "I-Like-Ike," red, white lettering and Eisenhower image, 9 x 26" **20.00**
Goldwater, stickpin, diecut plastic, figural elephant head
wearing eyeglasses, dark blue and white **4.00**

Goldwater, ticket, 1963 Fourth of July Rally, Washington
DC, glossy, red, white, and blue, black and white
Goldwater photo in center, 3 x 6¹/₂" **15.00**
Goldwater, tie clip, brass bar with spring clip on reverse,
diecut lettering on front, 1¹/₄" l **8.00**
Hoover, campaign ring, "Hoover 1928," silvered brass
with ornate designs on each band at top, red, white,
and blue enamel insert around date and name **18.00**
Hoover, lapel stud, white metal, black finish, elephant
with name on side. **8.00**
Hoover, pin, brass, "Hoover GOP," gray enamel elephant perching on white enamel ball **15.00**
Johnson, book, *A Texan Looks at Lyndon/A Study in
Illegitimate Power,* J Evetts Haley, 256 pp, paperback,
black and white photo on cover with insert photo of
author at top right corner, 1964, 4 x 6¹/₄" **50.00**
Johnson, flicker, multicolored, "LBJ For The USA," 1 side
with Johnson photo, other side with stars and stripes
in outline of USA design, encased in white metal
frame with bar pin on reverse **15.00**
Kennedy, John F, matchcover, "Kennedy For President,"
black and white photo with red, white, and blue
border. **30.00**
Kennedy, John F, pinback button, "Vote Kennedy For
President," red, white, and blue **18.00**
Kennedy, John F, tie clip, brass, inscribed "Kennedy,"
1960, 1¹/₂" l **35.00**
Kennedy, Robert F, button, black and white Kennedy
illus at bottom center on pink ground, "Fill the Faith
Gap In 68/Kennedy," 1968, 3" d **25.00**
Landon, pinback button, "Landon/Knox," yellow on
brown with attached yellow felt petal. **5.00**
Nixon, key fob, clear plastic, shield shaped, red, white,
and blue paper label and int with bluetone jugate
photos, attached brass chain and key ring. **15.00**
Nixon, pinback button, "Pat For First Lady," black and
white photo, red, white, and blue lettering **5.00**
Nixon, pinback button, red, white, and blue on white
ground, first name next to "Dependability/Integrity/
Capability/Knowledge" **4.00**
Nixon, poster, cardboard, "Nixon's The One," smiling
Nixon photo, Official Nixon Material–Feeley &
Wheeler Inc, New York, 13¹/₂ x 18" **15.00**

Nixon/Agnew, Campaign Poster, 1968, 21 x 13¹/₂", $20.00.

Nixon, sheet music, *Let's Sing For the President,* blue-tone Nixon photo on cover, 12 pp, ©1974 Henry Tobias Music Co, 9 x 12" 10.00

Nixon/Agnew, hand puppets, painted vinyl heads, each wearing fabric smocks with sewn-in hands, Nixon wearing blue tie, Agnew wearing red tie, 15" h 50.00

Republican, pinback button, red, white, and blue, attached silver fabric ribbon with blue "Vote Straight Republican/Tuesday Nov 2, 1948," 1³/₄" d 5.00

Roosevelt, Franklin D, newspaper, *Daily Mirror,* Apr 16, 1945, final edition, 20 pp, "FDR Is Laid To Rest," 1¹/₂ x 15" 25.00

Roosevelt, Franklin D, pamphlet, anti-FDR, red, white, and blue, 16 pp, 1936, 4 x 8³/₄" 15.00

Roosevelt, Franklin D, pinback button, "A Gallant Leader, Franklin D. Roosevelt" surrounding black and white images, ³/₄" d 5.00

Roosevelt/Willkie, magazine, *Sunday Mirror,* Nov 3, 1940, 20 pp, 11¹/₂ x 15³/₄" 25.00

Shriver, ring, gold-colored metal with diecut "Shriver" cut into top 8.00

Taft, Robert, pinback button, "Vote Taft," red, white, and blue, 1948 . . . . 15.00

Truman, Harry S, fan, *Philadelphia Evening Bulletin,* Democratic National Convention, Decker cartoon 1 side, "Welcome Delegates" other side, 1948 . . . . 30.00

Truman, Harry S, magazine, *Time,* Dec 31, 1945, Man of the Year issue 20.00

Truman, Harry S, ticket, White House dinner, May 27, 1946, handwritten guests' name and date, light yellow White House image in center, 2¹/₂ x 4" 25.00

Wallace, tie clasp, gold-colored metal with raised inscription "Wallace '68," 1968, 1³/₈" l 4.00

AUCTION PRICES – CAMPAIGN BUTTONS

Provenance Historical Americana, Americana Auction No. 7, March 9, 1999.

Coolidge–Dawes, black and white, jugate, "For President/Vice President, Coolidge/Dawes," ⁷/₈" d . . . **$20.00**

Cox, black and white, portrait above "James M Cox," 1¹/₄" d 259.00

Duff–Eisenhower, red, white, and blue, map outline of PA and "Re-Elect Duff with Ike," ⁷/₈" d 9.00

FDR–Truman, brown tone, artist portrait of candidates, "Roosevelt–Truman," 1¹/₂" d 231.00

Hoover, red, white, and blue, portrait and "Put Hoover On," ⁷/₈" d 67.00

Landon, green tone, portrait within rim inscription "Alf M Landon's Notification, Topeka, July 23, 1936," 1¹/₄" d 165.00

McCarthy, red and blue lettering on white ground, "Gee I like Joe" (GI Joe), 1¹/₄" d 99.00

Powell–Wallace, white lettering on black ground, "Powell & Wallace An Integrated Ticket," 1¹/₄" d 66.00

Stevenson–Kefauver, black and white, candidates pictured in TV screen, "TV Victory Committee," 2¹/₄" d 188.00

Willkie, black and white, portrait and inscription "Our Next President, Wendell Lewis Willkie," 3¹/₂" d 17.00

PORCELIER PORCELAIN

The Porcelier Manufacturing Company was incorporated on October 14, 1926, with business offices in Pittsburgh, Pennsylvania, and a manufacturing plant in East Liverpool, Ohio. In 1930 Porcelier purchased the vacant plant of the American China Company in South Greensburg, Westmoreland County, Pennsylvania.

Initially, Porcelier produced light fixtures. Electrical kitchen appliances were added by the mid-1930s. Some credit Porcelier with making the first all-ceramic electrical appliances. In the course of its history, Porcelier made over 100 patterns of kitchenware and over 100 different light fixtures.

Sears, Roebuck and Company and Montgomery Ward were among Porcelier's biggest customers. Many products appear with brand names such as Heatmaster and Harmony House.

In March 1954 Pittsburgh Plate Glass Industries bought the Porcelier plant and adjacent land. The company was dissolved in the summer of 1954.

Reference: Susan E. Grindberg, *Collector's Guide to Porcelier China,* Collector Books, 1996.

Collectors' Club: Porcelier Collectors Club, 21 Tamarac Swamp Rd, Wallingford, CT 06492.

Coffeepot, 3-pc, emb fruit and flower design **$50.00**

Coffeepot, 4-pc, Colonial pattern, with pot, dripper, lid, and china spreader, 11" h 300.00

Coffeepot, electric, field flowers decal, melon-ribbed bottom, pedestal base, glass lid 200.00

Lamp Base, basketweave pattern, 8¹/₄" h 60.00

Teapot, emb sailboat 1 side, anchor and life preserver around rim, 7¹/₄" h, 10" w 30.00

Teapot, green band, pink domed lid 40.00

Teapot, pastel flowers, silver trim, 6¹/₄" h 30.00

Teapot, ribbed, pink flamingo 50.00

Coffeepot, electric, basketweave pattern, wildflower decal, #5007, 13" h, $60.00.

POSTCARDS

In 1869 the Austrian government introduced the first government-issued postcard. The postal card concept quickly spread across Europe, arriving in the United States in 1873.

The period from 1898 until 1918 is considered the golden age of postcards. English and German publishers produced most of the cards during the golden age. Detroit Publishing and John Winsch were leading American publishers.

The postcard collecting mania that engulfed Americans ended at the beginning of World War I. Although greeting cards replaced many postcards on sales racks, the postcard survived. Linen cards dominated the period between 1930 and the end of the 1940s. Chromolithograph cards were popular in the 1950s and 60s. Postcards experienced a brief renaissance in the 1970s and 80s with the introduction of the continental size format (4 x 6") and the use of contemporary designs.

Are the stamps on postcards valuable? The answer is no 99.9% of the time. If you have doubts, consult a philatelic price guide. A postcard's postmark may be an added value factor. There are individuals who collect obscure postmarks.

References: J. L. Mashburn, *Black Postcard Price Guide, Second Edition*, Colonial House, 1999; J. L. Mashburn, *Fantasy Postcards*, Colonial House, 1996; J. L. Mashburn, *The Artist-Signed Postcard Price Guide*, Colonial House, 1993; J. L. Mashburn, *The Postcard Price Guide, Third Edition*, Colonial House, 1997; J. L. Mashburn, *Sports Postcard Price Guide*, Colonial House, 1998; J. L. Mashburn, *The Super Rare Postcards of Harrison Fisher With Price Guide*, Colonial House, 1992; Jane Wood, *The Collectors' Guide to Post Cards*, L-W Books, 1984, 1997 value update.

Periodicals: *Barr's Post Card News*, 70 S 6th St, Lansing, IA 52151; *Postcard Collector*, PO Box 1050, Dubuque, IA 52004.

Collectors' Clubs: Deltiologists of America, PO Box 8, Norwood, PA 19074; Postcard History Society, PO Box 1765, Manassas, VA 20108.

Note: *Barr's Post Card News* and the *Postcard Collector* publish lists of over fifty regional clubs in the United States and Canada. Prices listed are for postcards in excellent condition.

Valentine, 1950s, $2.00.

23rd Academy Awards Oscars, Mar 29, 1951, list of main awards on reverse, *All About Eve* best picture, blue sepia, 1950 . . . . **$20.00**

Advertising, American Legion Convention, Boston, Oct 6-9, 1930, multicolored scene of 2 soldiers shaking hands in front of monument and "Welcome Comrade" **100.00**

Advertising, Boy Bread, bakers standing beside steam engine auto with large loaf of Boy Bread on top, real photo, Foltz Studio, Savannah, Georgia, c1930 . . . . **600.00**

Advertising, Campbell's Tomato Soup, Campbell's Kids with adv text for sale on soup by Schmidt's Grocery, St Paul, Minnesota, black and white, on government postcard, 1937, used **225.00**

Advertising, Flexible Flyer, "The Sled That Steers," S L Allen & Co **15.00**

Advertising, Hershey's Ice Cream, real photo, family at dinner table, child feeding grandmother, adv text on back, monotone **175.00**

Advertising, RCA Victor Televisions, front view of Wing Co store in Pasadena, CA, linen, printed by Mellinger Studios, c1945 . . . . **200.00**

Advertising, Spanish Olive Oil, woman pouring oil, Spanish text, sgd, c1920 . . . . **100.00**

Advertising, Super Shell Gasoline, 1930, used **45.00**

Advertising, Werner's Bowling Alleys, Long Island, NY, woman and man bowling, linen, printed by Henry Bauman, c1940 . . . . **250.00**

Advertising, WPIX Channel 11, New York, real photo, Three Stooges Fun House, shows Stooges and Joe Bolton, sgd by Moe, Larry, and Curly, c1960 . . . . **500.00**

Boxing, Jack Dempsey knocking out Jess Williard, 1950 postmark, 3½ x 5½" **20.00**

Drummer Boy, black boy playing drums, published by Ires, Italy, sgd Roy, postmarked Jul 1937 . . . . **40.00**

Fraternal, Elks Lodge, "The Bugle," 1921, used **10.00**

Glow-in-the-Dark, 2 mermaids in moonlight, French, c1930 . . . . **225.00**

Help the Wounded, nurse and medic treating wounded, "St John Ambulance Association Malta Centre," 1928, used **85.00**

Illustrator, Campsi, Junyent, Gaspar, woman in wedding dress with lilies, French wedding outfitter adv, France, 1929, used **150.00**

Illustrator, Hohlweing, Ludwig, "Deutsche Lufthansa," winged man flying over Olympic stadium, German airline adv, issued for 1936 Berlin Olympics **225.00**

Illustrator, Mucha, Alphonse, woman with school child, design from Central Matice School diploma, published by Czech Retired Revolutionary Sailors, black and white, 1926 . . . . **350.00**

International Peace Week of Youth, Aug 3-10, 1924, dove with olive branch released over city, Utrecht, Holland, 1924 . . . . **125.00**

Lada, Art Deco dancer, adv text on back for performance of "Lada, The Supreme Concert Dancer" at the Brooklyn Academy of Music, 1920 . . . . **200.00**

Real Photo, Bailey's Ice Cream Shop, Pasadena, CA, ext view, c1935 . . . . **225.00**

Real Photo, Bermuda Clipper, cabin int view, "Aboard the USA Bermuda Clipper," black and white **200.00**

Left: Comic card, "The Broker," $150.00. Photo courtesy Postcards International. **Right: Real Photo, "Sheriff, 101 Ranch, Tex Cooper, 1933 Pioneer Days, Dallas World's Fair," sgd, "1933 and 1934 Century of Progress Chicago" on bottom, $85.00.** Photo courtesy Collectors Auction Services.

POSTERS

The full color poster arrived on the scene in the 1880s, the result of the lithographic printing revolution. Posters by Courier and Strobridge are considered some of the finest examples of American lithography ever printed. Philadelphia was the center of the poster printing industry in America prior to 1945.

Almost from its inception, collectors were fascinated with this colorful art form. Printers began overprinting their commercial runs and selling the extra posters through print dealers and galleries. Editions Sagot in Paris offered posters for sale featuring the art of Toulouse-Lautrec. Posters were an inexpensive advertising form and played a major role during World Wars I and II.

Scarce is a term that must be used very carefully when referring to posters. Print runs into the millions are known. Yet, most were destroyed. The poster collecting community was relatively small and heavily art focused until the 1970s.

Carefully check the date mark on movie posters. An "R", usually located in the lower right corner near the border in the white area, followed by slash and the date denotes a later release of a movie. These posters generally are not as valuable as posters associated with the initial release.

Reference: Janet Gleeson, *Miller's Collecting Prints and Posters,* Millers Publications, 1997.

Note: See Movie Memorabilia for additional listings.

Real Photo, boy in baseball uniform with catchers mitt, black and white.	35.00
Real Photo, Commander Byrd's polar exploration plane "The America".	500.00
Real Photo, Dare Devil Peggy's Famous Troupe of Diving Belles, circus attraction booth, British, c1935	150.00
Real Photo, dentist treating soldier, "Camp Hospital, Camp Kearny, California," c1925	100.00
Real Photo, Imperial Airways, "The Forward Cabin of an Imperial Airways Liner of the Heracles Class," Tuck, 1932, used	150.00
Real Photo, Japanese Rolling Ball game booth, c1925	200.00
Real Photo, Josephine Baker, wearing tuxedo and top hat, from "The Joy of Paris," sgd, Piaz Studios, 1933	450.00
Real Photo, Ku Klux Klan, members in clan outfits wandering around grounds, "Scene at Pontiac, Mich, Labor Day, 1925"	125.00
Real Photo, Larry Doby of the Cleveland Indians, batting pose, wearing baseball uniform, sgd, 1952, used	250.00
Real Photo, Pan American Clipper, "China Clipper at San Pedro, California," c1940	125.00
Real Photo, Princess Margarite holding rose, "Age 25 yrs, Weight 32 lbs, Measures 27 in," c1930	100.00
Real Photo, Red Sox, team and managers, black and white, 1959.	275.00
Real Photo, The Human Iceberg, daredevil being enclosed in block of ice, sgd "Freezingly Yours, Mano, The Human Iceburg," c1940	150.00
Real Photo, "Twelve Merit Certificate Winners in National Week Contest, The Dunbar Mutual Insurance Society, Cleveland," black and white, c1935	125.00
Red Cross Convention, dove wearing Red Cross shirt standing atop soldier's helmet, Japan, 1934	125.00
Uncle Sam, lynching Southern continent, cartoon scene, "Hemisferio accidental 1941"	125.00

"Alaska," Alaskans sailing in dec wooden boat with yellow sail beneath shadow of snow-capped blue and gray mountains, Sidney Laurence, Brown & Bigelow, St Paul, c1935, 40 x 30".	$650.00
"American Airlines, Arizona," towering green cactus in foreground with horseback riders in blue and purple on orange mounts, purple hills and white hacienda in background, yellow sky, orange lettering, 40 x 30"	450.00
"Aspen, Ski Capitol of the Americas," skier with mountain and chairlift in background, turquoise on black, white lettering, c1950, 38¾ x 25¼".	1,375.00
"Cole Bros. Circus," children in light blue and yellow riding on back of big brown hippo outside Big Top, red lettering, red and blue banner affixed to bottom, 34½ x 41".	450.00

Gold Mine Icicles, with Roger Maris product endorsement, 1960s, 11½ x 17½", $375.00.

"Colorado Tops the Nation," skier in brown and black shooting down steep slope, pink and pale yellow mountains in distance, light blue sky, light blue border, 1941, 29½ x 21½" **3,250.00**

"Dante Magic Review, Sim Sala Bim," duo-tone 4-sheet litho, Dante's smiling head over name boldly printed across poster, humorous images beneath, 1940s-50s, 79½ x 81" **1,375.00**

"Israel," woman in brown blowing a shofar over an image of an old building next to a modern Kibbutz, early Israeli travel poster, 27¾ x 18¾" **225.00**

"Majestic, White Star Line, The World's Largest Ship," orange-funneled ship sailing through blue waters under green sky, WJ Aylward, c1932, 29¼ x 19½" **700.00**

"New Orleans," colorful aerial view of New Orleans French Quarter, costume-clad revellers drop confetti on passing king of Mardi Gras parade, mostly green, yellow, pink, and blue, Beverdier, c1960, 35 x 23" **425.00**

"Pacific Line, South America via Bermuda, Havana & Panama Canal," man in tropical white suit and safari hat, woman in blue holding orange parasol and feeding multicolored parrot, colorful foliage, ship in background passing through canal's Miraflores Lock, 39½ x 25" **1,250.00**

"Ride a Schwinn Lightweight for Health and Pleasure, See the Schwinn Built," young man and woman on bicycles, lighthouse in background, yellow sky, Arnold Schwinn and Co, Chicago, 39½ x 24" **200.00**

Shredded Wheat, "For breakfast – so easy to prepare, Nourishing," cereal box, large hand pouring milk from creamer into cereal bowl, 10½ x 16" **60.00**

"Steam Power, New Haven," black and white photo montage, 2 train images, red lettering, 41¾ x 27½" **325.00**

"Symphonie powder stays on until you take it off," framed image of pretty girl smiling for photographer above product pkg and text, 20½ x 14½" **60.00**

"The Floyd's, Unique Entertainers," color litho, oval portraits of Walter and Mary Floyd imposed on red ground, Boston: Libbie Show Print, c1915, 15 x 19¾".... **200.00**

"The New 20th Century Limited, New York–16 Hours Chicago, New York Central System," Art Deco image of steel blue train traveling beside green water, burgundy, gray, and orange lettering, 1938, 41 x 27" **11,500.00**

Ringling Bros and Barnum & Bailey Circus, 17 x 24¼", $550.00.
Photo courtesy Collectors Auction Services.

"The Teamworker!," bee gathering nectar from red and green flower against black background, blue and yellow lettering, Mather & Co, Chicago, 1929, 43 x 34¼" **625.00**

"TWA, Disneyland, Fly TWA, Los Angeles," rocket with electric pink markings rising into sky, park attractions visible in orange, red, brown, green, and purple, tie-dyed purple and blue background, bright orange and pink lettering, David, 1955, 40¼ x 25" **550.00**

"Unguentine for Burns," sunburned woman wearing towel, applying salve to shoulders, cardboard litho, Lawrence Wilbur, Canada, 35 x 22½" **100.00**

"Visit Mexico," young Mexican woman, shaded by tropical foliage in shades of green, yellow, purple, and blue, carrying lush basket of colorful fruit, light blue lettering on red ground, Gonzalez Camarena, Offset Galas, Mexico, 36½ x 27⅞" **400.00**

"Washington, The City Beautiful, Pennsylvania Railroad," stylish woman wearing blue suit and pink shirt disembarking from train, admiring White House, Capitol, and Supreme Court buildings nestled among green trees, clear blue sky, orange and red lettering, Edward Eggleston, c1935, 40 x 25¼" **3,500.00**

"Women Work For Victory," Connecticut WPA, 3 women wearing orange and blue marching off to jobs, 1 in factory, 1 in office, 1 to farm, light brown background, screen print, 26 x 18" **1,375.00**

"Yeoward Line, Sunshine Cruises, To Lisbon, Madeira, Canary Islands," blue harbor and yellow crescent coastline dotted with houses, ship framed between brown palm trees forming green leafy canopy, yellow lettering, Cawthorne, 34⅝ x 25" **575.00**

POTTERIES, REGIONAL

There were thousands of pottery factories scattered across the United States. Many existed only for a brief period of time.

Recent scholarship by individuals such as Phyllis and Tom Bess on the Oklahoma potteries, Carol and Jim Carlton on Colorado pottery, Jack Chipman on California pottery, and Darlene Dommel on the Dakota potteries have demonstrated how rich America's ceramic heritage is. This is only the tip of the iceberg.

This is a catchall category for all those companies that have not reached a strong enough collecting status to deserve their own category. Eventually, some will achieve this level. Collectors collect what they know. Thanks to today's scholarship, collectors are learning more about these obscure potteries.

References: California: Jack Chipman, *Collector's Encyclopedia of California Pottery, Second Edition,* Collector Books, 1998; Michael L. Ellis, *Collector's Guide to Don Winton Designs,* Collector Books, 1998; Michael Schneider, *California Potteries,* Schiffer Publishing, 1995; Bernice Stamper, *Vallona Starr Ceramics,* Schiffer Publishing, 1995. Colorado: Carol and Jim Carlton, *Collector's Encyclopedia of Colorado Pottery,* Collector Books, 1994, out of print. North Dakota: Darlene Hurst Dommel, *Collector's Encyclopedia of the Dakota Potteries,* Collector Books, 1996, out of print. Oklahoma: Phyllis and Tom Bess, *Frankoma and Other Oklahoma Potteries, 3rd Edition,* Schiffer Publishing, 2000.

Collectors' Clubs: Arkansas: Arkansas Pottery Collectors Society, 2006 Beckenham Cove, Little Rock, AR 72212; Minnesota:

Nemadji Pottery Collectors Club, PO Box 95, Moose Lake, MN 55767; North Dakota: North Dakota Pottery Collectors Society, PO Box 14, Beach, ND 58621.

California, Ball Artware, figure, pheasant, 7½" h $30.00

California, Batchelder, bookends, pr, seated monk, unglazed, c1923, 4½" h 500.00

California, Batchelder, tile, medieval landscape, imp mark, 4" 225.00

California, Bellaire, candlesticks, pr, Jamaica line, sgd 175.00

California, Bellaire, figure, angels with harp, 15" d 400.00

California, Bellaire, figure, seated Bali woman, 8" h 800.00

California, Bellaire, lamp base, hp Japanese geisha girls, sgd, 18" d 200.00

California, Bellaire, plate, exotic pear shaped floral spray, sgd "Marc Bellaire," 10" d 65.00

California, Bellaire, vase, Mardi Gras line, 18" h 350.00

California, Cemar, figure, leaping deer, brown flocking on base, 11¾" h 65.00

California, Cleminsons, bobby pin holder, cov, "Bobbie Guard" 50.00

California, Cleminsons, butter, cov, Distelfink dec 50.00

California, Cleminsons, cleanser shaker, Katrina, ink stamp mark, 6½" h 45.00

California, Cleminsons, jar, cov, Chinaman, stamped mark 60.00

California, Cleminsons, wall pocket, chef, 7¼" h 15.00

California, Cleminsons, wall pocket, little house on top of world, stamped mark, 8" w 50.00

California, Freeman-McFarlin, figure, donkey with bee on nose, paper label, 5¼" h 30.00

California, Freeman-McFarlin, figure, owl with large eyes, 9" h 25.00

California, Haldeman, dish, figural swan, turquoise int, white ext, 5 x 7" 15.00

California, Haldeman, figure, dancing lady, 6" h 125.00

California, Haldeman, flower bowl, applied birds on branch, 5½" h 75.00

California, Haldeman, planter, shell, pink, incised mark, 5 x 9½" 40.00

California, Haldeman, rose bowl, applied roses, 4¾" h 45.00

California, Keeler, figure, canary, tail down, 6" h 15.00

California, Keeler, figure, cocker spaniel, begging, #735, in-mold mark, 6" h 45.00

California, Keeler, figure, ducks, pr, stamped mark 45.00

California, Keeler, figure, peacock, Exotic line, #701, 16" h 250.00

California, Keeler, figure, pheasant, 12¼" h 75.00

California, Keeler, figure, Siamese cat, #798 . . . . 25.00

California, Kindell, Dorothy, ashtray, "The Beach-combers," in-mold mark, 11" l 175.00

California, LaMiranda, lotus vase, in-mold mark, 6" h 35.00

California, LaMiranda, planter, water buffalo, 7 x 10" 60.00

California, Maddux, figure, cock-a-too, 11" h 65.00

California, Maddux, figure, fighting rooster, 10¾" h 40.00

California, Maddux, figure, flamingo, 10¾" h 85.00

California, Manker, bud vase, turquoise, incised "William Manker" with logo and "wm," 5¾" h 150.00

California, Manker, jar, cov, citron green, 6" h 75.00

California, Manker, vase, cylinder shaped, blended green to yellow glaze, 14" h 300.00

California, Manker, vase, fluted, powder blue ext, light rose int, 6" h 150.00

California, Manley, Jean, figure, seated boy holding duck, 4" h 65.00

California, McCarty Brothers, planter, Mexican children playing musical instruments, price for pr 25.00

California, McCulloch, Stewart, multicolored 45.00

California, Nichols, Betty Lou, nodders, pr, cat and mouse 300.00

California, Nichols, Betty Lou, planter, Olga, painted mark and copyright symbol, 8 x 11½" 400.00

California, Pacific, baby plate, divided, bunny design border, c1934, 9" d 45.00

California, Pacific, figure, stylized bird, satin white, circular in-mold mark 80.00

California, Pacific, flower holder, figural cockatoo, #3802, yellow 100.00

California, Pacific, planter, Jill, #906, pastel green, 5" h 45.00

California, Pacific, vase, #3602, ovoid, white and maroon, 10" h 175.00

California, Roselane, centerpiece, angel fish, Aqua Marine line, in-mold mark, 7½" h 85.00

California, Roselane, figure, Siamese cat, 9½" h 75.00

California, Roselane, figure, "Sparkler" deer, plastic eyes, c1965, 4 x 3½" 9.00

California, Roselane, figure, stylized deer 20.00

California, Ross, bank, elephant 70.00

California, Simmons, Robert, figure, boxer dog, 7¾ x 10" 30.00

California, Simmons, Robert, figure, doe and fawn, 5 x 7" 25.00

California, Twin Winton, ashtray, Hillbilly line 35.00

California, Twin Winton, cookie jar, Keystone Cop, wood finish, 12½" h 125.00

California, Twin Winton, figure, winking lion, 3¼" h 40.00

California, Twin Winton, pretzel bowl, Hillbilly line 45.00

California, Weil, vase, sailor boy, hp dec, c1943, 10¾" h 20.00

California, Will-George/The Claysmiths, figure, bird on branch, paper label, 2 x 5" 20.00

California, Will-George/The Claysmiths, figure, child artist, incised mark 100.00

California, Will-George/The Claysmiths, figure, child artist with model, incised mark, c1939, price for pr 60.00

California, Will-George/The Claysmiths, figure, young Pan, surrounded by forest creatures, stamped mark, 7" h 85.00

California, Miramar of California, covered casserole, turquoise, metal stand, #644, 1956, 8⅝" d, $18.00.

California, Marsh Industries, tidbit tray, turquoise, metal center handle, #T-31, late 1950s/ early 1960s, 14¹/₄" h, $20.00.

California, Will-George/The Claysmiths, pitcher, rooster shaped, stamped mark, 7" h 140.00
California, Willis, Barbara, bowl, leaf shaped, turquoise crackle on brown, incised mark, 12" l 200.00
California, Willis, Barbara, cigarette box, white crackle on brown, 4 x 4¹/₂" 160.00
California, Willis, Barbara, wall pocket, crescent shaped, light green crackle on brown, stamped mark, 5" h 150.00
California, Winfield, platter, hp center tulips, incised mark, 14" sq 150.00
California, Yona, wall plaques, pr, Egyptians, 11" h 75.00
Colorado, Broadmoor, lamp base, cream, swirl design, sgd by Cecil Jones, 15" h 200.00
Colorado, Broadmoor, planter, applied handles, red, hand thrown 125.00
Colorado, Denver White, wall plaque, train design, 8" 65.00
Colorado, Rocky Mountain, figure, poodle, 10" h 25.00
North Dakota, Dickinson Clay Products, ashtray, figural cowboy hat, brown, "North Dakota" on rim, 4¹/₂ x 5" 45.00
North Dakota, Dickinson Clay Products, ashtray, round, marine blue with white overglaze, 4¹/₄" d 40.00
North Dakota, Dickinson Clay Products, bookends, pr, mountain sheep, 4¹/₂ x 4¹/₄" 400.00
North Dakota, Dickinson Clay Products, dish, shell shaped, sea green, 1¹/₂ x 7¹/₄" 25.00
North Dakota, Dickinson Clay Products, paperweight, shield shaped, red, 2³/₄" 35.00
North Dakota, Dickinson Clay Products, vase, applied handles, metallic black, mkd "Dickota," 4³/₄" h 45.00
North Dakota, Dickinson Clay Products, vase, glossy orange glaze with gold and black overglaze, 4" h 50.00
North Dakota, Dickinson Clay Products, vase, peacock pink mottled glaze, 7¹/₂" h 65.00
North Dakota, Messer, bud vase, porcelain, hp cattails, 5" h 125.00
North Dakota, Messer, figure, Hereford bull, 3 x 4³/₄" 300.00
North Dakota, Messer, figure, prairie dog, 2¹/₄" h 100.00
North Dakota, Messer, salt and pepper shakers, pr, grain elevators, "Farmers Equity Exchange," 3¹/₂" h 100.00

North Dakota, Pine Ridge, ashtray, Cottier, geometric motif, 5¹/₂" d 100.00
North Dakota, Pine Ridge, bowl, Cottier, geometric motif, 2 x 9" 125.00
North Dakota, Pine Ridge, bowl, geometric motif, sgd "N Firethunder" 300.00
North Dakota, Pine Ridge, serving set, 10" h pitcher and four-3¹/₂" h tumblers, geometric motif, sgd "Ramona Wounded Knee" 600.00
North Dakota, Rushmore, bud vase, slip painted cattails on greenish white ground, 5" h 75.00
North Dakota, Rushmore, dish, slip painted cattails on greenish white ground, 11" l 75.00
North Dakota, Rushmore, figure, molded cowboy boots, 3¹/₂" h 30.00
North Dakota, Rushmore, vase, ruffled, hand thrown, green streaks, 4³/₄" h 40.00
North Dakota, WPA Ceramics, bowl, black and tan sgraffito, Native American motif, 3¹/₂ x 7" 700.00
North Dakota, WPA Ceramics, figure, beaver, incised mark, 3¹/₄ x 5" 250.00
North Dakota, WPA Ceramics, figure, Tom Tom the Piper's Son, 6¹/₂" h 700.00
North Dakota, WPA Ceramics, plate, cobalt blue sgraffito, Native American motif around sides, 9" d 800.00
North Dakota, WPA Ceramics, strawberry jar, hand thrown, turquoise 250.00
North Dakota, WPA Ceramics, vase, hand thrown, charcoal, sgd by Tony Lanz, 11" h 250.00
North Dakota, WPA Ceramics, vase, hand thrown, tan, horizontal lines on body, black on handles, 7" h 125.00
North Dakota, WPA Ceramics, vase, sgraffito wheat design, 5" h 350.00
Oklahoma, Cherokee, bowl, Indian motif animals around top, 12" d 20.00
Oklahoma, Cherokee, figure, quail, dated "11-10-81," 6" h 7.00
Oklahoma, Cherokee, figure, standing horse, dated "7 11-84," 6" h 10.00
Oklahoma, Creek, figure, Indian moccasin, gold sticker "Authentic Indian Pottery Made In Checotah, OK USA," 8" l 5.00
Oklahoma, Creek, figure, mallard, green, 5¹/₂ x 7¹/₂" 8.00
Oklahoma, Creek, figure, mallard, red and green, 7¹/₂ x 9" 15.00
Oklahoma, Creek, salt and pepper shakers, pr, figural teepee, 3" h 8.00
Oklahoma, Gracetone Pottery, figure, hound dog, cinnamon, 6" h 300.00
Oklahoma, Hammat Originals, figure, Chico the monkey, 12" h 35.00
Oklahoma, Hammat Originals, wall mask, Indian maiden, "Oklahoma" across headband, 4¹/₂" 15.00
Oklahoma, Sequoyah, ashtray, figural duck, #38, mkd "Evelyn Van Sequoyah 1939," 8" l 100.00
Oklahoma, Sequoyah, ashtray, figural turtle, mkd "Evelyn Van Sequoyah #1," 5¹/₂" l 50.00
Oklahoma, Sequoyah, pitcher, frog handle, mkd "Levida Going 1938 Sequoyah," 5" h 75.00
Oklahoma, Sequoyah, vase, straight neck, mkd "Winnie Simmer 1938-39 Sequoyah," 6¹/₂" h 45.00
Oklahoma, Synar, basket, woodpine and aqua, 7¹/₂" h 15.00
Oklahoma, Synar, lotus bowl, wintergreen, 5¹/₂" 25.00

Oklahoma, Synar, vase, pine cone dec, woodpine and
aqua, 11" h **15.00**
Oklahoma, Synar, vase, wheat dec, woodpine and
aqua, 10" h **15.00**
Oklahoma, Synar, wall pocket, wintergreen, 8" h **20.00**
Oklahoma, Tamac, garden dish, frosty pine, 12" l **15.00**
Oklahoma, Tamac, platter, flying duck, hp, Sportsman
Series, 15" l **45.00**
Oklahoma, Tamac, spoon rest, "For My Stirring Spoon,"
6" l **10.00**
Oklahoma, Tamac, vase, free form, frosty pine, 4½" h **20.00**
Oklahoma, Winart, decanter, pink with brown drip, 1 qt,
8" h **30.00**

PRAYER LADIES

Prayer Ladies are kitchen items in the shape of a woman wearing
an apron with a prayer printed on it. More often than not, the
woman has her eyes closed and hands folded in prayer.

Prayer ladies are found in a wide variety of forms, e.g., bud
vases, cookie jars, egg timers, napkin holders, salt and pepper
shakers, scouring pad holders, string holders, and toothpick holders. The most commonly found examples wear a pink dress.

Prayer Ladies date from the 1960s and 70s. Enesco, one of the
chief importers, called its line "Mother in the Kitchen."

Reference: April Tvorak, *Prayer Lady—Enesco Price Guide*, published by author, 1998.

Air Freshener, pink **$150.00**
Bank, pink **140.00**
Bell, blue **90.00**
Bell, pink **80.00**
Bud Vase, pink **125.00**
Candleholders, pr, pink **150.00**
Canister, pink **300.00**
Cookie Jar, blue **500.00**
Cookie Jar, pink **300.00**
Cookie Jar, white, blue trim **425.00**
Crumb Sweeper Set, brush and tray, pink **150.00**
Egg Timer, pink **130.00**
Flat Spoon Rest, blue **45.00**
Flat Spoon Rest, pink **35.00**
Flat Spoon Rest, white, blue trim **50.00**
Instant Coffee, blue **140.00**
Instant Coffee, pink **35.00**
Instant Coffee, white, blue trim **160.00**
Mug, blue **140.00**
Mug, pink **130.00**
Napkin Holder, blue **35.00**
Napkin Holder, pink **25.00**
Napkin Holder, white, blue trim **40.00**
Photo Holder, pink **130.00**
Planter, pink **125.00**
Ring Holder, pink **45.00**
Salt and Pepper Shakers, pr, blue **20.00**
Salt and Pepper Shakers, pr, pink **16.00**
Salt and Pepper Shakers, pr, white, blue trim **22.00**
Soap Dish, blue **45.00**
Soap Dish, pink **40.00**
Spoon Holder, blue **55.00**
Spoon Holder, pink **45.00**
Tea Set, teapot, creamer, and sugar, blue **400.00**

Clothes Sprinkler,
pink, 6½" h, $300.00.

Tea Set, teapot, creamer, and sugar, pink **250.00**
Toothpick Holder, blue **30.00**
Toothpick Holder, pink **20.00**
Toothpick Holder, white, blue trim **35.00**
Wall Plaque, pink **100.00**

PRECIOUS MOMENTS

During a visit to the Los Angeles Gift Show in 1978, Eugene
Freeman, president of Enesco, saw some cards and posters featuring the drawings of Samuel J. Butcher. At first, Butcher and Bill
Biel, his partner in Jonathan and David, were not thrilled with the
idea of having Butcher's art transformed into three-dimensional
form. However, after seeing a prototype sculpted by Yashei Fojioka
of Japan, Butcher and Biel agreed.

Initially twenty-one pieces were made. Early figures are darker
in color than those made today. Pieces produced between 1978
and 1984 and licensed by Jonathan & David Company have smaller heads than pieces relicensed by the Samuel J. Butcher Company
and Precious Moments. Jonathan & David closed in 1988.

The Enesco Precious Moments Club was established in 1981. In
1989, Butcher opened the Precious Moments Chapel in Carthage,
Missouri. In 1995 Goebel introduced hand-painted bronze minia-
tures. The year 1995 also saw Enesco launch its Century Circle
Retailers, a group of 35 retailers selling a limited edition line of
Precious Moments material.

References: Collectors Information Bureau, *Collectibles Market
Guide & Price Index, 17th Edition,* Collector's Information Bureau,
1999; Mary L. Sieber (ed.), *2000 Price Guide to Limited Edition
Collectibles,* Krause Publications, 1999.

Collectors' Club: Enesco Precious Moments Collectors' Club
(company-sponsored), PO Box 99, Itasca, IL 60143.

Note: For additional listings see Enesco and Limited Edition
Collectibles.

Bell, But The Greatest of These Is Love, S Butcher, 1992 . . . . **$40.00**

Bell, Jesus Is Born, S Butcher, 1981 . . . . 50.00
Bell, Prayer Changes Things, S Butcher, 1981 . . . . 55.00
Bell, Surrounded With Joy, #E-0522, S Butcher, 1983 . . . . 50.00
Figurine, A Friend Is Someone Who Cares, #530632 . . . . 50.00
Figurine, Blessum You, #727335 . . . . 25.00
Figurine, Don't Let the Holidays Get You Down,
  #522112 . . . . 65.00
Figurine, Faith Is the Victory, #521396 . . . . 115.00
Figurine, Get Into The Habit Of Prayer, #12203 . . . . 30.00
Figurine, Gliding Through the Holidays, #521566 . . . . 25.00
Figurine, I Get a Bang Out Of You, #12262 . . . . 35.00
Figurine, Lord, Keep Me On My Toes, #100129 . . . . 65.00
Figurine, Lord, Keep Me On the Ball, #12270 . . . . 40.00
Figurine, Lord, Turn My Life Around, #520551 . . . . 45.00
Figurine, Love Beareth All Things, E-7158 . . . . 30.00
Figurine, Make Me a Blessing, #100102 . . . . 60.00
Figurine, Money's Not the Only Green Thing Worth
  Saving, #531073 . . . . 60.00
Figurine, Mother Sew Dear, #E-3106 . . . . 25.00
Figurine, Not a Creature Was Stirring, #524484 . . . . 25.00
Figurine, Our First Christmas Together, #101702 . . . . 85.00
Figurine, Pretty As a Princess, #526053 . . . . 30.00
Figurine, Showers Of Blessings, #105945 . . . . 40.00
Figurine, Sometimes You're Next to Impossible, #530964 . . . . 35.00
Figurine, Summer's Joy, #12076 . . . . 70.00
Figurine, The Greatest Gift Is a Friend, #109231 . . . . 30.00
Figurine, The Lord Turned My Life Around, #520535 . . . . 40.00
Figurine, To Be With You Is So Uplifting, #522260 . . . . 40.00
Figurine, Trust In the Lord To the Finish, PM–842 . . . . 45.00
Figurine, You Deserve an Ovation, #520578 . . . . 30.00
Figurine, You Suit Me to a Tee, #526193 . . . . 25.00
Figurine, We're Pulling For You, #106151 . . . . 55.00
Figurine, Wishing You a Cozy Season, #521949 . . . . 50.00
Ornament, Baby's First Christmas, 1985 . . . . 35.00
Ornament, Blessed Are the Pure In Heart, 1984 . . . . 20.00
Ornament, Love Is Kind, 1984 . . . . 25.00
Ornament, Love Is the Best Gift of All, 1987 . . . . 35.00

Ornament, May God Bless You With a Perfect Holiday
  Season, 1984 . . . . 20.00
Ornament, Mouse With Cheese, 1982 . . . . 100.00
Ornament, Peace On Earth, 1984 . . . . 25.00
Ornament, Reindeer, 1986 . . . . 175.00
Ornament, Rocking Horse, 1986 . . . . 25.00
Ornament, Smile Along the Way, 1988 . . . . 30.00
Ornament, To My Forever Friend, 1988 . . . . 20.00
Ornament, Waddle I Do Without You, 1987 . . . . 20.00
Perfume Bottle, Precious Moments October Perfume,
  porcelain, light pink, "opal" birthstone, 6" h 18.00
Plate, Blessings From Me to Thee, Christmas Blessings
  Series, S Butcher, 1991 . . . . 50.00
Plate, Friend In the Sky, Precious Moments of Childhood
  Series, T Utz, Hamilton Collection, 1979 . . . . 50.00
Plate, God Loveth a Cheerful Giver, Classics Series,
  S Butcher, Hamilton Collection, 1993 . . . . 35.00
Plate, He Covers the Earth With His Beauty, Beauty of
  Christmas Series, S Butcher, 1994 . . . . 50.00
Plate, He Hath Made Everything Beautiful In His Time,
  Mother's Day Series, S Butcher, 1995 . . . . 50.00
Plate, He Is Not Here, Bible Story Series, S Butcher,
  Hamilton Collection, 1993 . . . . 30.00
Plate, Holly-Day Wishes, Holly-Day Greetings Series,
  1997, 3½" d 10.00
Plate, Love Is Kind, Inspired Thoughts Series, S Butcher,
  Enesco, 1984 . . . . 40.00
Plate, Loving Thy Neighbor, Mother's Love Series,
  S Butcher, Enesco, 1984 . . . . 40.00
Plate, Make a Joyful Noise, Easter Series, S Butcher,
  Enesco, 1993 . . . . 18.00
Plate, My Kitty, T Utz, Viletta China, 1982 . . . . 30.00
Plate, My Peace I Give Unto Thee, Christmas Love
  Series, S Butcher, Enesco, 1987 . . . . 45.00
Plate, Tell Me the Story of Jesus, Joy of Christmas Series,
  S Butcher, Enesco, 1985 . . . . 40.00
Plate, Unto Us a Child Is Born, Christmas Collection
  Series, Enesco, 1984 . . . . 40.00
Plate, Winter's Song, Four Seasons Series, S Butcher,
  Enesco, 1986 . . . . 40.00

PREMIUMS

A premium is an object given free or at a reduced price with the purchase of a product or service. Premiums divide into two groups: (1) point of purchase (you obtain your premium when you make the purchase) or (2) proof of purchase (you send proof of purchase, often box labels or seals, to a distribution point which then sends the premium to you).

Premiums are generational. The fifty-, sixty- and seventy-something generations think of radio premiums. The forty- and older thirty-something generations identify with cereal and radio premiums. Younger generations collect fast-food premiums.

Collectors place a premium on three-dimensional premiums. However, many of these premiums arrived in paper containers and envelopes and contained paper instruction sheets. A premium is considered complete only if it has its period packaging and everything that came with it.

Ovaltine's offer of a "Little Orphan Annie" music sheet was one of the earliest radio premiums. Jack Armstrong, Lone Ranger, and Tom Mix premiums soon followed. By the middle of the 1930s every child eagerly awaited the phrase "Now, an important word

Plate, Love Is The Best Gift Of All, Precious Moments Last Forever, S Butcher, Enesco, 1992, $30.00.

from our sponsor" with pad in hand, ready to write down the address for the latest premium offer. Thousands of radio premiums were offered in the 1930s, 40s, and 50s.

Cereal manufacturers found that the inclusion of a premium in the box was enough of an incentive to stimulate extra sales. Cereal premiums flourished in the post-1945 period. Although television premiums were offered, they never matched in numbers those offered over the radio.

The arrival of the fast-food restaurant and eventual competition between chains led to the use of premiums to attract customers. Many premiums were tied to television shows and movies. Although not a premium, fast-food packaging has also attracted the interest of collectors.

Not all premiums originated via cereal boxes, fast-food chains, radio, or television. Local and national food manufacturers and merchants used premiums to attract customers. Cracker Jack is the most obvious example.

References: Scott Bruce, *Cereal Box Bonanza: The 1950's,* Collector Books, 1995; Ted Hake, *Hake's Price Guide to Character Toys, 2nd Edition,* Avon Books, Gemstone Publishing, 1998; Jim Harmon, *Radio & TV Premiums,* Krause Publications, 1997; Robert M. Overstreet, *Overstreet Premium Ring Price Guide, Third Edition,* Gemstone Publishing, 1997; Loretta Rieger and Lagretta Bajorek, *Children's Paper Premiums in American Advertising: 1890-1990s,* Schiffer Publishing, 2000; Tom Tumbusch, *Tomart's Price Guide to Radio Premiums and Cereal Box Collectibles,* Wallace-Homestead, 1991, out of print.

Newsletter: *The Premium Watch Watch,* 24 San Rafael Dr, Rochester, NY 14618.

Note: See Cracker Jack, Fast-Food Collectibles, and McDonald's for additional listings.

REPRODUCTION ALERT

Bazooka Bubble Gum, Bazooka Joe Initial Ink Stamp Ring, brass ring with adjustable bands, circular compartment on top with raised image of Bazooka Joe, cap lifts off to reveal ink pad and rubber insert with raised initial "A," c1966, used **$145.00**

Beech-Nut Gum, photo, Chandu the Magician, black and white, 1930s, 8½ x 11" **75.00**

Big Boy, bank, vinyl, Big Boy figure wearing red and white checkerboard overalls, ©Marriott Corp 1973, 8½" h **50.00**

Boo Berry, figure, soft plastic, 1970s, 1¾" h **10.00**

Boo Berry, iron-on transfer, color, 3 x 3¼", MIP **10.00**

Boo Berry, Secret Compartment Ring, pink plastic, 1976. . . . . **75.00**

Cap'n Crunch, wiggle figure, red plastic, thin spring base, 1970s, 2½" h **10.00**

Cheerios, key chain, Lone Ranger 17th Anniversary 1933-1950, silvered brass, Lone Ranger riding Silver on front, "Official Seal/The Lone Ranger Lucky Piece" and Lone Ranger, Tonto, and silver bullet surrounded by horseshoe design on back, 1950 . . . . **30.00**

Cheerios, mask, Lone Ranger, full color painted art image of Lone Ranger cut out from back of cereal box, perforated eyes and string holes unpunched, neatly cut edges, 6¾ x 10¾" **45.00**

Cheerios, Space Shuttle Adventure Kit, booklet, shirt transfer sheet, peel-off emblem sticker, Columbia space shuttle pre-formed flying model kit with instructions, complete in orig 8½ x 10½" mailing envelope dated Jan 12, 1982 . . . . **25.00**

Cobakco, pinback button, metal, "Cobakco Safety Club– The Lone Ranger," blue and gold, 1" d **55.00**

Cocomalt, compass ring, brass luster base with adjustable brass bands holding inset plastic compass, 1936. . . . . **45.00**

Cream of Wheat, Buck Rogers Solar Scouts Member's Badge, brass, Buck with raised guns seated in spaceship, reverse inscribed "To My Solar Scout Pal" with facsimile signature, 1936, 1½" h **65.00**

Cream of Wheat, pinback button, Buck Rogers in the 25th Century member, Buck, rocket pistol, and spaceship on blue ground with yellow rim, with back paper, 1935, 1" d. **75.00**

Crest Toothpaste, Gel Man Ring, blue flexible rubber with 1988 Proctor & Gamble copyright on reverse, "Crest" on bottom edge of ring band, 2" h **12.00**

Devil Dogs, ring, brass bands with wing design, top with high relief head of bulldog with initial "A" above head, 1935 . . . . **40.00**

Freakies Cereal, figure, green vinyl, c1973, 1¾" h, MIP. **10.00**

Fruit Loops, Toucan Sam Secret Decoder, blue vinyl with movable circular wheel at center and small cutouts that reveal letter and number combinations, 1983, 2¼" h **18.00**

Gorman's Bread, badge, Speed Gibson's Flying Police, brass, blue accent paint, 1937, 1⅝" h **20.00**

Green Giant, Little Sprout doll, soft vinyl, movable head, 1970s, 6" h **20.00**

Hamburger Helper, Helping Hand figure, gold-painted plaster designed like 4-fingered glove with smiling face on palm, sealed in orig plastic bag, orig box, 1¼ x 2 x 3" **30.00**

Honeycomb, Honeycomb Kid Flicker Ring, close-up of kid with lasso/Kid riding a pair of buffalo, bright green plastic base **125.00**

Log Cabin Syrup, pull toy, litho tin, 5¾" h, 4¾" l, $500.00. Photo courtesy Wm Morford.

Jell-O, hand puppet, Mr Wiggle, hollow soft vinyl, dark red with black and white eye markings and black smiling opened mouth, complete with 11 x 14½" comic page from Sep 25, 1966 *Philadelphia Enquirer* offering puppet by sponsor Jell-O, ©1969 General Foods, 6" h **75.00**

Kellogg's, Don Winslow's Official Squadron of Peace Manual, with medal, creed sheet, and flyer offering DW Periscope, orig mailing envelope **150.00**

Kellogg's Frosted Flakes, wristwatch, quartz, smiling Tony the Tiger, black hands and numbers, brown leather band, ©1989 Kellogg Co **40.00**

Kellogg's, walkie-talkie, punch-out, orig brown envelope with instructions, c1945, 8¼ x 10½" **175.00**

Kentucky Fried Chicken, salt and pepper shakers, pr, figural Colonel Sanders, 1 white base, 1 black base, Starling Plastics Ltd, London, Canada, c1970, 4¼" h **40.00**

Kix, Lone Ranger Six-Gun Ring, 3-dimensional gray plastic gun with silvered metal grips, front edge with small opening for flint to produce sparks, brass base with saddle designs on each side and brand designs around top, 1947 .... **65.00**

Kool-Aid, Treasure Hunt Ring, silver luster with brass luster insert on top, shield-like design accented by letters and symbols with "1614," silvered outer edge of top depicts 10 additional symbols, unused **150.00**

Mary Jane Bread, pinback button, "Mary Jane Bread" and Roy Rogers, red and black, 1¼" d **50.00**

Mister Softee, flicker ring, "I Like Mr Softee" changes to portrait of Mister Softee's head and upper torso, silver plastic base, 1960s **45.00**

National Biscuit Co, bandanna, cotton, Straight Arrow, 1949, 18½" sq. **45.00**

National Biscuit Co, cavalry hat, Rin Tin Tin and Rusty Fighting Blue Devils, black pressed felt with gold cloth cord, image of Rusty with arm around Rinty on dark blue, silver, and gold patch on front, Arlington Hat Co, NY, medium, 1954, 11" d **70.00**

Ovaltine, Radio Orphan Annie Shake-up Mug, beetleware green plastic cup, image of Annie and Sandy, "For Extra Pep 'n Flavor We Drink Chocolate Flavored Ovaltine!," red top, 1940, 2¾ x 4¾", $55.00. Photo courtesy Past Tyme Pleasures.

National Biscuit Co, figure, Crunchy the Nabisco Spoonman, vinyl, purple, 1959, 1⅞" l **30.00**

Ovaltine, Radio Orphan Annie's SS 1935 Decoder **20.00**

Pop-Tarts, puppet, HR Pufnstuf, 1970 .... **80.00**

Post Cereal, ashtray, clear glass, Art Deco style stepped design, 3 rests, red and black decal with "Post Cereals/Post Flakes/Huskies/Whole Bran Shreds/Post's Bran Flakes," 1930s, 4½" d **20.00**

Post Cereal, Fireball Twigg Explorer Ring, silver luster adjustable base, large clear plastic dome on top covered by black and white sundial and compass needle **65.00**

Post Cereal, puzzle, cardboard, photo image of smiling Roy Rogers holding 2 collie puppies against western mountain background, ©1952 Frontiers Inc, unpunched, 4 x 5" **25.00**

Post Raisin Bran, badge, Hopalong Cassidy, litho tin, Hoppy image, 2" h **35.00**

Post Raisin Bran, tab, litho tin, Wild Bill Hickok image in black on red, blue, and yellow ground, neatly folded over, 1950s, 1¾" h **20.00**

Quaker, badge, Dick Tracy Junior Secret Service, brass shield with Tracy profile, 1930s **65.00**

Ralston, invisible ink and developer, Tom Mix, orig box with instruction sheet, writing manual, and 1938 premium catalog **275.00**

RCA Victor, television, brown plastic, 3 Tom Mix film strips. **50.00**

Reddy Kilowatt, magic gripper for loosening jar lids, light bulbs, etc, dark yellow rubber disk, image of Reddy Kilowatt as chef, red lettering, 1950s, 5¼" d **20.00**

Richfield Hi-Octane Gasoline, ink blotter, adv for Jimmie Allen radio program, red, white, and blue, 1938. .... **45.00**

Sears, pencil case, "Roy Rogers" and image on front, "First to Sears then to School" on back, red, black, and white, 4¼ x 8¼" **65.00**

Star-Kist Tuna, wristwatch, wind-up, Charlie Tuna holding sign "Sorry Charlie" on dial, blue numbers, gold accents, glow-in-the-dark hands, black leather band, 1970s **100.00**

Strollers Cigarettes, cigarette card, Tom Mix, #192, 1⅜ x 2½" **25.00**

Toddy, jigsaw puzzle, 1932 Olympic Games, color litho, orig envelope, 75 pcs, 13 x 10", $30.00.

Sugar Jets, ring, molded dark red plastic with high relief
Mickey Mouse head image against shield design,
name below on swirling banner **20.00**

Sun Herald and Examiner, pinback button, litho tin,
"Lone Ranger, Sun Herald and Examiner," 1⅛" d **60.00**

Zonkers, figure, Screaming Yellow Zonkers, solid vinyl,
bright yellow, 1970s, 1½" h **15.00**

PRESLEY, ELVIS

Elvis died on August 17, 1977. Or, did he? The first Elvis license material dates from the mid-1950s. Vintage Elvis dates prior to 1965.

Collectors divide Elvis material into two periods: items licensed prior to Elvis' death and those licensed by his estate, known to collectors as fantasy items. Some Elvis price guides refuse to cover fantasy pieces. Special items manufactured and marketed solely for Elvis fan club members are a third category of material and should not be overlooked.

Reference: Jerry Osborne, *The Official Price Guide to Elvis Presley, Second Edition,* House of Collectibles, 1998.

Collectors' Club: Elvis Forever TCB Fan Club, PO Box 1066, Miami, FL 33280.

Calendar Cards, "Elvis RCA Records" promotion, full-
color Elvis images, includes 1979 "Always Elvis,"
1980 "Elvis 25 Years on RCA Records," and photo of
Elvis singing and Elvis in costume holding microphone in front of Christmas tree, large doll and Col
Tom Parker dressed as Santa Claus, facsimile signature
and inscription "Seasons Greetings, Elvis And The
Colonel," 2¼ x 3⅞" **$20.00**

Coloring Contest Sheet, "Girls! Girls! Girls!" promotion,
paper picture of Elvis in boat with 6 women, 6 paints,
©Paramount, unused, 1962, 9 x 12" **25.00**

Dog Tag Necklace and Bracelet, chrome luster metal
with image of Elvis with sideburns, facsimile signature, includes name, Army code, and blood type, 12" l
silver-colored metal necklace, on orig glossy card
with blue lettering "Remembrance Bracelet," 1950s **35.00**

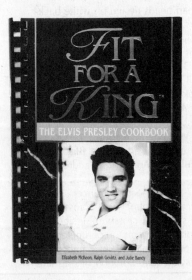

Cookbook, *Fit For a King, The Elvis Presley Cookbook,* $5.00.

Flicker Button, full figure images of Elvis singing with
guitar and microphone, red rim, ©1956 by Vari-Vue,
3" d **45.00**

Flicker Key Chain, plastic, full figure images of Elvis
singing and holding guitar and microphone, ©1956
by Vari-Vue, 2 x 2¾" **45.00**

Jewelry Picture Strip, perforated strip with 4 identical
black and white glossy images to be applied to cos-
tume jewelry unused, c1956, ⅞ x 4⅛" **18.00**

Wallet Photo, glossy paper, Elvis singing and playing
guitar, facsimile signature, 2½ x 3½" **30.00**

PRINTS

Prints serve many purposes. They can be reproductions of an artist's paintings, drawings, or designs, original art forms, or developed for mass appeal as opposed to aesthetic statement. Much of the production of Currier & Ives fits this last category. Currier & Ives concentrated on genre, urban, patriotic, and nostalgic scenes.

Prints were inexpensive, meaning they could be changed every few years. Instead of throwing them out, they went into storage. Most prints were framed. In today's market, check the frame. It could be more valuable than the print.

References: Jay Brown, *The Complete Guide to Limited Edition Art Prints,* Krause Publications, 1999; Janet Gleeson, *Miller's Collecting Prints and Posters,* Millers Publications, 1997; Martin Gordon, *Gordon's Print Price Annual,* Gordon Art Reference, published annually; Michael Ivankovich, *Collector's Value Guide to Early 20th Century American Prints,* Collector Books, 1998; Susan Theran, *Prints & Photographs: Identification and Price Guide,* Avon Books, 1993.

Periodicals: *Art On Paper,* 39 E 78th St, #501, New York, NY 10021; *InformArt,* 204 Playhouse Corner, Southbury, CT 06488; *Journal of the Print World,* 1008 Winona Rd, Meredith, NH 03253.

Newsletter: *The Illustrator Collector's News,* PO Box 1958, Sequim, WA 98382.

Note: For additional listings see Illustrators, Wallace Nutting, Nutting-Like Photographs, Maxfield Parrish, and Norman Rockwell.

Arms, John Taylor, "Early Morning, North River," etching
and aquatint, wide margins, 2nd state of 2, edition of
100, sgd in pencil lower right, 1921, 9½ x 7½" **$2,500.00**

Bellows, George, "The Irish Fair," lithograph, full margins, edition of 84, sgd and titled in pencil lower margin, sgd by printer "Bolton Brown" in pencil lower
left, 1923, 18⅞ x 21⅜" **925.00**

Benton, Thomas Hart, "Rainy Day," lithograph, full margins, edition of 250, sgd in pencil lower right, published by Associated American Artists, NY, 1938,
8¾ x 13⅜" **1,725.00**

Bone, Muirhead, "Manhattan Excavation," drypoint,
wide margins, 19th state of 19, edition of 151, sgd in
pencil lower right, 1928, 12⅜ x 10¼" **5,750.00**

Burchfield, Charles, "Summer Benediction," lithograph,
full margins, edition of 260, sgd in pencil lower right,
published by Print Club of Cleveland, ink stamp "Lugt
supplement 2049b" on verso, 1951, 12⅛ x 9⅛" **2,500.00**

Cook, Howard, "Engine Room," lithograph, full margins, edition of approx 35 from intended edition of 75, sgd, dated, and numbered "75" in pencil lower margin, 1930, 10 x 12¼" **2,250.00**

Curry, John Steuart, "The Missed Leap," lithograph, wide margins, edition of 250, sgd in pencil lower right, published by Associated American Artists, NY, 1934, 16⅞" x 9¾" **650.00**

Eby, Kerr, "Desert Freight," drypoint, full margins, 4th state of 4, edition of approx 75, sgd and inscribed "imp" in pencil lower right, 1922, 8⅞ x 14" **400.00**

Freeman, Mark, "Thunder Overhead," lithograph, full margins, sgd, titled, and numbered 25/60 in pencil lower margin, 1947, 16 x 20½" **850.00**

Geerlings, Gerald, "Where the West Begins," etching, full margins, 3rd state of 7, proof, sgd, titled, dated, and inscribed "1 only 3rd trial state" in pencil lower margin, 1932, 7⅞ x 9⅛" **2,175.00**

Griggs, Frederick L, "Anglia Perdita," etching, wide margins, 5th state of 5, edition of 50, sgd in pencil lower right, artist's ink stamp "Lugt supplement 760a" on verso, 1921, 10 x 7¼" **1,375.00**

Kent, Rockwell, "Twilight of Man," wood engraving, full margins, edition of 120, sgd in pencil lower right, 1926, 5½ x 8" **1,250.00**

Landeck, Armin, "12th Street Walls," drypoint, full margins, artist's proof, edition of 100, sgd, dated, and inscribed "Trial Print" in pencil lower margin, 1944, 8⅛ x 11⅝" **700.00**

Lozowick, Louis, "Oil Country," lithograph, full margins, edition of less than 200, printed by George Miller, NY, published by the American Artists Group, NY, ink stamp on verso, 1936, 12½ x 7½" **850.00**

Riggs, Robert, "Tank," lithograph, full margins, edition of several sgd impressions, sgd in pencil lower right, c1941, 14" sq **1,000.00**

Sloan, John, "Up the Line, Miss?," etching, full margins, 5th state of 5, edition of 80 from intended edition of 100, sgd, titled, and inscribed "100 proofs" in pencil lower margin, sgd by printer "Ernest Roth" in pencil lower left, 1930, 5½ x 7" **850.00**

Soyer, Raphael, "In Studio," lithograph, full margins, edition of 100, sgd, titled, and inscribed "100 Ed" in pencil lower margin, published by the American Artists School, NY, ink stamp on verso, 1935, 13½ x 9½" **750.00**

Sternberg, Harry, "Blast Furnace #1," etching and aquatint, 1" margins, edition of 250, sgd in pencil lower right, published by Associated American Artists, NY, 1937, 11⅞ x 8⅜" **925.00**

Wilbur, Lawrence N, "The East River," drypoint, full margins, artist's proof, edition of 65, sgd, titled, and inscribed "Artists Proof" in pencil lower margin, 1945, 9⅞ x 14" **575.00**

Wood, Grant, "Honorary Degree," lithograph, 1¼" margins, edition of 250, sgd in pencil lower right, published by Associated American Artists, NY, 1938, 12 x 7" **1,400.00**

PSYCHEDELIC COLLECTIBLES

Psychedelic collectibles describes a group of objects made during the 1960s and 70s that are highly innovative in their use of colors and design. American Indian tribal art, the artworks of Toulouse Lautrec and Alphonse Mucha, the color reversal approach of Joseph Albers, dancer Loie Fuller's diaphanous material, late 19th-century graphics, paisley fabrics, and quilts are just a few of the objects and techniques that are the roots of psychedelic design.

The period is marked by eclecticism, not unity—there were no limits on design. Psychedelic artists and manufacturers drew heavily on new technologies, e.g., inflatable plastic furniture. Coverings such as polyester and vinyl were heavily used.

Peter Max is the most famous designer associated with the psychedelic era. His artwork graced hundreds of objects. Although mass produced, some items are hard to find.

Reference: Susanne White, *Psychedelic Collectibles of the 1960s & 1970s,* Wallace-Homestead, 1990, out of print.

Book, *Love,* Peter Max, hard cover, trees, flowers and profile of pretty girl, 36 pp, black and white text on left, color art on right, based on teachings of Himalayan swamis, William Morrow & Co, NY, ©1970 Peter Max, 5¾ x 5¾" **$30.00**

Inflatable Pillow, Peter Max, clear soft vinyl with colorful butterfly and human heads design on white background, black borders, early 1970s, 15½ x 15½" **30.00**

Paper Dolls, "The Partridge Family, Susan Dey as Laurie," psychedelic design on front cover with diecut window over color photo of Dey, book contains 2 punch-out figures and punch-out headbands, 4 pp with outfits, 2 pp of text and black and white photos of Susan, Artcraft ©1972 Columbia Pictures, 8¼ x 12¼" **80.00**

Postcard, The Doors, Nov 16-18, 1967 concert at the Fillmore Auditorium, Winterland featuring The Doors, Procol Harem, Mt Rushmore, art by Jim Blashfield, Bill Graham #93, Fillmore Auditorium address on reverse, 4⅝ x 7" **35.00**

Poster, "Grateful Dead, Blue Cheer in Concert," Rick Griffin art, driver wearing helmet with crossbones coming out of it and skull and crossbone images on his sunglasses, skeleton heads form top perimeter, sgd lower right, July 11 "Shrine" date, 1980s authorized second printing by Psychedelic Solution of orig late 1960s poster, 15 x 22¾" **20.00**

Grant Wood, "Seed Time and Harvest," lithograph, wide margins, edition of 250, sgd and dated in pencil lower right, published by Associated American Artists, NY, 1937, 7⅜ x 12⅛", $3,500.00.

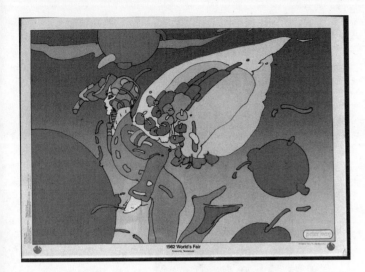

Poster, 1982 Knoxville World's Fair, Peter Max, $75.00.

Poster, The Doors, March 7-11 concerts at the Matrix in San Francisco, art by Victor Moscoso, bright orange, blue, and reddish-pink, photo on back of woman standing in archway, overall thin red lines create hypnotic effect, second printing, ©1967 Neon Rose, 14¼ x 20½" 100.00

Poster, "The Rolling Stones in Concert," Byrd art, Art Nouveau style nude pretty girl holding large billowing sheet behind her shoulders, blank area at bottom for listing concert times, ©1969 Stone Productions Ltd by Tea Lautrec Litho, San Francisco of California, 14 x 21½" 60.00

Program, "The Rolling Stones in Concert," Byrd cover art, Art Nouveau style cover art with nude pretty girl holding large billowing sheet behind her shoulders, 16 glossy pp with black and white and color photos and discography, ©1969 Stone Productions Ltd, 12" sq. 50.00

Scarf, Peter Max, silk, white with black border, colorful astrological design with figures, stars, and symbols in circle around Earth at center, early 1970s, 21" sq 70.00

PUNCHBOARDS

Punchboards are self-contained games of chance that are made of pressed paper and contain holes with a coded ticket inside each hole. After paying an agreed upon amount, the player uses a "punch" to extract the ticket of his choice. Cost to play ranged from 1¢ to $1.00.

Animal and fruit symbols, cards, dominos, and words were used as well as numbers to indicate prizes. While some punchboards had no printing, most contained elaborate letters and/or pictures.

Punchboards initially paid the winner in cash. In an effort to appease the anti-gambling crowd, some punchboards paid off in cameras, candy, cigar, cigarettes, clocks, jewelry, radios, sporting goods, toys, etc.

The 1920s through the 1950s was the golden age of the punchboard. An endless variety were made. Many had catchy names or featured pin-up girls. Negative publicity resulting from the movie *The Flim Flam Man* hurt the punchboard industry.

Value rests with unpunched boards. Most boards sell for $15 to $30, although some have broken the $100 barrier.

Reference: Norman E. Martinus and Harry L. Rinker, *Warman's Paper*, Wallace-Homestead, 1994.

Barrel of Cigarettes, 5¢ per punch, 1930s, 10⅛ x 14½". **$50.00**
Bars & Bells 135.00
Basketball, 1¢ per punch, WH Brady Co, Eau Clair, WI, 1930s, 6½ x 9" 15.00
Best Hand. 40.00
Big Game, fruit symbols 10.00
Bingo, 5¢ per punch 15.00
Bonus Extra, 25¢ per punch, 12¼ x 13" 40.00
California or Bust, 11 x 12" 25.00
Catch No. 100, 5¢ per punch, 2 x 2¾" 8.00
Cigarette Book Cover, 5¢ per punch, illus of Camel, Chesterfield, Lucky Strike, and other cigarette packages, Consolidated, late 1930s, 5 x 5" 30.00
Fast Money 40.00
Full of Tens, cash pay, 25¢ per punch. 25.00
Good Punching, 1950s, 9½ x 9⅞". 35.00
Knockout 100, 5¢ per punch, 2 x 2¾" 8.00
National Winner 20.00
Ninety Percenter, 5¢ per punch 18.00
Odd Pennies, 3¢ per punch, late 1920s, 6¾ x 8⅝" 65.00
Pick a Cherry, cash pay, cherry seals 20.00
Prize Golden Boy Charley, 25¢ per punch, 9 x 8½" 50.00
Professor Charley, 25¢ per punch, Superior, 1946, 9⅞ x 12¼" 15.00
Professor Smokes, 25¢ per punch 45.00
Put & Take, 1¢ to 5¢ per punch, 1920s, 5⅜ x 7" 25.00
Release 100, 5¢ per punch, 2 x 2¾" 8.00
Ship Ahoy, 10¢ per punch, 9 x 15⅜" 125.00
So Sweet 40.00
Speedy Tens 18.00
Take It Easy, colorful, nude 50.00
Tavern Maid, 5¢ per punch, c1938, 9⅝ x 13½" 55.00
War Games, 20" l 265.00

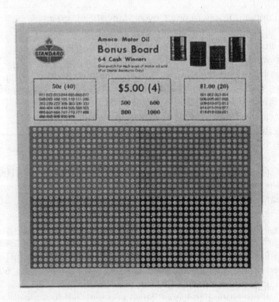

Amoco Motor Oil Bonus Board, Standard Oil, 10⅛ x 9¾", $30.00. Photo courtesy Collectors Auction Services.

PUPPETS

Oriental string puppets date from 1,000 B.C. Clay, leather, and terra-cotta puppets have been found in archeological sites in the Far East, Greece, and Persia.

Puppet shows and theaters were commonplace in Europe by the 18th century. The first marionette toys date from the late 19th century. In 1920 Tony Sarg designed the first commercial marionettes sold in the United States for New York's B. Altman Company. By the 1930s over half a dozen American firms were producing marionette toys.

Television shows from the 1940s and 50s such as *The Howdy Doody Show* and *The Mouseketeer Club* popularized the marionette. Two dozen different companies made marionettes. Hand puppets made their arrived on the toy scene.

Marionettes declined in popularity in the 1960s and 1970s.

Reference: Daniel E. Hodges, *Marionettes and String Puppets Collector's Reference Guide,* Antique Trader Books, 1998.

Finger Puppet, Joan Palooka, rubber puppet with slit in bunting for fingers to make baby move, with birth certificate dated Sep 25, 1952 noting Ham Fisher as godfather and instruction sheet, orig box with Ham Fisher artwork, National Mask and Puppet Corp, Brooklyn, NY, 9" h **$125.00**

Hand Puppet, boxers, pr, soft vinyl heads, fabric handcovers, 1 with charcoal fleshtone head with molded hair and red and white plaid fabric with green dots, other with ivory fleshtone head with molded crewcut and blue and white plaid fabric with red dots, 1960s, 8½" h **75.00**

Hand Puppet, Denny Dimwit, rubber head, striped fabric handcover, orange hands, early 1950s, 8" h **40.00**

Hand Puppet, Donald Duck, hard vinyl head, fabric handcover, printed design on front, yellow back, "Walt Disney Distributing Co" tag, mid-1970s, 11" h **20.00**

Hand Puppet, Dopey, soft vinyl head, fabric handcover, red hat, printed body design, stitched copyright tag, 1960s, 10½" h **25.00**

Hand Puppet, Droop-a-Long Coyote, vinyl head, green hat, light green fabric handcover, purple body with star, gun belt and gun, pink hands and feet, name at bottom, Ideal, ©Hanna-Barbera Prod Inc, 1960s, 9" h **35.00**

Hand Puppet, Knucklehead Smiff, vinyl head and handcover, ©1966 Paul Winchell, 10½" h **40.00**

Hand Puppet, Magilla Gorilla, vinyl head, purple hat with green band, blue fabric handcover with brown body accents, purple bowtie, shorts, and shoes, Ideal, ©Hanna-Barbera Prod Inc, 1960s, 10" h **30.00**

Hand Puppet, Martin and Lewis, painted soft rubber dual-image head, fabric handcover, early 1950s, 9" h **100.00**

Hand Puppet, Mr Ed, soft vinyl head, red and blue fabric handcover, ©1962 Mr Ed Co, 10" h **50.00**

Hand Puppet, Popeye, soft vinyl head, diecut thin vinyl arms, fabric handcover, internal voice box activated by cord loop, Mattel ©1967, 12" h **45.00**

Hand Puppet, Reddi Whip, painted soft vinyl head, striped fabric handcover, 1960s, 8" h **60.00**

Hand Puppet, Ricochet Rabbit, soft vinyl head, purple hat, yellow fabric handcover, green vest with red floral pattern, brown holster with yellow bullets and gun, Ideal, early 1960s, 11" h **45.00**

Ventriloquist Dummy, Danny O'Day, plastic head and hands, stuffed cloth body, with instructions, Juro Novelty Co, 1964, 30" h, $175.00. Photo courtesy Collectors Auction Services.

Hand Puppet, Soupy Sales, vinyl head, fabric handcover, yellow body with red design, classic image of Soupy with text "Soupy Sez Let's Do The Mouse," white felt hands, red tie with white polka dots, ©1965 Gund, 10" h **50.00**

Hand Puppet, Tin Man, Wizard of Oz, soft vinyl head, glossy gray vinyl handcover with "Japan" sticker, late 1960s, 10" h **12.00**

Marionette, Howdy Doody, hard plastic head, hands, and boot bottoms, movable mouth and eyes, cloth body, early 1950s, 15½" h **175.00**

Push Puppet, Jiminy Cricket, hard plastic, green base, silver foil sticker, Kohner Bros, 1960s, 3" h **18.00**

Push Puppet, Mickey Mouse, plastic, red shorts, yellow shoes, blue base, silver foil sticker, Kohner #3990, ©Walt Disney Productions, c1970s, 2½" h **25.00**

Push Puppet, Peter Pan, plastic, Kohner Bros, orig box, 1950s, 4¼" h **85.00**

Ventriloquist Dummy, Charlie McCarthy, composition, movable head and mouth operated by string on back of head, c1938, 12¼" h **80.00**

PURINTON POTTERY

Bernard Purinton founded Purinton Pottery, Wellsville, Ohio, in 1936. The company produced dinnerware and special order pieces. In 1940 Purinton moved to Shippenville, Pennsylvania.

Dorothy Purinton and William H. Blair, her brother, were the company's principal designers. Dorothy designed Maywood, Plaid, and several Pennsylvania German theme lines. Blair is responsible for Apple and Intaglio.

Purinton hand painted its wares. Because of this, variations within a pattern are common. Purinton made a complete dinnerware service including accessory pieces for each of its patterns.

The company utilized an open stock marketing approach. Purinton products were sold nationwide. Some were exported.

In 1958 the company ceased operations, reopened briefly, and then closed for good in 1959. Cheap foreign imports were the principal reason for the company's demise.

References: Jamie Bero-Johnson and Jamie Johnston, *Purinton Pottery,* Schiffer Publishing, 1997.

Newsletter: *Purinton Pastimes,* PO Box 9394, Arlington, VA 22219.

Apple, baker	$45.00
Apple, butter, cov	240.00
Apple, breakfast plate	20.00
Apple, cereal bowl	10.00
Apple, creamer and sugar	30.00
Apple, dinner plate	10.00
Apple, Dutch jug, 2 pint	20.00
Apple, marmalade	55.00
Apple, oil cruet, tall	55.00
Apple, pickle dish	40.00
Apple, relish, 3-part, ceramic handle	35.00
Apple, salad bowl	70.00
Apple, tumbler	10.00
Apple, vegetable, cov	35.00
Autumn Leaves, bowl	5.00
Autumn Leaves, coffee carafe	5.00
Blue Pansy, basket planter	15.00
Blue Pansy, teapot, angle handle, no lid	15.00
Brown Intaglio, beer mug	30.00
Brown Intaglio, butter, cov	40.00
Brown Intaglio, cereal bowl	25.00
Brown Intaglio, chop plate	30.00
Brown Intaglio, cookie jar, square, wooden lid	85.00
Brown Intaglio, creamer and sugar, no lid	20.00
Brown Intaglio, dinner plate	2.00
Brown Intaglio, dish, rect, 3-part	30.00
Brown Intaglio, fruit bowl	45.00
Brown Intaglio, mug	15.00
Brown Intaglio, salt and pepper shakers, pr, mini jug	20.00
Brown Intaglio, sugar, no lid	1.00
Chartreuse, beverage pitcher	25.00
Chartreuse, chop plate	20.00
Chartreuse, spaghetti bowl	175.00
Chartreuse, tumbler	15.00
Cherries, teapot, angle handle	115.00
Daisy, cruet	140.00
Daisy, flour canister	5.00
Daisy, sugar canister	20.00
Fruit, casserole lid	40.00
Fruit, Dutch jug	45.00
Fruit, Kent jug	30.00
Fruit, salt and pepper shakers, pr, miniature	40.00
Fruit, teapot, 4 cup	40.00
Fruit, teapot, 6 cup	42.00
Fruit, tumbler	25.00
Heather Plaid, Dutch jug	25.00
Maywood, candleholder, star	60.00
Maywood, sugar	20.00
Mt Rose, decanter, right handled	50.00
Mt Rose, Rebecca jug	17.00
Mt Rose, teapot, 2 cup	25.00
Mt Rose, teapot, 6 cup	70.00
Normandy Plaid, dinner plate	35.00
Normandy Plaid, Dutch jug, 2 pint	55.00
Normandy Plaid, oil and vinegar cruet	40.00
Normandy Plaid, teapot, 6 cup	40.00
Pennsylvania Dutch, beverage pitcher	500.00
Pennsylvania Dutch, honey jug	45.00
Provincial Fruit, teacup	45.00
Red Ivy, coffeepot	60.00
Red Ivy, creamer and sugar	35.00
Red Ivy, grease jar	65.00
Red Ivy, honey jug	25.00
Red Ivy, Kent jug	20.00
Red Ivy, teapot, 4 cup	55.00
Rooster, cookie jar	80.00
Shooting Star, honey jug	20.00
Shooting Star, vase	10.00
Sunflower, breakfast plate	190.00
Sunny, jardiniere	18.00
Tree, honey jug	110.00
Tulip and Vine, tureen	90.00
Turquoise Intaglio, cup	15.00
Turquoise Intaglio, dinner plate	20.00
Wildflower, honey jug	25.00
Yellow Ivy, Kent jug	15.00

Apple, teapot, 6 cup, 6¼" h, $75.00.

PUZZLES

Puzzles divide into two groups: (1) jigsaw and (2) mechanical. American and English collectors focus primarily on jigsaw puzzles. European collectors love mechanical puzzles.

The jigsaw puzzle first appeared in the mid-18th century in Europe. John Silbury, a London map maker, offered dissected map jigsaw puzzles for sale by the early 1760s. The first jigsaw puzzles in America were English and European imports and designed primarily for use by children.

Prior to the mid-1920s, the vast majority of jigsaw puzzles were cut from wood for the adult market and composition board for the children's market. In the 1920s the diecut, cardboard jigsaw puzzle evolved.

Avoid puzzles whose manufacturer cannot be determined, unless the puzzle has especially attractive graphics or craftsmanship. Diecut cardboard puzzles in excess of 500 pieces remain primarily garage sale items. Some collector interest exists for early Springbok puzzles.

References: *Dexterity Games and Other Hand-Held Puzzles,* L-W Books Sales, 1995; Chris McCann, *Master Pieces: The Art History of Jigsaw Puzzles,* Collectors Press, 1998; Harry L. Rinker, *Antique Trader's Guide to Games & Puzzles,* Antique Trader Books, 1997; Anne D. Williams, *Jigsaw Puzzles,* Wallace-Homestead, 1990, out of print.

Collectors' Clubs: Association of Game and Puzzle Collectors, PMB 321, 197M Boston Post Road West, Marlborough, MA 01752; National Puzzler's League, PO Box 82289, Portland, OR 97282.

Frame Tray, Baby Huey the Baby Giant Puzzle, Tuco Work Shops, Upson Co, Huey floating on his back while 2 ducks sit on his stomach and paddle, 10⅜ x 14⅜" $15.00

Frame Tray, Bonny Braids: Dick Tracy's New Daughter, #7319, Saalfield Publishing, 28 pcs, 10¼ x 11½" **35.00**

Frame Tray, Cheyenne, Milton Bradley, 1957, 14 x 10" **20.00**

Frame Tray, Dragon Wagon, Burger Chef adv, part of Timetraveler Funmeal Fest, 16 pcs, 1980, 9½ x 6⅝" **10.00**

Frame Tray, Li'l Abner, Jaymar Specialty Co, 35 pcs, 14 x 11" **20.00**

Frame Tray, Pip the Piper Frame Tray Puzzle, Whitman Publishing, photo of TV show characters, 17 pcs, 11⅜ x 14½" **15.00**

Frame Tray, Rusty Riley, Sta-N-Place, #18, Built Rite, Warren Paper Products, 24 pcs, 5 hidden animals and clown, ©1949, 12½ x 8¾" **15.00**

Frame Tray, The Big Sport, Dayton Tires adv, tire cartoon of man's head, 18 pcs, 1950s, 9 x 12" **15.00**

Jigsaw, 1933-34 Century of Progress World's Fair (untitled), hand cut, period packaging, 124 pcs, 6¼ x 8½" **35.00**

Jigsaw, A Canadian Landscape, Empire Jig Picture Puzzle, JR Brundage, diecut, 400+ pcs, Empire State Building sketch on box **8.00**

Frame Tray, Cisco Kid, Tip-Top Bread adv, Specialty Adv Service, 36 pcs, orig envelope and guide diagram, ©1953, 7¾ x 8½", $40.00.

Jigsaw, A Colonial Sweetheart, Big 10, Consolidated Paper Box Co, diecut, 280 pcs, orig box, mid-1930s, 10¼ x 15¼" **10.00**

Jigsaw, Acadia National Park, William Hodges, hand cut, photo of ocean surf on rocky Maine coast, 334 pcs, orig box, 1970s, 11 x 8" **35.00**

Jigsaw, Between Two Fires, Jig of the Week, University Distributing Co, #16, diecut, orig box and paper insert, 20 x 15" **12.00**

Jigsaw, Chess Players, Parker Brothers, hand cut, drawing room scene of gentlemen at game table, 200 pcs, 17 figurals, orig box, late 1930s, 14 x 10" **30.00**

Jigsaw, Children of American History Picture Puzzle, All-Fair Puzzle, EE Fairchild Corp, #680, Series 3, diecut, 2-puzzle set, each puzzle 9½ x 6¾" **12.00**

Jigsaw, Circus Picture Puzzles, Parker Brothers, diecut, set of 3, c1925, orig 8 x 11" box **35.00**

Jigsaw, Contentment Cottage, Full o' Cheer Picture Puzzles, hand cut, T Noel Smith country scene of cottage and garden by stream, 132 pcs, 9 figurals, 1930s, 12 x 9" **30.00**

Jigsaw, Dick Tracy Kiddies Jigsaw, Jaymar Specialty Co, diecut, 1950s, orig 8 x 10" box **35.00**

Jigsaw, Dr Kildare Jigsaw Puzzle, #4318, "We are going to call him Jimmy," #2, Milton Bradley, with color portrait for framing, 600+ pcs, guide picture on box, ©1962, 14 x 12" **20.00**

Jigsaw, Granny Goose Picture Puzzle, Madmar Quality Co, Series 318A, diecut, 3-puzzle set, fairy tale themes, Mary LeFetra Russel illus, 12 pcs each puzzle, cardboard box, 1930s, 7⅞ x 9⅞" **40.00**

Jigsaw, Guardians of Liberty, Joseph K Straus, hand cut, WWII scene of battleship and planes passing Statue of Liberty, TJ Slaughter artist, 482 pcs, mid-1940s, 16 x 20" **25.00**

Jigsaw, Home on Leave, Guild Picture Puzzle, Series T, Whitman Publishing Co, #2900, diecut, Hy Hintermeister illus of family relaxing in front of blazing hearth, 300+ pcs, 20 x 15¾" **30.00**

Jigsaw, Hospitality, Interlocking Picture Puzzle, Built-Rite, diecut, 350+ pcs, guide picture on box, 19⅝ x 15⅝" **5.00**

Jigsaw, Johnny's Machine, Little Golden Picture Puzzle, Whitman Publishing, diecut, book cover, guide picture on box, 1949 . . . . **15.00**

Jigsaw, Kaptain Kool and The Kongs, H-G Toys, diecut, 70 pcs, guide picture on box, c1977, 10 x 14" **10.00**

Jigsaw, Lariat Sam Puzzle, EE Fairchild Corp, diecut, 60 pcs, guide picture on box, c1978, 14 x 10" **15.00**

Jigsaw, Mediterranean Harbor (untitled), Parker Brothers, hand cut, young couple watching sunset and sailboats returning to mooring in small Mediterranean village, 1,305 pcs, 148 figurals, orig box, 37 x 29" **175.00**

Jigsaw, Pal O' Mine, Tuco, Upson, diecut, 320 pcs, orig box, c1940, 19½ x 15" **15.00**

Jigsaw, Pandora Picture Puzzles, Bunny Rabbit Series, Selchow & Righter, diecut, set of 3, c1940, orig 11 x 8" box **60.00**

Jigsaw, Portable Appliances, General Electric adv, kitchen scene with appliances, 104 pcs, with guide picture and plastic bag, c1960, 15 x 10½" **30.00**

Jigsaw, Port of Heart's Desire, Milton Bradley, hand cut, kneeling mother holding daughter, 168 pcs, orig box, 1920s, 8 x 10" **40.00**

Jigsaw, Eddie Cantor Jig-Saw Puzzle, Radio Stars Series No. 1, Einson-Freeman, 200+ pcs, 1933, 10 x 14³/₄", $30.00

Jigsaw, Pretty Country Scene, hand cut, box covered with Christmas paper depicting winter village and stagecoach scene, 15¼ x 11¼" **15.00**

Jigsaw, Proof Positive, Perfect Picture Puzzle, Consolidated Paper Box Co, #250-29, diecut, boy photographing dog holding fishing float, 375 pcs, 1950s, approx 19½ x 15½" **6.00**

Jigsaw, Santa Inez Valley, Milton Bradley, #4730, diecut, 568 pcs, orig box, mid-1930s, approx 22 x 16". **10.00**

Jigsaw, Secrets, United Artists, Movie Cut-Ups, #14, Mary Pickford and Leslie Howard, diecut, 304 pcs, wrapped in label from Pippins Cigars reading "It's A Pippins Jig," 10 x 13¼" **40.00**

Jigsaw, Sgt Pepper Band, The Beatles Yellow Submarine, Jaymar Specialty Co, diecut, 650 pcs, orig unopened box, ©1968 King Features Syndicate, 19 x 19" **5.00**

Jigsaw, Silver Moon, DeLuxe Picture Puzzle, Regent Specialties, Inc, diecut, approx 400 pcs, cardboard box, 1930s, approx 16 x 20" **15.00**

Jigsaw, Spoils of War, Madmar Interlox Puzzle, hand cut, Prussian officers enjoying leisurely evening of music and relaxation in European parlor, 755 pcs, orig box, 20 x 16" **65.00**

Jigsaw, Tarzan of the Apes Jig-Saw, Screen Books Magazine, Midwest Distributors, diecut, Johnny Weissmuller on elephant, paper envelope, 10³/₄ x 8½" . . . **150.00**

Jigsaw, The Circus, Dover Jig Picture Puzzle, Milton Bradley, #4728, diecut, 300+ pcs, guide picture on box, 1930s **15.00**

Jigsaw, The Flower Market, RW Bliss, hand cut, Van Vreeland print of Dutch flower market by canal, 200 pcs, period box, c1930, 9 x 12" **25.00**

Jigsaw, The Heart of Nature, hand cut, stream coursing through mountainous countryside, 101 pcs, dated Mar 12, 1933, 7 x 9" **40.00**

AUCTION PRICES – DEXTERITY PUZZLES

Hake's Americana & Collectibles, Hake's 1999 Small Collectibles Sale, a pre-priced, first come–first served sale.

Baby Bear, seated bear holding plate with sausage link, upper paws slotted, place miniature metal knife in 1 and fork in other, Montana merchant adv on bottom, Germany **$72.00**

Caricature Black Man, emb surface, coal-black man's head with white eyes and red lip line, place 5 white balls to form teeth, blue shirt, green ground, "Ike Simons Fine Clothing" adv on bottom, silvered rim, Germany **65.00**

Circus Seals, 4 performing seals, each with ball balanced on snout, place ball in each ball image, US Zone Germany, 1950s **28.00**

Monkey Face, emb surface, head fringed in fur, pellet eyes roll back and forth, place 4 balls into mouth line to form teeth, "Wagner's Home Bread, Detroit" adv on bottom, Germany **40.00**

Nesting Birds, emb surface, 2 bluebirds tending their nest, place 5 balls in nest as eggs, mirror on bottom, probably Germany **48.00**

Smiling Face, rotund man's face with cigar clenched between teeth, face rimmed in yellow sunflower-like leaves on pale blue ground, place 4 balls to form mustache, mirror on bottom, probably German. **58.00**

Tiger Head, close-up head recessed at each eye and at teeth for placement of 4 white balls, mirror bottom, Germany. **48.00**

PYREX

The origins of Corning Glass begin with Amory Houghton and the Bay State Glass Company, East Cambridge, Massachusetts, founded in 1851. In 1854 Houghton established the Union Glass Company, a leading producer of consumer and specialty glass, in Sommerville, Massachusetts. In 1864 Houghton purchased the Brooklyn Flint Glass Works and moved it to Sommerville. In 1868 Houghton moved his company to Corning, New York, and renamed it the Corning Flint Glass Works. After an initial period focused on producing tabletop glassware, the company's main product became hand-blown glass light bulbs.

In 1908 Dr. Eugene C. Sullivan established a research laboratory at Corning. Dr. William C. Taylor joined Sullivan that same year. In the early 1910s Sullivan and Taylor developed Nonex, a heat resistant glass. Dr. Jesse T. Littleton joined Corning around 1912 and began experiments on glass suitable for baking vessels.

Corning Glass created a consumer products business in 1915, launching a 12-piece Pyrex line. In 1920 Corning granted Fry Glass Company, Rochester, Pennsylvania, a license to produce Pyrex cooking glass under its Fry Oven Glass label. The 200-inch glass disk for the Hale telescope at the California Institute of Technology is one of the most famous uses for Pyrex.

References: Barbara Mauzy, *Pyrex*, Schiffer Publishing, 2000; Susan Tobier Rogove and Marcie Buan Steinhauer, *Pyrex By Corning*, Antique Publications, 1993, 1997-98 value update.

Cake Dish, red, 8¼" d **$8.00**
Casserole, cov, Cinderella, oval, 1½ qt **15.00**
Casserole, cov, Constellation, 1½ qt. **15.00**

Mixing Bowls, nesting set of 4, #404 yellow, #403 green, #402 red, and #401 blue, $30.00. Photo courtesy Ray Morykan Auctions.

Casserole, cov, Daisy, oval, divided, 1½ qt.	20.00
Casserole, cov, Empire Scroll, 1½ qt	15.00
Casserole, cov, Golden Bouquet, 1½ qt	15.00
Casserole, cov, Golden Leaf, 4 qt.	25.00
Casserole, cov, Golden Pine, 2 qt	15.00
Casserole, cov, Holiday, 1 qt	15.00
Casserole, cov, Medallion, with candle warmer, 2½ qt	20.00
Casserole, cov, Snowflake, 2½ qt.	20.00
Casserole, cov, Town & Country, 1½ qt	15.00
Chip and Dip Set, Golden Leaf	20.00
Deluxe Buffet Server, with double warmer, 2½ qt.	20.00
Dish, cov, divided, yellow, 1 1/2 qt	15.00
Dish, divided, Town & Country, 1½ qt	15.00
Flameware, beverage server, banded, 4 cup	10.00
Flameware, bowl, tab handles, 8 x 3".	10.00
Flameware, double boiler, #6762, 1 qt.	30.00
Flameware, percolator, #7759, 9 cup	20.00
Flameware, percolator, #7826, 6 cup.	20.00
Flameware, sauce pan, #832-B, 1 qt	10.00
Flameware, teapot, #8126, thin handle	20.00
Flameware, teapot, #8446, metal top and insert	10.00
Hostess Bowl, black with blue opal, 2½ qt.	15.00
Hostess Bowl, rose, 2½ qt.	10.00
Loaf Pan, #213, clear, metal stand with fruit design, 1981	15.00
Loaf Pan, flamingo pink, 1½ qt	8.00
Measuring Cup, 1 cup.	6.00
Meat Platter, 10½ x 14½".	12.00
Mixing Bowls, nesting set of 4, Cinderella, 1½ pt, 1½ qt, 2½ qt, and 4 qt.	35.00
Mug, white and green floral design	3.00
Nesting Bowl, Americana, #404.	12.00
Nesting Bowl, Butterprint, #402.	5.00
Nesting Bowl, Terra, #401	4.00
Nesting Bowl, yellow, #404.	10.00
Nesting Bowl, Yellow Dot, #402.	5.00
Nesting Bowl, yellow stripe, #403	8.00
Nursing Bottle, narrow neck, 4 oz	10.00
Percolator, Flameware, #7824, 4 cup, black handle	15.00
Pie Plate, clear, 10" d	8.00
Platter, white, oval, 13" l	8.00
Refrigerator Dish, Daisy, #503, 1½ qt.	10.00
Refrigerator Dish, Early American, 1½ cup.	5.00
Roasting Pan, cov, aluminum bottom, clear glass top, 15" l	30.00
Serving Dish, divided, Royal Wheat, 1½ qt.	15.00

QUILTS

In the 18th century quilting was used for garments. Quilted curtains and bedcovers also enjoyed widespread popularity. Lap quilts and covers were common during the Victorian era. World War I had a negative effect on quilting as women worked in factories during wartime. A quilting revival occurred in the late 1920s and 1930s. World War II ended this quilting renaissance.

A quilt exhibition at the Cooper Hewitt Museum in New York in 1971 reawakened interest in historic quilts and revitalized the art of quilt making. Many of today's contemporary quilts are done as works of art, never intended to grace the top of a bed.

Beginning in the 1920s, most patchwork quilts were made using silk-screened fabrics. Cherry Basket, Dresden Plate, Grandmother's Flower Garden, Nursery Rhyme blocks, and Sunbonnet Babies were popular patterns of the 1920-30s period.

Periodical: *Quilters Newsletter*, PO Box 4101, Golden, CO 80401.

Collectors' Clubs: American Quilter's Society, PO Box 3290, Paducah, KY 42002; The National Quilting Assoc, Inc, PO Box 393, Ellicott City, MD 21043.

Basket, appliquéd, 16 baskets, multicolor triangular patches, red handles, 66 x 72"	$175.00
Cross, pieced, red and white, 66 x 90".	110.00
Diamond in Square, pieced, blue and white print with some red-striped fabric, 74" sq.	500.00
Floral, trapunto, white on white, applied woven fringe, 82 x 86".	2,500.00
Floral Medallions, pieced, 30 stylized floral medallions in yellow, green, and red on white ground, ice cream cone border, 80 x 92"	500.00
Floral Wreaths, appliquéd, 16 floral wreaths and vining border in red, green, and goldenrod, 84" sq	350.00
Floral Wreaths, appliquéd, pink, green, and yellow on white ground, sawtooth edge, 74 x 76".	425.00
Flower Compotes, pieced, crib size, 30 compotes of flowers in pink, black, and blue calico with white, 32 x 40".	225.00

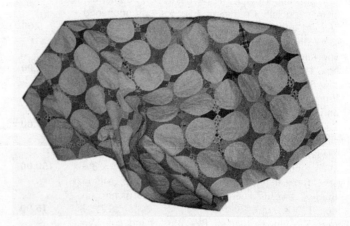

Circles, pieced, white circles on multicolor ground, sgd "Made by Ruth Hill" in corner on back, 75 x 68", $165.00. Photo courtesy Collectors Auction Services.

Oak Leaf Medallions, appliquéd, 10 stylized oak leaf medallions in red and green on white ground, all but 2 have yellow centers, printed label, replaced binding, 64 x 82" 400.00

Stars, pieced, crib or doll size, 30 stars in red and white, 28 x 35" 475.00

Stars, pieced, figural ground reversal design with multicolor printed stars alternating with white star ground, green and white stripe inner borders, green and white scalloped sawtooth border, 74 x 94" 450.00

Stars, pieced, multicolor prints with yellow centers, white ground, blue border, 68 x 76" 400.00

Sunbursts, pieced, 20 sunbursts in yellow, black, blue, and red in blue and orange grid, prints and solids, 68 x 84" 300.00

Victory Quilt, pieced, appliquéd, and embroidered, cotton, white, blue, yellow, and green cotton patches, center depiction of FDR flanked by portraits of Stalin and Churchill and other patriotic symbols, each set within large blue "V," inner field appliquéd and embroidered with American eagle and flags and legends "Remember Pear Harbor" and "Victory Is Our Goal," outer field with Allied flags, red crosses, and blue stars on white ground with star and diagonal line quilting, red, white, and blue-striped border, sgd "Mrs WB Lathouse, Warren, Ohio," c1945, 96 x 76" 5,000.00

Wrench, pieced, crib size, aqua and white, machine pieced, hand-quilted, 26 x 40".................. 125.00

RADIO CHARACTERS & PERSONALITIES

Radio's golden age began in the 1920s and extended through the 1950s. Families gathered around the radio in the evening to listen to a favorite program. American Movie Classics' *Remember WENN* television show provides an accurate portrayal of the early days of radio.

Sponsors and manufacturers provided a wide variety of material ranging from cookbooks to photographs directed toward the adult audience. Magazines devoted exclusively to radio appeared on newsstand racks.

When collecting radio material, do not overlook objects relating to the shows themselves. Props, publicity kits, and scripts are a few examples. Many Big Little Book titles also focused on radio shows.

Reference: Jon D. Swartz and Robert C. Reinehr, *Handbook of Old-Time Radio: A Comprehensive Guide to Golden Age Radio Listening and Collecting*, Scarecrow Press, 1993.

Periodical: *Old Time Radio Digest*, 10280 Gunpowder Rd, Florence, KY 41042.

Newsletter: *Hello Again,* PO Box 4321, Hamden, CT 06514.

Collectors' Clubs: Friends of Vic & Sade, 7232 N Keystone Ave, Lincolnwood, IL 60646; National Lum 'n' Abner Society, #81 Sharon Blvd, Dora, AL 35062; North American Radio Archives, 134 Vincewood Dr, Nicholasville, KY 40356; Pow-Wow (Nabisco Straight Arrow), PO Box 24751, Minneapolis, MN 55424; Radio Collectors of America, 28 Wolfe St, Unit #1, West Roxbury, MA 02132.

Note: For additional listings see Premiums.

Amos 'n Andy, compact, metal case with plastic lid insert, key chain attachment, 2 x 2", $475.00. Photo courtesy Collectors Auction Services.

Allen, Jimmie, Official Jimmie Allen Secret Signal Brass Whistle, flat mouthpiece accented by curved piece of brass with diecut and stamped image of airplane, 1½" l $85.00

Amos 'n Andy, doll, wood, jointed, green jacket, yellow pants, black tie, orange hat, 1930s, 5¾" h 200.00

Amos 'n Andy, poster, "Folks, Help Your Grocer 'An Help Yo' Self Shop Early/Soapy-Rich Rinso," 11 x 14" 110.00

Amos 'n Andy, sheet music, *The Perfect Song/Musical Theme of the Pepsodent Hour,* 8 pp, ©1937, 9 x 12" 25.00

Armstrong, Jack, Dragon's Eye Glow-in-the-Dark Ring, dark green oval stone, white plastic base with crocodile design on each band, 1940.................... 225.00

Armstrong, Jack, Secret Whistling Brass Ring, built-in siren whistle on top, adjustable bands with Egyptian symbols on sides, 1937 .... 55.00

Aunt Jemima Breakfast Club, creamer and sugar, cov, plastic, F&F Mold and Die.................... 150.00

Aunt Jemima Breakfast Club, pancake turner, metal, "Hurray It's Aunt Jemima" on handle 45.00

Benny, Jack, record set, 78 rpm, set of 4, comedy sketches, Top Ten Records, orig cov, 1947.................... 45.00

Burns, Bob, poster, "Laugh with Bob Burns/On the air for Lifebuoy," 10 x 14" 10.00

Little Orphan Annie, book, *Little Orphan Annie and Her Junior Commandos,* Whitman Better Little Book #1457, 1942 .... 35.00

Little Orphan Annie, comic strip book, *Little Orphan Annie Shipwrecked,* Cupples & Leon Co, ©1931 *Chicago Tribune*, 86 pp, hardcover, 7 x 8½" 35.00

Little Orphan Annie, greeting card, Christmas, folder, full color cover art of perplexed Santa with balloon caption wondering on the whereabouts of Annie and Sandy, inner right panels shows Christmas greeting and wishes for coming year 1961 with markers indicating street numbers for Mr and Mrs Harold Gray, 1960, 5 x 7" 75.00

Little Orphan Annie, nodder, painted hollow bisque figure and head mounted to body by inner elastic stringing, yellow hair, red dress with white trim, orange shoes, name incised across shoulders, 3¼" h 50.00

Little Orphan Annie, pin, "Radio Orphan Annie's Secret Society," star design surrounding center portrait, 1934, 1" d 15.00

Little Orphan Annie, Radio Orphan Annie Decoder Badge, center wheel with numerals and logo, orig brass luster, 1935, 1½" d 35.00

McCarthy, Charlie, eggcup, ceramic, black image with blue and red accents on orange and white cup, Japan, 1930s, 2¼" h, 1¾" d **75.00**

McCarthy, Charlie, game, Charlie McCarthy's Radio Party Game, 5 x 7" paper envelope with directions printed on side, complete with litho game card, spinning wheel, and playing pcs, ©1938 Standard Brands, Inc, 1930s. **30.00**

McCarthy, Charlie, greeting card, "Get Well! Talking Card," image of Charlie looking at viewer wearing beret and coat with red carnation, reverse has instructions directing user to pull narrow plastic strip to hear message "Please Get Well," 1930s, 4⅜ x 5½" **15.00**

McCarthy, Charlie, magazine, *Home Movies,* Vol 10, #10, Oct 1943, black and white photo on front showing Bergen threading film reel as Charlie and Mortimer look on, 32pp, 9 x 12" **15.00**

McNeill, Don, pinback button, "Himself Hide-Away Don McNeill," black and white photo and green lettering on white rim, 2¼" d **10.00**

Merman, Ethel, sign, cardboard, *Radio Star* magazine adv, 8½ x 12" **15.00**

Penner, Joe, sheet music, *Don't Never Do-o-o That,* black and yellow cov, ©TB Harms Co, 1934. . . . . . . **20.00**

Smith, Kate, pinback button, "Kate Smith's Philadelphia A&P Party, Nov 4, 1935/Hello Everybody," photo illus, black and red, 2¼" d **25.00**

The Shadow, figure, ceramic, classic pose of Shadow covering face with arm raised holding dagger in hand, mkd under base with blue letter "K" with crown above, 1930-40s, 7" h **175.00**

The Shadow, Glow-in-the-Dark Ring, cream colored plastic, raised full figure Shadow on each band topped by irregular shaped lump of blue plastic representing anthracite coal **200.00**

The Shadow, matchcover, Shadow silhouette, skull, and skeleton holding knife dripping blood on outside, The Shadow with 2 men behind bars and text "Crime Does Not Pay" with "Brought To You By 'blue coal' Dealer" on inside display, 1940s, 1½ x 4½" **50.00**

Helen Broderick and Victor Moore, window card, cardboard, NBC Blue Network, sponsored by National Biscuit Co, 16½ x 11½", $16.00. Photo courtesy Collectors Auction Services.

Just Plain Bill, jigsaw puzzle, Kolynos Dental Cream premium, orig envelope, 150 pcs, 12 x 9", $30.00.

The Shadow, Mystic Keys, cast iron, 1940 . . . . **90.00**

The Shadow, sticker, paper, "Tune In On The Show," used on envelopes sent out by the Blue Coal Co or its dealers, center text "The Shadow For The Best In Thrilling Radio Entertainment/Tune In Every Sunday Afternoon...," red, white, and blue, unused, 1930s, 2 x 2½" **50.00**

The Young Forty-Niners, map, full color US adventure map, illus, ©1933 Colgate-Palmolive-Peet Co, 20 x 31" **75.00**

Winslow, Don, salt and pepper shakers, pr, Winslow and Red Pennington, 1940s **35.00**

AUCTION PRICES – RADIO ORPHAN ANNIE

Past Tyme Pleasures, Absentee Auction, May 22, 1999. Prices include a 10% buyer's premium.

Decoder, "1935 Radio Orphan Annie's SS," brass, silver flash worn off outside rim, 1¼" d **$33.00**

Decoder, "1936 ROA SS," brass, badge-shaped with secret compartment, scuff marks on top of date, 1¼ x 1¾" **33.00**

Decoder, "1939 ROA Secret Code," Mysto-Matic decoder badge, plated brass, "ROA Secret Code–1939," 1¼" d **55.00**

Manual, "Radio Orphan Annie's Secret Society, 1937, Bigger and Better Than Ever," together with Sunburst brass decoder badge, 1937, 1¾ x 2" **83.00**

Pinback Button, celluloid, Annie and "Orphan Annie Loves Red Cross Macaroni," Parisan Novelty Co, Chicago, 1¼" d **55.00**

Shake-up Mug, green beetleware cup with Annie and Sandy, "For Extra Pep 'n Flavor We Drink Chocolate Flavored Ovaltine!," red lid, 1940, 2¾ x 4¾" **55.00**

Shake-up Mug, white beetleware cup with Annie and Sandy, "Leapin' Lizards! For a Swell Summer Drink There's Nothin' Like a Cold Ovaltine Shake-up – Eh, Sandy?," red lid, 1931, 2¾ x 4¾" . . . **44.00**

RADIOS

Marconi, who designed and perfected the transmission and reception instruments that permitted the sending of electrical messages without the use of direct communication, is considered the father of radio. By the end of the 1890s, the Marconi "Wireless" was being used for ship-to-shore communications.

Significant technological developments took place rapidly. By the mid-1920s the cost and quality of radios had reached a point where they were within the budget of most American households. The radio was transformed from a black box with knobs, dials, and a messy battery to a piece of stylized console furniture. The table-top radio arrived on the scene in the 1930s.

Although the transistor was invented in 1927, it was not until the post-1945 period that it was used heavily in the production of radios. Today transistors are a major subcategory of radio collecting. The transistor also made possible the novelty radio, another popular collecting subcategory.

The value of any radio is directly related to its playability. If components, parts, or tubes are missing or if the radio needs repair, its value is lowered by 50% or more. Parts are readily available to restore radios. In fact, the collecting of radio accessories, ephemera, and parts is increasing.

References: Marty Bunis and Robert Breed, *Collector's Guide to Novelty Radios, Bk II,* Collector Books, 1998; John H. Bryant and Harold N. Cones, *The Zenith Trans-Oceanic,* Schiffer Publishing, 1995; Marty and Sue Bunis, *Collector's Guide to Antique Radios, Fourth Edition,* Collector Books, 1997; Marty and Sue Bunis, *Collector's Guide to Transistor Radios, Second Edition,* Collector Books, 1996; Marty Bunis and Robert F. Breed, *Collector's Guide to Novelty Radios,* Collector Books, 1995; Harold Cones and John Bryant, *Zenith Radio: The Early Years, 1919-1935,* Schiffer Publishing, 1997; Chuck Dachis, *Radios By Hallicrafters, 2nd Edition,* Schiffer Publishing, 1999.

David and Betty Johnson, *Guide to Old Radios, Second Edition,* Wallace-Homestead, Krause Publications, 1995; Ken Jupp and Leslie Piña, *Genuine Plastic Radios of the Mid-Century,* Schiffer Publishing, 1998; Ron Ramirez, *Philco Radio: 1928-1942,* Schiffer Publishing, 1993; Norman R. Smith, *Transistor Radios: 1954-1968* (1998), *Zenith Transistor Radios* (1998), Schiffer Publishing; Scott Wood (ed.), *Evolution of the Radio, Vol. 1* (1991, 1994 value update), *Vol. 2* (1993), L-W Books Sales.

Periodicals: *Antique Radio Classified,* PO Box 2, Carlisle, MA 01741; *The Horn Speaker,* PO Box 1193, Mabank, TX 75147.

Newsletter: *Transistor Network,* 32 West Main St, Bradford, NH 03221.

Collectors' Clubs: Antique Wireless Assoc, 59 Main St, Holcomb, NY 14469; Hallicrafters Collectors Assoc, PO Box 521, Morgantown, IN 46160.

Addison, 5F "Theater," red Catalin, yellow grille bars
  and knobs, c1940 . . . . **$1,250.00**
Admiral, 5A32, clock radio, brown plastic, 1952 . . . . **35.00**
Air Castle, 10002, table model, plastic, 1949 . . . . **45.00**
Airline, 84BR-1542A, table model, plastic, 1953 . . . . **45.00**
Arvin, 240P, portable, plastic, center vertical slide rule
  dial, checkered grille, 1949 . . . . **40.00**
Automatic, table model, wood, 3 knobs, AC, 1975 . . . . **40.00**

Bendix, 626C, table model, plastic, 3 knobs, rear hand
  hold, AC/DC, 1947 . . . . **50.00**
Channel Master, Model 6511 "All Transistor Home
  Super," table model, green plastic case **50.00**
Coronado, 43-6951, console, wood, upper slanted slide
  rule dial, cloth grille covering, 4 knobs, AC, 1948 . . . . **75.00**
Crown, TR-380, transistor, coat pocket style, 1959 . . . . **25.00**
Determined Products Ltd, Snoopy on Doghouse, figural,
  white doghouse with red roof, Snoopy handle, ©1958
  United Features Syndicate, 1970s, 6¼" h **50.00**
DeWald, 565, portable, leatherette, inner slide rule dial,
  cloth grille, 1941 . . . . **35.00**
Emerson, 505, portable, leatherette, right front dial, per-
  forated grille, handle, 1946 . . . . **35.00**
Fada, C34, portable, leatherette, inner dial, vertical grille
  bars, flip-open front, 5 tubes, AC, 1939 . . . . **60.00**
Firestone, electric, burlap front with number selections,
  7" h, 10½" w **60.00**
Gabriel Industries, Mickey Mouse Boy's Transistor Radio,
  black plastic with diecut tin Mickey image on front,
  late 1950s, 5" h **75.00**
General Electric, 522, clock radio, ivory plastic, brown
  knob and dial, 1954 . . . . **35.00**
General Electric, K-41, table model, metal, right front
  dial, cloth grille, 2 knobs, AC, 1933 . . . . **85.00**
Hoffman, P-410, transistor, large dial, 1957 . . . . **60.00**
Lloyds, 7S43D, molded plastic and metal, leatherette
  case, orig box with instruction booklet, 7 x 4½ x 2" **20.00**
Magnavox, AM-62, portable, 1962 . . . . **15.00**
Majestic, 511, table model, white Bakelite, blue Catalin
  grille, 1938 . . . . **400.00**
Marx, Tom & Jerry, blue molded plastic, figural Tom head
  and full-size Jerry, black vinyl handle, orig earphones
  and box, ©M-G-M Inc, 1972, 4½" h **75.00**
Mitchell, 1257, clock radio, ivory, 1952 . . . . **40.00**
Motorola, 55B1, portable, electric **40.00**
Motorola, XP34GN, transistor, brown plastic, silver dial,
  Solid State AM/FM, orig box **20.00**
Norelco, L3X76T-01, transistor, 1961 . . . . **25.00**
Nuvox, transistor, olive green plastic, alligator leatherette
  carrying case, c1972, 10 x 4" **55.00**

Fada, Model 1000 "Streamliner," yellow Catalin, 1946, $825.00.
Photo courtesy Collectors Auction Services.

RCA Victor, Model 96-X-1, table model, Art Deco style
  white plastic case, 1939 . . . . **175.00**
Regal, 7251, table model, plastic, 1948 . . . . **50.00**
Sentinel, 284 "wavy grill," yellow Catalin, 1947 . . . . **750.00**
Silvertone, 11, clock radio, white, 1951 . . . . **35.00**
Sparton, 7-46, console, wood, 1946 . . . . **90.00**
Standard Oil/Amoco Gasoline, transistor, gas pump **20.00**
Sylvania, 4P14, transistor, 1961 . . . . **20.00**
Telechron, 8H59, clock radio, red plastic, 1948 . . . . **60.00**
Westinghouse, H-147, brown Bakelite, 1947 . . . . **40.00**
Zenith, G0725, table model, Bakelite, AM/FM, 1950 . . . . **40.00**

RAILROADIANA

Canals and railroads competed head to head for right-of-ways in the 1830s. By the early 1840s, the railroad was the clear victor. The Civil War showed the importance and value of railroads. Immediately following the war, America went on a railroad building spree. The transcontinental railroad was completed. Robber barons such as Gould and Vanderbilt created huge financial fortunes from their railroad activities. A period of mergers occurred as the 19th century came to a close.

The period from the 1880s through the end of World War II is considered the golden age of railroads. The Interstate Highway system, a car in every garage, and the growing importance of air transportation ended the steel highway's dominance. Poor management and a bloated labor force added to its decline.

In the 1970s the federal government became actively involved in railroad management through Amtrak and Conrail. Thousands of miles of track were abandoned. Passenger service, except for a few key corridors, disappeared. Mergers continued into the 1990s. Even Conrail became a victim of consolidation.

References: Stanley L. Baker, *Railroad Collectibles, 4th Edition,* Collector Books, 1990, 1999 value update; Richard C. Barrett, *The Illustrated Encyclopedia of Railroad Lighting, Volume 1: The Railroad Lantern,* Railroad Research Publications, 1994; Barbara J. Conroy, *Restaurant China: An Identification & Value Guide for Restaurant, Airline, Ship & Railroad Dinnerware, Vol. I,* Collector Books, 1998; Brad S. Lomazzi, *Railroad Timetables, Travel Brochures & Posters,* Golden Hills Press, 1995; Richard W. Luckin, *Butter Pat World: Transportation Collector's Guide Book,* RK Publishing, 1995; Richard W. Luckin, *Mimbres to Mimbreño: A Study of Santa Fe's Famous China Pattern,* RK Publishing, 1992; Richard W. Luckin, *Teapot Treasury and Related Items,* RK Publishing, 1987; Everett L. Maffet, *Silver Banquet II: A Compendium on Railroad Dining Car Silver Serving Pieces,* Silver Press, 1990; Douglas W. McIntyre, *The Official Guide to Railroad Dining Car China,* published by author, 1990.

Periodical: *The Main Line Journal,* PO Box 121, Streamwood, IL 60107.

Collectors' Clubs: Key, Lock and Lantern, Inc, PO Box 66, Penfield, NY 14526; Railroadiana Collectors Assoc, PO Box 4894 Diamond Bar, CA 91765.

Blotter, Burlington Route, 100th Anniversary 1849-1949,
  vintage passenger train and diesel streamliner, "Way
  to the Zephyrs and Vista-Domes" **$10.00**

Bond, Minnesota Western Railroad, Thirty Year Gold
  Bond, 30 coupons at both ends, unissued, 1924,
  16½ x 31¼" **60.00**
Book, *Copper Railroad Range,* listing different railroads,
  Tonnage, Conductor, Hancock, Calumet, Dol Bay,
  Laurium, etc, 200 pp, 1947, 8 x 13½" **100.00**
Demitasse Cup and Saucer, Southern Pacific Co, Prairie
  Mountain Wildflower, railroad backstamped **275.00**
Dinner Plate, Baltimore & Ohio Railroad, Shenango
  China, 9¼" d. **75.00**
Napkin, linen, Rock Island Railroad, logo at center,
  acorn and leaves border, dated "3-62" at bottom edge,
  20" sq. **20.00**
Pinback Button, C&O Railroad, Chessie, depicts sleep-
  ing kitten, back inscription "Compliments Of Chessie/
  Chesapeake & Ohio Railway," 1940s **15.00**
Pinback Button, Central Electric Railway Association,
  yellow, black, and white with white center band for
  inking of name, 1928 . . . . **10.00**
Pinback Button, Reading Lines Tour Party, blue and
  white, 1920s **10.00**
Pinback Button, Union Pacific Railroad, "Official Time
  Inspectors," black lettering with red, white, and blue
  shield symbol on white ground, 1920s **10.00**
Playing Cards, B&O Railroad, double deck, "11,000 miles
  of track serving the heart of industrial America," map of
  System, logo, and 2 trains, red, blue borders, 1943 . . . . **45.00**
Poster, "Go Union Pacific Railroad, Hoover Dam and
  Lake Mead," family motorboating in shadow of dam,
  brown cliffs strung with power cables, orange sky,
  green and red lettering, 1950s, 32½ x 24½" **525.00**
Poster, "Norfolk and Western Railway, A Century of
  Service," lavender colored modern engine steams
  above scene of early locomotive surrounded by peo-
  ple dressed in yellow, pink, blue, and red, Leslie
  Ragan, 1938, 28 x 22¼" **800.00**
Sign, "For Fast Dependable Through Service Order and
  ship by Railway Express Agency Incorporated," self-
  framed tin over cardboard, depicts train, cart, and
  early truck, mkd "The HD Beach Co Coshocton, O
  USA," 13¼" h, 19¼" w **1,000.00**
Stock Certificate, Chicago, St Paul, Minneapolis &
  Omaha Railway Co, 20 shares, depicts train in center
  of 2 ovals, brown border, 1922 . . . . **20.00**
Stock Certificate, The Northern Central Railway Co,
  Pennsylvania and Maryland, American Banknote Co,
  orange and white, 1924. . . . . **20.00**
Stock Certificate, The Pennsylvania Railroad Co,
  American Banknote Co, brown and white, 1931 . . . . **20.00**
Ticket Booklet, Burlington Route, carbonized, blue
  cover with logo and streamlined Zephyr, unused,
  1960s, 2¾ x 6½" **5.00**
Ticket Booklet, Missouri Pacific Lines, carbonized, cover
  depicts "Eagles" streamliner, unused, 1960s, 3 x 6½" **8.00**
Ticket Stub, Philadelphia Traction Co, blue paper, black
  inked image of 2 rail passenger cars on front, reverse
  has entwined initials of company printed on black on
  buff. **10.00**
Timetable, Northern Pacific, North Coast Limited, sum-
  mer, white cover with red and black logo, 1937 . . . . **15.00**
Timetable, Pennsylvania Railroad, maroon cover with
  white drawing of train, issued Feb 10, 1963 . . . . **10.00**

REAMERS

A reamer is a device used to extract juice from fruits. Reamers are collected primarily by composition, i.e., ceramic, glass, and metal. In an attempt to bring order to reamer collecting, Ken and Linda Ricketts and Mary Walker assigned reamers an identification number. These numbers are used by most collectors.

There are two basic types of reamers: (1) hand operated and (2) mechanical. Reamers were extremely popular in the period between World War I and II. Only a few were made in the post-1945 period, a result of the popularity of frozen juice concentrates and pre-packaged fruit juices.

In the early 1980s Edna Barnes reproduced a number of old reamers from molds belonging to the Jenkins Glass Company and Imperial Glass Company. These reproductions are marked with a "B" in a circle.

Reference: Gene Florence, *Kitchen Glassware of the Depression Years, Fifth Edition,* Collector Books, 1995, 1999 value update.

Collectors' Club: National Reamer Collectors Assoc, 47 Midline Ct, Gaithersburg, MD 20878.

Federal, glass, crystal, ribbed, horizontal tab handle	**$12.00**
Federal, glass, pink, ribbed, horizontal tab handle	**75.00**
Fry, glass, amber, straight side	**350.00**
Fry, glass, canary vaseline, straight side	**75.00**
Fry, glass, white opalescent, straight side	**12.00**
Germany, ceramic, parrot's head, blue, aqua, orange, yellow, and black on cream ground, 2-pc	**35.00**
Hazel Atlas, glass, Criss Cross, cobalt, 2-cup pitcher and reamer set	**250.00**
Hazel Atlas, glass, Criss Cross, crystal	**10.00**
Hazel Atlas, glass, Criss Cross, pink	**250.00**
Hazel Atlas, glass, pink, tab handle	**38.00**
Hazel Atlas, glass, yellow, 2-cup pitcher and reamer set	**400.00**
Japan, ceramic, clown, white with black, yellow, and orange polka-dots	**250.00**
Japan, ceramic, lemon shaped, 3-pc	**35.00**
Japan, ceramic, pear shaped, 3-pc	**25.00**
Japan, ceramic, raised grapevine dec, 2-pc pitcher and reamer set	**25.00**
Japan, ceramic, tab handle, flower and leaves dec	**10.00**
Japan, ceramic, white, diamond-point and floral dec, 2-pc	**25.00**

McKee, glass, white, emb "Sunkist," $10.00. Photo courtesy Ray Morykan Auctions.

Jeannette, glass, Jennyware, crystal	**10.00**
Jeannette, glass, dark jadite	**40.00**
Jeannette, glass, Jennyware, pink	**100.00**
Jeannette, glass, Jennyware, ultramarine	**125.00**
Jeannette, glass, light jadite	**35.00**
MacBeth-Evans, glass, white, "MacBeth-Evans Glass Co, Charleroi, Pa"	**200.00**
MacBeth-Evans, glass, clambroth, "MacBeth-Evans Glass Co, Charleroi, Pa"	**300.00**
Proctor Silex, electric, 8" h	**5.00**
"Radnt," glass, crystal	**100.00**
Sunkist, glass, caramel	**375.00**
Sunkist, glass, chalaine blue	**275.00**
Sunkist, glass, Crown Tucsan, milk glass	**350.00**
Sunkist, glass, light jadite	**45.00**
Sunkist, glass, white milk glass, block letters	**110.00**
US Glass, glass, green, slick handle, grapefruit	**475.00**

RECORDS

Thomas Edison is credited with the invention of the phonograph. In 1877 Edison demonstrated a phonograph he designed that played wax cylinder records. Although patenting his phonograph in 1878, Edison did not pursue the concept, preferring instead to concentrate on further development of the light bulb.

Alexander Graham Bell created the graphaphone, successfully marketing it by the end of the 1880s. Emile Berliner developed the flat disc phonograph in 1900. Discs replaced cylinders as the most popular record form by the end of the decade.

Initially records were played at a speed of 78 revolutions per minute (rpm). 45 rpm records became the dominant form in the late 1940s and 50s, eventually being replaced by the 33⅓ rpm format. Most phonographs, more frequently referred to as record players in the post-1945 period, could play 33⅓, 45, and 78 rpm records. The arrival of the compact disc in the early 1980s made the turntable obsolete.

Most records have relatively little value, especially those without their dust jackets or album covers. The more popular a song title, the less likely it is to have value. Many records were released in several pressings. Find out exactly which pressing you own. If a record is scratched or warped, its value disappears.

References: Mark Brown, Thomas Conner and John Wooley, *Forever Lounge,* Antique Trader Books, 1999; Les Docks, *American Premium Record Guide, 1900-1965: Identification and Value Guide to 78s, 45s and LPs, Fifth Edition,* Books Americana, Krause Publications, 1997; Anthony J. Gribin and Matthew M. Schiff, *The Complete Book of Doo-Wop,* Krause Publications, 2000; Fred Heggeness, *Goldmine Country Western Record & CD Price Guide,* Krause Publications, 1996; Fred Heggeness, *Goldmine's Promo Record & CD Price Guide, 2nd Edition,* Krause Publications, 1998; Ron Lofman, *Goldmine's Celebrity Vocals,* Krause Publications, 1994; Vito R. Marino and Anthony C. Furfero, *The Official Price Guide to Frank Sinatra Records and CDs,* House of Collectibles, 1993; R. Michael Murray, *The Golden Age of Walt Disney Records: 1933-1988,* Antique Trader Books, 1997.

Tim Neely, *Goldmine Christmas Record Price Guide,* Krause Publications, 1997; Tim Neely, *Goldmine Jazz Album Price Guide,* Krause Publications, 2000; Tim Neely, *Goldmine Price Guide to Alternative Records,* Krause Publications, 1996; Tim Neely (ed.), *Goldmine Price Guide to 45 RPM Records,* Krause Publications,

1996; Tim Neely, *Goldmine Record Album Price Guide,* Krause Publications, 1999; Tim Neely, *Goldmine Standard Catalog of American Records,* Krause Publications, 1998; Tim Neely and Dave Thompson, *Goldmine British Invasion Record Price Guide,* Krause Publications, 1997; Jerry Osborne, *Rockin' Records,* Antique Trader Books, 1998; Jerry Osborne, *The Official Guide to the Money Records,* House of Collectibles, 1998; Jerry Osborne, *The Official Price Guide to Country Music,* House of Collectibles, 1996; Jerry Osborne, *The Official Price Guide to Movie/TV Soundtracks & Original Cast Albums, Second Edition,* House of Collectibles, 1997; Jerry Osborne, *The Official Price Guide to Records, 14th Edition,* House of Collectibles, 2000.

Martin Popoff, *Goldmine Heavy Metal Record Price Guide,* Krause Publications, 2000; Ronald L. Smith, *Goldmine Comedy Record Price Guide,* Krause Publications, 1996; Charles Szabala, *Goldmine 45 RPM Picture Sleeve Price Guide,* Krause Publications, 1998; Neal Umphred, *Goldmine's Price Guide to Collectible Jazz Albums, 1949-1969, 2nd Edition,* Krause Publications, 1994; Neal Umphred, *Goldmine's Price Guide to Collectible Record Albums, 5th Edition,* Krause Publications, 1996.

Periodicals: *DISCoveries Magazine,* PO Box 1050, Dubuque, IA 52004; *Goldmine,* 700 E State St, Iola, WI 54990.

Collectors' Clubs: Assoc of Independent Record Collectors, PO Box 222, Northford, CT 06472; International Assoc of Jazz Record Collectors, PO Box 518, Wingate, NC 28174.

Acuff, Roy, *The Voice of Country Music,* LP, Capitol #ST-2276, 1965 .... $12.00
Alabama, *Wild Country,* LP, Plantation #PLP044, 1981 ...... 8.00
Allen, Steve, *Let's Dance,* LP, Coral #CRL0-57028, 1956 ..... 10.00
Amboy Dukes, *Marriage On the Rocks,* LP, Polydor #24-4012, 1970 .... 8.00
Andrews Sisters, *Club 15,* LP, Decca #DL-5155, 1950 ... 12.00
Arnold, Eddy, *Cattle Call,* LP, RCA Victor #LPM-2578, 1962 .... 8.00
Astaire, Fred, *Shoes With Wings,* LP, MGM #E03413, 1956 .... 15.00
Astro Jets, *Boom a Lay/Hide and Seek,* 45 rpm, Imperial #5760, 1961 .... 15.00
Autry, Gene, *Gene Autry Sings,* LP, Harmony #HS07399, 1968 .... 5.00
Baez, Joan, *From Every Stage,* LP promo, A&M #SP-8375, 1987 .... 50.00

Baker, LaVern, *Play It Fair/Lucky Old Sun,* 45 rpm, Atlantic #1075, 1956 .... 20.00
Bandits, *The Electric 12 String,* LP, World Pacific #T-1833, 1964 .... 6.00
Baxter, Les, *The Sacred Idol,* LP, Capitol #ST-1293, 1960 ..... 25.00
Beach Boys, *Surfin' Safari/409,* 45 rpm, Capitol #4777, 1962 .... 60.00
Beck, Jeff, *Wired,* LP, Epic #HE-43849, 1982 .... 12.00
Bee, Molly, *Swingin' Country,* LP, MGM #SE-4423, 1967 ..... 8.00
Bennett, Tony, *Because of You,* LP, Columbia #CL-6221, 1952 .... 25.00
Berry, Chuck, *Maybellene/Wee Wee Hours,* 45 rpm, Chess #1604, 1955 .... 35.00
Cadillacs, *Zoom/You Are,* 45 rpm, Josie #792, 1959 .... 20.00
Carpenters, *We've Only Just Begun/All of My Life,* 45 rpm, Vistone #2055, 1968 .... 12.00
Coachmen, *Mr Moon/Nothing at All,* 45 rpm, MMC #0110, blue vinyl, 1965 .... 40.00
Dee Jayes, *Bongo Beach Party/Mr Bongo Man,* Highland #1031, 1962 .... 30.00
Drifters, *Up On the Roof,* LP, Atlantic #8073, 1963 .... 50.00
Earth Wind & Fire, *Evil/Clover,* Columbia #45888, 1973 ...... 2.00
Euphoria, *Lost In Trance,* LP, Rainbow #1003, 1970s 85.00
Flatt & Scruggs, *Foggy Mountain Banjo,* LP, Columbia #CS-8364, 1961 .... 10.00
Four Imperials, *My Girl/Teenage Fool,* Chant #10067, 1958 .... 45.00
Frawley, William, *The Old Ones,* LP, Dot #DLP-3061, 1957 .... 15.00
Genesis, *A Trick of the Tail,* LP, Mobile Fidelity #MFSL-062, 1981 .... 10.00
Greenbaum, Norman, *I.J. Foxx/Rhode Island Red,* Reprise #0956, 1970 .... 3.00
Greensleeves, Eddie, *Humorous Folk Songs,* LP, Cameo #C-1031, 1963 .... 6.00
Haley, Bill & His Comets, *Rock Around the Clock,* LP, Decca #DL-8225, 1960 .... 15.00
Hi-Tones, *Raunchy Sounds,* LP, Hi #HL-31011, 1963 .... 6.00
Homer & Jethro, *They Sure Are Corny,* LP, King #639, 1959 .... 50.00
Jackson 5, *ABC/The Young Folks,* Motown #1163, 1970 ...... 5.00
Jacobs, Hank, *So Far Away,* LP, Sue #LP-1023, 1964 .... 35.00
Jones, Spike, *Dinner Music For People Who Aren't Very Hungry,* LP, Verve # MGV-4005, 1957 .... 15.00
Kai, Lani, *Beach Party/Little Brown Girl,* Keen #2023, 1958 .... 25.00
Kingsmen, *More Great Sounds,* LP, Wand #WD-659, 1964 .... 8.00
Lee, Peggy, *Benny Goodman and Peggy Lee,* LP, Columbia #CL-6033, 1949 .... 18.00
Lewis, Jerry Lee, *By Request,* LP, Smash, #MGS-27086, 1966 .... 6.00
Liberace, *Piano,* LP, Advance #7, 1951 .... 10.00
Little Feat, *Willin'/Oh, Atlanta,* Warner Bros #8420, 1977 .... 2.00
Magic Lantern, *Country Woman,* Charisma #100, 1972 ...... 5.00
McCartney, Paul, *Jet/Let Me Roll It,* Apple #1871, 1974 ...... 5.00
Monkees, *Valleri/Tapioca Tundra,* Colgems #1019, 1968 ..... 8.00
Nelson, Willie, *Texas In My Soul,* LP, RCA Victor #LPM-3937, 1968 .... 30.00
Nino & The Ebb Tides, *I Love Girls/Don't Look Around,* Recorte #413, 1959 .... 85.00
O'Brian, Hugh, *TV's Wyatt Earp Sings,* LP, ABC Paramount #ABC-203, 1957 .... 25.00

Bananarama, *Venus/White Train,* **45 rpm, London Records Ltd, 1986, $3.00.**

Elmo & Patsy, *Grandma Got Run Over By a Reindeer,* **45 rpm, CBS, 1984, $2.00.**

Ray-Vons, *Judy/Regina,* Laurie #3248, 1964 . . . . **60.00**

Righteous Brothers, *Back to Back,* LP, Philles #PHLP-4009, 1966 . . . . **6.00**

Shangri-Las, *Leader of the Pack,* LP, Red Bird #20-101, 1965 . . . . **50.00**

Talking Heads, *Live at the Roxy,* LP, Warner Bros #WBMS-104, 1979 . . . . **12.00**

Wells, Kitty, *Country Music Time,* LP, Decca #DL-4554, 1964 . . . . **6.00**

RED WING POTTERY

The Red Wing Stoneware Company, Minnesota Stoneware Company (1883-1906), and North Star Stoneware Company (1892-96) were located in Red Wing, Minnesota. David Hallem founded the Red Wing Stoneware Company in 1868. By the 1880s Red Wing was the largest American producer of stoneware storage vessels.

In 1894 the Union Stoneware Company was established as a selling agency for Minnesota, North Star, and Red Wing. Minnesota and Red Wing bought out North Star in 1896. In 1906 production was merged into one location and the Red Wing Union Stoneware Company created. The company made stoneware until introducing an art pottery line in the 1920s. During the 1930s Red Wing created several popular lines of hand-painted dinnerware that were sold through department stores, gift stamp redemption centers, and Sears.

In 1936 the company became Red Wing Potteries, Inc. Stoneware production ended in 1947. In the early 1960s the company began producing restaurant china. Financial difficulties that began in the 1950s continued. Red Wing ceased operations in 1967.

References: Dan and Gail DePasquale and Larry Peterson, *Red Wing Collectibles,* Collector Books, 1985, 1997 value update; B. L. Dollen, *Red Wing Art Pottery,* Collector Books, 1997; B. L. and R. L. Dollen, *Red Wing Art Pottery, Book II,* Collector Books, 1998; Ray Reiss, *Red Wing Art Pottery: Including Pottery Made for RumRill,* Property Publishing, 1996; Ray Reiss, *Red Wing Art Pottery Two,* Property Publishing, 2000; Ray Reiss, *Red Wing Dinnerware,* Property Publishing, 1997; Gary and Bonnie Tefft, *Red Wing Potters & Their Wares, Third Edition,* Locust Enterprises, 1996.

Collectors' Clubs: Red Wing Collectors Society, 2000 W Main St, Ste 300, Red Wing, MN 55066; The RumRill Society, PO Box 2161, Hudson, OH 44236.

Bob White, bread tray, 24" l **$100.00**
Bob White, butter, cov 75.00
Bob White, butter warmer, cov 60.00
Bob White, creamer and sugar 75.00
Bob White, hors d'oeuvres bird 65.00
Bob White, lazy susan 90.00
Bob White, plate, 10" d 25.00
Bob White, platter, 13" l 38.00
Bob White, relish tray, 3-pc 50.00
Bob White, salad bowl, 12" d 65.00
Bob White, tumbler 200.00
Candlesticks, pr, #397, white, 5¼" h 20.00
Compote, M5007, blue-gray, 4½" h 8.00
Ewer, #882, green, 4" h 12.00
Ewer, #1012, white, 7" h 18.00
Ewer, #1187, blue, 11¾" h 35.00
Ewer, #1510, brown, 7" h 10.00
Ewer, #1510, green, 7" h 20.00
Fondoso, batter pitcher 65.00
Fondoso, batter set try 50.00
Fondoso, casserole, 8½" d 75.00
Fondoso, chop plate, 14" d 35.00
Fondoso, coffeepot 50.00
Fondoso, coffee server 45.00
Fondoso, console bowl 40.00
Fondoso, cookie jar 50.00
Fondoso, creamer and sugar, large 65.00
Fondoso, cup and saucer 30.00
Fondoso, custard cup 30.00
Fondoso, dessert cup, ftd, 4" d 15.00
Pepe, beverage server, with lid 90.00
Pepe, bread tray, 24" l 75.00
Pepe, butter 80.00
Pepe, casserole, 4 qt 75.00
Pepe, creamer and sugar 75.00
Pepe, cruet, with stopper 160.00
Pepe, cup and saucer 30.00
Pepe, dish, 6" d 30.00
Pepe, gravy boat, cov 60.00
Pepe, lazy susan 90.00
Pepe, mug 65.00
Planter, #431, black, 3½" h 5.00
Planter, #1017, white, 3½" h 25.00
Planter, #1136, brown, 4½" h 40.00
Random Harvest, coffeepot, cov 30.00
Random Harvest, cup and saucer 6.00
Random Harvest, dessert bowl, 6¾" d 5.00
Random Harvest, dinner plate, 10¾" d 12.00
Random Harvest, salad plate, 8½" d 8.00
Random Harvest, soup bowl 10.00
Random Harvest, vegetable, oval 20.00
Rose Bowl, #276, gray, 3¼" d 10.00
RumRill, vase, #668, turquoise, 8½" h 55.00
Tampico, beverage server, cov 90.00
Tampico, butter, cov 80.00
Tampico, casserole, cov 75.00
Tampico, coffee cup 30.00
Tampico, creamer and sugar 75.00
Tampico, gravy boat, with lid 55.00
Tampico, pitcher, 1½ qt 70.00
Tampico, relish dish 50.00
Tampico, salad bowl, 12" d 65.00
Tile, "Minnesota Centennial, 1858-1958," green 45.00
Town and Country, bean pot 160.00

Town and Country, casserole **65.00**
Town and Country, casserole, individual **30.00**
Town and Country, creamer and sugar **35.00**
Town and Country, cruet, cov **40.00**
Town and Country, cup and saucer **25.00**
Town and Country, milk pitcher **65.00**
Town and Country, mixing bowl, 9" d **90.00**
Town and Country, mug **50.00**
Town and Country, mustard jar **50.00**
Town and Country, plate, 11" d **15.00**
Town and Country, relish tray, 7" l **25.00**
Town and Country, salad bowl, 13" d **55.00**
Town and Country, salt and pepper shakers, pr, large **45.00**
Town and Country, syrup pitcher **60.00**
Town and Country, teapot **110.00**
Tray, #1040, pink, 8 x 12" **8.00**
Vase, #157, green and white, 9½" h **45.00**
Vase, #402, red, 7¼" h **20.00**
Vase, #505, white, 7½" h **18.00**
Vase, #947, white, 10" h **10.00**
Vase, #1120, deer, maroon, 7¼" h **30.00**
Vase, #1202, purple, 9¼" h **25.00**
Vase, #1210, white, 10" h **30.00**
Vase, #1216, white, 8" h **12.00**
Vase, #1356, gray, 7½" h **20.00**
Vase, #1361, yellow, 8" h **18.00**
Vase, M1610-7½, green, 6" h **15.00**
Vase, elephant handles, 6" h **65.00**

REGAL CHINA

Regal China Corporation, Antioch, Illinois, was established in 1938. In the 1940s, Regal was purchased by Royal China and Novelty Company, a distribution and sales organization. Royal used Regal to make the ceramic products that it sold.

Ruth Van Tellingen Bendel designed Snuggle Hugs in the shape of bears, bunnies, pigs, etc., in 1948. She also designed cookie jars, other figurines, and salt and pepper shaker sets.

Regal did large amounts of decorating for other firms, e.g., Hull's Red Riding Hood pieces. Regal has not sold to the retail trade since 1968, continuing to operate on a contract basis only. In 1976 it produced a cookie jar for Quaker Oats; 1983 products include a milk pitcher for Ovaltine and a ship decanter and coffee mugs for Old Spice. Regal currently is a wholly owned subsidiary of Jim Beam Distilleries.

Reference: Harvey Duke, *The Official Price Guide to Pottery and Porcelain, Eighth Edition,* House of Collectibles, 1995.

Canister Set, Blue Willow, square jars, rounded covers,
  large flour smaller sugar, tea, and coffee **$175.00**
Cereal Canister, Old MacDonald **200.00**
Cinnamon Spice Jar, Old MacDonald **150.00**
Cloves Spice Jar, Old MacDonald **150.00**
Cookie Jar, Diaper Pin Pig **400.00**
Cookie Jar, Humpty Dumpty **300.00**
Cookie Jar, Quaker Oats **150.00**
Creamer, Alice in Wonderland, White Rabbit **400.00**
Creamer, Rooster **85.00**
Flour Canister, Old MacDonald **200.00**
Grease Jar, pig **150.00**

Nutmeg Spice Jar, Old MacDonald **150.00**
Popcorn Canister, Old MacDonald **275.00**
Salt and Pepper Shakers, pr, Alice, white and gold **500.00**
Salt and Pepper Shakers, pr, A-Nod to Abe **350.00**
Salt and Pepper Shakers, pr, boy and girl **75.00**
Salt and Pepper Shakers, pr, milk churns **40.00**
Salt and Pepper Shakers, pr, pig, 1 pc **100.00**
Snuggle Hugs, boy and dog, white **65.00**
Snuggle Hugs, Mary and Lamb, yellow, black tail **45.00**
Tea Canister, Old MacDonald **250.00**
Teapot, cov, duck head on lid **275.00**

ROBOTS

Robot toys of the late 1940s and early 1950s were friction or windup powered. Many of these lithographed tin beauties were made from recycled material. By the mid-1950s, most robots were battery powered. Japanese manufacturers produced several hundred models. Model variations are common, the result of manufacturers freely interchanging parts. Plastic replaced lithographed tin as the material of choice in the late 1960s.

Robot models responded to changing Space Age motifs. The Japanese Atomic Robot Man, made between 1948 and 1949, heralded the arrival of the Atomic age. Movies, such as *Destination Moon* (1950) and *Forbidden Planet* (1956), featuring Robbie the Robot, provided the inspiration for robot toys in the early and mid-1950s. Space theme television programs, e.g., *Lost in Space* (1965-1968), played a similar role in the 1960s. Ideal and Marx entered the toy robot market in the late 1960s.

Markings can be confusing. Many of the marks are those of importers and/or distributors, not manufacturers. Cragston is an importer, not a maker. Reproductions and fantasy items are a major problem in the late 1990s. Because of the high desirability and secondary market cost of robots such as Mr. Atomic ($10,000+), modern copies costing between $250 and $750 new are being made. Inexpensive Chinese and Taiwanese robots made in shapes that never existed historically are flooding the market.

References: Jim Bunte, Dave Hallman and Heinz Mueller, *Vintage Toys: Robots & Space Toys,* Antique Trader Books, 2000; Maxine A. Pinsky, *Marx Toys: Robots, Space, Comic & TV Characters,* Schiffer Publishing, 1996.

Periodicals: *Toy Shop,* 700 E State St, Iola, WI 54990; *Toy Trader,* PO Box 1050, Dubuque, IA 52004.

Answer Game Machine, Anico, battery operated, multicolor with keys 1 through 10, digital display, and
  control levers, orig box, 15" h **$400.00**
Answer Game Machine Robot, Idnida, tin, battery
  operated, orig box, 14½" h **550.00**
Astronaut, Daiya, metallic blue, yellow, silver, and red
  details, clear-domed helmet, air tanks, rifle with light
  and sounds, arm-lifting and walking movements, 14" h . . **1,100.00**
Atomic Man Robot, gray-green rect body, cylindrical
  head with open eyes and litho meters, silver details,
  cast arms, red feet, clockwork walking movement,
  orig box, 5" h **1,600.00**
Atom Robot, Yonezawa, friction, silver with red, blue,
  and yellow details, bump-and-go action, orig box **750.00**

Hi-Bouncer Moon Scout, Marx, battery operated, litho tin torso, plastic arms, orig box, 1960s, 11¹/₂" h, $900.00.

Chief Robot Man, Yoshiya, silver with green plastic chest, red metal arms, cream and red turning head with spinning antenna, directional movement, "ea-ea" sound, 12" h.............................. 1,500.00

Chief Smoky Robotman, Yoshiya, battery operated, silver and red, stop-and-go action, clicking sound, smoke comes out of head, orig box, 12" h................ 3,250.00

Conehead Robot, Yonezawa, metallic blue with red feet and arms, sparking eyes, rubber ears, cone-tip, and flat wrench arms, walking movement, 8¹/₂" h......... 3,250.00

Cragstan Astronaut, Yonezawa, friction, red with blue, white, and yellow details, walks, moves arms, clank clank sound, 9¹/₂" h........................... 1,250.00

Cragstan Robot, Yonezawa, tinplate, battery operated, silver body, red arms and chest, domed clear plastic head with visible mechanism, bump-and-go action, orig box, 10¹/₂" h.............................. 1,725.00

Cragstan Talking Robot, Yonezawa, red and white plastic, plastic wing-ears, control room in eyes, speaker in chest, orig box, 11" h........................... 1,500.00

Dino-Robot, Horikawa, battery operated, dark green with silver and red details, opening head with plastic monster head, opening mouth and light, walking action, orig box, 11" h......................... 1,500.00

Directional Robot, Yonezawa, battery operated, light metallic blue, lighted turning head, stop-and-go action, orig box, 11" h......................... 1,500.00

Door Robot, Alps, battery operated, light metallic blue, spinning clear plastic head, rotating color wheel in mouth, litho details, opening door in chest, rubber claws, remote controlled walking action, 9¹/₂" h....... 2,500.00

Dux Astroman, Germany, battery operated, green plastic with clear green chest showing gears and lights, clear helmet, antenna, white head, remote controlled bending, lifting, and walking action, orig box, 12" h....... 1,725.00

Fighting Robot, Horikawa, battery operated, metallic green with light on head, lit and moving firing gun, walking action, orig box, 11¹/₄" h.................. 1,150.00

Gear Chest Robot, tin, battery operated, gray, full view gear in chest, quick/slow/stop dial on head, 2 antennae on shoulders, cracks to chestplate, 11¹/₂" h........ 165.00

Giant Sonic Robot, Masudaya, battery operated, red with black head and arms, blue, yellow, and silver details, light-up face, forward and turning movement, train whistle sound from speaker in chest, orig box, 15" h 11,500.00

High-Wheel Robot, Yoshiya, battery operated, metallic blue with multicolor gears in torso, light-up face and chest, claw hands, adjustable antenna, remote control, orig box, 8³/₄" h 700.00

Inter-Planet Space Captain, Naito Shoten, blue helmet with teeth, cream body, black legs, red feet, rifle coils, clockwork walking action, orig box, 8" h........... 7,500.00

Lantern Robot, Linemar, battery operated, gray with litho radar, rivets, and other details, hinged hand with tray for baby powder to produce smoke, light-up eyes and red lantern, remote controlled walking action, orig box, instructions, and price tag on arm, 7³/₄" h........ 7,500.00

Mechanical Robot, Linemar, metallic blue with red lining and details, easel supports, coil antenna, flat arms, clockwork walking action, 6" h 300.00

Mighty Robot, N, litho tin, windup, blue-green with silver, red, and yellow details, sparking mechanism behind screen, clockwork walking movement, 1950s, 5¹/₂" h 100.00

Mighty Robot, Yoshiya, metallic blue with red chest and plastic arms, lighted clear plastic head with gears, bump-and-go action, 12" h....................... 4,000.00

Mr Atom Walking Robot, Advance Doll & Toy Co, red and gray plastic, battery operated, orig box, 18" h....... 500.00

Mr Mercury, Yonezawa/Marx, battery operated, gold body, gray arms and legs, red feet, domed head, control room in face, remote control for bending, lifting, and walking movements, orig box, 13" h............. 1,700.00

Mr Mercury, Yonezawa/Marx, battery operated, pink body with blue arms, black legs, red feet, domed head with control room in face, remote control for bending, lifting, and walking movements, 13" h 700.00

Mr Robot the Mechanical Brain, Alps, silver with black details, battery operated light-up hands, clockwork walking mechanism, orig box with instructions, 8" h ... 1,500.00

Non-Stop Lavender Robot, Masudaya, lilac with bright colored details, light-up face, red claws, walking and turning action, 14¹/₂" h 3,500.00

Offical Lost In Space Robot, AHI, silver plastic, stop-and-go action, orig box, 10" h 200.00

Planet Robot, KO, windup, walks forward, sparking action, with orig box and inserts, 1970s, 9" h....... 350.00

Planet Robot, Yoshiya, battery operated, metallic blue with red claws and feet, light-up head, spinning antenna, remote control, orig box, 9¹/₄" h........... 1,500.00

R-35 Robot, Linemar, battery operated, silver with multicolor details, blue cylindrical head, light-up eyes, red claws, remote control walking action, 7¹/₂" h........ 250.00

R-35 Robot, Modern Toys, litho tin, battery operated, walks forward and backward, arms swing, eyes light up, 1950s, 7¹/₂" h............................. 525.00

Radicon Robot, Masudaya, steel gray textured finish, red, eyes, spinning antenna, gauge, and blue light in chest, radio remote control forward, backward, and turning movement, 14½" h **8,000.00**

Robotank Z, Nomura, gray with multicolor detailing, red plastic arms, clear head, Japanese recordings, firing guns, and movements, orig box, 10½" h **400.00**

Robot Lilliput, KT, Occupied Japan, orange rect body, square head, red, black, and white details including eyes, eyebrows, teeth, meters, and rivets, articulated arms, clockwork walking movement, 6" h **6,000.00**

Robot St-1, Germany, pressed steel, windup, silver finish with red accents, coil antenna, walks, sparking action, 1950s, 7" h **450.00**

Smoking Spaceman, Linemar, battery operated, metallic gray with swirling light on head, light-up eyes, smoking action, walking movement, orig box, 12" h **1,600.00**

Space Commando, Nomura, gray with red details, walking mechanism, orig box, 7½" h **3,100.00**

Space Commando Space Man, Sonsco, blue-gray with yellow and red details, white helmet, antenna, remote control walking action, orig box, 7½" h **4,600.00**

Space Conqueror Man of Tomorrow, Daiyai, blue with yellow details, clear helmet, red laser, air tanks, walking, lifting, and firing movement, orig box, 11" h **1,900.00**

Space Fighter, Horikawa, brown with multicolor details, doors in chest for twin lasers, walking movement, 16" h **250.00**

Space Man, Nomura, battery operated, gray, red, and white, light-up helmet, antenna, rifle, flashlight, remote control walking action, orig box, 9" h **2,300.00**

Sparking Ratchet Robot, Nomura, metallic blue with black feet and hands, sparking window in chest, orig box, 8" h **1,500.00**

Super Robot, litho tin, battery operated, dark gray, opening chest doors reveal shooting guns, extensive graphics, large red shoes and eyes, 11½" h **150.00**

Swivel-O-Matic Astronaut, Horikawa, battery operated, metallic green, swiveling torso with pivoting lasers, walking action, orig box, 11½" h **250.00**

Target Robot, Masudaya, purple with red and yellow details, lights in mouth, light-up eyes, red claws, red circular target in chest, robot changes directions, forward turning movement, orig gun and dart, 15" h **6,300.00**

Television Spaceman, Alps, battery operated, metallic gray with TV screen in chest with lunar images, clear plastic head, radar and walking action, orig box, 14" h . . . **900.00**

Thunder Robot, Asakusa, battery operated, metallic brown with red feet, red plastic hands with lasers, spinning propeller, light-up eyes, walking action, orig box, 11" h **11,000.00**

Tremendous Mike Robot, Aoshin, orange with red arms and blue face, sparking mechanism behind TV screen in body, clockwork turn-and-go movement, lacking radar, 9¼" h **3,400.00**

Video Robot, Horidawa, blue with red and gold details, plastic head, arms, legs, and feet, screen in chest, orig box, 9½" h **300.00**

X-70 Tulip Head Robot, Nomura, lilac and silver, orange plastic arms, 3 lowering head panels reveal rotating camera and screen, walking action, orig box, 9" h **2,000.00**

Zoomer the Robot, Nomura, silver with black fittings, orig box, 8" h **1,100.00**

ROCK 'N' ROLL

In spite of its outward appearance, the rock 'n' roll field tends to be traditionalist. Material from short-lived new wave or punk groups of the 1970s, e.g., The Damned and Generation X, do not appear to be attracting large numbers of collectors.

Collectors are specializing. Memorabilia from the girl groups of the late 1950s and early 1960s has become hot. The field is trendy. Autographs, guitars, and stage costumes are three categories that have gotten hot, cooled off, and show signs of resurgence. Hard Rock Cafés have spread around the world, creating an international interest in this topic. The top end of this market is documented by the values received at rock 'n' roll auctions held in London, Los Angeles, and New York.

References: Mark A. Baker, *Goldmine Price Guide to Rock 'N' Roll Memorabilia,* Krause Publications, 1997; Marty Eck, *The Monkees Collectibles Price Guide,* Antique Trader Books, 1998; Joe Hilton and Greg Moore, *Rock-N-Roll Treasures,* Collector Books, 1999; Tom Shannon, *Goldmine KISS Collectibles Price Guide,* Krause Publications, 2000.

Collectors' Club: Kissaholics, PO Box 22334, Nashville, TN 37202.

REPRODUCTION ALERT: Records, picture sleeves, and album jackets, especially for the Beatles, have been counterfeited. Sound may be inferior. Printing on labels and picture jackets usually is inferior to the original. Many pieces of memorabilia also have been reproduced, often with some change in size, color, and design.

Note: See Autographs, Beatles, Elvis Presley, Psychedelic, and Records for additional listings.

Bill Haley and His Comets, song folio, 32 pp, words and music to 10 different songs, photos and biographies of band members, bluetone photo of Bill Haley on back cover, ©1956 Valley Brook Publications, 9 x 12". **$35.00**

Bono, Sonny, doll, poseable, complete with full color catalog folder featuring Sonny and Cher outfits, Mego, 1976, 12" h, 6 x 16½ x ½" box **50.00**

Brown, James, handwritten lyrics, *I Love You,* 10 lines with accompanying music in pencil on "James Brown Productions" music sheet, black ink inscription at top "Ted Wright Bobby Byrd," and "Try Me Music Inc ©1965". **925.00**

Clapton, Eric, electric guitar, Fender Squier Stratocaster, serial #CY98063282, black finish, double cutaway body, 22-fret rosewood fingerboard with dot inlays, 3 pickups, selector switch, 3 rotary controls, tremolo bridge, and white pickguard, sgd on pickguard in black marker **1,000.00**

Creedence Clearwater Revival, electric guitar, Fender Telecaster, serial #MN6149190, black finish, single cutaway body, 21-fret fingerboard, pickup, selector switch, 2 rotary controls, white pickguard, sgd in black marker by Doug Clifford and Stu Cook on pickguard, and John Fogarty on body in blue marker **400.00**

Dylan, Bob, harmonica, Hohner Marine Band, A key, used during 1993 world tour, matted with sheet music for *Blowing In the Wind,* with letter of provenance from Cesar Diaz, 16 x 19". **1,000.00**

Monkees, book, *Who's Got the Button?*, by William Johnston, illus by Richard Moore, Whitman Pub, Authorized TV Adventure, #1539, hard cover, 1968, $15.00.

Eldorados, The, record, *Crazy Little Mama,* LP, Vee-Jay Records 1001 . . . . **475.00**

Fleetwood Mac, concert poster proof, sgd, stiff paper, full color, for concert presented by Billy Graham at Oakland Stadium, Sat May 7, 1977, color tinted photo of band, bottom margin with white ink signatures by band members on black ground, 22 x 29" **50.00**

Grateful Dead, poster, stiff paper, #216, Fillmore West, Feb 5-8, 1970, featuring Grateful Dead, Taj Mahal, and Big Foot, image of running man with peeled skin body, pair of giant mushrooms, and archway with steps leading to outer space, Bill Graham, 14 x 22". **75.00**

Heart, album, *Heart,* Capitol Records, sgd on reverse in black felt-tip pen by members, 12¼ x 12¼" **35.00**

Hendrix, Jimi, poster, "Jimi Hendrix Band of Gypsies," full color glossy, image of Hendrix playing guitar with 1 hand raised in air, concert goers and large American flag with peace symbol in background, black, white, and red text, promoting the 1970 release recorded New Year's Eve at Fillmore East and issued on Capitol Records, 34½ x 57". **75.00**

Hendrix, Jimi, receipt sgd, for payment of $175 from Gerry Stickells, dated "24th July 1970," blue ink signature, matted with machine print photograph, 1970, 20 x 13½". **925.00**

Herman's Hermits, program, 16 pp, full color stiff paper cover featuring photo and text on each member, MGM adv on inside front cover, with 8½ x 11" order form for "Herman's Hermits Official Sweatshirt Personally Designed and Autographed by Herman, Himself," illus of customized sweatshirt with caricature and signature, 1960s, 10 x 13" **15.00**

Holly, Buddy, record, *Peggy Sue,* 45 rpm, Coral Records 9-61885 . . . . **300.00**

John, Elton, CD insert, sgd, *Candle In the Wind,* black ink inscription "With love Elton," with matted black and white machine print photograph of Princess Diana, 15 x 19". **350.00**

Joplin, Janis, autograph, black ballpoint signature, on reverse of notepaper mkd "International Hotel 6221 W Century Blvd, Los Angeles," dedicated "For Donna Love," and inscribed with love heart, 1968 . . . . **925.00**

Joplin, Janis, poster, stiff paper, "Neon Rose," for concert at Matrix, San Francisco, Jan 17-22, 1967, featuring Big Brother and The Holding Company, photo of Joplin and band in bright orange and blue, blue text on reddish-purple ground, 13¹³/₁₆ x 20" **15.00**

King, BB, guitar, Gibson Epiphone, red, felt-tip pen inscription on body **1,000.00**

Kiss, album, *Kiss Unmasked,* Casablanca, sgd on reverse in gold pen by orig members, with 22 x 32½" full color glossy poster and black and white order forms for Kiss merchandise items, 1980, 12¼" sq **75.00**

Kiss, comic book, Marvel Comics Super Special, Vol 1, #1, "Printed In Real Kiss Blood," shows Kiss donating blood, 8¼ x 11" **50.00**

Kiss, game, Kiss On Tour, American Publishing Corp, ©1978 Aucoin Management Inc, 9½ x 18½ x ¾" box **35.00**

Kiss, View-Master reels, set of 3, ©1979 Aucoin Management Inc, 4½" sq, MIP **15.00**

Madonna, album cover, sgd, *Like a Virgin,* blue felt pen signature, matted with 3 silver copies and 3 silver singles, framed, 35¼ x 18". **575.00**

Marley, Bob, album cover, sgd, *Exodus,* blue felt pen inscription "Rasta Live Bob Marley," matted and framed, 18½ x 18½". **3,150.00**

Martha and The Vandellas, record, includes *Come and Get These Memories,* Gordy Records 902, sgd on back cover **200.00**

McCartney, Paul, record, *Mary Had a Little Lamb/Little Woman Love,* Apple Records 1851, 45 rpm, illus sleeve **160.00**

Midler, Bette, autograph, PS, black and white, felt-tip pen signature, 8 x 10" **35.00**

Monkees, magazine, *TV Magazine,* Jan 1-7, 1967, "Mad Man-Made Monkees," 3-pp article with color photos, 5¼ x 7". **10.00**

Moody Blues, autograph, PS, black and white, group photo sgd in red ink by orig members, 8 x 10" **150.00**

Morrison, Jim, autograph, sgd "Morrison" in black ballpoint pen on blue album page, matted with gold copy of *Light My Fire,* and black and white photograph, 15¼ x 21". **975.00**

Nicks, Stevie, T-shirt, sky blue cotton with white trim, back with navy printed "Tusk Fleetwood Mac World Tour '79-'80," worn on stage, matted with color photograph, c1979, 24 x 32". **575.00**

Nirvana, promotional poster for album *In Utero,* sgd with first names in black felt pen by group members, framed, 33 x 24" **575.00**

Rolling Stones, album cover, *The Rolling Stones,* sgd on reverse in black ballpoint pen by orig members "To Kathy," matted and framed, 19¾" sq **700.00**

Rolling Stones, autograph, black and white machine print, sgd in blue or red ballpoint pen by orig members, matted and framed, c1960s, 5 x 5¼" **2,300.00**

Rolling Stones, program, 20 pp, black and white glossy paper, photos and profile of each band member, black and white group photo on front and back, Souvenir Publishing and Distributing Co, c1964, 10 x 12¾" **35.00**

Rolling Stones, sign, paper, black and white photo of band members, "Bill Wyman Plays and Praises Framus/The Rolling Stones," Wyman in center holding Framus guitar, 1960s, 19 x 25"............ **60.00**

Rolling Stones, song folio, *Big Hits (High Tide and Green Grass),* 24 pp, full color photos, Immediate Music Inc, 1966, 9 x 12"..................... **10.00**

Rydell, Bobby, sign, paper, countertop, 1 side with image of Rydell from waist up, other side with photos of 2 record albums, "Bobby Rydell/Cameo Records," imprint for "Frolics" MA record store, 7 x 7"........... **15.00**

Springfield, Buffalo, sign, rect, pressed aluminum, raised lettering and dark blue printed background, mkd "Scioto Sign-Kenton O.62," complete with letter of provenance from former manager Charlie Green, 1966 .. **1,725.00**

Springsteen, Bruce, harmonica, Hohner Marine Band, E key, matted with album cover for *Darkness on the Edge of Town,* sgd in black felt pen, 17 x 24"........ **1,950.00**

Streisand, Barbra, magazine, *Life,* May 22, 1964, 7-pp article, black and white photos, color cover........... **10.00**

Supremes, tickets, set of 7, for concert at KRNT Theater in Des Moines, IA, 1967...................... **925.00**

Wavy Gravy, book, *The Hog Farm and Friends,* chapters on "The Woodstock Exchange," and "The Last Fast Bus to Earth," ©1974 Pacific High School Inc, 5³/₄ x 10¹/₂"..... **35.00**

Woodstock, mailing card, stiff paper, full color, Art Nouveau style art, "Woodstock Music & Art Fair Presents an Aquarian Exposition/Aug 15-16-17," ©1969, 4¹/₂ x 7¹/₄"................................. **10.00**

ROCKWELL, NORMAN

Norman Rockwell was born on February 3, 1894. His first professional drawing appeared in *Tell Me Why Stories.* Rockwell was eighteen at the time. Rockwell is best known for his magazine covers, the most recognized appearing on *Boy's Life* and *The Saturday Evening Post* (over 320 covers). Advertising, books, and calendars are only a few of the additional media where his artwork appeared. His artistic legacy includes more than 2,000 paintings.

Rockwell is one of America's foremost genre painters. He specialized in capturing a moment in the life of the average American. His approach ranged from serious to humorous, from social commentary to inspirational. He used those he knew for inspiration. His subjects ranged from New England villagers to presidents.

Rockwell's artwork continues to be heavily reproduced. Do not confuse contemporary with period pieces. His estate continues to license the use of his images. Buy modern collectibles for display and enjoyment. Their long-term value is minimal.

Reference: Denis C. Jackson, *The Norman Rockwell Identification and Value Guide to Magazines, Posters, Calendars, Books, 4th Edition,* TICN, 1998.

Collectors' Club: Rockwell Society of America, 597 Saw Mill River Rd, PO Box 705, Ardsley, NY 10502.

REPRODUCTION ALERT

Note: For additional listings see Limited Edition Collectibles.

Blotter, Schmidt's Brewery, 1935, 6 x 3¹/₄".......... **$25.00**
Calendar, 1920, Painting the Kite, De Laval adv......... **325.00**

Cereal Box, Kellogg's Corn Flakes, girl with pigtails, 1954.................................... **40.00**

Limited Edition Bell, Looking Out to Sea, River Shore, 1981.................................. **100.00**

Limited Edition Figurine, Confrontation, Gorham, 1988 ..... **75.00**

Limited Edition Figurine, Grandpa's Guardian, River Shore, 1982 .... **175.00**

Limited Edition Figurine, Tiny Tim, miniature, Gorham, 1979..................................... **20.00**

Limited Edition Plate, Boy Fishing, Coca-Cola American Life Heritage Collection, Cavanagh Group International, 1996........................ **60.00**

Limited Edition Plate, Country Pride, On the Road Series (Curator Collection), Artaffects, 1984 .... **55.00**

Limited Edition Plate, Proud Parents, Rockwell American Sweethearts Series, Franklin Mint, 1978 .... **160.00**

Limited Edition Plate, Ready For School, Early Works Series, Fairmont China, 1980 .... **20.00**

Limited Edition Plate, Spring Recess, American Landscapes Series, Gorham, 1983 .... **60.00**

Limited Edition Print, Circus, Circle Fine Art **2,650.00**

Limited Edition Print, Fido's House, Circle Fine Art....... **3,600.00**

Magazine Cover, *The Saturday Evening Post,* Feb 18, 1922 ..... **85.00**

Magazine Cover, *The Saturday Evening Post,* Aug 30, 1952..... **40.00**

Paint By Number Set, No Peeking, Craft House, #15652, 12 x 16".................................. **10.00**

Playing Cards, Four Seasons, orig box, unopened **12.00**

Poster, Bell Telephone adv, lineman on pole............. **25.00**

Puzzle, *The Saturday Evening Post,* Runaway, Parker Brothers, #522, 11 x 14".................... **25.00**

Registration Card, Official Boy Scout's, bi-fold, Rockwell illus front cover of Boy Scout, Cub Scout, and Sea Scout with flags, scouting trail banner bottom illus, orig envelope, dated Feb 1947, 5 x 4" **15.00**

Sheet Music, *Lady Bird Cha Cha Cha,* Samuel Starr........ **20.00**

Window Cards, "American At Work," Red Wing Shoe Co, price for set of 4 .... **35.00**

Magazine Cover, *The Saturday Evening Post,* **Dec 2, 1922, sgd, $135.00.**

ROOKWOOD

In 1880 Cincinnatian Maria Longworth Nichols established Rookwood, a pottery named after her father's estate. She and a number of other Cincinnati society women designed and produced the first forms and decorative motifs.

Standard Ware was extremely popular in the 1880s and 90s. It was produced by applying an underglaze slip painting to a white or yellow clay body and then glazing the entire piece with a glossy, yellow-tinted glaze.

In 1904 Stanley Burt developed Vellum ware, a glaze that was a cross between high glaze and matte glaze. By 1905 a matte glaze replaced the company's high-glazed wares. Ombroso, a matte-glaze line, was introduced in 1910 to mark the company's 30th anniversary. In 1915 the company introduced a soft porcelain line featuring gloss and matte glazes.

By the early 1930s, the company was experiencing financial difficulties and filed for bankruptcy in 1941. A group of investors bought the company. A shortage of supplies during World War II forced ownership to be transferred to the Institution Divi Thomae Foundation of the Roman Catholic Archdiocese of Cincinnati in 1941. Sperti, Inc., operated the company for the Archdiocese. By the end of the 1940s the company was again experiencing financial difficulties.

In 1954 Edgar Heltman took over, shifting production to commercial ware and accessory pieces. Production ceased briefly in 1955. In 1956 James Smith bought the company from Sperti. Herschede Hall Clock Company bought Rookwood in 1959, moved its operations to Starksville, Missouri, and finally ceased operations for good in 1967.

Rookwood pieces are well marked. Many have five marking symbols: (1) clay or body mark, (2) size mark, (3) decorator mark, (4) date mark, and (5) factory mark.

References: Anita J. Ellis, *Rookwood Pottery: The Glaze Lines*, Schiffer Publishing, 1995; Ralph and Terry Kovel, *Kovels' American Art Pottery,* Crown Publishers, 1993; L-W Book Sales (ed.), *A Price Guide to Rookwood,* L-W Book Sales, 1993, 1999 value update.

Collectors' Club: American Art Pottery Assoc, PO Box 834, Westport, MA 02790.

Vase Lamp, Daffodil pattern, 27" h, $550.00. Photo courtesy Collectors Auction Services.

Candlesticks, pr, dolphins, twisted shaft and flaring bobeche under gunmetal glaze, flame mark, "XXI/2464," 11¾" h.............................. $725.00

Planter, Abel, Louise, wax matte, cobalt blue flowers on blue-green butterfat ground, flame mark, "XXV/2000" with encircled "A," 6 x 6½"............... 775.00

Potpourri Jar, Abel, Louise, wax matte, clusters of blue flowers and leaves on blue-green butterfat ground, with inner and outer lids, flame mark, "XX/V/1321E/A," 1925, 4 x 3½"...................... 875.00

Vase, Abel, Louise, bulbous, wax matte, fleshy dogwood blossoms on blue-green butterfat ground, flame mark, "XXVII/2969" with encircled "A," 1927, 7½ x 6½"..... 1,425.00

Vase, Asbury, Lenora, vellum, bulbous, yellow roses and green leaves on butter yellow ground, flame mark, "XXVII/914E/LA," 1927, 5¾ x 4½"................. 875.00

Vase, Diers, Ed, vellum, ovoid, stylized pink roses and blue stems on mint green ground, uncrazed, flame mark, "XXIII/913F/ED," 5½ x 3".................... 1,325.00

Vase, Epply, Lorinda, bulbous, purple and dark blue Art Deco flowers on ivory ground, 1933, flame mark, "XXXIII/LE," 5¾ x 4½"......................... 975.00

Vase, Hentschel, William, coupe shaped, squeezebag dec, Art Deco profile of woman, cactus, and chevroned abstract forms in brown and ivory on golden yellow ground, flame mark, "XXX/6112" with artist's initials, 8 x 7½".......................... 2,250.00

Vase, Hurley, ET, porcelain, 3 red seahorses and green algae on white ground, flame mark, "XLIII/02720/ETH.," 6½ x 3¾"................................ 1,750.00

Vase, Jensen, Jens, classical, wax matte, irises on blue-green butterfat ground, flame mark, "XXIV/614D" with artist's cipher, 11 x 5½"..................... 2,500.00

Vase, Lincoln, Elizabeth, classical, wax matte, green and brown pinecones on vermillion butterfat ground, flame mark, "XXVII/546C/LNL," 1927, 9½ x 4¾"...... 1,200.00

Vase, McDonald, MH, bulbous, wax matte, magnolia blossoms on shaded pink ground, flame mark "XXXVI/6211/MHM," 1936, 10½ x 6½"............. 2,300.00

Vase, McDonald, MH, jewel porcelain, landscape of blue and green trees, uncrazed, flame mark, "XL/892B/MHM," 11 x 5½"..................... 3,200.00

Vase, Schmidt, Carl, marine scenic vellum, bulbous, fishing boats on the ocean, flame mark, "XXVI/827" and artist cipher, 11 x 6"....................... 8,250.00

Vase, Steinle, Caroline, ovoid, wax matte, white wild roses and green leaves on shaded green and ivory butterfat ground, flame mark, "XXIII/514F/CS," 1923, 7 x 3¾"... 875.00

Vase, Todd, Charles, matte, band of stylized bumble bees on shaded pink and yellow butterfat ground, flame mark, "XX/1873/V/CST," 1920, 5¾ x 3¾"....... 1,100.00

Vase, Wilcox, Harriet, jewel porcelain, pink cherry blossoms on purple ground, flame mark, "XXIII/HEW839B," 9¼ x 3¼"........................... 2,100.00

Vessel, Lincoln, Elizabeth, faceted, wax matte, red cherry blossoms on blue and pink butterfat ground, flame mark, "XXII/2577/LNL," 1922, 3½ x 6"............. 650.00

ROSE BOWLS

A rose bowl is a small round or ovoid shaped bowl with a crimped, petaled, pinched, or scalloped opening at its top. It served as a container for fragrant potpourri or rose petals.

Rose bowls are found in a wide variety of material with glass being the most common. A favorite giftware accessory, rose bowls often incorporate the best design qualities and materials of their era. Rose bowls are found in virtually every type of art glass.

The popularity of rose bowls extended from the second half of the Victorian era through the 1950s. The form is still made today.

Reference: Johanna S. Billings, *Collectible Glass Rose Bowls*, Antique Trader Books, 1999.

Collectors' Club: Rose Bowl Collectors, PO Box 244, Danielsville, PA 18038.

Czechoslovakian, blue satin	$85.00
Czechoslovakian, large dot pattern, cranberry	85.00
Czechoslovakian, pink satin	85.00
Daisy & Button, amber	45.00
Daisy & Button, green crimped	10.00
Daisy & Plume, green	75.00
Dugan, Grape Delight, white carnival glass	100.00
Fenton, Beaded Melon, ivy green	45.00
Fenton, Beatty Honeycomb, green	40.00
Fenton, Burmese, leaf dec	65.00
Fenton, Burmese, purple painted roses	75.00
Fenton, Fine Dot, cranberry	140.00
Fenton, Hanging Heart, blue	160.00
Fenton, Hobnail, cranberry opalescent	75.00
Fenton, Hobnail, green opalescent, 1940-50	125.00
Fenton, Hobnail, mini blue opalescent	30.00

Fenton, Silver Crest line, Violets in the Snow dec, #7254-DV, mkd "Fenton" in oval and "Hand Painted By B. Doonan," 1975-80s, $20.00. Photo courtesy Ray Morykan Auctions.

Fenton, pink overlay	25.00
Fenton, Silver Crest, beaded melon	30.00
Fenton, Valtec Sunburst, green	20.00
Fostoria, American, 8" h	65.00
Imperial, Art Deco style, 5" h	15.00
Imperial, Star & File, carnival glass	100.00
LG Wright, Priscilla, crystal	25.00
LG Wright, squat, green opalescent Hobnail	45.00
Murano, lavender rose, crystal rigaree foot, c1960	65.00
Murano, spherical, lavender-pink, applied rigaree base	50.00
Northwood, Beaded Cable, marigold carnival glass	120.00
Northwood, Beaded Drape, white opalescent	50.00
Pink Satin, gold leaves dec, large	140.00
Venetian Glass, translucent pink, applied leaves on circular vine	165.00
Westmoreland, ruby pressed, c1970	90.00

ROSEMEADE

Rosemeade's origins began with Laura Taylor, a North Dakota studio potter who demonstrated her skills at the North Dakota Building at the 1939 New York World's Fair. Robert J. Hughes, president of the Greater North Dakota Association, saw Taylor's demonstration and organized the Wahpeton Pottery Company in 1940. Laura Taylor, a partner, was secretary/treasurer.

The company's products were marketed under the trade name Rosemeade in honor of Rosemeade Township, Taylor's birthplace. Vera Gethman and Taylor were the company's two principal designers. Glaze development fell under the watchful eyes of Howard Lewis and Taylor. The company produced a wide range of objects from commemorative and souvenir pieces to household and kitchenware.

In 1953 the company became Rosemeade Potteries. Howard Lewis left Rosemeade in 1956, replaced by Joe McLaughlin, who previously worked for Red Wing Potteries. McLaughlin began importing clay from Kentucky, introduced decal decoration, and incorporated the artistic designs of Les Kouba into the line.

Laura Taylor died in 1959. The company continued operating until 1961. Cheap Japanese copies made from molds cast from Rosemeade pieces and a new minimum wage law contributed to the company's closing. The salesroom remained open until 1964.

References: Darlene Hurst Dommel, *Collector's Encyclopedia of Rosemeade Pottery,* Collector Books, 2000; Harvey Duke, *The Official Price Guide to Pottery and Porcelain, Eighth Edition,* House of Collectibles, 1995.

Ashtray, attached dove, "North Dakota Peace Garden State"	$150.00
Ashtray, wheat motif, 2 rests, blue, 4¼" d	35.00
Bank, goldfish	500.00
Basket, pink, 4¼ x 5"	40.00
Bookends, pr, Art Deco wolfhounds	400.00
Cranberry Dish, cov, turkey, 4½" l	125.00
Figurine, cats, 2 x 2", price for pr	20.00
Figurine, Chinese ring-necked pheasant, 7 x 11½"	250.00
Figurine, doe, bronze, 7¼" h	50.00
Figurine, elephant	65.00
Figurine, hen pheasant, 3½ x 11½"	200.00
Figurine, Rocky Mountain goat on base, 2¾ x 2¾"	150.00
Figurine, skunks, 1½ and ¾", price for pair	20.00

Dish, wheat design, golden yellow, 6³/₄" l, $75.00.

Incense Burner, log cabin 65.00
Jam Jar, barrel shape 45.00
Jug, Minnesota Centennial, pink, 7" h 80.00
Nut Cup, 1³/₄ x 4³/₄" 20.00
Pin, prairie rose, 2 x 2" 375.00
Planter, deer on log, 4 x 5¹/₄" 50.00
Planter, dove, 4¹/₂ x 6" 140.00
Planter, peacock, 7¹/₂" h 175.00
Salt and Pepper Shakers, pr, chickens, 2¹/₂" h 65.00
Salt and Pepper Shakers, pr, dolphins, green, 2¹/₂" h 50.00
Salt and Pepper Shakers, pr, leaping deer 60.00
Salt and Pepper Shakers, pr, mice 60.00
Salt and Pepper Shakers, pr, Paul Bunyan, 2¹/₄" h 75.00
Salt and Pepper Shakers, pr, quail, feather top knot, 2¹/₂" h . . . 75.00
Salt and Pepper Shakers, pr, Scottish Terrier 50.00
Salt and Pepper Shakers, pr, tulips, pink, 2¹/₄" h 40.00
Spoon Rest, ladyslipper, 2¹/₂" l 50.00
Wall Plaque, fish, 3¹/₂ x 6" 175.00
Wall Pocket, leaf 50.00

ROSENTHAL

Philip Rosenthal established the Rosenthal factory in Selb, Bavaria, in 1879. The company flourished, providing figurals and tableware of high-quality workmanship that were simplistic in design. Between 1879 and 1936, Rosenthal acquired factories in Kronach, Marktredwitz, Selb, Waldenburg, Sophienthal, and Waldershof.

Following World War II, many of Rosenthal's factories were either lost or outdated. Philip Rosenthal II took control of the company, formed Rosenthal Porcelain AG, and began to rebuild. New designers were hired. Today Rosenthal plays a major role in the giftware market.

References: Ann Kerr, *Rosenthal,* Schiffer Publishing, 1998; Dieter Struss, *Rosenthal: Dining Services, Figurines, Ornaments and Art Objects,* Schiffer Publishing, 1997.

Note: The following figures are all marked "Rosenthal."

Angora Cat, white, Karner, #169, 4¹/₄" h, 9¹/₄" l **$450.00**

Bird on Stump, brown, gray, and white, K Himmelstoss,
    4¹/₂" h **80.00**
Borzoi, 4¹/₂" h, 11" l **200.00**
Boy Feeding Squirrel, 4¹/₂" h, 4" w **50.00**
Bulldog, 5" h, 6" l **325.00**
Cat, white, mkd "DR," #25194, 6¹/₂" h, 2¹/₂" l **60.00**
Child Feeding Fawn, #16652, 6¹/₂" h, 3" w **50.00**
Dachshund Puppy, Karner, #1247, 6" h **150.00**
Dancer, wearing mauve skirt, light yellow shawl, 9" h **400.00**
Doe and Fawn, L Rempel, #1638, 6¹/₄" h, 7¹/₄" l **130.00**
Flying Sea Gull, #154 1/3, 8" h, 11³/₄" wingspan **40.00**
Fox, G Kuspert, 5¹/₂" h, 4¹/₂" w **175.00**
German Shepherd Puppy, Karner, 1934, 5" h **125.00**
Kneeling Nude Woman, drinking water from her
    cupped hands, Ernst Wenck, #752/1, 7¹/₄" h **525.00**
Kneeling Nude Woman, white, F Klimsch, 12" h, 6" w **325.00**
Kneeling Nude Woman, white, mkd "LFG," 8¹/₄" h **250.00**
Laughing White Rabbit, 2" h **50.00**
Mallard Ducks, W Zugel, #341/2, 8" h, 10¹/₂" l **225.00**
Penguin, K Himmelstoss, 3¹/₄" h **70.00**
Pointer, H Fritz, 7" h, 8¹/₂" l **185.00**
Poodle, gray, Karner, 7¹/₂" h, 8" l **275.00**
Springer Spaniel with Pheasant, 5¹/₂" h, 9" l **275.00**
Terrier, #1243, 6" h **250.00**
Three Birds on Branch, gray and brown, 4¹/₂" h, 6" l **125.00**

ROSEVILLE POTTERY

George Young purchased the J. B. Owens Pottery, renaming it the Roseville Pottery, in 1892. Cooking utensils, cuspidors, flowerpots, and umbrella stands were among the company's earliest products. Around the turn of the century, Roseville purchased the Midland Pottery plant in Roseville (1898), moved the company's main office to Zanesville, Ohio, bought Peters and Reed, and acquired the Muskingum Stoneware plant (1901).

Rozane, the company's first artware line, evolved into a general term used to describe all the company's art or prestige lines. John Herold established Roseville's commercial artware department in 1903. Artware, including dresser sets, juvenile ware, tea sets, and smoker sets dominated production until the late 1910s.

Roseville closed two of its factories in 1910. Fire destroyed another in 1917. In 1918 Russell Young replaced his father as manager; Frank Ferrel replaced Harry Rhead as art director. Ferrel shifted the company's production into industrial artware, resulting in the introduction of more than eighty new lines.

In 1932 the firm became Roseville Pottery, Inc. The company experienced a major slump in sales following World War II. New industrial artware lines failed to halt the decline. Mosaic Tile Company bought the Roseville plant in 1954. Production of Roseville ceased.

References: Mark Bassett, *Introducing Roseville Pottery,* Schiffer Publications, 1999; Jack and Nancy Bomm, *Roseville In All Its Splendor,* L-W Book Sales, 1998; John W. Humphries, *Roseville By the Numbers,* published by author, 1999; Sharon and Bob Huxford, *The Collectors Encyclopedia of Roseville Pottery, First Series* (1976, 1997 value update), *Second Series* (1980, 1997 value update), Collector Books; Gloria and James Mollring, *Roseville Pottery,* published by authors, 2000; Randall B. Monsen, *Collectors' Compendium of Roseville Pottery and Price Guide, Vol. 1* (1995), *Vol. 2* (1997), Monsen and Baer.

Collectors' Clubs: American Art Pottery Assoc, PO Box 834, Westport, MA 02790; Rosevilles of the Past, PO Box 656, Clarcona, FL 32710.

REPRODUCTION ALERT: Cheap reproduction Roseville pieces are surfacing at auctions and flea markets. Distinguishing characteristics include glaze colors and crude decorative techniques.

Basket, Bushberry, blue, #372-10" $450.00
Basket, Freesia, green, raised mark, #390-7" 225.00
Basket, Gardenia, gray, rounded handle, #610-12" 110.00
Basket, Water Lily, pink, imp mark, #382-12" 165.00
Basket, Zephyr Lily, brown, #395-10" 225.00
Bookends, pr, Snowberry, blue, raised mark, 5½ x 5 x
  4½" 140.00
Centerbowl, Ferella, brown, flaring, attached flower
  frog, unmkd, 4½ x 10" 500.00
Centerbowl, Fucshia, brown, imp mark, 4 x 12½" 225.00
Cookie Jar, Zephyr Lily, blue, #5-8" 350.00
Ewer, Zephyr Lily, blue, raised mark, #140-12" 190.00
Fan Vase, Nude Panel, brown, RV ink mark, 8¼ x 5½" 450.00
Floor Vase, Bushberry, green, raised mark, 18" h 875.00
Floor Vase, Carnelian II, mottled pink and green glaze,
  unmkd, 18" h 1,975.00
Floor Vase, Cherry Blossom, pink, foil label, 16¾ x 10¾" . . 3,575.00
Floor Vase, Magnolia, green, raised mark, #100-18" 275.00
Floor Vase, Snowberry, blue, raised mark, 18" h 525.00
Hanging Basket, Freesia, brown, raised USA mark, 8" d 55.00
Jardiniere, Blackberry, unmkd, 9" h 1,425.00
Jardiniere, Clematis, blue, raised mark, #667-8" 250.00
Jardiniere, Futura, protruding shoulder, stylized yellow,
  green, blue and lavender leaves on burnt-orange
  ground, unmkd, 6 x 8½" 250.00
Jardiniere, Luffa, green, unmkd, 8" h 300.00
Jardiniere, Sunflower, unmkd, 10½ x 13" 1,000.00
Jardiniere and Pedestal, Baneda, pink, remnants of foil
  label, 8" h 1,875.00
Jardiniere and Pedestal, Florentine, unmkd, 10" h 275.00
Low Bowl, Freesia, brown, flaring rim, raised mark,
  #122-8" 65.00

Low Bowl, Zephyr Lily, buttressed handles, raised mark,
  #474-8" 110.00
Pillow Vase, Futura, 4-sided, pink and green glossy
  glaze, buttressed handles, emb geometric pattern,
  unmkd, 8½ x 6¼" 775.00
Pitcher, Pinecone, blue, imp mark, 10" h 775.00
Planter, Blackberry, oblong, 3½ x 13½" 475.00
Planter, Montacello, bulbous, brown, stylized floral pat-
  tern, unmkd, 5¼ x 7½" 360.00
Planter, Pinecone, 4-sided, blue, #468-8" 190.00
Planter, Teasel, spherical, ftd, imp mark, #343-6" 90.00
Planter, Vista, unmkd, 6½ x 5½" 375.00
Umbrella Stand, Primrose, brown, raised mark, 21 x 11" . . 1,325.00
Urn, Cosmos, blue, raised mark, 8" d 250.00
Urn, Foxglove, pink, imp mark, 8" h 250.00
Urn, Magnolia, brown, raised mark, #100-18" 275.00
Urn, Morning Glory, green, unmkd, 9¼ x 7" 325.00
Urn, Pinecone, brown, twig handles, scalloped rim, imp
  mark, #848-10" 225.00
Urn, Zephyr Lily, tall, blue, raised mark, #141-15" 190.00
Vase, Baneda, double gourd shaped, foil label, 9½ x
  7½" 825.00
Vase, Cherry Blossom, squat, pink, unmkd, 5¼ x 7" 600.00
Vase, Clematis, blue, #1111-15" 190.00
Vase, Falline, bulbous, brown, unmkd, 6½ x 6½" 650.00
Vase, Freesia, brown, flaring rim, raised mark, #122-8" 65.00
Vase, Futura, bullet shaped, 4 buttresses and geometric,
  matte blue, unmkd, 8 x 4" 350.00
Vase, Futura, flaring, green buttresses, orange ground,
  8½" h 300.00
Vase, Futura, tapering stepped neck, buttressed handles,
  green and orange glaze, 7¼" h 225.00
Vase, Imperial II, bulbous, raised border on collar, white
  rim, cobalt blue ground, unmkd, 9¾ x 5½" 1,500.00
Vase, Jonquil, 2-handled, unmkd, 6¾" h 400.00
Vase, Jonquil, flask shaped, unmkd, 4½ x 3½" 165.00
Vase, Lotus, red and pink, raised mark, #L3-10" 140.00
Vase, Montacello, bulbous, brown, 2-handled, stylized
  pattern, unmkd, 5¼ x 5½" 380.00
Vase, Montacello, corseted, brown, stylized pattern,
  black paper label, 4¼ x 5½" 360.00
Vase, Montacello, flaring, stylized floral pattern, unmkd,
  10½ x 6" 1,750.00
Vase, Montacello, milk can shaped, brown, stylized
  white pattern, unmkd, 6¼ x 7¼" 415.00
Vase, Morning Glory, squat bulbous, green, foil label,
  6¼ x 7½" 450.00
Vase, Nude Panel, bulbous, green, 3 cameo panels of
  dancing figures, RV ink mark, 10¼ x 5" 1,975.00
Vase, Savona, emb fruits and flowers, foil label, 10" h 275.00
Vase, Sunflower, bulbous, 2-handled, unmkd, 9¼ x 7" . . . 1,200.00
Vase, Sunflower, cylindrical, triangular handles, unmkd,
  5¾" h 325.00
Vase, Vista, tall, buttressed handles, 12 x 6" 1,000.00
Vase, Windsor, flaring, 2-handled, imp stylized leaf
  motif in green, mottled burnt-orange ground, unmkd,
  7½ x 4¼" 325.00
Vase, Wisteria, tapered, buttressed base, foil label,
  8¼" h 475.00
Vase, Zephyr Lily, blue, conical shaped, flaring but-
  tressed base, imp mark, #136-9" 110.00
Vase, Zephyr Lily, blue, squat base, flaring rim, imp
  mark, 12" d 225.00
Vessel, Blackberry, bulbous, 7" h 650.00

Vase, Bleeding Heart, #961-4, 4⅛" h, $75.00.

Vessel, Carnelian II, green, squat, flaring rim, unmkd, 10¼" h **250.00**

Vessel, Cherry Blossom, brown, squat, unmkd, 4" h **275.00**

Vessel, Ferella, ftd, unmkd, 4 x 5½" **475.00**

Vessel, Futura, spherical, on buttressed pentagonal base incised with polychrome circles on cobalt ground, unmkd, 8½ x 5½" **975.00**

Vessel, Imperial II, barrel shaped, mottled cobalt and turquoise glaze, unmkd, 8 x 6½" **725.00**

Vessel, Luffa, beaker shaped, brown, unmkd, 6¼" h **300.00**

Vessel, Morning Glory, green, squat, 2-handled, foil label, 4¼" **470.00**

Vessel, Sunflower, spherical, unmkd, 7¼ x 8" **1,550.00**

Wall Pocket, Clematis, #1295-8" **135.00**

Wall Pocket, Dahlrose, black paper label, 8" h **325.00**

Wall Pocket, Donatello, green, unmkd, 9¾ x 4½" **165.00**

Wall Pocket, Florane, RV ink mark, 10" h **100.00**

Wall Pocket, Magnolia, brown, raised mark, #1294 . . . . . . **190.00**

Wall Pocket, Primrose, brown, imp mark, 8" h **650.00**

ROYAL CHINA

Although the Royal China Company purchased the former E. H. Sebring Company (Sebring, Ohio) plant in 1933, extensive reno- vation delayed production until 1934. Initially, Royal China pro- duced mainly overglaze decal ware. Kenneth Doyle's underglaze stamping machine, developed for Royal China in 1948, revolu- tionized the industry, allowing for the inexpensive production of underglaze ware. By 1950 Royal China eliminated its decal ware.

The company produced a wide range of dinnerware lines. Colonial Homestead (early 1950s), Currier and Ives (1949/50), Old Curiosity Shop, and Willow Ware (1940s) are among the most popular. Royal Oven Ware was introduced in the 1940s.

In 1964 Royal China purchased the French-Saxon China Company, operating it as a wholly owned subsidiary. The Jeannette Corporation acquired Royal China in 1969. In 1970 fire destroyed the plant and Royal China's operations were moved to the French- Saxon plant, also located in Sebring, Ohio.

The company changed hands several times in the 1970s and 80s, being purchased by the Coca-Cola Bottling Company (1976), J. Corporation of Boston (1981), and Nordic Capitol of New York (1984). Each owner continued to manufacture ware under the Royal China brand name. Operations ceased in 1986.

Reference: Eldon R. Aupperle, *A Collector's Guide For Currier & Ives Dinnerware,* published by author, 1996.

Collectors' Club: Currier & Ives Dinnerware Collectors Club, RD 2, Box 394, Hollidaysburg, PA 16648.

Note: See Willow Ware for additional listings.

Blue Heaven, bread and butter plate, 6" d **$3.00**

Blue Heaven, casserole, cov **40.00**

Blue Heaven, custard cup **3.00**

Blue Heaven, dinner plate **5.00**

Blue Heaven, gravy boat **20.00**

Blue Heaven, pie plate **12.00**

Blue Heaven, platter, round **15.00**

Blue Heaven, small tab plate **12.00**

Blue Heaven, soup bowl, 8" d **6.00**

Blue Heaven, teapot **40.00**

Blue Heaven, vegetable **12.00**

Blue Heaven, water pitcher **30.00**

Colonial Homestead, flat soup **12.00**

Colonial Homestead, gravy boat **12.00**

Colonial Homestead, platter **12.00**

Colonial Homestead, serving plate, 12" d **25.00**

Colonial Homestead, vegetable, 10" d **20.00**

Currier & Ives, blue, ashtray **20.00**

Currier & Ives, blue, bread and butter plate **8.00**

Currier & Ives, blue, cake plate, tab handles **20.00**

Currier & Ives, blue, calendar plate **20.00**

Currier & Ives, blue, candle lamp with globe **150.00**

Currier & Ives, blue, casserole, cov **85.00**

Currier & Ives, blue, cereal bowl **18.00**

Currier & Ives, blue, chop plate, 12" d **35.00**

Currier & Ives, blue, creamer and sugar **30.00**

Currier & Ives, blue, cup and saucer **8.00**

Currier & Ives, blue, dinner plate, 10" d **8.00**

Currier & Ives, blue, fruit bowl, 5½" d **5.00**

Currier & Ives, blue, gravy and underplate **45.00**

Currier & Ives, blue, luncheon plate, 9" d **20.00**

Currier & Ives, blue, platter, oval, 13" l **30.00**

Currier & Ives, blue, salad plate **15.00**

Currier & Ives, blue, salt and pepper shakers, pr **40.00**

Currier & Ives, blue, soup bowl, 8" d **15.00**

Currier & Ives, blue, teapot, cov **125.00**

Currier & Ives, blue, vegetable, 9" d **30.00**

Currier & Ives, brown, pie baker **12.00**

Currier & Ives, red, cocoa cup **18.00**

Fair Oaks, creamer **8.00**

Fair Oaks, platter, oval **20.00**

Memory Lane, pink, butter, cov **15.00**

Memory Lane, pink, dinner plate **10.00**

Memory Lane, pink, saucer **2.00**

Old Curiosity Shop, bowl, 9" d **12.00**

Old Curiosity Shop, dinner plate, 10" d **15.00**

Old Curiosity Shop, platter **18.00**

Old Curiosity Shop, soup bowl **6.00**

Currier & Ives, blue, pie baker, 10" d, $24.00.

Old Curiosity Shop, sugar **12.00**
Orchid, pink, salad fork and spoon **10.00**
Orchid, pink, salt and pepper shakers, pr **10.00**
Orchid, pink, tray, round **20.00**
Rooster, bread and butter plate **4.00**
Star Glow, bread and butter plate **2.00**
Star Glow, gravy boat **15.00**
Star Glow, pie baker **12.00**
Star Glow, platter, oval, 13½" l **6.00**

ROYAL COPENHAGEN

In the mid-18th century Europe's royal families competed with each other to see who would be the first to develop a porcelain formula. In 1772 Franz Heinrich Muller, a Danish pharmacist and chemist, discovered a formula for hard paste porcelain. Muller submitted his samples to the Queen Dowager. She was so delighted that she christened his firm "The Danish Porcelain Factory." Although founded privately in 1775, the Danish monarchy fully controlled the firm by 1779. Three wavy lines were chosen as the firm's trademark to symbolize the seafaring tradition of the Danes.

The company proved a drain on the Danish monarchy's finances. In 1867 A. Falch purchased the company under the condition that he be allowed to retain the use of "Royal" in the firm's title. Falch sold the company to Philip Schou in 1882.

In 1885 Arnold Krog became art director of Royal Copenhagen and developed underglaze painting. Only one color is used. Shading is achieved by varying the thickness of the pigment layers and firing the painted plate at a temperature of 2,640 degrees Fahrenheit. Krog revitalized the company. In 1902 Dalgas became art director and introduced the blue and white Christmas Plate series in 1908.

Today the Royal Copenhagen Group also includes Bing and Grondahl. The firm is noted for its extensive dinnerware and giftware lines.

References: Robert J. Heritage, *Royal Copenhagen Porcelain: Animals and Figurines,* Schiffer Publishing, 1997; Rinker Enterprises, *The Official Price Guide to Collector Plates, Seventh Edition,* House of Collectibles, 1999.

Note: For additional references see Limited Edition Collectibles.

Bread and Butter Plate, Quaking Grass **$6.00**
Bread and Butter Plate, Tranquebar **15.00**
Bowl, Art Faience, 4¼" d **25.00**
Cream Soup and Liner, Quaking Grass **25.00**
Cup, Tranquebar **25.00**
Demitasse Cup and Saucer, Blue Fluted, price for set of 4 . . . . **60.00**
Dinner Plate, Tranquebar **30.00**
Dish, Blue Lace, ftd. **55.00**
Figurine, bird **55.00**
Figurine, boy kissing girl, 7" h **60.00**
Figurine, boy with calf **110.00**
Figurine, dachshund **75.00**
Figurine, dancing girl **85.00**
Figurine, frog on rock, #507 . . . . **40.00**
Figurine, mouse on sugar cube, #510. . . . . **45.00**
Figurine, owl, #834 . . . . **20.00**
Figurine, pan. **210.00**
Figurine, polar bear, 15" h **300.00**
Figurine, rainbow trout, #2676 . . . . **50.00**

Figurine, robin, #2238. . . . . **30.00**
Figurine, Siamese Cat, "Precious," #681 . . . . **25.00**
Figurine, wire-haired terrier, #2967 . . . . **20.00**
Fruit Bowl, Tranquebar **18.00**
Limited Edition Plate, Bringing Home the Tree, Christmas
   in Denmark Series, H Henrik Hansen, 1991 . . . . . **70.00**
Limited Edition Plate, Fano Girl, Christmas Series,
   K Lange, 1955 . . . . **145.00**
Limited Edition Plate, Indian Love Call, America's
   Mother's Day Series, S Vestergaard, 1988 . . . . **35.00**
Limited Edition Plate, Mermaid, Hans Christian
   Anderson Fairy Tale Series, S Vestergaard, 1985 . . . . **45.00**
Limited Edition Plate, Mother and Baby Rabbit,
   Motherhood Series, S Vestergaard, 1985 . . . . **30.00**
Limited Edition Plate, The Robins, Nature's Children
   Series, J Nielsen, 1993. . . . . **40.00**
Pitcher, Marselis, 1950s. **50.00**
Platter, Blue Fluted, 12" l **55.00**
Platter, Quaking Grass, oval. **50.00**
Soup Bowl, Quaking Grass **20.00**
Soup Bowl, Tranquebar, rimmed **30.00**
Sugar, open, Tranquebar **25.00**
Sweetmeat Dish, Tranquebar **30.00**
Trivet, Tranquebar **25.00**

ROYAL COPLEY

Royal Copley and Royal Windsor are tradenames of the Spaulding China Company. Royal Copley, representing approximately 85% of all Spaulding production, was sold mostly through chain stores. Royal Windsor items were sold to the florist trade.

Spaulding China, Sebring, Ohio, began operations in 1942. The company chose names that had an English air, e.g., Royal Copley and Royal Windsor. Even marketing terms such as Crown Assortment and Oxford Assortment continued this theme.

Birds, piggy banks, Oriental boy and girl wall pockets, and roosters were among Royal Copley's biggest sellers. The small birds originally retailed for 25¢. Pieces were marked with a paper label.

Cheap Japanese imports and labor difficulties plagued Spaulding throughout the post-war period. In 1957 Morris Feinberg retired, contracting with nearby China Craft to fill Spaulding's remaining orders. Initially Spaudling was sold to a Mr. Shiffman, who made small sinks for mobile homes. After being closed for several years Eugene Meskil of Holiday Designs bought the plant. The company made kitchen ware. Richard C. Durstein of Pittsburgh bought the plant in 1982.

References: Joe Devine, *Collector's Guide to Royal Copley plus Royal Windsor & Spaulding,* Bk I (1999), Bk II (1999), Collector Books; Mike Schneider, *Royal Copley,* Schiffer Publishing, 1995.

Newsletter: *The Copley Courier,* 1639 N Catalina St, Burbank, CA 91505.

Ashtray, bird on flower **$12.00**
Ashtray, leaf and bird **16.00**
Bank, chicken. **75.00**
Bank, pig **25.00**
Bank, pig with bowtie **40.00**
Bank, rooster, "Chicken Feed," 7" h **85.00**
Bank, teddy bear. **95.00**
Bud Vase, parrot on limb. **35.00**

Bud Vase, warbler	25.00
Figurine, chicken	30.00
Figurine, dove	20.00
Figurine, lark, blue tail	12.00
Figurine, mallard drake, 9" h	20.00
Figurine, oriental girl	12.00
Figurine, parrot	40.00
Figurine, pheasant	25.00
Figurine, pink bird on log	35.00
Figurine, rooster, white	90.00
Figurine, titmouse	25.00
Figurine, wren, green and tan	15.00
Figurines, pr, Chinese couple, 7¹/₂" h	25.00
Figurines, pr, pheasants	40.00
Head Vase, cocker spaniel	25.00
Head Vase, girl with pigtails	30.00
Head Vase, pirate	45.00
Pitcher, daffodil pattern	35.00
Planter, barefoot boy	55.00
Planter, Blackamoor lady, 8" h	36.00
Planter, Blackamoor man, 8" h	30.00
Planter, blue bird, blue and pink	20.00
Planter, boy leaning on barrel	20.00
Planter, cocker spaniel	30.00
Planter, crying girl, blue	12.00
Planter, deer and tree stump	15.00
Planter, dog and mailbox	30.00
Planter, duck, blue and brown	10.00
Planter, duck eating grass, 5" h	18.00
Planter, Dutch girl	30.00
Planter, gazelle	65.00
Planter, goat, pink	45.00
Planter, hen	40.00
Planter, hummingbird, blue	135.00
Planter, kitten on stump	35.00
Planter, kitten with ball of yarn	25.00
Planter, mother deer and fawn	15.00
Planter, nuthatch on tree	25.00

Planter, oriental boy, 5¹/₂" h	25.00
Planter, oriental girl	20.00
Planter, pink dogwood	12.00
Planter, poodle, black	25.00
Planter, poodle, green	30.00
Planter, rooster	20.00
Planter, Siamese cats	115.00
Planter, tanager	20.00
Planter, teddy bear and mandolin	50.00
Planter, wren on tree stump	20.00
Soap Dishes, pr, blue bird and red bird	15.00
Vase, doe and fawn	18.00
Vase, Essex	12.00
Vase, fish	12.00
Vase, fish, cylindrical	30.00
Vase, philodendron, ftd, 7¹/₂" h	15.00
Vase, praying angel	175.00
Vase, trailing leaf and vine	30.00
Wall Pocket, Amsterdam	20.00
Wall Pocket, angel	75.00
Wall Pocket, bird	35.00
Wall Pocket, Blackamoor	45.00
Wall Pocket, girl wearing hat	30.00
Wall Pocket, Huck Finn	30.00
Wall Pocket, man's head	35.00
Wall Pocket, oriental girl	25.00
Wall Pocket, rooster, black and white	55.00
Wall Pockets, pr, boy and girl	70.00
Wall Pockets, pr, colonial couple	90.00

ROYAL DOULTON

In 1815 John Doulton founded the Doulton Lambeth Pottery in Lambeth, London. The firm was known as Doulton and Watts between 1820 and 1853. Henry Doulton, John's second son, joined the firm in 1835. In 1887 he was knighted by Queen Victoria for his achievements in the ceramic arts.

Henry Doulton acquired the Niles Street pottery in Burslem, Staffordshire in 1877, changing the name to Doulton & Co. in 1882. This plant made high quality porcelain and inexpensive earthenware tableware. In 1901 King Edward VII granted the Royal Warrant of appointment to Doulton. "Royal" has appeared on the company's wares since that date.

Whereas production increased at the Burslem plant during the 20th century, it decreased at the Lambeth plant. By 1925 only twenty-four artists were employed, one of whom was Leslie Harradine, noted for his famed Dickens' characters. Commemorative wares were produced at Lambeth in the 1920s and 30s. Agnete Hoy, famous for her cat figures, worked at Lambeth between 1951 and 1956. Production at the Lambeth plant ended in 1956.

Although Royal Doulton made a full line of tabletop ware, it is best known for its figurines and character jugs. Most figurines were made at Burslem. The HN numbers, named for Harry Nixon, were introduced in 1913. HN numbers were chronological until 1949 after which each modeler received a block of numbers. Noke introduced the first character jugs in 1934. Noke also created series ware, a line that utilizes a standard blank decorated with a wide range of scenes.

Today the Royal Doulton Group includes John Beswick, Colclough, Webb Corbett, Minton, Paragon, Ridgway, Royal

Planter, kitten in basket, pastel colors, 8¹/₂" l, $35.00

Adderley, Royal Albert, and Royal Crown Derby. It is the largest manufacturer of ceramic products in the United Kingdom.

References: Jean Dale, *The Charlton Standard Catalogue of Royal Doulton Animals, Second Edition,* Charlton Press, 1998; Jean Dale, *The Charlton Standard Catalogue of Royal Doulton Beswick Figurines, Sixth Edition,* Charlton Press, 1998; Jean Dale, *The Charlton Standard Catalogue of Royal Doulton Beswick Jugs, Fourth Edition,* Charlton Press, 1997; Jean Dale, *The Charlton Standard Catalogue of Royal Doulton Beswick Storybook Figurines, Fifth Edition,* Charlton Press, 1999; Jean Dale and Louise Irvine, *The Charlton Standard Catalogue of Royal Doulton Bunnykins,* Charlton Press, 1999; Harry L. Rinker, *Dinnerware of the 20th Century: The Top 500 Patterns,* House of Collectibles, 1997.

Periodical: *Collecting Doulton,* Elescar Heritage Centre, Nr Barnsley, S York 274 8HJ UK.

Collectors' Clubs: Royal Doulton International Collectors Club, 701 Cottontail Ln, Somerset, NJ 08873 (company-sponsored); Royal Doulton International Collectors Club, 850 Progress Avc, Scarborough Ontario M1H 3C4 Canada.

Adrienne, cup and saucer	$6.00
Adrienne, dinner plate	6.00
Adrienne, platter	40.00
Brambly Hedge, cake plate	35.00
Brambly Hedge, coffeepot	80.00
Brambly Hedge, Dusty Dogwood	30.00
Brambly Hedge, Mr Apple	30.00
Brambly Hedge, Mrs Toadflax	45.00
Bunnykins, 60th Birthday	50.00
Bunnykins, Astro Bunnykins	90.00
Bunnykins, Be Prepared, 1987-96	40.00
Bunnykins, bowl, Camping	15.00
Bunnykins, cereal bowl, Mr Piggly	50.00
Bunnykins, Doctor, DB181	40.00
Bunnykins, Harry, DB73	65.00
Bunnykins, Home Run	60.00
Bunnykins, Schoolmaster	35.00
Bunnykins, Touchdown, DB29	110.00
Carlyle, sandwich tray, handled	60.00
Character Jug, Blacksmith, D6571	100.00
Character Jug, Graduate, The	65.00
Character Jug, King Arthur	250.00
Character Jug, Little Mester	100.00
Character Jug, Merlin	50.00
Character Jug, Punch and Judy	275.00
Character Jug, Robinson Crusoe	75.00
Character Jug, Saint George	130.00
Character Jug, Sam Johnson	85.00
Character Jug, Tam O'Shanter	35.00
Character Jug, Ugly Duchess	125.00
Chelsea Rose, gravy boat	60.00
Chelsea Rose, plate 8" d	10.00
Chelsea Rose, platter, 14½" l	50.00
Chelsea Rose, vegetable, oval	26.00
Chelsea Rose, vegetable, round	50.00
Chiltern, teacup and saucer	30.00
Clock, Winnie the Pooh	75.00
Coaching Days, berry bowl	30.00
Coaching Days, bowl, pedestal base	30.00
Coaching Days, creamer	40.00

Coaching Days, dish, oval	30.00
Coaching Days, mug, 3⅛" h	60.00
Coaching Days, pitcher, small	100.00
Coaching Days, punch bowl	400.00
Coaching Days, saucer	6.00
Coaching Days, teapot lid	50.00
Dog Plate, The Pointer	185.00
Dog Plate, The Scottie	250.00
Figure, Blithe Morning, HN2021	175.00
Figure, Broken Lance, HN2041	400.00
Figure, bulldog, HN1042	650.00
Figure, Buttercup, HN2399	65.00
Figure, Charlotte, HN2421	180.00
Figure, Choir Boy, HN2141	30.00
Figure, Cup of Tea, The, HN2322	210.00
Figure, Fair Lady, HN2193	145.00
Figure, Favourite, The, HN2249	140.00
Figure, flop-earred rabbit, flambé glaze	160.00
Figure, Lady Fayre, HN1265	650.00
Figure, Lizzie, HN2749	120.00
Figure, Monica, HN1467	80.00
Figure, My Love, HN2339	100.00
Figure, Penelope, HN 1901	300.00
Figure, Rose, HN1368	50.00
Figure, Snowballing, DS22	140.00
Figure, swimming duck, flambé glaze	100.00
Figure, Valerie, HN2104	75.00
Kirkwood, casserole, cov, red	90.00
Kirkwood, dinner plate, red	20.00
Old Colony, cup and saucer	7.00
Orchard Hill, soup	30.00
Thistle Down, bread plate	30.00
Thistle Down, gravy boat, ftd	35.00
Thistle Down, vegetable, oval	40.00
Toby Jug, Cliff Cornell	80.00
Toby Jug, Falstaff	25.00
Toby Jug, George Washington	50.00
Toby Jug, Mr Pickwick	135.00
Toby Jug, Rip Van Winkle	80.00
Tonkin, bread and butter plate, 6" d	12.00
Tonkin, cup and saucer	12.00
Tonkin, dinner plate	18.00

ROYAL WINTON

In 1885 Edward, Leonard, and Sidney, three brothers, were instrumental in founding Grimwade Brothers, also known as the Winton Pottery, a firm located in Stoke-on-Trent, Staffordshire, England. Several expansions followed including the purchase of the Winton Pottery Company and Stoke Pottery in 1900. The three firms were combined as Grimwades Limited.

In 1907 Grimwades acquired Atlas China of Stoke, Heron Cross Pottery of Fenton, Rubian Art Pottery, and Upper Hanley Pottery. The company specialized in the production of chinaware and earthenware household and toilet articles as well as British Royalty commemoratives.

In 1913 King George V and Queen Mary visited Winton Potteries. Although formal permission was not granted to use the "Royal" name, it appeared regularly in the company's advertisements following that date.

Royal Winton introduced its chintz patterns and relief wares in the 1930s. Royal Winton's golden age ended with the 1964 death of James Plant, Jr., who introduced a wide range of new chintz, luster, pastel, commemorative, and hand-decorated, artist-signed lines. Today the firm produces tabletop ware, giftware, and limited edition reissues of its chintz patterns.

References: Eileen Rose Busby, *Royal Winton Porcelain*, Glass Press, 1998; Muriel M. Miller, *The Royal Winton Collector's Handbook*, Francis Joseph, 1999.

Collectors' Club: Chintz World International, PO Box 50888, Pasadena, CA 91115.

Anemone, toast rack	$85.00
Beeston, cup and saucer	80.00
Castle Garden, vase	55.00
Countess, breakfast set	700.00
Crocus, plate	80.00
Crocus, side plate	40.00
Estelle, bonbon dish	50.00
Estelle, cup and saucer	25.00
Evesham, luncheon plate, 8" d	70.00
Evesham, sauceboat and liner	170.00
Evesham, vegetable, oval	110.00
Hazel, bread and butter plate, 6" sq	45.00
Hazel, celery dish	80.00
Hazel, creamer and sugar	95.00
Hazel, cup and saucer	100.00
Hazel, dessert bowl	55.00
Hazel, dinner plate, 10" d	140.00
Hazel, mustard, open	65.00
Hazel, plate, 12" d	140.00
Hazel, salad plate, 7" d	70.00
Hazel, teapot, ascot shape	400.00
Julia, cake plate, 1930s	110.00
Julia, creamer and sugar	200.00
Julia, dinner plate, 10½" d	40.00
Julia, trio	225.00
Marguerite, compote	100.00
Marguerite, jam pot	185.00
Marguerite, salad plate, 7" d	50.00
Old Cottage, biscuit barrel	100.00
Old Cottage, breakfast set	275.00
Old Cottage, cheese dish, cov	45.00
Old Cottage, creamer and sugar	60.00
Old Cottage, cup and saucer	80.00

Old Cottage, jug	215.00
Open Rose, bonbon dish, cov	125.00
Pekin, basket, 1951, 5½" h	115.00
Pekin, candy jar, 8" h	130.00
Pekin, relish platter	15.00
Petunia, toast rack	85.00
Pink Petunia, tennis set	30.00
Queen Anne, basket	140.00
Rose Brocade, butter dish	35.00
Rose Brocade, cup and saucer	15.00
Rose Brocade, tray	30.00
Rosebud, cake plate	55.00
Rosebud, cup and saucer	35.00
Rosebud, teapot	160.00
Rosebud, trio	30.00
Royalty, trio	110.00
Somerset, cup and saucer	115.00
Souvenir Plate, Provincetown	75.00
Souvenir Teapot, Manitoba	50.00
Summertime, bread and butter plate, 6" d	50.00
Summertime, cake plate	125.00
Summertime, compote, ftd	125.00
Summertime, creamer and sugar	125.00
Summertime, cup and saucer	85.00
Summertime, stacking tea set	600.00
Summertime, teapot, 2 cup	225.00
Summertime, tray	100.00
Summertime, vase	85.00
Sunshine, box	45.00
Sweet Pea, butter dish	250.00
Sweet Pea, compote	180.00
Sweet Pea, creamer	80.00
Sweet Pea, pitcher	65.00
Sweet Pea, sugar	65.00
Victorian Rose, nut dish	55.00
Welbeck, bread and butter plate, 6" d	35.00
Welbeck, butter dish	300.00
Welbeck, eggcup	30.00
Welbeck, luncheon plate, 8" d	40.00
Welbeck, nut dish	85.00
Welbeck, rimmed soup	35.00
Welbeck, tall mug	30.00
Yellow Tiger Lily, jug	35.00

Hazel, tray, $100.00.

SALEM CHINA

Biddam Smith, John McNichol, and Dan Cronin, formerly with Standard Pottery in East Liverpool, Ohio, founded the Salem China Company in Salem, Ohio, in 1898. Due to financial problems, it was sold to F. A. Sebring in 1918. Under the management of Frank McKee and Sebring's son, Frank Jr., the company became very successful through the sale of fine dinnerware, much of which was trimmed with 22K gold.

Viktor Schenckengost created many of Salem's shapes and designs during the 1930s and 40s. Salem China continued to manufacture dinnerware until 1967. Beginning in 1968, Salem was exclusively a distribution and sales business.

References: Susan and Al Bagdade, *Warman's American Pottery and Porcelain*, Wallace-Homestead, 1994; Harvey Duke, *The Official Price Guide to Pottery and Porcelain, Eighth Edition*, House of Collectibles, 1995.

North Star, pitcher, Constellation shape, designed by Viktor Schreckengost, 1966, 8¹/₈" h, $12.00.

SALT & PEPPER SHAKERS

The salt and pepper shaker emerged during the latter half of the Victorian era. Fine ceramic and glass shakers slowly replaced individual and master salts. These early shakers were documented by Arthur G. Peterson in *Glass Salt Shakers: 1,000 Patterns* (Wallace-Homestead, 1970).

Although pre–World War I figural salt shakers do exist, the figural salt and pepper shaker gained in popularity during the 1920s and 30s, and reached its zenith in the 1940s and 50s. By the 1960s, inexpensive plastic salt and pepper shakers had replaced their ceramic and glass counterparts.

Salt and pepper shaker collectors specialize. Salt and pepper shakers that included mechanical devices to loosen salt were popular in the 1960s and 70s. Depression era glass sets also enjoyed strong collector interest during that period. Currently, figural salt and pepper shakers are hot, having experienced a 100% price increase during the past five years.

References: Larry Carey and Sylvia Tompkins, *1003 Salt & Pepper Shakers* (1997), *1004 Salt & Pepper Shakers* (1998), *1005 Salt & Pepper Shakers* (1999), Schiffer Publishing; Melva Davern, *The Collector's Encyclopedia of Salt & Pepper Shakers: Figural and Novelty, Second Series*, Collector Books, 1990, 2000 value update; Helene Guarnaccia, *Salt & Pepper Shakers, Vol. 1* (1985, 1999 value update), *Vol. II* (1989, 1998 value update), *Vol. III* (1991, 1998 value update), *Vol. IV* (1993, 1999 value update), Collector Books; Mike Schneider, *The Complete Salt and Pepper Shaker Book*, Schiffer Publishing, 1993; Irene Thornburg, *Collecting Salt & Pepper Shaker Series*, Schiffer Publishing, 1998; Irene Thornburg, *The Big Book of Salt and Pepper Shakers Series*, Schiffer Publishing, 1999.

Collectors' Club: Novelty Salt & Pepper Shakers Club, PO Box 677388, Orlando, FL 32867.

Note: All shakers listed are ceramic unless noted otherwise. Prices are for sets. For additional listings refer to Depression Glass and individual ceramics and glass manufacturer's categories.

Basket Petitpoint, platter	$8.00
Boston, plate	2.00
Bryn Mawr, dinner plate	4.00
Century, berry bowl, 6" d	8.00
Century, bread and butter plate, 6¼" d	8.00
Century, cake plate, handled	8.00
Century, creamer and sugar	10.00
Century, plate, 7" d	8.00
Century, plate, 7½" d	10.00
Century, plate, 9" d	15.00
Century, platter, 13½" l	10.00
Century, soup bowl	12.00
Colonial Fireside, bowl	5.00
English Village, sauce dish	4.00
English Village, serving bowl	20.00
Godey Print, creamer	6.00
Hopscotch, creamer	5.00
Hopscotch, cup	8.00
Mary and Lamb, plate	20.00
Monticello, gravy boat	9.00
North Star, bread and butter plate	2.00
North Star, cup	8.00
North Star, dessert dish	3.00
North Star, dinner plate	5.00
North Star, platter, handled	6.00
North Star, saucer	2.00
North Star, vegetable	8.00
Riviera, platter, tab handle	8.00
Royal Rose, dinner plate, 10" d	10.00
Rust Tulip, bowl, 5¼" d	12.00
Rust Tulip, bread and butter plate, 6½" d	10.00
Rust Tulip, creamer and sugar	12.00
Rust Tulip, plate, 9¼" d	15.00
Rust Tulip, platter, 12" l	15.00
Rust Tulip, serving bowl	15.00
Rust Tulip, soup bowl	15.00
Tricorne Sailing, cup and saucer	12.00
Victorian Ladies, plate	4.00
Virginia, plate	2.00

Apple Basket, Occupied Japan	$15.00
Aunt Jemima and Uncle Mose, F&F Mold and Die Works, 5" h	50.00
Babies in Basket	75.00
Biker Hogs	6.00
Bird on Basket	8.00
Black Boy with Barrel	20.00
Black Poodles, Japan	12.00
Black Porter and Suitcase	70.00
Black Scotties, Japan	15.00
Black Uncle and Mammy	2.00
Blue Hill, Noritake	60.00
Bowlers	12.00
Boxers, red and black trunks	35.00
Boy and Girl Pigs	8.00
Bud Man	22.00
Budweiser Mirror	20.00
Bull, Holt-Howard	50.00
Bull and Cow	8.00
Bunnies, green, Van Telligen	35.00
Bunnies, Hallmark	3.00
Burger Chef, plastic	5.00

Tomatoes on Leaf Tray, Maruhon Ware, Occupied Japan, 1⁷/₈" h tomatoes, 5⁵/₈" l tray, $20.00. Photo courtesy Ray Morykan Auctions.

Cardinal Tuck, Goebel	55.00
Cat and Poodle in Basket, Japan	18.00
Charlie Brown and Lucy, sitting on couch	25.00
Chef, yellow, American Bisque, 4¹/₂" h	20.00
Chesterton, raindrops shape, Harker	20.00
Chicken and Sun	3.00
Chihuahua	70.00
Circus Horse and Wagon	18.00
Coca-Cola	15.00
Coffee Maker	5.00
Collies	18.00
Coors Beer	2.00
Country Pigs	5.00
Cow and Moon	8.00
Cucumber	1.00
Daisy Dorables, Holt-Howard	125.00
Dick Tracy and Junior	35.00
Dog, Staffordshire	20.00
Dog and Bone	10.00
Dog Detective	12.00
Dog on Bar Stool, Enesco	25.00
Donkey	10.00
Dr Dog and Patient	20.00
Duck Head	4.00
Dumbo, 3¹/₂" h	75.00
Dutch Boy and Girl	8.00
Eagle and Bell	5.00
Egg, plastic	5.00
Elephant, Japan	12.00
Feet	2.00
Flamingo	12.00
Floragold, Jeannette, glass	40.00
Flower and Fern, Shawnee	20.00
Foxes, brown	12.00
Frogs, Norcrest	10.00
Frying Pan	3.00
Giraffe Heads	10.00
Girl with Reindeer, Norcrest	20.00
Golf Ball	6.00
Goofy, Disney	12.00
Google Eyed Squirrel, 3" h	5.00
Guardian Service, aluminum	25.00
Guitar and Music Stand, plastic	8.00
Gumby and Pokey	20.00
Hillbillies in Barrels	15.00

Hocking, green banded, glass	10.00
Hummingbird, Avon	10.00
Husband and Wife, "What's Hers is Hers/What's His is Hers"	12.00
Ice Cream Cones	5.00
Kangaroo with 2 Babies	4.00
Kellogg's Snap and Pop	65.00
Kissin' Kousins	10.00
Lego Red Kettle	3.00
Lobsters	3.00
Love Birds	5.00
Maid and Butler, Kessler	10.00
Marywood, Noritake	50.00
Mice and Cheese, plastic	12.00
Model T, plastic, orig box	15.00
Monkey, Ceramic Arts Studio	20.00
Mouse and Cheese, Ceramic Arts Studios	40.00
Mr Peanut, glass	6.00
Mushroom, Japan	5.00
Noah's Ark	5.00
Owl, Fitz & Floyd	6.00
Paul Bunyan and Babe	18.00
Pineapple	6.00
Pink Spoon and Fork	10.00
Polished Brass Teapot	1.00
Rabbit and Carrot	10.00
Reclining Nude	20.00
Rosie the Robot	15.00
Rotisserie, plastic	200.00
Sandman	95.00
Santa and Reindeer	15.00
Seagram's Seven, plastic	8.00
Sheep, black and white	5.00
Ship, red and white, plastic	6.00
Sink and Range	6.00
Smiling Cat	4.00
Smokey Bear	100.00
Squirrel on Log	10.00
Steamship, 2¹/₄" blue or maroon smokestacks on 5¹/₂" l white ceramic hull holder with recessed top side, c1950s	45.00

Siamese Cats, Japan, 1960s, $8.00.

Strawberry **1.00**
Sultan and Harem Girl **95.00**
Swinging Cows **12.00**
Swiss Boy and Girl **8.00**
Swordfish **100.00**
Toaster **10.00**
Totem Pole **2.00**
Tropical Fish **20.00**
Vegetable Heads, gold trim, Vallona Star **30.00**
Washer and Dryer **15.00**
Whale, yellow and black **8.00**
Windmills **4.00**
Winking Cats **18.00**
Winking Watermelons **10.00**

SAND PAILS

Pre-1900 tin sand pails were japanned, a technique involving layers of paint with a final lacquer coating. Lithographed tin pails arrived on the scene in the first two decades of the 20th century.

The golden age of lithographed tin sand pails began in the late 1930s and extended into the 1960s. After World War II, the four leading manufacturers were J. Chein & Co., T. Cohn, The Ohio Art Company, and U.S. Metal Toy Manufacturing. Character-licensed pails arrived on the scene in the late 1940s and early 1950s. By the mid-1960s, almost all sand pails were made of plastic.

Many sand pails were sold as sets. Sets could include sand molds, a sifter, spade, and/or sprinkling can.

Reference: Carole and Richard Smyth, *Sand Pails & Other Sand Toys,* published by authors, 1996.

Collectors' Club: Ohio Art Collectors Club, 18203 Kristi Rd West, Liberty, MO 64068.

Chein, boys fishing from boat while riding large fish, red
    plastic handle, shield logo, 1950s, 8" h **$65.00**
Chein, circus theme, performing animals, 1960s, 5" h **125.00**

Ohio Art, Donald Duck, ©1939, $250.00.

Chein, kids at beach, little boy and girl playing under
    beach umbrella on both sides, red plastic handle,
    1950s, 8" h **65.00**
Chein, Story of Peter Rabbit, story written around sides
    with small illus inserted in text, light blue and pink
    ground, 1970s, 8" h **45.00**
Disney, characters from *Pinocchio* film, 1940, 6½" h **225.00**
Ohio Art, boy, puppy, and beach ball, plaid design
    around top and bottom, 1950s, 3" h **60.00**
Ohio Art, circus theme, ringmaster, lion, clown, and tiger **65.00**
Ohio Art, comic farmer strumming banjo for cows and
    pigs in pasture, 1970s, 5" h **55.00**
Ohio Art, drum majorette, boy pumping weights, and little girl handing out ice cream cones at circus,
    designed by Elaine Ends Hileman, 1950s, 8" h **100.00**
Ohio Art, Flipper, children with trick-performing dolphin, "World's Best Toys" logo, 1960s **90.00**
Ohio Art, garden, boy and girl playing in wheelbarrow
    on 1 side, girl chasing chicken and boy feeding lamb
    on other side, "World's Best Toys" logo, 1960s **125.00**
Ohio Art, kids in boat, anchor border, 1950s **150.00**
Ohio Art, kids on carousel, designed by Elaine Ends
    Hileman, #117, 1950s **150.00**
Ohio Art, Shirt Tales, TYG and Pammy, 1981 . . . . **25.00**
Ohio Art, tiger cubs playing in grass, 1960s, 8" h **140.00**
Ohio Art, various road signs and patch pockets on denim
    ground, 1970s, 8" h **45.00**

SCANDINAVIAN GLASS

Scandinavian Glass is a generic term for glassware made in Denmark, Finland, and Sweden from the 1920s through the 1960s and heavily exported to the United States. Collectors assign a high aesthetic value to Scandinavian glass. Focus at the moment is on key companies, e.g., Kosta Glasbruk and Orrefors, and designers such as Edward Held, Nils Landberg, Vicke Lindstrand, Tyra Lundgren, Ingeborg Lundin, Sven Palmqvist, Sven Erik Skawonius.

In the 1920s and '30s, Orrefors produced engraved crystal that combined Modern abstractionism with classicism. In the 1940s Orrefors' forms became heavier, decoration spare, and the inherent refractive properties of glass were emphasized. Designers at Kosta Glasbruk were moving in this direction in the 1930s. The 1950s saw an emphasis on simple light softly contoured forms. Following a period of "Pop" influence in the 1960s, Orrefors' pieces became sculptural in approach. It was also during this period that color entered the Scandinavian glass design vocabulary and design links were established between Scandinavian and Italian glass designers.

Currently, interest in Scandinavian glass is strongest in metropolitan regions in the Middle Atlantic States and West Coast. It is now regularly featured in 20th-Century Modern auction catalog sales across the United States.

Boda, vase, designed by Bertil Vallien, bottle shaped,
    sandblasted, lustered amber ext with polychrome
    applied rods and canes, etched signature and number,
    10½ x 5¼" **$725.00**
Flygsfors, vase, designed by Berndt, freeform, cobalt
    blue at base cased to colorless and red at pulled and
    pierced rim, base inscribed "Flygsfors 58 Berndt,"
    1958, 5½" h **200.00**

Gunnel Nyman, vase, ovoid, pink sommerso glass int, controlled submerged bubbles, acid-etched signature and "Nuutajarvi Notsjo," 8½ x 3½" **225.00**

Hadeland, vase, designed by Severin Brorby, flaring form, transparent olive glass with 6 applied freeform medallions, etched "Hadeland/7020/SB," 11 x 7½" **350.00**

Holmegaard, bowl, designed by Per Lütken, emerald green, closed-in rim, domed bottom, etched signature and number, 4½ x 12½" **200.00**

Kosta, bowl, designed by Paul Hoff, sandblasted clear glass with int dec of enameled yellow glass lemons, green leaves on ext, etched signature and "57585," foil label, 6 x 8" **450.00**

Kosta, vase, attributed to Vicke Lindstrom, heavy walled flattened ovoid form, colorless glass with int dec of aubergine spiral lines, base inscribed "Kosta LH 1384," c1955, 5½" h **450.00**

Kosta, vase, cut and etched blue crystal, heavy walled ovoid form, pale blue with ribbed sides, centered by bird on pine bough, c1960, 7¾" h **500.00**

Kosta, vase, designed by Vicktor Lindstrand, gourd shaped, black and white lines, etched "LH1257," 10½ x 2½" **110.00**

Kosta, vase, designed by Vicktor Lindstrand, tear shaped sommerso glass, cranberry int, striated white bands within clear glass body, unmkd, 6¾ x 4½" **500.00**

Kosta Boda, bowl, flaring form, mottled speckled violet, blue, and green ext, etched artist signature and number with foil label, 6½ x 9½" **110.00**

Kosta Boda, tray, designed by Bertil Vallien, ftd, square, colorless glass, various symbols centered by stylized blue face in square foot, highlighted with metal figure of man and applied red glass arc, base inscribed "Kosta Boda B Vallien 79365," c1965, 8½" **200.00**

L Fraucek, goblet, clear glass, int diagonal lines, acid etched "L Fraucek" and number, 3 x 3½" **150.00**

Orrefors, Ariel vase, designed by Edvin Ohrstrom, bulbous, raised neck on heavy walled colorless glass, int dec with alternating maroon stripes and elongated air trap bubbles, base inscribed "Orrefors Sweden Ariel No. 1903E Edvin Ohrstrom," c1945, 6" h **1,000.00**

Orrefors, bowl, cylindrical, cased glass with checkered and triangular cobalt and clear pattern, acid-etched "Orrefors/Ariel No. 167H/Ingeborg/Lunden," 5½ x 6½" . . **1,425.00**

Orrefors, bowl, flaring form, pale blue glass with controlled bubbles, acid-etched "Orrefors" with artist signature, 4 x 6" **550.00**

Orrefors, Graal bowl, designed by Edvard Hald, flared blue glass, int dec with colorless loops, applied disk foot inscribed "Orrefors Graal 2109-E6 Edvard Hald," c1940, 2¼" h, 6" d **1,375.00**

Orrefors, Graal vase, designed by Edvard Hald, heavy walled tear-shaped vessel of colorless glass, int dec with fish among seaweed in brown-green, inscribed "Orrefors Graal No. 9521Y II Hald," c1940, 5½" h **925.00**

Orrefors, Kraka bowl, designed by Sven Palmquist, controlled submerged bubbles in shaded blue to clear glass, etched "Orrefors 342," 3½ x·7" **1,100.00**

Orrefors, Kraka vase, designed by Sven Palmquist, elongated, heavy walled colorless glass, int dec with blue net and trapped bubbles on amber ground, sgd, "Orrefors Kraka No. 322 Sven Palmquist," c1950, 12½" h **1,400.00**

Orrefors, vase, 4-sided, green sommerso glass int, acid etched "Orrefors/NU 3538-2," 10 x 5" **225.00**

Orrefors, vase, sommerso glass, 3-sided, tapered form, green int, acid-etched "Orrefors/NU 35381," foil label, 15¼ x 3½" **500.00**

Stromberg, vase, heavy crystal, faceted, etched signature, 8½ x 4" **325.00**

Unknown Maker, decanter, 4-sided, dimples, flat stopper, unmkd, 13 x 6½" **150.00**

SCHOENHUT

In 1872 Albert Schoenhut, a German immigrant, founded his own company to manufacture a toy piano he perfected. The company quickly expanded its line including a host of musical percussion instruments, military toys, novelty toys, and children's play equipment. Beginning in the 1890s, Schoenhut's sons (there were six) started working for the company.

In 1902 Schoenhut purchased Fritz Meinecke's patent rights for a toy animal whose parts were held together by elastic. The first Humpty Dumpty Circus items appeared in 1903. In 1908 the Rolly Dolly was introduced. Schoenhut received a patent for a swivel, spring-jointed doll in 1911. Walking dolls were added in 1919 and sleep-eye dolls in 1921.

In the late 1920s Schoenhut manufactured a line of comic character jointed toys for George Borgfelt & Co. The Depression hit the company hard. Several new games, colorful wagons and pull toys, and a line of diecut, cardboard jigsaw puzzles were introduced. Schoenhut's catalog dropped from eighty-five (late 1920s) to thirty-nine pages (1934).

The company went into bankruptcy in 1935. Albert F. and his son Frederick Carl created the Schoenhut Manufacturing Company to continue making toy pianos. In 1950 Nelson Delavan purchased the manufacturing rights and reproduced several animals and personnel.

Reference: Carol Corson, *Schoenhut Dolls,* Hobby House Press, 1993; Elizabeth Stephan (ed.), *O'Brien's Collecting Toys, 9th Edition,* Krause Publications, 1999.

Collectors' Club: Schoenhut Collectors Club, 1003 W Huron St, Ann Arbor, MI 48103.

Note: All figures are in good condition unless noted otherwise.

Bear, brown, painted eyes, full size **$250.00**
Buffalo, cloth mane, glass eyes, full size 575.00
Camel, 2 humps, reduced size 300.00
Clown, 1-part head, full size 100.00
Donkey, glass eyes, full size 125.00
Elephant, glass eyes, full size 150.00
Elephant, painted eyes, full size 100.00
Elephant, reduced size 90.00
Giraffe, painted eyes, full size 200.00
Hippopotamus, glass eyes, full size 500.00
Horse, white, reduced size 175.00
Lady Acrobat, bisque head, full size 375.00
Leopard, painted eyes, full size 300.00
Lion Tamer, bisque head, full size 450.00
Pig, glass eys, full size 725.00
Poodle, carved mane, glass eyes, full size 900.00
Poodle, cloth mane, glass eyes, full size 275.00

Schoenhut Figures. Left: Hobo, 1-part head, full size, $300.00. Right: Clown, 2-part head, full size, $275.00. Photos courtesy Gene Harris Antique Auction Center, Inc.

Ringmaster, 1-part head, full size	375.00
Ringmaster, bisque head, full size	425.00
Ringmaster, reduced size	225.00
Sea Lion, painted eyes, full size	500.00
Tiger, reduced size	275.00
Zebra, painted eyes, full size	300.00

SCHOOP, HEDI

Hedi Schoop, born in Switzerland in 1906, was educated at Vienna's Kunstgewerbeschule and Berlin's Reimann Institute. In the early 1930s she and her husband, Frederick Hollander, a well-known composer, emigrated to America.

After arriving in Los Angeles, Schoop began making and marketing a line of plaster of Paris dolls dressed in contemporary fashions. Discovered by a representative of Barker Brothers, she was advised to scrap the textile clothing and do figures that were entirely ceramic.

Hedi's mother financed a plant in North Hollywood. Schoop employed many displaced European actors, dancers, and musicians as decorators. In 1942 the company became Hedi Schoop Art Creations. Business was strong in the late 1940s and early 1950s. The company introduced a line of TV lamps in the mid-1950s. A fire ended production in 1958. Schoop did not rebuild. Instead, she worked as a free-lance designer for several Los Angeles area firms. She retired permanently from the ceramics business in the 1960s, devoting her time after that to painting.

References: Jack Chipman, *Collector's Encyclopedia of California Pottery, Second Edition,* Collector Books, 1999; Mike Schneider, *California Potteries,* Schiffer Publishing, 1995.

Butterfly Bowl and Dish, ruffled edges	**$90.00**

Double Cornucopia Vase, purple ext with gold specks, dark pink int, #480, 4" h, 8¼" w	50.00
Fan Vase, ruffled rim, black with red and gold trim, 7" h, 11" w	40.00
Figurine, deer, mottled brown and gold, #291/2, 11" h, 9½" l	80.00
Figurine, kneeling oriental woman, wearing red dress with gold specks, holding black bowl, 11" h	60.00
Figurine, oriental girl and crying boy, girl wearing white kimono with green and brown flowers and trim, boy wearing white tunic with green and brown trim and green pants, each holding white basket, 9" h	125.00
Figurine, woman wearing white dress with brown and green trim, holding flowers and 2 baskets, 12" h	125.00
Figurines, pr, dancing girls with arms raised above their heads, matched pair each wearing long pink dress with swirled skirts and gold trim, 13" h and 12" h	90.00
Figurines, pr, Dutch boy and girl, wearing yellow	80.00
Figurines, pr, French couple, man wearing cobalt vest and green pants, woman wearing cobalt shawl and green dress, 13" h	150.00
Figurines, pr, hula dancers, grass skirts, wearing flowers in hair and leis	525.00
Figurines, pr, oriental couple, each carrying green and white lantern and wearing white pants and swirled green and white tunics	250.00
Figurines, pr, oriental couple, each holding lantern and wearing green tunic and pants with gold trim, 12" h	50.00
Flower Holder, ballerina, white with green dec, 9½" h	125.00
Flower Holder, dancing girl, mint green dress with cream sleeves and ruffled bottom, pink flower at waist, holding cream basket, 12" h	110.00
Flower Holder, Dutch boy, 10¼" h	30.00
Flower Holder, Dutch boy, wearing green jacket and pants, yellow hat and scarf, brown wooden shoes, 10½" h	15.00
Flower Holder, Dutch girl, wearing yellow and white dress, holding yellow jar, #62P, 9" h	45.00
Flower Holder, girl wearing cream dress with pink trim, holding pink flowers and basket, 9" h	90.00
Flower Holder, oriental woman holding fan, wearing white kimono with brown and yellow flowers and green trim, 11¼" h	55.00
Flower Holder, rooster, bisque body with glazed green comb and green, black, and white feathers, 12½" h	125.00
Flower Holders, pr, Comedy and Tragedy figures each with guitar and mask, gold and black, 12" h	175.00
Flower Holders, pr, oriental couple, man carrying 2 pots, woman holding fan, 12" h and 11" h	200.00
Flower Holders, pr, oriental woman holding fan, wearing white kimono with green trim, 11" h	20.00
Nut Dish, green wood nymph in leafy dish, cream and green, 6" h nymph, 11½" l dish	40.00
Planter Dish, #425, 3" h, 9¼" l, 5¼" w	25.00
Planter, girl holding book, wearing white dress and scarf with green polka dots, standing in front of large green book planter, 8½" h, 6½" w	55.00
Plate, Dalmatian, 7¼" sq	80.00
Plate, pink flowers and green leaves, gray ground, silver rim, 7¼" sq	35.00
TV Lamp, Comedy Tragedy, black and white masks on black base, gold trim	375.00

SCIENTIFIC INSTRUMENTS

Scientific instruments is a broad category that encompasses astrological, calculating, educational, engineering, mathematical, medical, nautical, surveying, and weather instruments along with supporting paper collectibles, e.g., books. Although 18th-and 19th-century instruments have been and remain the principal collector focus, interest is growing in post-1920 instruments, due in part to affordability.

English and European examples command a premium price. Completeness is a major value consideration. The period box is required for an object to be considered complete. Toy scientific kits, e.g., chemistry, electricity, erector, and microscope sets, especially by A. C. Gilbert Company of New Haven, Connecticut, are rising steadily in value.

The appearance of specialized shows, e.g., the Maryland Science and Microscope Society's annual April show and sale, indicates the depth and strength of the market.

Periodical: *Rittenhouse*, PO Box 151, Hastings on Hudson, NY 10706.

Newsletter: *Scientific, Medical & Mechanical Antiques*, PO Box 412, Taneytown, MD 21787.

Collectors' Clubs: Oughtred Society (slide rules), PO Box 99077, Emeryville, CA 94662; Zeiss Historical Society, 300 Waxwing Dr, Cranbury, NJ 08512.

Analytical Beam Balance, W Ainsworth & Sons Inc, Denver, CO, DLB type with chain weight and notched beam, case with glass sides, counter-poised removable door, drawer, 200-g capacity, 1/20 mg sensitivity, c1950, 18" l, 9" w, 18" h **$150.00**

Boyden's Hook Gauge, 4½ x 28¼" l mahogany frame on which 2-ft nickel silver gauge with brass hook moves, c1920. . . . . **150.00**

Microscope, Carl Zeiss, Jena, Germany, #83081, binocular, with angled binocular tubes, micrometer screw fine focus, quad nosepiece, detachable mechanical stage, square table, condenser, double mirror, 2 eyepiece caps, filters, stage accessories, japanned finish, 14⅝" h, 6" w, 8" l **550.00**

Microscope, Carl Zeiss, Jena, Germany, #180416, monocular, 13½" x 8" l tube with quad nosepiece, with fine focus on arm, rotating mechanical stage, adjustable condenser, double mirror, japanned and lacquered brass, with case, c1935 . . . . **200.00**

Miniature Surveyor's Level, "Gebr Wichmann/Max Hildebrand GMBH Freiberg-Sa.," 4⅛" h, with 7" w telescope and 2⅜" vial, eyepiece focus, tribrach base, tan enameled brass, c1930 . . . . **175.00**

Simplex Slide Rule, Albert Nestler, A-G Lahr 1/B, celluloid, clad mahogany, 4 logarithmic scales, trigonometric and linear, German silver cursor, c1920, 15" l, 1¾" w. **150.00**

Stadia Hand Transit, pat Nov 15, 1910, 10½" l telescope through 3" d compass/clinometer case, with 2" l needle, 1½" l hinged sight vanes, silvered compass card with 2 inset vials, floating clinometer dial, brass construction, black enamel finish, with sewn leather case, leveling adapter, and tripod, c1920 . . . . **325.00**

The Handy Shrinkage Rule, 24⅜" to 2', 24⅜ x 1½ x ⅛" thick boxwood with brass end covers, graduated on 4 edges, right and left hand, in 1/16" increments, c1930 . . . . . **30.00**

Wellsworth Worth-Black Amblyoscope, American Optical Co, Buffalo, NY, 6¼ x 5¾" overall with 2 black crackle finished, 1½" d sight tubes, measures eye muscle balance by superimposing hands onto clocks, birds into cages, circles into squares, etc, with 17 sets of celluloid slides, and orig labeled cardboard box, c1935 . . . . . . **60.00**

SEBASTIAN MINIATURES

Sebastian Miniatures, hand-painted, lightly glazed figurines, are the creation of Prescott W. Baston (1909-1984). He organized the Sebastian Miniature Company in 1940. Production initially was located in Marblehead, Massachusetts, eventually moving to Hudson, Massachusetts.

Sebastian Miniatures range in size from three to four inches. Production was limited. Baston also produced special commission advertising and souvenir figurines. Over 900 different figures have been documented. Pewter miniatures were introduced in 1969. In 1976, the Lance Corporation produced 100 of Baston's most popular designs for national distribution.

Prescott Baston died on May 25, 1984. His son, Woody, continued in his father's footsteps. The Sebastian Collectors Society plays a far greater role in determining secondary market pricing than normally expected from a collectors' club.

References: Collectors' Information Bureau, *Collectibles Market Guide & Price Index, 17th Edition*, Collectors' Information Bureau, 1999; Mary Sieber (ed.), *2000 Price Guide to Limited Edition Collectibles, 5th Edition*, Krause Publications, 1999.

Collectors' Clubs: The Sebastian Exchange Collectors Assoc, PO Box 10905, Lancaster, PA 17605; Sebastian Miniatures Collectors Society (company sponsored), 321 Central St, Hudson, MA 01749.

Lobsterman, #65, Marblehead label, 1974-75, $40.00.

Abraham Lincoln, #85-C/6002, 1982 . . . . $20.00
Amish Man, #70/6224, 1984 . . . . 18.00
Aunt Polly, #97/6135, 1981 . . . . 12.00
Baby Buggy of 1850, #172/6303, 1981 . . . . 20.00
Becky Thatcher, #96/6131, 1979 . . . . 18.00
Ben Franklin, #326/6218, 1976 . . . . 20.00
Building Days, pr, #375/376, 1979 . . . . 30.00
Colonial Carriage, #278/6215, 1979 . . . . 20.00
Colonial Glassblower, #277/6216, 1979 . . . . 15.00
Colonial Kitchen, #198/6251, 1984 . . . . 15.00
Colonial Overseer, #298, 1978 . . . . 15.00
Cranberry Picker, #162, 1950-75 . . . . 15.00
Croquet, #399, 1982 . . . . 12.00
Family Feast, #405, 1983 . . . . 45.00
Family Picnic, #380, 1980 . . . . 20.00
Family Reads Aloud, #387, 1981 . . . . 20.00
Farmer, #63-A/6226, 1981 . . . . 25.00
For You, #415/2958, 1983 . . . . 18.00
Franklin Delano Roosevelt, #86, 1983 . . . . 30.00
Girl with Cymbals, #43, 1942 . . . . 375.00
Grocery Store, #319/6223, post-1976 . . . . 15.00
Ichabod Crane, #140, 1949-75 . . . . 25.00
John and Priscilla Alden, #286/6323, 1980 . . . . 20.00
Lace Maker, #173/6301, 1981 . . . . 18.00
Little Nell and Her Grandfather, #106/6110, 1984 . . . . 10.00
Lobsterman, #65/6201, 1986 . . . . 18.00
Mayflower, #273/6255, 1976 . . . . 25.00
Mayflower, New Jersey Descendants, #273-D, 1970 . . . . . . 80.00
Mr Micawber, #50-A/6101, 1976 . . . . 35.00
Mr Pickwick, #58-A/6106, 1976 . . . . 35.00
Nathaniel Hawthorne, #110, 1948-75 . . . . 65.00
News Wagon, #477/3827, 1987 . . . . 25.00
Peggotty, #52, 1946-53 . . . . 30.00
Penny Shop–House of Seven Gables, #166/6122, 1979 . . . . 18.00
Phoebe–House of Seven Gables, #163, 1950-75 . . . . 65.00
Pilgrims, #72/6324, 1982 . . . . 12.00
Pope Paul VI, #343, 1965-75 . . . . 275.00
Rabbit/Jell-O, #230, 1954 . . . . 475.00
Sairey Gamp and Mrs Harris, #60-A/6108, 1976 . . . . 35.00
Self-Portrait, #391/2312, 1982 . . . . 18.00
Snow Days, Boy, #378, 1980 . . . . 12.00
Snow Days, Girl, #379, 1980 . . . . 18.00
Statue of Liberty, #466-A/3871, 1986 . . . . 50.00
Sverige Dalarna, #104, 1948-54 . . . . 80.00
Switching the Freight, #215/6236, 1979 . . . . 16.00
Uncle Sam, #357, 1981 . . . . 15.00
White House, #491, 1987 . . . . 70.00
Yankee Clipper Ship, #242/6254, 1986 . . . . 15.00

SEWING COLLECTIBLES

The ability to sew and to sew well was considered a basic household skill in the 18th century, 19th century, and first two-thirds of the 20th century. In addition to utilitarian sewing, many individuals sewed for pleasure, producing work ranging from samplers to elaborately embroidered table coverings.

The number of sewing implements, some practical and some whimsical, multiplied during the Victorian era. Crochet hooks, pincushions, and tape measures were among the new forms. Metals, including gold and silver, were used. Thimbles were a popular courting and anniversary gift. Sewing birds attached to the edge of the table helped the sewer keep fabric taut.

As America became more mobile, the sewing industry responded. Many advertisers used needle threaders, tape measures, and sewing kits as premiums. A matchcover-like sewing kit became a popular feature in hotels and motels in the post-1945 era. While collectors eagerly seek sewing items made of celluloid, they have shown little interest thus far for post-1960 plastic sewing items.

References: *Advertising & Figural Tape Measures,* L-W Book Sales, 1995; Elizabeth Arbittier et al., *Collecting Figural Tape Measures,* Schiffer Publishing, 1995; Wade Laboissonniere, *Blueprints of Fashion: Home Sewing Patterns of the 1940s,* Schiffer Publishing, 1997; Sally C. Luscomb, *The Collector's Encyclopedia of Buttons,* Schiffer Publishing, 1997; Wayne Muller, *Darn It!, The History and Romance of Darners,* L-W Book Sales, 1995; Glenda Thomas, *Toy and Miniature Sewing Machines* (1995), *Book II* (1997), Collector Books; Helen Lester Thompson, *Sewing Tools & Trinkets,* Collector Books, 1997; Debra J. Wisniewski, *Antique & Collectible Buttons,* Collector Books, 1997, 2000 value update; Estelle Zalkin, *Zalkin's Handbook of Thimbles & Sewing Implements,* Warman Publishing Co, 1988.

Newsletter: *That Darn Newsletter,* 461 Brown Briar Circle, Horsham, PA 19044.

Collectors' Clubs: International Sewing Machine Collectors Society, 551 Kelmore St, Moss Beach, CA 94038; Toy Stitchers, 623 Santa Florita Ave, Millbrae, CA 94030.

Note: See Thimbles for additional listings.

Advertising Tear Sheet, Vintage Imported Toy Sewing
    Machines, depicts assortment of models with descrip-
    tion and price for each, 1928, 9 x 3" $25.00
Booklet, *Short Cuts to Home Sewing,* 48 pp, ©1926 The
    Singer Sewing Machine Co, 5½ x 8⅜" 15.00
Button, shell, mother-of-pearl and abalone shell,
    carved, inlaid 1.00
Button, tin and pewter, japanned and painted, pewter
    includes molded, engraved, disc, etc 2.00
Catalog, American Thread Co, New York, NY, 20 pp,
    1921 . . . . 20.00
Catalog, The Fashion World, NY, Spring and Summer
    Fashions, 42 pp, 1925 . . . . 20.00
Clamp, inlaid wood and metal, marquetry box with
    locking drawer attached to metal clamp 225.00

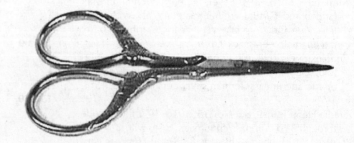

Embroidery Scissors, polished steel, c1950, 3½" l, $5.00. Photo courtesy Ray Morykan Auctions.

Clamp, steel, red box cushion and netting hook, heart shaped thumbscrew . . . . : **175.00**
Hemming Clamp, cast iron, dolphin with trefoil tail, acanthus leaf clamp, amorini thumbscrew **850.00**
Hemming Clamp, cut steel, red plush pincushion over drawer and dolphin, scrolled thumbscrew, orig box **1,800.00**
Hemming Clamp, iron, snake's head, needle-point pincushion, flat thumbscrew **175.00**
Hemming Clamp, ivory, carved, treasure chest with padock, die thumbscrew **225.00**
Mending Kit, Handy Pack, Art Deco **10.00**
Needle Book, Elsie the cow, mounted needles, 4¾ x 5¼" **6.00**
Pincushion, lusterware, c1930 . . . . **25.00**
Pincushion, metal, lady's slipper, feather, shell designs, Occupied Japan, c1937 . . . . **35.00**
Pincushion Clamp, pierced and carved bone **250.00**
Sewing Bird, brass, with pincushion and tall standard **175.00**
Sewing Clamp, polished steel, "The Mignon," maroon velvet pincushion, Germany **60.00**
Sewing Clamp, rosewood, fabric pincushion, Tunbridge **110.00**
Sewing Knife, White Sewing Machines adv, red plastic cover, steel blade, mkd "Gitz Razor-Nife" **5.00**
Spool Holder Clamp, Folk Art, ebony and ivory **375.00**
Tape Measure, Bokar Coffee Supreme, celluloid canister, depicts product can in brown and red on white ground, reverse panel with red and black lettering, cloth tape, c1920-30s **20.00**
Tape Measure, Boston Garter, celluloid canister, brown and orange on pink ground, brown lettering, depicts example hosiery garter plus its uses on stocking by seated man, reverse with multicolored depiction of lady standing at dressing table wearing dressing gown while holding "Velvet Grip Hose Supporter" **10.00**
Tape Measure, Levin's Auto Supply, celluloid canister, green lettering "Stores In Northern California" with "Van Ness Automotive Products," reverse with red and green Christmas wreath around complimentary greeting for 1940-1941 year, cloth tape **10.00**
Tape Measure, Penn Treaty Co, celluloid canister, white, black lettering on both sides for business in Glen Riddle, PA, c1930s **10.00**
Tape Measure, Sears Allstate Truck Tire Center, black plastic tire with domed plastic cover, red company name, metal tape, 1950-60s **10.00**
Tape Measure, Woolworth building, silvered tin canister with color celluloid insert on 1 side depicting Woolworth building towering above surrounding structures, cloth tape, mkd "Germany," 1930s **20.00**
Thimble, aluminum, Singer Sewing Machine **10.00**
Toy Sewing Machine, Casige, German, Carl Sieper, Gevelsberg, No. 0/1, nickel-plate **200.00**
Toy Sewing Machine, Damascus, American, orig box, c1935 . . . . **300.00**
Toy Sewing Machine, Eldredgette, American, c1930 . . . . **200.00**
Toy Sewing Machine, FW Müller, German, Berlin, No.15, dec cast iron, missing thread tension, c1930 . . . . . **275.00**
Toy Sewing Machine, Junior Miss, Artcraft Products, American, sheet metal on wooden pedestal, complete with table clamp and operating instructions, orig box, c1946 . . . . **110.00**
Toy Sewing Machine, Stitchwell, American, dec cast iron, orig wooden box, c1925 . . . . **325.00**
Yarn Swift, Mauchline Ware, Crystal Palace Sydenham **250.00**

SHAWNEE POTTERY

Addis E. Hull, Jr., Robert C. Shilling, and a group of investors established the Shawnee Pottery Company, Zanesville, Ohio, in 1937. It was named for an Indian tribe that lived in the area.

Shawnee manufactured inexpensive, high-quality kitchen and utilitarian earthenware. The company perfected a bisque drying method that enabled decorating and glazing to be achieved in a single firing. In the late 1930s and early 1940s, Shawnee supplied products to large chain stores. Valencia, a dinnerware and kitchenware line, was created for Sears.

Robert Ganz joined Shawnee as a designer in 1938, creating some of the company's most popular cookie jars, e.g., Puss 'n Boots and Smiley. Designer Robert Heckman arrived in 1945 and was responsible for the King Corn line and numerous pieces featuring a Pennsylvania German motif.

Hull left Shawnee in 1950. In 1954 John Bonistall became president and shifted production from kitchenware to decorative accessories. He created the Kenwood Ceramics division to market the remaining kitchenware products. Chantilly, Cameo, Elegance, Fernwood, Petit Point, and Touché are several art lines introduced in the late 1950s. The company prospered in the late 1950s.

A decision was made to cease operations in 1961. Bonistall purchased Shawnee's molds and established Terrace Ceramics, Marietta, Ohio.

References: Pam Curran, *Shawnee Pottery,* Schiffer Publishing, 1995; Jim and Bev Mangus, *Shawnee Pottery,* Collector Books, 1994, 2000 value update; Mark Supnick, *Collecting Shawnee Pottery,* L-W Book Sales, 1989, 2000 value update; Duane and Janice Vanderbilt, *The Collector's Guide to Shawnee Pottery,* Collector Books, 1992, 1998 value update.

Collectors' Club: Shawnee Pottery Collectors Club, PO Box 713, New Smyrna Beach, FL 32170.

Ashtray, boomerang shape, 13" l, 8" w **$10.00**
Ball Jug, Sunflower pattern **90.00**

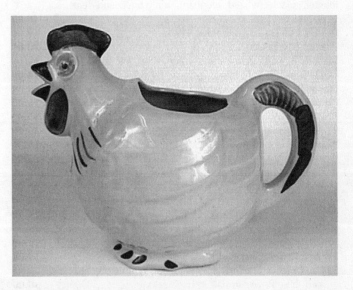

Pitcher, Chanticleer, 7½" h, $70.00. Photo courtesy Ray Morykan Auctions.

Bookends, pr, setter dogs, 4½" h **60.00**

Bowl, ruffled edge, 4-toed, mint green, 9" w **15.00**

Candlestick, green, #3026. **15.00**

Console Bowl, basketweave ext, #1417, 3½" h, 18" l **15.00**

Console Bowl, oblong, gray granite ext, pink int, 3¼" h, 11¼" l, 3¼" w. **12.00**

Console Set, #1417 bowl, pair of #1419 candleholders, price for 3-pc set. **30.00**

Corn on the Cob Dishes, price for 5. . . . . **110.00**

Dishes, triangular, 3 flying geese, "Souvenir of Sioux City IA" sticker, #403, 8¼" l, 5¼" w, price for pr **12.00**

Figurine, deer, white with pink ears and pink clover dec, 5" h, 4½" l **18.00**

Figurine, frog, green, 2" h **18.00**

Figurine, oriental boy, 5" h **12.00**

Flowerpot, attached saucer, blue and white swirled, #533, 3" h, 3½" w. **25.00**

Flowerpot, attached saucer, pink, 3¼" h, 4½" d **20.00**

Flowerpot, attached saucer, tulip shape, #466, coral pink, 5" h **25.00**

Flowerpot, brown, attached yellow saucer, #410, 4" h, 4" sq. **12.00**

Flowerpots, white, 3⅛" h, price for pr **15.00**

King Corn, butter dish, cov, #72. . . . . **85.00**

King Corn, casserole, cov, 5½" h, 11" l. **70.00**

King Corn, mixing bowl, #8, 3½" h, 8" d. **60.00**

King Corn, mug, 3½" h **50.00**

King Corn, platter, #96, 11¾" l, 8¼" w. **115.00**

King Corn, salt and pepper shakers, pr, 3" h. **40.00**

King Corn, salt and pepper shakers, pr, 5¼" h. **25.00**

Lamps, pr, Blackamoor heads, gold trim, 8" h. **75.00**

Pepper Shaker, Jack, 5¼" h **25.00**

Pie Bird, blue and pink, 5¼" h. **50.00**

Pie Bird, green wings, pink base, 5¼" h **45.00**

Pillow Vase, pebbled turquoise, peach, and white ext, 5" h, 7" w **10.00**

Pillow Vase, vertical ribs, #231, 6" h, 4¼" w. **10.00**

Pitcher Vase, white, scrolled handle, 3" h. **15.00**

Planter, black stylized bull, pink base and leaf planter, 4" h, 6½" l **30.00**

Planter, black stylized elephant, pink base and leaf planter **40.00**

Planter, boy leaning on fence, 4¼" h **10.00**

Planter, chuckwagon. **30.00**

Planter, elf sitting on shoe, green shoe, elf wearing white with purple trim. **18.00**

Planter, foot bridge, #756 . . . . **15.00**

Planter, gristmill, #769, 5½" h, 7" l. **15.00**

Planter, horse, red, #509, 7¾" h, 8" l **35.00**

Planter, oriental girl with urn, 6¼" h, 5" w **25.00**

Planter, pixie with wheelbarrow, 4" h, 5" w **18.00**

Planter, scallop shells, 6-sided, #154, 3" h, 6" w. **20.00**

Planter, truck, red cab, yellow trailer, #680 and #681 . . . . . . **65.00**

Planter, wishing well, 5½" h, 8" w **15.00**

Queen Corn, salt and pepper shakers, pr, 3¼" h. **25.00**

Salt and Pepper Shakers, pr, fruit, 4" h **35.00**

Salt and Pepper Shakers, pr, milk cans **20.00**

Salt and Pepper Shakers, pr, owl, 3¼" h **20.00**

Salt and Pepper Shakers, pr, Puss 'n' Boots. **30.00**

Salt and Pepper Shakers, pr, Smiley and Winnie Pig, red scarf, blue flower in hat, 3" h. **30.00**

Salt and Pepper Shakers, pr, Smiley Pig, peach bib, range size, 5" h. **125.00**

Teapot, hp blue flower, 5½" h, 8½" w **35.00**

Teapot, Sunflower pattern, 30 oz, 6¼" h. **40.00**

Teapot, Tom the Piper's Son **80.00**

Triple Bowl, handled, #517, 6¾" h, 7" w **20.00**

Vase, classic shape, yellow, 2 scrolled handles, pedestal base **25.00**

Vase, cylindrical, quatrefoil opening, textured burgundy ext, white int, 10" h. **30.00**

Vase, diamond quilted body with emb flowers at corners, 2-handled, yellow, #827, 7" h **18.00**

Vase, fluted, pink swirled, #502, 4" h, 5¼" w **15.00**

Vase, oblong, tapers to base, gray granite ext, pink int, #1026, 7¼" h, 6⅛" l **15.00**

Window Box, Cameo line, butterscotch ext, #2506, 4" h, 14" l. **10.00**

SHEET MUSIC

Sheet music is collected primarily for its cover art. The late 1880s through the early 1950s is considered the golden age of sheet music cover art. Every conceivable theme was illustrated. Leading illustrators lent their talents to sheet music covers.

Covers frequently featured a picture of the singer, group, or orchestra responsible for introducing the song to the public. Photographic covers followed the times. Radio stars, movie stars, and television stars appeared on sheet music covers to promote their show or latest screen epic.

Sheet music's popularity is closely related to the popularity of piano playing. When interest in piano playing declined in the 1950s, sheet music covers no longer exhibited the artistic and design creativity of former times. Collector interest in post-1960s sheet music, with the exception of TV show themes and rock 'n' roll sheets, is minimal.

Most sheet music is worth between $1.00 and $3.00, provided it is in near mint condition. In spite of this, many dealers ask an average $5.00 to $10.00 per sheet for mundane titles. Part of the reason for this discrepancy in pricing is the crossover influence of subject collectors. These collectors have little patience with the hunt. Not realizing how easy it is to find copies, they pay high prices and fuel the unrealistic expectations of the general dealer.

Further complicating the picture is the inaccurate, highly manipulative values in the Pafik and Guiheen price guide (Collector Books, 1995). The book has been roundly criticized, and rightly so, within the sheet music collecting community.

References: Debbie Dillon, *Collectors Guide to Sheet Music,* L-W Book Promotions, 1988, 1995 value update; Marion Short, *The Gold in Your Piano Bench* (1997), *Covers of Gold* (1998), *Hollywood Movie Songs* (1999), Schiffer Publishing.

Periodical: *Sheet Music Magazine,* 333 Adams St, Bedford Hills, NY 10507.

Newsletter: *The Rag Times,* 15522 Ricky Ct, Grass Valley, CA 95949.

Collectors' Clubs: National Sheet Music Society, Inc., 1597 Fair Park Ave, Los Angeles, CA 90041; Remember That Song, 5623 N 64th Ave, Glendale, AZ 85301; Sonneck Society for American Music & Music in America, PO Box 476, Canton, MA 02021.

Advisor: Wayland Bunnell, 199 Tarrytown Rd, Manchester, NH 03103.

Love Walked In, The Goldwyn Follies, tan wash, c1938, $25.00.

All's Well, Rainger/Robin, *Gulliver's Travels,* Fleischer cartoon drawings on film strip, 1939 . . . . **$15.00**

Alvin Twist, The, Bagdasarian, drawing of Alvin doing the twist, credit to Liberty Records, 1962 . . . . **8.00**

Apple Blossom Time, A Von Tilzer/Fleeson, *Buck Privates,* photo of Andrews Sisters in uniform saluting, 1920 . . . . **5.00**

A Trip Doesn't Care At All, Hilliard/Sigman, *Angel In the Wings,* magicians wand touching billboard, 1947 . . . . **3.00**

Ballad of Bonnie and Clyde, Murray/Callander, photo of Georgie Fame with tommy gun by old car, 1967 . . . . **3.00**

California Polka, The, Fitzsimmons, burlap background, large tilted inset photo of Ted Williams, 1946 . . . . **5.00**

Cow Cow Boogie, Raye/dePaul/Carter, *Swing Symphony,* Walter Lantz cartoon, cow at piano, rattlesnake, 1942 . . . . . **6.00**

Cuddle Up a Little Closer, Hoschna/Harbach, *Coney Island,* photo of Betty Grable and Cesar Romero, 1932 . . . . . **4.00**

Drink to Me Only With Thine Eyes, traditional arrangement by LC Johnson, Barbelle center drawing of angels in decorative oval frame, 1924 . . . . **4.00**

Flamingo, Grouya/Anderson, green and white photo of Duke Ellington at piano, 1966 . . . . **6.00**

Hokey Pokey, LaPrise/Macak/Mason/Baker, small figures dancing, head photos of The Sun Valley Trio, 1950 . . . . **3.00**

Hot Roasted Peanuts, Breau/C Tobias/H Tobias, comic peanut vendor with wagon, 1923 . . . . **6.00**

How Sweet You Are, A Schwartz/Loesser, *Thank Your Lucky Stars,* depicts heads of Bogart, Cantor, DeHavilland, and Lupino, 1943 . . . . **4.00**

If I Had My Life to Live Over, Vincent/H Tobias/Jaffe, night scene of people paddling canoe, left insert of Kate Smith, 1944 . . . . **5.00**

If I'm Dreaming, Burke/Dubin, *Sally,* photo of Marilyn Miller dancing, chorus line, 1929 . . . . **3.00**

Indian Love Call, Friml/Harvach/Hammerstein, Warner Bros logo on blue, 1924 . . . . **2.00**

Innamorata, Warren/Brooks, *Artists and Models,* photo of Dean Martin and Jerry Lewis at easel, 1955 . . . . **8.00**

Knee Deep In Stardust, Gaal/Shaw, photo of Kate Smith, 1941 . . . . **8.00**

Laura, Raksin/Mercer, right photo of Gene Tierney, inset lower left of Tommy Dorsey, 1945 . . . . **8.00**

Little Drummer Boy, Noel/Pelosi, red, white, and blue stylized drummer in uniform, Marlo Music, 1938 . . . . **4.00**

Lucky Cowboy, Robin/Rainger, large photo of Julie Gibson, hearts in background, 1937 . . . . **15.00**

Misty, Garner/Burke, blue cross-hatch pattern, 1955 . . . . **3.00**

My Best to You, Jones/Willadsen, curving staves, notes, small drawings of dancers and orchestra, left inset of Eddie Howard, 1942 . . . . **3.00**

Open Up Your Heart, Hamblen, border of tiny hearts, large center inset photo of McGuire Sisters, 1953 . . . . **3.00**

Ragamuffin, Janssen, 4/4 fox trot, running boy in raggedy clothes, 1920 . . . . **3.00**

Rock Me In My Swanee Cradle, Eleanor Young/Squires/ Parish, moon and house, river seen through curtained window, 1922 . . . . **6.00**

Shepherd of the Air, Gaskill, silhouette of Father Coughlin at radio mike, angels as clouds, doves, 1933 . . . . . **4.00**

Skylark, H Carmichael/Mercer, stylized birds and clouds, left inset photo of Bing Crosby, 1942 . . . . **6.00**

Somewhere My Love, Jarre/Webster, *Dr Zhivago,* large photo of Ray Conniff, full movie credits, Academy Award credit, 1966 . . . . **3.00**

Surrey With the Fringe on Top, Rodgers/Hammerstein, *Oklahoma,* photo of Shirley Jones and Gordon McRae in surrey, 1943 . . . . **10.00**

Thoroughly Modern Millie, Van Heusen/Cahn, drawing of Julie Andrews, Carol Channing, Mary Tyler Moore, small planes, and cars, 1967 . . . . **5.00**

Together, DeSylva/Brown/Henderson, *Since You Went Away,* head photos of Shirley Temple, Claudette Colbert, and Joseph Cotton, 1944 . . . . **4.00**

Whatever Lola Wants, Adler/Ross, *Damn Yankees,* Gwen Verdon in skimpy Lola costume, 1955 . . . . **8.00**

Where Is Love, Bart, *Oliver,* full color stars and scenes with blue border, cast list and photos on back, 1968 . . . . . . **5.00**

SHELLEY CHINA

Members of the Shelley family have manufactured ceramics in England's Staffordshire district since the mid-18th century. In 1872 Joseph Shelley and James Wileman formed Wileman & Co. Percy, Joseph's son, joined the firm in 1881. Percy hired designers and artists, significantly upgrading the company's product line.

Rowland Morris created Dainty White, the company's most successful popular dinnerware shape, around 1900. Frederick Rhead and Walter Slater also worked for the firm.

The company began making crest ware, miniature, and parian busts following World War I. Fine china was known as "Eggshell." In 1925 Wileman & Co. became Shelley. Hild Cowham and Mabel Atwell's nursery ware proved highly popular in the 1920s and 1930s. Tea wares added luster to Shelley's reputation. The Queen Anne octagonal shape is one of the best known.

Earthenware production ceased after World War II. Shelly concentrated on dinnerware. In 1966 Allied English Potteries acquired Shelley. It became part of the Doulton Group in 1971.

Reference: Robert Prescott-Walker, *Collecting Shelley Pottery,* Francis Joseph, 1999.

Collectors' Club: National Shelley China Club, 12010 38th Ave NE, Seattle, WA 98125.

Cup and Saucer, Dainty Blue pattern, $75.00.

Breakfast Set, blue heron design, #R782/A, cup, saucer, and 8" plate. **$125.00**

Breakfast Set, Eastern Star design, gold trim, cup, saucer, and 8" d plate **35.00**

Cigarette Jar, Begonia pattern, blue trim, #13427, 2" h, 2" d **35.00**

Creamer and Sugar, pink roses, turquoise scrolls, green leafy swags, #10243, scalloped bodies, mkd "Late Foley" **60.00**

Creamer and Sugar, Rosebud pattern, #272101, scalloped bodies **45.00**

Creamer and Sugar on Tray, white with gold trim, scalloped bodies, 7" l tray **125.00**

Cream Soup and Saucer, 2-handled soup, Georgian pattern. **50.00**

Cup and Saucer, basket of fruit design, gold trim **65.00**

Cup and Saucer, black and white checkerboard and swag borders. **15.00**

Cup and Saucer, Blue Rock pattern, Ludlow shape **45.00**

Cup and Saucer, Campanula pattern, dark purple trim, fluted cup. **115.00**

Cup and Saucer, Crochet pattern, gold trim, #13302. . . . . . . **65.00**

Cup and Saucer, Sheraton pattern, Gainsborough shape, #13289. . . . . **65.00**

Cup and Saucer, souvenir "Royal Palms, Bermuda," gold trim **20.00**

Cup and Saucer, Wild Flowers series, #13668 . . . . **40.00**

Cup and Saucer, Yellow Dainty pattern, solid yellow with black trim **70.00**

Eggcup, Wild Rose pattern, 3¼" h **45.00**

Juvenile Cup and Saucer, 2 dogs on cup, "The Babes In The Wood" on saucer **50.00**

Milk Jug, Yellow Dainty pattern, solid yellow with black trim, melon-ribbed body, 3¼" h **45.00**

Mint Dish, wild flowers on light green ground, square shape with scalloped rim and fan handles **100.00**

Plate, Dainty Blue pattern, 6" w. **40.00**

Plate, Dainty Blue pattern, 7" w. **70.00**

Plate, Dainty Blue pattern, 8⅛" w **45.00**

Plate, Dainty Blue pattern, 9¼" w **45.00**

Teacup and Bowl, scenic design with black handle and trim, #11349, 5¼" d bowl **15.00**

SILHOUETTE PICTURES

Silhouettes, named for Etienne de Silhouette, the French Minister of Finance responsible for their introduction, were popular in the 18th and early 19th centuries. They lost their appeal when the photograph arrived on the scene in the mid-19th century. Brief revivals occurred in the 1930s and 1950s, when silhouette stands were commonly found resort attractions.

In the 1920s, a new type of silhouette was introduced. This consisted of a black or colored picture that was painted on the back of a piece of flat or convex glass. A paper scenic, tinted, or textured foil background was used to enhance the picture.

Leading manufacturers included Art Publishing Co. (Chicago), Benton Glass Company (Benton, MI), The Buckbee-Brehm Company (Minneapolis), Newton Manufacturing (Newton, IA), Reliance Products (New York/Chicago), and West Coast Picture Company (Portland). Forms ranged from simple two-dimensional pictures to jewelry boxes and were popular promotional giveaways. Stock forms were imprinted with advertisements for local merchants.

Reference: Shirley Mace, *Encyclopedia of Silhouette Collectibles on Glass,* Shadow Enterprises, 1992.

Note: All examples listed are pictures with the silhouette painted on glass.

Boy fishing while dog watches, black silhouette, pressed flower background, Fisher **$18.00**

Butterflies and flowers, black and white silhouette, foil background, Reliance **25.00**

Colonial man and waving woman walking near tree, black silhouette, color background with thatched cottage, Benton **20.00**

Colonial woman holding parasol, walking with small boy and girl, color silhouette on white ground, Art Pub Co, 1930s **20.00**

Colonial woman seated at spinning wheel, black silhouette, foil ground, Art Pub Co #268, 1930s. **20.00**

Cowboys at campfire, black silhouette with red and white flames, color background of Rocky Mountains, Newton Mfg **20.00**

Dutch boy and girl with ducks and tulips, red, yellow, black, and white silhouette, color background of Dutch landscape with windmill, Forever, plastic frame, 1950 calendar, 4½" h, 5½" w **20.00**

Girl chasing doll-stealing dog, black silhouette, pressed flower background, Fisher **18.00**

"Good Night," man and woman kissing at iron gate, Buckbee-Brehm, 1932 . . . . **25.00**

"Happy in Her Garden," woman watering flowers, black silhouette with yellow flowers, white background, Plaquette Art Co **25.00**

Kittens at duck pond, black silhouette, white ground, Benton **25.00**

"Knitting," woman seated in armchair next to window with flowered drapes, she knits while kittens play with yarn, brown and black room silhouette, window looks out on village landscape background, with thermometer and 1951 calendar pad, Forever #6842, 6 x 8" **20.00**

Man and woman building snowman, black silhouette, color background with snowy landscape, Benton **25.00**

Colonial Couple, convex glass, copper frame, probably Benton Glass Co, c1940s, 3¹/₂ x 4¹/₂", price each, $18.00.

Parlor scene with woman playing piano while girl
dances, blue silhouette, white ground, Benton 60.00
"The Answer," girl mailing letter, black silhouette, white
ground, Buckbee-Brehm, c1930 . . . . 25.00
Two Scottie dogs playing tug of war, black silhouette,
white ground 20.00
White lace silhouette framing background color portrait
of Grecian woman, 1941, Donald Art Co 25.00
Woman and Afghan standing at river's edge, black silhouette, silver foil ground, Deltex, 1933 . . . . 45.00
Woman at spinning wheel, black silhouette, red, white,
and black background with kettle and brick hearth,
Newton Mfg, 1961 calendar 12.00
Woman walking Scottie while reaching for wind-blown
hat, city skyline in background, black silhouette, silver
foil ground, Deltex, 1933 . . . . 45.00

SILVER, PLATED & STERLING

Sterling silver contains 925 parts of silver per 1,000. The remaining 75 parts consist of additional metals, primarily copper, that add strength and hardness to the silver. Silver plate, developed in England in the late 1860s, is achieved through electrolysis. A thin layer of silver is added to a base metal, usually britannia (an alloy of antimony, copper, and tin), copper, or white metal (an alloy of bismuth, copper, lead, and tin).

Silver plated ware achieved great popularity in the period between 1880 and 1915. Alvin, Gorham, International Silver Company (the result of a series of mergers), Oneida, Reed & Barton, William Rogers, and Wallace are among the principal manufacturers.

Silverware can be divided into three distinct categories: (1) flatware, (2) hollowware, and (3) giftware. This category includes hollowware and giftware. Currently silverware collecting is enjoying a number of renaissances. Plated pieces from the late Victorian era, especially small accessories such as napkin rings, benefited from the Victorian revival of the 1980s. The return to more formal dining has created renewed interest in tabletop accessory pieces.

References: Janet Drucker, *Georg Jensen,* Schiffer Publishing, 1997; Penny Chittim Morrill and Carole A. Berk, *Mexican Silver: 20th Century Handwrought Jewelry & Metalwork, 2nd Edition,* Schiffer Publishing, 1999; Dorothy T. Rainwater, *Encyclopedia of American Silver Manufacturers, 4th Edition,* Schiffer Publishing, 1998.

Periodical: *Silver Magazine,* PO Box 9690, Rancho Santa Fe, CA 92067.

Note: See Flatware for additional silver listings.

SILVER PLATED

Candle Snuffer, Meriden, raised floral design $15.00
Child's Mug, Oneida, etched design 10.00
Cigar Holder, Graham Silver, champagne bottle form,
beaded rim, engraved "Cigars," 10¹/₂" h 80.00
Ice Bucket, Gorham, 2-handled, beaded rim, square
base 35.00
Salt and Pepper Shakers, pr, urn form, 4¹/₂" h 75.00
Soup Tureen, oval form with cast handles and reeded
edge, domed lid with reeded edge and flower-form
finial, reeded foot, monogrammed, 20th C, 12" h,
18" l 250.00
Tea Tray, oval, 2-handled, gadrooned rim, engraved
scrollwork bands, 30" l 150.00
Tray, oval with gallery, ball feet, 24" l 150.00
Water Pitcher, Meriden & Co, raised floral dec 50.00

STERLING

Basket, Frank W Smith Silver Co, made for Tiffany & Co,
#2219, shaped oval basket with sides pierced and
engraved with C-scrolls, flowers, foliage, and diaper-
work, shaped rim with applied molded scrollwork,
reticulated swing handle with scrolls and bellflowers,
4 extended scroll supports, early 20th C, 23 oz, 8" h,
10¹/₂" l $1,750.00
Bowl, Georg Jensen, Johan Rohde designer, #171, plain
circular bowl supported by ring of scrolling foliage
and berries on stepped circular base, 1925-30, 5¹/₂" h,
8" d 3,250.00
Candelabra, Shreve & Co, 5-lite, stepped circular bases,
baluster stem, 18" h, weighted base, price for pr 7,000.00
Centerpiece Bowl, M Buccellati, Milan, shaped oval
form with outset curved panels, 4 open cast scroll
supports, and 4 cast foliate scrollwork handles,
mid-20th C, 6" h, 18¹/₂" l 2,000.00
Centerpiece Bowl, Shreve & Co, circular bowl, self-ring
foot, raised base, steep sides curving at top to applied
wide flat horizontal reticulated border, 3¹/₂" h, 15¹/₂" d . . 1,500.00
Pitcher, Italian, made for Tiffany & Co, NY, octagonal
form with flat tapering sides, C-form wooden handle,
7¹/₂" h 1,200.00
Tea and Coffee Set, Durgin Division of The Gorham Co,
#40001 through #40005, 5-pc set consisting of cof-
feepot, teapot, open sugar bowl, cream pitcher, and
waste bowl, decagonal urn forms on conforming
pedestal bases, lids with fan-form finials, scroll handles, 24¹/₂" l #40007 matching oval tray with pierced
handles, dated 1930, 190 oz 3,750.00

SIZZLERS

Mattel produced Sizzlers between 1970 and 1978. Actually, Sizzlers disappeared during 1974, 1975, and 1977. George Soulakis and General Electric developed a nickel-cadmium rechargeable battery that could run for four to five minutes on a 90-second charge. Sizzlers had a hard plastic body and were painted in a variety of colors. Sizzler body types are divided into American cars, Grand Prix types, and exotics. Sizzler variants include Earthshakers, Hotline Trains, and Chopcycles.

Three different chargers were made: (1) a battery Juice Machine (resembling a 1970s gas pump), (2) a battery Goose Pump, revamped in 1978 as the Super Charger, and (3) the Power Pit, an AC charger (resembling a gasoline service station) that plugged into the wall.

Unrestored cars are worth between 20 and 25% of the value of the identical car in restored condition. Complete race sets and accessories still in period packaging are highly desirable.

Mattel failed to protect the Sizzler brand name. Contemporary Sizzlers are manufactured by Playing Mantis of South Bend, Indiana.

Reference: Mike Grove, *A Pictorial Guide to Sizzlers,* published by author, 1995.

Note: Prices listed are for cars in unrestored condition.

Anteater II, #9382, 1976 . . . . **$3.00**
Camaro Trans-Am, #6529, 1971 . . . . **15.00**
Chevy Camaro II, #9380, 1976 . . . . **8.00**
Corvette 4-Rotor, #9864, 1978. . . . . **20.00**
Dark Shadow, #2353, 1978 . . . . **10.00**
Double Boiler, #5885, 1972 . . . . **15.00**
Ferrari, #6551, 1970 . . . . **55.00**
Fireworks, #4943, 1973 . . . . **50.00**
Lamborghini Countach, #9863, 1978 . . . . **15.00**
Law Mill, #4948, 1973 . . . . **50.00**
Long Count, #9866, 1978 . . . . **15.00**
March F-1, #6535, 1971 . . . . **12.00**
Ram Rocket, #4945, 1973 . . . . **45.00**
Red Baron, #4947, 1973 . . . . **35.00**
Revvin' Heaven, #6504, 1970 . . . . **5.00**
Spoil Sport, #6520, 1971 . . . . **8.00**

SLOT CARS

Aurora Plastics Corporation, founded in March 1950, introduced a line of plastic model airplane kits in the fall of 1952. In December 1953, Aurora moved into a new plant in West Hempstead, Long Island, New York. Shortly thereafter Aurora began making a line of hobby craft products. In 1960 Aurora purchased K & B Allyn, a California manufacturer of gas-powered airplane motors.

Aurora launched the electric slot car in 1960. They were an overnight success. From their inception slot cars were noted for the attention paid to details—they looked like the real thing. The slot car's golden age extends from 1962 through the mid-1970s. New models, scales, and track sets and accessories appeared on a regular basis. However, by the mid-1970s, many of the Aurora slot car innovators no longer worked for Aurora. The company changed hands several times during the 1970s and 1980s. By the 1980s, Tyco assumed the leadership role in the slot car field.

References: John A. Clark, *HO Slot Car Identification and Price Guide,* L-W Book Sales, 1995; Thomas Graham, *Greenberg's Guide to Aurora Slot Cars,* Greenberg Books, 1995.

Periodicals: *HO Slot Car Journal,* PO Box 2051, Redmond, WA 98073; *Scale Auto Racing News,* 2608 Robert Rd, Arkansas Pass, TX 78336.

Newsletter: *H.O. USA Newsletter,* 435½ S Orange St, Orange, CA 92866.

Note: Prices listed are for slot cars in mint condition unless noted otherwise.

AFX, Andretti Race Set, with 4 cars **$90.00**
AFX, Dragster Dodge Fever **40.00**
AFX, Magna Traction Chevy Nomad. **30.00**
Atlas, Chevy Impala, MOC **60.00**
Aurora, Dino Ferrari, red **25.00**
Aurora, Ford FT 40, black, MIB **500.00**
Cox, Chaparral 2C, white plastic body, molded magnesium sidewinder frame, 16D motor, magnesium rims, #3, 1/24 scale, 1960 . . . . **300.00**
Cox, Chaparral 2D, white plastic body, molded magnesium sidewinder frame, 16D motor, magnesium rims, #65, 1/24 scale, 1960s. **250.00**
Eldon, Chaparral, factory white painted Lexan body, smoked windows, chrome plated steel chassis, inline motor, 1/24 scale, 1960s **75.00**
Eldon, Chaparral 2D, dark blue plastic body, smoked windows, plastic adjustable inline frame, 1/32 scale, 1960s **35.00**
Eldon, Porsche Carrera, silver plastic body, smoked windows, plastic adjustable inline frame, 1/32 scale **35.00**
Eldon, Porsche Carrera 6, factory painted silver Lexan body, smoked windows, chrome plated steel chassis, inline motor, 1/24 scale, 1960s **75.00**
Ideal, Dukes of Hazzard Police Car, near mint **10.00**

Aurora XLerators Speed Loop Racing Set, $25.00.

K&B (Aurora), Ferrari 275 LM, red plastic body, aluminum adjustable sidewinder chassis, 1/24 scale, 1966. . . . . **150.00**

K&B (Aurora), Ford Cobra Coupe, blue plastic body, adjustable aluminum sidewinder chassis, 1/24 scale, 1960s **300.00**

Monogram, Chaparral 2D, white plastic body, aluminum sidewinder frame, weighted style working wing, 1/24 scale, 1960s **250.00**

Monogram, Ferrari 275P, red plastic body, brass or aluminum inline chassis, drop wire guide arm, #22, X220 motor, 1/24 scale, 1960s. **275.00**

Revell, BRM, green or blue plastic body, adjustable aluminum inline chassis, 1/25 scale, 1960s. **50.00**

Revell, Chaparral 2C, white plastic body, adjustable brass inline chassis, 1/32 scale, 1960s **125.00**

Revell, Cobra, blue plastic body, adjustable aluminum inline frame, SP 500 motor, 1/32 scale, 1960s. **300.00**

Strombecker, Aston Martin "James Body," silver plastic body, suspended brass brackets with scorcher type motor, 1/32 scale, 1960s **200.00**

Strombecker, Braham F1, green plastic body, suspended scorcher type motor, 1/24 scale, 1960s. **250.00**

Tomy, Alpha Cubic, #22, MIB **80.00**

Tomy, Camel, #12 . . . . **200.00**

Tyco, HP7 Z-28 Camaro, yellow/brown, NM **10.00**

Tyco, Jam Car 5000 Slotless Slot Car, NM **10.00**

SLOT MACHINES

In 1905 Charles Frey of San Francisco invented the first three-reel slot machine, known as the Liberty Bell. An example survives at the Liberty Bell Saloon, an establishment owned by Frey's grandson in Reno, Nevada.

Although the Mills Novelty Company copyrighted the famous fruit symbols in 1910, they were quickly copied by other manufacturers. They are still one of the most popular slot machine symbols. The jackpot was added in 1928.

Early slot machines featured wooden cabinets. Cast-iron cabinets appeared in the mid-1910s. Aluminum fronts arrived in the early 1920s. Mechanical improvements, such as variations in coin entry and detection of slugs, occurred during the 1930s. Additional security devices to prevent cheating and tampering were added in the 1940s. The 1950s marked the introduction of electricity, for operation as well as illumination.

The 1920s and 30s is the golden age of slot machines. Machines featured elaborate castings, ornate decoration, and numerous gimmicks. Caille, Jennings, Mill, Pace, and Watling are among the leading manufacturers.

References: Jerry Ayliff, *American Premium Guide to Jukeboxes and Slot Machines, Third Edition,* Books Americana, 1991; Richard M. Bueschel, *Collector's Guide to Vintage Coin Machines,* Schiffer Publishing, 1995; Richard M. Bueschel, *Lemons, Cherries and Bell-Fruit-Gum: Illustrated History of Automatic Payout Slot Machines,* Royal Ben Books, 1995; Marshal Fey, *Slot Machines: A Pictorial History of the First 100 Years, Fourth Edition,* published by author.

Periodicals: *Antique Amusements, Slot Machines & Jukebox Gazette,* 909 26th St NW, Washington, DC 20037; *Coin Drop International,* 5815 W 52nd Ave, Denver, CO 80212; *Loose Change,* 1515 S Commerce St, Las Vegas, NV 89102.

Western Products, Reel Poker, 9¼" h, $550.00. Photo courtesy Collectors Auction Services.

AC Novelty, Multi-Bell, 1936 . . . . **$2,800.00**
Bally, Bally Bell, 5¢, 1938 . . . . **2,400.00**
Buckley, Bones, 5¢, 1936 . . . . **4,000.00**
Bull Durham, Triple Jack Gold Award, 1934 . . . . **2,800.00**
C&F, Baby Grand, 1932 . . . . **1,000.00**
Caille Bros, Dough Boy, 25¢, 1935 . . . . **850.00**
Jennings, Dutchess, 5¢, oak stand, 1934 . . . . **2,500.00**
Jennings, Rainbow, 1932 . . . . **1,000.00**
Jennings, Red Sun Chief, 25¢, matching light-up glass panel stand **3,000.00**
Jennings, Little Duke Jackpot, 10¢, 1933 . . . . **1,500.00**
Jennings, Silver Dollar Red Sun Chief, matching light-up glass panel stand **4,000.00**
Mills, Bonus, 5¢, 1937 . . . . **2,400.00**
Mills, Bursting Cherry, 25¢, matching light-up stand, 1938-42 . . . . **2,800.00**
Mills, "Copperfront," 5¢, cast-iron, 1938 . . . . **2,700.00**
Mills, Extraordinary Golden, 5¢, 1933 . . . . **1,400.00**
Mills, Futurity Golden, 5¢, 1936 . . . . **3,000.00**
Mills, Golden Nuggets, 25¢, matching light-up Golden Nugget stand **2,700.00**
Mills, Lions Head, 25¢, matching light-up stand, 1932. . . . **2,800.00**
Mills, Mystery, 10¢, 1962 . . . . **1,200.00**
Mills, Operator Bell, 25¢, 1922 . . . . **1,200.00**
Mills, Romanhead, 25¢, 1932 . . . . **2,800.00**
Mills, Silent Golden, 1932 . . . . **2,000.00**
Mills, Silent Gooseneck, 1931 . . . . **1,400.00**
Mills, Silver Place, 25¢. **2,800.00**
Pace, 3 Jacks, 1930 . . . . **750.00**
Pace, Comet Front Vender, 1934 . . . . **1,500.00**
Sega, Vest Pocket, 1¢, 1950s **1,000.00**
Superior Confection, Escalator Vender, 1934 . . . . **1,600.00**
Superior Confection, Gooseneck Gold Award, 1934. . . . . **1,600.00**
Superior Confection, Races, 5¢, 1935 . . . . **5,000.00**
Vendet, Midget, 5¢, 1932 . . . . **1,250.00**
Watling, Rol-A-Top Checkerboard, 10¢, 1947 . . . . **7,000.00**
Watling, Rol-A-Top, 5¢, 1935 . . . . **2,600.00**
Watling, Wonder Vender, 1934 . . . . **1,400.00**

SNACK SETS

A snack set consists of two pieces, a cup and a matching under-plate. Although glass was the most commonly used material, they also were made in ceramics and plastic. Dating back to the 1920s, the snack set achieved its greatest popularity in the 1950s and 60s. Snack sets were ideal for informal entertaining.

Most sets were sold in services consisting of four cups and four plates. Collectors pay a slight premium for a service of four sets in their period box. Some snack sets have become quite expensive, not because they are snack sets but because of their crossover value. Many chintz sets exceed $250.

Reference: Delores Long, *100 Glass Snack Sets,* published by author, 1998.

Newsletter: *Snack Set Searchers,* PO Box 158, Hallock, MN 56728.

Note: Prices are for sets consisting of one cup and one plate.

Bed Quilt, Anchor Hocking, red cup **$10.00**
Blossom, Federal. **8.00**
Blue Mosaic, Anchor Hocking, Fire-King line **10.00**
Button and Daisy, Indiana, avocado. **6.00**
Button and Daisy, Jeannette, avocado green **8.00**
Colonial Lady, Anchor Hocking, crystal cup **7.00**
Colonial Lady, Anchor Hocking, red cup **12.00**
Crystal Leaf, Federal **5.00**
Daisy, Hazel Atlas, Capri Blue. . , ... **18.00**
Dogwood, Hazel Atlas, white milk glass **6.00**
Fan, Anchor Hocking, green cup **10.00**
Feather, Jeannette, blue **10.00**
Feather, Jeannette, shell pink **18.00**
Gaiety, Federal **6.00**
Harvest, Indiana, carnival glass **25.00**
King's Crown, Indiana, amber **12.00**
Leaf, Jeannette **8.00**
Ring, Anchor Hocking, green. **10.00**

Rooster, Hazel Atlas, Gay Fad Studios **12.00**
Seashell, Hazel Atlas, Alpine, amethyst plate, white cup **15.00**
Snowflake, Indiana, crystal **8.00**
Tree of Life, Indiana, lavender flashed **10.00**
Turquoise Blue, Anchor Hocking, Fire-King **10.00**
Whitehall, Indiana, frosted **6.00**
Yorktown, Federal, iridescent. **6.00**

SNOW BABIES

Snow babies, also known as sugar dolls, are small bisque figurines whose bodies are spattered with glitter sand, thus giving them the appearance of being coated in snow. Most are German or Japanese in origin and date between 1900 and 1940.

The exact origin of these figurines is unknown. The favored theory is that they were developed to honor Admiral Peary's daughter, Marie, born in Greenland on September 12, 1893. The Eskimos named the baby "Ah-Poo-Mickaninny," meaning snow baby. However, it is far more likely they were copied from traditional German sugar candy Christmas ornaments.

Babies, children at play, and Santa Claus are the most commonly found forms. Animal figures also are known. It is estimated that over 1,000 snow baby figurines were made. Many collections number in the hundreds. Do not overlook paper items—snow babies also appeared on postcards and in advertising.

Reference: Mary Morrison, *Snow Babies, Santas, and Elves: Collecting Christmas Bisque Figures,* Schiffer Publishing, 1993.

All We Need Is Love, Department 56, #68860, MIB **$25.00**
Babies, 1 with penguin, other with deer, Avery
   Creations, 1994. . . . . **5.00**
Babies, 3 babies playing by igloo, Muray Kreiss & Co **25.00**
Babies, sitting under tree, 1 on elbows with feet in air,
   other looking at gift in lap, Department 56, #76715 . . . . . . **15.00**
Babies on Sleds, Germany. **100.00**
Baby, holding star, other arm in air, seated beside pen-
   guin, Department 56 . . . . **10.00**
Chick Coming Out, Department 56, 3¼" h. **10.00**

Homestead, Federal, $4.00. Photo courtesy Ray Morykan Auctions.

I Made This Just For You, Department 56, #6802-0, 1995, $15.00.

Crossing Starry Skies, Department 56, #6834-9 . . . . **20.00**
Easter Bunny, mkd "Easter 1997," Department 56, 4 x 4" **10.00**
Hold on Tight, Department 56, MIB **15.00**
Hugging Babies, Department 56, 4¼" h **20.00**
I'll Light My Way, box mkd "99 Christmas Collectibles
    Showcase at Walt Disney World Resort," 4½" h **65.00**
Jack Frost...A Touch of Winter Magic, Department 56,
    #6854-3 . . . . **75.00**
Let's Go See Jack Frost, 10-year anniversary, Department
    56, #68850, MIB **35.00**
Let's Go Skiing, Department 56, MIB **12.00**
No Snow Babies, man and woman skiing, Germany **95.00**
Reach for the Moon, Department 56, 6" h, MIB **18.00**
Skier, Japan, 2½" h **5.00**
So Much Work to Do, #6837 . . . . **20.00**
Somewhere In Dream Land, 7 x 8½", MIB **50.00**
There's Another One, Department 56, #6853-5 . . . . **15.00**
There's No Place Like Home, Winter Tales Series, orig box . . . **15.00**
Wait For Me, Department 56, retired 1994, MIB **50.00**
Why Don't You Talk to Me?, Department 56, #6801-2 . . . . . . **25.00**
Winken, Blinken, & Nod, Department 56, #6814-4 . . . . **55.00**

SNOW GLOBES

Snow globes originated in Europe in the mid-18th century. Manufacturing was primarily a cottage industry. Constantly gaining in popularity during the later decades of the Victorian era and the first three decades of the 20th century, the snow globe became extremely popular in the 1930s and early 1940s. Although the first American patent dates from the late 1920s, most globes sold in the 1930s were imported from Germany and Japan. They consisted primarily of a round ball on a ceramic or plastic base.

William M. Snyder founded Atlas Crystal Works, first located in Trenton, New Jersey, and later Covington, Tennessee, in the early 1940s to fill the snow globe void created by World War II. Driss Company of Chicago and Progressive Products of Union, New Jersey, were American firms making snow globes in the post-war period. Driss manufactured a series based on four popular characters (Davy Crockett, Frosty the Snowman, The Lone Ranger, and Rudoph the Red Nosed Reindeer); Progressive made advertising and award products.

The plastic domed snow globe arrived on the scene in the early 1950s. Initially German in origin, the concept was quickly copied by Japanese manufacturers. After a period of decline in the late 1960s and 70s, a snow globe renaissance occurred in the 1980s, the result of snow globes designed for the giftware market.

References: Nancy McMichael, *Snowdomes*, Abbeville Press, 1990; Connie A. Moore and Harry L. Rinker, *Snow Globes*, Courage Books, 1993.

Collectors' Club: Snowdome Collectors Club, PO Box 53262, Washington, DC 20009.

Anderson Concrete Corp, glass dome, hard plastic base,
    orange plastic concrete mixer trucks, painted view of
    skyline in background, Progressive Products, Union,
    NJ, c1950s, 1½ x 3 x 3" **$50.00**
Bowling Award, amber glass dome, oval black plastic
    base, 3 gold bowling pins and black ball with pin-
    point gold granules, "York County Lions, Team-High
    Average, 1959" on base, 3" h **35.00**

Cities Service, promotional giveaway salesman's sample, plastic, $225.00. Photo courtesy Collectors Auction Services.

Enchanted Forest, clear plastic dome, white plastic oval
    base, swan and bear wearing top hat emerging from
    fairytale castle-type box, made in Hong Kong for
    Maryland amusement park, c1960s, 2¼ x 3" **10.00**
Florida Orange Bird, plastic, Orange Bird symbol on end
    of teeter-totter that raises and lowers, painted back-
    ground of palm trees and ocean coastline, ©Walt
    Disney Productions, made in Hong Kong, 2¾" h **15.00**
New York World's Fair, glass globe, black hard plastic
    base, white replica Trylon and Perisphere, 1939, 3" h **50.00**
Seattle Expo, hard plastic dome, oval white plastic base,
    Space Needle replica in shades of tan with red
    accents on light blue ground, 1962, 3¼" h **15.00**
Shrine of the Little Flower, glass dome, dark brown
    ceramic base, plastic replica figure of Holy Mother
    holding infant Jesus, base decal mkd "Shrine Of The
    Little Flower/Royal Oak, Mich," 1930-40s, 3" d **10.00**
World War II Aircraft, glass dome, black enameled glass
    base, tan fighter plane on pedestal extending down-
    ward from wing tip, 3" d **35.00**

SOAKIES

Soakies, plastic figural character bubble bath bottles, were developed to entice children into the bathtub. Soakies, now a generic term for all plastic bubble bath bottles, originates from "Soaky," a product of the Colgate Palmolive Company.

Colgate Palmolive licensed numerous popular characters, e.g., Rocky and Bullwinkle, Felix the Cat, and Universal Monsters. Colgate Palmolive's success was soon copied, e.g., Purex's Bubble Club. Purex licensed the popular Hanna-Barbera characters. Avon, DuCair Bioessence, Koscot, Lander Company, and Stephen Reiley are other companies who have produced Soakies.

Soakies arrived on the scene in the early 1960s and have remained in production since. Most are 10" high. Over a hundred different Soakies have been produced. Many are found in two or more variations, e.g., there are five versions of Bullwinkle.

Reference: Gregg Moore and Joe Pizzo, *Collector's Guide to Bubble Bath Containers*, Collector Books, 1999.

Left: El Cabong, Purex, 1964, $45.00; Right: Atom Ant, Purex, 1965, $40.00.

Baloo, bright blue, tan and orange painted features, 1966, 7" h.......................$15.00

Batman, purple, blue, and yellow outfit, fleshtone face, ©1966 National Periodical Publications Inc, 10¼" h...... 50.00

Brutus, black beard and hair, red and white striped shirt, red trousers, Colgate-Palmolive, 10" h............... 35.00

Casper the Friendly Ghost, white, blue and pink accents, standing atop drum holding flowers in hand and heart shaped gift behind back, 1970s, ©Harvey Famous Cartoons, 9¾" h....................15.00

Creature From the Black Lagoon, ©1960s Universal Picture Co, 10" h.....................50.00

Dick Tracy, yellow outfit with black accents, Colgate-Palmolive, ©1965 News Syndicate, 10" h.............15.00

Dino, purple, Purex, ©Hanna-Barbera Prod, Inc, 1960s, 10⅝" h.....................15.00

Felix the Cat, black and white, name incised on chest, holding yellow bag of tricks with red polka dots, Colgate-Palmolive, 1960s, 9¾" h..............35.00

Frankenstein, black, gray shirt, pale green hands, ©1960s Universal Pictures Co, 10" h................50.00

Morocco Mole, brown, white accent shirt and eyes, blue vest, red cap, name incised on dark orange base, Purex, ©1960s Hanna-Barbera Prod, 6¾" h...........50.00

Mr Jinx, holding Pixie and Dixie, orange, black and white accents, Purex, 9¾" h.........................15.00

Paul McCartney, ©1965 NEMS Enterprises Ltd, 9½" h.......50.00

Smokey Bear, brown, white facial accents, blue pants and yellow hat, holding shovel, with red and foil sticker "Prevent Forest Fires," text repeated in French beneath English translation, Lander Co, Toronto, Canada, c1970, 10¾" h......................35.00

Spider-Man, red and blue, Colgate-Palmolive, ©1977 Marvel Comics Group, 8½" h..................15.00

Squiddly Diddly, arms folded, orange vest, white accent hat, name incised on base, Purex, ©1960s Hanna-Barbera Prod, 6¾" h...................50.00

Wendy, yellow hair and stars, red accent face, holding heart shaped gift behind back, name in relief on bottom, 1970s, ©Harvey Famous Cartoons, 7" h..........15.00

SODA POP COLLECTIBLES

In addition to Coca-Cola, Pepsi, and Moxie, there are thousands of soda brands, ranging from regional to national, attracting collector interest. In the 1920s Americans became enamored with buying soda in a bottle to consume at their leisure. Tens of thousands of local bottling plants sprang up across America, producing flavors ranging from cream to sarsaparilla. Some brands achieved national popularity, e.g., Grapette and Hires.

Capitalizing on the increased consumption of soda pop during World War II, manufacturers launched a major advertising blitz in the late 1940s and early 1950s. From elaborate signs to promotional premiums, the soda industry was determined to make its influence felt. The soda bubble burst in the early 1970s. Most local and regional bottling plants ceased operations or were purchased by larger corporations. A few national brands survived and dominate the market.

References: Donald A. Bull and John R. Stanley, *Soda Advertising Openers,* Schiffer Publishing, 2000; Tom Morrison, *Root Beer* (1992), *More Root Beer* (1997), Schiffer Publishing; Allan Petretti, *Petretti's Soda Pop Collectibles Price Guide, 2nd Edition,* Antique Trader Books, 1999; Jeff Walters, *The Complete Guide to Collectible Picnic Coolers & Ice Chests,* Memory Lane, 1994.

Periodical: *Club Soda,* PO Box 489, Troy, ID 83871.

Collectors' Clubs: The Cola Club, PO Box 158715, Nashville, TN 37215; Dr. Pepper 10-2-4 Collectors Club, 3100 Monticello, Ste 890, Dallas, TX 75205; Grapette Collectors Club, 2240 Hwy 27N, Nashville, AR 71852; National Pop Can Collectors, 19201 Sherwood Green Way, Gaithersburg, MD 20879; Painted Soda Bottle Collectors Assoc, 1055 Ridgecrest Dr, Goodlettsville, TN 37072.

Note: For additional listings see Coca-Cola, Moxie, and Pepsi-Cola.

Backbar Bottle, Orange Julep, label under glass.........$150.00

Bank, A&W Root Beer, figural bear, painted composition, brown head with tan muzzle, matching brown and tan trousers and feet, orange sweater and tam, coin slot in back of head, 6½" h.................. 75.00

Bottle Display Sign, Hires Root Beer, diecut cardboard, man and woman in boat, "Hires Root Beer Cools and Refreshes," 1930-40s, 10 x 12"................... 225.00

Box, Dr Pepper, cardboard, holds four 1-gal fountain syrup jugs, 1930s................... 55.00

Calendar, Dr Pepper, 1935, woman standing at ship rail holding bottle, "Yo! Ho!...Energy Up/Dr Pepper 5¢" above "At 10-2 & 4 O'Clock," December page only, "Looney's Laundry, phone 857" at bottom, framed under glass, 16 x 33"......................... 6,000.00

Calendar, Dr Pepper, 1965, paper, "Distinctively Different...," woman in white gown looking in mirror..... 85.00

Calendar Holder, Dr Pepper, 1950s, plastic and aluminum, partial pad.............................. 90.00

Can, Dad's Root Beer, cone top, 1 qt, 1940-50s.......... 150.00

Can, Dr Pepper, cone top, orig cap, 6 oz, empty........ 1,600.00

Carrier, Dr Pepper, metal, emb, holds 6 bottles.......... 450.00

Clock, Dr Pepper, bottle cap shaped, tin, light-up, c1950-60s, 15" d........................... 275.00

Toy Headband, Whistle Soda, paper, G Gamse & Bro Litho, 5¹/₂" h, 23¹/₂" l, $10.00. Photo courtesy Collectors Auction Services.

Clock, Royal Crown Cola, double bubble, white diamond center in red circle with "Royal Crown Soda," blue rim with white crowns, orig box, 1963 . . . . **1,250.00**

Cooler, Dr Pepper, airline style, complete with inner tray, 1950s, 9 x 18 x 16" **225.00**

Dispenser, Challenge Root Beer, wooden and stainless steel, barrel shaped, complete with 4 tag signs around barrel, c1940-50s, 20" h **300.00**

Display Bottle, Dr Pepper, plastic, 1950s, 4" h **575.00**

Display Bottle, Smile, orig orange and black paint, 1920-30s, 18" h **825.00**

Door Push, Dr Pepper, emb, "Drink Dr Pepper/frosty, man, frosty!," adjustable **150.00**

Drinking Glass, Bubble Up, clear glass, repeated design in green and red, c1950s, 4³/₄" h, 2³/₄" d **45.00**

Drinking Glass, Dr Pepper, clear, 2-color applied label, 1960s **90.00**

Fan Pull, Frosty Old Fashioned Root Beer, cardboard, 2-sided, 5" h **40.00**

Fan Pull, Pal, cardboard, 2-sided, 9" h **60.00**

Fan Pull, Squirt, diecut cardboard, squirt boy with "Drink Squirt," 2-sided **40.00**

Fan Pull, Whistle, diecut cardboard, boy seated on bottle neck, 1-sided, 1940-50s, 1¹/₂" h **250.00**

Hand Fan, Dr Pepper, front shows seated woman in long dress holding soda bottle, "Drink A Bite To Eat At 10-2 and 4 O'Clock," back shows drawing of man in top hat, "It's Economical," Earl Moran illus, 1930-40s **350.00**

Hat Badge, Dr Pepper, gold, curved, 1930-40s **800.00**

Ice Chest, Squirt, litho tin, repeating image of Squirt bottle and Squirt symbol figure on merry-go-round horse, upper perimeter with awning design carried through lid, ©1953 Squirt Co, 13¹/₂" h, 11¹/₂" d **50.00**

Kick Plate, Dr Pepper, porcelain, 1930-40s, 10 x 24" **425.00**

Kick Plate, NuGrape, emb tin, bottle on left, "Drink NuGrape Soda/Imitation Grape Flavor/A Favorite With Millions," 1930s, 12 x 30" **200.00**

Kick Plate, Whistle, emb tin, "Thirsty? Just Whistle/Morning-Noon-Night," c1939, 12 x 27" **250.00**

License Plate Attachment, Dr Pepper, tin, "Make Our City Safe," 1940s, 10" w **775.00**

Lighter, Dr Pepper, slim style, polished finish, red enamel painted logo, 1976 . . . . **150.00**

Measuring Cup, Hires Root Beer, glass, blue applied color label, 1940-50s **30.00**

Megaphone, Dr Pepper, heavy paper with metal ring at top, 1950s **350.00**

Menu Board, Dr Pepper, emb, 1970s, 20 x 28" **65.00**

Menu Board, Orange-Crush, tin, emb, "Drink Orange Crush, 1930s, 20 x 28" **450.00**

Ring, Dr Pepper, route salesman's, gold, old clock logo, size 9, 1930-40s **650.00**

Seltzer Bottle, Zetz 7-Up, 2-color applied label, black waiter on red ground **500.00**

Sign, 7-Up, diecut paper, 2-sided, "7UP The Uncola," full color Santa portrait within holly wreath, "The Man From Uncola" and yellow streamer band on each side inscribed "Give Unto Others," c1970s, 13¹/₂ x 13¹/₂" **45.00**

Sign, Bohemian Ginger Ale, diecut cardboard, "A Good Mixer," 1930s, 11 x 12¹/₂" h **75.00**

Sign, Cloverdale Soft Drinks, tin, beveled edge, easel back, string hanger, silver emb dots lettering, 1950s, 9 x 13" **40.00**

Sign, Dad's Root Beer, emb tin, "Have A Dad's Old Fashioned Root Beer," 1950s, 20 x 28" **110.00**

Sign, Double Cola, tin, emb, "Double Measure Double Pleasure/Drink Double Cola," bottle pouring soda into 2 glasses, 20 x 28" **550.00**

Sign, Dr Pepper, cardboard, woman with dog, winter background scene, "Smart life Dr Pepper," 15 x 25" **500.00**

Sign, Dr Pepper, emb cardboard, colorful clown above "Dr Pepper Distinctively Different," 1960s, 10 x 14" **125.00**

Sign, Dr Pepper, masonite and plastic, emb, "pick a pack," complete with hanger, bottom back brackets, and metal frame, 1960s, 12 x 16" **75.00**

Sign, Hires Root Beer, light-up, glass cover, "Drink Hires Here," 1940-50s, 16" d **2,500.00**

Sign, Hires Root Beer, tin, emb, "For Thirst And Pleasure," 1950, 41" d **575.00**

Sign, Howel's Root Beer, emb tin, "With that good Old Fashioned Flavor/5¢," 1940s, 20 x 28" **500.00**

Sign, Mountain Dew, tin, emb, "Ya-hooo! Mountain Dew/It'll tickle yore innards!," 1966, comical bearded man holding jug, 17 x 35" **500.00**

Sign, Nesbitt's, tin, "Nesbitt's California Orange Sold Here," 1940s, 13 x 18" **1,000.00**

Sign, NuGrape, cardboard, "Everybody likes a Change/Everybody likes...NuGrape Soda," boy and girl with 6-pack of soda, 1940s, 13 x 25" **100.00**

Sign, NuGrape, emb tin, diecut soda bottle, 1950s, 17" h **225.00**

Sign, Dr Pepper, cardboard, WWII era, 18¹/₂ x 28¹/₂", $375.00. Photo courtesy Collectors Auction Services.

Sign, Old Dutch Root Beer, emb tin, windmill illus,
1950s, 1½ x 3" **175.00**
Sign, Pop Cola, emb tin, soda bottle below "Drink,"
1940s, 10 x 27" **125.00**
Sign, Vernor's Ginger Ale, tin, "Drink Vernor's Ginger
Ale/deliciously different," bearded man seated on keg
holding large bottle, 1940-50s, 18 x 54" **600.00**
Sign, White Rock Sparkling Water, emb tin, woman
kneeling on rock in water, 1950s, 33 x 57" **550.00**
Syrup Jug, Dr Pepper, orig top and label, 1 gal, 1940-50s . . . **175.00**
Thermometer, Cheer Up, horizontal numerals above "A
Delightful Drink/Drink Cheer Up/A Real Super
Charged Beverage," 1930-40s **675.00**
Thermometer, Dr Pepper, "Drink Dr Pepper Good For
Life," bottle illus on yellow ground, 1939, 17" h **1,400.00**
Thermometer, Moxie, tin, "Drink Moxie/It's Always A
Pleasure To Serve You," 1952, 10 x 26" **1,200.00**
Thermometer, Nu-Grape, tin, diecut bottle, 1940s, 17" h **300.00**
Thermometer, Sun Crest, tin, emb diecut bottle, 1940s,
17" h **215.00**

Snow Globe,
California,
plastic, bank
base with
calendar,
#VNO355L,
Hong Kong,
4" h, $10.00.

SOUVENIRS

Novelty souvenirs featuring historical or natural landmarks with
identifying names were popular keepsakes prior to World War I.
Commemorative pieces include plates issued during anniversary
celebrations and store premiums, many of which featured calendars. Souvenirs tend to be from carnivals, fairs, popular tourist
attractions and hotels, and world's fairs.

The souvenir spoon arrived on the scene in the late 1880s. In the
1920s the demitasse spoon replaced the teaspoon as the favored
size. The souvenir spoon craze finally ended in the 1950s, albeit
the form can still be found today.

Plastic souvenir items dominate the post–World War II period.
Many pieces were generic with only the name of the town, site, or
state changed from one piece to another. In the late 1960s ceramic commemorative plates enjoyed a renaissance.

The vast majority of items sold in today's souvenir shops have
nothing on them to indicate their origin. Souvenir shops are gift
shops, designed to appeal to the universal taste of the buyer.

References: Pamela E. Apkarian-Russell, *A Collector's Guide to
Salem Witchcraft & Souvenirs,* Schiffer Publishing, 1998; Wayne
Bednersh, *Collectible Souvenir Spoons,* Collector Books, 1998;
Monica Lynn Clements and Patricia Rosser Clements, *Popular
Souvenir Plates,* Schiffer Publishing, 1998; Myra Y. and Eric B.
Outwater, *Floridiana,* Schiffer Publishing, 2000; Dorothy T.
Rainwater and Donna H. Felger, *American Spoons, Souvenir and
Historical,* Everybodys Press, Schiffer Publishing, 1977; Dorothy T.
Rainwater and Donna H. Felger, *Spoons From Around the World,*
Schiffer Publishing, 1992; David Weingarten and Margaret Majua,
Monumental Miniatures, Antique Trader Books, 1999; Laurence W.
Williams, *Collector's Guide to Souvenir China,* Collector Books,
1998.

Collectors' Clubs: American Spoon Collectors, 7408 Englewood
Ln, Raytown, MO 64133; Souvenir Building Collectors Society,
PO Box 70, Nellysford, VA 22958; Statue of Liberty Collectors'
Club, 26601 Bernwood Rd, Cleveland, OH 44122.

Note: See Advertising, British Royal Commemoratives, Circus,
Patriotic, Postcards, and World's Fair for additional listings.

Ashtray, Kansas, cast metal, relief design with flowers
and images symbolic of Kansas, enameled highlights,
oval, Japan **$8.00**
Ashtray, "New Smyrna Beach, Florida," cast metal, relief
design with alligator, turtle, flying fish, flowers, native,
and words in crest, 5 x 4" **12.00**
Ashtray, New York City, diecut metal, skyline above out-
line of state, Japan **8.00**
Bandanna, "Atom Bomb Proving Grounds," multicolor
image of mushroom cloud rising from test detonation
near Las Vegas, fringed edge, late 1940s, 27" sq **60.00**
Booklet, *Hollywood,* pictures movie sets, movie star
homes, Grauman's Chinese Theatre, etc, 1960s **4.00**
Booklet, *Sunny California, Los Angeles and Vicinity,*
42 pp, 5¼ x 8" **12.00**
Brochure, Hawaiian Islands, "Tourfax, for travel to and
through the Hawaiian Islands, 10 pp, black and light
red, 7¾ x 11" **35.00**
Coin, Port of Cincinnati, OH, orig presentation box,
1992 . . . . **12.00**
Creamer, Reagan inauguration, ceramic, Regan image
and "Ronald W. Reagan 40th President," c1981,
3¾" h **10.00**
Desk Clock, Cape Canaveral, molded clear acrylic panel
with LCD clock and calendar set in Westar symbol,
"Cape Canaveral February 1982" etched in white,
4" h, 3" w **35.00**
Figure, 3 natives in canoe, playing instruments, sitting
under 3½" h wooden diecut palm tree with hp red
coconuts, figures with wooden ball heads, straw hair,
dowel necks, and barrel shaped bodies, 6½" l canoe
with "Florida" in bright yellow, bottom stamped
"Japan" **20.00**
Handkerchief, Fort Meade, 1943, pink silk with pink
lace trim, 12 x 8" **5.00**
Handkerchief, Washington, DC, map of city and Capitol,
White House, Library of Congress, Lincoln Memorial,
Washington Memorial, Jefferson Memorial, Mount
Vernon, and cherry blossoms, light turquoise ground,
scalloped edge, 13 x 13½" **12.00**

Letter Opener, Hawaii, simulated carved lava handle with raised "Hawaii," stainless steel blade, 8" l **5.00**

Lighter, map of Virginia on 1 side, state bird and flower on other side, Mambro, Japan **20.00**

Magazine, *New York,* 60 pp, Statue of Liberty and blimp scene on cov, Manhattan Card Publishing Co, 1935, 7 x 10" **25.00**

Napkin Ring, Bunker Hill Monument, silver plated **20.00**

Pamphlet, "Going Away to Sunny California via Southern Pacific, Shasta Route" **12.00**

Pennant, "Fort McClellan," purple felt, yellow band, purple streamers, white lettering, multicolor Army emblem, aircraft, anti-aircraft gun, etc, 1940s, 29½" l **20.00**

Pennant, "Knott's Berry Farm Ghost Town, California," red felt, yellow streamers, white letters, multicolor scene with cowboy on horse, covered wagon, Knott's Berry Farm, and Ghost Town, early 1950s, 26" l **25.00**

Pillow, Alaska, silk, yellow fringe, "Mother" poem, illus of Eskimo with dog sled, Mt McKinley, gold prospecting, moose, and salmon **30.00**

Pillow, Georgia, white acetate, yellow fringe, illus of state map, tobacco leaf, barrel of peaches, wild turkey, speckled trout, state scenes, and University of Georgia graduate **15.00**

Pillow, Pike's Peak Region, pink acetate, black back, pink fringe, illus of summit of Pike's Peak, Royal Gorge, Seven Falls, and Balanced Rock **20.00**

Pinback Button, Bronx Zoo, multicolored, panda image, yellow rim, inscribed "New York Zoological Park," c1950s **15.00**

Pinback Button, Hawaii, "Aloha," tropical beach scene, back paper with "Compliments of Hawaii Promotion Committee/Honolulu, Hawaii," 1930s **50.00**

Pinback Button, "Souvenir Terrell Jacobs," black and white photo of animal trainer Jacobs and lion, 1930s, 1¾" d **25.00**

Pin Dish, San Diego Zoo, cast metal, raised design with zebra, monkey, seal, elephant, giraffe, and lion in center with bear, rabbit, pheasant, ostrich, and pelican around rim, Japan, 1940s, 5½ x 5" **40.00**

Pitcher, Old St Michaels Church, ceramic, church on front above "Old St Michaels Church, Built 1752 Charleston, SC," gold highlights, mkd on bottom "Hand Painted the Jonroth Studios Germany Imported for Eyschmidt's Art Shop Charleston, SC," 4½" h **25.00**

Plate, California, multicolor with floral border, center Capitol building surrounded by vignettes of other attractions and parks, state information on back, Vernon Kilns, 10¼" d **20.00**

Plate, State of West Virginia, ceramic, gold rim, Conrad Crafters, 9" d **10.00**

Pocket Mirror, Niagara Falls, multicolored scene, c1920s **50.00**

Pocket Mirror, Rockefeller Center, rect plexiglass cover over full color art image, white border margins accented by blue designs, c1940s **15.00**

Spoon, Cannes, silver plate, enameled Cannes shield on handle, 5¼" l **10.00**

Spoon, George Washington House, pictures Washington with birth and death dates, house, and knight's hood, mkd "Sterling Pat FA Whelan" **25.00**

Spoon, "Key West" in bowl, "Florida" on handle, sterling silver, 5⅜" l **30.00**

Spoon, "La Junta" engraved in bowl, "Colorado" on handle, sterling silver, 5⅜" l **20.00**

Spoon, "Old Point Comfort, VA," sterling silver, Watson Co, 3⅞" l **20.00**

Spoon, Philadelphia, Liberty Bell and "Philadelphia" on handle, sterling silver, 5½" l **12.00**

Spoon Rack and Spoons, wooden rack with 37 stainless spoons from various states and 1 gold-plated spoon from Niagara Falls, Canada **50.00**

Tablecloth, Minnesota, printed cotton, red, green, and yellow on white, graphics include man milking cow, cheese, canned vegetables, sailboat, hunter, fisherman, Indian and teepee, fish, bears, birds, Paul Bunyon, farmer, and bathing beauty, 36 x 30" **75.00**

Tape Measure, "Marlborough-Blenheim Hotel, Atlantic City, NJ," tin canister with celluloid insert of hotel **12.00**

Tape Measure, Rockefeller Center/Statue of Liberty, tin canister capped by multicolored celluloid on each side, inner cloth tape, c1930-40s **10.00**

Tea Tile, Bermuda, cork backing, 6" sq **5.00**

Tray, Estes Park, painted cork, pictures Rocky Mountains scene with deer, "Rocky Mountain National Park, Estes Park, Colorado," 1950, 17 x 11½" **8.00**

Vase, "Crystal Cave, Kutztown, Penna.," ceramic, tree with deer, squirrel, and mushrooms, paper label **5.00**

SPACE ADVENTURERS, FICTIONAL

Philip Francis Nowland and John F. Dille launched *Buck Rogers 2429 A.D.* in January 1929. The late 1930s was the golden age of this famous space explorer. Buck Rogers in the 25th Century, a television program airing between September 1979 and April 1981, created a renewed interest in Buck.

Flash Gordon was Buck Rogers' main rival in the 1930s. The 1940s was Flash's golden age. A second generation became hooked on Flash when the movie serials were repeated dozens of times on television in the late 1940s and 50s.

Americans were enamored by space in the early 1950s. Television responded with Captain Video and His Video Rangers, Flash Gordon, Rocky Jones Space Ranger, Space Patrol, and Tom Corbett, Space Cadet. A second generation of space adventure series, e.g., Lost in Space and Star Trek, was launched in the 1960s and 70s. Spinoffs such as Deep Space Nine and Babylon 5 have kept the legend of the space adventurer alive on television.

References: Dana Cain, *UFO & Alien Collectibles Price Guide,* Krause Publications, 1999; Frank M. Robinson, *Science Fiction of the 20th Century: An Illustrated History,* Collectors Press, 1999; Stuart W. Wells III, *Science Fiction Collectibles,* Krause Publications, 1999.

Collectors' Club: Galaxy Patrol, 144 Russell St, Worcester, MA 01610.

Note: For additional listings see Premiums, Space Toys, Star Trek and Star Wars.

Battlestar Galactica, Colorforms, 1978, unused **$12.00**

Battlestar Galactica, Cylon radio, plastic, figural Cylon warrior head, Vanity Fair, orig box, 1978, 3½ x 3½ x 5½" **55.00**

Battlestar Galactica, game, Milton Bradley, 1978 . . . . **18.00**

Buck Rogers, Colorforms, 1979, unused **10.00**

Buck Rogers, comic book, Famous Funnies, Eastern Color Printing Co, July 1941, Issue #2, 64 pp **550.00**

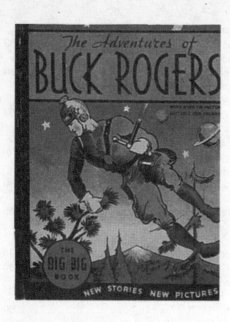

Big Big Book, *The Adventures of Buck Rogers,* 1938, 9¹/²" h, 7 ¹/²" w, $65.00. Photo courtesy Collectors Auction Services.

Planet of the Apes, costume, Caesar, Ben Cooper, 1973 . . . . . **35.00**
Planet of the Apes, model, Dr Zira, Addar, 1974 . . . . **18.00**
Planet of the Apes, playset, 4 hp hard plastic ape figures,
    5 green soft plastic army men, yellow army man with
    blue jeep, 2 horses, and bridge with 2 trees, Multiple
    Toymakers, c1974, orig unopened box **75.00**
Space: 1999, Moon Car, friction, hard plastic, 1976,
    5" l, MOC **50.00**
Tom Corbett Space Cadet, autographed cast photograph,
    black and white, image of Cadets in dormitory room
    at Academy standing at attention for Capt Strong,
    boldly signed in blue felt-tip pen, 8 x 10" **150.00**
Tom Corbett Space Cadet, lunch box, Aladdin, 1954 . . . . . . **150.00**

SPACE EXPLORATION

Collector interest in artifacts relating to the manned space program began in the early 1980s. After a brief fascination with autographed material, collectors moved to three-dimensional objects.

The collapse of the Soviet Union coupled with Russia's and several cosmonauts' need for capital has resulted in the sale of space memorabilia by several leading auction houses around the world. Everything from capsules to space suits are available for purchase.

This category focuses primarily on material associated with manned space flight. Collector interest in material from unmanned flights is extremely limited.

Reference: Stuart Schneider, *Collecting the Space Race,* Schiffer Publishing, 1993.

Activity Book, *Astronauts,* 4 pp, punch-outs for assembly
    of Redstone Rocket, Ground Control Center, launch-
    ing the Atlas, and Recovery of the Astronaut,
    Golden Press Funtime Book, ©1961, 7¹/⁴ x 13" **$50.00**
Badge, moon landing commemorative, celluloid, red,
    white, and blue design with black and white astronaut
    photo flanked by images of Earth and moon, 3¹/²" d **15.00**

Buck Rogers, costume, Ben Cooper, 1978, window box **18.00**
Buck Rogers, crayon box, cardboard, American Pencil
    Co, Buck and Wilma looking through porthole one
    side, Buck Rogers Crayon Ship other side, 2 x 4³/⁴ x ¹/²" **70.00**
Buck Rogers, member's pinback button, color image of
    Buck, rocket pistol, and spaceship on blue back-
    ground with yellow rim, Cream of Wheat premium,
    1935 . . . . **100.00**
Captain Marvel, frame tray puzzle, "No 1/One Against
    Many," illus of Billy Batson changing into Capt Marvel
    to take on 4 villains, complete, 1940s **30.00**
Captain Marvel, Magic Flute, Lee-Tex Rubber Products
    Corp, 1946, 4¹/²" l, MOC **90.00**
Captain Video, Supersonic Spaceships boxed set, 4 hard
    plastic spaceships, Lido Toy Co, early 1950s, orig win-
    dow box **150.00**
ET, lunch box, metal, with thermos, Aladdin, 1982 . . . . **18.00**
ET, Pizza Hut promotional drinking glasses, set of 4,
    1982, 6" h **10.00**
Flash Gordon, charm, plastic with brass luster Flash
    standing on small base, early 1950s **15.00**
Flash Gordon, paint book, Whitman, 1936, 96 pp, 11¹/⁴
    x 14" **65.00**
Flash Gordon, pencil box, cardboard, Flash and Dale
    battling Space-Dragon one side, Flash and Sand-Car
    other side, slide-out tray with orig pencil, rulers,
    crayons, etc, Eagle Pencil Co, 1951, 4¹/² x 8 x 1" **55.00**
Flash Gordon, pop-up book, *Flash Gordon Tournament
    of Death,* Blue Ribbon Press, 16 pp with 3 pop-ups,
    1935, 8 x 9" **450.00**
Lost in Space, cast photograph, black and white, stars'
    names and "20th Century Fox Television" logo, 1960s,
    8 x 10" **25.00**
Lost in Space, *TV Guide,* Vol. 13, #45, Nov 6, 1965,
    cover image of June Lockhart and Guy Williams float-
    ing in space **30.00**
Matt Mason, action figure, Calisto, Mattel, 1968, 6¹/⁴" h **300.00**
Matt Mason, frame tray puzzle, image of Major Mason
    traveling across lunar surface on space sled, Whitman,
    1968 . . . . **15.00**

Pinback Button, Apollo XI crew, Armstrong, Collins, and Aldrin, red, white, and blue, July 1969, 3¹/²" d, $30.00.

Bank, ceramic, figural astronaut, coin slot on backpack, red, white, and blue US flag sticker on reverse, rubber trap mkd "Ceramaster," 1969-70, 3 x 3½ x 6½" **50.00**

Booklet, *Astronaut John H Glenn Orbits the Earth for America February 20, 1962,* 12 pp, photos, distributed by US Government Printing Office, 7¾ x 10¼" **15.00**

Coloring Book, "Apollo Man on the Moon" **20.00**

Game, Lunar Landing Game, Lay's Packing Co **40.00**

Jigsaw Puzzle, "First on the Moon," 500 pcs, 11 x 16", Milton Bradley **30.00**

Jigsaw Puzzle, "Moon Map," Selchow & Righter, ©Rand McNally & Co, late 1960s, orig box, 1¼ x 8¼ x 12¼" **25.00**

Lamp, electric, shade and base covered in colorful fabric with scenes of astronauts blasting off, orbiting the moon, and performing their experiments on lunar surface, Saturn rocket shaped base **150.00**

Little Golden Book, *Exploring Space,* 1st ed, 24 pp, color illus, ©1958, 6½ x 8" **25.00**

Magazine, *National Geographic,* "First Explorers on the Moon," Dec, 1969, Apollo 11 Mission, bound insert 33⅓ record *Sounds of the Space Age from Sputnik to Lunar Landing* narrated by Col Frank Borman **25.00**

Model, Apollo-Soyuz, Revell, 1/96 scale, orig box **45.00**

Mug, white glass, single black replica of headline "Men Walk On The Moon" by *American News* Newspaper, 3" h, 3" d **25.00**

Newspaper, *The Washington Daily News,* Sun, Jul 20, 1969, first men on the moon headline **10.00**

Pennant, felt, "Wapakoneta, Ohio Home Of Astronaut Neil Armstrong," black and white paper photo, 20" l **25.00**

Pinback Button, "America's First Astronaut/Navy Lt Comdr Alan B Shepard," black and white photo, 1¾" d **25.00**

Stuffed Toy, Mercury Mouse, Dream Pets series, orig tag, Dakin, 7¼" h **75.00**

SPACE TOYS

Space toys divide into three basic groups: (1) astronauts and spacemen, (2) spacecraft (capsules, flying saucers, rockets, and satellites), and (3) tanks and vehicles. Robots are excluded. They have reached the level of independent collecting status.

The toy industry, especially the Japanese, responded quickly to the growing worldwide interest in manned space flight. The first lithographed tin toys arrived on the market in the late 1940s. Toys became increasingly sophisticated during the 1950s. The number of parts that lit up or made sounds increased.

Plastic became the principal construction material by the early 1970s. Production shifted from Japan to China and Taiwan, a move that collectors view as having cheapened the toys. The decline in public interest in the space program in the mid-1970s also led to a decline in the production of space toys. Most collectors focus on space toys made prior to 1970.

The period box is an essential component of value, often adding 25% to 40% to the toy's value. The artwork on the box often is more impressive than the toy itself. Further, the box may contain information about the name of the toy, manufacturer, and/or distributor not found on the toy itself.

References: Jim Bunte, Dave Hallman and Heinz Mueller, *Vintage Toys: Robots & Space Toys,* Antique Trader Books, 2000; Dana Cain, *UFO & Alien Collectibles Price Guide,* Krause Publications, 1999; Maxine A. Pinsky, *Marx Toys: Robots, Space, Comic, Disney & TV Characters,* Schiffer Publishing, 1996; Stuart W. Wells III, *Science Fiction Collectibles,* Krause Publications, 1999.

Periodicals: *Toy Shop,* 700 E State St, Iola, WI 54990; *Toy Trader,* PO Box 1050, Dubuque, IA 52004.

Note: For additional listings see Robots, Space Adventurers, Star Trek and Star Wars.

Aero Jet Range Rocket, plastic rocket, operates on energy pellets (included), flies 200-300 feet in air, orig box, Ranger Steel Products, 11½" h **$35.00**

Animal Jet, friction, litho tin and plastic, images of Huckleberry Hound, Quick Draw McGraw, and Woody Woodpecker on sides of space jet, sparkler, black rubber tires, Marubishi, Japan, 8¼" l **275.00**

Apollo 12 Space Capsule, friction, litho tin, TT, Japan, 1960s, 3 x 4 x 2½" **80.00**

Atomic Disintegrator, cap pistol, die cast with plastic grips, orig box, Hubley, 1950s, 7" l **525.00**

First Lunar Landing–Apollo 11, plastic model kit, Monogram #6872, sealed box, 1/48 scale, c1970 .... **25.00**

Flying Saucer with Space Pilot, battery operated, litho tin pilot, swivel lighted engine, space noise, revolving antenna and mystery action, orig box, KO, Japan **250.00**

Moon McDare, action figure, with accessories and instruction sheet, AC Gilbert, 12" h **30.00**

NASA Space Shuttle *Challenger*/Flying Jet Plane, battery operated, 12½ x 12½ x 4½" litho tin and plastic Boeing 747 and 7" l plastic space shuttle, plane moves on 3 wheels and then rises on black metal arm, blinking lights and engine lights **80.00**

Non-Fall Moon Rocket, blue, pink, red, and yellow, spinning astronaut at periscope, lights and turning actions, orig box, Masudaya, Japan, 9½" l........... **175.00**

Rocket Radio, with ear plug and orig box, Japan, c1960s, 4⅜" h................................ **110.00**

Rocket X-2, friction, litho tin rocket with sparkling action, MT, Japan, 7½" h **100.00**

Satellite Jumping Shoes, heavy steel shoes attached to base plate by 3 large coil springs, 1950s, 10" l **40.00**

Sonic Control Fly Ship X-3, battery operated, plastic, OK Toys, 1980s................................. **35.00**

Space Buggy, plastic model kit, Monogram, #PS194:200, 1/48 scale, sealed box, c1969 .... **65.00**

Space Ship, friction, litho tin, rubber tires, MSK, Japan, 9½" l, $150.00. Photo courtesy Collectors Auction Services.

Cragstan Myster Action Satellite, battery operated, litho tin, 1960s, $175.00. Photo courtesy Gene Harris Antique Auction Center, Inc.

Space Cap Gun, black plastic with metal trigger and flip-up roll caps compartment, Palmer Plastics, 5³/₄" l **25.00**

Space Copter on Parade, plastic and tin, windup, 3 attached satellites with spinning props, orig box, Yone, Japan, 8" l **70.00**

Space Dog, friction, red with black flapping ears, opening mouth, and ball eyes, orig box, Yoshiya, Japan, 8¹/₂" l **750.00**

Spacemen, ramp walkers, pr, MOC **15.00**

Space Ride, litho tin, lever action, 4 rockets spin and music plays when wound, Chein, 11¹/₂" h **600.00**

Space Taxi, plastic model kit, Monogram, #PS45:129, 1/48 scale, c1959 . . . . **60.00**

Space Whale Ship, windup, wobbling action, KO, Japan, 10" l, MIB **875.00**

Super Space Capsule, stop and go action, twin opening doors with astronaut, orig box, SH, Japan, 9¹/₂" h **125.00**

Twirly Whirly Rocket Ride, blue with multicolored details, bell, lifting and spinning mechanism, orig box, Alps, 13¹/₂" h **900.00**

US Space Missiles, plastic model kit, Monogram, #PS221:300, 1/128 scale, c1969 . . . . **30.00**

Walking Space Twins, ramp walkers, pr, MOC **25.00**

X-950 Rocket, friction, litho tin, sparkling action, Arnold, Germany, 10" l **275.00**

SPORTS COLLECTIBLES

This category includes memorabilia from sports that do not have separate categories, e.g., baseball, basketball, football, and hockey. The listings include amateur and professional material.

Sports memorabilia has attracted collector interest for two reasons. First, collectors grew tired of two-dimensional trading cards. They wanted three-dimensional material, especially items used to play the sport. Second, decorators began creating sports theme restaurants and bars in the 1980s. Collectors were amazed at the variety of material available.

When buying any game-related object, obtain a written provenance. Beware of sports autographs. The FBI reports that forgeries are as high as 70% and more in some sports categories. The only way to make certain the signature is authentic is to see the person sign it. One hot area in the late 1990s is trophies.

References: Mark Allen Baker, *Sports Collectors Digest Complete Guide to Boxing Collectibles,* Krause Publications, 1995; Roderick A. Malloy, *Malloy's Sports Collectibles Value Guide, Up-to-Date Prices For Noncard Sports Memorabilia,* Attic Books, Wallace-Homestead, 1994; J. L. Mashburn, *Sports Postcard Price Guide,* Colonial House, 1998; Kristian Pope, *Professional Wrestling Collectibles,* Krause Publications, 2000.

Periodical: *Boxing Collectors News,* 3316 Luallen Dr, Carrollton, TX 75007.

Collectors' Clubs: Antique Ice Skate Collectors Club, 70-104 Scott St, Meriden, CT 06450; Boxiana & Pugilistica Collectors International, PO Box 83135, Portland, OR 97283.

Note: For additional listings see Auto & Drag Racing, Baseball Cards, Baseball Memorabilia, Basketball Cards, Basketball Memorabilia, Football Cards, Football Memorabilia, Golf Collectibles, Hockey Cards, Hockey Memorabilia, Horse Racing, Olympic Memorabilia, and Tennis Collectibles.

Bowling, game, Hats Off Bowling Game, Transogram, 1944 . . . . **$30.00**

Boxing, book, *Jack Johnson–In the Ring–and Out,* sgd, dj, 1927 . . . . **825.00**

Boxing, casino chip, $25, MGM, Tyson/McNeeley **70.00**

Boxing, contract, sgd by Cassius Clay, William Morris Agency, dated April 25, 1963 . . . . **1,350.00**

Boxing, pinback button, "Joe Louis–World's Champion," sepiatone photo figure on white ground, dark brown lettering, c1930-40s **45.00**

Boxing, program, Evander Holyfield vs George Foreman, Apr 19, 1991 . . . . **50.00**

Boxing, program, Interservice Boxing Championship, 20 pp, 1953, 7³/₄ x 10¹/₂" **15.00**

Boxing, telephone card, Marciano vs Walcott, AT&T, 1997 . . . . **25.00**

Boxing, trading card, Adventure, Johnson, 1956 . . . . **35.00**

Boxing, trading card, All World, Sugar Ray Leonard, sgd, black signature **10.00**

Boxing, trading card set, Heroes of the Prize Ring, set of 20, 1993 . . . . **25.00**

Boxing, trading card set, Ideal Boxing Greats, set of 25 . . . . . . **20.00**

Ice Skating, book, *Wings on My Feet,* Sonja Henie, 1940 . . . . **35.00**

Ice Skating, pinback button, Ice Capades, Donna Atwood photo, black lettering on yellow ground, 1950s **12.00**

Ice Skating, program, Ice-Capades, black and white photos, colorful pin-up depiction of skater on cov, 1945 . . . . **8.00**

Ice Skating, sheet music, *Let's Bring New Glory to Old Glory,* from movie *Iceland* **15.00**

Ice Skating, skates, pr, child's, Dutch, plain blade, wooden footplate, leather straps, 1950s **40.00**

Ice Skating, skates, pr, child's, Rinkmaster, brown and black leather, steel blades, size 6, 1950s **40.00**

Karate, manual, Chuck Norris Karate Studios, sgd, black and white photos, 1973 . . . . **80.00**

Mountain Climbing, game, Mt Everest, Gabriel, "Climb the Highest Mountain," 1955 . . . . **25.00**

Ping Pong, clock, desk, wind-up, chrome luster finish metal case, glass over dial face image of elongated oval world globe, sweep second hand in image of tiny ping-pong ball at end of curved arc, hour hand has adjoined miniature ping-pong paddle that rotates back and forth, made in China **35.00**

Boxing, electric clock, "Joe Lewis World Champion," molded copper, United Self Starting, 12" h, $550.00. Photo courtesy Collectors Auction Services.

Pool, game, Skittle Pool, Aurora, 1972 . . . . **30.00**

Skiing, poster, "Ski Stowe Vermont, Mt Mansfield has Everything," Sascha Maurer, 39¹/₄ x 23¹/₄" **4,500.00**

Softball, program, "The King and His Court," 14 pp, 1945-55 . . . . **20.00**

Track, game, Track Meet, *Sports Illustrated,* 1972 . . . . **12.00**

Volleyball, game, Volley, Milton Bradley, "The Fast Action Random Shot Game," 1976. . . . . **10.00**

Wrestling, book, *Fall Guys,* Marcus Griffin, 1937 . . . . **20.00**

Wrestling, exhibit cards, set of 3, black and white photos of Rudy Kay, George Drake, and Zuma/Man of Mars in martian outfit, Exhibit Supply Co, 3¹/₄ x 5¹/₄" **15.00**

Wrestling, figure, Hulk Hogan, with stand, LJN, 8" h. **35.00**

Wrestling, game, Verne Gagne Wrestling, 1950s. **25.00**

Wrestling, magazine, *Sports Illustrated,* Danny Hodge cov, Apr 1, 1957 . . . . **12.00**

Wrestling, pennant, felt, Antonino Rocca, 1950s, 9 x 22¹/₂" **15.00**

Wrestling, *TV Guide,* Georgous George cov, Feb 25, 1950. . . . . **20.00**

STAMPS

Stamp collecting as a hobby was extremely popular throughout the middle decades of the 20th century. After a speculation period in the 1960s and 70s, when stamps became an investment commodity, the bubble burst in the 1980s. Middle- and low-end stamps experienced major price declines. To its credit, Scott Publishing adjusted the prices within its guides to reflect true market sales. Since this meant reducing the value for many stamps, the results sent shock waves through the market.

Stamp collecting is still in a period of recovery. Many question whether stamp collecting will ever recover its former popularity. Today's market is almost exclusively adult-driven. Investment continues to be the dominant collecting motivation. The overall feeling within the market is positive. Attendance is up at stamp shows. Modestly priced stamps are selling strongly. Interest in foreign issues is rising.

Condition, scarcity, and desirability (popularity) are the three pricing keys. Before researching the value of any stamps, carefully read the front matter of the book you are using, especially infor-

mation relating to catalog values, grade, and condition. Make certain you understand the condition grade being used for pricing. Most stamp collectors want examples graded at very fine or above.

Book values are retail value. Valuable stamps are far easier to sell than lesser valued stamps. Expect to have to discount commonly found stamps by 60% to 70% when selling them. It may make far more sense to use recently issued United States stamps for postage than to try to sell them on the secondary market.

Most catalogs provide unused and used (canceled) values. In some cases, the postmark and/or cancellation may have more value than the stamp.

The five-volume *Scott Standard Postage Stamp Catalogue* (Scott Publishing Co., 911 Vandemark Road, Sidney, OH 45365) is the basic reference used by most collectors to determine values. Volume 1 contains information about United States stamps. If the collection you are evaluating only contains United States stamps, also consult Marc Hudgeons' *The Official 2001 Blackbook Price Guide to United States Postage Stamps, 23rd Edition* (House of Collectibles, 2000).

Over the past few years, numerous advertisements from the International Collectors Society have appeared in newspapers and magazines offering stamps featuring prominent personalities issued by countries such as Grenada. These stamps are being printed specifically for sale to unknowledgeable collectors who believe they are purchasing a bargain and long-term collectible. Nothing is further from the truth. They are not the "Hot New Collectible" claimed by the International Collectors Society. Both philatelic and regular collectors are shunning these stamps now and will do so in the future.

Periodicals: *Linn's Stamp News,* PO Box 29, Sidney, OH 45365; *Scott Stamp Monthly,* 911 Vandemark Rd, PO Box 828, Sidney, OH 45365; *Stamp Collector,* 700 E State St, Iola, WI 54990.

Collectors' Club: American Philatelic Society, PO Box 8000, State College, PA 16803.

Note: David J. Maloney, Jr.'s *Maloney's Antique & Collectibles Resource Directory* (found at your local library) contains the names of many specialized collectors' clubs.

STANGL

Stangl Pottery is a continuation of Fulper Pottery. In 1928 Johann Martin Stangl, a former chemist and plant manager at Fulper Pottery, became president of the Fulper pottery located in Flemington, New Jersey. In 1929 he purchased Fulper. Stangl continued to produce some pieces under the Fulper trademark until around 1955. Stangl made inexpensive artware, dinnerware, and utilitarian ware.

In 1940 Stangl introduced a line of bird figurines, inspired by images from Audubon prints. Auguste Jacob designed and created the models for the birds. Initially, twelve birds were produced. A few out-of-production birds were reissued between 1972 and 1977. These are clearly dated on the bottom. When production ceased in 1978, over a hundred different shapes and varieties had been made. In addition, more than fifty dinnerware patterns were introduced between 1942 and 1968.

Johann Martin Stangl died in 1972. Frank Wheaton, Jr., bought Stangl and sold it to Pfaltzgraff Pottery in 1978. Pfaltzgraff ended production.

References: Harvey Duke, *Stangl Pottery*, Wallace-Homestead, 1992; Robert C. Runge, *Collector's Encyclopedia of Stangl Dinnerware*, Collector Books, 2000; Mike Schneider, *Stangl and Pennsbury Birds*, Schiffer Publishing, 1994.

Collectors' Club: Stangl/Fulper Collectors Club, PO Box 538, Flemington, NJ 08822.

BIRDS

Baltimore Oriole, #3402, stamp mark, 3" h	**$100.00**
Bird of Paradise, stamp mark, #3625, 15" h	**1,525.00**
Black Hole Warbler, #3810, stamp mark, 4" h	**100.00**
Bluejay, #3716, stamp mark, 10½" h, 7" w	**500.00**
Bluejay, #3715, stamp mark, paper label, 10" h, 10" w	**550.00**
Cardinal, #3444, stamp mark, 6½" h	**75.00**
Cockatoo, #3580, white, stamp mark, 9" h	**400.00**
Cockatoo, #3584, multicolored, stamp mark, 12½" h	**150.00**
Double Bluejays, #3717D, stamp mark, 13" h	**2,125.00**
Double Western Tanagers, #3750D, incised mark, 8" h, 7" w	**275.00**
Double White Wing Crossbills, #3754D, stamp mark, 8½" h	**400.00**
Flying Duck, #3443, blue-green, imp mark, 9" h, 13" w	**175.00**
Flying Duck, #3443, gray and blue, stamp mark, 9" h, 13" w	**200.00**
Key West Quail Dove, #3454, one wing up, multicolored, stamp mark, paper label, 9¼" h, 10½" w	**150.00**
Magpie Jay, #3758, stamp mark, 10½" h	**775.00**
Owl, #3407, stamp mark, 4½" h	**350.00**
Pheasants, #3491 male and #3492 female, stamp mark, 6½" h, 9" w, price for pair	**250.00**
Rooster and Hen, gray, #3445 and #3446, stamp mark, 9¾" h and 7" h, price for pair	**225.00**
Rooster and Hen, yellow, #3445 and #3446, mkd, 9¾" h and 7" h, price for pair	**250.00**
Scissortail Flycatcher, #3757, stamp mark, foil label, 11" h	**550.00**
Shoveler Duck, #3455, stamp mark, 12" h, 15" w	**1,125.00**
Western Bluebird, #3815, stamp mark, 6½" h	**300.00**

DINNERWARE

Blue Daisy, dinner plate	**$12.00**
Blue Daisy, mug and saucer	**9.00**
Blue Daisy, vegetable, 8½" d	**20.00**
Blue Tulip, bean pot	**30.00**
Blue Tulip, dinner plate, 10" d	**15.00**
Country Garden, coaster	**12.00**
Country Garden, creamer and sugar	**10.00**
Country Garden, cup and saucer	**8.00**
Country Garden, dinner plate, 10" d	**16.00**
Country Garden, eggcup	**15.00**
Country Garden, mug	**8.00**
Country Garden, pitcher	**10.00**
Country Garden, salad bowl, 12" d	**85.00**
Country Garden, salt and pepper shakers, pr	**12.00**
Country Garden, soup bowl, 7½" d	**25.00**
El Rosa, berry bowl	**10.00**
El Rosa, candy dish	**20.00**
El Rosa, plate, 11" d	**55.00**
Fruit, berry bowl, 5½" d	**12.00**
Fruit, chop plate, 12" d	**85.00**

Fruit, coffee mugs, set of 4	**175.00**
Fruit, dinner plate, 10" d	**12.00**
Fruit, gravy boat	**20.00**
Fruit, plates, cherries, 8" d, set of 4	**70.00**
Fruit, sugar	**15.00**
Fruit, tidbit tray	**15.00**
Garden Flower, bowl, tab handles	**6.00**
Garden Flower, bread and butter plate, 6" d	**12.00**
Garden Flower, creamer and sugar	**15.00**
Golden Blossom, berry bowl	**4.00**
Golden Blossom, creamer and sugar	**25.00**
Golden Blossom, dinner plate	**12.00**
Golden Blossom, luncheon plate, 8" d	**6.00**
Golden Blossom, salt and pepper shakers, pr	**12.00**
Golden Grape, berry bowl	**8.00**
Golden Grape, butter, cov	**15.00**
Golden Grape, dinner plate	**12.00**
Golden Grape, pitcher	**15.00**
Golden Grape, platter, kidney-shaped	**15.00**
Golden Grape, salt and pepper shakers, pr	**8.00**
Golden Harvest, chop plate, 14" d	**30.00**
Golden Harvest, creamer and sugar	**15.00**
Golden Harvest, dinner plate	**12.00**
Kiddieware, ABC cup	**45.00**
Kiddieware, ABC warming dish	**55.00**
Kiddieware, Little Quackers bowl	**20.00**
Kiddieware, Peter Rabbit plate	**125.00**
Magnolia, bread and butter plate, 6" d	**5.00**
Magnolia, butter pat	**16.00**
Magnolia, cup and saucer	**12.00**
Magnolia, dinner plate	**20.00**
Magnolia, gravy boat	**40.00**
Magnolia, platter, large	**30.00**
Magnolia, salt and pepper shakers, pr	**30.00**
Orchard Song, cup	**2.00**
Orchard Song, dinner plate	**15.00**
Orchard Song, platter, 12½" l	**30.00**
Prelude, cup and saucer	**20.00**
Prelude, dinner plate, 10" d	**30.00**
Prelude, salad plate, 8" d	**20.00**
Prelude, salt and pepper shakers, pr	**10.00**
Provincial, bread and butter plate	**5.00**
Provincial, dinner plate	**10.00**
Provincial, chop plate, 12" d	**55.00**
Provincial, mug	**12.00**
Provincial, oil and vinegar cruets, pr	**42.00**
Provincial, platter, round, 12⅜" d	**30.00**
Provincial, vegetable, 9¾" d	**25.00**
Sculptured Fruit, bowl	**15.00**
Sculptured Fruit, compote	**25.00**
Sculptured Fruit, creamer and sugar	**30.00**
Sculptured Fruit, cup and saucer	**18.00**
Sculptured Fruit, dinner plate	**12.00**
Thistle, cup and saucer	**10.00**
Thistle, dinner plate	**18.00**
Thistle, lug soup	**8.00**
Thistle, pitcher	**30.00**
Thistle, salad bowl, 10" d	**25.00**
Thistle, salad bowl, 12" d	**100.00**
Thistle, salt and pepper shakers, pr	**30.00**
Town and Country, blue, mug and saucer	**25.00**
Town and Country, brown, creamer and sugar	**30.00**

Town and Country, brown, pitcher and bowl, 1970s, 10³/₄" h pitcher, 14⁵/₈" d bowl, $100.00. Photo courtesy Ray Morykan Auctions.

GIFTWARE

Ashtray, Antique Coin, #5146	$10.00
Ashtray, Canada goose	12.00
Ashtray, pheasant, #3926C	12.00
Ashtray, Terra Rose	12.00
Bowl, ruffled, Antique Gold, #4061, 8" d	10.00
Cigarette Box, butterfly	50.00
Flowerpot, yellow tulip	20.00
Leaf Bowl, blue, Terra Rose	40.00
Vase, horse head, Terra Rose	325.00

STAR TREK

Gene Roddenberry's Star Trek appeared on TV beginning in September 1966 and ending on June 3, 1969. The show's initial success was modest. NBC reversed a decision to cancel the show in 1968 when fans rose in protest. A move to Friday evenings in its final season spelled doom for the show in the ratings war.

NBC syndicated Star Trek. By 1978 it had been translated in 42 languages and shown in 51 countries. Over 125 stations carried it in the United States. There were more than 350 local fan clubs.

The first Star Trek convention was held in 1972, drawing 3,000 fans. A dispute between the professional and fan managers of the convention resulted in two separate conventions in 1974. Before long, dozens of individuals were organizing Star Trek conventions around the country.

In 1979 Paramount released *Star Trek: The Motion Picture*. Its success led to additional films and television series starring the crew of the *Enterprise*. In September 1987 *Star Trek: The Next Generation* was launched. *Deep Space Nine* and *Star Trek: Voyager* followed. The *Generations* movie appeared in 1994 and *First Contact* in 1996.

References: Ursula Augustin, *Star Trek Collectibles: Classic Series, Next Generation, Deep Space Nine, Voyager*, Schiffer Publishing,

1997; Sue Cornwell and Mike Kott, *House of Collectibles Price Guide to Star Trek Collectibles, Fourth Edition,* House of Collectibles, 1996; Christine Gentry and Sally Gibson-Downs, *Greenberg's Guide to Star Trek Collectibles, Vol. 1* (1991), *Vol. 2* (1992), *Vol. 3* (1992), Greenberg Books, Kalmbach Publishing; Jerry B. Snyder, *A Trekker's Guide to Collectibles, 2nd Edition,* Schiffer Publishing, 1999.

Collectors' Clubs: International Federation of Trekkers, PO Box 242, Lorain, OH 44052; Starfleet, 200 Hiawatha Blvd, Oakland, NJ 07436; Star Trek: The Official Fan Club, PO Box 111000, Aurora, CO 80042.

Action Figure, Dr McCoy (Bones), blue shirt, black boots and pants, belt with communicator and phaser, Mego, ©1974 Paramount Pictures Corp, 8" h	$75.00
Action Figure, Klingon, brown and dark maroon outfit, belt holds phaser and communicator, Mego	50.00
Action Figure, Lt Uhura, red dress, with tricorder and life-like hair, Mego	75.00
Action Figure, Mr Spock, black and blue outfit, complete with belt, phaser, communicator, and tricorder, Mego	50.00
Action Figure, Scotty, red shirt, black pants and boots, belt with phaser and communicator, Mego, 8" h, MOC	75.00
Activity Book, *Star Trek Action Toy Book,* 16 stiff paper punch-out pages, Random House, ©1976 Paramount Pictures Corp, 8¹/₂ x 12"	20.00
Belt Buckle, Kirk and Spock, brass, enamel trim, 1979	10.00
Blueprints, set of 7, black and white paper sheets, official plans from the drawing board of Matt Jeffries, art director for TV series, Enterprise, Galileo, and hangar deck, 1968, 8¹/₂ x 11"	25.00
Book, *Trillions of Trilligs,* pop-up, Random House, hardback, 1977	10.00
Bop Bag, inflatable, full color image of Spock with space scene and Enterprise background, orig box, Azrak-Hamway International Inc, ©1975 Paramount Pictures Corp, 50" h	50.00
Calendar, 1976, Kirk and Spock cov, color stills inside, Ballantine Books, 1976	40.00
Certificate, parchment-like paper, black and white, "United Federation of Planets," includes inked "Star Date" and name of orig recipient plus facsimile signature of Gene Roddenberry, issued in 1968 with annual dues to Star Trek Interstellar Fan Club, 8¹/₂ x 11"	20.00
Cookie Jar, *USS Enterprise,* NCC-1701-A, Pfaltzgraff	30.00
Costume, Klingon, Ben Cooper, 1975	15.00
Costume, Mr Spock, plastic mask, 1-pc rayon/vinyl outfit, Ben Cooper, ©1978 Paramount Pictures Corp, orig box	20.00
Decanter, Mr Spock, figural, ceramic bust, Grenadier, ©1979 Paramount Pictures Corp, orig box, 9¹/₄" h	75.00
Drinking Glass, *USS Enterprise,* Dr Pepper, 6¹/₄" h	75.00
Fan Letter, Star Trek letterhead with black and white *Enterprise* on blue ground, welcomes recipient to "Star Trek Interstellar" and mentions "Inside Star Trek Official Fan Newsletter" with NBC reference "Twisting the Peacock's Tail," includes facsimile signature of Gene Roddenberry, late 1960s, 8¹/₂ x 11"	50.00
Game, Star Trek Game, "Star and Mission Cards" and 3-D Enterprise playing pcs, Milton Bradley, ©1979 Paramount Pictures Corp, MIB	50.00

Game, *Star Trek The Motion Picture*, Milton Bradley, 1979. . . . . **85.00**

Greeting Card, Kirk and McCoy with punch-out phaser gun, birthday greeting, mailing envelope, Random House, ©1976 Paramount Pictures Corp, 5 x 10" **20.00**

Jigsaw Puzzle, *Star Trek The Motion Picture*, 551 pcs, Aviva, 1979, 18 x 24" **25.00**

Key Chain, *Enterprise*, oval blue ground, Aviva, 1979 . . . . **4.00**

Kite, vinyl, images of *Enterprise* and Klingon cruiser, Hi-Flyer, ©1975 Paramount Pictures Corp, 36" l unopened pkg. **15.00**

Limited Edition Plate, "Beam Us Down Scotty," Hamilton/Ernst, 1986, 8½" d **45.00**

Lunch Box, *Star Trek The Motion Picture*, metal box, 6½" h purple plastic thermos, King-Seeley, ©1979 Paramount Pictures Corp **50.00**

Model, *USS Enterprise*, AMT, ©1966 Desilu Productions, 10 x 14½ x 2½" box **200.00**

Model, *USS Enterprise* Command Bridge, AMT, ©1975 Paramount Pictures Corp, 8½ x 10½ x 3" box **50.00**

Movie Viewer, black and red hard plastic viewer with 2 boxed films, Chemtoy Corp, ©1967 Desilu Productions Inc, on 5½ x 7½" blister card **50.00**

Napkins, set of 16, depicting Spock, Kirk, and McCoy, Tuttle Press, ©1976 Paramount Pictures Corp, sealed 6½ x 6½" pkg **15.00**

Pennant, felt, "Paramount Pictures Star Trek Adventure, Universal Studios Tour," multicolored, *Enterprise* and planet, 9 x 12½" **10.00**

Phaser Ray Gun/Space Flashlight, battery operated, black hard plastic with silver accents, click action noise, raised logo on side, Azrak-Hamway, ©1976 Paramount Pictures Corp, 3½" l **50.00**

Record, *William Shatner The Transformed Man*, 33⅓ rpm, Decca, 1970 . . . . **20.00**

Ring, McDonald's Happy Meal premium, blue plastic, emb designs on secret compartment lid, ©McDonald's, 1979, 1½ x 4". **25.00**

View-Master Reels, set of 3, *Star Trek The Motion Picture*, ©1979 Paramount Pictures Corp, MIP **15.00**

Water Pistol, *Star Trek The Motion Picture*, hard plastic, silver, Aviva Enterprises Inc, ©1970 Paramount Pictures Corp, MOC **20.00**

STAR WARS

Star Wars: A New Hope, George Lucas' 1977 movie epic, changed the history of film making. Luke Skywalker, Princess Leia, Hans Solo, Chewbacca, Ben (Obi-Wan) Kenobi, Darth Vadar, R2-D2, and C-3PO have become cultural icons. Their adventures in the *Star Wars* trilogy were eagerly followed.

Much of the success of the *Star Wars* trilogy is credited to the special effects created by Lucas' Industrial Light and Magic Company. John Williams' score and Ben Burtt's sound effects also contributed. Twentieth Century Fox granted a broad license to the Kenner Toy Company. Approximately 80% of *Star Wars* merchandise sold in Canada and the United States is made by Kenner. Almost every Kenner product was available in England, Europe, and other English-speaking countries through Palitoy of London.

The logo on the box is a good dating tool. Licensing rights associated with the release of *Star Wars* were retained by Twentieth Century Fox. Lucasfilm Ltd. owns the licensing rights to the sequels

and regained the right to the *Stars War* name before releasing *The Empire Strikes Back.*

References: Sue Cornwell and Mike Kott, *House of Collectibles Price Guide to Star Wars Collectibles, Fourth Edition,* House of Collectibles, 1997; Jeffrey B. Snyder, *Collecting Star Wars Toys 1977-1997,* Schiffer Publishing, 1998; Stuart W. Wells III, *The Galaxy's Greatest Star Wars Collectibles Price Guide,* Antique Trader Books, 1998.

Collectors' Club: Official Star Wars Fan Club, PO Box 111000, Aurora, CO 80042.

Action Figure, *Return of the Jedi*, Admiral Ackbar, 6th series **$30.00**

Action Figure, *Return of the Jedi*, AT-ST Driver, 7th series **30.00**

Action Figure, *Return of the Jedi*, Bib Fortuna, 6th series. **30.00**

Action Figure, *Return of the Jedi*, Nien Nunb, 6th series **35.00**

Action Figure, *Return of the Jedi*, Paploo, 7th series **40.00**

Action Figure, *Return of the Jedi*, Princess Leia Organa, combat poncho, 7th series. **60.00**

Action Figure, *Return of the Jedi*, Prune Face, 7th series **30.00**

Action Figure, *Return of the Jedi*, Rebel Commando, 6th series **30.00**

Action Figure, *Return of the Jedi*, Squid Head, 6th series. **30.00**

Action Figure, *Return of the Jedi*, Walrus Man, Tri-Logo series **60.00**

Action Figure, *Return of the Jedi*, Wicket W Warrick, 7th series **50.00**

Action Figure, *Star Wars*, Boba Fett, 2nd series **850.00**

Action Figure, *Star Wars*, Ben Obi-Wan Kenobi, white hair, 1st series **225.00**

Action Figure, *Star Wars*, Darth Vader, 1st series **200.00**

Action Figure, *Star Wars*, Hammerhead, 2nd series **130.00**

Action Figure, *Star Wars*, Jawa, cloth cape, 1st series **200.00**

Action Figure, *Star Wars*, Luke Skywalker X-Wing Pilot, 2nd series **150.00**

Action Figure, *Star Wars*, R2-D2, 1st series **150.00**

Action Figure, *Star Wars*, R5-D4, second series **135.00**

Action Figure, *The Empire Strikes Back*, AT-AT Commander, 5th series **50.00**

Action Figure, *The Empire Strikes Back*, Bespin Security Guard, black, 5th series **50.00**

Action Figure, *The Empire Strikes Back*, Bossk, 3rd series . . . **100.00**

Action Figure, *The Empire Strikes Back*, Cloud Car Pilot, 5th series **60.00**

Action Figure, *The Empire Strikes Back*, FX-7, 3rd series **100.00**

Action Figure, *The Empire Strikes Back*, Han Solo, Hoth outfit, 3rd series **75.00**

Action Figure, *The Empire Strikes Back*, Imperial TIE Fighter Pilot, 5th series. **100.00**

Action Figure, *The Empire Strikes Back*, Leia Organa, Bespin gown, 3rd series. **175.00**

Action Figure, *The Empire Strikes Back*, Luke Skywalker, Bespin fatigues, 3rd series **175.00**

Action Figure, *The Empire Strikes Back*, R2-D2, with sensorscope, 5th series **50.00**

Action Figure, *The Empire Strikes Back*, Yoda, orange snake, 4th series **75.00**

Action Figure, *The Power of the Force*, A-Wing Pilot, 8th series **100.00**

Action Figure, *The Power of the Force*, Barada, 8th series . . . **100.00**

Action Figure, *The Power of the Force*, Han Solo, carbonite chamber, 8th series **225.00**

Action Figure, *The Power of the Force,* Luke Skywalker, Stormtrooper outfit, 8th series **400.00**

Action Figure, *The Power of the Force,* Romba, 8th series **50.00**

Action Figure Accessory, storage case, *Star Wars,* black vinyl, holds 24 action figures, 1977, 3 x 8½ x 12" **50.00**

Activity Book, *Wicket the Ewok Watercolor Painting Set,* Craft Master, 1983 . . . . **30.00**

Bank, Darth Vader, *Return of the Jedi,* Adam Joseph Industries, 1983, MIB **50.00**

Chewbacca Bandolier Strap, *Return of the Jedi,* orig box, 1983 . . . . **30.00**

Costume, Darth Vader, *Star Wars,* Ben Cooper, orig box, size medium **65.00**

Costume, R2-D2, *The Empire Strikes Back,* Ben Cooper, orig box, 1980 . . . . **50.00**

Dixie Cups, 5 oz, 100 full color cups with scenes from *Return of the Jedi,* orig box **50.00**

Jigsaw Puzzle, *Star Wars,* "Attack of the Sand People," 140 pcs, orig box, 14 x 18" **15.00**

Light Saber, *Return of the Jedi,* plastic, "The Force Light Saber," 1984, 43" l **50.00**

Model Kit, *Star Wars,* Darth Vader, MPC, battery operated, orig box, 1978 . . . . **85.00**

Model Kit, *Star Wars,* R2-D2, MPC, orig box, 1977 . . . . **50.00**

Necklace, *Star Wars,* C-3PO, cast metal figure with movable arms on gold finish chain, c1977, MIP **20.00**

Pillow, R2-D2, stuffed, silver, white, blue, and red, 1977, 9" h **50.00**

Playset, Bespin Freeze Chamber, Kenner's micro collection, 1983, MIB **85.00**

Playset, Hoth Ice Planet Set, *The Empire Strikes Back,* orig box, 1980 . . . . **125.00**

Playset, Hoth Wampa Cave, *The Empire Strikes Back,* Kenner's micro collection, 1982, MIB **140.00**

Playset, Turret & Probot Playset, orig box, JC Penney exclusive, 1980 . . . . **150.00**

Radar Laser Cannon, *The Empire Strikes Back,* orig box, 1982 . . . . **25.00**

Stuffed Toy, Wicket W Warrior, Kenner, orig box, 1984, 15½" h **50.00**

Telephone, Darth Vader Speaker Phone, figural, American Telecommunications Corp, 1983, 14" h **150.00**

Vehicle, AST-5 Armored Sentinel Transport, *Return of the Jedi,* 1983, MIB **25.00**

Vehicle, Millennium Falcon, *The Empire Strikes Back,* 1981, MIB **65.00**

Vehicle, Rebel Transport Vehicle, *The Empire Strikes Back,* orig box, 1982 . . . . **125.00**

Vehicle, Speeder Bike, *Return of the Jedi,* 1983, MIB **25.00**

Vehicle, TIE Fighter, *Star Wars,* flashing laser light, no sound, orig box, 1978 . . . . **50.00**

Vehicle, Y-Wing Fighter, *Return of the Jedi,* orig box **65.00**

STEIFF

Giegen on the Benz, Bad Wurtemburg, Germany, is the birthplace and home of Steiff. In the 1880s, Margarette Steiff, a clothing manufacturer, made animal-theme pincushions for her nephews and their friends. Fritz, Margarette's brother, took some to a county fair and sold them all. In 1893 an agent representing Steiff appeared at the Leipzig Toy Fair.

Margarette's nephew, Richard, suggested making a small bear with movable head and joints. It appeared for the first time in Steiff's 1903 catalog. The bear was an instant success. An American buyer placed an order for 3,000. It was first called the "teddy" bear in the 1908 catalog.

In 1905 the famous "button in the ear" was added to Steiff toys. The first buttons were small tin circles with the name in raised block letters. The familiar script logo was introduced in 1932, about the same time a shiny, possibly chrome, button was first used. Brass ear buttons date after 1980.

The earliest Steiff toys were made entirely of felt. Mohair plush was not used until 1903. When fabrics were in scarce supply during World War I and World War II, other materials were used. None proved successful.

By 1903-04 the Steiff catalog included several character dolls. The speedway monkey on wooden wheels appeared in the 1913 catalog. Character dolls were discontinued in the mid-1910s. Cardboard tags were added in the late 1920s. Teddy Babies were introduced in 1929.

Steiff's popularity increased tremendously following World War II. A line of miniatures was introduced. After a period of uncertainty in the 1970s, due in part to currency fluctuation, Steiff enjoyed a renaissance when it introduced its 1980 Limited Edition "Papa" Centennial Bear. More than 5,000 were sold in the United States. Steiff collectors organized. A series of other limited edition pieces followed. Many credit the sale of the "Papa" Bear with creating the teddy bear craze that swept America in the 1980s.

References: Jürgen and Marianne Cieslik, *Button in Ear: The History of Teddy Bear and His Friends,* distributed by Theriault's, 1989; Jürgen and Marianne Cieslik, *Steiff Teddy Bears,* Steiff USA, 1994; Edith and Johan Koskinen, *Steiff Price Guide,* Gold Horse Publishing, 1999; Margaret Fox Mandel, *Teddy Bears and Steiff Animals* (1984, 2000 value update), *Second Series* (1987, 2000

Drinking Glass, The Star Wars Trilogy, Darth Vader, Coca-Cola and Burger King promotion, 1977, 5½" h, $10.00. Photo courtesy Ray Morykan Auctions.

value update), Collector Books; Margaret Fox Mandel, *Teddy Bears, Annalee Animals & Steiff Animals, Third Series*, Collector Books, 1990, 2000 value update; Linda Mullins, *Teddy Bear & Friends Price Guide, Fourth Edition*, Hobby House Press, 1993; Christel and Rolf Pistorius, *Steiff: Sensational Teddy Bear, Animals & Dolls*, Hobby House Press, 1991.

Collectors' Clubs: Steiff Club USA (company sponsored), 31 E 28th St, 9th Flr, New York, NY 10016; Steiff Collectors Club, Franklin Park Mall, 5001 Monroe St, Toledo, OH 43623.

Beepo Dachshund, brown and tan mohair, straw stuffed, glass eyes, jointed with swivel head, open mouth with felt tongue, red leather collar, script button with yellow flag, paper collar tag, 1950-60, 5" l **$150.00**

Bulldog, blonde plush, poseable wire ears, articulated head, wooden eyes, dewlap jaws, small repair at tail, c1958, 24" h, 25" l **625.00**

Cockie Cocker Spaniel, brown and white mohair, straw stuffed, swivel head with glass eyes, red leather collar, squeaker, 1950-60, 11" h, 13" l **50.00**

Collie, long and short mohair, straw stuffed, open mouth with felt tongue, glass eyes, 1960s, 7" h, 8" l **70.00**

Donkey, tan mohair, cropped mohair face, straw stuffed, black tipped ears, black eyes, script button, 1950-60, 8" h, 9½" l **30.00**

Elephant, reclining, wooden teeth, glass eyes, thick mane **1,375.00**

Elephant, tan plush, realistic knee wrinkles, toenails, large floppy ears, smiling face, c1960, 25" h, 50" l **500.00**

Floppy Cockie, soft stuffed, felt eyes, int bell, script button, 1950-60, 12" l **50.00**

Giraffe, large orange and tan plush, glass eyes, articulated neck, restitching on ear, 59" h. **1,500.00**

Lamb, white and tan mohair, snubbed felt-lined tail, green and black glass eyes, felt ears, blue ribbon with bell, 1950-60, 4" h **25.00**

Lea Lioness, mohair, straw stuffed, orange glass eyes, 1950-60, 4" h **30.00**

Leopard, mohair, straw stuffed, green and black glass eyes, script button, 1950s, 12" l **125.00**

Lizzy Lizard, airbrushed velvet, with button, 8" l. **300.00**

Monkey Cart Toy, monkey steering 4-wheeled cart, c1938, 9" l **350.00**

Panda Bear, black and white mohair, straw stuffed, swivel head, orange glass eyes, red collar with bell, paper collar tag, 1950s, 5¾" l **150.00**

Pelican, beige mohair, felt beak and feet, glass eyes, with button and tag, 9½" h **400.00**

Pug, brown and black mohair, straw stuffed, glass eyes, 1950-60, 6¼" h **50.00**

Running Rabbit, tan and white mohair, brown tipped ears, straw stuffed, glass eyes, felt lined ears, script button and partial yellow tag, 1950-60, 7" l **90.00**

Seated Rabbit, tan and gray, swivel head, large brown glass eyes, inner mohair ears, 1950-60, 8" h **50.00**

Sparrow, mohair, horse hair wings and tail, wire feet, 4" h **300.00**

Tiger, mohair, straw stuffed, green and black glass eyes, 1950-60, 9" l **125.00**

Xorry Desert Fox, mohair, straw stuffed, black velvet backed ears, glass eyes, script button, 1960s, 6½" l **80.00**

STEMWARE

There are two basic types of stemware: (1) soda-based glass and (2) lead- or flint-based glass, also known as crystal. Early glass was made from a soda-based formula, which was costly and therefore available only to the rich. In the mid-19th century, a soda-lime glass was perfected, which was lighter and less expensive, but lacked the clarity and brilliance of crystal glass. This advance made glassware available to the common man.

The principal ingredients of crystal are silica (sand), litharge (a fused lead monoxide), and potash or potassium carbonate. The exact formula differs from manufacturer to manufacturer and is a closely guarded secret. Crystal can be plain or decorated, hand blown or machine made. Its association with quality is assumed.

There are three basic methods used to make glass—free blown, mold blown, or pressed. Furthermore, stemware can be decorated in a variety of ways. It may be cut or etched, or the bowl, stem or both may be made of colored glass. The varieties are as endless as the manufacturers. Notable manufacturers include Baccarat, Fostoria, Lenox, Orrefors, and Waterford.

References: Tom and Neila Bredehoft, *Fifty Years of Collectible Glass: 1920-1970, Vol. II*, Antique Trader Books, 1999; Gene Florence, *Stemware Identification: Featuring Cordials With Values, 1920s-1960s*, Collector Books, 1997; Bob Page and Dale Frederiksen, *Crystal Stemware Identification Guide*, Collector Books, 1998; Bob Page and Dale Frederiksen, *Seneca Glass Company: 1891-1983*, Replacements, Ltd., 1995; Harry L. Rinker, *Stemware of the 20th Century: The Top 200 Patterns*, House of Collectibles, 1997.

Note: See individual manufacturers' categories for additional listings.

Champagne, Apple Blossom #3130, yellow, Cambridge **$28.00**

Champagne, Bouquet, crystal, Fostoria. **18.00**

Champagne, Buttercup, crystal, Fostoria. **20.00**

Champagne, Corsage, crystal, Fostoria **18.00**

Champagne, Decagon, amethyst, Cambridge **25.00**

Champagne, Dolly Madison cutting, Fostoria **15.00**

Champagne, Florentine, crystal, Fostoria **15.00**

Champagne, Fuchsia, crystal, Fostoria **20.00**

Champagne, Holly, crystal, Fostoria **15.00**

Champagne, June, crystal, Fostoria, 6" h. **20.00**

Champagne, June, yellow, Fostoria, 6" h. **20.00**

Champagne, Laurel cutting, Fostoria **15.00**

Champagne, Meadow Rose, crystal, Fostoria **20.00**

Champagne, Morning Glory etching, Fostoria, 5½" h **20.00**

Champagne, Navarre etching, pink, Fostoria. **25.00**

Champagne, Nouveau etching, smoke, Fostoria **25.00**

Champagne, Revere cutting, Fostoria **15.00**

Champagne, Romance, Fostoria. **15.00**

Champagne, Rose cutting, crystal, Fostoria, 5" h **20.00**

Champagne, Rose Point #3121, Cambridge **30.00**

Champagne, Versailles, blue, Fostoria. **35.00**

Champagne, Versailles, pink, Fostoria. **25.00**

Champagne, Versailles, yellow, Fostoria **20.00**

Champagne, Willow etching, crystal, Fostoria. **12.00**

Claret, Nouveau etching, smoke, large, Fostoria **25.00**

Claret, Romance, Fostoria. **55.00**

Cocktail, Buttercup, crystal, Fostoria. **20.00**

Cocktail, Century, crystal, Fostoria **18.00**

Cocktail, Chintz, crystal, Fostoria. **25.00**

Champagne,
Navarre etching,
crystal, Fostoria,
$25.00.

Ice Tea Tumbler, Nouveau etching, smoke, Fostoria......... 25.00
Ice Tea Tumbler, Rose cutting, crystal, Fostoria 25.00
Ice Tea Tumbler, Spiral Flutes, green, flat, Duncan &
 Miller 65.00
Ice Tea Tumbler, Willowmere etching, crystal, Fostoria 30.00
Juice Tumbler, Decagon, royal blue, Cambridge 30.00
Juice Tumbler, Holly, crystal, Fostoria 18.00
Juice Tumbler, June, crystal, ftd, Fostoria, 4½" h 25.00
Juice Tumbler, June, yellow, Fostoria...................... 30.00
Juice Tumbler, Meadow Rose, crystal, ftd, Fostoria 20.00
Juice Tumbler, Romance, crystal, Fostoria................. 20.00
Mushroom Tumbler, Caprice #184, pistachio,
 Cambridge, 12 oz 150.00
Mushroom Tumbler, Caprice #188, moonlight blue,
 Cambridge, 12 oz 60.00
Mushroom Tumbler, Portia #3400/38, Cambridge, 12 oz..... 45.00
Mushroom Tumbler, Rose Point #3400/38, Cambridge,
 12 oz 85.00
Old Fashion, American, Fostoria 12.00
Old Fashion, Baroque, blue, Fostoria 85.00
Old Fashion, Caprice #310, moonlight blue, Cambridge.... 125.00
Oyster Cocktail, Caprice #300, pink, Cambridge 85.00
Oyster Cocktail, Chintz, crystal, Fostoria 25.00
Oyster Cocktail, Corsage, Fostoria 15.00
Oyster Cocktail, June, crystal, Fostoria 25.00
Oyster Cocktail, Romance, crystal, Fostoria 25.00
Oyster Cocktail, Rose Point #3121, Cambridge........... 65.00
Oyster Cocktail, Trojan, yellow, Fostoria................. 20.00
Oyster Cocktail, Versailles, blue, Fostoria 45.00
Parfait, Rose Point #3121, Cambridge.................. 95.00
Parfait, Trojan, yellow, Fostoria 45.00
Sherbet, American Lady, crystal, Fostoria 10.00
Sherbet, Baroque, crystal, Fostoria 10.00
Sherbet, Caprice #300, crystal, low, Cambridge 18.00
Sherbet, Caprice #300, crystal, tall, Cambridge, 6 oz 12.00
Sherbet, Caprice #300, moonlight blue, low, Cambridge..... 30.00
Sherbet, Decagon, Willow Blue, low, Cambridge 25.00
Sherbet, Holly, crystal, low, Fostoria.................. 15.00
Sherbet, Jamestown, amber, Fostoria 8.00
Sherbet, Jamestown, blue, Fostoria.................... 15.00
Sherbet, Jamestown, green, Fostoria 12.00
Sherbet, Jamestown, red, Fostoria..................... 15.00
Sherbet, June, crystal, low, Fostoria 20.00
Sherbet, June, yellow, low, Fostoria 20.00
Sherbet, Laurel cutting, low, Fostoria 15.00
Sherbet, Navarre etching, crystal, low, Fostoria 20.00
Sherbet, Romance, crystal, low, Fostoria............... 15.00
Sherbet, Versailles, blue, low, Fostoria 25.00
Sherbet, Versailles, pink, tall, Fostoria................. 40.00
Sherbet, Versailles, yellow, low, Fostoria............... 18.00
Sherbet, Willow etching, crystal, low, Fostoria 15.00
Sherry, Portia #7966, Cambridge, 2 oz................. 50.00
Sundae, American, Fostoria 8.00
Tumbler, Baroque, blue, ftd, Fostoria.................. 30.00
Tumbler, Caprice #300, crystal, ftd, Cambridge, 5 oz 18.00
Tumbler, Decagon, amethyst, ftd, Cambridge, 2½ oz 25.00
Tumbler, Diane #498, Cambridge, 12 oz................ 55.00
Tumbler, Fuchsia, crystal, Fostoria, 5¼" h............. 20.00
Tumbler, Romance, ftd, Fostoria, 5 oz 15.00
Tumbler, Romance, ftd, Fostoria, 12 oz 25.00
Tumbler, Rose Point #3121, Cambridge, 9 oz........... 40.00
Tumbler, Versailles, yellow, Fostoria, 2½ oz 40.00
Water Goblet, American Lady, crystal, Fostoria 15.00
Water Goblet, Baroque, blue, Fostoria 25.00

Cocktail, Corsage, crystal, Fostoria..................... 20.00
Cocktail, Decagon, amethyst, Cambridge................ 25.00
Cocktail, Decagon, Willow Blue, Cambridge 25.00
Cocktail, Dolly Madison cutting, Fostoria............... 15.00
Cocktail, Fuchsia, crystal, Fostoria 20.00
Cocktail, Holly, crystal, Fostoria...................... 20.00
Cocktail, June, crystal, Fostoria 30.00
Cocktail, June, yellow, Fostoria 35.00
Cocktail, Laurel cutting, Fostoria 15.00
Cocktail, Lido, blue, Fostoria 25.00
Cocktail, Navarre etching, crystal, Fostoria............. 20.00
Cocktail, Romance, Fostoria 18.00
Cocktail, Versailles, blue, Fostoria 45.00
Cocktail, Versailles, yellow, Fostoria................... 30.00
Cocktail, Willowmere etching, crystal, Fostoria.......... 20.00
Cordial, Blossom Time #3675, Cambridge 75.00
Cordial, Caribbean, crystal, Duncan & Miller............ 75.00
Cordial, Carmen #3500, Cambridge.................... 90.00
Cordial, Corsage, Fostoria 50.00
Cordial, Fuchsia, crystal, Fostoria..................... 40.00
Cordial, Heather, crystal, Fostoria 40.00
Cordial, Holly, crystal, Fostoria 40.00
Cordial, Manor, yellow, Fostoria...................... 75.00
Cordial, Romance, crystal, Fostoria 50.00
Cordial, Victorian, cobalt, Fostoria.................... 45.00
Double Old Fashion, Navarre etching, Fostoria.......... 75.00
Goblet, Dolly Madison cutting, low, Fostoria 15.00
Goblet, Holly, crystal, low, Fostoria 25.00
Ice Tea Tumbler, Baroque, blue, ftd, Fostoria........... 30.00
Ice Tea Tumbler, Buttercup, crystal, Fostoria 25.00
Ice Tea Tumbler, Caprice #300, crystal, ftd, Cambridge 20.00
Ice Tea Tumbler, Chintz, crystal, Fostoria.............. 25.00
Ice Tea Tumbler, Jamestown, blue, flat, Fostoria......... 20.00
Ice Tea Tumbler, Jamestown, blue, ftd, Fostoria......... 20.00
Ice Tea Tumbler, Jamestown, pink, ftd, Fostoria......... 20.00
Ice Tea Tumbler, Jamestown, red, flat, Fostoria 25.00
Ice Tea Tumbler, June, crystal, Fostoria 25.00
Ice Tea Tumbler, June, yellow, Fostoria 25.00
Ice Tea Tumbler, Meadow Rose, crystal, Fostoria........ 25.00
Ice Tea Tumbler, Midnight Rose, crystal, Fostoria........ 25.00

Water Goblet, Baroque, crystal, Fostoria. **15.00**
Water Goblet, Buttercup, crystal, low, Fostoria **25.00**
Water Goblet, Buttercup, crystal, tall, Fostoria **25.00**
Water Goblet, Caprice #300, crystal, Cambridge, 9 oz **18.00**
Water Goblet, Chintz, crystal, Fostoria, 7½" h **30.00**
Water Goblet, Decagon, green, Cambridge **30.00**
Water Goblet, Decagon, royal blue, Cambridge **35.00**
Water Goblet, Decagon, Willow Blue, Cambridge **35.00**
Water Goblet, Jamestown, amber, Fostoria **10.00**
Water Goblet, June, crystal, Fostoria. **25.00**
Water Goblet, June, yellow, Fostoria **25.00**
Water Goblet, Laurel cutting, Fostoria **18.00**
Water Goblet, Midnight Rose, crystal, Fostoria **25.00**
Water Goblet, Nouveau etching, smoke, Fostoria **25.00**
Water Goblet, Revere cutting, Fostoria **18.00**
Water Goblet, Rose cutting, crystal, Fostoria. **25.00**
Water Goblet, Spiral Flutes, green, Duncan & Miller. **15.00**
Water Goblet, Versailles, yellow, Fostoria **25.00**
Water Goblet, Willow etching, crystal, Fostoria **18.00**
Whiskey, Apple Blossom, green, ftd, Cambridge, 2 oz. **85.00**
Whiskey, Apple Blossom, yellow, ftd, Cambridge, 2 oz **65.00**
Whiskey, June, yellow, ftd, Fostoria **65.00**
Wine Goblet, Buttercup, crystal, Fostoria **30.00**
Wine Goblet, Caprice #6, moonlight blue, Cambridge, 3 oz . **200.00**
Wine Goblet, Chintz, crystal, Fostoria **45.00**
Wine Goblet, Decagon, pink, Cambridge. **35.00**
Wine Goblet, Diane #3122, Cambridge, 3½ oz, 6¾" h **45.00**
Wine Goblet, Fuchsia, crystal, Fostoria **25.00**
Wine Goblet, Jamestown, red, Fostoria **20.00**
Wine Goblet, June, yellow, Fostoria, 2½ oz **55.00**
Wine Goblet, Laurel cutting, Fostoria **15.00**
Wine Goblet, Versailles, blue, Fostoria **85.00**
Wine Goblet, Willow etching, crystal, Fostoria **25.00**

STEUBEN GLASS

Frederick Carder and Thomas Hawkes founded the Steuben Glass Works in 1903. Initially Steuben made blanks for Hawkes. The company also made Art Nouveau ornamental and colored glass. Steuben Glass had trouble securing raw materials during World War I. In 1918 Corning purchased Steuben Glass from Carder and Hawkes. Carder became art director at Corning.

Steuben experienced numerous financial difficulties in the 1920s, reorganizing several times. When Corning threatened to close its Steuben division, Arthur Houghton, Jr., led the move to save it. Steuben Glass Incorporated was established. All earlier glass formulas were abandoned. The company concentrated on producing crystal products.

In 1937 Steuben produced the first in a series of crystal pieces featuring engraved designs from famous artists. Despite production cutbacks during World War II, Steuben emerged in the post-war period as a major manufacturer of crystal products. The company's first crystal animals were introduced in 1949. Special series, incorporating the works of Asian and British painters, and a group of 31 Collector's pieces, each an interpretation of a poem commissioned by Steuben, were produced during the 1950s and 60s.

Reference: Thomas P. Dimitroff, et al., *Frederick Carder and Steuben Glass*, Schiffer Publishing, 1998.

Bowl, colorless glass, flattened extended rims, incised
  "S" on base, 7½" d, price for set of 12 . . . . **$550.00**

Vase, spiral design, fleur-de-lis mark, 11½" h, $275.00.

Bowl, gold aurene on calcite, flared scalloped rim int
  with iridescent gold, 2" h **175.00**
Bud Vase, crystal, catalog #7947, designed by Don Wier,
  elongated neck on swollen base with applied ball and
  scroll dec, base inscribed "Steuben," 1947, 6¾" h **200.00**
Bud Vase, cylindrical form, raised on flattened disk foot,
  inscribed "Aurene," 7¾" h **250.00**
Figurine, chick, inscribed "Steuben," G Thompson, 4" h **200.00**
Figurine, owl, looking right, frosted eyes, inscribed
  "Steuben," D Pollard design, 5½" h **225.00**
Flatware, catalog #7478, 24 pcs, 12 forks and spoons,
  colorless lead glass handles on silver, unsgd, some pcs
  mkd "H," c1930 . . . . **1,000.00**
Grotesque Bowl, catalog #7543, 3-lined pillar-molded
  floriform body, colorless crystal ruffled rim, 6¾" h **225.00**
Perfume, Cluthra, catalog #7327, hexagonal faceted
  form, off-white rising to black cluthra glass, raised
  neck topped with angular colorless glass stopper,
  fleur-de-lis mark, 6" h **500.00**
Sculpture, Thistle Rock, cut and polished glass rock sup-
  porting golden thistle, base inscribed "Steuben,"
  velvet-lined red leather case, Vermeil, 7" h **2,175.00**
Vase, celeste blue, rib-form flared, raised disk on foot,
  recessed, polished pontil, fleur-de-lis mark at base,
  7" h **325.00**
Vase, Cluthra, catalog #2683, rose pink, broad oval
  body with flared rim, white on colorless surround,
  fleur-de-lis mark on base, 10½" h **1,375.00**
Vase, trumpet shape, light amethyst with fleur-de-lis
  mark on round polished base, set in wrought iron leaf
  form base, Carder, 11½" h vase **250.00**
Wine Goblets, catalog #7737, set of 11, designed by
  Sidney Waugh, trumpet shaped, wide angular
  teardrop stems, orig gray fitted box, 7¼" h **625.00**
Wine Goblets, catalog #7846, set of 6, designed by
  Arthur A Houghton Jr, crystal, flared cylindrical vessel
  with knobbed stem and square base, small "S"
  inscribed on base, c1939, 7¹/₁₆" h **250.00**

STOCKS & BONDS

A stock certificate is a financial document that shows the amount of capital on a per share basis that the owner has invested in a company. Gain is achieved through dividends and an increase in unit value. A bond is an interest bearing certificate of public or private indebtedness. The interest is generally paid on a fixed schedule with the principal being repaid when the bond is due.

Joint stock companies were used to finance world exploration in the 16th, 17th, and 18th centuries. Several American colonies received financial backing from joint stock companies. Bonds and stocks help spread financial risk. The New York Stock Exchange was founded in the late 18th century.

In the middle of the 19th century, engraving firms such as the American Bank Note Company and Rawdon, Wright & Hatch created a wide variety of financial instruments ranging from bank notes to stock certificates. Most featured one or more ornately engraved vignettes. While some generic vignettes were used repeatedly, vignettes often provided a detailed picture of a manufacturing facility or product associated with the company.

Stocks and bonds are collected primarily for their subject matter. Date is a value factor. Pre-1850 stocks and bonds command the highest price provided they have nice vignettes. Stocks and bonds issued between 1850 and 1915 tend to be more valuable than those issued after 1920. Unused stock and bond certificates are less desirable than issued certificates. Finally, check the signatures on all pre-1915 stocks. Many important personages served as company presidents.

References: Norman E. Martinus and Harry L. Rinker, *Warman's Paper,* Wallace-Homestead, Krause Publications, 1994; Gene Utz, *Collecting Paper,* Books Americana, 1993.

Periodical: *Bank Note Reporter,* 700 E State St, Iola, WI 54990.

Collectors' Clubs: International Bond and Share Society, 15 Kyatt Pl, PO Box 430, Hackensack, NJ 07602; Old Certificates Collector's Club, 4761 W Waterbuck Dr, Tucson, AZ 85742.

BONDS

Black Cross Navigation & Trading Co, $25 bond, orange
  border, 1925 . . . . **$875.00**
Converse Rubber Shoe, $1,000 sinking fund convertible
  gold bond, orange, eagle with shield and Liberty cap,
  sgd by MM Converse, 1922 . . . . **250.00**
Delaware & Hudson Railroad Co, $1,000, 2 women and
  farm scene vignette, 1963 . . . . **5.00**
General Motors Corp, $1,000, streamlined car, truck,
  locomotive, 3 heads, and factory building vignette,
  coupons, issued, 1954 . . . . **15.00**
Republic of China, $1,000, US secured sinking fund
  bond, blue with blue security underprint, hillside
  pagoda, 1937 . . . . **550.00**

STOCKS

Abercrombie & Fitch, 350 shares, pair of Indians on cliff
  watching deer, issued to and sgd by Ezra H Fitch,
  1924 . . . . **$775.00**
Albert F Remy Co, 5 shares, green, red seal, rotund and
  mustached policeman, issued and sgd by Albert F
  Remy, 1931 . . . . **250.00**

American League Base Ball Club of Chicago, Chicago
  White Sox, 200 shares, eagle atop rock, gold seal and
  underprint, issued to Grace Comisky, 1941 . . . . **450.00**
Armstrong Rubber, 24 shares, green, busy city street
  scene with early automobiles and trucks, 1945 . . . . **200.00**
Bach Aircraft, 25 shares, blue, corporate logo with
  "Safety–Economy–Comfort," 1929 . . . . **450.00**
Coca-Cola Bottling Works, 2 shares, Chattanooga, TN,
  gold seal and underprint, maiden with hat at left,
  1924 . . . . **550.00**
Fort Wayne & Jackson Railroad Co, blue and white, 1972 . . . . . **12.00**
Fraser Pencil, 334 shares, blue, 45 pencils that radiate in
  sunburst pattern vignette, sgd by Fraser, 1920 . . . . **450.00**
Houdini Picture Co, 30 shares, voting trust certificate,
  green borders, security underprint, 1921 . . . . **200.00**
Lehigh Valley Railroad Co, orange and white, 1971 . . . . **10.00**
Pickwick Airways, 10 shares, orange, woman flanked by
  2 tri-motor airplanes, 1930 . . . . **775.00**
Ringling Bros and Barnum & Bailey Combined Shows, 4
  shares, pink border, multicolored circus figures, 1971 . . . . **375.00**
Seaboard Airways, 10 shares, orange, eagle with out-
  stretched wings, 1931 . . . . **475.00**
Stutz Motor Car of America, 10 shares, winged Stutz
  logo flanked by 2 women, 1937 . . . . **400.00**
Taxicar, 100 shares, light green, old fashioned truck and
  cars entering and leaving building, 1923 . . . . **375.00**
The New York, Chicago, and St Louis Railroad Co,
  Nickel Plate Road, brown and white, 1960 . . . . **8.00**
Wyoming Teapot Oil Syndicate, 50 shares, gold under-
  print and corporate seal, oil towers and tanker cars,
  1923 . . . . **175.00**

STRING HOLDERS

Commercial cast-iron string holders, designed to assist merchants and manufacturers in the wrapping of packages, date to the middle of the 19th century. Smaller household models appeared as the century ended.

The 1920s through the 1950s is the golden age of the household string holder. Several Depression glass patterns included a string holder. Hull's Little Red Riding Hood series included an example. Ceramic and chalkware string holders in the shape of a human face, animal, and fruit were common, often selling for less than fifty cents at a five-and-dime store.

Most string holders are unmarked. Many examples were imported from Japan. A few, e.g., Universal Statuary Company, are American made.

Several mail order catalog companies offered reproduction and new ceramic string holders. Do not confuse them with their historic antecedents.

References: Ellen Bercovici, Bobbie Zucker Bryson and Deborah Gillham, *Collectibles for the Kitchem, Bath & Beyond,* Antique Trader Books, 1998; Sharon Ray Jacobs, *A Collector's Guide to Stringholders,* L-W Book Sales, 1996.

Apple, chalkware, red, 9" h, 6¼" w **$30.00**
Apple, chalkware, red and yellow apple with bunch of
  strawberries and green leaves, 9" h **25.00**
Apple with Worm House, chalkware **90.00**
Baby Heads, pr, chalkware, 1 crying, 1 laughing, 4¼" h,
  3¼" w, price for pr **65.00**

Prayer Lady, ceramic, pink, 6¹/₂" h, $150.00

Barn Owl, ceramic, scissors form eyeglasses, Babbacombe, England. **40.00**

Bart the Monkey, chalkware, 6" h. **25.00**

Black Man's Head, chalkware, smiling face, wearing straw hat, 6¹/₂" h **140.00**

Canister, tin, white with black design around bottom of knitting woman in rocking chair and cat playing with ball of yarn, 4¹/₂" h, 4¹/₄" d **12.00**

Cat, chalkware, brown cat with green eyes holding red ball of yarn, 7" h, 4³/₄" w **40.00**

Cat Snip, ceramic, white, full figure cat holding oversized ball of yarn, paw holds scissors, Fitz and Floyd, "FF Japan" sticker **100.00**

Cozy Kitten, ceramic, Siamese cat head, plaid bow holds scissors, Holt-Howard. **65.00**

Dutch Girl Head, ceramic, wearing red hat **35.00**

Dutch Girl Head, chalkware, green hat **110.00**

Fish and Boy, ceramic, oversized white fish with fisherman boy resting in its mouth, tail holds scissors, mkd "Fitz and Floyd, Inc MCMLXXVIII" **75.00**

Fox Head, scissors form eyeglasses, Babbacombe Pottery, England, 7¹/₂" h, 5" w **50.00**

Hawaiian God, ceramic, white, mkd "Japan, R-95, Dromid of Hawaii," 7¹/₄" h **8.00**

Heart, ceramic, "You'll always have a pull with me," Cleminsons **100.00**

Japanese God, ceramic, white, mkd "Ichiban, Japanese Steakhouse" on back, OMC Japan sticker, 9" h **15.00**

Lady with Flower Basket, ceramic, Japan, 6" h, 4⁷/₈" w **90.00**

Mammy, ceramic, wearing red bandanna and white dress with green and brown plaid design **125.00**

Mammy, ceramic, wearing white dress, mkd "NS Co USA" **100.00**

Mexican Man, chalkware **125.00**

Mexican Señorita Head, chalkware, mkd "Universal Stat Co ©1949," 8" h, 7" w **135.00**

Mother and Child, ceramic, white, Japan, 6" h, 4" w **10.00**

Mouse and Cheese, ceramic, mouse sitting on oversized cheese wedge, scissor holder, Babbacombe, England **40.00**

Mouse, ceramic, dressed as girl, Japan **85.00**

Nubian Lady Head, chalkware, red turban, 6¹/₂" h, 5¹/₂" w. **100.00**

Pear, chalkware, yellow with red accents, 8" h, 5¹/₂" w **40.00**

Prince Pineapple, chalkware, 6⁷/₈" h, 4⁵/₈" w **50.00**

Sailor Boy, chalkware, eyes looking left, mkd "1942 by Universal Sta Co," 7¹/₂" h, 6" w. **400.00**

Sailor Boy Head, chalkware, with pipe. **60.00**

Scottie Dog Head, chalkware, beige with black details, 6¹/₂" h, 4¹/₄" w **110.00**

Strawberry Face, chalkware **90.00**

Tomato Head Chef, chalkware **175.00**

Tuxedo Cat, ceramic, black and white cat head, pink bow holds scissors. **30.00**

STUFFED TOYS

The bear is only one of dozens of animals that have been made into stuffed toys. In fact, Margarette Steiff's first stuffed toy was not a bear but an elephant. The stuffed toy animal was a toy/department store fixture by the early 1920s.

Many companies, e.g., Ideal and Knickerbocker, competed with Steiff for market share. Following World War II, stuffed toys became a favorite prize of carnival games of chance. Most of these toys were inexpensive imports from China and Taiwan.

Many characters from Disney animated cartoons, e.g., *Jungle Book* and *The Lion King,* appear as stuffed toys. A major collection could be assembled focusing solely on Disney-licensed products. The 1970s stuffed toys of R. Dakin Company, San Francisco, are a modern favorite among collectors.

The current Beanie Baby craze has focused interest on the miniature stuffed toy. As with any fad, the market already is flooded with imitations. The Beanie Baby market is highly speculative. Expect a major price collapse in a relatively short period of time.

References: Dee Hockenberry, *Collectible German Animals Value Guide: 1948-1968,* Hobby House Press, 1988; Carol J. Smith, *Identification & Price Guide to Winnie the Pooh Collectibles, I* (1994), *II* (1996), Hobby House Press.

Periodical: *Soft Dolls & Animals,* 30595 Eight Mile, Livonia, MI 48152.

Note: For additional listings see Beanie Babies, Steiff and Teddy Bears.

Bambi, California Stuffed Toys, dark brown and tan, tan spots on back, blue ribbon around neck, ©Walt Disney Productions **$10.00**

Beethoven, Dakin, ©Universal Studios, 9" l **4.00**

Benji, unknown maker, light tan plush, 1977, 11" h **30.00**

Christopher Robin, Gund, vinyl head, removable shirt and pants, 1960s, 4¹/₂ x 7 x 18" **50.00**

Cocker Spaniel, Character Novelty, dark brown mohair, jointed head, black steel eyes, metal nose, embroidered mouth, 29" h **60.00**

Cocker Spaniel, Knickerbocker, brown, swivel head, clear and black glass eyes, felt tongue, red plastic collar with bells, fabric tag, 1950s **80.00**

Elmer the Elephant, Japan, plush, molded rubber face, velveteen inner ears and feet, 1940s, 4¹/₂ x 6 x 8¹/₂". **50.00**

Ginger Bread Man, Knickerbocker, tan plush, 12" h **65.00**

Happy Herbert the Frog, Dakin, plush **15.00**

Mickey Mouse Drum Major, green jacket, yellow hands, red papier-mâché shoes, $100.00.

SUPER HEROES

Early super heroes such as Batman and Superman were individuals who possessed extraordinary strength and/or cunning, yet led normal lives as private citizens. They dominated the world of comic books, movie serials, newspaper cartoon strips, radio, and television from the late 1930s through the end of the 1950s. Captain Marvel, Captain Midnight, The Green Lantern, and Wonder Woman are other leading examples of the genre.

The 1960s introduced a new form of super hero, the mutant. The Fantastic Four (Mr. Fantastic, The Human Torch, The Invisible Girl, and The Thing) initiated an era that included a host of characters ranging from Spiderman to The Teenage Mutant Ninja Turtles. Most mutant super heroes are found only in comic books. A few achieved fame on television and the big screen.

In the 1990s comic book storytellers and movie directors began blurring the line between these two distinct groups of super heroes. The death of Superman and his resurrection as a person more attune with the mutant super heroes and the dark approach of the Batman movies are two classic examples.

Collectors prefer three-dimensional objects over two-dimensional material. Carefully research an object's date. Age as a value factor plays a greater role in this category than it does in other collectibles categories.

References: Bill Bruegman, *Superhero Collectibles*, Toy Scouts, 1996; Jim Marshall, *Super Hero Toys*, Schiffer Publishing, 1999; Alan J. Porter, *Batman Unauthorized Collectors' Guide*, Schiffer Publishing, 1999.

Newsletter: *The Adventures Continue* (Superman), 935 Fruitsville Pike, #105, Lancaster, PA 17601.

Collectors' Clubs: Air Heroes Fan Club (Captain Midnight), 19205 Seneca Ridge Ct, Gaithersburg, MD 20879; Batman TV Series Fan Club, PO Box 107, Venice, CA 90294; Rocketeer Fan Club, 10 Halick Ct, East Brunswick, NJ 08816.

Note: For additional listings see Action Figures, Comic Books, and Model Kits.

Huckleberry Hound, Knickerbocker, ©Hanna-Barbera, plush, vinyl face, 1959, 9" h 30.00

King Kong, Mattel, corduroy covered body, felt with vinyl face, holding 2³/₄" hard vinyl boy in right arm, pull-string talker, ©1966 RKO General Inc, Mattel Inc, 13³/₄" h 175.00

Mama Chicken and Babies, Dakin, 5" h 20.00

Mercury Mouse, Dakin, velveteen and felt fabric, from "Dream Pet" series, orig string tag, 1960–70s, 7" h 75.00

Odie, Dakin, plush, wearing blue and white jogging outfit, with stuffed bone attached by velcro in mouth, 1983, 10" h 15.00

Opus the Penguin, Dakin, plush, tag reads "1984 Washington Post Writers Group, R Dakin & Co," 12" h 6.00

Paddington Bear, Eden Toys, 14" h 5.00

Paploo the Ewok, Kenner, orig box and tags, 1984, 15¹/₂" h 50.00

Peck-Peck Bird, Schuco, mohair, metal form, black metal eyes, tan metal beak, black or tan metal feet, assorted colors, 2¹/₂" h, 4¹/₂" l 150.00

Pooky, Dakin, 8" h 15.00

Seal, Dakin, Nature Babies Collection, white, 1976, 10" h 3.00

Shari Lewis's Lamb Chop, Knickerbocker, white plush body, red felt hands, tan flannel ears, 13" h 25.00

Super Rufus Dream Pet, Dakin, green cloth covered body, gray plush ears, black felt mask, black felt nose, red felt "R" on chest, wearing blue fabric cape with applied white cloth lightning bolt on back, attached string tag on ear, 1970s, 3¹/₄ x 3¹/₂ x 5" 15.00

Thumper, Knickerbocker, gray, beige, and white, pink tongue, ©Walt Disney Productions, 11" h 3.00

Tiger, Gund, plush, yellow neck ribbon, 19" h 40.00

Tiger, Petz, mohair, glass eyes, chest button, 7" h 18.00

Turtle, Schuco, beige plush, cardboard form, airbrushed design, pipe cleaner legs, black metal eyes, c1950, 2" h 150.00

Woody Owl, Dakin, #2286 . . . . 40.00

Yogi Bear, Knickerbocker, tag reads "A Huckleberry Hound Toy, Knickerbocker, 1959," 18" h 60.00

Aquaman, outfit, 1-pc stretch fabric suit, rubber and plastic face mask, conch horn, belt with knife sheath, knife, fins, trident, and swordfish sword, Ideal, 1966 . . . . . $70.00

Batman, coloring book, Whitman #1140, front and back cover images of Robin steering Batboat as Batman gets ready to jump off bow into heavy surf, 128 pp, 1966, 8 x 10³/₄" 30.00

Batman, *Life* magazine, Vol 16, #10, March 1966, cover photo of laughing Batman jumping into air against bat signal background 40.00

Batman, lunch box, emb metal, Batman punching villain, Robin, Batmobile, and bat signal in background, with thermos, Aladdin, 1966 . . . . 300.00

Batman, miniature license plate, emb tin, yellow on black, c1966, 2¹/₄ x 4" 30.00

Batman, notebook, vinyl, yellow with multicolor image of smiling Batman on front, 1966, 10 x 12" 60.00

Batman, pinback button, celluloid, "Deputy Crime Fighter/Batman and Robin," multicolor, Batman and Robin in center star design against red background, Riddler, Joker, and Penguin around bottom rim, 1966, 3¹/₂" d 25.00

Superman, Soaky Bottle, Colgate-Palmolive, 1965, $50.00.

Batman, *TV Guide*, #678, March 26, 1966, cover photo of Adam West as Batman throwing punch with large red "Pow" **50.00**

Batman, Duncan yo-yo, plastic, black with colorful Batman decal on 1 side, Batman and Robin decal other side, 2¼" d, in 1½ x 2½ x 2¾" clear plastic display case. **10.00**

Captain America, Cosmic Ray Light Gun, plastic, white and orange gun/flashlight with blue Captain American image on handle, Larami #9363-3, ©1974 Marvel Comics Groups, on blister card **30.00**

Captain Marvel, drinking glass, image of Capt Marvel against blue background, Pepsi series ©1976 DC Comics Inc, 6¼" h. **15.00**

Captain Midnight, 1947 Secret Squadron Manual, 4½ x 6". **75.00**

Captain Midnight, 1957 Secret Squadron Membership Card, filled-in **35.00**

Captain Midnight, Flight Patrol Reporter, Spring 1939 newspaper, Vol 1, #1, folded for mailing, 16½ x 10" **125.00**

Captain Midnight, Secret Squadron emblem, 2¼" d ... **40.00**

Captain Midnight, Secret Squadron Membership Kit, inclues manual, dart decoder, member card, and cover letter, orig mailing envelope with hand-penned messages. **250.00**

Captain Midnight, shake-up mug, plastic, orange, emb design. **95.00**

Green Hornet, flicker ring, multicolor flicker image of Kato in civilian clothes and in costume in front of Black Beauty, plastic base with silver luster, c1966 ...... **25.00**

Green Hornet, mug, white glass with black and green character images on 1 side and logo on other, ©1966, 3" h **45.00**

Green Hornet, pinback button, litho, "Official Green Hornet Agent," green and black silhouette of Green Hornet, Kato, and car, ©1966, 4" d **30.00**

Green Hornet, playing cards, card backs have Green Hornet against light green pattern background, various black and white action scenes from TV show on fronts, white box with green, red, and gray image of Green Hornet running with Kato and car in distance, Ed-U Cards, ©1966, complete and unused **30.00**

Green Hornet, View-Master reel set, #B488, with 4 x 4" story booklet, ©1966. .... **40.00**

He-Man, game, Battle For Eternia, Mattel, 1985 .... **25.00**

Incredible Hulk/Spider-Man, play set, diecut cardboard figures of Spider-Man, Hulk, 9 villains, and apartment and Daily Bugle buildings, case unfolds into city scene, orig sealed box with image of rooftop battle between Marvel heroes and villains on front, Tara Toy Corp, ©1969 Marvel Comics Group, 6 x 16 x 2" **40.00**

Phantom, book, *The Son of the Phantom*, hard cov, Whitman, black and white illus, dj, 248 pp, ©1946 King Features Syndicate Inc, 5½ x 8" **18.00**

Phantom, game, The Phantom Ruler of the Jungle Game, Transogram, 1965 .... **110.00**

Spider-Man, game, Milton Bradley, box cover shows Spider-man in fight with "Marvel Super Heroes," 1967 .... **50.00**

Spider-Man, View-Master reels, 2 talking sets, each with 3 reels, record, and story booklet, "Spider-Man" and "The Amazing Spider-Man Versus Doctor Octopus," in sealed boxes, late 1970s **15.00**

Superman, 3 balloons, uninflated red, cream, or blue, each with black art image of Superman flying above logo, ©1966 National Periodical Publications Inc **12.00**

Superman, drinking glass, Polomar Jelly, "To the Rescue," gray and red, 5¾" h **70.00**

Superman, drinking glass, Superman rescuing bus from flood, pulling chariot with people, flying with man, ©1964 National Periodical Publications Inc, 5½" h **40.00**

Superman, lighter, polished chrome with engraved logo, black plastic case, Zippo, 1996 .... **25.00**

Superman, lobby card, features Kirk Alyn as Superman, Phyllis Coates as Lois Lane, and Tommy Bond as Jimmy Olsen, 1950, 11 x 14". **50.00**

Superman, lunch box, emb metal, Superman flying over skycrapers, with thermos, Thermos, 1967 .... **800.00**

Superman, magazine, *Superman-Tim,* Nov 1945, 16 pp, cover shows Tim dressed in football gear **40.00**

Superman, pinback button, celluloid, "Supermen Of America," center Superman image below "Strength," "Courage," and "Justice," 1939, 1¼" d **75.00**

Superman, pinback button, litho tin, Superman image, reverse text "Read Superman Action Comics Magazine," c1939, ⅞" d **125.00**

Superman, pinback button, Pep cereal premium, 1943 ...... **20.00**

Superman, toy, Kryptonite Rock, orig box, 1977 .... **20.00**

Superman, toy, Superman with Plane, windup, litho tin, red, Superman rotates over rear of airplane then flips plane over, Marx, 1930s **1,300.00**

Superman, *TV Guide*, #26, Sep 25, 1953, George Reeves cov, article "How They Make Superman Fly" **200.00**

Superman, valentine, diecut, image of Superman and little boy with "I'm Not A Bit Like Superman, Can't Hear Through Walls Of Brick, So If You Like Me Valentine, Come Out And Say So Quick!," 1940. .... **35.00**

Wonder Woman, lunch box, vinyl, image of Wonder Woman with clenched fists on yellow background, with thermos, Aladdin, 1977 .... **115.00**

Wonder Woman, marionette, hard plastic body with vinyl head, attached hand control unit, Madison Ltd, ©1977 DC Comics Inc, with orig 8½ x 11 x 3½" window box. **40.00**

Wonder Woman, pinback button, "Wonder Woman, Official Member Super Hero Club," #14 in numbered series, Button World Mfg, 1966, 3½" d **12.00**

SWANKYSWIGS

A Swankyswig is a decorated glass container used as packaging for Kraft Cheese which doubled as a juice glass once the cheese was consumed. The earliest Swankyswigs date from the 1930s. They proved extremely popular during the Depression.

Initial designs were hand stenciled. Eventually machines were developed to apply the decoration. Kraft test marketed designs. As a result, some designs are very difficult to find. Unfortunately, Kraft does not have a list of all the designs it produced.

Production was discontinued briefly during World War II when the paint used for decoration was needed for the war effort. Bicentennial Tulip (1975) was the last Swankyswig pattern.

Beware of Swankyswig imitators from the 1970s and early 1980s. These come from other companies, including at least one Canadian firm. Cherry, Diamond over Triangle, Rooster's Head, Sportsman series, and Wildlife series are a few of the later themes. In order to be considered a true Swankyswig, the glass has to be a Kraft product.

References: Gene Florence, *Collectible Glassware From the 40's, 50's, 60's, 5th Edition,* Collector Books, 2000; Jan Warner, *Swankyswigs, A Pattern Guide Checklist, Revised,* The Daze, 1988, 1992 value update.

Collectors' Club: Swankyswig's Unlimited, 201 Alvena, Wichita, KS 67203.

1964 World's Fair, 1910 Buick, blue, 3¾" h	**$6.00**
1964 World's Fair, 1913 Chevrolet, rust, 3¾" h	**6.00**
1964 World's Fair, 1914 Maxwell, green, 3¾" h	**6.00**
1964 World's Fair, 1914 Studebaker, red, 3¾" h	**6.00**
Antique, blue teapot, 3¾" h	**5.00**
Bustling Betsy, green, 3¾" h	**5.00**
Bustling Betsy, light blue, 3¾" h	**5.00**
Bustling Betsy, red, 3¾" h	**5.00**
Bustling Betsy, yellow, 3¾" h	**5.00**
Cornflower #2, light blue, 3½" h	**4.00**
Cornflower #2, red, 3½" h	**4.00**
Cornflower #2, yellow, 3½" h	**4.00**
Forget Me Not, blue, 3½" h	**4.00**
Forget Me Not, red, 3½" h	**4.00**
Kiddie Cup, bird and elephant, red	**5.00**
Kiddie Cup, bird and rabbit, orange	**5.00**
Kiddie Cup, black cat, 2 dogs	**10.00**
Kiddie Cup, daisies, red, white, and green	**5.00**
Kiddie Cup, duck and horse, black	**5.00**
Kiddie Cup, geese, red, yellow, and blue	**10.00**
Kiddie Cup, pig and bear, light blue	**5.00**
Kiddie Cup, red band	**3.00**
Kiddie Cup, red ships, blue anchor	**10.00**
Kiddie Cup, rooster head, red	**18.00**
Kiddie Cup, squirrel and deer, brown	**5.00**
Kiddie Cup, stars, black	**4.00**
Kiddie Cup, triangle in circle, green	**5.00**
Posey Tulip, 3½" h	**5.00**
Purple Posey, violet, 3½" h	**6.00**
Red and White Checkerboard, 3½" h	**25.00**
Tulip #1, black, 3½" h	**4.00**
Tulip #1, blue, 3½" h	**4.00**
Tulip #1, green, 3½" h	**4.00**
Tulip #1, red, 3½" h	**4.00**
Tulip #3, dark blue, 3¾" h	**4.00**

SWAROVSKI CRYSTAL

Daniel Swarovski founded D. Swarovski & Co. in Georgenthal, Bohemia, in 1895. Initially the company produced high quality abrasives, crystal stones for the costume jewelry industry, and optical items. The company continues to produce several accessory and jewelry lines including the inexpensive Savvy line and the high-end Daniel Swarovski boutique collection.

In 1977 Swarovski introduced a line of collectible figurines and desk items. A crystal mouse and a spiny hedgehog were the first two figurines. Swarovski figurines have a 30% or more lead content. In 1987 the International Swarovski Collectors Society was formed. Swarovski produces an annual figurine available only to Society members. Every three years a new theme is introduced, e.g., "Mother and Child," three annual figures featuring a mother sea mammal and her offspring.

Initially Swarovski crystal figurines were marked with a block-style SC. In 1989 Swarovski began using a mark that included a swan. Swarovski was included in the mark on larger pieces. Pieces made for the Swarovski Collectors Society are marked with an SCS logo, the initials of the designer, and the year. The first SCS logo included an edelweiss flower above the SCS.

Regional issues are common. Some items were produced in two versions, one for Europe and one for the United States. Many items with metal trim are available in rhodium (white metal) or gold.

A Swarovski figurine is considered incomplete on the secondary market if it does not include its period box, product identification sticker, and any period paper work. Society items should be accompanied by a certificate of authenticity.

Today the Daniel Swarovski Corporation is headquartered in Zurich, Switzerland. Production and design is based in Wattens, Austria. Swarovski has manufacturing facilities in 11 countries, including a plant in Cranston, Rhode Island. The company employs more than 8,000 people worldwide.

Be alert to Swarovski imitations with a lower lead content which often contain flaws in the crystal and lack the Swarovski logo.

References: Jane Warner, *Warner's Blue Ribbon Book on Swarovski: Beyond Silver Crystal,* published by author, 1999; Tom and Jane Warner, *Warner's Blue Ribbon Book on Swarovski Silver Crystal, Fourth Edition,* published by authors, 1999.

Newsletters: *The Crystal Report,* 1322 N Barron St, Eaton, OH 45320; *Swan Seekers News,* 9740 Campo Rd, Ste 134, Spring Valley, CA 91977.

Collectors' Club: Swarovski Collectors Society (company sponsored), 1 Kennedy Dr, Cranston, RI 02920.

Baby Giraffe, #7603000002	**$175.00**
Candleholders, pr, 7600NR102, 3" h	**175.00**
Cockerel, #7674000001	**60.00**
Diary, Crystal Memories, #9460000055, retired	**35.00**
Dolphins, Mother and Child series, D01X901, 1990	**1,000.00**
Elephant, Inspiration Africa series, D01X931, 1993	**1,100.00**
Flower Pot, Crystal Memories, #9460000075	**30.00**
Fox, #7629NR70, 1987-99	**65.00**
Fox Running, #7677NR055, retired 1996	**60.00**
Freight Car, Crystal Memories, #9460000082	**30.00**
German Shepherd, #7619000007	**75.00**
Grizzly, #7637000006	**250.00**
High-Heeled Shoe, Crystal Memories, #9460000031	**35.00**

Baby Elephant, $155.00.

Hot Air Balloon, Crystal Memories, #9461000004	75.00
Inkwell with Quill, Crystal Memories, #9460000060	35.00
Julia, Julia's World series, #9540NR000011, 1990-92	40.00
Lantern, Crystal Memories, #9460000023, retired	35.00
Leopard, African Wildlife series, #7610002000, introduced 1997	175.00
Lovebirds, Caring and Sharing series, D01X861, 1987	3,500.00
Mother Goose, #7613NR00001, 1993-99	55.00
Puppet Clown, #7550NR000003, 1997	85.00
Rocking Horse, Crystal Memories, #9460000068	35.00
Sali, Julia's World series, #9540NR000012, 1990-92	40.00
Star Ornament, 1991	350.00
Suncatcher Ball, 8000 series, 30mm	20.00
Suncatcher Prism, 8000 series, 137mm	25.00
Tennis Racket, Crystal Memories, #9460000048, retired	30.00
Toucan, Feathered Friends series, #7670NR000001	100.00
Toucan "Up in the Trees," #7621NR000002, retired 1992	175.00
Typewriter, Crystal Memories, #9460000076	40.00
Umbrella, Crystal Memories, #9460000008, retired	30.00
Watering Can, Crystal Memories, #9460000007, retired	30.00
Wedding Cake, Crystal Memories, #9460000095	55.00

SYRACUSE CHINA

Syracuse China traces its origins to W. H. Farrar, who established a pottery in Syracuse, New York, in 1841. The plant moved from Genessee Street to Fayette Street in 1855 and operated as the Empire Pottery. The Empire Pottery became the Onondaga Pottery Company after a reorganization in 1871, retaining that name until 1966 when the company became the Syracuse China Company. Few noticed the change because Onondaga Pottery had marketed its dinnerware under a Syracuse China brand name since as early as 1879.

Onondaga introduced a high-fired, semi-vitreous ware in the mid-1880s that was guaranteed against crackling and crazing. In 1888 James Pass introduced Imperial Geddo, a translucent, vitrified china. By the early 1890s, the company offered a full line of fine china ware.

Onondaga made commercial as well as household china. In 1921 a new plant, devoted exclusively to commercial production, was opened. In 1959 Onondaga Pottery acquired Vandesca—Syracuse, Joliette, Quebec, Canada, a producer of vitrified hotel china. In 1984 Syracuse China absorbed the Mayer China Company.

After manufacturing fine dinnerware for 99 years, Syracuse China discontinued its household china line in 1970, devoting its production efforts exclusively to airline, commercial, hotel, and restaurant china.

References: Cleota Reed and Stan Skoczen, *Syracuse China,* Syracuse University Press, 1997; Harry L. Rinker, *Dinnerware of the 20th Century: The Top 500 Patterns,* House of Collectibles, 1997.

Airlite, bowl, eagle logo with "AA" and stars, made for American Airlines, 6" d	$125.00
Bracelet, bread and butter plate, 6¼" d	5.00
Bracelet, coffeepot, no lid	50.00
Bracelet, cream soup and saucer	25.00
Bracelet, demitasse cup and saucer	15.00
Bracelet, fruit bowl, 5" d	8.00
Bracelet, luncheon plate, 9" d	10.00
Bracelet, soup bowl, flat, 8⅞" d	12.00
Bracelet, sugar, cov	20.00
Bracelet, vegetable, oval, 10¼" l	35.00
Briarcliff, dinner plate, 10" d	12.00
Briarcliff, serving platter	25.00
California Poppy, dinner plate, 9" d	20.00
California Poppy, dinner plate, 10" d	18.00
California Poppy, bowl, 5" d, 1" h	15.00
California Poppy, serving bowl, 9" d, 2½" h	40.00
California Poppy, soup plate, 9" d	30.00
Coralbel, platter	20.00
Dogwood, berry bowl, 4½" d	12.00
Dogwood, bread and butter plate, 6⅜" d	8.00
Dogwood, creamer, 3¾" h, 3½" l	20.00
Dogwood, plate, 7¼" d	12.00
Dogwood, plate, 8¾" d	15.00
Dogwood, plate, 9" d	18.00
Dogwood, soup plate, 9" d	20.00
Eden Roc, plate, mkd "94f," 7" d	10.00
Evening Star, plate, 8" d	3.00
Glendale, plate, 7⅛" d	8.00
Grandma Moses, plate, mkd "Grandma Moses, Taking in the Laundry, International Limited Edition, Syracuse China USA, Copyright Grandma Moses Properties, Inc," 12" d	40.00
Lynnfield, plate, 10" d	5.00
Meadow Breeze, cup and saucer	12.00
Oakleigh, bow, 5¼" d, 4" h	8.00
Oakleigh, plate, "Eldredge," mkd "97J," 7" d	15.00
Oakleigh, plate, 7" d	3.00
Oakleigh, plate, 9½" d	15.00
Old Ivory, creamer and open sugar	30.00
Old Ivory, cream soup, 5" d, 2" h	10.00
Restaurant Ware, plate, cowboy on bucking bronco, mkd "Syracuse China Eono-Rim" 8¾" d	50.00
Restaurant Ware, plate, Indian on horseback overlooking canyon, mkd "Syracuse China 93-A USA," 9" d	50.00
Restaurant Ware, plate, Petroleum Club, Wichita, KS, 7¼" d	5.00

Bracelet: 9³/₄" d dinner plate, $12.00; cup and saucer, $15.00.

Restaurant Ware, plate, pink flowers, mkd "Trend
  Syracuse China 96-E USA," 7³/₄" d 5.00
Restaurant Ware, plate, Southern Pacific Lines, mkd
  "2M," 8³/₄" d 80.00
Restaurant Ware, plate, western bull, mkd "Syracuse
  China Econo-Rim," 8³/₄" d 25.00
Roxbury, bowl, mkd "3CC" 6" d, 2¹/₂" d 12.00
Roxbury, cup and saucer 12.00
Roxbury, plate, mkd "4G" 6.00
Sherwood, dinner plate 6.00
Sherwood, salad plate 5.00
Stansbury, soup bowl, gold rim, 8" d 25.00
Strawberry Hill, bread and butter plate, 6¹/₂" d 4.00
Strawberry Hill, platter, 12¹/₂ x 10" 30.00
Sundown, dinnerware set, 8 pcs, 10" dinner plate, 7³/₈"
  salad plate, 6³/₈" grapefruit bowl, 5¹/₈ x 2" fruit bowl,
  3¹/₄ x 3" coffee mug, 5¹/₂" saucer, 4 x 2¹/₄" soup cup,
  4¹/₂" soup liner 275.00

TAYLOR, SMITH & TAYLOR

Around 1900 Joseph G. Lee, W. L. Smith, John N. Taylor, W. L. Taylor, and Homer J. Taylor founded the firm that eventually became Taylor, Smith & Taylor. The Taylors purchased Lee's interests in 1903, only to sell their interests to the Smiths in 1906. The company's plant was located in Chester, West Virginia, the corporate offices in East Liverpool, Ohio.

Taylor, Smith & Taylor made a wide range of plain and painted semi-porcelain wares, e.g., dinnerware, hotel and restaurant ware, and toilet sets. Lu-Ray (introduced in 1930), Pebbleford, and Vistosa are three of the company's most popular dinnerware shapes. In the 1960s a line of cooking and oven ware was produced. Special commission work ranged from dinnerware premiums for Mother's Oats to Gigi and Holly Hobbie plates for American Greetings Corp.

Anchor Hocking purchased Taylor, Smith & Taylor in 1973. The plant closed in January 1982.

References: Susan and Al Bagdade, *Warman's American Pottery and Porcelain*, Wallace-Homestead, 1994; Harvey Duke, *The Official Identification and Price Guide to Pottery and Porcelain, Eighth Edition*, House of Collectibles, 1995; Kathy and Bill Meehan, *Collector's Guide to Lu-Ray Pastels*, Collector Books, 1995; 1998 value update.

Calendar Plate, gold design on pink, 1957, 10" d **$12.00**
Calendar Plate, gold design on white, 1958, 10" d **15.00**
Calendar Plate, gold design on white, 1960, 10" d **10.00**
Conversation, Cockerel, dinner plate, 10¹/₄" d **8.00**
Conversation, Cockerel, platter, 13¹/₄" l **35.00**
Conversation, Coffee Tree, 5-pc place setting consisting
  of 10" dinner plate, 8" soup bowl, 5¹/₂" fruit bowl, and
  cup and saucer **15.00**
Conversation, King O'Dell, bread and butter plate, 6¹/₄" d **5.00**
Conversation, King O'Dell, sauce dish, 5¹/₂" d **5.00**
Empire, Dutch Tulip, water jug, 7¹/₂" h **25.00**
Empire, floral decal, grill plate **3.00**
Empire, floral rim, platter, 13¹/₂" l **20.00**
Empire, gold floral band dec, gravy boat and liner **15.00**
Empire, pink floral decal, berry bowl, 5¹/₄" d **2.00**
Empire, pink floral decal, bread and butter plate, 6¹/₄" d **3.00**
Empire, pink floral decal, creamer, 2¹/₂" h **6.00**
Empire, pink floral decal, cream soup, 2-handled, 7¹/₄" w **8.00**
Empire, pink floral decal, luncheon plate, 7¹/₂" d **5.00**
Empire, pink floral decal, sugar bowl **10.00**
Ever Yours, Autumn Harvest, bread and butter plate,
  6³/₄" d **2.00**
Ever Yours, Autumn Harvest, carafe, 9¹/₄" h **15.00**
Ever Yours, Boutonniere, butter, cov **35.00**
Ever Yours, Boutonniere, casserole, cov, oval, 10¹/₈" l **30.00**
Ever Yours, Boutonniere, salt and pepper shakers, pr, 2" h **15.00**
Ever Yours, Weathervane, 4-pc place setting consisting of
  10" dinner plate, 5¹/₄" bowl, cup, and saucer **15.00**
Fairway, Center Bouquet, cup and saucer **15.00**
Fairway, Center Bouquet, dinner plate, 9" d **30.00**
Fairway, Center Bouquet, salad plate, 7" d **15.00**
Fairway, Dogwood, dinner plate **5.00**
Holly Spruce, 12-pc snack set consisting of 4 each
  8" plates, cups, and saucers **20.00**
Laurel, pink rose decal, berry bowl **2.00**
Laurel, pink rose decal, blue rim, soup bowl, 7¹/₂" d **3.00**
Laurel, pink rose decal, cup and saucer **5.00**
Laurel, pink rose decal, dessert plate, 6" d **3.00**
Laurel, pink rose decal, dinner plate, 9¹/₄" d **8.00**
Laurel, pink rose decal, platter, oval, 11" l **12.00**
Laurel, pink rose decal, salad plate **3.00**
Laurel, pink rose decal, sauce dish, 5¹/₄" d **3.00**
Laurel, pink rose decal, serving bowl, 8¹/₂" d **14.00**
Laurel, pink rose decal, vegetable, oval, 9¹/₂" l **15.00**
Laurel, Silhouette, cup and saucer **20.00**
Laurel, Silhouette, dinner plate, 9" d **12.00**
Lu-Ray, blue, serving bowl, oval, 10¹/₂" l **20.00**
Lu-Ray, cream, plate, 9" d **11.00**
Lu-Ray, pink, platter, 13" l **15.00**
Lu-Ray, yellow, saucer **2.00**
Pebbleford, pink, dessert plate **3.00**
Pebbleford, pink, dinner plate, 10¹/₄" d **4.00**
Pebbleford, pink, fruit bowl, 5¹/₈" d **4.00**
Pebbleford, pink, platter, 11¹/₄" l **15.00**
Pebbleford, Reveille, cup and saucer **3.00**
Pebbleford, Reveille, dinner plate, 10" d **6.00**
Pebbleford, Reveille, fruit bowl **2.00**

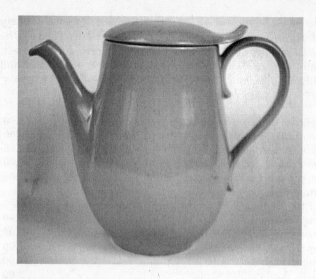

Pebbleford, turquoise, coffee server, 1952-65, 7⁷/₈" h, $20.00.

Pebbleford, Reveille, platter, oval, 12" l, 9" w **15.00**
Pebbleford, Reveille, platter, oval, 13¹/₂" l **18.00**
Pebbleford, Reveille, serving bowl, 8¹/₂" d **10.00**
Pebbleford, turquoise, dinner plate, 10¹/₄" d **8.00**
Taylorstone Classic, Cathay, cup and saucer **4.00**
Taylorstone Classic, Cathay, dessert plate, 6⁵/₈" d **3.00**
Taylorstone Classic, Cathay, dinner plate, 10¹/₂" d **2.00**
Taylorstone Classic, Cathay, soup bowl, 7³/₄" d **5.00**
Versatile, creamer and covered sugar **25.00**
Versatile, Daisy, dinner plate, 9¹/₄" d **3.00**
Versatile, Dwarf Pine, bowl, 5¹/₈" d **4.00**
Versatile, Dwarf Pine, bowl, 6³/₄" d **4.00**
Versatile, Dwarf Pine, platter, 13¹/₂" l **15.00**
Vistosa, egg cup, green **80.00**
Vistosa, teapot, yellow, 6¹/₂" h **30.00**
Vogue, flowerpots dec, dinner plate, 9¹/₄" d **5.00**

TEAPOTS

Tea drinking was firmly established in England and its American colonies by the middle of the 18th century. The earliest teapots were modeled after their Far Eastern ancestors. Teapot shapes and decorative motifs kept pace with the ceramic and new design styles of the 19th century. The whimsical, figural teapot was around from the start.

Teapots were a common product of American ceramic, glass, and metal manufacturers. The "Rebekah at the Well" teapot appeared in the mid-1850s. Hall China of East Liverpool, Ohio, was one of the leading teapot manufacturers of the 1920s and 30s. Figural teapots were extremely popular in the 1930s. The first etched Pyrex teapot was made in the late 1930s.

References: Tina M. Carter, *Collectible Teapots*, Antique Trader Books, 2000; Garth Clark, *The Eccentric Teapot: 400 Years of Invention*, Abbeville Press, 1989.

Periodical: *Tea Talk*, PO Box 860, Sausalito, CA 94966.

Note: All teapots listed are ceramic. See Chintz, Hall China, and individual manufacturers for additional listings.

Ambassador, country garden style, yellow rose finial, spring flowers on pot, mkd "Ambassador Ware," England, 6" h **$15.00**
Arthur Wood & Sons, Staffordshire, England, Blue Chintz, 8" h, 10¹/₂" w **55.00**
Arthur Wood & Sons, Staffordshire, England, Green Chintz **77.00**
Blue Danube, #25/20, 6¹/₂" h, 9" w **60.00**
Burleigh Ware, North Staffordshire, Blue Calico pattern, 3¹/₂" h, 9¹/₂" w **55.00**
Eastenders, Queen Victoria Pub, figural **18.00**
German, Blue Onion, 10" h **40.00**
Hall, McCormick, burgundy, ceramic infuser **40.00**
Harker, Apple, Hot Oven Ware **80.00**
Lefton, Violet Chintz **100.00**
Lipton, blue **45.00**
Lipton, green **70.00**
Lipton, maroon **45.00**
Metlox, Homestead Provincial **45.00**
Nippon, 1000 Faces **30.00**
Occupied Japan, white flowers on turquoise ground, 4³/₈" h, 7³/₄" w **25.00**
Pfaltzgraff, Tea Rose pattern, 5¹/₂" h, 10¹/₂" l **85.00**
Porcelier, raised sailboats, 6 cup, 7⁵/₈" h, 9¹/₂" w **40.00**
Price Kensington, England, #2847, green and ivory, gold finial and trim, 6" h, 8" w **25.00**
Price Kensington, England, Pansy **30.00**
Price Kensington, England, Pink Flower **25.00**
Purinton, red flower, individual size **40.00**
Pyrex, glass, 6 cup, #8336 . . . . **15.00**
Ray Silver Co, pewter **30.00**
Reed & Barton, silver plate, cherub design, 7¹/₄" h, 5¹/₄" w **65.00**
Robinson, Blue Pagoda, mkd "Robinson Design Group– 1989–Japan," **10.00**
Robinson, floral pattern on ivory ground, mkd "Robinson Design Group–1989–Japan," 6" h, 9" w **15.00**
Roseville, Zephyr Lily, #7-7 . . . . **675.00**
Royal Caldone, Hanley, Stoke-on-Trent, Daisy Rose, 6 cup **18.00**
Royal Caldone, Hanley, Stoke-on-Trent, Floral Bouquet, 6 cup **15.00**
Royal Caldone, Hanley, Stoke-on-Trent, Olde Rose, 6 cup **15.00**
Royal Caldone, Hanley, Stoke-on-Trent, Pansies **30.00**
Royal China, Blue Heaven **40.00**
Royal Doulton, Dr Scholls Foot Comfort Service, ivory with yellow, blue, and black trim, 6" h, 7" w **25.00**
Royal Doulton, Moonstone **20.00**
Sadler, Harrods Westie, 6 cup **45.00**
Sadler, Ivy Leaves, 6 cup **25.00**
Sadler, Medallion, gold finial and trim, 6 cup **20.00**
Sadler, Tulip, gold trim, 6 cup **15.00**
Sadler, Victoria, gold trim, 6 cup **15.00**
Sadler, Violets, gold trim, 6 cup **20.00**
Seltmann, butterflies and flowers dec, #23312, mkd "Seltmann Weider Bavaria Liane," 6" h, 10" w **16.00**
Shawnee, King Corn, #75, 30 oz **100.00**
Shawnee, Rosette, burgundy, 5 cup, 6¹/₂" h, 8¹/₂" w **25.00**
Shelley, Red Duchess **160.00**
Silvestri, Frog, 3-pc stacking set, 7" h **30.00**
Souvenir, figural Scottie dog, "Souvenir of Battle Creek," 1950s, 9" h **45.00**

Souvenir, mammy baking cookies, lobster, woman, and boat, "Souvenir of Beloxi, Ocean Springs, Bay St Louis, Pass Crestian, and Golf Port," 6" h, $85.00. Photo courtesy Collectors Auction Services.

Staffordshire, purple pansies dec, 3-pc stacking set, 6" h, 6" w	20.00
Wedgwood, Countryside, 8½" h, 9½" w	80.00
Weller, Utility Ware, Pumpkin, gourd-shaped, tan with green handle and lid, 6" h, 9" w	50.00

TECO POTTERY a.k.a. The Gates Potteries

In 1881 William Gates founded the Spring Valley Tile Works, Terra Cotta (Crystal Lake), Illinois. Renamed the Terra Cotta Tile Works in 1885, the plant was destroyed by fire in 1887. The plant was rebuilt and the firm became the American Terra Cotta and Ceramic Company.

In 1902 the company introduced Teco ("te" from terra and "co" from cotta), its art pottery line. Experimental pieces date as early as 1895. The firm employed a large number of artists and architects as designers. Many pieces were designed for specific architectural projects. Glaze experiments were continuous. In 1911 the company's shape vocabulary exceeded 500 pieces.

The 1929 stock market crash led to the demise of the company. George Berry purchased the buildings in 1930 and created the American Terra Cotta Company to make architectural terra cotta, ornamental pottery, and decorative ceramic wares. In 1972 American Terra Cotta Company merged with TC Industries.

Reference: Ralph and Terry Kovel, *Kovel's American Art Pottery,* Crown, 1993.

Collectors' Club: American Art Pottery Assoc, PO Box 834, Westport, MA 02790.

Ikebana Vase, emb lotuses under leathery matte green glaze with gunmetal accents, stamped "Teco," 11½ x 5½"	$7,500.00
Jardiniere, hemispheric, 4 buttressed legs, stamped "Teco," 7 x 11"	6,500.00
Pitcher, corseted with wishbone handle, smooth matte green glaze, stamped "Teco," small firing flaw to handle, 9 x 3½"	1,100.00

Vase, beaker shaped, buttressed handles, matte green glaze, stamped "Teco," 8 x 5½"	2,500.00
Vase, bottle shaped, 2 full-height buttresses, mottled matte green glaze, stamped "Teco/435," 7¼ x 4¼"	1,500.00
Vase, bottle shaped, aventurine, mirrored black, gold, and amber microcrystalline flambé glaze, stamped "Teco," 10½ x 3¾"	3,000.00
Vase, F Moreau, buttressed, tulip shaped, smooth matte green glaze, stamped "Teco/463," 12 x 5"	4,000.00
Vase, gourd shaped, buttressed handles, cut-out forms and emb with oriental floral pattern under matte green glaze, stamped "Teco/113," 6½ x 5½"	2,500.00
Vase, ovoid, 4 double buttressed legs, smooth matte blue glaze, stamped "Teco/127," 9 x 4"	2,500.00
Vase, ovoid, 4 lobes, smooth matte green glaze, stamped "Teco," 5½ x 3½"	1,000.00
Vase, ovoid "rocketship," 4 swag buttressed legs, mauve matte glaze, stamped "Teco," 9 x 4"	7,500.00
Vase, spherical, 4 flaring buttress feet, matte green glaze, stamped "Teco/339," 12½ x 10½"	7,750.00
Vase, squat base, tall neck, green and charcoal matte glaze, stamped "Teco," 16½ x 8"	1,250.00
Vessel, dimpled, dark speckled matte green and charcoal glaze, incised "Teco/519," 3¾ x 3¼"	600.00
Wall Pocket, emb stylized leaves under smooth matte green glaze, stamped "Teco/156A," 16¾ x 6½"	1,750.00

TEDDY BEARS

The teddy bear, named for President Theodore Roosevelt, arrived on the scene in late 1902 or early 1903. The Ideal Toy Corporation (American) and Margarette Steiff (German) are among the earliest firms to include a bear in their stuffed toy lines.

Early teddy bears are identified by the humps in their backs, elongated muzzles, jointed limbs, mohair bodies (some exceptions), and glass, pinback, or black shoe button eyes. Stuffing materials include excelsior, the most popular, kapok, and wood-wool. Elongated limbs, oversized feet, felt paws, and a black embroidered nose and mouth are other indicators of a quality early bear.

Teddy bear manufacturers closely copied each other. Once the manufacturer's identification label or marking is lost it is impossible to tell one maker's bear from another.

America went teddy bear crazy in the 1980s. A strong secondary market for older bears developed. Many stuffed (plush) toy manufacturers reintroduced teddy bears to their line. Dozens of teddy bear artisans marketed their hand-crafted creations. Some examples sold in the hundreds of dollars.

The speculative fever of the 1980s has subsided. Sale of the hand-crafted artisan bears on the secondary market has met with mixed results. While the market is still strong enough to support its own literature, magazines, and show circuit, the number of collectors has diminished. Those that remain are extremely passionate about their favorite collectible.

References: Milton Friedberg, *Teddy Bears and Stuffed Animals: Hermann Teddy Originals, 1913-1998,* Schiffer Publishing, 1999; Ann Gehlbach, *Muffy VanderBear,* Hobby House Press, 1997; Dee Hockenberry, *The Big Bear Book,* Schiffer Publishing, 1996; Edith and Johan Koskinen, *Teddy Bear Identification and Price Guide,* Gold Horse Publishing, 1999; Margaret Fox Mandel, *Teddy Bears and Steiff Animals* (1984, 2000 value update), *Second Series*

(1987, 2000 value update), Collector Books; Margaret Fox Mandel, *Teddy Bears, Annalee Animals & Steiff Animals, Third Series*, Collector Books, 1990, 2000 value update; Linda Mullins, *American Teddy Bear Encyclopedia*, Hobby House Press, 1995; Linda Mullins, *Teddy Bear & Friends Price Guide*, Hobby House Press, 2000; Jesse Murray, *Teddy Bear Figurines Price Guide*, Hobby House Press, 1996; Cynthia Powell, *Collector's Guide to Miniature Teddy Bears*, Collector Books, 1994; Carol J. Smith, *Identification & Price Guide to Winnie the Pooh Collectibles*, *I* (1994), *II* (1996), Hobby House Press; Ken Yenke, *Teddy Bear Treasury*, Collector Books, 1999.

Periodicals: *Teddy Bear & Friends*, 741 Miller Dr SE, Ste D2, Harrisburg, PA 20175; *Teddy Bear Review*, 170 Fifth Ave, 12th Flr, New York, NY 10010.

Collectors' Clubs: Good Bears of the World, PO Box 13097, Toledo, OH 43613; Teddy Bear Boosters Club, 19750 SW Peavine Mtn Rd, McMinnville, OR 97128.

Note: See Steiff and Stuffed Toys for additional listings.

Chilturn, blonde, stuffed, fully jointed, glass eyes, felt pads, 11" h $75.00

Eduard Creamer, Germany, long curly gold mohair, fully jointed, shaved muzzle, glass eyes, open rose felt mouth, tan embroidered nose, cream felt pads, excelsior stuffing, 1930s, 32" h 1,900.00

Hermann, shaggy beige mohair, fully jointed, cream mohair plush muzzle, cream felt pads, black embroidered nose, mouth, and claws, excelsior stuffing, mid-20th C, 19" h 125.00

Ideal, yellow mohair, fully jointed, black steel eyes, black nose and mouth, kapok and excelsior stuffing, early 20th C, 12" h 200.00

Ideal, yellow mohair, fully jointed, excelsior stuffing, c1930, 11" h 150.00

Ideal, yellow mohair, fully jointed, glass eyes, excelsior stuffing, orig cotton romper suit, c1920s, 17" h 500.00

Knickerbocker Style, green mohair, straw and soft stuffed, fully jointed with swivel head, brown and black glass eyes, velvet pads, 1930-40s, 16½" h 175.00

Merrythought, black mohair, fully jointed, glass eyes, shaved muzzle, black embroidered nose, mouth, and claws, black felt pads, "I Growl" tag, 1930s, 23" h 1,250.00

Merrythought, curly cream mohair, fully jointed, glass eyes, shaved muzzle, yellow embroidered nose, mouth, and claws, cream felt pads, 1930s, 15" h 625.00

Schuco, yellow mohair, fully jointed, glass eyes, embroidered nose and mouth, excelsior stuffing, felt pads, "I Growl" tag on chest, 1920s, 12" h 345.00

Schuco, Yes/No Bear, yellow mohair, fully jointed, black steel eyes, embroidered nose and mouth, excelsior stuffing, rayon pads, c1921, 12" h 450.00

Steiff, gold mohair, fully jointed, glass eyes, excelsior stuffing, felt pads, c1951, 11½" h 200.00

Tara Toys, Ireland, light gold mohair, fully jointed, plastic eyes, Rexine pads, mouth opens and closes by squeezing knobs on back of head, cloth label sewn in foot seam, 1950s, 16" h 175.00

Unknown Maker, American, cream mohair, jointed arms, light bulb eyes, tan embroidered nose and mouth, excelsior stuffing, brown felt pads, 24" h 425.00

TELEPHONES & RELATED MEMORABILIA

Until the mid-1990s, telephone collecting centered primarily on candlestick telephones and single, double, and triple wall-mounted, oak case telephones. Avant-garde collectors concentrated on colored, rotary-dial telephones from the Art Deco period. The Automatic Telephone Company (General Telephone) and Western Electric (Bell System) were the two principal manufacturers of this later group. Kellogg, Leich, and Stromberg Carlson also made colored case telephones.

Recently collector interest has increased in three new areas: (1) the desk sets of the late 1930s and 40s, typified by Western Electric Model 302 A-G dial cradle telephone (1937-1954 and designated the "Perry Mason" phone by collectors), (2) colored plastic phones of the 1950s and 60s, e.g., the Princess, and (3) figural telephones, popular in the late 1970s and throughout the 1980s.

References: James David Davis, *Collectible Novelty Phones*, Schiffer Publishing, 1998; Kate Dooner, *Telephone Collecting: Seven Decades of Design*, Schiffer Publishing, 1993; Kate Dooner, *Telephones: Antique to Modern, 2nd Edition*, Schiffer Publishing, 1998; Richard D. Mountjoy, *One Hundred Years of Bell Telephone*, Schiffer Publishing, 1995.

Collectors' Clubs: Antique Telephone Collectors Assoc, PO Box 94, Abilene, KS 67410; International Phone Card Collectors, PO Box 632, Millwood, NY 10546; Mini-Phone Exchange, 5412 Tilden Rd, Bladensburg, MD 20710; Telephone Collectors International, 3207 E Bend Dr, Algonquin, IL 60102.

TELEPHONE

AT&T, candlestick, brass, base mkd "Pat in USA/Jan 26 15/Jan 1 18/May 7 18/Sep 21 20," top of stick mkd "51AL," orig tag with "Property of American Tel & Tel" . . $300.00

Automatic Electric Co, Monophone, black Bakelite 100.00

Bell System, Model 1702B, Princess, olive green, push button, early 1960s 150.00

Electric General Co, oak wall phone, orig finish 225.00

Ericsson LM, wall telephone, black metal, 2 earpieces, one hangs on each side, silvered metal dial, stamped on back "DBR 1201-1 26 61 Made in Sweden," 6" h, 2¼" d 150.00

Lineman, metal, stamped on handle "D-81760" and on back of dial "54-B," 9½" l 85.00

Novelty, Smurf, figure on top spins when numbers are dialed, ©Peyo 1982, 9" h 15.00

Western Electric, candlestick, stamped "Western Electric, made in USA, patented in USA, Jan 26 15," cloth covered cord 150.00

Western Electric, in-house style, Model 302, ivory colored plastic 200.00

Western Electric, Model 500, rotary desk set, bright yellow, hard-wired handset cord and matching line cord 25.00

TELEPHONE RELATED

Booklet, *The Telephone in America*, illus, 64 pp, 1934, 6 x 9" $8.00

Candy Container, glass, figural candlestick telephone, "Miniature Dial Telephone, Victory Glass Co, Jeannette, PA" label on bottom, 4¾" h 50.00

Cookie Jar, figural phone, Clay Art 25.00

Telephone Card, F-R-I-E-N-D-S, 15 minutes, $15.00.

Directory, 1931 Tulsa, OK, published by Southwestern Bell Telephone Co, 160 pp. **40.00**

Lighter/Clock/Lamp combination, figural telephone, lighter coil in mouthpiece, metal lamp shade, Boye Corp, Brooklyn, NY, clock movement by Lanshire, Chicago, IL, 1940s-50s **190.00**

Pinback Button, celluloid, red, white, and blue shield in center with "Independent Local and Long Distance Telephone," "The Williams Telephone & Supply Co, Cleveland, O" around outside, 1¼" d **15.00**

Salt and Pepper Shakers, pr, figural telephones, souvenir of Arizona, Grand Canyon State **5.00**

Sign, "Bell System" in middle of central bell, "Michigan Bell Telephone Company, American Telephone & Telegraph Company" in outer circle, enameled iron, dark blue and white, 11" d **200.00**

Sign, "Public Telephone," porcelain, circle with telephone and "Independent," blue and white, 1940-50s, 18" sq **125.00**

Sign, "Telephone," porcelain, blue and white, 9⅞ x 2⅜" **50.00**

Telephone Card, American National Phone Card/ANPC (ANP), Betty Boop and Popeye, jumbo 5 x 7" **8.00**

Telephone Card, AmeriVox, John F and Jacqueline Kennedy, $21 value **25.00**

Telephone Card, Frontier Communications (FRO), Tekno Comix Neil Gaiman's "Mr Hero" **8.00**

Telephone Card, Pacific Bell (PAC), 1957 Thunderbird **12.00**

Telephone Card, Score Board Inc (SBI), Drew Bledsoe, $2 value **2.00**

Telephone Card, Sprint (SPR), Mickey Mantle, 5 minutes **12.00**

Telephone Card, TotalTel (TTT), Cigar Aficionado/Demi Moore, 10 minutes **20.00**

TELEVISION CHARACTERS & PERSONALITIES

Television programming is only fifty years old. Prior to World War II, television viewing was largely centered in the New York market. In 1946 the first network was established, linking WNBT, NBC's New York station, with Schenectady and Philadelphia.

Networks were organized, and programming ordered. By 1949 Americans were purchasing televisions at the rate of 100,000 units a week. In 1955 one-third of all American homes had a television. In the mid-1980s virtually every home included one or more sets.

The 1950s and 60s are the golden age of television licensing. Many early space and western programs licensed over fifty different products. The vast majority of the licensed products were directed toward the infant and juvenile markets.

Television licensing fell off significantly in the 1970s and 80s, the result of increased adult programming, higher fees, and demands by stars for a portion of the licensing fees. Most television shows have no licensed products.

References: Paul Anderson, *The Davy Crockett Craze,* R & G Productions, 1996; Tim Brooks and Earle Marsh, *The Complete Directory to Prime Time Network and Cable TV Shows: 1946–Present, Seventh Edition,* Ballantine Books, 1999; Dana Cain, *Film & TV Animal Star Collectibles,* Antique Trader Books, 1998; Greg Davis and Bill Morgan, *Collector's Guide to TV Memorabilia: 1960s & 1970s, Second Edition,* Collector Books, 1998; Marty Eck, *The Monkees Collectibles Price Guide,* Antique Trader Books, 1998; Glenn Erardi, *Guide to Tarzan Collectibles,* Schiffer Publishing, 1998; Ted Hake, *Hake's Guide to TV Collectibles,* Wallace-Homestead, Krause Publications, 1990; Jack Koch, *Howdy Doody,* Collector Books, 1996; Cynthia Boris Liljeblad, *TV Toys and the Shows That Inspired Them,* Krause Publications, 1996; Kurt Peer, *TV Tie-Ins: A Bibliography of American TV Tie-In Paperbacks,* Neptune Publishing, 1997; Christopher Sausville, *Planet of the Apes Collectibles,* Schiffer Publishing, 1998; Dian Zillner, *Collectible Television Memorabilia,* Schiffer Publishing, 1996.

Periodicals: *Big Reel,* PO Box 1050, Dubuque, IA 52004; *The TV Collector,* PO Box 1088, Easton, MA 02334.

Note: For additional listings see Autographs, Cartoon Characters, Coloring Books, Comic Books, Cowboy Heroes, Hanna-Barbera, Games, Little Golden Books, Lunch Boxes, Movie Memorabilia, Pez, Space Adventurers, Star Trek, Super Heroes, TV Guide, Warner Brothers, and Whitman TV Books.

Addams Family, postcard, full color glossy photo of cast members including Wednesday holding headless doll, Pugsley holding octopus, and Uncle Fester holding homemade bomb, reverse has brown and white illus of Thing painting the Addams Family name with text referring to Addams Family 8 x 10" photos that were available for 50 cents each, mkd "Filmways TV Productions Inc, 1960s," 3½ x 5½" **$15.00**

A-Team, Mr T Club Membership Outfit, Imperial Toy Corp, #8583, ©1983, $12.00.

Adventures In Paradise, record, $33\frac{1}{3}$ rpm, full color cover photo of Adam Troy's schooner "The Tiki," reverse includes text on the program, ABC-Paramount Records, c1960, $12\frac{1}{4} \times 12\frac{1}{4}$" **35.00**

Adventures In Paradise, sheet music, 4 pp, *A TV Musical Theme*, black and white cover photo of Gardner McKay as Adam Troy, metallic green border, ©1960 20th Century Music Corp, 9 x 12" **35.00**

Andy Griffith Show, comic book, #1341, Four Color Series, Dell, ©1962 Mayberry Enterprises **50.00**

Battlestar Galactica, *TV Guide*, #1329, Sep 16, 1978, for Washington-Baltimore Edition, color cover shows 3 cast members in background with planets and stars **30.00**

Beverly Hillbillies, boxed set of 5 puzzles, Jaymar **115.00**

Beverly Hillbillies, song folio, *Beverly Hillbillies/The Clampett Family Song Book*, 32 pp, Alfred Music Co, 1963 Filmways TV Productions Inc, 9 x 12" **15.00**

Bewitched, autograph, PS, Dick Sergeant, Elizabeth Montgomery, and Erin Murphy, black and white glossy, blue felt-tip pen signature "Best Wishes Erin Murphy," 8 x 10" **50.00**

Bixby, Bill, The Magician TV Magic Set **50.00**

Bonanza, Hoss and His Horse Figure Set, 18 accessories, orig 17 x 9" box, 1966 . . . . . **180.00**

Bozo, doll, stuffed, white vinyl head, blue body with white polka dots, orange, red, and black accents, white hands, yellow feet, Knickerbocker, ©1973 Larry Harmon Productions, $11\frac{1}{2}$" h **18.00**

Bozo, record, *Bozo Under the Sea*, 78 rpm, full color cover showing Bozo greeting fish, 38-pp story album, ©1948 Capitol Records, $10\frac{1}{2} \times 12$" **20.00**

Bozo, talking hand puppet, orig box, Mattel, 11 x 7" **125.00**

Brady Bunch, activity book, *The Brady Bunch Sticker Fun*, 12 pp, Whitman, ©1973 Paramount Pictures Corp, $10\frac{1}{4} \times 12$" **50.00**

Brady Bunch, paper dolls, Whitman, ©1973 Paramount Pictures Corp, $10 \times 12\frac{3}{4}$" **35.00**

Brady Bunch, *TV Magazine*, Florence Henderson/Brady Bunch cov, 1970 . . . . . **25.00**

Captain Kangaroo, squeeze toy, vinyl, Captain with bunny in pocket **100.00**

CBS, pinback button, black lettering on yellow ground, c1960s, $2\frac{1}{2}$" d **8.00**

Charlie's Angels, 3-D Viewer on card, 24 scenes, Kenner, 1973, 7 x 12" **50.00**

Charlie's Angels, doll, Kris/Cheryl Ladd, poseable, long life-like rooted blonde hair, wearing white jumpsuit, blue boots, green scarf, ©1977 Spelling-Goldberg Productions, $8\frac{1}{2}$" h, MOC **35.00**

Charlie's Angels, doll, Sabrina/Kate Jackson, poseable, wearing red jumpsuit, blue boots, and scarf, Hasbro, ©1977 Spelling-Goldberg Productions, $8\frac{1}{2}$" h, MOC **35.00**

Chips, wallet, vinyl, tan, "California Highway Patrol" badge design, Imperial Toy Corp, ©1981 MGM Inc, $4\frac{1}{2} \times 7\frac{1}{4}$", MOC **8.00**

Columbo, game, Columbo Detective Game, Milton Bradley, ©1973 Universal Television **15.00**

Como, Perry, pinback button, "The Perry Como Sunshine Show," orange and yellow sunflower design around brown and white portrait illus in center, "GTE Presents" text at rim with show name, date April 10, and CBS-TV, 1960-70s, 4" d **8.00**

Davy Crockett, Fess Parker, charm bracelet on photo card, Disney **35.00**

Davy Crockett, plate, white, center dark brown image of Davy staring down at bear above facsimile signature, ©Walt Disney Prod, c1955, 7" d **60.00**

Davy Crockett, Walt Disney's Davy Crockett Pocketknife, cream colored celluloid grip, black, white, and red art image on 1 side with small inset circular photo of Davy against long rifle and tomahawk, ©Walt Disney Prod, $\frac{3}{8} \times 2\frac{1}{4}$" **45.00**

Death Valley Days, model kit, 20 Mule Team, plastic, Pacific Coast Borax Co premium, MIB **35.00**

Dick Van Dyke, coloring book, Dick, Laura, and Richie on cov, Artcraft, 1963 . . . . . **200.00**

Douglas, Jack, ashtray, smoked glass, blue and bright gold designs, center text "Created By Jack Douglas" surrounded by 6 TV screen designs featuring different illus and logos including "Sundown, League Boots, I Search For Adventure, Bold Journey, Golden Voyage, and Kingdom of the Sea," 1950s, 7 x 9" **15.00**

Dr Kildare, nodder, orig box with insert **125.00**

Dragnet, talking police car, plastic, crank handle, complete with instructions, orig box, Ideal, 1955, 15" l **250.00**

Dukes of Hazzard, General Lee Car, cast metal, 1/25 scale, Confederate flag on roof, black and white "01" on doors, Ertl, #1791, ©1981 Warner Bros, 8" l **125.00**

Ellery Queen, comic book, *Ellery Queen Detective*, #1289, Four Color Series, Dell, 1961 . . . . . **15.00**

Flipper, bank, figural, soft plastic, in upright position on wave shaped base, mkd "Flipper," ©ITF-MGM, 1960s, $5\frac{1}{2} \times 6 \times 16\frac{1}{2}$" **35.00**

Flipper, game, Flipper Flips, Mattel, 1965, $9\frac{1}{2} \times 19\frac{1}{2} \times \frac{3}{4}$" box **40.00**

Flipper, Stardust Velvet Art by Numbers, Hasbro, MIB **60.00**

Flying Nun, doll, orig box, Hasbro, $2\frac{1}{2} \times 5\frac{1}{2}$" **85.00**

Gentle Ben, thermos, metal, full color illus, yellow cup, Aladdin, ©1968 Ivan Tors Films, $6\frac{1}{2}$" h **35.00**

Get Smart, game, Get Smart the Exploding Time Bomb Game, Ideal, ©1965 Talent Associates, $10 \times 19\frac{3}{4} \times 2$" box **75.00**

Gilligan's Island, pencil tablet, full color photo of Gilligan and Skipper on cov, 24 pp, unused, 1960s, 8 x 10" **15.00**

Gleason, Jackie, magazine, *Golf Digest*, Vol 11, #10, Nov 1960, 4-pp article "Jackie Gleason, Broadway's Biggest Golf Buff," $5\frac{1}{2} \times 8\frac{1}{4}$" **15.00**

Gleason, Jackie, magazine, *TV Digest*, Vol 5, #29, Jul 21, 1951, Philadelphia area publication, $5\frac{1}{2} \times 8\frac{1}{2}$" **15.00**

Gleason, Jackie, pinback button, "Jackie Gleason the Bus Driver," black and white Gleason portrait on light orange ground, yellow ribbon below accented by gold plastic 4-leaf clover, 1955 VIP Corp copyright on curl, $1\frac{1}{4}$" d **20.00**

Green Hornet, whistle, hard plastic, "Official Replica of the Hornet's Sting," Chicken of the Sea premium, with orig mailing envelope and order blank, 1967, 3" l **250.00**

Gunsmoke, autograph, PS, Ken Curtis as Marshal Matt Dillon, blue ink inscription "To Frances, Sincere best wishes, Ken Curtis," 1960-70s, $4\frac{3}{4} \times 6\frac{3}{4}$" **35.00**

Gunsmoke, record, *From the CBS-TV Production Starring James Arness*, 45 rpm, *Whoopee Ti-Yi-Yo* on reverse, sung and played by The Prairie Chiefs, 7 x 7" paper sleeve, RCA Victor Bluebird **15.00**

Happy Days, Fonz AM Radio, juke box style, 1976 . . . . . **60.00**

Happy Days, pinback button, "The Fonz For President," bluetone photo on white ground, $1\frac{3}{4}$" d **15.00**

Hawaiian Eye, flicker necklace/mirror, 2½" d pendant with goldtone metal frame, attached 12" l matching goldtone metal necklace, black and white flicker insert changes from "Hawaiian Eye Starring Troy Donahue" to Donahue portrait, c1962 . . . . **20.00**

Hogan's Heroes, comic book, #1, Jun 1966, Dell **15.00**

Hogan's Heroes, game, Hogan's Heroes Bluff Out Game, Transogram, ©1966 Bing Crosby Productions Inc, 9 x 17½ x ¾" box **50.00**

Hogan's Heroes, record, *Hogan's Heroes Sing the Best of World War II*, 33 rpm, 1960s **15.00**

Honeymooners, watch, 1¼" d black plastic case with matching black vinyl straps, black and silver photo of Gleason against blue ground, numerals, yellow hands and Show Time logo in pink, with warranty paper, issued by Show Time cable channel, Criterion, c1985 . . . . . **15.00**

Howdy Doody, can, Frosty Snow Spray, metal canister with cap, front picture of Howdy offering "20 Free Stencils with purchase of this can," Howdy image with "Howdy Doody as seen on NBC TV," ©California National Products Inc, c1950s, 7" h, 2¾" d **35.00**

Howdy Doody, Doodle Slate, diecut cardboard backing sheet holding pointed wood stylus, Howdy at top center, Mr Bluster and Dilly Dally at lower corners, Kagran, c1951-56, 9 x 11" **35.00**

Howdy Doody, ear muffs, brown soft plush inner surface, hard plastic insert with full raised-dimension Howdy Doody face image, elastic black fabric border, adjustable metal spring band, 1950s **35.00**

Howdy Doody, figure, enamel painted wooden body, composition head, "Howdy Doody/Bob Smith" on chest, 12½" h **225.00**

Howdy Doody, ice cream wrapper, Clarabell Banana Bar, red, white, and blue Clarabell image, top margin inscription "Save These Bags," reverse has offer for "Rocket Express" combination shaker and cup for milk drinks, Doughnut Corp of American premium, front bottom margin imprinted for Rivers Ice Cream Co, MA, Kagran, 1951-56, 3½ x 5½" flattened size **15.00**

Howdy Doody, lunch box, metal, front scene of Howdy and friends preparing meal at western "Chuck Wagon," reverse scene of Howdy pointing to opened picture book of 4 historic western events, Adco, c1954, 6½ x 9 x 4" **175.00**

Howdy Doody, Make It Yourself Bee-Nee Kit, Kagran, orig 4¼ x 6¼" box **65.00**

Howdy Doody, Ovaltine mug, hard plastic, red, full color portrait decal with black and white caption "Be Keen–Be Keen Drink Chocolate Flavored Ovaltine!," c1948-51, 3" h **35.00**

Howdy Doody, plate, center Howdy Doody in cowboy outfit, sgd "Smith Taylor USA" on back, 8½" d **40.00**

Howdy Doody, poster, paper, "Be Sure To Save All Howdy Doody Bags For Swell Prizes," Kagran, c1951-56, 10½ x 14" **50.00**

Howdy Doody, prize catalog, *Howdy Doody Ice Cream Club*, 12 pp, illus, introductory message from Howdy to ice cream club members, words and music for Howdy Doody Club Song, point value listing for various ice cream products pictured on back cov, c1951-56, 4 x 5" **50.00**

Howdy Doody, Sip-A-Mug, plastic, translucent red, thin plastic lid centered by raised Howdy face image, 1950s, 3" h **15.00**

Howdy Doody, Summer-Fall-Winter-Spring Embroidery Kit, Kagran, with instructions, unused, orig 1 x 12¼" box **60.00**

Howdy Doody, Tuk-A-Tab mask, stiff paper sheet holding punch-out parts for tab and slot assembly, Poll Parrot premium, Bob Harris, c1948-51, 12 x 15" **50.00**

Howdy Doody, Xylo Doodle Magic Piano, plastic, with instruction sheet, orig box **325.00**

HR Puff N Stuff, Witchie Poo doll, orig box, My Toy, 1970 . . . . **1,375.00**

I Dream of Jeannie, doll, life-like rooted hair, plastic purse, display stand, poseable, Remco, ©1977 Screen Gems, 6½" h, 4 x 10½ x 1¼" box **75.00**

I Love Lucy, magazine, *TV Show*, Lucy and Desi on cov, 1953 . . . . **35.00**

Kojak, repeater cap pistol, cast metal, dark gray finish, black hard plastic grips, raised "Kojak" name above trigger, Lone Star Products Ltd, England, ©1977 Universal City Studios Inc, 5½" l, 4 x 5½ x 1½" box **15.00**

Kukla, Fran and Ollie, Tri-Vue Film Card, color photos from show, red and white "Land of Enchantment" envelope, ©1953 Burr Tilstrom, 3½ x 5½" **15.00**

Land of the Giants, coloring book, Whitman, 1969 . . . . **25.00**

Lassie, biscuit tin, Lassie and Timmie photos, 5" l **150.00**

Lassie, contract, sgd, 2 pp, orig carbon copy contract dated Oct 15, 1958 for June Lockhart, inked signatures of June Lockhart and Sherman A Harris, 8½ x 11" **50.00**

Lassie, greeting card, Christmas, front color photo of Lassie about to receive bone from Timmy with elderly man holding present, black felt-tip signature "Best Wishes Jon Provost," text on reverse, c1957, 5 x 12" **15.00**

Lassie, tie bar and cuff links set, cast metal, gold luster and painted accents on raised designs, 1¾" tie bar of Lassie accented in reddish brown and white and Timmy with tan hair, yellow shirt, and blue pants, ¾" d cuff links depicting Lassie with name incised on rim design, 1950s **35.00**

Lassie, wallet, vinyl, brown, Campbell's Soups premium, complete and unused in orig mailing envelope, c1959, 3¼ x 4¼" **35.00**

Lewis, Shari, costume, Charlie Horse, rayon, 1-pc, thin molded plastic mask, Halco, ©1961 Tarcher Productions Inc, 9 x 11 x 3½" box **15.00**

Little House on the Prairie, costume, Laura, Ben Cooper **30.00**

Little Rascals, coloring book, 112 pp, Saalfield, ©1957 California National Products Inc **25.00**

Little Rascals, pencil case, red enamel painted tin, hinged lid, black and white depiction of Jackie character on lid, Wallace Pencil Co, 1920-30s, 8 x 2 x ¾" **40.00**

London, Gene, photo, Gene London at desk and Pixanne flying through air, facsimile signatures, 1950-60s, 8½ x 11" **15.00**

London, Gene, pinback button, black and white photo on blue ground, white text "I Am A Gene London Fan/Channel 10," Philadelphia Badge Co Inc, 1950-60s, 3" d **15.00**

Magnum PI, click gun with handcuffs, hard plastic, black, silver metal keys, Ja-Ru, ©1981 Universal City Studios Inc, MOC **10.00**

Man From UNCLE, record, *More Music From the Man From UNCLE*, 33⅓ rpm, front cover shows Illya and Solo with woman in red dress, all inside a destroyed MG, black and white photos from the show on back, ©1966 RCA Victor, 12¼ x 12¼" **10.00**

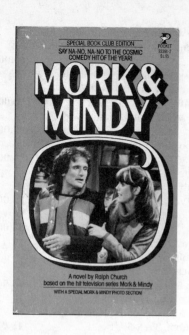

Mork & Mindy, paperback book, by Ralph Church, Pocket Books #83381-2, NY, ©1979, $5.00.

M*A*S*H, action figure, Hot Lips, MOC **40.00**
M*A*S*H, drinking glasses, set of 4, 4077th logo, 1983 . . . . . **25.00**
M*A*S*H, matchcover, M*A*S*H 4077th Official Products, black and white photo on 1 side, army green M*A*S*H logo on other side, DD Beam & Sons California Inc, ©1971 20th Century Fox Film Corp, with inside order form from "Strikin' It Rich" Co, 1½ x 1⅞" **14.00**
M*A*S*H, pinback button, olive green helicopter on red ground, yellow lettering "M*A*S*H 4077th," 1981 20th Century Fox Film copyright on curl, 1¾" d **15.00**
M*A*S*H, Radar's Teddy, stuffed, plush, brown, wearing green T-shirt with white text, M*A*S*H logo and red cross, attached cardboard tag, California Stuffed Toys, ©1983 20th Century Fox Film Corp, 7 x 8 x 9" **15.00**
Miss Piggy, bank, ceramic, painted and glazed, wearing blue dress and gloves, pink shawl, red flower, and yellow ring on finger, ©Henson Associates, 1980s, 3½ x 4 x 8" **35.00**
Mister Ed, autograph, PS, blue felt-tip signatures "With Love Connie Hines 'Carol'/Best Wishes Alan Young 'Wilbur,'" black and white, 8 x 10" **35.00**
Mister Ed, game, Mister Ed The Talking Horse Game, Parker Bros, ©1962 The Mister Ed Co, 9 x 17¼ x 1½" box **35.00**
Moore, Mary Tyler, record, *Million Sellers*, 33⅓ rpm, front cover photo of Mary Tyler Moore in gold lamé bathing suit, Tops Records, 1950s, 12¼ x 12¼" **35.00**
Munsters, magazine, *Drag*, Herman in Dragula roadster on cov, Feb 1966. . . . . **125.00**
My Favorite Martian, coloring book, #1148, 128 pp, Whitman, 1964 . . . . **50.00**
Nanny and the Professor, Colorforms, 1970 . . . . **25.00**
NBC, postcard, issued as souvenir "Of The Behind The Scenes Tour Of The NBC Studios," full color peacock design with 1967 Fall program schedule, 5½ x 8½" **15.00**
Our Gang, book, *A Story of Our Gang*, "Romping Through The Hal Roach Comedies," 20 pp, color photos, Whitman, 1929 . . . . **30.00**
Outer Limits, game, The Outer Limits Game, Milton Bradley, ©1964 Daystar, 9½ x 19 x 1½" box **75.00**

Patrick, Butch, autograph, PS, Patrick as Eddie Munster holding wolfman doll, blue felt-tip pen signature "Butch Patrick/Eddie," black and white glossy, 8 x 10" **50.00**
Patty Duke, fan club photo, black and white, Patty and Cathy and "Thanks for Watching," 5 x 3" **15.00**
Pinky Lee, View-Master reel, "7-Day," with illus sleeve and booklet, 1955 . . . . **15.00**
Police Woman, doll, Angie Dickinson, Sgt Pepper, 1976, 9" h, MIB **40.00**
Rat Patrol, coloring book, Saalfield, 1966. . . . . **60.00**
Rin Tin Tin, advertisement, "Official Rin Tin Tin Cavalry Bugle, 50 cents & 1 Nabisco Shredded Wheat box top," green and gray, 1956. . . . . **12.00**
Roy Rogers, magazine, *Jack & Jill*, Roy and Trigger cov and article, 1961. . . . . **35.00**
Sales, Soupy, game, Soupy Sales Sez Go-Go-Go, Milton Bradley, ©Soupy Sales, 1960s, 9½ x 19 x 1½" box **50.00**
Sales, Soupy, souvenir program, 16 pp, for appearance at The Paramount Theater in NY, photos and text on Soupy and musical performers of show including Little Richard and The Hollies, c1965, 9 x 12" **15.00**
Sgt Bilko, poster, Camel cigarettes adv, "Star of TV's best comedy show," matted. **115.00**
Sheena Queen of the Jungle, postcard, black and white glossy, full figure photo on front of Irish McCalla in costume, facsimile printed message thanking viewers and mentioning that many have asked for "A Sheena Horn," reverse has printed station identification for WPIX, NY, with 1956 postmark, 3½ x 5½" **50.00**
Six Million Dollar Man, action figure accessory, backpack radio, hard plastic, with helmet and ear plug, ©1975 Universal City Studios Inc, 6¼ x 6½ x 2¼" box **35.00**
Six Million Dollar Man, Action Play Doh Set, Kenner, 1973, MIP. **35.00**
Six Million Dollar Man, bank, hard vinyl, Steve Austin wearing orange suit busting through red brick wall on gray base, Animals Plus Inc, ©1976 Universal City Studios Inc, 4 x 4 x 10" **15.00**
Six Million Dollar Man, playset, Mission Control, Kenner, ©1976 Universal City Studios Inc, 12 x 15½ x 5" box **35.00**
Skelton, Red, record, *The Pledge of Allegiance By Red Skelton From the Red Skelton Hour, Jan 14, 1969*, Burger King premium, 6 x 6" **10.00**
Sonny & Cher, postcard, smiling full figure Sonny & Cher on front wearing gold outfits for show at Harrah's, Lake Tahoe, reverse lists concert dates for other performers in Reno and Tahoe, c1978, 4 x 8" **10.00**
Soupy Sales, flicker ring, silvered plastic, black, white, and red, 1960s **20.00**
Space:1999, moon car, plastic, friction, Azrak-Hamway, ©1976 ATV Licensing Ltd, 3½ x 6½ x 7½", MOC **50.00**
Starsky & Hutch, walkie-talkies, LJN, orig box **420.00**
Taxi, ticket, stiff yellow paper, black text "Taxi—A Hilarious New Comedy," for Fri Aug 18, 1978, 2½ x ⅜" **10.00**
The Real McCoys, comic book, #01689-207, Dell, ©1962 Brennan-Westgate Productions **15.00**
Three Stooges, book, *Magic Re-Color Book*, spiral-bound cardboard cov, six 6 x 9½" pp, Fun Bilt Toys, ©1959 Norman Maurer Productions, 9 x 10½" **35.00**
Three Stooges, Little Golden Record, 45 rpm, *Moe, Larry & Curly-Joe The Music Wreckers*, in 7 x 8" stiff paper jacket, ©1959 Norman Maurer Productions **25.00**

Three Stooges, Talking Phone Pal, orig box **65.00**

Walker, Clint, autograph, PS, black marker inscription "Best wishes/Clint Walker/Cheyenne," black and white, 1955-58, 8 x 10" **15.00**

Welcome Back Kotter, doll, John Travolta Superstar, poseable, box includes pin-up photo on back with facsimile signature, Chemtoy Corp, ©1977, 11½" h, 9 x 13 x 2" box **35.00**

Welcome Back Kotter, poster, "The Sweathogs From 'Welcome Back, Kotter'," full color, glossy, Dargis Associates Inc, ©1976 The Wolper Organization Inc, 22 x 35" **15.00**

Welcome Back Kotter, ticket, orange, black text, for Fri Aug 18, 1978 show at ABC TV Center, Hollywood Theater, 2¼ x 4¼" **10.00**

Welk, Lawrence, game, Crusade Lawrence Welk's All Star Acts Kit, color photo of Welk on box lid plus blue-tone and redtone photos on sides of other celebrities including Bob Hope, Frank Sinatra, Paul Newman, Ed Sullivan, and Art Carney, Games For Industry Inc, 1967, 9 x 17 x 2" box **35.00**

Wild Wild West, magazine, *TV Tab*, 24 pp, supplement to *Rochester NY Democrat & Chronicle Sunday Newspaper*, Aug 1-7, 1965, front cover shows full color caricature of Ross Martin and Robert Conrad, 7½ x 10½" **15.00**

Zorro, pinwheel, plastic, wooden pole, Disney **40.00**

AUCTION PRICES – TV CHARACTERS

TV Toyland, Auction #4, June 4, 1999. Prices include a 15% buyer's premium.

Chips, highway patrol chase car with figure, orig box, 1981 . . . . **$40.00**

Clutch Cargo, coloring book, Saalfield **87.00**

Danny Thomas Show, Angela Cartwright frame tray puzzle, Saalfield, sealed, 1962 . . . . **230.00**

Davy Crockett, Fess Parker, charm bracelet on photo card, Disney **35.00**

Dobie Gillis, shoe-boots, orig photo box with Maynard and Dobie and "Star of TV Show" **259.00**

Dragnet, talking police car, Ideal, 15" plastic car, turn crank to talk, instructions, dome, playset-type accessories, orig box, 1955 . . . . **250.00**

Dukes of Hazzard, dashboard and Fuzz detector toy, Illco, generic mailing box, 12 x 6" **199.00**

Green Acres, board game, Standard Toykraft **253.00**

Hogan's Heroes, stockade set, miniature army figures and vehicles, sealed on photo card with Hogan and 3 cast members, 1977, 7 x 12" **82.00**

Lassie, charm bracelet, "Lassie 55-56 Emmy Award Winner," display window box **352.00**

Lost in Space, robot, Mexican, speaks Spanish **1,200.00**

Munsters, Herman Munster vinyl doll, Remco, 1964, 7" h **120.00**

Partridge Family, concert poster, David Cassidy on "boxing style" poster, "Watch the Partridge Family every Friday TV 27 - Madison Stat July 17, 1971," 15 x 22" **611.00**

Rin Tin Tin, fan club kit, Fort Apache letter, personalized black and white cast photo, envelope with logo **35.00**

Welcome Back Kotter, Barbarina and Horshack wind-up action bank, Fleetwood, 1975 . . . . **50.00**

Wyatt Earp, wallet, Hugh O'Brien, 1957 . . . . **80.00**

TELEVISION LAMPS

"You will go blind if you watch television in the dark" was a common warning in the early 1950s. American lamp manufacturers responded by creating lamps designed to sit atop the television set and provide the correct amount of indirect lighting necessary to preserve the viewer's eyesight.

The need was simple. The solutions were imaginative and of questionable taste in more than a few cases. Most television lamps were ceramic and back-lit. Motifs ranged from leaping gazelles to a prancing horse with a clock in the middle of his body graced by a red Venetian blind, pagoda-like shade.

References: Leland and Crystal Payton, *Turned On: Decorative Lamps of the Fifties*, Abbeville Press, 1989; Tom Santiso, *TV Lamps*, Collector Books, 1999; Calvin Shepherd, *'50s TV Lamps*, Schiffer Publishing, 1998.

Basset Hound, ceramic, Maddux of California, 11½" h **$65.00**

Basset Hound, painted plaster, brown, 9" h **45.00**

Big Horn Sheep, planter, golden yellow and green, 8" h **40.00**

Boxer Dogs, Claes, 1956, 13" h **85.00**

Bull, Maddux of California, #859, black, 11½" h **60.00**

Chinese Couple on Junk, Fuhry and Sons, 16½" l **85.00**

Colonial Man and Woman, candy dish, 12½" h **85.00**

Comedy and Tragedy Masks, Royal Haeger, 9½" h **50.00**

Covered Wagon, Marcia of California, 11" l **55.00**

Covered Wagon and Horses, 10" l **50.00**

Crane In Flight, California Original **75.00**

Crowing Rooster, white, gold highlights, Lane, 15" h **65.00**

Crowing Rooster on Fence, Lane **100.00**

Deer and Fawn Head, brown, fiberglass shade **75.00**

Deer and Fawn Head, stylized, Gilner Co, 13" h **50.00**

Dolphin Trio, green, gold trim, Enchanto of California, 12" h **60.00**

Donkey, planter, wood base, Royal Haeger **100.00**

Fawn, candy dish, Lane, 1959 . . . . **65.00**

Flamingo, candy dish, Lane, 1957, 14" h **350.00**

Frogs on Lily Pad, Royal of California, 7" h **45.00**

Horn Vase, rose dec, 11½" h **50.00**

Horse, candy dish, Lane, 13½" h **80.00**

Horse, white, Maddux of California, 12½" h **65.00**

Horse, woman rider shooting deer, gold trim, 10" h **85.00**

Horse Head Trio, Kron, 11" h **125.00**

Leaf, gold trim, Lanell of California, 9½" h **45.00**

Leaping Fawn, planter, green, 8" l **50.00**

Leaping Horse, planter, Art Deco style, green **70.00**

Leaping Horse, planter, black and white, Maddux of California **65.00**

Matador, Lane, 15½" h **90.00**

Mermaid on Shell, Cali-Co of California, 8½" h **45.00**

Nordic Ship, bisque, airbrushed, light green, gold trim **75.00**

Oriental Couple and Pagoda, painted plaster, Silvestri Bros, 9½" h **65.00**

Paddle Boat, planter, green, gold trim **75.00**

Palomino Horse, Maddux of California, 12½" h **65.00**

Panther, black, Kron, 15" l **80.00**

Panther, candy dish, black, 14" l **65.00**

Panther, white, Kron, 16½" l **95.00**

Pea Fowl, Royal Fleet of California, 10" h **50.00**

Pitcher, hp floral dec, 13" h **45.00**

Poodles, candy dish, pink, Lane, 13" h **150.00**

Pug and Poodle, Kron, 13" h **125.00**

Gazelle, chalkware, red, brown, and gold, 1950s, $60.00.

Racing Greyhounds, 9" h. **60.00**
Rearing Horse with Fence, California Original, L0431. . . . . . . **90.00**
Roadrunner, multicolored, green base, Maddux of
  California, 9½" h. **70.00**
Sailboat, basketweave sails, Comer Creation, 10" h. **35.00**
Sail Fish, candy dish, Lane, 14" h. **95.00**
Shell, iridescent, Maddux of California, 10" h. **65.00**
Siamese Cats, black and cream, Claes, 1954, 12" h **50.00**
Siamese Cats, black and white, Lane, 12" h **45.00**
Swan, planter, blue base, Maddux of California **100.00**
Tiger, Modernera Lamp Los Angeles, 7½" h **55.00**
Triple Horse Heads, Kron, 11½" h **100.00**
Tulip Vase, Ceramic Arts of California, 9½" h **50.00**
Tulip Vase, Esco-lite, 9" h. **45.00**
Unicorn, white, gold trim, 14½" h **55.00**
Vase, emb dragon design, Walco, 10" h **60.00**
Vase, Royal Haeger, 7½" h **40.00**
Wagon Wheel, 11½" h **45.00**
Zebra, gold and black, 12" l **40.00**

TELEVISIONS

Television sets are divided into three groups: (1) mechanical era sets, 1925 to 1932, (2) pre–World War II sets, 1938-1941, and (3) post-1946 sets. Mechanical era sets, also known as radiovisors, were used in conjunction with the radio. Reception was limited to the Chicago and New York area.

The electronic picture tube was introduced in 1938. The smaller the tube, the older the set is a good general rule. Early electric sets provided for a maximum of five channels, 1 through 5. Many sets made prior to 1941 combined the television with a multiband radio. Fewer than 20,000 sets were produced. Many of the sets were sold in kit form.

Production of television sets significantly increased following World War II. Channels 6 to 13 were added between 1946 and 1948. Channel 1 was dropped in 1949, replaced with V.H.F. channels 2 through 13. The U.H.F. band was added in 1953.

Collectors focus primarily on the black and white sets from the 1940s and 1950s. There is some interest in color sets made prior to 1955. Brand and model numbers are essential to researching value. Cabinet condition also is critical to value, sometimes more

important than whether or not the set is operational. Sets made after 1960 have more reuse than collectible value.

References: Bryan Durbal and Glann Bubenheimer, *Collector's Guide to Vintage Televisions,* Collector Books, 1999; Scott Wood (ed.), *Classic TVs With Price Guide: Pre-War Thru 1950s,* L-W Book Sales, 1992, 1997 value update.

Periodical: *Antique Radio Classified,* PO Box 2, Carlisle, MA 01741.

Collectors' Club: Antique Wireless Assoc, 59 Main St, Holcomb, NY 14469.

Admiral, P17E31, painted metal tabletop, top handle,
  1959. . . . . **$35.00**
Air King, A-1016, console, square lines, drop-down door
  at center, 16" screen **50.00**
Ansley, 701, Beacon, wooden tabletop, 13-channel
  tuner, grill cloth and mesh panels, 4 knobs at bottom,
  1948, 10" screen **75.00**
Bendix, 3051, console, square lined, 3 knobs below
  screen, 16" screen **35.00**
CBS-Columbia, 2-C3, console, French Provincial style,
  double doors, 1950, 20" screen **20.00**
Crosley, 9-4-7, wooden tabletop, metal mesh around
  screen, continuous tuner control and window to right,
  1949, 12" screen **35.00**
DeWald, ET-171, console, pull-out phono, 1951,
  17" screen **45.00**
Emerson, 614, Bakelite tabletop, porthole-style screen,
  ribs across front and sides, 1950, 10" screen **75.00**
Fada, S20C10, console, screen on left, 4 knobs behind
  door, 1951, 20" screen **20.00**
General Electric, 835, tabletop, metal mesh grill,
  10" screen. **50.00**
Hallicrafters, T-506, wooden tabletop, 12-channel push-
  button tuner, 1949, 7" screen **150.00**
Motorola, 17T5, Bakelite tabletop, 2 knobs under
  screen, 1952, 17" screen **35.00**

Motorola, wooden tabletop, plastic knobs, with brochure, 9½" h, 16" w, 16½" d, $175.00. Photo courtesy Collectors Auction Services.

Motorola, VK-106, console, stepped-up top in center, forward screen, 1948, 10" screen **125.00**

Norelco, PT 200, console, fixed plastic projection screen, 1948 . . . . **50.00**

Olympic, 3K119, console, screen in center, 4 spindle legs, 1962 . . . . **10.00**

Philco, 51-T1601, metal tabletop, rounded top, screen over 4 knobs, 1951 . . . . **15.00**

Philco Predicta, 3408, The Debutante, metal body, cloth grill, 1960, 17" screen **400.00**

RCA, 8T-241, tabletop, blonde, 1940s **50.00**

RCA, 9T246, metal tabletop, grill around screen, imitation mahogany finish, 1949, 10" screen **25.00**

RCA, portable, 8½ x 6¼ x 12", 9" screen **125.00**

Sentinel, 402, console, 4 knobs below screen, 10" screen **50.00**

Silvertone, 112, wooden tabletop, 1950, 12" screen **35.00**

Sony, TV5-503W, metal and plastic transistor TV, screen to left, controls to right, 1963 . . . . **25.00**

Sparton, 4931, console, 5 knobs below screen, 1949, 10" screen **75.00**

Stewart-Warner, 9126, wooden tabletop, 2 knobs below screen, 1951, 17" screen **15.00**

Stromberg-Carlson, TC-125-LA, console, controls at bottom left and right, 1949, 12" porthole-style screen **85.00**

Sylvania, 247, console, 4 knobs below screen, 16" screen **25.00**

Westinghouse, H-181, double-door highboy, 1948, 10" screen **125.00**

Westinghouse, H-661C12, console, double doors, 1949, 12" screen **55.00**

Zenith, G2340, console, porthole-style screen, 1950, 12" screen **125.00**

Zenith, L2894H, Stratosphere, 27" screen **100.00**

Zenith, Spirit of '76, black and white, minuteman on both sides with Declaration of Independence signatures, top stamped "Spirit of '76," 10" screen **15.00**

TEMPLE, SHIRLEY

Born on April 23, 1928, in Santa Monica, California, Shirley Temple was the most successful child movie star of all time. She was discovered while attending dance class at the Meglin Dance Studios in Los Angeles. Fox Film's *Stand Up and Cheer* (1934) was her first starring role. She made a total of twelve pictures that year.

Gertrude George, Shirley's mother, played a major role in creating Shirley's image and directing her licensing program. Requests for endorsements and licenses were immediate. Hundreds of products were marketed.

By 1935 Temple was the number one box office star, a spot she retained through 1938. In 1940 Temple starred in *The Blue Bird* and *Young People,* her last films for Fox. She immediately signed a $100,000-a-year contract with MGM and starred in *Kathleen* in 1941, her first teenage/adult movie role. Shirley married for the first time in 1945. She retired from films in 1950, the same year she divorced her husband and married Charles Black.

In 1957 Shirley was host of the *Shirley Temple Storybook.* In the 1960s Shirley Temple Black became active in Republican politics. After serving as a U.S. Delegate to the United Nations and Ambassador to Ghana, she became Chief of Protocol in Washington. Her final government service was as Ambassador to Czechoslovakia in 1989.

References: Edward R. Pardella, *Shirley Temple Dolls and Fashion, 2nd Edition,* Schiffer Publishing, 1999; Dian Zillner, *Hollywood Collectibles: The Sequel,* Schiffer Publishing, 1994.

Book, *Shirley Temple at Play;* color photos, 20 pp, Saalfield, 1935 . . . . **$55.00**

Book, *The Littlest Rebel,* black and white photos, full color scene on back cov, Saalfield, #1115, 4½ x 5¼" **40.00**

Creamer, cobalt blue glass, white face **45.00**

Doll, composition, jointed, ringlet hair, sleep eyes, fabric dress and matching cap, knit anklets, shoes, back of head emb "Shirley Temple/©Ideal N&T Co," 22" h **800.00**

Doll, vinyl, jointed, rooted blonde hair, fixed hazel eyes with lashes, open mouth with painted teeth line, sheer fabric dress with double-ply skirt, fabric stockings and panty brief, back of head mkd "©1972/Ideal Toy Corp/ST-14-H-213," back of doll mkd "1972 ©Ideal /2-M-5534," 16¾" h **80.00**

Figurine, white salt, wearing maroon flocked dress, performing curtsey, 1930s, 6½" h, on 2 x 2" base **50.00**

Hair Bow, Bakelite, cameo portrait of Shirley on oval red ground with silvered tin rim in center of dark red bow, metal hair clip, 2¼" l **75.00**

Handkerchief, sheer white linen-type fabric, brown, orange, and green border spaced in white, Temple portrait on each corner in brown with orange accent, c1935, 9½" sq **50.00**

Jewelry Box and Catalog, black and white photo image and facsimile signature on lid, ST Jewelry Inc "Dangles For Bracelets" catalog has image of Shirley on cov, features short verses describing 12 bracelet charms, mid-1930s, ½ x 3 x 3" **60.00**

Mug, cobalt blue glass, white face **70.00**

Paper Dolls, Whitman, 1976, 10 x 13" **25.00**

Photograph, Shirley wearing Santa outfit, bluetone with starry night sky background, fleshtone tint on face and hair curls, mid-1930s, 8 x 10" **15.00**

Pin, oval tinted real photo of Shirley surrounded by mint luster brass frame surrounded by scalloped pink celluloid border, 1930s, 1⅛" h **175.00**

Life Magazine, Mar 30, 1942, $25.00.

Pinback Button, browntone photo with pale orange hair ribbon accents, "The World's Darling/Genuine Shirley Temple Doll," open back with Whitehead & Hoag backpaper, "©Ideal Novelty & Toy Co" on rim, 1¼" d **70.00**

Postcard, sepia photo, 20th Century-Fox brown logo at each lower margin corner, reverse with left panel text in English "Shirley" and "Miss Broadway," remaining text in Czechoslovakian, 1930s, 3½ x 5½" **25.00**

TENNIS COLLECTIBLES

Tennis came to America in the mid-1870s. After a tennis craze in the 1880s, the sport went into a decline. International play led to a revival in the early 1900s. The period from 1919 to 1940 is viewed by many tennis scholars as the sport's golden age.

Tennis collectibles are divided into two periods: (1) pre-1945 and (2) post-1945. There is little collector interest in post-1945 material. There are three basic groups of collectibles: (1) items associated with play such as tennis balls, ball cans, rackets, and fashions, (2) paper ephemera ranging from books to photographs, and (3) objects decorated with a tennis image or in a tennis shape. Because tennis collecting is in its infancy, some areas remain highly affordable (rackets) while others (tennis ball cans) already are in the middle of a price run.

Reference: Jeanne Cherry, *Tennis Antiques & Collectibles*, Amaryllis Press, 1995.

Collectors' Club: The Tennis Collectors Society, Guildhall Orchard, Mary Lane North, Great Bromley, Essex, Colchester, CO7 7TU UK.

Autograph, PS, black and white image of Don Budge, sgd in blue, with certificate of authenticity, 8 x 10" **$20.00**

Autographed Wilson Tennis Ball, Chris Evert, in clear plastic case, with certificate of authenticity **15.00**

Ball Box, Kingcraft Lillywhite Frowd Tennis Balls, with 4 of 6 orig balls **55.00**

Ball Cans, Pennsylvania Centre Court, $50.00, and Wright & Ditson, $30.00.

Ball Can, Cortland "Championship," blue, white, and green, opened **55.00**

Ball Can, Dunlop "Championship," Vinnie Richards, keywind, yellow and black on red, opened, with 1 orig ball, 1940s **135.00**

Ball Can, Penn-Craft "All Court," red, white, and black, opened, with 2 unused balls, c1950 . . . . **145.00**

Ball Can, Spalding "Poncho Gonzalez," red, white, and black, opened **60.00**

Ball Can, Wilson "Championship," keywind, blue, white, and copper-colored, opened, with 3 orig balls **185.00**

Ball Can, Wilson "Championship," yellow and red, unopened, early 1970s **12.00**

Ball Can, Wilson "Match-Point," keywind, red, black, and yellow, unopened **115.00**

Book, *Psych Yourself to Better Tennis*, Walter A Luszki, Wilshire Book Co, 145 pp, 1974, soft cov **6.00**

Dexterity Puzzle, glass front with tin rim, emb multicolor image of 3 children in Victorian dress playing lawn tennis and "DRGM 116769," 4 white balls, mirror on back, 1¹³⁄₁₆" d **40.00**

Drinking Glasses, boxed set of 6, "Wilson Championship" ball can dec in red, yellow, black, and white, early 1970s **55.00**

Lawn Tennis Tape Measure, leather, paper label on front shows court layout with measurements, measure retracts **210.00**

Pin, enameled, Robertsons Golly Tennis Player, "REV GOMM Birmingham" on back, 1950s **30.00**

Postcard, Bill Tilden, black and white image of Tilden making forehand shot, unused, c1920s **65.00**

Postcard, "Coral Beach Tennis Club, Bermuda," chrome finished card, postmarked 1956 . . . . **5.00**

Program, Wimbledon, June 28, 1954, cover image of Tony Trabert, photos of 1953 winners **20.00**

Racquet, Dunlop, "McEnroe," wooden, tight orig strings, 4⅜" grip **30.00**

Racquet, Volkl, C9 Pro, wooden, 4⅜" grip, with cov **100.00**

Racquet, Wilson, T3000, steel, 4½" grip **18.00**

Racquet, Wright & Ditson, Champion, scored grip **30.00**

Salt and Pepper Shakers, pr, figural tennis player holding racket salt, yellow tennis ball pepper **15.00**

THIMBLES

By the middle of the 19th century, the American thimble industry was able to produce finely worked thimbles. Gold and silver thimbles were restricted to the upper class. Utilitarian thimbles were made of brass or steel. In 1880 William Halsey patented a process to make celluloid thimbles. Aluminum thimbles made their appearance in the second quarter of the 20th century.

A thimble was one of the few gifts considered appropriate for an unmarried man to give to a lady. Many of these fancy thimbles show little wear, possibly a result of both inappropriate sizing and the desire to preseve the memento.

Advertising thimbles were popular between 1920 and the mid-1950s. Early examples were made from celluloid or aluminum. Plastic was the popular post-war medium. The first political thimbles appeared shortly after ratification of the 19th amendment. They proved to be popular campaign giveaways through the early 1960s.

References: Averil Mathis, *Antique and Collectible Thimbles and Accessories*, Collector Books, 1986, 1997 value update; Estelle Zalkin, *Zalkin's Handbook of Thimbles & Sewing Implements*, Warman Publishing, 1988.

Newsletter: *Thimbletter,* 93 Walnut Hill Rd, Newton Highlands, MA 02161.

Collectors' Clubs: Thimble Collectors International, 2594 E Upper Hayden Lake Rd, Hayden, ID 83835; The Thimble Guild, PO Box 381807, Duncanville, TX 75138.

Note: For additional sewing listings refer to Sewing Items.

Bisque, kewpie dec, dated 1996 . . . . **$15.00**
Bone China, "Always Coca-Cola" logo, England **5.00**
Bone China, Pansy, Healacraft, England **15.00**
Bone China, Siamese cat head and "Siamese," mkd "Fine Bone China, England" **18.00**
Celluloid, Tastykake adv, size 8 . . . . **5.00**
China, American Fashion Circa 1890, orig box, Avon, 1982 . . . . **7.00**
China, American Fashion Circa 1923, orig box, Avon, 1982 . . . . **9.00**
China, Baby Animals of the World, Baby Badgers, World Wildlife Fund, Franklin Mint, 1981 . . . . **25.00**
China, Blomen Van Nederland, Crocus, Franklin Mint, 1978 . . . . **10.00**
China, Delft dec with blue peacock on branch surrounded by floral wreath, Majestic **15.00**
China, Friends of the Forest, Otter, Franklin Mint, 1982 . . . . . **12.00**
China, Gone With the Wind, Scarlett **15.00**
China, Osborne pattern, Wedgwood **55.00**
China, owl, Collector's Club issue, sgd by artist, Oakley China, England **12.00**
China, Pampers Nappies adv, England **3.00**
China, red and gold dragon, gold trim, mkd "Rockingham, England" **18.00**
China, rose-covered cottage scene, mkd with H&S logo **25.00**
China, scalloped edge, forget-me-not bouquet tied with pink ribbon, mkd "Retsch Germany" **20.00**
China, ship and "Sault Ste Marie, Michigan" **5.00**
China, Sunbonnet Babies baking, mkd "Downs Ltd Ed 2500" **26.00**
Cloisonné, bird and flowers dec on brown ground, gold top and band, blue int **18.00**
Gold, monogrammed, mkd with thimble in star and "10K," Waite Thresher **50.00**
Pewter, cow on top, Lancaster area, PA **10.00**
Porcelain, American Lighthouse set, lighthouse-shaped wood shelf with 24 thimbles, Lenox **100.00**
Porcelain, blue castle logo and "Haviland Limoges France" on outside and inside **25.00**
Porcelain, cobalt blue net with gold accents, mkd with LFZ (Lomonosov Porcelain Factory) logo and made in Russia mark **12.00**
Sterling Silver, inlaid mother-of-pearl flower with brass center and black ground on front, back with alternating vertical stripes in mother-of-pearl and black **18.00**
Sterling Silver, paneled bands, size 11 . . . . **20.00**
Sterling Silver, red top, scrolled band, mkd "sterling Germany 6" **40.00**
White Milk Glass, hp gray and black cat with green eyes and orange collar, sgd "GTB" **8.00**

TIFFANY

Charles L. Tiffany and John B. Young founded Tiffany & Young, a stationery and gift store, in 1837. In 1841 Tiffany & Young became Tiffany, Young & Ellis. The name was changed to Tiffany & Company in 1853.

In 1852 Tiffany insisted that its silver comply with the English sterling silver standard of 925/1000. Charles Lewis Tiffany was one of the leaders in the fight that resulted in the federal government adopting this standard, passing a 1906 statute that set 925/1000 as the minimum requirement for articles marked "sterling."

During the 1850s Tiffany & Company produced some electroplated wares. Production increased significantly following the Civil War. The manufacture of electroplated ware ended in 1931.

Tiffany incorporated as Tiffany & Co., Inc., in 1868, the same year the company acquired the Moore silverware factory. Tiffany's silver studio became America's first school of design. Beginning in 1868, Tiffany silverware was marked with "Tiffany & Co." and the letter "M" for Edward C. Moore, head of the studio. The company continued to mark its silverware with the initial of its incumbent president until the practice was discontinued in 1965.

Tiffany's jewelry, especially its botanical brooches and use of semi-precious gemstones, captured the world's attention at the Paris Exposition Universelle in 1878. Louis Comfort Tiffany, son of Charles Tiffany, became the company's first Design Director. Under his leadership, the company manufactured a wealth of Art Nouveau objects, especially jewelry and lamps.

Recognized as one of the world's most respected sources of diamonds and other jewelry, Tiffany craftsmanship extends to a broad range of items including fine china, clocks, flatware, leather goods, perfume, scarves, silver, stationery, and watches. Tiffany opened its New York Corporate Division 1960. The Vince Lombardi Trophy for the National Football League Super Bowl Championship is one of its most famous commissions.

References: John A. Shuman III, *The Collector's Encyclopedia of American Art Glass,* Collector Books, 1988, 1999 value update; Moise S. Steeg, Jr., *Tiffany Favrile Art Glass,* Schiffer Publishing, 1997; Kenneth Wilson, *American Glass 1760-1930: The Toledo Museum of Art,* 2 vols., Hudson Hills Press and The Toledo Museum of Art, 1994.

REPRODUCTION ALERT: Brass belt buckles and badges marked "Tiffany" have been widely reproduced.

BRONZE

Cigar Box, gilt-bronze and enamel, rect form, Zodiac pattern, multicolored enameling to each medallion, partial cedar liner, base stamped "Tiffany Studios New York 1655," 2½" h, 6½" w, 6" deep **$1,600.00**
Note Paper Holder, gilt-bronze and enamel, rect form, geometric pattern border in relief, red, blue, and green enamel inlay, imp "Louis C Tiffany Furnaces nc Favrile 610," c1925, 7⅝" l, 4⅛" w **250.00**
Tazza, gilt-bronze and enamel, circular dish on short standard raised on spreading circular foot, Greek key and stylized foliate motif with oval green enamel insets on rim, imp "Tiffany Studios New York," 2½" h, 7¼" d **700.00**
Thermometer, etched metal and glass, grapevine pattern, beaded border, green patina and green slag glass with easel stand, imp "Tiffany Studios New York," 8¾" h **1,500.00**

Tray, gilt-bronze and enamel, rect form, dots and dashes border with stylized flower corners, yellow, green, and blue enamel, stamped "Louis C Tiffany Furnaces Inc 313," 4¾ x 2½" **300.00**

GLASS

Bowl and Undertray, gold iridescent, 8-ruffled sides with conforming undertray, polished pontils, base mkd "LCT," 5¾" d **$500.00**

Bud Vase, slender iridescent gold glass cylinder, 6 elongated green leaves rising from base, inscribed "LCT," inserted into open scrolled bronze mount stamped "Tiffany Studios New York 714," 16" h **1,000.00**

Cabinet Vase, oval body, flared rim, iridescent blue at base rising to gold, 8 pulled swirled dec, polished pontil, base mkd "LCT J9320," 2⅞" h **525.00**

Compote, iridescent gold, 2 engraved butterflies within, gilded pedestal foot inscribed "LC Tiffany Favrile 1149," 4" h **1,150.00**

Open Salt, broad shouldered, iridescent blue with 8 pulled prunts, base inscribed "LCT Favrile X620," 2⅛" d **800.00**

Paperweight, crystal, pyramid shaped, bottom etched "Atlanta 100–1984 Arthur Andersen & Co, 4½ x 3" **20.00**

Shade, amber glass, honeycomb pattern, iridescent gold with onion skin at rim, top rim mkd "LCT," 7½" d **1,150.00**

Vase, bulbous, 10-ribbed, iridescent blue, flared rim and applied ribbed base, sgd "LC Tiffany-Favrile 1524 3333 P," c1920, 9" h **2,400.00**

Wine Glass, bulbous body tapering to base, iridescent amber glass with applied trailing prunts, polished pontil, base mkd "LCT G1696," 4" h **175.00**

LAMPS

Lamp, octagonal form, cream colored glass rising to bulbed top, caramel and gold pulled petal design dec, set in fitted gilt bronze and wooden base, 8" h . . . **$1,150.00**

Table Lamp Base, dark patina on textured surface, 4 curved socket arms over 6-sided baluster shaped standard, domed base, imp "Tiffany Studios New York 532," 23½" h **2,250.00**

STERLING SILVER

Alarm Clock, 8 day, case inscribed "Mother/1918 Sept 16, 1943/From/Junior/Alfred/Oliver," Tiffany & Co **$200.00**

Ballpoint Pen, #925, blue ink, wing-etched design, made in Germany, Tiffany & Co **45.00**

Bookmark, figural leaf, 3⅛" l **30.00**

Bowl, "VCD" monogram on front, mkd "Tiffany & Co Makers Sterling Silver 925-1000," 2½" h, 5¼" d, approx 8.3904 troy oz **125.00**

Bud Vase, trumpet form, elongated neck, spherical form body, mkd "Tiffany & Co 23635" **100.00**

Card Tray, ornate script in center, 6⅛ x 4", approx 3.5 troy oz **65.00**

Flatware Set, 12 pcs, Flemish pattern, 2 knives, two 7" forks, four 7¼" forks, 4 soup spoons, no monogram, mkd "Sterling, Pat 1911" **550.00**

Kiddush Beaker, c1920, 3¾" h, 2⅞" d **150.00**

Ladle, Flemish pattern, back of handle mkd "Tiffany & Co, Sterling, Pat 1911, M," 2 x 2⅜" bowl, 7¼" l, approx 3.52 troy oz **100.00**

Necklace, 46 beads strung on sterling chain, tag mkd "Tiffany & Co" on front, "925" on reverse, 18" l **80.00**

Nutcracker, Chrysanthemum pattern, 5½" l, approx 8 troy oz **550.00**

Salt Dip, mkd "Tiffany & Co 25005," 1½ x 1½" **50.00**

TIFFIN GLASS

J. Beatty and Sons built a large glass works in Tiffin, Ohio, in 1888. In 1892 Tiffin Glass Company became part of the U.S. Glass Company, a combine based in Pittsburgh, Pennsylvania.

During the Depression, Tiffin made hundreds of patterns, its output twice that of Cambridge and A. H. Heisey. Tiffin purchased Heisey blanks to meet its production requirements. The company's famed "Lady Stems" were made between 1939 and 1956.

Tiffin's profits carried many other plants in the U.S. Glass Company. Several plants making inexpensive glassware were closed or sold during the Depression. By 1951 Tiffin was the only U.S. Glass plant remaining in operation. U.S. Glass Company purchased Duncan & Miller in 1955. In 1962 U.S. Glass declared bankruptcy and closed the Tiffin factory.

Production resumed under the name "Tiffin Art Glass Corporation," a firm created by former Tiffin employees. Tiffin Art Glass produced high quality, etched stemware and glass accent pieces. The company also offered a pattern matching program, annually manufacturing retired patterns.

Tiffin purchased the molds and equipment of the T. G. Hawkes Cut Glass Company, Corning, New York, in 1964. Continental Can purchased the Tiffin factory in 1966, selling it in 1968 to the Interpace Corporation, a holding company of Franciscan china. Tiffin was sold once again in 1980, this time to Towle Silversmiths. Towle began importing blanks from Eastern Europe. In 1984 Towle closed the Tiffin factory and donated the land and buildings to the city of Tiffin. Jim Maxwell, a former Tiffin glass cutter, bought the Tiffin molds and equipment. The Tiffin trademark is now a registered trademark of Maxwell Crystal, Inc. In 1992 Maxwell placed four Hawkes and Tiffin patterns back into production.

References: Fred Bickenheuser, *Tiffin Glassmasters, Book I* (1979, 1994-95 value update), *Book II* (1981, 1994-95 value update), *Book III* (1985), Glassmasters Publications; Ed Goshe, Ruth Hemminger and Leslie Piña, *'40s, '50s & '60s Stemware by Tiffin*, Schiffer Publishing, 1999; Ed Goshe, Ruth Hemminger and Leslie Piña, *Depression Era Stems & Tableware: Tiffin*, Schiffer Publishing, 1998; Ruth Hemminger, Ed Goshe and Leslie Piña, *Tiffin Modern: Mid-Century Art Glass*, Schiffer Publishing, 1997; Kelly O'Kane, *Tiffin Glassmasters: The Modern Years*, published by author, 1998; Bob Page and Dale Fredericksen, *Tiffin Is Forever: A Stemware Identification Guide*, Page-Fredericksen, 1994; Leslie Piña, *Tiffin Glass: 1914-1940*, Schiffer Publishing, 1997; Harry L. Rinker, *Stemware of the 20th Century: The Top 200 Patterns*, House of Collectibles, 1997.

Collectors' Club: Tiffin Glass Collectors' Club, PO Box 554, Tiffin, OH 44883.

Byzantine, cocktail, #15048, yellow **$15.00**
Byzantine, cocktail, crystal **15.00**
Byzantine, decanter, yellow **600.00**
Byzantine, juice tumbler, crystal **15.00**
Byzantine, low sherbet, crystal **12.00**
Byzantine, plate, crystal, 8½" d **5.00**

Classic, wine, 4¹⁵/₁₆" h, $30.00.

Byzantine, plate, yellow, 7" d 15.00
Cadena, cordial, topaz 80.00
Cadena, decanter, #185, yellow 450.00
Cadena, low sherbet, topaz 15.00
Cadena, wine, topaz 35.00
Carmel, cereal canister, screw lid, 48 oz 725.00
Cherokee Rose, claret, #17399 . . . . 50.00
Cherokee Rose, low sherbet, #17403 . . . . 20.00
Cherokee Rose, saucer champagne, #17399 . . . . 25.00
Cherokee Rose, sherbet, #17403 . . . . 20.00
Cherokee Rose, sherry, #17399 . . . . 40.00
Cherokee Rose, water goblet, #17399, 9 oz 30.00
Cherokee Rose, water goblet, 9 oz 30.00
Classic, bud vase, crystal, 10½" h 65.00
Classic, decanter, #14179, crystal 500.00
Classic, pitcher, flat, crystal 225.00
Cordelia, cocktail, crystal 10.00
Cordelia, sherbet, crystal, 3" h 8.00
Flanders, champagne, crystal 15.00
Flanders, console bowl, pink 275.00
Flanders, creamer, flat, pink 225.00
Flanders, cup and saucer, crystal 45.00
Flanders, cup and saucer, yellow 100.00
Flanders, decanter, #185, yellow 500.00
Flanders, goblet, pink, with pink stem, 7" h 75.00
Flanders, pitcher, ftd, pink, 64 oz 500.00
Flanders, plate, pink, 8¼" 20.00
Flanders, stemmed compote, blown, pink 750.00
Flanders, tray, center handle, pink 300.00
Flanders, water goblet, pink 75.00
Fuchsia, bud vase, 6½" h 30.00
Fucshia, champagne, crystal 18.00
Fuchsia, cocktail, crystal 18.00
Fuchsia, console bowl, flared, 12⅝" d 135.00
Fuchsia, cordial, 1 oz 80.00
Fuchsia, cordial, crystal 55.00
Fuchsia, low sherbet, crystal 18.00
Fuchsia, parfait, 5¹⁵/₁₆" h 35.00
Fuchsia, saucer champagne 18.00
Fuchsia, sherbet 18.00
Fucshia, tumbler, 12 oz, 6⁵/₁₆" h 30.00
Fucshia, water goblet, 7½" h 25.00

Fuchsia, water goblet, crystal 20.00
Fuchsia, wine, 5¹/₁₆" h 35.00
Fuchsia, wine, #15083, 5¹/₁₆" h 30.00
Fucshia, wine, crystal 45.00
June Night, claret, 6¼" h 40.00
June Night, cordial, 5¼" h 60.00
June Night, iced tea tumbler, 6⅝" h 35.00
June Night, juice tumbler, 5¼" h 25.00
June Night, parfait, 6⅝" h 60.00
June Night, plate, crystal, 8" d 12.00
June Night, sherbet, crystal 15.00
June Night, sherry, crystal 40.00
June Night, water goblet, 7⅞" h 30.00
June Night, water goblet, crystal 25.00
King's Crown, candy dish, cov, flat 100.00
King's Crown, compote, 12" d 150.00
King's Crown, creamer and sugar 35.00
King's Crown, crimped bowl, cranberry flashed, 4½" h,
   11½" d 125.00
King's Crown, oil lamp, no hardware, 5½" h 100.00
King's Crown, ruffled bowl, 11½ d" 225.00
King's Crown, salad bowl, 9¼" d 85.00
King's Crown, tidbit, ruffled, pedestal base 225.00
King's Crown, tumbler, cranberry flashed, 13 oz, 5½" h 20.00
King's Crown, wine, cobalt 15.00
King's Crown, wine, cranberry flashed, 2 oz 8.00
Le Fleur, pitcher, cov, yellow 650.00
Persian Pheasant, cordial, crystal 45.00
Persian Pheasant, sherbet, crystal 20.00
Twilight, soda, #17501, ftd, 10 oz 20.00
Twilight, cocktail, #17507 . . . . 25.00

TONKA

Mound Metalcraft, located on the banks of Lake Minnetonka in Mound, Minnesota, was incorporated in September 1946 to manufacture garden tools and household products. Absorbing the toy business of L. E. Streeter Company, Tonka introduced two pressed steel toys at the 1947 New York Toy Fair. By 1949 the line included fourteen different products including a doll hospital bed.

In 1956 Mound Metalcraft changed its name to Tonka and introduced its line of Hi-Way trucks. Tonka gained a reputation for producing nicely designed, realistic-looking vehicles.

In 1961 Tonka purchased a plastics company and began producing plastic accessories for its vehicles. Tonka acquired Kenner in 1988. Hasbro purchased the combined company in 1991.

The year 1963 is the major divider between younger and older Tonka collectors. Restoration of early examples is common and often unreported by the seller. Beware.

Reference: Don and Barb DeSalle, *Tonka Trucks: 1947-1963*, L-W Book Sales, 1994, 1999 value update.

Note: Prices listed are for vehicles in mint condition and mint in box sets.

Air Force Ambulance, #402, 1966 . . . . $275.00
Allied Van Lines, #400, 1953 . . . . 300.00
Army Tractor, #250, 1964 . . . . 150.00
Army Troop Carrier, #380, 1964 . . . . 175.00
Blue Pickup, #02, 1957 . . . . 325.00
Bulldozer, #300, 1963 . . . . 100.00
Doughboy Feeds Stake Truck, 1961 . . . . 400.00

Green Giant Brands Truck, pressed steel, rubber tires, 24" l, $175.00. Photo courtesy Collectors Auction Services.

Dump Truck with Sandloader, #616, 1963	175.00
Eibert Coffee Metro Van, 1954	600.00
Gambles Pickup, 1960	225.00
Giant Dozer, #118, 1961	225.00
Golf Club Tractor, #101, 1961	225.00
Hydraulic Dump Truck, #520, 1962	150.00
Jeep Wrecker, #375, 1964	200.00
Pickup with Camper, #530, 1963	250.00
Platform Stake Truck, #03, 1958	350.00
Powerlift Truck and Trailer, #200, 1948	400.00
Ramp Hoist, #640, 1963	500.00
RCD Fast Freight Semi, 1954	850.00
Set, Aerial Sandloader, #825-5, dump truck and aerial sandloader, 1955	700.00
Set, Builders Supply Fleet, #875-6, lumber truck with load, red pickup, and stake truck bed, 1956	1,500.00
Set, Construction, #2190, cement mixer, dump truck, bulldozer, 11-wheel spread pack, and dozer loader, 1962	600.00
Set, Hi-Way Construction, #B207, lime green, dump truck, equipment trailer, drag line, and road grader, 1959	1,250.00
Set, Outdoor Living, #2140, jeep surry, jeep runabout with 4 suitcases, Tonka clipper, and camper, 1963	550.00
Set, Paving Department, #B218, dump truck, #100 dozer, cement truck, road grader, and 2 signs, 1960	850.00
Set, Sanitary Service, #B203, sanitary truck, 2 refuse containers, and scoop, 1959	1,250.00
Set, Super Service, #2130, wrecker, jeep, ser-vi-car, stake trailer, and box trailer, 1962	500.00
Set, Timber Company, #B201, power boom loader, timber truck, 4 logs, and 4 beams, 1960	1,750.00
Set, Tonka Farm, #B202, stock rack truck, wood corral, and 6 animals	850.00
Set, Tonka Trailer Fleet, #675, red cab, blue cab, carryall trailer, grain hauler trailer, livestock van, log trailer, and steel carrier, 1953	1,000.00
Set, Tonka Truck–Trailer Rental, #B204, pickup, stake truck, box trailer, and stake trailer, 1957	700.00
Set, Trailer Sales, #B206, pickup, sportsman, horse trailer, stake trailer, box trailer, and boat with trailer, 1961	650.00
Standard Tanker, 1961	700.00
Stock Rack Farm Truck, #32, 1957	550.00
Suburban Pumper, #46, 1958	225.00
Swanson Bros Moving Van, 1963	700.00
Tonka Air Lines, 1963	350.00
Tonka Cargo King, #30, 1956	250.00
Tonka Freighter, 1956	225.00
Tonka Marine Service, #41, 1960	500.00
Tonka Service Van, #103, 1961	200.00
Utility Dump, #301, 1962	250.00
Wheaton Van Lines Semi, 1959	600.00

TOOLS

From the 1920s through the end of the 1950s, the basement workshop was a standard fixture in many homes. Manufacturers quickly developed hand and machine tools for this specific market. The do-it-yourself, fix-it-yourself attitude of the late 1940s through the 1960s resulted in strong tool sales.

Tool collectors collect primarily by brand or tool type. Most focus on tools made before 1940. Quality is critical. Most collectors want nothing to do with cheap foreign imports. Interest is building in power tools and some specialized tool groups, e.g., Snap-on Tools.

References: Ronald S. Barlow, *The Anique Tool Collector's Guide to Value*, L-W Book Sales, 1999; Herbert P. Kean and Emil S. Pollak, *A Price Guide to Antique Tools, 2nd Edition*, Astragal Press, 1998; Herbert P. Kean and Emil S. Pollak, *Collecting Antique Tools*, Astragal Press, 1990; Kathryn McNerney, *Antique Tools*, Collector Books, 1979, 1998 value update; Emil and Martyl Pollak, *A Guide to American Wooden Planes and Their Makers, Third Edition*, Astragal Press, 1994; R. A. Salaman, *Dictionary of Tools*, Charles Scribner's Sons, 1974; John Walter, *Antique & Collectible Stanley Tools, Second Edition*, Tool Merchants, 1996; Jack P. Wood, *Early 20th Century Stanley Tools*, catalog reprint, L-W Book Sales, 1996 value update; Jack P. Wood, *Town-Country Old Tools and Locks, Keys and Closures*, L-W Books, 1990, 1999 value update.

Collectors' Clubs: Early American Industries Assoc, 167 Bakersville Rd, South Dartmouth, MA 02748; Tool Group of Canada, 7 Tottenham Rd, Don Mills, Ontario MC3 2J3 Canada.

Basin Wrench, "Andree," patented May 10, 1921, 8" l	$30.00
Bell Faced Claw Hammer, Stanley, c1920s, 13" l	50.00
Bench Rule, Simplified Rule Co, Philadelphia, PA, stainless steel, patented July 28, 1931, 6" l	12.00
Bench Vise, Stanley #753, cast iron, 2" steel jaws, stationary base, 1920s	40.00
Bull Nose Rabbet Plane, Stanley #75, cast iron, 4" l	40.00
Cabinet Scraper, Stanley #82, cast iron, maroon hardwood handle, post 1942, 14½" l	25.00
Carpenter's Rule, Stanley #61, lacquered boxwood with brass trim, 4-fold, 2' l	15.00
Combination Square, LS Starrett Co, Athol, MA, c1920s, 12" l	100.00
Defiance Bit Brace, Stanley #1253, iron, red-lacquered hardwood handles, 12" l	12.00
Defiance Smooth Plane, Stanley #1204, cast iron, red-lacquered hardwood handle, 9" l	12.00
Double Cutter Spoke Shave, Stanley #60, cast iron, 1920s, 11" l	75.00

Draw Knife, Montgomery Ward, "Lakeside Quality,"
   1920s, 8" l blade, 12½" l overall **35.00**
Flow Rule Slide Rule, Foxboro Co, Foxboro, MA, for
   pipe calculations, orig box, late 1940s, 12½" l **300.00**
Hand Drill, Millers Falls Co #77A, gear-driven, orig car-
   ton, unused, 1930s, 12½" l **55.00**
Hand Drill, Peck, Stow & Wilcox Co #517, hollow han-
   dle, gear-driven, orig box, c1950s, 12" l **35.00**
Hande Nut Wrench, H&E Wrench Co, New Bedford,
   MA, patented Sep 20, 1921, 10" l **45.00**
Pivot Head Nut Wrench, Any Angle Wrench Co, Lima,
   OH, with push-button release, patented 1916, 8" l **55.00**
Rabbet Plane, Stanley #190, cast iron, 8" l **40.00**
Right Angle Ratchet Screwdriver, Goodell-Pratt Co #668,
   for use in tight spaces, orig box, patented Sep 16,
   1925, 4" l **75.00**
Screwdriver, Stanley #31, "Baby Hurwood," nickeled
   steel shank, hardwood handle, 1930s, 4⅛" l **10.00**
Seattle Quick Adjust Pipe Wrench, Becklin Wrench Co,
   patented Mar 16, 1920, 14" l **225.00**
Self-Adjusting Pipe Wrench, Hoe Corp, Poughkeepsie,
   NY, pivoting head, patented Feb 21, 1922, 6" l **60.00**
Slide Adjust Pipe Wrench, H&E Wrench Co, New
   Bedford, MA, patented Mar 27, 1923, 13" l **170.00**
Smooth Plane, Stanley #2, cast iron, rosewood handle
   and knob, 7" l **370.00**
Tape Measure, Stanley #1266, nickel plated steel,
   1940s, 6' l **18.00**
Wakco Weight Slide Rule, Warren-Knight Co,
   Philadelphia, PA, #1373-C, for large weights calcula-
   tions, with orig instructions, dated 1951, 12½" l **165.00**
Wedge Bench Clamp, Self-Adjusting Clamp Co,
   Westfield, NJ, cast iron, patented Oct 28, 1919, 12" l **35.00**
Wrench, US Wrench Co, Philadelphia, PA, "Bohn
   Quickfit," nickel plated, patented 1924, 5½" l **45.00**

TOOTHPICK HOLDERS

When is a toothpick holder not a toothpick holder? When it is a
match holder, miniature spoon holder for a toy table setting, a salt
shaker with a ground-off top, a small rose bowl, shot glass, an individual open sugar, a vase, or a whimsy. A toothpick is designed to
hold toothpicks. Toothpicks have a flat bottom and allow enough
of the toothpick to extend above the top so one can be extracted
with no problem. If the toothpicks do not extend above the top or
stand erect, chances are the object is not a toothpick holder.

References: Neila Bredehoft, et al., *Glass Toothpick Holders*,
Collector Books, 1999; William Heacock, *Encyclopedia of
Victorian Colored Pattern Glass, Book 1, Toothpick Holders From
A to Z, Second Edition*, Antique Publications, 1976, 1992 value
update; National Toothpick Holders Collectors Society, *Toothpick
Holders: China, Glass, and Metal*, Antique Publications, 1992.

Collector's Club: National Toothpick Holders Collectors Society,
PO Box 417, Safety Harbor, FL 34695.

Bone China, Japan, Santa head, 2" h **$3.00**
Carnival Glass, Imperial, red and gold, orig paper label,
   2½" h **10.00**
Carnival Glass, vaseline, holly berry vine and leaf
   around middle, 3 beaded rows on rim, middle, and
   bottom, 2⅜" h **18.00**

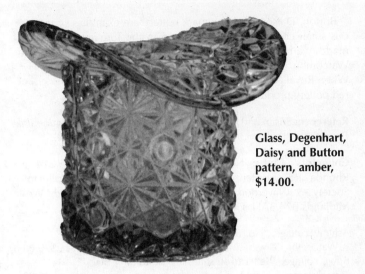

Glass, Degenhart, Daisy and Button pattern, amber, $14.00.

Ceramic, Japan, flamingo, base mkd "Florida," 3⅛" h **10.00**
Ceramic, Occupied Japan, colonial couple, 1½" h **15.00**
Ceramic, Occupied Japan, man playing violin, 3½" h **10.00**
Ceramic, Occupied Japan, vase, raised Dragonware
   style, 3" h **20.00**
Glass, Boyd, daisy pattern, cobalt blue, 2½" h **5.00**
Glass, Daisy & Button, ftd, 2¾" h **3.00**
Glass, Degenhart, floral design around edges, persim-
   mon, 2½" h **10.00**
Glass, Fenton, green frosted, 3¾" h **20.00**
Glass, Fire-King, figural mug, ruby stained, 2" h **8.00**
Glass, Imperial, End Of Day, cornucopia on pedestal,
   2½" h **10.00**
Glass, Moon & Star, amber, 2" h **15.00**
Porcelain, Enesco, dog standing atop brown and black
   boot, "Enesco Japan" foil label, 2½" h, 3" w **8.00**
Porcelain, Japan, bear cub with beehive, mkd "T-1554
   Japan," 3½" h, 2½" w **3.00**
Porcelain, Japan, kitten and yellow hat, mkd "T-1554
   Japan," 3½" h, 2½" w **3.00**
Pressed Glass, eagles and stars, green, 2½" h **18.00**
Sterling Silver, urn, flattened rim, 2" h **10.00**
Stoneware, figural swan, 2¾" h **10.00**

TORQUAY POTTERY

Pottery manufacturing came to the Torquay district of South
Devon, England, in the 1870s following G. J. Allen's discovery of
a red terra-cotta potting clay in 1869. Allen organized the
Watcombe Pottery, producing a wealth of art pottery terra-cotta
products.

In 1875 Dr. Gillow founded the Torquay Terra-Cotta Company.
Its products were similar to those of Watcombe Pottery. It closed in
1905, only to be reopened by Enoch Staddon in 1908. Staddon
produced pottery rather than terra-cotta ware.

John Philips established the Aller Vale Pottery in 1881. The company specialized in souvenir pieces. Designs were painted on
pieces with a thick colored slip that contrasted with the color of
the ground slip coat. This "motto" ware achieved widespread popularity by 1900. In 1902 Aller Vale and Watcombe merged and
became Royal Aller Vale and Watcombe Art Potteries. The new
company produced commemorative and motto ware.

Burton, Daison, and Longpark pottery are examples of numerous small companies that sprang up in the Torquay District and made wares similar to those produced by Aller Vale and Watcombe. Longpark, the last of these companies, closed in 1957. When Royal Aller Vale and Watcombe closed in 1962, the era of red pottery production in Torquay ended.

Reference: Susan and Al Bagdade, *Warman's English & Continental Pottery & Porcelain, 3rd Edition,* Krause Publications, 1998.

Collectors' Clubs: North American Torquay Society, 214 N Rhonda Rd, McHenry, IL 60050; Torquay Pottery Collectors Society, 5 Claverdon Dr, Little Aston, Sutton Coldfield, West Midlands B74 3AH, UK.

Ashtray, cottage, "No road is long with good company," Watcombe, 5" w	**$20.00**
Bowl, cottage, "Better to sit still than rise to fall," black backstamp, 3³/₄" w, 1³/₈" h	**30.00**
Candleholder, cottage, "A safe conscience makes a sound sleep," 2³/₄" h, 4" d	**100.00**
Creamer, cottage, "Plymouth #2" and "Du'ee elp yerzel," Watcombe, 3" h, 3" d	**25.00**
Creamer, sailboat and seagulls, "Mousehole" on 1 side, "Fresh milk today" on other side, Wattcombe	**10.00**
Dish, "Do not stain today's blue sky with tomorrow's clouds," Watcombe, 6¹/₂" l	**40.00**
Dish, "Kind words are the music of the world," 6¹/₄" d	**65.00**
Jug, seagulls flying over waves, "Torquay"	**15.00**
Jug, thistle, "The deils aye kind tae his ain," Longpark, 1926-37, 3¹/₂" h, 2³/₄" d	**30.00**
Match Holder, slip ware design with motto "Match for any man," 3¹/₂" h	**75.00**
Mug, "Say little but think much," Babbacombe	**20.00**
Mustard Pot, cov, seagull, "Teignmouth," 3³/₄" h	**30.00**
Perfume Bottle, "W Toogood's Ltd Dovon Violets Perfume London England," pinched sides, 2¹/₂" h	**35.00**
Pin Tray, cottage, "Put a stout heart to a steep hill," 3¹/₄ x 5¹/₄"	**45.00**
Teapot, "Daunt'ee put yerzel out a tha way"	**30.00**
Teapot, Niagara Falls and "Down your sorrows in a cup of tea," 3³/₄" h, 6¹/₂" w	**50.00**
Teapot, "Unless the Kettle Boiling B, Filling the teapot spoils the T"	**55.00**

Cheese Dish, cottage, "Cheese" on cover, 4" h, 6" l, $50.00.

TOYS

Toys drive the 20th-century collectibles market. The standards for condition, scarcity, and desirability established by the toy community are now being applied throughout the antiques marketplace.

The toy market of the 1990s is highly sophisticated. In fact, some question if there is a single toy market any longer. Many categories within the toy market have broken away and become independent collecting categories. This category covers manufacturers and toy types still located within the general toy category.

Currently, the post-1945 period is the hot period among toy collectors. Prices for pre-1920 cast-iron and penny toys are stable and, in some cases, in decline. Pressed steel dominates vehicle collecting with a small cadre of collectors beginning to look at plastic. Diecast toys, the darlings of the 1970s and 80s, have lost some of their luster. Vehicles remain the toy of choice among collectors aged thirty-five and above. Young collectors focus on action figures and licensed toys.

With so many toys of the post-1945 era of Far Eastern origin, the national collecting prejudice for toys made in one's own country has diminished. What it is rather than where it was made is the key today. One result is a lowering of quality standards for more recently issued toys. The pre-1960s toy market remains heavily quality-driven.

The contemporary toy market is cursed by two groups of individuals—toy speculators and toy scalpers—whose activities badly distort pricing reality. Toy speculators hoard toys, thus upsetting the traditional supply and demand cycle. Toy scalpers created artificial shortages for modern toys. They accept no financial or moral responsibility for their actions when the speculative bubble they created bursts. And, it always does.

References: General: Sharon and Bob Huxford (eds.), *Schroeder's Collectible Toys: Antique to Modern Price Guide, Sixth Edition,* Collector Books, 1999; Sharon Korbeck and Elizabeth A. Stephan (eds.), *2000 Toys & Prices, 7th Edition,* Krause Publications, 1999; Elizabeth Stephan (ed.), *O'Brien's Collecting Toys, 9th Edition,* Krause Publications, 1999.

Generational: Ronald S. Barlow (ed.), *The Great American Antique Toy Bazaar, 1879-1945: 5,000 Old Engravings from Original Trade Catalogs,* Windmill Publishing, 1998; Tom Frey, *Toy Bop: Kid Classics of the 50's & 60's,* Fuzzy Dice Productions, 1994; March Rich, *100 Greatest Baby Boomer Toys,* Krause Publications, 2000; Carol Turpen, *Baby Boomer Toys and Collectibles, Second Edition,* Schiffer Publishing, 1998.

Juvenile: *Price Guide to Pull Toys,* L-W Book Sales, 1996; *Tops and Yo-Yos and Other Spinning Toys,* L-W Book Sales, 1995.

Lithograph Tin: Alan Jaffe, *J. Chein & Co.,* Schiffer Publishing, 1997; Lisa Kerr, *American Tin-Litho Toys,* Collectors Press, 1995; Lisa Kerr, *Ohio Art: The World of Toys,* Schiffer Publishing, 1998; Maxine A. Pinsky, *Greenberg's Guide to Marx Toys, Vol. I* (1988) and *Vol. II* (1990), Greenberg Publishing.

Miscellaneous: Jose E. Alvarez, *The Unofficial Guide to Transformers: 1980s Through 1990s,* Schiffer Publishing, 1999; Robert E. Birkenes, *White Knob Windup Collectible Toys,* Schiffer Publishing, 1998; Raymond V. Brandes, *Big Bang Cannons,* Ray-Vin Publishing, 1993; Christopher Cook, *Collectible American Yo-Yos, 1920s-1970s,* Collector Books, 1997; Patty Cooper and Dian Zillner, *Toy Buildings: 1880-1980,* Schiffer Publishing, 2000; James L. Dundas, *Collecting Yo-Yos,* Schiffer Publishing, 2000; James L. Dundas, *Toys That Shoot and Other Neat Stuff,* Schiffer Publishing,

1998; David Gould and Donna Crevar-Donaldson, *Occupied Japan Toys With Prices,* L-W Book Sales, 1993; Morton A. Hirschberg, *Steamtoys,* Schiffer Publishing, 1996; Jay Horowitz, *Marx Western Playsets,* Greenberg Publishing, 1992; Don Hultzman, *Collector's Guide to Battery Toys,* Collector Books, 1998; Charles M. Jacobs, *Kenton Cast Iron Toys,* Schiffer Publishing, 1996; Kathy and Don Lewis, *Talking Toys of the 20th Century,* Collector Books, 1999; L. H. MacKenzie, *Squeaky Toys,* Schiffer Publishing, 1998; Anthony Marsella, *Toys From Occupied Japan,* Schiffer Publishing, 1995; Jack Matthews, *Toys Go to War: World War II Military Toys, Games, Puzzles & Books,* Pictorial Histories Publishing, 1994; Albert W. McCollough, *The New Book of Buddy "L" Toys, Vol. I* (1991), *Vol. II* (1991), Greenberg Publishing; Brian Moran, *Battery Toys, 2nd Edition,* Schiffer Publishing, 1999; Harry A. and Joyce A. Whitworth, *G-Men and FBI Toys and Collectibles,* Collector Books, 1998.

Plastic: Bill Hanlon, *Plastic Toys: Dimestore Dreams of the '40s & '50s,* Schiffer Publishing, 1993.

Vehicles: Rich Bertoia, *Antique Motorcycle Toys,* Schiffer Publishing, 1999; Don and Barb DeSalle, *The DeSalle Collection of Smith-Miller & Doepke Trucks,* L-W Book Sales, 1997; Charles F. Donovan, Jr., *Renwal, World's Finest Toys: Vol. 2, Transportation Toys & Accessories,* published by author, 1996; Edward Force, *Corgi Toys,* Schiffer Publishing, 1984, 1997 value update; Edward Force, *Dinky Toys, 4th Edition,* Schiffer Publishing, 1999; Edward Force, *Solido Toys,* Schiffer Publishing, 1993; Sally Gibson-Downs and Christine Gentry, *Motorcycle Toys,* Collector Books, 1995.

Kurt Guile, Mike Willyard and Gary Konow, *Wyandotte Toys Are Good and Safe: 1920-1957,* Wyandotte Toys Publishing, 1996; Ken Hutchison and Greg Johnson, *The Golden Age of Automotive Toys: 1925-1941,* Collector Books, 1996; Dana Johnson, *Collector's Guide to Diecast Toys & Scale Models, 2nd Edition,* Collector Books, 1998; Douglas P. Kelly, *The Die Cast Price Guide Post-War: 1946 to Present,* Antique Trader Books, 1997; Bill Manzke, *The Unauthorized Encyclopedia of Corgi Toys,* Schiffer Publishing, 1997; Kurt M. Resch, *A World of Bus Toys and Models,* Schiffer Publishing, 1999; David Richter, *Collector's Guide to Tootsietoys, Second Edition,* Collector Books, 1996; Elizabeth Stephan (ed.), *O'Brien's Collecting Toy Cars & Trucks, 3rd Edition,* Krause Publications, 2000; Gerhard G. Walter, *Tin Dream Machines: German Tin Toy Cars and Motorcycles of the 1950s and 1960s,* New Cavendish, 1998.

Periodicals: *Antique Toy World,* PO Box 34509, Chicago, IL 60634; *Master Collector,* 225 Cattle Baron Parc Dr, Fort Worth, TX 76108; *Toy Shop,* 700 E State St, Iola, WI 54490; *Toy Cars & Vehicles,* 700 E State St, Iola, WI 54990; *Toy Trader,* PO Box 1050, Dubuque, IA 52004.

Collectors' Clubs: Antique Toy Collectors of America, Two Wall St, 13th Flr, New York, NY 10005; Canadian Toy Collectors Society, 91 Rylander Blvd, Unit 7, Ste 245, Scarborough, Ontario M1B 5M5 Canada.

Maloney's Antiques & Collectibles Resource Directory by David J. Maloney, Jr., lists many collectors' clubs for specific types of toys. Check your local library for the most recent edition.

Note: For additional toy listings see Action Figures, Barbie, Bicycles, Breyer Horses, Cap Guns, Cartoon Characters, Coloring Books, Construction Toys, Cowboy Heroes, Disneyana, Dolls, Ertl, Farm Toys, Fisher-Price, Games, GI Joe, Hanna-Barbera, Hess

Trucks, Hot Wheels, Matchbox, Model Kits, Monsters, Occupied Japan, Paint By Number Sets, Paper Dolls, Pedal Cars, Premiums, Puppets, Puzzles, Radio Characters and Personalities, Robots, Sand Pails, Sizzlers, Slot Cars, Space Adventurers, Space Toys, Star Trek, Star Wars, Steiff, Stuffed Toys, Super Heroes, Teddy Bears, Television Characters & Personalities, Tonka, Toy Soldiers, Toy Train Accessories, Toy Trains, View-Master, and Warner Brothers.

AC Gilbert, Stutz Bearcat, windup, litho tin, 9½" l **$1,250.00**

Alps, Arthur A-Go-Go Drummer, battery operated, cloth and vinyl, bangs tune using animated arms, body sways, orig box, 9½" h 350.00

Alps, Bozo Clown Drummer, windup, litho tin, beats tune on drums while shaking head and body side to side, 1950s, 8" h 225.00

Alps, Busy Housekeeper Bear, battery operated, plush bear, moves forward and back, turns head while vacuuming, orig box, 8½" h 300.00

Alps, Charlie Drumming Clown, battery operated, litho tin, plastic, and cloth, clown hits snare drums and small cymbal with drumstick while playing with his feet, head moves and nose lights up, orig box, 10" h 250.00

Alps, Fishing Polar Bear, battery operated, plush bear on litho tin base, lifts pole out of pond with fish on line, reaches down, grabs fish, puts fish in basket and laughs with lighted eyes, orig box, 10½" h 350.00

Alps, Frankie the Roller Skating Monkey, battery operated, remote control, plush, skates forward and reverse, orig box, 12" h 115.00

Alps, Little Baseball Player, windup, hard vinyl, wearing red, white, and blue uniform with orange accents, vibrates as its head moves up and down, 1960s, 2 x 2½ x 5½" box 35.00

Alps, Mechanical Turkey, windup, litho tin, plush, and plastic, advances with strutting stride, lifts head, simulated turkey sounds, orig box, 7" h 115.00

Alps, Bunny the Magician, battery operated, 5 actions, 1950s, 14½" h, $300.00.

Asahi, Japan, race car, battery operated, 8¹/₂" l, $85.00.

Alps, Monkey on a Picnic, battery operated, plush monkey on litho tin base, eats banana and drinks from can of soda, leans backward, squeaks and pats stomach until he begins eating again, orig box, 9" h **350.00**

Arcade, Ford Model T Coupe, cast iron, black, gold accents, white tires, 1920s, 2¹/₂ x 6¹/₂ x 3³/₄" **200.00**

Arnold, US Zone Germany, Motorcycle Rider, litho tin, sparkling headlight, orig box, 1940s, 7¹/₂" l **600.00**

Arnold, US Zone Germany, Santa Claus, windup, litho tin, orig box, 4" h **725.00**

Asahi, Japan, Rescue Helicopter, windup, litho tin, red body, pink celluloid blades, repeated "Rescue" name on sides, with key, 1950s, 5³/₄" l **50.00**

ATC, Japan, 1962 Chevy, friction, black rubber tires, 1960s, 11³/₄" l **950.00**

ATC, Japan, Lucky Car, windup, litho tin, black rubber tires, wheels set for turning only, bell rings, 1950s, 6¹/₂" l **125.00**

Avalon, Roy Rogers Paint By Number Oil Painting Set, complete with 2 paintings, 12 paint vials, orig box **300.00**

Bandai, 1960 Cadillac, friction, enamel body, litho tin int, black rubber tires, 11¹/₄" l. **150.00**

Bandai, Buick, battery operated, litho tin, green, silver bumpers, headlights, and hood ornaments, 1950s, orig box, 2¹/₂ x 6 x 2". **50.00**

Bandai, Ferrari, friction, litho tin, plastic steering wheel, 1950s, 3 x 8 x 1³/₄ **75.00**

Bandai, Ford Thunderbird, friction, litho tin, convertible, cream, black, white, red, and yellow int, clear plastic windshield, steering wheel, litho tin "Thunderbird" license plate, 1959, 3 x 8 x 2" **75.00**

Bandai, MG Car, friction, enamel finish, black rubber tires, orig box, 1950s, 10¹/₂" l **350.00**

Bandai, Vespa Silver Pigeon, friction, enamel over tin, 1950s, 9¹/₂" l **350.00**

Buddy L, Greyhound Bus, pressed steel, blue and white, large scale, clockwork mechanism **275.00**

Buddy L, Texaco Gasoline Tanker, pressed steel, hollow vinyl wheels, hard plastic grille, Texaco decal on sides with "Tour With Texaco/Sound Your Horn/The Road Is Yours," 1960s, 5 x 24 x 6¹/₂". **75.00**

Chein, Beach Toy Set, litho tin, colorful animal molds, sifter, and shovel, with orig sieve, 8¹/₂ x 11" **225.00**

Chein, Three Little Pigs Washer, litho tin, complete with wringer and pedestal feet base, 8" h **350.00**

CK, Japan, Magic Boat, celluloid, green, yellow, black, and pink, with flag and cannon attachments, orig box, 1¹/₂ x 2¹/₄ x 1¹/₄". **25.00**

Corgi, Bentley Continental, model 224-1, 1/43 scale, cream over pale green, 1961 . . . . **30.00**

Cragstan, Beach Buggy with Surfboard, battery operated, plastic buggy with visible engine, advances with bump-n-go action, blinking lights, surfboard, rocking body, orig box, 11" l **200.00**

Cragstan, Ford Thunderbird, battery operated, remote control, litho tin dash, top retracts into trunk, orig box, 11¹/₄" l **200.00**

Cragstan, US Military Vehicle Set, litho tin, includes tank, ambulance, cargo truck, officers' car, jeep, and cannon, orig box, 7¹/₂ x 13¹/₂". **250.00**

Daiya, Japan, turtle, windup, litho tin head and shell, black hard plastic underside, walks in circles as head moves side to side, flips over, 1960s, orig box, ¹/₂ x 6 x 2¹/₄" **15.00**

Dayton Toys, Mickey Mouse Wagon, steel construction, black rubber tires, 1930s, 22¹/₂" l **700.00**

Dinky, Atlantean Bus, diecast metal, double decker bus with "BP" decals on sides, black rubber wheels **25.00**

Dinky, Jaguar SS, model 38f-2, 1/43 scale, blue, gray int. **45.00**

Distler, US Zone Germany, 1953 Packard Convertible, windup, litho tin dash, black rubber tires, nickel trim, 3-speeds forward, 1 reverse, 1940-50s, 10¹/₂" l **225.00**

DTC, Japan, Very Important Person Car, friction, litho tin int and people, black rubber tires, man stands and waves his hat, orig box, 7³/₈" l **175.00**

Germany, Bomber Airplane, litho tin, clockwork mechanism, lead cap bombs drop from wings when activated, painted olive green, wings read "D-O LAF" with image of swastika on tail fin, composition figure seated in cockpit, 14¹/₂" wingspan **750.00**

Germany, Powerful Katrinka, windup, litho tin, wheelbarrow raises and lowers as Katrinka moves forward, 1920-30, 5¹/₂" h **1,500.00**

Germany, Snake, windup, painted wood body, travels forward as front half moves back and forth, tail segment wiggles back and forth, 1920s, 13" l **75.00**

Girard, 1934 Pierce Arrow, pressed steel, light green, orange running boards and cream top, electric head lights and tail light, clockwork mechanism, 13¹/₂" l **425.00**

Buddy L, Texaco Fire Engine, metal, real siren, bell, water deluge gun, extension ladder, and hoses, orig box and instructions, 24" l, $600.00. Photo courtesy Collectors Auction Services.

Chein, bird, windup, litho tin, 3" h, $45.00. Photo courtesy Collectors Auction Services.

Globe, Police Motorcycle with Side Car, cast iron, painted red, seated policeman driver and rider in side car, 2-cylinder Indian model engine trimmed in silver, yellow spoke wheels, rubber tires, c1930s, 8¾" l **875.00**

Haji, Japan, Fighter Plane, friction, litho tin, "USAF/FU-881," red, white, blue, silver, and yellow, 1950s, 4½ x 5¼ x 2¼" **15.00**

Hasbro, Pete the Pepper with Mr Potato Head, complete with figures and accessories, full color instruction sheet, orig box, 6 x 9 x 3" **15.00**

Hong Kong, Motor Scooter, plastic, complete with windscreen, mounted rear spare, detachable full figure driver, orig box, 6½" l **175.00**

House of Campbell, Toyville Garage, litho paper over chipboard, includes 2 small gas pumps with shoestring hoses, 1930s, 4⅜ x 4⅝ x 10⅜" **100.00**

Hubley, Auto Transport, diecast, transport trailer holding 4 plastic sedans, conventional cab model painted red overall, silver grille and fenders, orig box, 14" l **250.00**

Hubley, Farm Set, diecast, painted red, emb "Hubley Jr," large rubber tread tires with yellow hubs, orig box, 7" l **110.00**

Hubley, Farm Tractor, diecast, painted red, steerable wheel and spring action seat, rubber tires with spoke wheels, orig box, 9" l **225.00**

Hubley, Fish Hatchery Truck, diecast, red, silvered bumper and grilles, features plastic transport tank with net and fish figures, orig box, 10" l **350.00**

Hubley, Kiddie Toys, diecast, includes sports car, airplane, farm tractor, and stake truck, orig box, 12 x 13" . . . **375.00**

Hubley, P-38 Fighter Plane, cast metal, red top half, silver bottom half, retractable land gear with black rubber wheels, nickel-plated propellers, 1950s, 9 x 12½ x 2½" **75.00**

Hubley, Poultry Truck, diecast, red and white, nickeled bumper, flat bed with 3 chicken crates filled with plastic figures, orig box, 10" l **275.00**

Hubley, Power Shovel and Front End Loader, diecast, painted yellow, shovel with red bucket and extension arm, loader has red scoop, each with rubber tread belt traction, orig box, 15¾" l **600.00**

Hubley, Road Scraper, diecast, painted yellow, with silvered scraper and rubber tires, orig box, 10" l **275.00**

Hubley, Sky View Yellow Cab, painted orange, black striping and running boards, silver highlights throughout, rear folding luggage rack, rubber tires, sides stenciled "Yellow Cab," orig seated driver with painted face, c1938, 8½" l **525.00**

Hubley, Sports Car, diecast, yellow, 2-seat convertible, opening front and rear hoods, spare tire housed in trunk, orig box, 12¾" l **925.00**

Hubley, Sports Car, diecast, yellow, black removable top, rubber tires, chromed bumpers, silver and black int, orig box, 9" l **225.00**

Hubley, Stockyard Truck, diecast, red, silver bumper and grille, yellow stake van body tilts down automatically for unloading animals, orig box, 10¼" l **200.00**

Hubley, Tractor Loader, diecast, painted orange, silvered scoop raises and lowers, large rubber traction tires, steering wheel turns front tires, orig box, 12" l **150.00**

Hullco Toys, US Gas Pump, litho tin meter and painted base, turn crank until meter reads full, 1920-30s, 7⅜" h **200.00**

Ideal, Motorific Tow Truck, battery operated, hard plastic, orange, "Towing Road Service" sticker on each side, raised "GMC" on front grille, ©1966, 2½ x 6 x 3" **25.00**

Ideal, Pirate Ship, hard plastic, complete with accessories, 1960s, 7 x 14 x 9½" box **50.00**

Ideal, Yo Gun, hard plastic, raised text on each side, complete with 40" l string with soft plastic yellow ball attached to end, 1960s, 7" l **15.00**

Irwin, Build Your Own Helicopter Kit, 27 pcs, gyro-friction motor, instructions, orig box **135.00**

Japan, Delivery Truck, friction, litho tin, "Switch To Rail Express/Air Express/Safe Swift Sure" on each side, red, white, and blue int, 1950s, 1½ x 3½ x ¾" **15.00**

Japan, Dolly Seamstress, battery operated, litho tin, cloth, and vinyl, girl sits at sewing machine and operates foot pedals while pushing material under moving needle while changing lighted pattern appears, orig box, 7" h **250.00**

Japan, Ford Delivery Wagon, friction, litho tin, blue-green, decals on sides read "Flowers for Gracious Living," doors with oval tin plate, elephant decal reads "Ford Lasts Longer," orig box, 12" l **2,000.00**

Japan, Jolly Bear the Drummer Boy, battery operated, litho tin, lighted eyes, bear drums tune using metal stick, remote control action, orig box, 7½" h **250.00**

Japan, Jumbo the Elephant, friction, litho tin, large rolling eyes, rubber trunk, tusks, and tail, orig box, 6½" l **250.00**

Japan, King of the Rancher, windup, litho tin, cowboy swings metal lasso, orig box, 4" l **135.00**

Japan, Mechanical Range Rider, windup, litho tin, cowboy on horseback, rocking action, hat jostles back and forth, orig box, 6½" h **150.00**

Japan, MG car, friction, litho tin, red, black, white, blue, and yellow int, "MG" logo on grille and spare tire on back, 1950s, 1¾ x 4 x 1¼" **50.00**

Japan, Poor Pete, windup, celluloid, black boy wiggles as bulldog bites his rear, 1930s **450.00**

Japan, Robot on Tricycle, windup, soft plastic robot figure and bike frame, litho tin bell on back, robot's head moves, 1960s, 2½ x 4½ x 4½" **75.00**

Occupied Japan, trapeze toy, windup, celluloid figure, wire frame, mkd "My Friend" in globe on acrobat's back, inspection sticker on leg, 1930s, 8¼" h, $60.00.

Japan, Space Navigator Telescope, tin body, painted black end caps, paper label, illus of speeding rocket, Saturn, and stars, 1950s, 3¼" l, ¾" w, ¾" d, extends to 5' **15.00**

Japan, Traffic Policeman, battery operated, litho tin, vinyl, and cloth, waves arms and blows whistle, turns and stops traffic when light changes, orig box, 14" h **300.00**

Japan, Whistle, litho tin, figural airplane, blue, white, and orange, with working whistle attachment on plane int, 1930s, 2½" l **50.00**

Japan, Yamato Battleship Putt-Putt Boat, litho tin, gun turrets on deck with small pair of airplanes, with small tube and tin candleholder, 1960s, orig box, 2 x 6¾ x 2" **50.00**

JDP, France, French Town-Car, windup, litho tin, black, blue and light blue striping, doors open, front wheel steering, 1920s, 10½" l **1,900.00**

Keystone Mfg, Mickey Mouse Movie Projector, enamel paint over pressed steel, hand-cranked electric lamp, missing film track at lens opening, 1930s, 5⅜ x 11½" base, 11¾" h **115.00**

Kingsbury, Blue Bird Speed Record Racer, windup, enamel finish, black rubber tires, 1930s, 18½" l **500.00**

KO, Japan, Flying Saucer with Space Pilot, battery operated, swivel lighted engine, space noise, revolving antenna and mystery action, orig box **250.00**

KO, Japan, Space Snow Tractor, windup, litho tin, advances with spinning rear propeller and mystery action, orig box, 6" l **400.00**

Kohler, Germany, rooster, windup, litho tin body, felt red comb and green tail feathers, bobs when wound, 1960s, 1½ x 3½ x 3¾" **15.00**

Lindstrom, Sweeping Mammy, windup, litho tin, Mammy vibrates and makes sweeping motions with broom, orig box, c1935, 8" h **500.00**

Linemar, 1954 Chevrolet, friction, tin, painted gray, black roof and wide white stripes, chrome trim throughout including bumpers, front grille and hood ornament, yellow, blue, and brown striped seating, tinted windows, rubber tires with chrome painted hub caps, orig box, 11¼" l **1,250.00**

Linemar, Automatic Dock Yard Crane, windup, litho tin, illus of ships on sides of dock platform base, 1950s, orig box, 3 x 8½ x 7" **75.00**

Linemar, Football Player, windup, litho tin, advances with shifting body and moving right leg, 6" h **225.00**

Linemar, Little Audrey, windup, litho tin, spring bobbing head, hops forward, 5" h **450.00**

Linemar, Mickey riding tricycle, litho tin tricycle with bell, celluloid seated Mickey, clockwork mechanism activates pedal action, ©Walt Disney Productions, 3⅝" l **325.00**

Linemar, Playful Pluto, windup, litho tin, tail spins and head nods, 1950s, 5¾" l **175.00**

Linemar, Sleeping Baby Bear, battery operated, plush, sits up in bed and stretches arms, opens mouth, closes eyes, and makes yawning sound, then goes back to sleep, orig box, 9" l **400.00**

Linemar, Super Susie, battery operated, plush bear on litho tin base, rings up items on lighted cash register as she pushes them along on moving conveyer belt, orig box, 9" h **750.00**

Linemar, Telephone Bear, battery operated, litho tin, plush bear sits behind desk writing, answers phone and makes speaking noise while nodding head, orig box, 8" h **350.00**

Lupor, Police Patrol Car No. 7, friction, litho tin, siren noise, 1950s, 7" l **100.00**

Marx, Acrobatic Marvel, litho tin, clockwork mechanism activates rocking motion, orig box, 13½" l **200.00**

Marx, Army Military Model 45 Revolver, clicking noise, 8" l **80.00**

Marx, Busy Miners, windup, litho tin, mining cart moves up and down track, orig box, 1930s, 16⅜" l **325.00**

Marx, Deluxe Pickup Truck, pressed steel, nickel grille, litho tin tires, electric headlights, orig box, 1940s, 14¼" l **925.00**

Marx, Donald Duck Duet, windup, litho tin, Goofy dances jig as Donald pounds drum, orig box, c1945, 10¼" h **875.00**

Marx, Funny Flivver, windup, litho tin, clear plastic windshield, c1925, 3 x 7 x 5½" **175.00**

Marx, Highway Express Truck, pressed steel and litho tin, nickel grille, metal tires, 1940s **450.00**

Marx, Honeymoon Express, windup, litho tin, streamlined passenger train, complete with litho tin attachments, 1950s, orig box, 9½ x 2" **175.00**

Marx, Metal Sink With Running Water, pink litho tin sink with black and red accents, metal faucet attachment, red plastic accessories, separate pink litho water tank attaches to back of sink, orig box, 1950s, 10 x 5½ x 12" **35.00**

Marx, Police Squad Motorcycle, windup, litho tin, sparking action, siren makes noise, orig box, 1950s, 8 x 5½" **650.00**

Marx, Prehistoric Times Playset, complete with pcs and 20 pp prehistoric history booklet, 1961, 11½ x 24 x 4½" **175.00**

Marx, Ring-A-Ling Circus, windup, litho tin, graphics on base depict circus animals and performers, animals respond to ringmaster as they encircle him, 1920-30s, 7⅞" h **1,000.00**

Marx, Rollover Plane, litho tin, friction powered airplane with actions, orig box, 6" wingspan **375.00**

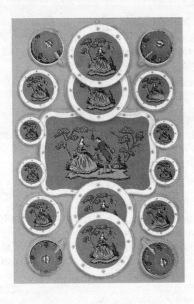

Ohio Art, Dixie Belle toy dishes #414, litho metal, 17 pcs, 1962, $75.00.

Marx, Rookie Cop, windup, litho tin, motorcycle wobbles back and forth while in motion, orig box, 1930s, 8¼" l **575.00**

Marx, Shuttle Choo-Choo Train, windup, litho tin track and scenery, 1950s, 20½ x 10" **100.00**

Marx, Sparkling Soldier Motorcycle, windup, litho tin, orig box, 1930s, 8¼" l **675.00**

Marx, Target Game, litho tin target, complete with black tin spring loaded pistol and 2 rubber tipped darts, orig box, 9½" sq. **75.00**

Marx, Tricky Motorcycle, windup, litho tin, orig box, 1940s, 4⅜" l **275.00**

Marx, Turnover Tank No. 3, windup, litho tin, tank rears up as it rolls forward, turns over, and continues, orig box, 1930-40s, 7½" l **200.00**

Marx, Yellow Cab, windup, litho tin, black rubber tires, orig box, 1950s, 11" l **325.00**

Mattel, Dream Car, friction, bright orange and red plastic, metal bumpers and trim, black rubber tires, orig box, 1950s, 10" l **150.00**

Mattel, Music Box Carousel, windup, litho tin and plastic, crank action, horses and riders move up and down as they circle, orig box, 1953 . . . . **110.00**

Modern Toys, Mercedes Benz Stunt Car, battery operated, litho tin, "Shell/STP/Firestone" logos on car with checkered flag, skull and crossbones, cat, and eyeballs designs, attached stunt roll bars, flips over, 1960s, 3 x 7 x 2½" **75.00**

Modern Toys, Motorcycle General, friction, litho tin, 8½" l **550.00**

Modern Toys, Neptune Tugboat, litho tin, battery operated, colorful graphics on upper deck cabin and pilot's house with surrounding railing, 14" l **75.00**

Movie Jektor Co, Mickey Mouse Movie Jektor, electric light bulb projects image through color paper strips, hand-crank operation, complete with 2 color cartoon strips, missing cord, orig box, 1930s, 10 x 9½ x 6" **150.00**

MT, Japan, Playful Puppy with Caterpillar, battery operated, plush puppy on litho tin base, barks and moves head side to side while following squiggling caterpillar, orig box, 7" l **150.00**

Nylint, Austin Western Telescoping Crane Truck, pressed steel, steering wheel controls front and rear wheels, 1950s, 7 x 21 x 9". **175.00**

Nylint, Naval Defense Motorized Gun, enamel over pressed steel, black rubber tires, spring loaded barrel shoots shells, 1950s, 21½" l **125.00**

Occupied Japan, Ape, windup, black plush body, celluloid hands and face, litho tin feet, pinkish-fleshtone with black accents, advances forward as arms move, 1940s, 4 x 2½" **35.00**

Occupied Japan, Baseball Catcher, windup, celluloid, moves in erratic motion while looking up for ball, orig box, 6" h **150.00**

Occupied Japan, Circus Elephant, windup, celluloid, hp features, balances twirling umbrella as head shifts side to side, orig box, 7½" h **475.00**

Occupied Japan, Crazy Car, windup, litho tin, moves in erratic motions as cowboys holds onto steering wheel, 5" l **275.00**

Occupied Japan, Make-up Anny, windup, celluloid, hp features, looks into mirror and shakes head back and forth while patting makeup on herself, orig box, 5½" h . . . **500.00**

Occupied Japan, Roly Poly Twister, windup, litho tin base revolves in roly poly action, 2 molded celluloid figures holding onto center pole twist separately from base, 5½" h **450.00**

Occupied Japan, Squirrel, windup, litho tin, advances in erratic motions, orig box, 4" l **150.00**

Remco, Exploding Booby Trap Land Mine, spring-loaded firing mechanism, from "Monkey Division Jungle Guerrilla Warfare" series, complete with attached trip string, 1964, 2½ x 5 x 7½" **35.00**

Rich Industries, Tower Garage, silkscreen and mason board construction, top of tower, clock hands, and rack lift, includes billboard sign and 3 plastic cars, 1950s, 27 x 11¾" base **350.00**

Schuco, Ralle Porsche 911R Racer, battery operated, plastic, lever shifts for forward and reverse actions, complete with 4 spare tires, functional jack, wrench, and road sign, orig box **200.00**

SH, Japan, Busy Robot, battery operated, litho tin and plastic, robot walks then dumps wheelbarrow, 11" h **650.00**

SL Allen Co, Mickey Mouse Flexible Flyer Sled, 1930s, 27¾" l **300.00**

SM, Japan, Tom Tom Canoe, friction, litho tin, Indian paddles canoe and beats on tom tom, orig box, 1950, 9½" l **750.00**

SSS, Japan, 1954 Ford, friction, litho tin, black rubber tires, siren noise, Ford logo script on front fenders, 1950s, 4¼" l **40.00**

SSS, Japan, 1961 Cadillac Convertible, battery operated, enamel on tin, litho tin int, front steering wheel, flocked seats and floor, black rubber tires, hood and trunk open, orig box, 1960s, 17¼" l **2,750.00**

SSS, Japan, Auto Hauler, friction, enamel over steel, back end opens to load cars, 1950s, 9½" l **35.00**

Strauss, Tip Top Porter, windup, litho tin, black porter pushes cart, 5½" h, 6" l **175.00**

Structo, Bearcat Roadster, pressed steel, orange, windshield and simulated top folded behind open seat, spare tire mounted on rear, clockwork mechanism activates intricate undercarriage gearing, 15" l **775.00**

Slik Toy, Lansing Foundry, tractor and manure spreader, red, rubber wheels, "MM" (Minneapolis-Moline) on sides, mkd "Made USA, 11," $45.00.

Structo, dump truck, pressed steel, red, side levers used for dumping load, open bench seat, Mack-type cab, metal wheels, 17½" l............................ 200.00

Structo, farm tractor, red and green, large spoke wheels, cast iron front wheels, includes trailer wagon, clockwork activated tractor, 10" l..................... 300.00

Structo, Hydraulic Dump Truck, pressed steel, orange cab, metallic green bed, orange dump door opens and closes, solid black rubber tires, lever operates hydraulic bed which raises bed into air, c1960, 6½ x 20 x 7"................................ 50.00

Structo, Ready-Mix Concrete Truck, pressed steel, barrel rotates and produces clicking noise, 1950s, 6½ x 21 x 9".................................... 75.00

Structo, US Army Missile Launcher Truck, pressed steel, green, yellow plastic int, extending outriggers on back and swivel bed, 3 separate spring-loaded launching tubes, metal holding rack with 3 suction cup darts, each side of bed mkd "US Army Missile Launcher" with star design, 1960s, 6 x 16 x 7"................ 50.00

Sun Rubber, Mickey Mouse Fire Department, rubber, white rubber tires, 1940-50s, 6½" l................ 85.00

Suzuki, Japan, Bell Cycle Rabbit, litho tin cycle with attached bell, rabbit and squirrel illus on wheels, soft plastic rabbit wearing red shirt, blue pants, yellow hat, blue balloon attached to handlebars, 1960s, orig box, 2¼ x 6 x 2¼"............................... 50.00

Tenko, Denmark, Ferguson Tractor, diecast, black rubber tires, 1960s, 4¾" l.............................. 95.00

Tipp Co, Germany, Grand Touring Limo, windup, litho tin tires and graphics, maroon and tan with red striping, emb rear seat, chauffeur, 1920s, 12¼" l......... 2,750.00

TM, Japan, Baby Pontiac, windup, enamel on tin, nickel grille, orig box, 1940s, 3⅜" l.................... 125.00

TM, Japan, Chevy Camaro, friction, nickel grille bumpers and window trim, 10⅞" l.................. 250.00

TN, Japan, Cadillac, battery operated, litho tin, metal white walls, nickel trim, electric headlights, 1950s, 13½" l.................................... 1,100.00

TN, Japan, Marvelous Car with Lights, battery operated, litho tin, orig box, 1950s, 11" l.................. 550.00

TN, Japan, Neptune Tug Boat, battery operated, litho tin, whistle, chug noise, light, and shaking action, orig box, 15¼" l................................ 85.00

TN, Japan, Newt-Puppy, windup, litho tin, puppy rings bell, shifts head, and swings newspaper, orig box, 6½" h.................................... 325.00

Tomy, Super Power Gas Station, battery operated, plastic, black rubber tires, pressing gas nozzle activates motor which spins rear wheels, orig box, 7¼" h....... 125.00

TPS, Japan, Coney Island Scooter, windup, litho tin, vinyl headed driver navigates track, 10 x 10" platform, orig box.................................. 225.00

TPS, Japan, Monkey Golfer, windup, litho tin, rubber ears, body twists in golfing position and strikes ball which travels across ramp into hole, orig box, 8" h..... 325.00

TPS, Japan, Pango Pango African Dancer, windup, litho tin, black native holding shield and spear, vibrating action, neck moves back and forth in dancing motion, 6½" h.................................... 250.00

TPS, Japan, Toddl'n Baby, windup, litho tin and plastic, felt clothes, waddles back and forth, orig box, 6½" h.... 150.00

TPS, Japan, Wagon Fantasyland, windup, litho tin, rocking monkey driver and 2 twirling squirrels on leaf being pulled by snail, orig box, 12" l............ 200.00

Unique Art, Lincoln Tunnel, windup, litho tin, cars, buses, and trucks on track, 24" l.................. 225.00

Unique Art, Motorcycle Policeman, windup, litho tin, 1930s, 8½" l................................ 450.00

Unique Art, Rodeo Joe Crazy Car, windup, litho tin, erratic actions as cowboy driver with metal hat hangs onto steering wheel, 8" l..................... 225.00

Usagiya, Japan, Friction Fire Engine, friction, litho tin, bright red, black, white, red, blue, and yellow accents, 5 litho tin firemen, ladder extends to 10", orig box, 1960s, 2 x 7½ x 3¼"..................... 75.00

Viceroy Sunruco, Canada, Mickey's Tractor, rubber, Mickey's head swivels, 1950s, 4¾" l.............. 150.00

Western Germany, Jonny Rope Climber, litho tin, pull on both rings and Jonny climbs rope, orig box, 1940-50s, 7" l.................................... 100.00

Western Germany, Somersault Clown, windup, cloth outfit, celluloid face, hp features, orig box, 6" h........ 110.00

Wolverine, Texaco Service Station, litho tin garage and driveway, plastic accessories, 1950-60s.............. 325.00

TN, Japan, Bartender, 6 actions, 1960s, 11½" h, $40.00.

Wyandotte, ride-on truck, pressed steel, rubber tires, missing bell, repainted, 16" h, 31" l, $55.00. Photo courtesy Collectors Auction Services.

W Toy, Japan, Duckmobile, litho tin, celluloid Donald Duck figure peering from moon roof, friction powered action causes Donald to duck back into car and reappear through roof, 6⁵/₈" l 425.00

Wyandotte, Shell Gas Station & Garage, litho tin, complete with 2 pressed steel cars, c1937, 7¹/₂ x 15³/₄" 1,450.00

Wyandotte, Station Wagon, pull toy, litho tin, black rubber tires, doors open, "Toytown Estate" on door, orig box, 21" l 1,600.00

Wyandotte, Wyandotte Van Lines, litho tin trailer, pressed steel cab, black rubber tires, 1950s, 8" l 125.00

Y, Japan, Teddy the Champ Boxer, battery operated, litho tin, plush bear, moves forward and reverse while swinging wildly at punching bag, head and eyes move, orig box, 9" h 400.00

Yamaichi, Japan, Overland Freight Service Transport Van, friction, litho tin, cream and red cab with company name in yellow and white, door opens on back, 1950s, 2¹/₂ x 7 x 3" 75.00

Yone, Japan, Copter on Parade, windup, litho tin and plastic, 3 helicopters attached by rod, advances with spinning plastic props and litho tin saucer umbrella tops, orig box, 7" l 250.00

Yone, Japan, Hopping Monkey, windup, litho tin, orange, yellow muzzle, wearing red, white, and blue striped hat and shirt, brown plastic feet, black rubber tail, 1960s, 2 x 4 x 2¹/₂" 15.00

Yone, Japan, US Army Jeep, friction, litho tin, green, illus of field phone and radar screen, litho tin gas tank and tire on back, retractable windshield, soldier figure from waist up, working mechanism produces siren noise, orig box, 3 x 6¹/₄ x 3" 50.00

Yonezawa, Drinking Dog, battery operated, litho tin, plush dog, pours from Cragstan Milk bottle and drinks, eyes light up, orig box, 8" h 200.00

Yonezawa, Mr Fox the Magician, battery operated, litho tin and plush, fox magician lifts hat to reveal rabbit, points to it, lifts again and rabbit is gone, complete with cape and glasses, orig box, 10" h 650.00

TOY SOLDIERS

Toy soldier is a generic term. The category includes animal, civilian, holiday, and western figures in addition to military figures. Military figures are preferred.

The earliest toy soldiers were two-dimensional paper soldiers, often printed in sheets that were cut apart for play. Hilperts of Nuremberg, Germany, introduced the first three-dimensional toy soldiers near the end of the 18th century.

Britains and Mignot are the leading manufacturers of 20th-century toy soldiers. Mignot offered models of more than 20,000 different soldiers in the 1950s. Britains introduced its first hollow-cast figures in 1893. Many figures had movable arms. Britains quality is the standard by which collectors judge all other mass-produced figures.

The American dime store soldier arrived on the scene in the 1930s and remained popular through the early 1950s. Barclay and Manoil dominated the market primarily because of their realistic castings and originality of poses. Pre-1941 Barclay soldiers have helmets that are glued or clipped on.

Recently adult collectors have been speculating heavily in limited production toy soldiers made by a small group of toy soldier craftsman. Others are buying unpainted castings and painting them. The result is an increased variety of material on the market. Make certain you know exactly what you are buying.

Toy soldier collectors place a premium of 20% to 40% on set boxes. Beware of repainted pieces. Undocumented touch-up is a major problem in the market.

References: Norman Joplin, *The Great Book of Hollow-Cast Figures,* New Cavendish Books, 2000; Richard O'Brien, *Collecting American-Made Toy Soldiers, No. 3,* Books Americana, 1997; Richard O'Brien, *Collecting Foreign-Made Toy Soldiers,* Krause Publications, 1997; Edward Ryan, *Paper Soldiers: The Illustrated History of Printed Paper Armies of the 18th, 19th & 20th Centuries,* Golden Age Editions, 1995, distributed by P.E.I. International; Joe Wallis, *Armies of the World, Britains Ltd. Lead Soldiers 1925-1941,* published by author, 1993.

Periodicals: *Old Toy Soldier,* 209 N Lombard, Oak Park, IL 60302; *Plastic Warrior,* 815 North 12th St, Allentown, PA 18102; *Toy Soldier Review,* PO Box 4809, North Bergen, NJ 07047.

Collectors' Club: Toy Soldier Collectors of America, 5340 40th Ave N, St Petersburg, FL 33709.

American Alloy, soldier marching **$70.00**
American Metal Toys, Anti-Aircraft gunner, kneeling **100.00**
American Metal Toys, bull **18.00**
American Metal Toys, farmer **15.00**
American Metal Toys, farmer's wife **18.00**
American Metal Toys, horse, copper colored, "228" **12.00**
American Metal Toys, machine gunner, prone **125.00**
American Metal Toys, mule **12.00**
American Metal Toys, nurse in white with black bag **90.00**
Arcade, tank and cannon, firing mechanisms work **190.00**
Auburn Rubber, hen **8.00**
Auburn Rubber, Marmon-Harrington tank **40.00**
Auburn Rubber, officer on horse **45.00**
Auburn Rubber, pig **12.00**
Auburn Rubber, stretcher bearer **35.00**
Auburn Rubber, US Infantry private, marching, port arms **18.00**
Auburn Rubber, wounded soldier lying down **40.00**

Britains, Bikanir Camel Corps, #123, c1920, $75.00.

Barclay, aviator 25.00
Barclay, boy skater 15.00
Barclay, cowboy with 2 guns 20.00
Barclay, drummer, short stride, tin helmet 25.00
Barclay, fireman with axe 30.00
Barclay, flagbearer, long stride, tin helmet 30.00
Barclay, girl on sled 20.00
Barclay, Indian chief with tomahawk and shield 12.00
Barclay, Indian with bow and arrow 15.00
Barclay, jockey on silver horse, #8 . . . . 35.00
Barclay, knight with shield 18.00
Barclay, minister holding hat 20.00
Barclay, mounted cavalryman, brown horse, blue uniform . . . 25.00
Barclay, newsboy 15.00
Barclay, nurse, kneeling 25.00
Barclay, officer with sword, long stride, tin helmet 25.00
Barclay, Renault tank, c1937, 4" l 45.00
Barclay, standing cow 12.00
Barclay, standing horse 15.00
Britains, #1893, Royal Indian Army Service Corps, 7 pcs, 1940 . . . . 225.00
Britains, #1901, Capetown Highlanders, 8 pcs, c1940 . . . . . 175.00
Britains, #2010, Parachute Regiment, 8 pcs, 1950s 175.00
Britains, #2017, Ski Troups, 4 pcs, c1950 . . . . 550.00
Britains, #2033, US Infantry Marching, steel helmets, 7 pcs, 1960s 100.00
Britains, #2073, RAF, 8 pcs, 1950s 250.00
Britains, #2100, Venezuelan Cadets, 20 pcs, 1960s 600.00
Grey Iron, bugler at attention 6.00
Grey Iron, calf 12.00
Grey Iron, black man digging 30.00
Grey Iron, conductor 12.00
Grey Iron, cowboy 20.00
Grey Iron, goose 10.00
Grey Iron, grenade thrower 45.00
Grey Iron, Indian brave shielding eyes 30.00
Grey Iron, knight in armor 25.00
Grey Iron, man in traveling suit 12.00
Grey Iron, pirate with sword, green 30.00
Grey Iron, postman 12.00
Grey Iron, Red Cross officer with arm band 40.00
Grey Iron, sailor in white 18.00
Grey Iron, US Doughboy charging 20.00

Grey Iron, US Doughboy sentry 25.00
Grey Iron, US Infantry, port arms 25.00
Grey Iron, US machine gunner 20.00
Grey Iron, woman with basket 15.00
HB Toys, Indian with knife 25.00
HB Toys, mounted Indian 40.00
Manoil, aviation mechanic with propellor, silver prop 140.00
Manoil, aviator carrying bomb sight 50.00
Manoil, bench 12.00
Manoil, blacksmith making horseshoes 25.00
Manoil, bomb thrower, 3 grenades in pouch 25.00
Manoil, cannon, wood wheels, gray 20.00
Manoil, carpenter with square 65.00
Manoil, doctor, white with red cross 25.00
Manoil, field doctor, crawling 65.00
Manoil, girl picking berries 55.00
Manoil, hound, tan with brown spots 25.00
Manoil, marine, second version 25.00
Manoil, navy gunner 35.00
Manoil, nurse 25.00
Manoil, policeman 25.00
Manoil, scarecrow with top hat 25.00
Manoil, seated machine gunner 35.00
Manoil, soldier with gas mask and flare pistol 30.00
Marx, 50-caliber machine gun 15.00
Marx, Anti-Aircraft gun 10.00
Marx, Indian Sikh 8.00
Marx, infantry 1st Lieutenant 12.00
Marx, pilot with papers 12.00
Marx, sharpshooter with rifle, brown uniform 20.00
Marx, US Calvary 10.00
Metal Cast, US cavalry, mounted, black and white horse . . . 35.00
Metal Cast, US Infantry private, rifle at slope 25.00
Molded Products, aviator with X-type front harness 12.00
Molded Products, cow, black and white 10.00
Molded Products, flagbearer, WWII helmet 15.00
Molded Products, horse, black and white 8.00
Molded Products, Indian standing with arms folded 10.00
Molded Products, soldier marching, WWI helmet 12.00
Molded Products, soldier with Anti-Aircraft gun, WWII helmet 15.00
Molded Products, soldier with parachute 15.00
Playwood Plastics, flagbearer 15.00
Playwood Plastics, gunner and machine gun 15.00
Playwood Plastics, parade soldier with pack 12.00
Playwood Plastics, soldier with gas mask and flare gun . . . 15.00
Slik-Toy, mortar man 9309 . . . . 65.00

TOY TRAIN ACCESSORIES

Toy train accessories and boxed train sets are two of the hottest toy train collecting categories in the 1990s. Toy train accessories divide into two main groups: (1) those made by toy train manufacturers and (2) those made by others. Many of the latter were in kit form.

As with toy trains, toy train accessories are sized by gauge. An HO building on a Lionel train platform appears very much out of place. O and S gauge accessories are the most desired. The period box adds 15% to 25% to the value.

Bachmann Brothers, a manufacturer of eyeglasses, produced its first plastic train accessory, a picket fence, in 1949. A log cabin followed in 1950. By the mid-1950s Bachmann's Plasticville O/S gauge buildings were found on the vast majority of America's toy train platforms. An HO line was introduced in 1955, an N gauge line in 1968. Plasticville houses are marked with a "BB" on a banner in a circle.

Bachmann ended a challenge to its market supremacy by Unlimited Plastics' Littletown when it acquired the company in 1956. Bachmann carefully stores its Plasticville dies, giving it the ability to put any model back into production when sufficient demand occurs.

References: Frank C. Hare, *Plasticville, 3rd Edition,* Kalmbach Publishing, 1993, out of print; Alan Stewart, *Greenberg's Guide to Lionel Trains, 1945-1969, Vol VI: Accessories,* Kalmbach Publishing, 1994.

AMERICAN FLYER

Animated Station, K766, S gauge, 1953-55	$200.00
Automatic Highway Flasher, 760, S gauge, orig box, 1949-56	35.00
Double Trestle Bridge, 754, S gauge, 1950-52	110.00
Figure 8 Layout, 6, includes 4 straight, 4 half straight, 18 curved, and one 90° crossover, 1953	40.00
Floodlight Tower, 774, S gauge, illuminated, 1951-56	75.00
Operating Stockyard Set, 771, with 736 Cattle Car, S gauge, 1950-54	135.00
Remote Uncoupler, 705, S gauge, with converter, 1946-47	8.00
Remote Uncoupling Track, 675, S gauge, orig box, 1939	10.00
Rerailer, 728, S gauge, 1956	25.00
Reverse Loop Relay, 695, S gauge, with two 707 and one 690 track terminal and 2 orig fiber pins, 1955-56	85.00
Transformer, 18B, 190 watts, dual control, with circuit breakers, c1953	125.00
Transformer, 30B, 300 watt, dual control, orig box, 1953-55	175.00
Trestle Bridge, 750, S gauge, black, silver, and metallic blue, orig box, 1945-56	125.00
Trestle Bridge with Beacon, 753, S gauge, 1952	75.00
Whistling Billboard, 568, S gauge, dark green base, 1956	60.00

LIONEL

Automatic Gateman, 145, O gauge, orig box, 1950-66	$50.00
Barrels, set of 6, 362-78, O gauge, orig box, 1952	20.00
Floodlight Tower, 195, 1957-69	75.00
Freight Shed, 256, illuminated, orig box, 1950-53	55.00
Girder Bridge, 214, HO gauge, US Steel, orig box, 1953-69	25.00
Lamp Post, 71, crackle gray, orig box, 1949-59	15.00
Radar Antenna, 197, O gauge, orig box, 1957-59	90.00
Railroad Control Tower, 192, orig box, 1959-60	250.00
Remote Control Switches, pr, 022, O gauge, electric, orig box, 1946-49	125.00
Rheostat, 95, orig box, 1934	20.00
Rocket Launcher, 175, O gauge, orig box, 1958-60	250.00
Rotary Beacon, 394, aluminum, green tower frame, orig box, 1949-53	75.00
Rotary Beacon, 494, silver, orig box, 1954	50.00
Rotating Beacon Cap, 394-37, orig box, 1953	30.00
Station Platform, 156, O gauge, orig box, 1939-40	150.00
Transformer, KW, 190 watt, 1950	150.00
Trestle Set, 110, O gauge, orig box, 24 pcs, 1955-69	25.00
Water Tank, 138, orig box, 1953-57	125.00
Water Tower, 193, orig box, 1953-55	100.00
Whistle and Reverse Controller, 167, O gauge, orig box, 1945	12.00

Plasticville, Railroad Signal Bridge, SG-3, 1952, $30.00.

PLASTICVILLE

5 and 10 Cent Store, CS-5, orig box	$55.00
Airport Hanger Kit, AP-1, orig box	25.00
Barn Kit, BN-1, orig box	15.00
Bridge and Pond Unit, BL-2, orig box	15.00
Cathedral, 1904, orig box	30.00
Cattle Loading Pen, 1623, orig box	60.00
Citizens with Paint Kit, 1619, orig box	20.00
Colonial Church, 1803, orig box	30.00
Dairy Barn, 1622, orig box	20.00
Diner, DE-7, orig box	36.00
Gas Station, 1800, orig box	60.00
Hospital Kit, #HS-6, orig box	15.00
Independence Hall, 1776, orig box	40.00
New England Rancher, MH-2, orig box	30.00
Ranch House, RH-1, orig box	40.00
School House, SC-4, orig box	15.00
Set of Road Signs, 12-A, orig box	10.00
Super Market Kit, SM-7, orig box	55.00
Switch Tower, SW-2, orig box	15.00
Trestle Bridge, BR-2, orig box	12.00
Turnpike Interchange, 1900, orig box	80.00
Windmill, 1408, orig box	25.00

TOY TRAINS

The mid-1920s through the late 1950s is the golden age of toy trains. American Flyer, Ives, and Lionel produced electric model trains that featured highly detailed castings and markings. A slow conversion to plastic occurred within the industry in the late 1950s and early 1960s. Most collectors shun plastic like the plague.

Trains are collected first by company and second by gauge. Lionel is king of the hill, followed by American Flyer. As a result, O, O27, and S are the three most popular gauges among collectors. Collector interest in HO gauge trains has increased significantly in the past five years. Many toy train auctions now include HO trains among their offerings. Interest is minimal in N gauge.

The 1990s witnessed several major shifts in collecting emphasis. First, post–World War II replaced pre-World War II trains as the hot chronological collecting period. Pre-1945 prices have stabilized. In the case of cast-iron trains, some decline has been noted. Second, accessories and sets are the hot post-1945 collecting areas. Prices on most engines and rolling stock have stabilized.

Third, the speculative bubble in mass-produced trains of the 1970s and 1980s has burst. With some exceptions, most of these trains are selling below their initial retail cost on the secondary market. Fourth, adult collectors currently are investing heavily in limited edition reproductions and special model issues. These pieces have not been strongly tested on the secondary market. Fifth, there are initial signs of a growing collector interest in HO material, primarily the better grade German trains, and inexpensive lithographed tin windup trains.

References: General: Tim Blaisdell and Ed Urmston Sr., *Standard Guide to Athearn Model Trains,* Krause Publications, 1998; John Grams, *Toy Train Collecting and Operating,* Kalmbach Publishing, 1999; *Greenberg's Pocket Price Guide, American Flyer S Gauge,* Kalmbach Publishing, 1999; *Greenberg's Pocket Price Guide, Lionel Trains, 1901-2000,* Kalmbach Publishing, 1999; *Greenberg's Pocket Price Guide: Marx Trains, 7th Edition,* Kalmbach Publishing, 1999; *Greenberg's Roadname Guide to O Gauge Trains,* Kalmbach Publishing, 1997; Peter H. Riddle, *America's Standard Gauge Electric Trains,* Antique Trader Books, 1998; Elizabeth Stephan (ed.), *O'Brien's Collecting Toy Trains, 5th Edition,* Krause Publications, 1999.

American Flyer: Greenberg Books, three-volume set.

Lionel: Greenberg Books, four volumes dealing with Lionel trains made between 1901 and 1942, seven volumes covering the 1945 to 1969 period, and two volumes for the 1970 to 1991 period. Also check Lionel Book Committee, Train Collectors Association, *Lionel Trains: Standard of the World, 1900-1943, Second Edition,* Train Collectors Association, 1989.

Miscellaneous: Greenberg Books has one or more price guides for Athearn, Kusan, Ives, Marx, and Varney.

Note: For a complete list of toy train titles from Greenberg Books, a division of Kalmbach Publishing Co., write PO Box 1612, Waukesha, WI 53187, and request a copy of their latest catalog. If you are a serious collector, ask to be put on their mailing list.

Periodicals: *Classic Toy Trains,* PO Box 1612, Waukesha, WI 53187; *LGB Telegram,* 1573 Landvater, Hummelstown, PA 17036; *O Gauge Railroading,* PO Box 239, Nazareth, PA 18064.

Collectors' Clubs: American Flyer Collectors Club, PO Box 13269, Pittsburgh, PA 15243; The Ives Train Society, PO Box 59, 6714 Madison Rd, Thompson, OH 44086; LGB Model Railroad Club, 1854 Erin Dr, Altoona, PA 16602; Lionel Collectors Club of America, PO Box 479, LaSalle, IL 61301; Marklin Club–North America, PO Box 510559, New Berlin, WI 53151; The National Model Railroad Assoc, 4121 Cromwell Rd, Chattanooga, TN 37421; Toy Train Operating Society, 25 W Walnut St, Ste 308, Pasadena, CA 91103; Train Collectors Assoc, PO Box 248, Strasburg, PA 17579.

AMERICAN FLYER

Automatic Unloading Car, 715, S gauge, American Flyer Lines, 1946-54	**$115.00**
Baggage Car, 951, S gauge, 1953-56	**30.00**
Boxcar, 637, S gauge, MKT, 1949-53	**40.00**
Boxcar, 25082, S gauge, New Haven, with hayjector, orig track trips, instructions, and box, 1961-64	**95.00**
Caboose, 24634, S gauge, American Flyer Lines, 1963-66	**45.00**
Coach Car, 495, O gauge, orig box	**65.00**
Coach Car, 655, S gauge, Silver Bullet, 1953	**125.00**
Coal Dump Car, 719, S gauge, CB&Q, 1950-54	**125.00**

Engine and Tender, 283, S gauge, Pacific, 1954-57	**135.00**
Engine and Tender, 308, S gauge, Atlantic, 1954-55	**50.00**
Engine and Tender, 21004 and 21404, S gauge, Switcher, PPR, 1957	**525.00**
Engine and Tender, 21130, S gauge, Hudson, 1962-63	**275.00**
Flatcar, 605, S gauge, American Flyer Lines, with log load, 1953	**30.00**
Flatcar, 24566, S gauge, New Haven auto transport, 1961-66	**215.00**
Floodlight, 24529, S gauge, Erie, depressed center, 1958	**35.00**
Gondola, 641, S gauge, American Flyer, 1949-51	**160.00**
Gondola, 24103, S gauge, Norfolk & Western, 1958	**25.00**
Gondola, 24125, S gauge, Bethlehem Steel, 1960-65	**30.00**
Hopper Car, 24230, S gauge, Peabody, 1961-64	**45.00**
Milk Car, 3212, O gauge, 1938	**100.00**
Observation Car, 663, S gauge, American Flyer Lines, lighted int, 1950-52	**40.00**
Operating Boxcar, 734, S gauge, 1950-54	**90.00**
Switcher Engine, 31004, HO gauge, PPR, slantback	**80.00**
Tank Car, 24329, S gauge, Hooker, 1961	**50.00**
Train Set, 474 and 475, S gauge, Alco AA Silver Bullet, 1953-55, price for 2-pc set	**375.00**

DORFAN

Baggage Car, 770, standard gauge, American Railways Express, lighted int	**$80.00**
Coach, 772, standard gauge, Washington, lighted int	**70.00**
Engine, 51, electric, O gauge	**200.00**
Lumber Car, standard gauge, eight wheel, 1930s	**425.00**
Observation Car, 773, standard gauge	**50.00**
Pullman Cars, 2 Boston and 1 Seattle, lighted int, 1920s, price for 3	**160.00**
Tank Car, "Indian Refining Co LRCX84"	**45.00**
Tank Car, "UTLX 29325," standard gauge	**200.00**
Train Station, 426, lighted, orig box, 1930s	**500.00**

IVES

Caboose, 67, O gauge	**$25.00**
Gravel Car, 128, O gauge, NYC & HR, 1910-12	**25.00**
Observation Car, 136, O gauge, peeling paint, minor rust, 1926-30	**25.00**
Parlor Car, 135, O gauge, peeling paint, minor rust, 1926-30	**25.00**
Train Set, 501, O gauge, 3251 Engine, 550 Baggage Car, and 552 Parlor Car, restorable condition, 1920s	**75.00**
Train Set, 510, O gauge, 3251 Engine, 63 NYC & HR Gravel Car, 64 Pennsylvania Lines Boxcar, and 67 Caboose, peeling paint, minor rust, 1920s	**160.00**
Train Set, 1800 Yankee Flyer, O gauge, 1810 Engine, two 1811 Pullman Cars, 1012 Station Transformer, 8-pc track, orig box, 1930s, MIB	**475.00**
Train Station, 117, 1923-28	**225.00**

LIONEL

Animated Hobo Gondola, 3444, O gauge, 1957	**$100.00**
Boxcar, 514, standard gauge, cream and orange, 1929	**200.00**
Boxcar, 2458, O gauge, Pennsylvania, automatic, 1945	**85.00**
Boxcar, 3464, O gauge, NYC, 1952	**25.00**
Boxcar, 3854, O gauge, Pennsylvania, operating, black doors, 1946	**700.00**
Boxcar, 6454, 027 gauge, Erie, 1950	**50.00**
Boxcar, 6464-275, O gauge, State of Maine, 1955	**95.00**

Lionel Train Sets. Top: Boston and Maine "Flying Yankee" Streamliner, 267W, orig boxes, $1,500.00; Bottom: Freight Train, 269E, orig boxes, $1,000.00. Photos courtesy Skinner, Inc., Boston, MA.

Brakeman Car Set, 3424, O gauge, 1956 . . . . **100.00**
Caboose, 6017-185, 027 gauge, gray, 1959 . . . . **75.00**
Cattle Car, 513, standard gauge, 1927 . . . . **190.00**
Cattle Car, 3656, O gauge, operating, black letters, 1950 . . . **300.00**
Crane 6828-100, O gauge, orig boxes, 1960 . . . . **250.00**
Engine, 247, 027 gauge, B&O, 2-4-2, 1959 . . . . **125.00**
Engine, 390E, standard gauge, 2-4-2, 1929 . . . . **800.00**
Engine and Tender, 225E and 2225W, O gauge, 2-6-2,
    gunmetal gray, 1939-40 . . . . **325.00**
Engine and Tender, 1664 and 1689W, 027 gauge, 2-4-2,
    1938 . . . . **135.00**
Flatcar, 511, standard gauge, with load, 1927 . . . . **130.00**
Flatcar, 811, O gauge, with load, maroon, 1926 . . . . **90.00**
Flatcar, 3419, O gauge, with helicopter, 1959 . . . . **150.00**
Flatcar, 3619, O gauge, with helicopter, orig box, 1962 . . . **170.00**
Flatcar, 6111, 027 gauge, with pipes, 1955 . . . . **50.00**
Flatcar, 6175, 027 gauge, with rockets, 1958 . . . . **100.00**
Flatcar, 6430, O gauge, with piggyback van, 1956 . . . . **90.00**
Flatcar, 6501, O gauge, with boat, orig box, 1962 . . . . . . **225.00**
Flatcar, 6801-50, O gauge, with yellow boat, 1957 . . . . . . **140.00**
Flatcar, 6801-75, O gauge, with blue boat, orig box,
    1957 . . . . **110.00**
Flatcar, 6825, O gauge, with girder bridge, 1959 . . . . **80.00**
Floodlight Car, 820, O gauge, green, orig box, 1931 . . . . . **175.00**
Floodlight Car, 2620, O gauge, gray hood, 1938 . . . . . . **100.00**
Girder Flatcar, 6418, O gauge, 16 wheel, 1955 . . . . **150.00**
Gondola, 512, standard gauge, 1927 . . . . **140.00**
Gondola, 2812, O gauge, apple green, 1938 . . . . **80.00**
Gondola, 6462-25, O gauge, NYC, black, 1954 . . . . **25.00**
Hopper Car, 216, standard gauge, dark green, 1926-40 . . . . **375.00**
Hopper Car, 516, standard gauge, with coal, 1928 . . . . **300.00**
Hopper Car, 6436, O gauge, N&W, 1955 . . . . **35.00**
Hopper Car, 6456, O gauge, maroon, orig box, 1948 . . . . . . **40.00**
Lumber Car, 3461, O gauge, operating, 1949 . . . . **100.00**
Missile Launcher Car, 3349, O gauge, 1960 . . . . **80.00**
Passenger Cars, O gauge, 600 Pullman, 601 Observation,
    and 602 Baggage, gray and red, 1933, price for 3 pcs **300.00**
Refrigerator Boxcar, 514R, standard gauge, cream with
    peacock roof, 1929 . . . . **350.00**
Refrigerator Boxcar, 6472, O gauge, 1950 . . . . **40.00**
Satellite Launcher Car, 3519, O gauge, remote, 1961 . . . . . **70.00**
Savings Bank Car, 6050-100, 027 gauge, Swift, red, 1963 . . . **50.00**
Searchlight Car, 3520, O gauge, orig box, 1952 . . . . **75.00**

Searchlight Car, 6520, O gauge, operating, green gener-
    ator, orig box, 1949 . . . . **475.00**
Searchlight Extension Car, 3650, O gauge, orig box, 1956 . . **100.00**
Tank Car, 515, standard gauge, Sunoco, terra cotta, 1927 . . . **215.00**
Tank Car, 6315, O gauge, Gulf, orange, 1956 . . . . **90.00**
Tank Car, 6465, 027 gauge, Sunoco, 1948 . . . . **30.00**
Train Set, 1063E, Lionel Junior, 1930s **450.00**
Train Set, 1591, Marine Corps **1,200.00**
Train Set, 1595, Marine Corps **1,600.00**
Train Set, 2379 Engine, Rio Grande, Super O gauge,
    1957 . . . . **1,400.00**
Transport Car, 6500, O gauge, Beechcraft Bonanza, orig
    box, 1962 . . . . **150.00**

TRANSPORTATION

America is a highly mobile society. America's expansion and growth is linked to its transportation system, whether road, canal, rail, or sky. Few communities have escaped the impact of one or more transportation systems. As a result, transportation memorabilia has a strong regional collecting base.

Further, collectors are fascinated with anything relating to transportation vehicles and systems. This is a catchall category for those transportation categories, e.g., bus, canal, and trolley, not found elsewhere in the book.

References: Kurt M. Resch, *A World of Bus Toys and Models,* Schiffer Publishing, 1999; Alex Roggero and Tony Beadle, *Greyhound: A Pictorial Tribute to an American Icon,* Motorbooks International, 1995.

Collectors' Clubs: Bus History Assoc, 965 McEwan, Windsor, Ontario N9B 2G1 Canada; International Bus Collectors Club, 1518 "C" Trailee Dr, Charleston, SC 29407; National Assoc of Timetable Collectors, 125 American Inn Rd, Villa Ridge, MO 63089.

Note: For additional listings see Automobiles, Automobilia, Aviation Collectibles, Bicycles, Ocean Liner Collectibles, and Railroad Collectibles.

Badge, Taxi Driver, Cab Owner #639, Toronto, 1949,
    1⁷/₈ x 1⁷/₈" **$50.00**
Badge, Taxi Driver #43, City of Sydney, Nova Scotia,
    1986 . . . . **10.00**
Badge, Tucson Cab #5, raised image of old car accented
    with green and white enamel **10.00**
Booklet, *Seattle City Guide,* trolley and motor coach
    map centerfold, lists various points of interest, 102 pp,
    Newman-Burrows Co, 1942, 4 x 6¹/₂" **30.00**
Cap, taxi driver's, tan cotton twill removable top, black
    wicker vented sides, patent leather visor, white metal
    badge with eagle and raised applied letters, size 7¹/₄" **20.00**
Jacket, Greyhound bus driver's, blue, 2 Greyhound logo
    buttons on front, blue stripes around cuffs, 2 flap
    pockets and 1 slot pocket on front, 2 int slot pockets,
    Howard Uniforms, size large **20.00**
Lighter, Plymouth Rapid Transit System, brushed finish
    with 5-color enamel-painted engraved logo, white
    and gold box, Zippo, 1970 . . . . **125.00**
Map, Baltimore MD trolley schedule, map of street cars,
    motor coaches, and trackless trolley of the Baltimore
    Transit Co, issued Jul 2, 1945, 16 x 20" **8.00**

Map, The Greyhound Lines, paper, Reserve Litho & Ptg. Co, Cleveland, April 1937, 20 x 30", $50.00. Photo courtesy Collectors Auction Services.

Map, Greyhound Bus Lines, flags of the United Nations, Army, Navy, and Marines insignias, 1942 . . . . **10.00**

Map, Honolulu bus route, 1966. . . . . **10.00**

Map, London bus map, central area, color map of bus routes on side, list of bus routes on reverse, 1934 . . . . **10.00**

Map, Philadelphia, depicts street car, bus, and subway-elevated lines, city wide information, places of interest, hours of service, map indexes, multicolored, Philadelphia Transportation Co, Philadelphia, PA, 24 x 32" **30.00**

Newspaper, *Public Service News*, Kansas City, MO, Dec 10, 1947, information on how to ride buses and street cars, shopping downtown stores, and theater news, 8½ x 7" **5.00**

Postcard, 3rd Lower Canal view, Holyoke, MA, #1453, Metropolitan News Co, MA and Germany **3.00**

Postcard, Gray Line Bus, depicts Gray Line bus in the Redwoods above printed inscription "Gray Line Bus and Big trees, Muir Woods, California Muir Woods, 5-52," 5½ x 3½" **8.00**

Postcard, Schuylkill Canal view, Norristown, PA, ... **20.00**

Sign, Bournemouth England Taxi #8, porcelain, city symbol above "Bournemouth 8," 1930-40s, 7 x 4½" **40.00**

Sign, City Cab Service, diecut metal, 2-sided, "3 Taxis" above "City Cab Service/UN.1-8271," c1950-60, 14¼" h, 17¼" w **40.00**

Sign, Greyhound Lines, porcelain, 2-sided, oval, c1940s, 36 x 20" **475.00**

Sign, The London Bus, London Ales adv, 7¾ x 11" **18.00**

Timetable, Bangor and Aroostook Bus and Passenger Train Schedules, lists bus schedules and stops from Bangor to Fort Kent as well as train stops from Bangor, Pesque Island, Ashland, and Fort Kent, also rail schedules between Northern Maine Junction and Caribou, dated Oct 30, 1960 . . . . **12.00**

Timetable, Santa Fe Coordinated Rail-Bus Timetable for California, 1938 . . . . **5.00**

Timetable, Vermont Transit Bus Co, 1941 . . . . **8.00**

Toy, Continental Trailways Bus, friction, litho tin, "27505 Silver Eagle Express," 10¾ x 3" **60.00**

Toy, Greyhound bus, windup, Keystone, 18½" l **100.00**

Trolley Card, Chesterfield Cigarettes, Gary Cooper holding cigarette pack with "Gary Cooper/The Story of Dr Wassell/For My Taste/It's Chesterfield, 1940s **40.00**

Trolley Card, Chesterfield Cigarettes, women in various sports outfits smoking cigarettes, 11 x 21". **35.00**

Trolley Card, Fox DeLuxe Beer, center bottle illus in front of banner with "Balanced Flavor," "Full 32 oz Quart/Economy Package/5 Full Glasses". **125.00**

Trolley Card, Wrigley's Double Mint Gum, cartoon baby with wings wearing banner with "1933" and holding gum pack, 11 x 21" **18.00**

TV GUIDE

TV Guide first appeared as *Tele-Vision Guide* on June 14, 1948. Its title was shortened to *TV Guide* on March 18, 1950. Published in New York, *Tele-Vision Guide* was one of a number of regional weekly, digest-sized TV log magazines.

Walter Annenberg bought *TV Guide* near the end of 1952 and went national with the April 3, 1953, issue whose cover featured a picture of Lucy Ricardo (Lucille Ball) and baby Ricky.

Value rests primarily with cover images. Issues #26 (9/25 to 10/1,1953) with George Reeves as Superman and #179 (9/1-7/56) with Elvis are two of the most sought-after issues. Occasionally an inside story is the key. The April 19-25, 1969, issue includes a story of the Beatles. Early fall premier issues command a small premium. Condition is critical. The survival rate is high. Collecting emphasis rests primarily with issues pre-dating 1980.

Reference: Ron Barlow and Ray Reynolds, *The Insider's Guide to Old Books, Magazines, Newspapers, Trade Catalogs*, Windmill Publishing, 1995.

Periodical: *PCM (Paper Collectors' Marketplace)*, PO Box 128, Scandinavia, WI 54977.

1953, Oct 30, Beulah Witch and Friends, #31 . . . . **$15.00**

1954, Jan 1, Bing Crosby. **20.00**

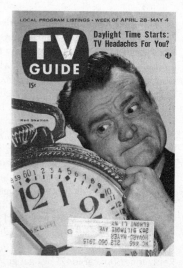

Left: 1953, Apr 10, Vol 1, #2, *Dragnet* **star Jack Webb, $25.00; Right: 1956, Apr 28, Vol 4, #17, Red Skelton, $12.00.**

1954, Mar 26, Jackie Gleason **20.00**
1954, Apr 9, Milton Berle and Charles Applewhite **20.00**
1954, Jun 25, Buffalo Bob Smith and Howdy Doody **80.00**
1954, Jul 17, Roy Rogers **80.00**
1955, Oct 1, Mickey Mouse and Disney characters **40.00**
1955, Dec 31, Cleo the dog of The Peoples Choice, #144 . . . . **20.00**
1958, Oct 11, Fred Astaire and Barrie Chase, #289 . . . . **10.00**
1959, May 23, Bob Hope **4.00**
1961, May 20, The Real McCoys **5.00**
1961, Route 66, Martin Milner and George Maharis **50.00**
1963, Nov 16, James Franciscus/Dean Jagger of Mr
  Novak, #555 . . . . **10.00**
1963, Dec 7, John McIntire of Wagon Train, Robert
  Fuller, #558 . . . . **20.00**
1963, Dec 14, Rosemary Clooney, Frank Sinatra, Dean
  Martin, Kathryn and Bing Crosby, #559 . . . . **20.00**
1963, Dec 28, Patty Duke, #561 . . . . **20.00**
1964, Feb 15, Mr and Mrs Andy Williams, #568 . . . . **10.00**
1964, Feb 22, David Janssen of The Fugitive, #569 . . . . **25.00**
1964, Apr 25, Danny Thomas, #578 . . . . **10.00**
1965, Feb, Beverly Hillbillies **10.00**
1967, Jul, Rat Patrol **25.00**
1968, Sep 14, Fall Preview, #807 . . . . **25.00**
1968, Nov, Mod Squad **25.00**
1969, Sep 13, Fall Preview, #859 . . . . **10.00**
1971, Jan 30, Bonanza, James Arness, Vol 19, #5 . . . . **8.00**
1978, Jul 15, Black Sheep Squadron, Robert Conrad **5.00**
1979, May 5, The Paper Chase, James Stephens and John
  Houseman **5.00**

TYPEWRITERS

E. Remington & Son's Sholes & Glidden typewriter, introduced in 1874, was the first commercially produced typewriter in the United States. The keyboard consisted only of capital letters.

The earliest typewriters are known as blind models, i.e., the carriage had to be lifted away from the machine to see what had been written. Five major manufacturers joined forces in 1893 to form the Union Typewriter Company. Their monopoly was soon challenged by L. C. Smith & Brothers and the Underwood Typewriter Company. These companies led the field in typewriter innovation in the pre-1940 period.

Electric typewriters appeared briefly in the 1900s. It was not until the 1930s that IBM introduced the first commercially successful electric typewriter. The electric typewriter replaced the manual typewriter by the late 1960s, only to lose its market position to the home computer in the late 1980s.

Advanced typewriter collectors focus primarily on pre-1920 models. Post-1920 typewriters with unusual features are the exception. The keyboard is a good barometer. If the letter placement, i.e., QWERTY, is the same as a modern typewriter or computer keyboard, chances are strong the machine has little value.

Europe, particularly Germany, is the center of typewriter collecting. The number of American collectors remains small.

References: Michael Adler, *Antique Typewriters: From Creed to QWERTY*, Schiffer Publishing, 1997; Darryl Rehr, *Antique Typewriters & Office Collectibles*, Collector Books, 1997.

Newsletters: *Ribbon Tin News*, 28 The Green, Watertown, CT 06795; *The Typewriter Exchange*, PO Box 52607, Philadelphia, PA 19115.

Collectors' Club: Early Typewriter Collectors Assoc, PO Box 641824, Los Angeles, CA 90064.

Advertising Tear Sheet, IBM, "Business large and small, in all parts of the country, are enthusiastic in their praise of the International All-Electric Writing Machine," text about machine's speed, feather-light touch, and ability to create 20 carbon copies at once, dated Apr 1940 . . . . **$10.00**
Advertising Tear Sheet, Star Branch Typewriter Ribbons, Webster Co, black and white ribbon tin on sepiatone ground, red lettering, 1927, 6½ x 9½" **2.00**
Book, *The Wonderful Writing Machine*, Bruce Bliven Jr, 236 pp, Random House, 1st printing, 1954, compliments The Royal Typewriter Co, dj, 6 x 9¼" **12.00**
Pin, Royal Typewriters, "Proficiency Club Accuratio Premium" in shield below crown **5.00**
Ribbon Tin, Carter's Ideal, waterlily and dragonfly graphics, 2½" d **6.00**
Ribbon Tin, Copper Chief, 2½" d **15.00**
Ribbon Tin, Elk **5.00**
Ribbon Tin, Fine Service, airplane graphics, 2⅝" sq **10.00**
Ribbon Tin, Kleenertype **6.00**
Ribbon Tin, LC Smith, airplane graphics **15.00**
Ribbon Tin, Rainbow **10.00**
Toy, Berwin, litho tin, gold and red keys, black trim, complete with ribbon, orig instructions **6.00**
Toy, Marx, Junior Typewriter, litho tin, hard molded plastic, orig box **15.00**
Typewriter, Corona Four, black metal **30.00**
Typewriter, Densmore, #4, ball bearing, black paint finish . . . **425.00**
Typewriter, IBM, Model 11, electric, 14" carriage **50.00**
Typewriter, Olivetti Praxis 48, electric **60.00**
Typewriter, Olympia SM Deluxe, manual, gray and white keys, plastic cover and instructions, Germany **10.00**
Typewriter, Remington Rand, Model 5 . . . . **15.00**
Typewriter, Remington Streamliner, manual, portable **20.00**
Typewriter, Royal, touch control, magic margin lever **12.00**
Typewriter, Royal Quiet DeLuxe, orig case, complete with manual, 1940s **35.00**
Typewriter, Simplex, Model D, 8¾ x 5½" **15.00**
Typewriter, Smith-Corona, Model 5A, #SL500, built-in carrying handle, gray case **15.00**

Remie Scout, 1932, $200.00. Photo courtesy Auction Team Köln.

Typewriter, Smith-Corona Floating Shift, portable, black, #4A293000, with case. **40.00**
Typewriter, Underwood Noiseless, portable **10.00**

AUCTION PRICES – TYPEWRITERS

Auction Team Köln (Köln, Germany), Office Antiques, November 27, 1999. Prices include a 20.17% premium (17.39% buyer's premium and 16% tax) and have been rounded to the nearest whole US dollar.

Correspondent, export version of the Rofa Model IV, 1923. . . . . **$727.00**
Hermes 2000 (Hebrew), c1958 . . . . **469.00**
Imperial Model D, 1919. . . . . **218.00**
International Electromatic, IBM, 1930. . . . . **119.00**
Mignon Model 4, 1923 . . . . **331.00**
Monarch Pioneer, 1932 . . . . **99.00**
National No. 5, c1920. . . . . **232.00**
Odoma, 1921 . . . . **496.00**
Panwriter, Japan, c1950 . . . . **429.00**
Rem-Blick, 1928 . . . . **331.00**
Remington Noiseless No. 6, 1925. . . . . **132.00**

UNIVERSAL POTTERY

In 1926 the Atlas China Company (Niles, Ohio) and the Globe Pottery Company (Cambridge, Ohio), both owned by A. O. C. Ahrendts, were consolidated and renamed the Atlas Globe China Company. Financial pressures resulted in another reorganization in the early 1930s. The factory in Niles closed. Globe was liquidated, its assets becoming part of the Oxford Pottery, also owned by Ahrendts.

In 1934 the company became Universal Pottery. Universal made baking dishes, a fine grade of semi-porcelain dinnerware, and utilitarian kitchenware. Tile manufacturing was introduced in 1956, and the company became The Oxford Tile Company. It continued to make dinnerware until 1960. Universal Promotions distributed Universal. It subcontracted with Hull, Homer Laughlin, and Taylor, Smith & Taylor to continue manufacturing Universal patterned pieces with a Universal backstamp into the 1960s.

Reference: Timothy J. Smith, *Universal Dinnerware and Its Predecessors*, Schiffer Publishing, 2000..

Ballerina, bowl, tab handles, jade green, 7" w **$5.00**
Ballerina, bread and butter plate, dove gray **4.00**
Ballerina, butter, jade green. **35.00**
Ballerina, cake plate, tab handles, chartreuse, 11½" w **18.00**
Ballerina, cake plate, tab handles, jade green, 11½" d **18.00**
Ballerina, chop plate, dove gray, 13" w **12.00**
Ballerina, creamer and open sugar, forest green **10.00**
Ballerina, creamer and sugar, periwinkle **15.00**
Ballerina, cup and saucer, black **6.00**
Ballerina, cup and saucer, jade green. **6.00**
Ballerina, dinner plate, dove gray, 10" d. **5.00**
Ballerina, French casserole, chartreuse, 5" w **12.00**
Ballerina, gravy boat, jade green **12.00**
Ballerina, gravy boat and liner, yellow **10.00**
Ballerina, luncheon plate, brown, 9" d **8.00**

Ballerina, luncheon plate, jade green, 9" d **4.00**
Ballerina, luncheon plate, perriwinkle, 9" d **8.00**
Ballerina, pitcher, ice lip, jade green **55.00**
Ballerina, salt and pepper shakers, pr, burgundy salt, dove gray pepper. **10.00**
Ballerina, serving bowl, periwinkle **15.00**
Ballerina, soup bowl, tab handles, burgundy, 7" w **6.00**
Ballerina, tea set, teapot, creamer, and sugar **25.00**
Ballerina, tidbit tray, dove gray. **15.00**
Ballerina, utility bowl, dove gray, 5¼" d. **20.00**
Ballerina, utility bowl, jade green, 5¼" d **20.00**
Ballerina Iris, cake plate, tab handles, 11½" w **25.00**
Ballerina Iris, platter, tab handles, 12" w. **25.00**
Ballerina Largo, soup bowl, tab handles, 7" w **4.00**
Ballerina Magnolia, berry bowl, 5½" d. **2.00**
Ballerina Magnolia, bowl, 6½" w. **4.00**
Ballerina Magnolia, coffeepot **15.00**
Ballerina Magnolia, creamer **8.00**
Ballerina Magnolia, cup and saucer. **5.00**
Ballerina Magnolia, dinner plate, 10⅛" d **7.00**
Ballerina Magnolia, gravy boat **12.00**
Ballerina Mist, coffee server. **30.00**
Ballerina Mist, creamer **12.00**
Ballerina Mist, cup and saucer. **3.00**
Ballerina Mist, dessert plate, 6" d. **5.00**
Ballerina Mist, dinner plate, 10" d **8.00**
Ballerina Mist, mixing bowl, 7½" d, 4" h **10.00**
Ballerina Mist, pitcher, 7½" h. **20.00**
Ballerina Mist, salt and pepper shakers, pr, 2⅞" h. **15.00**
Ballerina Mist, serving bowl, 9" d **10.00**
Ballerina Mist, soup bowl, tab handles, 7" w **12.00**
Ballerina Mist, vegetable, cov **18.00**
Ballerina Rose, ball jug, ice lip, 7" h **15.00**
Ballerina Rose, bowl, coupe shape, 7" d **8.00**
Ballerina Rose, bread and butter plate, 7½" d. **7.00**
Ballerina Rose, butter, ¼ lb **25.00**
Ballerina Rose, cup. **6.00**
Ballerina Rose, luncheon plate, 9¾" d **12.00**
Ballerina Rose, soup bowl, tab handles, 7" w **10.00**

Ballerina, chop plate, tab handles, forest green, 13" w, $12.00.

Ballerina Rose, teapot **25.00**
Ballerina Woodvine, berry bowl, 5½" d **2.00**
Ballerina Woodvine, casserole, cov, 10" w **25.00**
Ballerina Woodvine, luncheon plate, 9⅛" d **25.00**
Ballerina Woodvine, soup bowl, tab handles, 7" w **6.00**
Bittersweet, casserole **20.00**
Bittersweet, grease jar **15.00**
Bittersweet, jug, cov **18.00**
Bittersweet, pitcher **15.00**
Bittersweet, salt and pepper shakers, pr **15.00**
Bittersweet, salt and pepper shakers, pr, range size **20.00**
Bittersweet, stack set **50.00**
Bittersweet, tilt pitcher **55.00**
Calico Fruit, bowl, 4" d **12.00**
Calico Fruit, cake plate **28.00**
Calico Fruit, casserole **18.00**
Calico Fruit, drip jar, cov **25.00**
Calico Fruit, grill plate **15.00**
Calico Fruit, pie plate **32.00**
Calico Fruit, pitcher, hook lid **35.00**
Calico Fruit, refrigerator bowl, cov **18.00**
Calico Fruit, shaker **8.00**
Calico Fruit, utility bowl **15.00**
Cattail, bread and butter plate **4.00**
Cattail, casserole, cov **65.00**
Cattail, cracker jar, cov, 9" h **40.00**
Cattail, creamer **15.00**
Cattail, dinner plate **10.00**
Cattail, gravy and underplate **55.00**
Cattail, mixing bowl, 7" d **15.00**
Cattail, nesting bowls, 6", 7¼", and 8¾" d, set of 3 . . . . **30.00**
Cattail, pie plate **12.00**
Cattail, platter, oval, 15" l **15.00**
Cattail, salad fork and spoon **30.00**
Cattail, soup bowl **10.00**
Cattail, teapot **40.00**
Cattail, vegetable, 9½" **18.00**
Circus, bowl, 6½" d **18.00**
Circus, casserole, cov **25.00**
Circus, luncheon plate, 9" d **12.00**
Circus, milk pitcher, 5" h **30.00**
Circus, mixing bowl, 7" d **25.00**
Circus, mixing bowl, 9" d **35.00**
Circus, platter, oval, handled, 13" l **18.00**
Hollyhock, chop plate **25.00**
Hollyhock, dessert plate **5.00**
Hollyhock, dinner plate **7.00**
Hollyhock, saucer **3.00**
Hollyhock, vegetable **18.00**
Moss Rose, berry bowl, 5⅜" d **2.00**

U.S. GLASS

United States Glass resulted from the merger of eighteen different glass companies in 1891. The company's headquarters were in Pittsburgh. Plants were scattered throughout Indiana, Ohio, Pennsylvania, and West Virginia.

Most plants continued to manufacture the same products that they made before the merger. Older trademarks and pattern names were retained. Some new shapes and patterns used a U.S. Glass trademark. New plants were built in Gas City, Indiana, and Tiffin, Ohio. The Gas City plant made machine-made dinnerware,

kitchenware, and tabletop items in colors that included amber, black, canary, green, and pink. The Tiffin plant made delicate pressed dinnerware and blown stemware in crystal and a host of other colors. U.S. Glass' main decorating facility was in Pittsburgh.

During the first three decades of the 20th century, several plants closed, the result of strikes, organizational mismanagement, and/or economic difficulties. In 1938, following the appointment of C. W. Carlson, Sr., as president, the corporate headquarters moved from Pittsburgh to Tiffin. Only the Pittsburgh and Tiffin plants were still operating. Carlson, along with C. W. Carlson, Jr., his son, revived the company by adding several new shapes and colors to the line. The company prospered until the late 1950s.

By 1951 all production was located in Tiffin. U.S. Glass bought the Duncan and Miller molds in 1955. Some former Duncan and Miller employees moved to Tiffin. U.S. Glass created a Duncan and Miller Division.

C. W. Carlson, Sr., retired in 1959. U.S. Glass profits declined. In 1962 U.S. Glass was in bankruptcy. Production resumed when C. W. Carlson, Jr. and some former Tiffin workers founded Tiffin Art Glass Corporation.

Reference: Gene Florence, *Collector's Encyclopedia of Depression Glass, Fourteenth Edition,* Collector Books, 2000.

Cherryberry, comport, 5¾" d, 3¾" h, green **$25.00**
Cherryberry, deep berry bowl, 7½" d, iridescent **20.00**
Cherryberry, sherbet plate, 6" d, green **10.00**
Floral and Diamond Band, berry bowl, 8" d, green **20.00**
Floral and Diamond Band, butter, cov, green **90.00**
Floral and Diamond Band, compote, 5½" h, pink **20.00**
Floral and Diamond Band, creamer, 4¾" h, green **35.00**
Floral and Diamond Band, ice tea, 5" h, pink **55.00**
Floral and Diamond Band, luncheon plate, 8" d, green **75.00**
Floral and Diamond Band, pitcher, 42 oz, 8" h, green **90.00**
Florida, creamer, emerald green **20.00**
Florida, luncheon plate, emerald green **25.00**

Florida, berry bowl, individual size, emerald green, $15.00.

Florida, sugar, emerald green. **25.00**
Flower Garden, ashtray, blue. **300.00**
Flower Garden, candy, flat, teal. **200.00**
Flower Garden, candy, heart shape, yellow **1,500.00**
Grapefruit Reamer, transparent green, tooth chips. **500.00**
Lamps, pr, Art Deco motif, frosted white. **175.00**
Lamps, pr, Art Deco motif, opaque blue, square base **350.00**
Powder Jar, Annette, frosted pink **200.00**
Powder Jar, Curtsy, frosted pink **140.00**
Powder Jar, elephant, trunk down, frosted pink. **135.00**
Powder Jar, lovebirds, frosted green **125.00**
Primo, cake plate, 3-ftd, 10" d, green. **25.00**
Shaggy Daisy, cake plate, 3-ftd, 10" d, pink. **25.00**
Shaggy Rose, cake plate, 3-ftd, 10" d, green. **20.00**
Strawberry, butter, green **165.00**
Strawberry, salad plate, 7½" d, pink. **20.00**

VALENTINES

The valentine experienced several major changes in the early decades of the 20th century. Fold or pull out, lithograph novelty, mechanical action, and postcard valentines replaced lacy valentines as the preferred form. Diecut cards became common. Chromolithography brightened the color scheme.

The candy, card, flower, and giftware industry hopped aboard the valentine bandwagon big time following 1920. Elementary schools introduced valentine exchanges when inexpensive mass-produced valentine packs became available. Companies and stars licensed their images for valentine use.

Valentine collectors specialize. Many 20th-century valentines, especially post-1945 examples, are purchased by crossover collectors more interested in the card's subject matter than the fact that it is a valentine. Valentine survival rate is high. Never assume any post-1920 valentine is in short supply.

References: Robert Brenner, *Valentine Treasury,* Schiffer Publishing, 1997; Dan and Pauline Campanelli, *Romantic Valentines,* L-W Book Sales, 1996; Katherine Kreider, *One Hundred Years of Valentines,* Schiffer Publishing, 1999.

Collectors' Club: National Valentine Collectors Assoc, PO Box 1404, Santa Ana, CA 92702.

Greeting Card, beautiful woman with flowers, "Thou Art My Heart's Desire," diecut, opens, emb, printed color, 4½ x 7¼". **$20.00**
Greeting Card, boy and girl playing tennis with hearts, diecut, emb, printed color **20.00**
Greeting Card, boy with heart, diecut, opens, emb, gold highlights, printed color. **8.00**
Greeting Card, Cupid on letter, diecut, opens, cut paper lace, printed color, 6 x 6¼". **20.00**
Greeting Card, Cupid with instrument, easel back, diecut heart, add-on parchment paper, easel repaired, printed color, 7½" h. **20.00**
Greeting Card, Dutch boy and girl in wooden shoe boat, eyes move, mechanical, printed color, Sam Gabriel, 5¾" h. **8.00**
Greeting Card, elephant 1-man band, diecut, printed color, German, 8 x 10½". **25.00**
Greeting Card, fox with chenille tail, fold down to girl with umbrella, diecut, stand-up, printed color, 7½". **20.00**

Greeting Card, mechanical, 1930s, 4 x 6", $6.00.

Greeting Card, genie holding plate, easel back, diecut honeycomb, turban folds out, printed color, German, 6¾" h **25.00**
Greeting Card, girl on dog, diecut, easel back, printed color, German, 4¾ x 5½" **12.00**
Greeting Card, girl with garland of flowers, heart shaped, border opens, diecut, printed color, 5½" h **12.00**
Greeting Card, man and woman with horses in rain, diecut, opens, emb, printed color. **10.00**
Greeting Card, woman reading letter, diecut, opens, Cupid beside, printed color **10.00**
Greeting Card, woman with flying hearts, opens, printed color, Schmucker. **8.00**
Postcard, girl in tennis outfit hitting heart shaped ball across net, "Valentine Greetings," #407, Germany **2.00**
Postcard, heart between 2 doves and ribbon, "To My Valentine," emb **2.00**
Postcard, seated Cupid playing guitar, butterfly and floral illus, "To My Valentine" **3.00**
Postcard, "You Have The Key To My Heart" **2.00**

VAN BRIGGLE POTTERY

Artus Van Briggle established the Van Briggle Pottery Company in 1900. His pottery won numerous awards including one from the 1903 Paris Exhibition.

Following Van Briggle's death in 1904, his wife, Anne, became president of the company, reorganized, and built a new plant. Van Briggle produced a wide range of products including art pottery, garden pottery, novelty items, and utilitarian ware. Artware produced between 1901 and 1912 is recognized for its high quality of design and glaze. Van Briggle's Lorelei vase is a classic.

A reorganization in 1910 produced the Van Briggle Pottery and Tile Company. By 1912 the pottery was leased to Edwin DeForest Curtis who in turn sold it to Charles B. Lansing in 1915. Lansing sold the company to I. F. and J. H. Lewis in 1920, who renamed the company Van Briggle Art Pottery. Kenneth Stevenson acquired the company in 1969. He continued the production of art pottery, introducing some new designs and glazes. Upon his death in 1990, Bertha (his wife) and Craig (his son) continued production.

The Stevensons use a mark similar to the interlocking "AA" mark used by Artus and Anne. Because they also make the same shapes and glazes, novice collectors frequently confuse newly made ware for older pieces. Because the Stevensons only selectively release their wholesale list, discovering which older shapes and glazes are in current production is difficult.

Prior to 1907 all pieces had the "AA" mark and "Van Briggle." These marks also were used occasionally during the 1910s and 20s. "Colorado Springs" or an abbreviation often appears on pieces made after 1920. Some early pieces were dated. Value rises considerably when a date mark is present.

Reference: Richard Sasicki and Josie Fania, *Collector's Encyclopedia of Van Briggle Art Pottery*, Collector Books, 1993, 1999 value update.

Collectors' Club: American Art Pottery Assoc, PO Box 834, Westport, MA 02790.

REPRODUCTION ALERT: Van Briggle pottery is still being produced today. Modern glazes include Midnight (black), Moonglo (off-white), Russet, and Turquoise Ming.

Bookends, pr, Indian heads, Persian Rose glaze, 5½" h **$150.00**
Bookends, pr, owl, Persian Rose glaze, imp AA mark, c1920, 5" h, 5" w **150.00**
Bowl, emb leaves at closed-in rim, matte turquoise glaze, incised "AA/Van Briggle," c1920, 6¼" h, 10½" d **575.00**
Bud Vase, emb flowers, pedestal foot, shaded blue-green matte glaze, 7¼" h **100.00**
Bud Vase, Persian Rose glaze **30.00**
Bud Vase, rolled rim, elongated narrow cylindrical neck, flat spreading foot, shaded blue and turquoise matte glaze, incised "AA/20," 7¼" h, 2½" d **300.00**
Cabinet Vase, bulbous, emb crocuses, Persian Rose glaze, incised "AA/Van Briggle," 1920s, 2½" h, 2½" d **125.00**
Cabinet Vase, spherical, emb butterflies, Persian Rose glaze, incised "AA/Van Briggle/O," 3" h, 3½" d **175.00**
Cabinet Vase, squat, emb stylized leaves, shaded purple and green matte glaze, incised "AA/Van Briggle/ USA," 2" h, 3" d **150.00**
Candlestick, faceted, Persian Rose glaze, incised "AA/Van Briggle/Colo Spgs," pre-1932, 10¼" h, 5½" w **160.00**
Centerbowl, low bowl with emb dragonflies, flower frog emb with 3 perched frogs, shaded blue and turquoise matte glaze, bowl incised "AA/Van Briggle/20," frog incised "AA," 8½" d bowl, 5" d frog **250.00**
Centerbowl, oval low bowl with 2 emb sides and large figural swan flower frog, blue-green matte glaze, mkd, 14¾" w bowl, 8¼" h swan **100.00**
Centerbowl, shell-shaped bowl with emb mermaid and flying fish, with flower frog, Persian Rose glaze, bowl incised "AA/Van Briggle/Colo Spgs," 14" d bowl, 6¼" d frog **500.00**
Chamberstick, tall shaft, Persian Rose glaze, incised "AA/1920," 7½" h, 5½" d **175.00**
Console Set, tulip-shaped bowl and pr of candlesticks, white, incised "AA/Van Briggle/Colo Spgs" **50.00**
Figurines, pr, Indian brave and squaw with papoose, turquoise and blue matte glaze, imp "AA," 12½" h **275.00**
Gondola Vase, Persian Rose glaze **50.00**
Low Bowl, emb broad leaves, matte turquoise glaze, incised "AA/Van Briggle/20," 3½" h, 7¾" d **250.00**

Low Bowl, Persian Rose glaze **35.00**
Paperweight, figural rabbit, Persian Rose glaze, incised "AA," 2½" h, 2¾" w **125.00**
Vase, bulbous, emb butterflies, brown matte glaze, incised "AA/Van Briggle,/USA," 3¾" h, 3½" d **175.00**
Vase, cylindrical neck, bulbous base, emb violets and leaves, matte purple glaze, incised "AA/Van Briggle /20," 1920, 4" h, 3" d **150.00**
Vase, cylindrical neck, bulbous base, emb violets and leaves, matte turquoise glaze with brown clay showing through, incised "AA/Nunn/1920," 4" h, 3" d **250.00**
Vase, emb dragonflies, shaded blue-green matte glaze, 7" h **125.00**
Vase, flower-shaped, white **25.00**
Vase, ovoid, closed-in rim, emb tulips, shaded green and brown matte glaze, incised "AA/Van Briggle/USA," 9¼" h, 4¼" d **350.00**
Vase, tall cylindrical form, emb stylized leaves, 3 buttresses at rim, Persian Rose glaze, incised "AA/Van Briggle/20," 10¾" h, 4½" d **300.00**
Vase, tapered cylindrical neck, bulbous base, emb quatrefoils and leaves, Persian Rose glaze, incised "AA/ Van Briggle/Colo Spgs," 9¼" h, 7¼" d **325.00**
Vessel, squat, 2-handled, shaded blue-green matte glaze **55.00**
Vessel, squat, emb acorns and oak leaves, turquoise matte glaze, incised "AA/Van Briggle/9," 3¼" h, 5" d **225.00**
Vessel, squat, emb tulips, Persian Rose glaze, incised "AA/Van Briggle/Colo Spgs," 4½" h, 7" d **225.00**
Wall Pocket, cone-shaped, emb papyrus, Persian Rose glaze, incised "AA/Van Briggle/Colo Spgs," 10¾" h, 5½" w **250.00**

VENDING MACHINES

Vending machines were silent salesmen. They worked 24 hours a day. Thomas Adams of Adams Gum is created with popularizing the vending machine. In 1888 his Tutti-Frutti gum machines were placed on elevated train platforms in New York City. The wedding of the gumball and vending machine occurred around 1910.

Leading vending machine manufacturers from its golden age, 1920 through the end of the 1950s, include Ad-Lee Novelty, Bluebird Products, Columbus Vending, Northwestern, Pulver, Volkmann, Stollwerck and Co., and Victor Vending. Figural machines and those incorporating unusual mechanical action are among the most desirable.

Today's vending machine collectors collect either globe-type machines or lithograph tin counter-top models dating prior to 1960. While period paint is considered an added value factor, retention of period decals and labels and workability are the main value keys. Since the average life of many vending machines is measured in decades, collectors expect machines to be touched up or repainted.

Vending machines are collected either by type or by material dispensed. Crossover collectors can skew pricing.

References: Richard M. Bueschel, *Collector's Guide to Vintage Coin Machines,* Schiffer Publishing, 1995; Richard M. Bueschel, *Guide to Vintage Trade Stimulators & Counter Games,* Schiffer Publishing, 1997; Bill Enes, *Silent Salesmen: An Encyclopedia of Collectible Gum, Candy & Nut Machines,* published by author, 1987; Bill Enes, *Silent Salesman Too: The Encyclopedia of Collectible Vending Machines,* published by author, 1995.

Northwestern Deluxe Penny/Nickel Machine, red porcelain, with key, 1936, 17½" h, $275.00. Photo courtesy Collectors Auction Services.

VENETIAN GLASS

Italian glass is a generic term for glassware made in Italy from the 1920s into the early 1960s and heavily exported to the United States. Pieces range from vases with multicolored internal thick and thin filigree threads to figural clowns and fish.

The glass was made in Murano, the center of Italy's glass blowing industry. Beginning in the 1920s many firms hired art directors and engaged the services of internationally known artists and designers. The 1950s was a second golden age following the flurry of high-style pieces made from the mid-1920s through the mid-1930s.

Reference: Rosa Barovier Mentasti, *Venetian Glass: 1890–1990,* Arsenale Editrice, 1992, distributed by Antique Collectors' Club.

Newsletter: *Vertri: Italian Glass News,* PO Box 191, Fort Lee, NJ 07024.

Collectors' Club: Murano Glass Society, 32040 Mt Hermon Rd, Salisbury, MD 21804.

Advance Big Mouth Peanut Vendor, 1¢, glass globe, c1925, restored $400.00
Asco Hot Nut Vendor, 5¢, 21" h, restored 500.00
Coca-Cola, Cavalier 72, holds twelve 6-oz bottles, "Have a Coke" lens lights up after money is deposited, 1950s, 56½" h, 24½" w, 21⅞" deep, restored 4,275.00
Eagle Gumball, 25¢ 50.00
Eldridge Nut Vendor, peanuts or candy, aluminum, 8½" h, 4½" w, 4" d 400.00
Eveready Sandwich Vendor, 21 individual coin-operated compartments, 1930s 1,750.00
Hawkeye Vendor Gumball Machine, 1¢, 1930s 400.00
Hospeco Condoms, wall mount, aluminum, white, "Hospeco Health Guards Condoms/50 Cents/For Your Protection/The Modern Preshaped Condom" 45.00
Mills Automatic Tab Gum Vendor, aluminum, hammerstone green, c1936 .... 300.00
Mills Wilbur Succhard Chocolate Vendor, 1930s, 14" h, 9" w, 4" d, restored 975.00
Mutoscope Card Vendor, black motif with matching cards, lighted top, 1940s 1,500.00
Norelco Shavendor, 25¢, "Sanitized Electric Shave," dispenses after-shave lotion upon completion, wall mount, orig box, 11 x 14 x 7" 1,750.00
Northwestern Merchandiser, 1¢, glass globe, c1931, 16" h, restored 400.00
Northwestern Peanut, 1¢, porcelain base, emb frosted globe, 1930s, 15" h 400.00
Northwestern Super 60 Gumball 60.00
Pocket Combs, 10¢, metal, white, 32" h 175.00
Regal Vendor, 5¢, glass globe, orig mints inside, 1940s 300.00
Silver King Buffalo Target Penny Shoot & Gum Vendor, 1¢, 1940-50s, 17" h, 22" l, 9" w 800.00
Silver King Gumball Machine, 5¢, 1945 .... 325.00
Silver King Hot Nut, red hobnail glass globe, c1947, 15" h 500.00
Silver King Hunter Duck Penny Shoot & Gum Vendor, 1¢, insert penny and shoot at 3 ducks, pull plunger to receive gumball, 1940-50s, 17" h, 22" l, 9" w 500.00
Victor Extender Gumball Machine, Model V, cast iron, 1¢, 1941 .... 325.00
Victor Topper Gumball Machine, 1¢, 1950s, restored 250.00

Ansolo Fugo, attributed to, hanging light fixtures, pr, short yellow, red, and blue canes on lattimo ground, unmkd, 13 x 6" $875.00
Antonio DaRos, vase, block shaped, sommerso glass, off-center opening, cobalt, red, and yellow, unmkd, 10¼ x 6¼" 1,100.00
Barovier, Aurato vase, tear shaped, flaring split rim, amethyst and milk glass with gold foil, unmkd, 10 x 5½" 1,975.00
Bruno Saetti, vase, Seguso, rooster, eggplant spots and applied red glass features, on clear base with blue canes, etched "Bruno Saetti/A Seguso/Murano," 13 x 4¾" 1,750.00
Dino Martens, Oriente dish, leaf shaped, fused sections of orange-yellow, aubergine, white, turquoise, and aventurine with transparent red, green, and blue within colorless clipped and folded surround, 2½" h, 7½" l 425.00
Dino Martens, Oriente vase, ftd, flaring, multicolored opaque glass patchwork, post-factory drilled as lamp base, unmkd, 16¾ x 7½" 1,500.00
Dino Martens, vase, Aureliana Toso, corseted, mezza filigrana white, red, and clear glass, unsgd, 1954, 10 x 5¾" 300.00
Dominick Labino, sculpture, "Emergence" series, vertical expression in crystal, internal veils of pink and orange centering four bubbles at core, base inscribed "T. Labino 9-1971," 1971, 9¼" h 5,000.00
Dominick Labino, vase, elongated oviform, everted rim, 2 shaped handles, heavy walled, blue swirled glass, cased to ruby int, base inscribed "Labino 5-1971," 6¾" h 400.00
Dominick Labino, vase, urn shaped, 2 attached handles of lightly iridized ruby colored glass, base inscribed "Labino 1-1972," 5¼" h 550.00
Fornasetti, dinner plates, set of 7, "12 mesi/12 soli," different images in black on white ground, 5 depicting sun and 2 depicting moon, ink mark "Fornasetti/Milano," 10" d 600.00
Fornasetti, dinner plates, set of 8, image of Roman man and woman in chariot drawn by 6 horses on gilded ground, orig box, ink mark "Fornasetti/Milano Made Exclusively for Saks Fifth Avenue," 4" d 200.00

Pauls Products, dancers, red translucent glass with applied clear ornamentation, embedded with gold flecks, clear swirled rib and gold fleck base, each with "Pauls Products, Made in Italy" paper label, 9" h, price for pr, $600.00. Photo courtesy Jackson's Auctioneers & Appraisers.

Gambone, decanter, teal lattice band on body, neck, and stopper on white matte ground, ink mark "Gambone/ Italy," 12 x 4" 450.00

Lino Tagliapietra, vase, flattened oviform, extended neck of opaque white with black powder cased to colorless glass, medial red band and transparent cobalt blue glass, base inscribed "Lino Tagliapietra Efferte International Murano 1986 23/100 Italy," 11¼" h 925.00

Murano, ashtray, black amethyst with copper swirl, mkd "Venetian Weil Murano Italy," orig box, 3¼" d, price for set of 4 . . . . 300.00

Murano, bowl, attributed to Seguso, figural orange, heavy walled, applied green stem and leaf, ext orange peel texture, overall gold inclusions, scalloped red foil label, 7" d 300.00

Murano, bowl, figural duck, dark to light honey amber, white highlights and clear glass along edge of wings, black applied eyes and beak, polished glass bottom, 3½" h, 9¼" w 45.00

Murano, chandelier, clear glass with 4 electrified arms, opaque pink and blue flowers, unmkd, 18 x 15" 150.00

Murano, cigarette lighter, amber and gold, "Genuine Venetian Glass, Made in Italy" sticker, 4½" h 30.00

Murano, decanter, clear with chartreuse pulled canes on body, spherical opaque chartreuse stopper, foil label, 18 x 4" 55.00

Murano, dish, arrowhead shaped, green, red, blue yellow, and glittery copper, 9½" l, 7½" w 10.00

Murano, dish, figural swan, blue, orange, and yellow, clear neck, small rifts on tail simulate feathers, 6½" h 25.00

Murano, dish, latticed strands with pink, blue, yellow, red, burgundy, and green interspersed ribbons swirling from center to outside wide latticed clear glass bands, clear ftd base with gold glitter inclusions, 2¼" h, 5" w 50.00

Murano, figurine, apple, attributed to Alfredo Barbini, controlled bubbles with aventurine int, orig foil label, 4" h 35.00

Murano, figurine, clown, "La Commedia dell'arte," lattimo, black and red glass and gold foil, 12½ x 6" 775.00

Murano, figurine, dancing girl, teal and white with gold flecks in clear glass, swirled base, 10½" h 200.00

Murano, figurine, elephant, clear with encased blue and green, 5" h 15.00

Murano, figurine, pheasant, possibly Savatini & Co, shades of pink and cranberry with gold deposits throughout, 67" h 65.00

Murano, figurine, rooster, hand blown, candy apple red with gold flecks, 16" h 20.00

Murano, figurine, seated cat, clear with encased purple, 5" h 20.00

Murano, goblets, set of 4, hand blown, gold, Coin Dot pattern, 10" h 45.00

Murano, lamps, pr, figural couple in blue and white period costume with gold foil dec, each encased in freeform crystal block with trapped bubble highlights, supported by applied dome base, metal lamp fittings, 18½" h 975.00

Murano, paperweight, pear, hand blown, green leaf and stem, int gold spray, "Genuine Venetian Glass, Made in Murano Italy" paper label, 6" h, 10½" d 45.00

Murano, vase, black and silver glass, raised and flattened rim on ovoid black amethyst body with silver foil dec cased to colorless ext, polished pontil, 7¼" h 350.00

Murano, vase, transparent orange cased with crystal, stretch and swirled body, 9½" h 10.00

Paolo Venini, vase, filigrana, flaring, white and clear glass, unsgd, 10 x 6" 90.00

Raymor, vase, cylindrical, abstract fish on striped white and yellow ground, ink mark "R729/Raymor/Italy," 11 x 3¾" 225.00

Salviati, decanter, flask shaped, clear and red glass, spherical stopper, "Salviati & C/Murano" clear label, 12 x 6¼" 75.00

Salviati, figurine, angel, holding songbook in hands, gold flocks on hair, hands, and songbook, orig paper label, 9½" h 30.00

Tapio Wirkkala, decanter, Venini, beaker shaped, purple filigrana glass, clear glass cylindrical stopper, etched "Venini/Italia/TW," 9 x 5" 275.00

Unknown Maker, basket, pink with infused gold, applied flower and leaves on handle, 5" h, 4½" d 30.00

Unknown Maker, bottle, cylindrical, red band on green ground, "Fornesa de Muran a l'Insegna del Moreto Made In Italy/GF" foil label, 18 x 3" 450.00

Unknown Maker, bowl, free-form flaring, sommerso glass, amber with controlled bubbles, unmkd, 4 x 10" 55.00

Unknown Maker, bowl, stylized shell, aqua, gold int, 4¾" w, 2¾" h 25.00

Unknown Maker, candlestick, clear swan base, tail supports red bowl and holder, 5½" h 110.00

Unknown Maker, earrings, pr, translucent swirled pink with white stripes, brass clip-on backs, orig card mkd "Perla Veneziana-Made in Italy" 5.00

Unknown Maker, figurine, dolphin, gold and clear flecked yellow and black eyes, teal base, 4½" h 40.00

Unknown Maker, hatpin, millefiori ball with wide gold swirl, roses, and blue flowers, ½" d 50.00

Unknown Maker, lamp, Art Deco style, bulbous bottom, long stem neck with 6 drops of applied glass equally spaced around perimeter, teardrop shaped gold dust trim, 39½" h 75.00

Venini, bottle, bulbous, opaque blue glass, missing stopper, etched "Venini/Murano/Italia," 4³/₄ x 3¹/₄" **20.00**
Venini, ceiling lamp, Massimo Vignelli, lattima white glass fused to transparent horizontal face of blue, green, aubergine, and colorless stripes, mounted to socket fixture, 1954, 19¹/₂" h **800.00**
Venini, Fazzoletto vase, camichato slumped handkerchief bowl of lattimo white cased to cornflower blue, stamped "Venini/Murano/Italia," 4¹/₂" h **325.00**
Venini, Pezzato vase, orange, red, and yellow patchwork, acid-etched "Venini/Italia," 8³/₄ x 4¹/₂" **4,000.00**
Venini, Tessuto vase, Murano, attributed to Carlo Scarpa, elongated neck on ovoid form, black and turquoise vertical fused canes, polished pontil, foil label mkd "Venini SA Murano," 14¹/₄" h **2,000.00**

AUCTION PRICES – VENETIAN GLASS

Jackson's Auctioneers & Appraisers, Decorative Arts, May 29, 1999. Prices include a 12% premium and have been rounded to the nearest whole dollar.

Deer, amber, blue, and silver foil encased in crystal, "Made in Murano, Italy" red label, probably Seguso, 9" h **$90.00**
Dolphin, clear crystal with shaded electric blue back decorated with bullicante, free-form base, 13" h **90.00**
Ducks, ice blue with gold foil-dec clear accents, 5¹/₂" h, price for pair **34.00**
Fish, front half internally dec in red, rear in silver foil, clear fins, gray glass base, each with "Made in Italy Murano" red and silver foil label, 9" h, price for pr **196.00**
Flamenco Dancer, crystal internally dec with gold flecks, ice blue trim and ornamentation, bell-shaped foot, 9" h **112.00**
Penguin, gray and deep amber, wearing ice blue top hat, 11" h **34.00**

VERNON KILNS

In 1912 George Poxon established Poxon China in Vernon, California. Initially the company made tiles. Following World War I production shifted to earthenware dishes and hotel and restaurant ware. In 1928 George Poxon turned the company over to his wife Judith and her brother James Furlong. The company was renamed Vernon China.

In 1931 Faye G. Bennison bought Vernon China and changed the name to Vernon Kilns. Initially the company produced decal ware utilizing older Vernon China/Paxon shapes. An earthquake in 1933 shattered most of the company's inventory and did extensive damage to the kilns. This proved a blessing in disguise as Vernon Kilns introduced numerous new shapes and pattern lines. Art ware also was introduced, remaining in production until 1937.

In 1940 Vernon Kilns signed a contract with Walt Disney Productions to make figures of the characters from *Dumbo, Fantasia,* and *The Reluctant Dragon.* Specialty transfer print ware was introduced in the 1930s. The late 1940s and early 1950s saw the production of hundreds of commemorative patterns and series such as Moby Dick and Our America.

The Coronada shape line was introduced in 1938, Melinda in 1942, San Marino in the mid-1940s, and Anytime in 1955. Hand-painted Organdie and Brown-Eyed Susan were popular patterns.

In January 1958 a decision was made to close the company. Metlox Potteries, Manhattan Beach, California, bought the molds, modified some, and continued production of Anytime, Barkwood, Brown-Eyed Susan, Organdie, Sherwood, and Tickled Pink for a year. Although the Vernon Kilns plant closed, the corporation remained alive until it was legally dissolved in 1969.

References: Susan and Al Bagdade, *Warman's American Pottery and Porcelain,* Wallace-Homestead, Krause Publications, 1994; Harvey Duke, *The Official Price Guide to Pottery and Porcelain, Eighth Edition,* House of Collectibles, 1995.

Newsletter: *Vernon Views,* PO Box 945, Scottsdale, AZ 85252.

Arcadia, pitcher vase **$10.00**
Ashtray, Georgia map **12.00**
Brown Eyed Susan, creamer and sugar **18.00**
Brown Eyed Susan, dinner plate, 9¹/₂" d **5.00**
Brown Eyed Susan, salad plate **6.00**
Brown Eyed Susan, tea set, teapot, creamer, and open sugar **45.00**
Chatelaine, salt and pepper shakers, pr **8.00**
Chintz, bread and butter plate, 6¹/₄" d **10.00**
Chintz, cereal bowl **8.00**
Chintz, cup and saucer **20.00**
Chintz, dinner plate, 10¹/₂" d **25.00**
Chintz, teapot **150.00**
Coral Reef, chowder, cov **200.00**
Coral Reef, salt and pepper shakers, pr **100.00**
Desert Bloom, coffee server **40.00**
Dolores, gravy boat **30.00**
Dolores, salad plate, 7¹/₂" d **12.00**
Dolores, vegetable **20.00**
Early California, chop plate, turquoise, 12¹/₄" d **15.00**
Early California, cup and saucer, turquoise **8.00**
Early California, luncheon plate, orange, 9¹/₂" d **5.00**
Early California, mixing bowl, turquoise, 9" d **45.00**
Early California, teapot, turquoise, 6¹/₂" h **65.00**
Early California, vegetable, dark blue, 8⁷/₈" d **15.00**
Fantasia, console bowl, rect, emb dancing mushrooms design, blue, 2¹/₂" h, 12" l **100.00**
Fantasia, salt and pepper shakers, pr **150.00**
Figurine, Dumbo, #40, 1941, 4" h, 6" l **75.00**
Figurine, sprite #6, 1940 . . . . **225.00**
Figurine, sprite #7, 1940 . . . . **235.00**
Fruitdale, bread and butter plate, 6¹/₂" d **12.00**
Fruitdale, creamer **30.00**
Fruitdale, luncheon plate, 9¹/₂" **30.00**
Gingham, bowl, 8" d **12.00**
Gingham, coffee mug **12.00**
Gingham, pitcher, 1 qt **18.00**
Gingham, ramekin, cov **30.00**
Gingham, relish platter **30.00**
Gingham, tea cup **4.00**
Gingham, tidbit, 12" h **30.00**
Gingham, tumbler, 5¹/₂" h **30.00**
Hawaiian Flowers, chop plate, 12¹/₂" d **70.00**
Hawaiian Flowers, creamer and sugar **55.00**
Hawaiian Flowers, saucer **4.00**
Hawaiian Flowers, vegetable, pink **18.00**

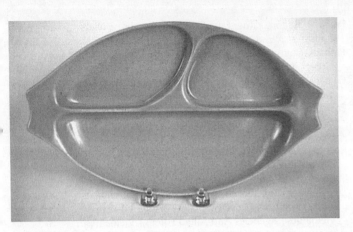

Heavenly Days, relish, coupe shape, 3-part, turquoise, 12³/₄" l, $22.00. Photo courtesy Ray Morykan Auctions.

Heavenly Days, vegetable, oval, divided	20.00
Homespun, bread and butter plate, 6¼" d	3.00
Homespun, casserole, cov	25.00
Homespun, chop plate, 12¼" d	25.00
Homespun, coffee mug	35.00
Homespun, cup and saucer	6.00
Homespun, luncheon plate, 9" d	8.00
Homespun, flat soup	12.00
Homespun, platter, oval, 13" l	20.00
Homespun, salad plate	5.00
Homespun, salt and pepper shakers, pr	15.00
Homespun, soup bowl, tab handles	12.00
Homespun, vegetable, 8⁷/₈" d	15.00
Mayflower, butter	135.00
Mayflower, casserole, cov	200.00
Mayflower, chop plate	40.00
Mayflower, dinner plate	8.00
Mayflower, flat soup, 8⁵/₈" d	25.00
Mayflower, gravy boat	30.00
Mayflower, platter, oval, 13³/₄" l	25.00
Mayflower, salad plate	8.00
Mayflower, teapot	115.00
Mayflower, water pitcher, 2 qt, 11½" h	125.00
Modern California, cup and saucer, orchid	7.00
Modern California, luncheon plate, orchid, 9½" d	6.00
Modern California, platter, orchid, 16" l	15.00
Modern California, sugar, sand	12.00
Monterey, salver	15.00
Monterey, sugar	15.00
Monticello, demitasse cup and saucer	15.00
Native California, butter, blue	80.00
Native California, cereal bowl, tab handles, yellow, 7¼" w	18.00
Native California, luncheon plate, yellow, 9¼" d	12.00
Native California, flat soup, pink	15.00
Native California, vegetable, oval, blue, 9½" l	20.00
Native California, vegetable, oval, green, 9½" l	18.00
Organdie, berry bowl, 5½" d	6.00
Organdie, carafe	30.00
Organdie, chop plate, 12¼" d	10.00
Organdie, dinner plate, 10¾" d	5.00
Organdie, eggcup	20.00
Organdie, flowerpot	45.00

Organdie, meat platter	12.00
Organdie, salt and pepper shakers, pr	15.00
Organdie, soup bowl, handled	4.00
Organdie, teapot	30.00
Organdie, tumbler	12.00
Organdie, tumbler, 5½" h, set of 4	45.00
Organdie, vegetable, divided	25.00
Planter, figural bird, 7½" l, 5¾" h	25.00
Raffia, berry bowl, handled, 5½" d	5.00
Raffia, bowl, 7" d	10.00
Raffia, bread and butter plate	3.00
Raffia, chop plate, 13" d	20.00
Raffia, cup and saucer	4.00
Raffia, dinner plate	5.00
Raffia, pitcher, 6½" h	18.00
Raffia, platter, oval, 9½" l	8.00
Raffia, platter, oval, 11" l	15.00
Raffia, platter, oval, 13½" l	12.00
Raffia, teapot	50.00
Raffia, vegetable, divided	12.00
Rio Chico, butter	25.00
Rio Chico, chop plate, 16½" d	30.00
Rio Chico, cup and saucer	16.00
Rio Chico, teacup and saucer	12.00
Rio Chico, vegetable, 9" d	15.00
Salamina, berry bowl, 5½" d	60.00
Salamina, bread and butter plate, 6½" d	70.00
Salamina, chop plate, 12¼" d	90.00
Salamina, chop plate, 14" d	275.00
Salamina, cup and saucer	80.00
Salamina, dinner plate, 10½" d	75.00
Salamina, luncheon plate, 9½" d	45.00
Salamina, pitcher, 1 pt	100.00
Salamina, salad plate, 7½" d	65.00
Salamina, vegetable, 8" d	250.00
Souvenir Cup and Saucer, Naval Academy	60.00
Souvenir Plate, Douglas Aircraft, 1940s	40.00
Souvenir Plate, Hollywood, CA	100.00
Souvenir Plate, Knotts Berry Farm, 1949	20.00
Souvenir Plate, University of Minnesota	20.00
Tam O'Shanter, casserole, cov	30.00
Tam O'Shanter, coffee carafe	30.00
Tickled Pink, pitcher	15.00
Tickled Pink, relish, 3-part	20.00
Tickled Pink, vegetable, oval, divided	15.00

VIETNAM WAR

The Vietnam War divided America. As a result, there are two distinct groups of collectibles: anti-war demonstration and military.

Destabilization followed the withdrawal of the French from Indo-China. In the early 1960s American military advisors were in South Vietnam assisting the country's military. In May 1962 President Kennedy sent 1,800 U.S. Marines to Thailand to protect it from a possible invasion by communist forces from Laos. On June 16, 1962 two U.S. Army officers were killed north of Saigon. On November 1, 1963, the government of President Diem was overthrown by South Vietnamese armed forces. America recognized the new government on November 7, 1963.

America increased its military and economic aide to South Vietnam in 1964. Mounting casualties during 1965 spurred protests. By the end of 1966, the United States had 400,000 troops in South Vietnam. The casualty count was over 6,600 killed and 37,500 wounded. Nguyen Van Thieu was elected president in 1967 amid charges of election fraud. Dissent continued to mount, reaching a fever pitch in the late 1960s and 70s. North Vietnam launched the Tet offensive on January 30, 1968.

Although Nixon reduced the U.S. troop commitment in 1969, major anti-war demonstrations took place in October and November. America continued to disengage from Vietnam. By December 1971 American troop strength dropped to 184,000. On March 30, 1972, North Vietnam crossed the DMZ and entered South Vietnam from Cambodia.

A peace agreement was signed on January 22, 1973. It proved ineffective. The South Vietnamese government fell to the North in 1975. America's presence in Vietnam ended. President Ford offered amnesty to deserters and draft evaders in September 1974. A general pardon was issued in 1977.

References: Richard J. Austin, *The Official Price Guide to Military Collectibles, Sixth Edition,* House of Collectibles, 1998; Jim Fiorella, *The Viet Nam Zippo: 1933–1975,* Schiffer Publishing, 1998; Ron Manion, *American Military Collectibles,* Antique Trader Books, 1995.

Newsletter: *Vietnam Insignia Collectors Newsletter,* 501 West 5th Ave, Covington, LA 07433.

Belt, 101st Airborne, brown rubberized canvas with matching keeper, complete with orig stamped brass buckle. **$65.00**
Book, *Lords of the Leaf,* WJ Weigert, Hearthstone Press, 1988, 163 pp, dj **2.00**
Booklet, *Survival,* FM 21-76 275, Department of the Army field manual, soft cover, 1970. . . . . **10.00**
Bracelet, "Missing In Action/Commander James Hickerson/ 12-22-67" **14.00**
Cap, USMC, olive drab cotton, stitched visor, soldier's name stamped on underside of visor, 2 metal vents on each side, dated 1968, size extra small. **10.00**
Dagger, Viet Cong, handmade blade, leather sheath and handle, 14½" l **25.00**
Helmet, American GI, camouflage cover with liner and head strap **35.00**
Lighter, front engraved "Old Reliable Express Company, 9th S&T BN, Camp Bearcat 1966-1967," back engraved with 9th patch and "9th Inf Div Vietnam" **30.00**
Magazine, *Life,* May 12, 1972, "Vietnam Retreat," soldier carrying another soldier over shoulder on cover **4.00**
Magazine, *Life,* May 26 1967, Big Lew Walt "The Marines' Marine" on cover **3.00**
Magazine Pouch, olive drab canvas, holds 3-30 round AK magazines, 7 pockets, dated 1964 . . . . **25.00**
Newspaper, *Vietnam Courier,* Aug 28, 1967, published in Hanoi, 7 photos, 11 x 15" **5.00**
Paperback Book, *History of the Vietnam War by Black Veterans,* Wallace Terry, Ballantine Books, 1985 . . . . **3.00**
Paperback Book, *Valley of the Shadow,* Captain Ed Y Hall, US Army, Honoribus Press, 1986, 270 pp. **5.00**
Patch, 1st Cavalry, 3½" w, 5¼" l **18.00**
Patch, 101st Airborne Screaming Eagles, 2½ x 3" **10.00**
Patch, 605 Transport Company, 2¼ x 2¾". **10.00**
Pillow Cover, silk, embroidered tiger, 1968, 17 x 14" **15.00**
Pinback Button, "Peace Now," center white dove on blue ground, white lettering, 2¼" d **6.00**

Pinback Button, "The Establishment 'Bombs, Bullets, Bullshit,'" 3½" d **5.00**
Pinback Button, "War Is Unhealthy For Children And Other Living Things," 3½" d **10.00**
Pinback Button, white doves, "Vietnam Moratorium" on blue ground, 4½" d **5.00**
Postcard, sent from North to South, written Jan 27th, 1957, from Thach Da, Yen Lang District, Vinh Phuc Province, arrived in Hanoi Feb 14, 1957 . . . . **20.00**
Record, *Hello Vietnam,* LP, The Lonesome Valley Singers, Diplomat Records 2376. **3.00**
Surrender Pass, flags of Allies on front, reverse shows soldier embracing former enemy who has surrendered with "Safe-Conduct Pass To Be Honored By All Vietnamese Agencies And Allied Forces," Vietnamese text **18.00**
TV Guide, Sep 29-Oct 5, 1973, #1070, "The War In Vietnam–What Happened vs What We Saw" **3.00**

VIEW-MASTER

William Gruber, a Portland, Oregon, piano tuner, and Harold Graves, president of Sawyer's, a Portland photo-finishing and postcard company, were the two principals behind View-Master. On January 20, 1939, a patent was filed for a special stereoscope utilizing a card with seven pairs of views. Sawyer, Inc., manufactured and sold View-Master products.

The Model A viewer, with its flip front opening and straight viewing barrels, was introduced in 1939. It was replaced by an improved Model B viewer in 1943. The more familiar Model C square viewer arrived in 1946 and remained in production for eleven years.

By 1941 there were more than 1,000 View-Master sales outlets. During World War II, View-Master made special training reels for the United States Navy and Army Air Corps. View-Master's golden years were 1945 to 1960. Hundreds of new reels appeared. The three-pack set was introduced.

In 1966 General Aniline and Film Corporation (GAF) purchased Sawyer's. GAF introduced new projects and the 3-D talking View-Master. Arnold Thaler purchased View-Master in 1980, only to sell it to Ideal. When Tyco acquired Ideal, View-Master was part of the purchase. Today, the View-Master brand name is owned by Mattel, the result of its purchase of Tyco in 1997.

References: Sharon Korbeck and Elizabeth Stephan (eds.), *2000 Toys & Prices, 7th Edition,* Krause Publications, 1999; John Waldsmith, *Stereo Views: An Illustrated History and Price Guide,* Wallace-Homestead, 1991.

Collectors' Club: National Stereoscopic Assoc, PO Box 14801, Columbus, OH 43214.

ACCESSORIES

Projector, GAF Talking View-Master Projector **$30.00**
Viewer, Cabbage Patch Kids, 1984, MIB. **15.00**
Viewer, ET View Master projector, Stereo Products, battery operated, 1982-83 . . . . **5.00**
Viewer, Sawyer's, Bakelite and metal, mkd "Junior Luma Ray f3-70mm" around lens **15.00**
Viewer, Sawyers Deluxe Stereoscope and projector, 1940-50s **55.00**

Single Reel,
Hopalong Cassidy,
#955, $5.00.

REEL SETS

Alf, 1987	$5.00
Bambi, B400	10.00
Benji	4.00
Brave Eagle, #933, 1956	3.00
Buckaroo Banzai, #4056, 1984	8.00
Cat From Outer Space, J22	8.00
Charlie Brown Summer Fun, B548, 1972	6.00
Close Encounters of the Third Kind, 1977	25.00
Conquest of Space, 1968	8.00
Coronation of Queen Elizabeth II, #405	2.00
Emergency, B597	20.00
Flintstones, B514, 1962	6.00
Freedomland, 1960	70.00
Grand Canyon Talking View-Master Reels	8.00
Heidi, 1958	6.00
Indian Tribal Ceremonial, 1948	6.00
James Bond 007, Live and Let Die, B393, 1973	15.00
Lancelot Link Secret Chimp, B504	16.00
Little Black Sambo, FT8, 1948	18.00
Man In Space, B6571	5.00
Marineland	10.00
Masters of the Universe, #2, 1985	1.00
Mighty Mouse, B5261	10.00
Moon Landing, 1969	15.00
Mt Lassen Volcanic National Park, California, #256	6.00
Peanuts, B536, 1966	10.00
Pebbles & Bamm-Bamm, 1964	8.00
Pee-Wee's Playhouse, 1987	5.00
Pipi Longstocking, B322	4.00
Scooby Doo Talking View-Master Reels, "That's Snow Ghost," 1972	15.00
Secret Squirrel and Atom Ant, #B535	12.00
Sesame Street, 1984	2.00
Snoopy and the Red Baron, 1969	10.00
Tarzan, #978, 1955	8.00
The Birth of Jesus, B875	4.00
The Black Hole, #35	9.00
The Christmas Story, B383	3.00
The Love Bug, 1968	6.00
Tournament of Thrills, 1970	3.00
Tron, M37, 1982	10.00
US Spaceport, #J79	10.00
Voyage to the Bottom of the Sea, B483	12.00
Zorro, #4691, 1958	30.00

SINGLE REELS

Aladdin and the Wonderful Lamp, FT-50B, 1951	$3.00
Bugs Bunny and Elmer Fudd, #800, 1951	8.00
Bullfight, #720, 1953	6.00
Cisco Kid, #960, 1950	10.00
Dells of the Wisconsin River, #124	1.00
Disneyland, Main Street USA, A1751	5.00
Dracula, 1976	5.00
Gene Autry, "Gene and His Wonder Horse Champion," #950, 1950	9.00
Glacier National Park, Montana, #47	2.00
Niagara Falls, Ontario, #375	2.00
Royal Canadian Mounted Police, #705	2.00
Roy Rogers, "King of the Cowboys," #945, 1957	10.00
Rudolph the Red-Nosed Reindeer	8.00
San Francisco, California, #188	1.00
Shenandoah National Park, #261	1.00
The Eskimos, Alaska, #309	2.00
The Matternhorn, Zermatt Switzerland, #2001, 1948	1.00
Tom & Jerry, #810, 1957	1.00
White Mountains, New Hampshire, #265	1.00
Wizard of Oz, B3611, 1957	18.00
Wonders of the Deep, #990-A, 1954	2.00

WADE CERAMICS

In 1958 A. J. Wade, George Wade and Son, Wade Heath & Co., and Wade (Ulster) combined, formed The Wade Group of Potteries, and went public.

George Wade and Son, located at the Manchester Pottery in Burslem, is the best known of the group. Prior to World War I, the company made industrial ceramics, concentrating heavily on the needs of the textile industry. After the war, the company made insulators for the electrical industry.

A. J. Wade, George's brother, established a firm to market glazed tiles and faience fireplace surrounds. A. J. Wade became a partner in Wade, Heath & Co., a manufacturer of Rockingham jugs, teapots, etc. In 1935 Colonel G. A. Wade, a son of George Wade, gained control of A. J. Wade's two companies. Previously, in 1926/28, Col. Wade assumed control of George Wade and Son.

In the late 1920s, George Wade and Son introduced a line of moderately priced figurines. They did so well the company added a line of animals. Production of these figurines ceased during World War II when the company shifted to wartime production.

In 1938 Wade, Heath & Co. acquired the Royal Victoria Pottery. A line of tableware was introduced. A license was acquired from Disney to produce character figurines. Although heavily devoted to wartime production in the early 1940s, the company did manufacture a line of utilitarian dinnerware and tea ware.

In 1950 Wade (Ulster) was established. Located in Portadown, Northern Ireland, the company produced industrial ceramics.

The ceramic giftware industry went into decline in the 1960s. The Wade Group focused on industrial production. When the giftware industry revived in the 1970s, The Wade Group returned to the market. Wade Heath & Co. devotes its efforts to commission and special contract orders, serving a large number of clients ranging from breweries to tobacco companies. In 1969 Wade (PDM) was established within The Wade Group to deal with promotional items, working with glass, plastic, and tin, in addition to ceramics.

Wade is best known in the United States through its Red Rose Tea premiums. These are made by George Wade & Son. Different sets are made for the American and Canadian market. Some figures are based on figures in the "Whimsies" line. Do not confuse the two. Whimsies are slightly larger.

References: Donna S. Baker, *Wade Miniatures*, Schiffer Publishing, 2000; Pat Murray, *The Charlton Standard Catalogue of Wade, Vol. One: General Issues, Third Edition* (1999), *Vol. Two: Decorative Ware, Second Edition* (1996), *Vol. Three: Tableware, Second Edition* (1998), *Vol. Four: Liquor Products, Third Edition* (1999), Charlton Press; Pat Murray, *The Charlton Standard Catalogue of Wade Whimsical Collectables, Fourth Edition*, Charlton Press, 1998; Ian Warner and Mike Posgay, *The World of Wade, Collectable Porcelain and Pottery* (1988, 1993 value update), *Book 2* (1995), Antique Publications.

Collectors' Clubs: The Official International Wade Collectors Club (company-sponsored), Royal Works, Westport Rd, Burslem, Stoke-on-Trent, ST6 4AP UK; Wade Watch, 8199 Pierson Ct, Arvada, CO 80005.

Ashtray, Dunhill, square, black with maroon and gold
 "Dunhill, London–Paris–New York" panel each side,
 5" sq, 1⁷⁄₈" h **$30.00**
Coffee Cup, yellow with rose decal **15.00**
Condiment Set, Bramble, 4³⁄₄" h cov mustard, 2¹⁄₂" h salt
 and pepper shakers, price for 3-pc set **40.00**
Creamer, Harvest Ware, copper luster **35.00**
Cup, commemorative, Elizabeth II **10.00**
Decanter, Royal Salute Scotch Whiskey, blue, emb
 knight on horseback and "Chivas," 4¹⁄₂" h **45.00**
Dessert Plate, yellow with rose decal, 6¹⁄₂" d **10.00**
Figurine, 3-story vine-covered house, 2-pc **20.00**
Figurine, angel fish **5.00**
Figurine, barrister, 3" h **45.00**
Figurine, bull, 1³⁄₄" h, 2" l **55.00**
Figurine, camel **4.00**
Figurine, elephant, Red Rose Tea premium **2.00**
Figurine, gingerbread man, 1¹⁄₂" h **15.00**
Figurine, golden retreiver **4.00**
Figurine, hippo, Red Rose Tea premium **3.00**
Figurine, kangaroo **4.00**
Figurine, koala, Red Rose Tea premium **3.00**
Figurine, lion, Red Rose Tea premium **4.00**
Figurine, mouse, 1¹⁄₂" h **15.00**
Figurine, Nursery Collection, Ole King Cole **4.00**
Figurine, poodle, Red Rose Tea premium **3.00**
Figurine, rabbit, Red Rose Tea premium **8.00**
Figurine, rhino, Red Rose Tea premium **3.00**
Figurine, tiger, Red Rose Tea premium **3.00**
Figurine, Tommy Tucker, mkd on back, 3¹⁄₄" h **30.00**
Figurine, Welsh Corgi **12.00**
Figurine, zebra **4.00**
Figurines, dogs, Happy Family, mother and 2 puppies,
 1¹⁄₄ to 2" h, price for 3-pc set **45.00**
Figurines, elephants, man riding largest elephant, blan-
 ket on back of other 2, 1¹⁄₂" to 2" h, price for 3-pc set **175.00**
Figurines, English Village, 6 buildings, 1¹⁄₂ to 2" h, price
 for set **70.00**
Figurines, pr, Tom and Jerry, 1973-79, 3³⁄₄" h Tom, 2" h
 Jerry, orig box **80.00**
Mug, figural elephant head, trunk forms handle, 4" h **55.00**
Mug, Nelson's Column Trafalgar Square, 3¹⁄₂" h **8.00**
Petfaces, 2 Pekingese dog faces, orig box **35.00**

Pin Tray, black with white horse figurine, 4" d **18.00**
Pin Tray, dark green with white duck figurine, 4" d **15.00**
Pipe Holder, dog figurine on green base, 3¹⁄₄" h **20.00**
Pitcher, copper luster, shamrocks dec, 6" h **45.00**
Pitcher, Cutty Sark, 7" h **20.00**
Pitcher, grouse on both sides **50.00**
Planter, Viking boat, "Isle of Man" sticker, 7¹⁄₄" l **15.00**
Souvenir Plate, "Dominion of Canada," 9¹⁄₂" d **15.00**
Teapot, English Life, Conservatory **20.00**
Teapot, English Life, Post Office **20.00**
Whiskey Pourer, Beefeater Gin, figural Beefeater, mkd
 "Wade" and "Renoir," 3" h **15.00**

WAGNER WARE

In 1891 Milton M. and Bernard P. Wagner established the Wagner Manufacturing Company in Sidney, Ohio. William, a third brother, soon joined the company. In order to add a line of skillets, Milton and Bernard purchased the Sidney Hollow Ware Foundry in 1903, placing William in charge. Finding the two companies in direct competition, Sidney Hollow Ware was sold and William bought into the main company as a partner. Louis, a fourth brother, joined the company a short time later.

Wagner Manufacturing made brass casting and cast-iron hollow ware, some of which was nickel plated. Wagner was one of the first companies to make aluminum cookware. The line included cake and ice cream molds, coffeepots, percolators, pitchers, scoops, spoons, and teapots. The company won numerous awards for its aluminum products between 1900 and 1940.

Several generations of Wagners were involved in the company management as individuals died and passed stock interests to their sons. In 1953 Philip Wagner, one of Milton Wagner's sons, was serving as president. He made it known he wanted to sell the company. Cable Wagner, William Wagner's son, purchased the Wagner Hotel Company. Randall Company of Cincinnati, Ohio, purchased the balance.

In 1957 Randall's Wagner Division purchased the Griswold Cookware line from McGraw Edison. Textron of Providence, Rhode Island, acquired the Randall Company in 1959. Textron's Wagner Division acquired the Durham Manufacturing Company of Muncie, Indiana, a manufacturer of casual leisure furniture for household use. In 1969, Textron sold its household line to General Housewares Corporation, a holding company. The sale included all patent and trademark rights for Griswold and Wagner.

Reference: David G. Smith and Charles Wafford, *The Book of Griswold & Wagner: Favorite Piqua, Sidney Hollow Ware, Wapak, 2nd Edition*, Schiffer Publishing, 2000.

Newsletter: *Kettles 'n Cookware*, PO Box 247, Perrysburg, NY 14129.

Bailed Griddle, #0, stylized logo **$100.00**
Bundt Pan **250.00**
Casserole, cov, with stand, Magnalite, #1052 . . . . **65.00**
Cheese Slicer, #300 . . . . **80.00**
Chef Skillet, #1386, 9" d **15.00**
Chicken Pan, cov, #1400, square **125.00**
Deep Fat French Frier, #1265, mkd "Wagner Ware
 Sidney O," 7¹⁄₂" d **40.00**
Display Rack, wood, cast iron tag in front, stylized logo,
 holds complete set 2-14 . . . . **550.00**

Drip Drop Roaster, cov, #8, bottom mkd "Wagner Ware Sidney-O-Round Roaster 248D"	**18.00**
Favorite Skillet, #2	**175.00**
Glass Lid, #6	**25.00**
Juicer, aluminum	**25.00**
Kettle, aluminum	**200.00**
Krusty Korn Kob Pan, 13 x 6"	**15.00**
Lamb Mold, black iron or nickel-plated	**115.00**
Omelette Pan	**50.00**
Popover Pan, 3 cup	**375.00**
Roaster Trivet, #7, aluminum, oval	**35.00**
Sandwich Toaster, wood handles, #1455	**275.00**
Sizzle Server	**25.00**
Sizzling Platter, #4342, Magnalite, orig oak handles	**25.00**
Skillet, #0	**55.00**
Skillet, #2	**65.00**
Skillet, #2, Wertz & Singer	**175.00**
Skillet, #4	**50.00**
Skillet, #8, center logo	**25.00**
Skillet, #9, "Sidney"	**40.00**
Skillet, #9, with heat ring	**55.00**
Skillet, #12	**100.00**
Skillet Lid, #7	**85.00**
Turks Head	**650.00**

WALLACE CHINA

The Wallace China Company, Vernon, California, was founded around 1931. The company made vitrified, plain and transfer printed wares for the hotel, institution, and restaurant markets. Willow ware in blue, brown, green, and red transfers was produced during the 1930s and 1940s.

Wallace China is best known for its Westward Ho houseware line, the result of a 1943 commission from the M. C. Wentz Company of Pasadena. Wentz wanted restaurant barbecue ware. Till Goodan, a well-known western artist, created three patterns: Boots and Saddles, Pioneer Trails, and Rodeo. His name is incorporated in most designs. A three-piece Little Buckaroo Chuck set for children and the El Rancho and Longhorn dinnerware patterns also were designed by Goodan.

In 1959 Shenango China Company acquired Wallace China. Wallace China operated as a wholly owned subsidiary until 1964 when all production ceased.

References: Jack Chipman, *Collector's Encyclopedia of California Pottery, Second Edition,* Collector Books, 1998; Harvey Duke, *The Official Price Guide to Pottery and Porcelain, Eighth Edition,* House of Collectibles, 1995.

Desert Ware, bowl, 5" d	**$12.00**
Desert Ware, bread and butter plate, 6" d	**6.00**
Desert Ware, mustard, cov, 3 1/2" h	**25.00**
Desert Ware, plate, oval, 7" l	**8.00**
Desert Ware, platter, oval, 12" l	**10.00**
El Rancho, bowl, 3 7/8" d	**30.00**
El Rancho, bowl, 4 3/4" d	**30.00**
El Rancho, bowl, 6 1/2" d	**75.00**
El Rancho, bread and butter plate, 6 1/4" d	**40.00**
El Rancho, coffee cup	**25.00**
El Rancho, dinner plate, 10 1/2" d	**80.00**
El Rancho, luncheon plate, 9" d	**45.00**
El Rancho, platter, oval, 9 1/8" l	**55.00**
El Rancho, salad plate, 7 1/4" d	**40.00**

El Rancho, saucer	**30.00**
El Rancho, soup bowl, 9" d	**40.00**
Shadowleaf, green, butter pat	**12.00**
Shadowleaf, green, coffee cup	**6.00**
Shadowleaf, green, dinner plate, 10" d	**20.00**
Shadowleaf, green, grill plate	**25.00**
Shadowleaf, green, salad plate, 8" d	**25.00**
Shadowleaf, green, sugar, cov, 4" h	**70.00**
Shadowleaf, green, syrup, 3 1/4" h	**15.00**
Shadowleaf, red, bread and butter plate, 5 1/2" d	**12.00**
Shadowleaf, red, coffee cup	**10.00**
Shadowleaf, red, dinner plate, 10 1/2" d	**75.00**
Shadowleaf, red, gravy boat	**20.00**
Shadowleaf, red, luncheon plate, 9" d	**20.00**
Shadowleaf, red, salad plate, 8" d	**20.00**
Shadowleaf, red, soup bowl, 6 1/2" d	**15.00**
Westward Ho, Boots & Saddle, chop plate, 13 1/4" d	**175.00**
Westward Ho, Boots & Saddle, coffee cup	**60.00**
Westward Ho, Boots & Saddle, dinner plate, 10 1/2" d	**100.00**
Westward Ho, Boots & Saddle, nesting bowl, 10 3/4" d	**425.00**
Westward Ho, Boots & Saddle, salad plate, 7" d	**75.00**
Westward Ho, Boots & Saddle, salt and pepper shakers, pr, 5" h	**110.00**
Westward Ho, Boots & Saddle, vegetable, 9" d	**160.00**
Westward Ho, Boots & Saddle, water pitcher	**300.00**
Westward Ho, Chuck Wagon, bowl, 4" d	**25.00**
Westward Ho, Chuck Wagon, bowl, 5" d	**30.00**
Westward Ho, Chuck Wagon, bread and butter plate, 6" d	**35.00**
Westward Ho, Chuck Wagon, coffee cup	**35.00**
Westward Ho, Chuck Wagon, creamer	**60.00**
Westward Ho, Chuck Wagon, cup	**55.00**
Westward Ho, Chuck Wagon, dinner plate	**65.00**
Westward Ho, Chuck Wagon, platter, 13" l	**125.00**
Westward Ho, Chuck Wagon, salad plate, 7" d	**35.00**
Westward Ho, Chuck Wagon, saucer	**15.00**
Westward Ho, Little Buckaroo, cereal bowl	**80.00**
Westward Ho, Longhorn, bowl, 4 7/8" d	**75.00**
Westward Ho, Longhorn, demitasse cup	**100.00**
Westward Ho, Pioneer Trail, dinner plate, 10 1/2" d	**80.00**

Westward Ho, Pioneer Trail, chop plate, 13" d, $175.00.

Westward Ho, Pioneer Trail, pitcher **475.00**
Westward Ho, Rodeo, cereal bowl. **60.00**
Westward Ho, Rodeo, coffee cup. **60.00**
Westward Ho, Rodeo, dinner plate **100.00**
Westward Ho, Rodeo, luncheon plate, 9" d **145.00**
Westward Ho, Rodeo, nesting bowl, 8³/₈" d **250.00**
Westward Ho, Rodeo, salad plate, 7" d **55.00**
Westward Ho, Rodeo, salt and pepper shakers, pr, 3¹/₂" h **80.00**
Westward Ho, Rodeo, salt and pepper shakers, pr, 5" h. **85.00**
Westward Ho, Rodeo, saucer, 6¹/₂" d **30.00**

WALL HANGINGS

This is a catchall category for the myriad of objects that hung on living room, dining room, bedroom, and kitchen walls since 1945. Looking at 1960 Sperry and Hutchinson S & H Green Stamps Distinguished Merchandise Ideabook, one finds oval framed hand-colored fruit prints, Syrocco Baroque-style scones, fruitwood cutout wall plaques featuring Early American scenes, a brush-stroked reproduction print of Romney's Miss Willoughby, and a Mirro five-piece coppertone mold set.

Whether a pair of 1950s' plaster Balinese dancers in pink costumes or a late 1960s' abstract bird made from teakwood and copper, period defining wall hangings are attracting strong collector and decorator interest.

Hanger, bamboo slats, multicolored scene of lake, mountains, and trees with flowers, backs stamped "Patent No. 42015/18, Made in Japan," c1930-40s, 10 x 20" **$20.00**
Plaque, Burwood Products, ballet dancers, plastic, 18¹/₂" h and 13¹/₂" h **10.00**
Plaque, Egyptian motif, solid brass, Nefertiti and Pharoah in relief, copper and gold plated accents on hand-wrought ground, 13¹/₂ x 18" **30.00**
Plaque, fish, chalkware, black, gold fins and tail. **8.00**

Plaque, fruit and nut, painted antique burgundy, red, green, and brown, 16" l **15.00**
Plaque, mermaids with bubble, porcelain, attached black metal screen, 8 x 6" **70.00**
Plaque, Mother Goose and 3 ducklings, chalkware, mkd "Miller," 1965, 12 x 5" h Mother Goose, 3¹/₂" h ducklings **25.00**
Plaque, Napco, #06497, hen and rooster, 6¹/₄ x 6¹/₄" **20.00**
Plaque, Napco, butterflies, 1960 . . . . **6.00**
Plaque, Nubian man and woman, plaster, 1960s, 10¹/₂" h **25.00**
Plaque, rooster, black metal, 1950 . . . . **8.00**
Plaque, Syroco, cherubs, gold colored, #7138, #7139, #7140, and #7141, 11" h, set of 4 . . . . **30.00**
Plaque, Syroco, poodle and cat, 1950s, 20¹/₂" h **20.00**
Plaques, pr, Roseville, Burmese faces, matte green crystalline glaze, raised mark, #72B and #82B, 8 x 5¹/₂", price for pr **250.00**
Sculpture, King and Queen from card deck, rock, stones, twine, and tiles on masonite, wooden frame, 1960, 12¹/₂ x 36" **20.00**
Sculpture, Paul Evans, bronze, 3 diamond shaped sections in gold and white, black accents, 30 x 11". **6,000.00**
Tapestry, Marlene Hoffmann for Galleria 70, "Guahiva," woven wool, orange, black, and white, 1970s, 117 x 67" **300.00**

WALL POCKETS

The earliest American wall pockets were made by folk potters in Virginia's Shenandoah Valley. The flower wall pocket became a standard household form in the 1920s and remained popular through the end of the 1940s.

When the post-war Modern design styles became popular, wall pockets were out. The wall pocket regained some of its former popularity in the 1960s and 1970s. Import companies, such as ENESCO, included wall pockets in their catalogs. These new examples stimulated interest in collecting older ones.

References: Joy and Marvin Gibson, *Collector's Guide to Wall Pockets: Book II,* L-W Book Sales, 1997; Marvin and Joy Gibson, *Collectors Guide to Wall Pockets: Affordable & Others,* L-W Book Sales, 1994; Betty and Bill Newbound, *Collector's Encyclopedia of Wall Pockets,* Collector Books, 1996, 1998 value update.

Collectors' Club: Wall Pocket Collectors Club, 1356 Tahiti, St Louis, MO 63128.

Note: Wall pockets are ceramic unless noted otherwise.

Bird, figural, Czechoslovakian **$20.00**
Bird on Cuckoo Clock, figural, Japan, 1950s, 6" h. **25.00**
Bird on Fan, figural, "Bradley Exclusives" sticker, 5" h, 5¹/₄" w **45.00**
Chintz, Florence pattern, Royal Winton **160.00**
Chintz, Julia pattern, Royal Winton **75.00**
Cocker Spaniel, figural, Royal Copley **18.00**
Covered Bridge, figural, Lefton. **45.00**
Cup and Saucer, figural, marbleized green plastic, mkd "Irwin Made in USA". **25.00**
Dancing Girl, figural, Hedi Schoop style **30.00**
Dutch Shoe with Tulip, figural, 4¹/₂" l **15.00**
Fan, figural, green, McCoy, 1956 . . . . **60.00**

Plaques, Napco, fruit, pear, apple, orange, and grape, Japan, price for set, $10.00. Photo courtesy Ray Morykan Auctions.

Pocket, Dahlrose pattern, Roseville, 8¹/₈" h, $325.00.

Flower, figural, pink with yellow center, unmkd, 5" h,
5" w **25.00**
Frying Pan, figural, Cleminsons **25.00**
Frying Pan, figural, "Too many cooks spoil the broth,"
Lefton **45.00**
Gloved Lady, figural, Royal Copley **25.00**
Hat, figural, Royal Copley **40.00**
Head of Christ, white porcelain, Holy Water font, mkd
"Bavaria, HW 162/0," 6" h, 4" w **40.00**
Head Vase, figural, black lady, Relco #8A170, 6¹/₄" h **25.00**
Head Vase, figural, girl's head, Napco #S240C, 4¹/₂" h,
4¹/₄" w. **40.00**
Head Vase, figural, mkd "Jean #D-231," 7" h **30.00**
Home Sweet Home, Cleminsons **65.00**
Hunter and Dog, figural, Inarco #E-3923, 13" h **20.00**
Kettle, figural, "...the kitchen is the Heart of the Home,"
Cleminsons, 7¹/₄" h **30.00**
Key, figural, "Welcome Guest," Cleminsons, 7¹/₄" h. **35.00**
Kissing Dutch Boy and Girl, figural, tulip at top, unmkd,
7¹/₂" h **20.00**
Lily, figural, yellow, McCoy, 1948, 7¹/₂" h **90.00**
Little Boy and Girl, figural, Napco **110.00**
Little Girl, with huge bow, figural, Napco. **55.00**
Picture Frame, square frame with emb flowers, girl hold-
ing lamb in center, Shawnee, #586, 5" h **25.00**
Pink Stork and Baby, figural, mkd "Hand Decorated
Shafford," 4¹/₂" h, 5" w. **55.00**
Pocket, cased glass, white int, orange swirled ext with
back trim, Czechoslovakian, 5³/₄" h, 4¹/₂" w **15.00**
Pocket, emb daffodils, turquoise, McCoy, 7" h **30.00**
Pocket, light blue with black ribs and emb flowers **25.00**
Pocket, white ground, pink and blue flowers, gold scroll-
work and trim, 5¹/₄" h, 4¹/₂" w **30.00**
Pocket, Woodrose pattern, Weller **35.00**
Sailfish, figural, Lefton, #60421 . . . . **40.00**
Snail, figural, LaMiranda Pottery, 4" h **35.00**
Straw Hat and Poodles, figural, Tilso, 5" h, 2¹/₄" w. **35.00**
Strawberry, figural, 4³/₄" h, 6" w **18.00**
Teapot, figural, pink spout, handle, and flower, blue
fruit, green leaves, Shawnee, 3¹/₂" h, 6¹/₄" w **15.00**
Telephone, figural, 8¹/₂" h, 3³/₄" w. **12.00**
Toucan Bird, fruit and leaves, figural, Japan, 5" h, 5" w **65.00**
Vase, figural, rect with flared rim, emb oriental tree with
applied leaves, Weil Ware, 4¹/₄" h, 5¹/₂" w **25.00**

WARNER BROTHERS

The Warner Brothers Animation Studio, located initially in a bungalow dubbed Termite Terrace, produced over 1,000 six- and
seven-minute theatrical cartoons between 1930 and 1969.
Cartoon Hall of Fame characters who appeared in these shorts
included Bugs Bunny, Daffy Duck, Elmer Fudd, Porky Pig, the
Road Runner, Sylvester, the Tasmanian Devil, Tweety, Wile E.
Coyote, and Yosemite Sam. Creative artists include Tex Avery, Bob
Clampett, Friz Freleng, Chuck Jones, and Bob McKimson. The
voice of Mel Blanc gave a distinct personality to each character.

During the 1940s and 50s Warner Bros. characters appeared on
movie screens and in comic books and newspapers. The launching of The Bugs Bunny Show on ABC in 1960 introduced them to
a new audience. In the 1970s and 80s the Warner cartoons were
shown at film festivals and made available on video cassette and
laser disc.

Warner found it owned a licensing goldmine. Warner Bros.
stores appeared in shopping malls in the early 1990s. Warner Bros.
continues to pursue a vigorous licensing program.

Although third in popularity behind Disney and Hanna-Barbera
in cartoon collectibles, Warner Bros. collectibles have established
a strong collecting niche. Collectors are advised to look beyond
the superstars at characters such as Bosco, Foghorn Leghorn, Pepé
Le Pew, and Speedy Gonzales.

References: Debra S. Braun, *Looney Tunes Collectibles*, Schiffer
Publishing, 1999; David Longest, *Cartoon Toys & Collectibles*,
Collector Books, 1999.

Advertising Tear Sheet, Bugs Bunny, "Brach's Easter
Candies" above Bugs Bunny holding large ladle with
dripping chocolate syrup in front of basket filled with
candy, 1958, 10 x 14" **$10.00**
Alarm Clock, Tweety in plastic nest, digital, Westclox,
1996, 5 x 5¹/₂". **10.00**
Bank, Porky Pig, figural, metal, standing next to tree, on
base with name on front, 1947, 3⁵/₈" h **175.00**
Bank, Tweety, holding large hammer, plastic, Applause,
orig box, 8 x 6". **8.00**
Bobbing Head, Scooby Doo, plastic, 1997. . . . . **10.00**
Book, *Bugs Bunny and the Secret of Storm Island*, Leon
Schlesinger, Dell Fast Action Story, 1942. . . . . **12.00**
Book, Elmer Fudd, *Gone Fishin'*, Dell, 1953 . . . . **8.00**
Coloring Book, Bugs Bunny, Whitman, #1147, Bugs tak-
ing picture of Elmer Fudd who is balancing carrot on
his nose, 128 pp, 1963, 8 x 10⁷/₈" **15.00**
Comic Book, Elmer Fudd, Dell, #977, 1959. . . . . **2.00**
Cookie Cutters, set of 4, Porky Pig, Bugs Bunny, Tweety,
and Sylvester, red, Wilton Enterprises, 1988 . . . . **6.00**
Cookie Jar, Bugs Bunny, "What's up Doc?," mkd "TM
1993 Warner Bros Inc, Certified International Corp,
Taiwan," 11" h. **40.00**
Cup, Bugs Bunny, plastic. **10.00**
Doll, Speedy Gonzalez, stuffed, yellow hat, orange shirt,
hands, and feet, red scarf, 1971, 14" h **35.00**
Drinking Glasses, Porky Pig, Bugs Bunny, Yosemite Sam,
and Road Runner, Pepsi series, 1973, price for set of 4 . . . . **10.00**
Fan Picture, set of 8, paper, smiling Bugs Bunny with car-
rot leaning against tree, Daffy Duck, Foghorn
Leghorn, Porky Pig, Speedy Gonzalez, Elmer Fudd,
Tweety, and Sylvester, ©Warner Bros–Seven Arts Inc,
c1950s, 8¹/₂ x 11" **35.00**

Hot Water Bottle, Sylvester and Tweety Bird, Duarry, Spain, mid-20th C, 12³/₄" h, $65.00.

Figure, Road Runner, hard plastic, soft rubber head, cheeks make "beep beep" sound when pressed, "R Dakin & Co, San Francisco" orig tag, 1950s, 9" h **10.00**

Figure, Speedy Gonzalez, vinyl, dark brown, yellow hat, red cloth kerchief, green shirt, and white pants, gray plastic base with black "Have A Speedy Recovery!," Dakin Goofy Grams series, 1970, 7½" h **15.00**

Figurine, Porky Pig, ceramic, smiling and waving, blue jacket, orange bow tie, light blue cap, orange base, mkd "©Warner Bros Inc, 1975 Japan," 4¼" h **15.00**

Gumball Machine, Bugs Bunny, standing, with carrot in hand, Superior Toy & Mfg, 1988, 9½" h **4.00**

Lunch Box, Looney Tunes characters on TV screen with knobs, replaced handle, American Thermos, 1959 .... **30.00**

Mug, Bugs Bunny, blue, Fiestaware, Homer Laughlin **8.00**

Mug, Tazmanian Devil, ceramic, mkd "Warner Bros Inc, 1989, The Good Company, Woodland Hills CA 91367" **2.00**

Neck Tie, child's, Elmer Fudd, wearing red pants, white vest, yellow jacket and hat on blue ground with "Elmer" below, 9" l **15.00**

Night Light, Scooby Doo, ceramic, Warner Bros Studio, 7" h **20.00**

Pinback Button, Bugs Bunny, "Help Crippled Children," smiling Bugs Bunny face on orange ground, purple lettering, 1958, 1¼" d **3.00**

Planter, Bugs Bunny, full figure smiling Bugs holding hand to chest, standing next to brown log, blue with pink accents, 1940s, 3 x 6 x 7" **35.00**

Plate, Scooby Doo, "Scooby Snacks," sea-mist green, Fiestaware, Homer Laughlin, 10" d **18.00**

Plate, Tweety, "Happy 50th Birthday Tweety," #Y7454, center Tweety surrounded by Looney Tunes characters in party scene, gold rim, 1993 .... **40.00**

Record, *Bugs Bunny and Tweetie Pie I Taut I Taw A Puddy-Tat*, 78 rpm, yellow vinyl **20.00**

Salt and Pepper Shakers, pr, Bugs Bunny holding "Duck Season" sign, Elmer Fudd holding rifle, 5½" h Bugs Bunny, 4³/₄" h Elmer **15.00**

Salt and Pepper Shakers, pr, Yosemite Sam, ceramic **12.00**

Snow Globe, Elmer Fudd, Daffy Duck, and Bugs Bunny, "Rabbit Season/Duck Season," plays *A Hunting We Will Go*, Goebel, 6" h, 7" d **15.00**

Squeak Toy, Sylvester, hands behind back, Reliance Prod Corp, 1978, 7" h **8.00**

Thermos, Porky's Lunch Wagon, red plastic cap, 1959, 8" h **75.00**

Tie Tack, Road Runner, cloisonné, Howard Eldon of California, 1970s, 1" h **5.00**

Tray, Tweety and Sylvester, Bugs Bunny, Porky Pig, Roadrunner, and Daffy Duck on white ground, banded rim, Fabcraft, 1974, 11³/₄" d **6.00**

View-Master Reel, Bugs Bunny and Elmer Fudd, "The Hunter," #800 .... **8.00**

Watch, Speedy Gonzalez, full figure smiling Speedy image, diecut yellow gloved hands, vinyl band, Hong Kong, 1970s **75.00**

Whitman Big Little Book, *Bugs Bunny: The Last Crusader*, #5772-2 .... **10.00**

WATCHES

Watches divide into three main collecting categories: (1) character licensed, (2) pocket, and (3) wrist. Character licensed watches arrived on the scene in the late 1930s. Although some character pocket watches are known, the vast majority are wristwatches. Collectors divide character watches into two types: (a) stem wound and (b) battery operated. Because they are relatively inexpensive to make, battery-operated licensed watches are frequently used as premiums by fast-food companies.

Pocket watches are collected by size (18/0 to 20), number of jewels in the movement, open or closed (hunter) face, case decoration, and case composition. Railroad watches generally are 16 to 18 in size, have a minimum of 17 jewels, and adjust to at least five positions. Double check to make certain the movement is period and has not been switched, a common practice.

The wristwatch achieved mass popularity in the 1920s. Hundreds of American, German, and Swiss companies entered the market. Quality ranged from Rolex to Timex. Again, collectors divide the category into two groups: (a) stem wound and (b) battery operated.

In the early 1990s a speculative Swatch watch collecting craze occurred. The bubble burst in the late 1990s. Prices have fallen sharply. The craze had a strong international flavor.

Watch collecting as a whole enjoys one of the strongest international markets. On this level, brand name is the name of the game. Watches are bought primarily as investments, not for use.

References: Hy Brown, *Comic Character Timepieces*, Schiffer Publishing, 1992; Gisbert L. Brunner and Christian Pfeiffer-Belli, *Wristwatches, 3rd Edition*, Schiffer Publishing, 2000; Frank Edwards, *Swatch: A Guide for Connoisseurs and Collectors*, Firefly Books, 1998; Edward Faber and Stewart Unger, *American Wristwatches, Revised*, Schiffer Publishing, 1997; Heinz Hample, *Automatic Wristwatches from Germany, England, France, Japan, Russia and the USA*, Schiffer Publishing, 1997; Robert Heide and John Gilman, *The Mickey Mouse Watch*, Hyperion, 1997; Helmut Kahlert, Richard Mühe, and Gisbert L. Brunner, *Wristwatches: History of a Century's Development, 4th Edition*, Schiffer Publishing, 1999; Cooksey Shugart, Richard E. Gilbert, and Tom

Engle, *Complete Price Guide to Watches, 20th Edition*, Cooksey Shugart Publications, 2000.

Periodical: *International Wrist Watch*, PO Box 110204, Stamford, CT 06911.

Newsletter: *The Premium Watch Watch*, 24 San Rafael Dr, Rochester NY 14618.

Collectors' Clubs: National Assoc of Watch & Clock Collectors, 514 Poplar St, Columbia, PA 17512; The Swatch Collectors Club, PO Box 7400, Melville, NY 11747.

Character, Archie, Mohertus Trading Co, NY, metal bezel, diamond tooled, stainless steel back, red vinyl band, orig box, 1960s $100.00

Character, Batman, Fossil, bat symbol on face, sweep second hand, leather band, 1989 . . . . 55.00

Character, Congo the Movie, digital, battery operated, face depicts ape's eye, blue vinyl band with printed "We Are Watching You," orig box 20.00

Character, Daisy Duck, US Time, 1⅛ x 1½" chromed metal case, color illus of Daisy on dial with hands pointing to red numerals on pink ground, orig red vinyl straps, 1947 . . . . 100.00

Character, "Dale Evans Queen of the West," Ingraham, white face, polished case, colorful Dale Evans depiction on face, light tan leather wrist band, western style buckle and tip, attached to orig display card in box bottom, 1951 . . . . 135.00

Character, Dudley Do-Right, 17j, 1¼" d chrome case with brushed silver face, colorful image of smiling Dudley wearing red Mountie hat, attached brown leather band 175.00

Character, Flintstones, quartz, gold plated case, stainless steel back, brown leather band 10.00

Character, Lion King, Timex, goldtone case, emb "Lion King" on leather band, orig box 25.00

Character, Roman Gabriel, display box in sliding clear plastic sleeve displays full color photo Gabriel image dial face, letters of his name serve as hour numerals, made in Switzerland for Roman Gabriel 18 of Los Angeles, orig warranty papers, 1970-80s 50.00

Character, Splash Mountain, Disneyland employee's, 1¼" d dial, black text "Limited Edition Cast Member Watch" with Splash Mountain logo, dial illus of Brer Rabbit, Bear, and Fox with water, log, and text "Disneyland Splash Mountain 1989" 75.00

Character, Star Wars Official Wristwatch, Bradley, black plastic case with metal dial with color photo of R2-D2 and C-3PO against black and white galaxy ground, white and orange hands, silvered metal and black vinyl band, orig warranty papers and plastic case, ©1980 20th Century Fox Film Corp 35.00

Character, Underdog, A&M, 1⅛" d chrome accent case, white face with full figure image of Underdog with red second hand, black vinyl simulated alligator skin band, ©1984 Pat Ward 50.00

Fob, Adam Eidemiller Construction, Greensburg, PA 50.00

Fob, Allis-Chalmers, bulldozer, leather strap, Metal Arts Co, 1950s 55.00

Fob, American Legion, depicts General Pershing image and name, "1939 Chicago" below, blue and white enamel American Legion Auxilary logo 10.00

Fob, "Case" on front, back mkd "JI Case Co Wheel and Crawler Tractors and Equipment," leather strap, 1950s 35.00

Fob, Industrial Brown Hoist Corp, Bay City, MI, 1½" l 12.00

Fob, Latrobe Construction Co, Latrobe, PA, triangle shaped, horse head above "Sukawa" 65.00

Fob, "State of Ohio," porcelain, blue and white, on gold colored 4-leaf clover 10.00

Fob, Union Boiler Co, "UB" intertwined, enamel on white ground, reverse mkd "Union Boiler Co, General Contractors Tro, W Va By Geo Mtts, O" 10.00

Fob, Western PA Fireman's Convention, in Vandergrift, PA, reverse mkd "Geo G McMurtry Fire Dept No. 1 Vandergrift Fire Dept No. 2," 1935 . . . . 20.00

Novelty, "Time For Peace," Sheffield, 1½" d brass luster case, green glow-in-the-dark lettering, sweep second hand designed like peace symbol, 1970 . . . . 75.00

Novelty, western saddle, Gabriel, brown plastic 2 x 2½" curved saddle accented by tiny silver studs with miniature metal stirrup attached to each side, fits over wrist when secured by fabric strap with metal buckle, clear crystal case over silver luster dial face accented by gold hour numerals and matching time hands, red sweep second hand, 1960s 50.00

Pocket Watch, Buster Brown Shoes, Photorific, JH1000, 1⅞" d chrome case with 1½" d dial art of Buster winking at viewer next to smiling Tige, attached black vinyl strap, orig case, 1960s 50.00

Pocket Watch, Elgin, 17j, Model 3, size 12, ¾ plate, open face, pendant set, pillow style case mkd "Elgin Giant Watch Case Co, Elgin, USA Guaranteed 14K Gold Filled, 25 Years Double Stock," 1920s 100.00

Pocket Watch, Waltham, 15j, X27900, mkd "Keystone Watchcase J Boss 20 Years," dated Jun 23, 1922 . . . . 70.00

Swatch, Back Stage, 1992 . . . . 20.00

Swatch, Banana, MIB 15.00

Swatch, Breakdance, designed by Keith Haring, 1985 . . . . . . 325.00

Swatch, Daiquiri, yellow leather strap 20.00

Swatch, Expo 86 . . . . 18.00

Swatch, Film No. 4, GB168, designed by Yoko Ono, 1996 . . . . 50.00

Swatch, Fiorenze Wave Tour, #600 . . . . 110.00

Swatch, Fire Signal, BR001F, 1986-87 . . . . 12.00

Swatch, McGregor 100.00

Swatch, Medichi, 1985 . . . . 115.00

Swatch, Mezza Luna, 1986, MIB 50.00

Swatch, Nine to Six, GB 117 . . . . 20.00

Swatch, Point of View, 1995 . . . . 50.00

Swatch, Red Island, red leather strap 12.00

Swatch, Riding Star, 1993 . . . . 25.00

Swatch, Scribble, 1993, MIP 25.00

Swatch, Sebastian Coe, Olympic series, GZ147, 1997 . . . . . . 20.00

Swatch, Sheherazade, 1985 . . . . 20.00

Swatch, Squiggly, 1984 . . . . 40.00

Swatch, Technosphere, 1985 . . . . 50.00

Swatch, Watching Breakfast 25.00

Swatch, White Out, 1986 . . . . 50.00

Swatch, Yamaha Racer, 1985 . . . . 55.00

Wristwatch, Benrus, 10K, rolled gold plate bezel, stainless steel back, lizard band, 1940s 20.00

Wristwatch, Bulova, 1" d goldtone case, white face with gold numerals, separate second dial, replaced strap 65.00

Wristwatch, Bulova Accutron, 14K, Boeing logo at 12 o'clock, case inscribed with presentation message 125.00

Wristwatch, Croton, 14K, white gold with diamonds, crowned shield on face with "C" inside and "Croton Nivada Grenchen Aquamatic 360 El Gort-Klaatuu Barada Nektuu," letter "J" on back with arrow beside "14kt," orig box, 1950s **150.00**

Wristwatch, Elgin, type A-11, 25mm d black face, white hands and numerals, yellow tinted lens, imp specs, expandable band, dated 1943 . . . . **130.00**

Wristwatch, Gruen, lady's, Art Deco style, 14K, white gold filled, silver metal dial, Breguet black numerals, blue steel "moon style" hands, 60-minute checkered outer dial, etched filigree case, 1920s. **55.00**

Wristwatch, Hamilton, 10K, gold filled, leather band, Anheuser-Busch Beer logo above 6 o'clock. **35.00**

Wristwatch, Hamilton, 17j, 10K, gold filled, 1940s. **60.00**

Wristwatch, Hamilton, 17j, 10K, yellow rolled gold bezel, stainless steel back, gold numerals interspaced by round cut diamonds, brown leather band. **95.00**

Wristwatch, Longines, "Admiral," self-winding, stainless steel **90.00**

Wristwatch, Longines, men's, 17j, 10K, gold filled, gold applied numerals and markers, orig dial mkd "T Swiss T," manual wind, replaced strap **75.00**

Wristwatch, Lord Elgin, #1584N, 23j, 10K, gold filled, autowind **20.00**

Wristwatch, Omega, #620, 17j, 14K gold, rect, brushed finish case with polished sides **200.00**

Wristwatch, Seiko, man's, chronograph, white dial with date, hour, minutes, and seconds, black bezel, 2-tone gold colored band. **100.00**

Wristwatch, Wittnauer, 17j, swiss movement, 1940s. **65.00**

WATERFORD CRYSTAL

Waterford Crystal, Waterford, County Waterford, Ireland, traces its lineage to a crystal manufacturing business established by George and William Penrose in 1783. Although this initial effort to manufacture crystal and other glassware in Waterford only lasted sixty-eight years, the items produced enjoyed an unequaled reputation.

The end of flint glass production in Dublin around 1893 marked the demise of almost three centuries of glassmaking in Ireland. In 1902 sand from Muckish in Donegal was brought to the Cork Exhibition where London glass blowers used a small furnace and made drinking glasses cut in an "early Waterford style." This attempt to create an interest in reviving glassmaking in Ireland failed.

In 1947, almost fifty years later, a small glass factory was established in Ballytuckle, a suburb of Waterford, located approximately one-and-one-half miles from the site of the Penrose glasshouse on the western edge of the city. Apprentices were trained by immigrant European craftsmen displaced by World War II.

The management of Waterford Crystal dedicated its efforts to matching the purity of color, inspired design, and the highest quality levels of 18th- and 19th-century Waterford glass. Capturing the brilliance of the traditional, deeply incised cutting patterns of earlier Waterford pieces provided an additional challenge.

Waterford Crystal continued to grow and prosper, eventually moving to a forty-acre site in Johnstown, near the center of Waterford. In the early 1980s computer technology improved the accuracy of the raw materials mix, known in the crystal industry as the batch. Improvements in furnace design and diamond cutting wheels enabled Waterford craftsmen to create exciting new intri-

cate glass patterns. Two additional plants in County Waterford helped the company meet its manufacturing requirements.

Waterford Crystal stemware consists of essentially twelve stem shapes with a variety of cutting patterns which expand the range to over thirty suites. Many popular patterns have been adapted for giftware, providing an opportunity to acquire matching bowls, vases, and other accessories. In addition to producing stemware, giftware, and lighting, Waterford Crystal also executes hundreds of commissioned pieces. All Waterford Crystal can be identified by the distinctive "Waterford" signature on the base.

References: Bob Page and Dale Frederiksen, *Crystal Stemware Identification Guide,* Collector Books, 1998; Harry L. Rinker, *Stemware of the 20th Century: The Top 200 Patterns,* House of Collectibles, 1997.

Alana, champagne, 4¹/₈" h **$25.00**
Alana, claret, 5⁷/₈" h **25.00**
Alana, cocktail, 4" h **20.00**
Alana, cordial, 3¹/₂" h **20.00**
Alana, highball, 5" h **25.00**
Alana, old fashion. **20.00**
Alana, sherry, 5¹/₈" h **30.00**
Alana, shot glass **20.00**
Araglin, champagne, fluted **20.00**
Araglin, claret, 7¹/₈" h **20.00**
Araglin, cordial. **20.00**
Araglin, old fashion. **20.00**
Araglin, sherry **20.00**
Ashling, champagne, 4¹/₈" h **30.00**
Ashling, champagne, fluted **30.00**
Ashling, claret, 5⁷/₈" h **35.00**
Ashling, cordial, 3¹/₂" h **25.00**
Ashling, old fashion **30.00**
Ashling, sherry **30.00**
Castlemaine, champagne, fluted, 8³/₈" h **20.00**
Castlemaine, claret, 7¹/₈" h **20.00**
Castlemaine, cordial, 4⁵/₈" h **20.00**
Castlemaine, old fashion, 3¹/₂" h **20.00**
Castlemaine, sherry. **20.00**
Clare, champagne, 4¹/₈" h **40.00**
Clare, claret, 5⁷/₈" h. **45.00**
Clare, cocktail, 4" h. **35.00**
Clare, old fashion, 3³/₈" h. **40.00**
Clare, sherry, 5¹/₈" h. **35.00**
Clare, wine. **40.00**
Colleen, short stem, brandy, 5" h **35.00**
Colleen, short stem, champagne, 3³/₈" h **30.00**
Colleen, short stem, champagne, fluted, 6" h **35.00**
Colleen, short stem, cocktail, 3⁵/₈" h. **30.00**
Colleen, short stem, cordial, 3¹/₄" h **20.00**
Colleen, short stem, highball **25.00**
Colleen, tall stem, brandy, 5³/₈" h **30.00**
Colleen, tall stem, champagne. **35.00**
Colleen, tall stem, claret, 6¹/₂" h **35.00**
Colleen, tall stem, cocktail **25.00**
Colleen, tall stem, cordial, 3⁷/₈" h **20.00**
Colleen, tall stem, highball **25.00**
Colleen, tall stem, wine. **35.00**
Curraghmore, champagne, 5¹/₂" h. **40.00**
Curraghmore, claret, 7¹/₈" h **40.00**
Curraghmore, cordial, 4³/₄" h **30.00**
Curraghmore, old fashion **35.00**

Curraghmore, sherry, 6¼" h	35.00
Curraghmore, wine, 6¼" h	40.00
Glenmore, champagne, 4¾" h	30.00
Glenmore, claret	30.00
Glenmore, cocktail, 4¼" h	30.00
Glenmore, cordial, 3¾" h	25.00
Glenmore, old fashion, 3½" h	30.00
Glenmore, sherry, 5½" h	30.00
Glenmore, wine	30.00
Kenmare, champagne, 4¾" h	30.00
Kenmare, claret	30.00
Kenmare, cocktail, 4⅝" h	30.00
Kenmare, iced tea	45.00
Kenmare, jug	100.00
Kenmare, old fashion, 3½" h	30.00
Kenmare, sherry, 5⅜" h	30.00
Kenmare, wine	30.00
Kildare, champagne	20.00
Kildare, claret, 6½" h	20.00
Kildare, cordial, 4" h	20.00
Kildare, iced tea, ftd	30.00
Kildare, juice	25.00
Kildare, old fashion	20.00
Kildare, sherry, 5¼" h	20.00
Kildare, tumbler	25.00
Kildare, water goblet	20.00
Kinsale, champagne, 4¾" h	35.00
Kinsale, claret, 6" h	45.00
Kinsale, cocktail, 4¾" h	30.00
Kinsale, iced tea	45.00
Kinsale, old fashion, 3⅝" h	35.00
Kinsale, sherry, 5⅜" h	30.00
Kinsale, water goblet, 6¾" h	45.00
Kinsale, wine	40.00

WATT POTTERY

In 1886 W. J. Watt founded the Brilliant Stoneware Company in Rose Farm, Ohio. The company made salt-glazed utilitarian stoneware. Watt sold his business in 1897. Between 1903 and 1921 Watt worked for the Ransbottom Brothers Pottery in Ironspot, Ohio. The Ransbottoms were Watt's brothers-in-law.

In 1921 Watt purchased the Globe Stoneware Company in Crooksville, Ohio, renaming it the Watt Pottery Company. Watt made stoneware containers between 1922 and 1935.

In the 1930s Watt introduced a line of kitchenware designed to withstand high oven temperatures. Pieces were rather plain with decoration limited to a white and/or blue band. The mid-1940s' Kla-Ham'rd series featured pieces dipped in a brown glaze.

Watt's Wild Rose pattern, known to collectors as Raised Pansy, was introduced in 1950. Production difficulties resulted in a second pattern design, marketed as Rio Rose but called Cut Leaf Pansy by collectors.

Watt introduced new patterns each year during the 1950s. Although Watt sold patterns under specific pattern names, collectors group them in a single category, e.g., Starflower covers Moonflower and Silhouette. Watt introduced its Apple series in 1952, producing pieces for approximately ten years. Several variations were produced. The Tulip and Cherry series appeared in the mid-1950s. Rooster was introduced in 1955. The Morning Glory series arrived in the late 1950s followed by the Autumn Foliage in 1959. Lines introduced in the 1960s met with limited success.

Watt also made advertising and special commission ware. Pieces marked Esmond, Heirloom, Orchard Ware, Peedeeco, and R-F Spaghetti may have Watt backstamps. Watt was not evenly distributed—50% of the company's products were sold in New York and New England, 25% in the greater Chicago area, a small amount distributed by Safeway in the southern and western states, and the balance throughout the midwest and northeast.

On October 4, 1965, fire destroyed the Watt Pottery Company factory and warehouse. Production never resumed.

References: Sue and Dave Morris, *Watt Pottery*, Collector Books, 1993, 1998 value update; Dennis Thompson and W. Bryce Watt, *Watt Pottery*, Schiffer Publishing, 1994.

Collectors' Club: Watt Collectors Assoc, PO Box 1995, Iowa City, IA 52244.

Note: See Yellow Ware for additional listings.

Apple, bean pot, cov, 3-leaf	**$165.00**
Apple, bowl, #6, adv	70.00
Apple, bowl, #8	50.00
Apple, bowl, #73	45.00
Apple, canister, cov, #72	450.00
Apple, casserole, #73, 3-leaf	30.00
Apple, chip and dip set, #96 and #120 bowls with wire rack	185.00
Apple, creamer, #62	100.00
Apple, French casserole, cov, individual	250.00
Apple, grease jar	275.00
Apple, ice bucket	265.00
Apple, mixing bowl, #8, adv	75.00
Apple, mixing bowl, #13, 2-leaf, 6½" d	35.00
Apple, mixing bowls, #04, #05, #06, and #07, price for 4-pc set	225.00

Apple, pitcher, #17, 3-leaf, ice lip, $160.00. Photo courtesy Gene Harris Antique Auction Center, Inc.

Apple, mixing bowls, ribbed, #7 and #8, 3-leaf, price for
 pr **100.00**
Apple, nesting bowls, #63, #64, and #65, 3-leaf, price
 for set of 3 . . . . **200.00**
Apple, pie plate, #33, adv **100.00**
Apple, pitcher, #15, 3-leaf **75.00**
Apple, pitcher, #15, 3-leaf, Coon's Corner adv **115.00**
Apple, platter, 3-leaf, 15" d **200.00**
Apple, salad bowl, #73, 3-leaf, green band **60.00**
Apple, salt and pepper shakers, pr, hourglass, adv **150.00**
Apple, spaghetti bowl, #39, 13¼" d **75.00**
Autumn Foliage, bowl, #6, ribbed **20.00**
Autumn Foliage, bowl, #7 . . . . **15.00**
Autumn Foliage, chip bowl, #120 . . . . **55.00**
Autumn Foliage, nesting bowls, ribbed, #04, #05, #06,
 price for 3-pc set **100.00**
Autumn Leaf, pitcher, #15, adv, 5½" h **75.00**
Cherry, bowl, #39 . . . . **55.00**
Cherry, pitcher, #15 . . . . **300.00**
Double Apple, baker, cov, #96 . . . . **125.00**
Double Apple, dip bowl, #120 . . . . **70.00**
Eagle, bowl, #73 . . . . **185.00**
Eagle, cereal bowls, set of 6 . . . . **375.00**
Eagle, mixing bowls, ribbed, #5, #6, #7, and #8, price
 for 4-pc set **400.00**
Esmond Fruit, canister set, 4 wedge-shaped canisters on
 wooden turntable base, wooden lid **35.00**
Esmond Fruit, cookie jar, #34, wooden lid **135.00**
Kla-Ham'rd, pitcher, #43-14, 2-tone, 7" h **20.00**
Moon & Stars, bowl, #9 . . . . **40.00**
Moon & Stars, custard cup **70.00**
Open Apple, spaghetti bowl, #39 . . . . **300.00**
Rio Rose, batter pitcher, cov, 3½" h **150.00**
Rio Rose, bowl, #5 . . . . **45.00**
Rio Rose, bowl, #8 . . . . **40.00**
Rio Rose, bowl, #39 . . . . **45.00**
Rio Rose, cup and saucer **45.00**
Rio Rose, platter, 15" d **85.00**
Rooster, bowl, #5 . . . . **80.00**
Rooster, bowl, #77 . . . . **80.00**
Rooster, creamer, #62, 4" h **250.00**
Rooster, ice bucket, voc. **175.00**
Rooster, mixing bowl, #9 . . . . **65.00**
Rooster, pitcher, #15 . . . . **80.00**
Rooster, salt and pepper shakers, pr, hourglass, adv **190.00**
Starflower, bowl, #7 . . . . **50.00**
Starflower, bowl, #8, adv **55.00**
Starflower, cereal bowl, #74 . . . . **30.00**
Starflower, ice bucket, cov, 5-petal, 7" h, 8" d **190.00**
Starflower, mixing bowl, #9 . . . . **30.00**
Starflower, mug, #501 . . . . **65.00**
Starflower, pie plate, 4-petal, #33 . . . . **175.00**
Starflower, pitcher, #15, 5¼" h **75.00**
Starflower, pitcher, #16, 7" h **80.00**
Starflower, pitcher, #17, 5-petal **75.00**
Starflower, salt and pepper shakers, pr, range size **200.00**
Starflower, spaghetti bowl, #39 . . . . **110.00**
Swirl, bowl, #8, turquoise, 8¼" d **15.00**
Teardrop, bean pot, cov. **65.00**
Teardrop, milk pitcher, #15, 5½" h **75.00**
Teardrop, mixing bowls, #5, #6, and #7, price for set of 3 . . . **100.00**
Teardrop, pitcher, #15 . . . . **70.00**
Tulip, bowl, #15, adv **65.00**
Tulip, mixing bowl, #65, 8½" d **75.00**

WEDGWOOD

In 1759 Josiah Wedgwood established a pottery near Stoke-on-Trent at the former Ivy House works in Burslem, England. By 1761, Wedgwood had perfected a superior quality inexpensive clear-glazed creamware which proved to be very successful.

Wedgwood moved his pottery from the Ivy House to the larger Brick House works in Burslem in 1764. In 1766, upon being appointed "Potter to Her Majesty" by Queen Charlotte, Wedgwood named his creamware "Queen's ware." The Brick House works remained in production until 1772.

Wedgwood built a new factory in Etruria in 1769, the same year he formed a partnership with Thomas Bentley. Wedgwood's most famous set of Queen's ware, the 1,000-piece "Frog" Service created for Catherine the Great, Empress of Russia, was produced at the Etruria factory in 1774.

By the late 1700s, the Wedgwood product line included black basalt, creamware, jasper, pearlware, and redware. Moonlight luster was made from 1805 to 1815. Bone China was produced from 1812 to 1822, and revived in 1878. Fairyland luster was introduced in 1915. The last luster pieces were made in 1932.

In 1906 Wedgwood established a museum at its Etruria pottery. A new factory was built at nearby Barlaston in 1940. The museum was moved to Barlaston and expanded. The Etruria works was closed in 1950.

During the 1960s and 1970s Wedgwood acquired many English potteries, including William Adams & Sons, Coalport, Susie Cooper, Crown Staffordshire, Johnson Brothers, Mason's Ironstone, J. & G. Meakin, Midwinter Companies, Precision Studios and Royal Tuscan. In 1969 Wedgwood acquired King's Lynn Glass, renaming it Wedgwood Glass. The acquisition of Galway Crystal Company of Galway, Erie, followed in 1974.

In 1986 Waterford and Wedgwood merged. The Wedgwood Group, now a division of Waterford Wedgwood, consists of six major divisions: Wedgwood, Coalport, Johnson Brothers, Mason's Ironstone, Wedgwood Hotelware, and Wedgwood Jewellery. The Wedgwood Group is one of the largest tabletop manufacturers in the world. It is a public company comprising eight factories and employing 5,500 people in the United Kingdom and overseas.

References: Susan and Al Bagdade, *Warman's English & Continental Pottery & Porcelain, 3rd Edition,* Krause Publications, 1998; Maureen Batkin, *Wedgwood Ceramics: 1846-1959,* Richard Dennis (England), 1996; Robin Reilly, *Wedgwood: The New Illustrated Dictionary, Revised,* Antique Collectors' Club, 1995; Harry L. Rinker, *Dinnerware of the 20th Century: The Top 500 Patterns,* House of Collectibles, 1997; Harry L. Rinker, *Stemware of the 20th Century: The Top 200 Patterns,* House of Collectibles, 1997.

Collectors' Clubs: The Wedgwood Society of Great Britain, 89 Andrewes House, Barbican, London ECY 8AY, U.K.; Wedgwood Society of New York, 5 Dogwood Ct, Glen Head, NY 11545.

Bank, brown earthenware, molded cylindrical brick
 building, inscribed on foot rim "Wedgwood–Etruria
 1769 The Round House," c1969, 4¾" h **$200.00**
Bicentennial Goblet, jasper diceware, applied white
 portraits of Washington and Jefferson on light blue
 ground, floral festoons and foliate trim, green banded
 trim and quatrefoils, limited edition of 200,
 imp mark, 1976, 4¾" h **700.00**

Biscuit Jar, cov, yellow jasper, black jasper relief of classical figures below fruiting grapevine garlands terminating at lion and ring masks, silver plated rim, handle, and cover, imp mark, c1930, 5³/₄" h **750.00**

Bookends, pr, designed by Doris Lindner, allover moonstone and white colored glazes, printed and imp marks, c1937, 6¹/₂" h **1,250.00**

Bookends, pr, designed by Erling Olsen, Art Deco style, allover red ground, imp mark, c1932, 6⁵/₈" h **1,850.00**

Bowl, designed by Therese Lessore, Queen's ware, silver luster and puce enamel dec scenes of female bathers disrobing, artist signed and imp mark, c1920, 5¹/₂" d . . . **1,150.00**

Bowl, ftd, yellow jasper, applied black classical and foliate relief, imp mark, 20th C, 8¹/₈" d **525.00**

Bowl, "Thomas Hart Benton America Bowl," Queen's ware, reproductions of his lithographs surrounding body, limited edition of 200, printed mark, 1985, 12¹/₄" d **425.00**

Box, cov, crimson jasper, square form, applied white classical figures and floral dec, imp mark, c1920, 4" w . **1,150.00**

Candlesticks, pr, yellow jasper, black classical and arabesque floral relief, imp mark, c1930, 6" h **700.00**

Cup, cov, light blue jasper, applied white arabesque floral and foliate relief, cupid finial, imp mark, 1973, 8⁵/₈" h **315.00**

Dish, attributed to Millicent Taplin, caneware, purple luster dec, hp foliate design, printed mark, c1930, 12¹/₂" d **375.00**

Dish, crimson jasper, diamond shaped, applied white classical and foliate relief, imp mark, c1920, 5³/₄" l **800.00**

Figure, Queen Elizabeth II, black basalt, seated figure with inscription "To Commemorate the Coronation of her Majesty Queen Elizabeth II, June 2nd 1953 AD," Kenneth White Studio imp mark, artist signature, and numbered, c1953, 9¹/₄" h **85.00**

Jardiniere, crimson jasper, cylindrical form, applied white classical Muses below fruiting grapevine festoons terminating at lion masks, imp mark, c1920, 7" h **2,500.00**

Jardiniere and Stand, crimson jasper, applied white classical relief, imp mark, c1920, 3¹/₂" h **1,750.00**

Lamp Base, designed by Norman Wilson, Moonstone, imp and printed mark, mid-20th C, 16¹/₂" h **175.00**

Mug, attributed to Harry Barnard, olive green jasper, slip dec verse "Who lives a good life is sure to live well" between drapery swag and acanthus leaf borders, imp mark, c1920, 5¹/₄" h **425.00**

Mustard Pot, yellow jasper, applied black fruiting grapevine festoons terminating at lion masks and rings, imp mark, 20th C, 3" h **175.00**

Plaque, "Beloved of the Great Enchantress," black basalt with gilt dec, limited edition of 250, imp mark, 1973, 8 x 8¹/₂" **350.00**

Plate, bone china, golfer, powder green border, mid-20th C, 10⁵/₈" d **115.00**

Plate, jasper diceware, commemorating 250th anniversary of birth of Josiah Wedgwood, white portrait and foliate borders, green ground with applied lilac quatrefoils, limited edition of 250, printed and imp marks, c1980, 9" d **850.00**

Table Clock, light blue jasper, Art Deco style, circular form, oval medallion to either side with white classical figure in relief, 20th C, 5⁵/₈" h **115.00**

Tea Set, 3 pcs, dark blue jasper, applied white relief for Coronation of Edward VIII, imp mark, 8³/₄" l covered teapot, 5¹/₈" creamer, and 4¹/₄" covered sugar bowl, c1937 . . . . **400.00**

Vase, cov, "Athena," jasper diceware, white classical and foliate relief on royal blue ground, green banded trim and quatrefoils, limited edition of 200, imp mark, 1976, 9¹/₄" h **925.00**

Vase, blue transfer printed fallow, imp and printed mark, c1929, 9¹/₂" h **115.00**

Vase, crimson jasper, bulbous, applied white classical relief, imp mark, c1920, 4³/₄" h **925.00**

Vase, designed by Louis Powell, earthenware, stylized silver luster foliate designs on white ground, artist signed and imp mark, c1930, 7⁵/₈" h **300.00**

Vase, Moonstone, silver luster dec, tapering sides with floral and foliate design, printed mark, c1930, 9¹/₄" h **115.00**

Vase, stoneware, brown body with glazed top and white club form spout, imp potter's monogram for J Dermer and Factory mark, mid-20th C, 11¹/₄" h **850.00**

Vase, stoneware, square bottle form with flaring rim, imp artist monogram for M Dillon and Factory, c1980, 5" h . . . **500.00**

Vase, Veronese ware, green hound with silver luster floral design, imp mark, c1935, 8¹/₂" h **150.00**

Vase, yellow jasper, applied black fruiting grapevine and foliate relief, imp mark, 20th C, 7¹/₈" h **350.00**

WELLER

Samuel Augutus Weller established the Weller Pottery Company in Fultonham, Ohio, in 1872. In 1888, Weller moved operations to Zanesville. By 1890 a new plant was built.

During a visit to the 1893 Columbian Exposition in Chicago, Weller saw Lonhuda ware. He bought the Lonhuda Pottery and brought William Long, its owner, to Zanesville to supervise production at Weller. When Long resigned in 1896, Weller introduced Louwelsa Weller, based on Long's glaze formula.

Weller purchased the American Encaustic Tiling Company plant in 1899. By 1900 Weller enjoyed a virtual monopoly on mass-produced art pottery. Soon Weller was exporting large amounts of pottery to England, Germany, and Russia.

In the 1910s Japanese potteries made almost exact copies of Weller products that sold in the American market for half the cost. Weller increased its production of ware for the floral and garden industries to offset the financial losses.

Weller purchased the Zanesville Art Pottery in 1920 and incorporated. Several new lines were introduced in the late 1920s. Weller's son-in-law became president in 1932. Divorce from his wife forced him to leave the company. The divorce settlement entitled him to reproduced Zona dinnerware, which he took to Gladding, McBean.

In 1945 Essex Wire Corporation leased space in the Weller factory. By 1947 Essex Wire bought the controlling stock of the company. The factory closed in 1948.

References: Sharon and Bob Huxford, *The Collectors Encyclopedia of Weller Pottery,* Collector Books, 1979, 1999 value update; Ralph and Terry Kovel, *Kovels' American Art Pottery,* Crown Publishers, 1993.

Collectors' Club: American Art Pottery Assoc, PO Box 834, Westport, MA 02790.

Umbrella Stand, Ardsley, 1920-28, 19" h, $550.00. Photo courtesy Gene Harris Antique Auction Center, Inc.

Basket, Florenzo, stamped mark, 5" w **$60.00**
Basket, Warwick, ruffled rim, kiln mark, 7" w **65.00**
Basket Planter, Roma, roses dec, unmkd, 10" w **50.00**
Bud Vase, Alvin, 6½" h **55.00**
Bud Vase, Cloudburst, lustered speckled gold glaze,
    unmkd, 6" h **60.00**
Cabinet Vase, LaMar, bulbous, 2½" h **50.00**
Candelabra, Woodcraft, owl figurine at top, 2-lite,
    stamped "Weller," 15" h **450.00**
Candlesticks, Oak Leaf, blue, 2½" d **65.00**
Candlesticks, pr, Ardsley, kiln mark, 3" h **80.00**
Centerbowl, Glendale, seagull dec, with nest shaped
    flower frog, 15" d bowl **425.00**
Console Bowl, Glendale, with flower frog, ink stamp
    mark, 15¼" d bowl **500.00**
Console Set, Hobart, 8-sided faceted rect centerbowl,
    dome flower frog with emb daisies, and pr of faceted
    candlesticks, lavender and teal glazes. **60.00**
Console Set, Hobart, large scalloped centerbowl in
    shaded lavender and teal matte glaze, figural flower
    frog in matte lavender glaze, and pr of low candle-
    sticks in matte teal glaze, 15½" d bowl, 8" h flower
    frog, 3" h candlesticks **175.00**
Console Set, Marvo, brown, flaring centerbowl and pr of
    low candlesticks, unmkd, 10" d bowl, 5½" d candle-
    sticks **150.00**
Cornucopia Vase, Cameo, blue, 7" h **40.00**
Double Bud Vase, Glendale, green, emb birds and fruit,
    4¾" h **90.00**
Jardiniere, Blue Ware, ladies dancing and playing instru-
    ments, imp "Weller," 7½" d **250.00**
Jardiniere, Copra, pansies dec, unmkd, 10" h, 8" d **175.00**
Jardiniere, Velva, green, 4¾" h **75.00**
Lamp Base, Baldin, stamped "Weller," 9" h **200.00**
Pillow Vase, Malvern, red, stamped mark, 8" h **110.00**
Pillow Vase, Patra, 2-handled, 6½" h **70.00**
Pitcher, Delsa, green, 6½" h **30.00**
Pitcher, Roba, purple, imp mark, 6" h **50.00**
Pitcher, Roma, poppy dec, 7¼" h **85.00**
Pitcher, Zona, bulbous with emb panels of leaves and
    frolicking ducks, olive green on ivory ground, ink kiln
    mark, 7¾" h **200.00**

Planter, Golbrogreen, unmkd, 4¾" h, 8½" d **25.00**
Planter, Oak Leaf, green, ovoid, stamped mark, 9½" w **60.00**
Planter, Woodrose, bucket shape, brown with yellow
    roses, 8¼" h **150.00**
Planter, Zona, rect, pink flowers on scrolled ground,
    stamped "Weller, 15" w, 6¼" h **275.00**
Umbrella Stand, Marvo, emb foliage, lavender and gray
    matte glaze, paper label, 19¾" h, 11" d **400.00**
Vase, 6-sided, matte green glaze, unmkd, 5" h, 3" w **225.00**
Vase, Florenzo, flaring basket form, 7¼" h **75.00**
Vase, Florenzo, scalloped and flaring rim, 7" h **80.00**
Vase, Goldenglow, asymmetrical handles, 9" h **100.00**
Vase, Ragenda, emb swirl dec, matte raspberry glaze,
    unmkd, 9½" h **150.00**
Wall Pocket, Blue Drapery, stamped "Weller," 7½" h **125.00**
Wall Pocket, emb polychrome dec with woman in gar-
    den, teal ground, unmkd, 7½" h **125.00**
Water Jug, Ollas, gourd shape, orange wash, 11¼" h **15.00**

WESTERN COLLECTIBLES

This category divides into three parts: (1) items associated with working cowboys and cowgirls such as horse tack, wagon trail memorabilia, everyday work clothes, dress duds, and rodeo memorabilia; (2) material related to the western dude ranch, and (3) objects shaped like or portraying images associated with the American West. It does not include items associated with literary, movie, and television characters.

Americans went western crazy in the 1950s, partially the result of the TV western. Western maple furniture was found in living rooms, dens, and children's bedrooms. Western motifs from riders on bucking horses to Mexicans taking siestas beneath cactus decorated everything from dinnerware to linens. The western revival of the early 1990s reawakened collector interest in this western motif material from the 1950s. As the decade ends, the craze seems to be abating, largely the result of high prices asked by dealers for commonly found items.

References: Judy Crandall, *Cowgirls: Early Images and Collectibles,* Schiffer Publishing, 1994; Michael Friedman, *Cowboy Culture, 2nd Edition,* Schiffer Publishing, 1999; Dan and Sebie Hutchins, *Old Cowboy Saddles & Spurs: Identifying the Craftsmen Who Made Them, Sixth Annual,* Horse Feathers Publishing, 1996; William Manns and Elizabeth Clair Flood, *Cowboys: The Trappings of the Old West,* Zon International, 1997; Joice Overton, *Cowboy Equipment,* Schiffer Publishing, 1998; Jim and Nancy Schaut, *Collecting the Old West,* Krause Publications, 1999; Jeffrey B. Snyder, *Stetson Hats and the John B. Stetson Company, 1865–1970,* Schiffer Publishing, 1997.

Periodical: *American Cowboy,* PO Box 6630, Sheridan, WY 82801.

Newsletter: *Cowboy Guide,* PO Box 6459, Santa Fe, NM 87502.

Collectors' Club: National Bit, Spur & Saddle Collectors Assoc, PO Box 3098, Colorado Springs, CO 80934.

Ashtray Stand, metal, figural cowboy boot with spurs,
    29" h **$30.00**
Autograph, Ben Johnson, PS, holding lasso and seated
    on horse, "Roper" at bottom, full color, 8 x 10" **30.00**

Poster, Tim McCoy's Wild West and Rough Riders, "The Indian Village," multicolored litho, mkd "Litho in USA #1414½," Tooker-Moore Litho Co, NY, 20½ x 27", **$1,875.00.** Photo courtesy Collectors Auction Services.

Autograph, Zack Miller of 101 Ranch, PS, "To Bill Brinkley/...Zack Miller," black and white, dated 1937, 19½" h, 16½" w **225.00**

Belt, cowhide, "Sitting Bull Chief of the Sioux, Remington" on front of buckle, "A gift from WF Cody Buffalo Bill" on reverse, Rare Stones Tiffany, Broadway, NY, 1970s **1,650.00**

Belt Buckle, calf roper with "National Finals Rodeo NFR 1985 Hesston" on front, "Third Edition Anniversary Series Limited Miniature Collector's Buckle Designed and Signed by Fred Fellows" on reverse, 2 x 2½" **4.00**

Belt Buckle, Hesston National Rodeo Finals, 1981 . . . . **12.00**

Book, *Western Roundup*, Dell, #13, black and white photo of Gene Autry inside front cover, Roy Rogers photo on back cover, 1956 . . . . **12.00**

Book, *Winchester Western Game Cooking Guide*, recipes and game care tips, 1979 . . . . **12.00**

Booklet, *Life Story of Pawnee Bill*, 32 pp, illus, c1920s, 6 x 8¾" **125.00**

Booklet, *Rifle Queen*, Isabelle Sayers, Ostrander, OH, illus, short biography of Annie Oakley, ©1973, 39 pp, 8½" h, 5½" w **110.00**

Bootjack, aluminum, 101 Ranch, cow head, 11½" l **80.00**

Catalog, Lawrence Leather, Portland, OR, 1960s, 8½ x 11" **25.00**

Catalog, O J Snyder Saddlery, 1535 Larimer St, Denver, CO, 56 pp, 1920s, 10" h, 6⅞" w **75.00**

Clock, Sessions, cowboy riding bucking horse, 14" h **400.00**

Comic Book, Bill Boyd Western Comic Annual, #5, L Miller & Co, 1960s **20.00**

Cowgirl Outfit, child's, Dale Evans, brown and yellow vest, shirt, and skirt with sewn-on initials, "DE" on each side, with tooled boots mkd "BF Goodrich" on heels and "Biltwel" inside, 1950s **135.00**

Cup Holder, metal, 4 hooks, cowboy on horse roping cattle with fence in background, 18 x 11" **18.00**

Gauntlets, leather, embroidered horseshoe motif, fringed design sewn in, metal buttons at edge **325.00**

Gauntlets, leather with glass beads, flower and fruit motif, fringed, early style lining, 14" l, 7½" w **450.00**

Holster Rig, leather, belt with tooled flower and steer-head design and 12-bullet holder with 12.44 caliber WCF bullets, holster with tooled floral design and engraved Mexican silver diamond-shaped conch, Mexican silver engraved belt buckle, leg ties, 10" l holster **325.00**

Letter, sgd by Zack T Miller of 101 Ranch, to sell shares of ranch to pay mortgage, sent to Donald A DeWees, orig envelope, 1934, 8½ x 11" **80.00**

Magazine, *Life*, John Reed Jr on cover, Jan 18, 1923 . . . . **15.00**

Membership Card, Old Time Cherokee Strip Cow Punchers Assoc, dues paid until Dec 31, 1925, sgd by JC Miller, President, with envelope, 2½" l, 4" w **400.00**

Photograph, Col Tim McCoy Wild West Show, performers in full costume, black and white, 11¾" h, 20" w **225.00**

Photograph, Downie Bros Circus, Circus Fans Association Convention, Norwich, CT, Jun 14, 1934, includes cowboys and cowgirls from Wild West show, photo by EJ Kelty, 12¾" h, 21¾" w **225.00**

Photograph, Old Timers Cowboy Reunion, Miller Bros 101 Ranch, panoramic view, list of men at second annual reunion of the Cherokee Strip Cow Punchers Assoc at 101 Ranch, Sep 1-5, 1921, attached to back, 2 membership cards attached to top, both sgd by Joe C Miller, dues paid until Dec 31, 1925, 7½ x 46" **400.00**

Photograph, Wenona, lady sharpshooter for 101 Ranch show, FW Glasier, Brockton, MA, 1925, 8 x 10" **150.00**

Pinback Button, National Western Stock Show, Denver, CO, 1958, 1¼" d **8.00**

Pipe, figural buffalo head with glass eyes, debossed "Bruyere Garantie" **45.00**

Pitcher and Tumbler Set, ceramic, Wild West collection, Elizabeth Studios, dark chocolate hp designs of long cattle, various brands, and horseshoes on creamy white ground, 9¾" h pitcher, three 5½" h tumblers **30.00**

Plate, decal commemorating Salinas Rodeo, Jul 13-16, 1939, mkd "Mayer China Eastern Pattern Copyright," 6" d **20.00**

Postcard, Joe Morrows Wild West Show, 3¼" h, 5½" w **18.00**

Postcard, rider on bucking steer at Calgary Stampede, real, black and white photo with sepiatone finish, mkd "E19, Al Butcher Bucked Off His Steer Oliver," unused, 1940, 5½ x 3½" **10.00**

Postcard, Tex Cooper photo with "Tex Cooper The Famous 101 Ranch, Cowboy Box 52 Maryland, Okla" above "Sheriff/Pioneer Days Centennial Dallas 1836-1936," "1933 A Century of Progress," and "1934 Century of Progress" on bottom, sgd "To OH Anderson from Tex Cooper, 101-Ranch 11-6-36," 5½" l, 3½" w **80.00**

Program, 35th Annual Frontier Days, 64 pp, 10¾" h, 7¾" w **165.00**

Program, Iowa 27th Championship Rodeo, Sidney, Iowa, Aug 15-19, 1950 . . . . **10.00**

Program, Miller Bros 101 Ranch, Jun & Jul 1927, 10 x 7" . . . **190.00**

Record, *Smiley Burnett and His Rodeo Songaree*, LP, Cricket Records CR 11, Smiley on cover with horse, 1958 . . . . **8.00**

Record, *The Rodeo Song*, Gary Lee and Showdown, LP **5.00**

Rifle Case, leather, fits large Weatherby or Winchester Model 70-type rifle with scope, brass strap holders, stamped "HH Heiser maker, Denver Colo, 839" **225.00**

Roster, Cherokee Strip Cow Punchers Assoc, Sep 1938,
  report of 17th Annual Reunion, 32 pp **150.00**
Roughout Vest, 4 floral shaped leather buttons, Indian
  design on right side, brass rivets mkd "101 Ranch,"
  teepees and fire designs above "101 Ranch," c1922 . . . . . **450.00**
Scarf, silk, Pendleton Rodeo, "Fan 'em Cowboy," teepee
  around corner, bucking bronco at corner edge,
  25½" sq **50.00**
Statue, adv, cowboy, chalkware on wood base with cast
  iron wheels, "Guns and Ammunition" on base **725.00**

AUCTION PRICES – WESTERN COLLECTIBLES

Collectors Auction Services, Western Americana Catalogue
Sale #23, May 29, 1999. Prices include a 10% premium and
have been rounded to the nearest whole dollar.

Painting on Velour, Indian on horse, with Indian
  symbols, slight soiling, 46½" h, 41½" w **$83.00**
Picture, stand-up, Poncho Villa men with
  Winchesters, celluloid over metal, sgd "GF
  Fschswei" at bottom edge, small faint paint
  speckles, scratches and staining, 9" w **72.00**
Print, "#2608 A Daughter of the Prairies, ©1907 by
  the Osborne Co," cowgirl and horse on plains,
  some spotting, 4" light scratch at middle, slight
  creases at eges, 16½" h, 20½" w **259.00**
Shooting Gallery Target, 3 red-painted metal targets
  on mounting bracket, all spring-loaded, 2 stay
  down after being hit until released, surface rust to
  bracket and springs, paint chips to target, overall
  soiling, 3½" h, 10" w, 3¾" d **55.00**
Watch Fob, "Lykes & Fernandez Havana, Cuba
  Agents for The Famous Heiser Saddles USA," saddle shaped metal fob with leather band, ornate
  floral pattern on saddle, soiling and wear to
  band, 3¼" h, 1¾" w **143.00**

WESTMORELAND

Westmoreland, Jeannette, Pennsylvania, traces its history to the
East Liverpool Specialty Glass Company and the influence of
Major George Irwin. Irwin was instrumental in moving the com-
pany from East Liverpool, Ohio, to Jeannette, Pennsylvania, to take
advantage of the large natural gas reserves in the area. Specialty
Glass, a new Pennsylvania Company, was established in 1888.
When the company ran out of money in 1889, Charles H. and
George R. West put up $40,000 for 53% of the company's stock.
The name was changed to Westmoreland Specialty Company.

Initially Westmoreland made candy containers and a number of
other glass containers. In 1910 the company introduced its
Keystone line of tableware. Charles West had opposed the move
into tableware production, and the brothers split in 1920. George
West continued with the Westmoreland Specialty Company,
changing its name in 1924 to the Westmoreland Glass Company.

Westmoreland made decorative wares and Colonial-era reproductions, e.g., dolphin pedestal forms, in the 1920s. Color, introduced to the tableware lines in the early 1930s, was virtually gone
by the mid-1930s. Amber, black, and ruby were introduced in the
1950s in an attempt to bolster the line.

In 1937 Charles West retired and J. H. Brainard assumed the
company's helm. Phillip and Walter Brainard, J. H.'s two sons,
joined the firm in 1940. In an effort to cut costs, all cutting and
engraving work was eliminated in the 1940s. Grinding and pol-
ishing of glass ceased in 1957. No new molds were made until the
milk glass surge in the early and mid-1950s.

The milk glass boom was over by 1958. While continuing to
produce large quantities of milk glass in the 1960s, Westmoreland
expanded its product line to include crystal tableware and colored
items. The effort was unsuccessful. Attempts to introduce color into
the milk glass line also proved disappointing. The company kept its
doors open, albeit barely, by appealing to the bridal trade.

In the search for capital, an on-site gift shop was opened on
April 12, 1962. The shop produced a steady cash flow. Shortly after
the shop opened, Westmoreland began selling seconds. Another
valuable source of cash was found.

By 1980 J. H. Brainard was searching for a buyer for the company. After turning down a proposal from a group of company
employees, Brainard sold Westmoreland to David Grossman, a St.
Louis–based distributor and importer, best known for his Norman
Rockwell Collectibles series. Operations ceased on January 8,
1984. Most of the molds, glass, historic information, catalogs, and
furniture were sold at auction.

References: Lorraine Kovar, *Westmoreland Glass, 1950–1984*
(1991), *Vol. II* (1991), *Vol. III: 1888–1940* (1998), Antique Publications; Chas West Wilson, *Westmoreland Glass,* Collector Books,
1996, 1998 value update.

Collectors' Clubs: National Westmoreland Glass Collectors Club,
PO Box 100, Grapeville, PA 15634; Westmoreland Glass Society,
1144 42nd Ave, Vero Beach, FL 32960.

Note: All items are white milk glass unless noted otherwise.

Beaded Edge, bread and butter plate **$3.00**
Beaded Edge, cup, grape **12.00**
Beaded Edge, dessert plate, hp fruit, 7" d **12.00**
Beaded Edge, plate, 7⅜" d, plum **12.00**
Beaded Edge, salad plate, fruit center, 7" **10.00**
Beaded Edge, saucer, pear **5.00**
Beaded Edge, tumbler, strawberry **15.00**
Beaded Grape, cake stand, ftd, 9½" d **70.00**
Beaded Grape, wedding bowl, cov, large, roses and
  bows dec **90.00**
Della Robia, candy jar, cov, scalloped edge **100.00**
Early American, cup and saucer, crystal **40.00**
English Hobnail, box, cov **20.00**
English Hobnail, champagne, crystal **10.00**
English Hobnail, cocktail, round foot, 3 oz, crystal **8.00**
English Hobnail, cocktail, round foot, 3 oz, ice blue **50.00**
English Hobnail, cocktail, square foot, crystal **12.00**
English Hobnail, cologne and powder set, #555,
  blue milk glass **300.00**
English Hobnail, cup and saucer, crystal **10.00**
English Hobnail, ginger ale tumbler, square foot, crystal **8.00**
English Hobnail, goblet, round foot, 6" d, crystal **10.00**
English Hobnail, juice tumbler, flat, ice blue **35.00**
English Hobnail, lamp, electric, 6" h, crystal **45.00**
English Hobnail, lamp, electric, 6" h, white **40.00**
English Hobnail, plate, 5½" d, crystal **8.00**
English Hobnail, plate, 8" d, amber **10.00**

Ring & Petal, bowl, flared, low ftd, amber, 4³/₄" h, 10" d, $30.00.
Photo courtesy Ray Morykan Auctions.

English Hobnail, plate, 8" d, crystal	6.00
English Hobnail, plate, 8" d, ice blue	30.00
English Hobnail, powder jar, cov, 5½" d, canary yellow	200.00
English Hobnail, sherbet, low, ftd, crystal	10.00
English Hobnail, sherbet, tall, square foot	12.00
English Hobnail, tumbler, flat, 9 oz, crystal	10.00
English Hobnail, tumbler, flat, 12 oz, crystal	12.00
English Hobnail, water goblet, round foot, crystal	10.00
English Hobnail, water goblet, round foot, ice blue	75.00
English Hobnail, wine, crystal	12.00
Old Quilt, candy, cov	20.00
Old Quilt, celery, ftd	40.00
Old Quilt, cheese dish, cov	55.00
Old Quilt, shaker, squat, 3½" h	12.00
Old Quilt, water goblet	18.00
Paneled Grape, appetizer set, 2-pc	45.00
Paneled Grape, ashtray, square, large	18.00
Paneled Grape, ashtray, square, small	8.00
Paneled Grape, banana stand	160.00
Paneled Grape, basket, scalloped foot, 10½"	90.00
Paneled Grape, bowl, lipped, 8½" d	90.00
Paneled Grape, bowl, ruffled	24.00
Paneled Grape, cake salver, pedestal, 11" d	50.00
Paneled Grape, candy, cov, 6¼", roses and bows dec	30.00
Paneled Grape, celery, 6" l	35.00
Paneled Grape, creamer and sugar, individual	25.00
Paneled Grape, cup and saucer	20.00
Paneled Grape, gravy boat and liner	40.00
Paneled Grape, pitcher, 8" h	35.00
Paneled Grape, punch stand	135.00
Paneled Grape, salt and pepper shakers, pr	25.00
Paneled Grape, soap dish	125.00
Paneled Grape, vase, 8½" h, roses and bows dec	30.00
Paneled Grape, wall pocket	135.00
Paneled Grape, water goblet	15.00
Ring & Petal, candlestick, 3³/₄" h, green satin mist	15.00
Ring & Petal, cake plate on stand, 11"	85.00

WHEATON

Wheaton Glass, a division of Wheaton Industries, Millville, New Jersey, manufactured commemorative bottles, decanters, and flasks between 1967 and 1974. Series included American Military Leaders (1974), Christmas, Great Americans (1969), Movie Stars, Patriots (1972), Presidential (1969), and Space. Wheaton bottles were sold by franchised dealers, at Grandma Wheaton's Shop (Millville), and through mail order (Collectors Guild and Bathsheba's Bottle Book).

Wheaton Industries assigned production to the Wheaton Historical Association in 1974. Series production continued from 1975 to 1982. Editions were limited, approximately 5,000 bottles, and made on a semi-automatic bottle making machine rather than the fully automated equipment employed by Wheaton Industries. The Millville Art Glass Co. obtained a licensing agreement from the Wheaton Historical Association and added a few new bottles to the Christmas and Presidential series.

In 1996 Wheaton Glass was sold and renamed Lawson-Mardon-Wheaton.

Wheaton Glass also manufactured copycats (stylistic copies) of 19th-century bottles and flasks between 1971 and 1974. Most were marked "Nuline," "W," or "Wheaton, NJ" on the base. Amber, amethyst, blue, green, milk, and ruby were the colors used.

Reference: Lois Clark, *Wheaton's,* published by author, 1998.

Collectors' Club: Classic Wheaton Club, PO Box 59, Downingtown, PA 19335.

American Miniatures, A Lancaster's Indian Vegetable Jaundice Bitters, amethyst	$25.00
American Miniatures, Ball and Claw Bitters, blue	25.00
American Miniatures, Dr Fisch's Bitters, blue	20.00
American Miniatures, EC Booz Old Cabin Whiskey, amethyst	10.00
American Miniatures, Frank's Safe Kidney & Liver Cure, amber	15.00
American Miniatures, Old Doc's Cure, blue	15.00
American Miniatures, RIP, casket, poison, ruby	30.00
American Miniatures, RIP, casket, poison, topaz	18.00
American Miniatures, Straubmuller's Elixer, blue	10.00
American Miniatures, Straubmuller's Elixir, ruby	15.00
Astronaut Decanter, Apollo 12, ruby	15.00
Astronaut Decanter, Apollo 14, blue	12.00
Astronaut Decanter, Apollo 17, amethyst	10.00
Bank, Federal Savings Vault, blue	45.00
Bank, Uncle Sam, green	15.00
Colonial Antique Series II, Liberty Bell, green	8.00
Commemorative, Frank H Wheaton St Birthday, topaz	10.00
Great Americans, Alexander Bell, amber	12.00
Great Americans, Betsy Ross, decanter, ruby	12.00
Great Americans, Charles Lindbergh, blue	12.00
Great Americans, John Paul Jones, green	10.00
Great Americans, Paul Revere, amethyst	8.00
Great Americans, Will Rogers, topaz	15.00
Ink, umbrella shaped, ruby	25.00
Mini-Presidential Decanter, James E Carter Jr, blue	25.00
Political Campaign, 1968 Democratic Donkey, green	10.00
Presidential Decanter, Abe Lincoln, topaz	12.00
Presidential Decanter, Franklin D Roosevelt, green	15.00
Presidential Decanter, George Washington, clear	8.00